1970

This book may be kept

THE GROWTH OF LITERATURE
VOLUME III

THE
GROWTH OF LITERATURE

BY

H. MUNRO CHADWICK

AND

N. KERSHAW CHADWICK

VOLUME III

PART I

THE ORAL LITERATURE OF THE TATARS

PART II

THE ORAL LITERATURE OF POLYNESIA AND A NOTE ON THE ORAL LITERATURE OF THE SEA DYAKS OF NORTH BORNEO

PART III

NOTES ON THE ORAL LITERATURE OF SOME AFRICAN PEOPLES

PART IV

A GENERAL SURVEY

CAMBRIDGE
AT THE UNIVERSITY PRESS
1940
REPRINTED
1968

Published by the Syndics of the Cambridge University Press
Bentley House, 200 Euston Road, London, N.W. 1
American Branch: 32 East 57th Street, New York, N.Y. 10022

PUBLISHER'S NOTE

Cambridge University Press Library Editions are re-issues of out-of-print
standard works from the Cambridge catalogue. The texts are unrevised
and, apart from minor corrections, reproduce the latest published edition.

Standard Book Number: 521 07424 x
Library of Congress Catalogue Card Number: 33–6470

First published 1940
Reprinted 1968

First printed in Great Britain at the University Press, Cambridge
Reprinted in Great Britain by John Dickens & Co. Ltd, Northampton

To our dear friend
DR A. C. HADDON
AND
to the memory of
JOHN ROSCOE
W. WYATT GILL, J. PERHAM
W. W. RADLOV
AND OF ALL THE
MISSIONARIES and TRAVELLERS
TO WHOSE WORK WE ARE INDEBTED
IN THIS VOLUME

CONTENTS

A NOTE ON THE ORAL LITERATURE OF THE IBAN OR THE SEA DYAKS OF NORTH BORNEO

PART III. NOTES ON THE ORAL LITERATURE OF SOME AFRICAN PEOPLES

Part IV. A GENERAL SURVEY

The bliss that one enjoys in attaining
heaven is scarcely equal to that which
one derives from reading this work.
                    Mahābhārata.

PREFACE

IN the Preface to the first volume we explained that the primary object of this work was to find an answer to the question whether it is possible to trace the operation of any general principles in the growth of literature. And we expressed our intention of approaching the question by a comparative study of the literary genres found in various countries and languages and in various periods of history.

At the same time we pointed out that for such comparative study the modern literatures of the West offer only a very limited amount of material. Owing to the constant interaction of these literatures upon one another for several centuries past, and before that to the common influence of Latin upon all of them, they have had little chance of independent development. The most valuable material for our purpose comes from ancient records unaffected, or only partially affected, by the influence of Latin or other languages of wide circulation, and from isolated or backward communities of the present day which are still but little affected by cosmopolitan literature.

The plan therefore which we set before ourselves was to examine a number of literatures, some ancient and some modern. In making our selection the guiding consideration was to find such literatures as would seem to be at least partly independent.

With this object in view we have confined our attention in general to modern literatures which are—or were until recently—unwritten, and to ancient literatures which seem to be largely derived from oral tradition. In Vol. II we have seen that a written and an oral literature may exist side by side in the same community; and in such cases we have limited our attention to the latter.

The connection between literature and writing is accidental, and belongs to a secondary phase in the history of literature. In general, however, oral literature tends to give way to written literature with the advance of civilisation, though it may persist, and within certain limitations even flourish, among the backward elements of civilised peoples. It is to peoples in what is commonly called a barbaric phase of culture and to the backward elements among more advanced peoples that our attention has been given. On the other hand, for reasons stated in the Preface to Vol. I, we have not concerned ourselves with the beginnings of literature or with those primitive phases of culture in which it first originated.

The comparative study of oral literature has received very little attention in the past, except in specific subjects and within limited areas. Consequently the extent of the subjects which come within its scope is by no means generally recognised. Nothing but a most inadequate impression can be obtained from the oral literatures of Western Europe, which consist of little more than folktales, folksongs and ballads. To oral literature which is cultivated under favourable conditions these bear the same relationship as popular songs do to the (written) literature of a civilised people, taken as a whole. From Eastern Europe, where a large amount of heroic narrative poetry is still current, the material is much richer. But among all modern Christian and Mohammedan peoples oral literature is practically limited to poems and stories intended for entertainment and to songs for use at social celebrations, such as weddings. In general it has been discarded by the more educated and intellectual elements in society. And consequently oral literature of more serious character—didactic or informative—has been displaced by written (ecclesiastical or secular) literature. For oral literature of this kind we must turn to peoples who are still, or were until recently, heathen, and to the records of ancient peoples. It is fortunate that, as we saw in Vol. I, the ancient literatures of our own islands and of Iceland have preserved a good deal, which was committed to writing before native thought died out.

It will be seen that oral poetry is as comprehensive as written poetry in its range of forms and subjects, and that most of these are widely distributed. Poetry indeed is in general an inheritance from oral literature.

On the other hand oral prose literature seems usually to be much more limited in its range. Ancient Indian prose which is believed to be of oral origin shows a good deal of variety; but most of the oral literatures which we have examined apparently preserve little prose, except narratives and perhaps laws. It is to be remarked, however, that the material is commonly less accessible than in the case of poetry.

In Vol. I we examined the ancient literatures of Europe which come within the scope of our survey. In Vol. II we examined two modern European oral literatures and two ancient Asiatic literatures. For the principles followed in the selection of these literatures we may refer to the Preface to the latter volume.

The modern literatures examined in Vol. II are those of peoples which have been Christian for many centuries. Consequently they

comprise little more than literature (poetry and prose) which is intended
for entertainment or for social celebrations. More serious matter—the
'literature of thought'—is very poorly represented. Such subjects are
left to the ecclesiastical (written) literature current in those countries—
literature which does not come within the scope of our survey. On
the other hand the ancient literatures, in both Vol. I and Vol. II, embrace
literature of thought, as well as that of entertainment and of celebration.
This is true to a large extent, as we have seen, even of the Christian
literatures examined in Vol. I.

In the present volume we have examined the oral literatures of the
Tatars and the Polynesians and of five African peoples. The material
at our disposal for the study of the latter has not been sufficient for
anything like a comprehensive survey; and consequently we have had
to content ourselves with notes on the African literatures. We have also
included a note on certain features in the oral literature of the Sea-Dyaks
(in Borneo), which are of special interest.

The selection, it will be seen, has been made from widely distant
regions and from peoples living under such diverse conditions as those
of the steppe, ocean, desert and forest.

Two of the African peoples selected—the Abyssinians and the
Tuareg—have long been Christians or Mohammedans. Their oral
literatures therefore, like those of the Russians and the Yugoslavs, are
concerned in the main with entertainment and social celebration, though
a good deal of occasional poetry, mostly of an ephemeral character,
has also been recorded. As in Russia and Yugoslavia, more serious
themes are left to the written literatures, ecclesiastical or other, which
are current among those peoples. This is in general true also of those
communities of the Tatars and the Galla which are Mohammedan, in
so far as their Mohammedanism is not merely superficial.

The Polynesians and the other African peoples—the Yoruba and
the Northern Bantu (apart from one or two coastal communities)—
were wholly heathen and ignorant of writing until recently; and the
same may be said of the Sea Dyaks and of many communities among
the Tatars and the Galla. The oral literatures of these peoples are concerned with native learning, as well as with entertainment and celebration. In some cases also occasional poetry has been recorded.

The oral literature of the Tatars is of great interest and variety;
yet no account of it seems ever to have been given before in English.
Indeed we do not know of any comprehensive treatment of it in any

language. A large amount of interesting material, however, has been collected, especially by W. W. Radlov, who was a Russian official in Central Asia during the latter part of last century, and to whose writings we are indebted for a considerable proportion of our information.

Those who have studied the European literatures treated in Vols. I and II will not in general find the oral literature of the Tatars particularly strange, despite the fact that we are here concerned with nomadic peoples. The Kara-Kirghiz have a well developed heroic narrative poetry, which will compare favourably with that of the Russians and the Yugoslavs; other communities cultivate saga in place of narrative poetry. Less familiar to us are the numerous stories which we have described as 'non-heroic'. Many of these are concerned with journeys to Heaven or the Underworld, which are connected with—or at least influenced by—the theology or manticism of the heathen Tatars. The manticism itself, commonly known as 'shamanism', is perhaps less peculiar than is popularly supposed. It has much in common with the manticism of ancient Europe; but the artistic or histrionic side is cultivated to an unusual degree, especially in representations of the seer's visits to Heaven or the Underworld.

For the oral literature of Polynesia also no comprehensive survey has ever been made before. But a great deal of very interesting material has been collected in various islands, and has been the subject of much careful study, especially in New Zealand and Hawaii. Perhaps the most interesting collections of all are those made about seventy years ago by the Rev. W. Wyatt Gill in the small island of Mangaia, in the Cook Group.

Polynesian literature differs greatly from those which we have already discussed. This is of course only what might be expected in view of the remoteness of the area and its backwardness in material culture. But the literature shows a wealth and variety which we should not expect from such conditions, or from the smallness of the population. It would seem indeed that the Polynesians are more intensely devoted to the cultivation of literature, and especially of poetry, than any other people.

In spite of the immensely wide distribution of the Polynesian languages, the literature everywhere has much in common. The direct influence of the sea is of course an all-important factor. The clear line of division between 'heroic' and 'non-heroic', which we have found among all other peoples, seems hardly to be traceable in this region. Stories of supernatural adventure, and especially of visits to Heaven and the Underworld, as among the Tatars, are current everywhere;

and many of them are told of the same (legendary) persons throughout Polynesia. The *tohungas*, or men of learning, are an influential class in all the larger communities. The intensive cultivation of poetry is also general; but there are great differences between one island (or group of islands) and another. The poetry of Tonga and New Zealand is much more easily intelligible to us than that of Tahiti or Mangaia. It is in these latter islands that we have met for the first time with what may fairly be called drama—of which we have found only somewhat uncertain traces elsewhere. In other respects also the records from the same islands suggest a strange world of unreality—a kind of fairyland or opera scene—for which we know no parallel.

In the note on the Sea Dyaks we have confined our attention to recitations or songs which are sung at certain festivals and at funerals. Materials for the study of the literature as a whole are not accessible to us, and have probably never been collected; but we wish to call special attention to these recitations, which are among the most outstanding achievements of oral literature known to us. They are chiefly occupied with journeys to Heaven or the Underworld, or with visits of deities to earth; but they are remarkable, like the recitations of the Tatar shaman, for their high artistic standard. They can hardly be called dramatic in the strict sense; but they show a curious combination of narrative with quasi-dramatic speech-poetry.

The five African literatures which we have selected belong to peoples of different races and languages. Both the Galla and the Tuareg indeed are Hamitic peoples; but they have been separated from one another probably for many thousands of years. The only real contact is between the Galla and the Abyssinians, who are neighbouring peoples—and perhaps much mixed—but separated by language and religion.

In Africa we have made no attempt at an exhaustive survey for any of the literatures. We have restricted ourselves to noting certain features which seemed to us important or distinctive. In doing so, however, we have been struck by the poverty of material much more than by any peculiar features. It is true that for the Galla and the Yoruba little seems to have been published, while the published material for the other (selected) literatures is very scattered and sometimes difficult of access. For other African peoples there are of course many collections of oral literature which we have not studied. But when all such allowances have been made, we do not think that the poverty which we have noted can be explained in this way.

It is in the literature of entertainment that the deficiency is most striking. Saga seems to be current among all the peoples we have surveyed; and very good specimens have been recorded from the Bantu, and perhaps also from the Yoruba. But the amount recorded is everywhere very small—apart from 'animal tales'. More remarkable is the fact that we have nowhere found any clear examples of 'speech-poetry'—which is current among all the other peoples included in our survey. Such poetry is of course of the utmost importance in the history of literature. It involves the cultivation of an imaginative faculty, which enables an author to express reflections and emotions appropriate, not to himself or to his own circumstances, but to some other character, real or fictitious. Yet in view of the care and skill devoted to speeches in animal tales, it is difficult to believe that such poetry is unknown in Africa. All the other kinds of poetry which are commonly found elsewhere seem to occur also here; but, apart from poetry of celebration and occasional poetry in North Africa, they are but sparsely represented.

In general African literature does not convey the impression of unfamiliarity which we get in Polynesia. Such special features as we have noted are not without parallels elsewhere. The most striking is the *Ahal* of the Tuareg; but analogies for this may be found in medieval Provence. Affinities with Hebrew literature, whether real or super-ficial, may be traced among the heathen Galla. The literature of the Bantu, so far as our material goes, is not very remote from the ancient European literatures in their less advanced phases.

The last part of this volume, from p. 697, consists of a survey of the results arising from the examination of the various literatures.

It is to be noted first that the chief elements occur everywhere, or almost everywhere, though in varying degrees of prominence. Every literature has of course distinctive characteristics, positive or negative, of its own; but in estimating these care must be taken to distinguish, as far as possible, between characteristics which apply truly to the literature current at a given time and characteristics, especially negative characteristics, which may be due to accidents of transmission. Thus poetry connected with heathen worship may be neglected by a collector who is a Christian missionary; a century later all trace of its existence may be lost. But it is in relation to ancient literatures that this con-sideration is of most importance. Certain literatures, e.g. Sanskrit and Hebrew,[1] seem to owe their preservation wholly to ecclesiastical circles.

[1] In a sense of course this is true also of Anglo-Saxon and other ancient literatures. But the two cases are different. Here secular works were preserved as separate (written) entities in the libraries of religious houses. In India and Palestine such secular literature as has survived is incorporated in ecclesiastical works.

If one were to take the literature which has survived as an index to the whole of the literature, secular and religious, current in India or Palestine at certain dates in the past, the result would obviously be absurd.[1] It is only from modern oral literatures and from such ancient literatures as have been preserved under more favourable conditions that one can form a reasonable estimate of the current literature of a community as a whole. Such literatures as Sanskrit and Hebrew, as we have them, convey a wrong impression of the literatures of their peoples as a whole; yet they are valuable not only for their wealth of ecclesiastical material—which is largely of oral derivation—but also for the fragments and traces of secular literature which they preserve.

We have classified the material in each literature throughout our survey according to certain 'categories' on the basis of subject matter, irrespective of form. Some of these categories are of a personal character, relating to individuals, while others are of general, or more or less general, reference. A brief discussion of these categories will be found in Part IV, Ch. I (p. 702 ff.).

A few remarks will be sufficient here. In literature relating to (human) individuals we have usually distinguished between two elements, which we call 'heroic' and 'non-heroic', and which represent corresponding elements in the life of barbaric societies. The former is concerned with the 'hero' or warrior, usually a princely warrior, and has its origin in military or princely circles. The latter is of mantic provenance, and the interest is most commonly, though not always, centred in a seer; frequently also it has a communal or religious interest. These subjects are noticed briefly in Ch. I of Part IV, and discussed more fully in Ch. III. To periods in which the heroic element is dominant we apply the term 'Heroic Age'.

The non-heroic element is the essentially intellectual part of a barbaric community, and its activities may be seen in literature of general reference—antiquarian, gnomic, mantic—as well as in stories or poems relating to individuals. We have not thought it necessary to discuss

[1] Some critics hold that we ought to have given a complete account of each literature as we have it, so as to emphasise the differences, as well as the affinities between the various literatures, and more especially perhaps between Oriental and Western literatures. We have followed this course only in (modern) literatures for which no other account is available. It would have been futile to do so for literatures, like Sanskrit and Hebrew, which have frequently been treated by scholars far better qualified than we are. The criticism seems to be based on a misconception not only of the object of our survey, but also of the difference between literature preserved from the past, say in ecclesiastical circles, and literature current in the past among all classes. It is the latter of course which we are trying to trace.

the latter in Part IV, except by way of comparison with heroic stories. We have also dealt only very briefly with 'post-heroic' literature, which is in general the literature of the phase of transition from barbaric to civilised—when the seer is giving place to the (secular) legislator and philosopher. From ancient times much interesting material, Greek and Norse, dating from this phase has been preserved, as we saw in Vol. I; but modern oral literatures have not added much. We have no doubt that such literature is current in Africa and elsewhere; but apparently it has seldom been thought worth recording.

Literature relating to unspecified (nameless) persons belongs for the most part to peasant society. Its origin, however, is by no means uniform; much of it is vagrant—carried from one land to another apparently by travellers and traders.

For the remaining categories it must suffice to refer to p. 704f. and to Chs. VI–IX of Part IV. Here we would only remark that both gnomic philosophy and mantic philosophy are to be traced back to barbaric times. Gnomic philosophy is usually—not always, according to traditional belief—based upon experience and observation; mantic philosophy is derived either by revelation or inspiration from some external power (usually a deity) or from some power within the seer himself. But the two philosophies are combined among some peoples, while among others they belong to different milieus. It will be seen that we have not found very much gnomic literature among modern peoples, though it seems to be known wherever heathen thought survives. The conditions most favourable to such literature are apparently those of the ('post-heroic') phase of transition from barbarism to civilisation. It will also be seen that antiquarian learning (i.e. knowledge of the far past) is often of mantic origin; but during the transitional phase inspiration tends to be transferred from the substance to the form of poetry.

We would call attention to the fact that, with the reservations stated above, the categories[1] which we have specified are to be found in all the literatures included in our survey, and that within these categories

[1] To carry out our classification with complete consistency, we ought perhaps to have recognised one more category—of 'literature relating to animals, etc.'. In point of fact such literature seems to occur everywhere, whether in the form of 'animal-tales' or in descriptions of animals. But within the scope of our survey it is only among certain African peoples that we have found an intensive cultivation of it; and we think it will be enough here to refer to the examples given on p. 607 ff. Other examples will be found in the first two volumes, especially in Vol. II, p. 571 ff., and in the various chapters on 'descriptive' poetry.

the various literatures tend to follow the same lines.[1] The chief reservation is that, as we have already noted, native learning tends to be displaced by the sacred scriptures among peoples which have long been Christian or Mohammedan.

In discussing literature which relates to persons it is often necessary to employ a system of classification which is not based upon subject matter. We have to distinguish between narrative, speech-poetry, didactic matter, poetry of celebration and appeal, and occasional poetry—which, for the sake of brevity, we call Types A, B, C, D, E. A more precise definition of these types will be found on p. 696; and their distribution in relation to the 'categories' is discussed in Ch. II of Part IV.

We have little doubt that the origin of poetry—i.e. 'sung speech', as against 'spoken speech'—is to be found in Types D and E, which in their very simplest forms are not always clearly distinguishable. But beyond this we are not prepared to speculate on the problem. The origin of narrative poetry is discussed in the same chapter; the characteristics of heroic narrative poetry in Ch. IV.

We are under the impression that the twofold system of analysis, by categories and types, which we have employed, enables us to obtain a more or less complete conspectus of the varieties of literature current in barbaric communities—making allowance of course for defective information and oversights. There are certain varieties, however, which we have been criticised for neglecting.

Folktales and folksongs have been noticed, along with other 'nameless' stories and poems, in Ch. V of Part IV and in the various chapters throughout the work from which this chapter is derived. Further, the influence of folktales upon heroic and other stories has been noticed incidentally in the various chapters on 'unhistorical elements'. But we have not thought it necessary to devote special sections to these subjects. Our survey is concerned with the native literatures of various selected peoples, whereas folktales[2] are vagrants, who get a lodging everywhere, and consequently cannot be treated adequately except in

[1] For some examples of parallelism in individual works we may refer to pp. 151, 672 in this volume; cf. also p. 556 with Vol. II, p. 557. But we regard the similarity in general characteristics (e.g. in antiquarian, gnomic and mantic literature) as more important than resemblances between individual works.

[2] This is true of folksongs only to a slight extent. But it is our treatment of folktales, not folksongs, which has been criticised.

an 'international' survey, which will take account of all their local variants. We are not at all inclined to deny their influence upon native literature, though it is quite likely that in stories here and there we have overlooked it. But at the same time we must point out that owing to their accessibility—they are almost the only form of oral literature current in civilised lands—folktales tend to receive a somewhat disproportionate amount of attention. For the study of ancient literatures they have without doubt a certain value, as contributing to the elucidation of individual stories relating to barbaric times; but this value is not to be compared with that of the oral literature, taken as a whole, of a people which has no writing.

We have also been criticised, and perhaps with better reason, for neglect of ritual literature. Hymns have been noticed in the theological chapters, ritual directions in the gnomic chapters, and poetry of social ritual in those which are concerned with unspecified individuals; but the material has usually been treated very briefly. It is only in rituals which supply interesting illustrations of literature or thought, and which are unknown or very little known in this country, that we have entered into details; instances will be found below, pp. 199 ff., 353 ff., 484 ff., and in Vol. II, p. 228 ff. A large amount of material for the study of ritual may of course be found in the Brāhmanas and the Book of Leviticus; but we doubt whether it has much bearing on the history of literature, or whether it would be of any great interest to the majority of our readers.

It is quite possible, however, that some readers will think we have unduly neglected the subject of dramatic ritual. There is some definite evidence for this in the Yajurveda and the Brāhmanas, as well as among the Polynesians and the Bantu; and we have little doubt that it was widespread in ancient Europe and elsewhere, though most of the evidence is of somewhat uncertain character. But we have not found anything which can properly be called dramatic literature, except in certain Polynesian islands. Such literature may have existed in barbaric times in ancient Europe; but, if so, it has left only slight and doubtful traces—though the ritual itself may well have influenced literature indirectly.

Again, it may be thought that we ought to have included the ancient records of Egypt and the Near East in our survey;[1] and in point of

---

[1] The same may of course be said of other literatures, e.g. Arabic and Chinese. A knowledge of these would have been most useful to us. The literatures of North Africa have doubtless been much influenced by the former, that of the Tatars perhaps

fact we have been criticised for not paying sufficient attention to the documents found at Ras Shamra. Our reply is that we are not prepared to embark upon subjects in which the knowledge required for such work as ours is accessible only to specialists. It is true that Mesopotamian and Egyptian records carry the history of literature back thousands of years beyond the earliest date at which we begin; but they are products of a more advanced phase of civilisation and of communities in which writing had been employed from the fourth millennium or earlier.[1]

Another criticism which has been passed upon our work is that, under the influence of 'Homer', we have paid too much attention to narrative poetry. We fear that this criticism is to some extent justified. One of the objects, though not the primary object, of our survey is to see how far one literature can contribute to the understanding of another, and perhaps especially how far modern oral literatures can throw light upon ancient literatures. Narrative poetry in those literatures which possess it tends to dominate and influence all other kinds of poetry, though some literatures, e.g. Greek and Norse, break away from this influence in course of time. And we are under the impression that on the whole it is in such literatures that the majority of our readers will be chiefly interested.

We admit that we have paid more attention to narrative poetry than to saga, and indeed to poetry of all kinds than to prose. But we are not entirely to blame for this—the explanation lies rather in the nature of the material itself. The prose material, as we have it, is inferior to the poetic material. The form in which we have poetry, both ancient and modern, is presumably the form—or at least a form—in which it was recited; but we doubt if this is usually true of sagas, except those from Iceland. We suspect that the great majority of sagas which we have seen, both ancient and modern, are abbreviated versions, or even mere summaries, of the sagas which were actually recited. We do not think that a comparative study of saga could be satisfactorily carried out in detail within the areas which we have surveyed.

At the conclusion of a work of this kind it is hardly necessary to state that the authors themselves are well aware of numerous defects and obscurities at least as serious as any of those which have met with by the latter. But we stated in the Preface to Vol. I that we were not prepared to embark upon undertakings which we should never be able to carry out. We did not set out to eat up the whole farmyard.

[1] The records include much ritual matter, including dramatic ritual, which may well throw light upon the ritual literature of less advanced peoples.

criticism. But it may not be out of place here to call attention to a few of the outstanding problems with which we feel that we have not been able to cope satisfactorily.

In the first place we would repeat what we have said above about the dearth of material from Africa. In all the areas we have selected there seems to be a shortage of saga and an absence of speech-poetry; in Central Africa material of all kinds is deficient in quantity. We should like to know whether this shortage is due to neglect of the cultivation —or preservation—of literature by the peoples themselves, or to insufficient activity, or to difficulties of any kind, in the collection of material.

Next, we would emphasise the need for ascertaining to what extent (oral) literature is cultivated by women in barbaric communities. In Vol. II we suggested that parts of the Books of Samuel are of feminine provenance; and the incredulity with which this suggestion was greeted by more than one critic—on general, not specific, grounds—would seem to indicate that it was regarded as something quite unreasonable. Yet it will be seen in the course of this volume that among some peoples the cultivation of literature is largely, if not mainly, in the hands of women; and we suspect that in general women have more scope for such activities in barbaric than in civilised communities. We should not be greatly surprised if this question should turn out to be rather closely connected with the preceding one. At all events it is desirable that women collectors should try to get into touch with African women before the native literatures have wholly disappeared. So far as we are able to ascertain, not much investigation has been made from this side.

Next, we have to confess that we are by no means satisfied with the references to music throughout our survey. In particular we are sometimes far from clear about the distinction drawn by some of our authorities between 'singing' and 'chanting', and also about the character of both the vocal and the instrumental music where recitations are accompanied upon a stringed instrument. Precise information upon such questions should not be impossible to obtain; but it is difficult of access to non-specialists.

Among other questions which specially call for comparative study we may mention the nature and extent of education in barbaric communities and the whole subject of inspiration, especially the 'call' of the seer. The latter subject has been much studied from the pathological side; but what is most wanted is a collection of the evidence from ancient and modern records, including, where possible, the seers' own accounts of their experiences.

Lastly, there is a question which is not a problem in itself, but arises frequently in connection with various subjects: "Is this story, or idea, or form of poetry, etc. a native development in each community, or has it spread from one people to another?" Folktales travel far and wide. Musical instruments, and doubtless also various forms of music, are acquired by one people from another. We suspect the same to be true of ritual practices and of ideas such as that of a coming destruction of the world. But is a type of poetry, say narrative poetry, derived by one people from another, or does it originate independently everywhere or in different centres? So also with the idea of a community of deities, modelled on a human community—is it of native growth or imported? It is hoped that our survey may help towards the formulation and insulation of a number of problems of this kind, and supply data which may lead to their solution. Probably not one of the literatures we have examined—not even the Polynesian—is of purely native growth. In the North African literatures the native element may be quite small.

Every oral literature may be regarded as consisting of a native nucleus, augmented from time to time by new elements of extraneous origin. But opinions may differ as to the interpretation of 'native'. May not the nucleus itself consist wholly or mainly of extraneous elements which have been assimilated long ago, and have had time to assume a distinctive form? In support of this view it may be urged that the material culture of any given people consists in the main of elements of extraneous origin—livestock, cereals, implements—which have been naturalised and adapted to its needs. But against this stands the fact that the literatures of two neighbouring peoples, who speak different languages, usually differ far more widely than their material cultures.

The singing of dirges or elegies for the dead, commonly by a female relative, is found probably among all the peoples included in our survey. Is the custom a 'natural' growth, which has sprung up independently everywhere, or a fashion which has spread from one centre? Speculation upon the origin of names, places, peoples and customs is probably current everywhere. But does it arise independently, or does one people learn it from another? Gnomes may be derived partly from descriptions, partly from precepts, and the latter may be derived from commands. But what is to be said about the very widespread custom of constructing a series of gnomes in poetic form?

We do not think that the time has yet come for giving a dogmatic answer to such questions. Data must first be collected. But we do think it is time that the science of literature should be recognised as an essential branch of anthropological study. Man's intellectual activities deserve attention quite as much as his material culture or social organisation. Yet, whereas the study of the latter subjects has made immense progress in recent times, that of the former is still generally ignored. By way of experiment we have put forward a scheme, which is based on a survey of the native (oral) literatures of certain selected peoples. If this scheme itself is not approved, it may perhaps pave the way for some alternative scheme, which will meet with more approval.

May we call the attention of readers to the fact that the Lists of Abbreviations printed on pp. 219 ff., 467 ff., 497, 531 ff., 637 ff., 649 and 678 ff. are intended merely for convenience of reference, in order to avoid constant repetitions? They are not intended as bibliographies. It would of course have been quite impracticable to attempt anything of the kind in such a book as this. We may also repeat here what we said in the Prefaces to the previous volumes, that we have made no attempt to consult the voluminous modern literature bearing upon these subjects. If we had done so, we should doubtless have avoided many errors and inaccuracies, and our work, so far as it went, would have profited greatly thereby; but it would never have seen the light. We have read some books which happen to have come in our way; and to some of these we refer occasionally.

At the same time we much regret that very little recent literature relating to the Tatars has been accessible to us. We believe that a good deal has been published in recent years; but the books are not purchasable in this country. We fear also that in Parts II and III, owing to the length of time that our work has been in preparation, we have probably overlooked a number of recent publications. The important works of the late R. W. Williamson and most of the publications of the Bernice P. Bishop Museum have appeared since Part II was first drafted.

The translations in Part I have been made from the original Tatar texts by the author responsible for this Part, except in a few cases where no original texts were accessible. She has availed herself, however, of the invaluable help afforded by Radlov's translations. In Part II she has depended almost entirely upon published translations; only in a few instances, where these seemed to be extremely free, she has ventured to give renderings of her own in place of them. We appreciate fully the value of a knowledge of the original languages, especially for those literatures which are discussed in detail; but such knowledge can be acquired only to a limited extent in a survey which covers so wide a field. The Polynesian languages differ from one another a good deal; and for the translation of the poetry, which has an extremely specialised diction and is highly allusive, it is better to trust to the work of expert linguists, especially as very few aids are available. In Part III, where five wholly different languages are involved, and in the Note on the Sea Dyaks, we have been entirely dependent upon published translations. For the literature of the Sea Dyaks no original texts are available, so far as we know.

In conclusion we must record the deep sense of obligation which we feel to the late Canon John Roscoe for the kindness with which he put at our disposal his unrivalled knowledge of the Northern Bantu, and for the trouble which he took on our behalf. We are greatly indebted to the Hon. F. R. Rodd for reading the proofs of the section relating to the Tuareg, and to both him and his brother, the Hon. P. Rodd, for interesting information which they have given us from time to time. We are also greatly indebted to Miss Dora Newell, who has read the proofs of Part II, and given us the benefit of her intimate knowledge of Samoa. Dr E. J. Lindgren has generously supplied us with publications and other information relating to shamans, which would not otherwise have been accessible to us. From Dr A. C. Haddon we have received many valuable references and the same constant help and encouragement as in our previous works.

We wish also to express our thanks to Mrs E. J. Osmond for interesting reminiscences of Mangaia in the early days of the Missions; to the London Missionary Society, and especially the Librarian, Mr D. Chamberlin, for the special privileges most kindly granted us in the use of the Library; to Dr S. M. Manton for instructive pictures of ceremonies in Bali; and to Mr T. W. Fraser for interesting personal observations of the Southern Bantu. For help most kindly rendered to us in various ways we are indebted also to Te Rangi Hiroa (Professor P. H. Buck), Professor C. G. Seligman, Professor S. Konovalov, Mr L. C. G. Clarke and Professor D. S. Robertson. Our thanks are also due to the Editor and staff of *The Illustrated London News* for the trouble they have kindly taken on our behalf.

Most of all we have to thank Dr C. E. Wright and Mrs R. C. Wright, who have read the whole of the volume in proof, and whose helpful criticism has been of the greatest value to us. We are under special obligations to Dr Wright, who has most kindly read the whole of our three volumes for us. The greater part of the present volume has also been read by Miss H. R. Ellis, to whom we are indebted for similar services.

To the University Library and its staff we are under the same obligations as in the past. To the Syndics of the Cambridge University Press, and also to the staff, we must repeat the thanks which we expressed in the Prefaces to the previous volumes.

N. Kershaw Chadwick is responsible for Parts I–III (pp. 1–679) of this volume, as also for Part I of Vol. II. The distribution of the work in Vol. I was explained in the Preface to that volume. The Index to Parts I–III of this volume has been prepared by Mr G. V. Carey, to whom both authors wish to express their cordial thanks for the care which he has taken with it.

H. M. C.
N. K. C.

December, 1938

PART I

THE ORAL LITERATURE OF THE TATARS

Turkistánning yerinda khâli imas erânlar.
Har bir kulach yerinda yatur mardán erán lar.

"In the land of Turkistán there is no lack of heroes.
In every fathom of its soil there lie heroic men."
(Old verse.)[1]

[1] R. B. Shaw, *Sketch of the Turki Language*, p. 13.

CHAPTER I

INTRODUCTION

UNDER the term Tatars we propose to consider the peoples of Asia who speak various dialects of the Turkish language, who do not inhabit towns, and who have no native written literature. Roughly speaking, our survey will include the Turkish tribes of the Altai, Sayan, and Tien Shan mountains, the valleys of the upper Yenisei, the Ob, and Irtish, the intervening steppes, and those of the Aral and Caspian basins, and the Turkoman tribes of northern Persia. Unfortunately the lack or inaccessibility of material relating to the Yakut, who are chiefly to be found in the valley of the Lena, precludes our including these most interesting people, to whom we can refer only incidentally. Our study takes as its starting point the cultural state of the Tatars when the great travellers of last century visited them and recorded their oral literature as it was current at that time, before the changes which have been brought about in central and northern Asia by the Russian Revolution. The political geography of the present régime, and the extensive spread of education, with the inevitable change of outlook and loss of native traditional culture are, of course, ignored here. The changes which have taken place throughout Siberia during the last twenty years are so extensive that we have felt it safer for the most part to speak of the native literature and native minstrelsy in the past tense; but we do not doubt that much still remains unchanged, at least among the nomads of the steppe and in the more inaccessible parts of the mountains.

The Turkish-speaking peoples are commonly divided into two large classes—the eastern and the western Turks. The western Turks include the Turks as far east as Persia and Afghanistan, and consist of the Osmanli and Turkoman stocks. Of these the Turkomans alone come within our range, as the Osmanli Turks have had a written literature for many centuries. According to Czaplicka's classification[1] the eastern Turks include the people of Turkestan and Central Asia as far as Mongolia, as well as the Crimea and Volga Tatars, who belong to this group both linguistically and historically. The eastern Turks dwelling in Asia are further subdivided into (1) the Iranian Turks, including the

[1] *Turks*, p. 20 ff.

Turks of Turkestan and some of the Turks of the Caspian steppe country who have come under 'Iranian' influence for many centuries; and (2) the 'Turanian Turks', including most of the Turks (Tatars) of the Steppe, southern Siberia, Jungaria, and northern Mongolia.[1] Owing to the mountain barriers of Central Asia, these Turks are believed to have been less subject to foreign influence than the first group. We think it certain, however, that their cultural debt in the past to China and Tibet has been underestimated, and in recent years also the cultures of Tibet and Russia have exercised considerable influence.

As the greater part of the literature available for our study is contained in Radlov's collections, we have adopted his classification, based on linguistic data, into the following groups, each of which is characterised by its own peculiar type of literary productions.

(1) The Tatars occupying the steppes and valleys of the Upper Yenisei and the slopes of the Sayan Mountains. For the sake of brevity we shall refer to these tribes as the Abakan group, as the greater part of the literature of this group was collected from the Tatars in the neighbourhood of the Abakan steppe. But it is to be understood that the term is used merely for the sake of convenience in the following pages, and is not to be pressed to its geographical limits. These tribes were largely shamanists and horse nomads till the Russians undertook vigorous measures of colonisation during the early part of last century. They have mostly either died out, or become absorbed in and assimilated to the Russians.

(2) The Kara-Kirghiz, most of whom are to be found on the slopes of the Tien Shan Mountains, especially round Lake Issyk-Kul. Some are believed to linger still in the valley of the Upper Yenisei, which is generally regarded as their former home (see p. 7 below). They are partly agriculturalists, but the majority are nomads, rich in flocks of horses and sheep. They are nominally Mohammedans,[2] but they know little of the Prophet or the Koran, and the more easterly of the tribes are said to be almost wholly ignorant of both (cf. p. 89 below).

---

[1] This classification differs somewhat from that of Vambéry (*Türkenvolk*, p. 85), who divided the 'Eastern Turks' into (1) Siberian Turks, including most of the tribes in the areas of the Lena, the Yenisei, and the Tobol; (2) the Turks of Chinese Turkestan and of the southern steppes; (3) the Volga Turks; (4) the Tatars round the shores of the Black Sea.

[2] In speaking of the religion of the various Tatar peoples, it must be understood that we are referring to the faith which they held at the time when the literature which we are about to study was recorded, and before the full effects of the Russian Revolution with its anti-religious campaign were felt.

(3) The Altai, including the Chern, or Black Forest Tatars, and the Teleut; and some smaller tribes in this region, such as the Kirei and the Kumandists. These tribes are almost wholly shamanists, though the Teleut were nominally converted to Islam as early as the seventeenth century, and the Kirei, now Mohammedans, were Nestorian Christians from the eleventh to the thirteenth centuries. The Tatars of this group are generally regarded as freer from foreign influence than other Tatars of Central Asia, and as retaining old Turkish customs and beliefs in their purest form. They practise agriculture where conditions permit; but the majority of the Tatars of the Altai are nomads or hunters.

(4) The Kazaks who inhabit the steppes in the northern and eastern part of the Aral-Caspian basin and the Orenburg district of Russia. They are frequently called Kirghiz, and the Russians call them Kirghiz-Kazaks. The word *Kazak* is believed to mean simply 'riders'. The name is first mentioned by the Persian poet Firdausi (1020), who refers to the '*kazaks*' as mounted and armed steppe marauders. These tribes are divided into three hordes, a division which was made by their *khan*, or prince, Tyavka, in the thirteenth century for administrative purposes. The Great Horde, as it is called, inhabits the steppe between the Sea of Aral and the mountains to the east of Lake Balkash; the Middle Horde that between the Tobol and the Irtish and the Syr Daria; the Little Horde that between the Sea of Aral and the lower Volga. The great majority have been nomads until recent times, though in the south and west they have been gradually adopting the mode of life of the Russian settlers for over a century. Their conversion has been a gradual process, and although Islam was introduced at an early date among the southern tribes, it was only adopted by the majority of the people when Kuchum Khan gave support to Mohammedan missionaries in the seventeenth century.

(5) The Tatars of the valleys of the Ob and Irtish, the majority of whom are generally designated roughly as the 'Tobol Tatars', though the name is as arbitrary as that of the Abakan group referred to above. They are the most consistently settled of all the Tatars in their mode of life, being chiefly occupied in agriculture and trade. They are mostly Mohammedans, though a small number have been Christians since 1720.

(6) Finally there are the Turkomans, who inhabit the steppe to the north of Persia and Afghanistan, between the Caspian Sea and the Oxus. A large proportion are still nomadic horse breeders, though since their subjugation by the Russians in 1881 they are gradually adopting agriculture and a more settled mode of life. They are all Mohammedans.

Little is known of the history of the Tatars, beyond their relations with the Chinese in the east, and their connections with Europe in the west. Among European writers they have generally not been clearly distinguished from the Mongols and the Tungus.[1] All our information goes to prove, however, that the civilisation of the Tatars was on a higher level in the past than in modern times. The ancient settled civilisation on the Yenisei, which has been brought to light by archaeologists, and which appears to extend through the whole of the first millennium before our era,[2] is generally attributed, rightly or wrongly, to the ancient Tatars. More important for our purpose, because more recent, are the traces left by the Uigurs, a certainly Turkish people who occupied first northern and western Mongolia and later the deserts and oases to the south-west during the first millennium of our era. The Uigurs were a highly civilised town-dwelling people, with an alphabet and a literature of their own. They enjoyed trade relations with both India and China. Their royal house, with its capital at Karakoram in northern Mongolia till 840, and after that in Chinese Turkestan at Kucha and elsewhere, professed Buddhism and Manichaeism at various periods before the tenth century. The conversion of their *khagan*, or ruler, to Manichaeism, and the resulting introduction of Manichaeism among the Uigurs took place in 763.[3] Even after the destruction of the Uigur power on the Orkhon in 840, and the shifting of their centre to Chinese Turkestan, their influence extended throughout the deserts and oases of Gobi and the Taklamakan, and the Tarim basin, and the great mountains to the west. As late as the thirteenth century one branch of the Uigurs still had their summer palace on the slopes of the Tien Shan Mountains.

This Uigur civilisation, derived in the main from the indigenous Indo-European speaking peoples who occupied the Turfan and Tarim basins, and the district of Khotan further south, for centuries before the southward movement of the Uigurs, cannot have failed to exercise a strong influence on the nomads who lived in the neighbouring mountains—an influence which was certainly none the less potent because it is now difficult to gauge. It is very necessary that we should keep this factor constantly in mind in our consideration of the oral literature of

---

[1] See A. B. Boswell, *S.R.* VI (1927–8), p. 68 ff.

[2] See Minns, *A.J.* x (1930), p. 1 ff. and the references there cited.

[3] Chavannes and Pelliot, *J.A.* 1913 (1), pp. 191 f.; 193 ff.; 303 ff.; 317; cf. Burkitt, pp. 50, 97 f. For a sketch of the history and culture of Kucha, see S. Lévi, *J.A.* 1913 (2), p. 311 ff. For a discussion of foreign elements in early Turkish culture, see Brockelmann, *A.M.* 1925, p. 110 ff.

the nomads. It is easy to underrate the importance of a great people and a great civilisation which disappeared from the map a thousand years ago, and which has been almost forgotten by history. The cultural influence of the Uigurs has never been fully appreciated by Western historians; but in this respect the native traditions are a surer guide than the pages of our historians. We shall see that in the chief epic Cycle of the Turks the leading place in the civilisation of the East is assigned to the Uigurs, whose high material culture, progressive policy, and peace-loving habits are a constant source of wonder to the nomad Kirghiz minstrel.

The original home of the Kara-Kirghiz is generally thought to have been on the head waters of the Yenisei. The final stage of their southward movements is believed to have taken place in the seventeenth century, owing to the Russian advance in Siberia.[1] The previous stages of these movements, however, are assigned to a much earlier date. The Kirghiz have been identified with a powerful people known to Chinese annals as the *Hakas*, or, more correctly, perhaps, the *K'ic-gia-sze*,[2] who seem to have occupied the regions round the source of the Yenisei during the ninth century, and who destroyed the Uigur power with its centre at Karakoram on the Orkhon in northern Mongolia in 840;[3] and the Kara-Kirghiz are more particularly identified with the branch of these powerful Turkish warriors which moved south-westwards from the source of the Yenisei in the tenth century.[4] The early Turkish activities which broke the Uigur power in the north are something more than the raids of barbarian warriors, and a careful study of their policy and actual achievements—so far as our evidence allows of such a study[5]—makes it clear that even the mountain Turks were capable at this time of care-fully planned movements, a deliberate policy, and organised warfare. They must, in fact, have been a far more highly civilised people than the Kirghiz of more recent times. Radlov, indeed, held that the love of 'epic'[6] poetry, shared in modern times by the Kara-Kirghiz and the Abakan Tatars, is probably of common origin, and belonged originally to the *Hakas* on the Yenisei.[7] This is more problematical, but is perhaps

---

[1] Radlov, *Proben* v, p. v; cf. Czaplicka, *Turks*, p. 48; cf. also Venyukov (Michell, p. 273).

[2] Radlov, *loc. cit.*

[3] See above.   [4] Radlov, *loc. cit.*

[5] See Chavannes and Pelliot, *J.A.* 1913 (1), p. 285 ff.

[6] By the term 'epic' Radlov evidently meant long narrative poems of adventure, whether relating to natural or supernatural persons and events. See Chapters II, III below.   [7] *Proben, loc. cit.*; cf. Czaplicka, *Turks*, p. 69.

supported by the similarity in form of the poetry of both the Kara-Kirghiz and the Abakan Tatars to that of the Tatars of the Altai who lie between.[1]

If this theory of a northern origin is correct—and there seem no grounds for doubting it—the Kara-Kirghiz must from early times have been near neighbours of the Buryat, a Mongol people living at that time (and still living to-day) around Lake Baikal. This might help to account in part for the confusion which prevails to some extent as to the exact distinction between the Kara-Kirghiz and the Buryat. The original distinction would, in fact, be partly lost if, as is generally believed, a section of the Buryat had already migrated southwards to the shore of Lake Issyk-Kul at the foot of the Alatau Mountains before the south-ward movement of the Kara-Kirghiz to this region. *Buryat* or *Burut* (*Pulut*) is the name by which the Kara-Kirghiz are known among the Chinese and the Kalmuck in modern times, while Russian writers (e.g. Valikhanov[2] and Venyukov) generally refer to them as *Dikokammenoi*. The Burut (Buryat) proper, however, are not Tatars at all, but Mongols. The most likely explanation of the confusion seems to be, therefore, that by this name the Chinese correctly denoted certain Mongol tribes dwelling round Lake Issyk-Kul before the migration of the Kirghiz from the Yenisei during the seventeenth and eighteenth centuries, and earlier, and that the name continued to be used afterwards both of the original inhabitants and of the later immigrant tribes. The confusion is an unfortunate one, however, as these tribes have yielded a rich harvest of literature and of evidence for native customs, which are variously cited as illustrating Mongol and Tatar tradition,[3] thus adding still greater confusion to the baffling Mongol-Tatar overlap in the mountain districts of Jungaria and Chinese Turkestan, and the Tien Shan Mountains.

[1] See further *Kogutei*, p. 7.

[2] Valikhanov was the son of a Kirghiz chief in the Russian service, and himself an educated gentleman and a valuable authority on Kirghiz matters. See R. B. Shaw, *J.A.S.B.* XLVI (1877), p. 243; cf. also p. 16, footnote 1 below.

[3] We may refer, for example, to the brief but interesting illustrated article by Kurt Lubinski, which has reference to the 'Oirot on the Mongolian-Siberian borders'. According to Czaplicka, the Oirot are Tatars (*Turks*, p. 96, and cf. *H.S.A.R.* I, p. 156—also largely her work), while most modern ethnologists class them among the western Mongols or Kalmucks. In the Kara-Kirghiz Cycle of *Manas*, the Oirot are identified with the Nogai. Now the Nogai is an alternative name generally applied to the western Mongols or Kalmucks; but the Nogai form the principal personnel of the *Manas* poems, which are the 'national' epics of the Kara-Kirghiz, and composed in a Tatar dialect. See further, Poppe, *A.M.* VIII, p. 183 ff., and the references there cited.

Something of the splendour and formality which prevailed at the nomad courts from the time of Jenghiz Khan to the seventeenth century can be gleaned from the works of the medieval travellers who visited them on diplomatic and missionary enterprises, as well as from the later records of Russian historians. These records do not, of course, always distinguish clearly between Tatar, Tungus, and Mongol,[1] but it is doubtful how far the distinction itself held good at this period, apart from the immediate families of the chief leaders and rulers, whose subjects consisted of all the peoples of the western steppe, and many of the eastern also. It is probable that the actual Mongol race formed the smallest element[2] in the great hordes which rolled together like a vast snowball under the genius and leadership of Jenghiz Khan and his immediate followers. The predominant element among those with whom the European travellers came into contact were doubtless Turks, as those who conquered China were certainly Tungus.

The devastating effects of the 'Tatar' invasions on eastern Europe have blinded us to the great intellectual achievements of their leaders, both in organisation and in the science of war, though their religious tolerance in an age when Europe was given up to fanaticism has long been recognised.[3] Their social polish was equally striking. A letter of condolence sent by Mamai Khan to Ivan the Terrible on the death of his father, Vasily III, is remarkable for its good taste and a certain cultivated character.[4] Medieval travellers, such as Pian de Carpini, Ibn Batuta, and William of Rubruck, all afford the strongest testimony to the tolerance and courtesy with which they were treated by the nomad princes, and still more to the elaborate etiquette observed in their courts. The records of Russian envoys to the court of Altyn Khan and neighbouring Mongol princes in the seventeenth century lay equal stress on the elaborate ceremonial, and the love of display.[5] We shall see when we come to examine the narrative poems that great attention is paid to detailed descriptions of even unimportant and everyday matters, such as feasting and the arrival of guests, and the most trivial movements and actions of royal persons. The narratives of the medieval travellers and those of the Russian envoys of the seventeenth century, notably that of Spathary, make it quite clear that this minute and meticulous etiquette is by no means a piece of poetical embroidery, but

---

[1] See Boswell, *S.R.* VI (1927–8), p. 68.   [2] See Czaplicka, *S.Y.* p. 54.
[3] Bury is probably the only historian who has done full justice to this aspect of Tatar culture.
[4] See Karamzin VII, p. 315.   [5] See Baddeley II, p. 204 ff.

a faithful reflection of the custom of barbaric courts, where such trifling matters are invested with all the dignity of a function, if not of an actual ritual. We shall have more to say on this subject also in a later chapter (p. 72 below).

Among the Turkomans the chief is known as a *khan*, and his dependent chiefs, who appear to be regarded as his personal servants, and to correspond to the Anglo-Saxon *þegnas*, are known as *naib*. The military leaders are known as *sirdars*, and are selected according to efficiency and merit, developing eventually into *ak-sakols*, or elders, along with the wealthiest and most influential men of the tribe. The Kazaks are governed by sultans, whose title is hereditary, and who are subordinate to the *khan*, chosen only from the sultans of purely aristocratic lineage.[1] The Kara-Kirghiz tribes are governed by *manaps*, or elders, originally elected, but now hereditary. There are also *bis* who administer the laws, and *batyrs* who are the leaders of the military expeditions. Above the *manap* is the *aga-manap*,[2] who is the head of a confederation of tribes.

Succession is through the male line, though the nature of their traditions suggests that formerly it was through the female.[3] A child of the Kysyl Tatars, when questioned as to his name, also adds (1) his mother's name, (2) his uncle's name, (3) his father's name, in this order.[4] In the absence of written records, great importance is attached to the preservation of the genealogies.[5] Rigid distinctions are made between those sultans who have inherited the blood of the khans without intermixture, and those who are descended from khans by alliance with inferior blood.[6] Vambéry tells us that when two Kirghiz meet, the first question asked is: "Who are thy seven fathers—ancestors?" The person addressed, even if a child in his seventh year, has always his answer ready, for otherwise he would be considered as very ill-bred.[7] The status of women is probably higher than may at first sight appear, though a large part of the heavy work falls to their share. Their position generally is said to be more honourable than among the settled Turks,[8] and would seem to resemble that of the desert Tuareg (see p. 656f. below). The Orkhon inscriptions also point

---

[1] Levchine, p. 398.
[2] Vambéry, *Türkenvolk*, p. 266; cf. Czaplicka, *Turks*, p. 49.
[3] Michell, p. 273f.
[4] Radlov, *Proben* II, p. 645, l. 1281 ff.
[5] Levchine, p. 147.   [6] *Ib.* p. 348.
[7] *Travels*, p. 369; cf. *Türkenvolk*, p. 285.
[8] Vambéry, *Türkenvolk*, p. 268; cf. also Barthold, p. 15.

to the high status of women among the Uigurs in the eighth century. Here the *khaghan* (*khan, kan*), in speaking of his father and mother, gives to the latter the title of 'the Wise (Regent) of the Clan'. When her husband dies, leaving behind two infant sons, the upbringing of the boys is apparently left exclusively in the care of the mother.[1]

We know little of the nature of the personal relationship existing between lord and man, but in regard to payment and property it would seem to be not unlike that which existed between a Teutonic chief and his followers. The chief's immediate followers who surround his person form a bodyguard and court, while he in turn provides for their material needs. An interesting instance of the excellent understanding which subsists between the Turkomans in this matter is mentioned by Fraser who, however, evidently misunderstood the incident himself. Having given a *naib* 50 ducats for a horse he was disgusted to find that the chief, on hearing of the sale, demanded the money from his servant, and deliberately dividing the gold into shares, kept 12 for himself, gave 7 to one of his own sons, 5 to another, and so on till only 4 were left; these he graciously gave back to the *naib*, who received it as a high mark of favour. '"What of it?" was the naib's reply to my burst of indignant astonishment at hearing the story; "is not all I have from the Khan? If I eat a hundred tomauns of his goods, he says nothing to me; I am very well off with what I have got, for, after all, the horse was a present to you, sir, and no doubt the Khan will make it up to me in some way or other." I was as much amused as provoked with this affair, and spoke to the Meerza of it in high terms of disgust. "Ah!" replied he, "great men do these sort of things often: the Naib says true; who can tell but tomorrow he may give him a horse worth sixty tomauns?"[2]

Some such elementary system of banking, which may be called 'accumulating credit' with a chief, is very necessary in a community where money can be of little value, and may well be a source of danger to its possessor. The situation was neatly explained to Levchine by an old Kazak-Kirghiz, who declared that it would be futile for him to sell his vast herds of horses, for he had no need of money which he would have to hide away in a chest, whereas when his herds galloped over the steppe, everyone gazed at them and realised the wealth of their owner.[3]

The material culture of the steppe nomads of modern times is not on a high level. They have no more permanent architecture than a tent; no industries; little agriculture, and that only in isolated districts; and, as

[1] Barthold, *loc. cit.*   [2] Fraser II, p. 325 f.
[3] Levchine, p. 348 f.

we have seen, no trade which can be regarded as organised. The way of life and the mental outlook are barbaric. The picture of the Kazaks given by Levchine[1] is probably not exaggerated, and is equally appropriate to the more virile of the nomads elsewhere—faithless and greedy, inactive in peace, incapable and ignorant of the art of war, though much given to surprise raids, unable to act in concert, but courageous and full of personal initiative—not so much warriors as brigands, whose sole object is booty, and who depart instantly from the neighbourhood of their enemies when this object is obtained. It is perhaps the form of barbarism most widely prevalent among people who have not a large hereditary aristocracy. Yet it is clear that these people are not without their own standards of conduct, and the qualities which go to make a gentleman. The 'aristocratic pride' of the Kirghiz is said to be particularly remarkable,[2] and O'Donovan was evidently impressed during his sojourn among the fiercest of the Turkomans by the refinement and courtesy of their behaviour to their friends and to one another.[3]

By far the most important factor in the life of the Asiatic nomad is his horse, which he undoubtedly regards as his most precious possession. The Turkomans in particular are said to be fond of telling stories and singing songs of their horses. These are said to be in reality wonderful creatures, and prized by the owner more than his wife, his children, even more than his own life.

"It is of interest to mark with what carefulness he brings him up", writes Vambéry, "how he clothes him to resist cold and heat, what magnificence he displays in the accoutrements of his saddle, in which he, perhaps in a wretched dress of rags, makes a strange contrast with the carefully decorated steed. These fine creatures are well worth all the praise bestowed upon them, and the stories recounted of their speed and powers of endurance are far from being exaggerated."[4]

In illustration of these observations by Vambéry regarding the Turkomans, we may refer to a passage in the Sagai poem of *Khan*[5] *Märgän*, in which a certain Altyn Aira begs a boon of the hero. At first Khan Märgän is silent, but is reassured when Altyn Aira says:

> It is not your horse for which I ask,
> It is a man whom I beg of you.
> Will you give him, my friend?

[1] Levchine, p. 339 ff.
[2] Vambéry, *Travels*, p. 369; cf. what Levchine says (p. 348) of the Kazaks.
[3] O'Donovan II, p. 315.   [4] Vambéry, *Travels*, p. 319 f.
[5] The form *kan*, dialect of *khan*, is retained by Radlov in many titles.

Then without further hesitation Khan Märgän replies:

I will give him, friend.[1]

It is a noticeable feature of the Tatar poems, as of the Russian *byliny*,[2] that while the hero may, and often does, forget his heroic quest in the pleasures of eating and drinking, the horse is never at fault, and invariably recalls him to his senses. Over and over again it is the horse which saves the situation. The horse may indeed be said to be the true hero of the Abakan narrative poems.

The superiority of the Tatar horses and horsemanship has rendered their more civilised neighbours to the south an easy prey to their raids. The Turkomans are said to be the hardest riders and the fiercest marauders of the west,[3] while the Great Wall of China and the Chinese Annals and poetry afford eloquent testimony to the raiding propensities of the nomads of the east,—whether Turks, Mongols, or Tungus. Even in the fifties of last century, when Atkinson visited the camp of a Kirghiz sultan, he found that the men had just returned from a successful raid, bringing enormous plunder, and celebrating the event with much drinking and feasting.[4] When Vambéry made his famous journey to Khiva, the caravan elected to travel through a desert so arid that some of the members perished from thirst, rather than travel by the shorter and more convenient route infested by Turkoman robbers, whose proud boast it was that not one Persian could cross their frontier without a string round his neck.[5] The leaders of their raids and marauding expeditions were generally chosen for their personal prestige, and he who showed himself competent in organising a successful expedition soon collected a considerable comitatus.[6]

In considering the intellectual development and the cultivation of oral literature among the Tatars, some caution is necessary, owing to the custom among the richer chiefs, notably those of the Kirghiz and the Turkomans, of keeping a mullah, or educated Mohammedan scholar, in their camps. Atkinson noticed that among the Kirghiz of Jungaria on the slopes of the Alatau Mountains, every sultan and chief had his mullah, who was a very important person in the tribe.[7] In 1878, the late Prof. Bateson met a Russian acting as scribe to the Kazak chief in

[1] Radlov, *Proben* II, p. 69.   [2] Cf. Vol. II, p. 84.
[3] Vambéry, *Travels*, p. 317.   [4] Atkinson, p. 571; cf. *ib*. p. 563.
[5] *Encycl. Brit., s.v. Turks.*
[6] A vivid picture of the procedure by which a comitatus was collected among the Turkomans for a raid is given by Fraser I, p. 377.
[7] Atkinson, p. 571.

an *aul*, or camp, among the Kazaks of the Middle Horde.[1] Vambéry
noted that among the Kazaks in the Khanate of Bokhara, the wealthy
'bays' (i.e. *begs*) were accustomed to search the cities for mullahs to
exercise the functions of teachers, chaplains, and secretaries at a fixed
salary, payable in sheep, horses, and camels,[2] and he mentions that it
was customary among the Turkomans for a chief to receive the *fatiha*,
or Mohammedan benediction, from a mullah before setting out on his
forays.[3] It was in the disguise of a learned Mohammedan dervish that
Vambéry sojourned, an honoured guest, among the fiercest tent-
dwelling Turkoman slave-raiders on the frontiers of Khiva, where he
was frequently forced to try conclusions with the resident mullah.

On the other hand it would be a great mistake to suppose that
Mohammedan culture has wholly superseded the native tradition, even
among those Tatars who have embraced Islam. Indeed among the
nomadic tribes it cannot be said to have penetrated very far. According
to Vambéry, in 1864 only one in a thousand could read or write,[4] and
Venyukov reckoned the same proportion among the Kara-Kirghiz.[5]
Broadly speaking it is certainly true that among the nomadic peoples of
Central Asia written literature is wholly unknown. Education and
writing have no doubt made considerable progress during recent years
in these parts, as elsewhere in the Soviet Republics; but in general the
nomadic and semi-nomadic population is doubtless everywhere still
illiterate.

Oral literature, on the other hand, is universal, and possesses great
vitality. In the art of extemporisation especially the Tatars are past
masters, as the literature which we are about to study will demonstrate.
But the art of memorisation is also cultivated among them, and an anecdote
related of the Kazaks to Vambéry by a distinguished mullah bears
striking testimony to the ready and retentive memory of the nomad.
The mullah was enjoying the hospitality of a chief of the Sargan tribe,
and in the evening after supper he proceeded to relate stories, into one
of which he inserted a poem in the Kalmuck language. On returning
to the same neighbourhood after a lapse of six years, he was not a little
surprised to hear the same story and the same poem recited exactly,
word for word, by a youth who appeared to him to be a stranger.
Upon enquiry, he learnt to his astonishment that the youth had heard
it as a nine-year-old boy from the mullah himself on his previous visit,

---

[1] Bateson, p. 197.   [2] Vambéry, *Travels*, p. 369.
[3] *Ib.* p. 317.
[4] *Ib.* p. 322.   [5] Michell, p. 287.

and retained it faithfully in his memory, despite the fact that the poem was in a foreign language.[1] Even if we make some allowance for possible exaggeration, or for exceptional powers on the part of the youth, the anecdote is interesting as showing that the powers of memory were highly valued and cultivated among these people.

The Turkomans are said to be especially pre-eminent in the art of memorisation. Their professional reciters are as remarkable for their highly specialised memories, and the verbal exactitude of their traditions, as the poets of the Kara-Kirghiz for their facility in improvisation. In the preservation of the past history of their tribes also the Turkomans are said to excel. Valikhanov refers further to Kirghiz tribes in the neighbourhood of Jungaria as notable for the preservation of their tribal and genealogical traditions, which are transmitted from generation to generation by the elders of the tribe, as well as by their poets.[2]

The eastern Tatars in general, however (including the Siberian Tatars, the Kara-Kirghiz, etc.), are said to be far inferior to the Kazaks with regard to historical traditions, and the Tobol and Kazan Tatars are also said to be deficient in this respect.[3] Even such traditions as we find among the Kirghiz and the Abakan Tatars are difficult of verification, owing to our limited knowledge of the history of these people from outside sources. It is clear that Chinese historians have laboured under the same difficulty in attempting to write the history of the Kirghiz and the Kalmucks (cf. p. 119 below). There can be no doubt, however, that traditions are orally transmitted over great distances, and through considerable periods of time. A certain hero Kangza, unknown to history, is said to figure largely in the traditions of the Teleut (Radlov),[4] the Altaians (Verbitski), and the Abakan Tatars (Katanov).[5] The story of the Russian conqueror of 'Siberia', Ermak Timofeevich (cf. Vol. II, p. 59 above), is found with slight variations among the Tatars of the Ob and the Irtish.[6] Episodes from early Nogai and Kazak stories have been heard among the Turkomans; and conversely the great Turkoman

---

[1] Vambéry, *Travels*, p. 292f.   [2] Michell, p. 95.

[3] Czaplicka, *Turks*, p. 56.

[4] See Radlov, *Proben* I, p. 218f.

[5] Czaplicka, *Turks*, p. 56. This hero is mentioned occasionally in Katanov's collection; but the stories in which he figures are too brief to afford much evidence of value—hardly more than brief anecdotes. We suspect that the name is corrupt—for Kan Gzak(?). The latter name occurs in the medieval Russian work, the *Slovo o Polky Igorevê*, as the name of one of the leaders of the Polovtsy.

[6] Radlov, *Proben* IV, pp. 11, 179, 263.

robber and hero Kurroglou is celebrated in songs of the Kazaks.[1] We shall see other examples of the travelling of stories from one part of Central Asia to another in the course of the following pages. It may be added that many legends relating, e.g. to the Kirghiz, are considered indecent by the present generation, which suggests that they have been handed down in their original form; and many words and phrases have been preserved in these traditions which are now obsolete.[2]

In attempting to study the oral literature of the Tatars we have encountered great difficulty, owing to the inaccessibility of much of the material. Scholars of eastern Europe have long been aware of the interest and importance attaching to the native poetry and traditions of the various races of Siberia. As early as 1842 Chodzko published a collection of sagas and poetry relating to the Turkomans and the Tatars of Astrakhan.[3] From 1866–1872 the Russian traveller and oriental scholar Radlov collected and published a series of sagas and poetry relating to the Tatar tribes of the mountains and steppes of Central Asia. Their work is of great value, and has never been superseded. Other collections have also been published, many of them, unfortunately, inaccessible to us. References to these will be found in such bibliographies as those of Czaplicka, *Turks*; Holmberg, *Siberian Mythology*, etc. Under the U.S.S.R. there is probably greater activity in recording the native oral literature of the Siberian peoples than at any previous time; but unfortunately most of this material also has been inaccessible to us.[4]

By far the most important of the collections which have come under our observation are those of Radlov.[5] His work has, however, two

---

[1] So Valikhanov (Michell, p. 100). Some interesting evidence for the historicity of the heroic narratives of the Kara-Kirghiz is given by this writer (*loc. cit.*). Owing to his Kirghiz origin (see p. 8, footnote 2 above), Valikhanov was in an exceptionally favourable position, so far as the critical standards of the time—the middle of last century—permitted, to assess the historical value of the Kirghiz traditions, and to equate them with Russian records.

[2] Valikhanov (Michell, p. 95 ff.). For some remarks on the antiquity of these traditions, see *ib., loc. cit.*

[3] *Specimens of the Popular Poetry of Persia.*

[4] A large number of books which appear to contain collections of native oral literature of the various Siberian peoples are appearing in the catalogues of the various Russian booksellers of Leningrad and Moscow; but our efforts to procure copies of these, by applying directly both to the firms and to their agents, have met with only slight success.

[5] *Proben.* (For full title, see List of Abbreviations at the close of the present volume.) In citing this work, as we shall constantly have occasion to do throughout

serious drawbacks. In the first place little information is given as to the authors or reciters of the poems, or the circumstances in which they were recorded. We are therefore almost wholly ignorant of the literary environment of most of his material. In the second place—and this is perhaps a natural corollary to the above—it is clear that while the collections entered under the names of the various tribes represent the highest literary achievement of these tribes, and the literary forms in which they excel, they do not represent the whole scope of their literary activity. For example, Radlov's collection from the tribes of the Abakan Tatars and the Kara-Kirghiz consists almost exclusively of long narrative poems. Yet he tells us in his introduction to Vol. v that many other (e.g. lyric) forms of poetry were also current among them; and this we know also from Katanov's collection.[1] Radlov's collection in the *Proben* from the Altai and from the Teleut consists principally of brief poems, most of them hardly above the level of folk-tales; yet we know from Radlov himself that these people possessed a fine body of shamanist literature (cf. p. 132 f. below). They also possessed a fine body of heroic traditional literature, as we shall see; and this appears to be true also of the inhabitants of the Sayan Mountains.[2]

The evidence of Radlov's texts leaves no room for doubting, however, that the most highly cultivated form of literature among the Tatars of modern times is narrative poetry, both heroic and non-heroic, and dramatic ritual poetry. Our finest specimens of narrative heroic poetry have been recorded from the Kara-Kirghiz, and are contained in Radlov's *Proben*, Vol. v. The best and longest non-heroic poems were recorded from the same tribes, and from the Abakan and Jüs Steppes and the neighbouring regions on the Upper Yenisei, and these last are contained in *Proben*, Vol. ii;[3] but briefer non-heroic poems were also recorded from the Tatars of the Altai and Sayan Mountains. Our only text of dramatic poetry which can lay claim to anything like completeness is the great dramatic monologue recited by the shaman of

the following chapters, we have, for the convenience of our readers, given our citations of volume and page, not to the original Turkish texts, but to the parallel volumes translated into German.

[1] See p. 18 below; and cf. the List of Abbreviations (*s.v.* Katanov) at the close of the present Part.

[2] *Ib.* pp. 56, 170; cf. Katanov (see List as above).

[3] For the sake of convenience and brevity the contents of this volume are referred to throughout the following chapters as the 'Abakan' poems, though it is to be understood that the Abakan poems form only a portion of the whole. Cf. p. 4 above.

the Altai Tatars, and recorded by the missionaries of the Altai Mission, and included by Radlov in a German translation in *Aus Sibirien*, Vol. II. Panegyric and elegiac poetry are also widespread, and occasional poetry appears to be universal. Of these, however, our collections contain relatively few examples, owing doubtless to their ephemeral character, though a saga Cycle from the Turkomans, recorded by Chodzko, contains many specimens. Saga is found chiefly on the western steppe, and in the valleys of the Ob and Irtish. The third volume of the *Proben* contains a fine collection of sagas and some narrative poetry from the Kazaks. The sagas from the Ob and Irtish, less ambitious in character, are contained in *Proben*, Vol. IV.

It should be added that by no means all the texts contained in Radlov's collection have been included in our survey, which is primarily concerned only with volumes I–V inclusive. Since Radlov's collection is now very rare and not easily accessible, it may interest the reader to have some idea of the contents of the remaining volumes. Vol. VI contains texts from the Taranchi Tatars; Vol. VII, texts from the Crimea; Vol. VIII, texts from the Osman Turks; Vol. IX, texts from the Uryankhai (Soyot), Abakan Tatars, and the Karagasy; Vol. X, texts from Bessarabia. The texts of volumes IX and X were not collected by Radlov himself but by Katanov and Moshchov respectively. Several of the volumes have translations in Russian and German, but Vol. IX is, we believe, the only one which contains material sufficiently free from the influence of foreign tradition to be of importance for our study. With a few exceptions the literature of the Volga and Crimean Tatars has been omitted from our study, because it was felt that the close proximity to Russia rendered the evidence less valuable for the student of Tatar literature. The literature of the Turks of Turkestan has also been omitted. These people have lived for centuries in close contact with the more civilised countries of the south, and have consequently long been familiar with the art of writing or with written literature. We regret, however, the omission of Katanov's collection (Vol. IX) from our survey. Unfortunately, this volume is not easily accessible to us.[1] Unlike Radlov's collection from the 'Abakan' Tatars, the collection of Katanov contains sagas as well as poems—the latter in general much shorter than those of Radlov. It also contains riddles, interpretations of dreams, anecdotes, folk-tales, legends, shaman's prayers, etc. Unlike Radlov's texts from these tribes also, many of the poems are strophic. The

---

[1] We have only been able to consult it occasionally in the British Museum.

volume contains much poetry and prose interspersed, though prose also appears independently. We hope that the omission of Katanov's volume from consideration in the following pages is not important in view of the fact that similar texts are included by Radlov in *Aus Sibirien*, which records his own travels in Siberia. The following pages will be primarily concerned, therefore, with the literature of the Turkomans and of the Siberian and Central Asiatic Turks of the steppes and mountains.

In attempting to present this material to English readers, our task is peculiarly difficult. As Radlov points out,[1] the translation can only reproduce a feeble picture of the original, since many of the expressions which are introduced in the original merely for the sake of rhyme and rhythm appear otiose in the translation. The concepts of the Turkish minstrel belong to a language of totally different affinities from those which are familiar to the English reader. It must inevitably be that something is lost, in some instances perhaps even misinterpreted in the transition, especially in regard to the poetry which relates to the world of shamanistic ideas—a world of thought which is far less familiar to us than that of heroic poetry and saga. It is in the hope of introducing this little known and peculiarly interesting literature to others, who may have time and opportunity to acquire a more intimate knowledge and a wider range of texts than have been possible to us, that we have ventured to put before the reader the following slight and tentative preliminary study.

A word must be said on the subject of metre. According to Radlov,[2] the original Turkish metres were characterised by alliteration, acrostics, and internal rhyme. These original metres have been lost, and in their place we have metres strongly influenced by Persian poetry with final rhymes. This modern Turkish metre is divided into two classes, known among the Kazak-Kirghiz[3] as *ölöng* and *jyr*. The *ölöng* consists of four-line strophes, of which the first, second, and fourth lines have end-rhyme.[4] Each line consists of three feet, and each foot has a sharp accent on the first and last syllable. The caesura between the feet must always fall between two words. The rhyme generally extends to the last

[1] Radlov, *Proben* v, p. xx.
[2] *A.S.* I, p. 501 ff.; *Proben* III, p. xxii.
[3] Radlov, like many other writers, refers to the Kazak as 'Kirghiz', as distinct from the Kara-Kirghiz, or 'Dikokammenoi' (see p. 8 above).
[4] In the Kashgar MS. of poems which was written in 1073 (see p. 65 below) the third line (or half-line) is the one which most commonly rhymes with the first and second, while the fourth is generally, though not invariably, unrhymed.

three syllables, but it often consists merely of assonance. Each of these couplets or quatrains—according to the manner of printing the lines—is complete and independent, and often forms a song by itself.[1] This metre is chiefly used for brief improvised songs and occasional poetry, but is rarely used for narrative poetry of great length. It is the prevailing metre for literary compositions (i.e. those written or printed in books or composed under the influence of written literature). Radlov tells us that the poetry of the Kara-Kirghiz is always sung; and he adds that he has heard some fourteen to fifteen different melodies for the *ölöng*, which is always accompanied by an instrument with two strings resembling the Russian *balalaika*.[2]

The metre to which Radlov refers as *jyr*,[3] like the metre of the Abakan poems,[4] is less subject to strict rule than the *ölöng*. It consists for the most part of three feet, but often only of two, each containing from two to four syllables quite irregularly. An end-rhyme is prevalent, and there is a tendency for groups of approximately equal lines to fall together. In the more finished poetical production, such as many passages in the Kara-Kirghiz poems, a fixed final rhyme often recurs through a number of consecutive lines, and consecutive assonances are still more frequent. This is said to be due in a large measure to the structure of the language.[5] In addition a regular repetition of a refrain line is common. Often the *jyr* are formed of pairs of rhymes, or of interwoven rhymes. In *jyr* it is said that there often appear traces of the original Turkish laws of rhythm,[6] e.g. alliteration, acrostic verse, and internal rhyme. This occurs most frequently in the oldest gnomic poetry, such as the brief poem recorded by Radlov, on the first page of the *Proben*, Vol. III.

This non-strophic metre, with no regular system of rhyme—though end-rhyme is frequent—is employed by professional poets almost everywhere for narrative purposes, especially among the Kara-Kirghiz,

[1] We may compare the brevity and popularity of the Japanese short poem known as the *tanka*.

[2] Radlov, *A.S. loc. cit.* Cf. *Wörterbuch, s.v. ölöng*.

[3] Radlov translates (*Wörterbuch, s.v.*) *jyr, jir*, as 'song'. The word appears to be used in a wide sense. According to Valikhanov it is also used by the Kara-Kirghiz ('Nogai') to denote "tales of olden times" in the form of narrative poetry, which are "perpetuated by a special class of bards". From what Valikhanov says later it is clear that he is referring to poems of the *Manas* Cycle. See Michell, p. 98.

[4] See Radlov, *Proben* III, p. xxiv.

[5] See N. K. Dmitrêv, in the Introduction to *Kogutei*, p. 31.

[6] Radlov has made a study of the traces of the ancient metrical system surviving in the modern poetry of the 'Abakan' Tatars. See *Zeitschrift für Völker-Psychologie* IV, p. 85.

and the Altai and Abakan tribes. It may be fairly said to be the dominant metre for oral narrative poetry among the Tatars as a whole. Indeed among the Kara-Kirghiz it is so much in the ascendant that it is employed even for heroic elegiac poetry by people who are said to be unfamiliar with narrative poetry (cf. p. 61 below). Among the Kazaks also this metre is in common (not invariable) use for narrative poetry.

It is held by Dmitrêv that the *ölöng* represents the most ancient type of Turkish versification,[1] though we have seen that this was not the view of Radlov.[2] Its wide range and general popularity may be adduced in support of this view. It is, indeed, said to be not unknown even for narrative poetry among the Abakan tribes and the Kara-Kirghiz, though unbroken flow of unrhymed lines, the typical 'narrative metre' (*jyr*) of these people, is tending to oust it, and both here and among the Kazaks is more general for narrative purposes. In our view it may be argued that the great popularity of the four-line strophe in Kazak and western poetry as a whole tends to support a more recent derivation of this metre from 'book poetry'. The prevalence of the refrain, and of formulae occupying a whole line, and repeated at regular intervals, points in the same direction.

There can be no doubt that the two forms are struggling for mastery, both in east and west. In the east the evidence suggests that the 'narrative' metre (i.e. the unrhymed, non-strophic) is gaining ground; but it would be unsafe to predict from the amount of material before us. The preponderance of narrative poetry from the eastern Tatars in Radlov's collection must not blind us to the very prevalent custom of extemporising brief strophic poems, which have not been recorded because of their ephemeral character and purely personal interest. On the other hand, if the 'narrative metre' is not an 'original' and 'native' one, where does it come from, and how has it come to be so widely applied to narrative poetry?

In the west, the struggle for mastery between the two metres is aptly evidenced by the Kazak narrative heroic poem of *Kenä Sary*, of which we have two versions, side by side, one in strophic, and one in 'narrative' metre. The latter version is in a fragmentary condition. This evidence rather suggests the encroachment of the lyric metre on the

---

[1] See N. K. Dmitrêv, *J.A.* (1926), p. 305. For a recent discussion by the same author of the metres and rhythms of the oral literature of the Altai Tatars, see Introduction to *Kogutei*, p. 25 ff.

[2] See Radlov, *Proben* III, p. xxii ff.

epic. We shall see later (p. 48 below) that the general form of Kazak narrative, and more especially the relationship of the 'strophic' to the 'narrative' metre, and of both to prose, supports this conclusion. The identity of the strophic metres with the metre of Turkish 'book' poetry, and the influence of Mohammedan culture among the western Tatars generally, suggests that the strophic metre is reinforced from written sources, whether directly or through minstrels trained in a foreign or educated tradition, and Radlov's observation of the archaic metres still retained in ancient texts is of the utmost importance in this connection. The widespread use of the brief strophic form for occasional poetry need cause no surprise, in view of the facilities offered by this form, and we ourselves have no doubt that Radlov was right in regarding the *jyr* as older than the *ölöng*. A study of Yakut metre would be relevant to this question, owing to the conservative character of Yakut poetry, and when Yakut texts are more easily accessible we have no doubt that they will be of great assistance in solving the problem.

Finally some reference is necessary to the musical instruments in use among the Tatars, though we can only mention one or two of the commonest. There can be no question that for the accompaniment of narrative poetry stringed instruments of some kind or other are in general use. The most elaborate of these is perhaps the *chatigan* (*jädigän*). We shall refer later to the love of the Sagai tribes for the *chatigans*, and their reluctance to sell them (p. 178 below). This instrument—a kind of zither—consists of a long cylindrical or oblong box without a lid, sometimes hollowed out of a single piece of wood. The box is, as it were, laid bottom upwards, and the strings are stretched along the outside of the bottom. There are generally five to eight strings in the modern *chatigan*,[1] but in the past it was probably a more ambitious instrument, for in the poems the static description is the 'forty-stringed *chatigan*'. A *chatigan* brought by Czaplicka from Siberia is in the Pitt-Rivers Museum at Oxford. This specimen[2] has six wire strings of equal length, variety of pitch being given by movable knuckle-bones of the reindeer, placed one under each string. The instrument is played by plucking the strings with the fingers of each hand. Probably the instrument is a rude imitation of a Russian *gusli*, though the shape is, of course, very different.

Various other stringed instruments are also in common use for the accompaniment of narrative and other forms of poetry. These generally

[1] Czaplicka, *S.Y.* p. 237.
[2] It is about a yard long, 8 inches wide, 6 inches high.

resemble in a varying degree some kind of fiddle or lute. The Turkomans commonly make use of a Russian *balalaika*, or two-stringed instrument somewhat like a guitar. Vambéry refers to the two-stringed *dütara* of the Turkomans (see p. 176 below), and Valikhanov knew an instrument resembling a *balalaika* among the Kirghiz,[1] which is believed to be derived from the *domra*.[2] Similar instruments are mentioned by Radlov as in use for the accompaniment of the *ölöng*[3] (see above). Verbitski refers to a similar instrument as used by the shamans of the Altai in addition to the drum,[4] and Troshchanski mentions a similar instrument among the Yakut.[5]

An instrument known as a *kobuz*[6] is also widely used to accompany the recitation of poetry. Levchine gives a detailed description of this instrument as used among the Kazaks. He describes it as a kind of violin, but open in front, and concave, and having usually three thick strings of horse-hair. It is played by means of a short bow, and held between the knees.[7] Among these people the *kobuz* is the most important accessory of the *baksha*, who acts as the diviner, seer, and sacrificing priest among the Mohammedan peoples of the western steppe (cf. p. 210 f. below). Verbitski also speaks in one place of the *kabys* or *komus* as a two-stringed instrument in use among the people of the Altai to accompany the recitation of their heroic tales; but elsewhere he defines the *komus* as the stringed instrument resembling a Russian *balalaika* used among the Altai tribes "by the shamans only".[8] The Soyot tribes are said to use the term *komus* for a Jew's-harp, which the Yakut also call *homus*,[9] while the Kirghiz are said to use the term *kobuz* of a shaman's drum.[10]

The Jew's-harp and the reed-pipe or flute are also widespread favourites. These have, of course, little to do with the recitation of poetry, though both appear to be used sometimes in mantic performances, especially to conjure spirits. The drum or tambourine is very general almost everywhere where the shaman is still found. In general,

---

[1] Michell, p. 81.
[2] Lavignac, v, p. 2497.
[3] Radlov, *A.S.* i, p. 504.
[4] Czaplicka, *A.S.* p. 216.
[5] *Ibid.*
[6] Radlov, *A.S.* i, p. 504.
[7] Levchine, p. 385.
[8] See Czaplicka, *A.S.* p. 216.
[9] Czaplicka, *A.S.* p. 216.
[10] *Loc. cit.*

however, the stringed instruments are used for the accompaniment of narrative poetry, the drum and tambourine, and, to a lesser extent, perhaps the pipe[1] and the Jew's-harp[2] in mantic performances, especially those of the shaman.

[1] The evidence for the uses of the reed-pipe for mantic purposes is chiefly literary; see *Proben* I, p. 202; II, pp. 268, 440 ff.; III, p. 145 f.

[2] Among the Uryankhai and among the Buryat of Irkutsk—the latter, of course, Mongols—the Jew's-harp is called a *khur*, and is said to be used by the shamans only. See Czaplicka, *A.S.* p. 216. Czaplicka appears to distinguish here between the Uryankhai and the Soyot; for these tribes see above. Elsewhere (*Turks*, p. 59) she mentions that the Uryankhai are sometimes called Soyot.

CHAPTER II

HEROIC POETRY AND SAGA

NARRATIVE poetry is widespread and highly cultivated throughout the Tatar tribes of the mountains and steppes of Central Asia. Its development is, however, by no means uniform. Heroic narrative poetry is found in its most highly developed form among the Kara-Kirghiz of the Tien Shan Mountains, especially in the neighbourhood of Lake Issyk-Kul, and is said to be cultivated also among the Yakut, though we have no texts of the latter.[1] Non-heroic narrative poetry of an almost equally elaborate form has been recorded in great quantities from the tribes on the steppes and in the valleys of the tributaries of the Upper Yenisei. The two forms are by no means kept rigidly apart. The poetry of the Kara-Kirghiz is distinguished by the liberal introduction of themes which are connected with the spiritual life of the people, while the form and style of the poetry of the tribes on the Yenisei are derived directly from heroic poetry, or are at least such as we are accustomed to associate with heroic poetry. Elsewhere also heroic and non-heroic forms and themes are combined in the same poems. Among the Tatars of the Altai and the Sayan Mountains this combined form is characteristic of much of the best narrative poetry, while among the Kazaks and the Tatars of the Ob and the Irtish a similar form is also characteristic of the prose saga.

The narratives vary greatly in form and length, those of the Altai and Sayan Mountains being in general shorter and much simpler in theme than those of the Tien Shan Mountains or the valley of the Yenisei. Again the proportion of narrative poetry to saga differs considerably in the different areas. Among the Kazaks the form of pure narrative poetry with no prose intermixture appears to be exceptional, though by no means unknown; among the Kara-Kirghiz narrative poetry is universal, and saga is rare. The different areas have, to a great extent, different ranges of theme, which overlap only to a very limited extent. In the present chapter we shall confine our attention to narrative poetry and saga which are primarily heroic in character.

The heroic poetry of Central and Northern Asia appears to be a purely native development, directly inspired by heroic conditions of life,

[1] See, however, p. 66 below.

though the themes relate for the most part to past times. We hear of Yakut poetry relating to events of the seventeenth century (cf. p. 43 below), and in the poetry of the Kara-Kirghiz the prominence of the Uigur state and its high prestige leave no room to doubt that certain elements in the traditions are derived from a period prior to Jenghiz Khan, in whose time the influence of the Uigurs was still powerful. Other features to be discussed later suggest that these poems assumed something of their present form during the religious wars of the seventeenth and eighteenth centuries. But the Tatar Heroic Age continued in some measure down to our own times, and it is undoubtedly this close association of the poems with actual heroic conditions of life in modern times which, despite much which is crude and childish, gives to Tatar heroic narrative genuine literary value in addition to its historical and ethnographical interest.

In the heroic poetry of the Tatars generally, the themes treated are similar to those which we have found in the heroic narrative poetry of other peoples. Among the commonest are raids, single combats, the theft of large herds, revenge and counter-attack, wooings and marriages, the birth and remarkable childhood of heroes, sports, especially horse-racing and wrestling, long journeys and the sundry adventures of a nomadic life. In the poetry which relates to both the actual and the spiritual experiences of heroes, heroic and supernormal adventures are skilfully interwoven, as they are in the *Odyssey*. Poetry of this kind forms a very large proportion of the whole of the narrative poetry of Central Asia. In such poetry supernatural elements are not rare, and visits to the Underworld are a common feature. In the purely heroic poems, on the other hand, supernatural features form only a small proportion of the whole, apart from the love of exaggeration which is general in the literature of barbaric peoples. In such poems the temper is as sober as that of the *Iliad*, and strikingly similar.

The most important body of Tatar heroic narrative poetry or epic is that which was recorded by Radlov from the Kara-Kirghiz last century. Whether for the length and advanced form of the poems, the naturalism of the subjects, or for the realism and polished character of the style, Kirghiz poetry far surpasses the heroic poetry of any of the other Tatar peoples which has come under our notice. In this chapter, therefore, we shall concentrate chiefly on the Kara-Kirghiz epics, and our account of the characteristic features of style will be based chiefly on them. In general, however, it may be said that this analysis of style will hold good both for the heroic poetry and prose saga of the Tatars as a whole, and also for much of the non-heroic poetry, notably for that of the Abakan tribes on the Yenisei, whose poetry constitutes the most important body of non-heroic literature which we possess from these peoples.

The Kara-Kirghiz are said to specialise in epic poetry almost to the exclusion of saga and lyric,[1] and to pay especial regard to finished and polished diction.[2] That these qualities are the result of deliberate artistic effort on the part of the poet, and appreciated as such by his audience, is clear from Radlov's introduction to the volume which contains these texts.[3] Moreover the poetic tradition appears to be quite native to the people. The themes are on native subjects, and the heroes belong almost exclusively to the past history of the Kara-Kirghiz themselves. They rarely overlap with those of the Abakan or Altai Tatars, or with those of the Turkomans, though some of their most important heroes appear also in the heroic narratives of the Kazaks.

An individual feature of the poetry of the Kara-Kirghiz, and one which shows the advanced character of the tradition, is its tendency to fall into Cycles. In this respect it offers a contrast to the poems of the Abakan Tatars represented in Radlov's own collection, which are all independent. The Abakan Tatars share with the Teleut and the Altai Tatars many tales which relate to a certain hero Kangza. The Abakan texts of Kangza[4] have not been translated, however, and this volume appears to be rare. The texts relating to Kangza are very brief (cf. p. 15 above).

Radlov grouped the narrative poems which he recorded from the Kara-Kirghiz into three Cycles, relating to the Mohammedan hero Manas, and the two heathen heroes, Joloi and Er Töshtük. Of these the first is by far the largest, and in many respects the most important. Radlov gives seven poems belonging to this group. They relate the birth of Manas of the Sary-Nogai tribe, the greatest of the Kara-Kirghiz heroes, his early years, his contest with the Uigur hero Er Kökchö and his warfare with the Kalmucks, his marriage with Kanykäi, the daughter of Temir Khan, his death and burial, and his resuscitation.

Manas is not the central figure of all the poems in which he plays a part, together with his comitatus or bodyguard of 'forty friends'. The second poem of the Cycle relates for the most part the conversion of the hero Alaman Bet to Mohammedanism, and his desertion of the hero

---

[1] *Proben* v, p. v.   [2] *Ib.* p. iii.   [3] Cf. p. 179 f. below.

[4] The Abakan texts of Kangza occur in Katanov's collection of texts from this region. His collection forms the ninth volume of Radlov's *Proben*. The volume containing translations appears never to have been published. See p. 18 above.

Kökchö to follow Manas. Alaman Bet is the foremost person in this poem, and Manas does not figure in it till more than half-way through. A large part of the story of *Bok Murun* is occupied with the funeral feast and games arranged by Bok Murun on the death of his father. Here also it is only in the latter part of the poem that Manas becomes the leading figure, and the poem ends with the death of the heathen prince Joloi of the Kara-Nogai in single combat at Manas' hands.

The first poem contains an account of the birth and childhood of the hero. In the opening lines we have a list of his immediate ancestors, and a brief mention of the exact locality of his home and parentage. His father, we are told, is Jakyp Bai, the son of Kara Khan, and his home is on the Chungkar-uja, presumably in the neighbourhood of Jungaria. Jakyp Bai, or Jakyp Khan—for both titles are given to him variously—complains to God that since he married he has had no child, and prays that he may have a son:

> A hero to destroy the Noigut,
> With their decorated stirrups and blue foot-gear;
> A hero to destroy the men of Kokand,
> With their saddles shaped like birds' heads, and their blue coats;
> A hero to destroy the Sarts,
> With their galled asses and their spindle-whorls;
> A hero to destroy the Kazaks,
> With their filthy saddle-cloths, and their steel lances;
> A hero to destroy the Kirghiz,
> Who never cease begging, and are insatiable.[1]

His prayer is heard, and a son is born to him of great promise. Jakyp prepares a feast, and all the guests prophesy good things for the child. The four great prophets bestow on him the name Manas; the seven envoys from Yarkand eat heartily at the feast, and—

"Fiercely will Manas tread Jelmogus[2] underfoot," said they.

Likewise from China come forty envoys. They also eat heartily at the feast, and—

"He will destroy the Chinese," said they.

The ten envoys of the Nogai Tatars sit eating meat, and—

"Fiercely will Manas trample underfoot," said they.

Already while he is still in his cradle Manas begins to speak, and his father forthwith brings him a yellow horse and saddles it, and calling

---

[1] *Proben* v, p. 2, ll. 29 ff.   [2] For *Jelmogus*, see p. 86 below.

to him one Bakai Khan, who seems to be in the position of a fosterer to the hero, he tells him that his son is ready to mount and ride afar, to pass through Medina, and the mighty Bokhara, and to strive with many mighty rulers. Bakai Khan is therefore to wait upon Manas, cook his food, make his fire, teach him what is unseen and unknown, and accompany him on his journeys, and, when he grows to man's estate, teach him the way to salvation by means of the Koran. The brave hero and his companions set out accordingly. At the age of ten Manas shoots an arrow as well as a lad of fourteen:

> When he grew to be a prince, he overthrew princely dwellings;
> Sixty stallions, a hundred horses,[1]
> He drove thither from Kokand,
> Eighty mares,[2] a thousand kymkar[3]
> He brought from Bokhara;
> The Chinese settled in Kashgar
> He drove away to Turfan;[4]
> The Chinese settled in Turfan
> He drove yet farther to Aksu.[5]

By such graphic catalogues the poet makes us acquainted with the sphere of Manas' military activities, and the features of the surrounding peoples which have made most impression on the Kirghiz imagination. On the west the hero evidently enriched himself with the horses of the Kazaks, driving them up the valley of the Jaxartes from Russian Turkestan. On the east he enriched himself at the expense of the Chinese traders in the wealthy cities fringing the Taklamakan Desert in Chinese Turkestan. The mountains separating these two wealthy regions served the hero as a natural fortress from which he was able to enrich himself at the expense of both.

With this brief and disjointed poem the minstrel introduces us to the greatest hero of Kara-Kirghiz epic poetry. Radlov apologises for the defects of the poem, which he attributes to the fact that the poet, in his opinion, had no account of the birth and childhood of Manas in his

---

[1] A *kunan*, a three-year-old foal.
[2] A *baital*, a young mare which has not yet foaled.
[3] The word in the Kirghiz text is *kymkap*. It does not appear in Radlov's *Wörterbuch*, which is no doubt why the original word is also kept in his translation, perhaps with a misprint (for *kymkar*). The number of technical terms used of horses of every kind, age, colour, and type, is one of the major difficulties which confront the translator of Kirghiz.
[4] One of the oases in the north of the Tarim basin.
[5] A city still farther to the north-east.

répertoire, but composed one on the spur of the moment in answer to some questions which Radlov put to him on the subject.[1] The story contains hints of much which is to be more fully developed in the later poems of the same hero—his profession of the Mohammedan faith; his predatory raids and aggressive warfare; his enmity with the Kalmucks and the Chinese; his feud with Kongyr Bai, who is sometimes represented as a Chinese ruler from Peking, sometimes as a local prince, 'Lord of Kashgar and Kokand', and collector of imposts on behalf of his over-lord.

The hero of the second poem in the *Manas* Cycle recorded by Radlov is Alaman Bet, to whom is applied the static epithet 'tiger-like'. By race he is a Mongol, an Oirot, i.e. a Kalmuck, and by birth a heathen; but the poem opens with an account of his conversion to the Moham-medan faith by the Uigur prince, Er Kökchö. During the first part of the poem Alaman Bet is an honoured guest in the retinue of Er Kökchö; but his high prestige arouses the jealousy of the rest of the retinue, and his familiarity with Er Kökchö's wife affords a fitting pretext for his dismissal. This familiarity is merely hinted at here; but a reference to the story in the poem *Joloi*[2] makes it clear that this intrigue is an accepted tradition among the Kara-Kirghiz. The second part of the poem tells us how Alaman Bet, on leaving the camp of Er Kökchö, goes to join Manas, with whom he swears brotherhood, and whose service he never afterwards leaves. The poem is full of interesting and intimate glimpses into local customs and native types. In particular we would call attention to the account of Er Kökchö's hawking on the shore of Lake Issyk-Kul, and of his meeting with Alaman Bet whom he sights on horseback on the opposite shore, the high black Kalmuck lambskin cap on his head, and to the first lesson in the Kalmuck speech which the latter at once gives to his new friend. Other picturesque passages in this vivid poem will be referred to later.

The third poem of the Cycle in Radlov's collection relates the battle between Manas and Er Kökchö, the marriage between Manas and Kanykäi, and the death and resuscitation of Manas himself. The poem opens with a panegyric on the hero, which occupies 84 lines, before the narrative proper begins. This third poem is not well constructed, and the course of the narrative is not by any means always clear. The battle between Manas and Er Kökchö is poorly motivated. Radlov regards it as the natural consequence of the action of Alaman Bet as described in the last poem; but this is not the only interpretation which might be

---

[1] *Proben* v, p. xiii.   [2] *Ib.* p. 515, l. 4843 ff.

put on the narrative, since we have heard in the earlier poem of Manas' aggressive policy, which is doubtless the true cause which first leads Er Kökchö to seek alliance with Alaman Bet. Moreover the poet lays great stress throughout the poem on Manas' subservience to the 'White Tsar' of Russia, and it is probably owing to support from Russian Turkestan that Manas feels himself in a position to attack the Uigurs. Radlov suspected that the emphasis laid on Manas' loyalty to Russia was intended as a compliment to himself. It is, however, to be doubted if the motif was actually invented for this purpose, for it is easy to see that Russian Turkestan and the fierce hill nomads had everything to gain by mutual aid against the powerful Uigur confederacy, backed now by Chinese, now by Tibetan support.

Whatever the true political situation in the background, however, the heroic minstrel characteristically represents the relations between Russians, Kirghiz, and Uigurs as purely personal. Manas rides forth to attack his enemy Er Kökchö in single combat, and the vaunting threats, the jibes, and the series of encounters which take place between them are described in great detail. In the first encounter, which is a wrestling match, Manas is naturally victorious; but when the more civilised Uigur, Er Kökchö, proposes a test by the firing of flint-locks, Manas' aim comes nowhere near him, and Er Kökchö stands laughing at his opponent as he himself takes only too sure an aim, and Manas flees wounded on his horse. Er Kökchö seeks to apply healing herbs to Manas' wound, but the Kirghiz turns and treacherously slays his horse— an act of bad faith not rare among heroes.

A brief account of Manas' visit of homage to the 'White Tsar' is next given, after which we have a detailed picture of a Kirghiz betrothal and marriage. Manas' father, Jakyp Bai, goes to woo Kanykäi, the daughter of Temir Khan, on behalf of his son. His suit is acceptable to Temir, and Manas comes later to take his bride with all the show of force and coarse arrogance characteristic of Kirghiz custom and Kirghiz heroes, while Kanykäi at first resists her violent lover with all the show of resolution proper to a high-born Kirghiz maiden. All is arranged to the satisfaction of both parties; but one Mengdi Bai, a man of Temir's following, who is described as Temir's orator, and as a slanderer by nature, determines to prevent the contract, and suborns two robbers to poison Manas as the wedding-party are on their homeward journey. The third part of the poem contains an account of Manas' death and of his ultimate resuscitation and restoration to health and normal life. It is a strange poem on the whole, and this last part in particular is difficult to understand. We shall see later in Chapter VIII below that there is reason to believe that a number of variant versions have been combined without any great skill, or care to avoid contradictions and overlapping, and that this is probably the chief cause of obscurities in the narrative.

The next poem, *Bok Murun*, is devoted to a magnificent funeral feast, followed by horse-racing and sports. The feast is given by the hero, Bok Murun himself, in honour of the memory of his father, Khan Kökötöi. At the opening of the poem Bok Murun sends his five sons to the surrounding peoples with an invitation to attend the games —an invitation couched practically in terms of a threat to absentees. The enumeration of the heroes to whom the invitations are to be sent constitutes a heroic catalogue closely analogous to that of the Achaean ships in Homer, and comprises what we may regard as a comprehensive list of the heroes celebrated in Kirghiz heroic poetry, including such famous names as Manas, Joloi, Jamgyrchi, Er Töshtük, Er Kökchö, and many others. This is followed by a further catalogue of the neighbouring tribes and peoples through whom Bok Murun proposes to make a raid in order to equip himself with all that is necessary for the coming feast. The great problem before the host is the ordering of the guests and the allotment of shares, for the Moslems and the heathen are constantly at one another's throats. In this contingency Bok Murun consults his spiritual father, Er Koshoi, the great Mohammedan prince, who is constantly referred to throughout the poems as having "opened the gate of Paradise, and cleared the road to the shut bazaars", from which we may assume that he is something of a diplomatist, and has taken the lead in adopting Mohammedanism, and allying himself with Russian Turkestan. Er Koshoi points out that Manas is the best person to keep the heathen in check—has he not just routed the formidable Buryat?—and Manas accordingly appoints the feast and races for the coming autumn.

As the heroes arrive, the minstrel, by a skilful device common to heroic literature,[1] represents the crowd of onlookers as speculating which of the horses will win the race, and this gives an opportunity for the introduction of a catalogue of heroic steeds and their several characteristics extending over 121 lines. The first race is run between Er Töshtük and Joloi's aged wife Ak Saikal, and is won by the hero by

---

[1] For parallels we may refer to the catalogue of heroes in early Irish literature cited in Vol. I, p. 281 ff., and to the *Iliad*, Book XXIII.

supernatural means. A wrestling match next takes place between the aged Er Koshoi and the heathen Joloi, and after a preliminary reverse the Moslem brings the mighty Joloi down. Kongyr Bai, the Prince of China, next comes forward, lance in rest, and carries off the prize of sixty horses, but is pursued and unhorsed by Manas. Other contests follow, in all of which the Moslems are victorious. The latter part of the poem, which is only very loosely connected with the preceding events, relates to a series of raids led by Manas against Er Kökchö and the hero Joloi, in which the latter hero is killed by Manas, and his two sons Oekum Bolot and Törö Bek are slain by Alaman Bet.

The poem of *Kös Kaman* is incomplete. The early part of the story is related with care and in great detail, but the latter part is hurried, and so defective that it is not easy to unravel the exact sequence of events. The subject of the poem is a circumstantial and somewhat varying version of the events related in the latter half of the third poem in the Cycle—the marriage of Manas to Kanykäi, and the death of the hero at the hands of the Kalmucks. The poem opens with an account of Manas' visit to Kanykäi, and her reception of her lover—a scene which differs considerably from the one in the version already alluded to. In *Kös Kaman* we have a delightful and dignified picture of Kanykäi as hostess, as she and her attendant maidens receive their guests. Having set out the brandy, they enter Kanykäi's brightly coloured tent, and she and her maidens present Manas and his followers with corslets brought on wagons from far Kashgar, and fine shirts and hose. They draw on to the feet of their guests long boots reaching to the saddle, and brought on a wagon from Tashkent:

> One took his white steed,
> One opened the door,
> One secured it after the fashion of the Sarts.
> Out of the great golden chest
> They brought strong brandy,
> The 'forty friends' took their seats;
> And when the 'forty friends' were seated,
> Strong brandy was set before them.[1]

The poem goes on to relate a raid of Manas and Alaman Bet against the Kalmucks, and the treacherous visit of a Kalmuck chief to Manas' home in which the hero is slain, though he is revived later by Kanykäi, with the help of a 'prince of Mecca'. The last part of the poem is again difficult to follow, and it would seem that the poet relates in a soliloquy

---

[1] *Proben* v, p. 210, l. 111 ff.

yet another variant version of the wooing of Kanykäi by Manas, and his raid against the Kalmucks.

The two last poems in the Cycle relate to Manas' son Semätäi, and to his grandson Seitäk. Semätäi is born after the death of his father, and his grandfather and cousins plot to murder him, in order that he may not inherit Manas' possessions; but with the help of his mother, Kanykäi, and his maternal grandfather, Temir Khan, the hero escapes and returns at a later time to slay his cousins and old Jakyp Bai, his grandfather on his father's side. The last poem of the Cycle falls naturally into two parts. The first part relates to the closing years of the life of Semätäi, and his murder at the hands of two Kalmucks, one of whom is the son of Alaman Bet. The second part of the poem relates to the birth of Semätäi's son Seitäk, who is posthumous like his father, and to his vengeance for his father's murder. It is Kanykäi herself who strikes the death-blow and drinks the blood of her enemy, a piece of savagery which is the more striking since she is the Kirghiz ideal woman, courteous, gentle, hospitable, wise, and capable. Seitäk settles in the old home of Manas, and lives there as 'ruler of everything between Talas and Tashkent', and so fittingly brings to a conclusion this great Cycle which we have followed through four generations.

The second great poem or Cycle in Radlov's collection is that of the hero Joloi, the Kara Nogai or Oirot prince, son of Nogai Bai, a prince of the 'Ten tribes of the Nogai'. Joloi is a less elevated figure of the heroic ideal than Manas. He is of great size, and so strong that he can overcome whole troops single-handed. This he rarely does, however, as in consequence of his inordinate appetite,[1] he is generally only aroused with difficulty from a drunken sleep by his wife Ak Saikal, or his horse Ach Budan. Ak Saikal generally fights at his side, and displays great activity and strength in battle. She is the heroine of the early episodes of the *Joloi* Cycle even more than Joloi is the hero.

The poem *Joloi* may fairly be called an epic, for the various episodes which Radlov has presented to us follow one another in close sequence, making a coherent and well-ordered narrative. At the opening we see the somewhat ignoble hero, lying on the ground replete, wholly indifferent to the theft of his father's thousand horses and the appeals of

---

[1] It is interesting to compare Levchine's account of the custom of 'heroic eating' among the Kazaks. "Beaucoup de Kirghiz", he writes, "prennent plaisir à contempler les exploits de certains mangeurs fameux qui viennent aux fêtes pour jouir doublement de leur gloire, en engloutissant des quantités incroyables de viande et de koumys" (Levchine, p. 371).

his family. At length by the efforts of his sister Kardygach and his sister-in-law he mounts his famous steed Ach Budan and sets out in pursuit, and finally succeeds in slaying Ak Khan, who has stolen the horses, and in seizing his wife Ak Kanysh. His wonderful horse also carries off for him Ak Saikal, the daughter of a mighty chief Angychal, and she becomes his wife. The poem relates a number of interesting episodes. We hear of the marriage of Joloi's sister Kardygach to the Kalmuck prince Karacha, and of their usurpation of Joloi's principality while the hero is imprisoned by the Kalmuck prince Urum Khan, the overlord of Kongyr Bai, whom we have seen as a Chinese envoy in the *Manas* Cycle. We hear also of the birth of Joloi's son Bolot in Joloi's absence, of the attempts of Kardygach and Karacha to slay the child, of his rescue and upbringing in the *aul*, or nomadic settlement of an old chief Köchpös Bai, by Joloi's two wives, who adopt him as their son, and of his subsequent rescue of his father. The poem ends with Bolot's marriage. Nothing is said here of his death at the hands of Alaman Bet.

The latter part of the poem is largely occupied with an account of the sacrificial feast held by Köchpös Bai and Bolot, and of the supernatural experiences of Bolot in the company of a certain Kara Chach, who is described as Bolot's 'sister' and Köchpös Bai's shepherdess. She is evidently an accomplished *shamanka*, or female shaman, for she wards off the powers of darkness which threaten Bolot's life, and convoys him safely through the perils of the Underworld, and again back to earth. The latter part of the poem is indeed wholly non-heroic in character, being concerned almost exclusively with religious ritual and supernatural and spiritual experiences. We shall therefore consider this portion more fully in the chapter relating to 'Non-heroic Poetry and Saga'.

Even from this brief summary it will be seen that the feminine interest is very strongly represented in *Joloi*. Indeed, the whole course of events from start to finish is determined by Joloi's two wives. The friendship and complete co-operation of these two women is one of the most striking features of the poem. Both Ak Kanysh and Ak Saikal are jointly referred to as the mothers of Bolot,[1] while an obscure passage relating to the aged wife of Köchpös Bai[2] appears to treat her also as one of his 'mothers', though she is, in reality, his foster-mother. Ak Saikal by her prowess, and Ak Kanysh by her prudence, are the real heroines of the poem. Ak Saikal saves her husband again and again from his enemies, and when his own stupidity places him beyond her aid, Ak Kanysh brings up his son in safety and tutors him to a vengeance which

[1] *Proben* v, p. 465.   [2] *Ib.* p. 470, l. 3341 ff.

is skilfully engineered by the two women together, and of which Bolot is only the conventional instrument. They, like Kanykäi, beg and obtain the privilege of administering the death-stroke to their captured enemy. An interesting feature of the poem is the manner in which the centre of interest and sympathy shifts from one group of people to another; from Joloi's home to the court of Urum Khan, and back again, from the place where Joloi lies imprisoned, to the *yurt* of his wives tending the flocks; from there to the home of Köchpös Bai, Bolot's adopted parent, to return for the dénouement to the land of the Kalmucks, and then, after Joloi's deliverance, back to Köchpös Bai. The skill with which the parallel threads are carried on and interwoven is hardly second to that which we find in the *Odyssey*.

The third poem of the Kara-Kirghiz which Radlov gives us is that of *Er Töshtük* ('the hero Töshtük'). This story is known also to other Tatars, where he appears in prose saga (cf. p. 109 ff. below), and where his name is preserved in the form *Jirtüshlük*,[1] and *Jär-Tüshtük*, 'the earth-sinker'.[2] This story, like that of *Joloi*, is presented to us in epic form; but it is wholly occupied with the life-history of a man whose experiences are spiritual rather than material, and whose principal adventures take place underground in the spirit world. We shall therefore reserve fuller treatment of this poem till we come to the chapter on 'Non-heroic Poetry and Saga'. It may, however, be mentioned here that the underground adventures of the hero are similar in many respects to the ordinary heroic adventures of Manas and Joloi, and it is clear from references to the hero himself, and to his famous horse Chal Kuiruk in the Cycles of *Manas* and *Joloi*, that Er Töshtük is also a well-known figure in heroic story. We may refer, e.g. to the poem of *Bok Murun*,[3] where Er Töshtük is brought into relation with Manas and Alaman Bet, and where he is represented as running a race with Joloi's wife.

The three Kara-Kirghiz Cycles overlap to some extent. Er Töshtük, as we have seen, appears in both the *Manas* Cycle and in a long separate poem of which he is himself the hero. Joloi, himself also the hero of a separate poem, is found in opposition to Manas, and it is clear from other references that their orbits intersect.[4] Joloi's son Bolot and his wife Ak Saikal are present at Bok Murun's games. Joloi's great enemy, the Kalmuck Karacha, also feels the heavy hand of Alaman Bet.

---

[1] *Proben* IV, p. 443; cf. V, p. xii.   [2] *Ib.* V, p. xiv.
[3] *Ib.* pp. 162, l. 698 ff.; 169, l. 925 ff.; 173, l. 1034 ff.; 514, l. 4821 ff.; etc.
[4] See e.g. *Proben* V, p. 51, l. 1501 f.; *ib.* p. 146, l. 139 ff.; p. 167, l. 841 ff.

Kongyr Bai, the Chinese tax-collector of the *Manas* Cycle, is sent in *Joloi* by Urum Khan to escort Ak Saikal from the Kalmucks to her own home. Moreover, it is clear that other heroes mentioned in the three Cycles before us are themselves the centres of Cycles of stories to which allusions are constantly made. We hear frequently of Er Koshoi,

> Who opened the closed holy doors of Paradise,
> Who opened the closed doors of the bazaars.[1]

We have no doubt therefore that Er Koshoi is credited with the introduction of Islam among the Nogai, and that he is also the hero of a poem or Cycle of his own. Indeed, he himself gives us a catalogue of the enterprises in which he has taken part, and from the allusive nature of the references it is clear that the audience is expected to be familiar with the stories.

Again, allusions are made frequently in the poems of the Kara-Kirghiz to Jamgyrchi, a Nogai ruler,[2] whose sphere of influence is a constant menace to Er Kökchö, and who is regarded by Manas as a foe of equal standing. There can be no doubt that he also is the hero of Kara-Kirghiz poems which celebrate him as an individual hero. We shall see as we proceed that the encounters of Jamgyrchi and Er Kökchö are also the subject of heroic narrative among the Kazaks.

In general the Cycles of the Kara-Kirghiz draw their themes directly from life. The lives and adventures of the heroes and heroines are portrayed in a natural setting, and allowing for a certain amount of exaggeration or poetical exaltation, and what we may term the heroic manner, their habits and actions are described for the most part with simple realism. Their faculties and bodily strength are those of mortals. Their journeys, unlike those of the heroes and heroines of the poems from the Abakan and neighbouring steppes to be considered later, are confined to the regions of earth, and do not take them further from home than might be expected of great men on superb steeds. The characterisation of the poems is equally convincing, though, as befits epic poetry at its best, there is no subtlety. The characters are presented quite naturally, partly by the wealth of detail, partly by the unerring selective power of the narrator. As an example of the briefer method of characterisation applied to the minor characters we may refer to the passage which describes how Ak Erkäch, the wife of the Uigur prince Er Kökchö, sees the Kalmuck hero Alaman Bet riding towards the house,

[1] Cf. e.g. *ib.* p. 18, l. 394ff.; *ib.* p. 142, l. 27ff.
[2] E.g. *ib.* p. 75.

and which shows her busily arranging her toilet and preparing to meet
him:

> Ak Erkäch, the high-born beauty,
> —Her gaily adorned head-dress
> She set upon her head,
> She parted her hair to the right,
> And arranged it on the right side;
> She parted her hair to the left,
> And arranged it on the left side.
> Her golden snood
> She fixed to the end of the moon,
> Her silver snood
> She fixed to the end of the sun;[1]
> Like a puppy she sidled,
> Like a puppy she whimpered,
> Displayed her teeth in laughter,
> Scattered fragrance by her breathing,
> Frisked like a young lambkin,
> Her ringlets fell to her shoulders.
> Ak Erkäch, the prince's daughter,
> Passed out through the door,
> And Alaman Bet, her hero,
> She encountered on her way.[2]

It is not difficult to picture to ourselves this frivolous and excitable
woman, and we are fully prepared for the intrigue which follows, and
the resulting breach between Ak Erkäch's elderly husband and the
gallant young Kalmuck hero.

In the poems of this Cycle, as in the Russian *byliny*, there seems to be
no fixed rule or precedent as to the limits of the incidents to be treated
in a single poem. The poem on the birth of Manas is more or less
restricted to the subject suggested by the title. The poem on the
conversion of Alaman Bet, his dismissal by Er Kökchö, and his subsequent compact with Manas, forms a complete unity of incident. On
the other hand the incidents of the third poem—the battle between
Manas and Kökchö, etc.—are only loosely connected in the poem as we
have it. Any of the incidents might have been omitted, or any incidents
from other poems added without alteration to the structure. It seems
clear that the Kara-Kirghiz minstrel, like the reciter of the Russian
byliny, selects his incidents according to his own mood, and according

---

[1] These are probably metal ornaments shaped like a sun, a crescent, etc., worn
by the women.
[2] *Proben* v, p. 38, l. 1023 ff.

to the temper of his audience, from the wealth of relevant incident in his répertoire. And this is done with very varying talent and constructive ability, and also with varying success according to the minstrel's mood.

From this brief account of the poems it will be seen that the *Manas* Cycle is a collection of individual epic poems, each concerned with the deeds of a different hero or group of heroes. This is true also of the poems of the Abakan Tatars; but there is a difference. Whereas the latter are all wholly, or almost wholly independent of one another, the distinctive feature about the Kara-Kirghiz poems is that the personnel of the various poems overlap. They are all contemporaries, and most, if not all, are known to one another. Practically all the heroes of the *Manas* Cycle figure in most of the poems, but with varying degrees of prominence. The *Manas* Cycle is, in reality, a picture of the life and activities of the chief heroes of a certain branch of the Nogai Tatars at a given period.

In view of the overlapping of the characters to which reference has been made above, it might be supposed that the poems *Joloi* and *Er Töshtük* ought to be included in the *Manas* Cycle equally with the poem on *Bok Murun and his Sons*; but this is hardly the case. Although Er Töshtük figures in the poem devoted to *Bok Murun*, his rôle is but slight; and although Manas figures in the poem *Joloi*, it is abundantly clear that for the minstrel's present purpose Joloi is the more interesting and important figure—for the moment his hero, whereas Manas, however great his actual prestige, is moving for the nonce on the outer orbit of Joloi's sphere. The Kara-Kirghiz poems indeed stand midway between the poems of the Abakan group on the one hand, each of which as we have said, is completely independent, and the Russian *byliny* on the other, each of which contains the adventures of an individual hero, but which are linked by the central though somewhat impassive figure of Prince Vladimir. In the Manas poems the central figure is far from being impassive. He is at times himself the central figure, and very active, though in certain poems the most active heroes are his relatives, friends, or followers, and the most important deeds are not always performed by the hero himself.

It would seem that in the Manas poems we have a 'Cycle' in the making. A petty prince of the Sary-Nogai is in process of acquiring a literary prestige which is doubtless in excess of such political or military influence as he may have actually possessed. This literary prestige is undoubtedly to be ascribed to the minstrels of the Kara-Kirghiz. We have seen that the minstrels also attach great importance to the conversion of Manas' sworn brother, Alaman Bet, to Mohammedanism, and to the devotion of Er Kökchö and Er Koshoi to Islam. There can be little doubt, therefore, that the Mohammedan influence in the Cycle, however superficial and recent, is strong, and it is very probable that it is to the influence of Mohammedan minstrels that Manas owes something of his prestige, and the Cycle such unity as it possesses. To be more specific, it would seem to be not improbable that such leaders as adopted Mohammedanism would gain a certain amount of political support from Russian Turkestan, which would enable them to acquire wealth and prestige above their neighbours—the surest way to the support and adulation of the professional minstrel.

The poems discussed above share in general those features which we have seen to be characteristic of heroic poetry elsewhere. In fact the resemblance both in form and style is surprisingly close. Granted the unfamiliarity of the environment, and of experiences incidental to a nomadic, as opposed to a settled, existence, the types of characters depicted and the action of the poems are closely analogous to those of the Homeric poems and of *Beowulf*. The literary features are also very much the same. We have the same wealth of description and leisurely narrative, the same love of epic formulae and static epithets, the same bizarre and picturesque splendour of the scenes.

In particular the minstrel loves to dwell on minute descriptions, and to expand his narrative by means of repetitions and the introduction of long speeches and catalogues, the latter often included in the speeches themselves. These not infrequently occupy several pages, and some examples have already been referred to. Dialogue of the kind which reflects the casual discourse of daily life, or the *stichomuthia* of Greek tragedy is unknown, as elsewhere in heroic poetry; but formal councils are not rare. We may refer to the deliberations which take place before Bok Murun's games, and note the leisurely manner in which the heroes express themselves at length. Interruption or 'cutting short' is unknown, and the decorum of conversation is always preserved. The exact words spoken on all occasions are so consistently reported that we are even given the exact words of the Kalmuck and Mohammedan greetings, though the minstrel feels the necessity of translating the words to his audience. The lessons in Kalmuck idiom which Alaman Bet gives to Er Kökchö,[1] and which the Kalmuck messenger from the Crimea gives to Kyrgyn Chal,[2] give the audience also the instruction which will stand

---

[1] *Proben* v, p. 8 f., l. 63 ff.   [2] *Ib.* p. 217, l. 345 ff.

them in good stead on similar occasions. The first meeting between Alaman Bet and Er Kökchö is described as follows:

> Alman Bet, the Tiger-like,
> —On his head a high black cap—
> Came riding towards him.
> When Kökchö saw him terror seized him.
> Alman Bet looked on Kökchö:
> "Altai! Altai!" cried he,
> "Jaby! Jaby!" cried he,
> "Möndü! Möndü!" cried he,
> "Kalakai kashka!" cried he,
> "Bichik solon!" cried he....

Thereupon Kökchö answers:

> "I do not understand your speech."
> Then thou spakest, Alman Bet:[1]
> "When I say 'Altai, Altai',
> I ask after your welfare;
> When I say 'Jaby, Jaby',
> I ask after your health;
> When I say 'Kalakai kashka',
> I ask: 'Have you a prince?'
> When I say: 'Bichik solon',
> I ask: 'Have you a lord?'"[2]

The speeches frequently repeat the narrative, which is then given in the identical words which have just been spoken. By this means speeches are utilised very widely for lengthening the narrative by repetition—always a favourite device of heroic narrative poetry. Among the Kara-Kirghiz the actual narrative and descriptions are frequently expressed in the form of speeches. An interesting instance of this is the detailed description which Joloi's sister-in-law gives to the hero of some food which she has prepared for him to give to his son Bolot, narrating the various processes in the preparation of the food, so that what is in effect a cookery recipe is transformed into a narrative of action conveyed in the form of a speech:

> In the year now past,
> I slaughtered a thousand mares, Khan Joloi.
> All the flesh of these thousand mares
> I cut into very narrow strips;

---

[1] This particular idiom introducing reported speech occurs also in the Russian *byliny*.
[2] *Proben* v, p. 8, l. 63 ff.

> I laid them in salt for six days,
> Then I pounded spices very fine,
> Strewed them on the meat.
> In the sun I dried it hard,
> Then I ground it in the mill,
> That it should not be coarse grained;
> Then I sieved it through a silken sieve,
> Brought out pestle and mortar,
> Assembled women and maidens,
> And had it pounded still more finely;
> Put it in a leather bag,
> Placed it in a leather satchel,
> Hung it up beside the fire,
> Bound it to the side of the cauldron.[1]

As in the Homeric poems the movements and actions of heroes and their wives are presented to us with great fulness. When a hero starts on a journey every detail of his movements is minutely set forth. He rises from his seat, he goes towards the door, he or his wife unfastens his horse from the post, and the process of saddling and bridling is meticulously related—not a strap is omitted, not a buckle is left to the imagination. Finally he mounts, he seizes his whip, and away he goes. The elaborate account of the preparations made by Manas and his followers for the journey to the funeral feast and games held by Bok Murun affords a lively picture of the bustle of a Kirghiz camp on the move:

> Bring horses for riding...
> Bring the cauldron hastily.
> To-day is the day for riding.—
> Our golden tent of white camel hair,
> Bind it up, fold it tightly...
> Lay on my white steed[2]
> My leopard-skin saddle cloth.
> On his head place a red bridle,
> Tie on him the blue falconer's drum,
> Bring him to me by the leading rein,
> And the golden white tent
> Bind well and truly to my pack-horse.[3]

The diction of the poems is very conventional. Static adjectives are universally used; e.g. 'high horse', 'red sun', 'golden bed, table', etc. Every hero is distinguished by a static epithet, e.g. 'Alaman Bet, the

[1] *Proben* v, p. 503, l. 4439.
[2] For *kunan*, see p. 29, footnote 1 above.   [3] *Ib.* p. 153, l. 372 ff.

tigerlike', 'Adshu Bai with sharp tongue', 'Er Joloi with a mouth like a drinking horn'; and many others occur in the numerous catalogues of the members of Manas' retinue. A phrase commonly applied to a hero is 'he whom no horse can carry'. To every hero is attached the name of his horse as we attach a surname, e.g. 'Alaman Bet of the Yellow Piebald'. Even cities and nations are also designated by a static descriptive phrase, e.g. 'Bokhara with six gates', 'the Russians with hairy mouths' (a reference to the Russian custom of wearing beards), 'the jabbering Chinese whose language no-one understands', 'the stinking Kalmucks with round tasselled caps, who cut up pork and tie it to their saddles', 'the Sarts who love their asses as if they were horses, and who carry their bread in their bosoms'. A vast number of static phrases are used as a standardised currency to supply the required expression for all occasions, and many of these are not to be understood literally, as when a promising baby hero is born and we are told that the upper half of him is of gold, the lower half of silver; and that he pronounces the word 'mother' at the end of two days, and 'father' at the end of seven. Finally it may be mentioned that here, as in heroic poetry elsewhere, a large number of motifs are also static and recur constantly in analogous circumstances. Formal speeches, such as warnings and lamentations, are sometimes couched in figurative or allegorical language, and are introduced with a certain deliberativeness: 'Ak Saikal now stood up and raised her voice', or 'spoke loudly'.[1]

Before leaving the narrative poetry of the Tatars, a word may be said of the poems of the remaining groups. Among the Tatars of the Altai and Sayan Mountains, narrative poetry is widespread, and relates in general to princes and aristocratic or famous heroes.[2] It would seem probable that a large body of heroic narrative poetry has been flourishing among these peoples in comparatively recent times,[3] though little beyond the few short examples in Radlov's collection has been accessible to us. Heroic narrative poetry appears to flourish also among the Yakut on the R. Kolyma, though very little information on this subject has been at our disposal. From incidental remarks in the narrative of Shklovsky, we learn that these people have epics relating to the great Yakut leader Djennik, under whom they revolted in the seventeenth century. These epics are said to be remarkable for their richness and wealth of imagery, and for their realistic detail[4] (cf. p. 122 below). The operation of flaying is described with great

[1] *Proben* v, p. 410, l. 1299.　　　　[2] *Kogutei*, p. 7.
[3] *Ib. loc. cit.*　　　　[4] Shklovsky, p. 209.

minuteness, details even being given as to what kind of knives were used. Unfortunately, however, we have no texts, and we do not know if any have been recorded.[1]

Both narrative poetry and saga are found among the Kazak-Kirghiz. The examples in Radlov's collection sometimes consist of pure narrative poetry, such as *Sain Batyr*, but more often of a combined form of narrative poetry and saga. The latter form appears to be practically confined to the Kazaks, among whom it has been developed to a high degree of artistic excellence. All the narratives from the Kazaks which we are about to consider, with the exception of *Sain Batyr*, are of this class.

Sain Batyr,[2] which is proper to the Little Horde, was obtained by Radlov from a MS. It consists of 1882 lines, and relates to the warfare between the Nogai and the Kalmucks, and is closely akin, both in theme and style, to the poems of the *Manas* Cycle. The hero, a Nogai Tatar, goes to assist a certain Kublanda, a hero of the Kara-Nogai, in his encounters against the Kalmucks, but is abandoned in the thick of the fight by his own followers and by Kublanda himself, and is left on the field sorely wounded. His retainers ride home and report him dead, but his wife and mother ride to the spot where the hero lies, and under their care he soon recovers from his wounds. They themselves are captured by the Kalmucks; but at this point his two sons ride to Kublanda to beg his help, and the three together attack the Kalmucks, and with the help of Sain overcome them and rescue the two women. It is difficult in this brief summary to do justice to the admirable proportions and literary quality of this narrative, which has all the heroic characteristics of the Kara-Kirghiz poems, together with the skill in managing episodes and multiple characters which we shall see to be the special prerogative of the Abakan poems. As already stated, Sain is the only example in Radlov's collection of a Kazak narrative poem with no prose intermixture, but its excellent qualities make it improbable that it is an isolated example of its kind, and its affinities with the poetry of the Kara-Kirghiz can hardly be accidental. We shall see presently that certain stories and heroes of the latter are known also to Kazak tradition, and it seems probable that Sain is a Sary-Nogai hero, and even that the poem itself has been introduced to the répertoire of the Kazaks from the Sary-Nogai, or some other branch of the Kara-Kirghiz.

Perhaps the most famous Kazak narrative is *Kyz-Zhibek*, which is best described as a heroic romance. This story is current in a number of variant versions, and perhaps in a number of variant forms. It is not

---

[1] Cf. however p. 66 below.   [2] *Proben* III, p. 205 ff.

contained in Radlov's collection, and the only version which we have seen is a Russian translation in the characteristic Kazak form of alternating prose and poetry. The poetry far exceeds the prose, however, and comprises both narrative and speeches, often repeating what has been narrated in prose immediately before. The prose thus serves to some extent as an introduction and commentary, and may not be an original feature of the work, though, as we shall see, the form is the one most usually found among the Kazaks. The late Prof. William Bateson, writing from the bank of the Shu River near Lake Balkash in the Great Horde in 1887, mentions that he had 'found a copy of a national song of an epic sort, telling of the loves of *Talighun and Djupek*, and of a war with the Kalmucks', which manifestly refers to Kyz-Zhibek and her first husband Tulegen, and which suggests that the version referred to may have been wholly poetical in form. Bateson further adds that he bought the copy for 1*s*. 8*d*., so we may presume that written versions were no longer rare at that time.[1] The story was current in oral form long before this, however, as we know from the testimony of old Kazaks, who heard Kyz-Zhibek from the lips of their grandfathers, and from the old *akin*, or native singers of extempore poetry. Russian scholars attribute it on internal evidence to the fourteenth or fifteenth century.[2]

The story relates to the wooing of the heroine Kyz-Zhibek, whose *aul*, or camp, is on the R. Yaïk, by a young chief of the Little Horde named Tulegen. Tulegen first hears of Zhibek from a merchant sojourning in his father's *aul*, and sets off to find her. Her father's chief counsellor, who is described as his 'vizier', befriends Tulegen, and introduces him to Zhibek. The two are united, and Tulegen stays three months in Zhibek's *aul*; but Zhibek has already been betrothed to a hero named Bekezhan, by her father, and her rejected lover causes Tulegen to be murdered by robbers as he is returning to Zhibek after visiting his

---

[1] Bateson, p. 166. Bateson's copy may have been one of the versions which were written down in Arabic script in Kazan during the nineteenth century. At the end of this century the famous native poet and scholar Zhusupbek twice worked over the oral narrative; and the Russian translation referred to above, which was presented to us by the kindness of Prof. Minns, was made by the famous Kazak poet Saken Sefullin from Zhusupbek's version. See the Introduction to *Kyz̧-Zhibek*, p. 3 ff. It is impossible for us with our limited resources to gauge how much is due to Zhusupbek, but the internal evidence of the version before us makes it extremely improbable, as the editors point out (*loc. cit.*), that the character of the original narrative has been substantially changed.

[2] Kyz-Zhibek, *loc. cit.*

father in his old home. In revenge Zhibek's brothers kill Bekezhan. Eight years later Tulegen's younger brother Sansyzbay goes to seek tidings of him and learns of his death. Following Tatar custom he seeks the hand of his brother's widow, but her father has again betrothed her, this time to a Kalmuck khan. Zhibek, however, sits weeping in her *yurt* while the wedding festivities are in progress, and on learning of Sansyzbay's arrival, she rides away over the steppe to meet him on one of the khan's horses. The khan pursues the fugitives, and a fierce combat takes place between himself and Sansyzbay; but the khan is slain, and in the battle which ensues between his Kalmuck followers and the followers of Zhibek's father, the latter are victorious, and the bride and bridegroom are happily united.

The examples of heroic narrative which Radlov cites from the Great and Middle Hordes consist, like *Kyz-Zhibek*, of prose and poetry interspersed in varying degrees. In the poem *Kosy Körpösh*, the narrative, which runs to 36 pages, consists almost wholly of poetry. The poem, like the latter, may be best described as a heroic romance; but the setting follows the conventional lines of Tatar heroic poetry elsewhere, and the romantic element may have been developed under foreign (Mohammedan) influence. The hero, Kosy, and the heroine are betrothed in infancy; but the hero's father dies soon afterwards, and his wife and son are reduced to penury. The heroine's father regrets the betrothal, and seeks to marry his daughter to a neighbouring chief; but the hero, by the advice of an old woman, seeks his betrothed in the disguise of a beggar, and wins her love. The frustrated bridegroom seeks to kill Kosy, but in this version he is himself slain by the heroine, who is happily united to her lover. In a version of the same story from the Baraba Tatars, however, the bridegroom chosen by the heroine's father succeeds in killing Kosy, and the heroine stabs herself on the dead body of her lover.

The Kazak version is composed almost wholly in the form of narrative poetry. Only two prose passages are introduced into the poem, and one is added at the end. It is interesting to note that a variant of this version is published in Berezin's *Chrestomathie* (pp. 70–162) which apparently consists wholly of verse,[1] while the other version from the Baraba Tatars, to which we have just referred, consists of mingled prose and verse, the latter being confined to the speeches (cf. p. 49 below). In both the Kazak and the Baraba versions the poetry is exclusively strophic, and in the former the refrain is used with a persistence which

[1] See Vambéry, *Türkenvolk*, p. 297 f.

strikes us as strange and distracting in a long narrative poem. This feature, and the excessive use of repetitions, give a lyrical tone to the poem, which again is disturbing in a lengthy narrative. The whole gives the impression of a hybrid ballad.

Three other heroic narratives of considerable length are recorded by Radlov from the Kazaks, and, like *Kyz-Zhibek*, they consist of alternate passages of verse and prose. Of these *Er Kökshü* and *Dshelkildäk* consist of rather more prose than verse, while *Er Targyn* contains a preponderance of verse, which sometimes continues in an uninterrupted flow for several pages. *Er Kökshü* and *Er Targyn* are typical heroic narratives, while *Dshelkildäk* contains a considerable proportion of non-heroic matter.

The opening of *Er Kökshü*[1] is somewhat obscure in the Kazak version. The story seems to be somewhat as follows. Er Kökshü, who is here represented as a young man, and the head of ten tribes of the Nogai, is raided after the death of Örmön Bet by Dshangbyrshy, himself the chief of a thousand followers. Er Kökshü's 'spiritual kinsman',[2] Manasha, who is the head of 'forty friends', also takes part in the battle. When all their men have perished, Er Kökshü and Dshangbyrshy decide not to fight themselves, and they accordingly drive off the animals, dividing the booty between them. Er Kökshü finds that his 'spiritual kinsman' Manasha has been wounded in the forehead by an arrow, and this he withdraws and applies healing medicines. He himself however dies of his wounds, and is buried by Manasha, who thereupon seizes his share of the booty, cheating Er Kökshü's son and heir, Kosai. The rest of the story relates the adventures of Kosai, his efforts to avenge his father, and finally the death of Temir Bai, the son of Dshangbyrshy, at his hands.

The similarity of these names to those of the Kara-Kirghiz heroes cannot be fortuitous. The name of the hero, together with Dshangbyrshy and Manasha, is manifestly identical with Er Kökchö, Jamgyrchi, and Manas, while Örmön Bet must be Alaman (Alman) Bet. The hostile relations between Er Kökchö and Jamgyrchi also reappear in the Kazak story. In spite of obscurities and differences of detail, the relations of the three great heroes—Er Kökshü, Manasha, and Dshangbyrshy—appear to be substantially the same as in the Kara-Kirghiz poems, where Er Kökchö is harassed by the depredations of his neighbours, Manas

---

[1] *Proben* III, p. 112 ff.
[2] From the Kara-Kirghiz Cycle of *Manas* (Manasha) we know that Manas and Er Kökchö are both Mohammedans.

on the one hand, and the powerful Jamgyrchi on the other. In the Kazak story, however, Er Kökshü is still a young man. The story of *Er Targyn* takes place during the lifetime of Örmön Bet, and therefore a trifle earlier than Er Kökshü. It is a typical story of adventure. The Kirghiz hero Er Targyn, having slain a man of his own people, flees to the Nogai, where by his bravery he rises to be the leader of the khan's troops. Having eloped with the khan's daughter he joins Örmön Bet, the prince of the Nogai, and routs the Kalmucks, and obtains the daughter of Örmön Bet as his second wife. The story of *Dshelkildäk* relates to the misfortunes of the family of the brother of Nörmön (?Örmön) Bet at the hands of a heathen prince, Telägäi, who is also a great magician and controller of the weather, and it also tells of their rescue, and the death of Telägäi at the hands of the youthful hero Dshelkildäk. Although the kernel of the story is a raid, and the vengeance of the injured, and although the style is heroic throughout, the victories on both sides are achieved as much by magic as by valour.

One of the most interesting, and at the same time the most problematical, features of these Kazak stories is the relationship of the poetry to the prose. Much of the prose has all the appearance of a paraphrase from heroic narrative poetry. Sometimes the corresponding passage in poetry actually overlaps the prose paraphrase, as in *Er Kökshü*, p. 116, and as is common in *Kyz-Zhibek*. More frequently, however, the poetical passage on which the prose appears to be based is omitted, as e.g. in *Dshelkildäk*, p. 136. Other prose passages, such as the dialogues in *Er Targyn*, pp. 155 and 169, are wholly foreign to the style of epic poetry, and have manifestly been composed directly for the place which they now occupy. In these formal characteristics the stories bear a close resemblance to the early Norse *Hervarar Saga*, Ch. XII ff., and it seems probable that all our texts are based on narrative poems which have been in part forgotten, or which are giving way under the influence of saga. On the other hand many of the poems contained in the sagas, more especially the speech poems, would seem either to be independent poems inserted into the sagas at appropriate points, or else to have been composed directly for their present context. This is probably the case in regard to the poems in *Er Targyn*, pp. 171 ff. and 180 ff. It is to be noted that whereas the poetry which appears to be original epic material consists of both narrative and speech poems, the poetry which appears to be either independent, or composed for the place which it now occupies, consists almost wholly of speeches.[1]

---

[1] It would be of interest to our study of the relationship of the poetry to the prose in these and other narratives to be considered presently if we could know more

The form of narrative which we have seen to be characteristic of the Kazaks, and which consists of mingled prose and verse, and of prose narrative interspersed with speech poems, is characteristic also of the Tatars of the Ob and the Irtish. Examples are *Kosy Körpöẕ, Idägä Pi, Toktamysh Khan*, and *Kur's Son*. The last is a heroic prose narrative from the Tobol Tatars, containing a number of speeches in verse, and is distinguished from the rest by being signed with the narrator's name.[1] It is to be suspected that the story is of foreign origin. We have already seen that the story of *Kosy Körpöẕ*[2] is found also in the form of a narrative poem among the Kazaks. In the Baraba version the narrative is confined to prose, while most of the speeches are in verse, and where poetry is employed in heroic narrative this seems to be the usual custom among the Tatars of this region.

The story of *Idägä Pi*[3] from the Baraba Tatars relates the life and adventures of the hero Idägä Pi in the service of Toktamysh Khan. He incurs the enmity of Toktamysh and is forced to flee, and the story passes on to relate the downfall of Toktamysh at the hands of Idägä Pi's son Myradyl, the quarrel between Myradyl and his father, Myradyl's usurpation of the throne of Toktamysh, and the final vengeance of Toktamysh's son Ismail. The same story is related in a variant form among the Kurdak Tatars.[4]

By far the most elaborate development of heroic saga with which we are familiar is the Turkoman prose Cycle of Kurroglou, which was written down by the traveller Chodzko from the dictation of native

of the relationship of poetry to prose in the various versions of the story of the ancient hero Kesar, king of Ling, who figures in oral prose narratives and poems throughout Tibet, Mongolia, and Ladakh. Mongolian prose versions of the story are in existence in a written form; Tibetan poetic and prose versions in oral form. What may be called the 'classic' form of the story, as it is found in central Tibet, has the form of epic poetry; while the version published by Francke from Lower Ladakh is chanted to-day by the Bedas, or groups of village minstrels and entertainers, in a form of poetry largely interspersed with prose. Similarly the shorter episodic narratives from the same story or cycle, which Francke regards as originating in the lateral valleys of Ladakh, are composed in a form of mingled prose and verse. See A. H. Francke, *Tibetische Hochzeitslieder* (Darmstadt, 1923), p. 1; *Ib. A History of Western Tibet* (London, 1907), p. 53; C. Bell, *The People of Tibet* (Oxford, 1928), p. 10; A. David-Neel and the Lama Yongden, *The Superhuman Life of Gesar of Ling* (London, 1933). Cf. also the prose version edited from a version printed at Pekin by I. J. Schmidt under the title of *Bogda Gesser Chan* (St Petersburg, 1836).

[1] *Proben* IV, p. 328. [2] *Ib.* p. 12 ff.
[3] *Ib.* p. 35 ff. [4] *Ib.* p. 164 ff.

rhapsodists during a sojourn of eleven years on the shores of the Caspian and in northern Persia, and which was translated into English by the same author.[1] This Cycle consists of narratives of the life and adventures of Kurroglou, a great bandit hero and accomplished minstrel who is believed to have lived in the latter half of the seventeenth century (cf. p. 122 below). It is divided into thirteen *mejjliss* (lit. 'meetings', or rhapsodies) which are self-contained prose narratives related independently, and which are said to last as long as the narrator may think advisable.[2] These thirteen *mejjliss* fill in all 327 pages in the English translation.

In scope and form the Cycle of Kurroglou bears a close analogy to the Kara-Kirghiz Cycle of Manas. Like the latter it contains a number of heroic stories, all of which relate to the great hero, though here also it cannot be said that he is in every case the most prominent person in the story. It would seem that in the Turkoman Cycle, as is probably the case also in the *Manas* Cycle, a number of adventures, originally proper to a number of different heroes, have been swept up in the course of time into the Cycle of the chief hero, thus contributing their quota to the great Turkoman classic. Like the Kara-Kirghiz stories also, those of Kurroglou begin with the childhood and early years of the hero, and cover a lifetime; but while the former continues with an account of the hero's son and grandson, the Kurroglou Cycle ends, at least in Chodzko's record, with the hero's death.

The stories told of Kurroglou and his troop of bandits consist largely of accounts of plundering expeditions, the object of attack being most frequently the merchant caravans encamped in the meadows below Kurroglou's mountain stronghold. Other favourite themes are the hero's visits in the disguise of a minstrel to the tents of his enemies; or to the harems of the Persian rulers, whence he carries off their daughters to fill his own harem. He is not always victorious, and when honourably defeated, as he is on one occasion by a merchant who challenges him to single combat, he is unscrupulous and treacherous in his mode of vengeance. Sometimes the heroes of the adventures are the members of Kurroglou's retinue, as, for instance, in the account of how Ayvaz, his adopted son, goes to steal game from the park of the pasha of Tokat. In the account of how Hamza the scullion steals Kurroglou's horse Kyrat, Kurroglou himself cuts but a sorry figure, though he is restored to his horse and his heroic dignity at the conclusion of the story. The Turkoman *mejjliss* contain a large number of songs, most of which are

[1] See List of Abbreviations.   [2] Chodzko, p. 13.

attributed to the hero Kurroglou himself, though some are attributed to his son Ayvaz and to others of his retinue. Kurroglou is indeed represented as a most accomplished poet and musician, and as celebrating every important occurrence in song. Every situation of excitement or emotion calls forth from him a series of extempore compositions. Whenever he speaks formally he finds poetry a more natural medium than prose.

The Cycle of Kurroglou is a typical specimen of heroic literature. The stories are all stories of adventure, and their object is simply to entertain. The milieu is that of a heroic society, in most respects just such as travellers among the Turkomans describe the native society to have been during the early part of last century. The narratives are all anonymous, and are carried on by oral tradition, partly to the accompaniment of a stringed instrument. In style too the narratives conform to the standards of heroic saga. The particular is related in preference to the general, with fulness of description and elaboration of details. Speeches are introduced very freely even on the most trivial matters.

Though individualistic throughout, the Kurroglou Cycle cannot claim to be wholly aristocratic. The hero himself was the son of the master of the stud of Sultan Murad, and though this might be regarded in itself as an office of some honour, his followers are undoubtedly plebeian, being drawn from among grooms, shepherds and artisans. His adopted brother is a merchant and his adopted son, the son of a butcher.[1] Nor is the rude plebeian side glozed over by the reciter. The descriptions of Kurroglou's enormous appetite and coarse table manners, and his powers of drinking[2] recall those of the Kirghiz hero Joloi, while even a merchant can upbraid him justly with ungentlemanly conduct towards his enemies.

"Hold back thy arm, Kurroglou!...I have heard a great deal about thee, but I have seen thee now, and thou dost not deserve thy fame. A brave man gives timely warning to his enemy; it is a woman's part to fight without warning and to kill by stealth."[3]

It is probable that while some of the plebeian features of the Kurroglou Cycle are original, others may be adventitious. The liberal introduction of humour is akin to that of many of the Irish sagas and to that of the Russian *bylina* of Vasili Buslaev. We refer to such passages as the consternation which is caused to the onlookers by the capacity of the hero's appetite, which consumes not only vast quantities of rice, but the bag in which it has been carried; to the terror inspired

[1] See Chodzko, p. 41f.   [2] *Ib.* pp. 48, 103, etc.   [3] *Ib.* p. 184f.

by the length of his moustaches; to the ague which keeps his retinue in bed for a twelvemonth, and which is caused by terror at sight of his enemy's head poised on his lance. Such humour is alien to the high seriousness of heroic narratives composed for an aristocratic audience. In its general conduct and outline, however, the Kurroglou Cycle accords closely with the aristocratic standards which we have seen to be characteristic of heroic poetry and saga elsewhere. The virtues most in favour are courage, loyalty, generosity; and the profession of freebooter and predatory warrior is followed by all. Riches and spectacular display in personal ornaments and weapons are highly prized. The heroic code of honour is generally recognised even though not always adhered to. Kurroglou himself possesses in a superlative degree the first polite accomplishment of a gentleman of Asiatic heroic society—the ability to carry on a conversation by means of extempore songs. This accomplishment is also shared in a lesser degree by other heroes in these sagas.

Above all the prominence of the horse accords with the highest standards of Turkoman ideals. Kurroglou's horse Kyrat, even more than its master, is the true hero of the Cycle, coveted as it is by potentates, and loved and admired by all. Kurroglou hardly seems to have an existence apart from his horse, whom he loves as his own soul. When he finds his steed dying he gladly gives himself up to his enemies, unwilling to live an hour after his faithful and beautiful companion.

The Altai and Teleut Tatars share with the Abakan Group an interesting series of sagas relating to the Mongol (Kalmuck) princes of Chinese Turkestan and Jungaria in the seventeenth and eighteenth centuries. These sagas are simple and direct in style, and, unlike those which we have mentioned above, they appear to be comparatively free from the influence of heroic poetry. The Sagai saga of *Sunu Mattyr*,[1] although quite brief—five and a half pages—falls naturally into three parts. In the early part of the saga we are shown the relations of the Kirghiz under the resident official Kongyr Targa, with their overlords in the Altai under Kongdaijy Khan.[2] When Kongyr Targa grows old, his people refuse to follow his advice and withhold their tribute from the Altai, and slay the officers sent to collect it. The Kongdaijy sends a punitive expedition and drives all the people from their homes. This part of the saga is post-heroic, told in summary form by a narrator with a defined political horizon and an antiquarian tendency.

[1] *Proben* II, p. 380 f.; cf. *ib. A.S.* I, p. 185 f.
[2] The word *kongdaijy* is in reality a title.

The second part of the story is purely heroic. It relates the slaying of a tiger with a single iron-tipped arrow by the Kongdaijy's seven-year old heroic son Sunu Mattyr. Later on his rivals, full of jealousy and treachery, accuse him of immorality and violence with their women, and persuade his father to have him thrown into a deep pit. He is ultimately resuscitated to vindicate his father's independence by his prowess against the 'Mongols'. The several motifs included in this portion of the story, including the last rally of the hero, who is believed to have been dead for some time, are all familiar to us from other stories of the Altai, the Kara-Kirghiz and the Abakan groups.

The third part is occupied with the adventures of Amyr Saran, who is here said to be another son of the Kongdaijy.[1] He leads the Kirghiz tribes to the edge of a lake where he bids them settle. He then insults the Mongol Khan[2] by refusing to marry his daughter and slaying a thousand of his soldiers. After this he flees to the White Tsar, but the 'Mongol Khan' insists that he shall be executed. The end is obscure, and much of the narrative is weak and unmotivated.

A comparison of this rather invertebrate story with the versions cited by Radlov elsewhere, both from the Sagai[3] and other tribes, emphasises the impression that what has come down to us is merely a disintegrated tradition of what must have been an extensive and perhaps elaborate Cycle of oral traditions. We do not know of any parallel version to the first part of the Sagai saga; but a Teleut version of the second part exists as an independent saga.[4] The Teleut version is simpler and clearer in the main than the Sagai version, though the end appears to have been confused and forgotten. According to the Teleut, Shünü (Sunu) was the youngest son of Kongodoi, an Oirot (Jungarian) prince, and the jealous rivals who plotted against him were his three younger brothers. In this version they persuade his father to destroy him, for fear that, with his great strength, he will destroy his father—a much simpler motive than that of the Sagai version. Moreover, in the Teleut narrative Shünü ultimately leaves home in consequence of an attempt on the part of his father to poison him. He is said to have joined his uncle, Ajykku Khan

---

[1] Cf. however, p. 121 below. From Baddeley's Genealogical table (G) it would seem probable that Amyr Saran was not the son but the great grandson of the Kongdaijy—if, indeed, this is a proper name, and not a title or term of relationship.

[2] The Mongol Khan is probably to be identified with the Chinese Emperor Kienlung. See Radlov, *A.S.* I, p. 171. Cf. Baddeley I, Genealogical Table G.

[3] Cf. Radlov, *A.S.* I, p. 167 ff.

[4] *Proben* I, p. 206 ff.; cf. Radlov, *A.S.* I, p. 169 ff.

(i.e. Ayuki, the Torgut prince), then living on the borders of Russia,[1] and to have distinguished himself in fighting on his behalf against the Russians.

In bringing together the several variants of this Cycle with a view to gauging its historical value in a later chapter, mention should be made here of a brief saga—hardly more than an anecdote—obtained by Radlov from the Altai,[2] which clearly refers to the same circle of events as those related in the previous sagas.

"The Oirot Kan dies and Amyr Sanaga rules over the people. In the Altai dwells the prince Chagan Narattan. Chagan Narattan fights Amyr Sanaga. They come to battle at the river Tscharysch. Chagan Narattan takes to flight before the battle is decided, and takes refuge with sixty-two men in a cave on the Katunja. The men of the Altai drive Amyr Sanaga over the Irtish, but when they do not find Chagan Narattan among the dead they go to look for him and eventually find him. He wants to escape again, but is captured at the river Bitutkan, which obtained its name from this event. The men of the Altai, angered at Chagan Narattan's cowardice, said to him: 'You have forsaken us in war, so we forsake you in peace. You are our leader no more.'"[3]

These sagas, brief and slight though they are, are worthy of consideration, as representing oral historical tradition carried on independently of written records. The history of the ruling Kalmuck princes of the Jungarian line is fairly well known from the sixteenth century down to our own time from Mongolian and Russian records,[4] and a comparison of these with the oral records given above affords the only important material to be found in Radlov's works for the study of the oral transmission of historical tradition among a nomadic people, as we shall see (p. 118 ff. below). At the same time these sagas offer interesting material for the study of variant texts, and of the intrusion of motifs common to folk-tales.

The story of *Taska Mattyr*, recorded by Radlov from the Kuärik Tatars,[5] differs greatly, both in form and style, from the sagas which we have been considering. It is a long and elaborate narrative after the manner of the Abakan poems. It relates to the adventures of a champion Taska Mattyr in the service of Üdsäng Päg, by whom he is sent to convey the tribute due from Üdsäng Päg himself to the Mongol Khan. The Mongol Khan in his turn sends the hero on a further

[1] See Howorth, I, p. 564 ff.
[3] *Loc. cit.*
[4] See Baddeley, *passim.*
[2] *A.S.* I, p. 172.
[5] *Proben* II, p. 700 ff.

mission, in the course of which he pays a visit to a supernatural country which is entered through a hole in a mountain, and which obviously bears a close relationship to the countries with a similar access in other stories and poems of the Tatars, and generally represents the land of the dead. When at last the hero returns to the court of Üdsäng Päg he has been away so long that he is not recognised till he plays his old familiar tunes on the *chatigan*, or Kirghiz zither.

This saga gives a vivid picture of the manners and relations of the Kirghiz of the Kara Jüs and the Mongols during the period to which the two last sagas also have reference. We see the khans enforcing the personal attendance of their tributary chiefs or their official deputies every three years; the long journey involved; the Kirghiz bivouac and the brewing of the evening tea; the Mongol Khan leaning on his bamboo staff; his wily manner of making these emissaries execute difficult tasks for him, and the long absence from home which these tasks sometimes entail. We see the ideal heroic prince in Üdsäng Päg, bold, cruel, unscrupulous, able, generous, a good master, a splendid hunter, an intrepid fighter. We see the ideal heroic adventurer in Taska Mattyr, who can shoot and hunt and follow a track better than anyone; who is brave, loyal, successful, and an accomplished musician; and who knows forty melodies and can also extemporise on the *chatigan*. The saga is composed in a leisurely and elaborate style with all the characteristics of heroic poetry highly developed, and neither the diction nor the syntax are those of prose. It is, however, a unique example of its kind among the prose narratives recorded by Radlov, and nothing is said of its history, or the milieu in which it circulates.

In addition to the narrative poetry and saga already considered, the Tatars possess a great wealth of oral poetry of a slighter character. Heroic poetry in the form of speeches in character is common. As we have seen, it occurs frequently in sagas. It is found also independently, and has been recorded especially among the Tatars of the Irtish and the Ob. A large number of poems of this type are attributed to well-known historical persons, but it is improbable that the majority are really personal poems composed by the heroes named. The range of names represented, the impersonal nature of the contents in general, the elaborate and finished style, the artificial, often strophic form and regularity of refrain, and the persistence of the conventional framework all suggest a traditional literary form rather than a spontaneous personal impulse.

An example of a *tolgaw* ('lament') on the taking of Kazan by the Russians in A.D. 1552, which was recorded by Chodzko from the recitation of a Tatar of Astrakhan in 1830,[1] must undoubtedly belong to this class. It purports to be the lament of a Tatar prince, Batyr Shorah, who perished in the marshes during an attempt to relieve the siege. From the nature of the contents, however, which refer specifically to the manner of his death, it is clear that it must have been composed by some other person after the event. This makes it probable that a fragment from another *tolgaw* on the same historical event, which follows immediately in Chodzko's collection,[2] is also a poem of similar origin.

Many examples of poems which celebrate historical persons are extant from the northern Tatars. A strophe has survived[3] from a forgotten *Song of Kuchum Khan* in which the hero is represented as reflecting on his achievements and thinking with affection of his archers. In another poem of seven strophes,[4] Khotsash, one of Kuchum Khan's heroes, is represented as recalling in old age the good things of his youth—brandy and mead, rich clothing and horses, and the love of the maid Känikä. Another poem purports to be spoken by Myrsa Tus, a younger brother of the 'hero Mamai'.[5] These two poems have elaborate strophic forms and refrains. In *Toktamysh Khan*,[6] Toktamysh is represented as holding converse with the noble Myratym and the sage Chänbai.

Speech poems of Type C[7] are commonly used as a framework in which to incorporate material which in substance belongs properly to the literature of learning and of celebration. A somewhat elaborate poem sung among the Kurdak tribes of the northern Tatars which purports to be spoken by the hero Atulu Batyr,[8] is obviously composed to convey information of a gnomic and descriptive character. A dialogue poem in which the mother of Murat Pi questions her son as he sets out for battle thinly veils a didactic tendency under a cloak of personal solicitude.[9] The poem *Karaza*[10] is spoken by a Tatar chief whose two sons have fallen in battle against Ermak the Cossack. The poem is an elegy on the two dead sons, and may of course have come down to us from the seventeenth century; but its finished form and careful structure make it more likely that it is a product of a later era.

[1] Chodzko, p. 362f.
[2] *Ib.* p. 364 (no. III).
[3] *Proben* IV, p. 141; cf. *A.S.* I, p. 157.
[4] *Proben* IV, p. 209f.
[5] *Ib.* p. 212f.
[6] *Ib.* p. 241 ff.
[7] For the 'Types', see p. 696.
[8] *Proben* IV, p. 210f.
[9] *Ib.* I, p. 220f.
[10] *Ib.* IV, p. 328.

There can be no doubt that the northern Tatars, and perhaps the Turkomans also, have developed to a special degree a literary form in which speech poems are represented as uttered by great heroes of the past. It is probable therefore that this form, which may well have begun as personal poetry, soon developed into a literary convention, and that the majority of heroic speech poems were composed long after the time of the men who are represented as speaking. These poems generally begin with a formula, such as 'Khotsash the hero speaks', or 'Atulu the hero speaks', or

> One day Jan-Bai spoke to Idägä.
> Kämal's son, Jan Bai spoke.[1]

Or:

> Among those who dwell on the Tobol
> Speaks Ak Buga the hero.[2]

The same form is frequently used in connection with heroes who are less illustrious, but who may nevertheless have had a historical existence. E.g.

> Bi Agysh speaks:
> O you beloved Nogai, etc.[3]

Or again:

> The lord of Januar Bos,
> Äbil Kasym, the prince, speaks.[4]

Such poems generally consist of a single speech or dialogue. They are free from prose passages. In form they resemble closely such Anglo-Saxon poems as the *Seafarer* and the *Wife's Complaint*. The contents, however, are purely heroic, and the interest is exclusively masculine.

Turning to the Tatar tribes farther south, we have noted that among the Kazaks and neighbouring peoples an individual form of heroic narrative has developed in which prose and poetry, the latter consisting principally though not exclusively of speeches, are combined in varying degrees. Among the same people also we have found poetry of this type in which a brief prose introduction and conclusion is commonly added to speech poems to indicate the setting. In such poems brief prose passages are also occasionally added in the body of the poem where the reciter feels the necessity of greater explicitness. The type is a common one, and is found among both the Kazaks and the Teleut. From the former we may cite *Täti*, which consists of the speech of a

---

[1] *Proben* IV, p. 165. [2] *Ib.* p. 236.
[3] *Ib.* p. 334. [4] *Ib.* p. 237.

dying Kazak chief who has been treacherously clothed in a poisoned coat by his enemy; *Köigüldü*, the boasting speech of a hero before he rides to avenge his brother who has been wounded by the Kalmucks; and *Mandyk's Son*, which consists of three separate speeches, joined by brief prose passages.[1] The analogy of such poems to those contained in the early Norse collection of the Elder Edda[2] is very striking.

At least one example of heroic poetry of this type is recorded also from the Kara-Kirghiz.[3] A short prose introduction relates the murder of Kul Myrsa by a rich man in whose house he is staying, and the arrival of the father Kubat in search of his son. The rich man tells Kubat that he has not seen his son; but his daughter waits by the wayside for Kubat, and then sings an elegy of twenty-four lines for his son, in which she relates how he has come by his end. A few lines of prose at the conclusion relate the vengeance of Kubat.

The composition of heroic panegyric and elegiac poetry is common among the Tatars. Travellers speak constantly of the presence of minstrels at the feast, and of their extempore composition in honour of host and guests. Radlov was present at a Kirghiz feast at which the chief, in his delight at the panegyric of a famous minstrel who was present, flung his satin cloak from his own shoulders and bestowed it upon the poet.[4] Parallels to this incident are common in Europe in the Viking Age (cf. vol. I, p. 346). Venyukov mentions that in 1860 a Kirghiz poet who was attached to the Russian expeditionary column was held in high esteem among his tribesmen as their chief poet. 'When the chief of the expedition gave an entertainment to the Kirghizes...this poet loudly and eloquently extolled the virtues of the giver of the feast—probably with a view to a noble largesse'.[5] Among the Kazaks also the late Prof. Bateson was made the subject of extempore panegyric poetry.[6]

The same practice is referred to in the Abakan prose narrative of *Taska Mattyr*, where we are told that at the feast given by the usurping prince Üdsäng Päg, "all began to eat, and Üdsäng Päg went among them and said: 'Sing!' and they sang and praised Üdsäng Päg."[7]

Chodzko tells us that among the Turkomans a minstrel who has

---

[1] *Proben* III, p. 100 ff.   [2] See Vol. I, pp. 9, 19.
[3] *Proben* V, p. 602 f.
[4] Radlov, *A.S.* I, p. 488; cf. also p. 185 below.
[5] Michell, p. 291.   [6] Bateson, p. 166.
[7] *Proben*, II, p. 703.

recited the deeds and poems of Kurroglou invariably concludes with a panegyric composed by himself or another, praising the person who is to pay him for his trouble.[1]

Several examples of panegyric poems are published by Radlov. We may refer to the Kazak address of twelve lines in praise of Abylai Khan.[2] A poem of three strophes which is sung as a prelude to the Teleut story of *Ak Köbök* is virtually an independent panegyric poem, but we have no evidence that it was sung apart from its present context.[3] Again, in the same saga, a poem of four strophes is sung by village girls in praise of the hero.[4]

An interesting and unusual example of panegyric poetry occurs in the Baraba version of the saga of *Ak Köbök*.[5] A smith, Kützömöz, has forged a sword for the hero which is highly approved. When Kützömöz demands his reward, Ak Köbök stands up and praises him in a typical heroic panegyric poem of twelve lines, of which the first six consist of remarks on the strength and efficiency of Kützömöz, while the last six invoke blessings and riches on him. It is a curious inversion of the usual practice to find a hero praising an artisan, but the smith is a person whose work is of unique importance to warriors, and the high status of Kützömöz may be inferred from the fact that he is mentioned by name.

A number of Turkoman panegyrics are extant which are attributed to the hero Kurroglou. The following is interesting, not only as being attributed to the hero himself, but also as having been apparently committed to memory by him; for in reference to a service which a certain Mustapha-beg had once performed for him Kurroglou says later: "I composed then a song to his honour, and I do not know why, but it comes to my recollection at the present moment. Bring my guitar; I'll sing it to thee...." Kurroglou tunes his guitar, and sings:

'Like a man, like a true warrior, he came and fought. Mustapha-beg is of noble blood. Under the blows of his sword the rocks cleave. Mustapha-beg is the son of a noble father.... He is master of forty thousand men always ready at his first signal. Clad in armour, in iron dresses with blood-shot eyes,[6] they eat his broth and his *pillaw*. Mustapha-beg is son of the Pakiar. Is there any father that can boast of five such sons? He is fit to be any hero's companion. He deserves to be

---

[1] Chodzko, p. 344.   [2] *Proben* III, p. 92.
[3] *Ib.* I, p. 224.   [4] *Ib.* p. 231.   [5] *Ib.* IV, p. 60.
[6] According to the opinion of oriental physiognomists blood-shot eyes are a sign of valour (Chodzko). In the *Mahabharata* also heroes have red eyes.

my brother. Mustapha-beg is the son of a nobleman. Shouting, he cuts his way through the enemy's ranks; he darts an unerring arrow from his bow, and pushes Kurroglou into a river. Mustapha-beg is the son of a nobleman.'"[1]

Kurroglou is also said to have composed a beautiful panegyric on his enemy, Reyhan Arab, which is incorporated in the story of Reyhan Arab's death at the hands of the hero.[2]

The practice of composing panegyric poetry on horses,[3] dogs, weapons, and other favourite adjuncts of heroic life is frequently referred to, both by travellers and in the heroic narratives themselves. Sir Alexander Burnes mentions the practice among the Turkomans of singing songs in honour of their horses.[4] Radlov quotes a Kazak poem of eight strophes which is at once a panegyric and an elegy on a favourite hawk which a dog has killed.[5] In the Teleut saga of *Ak Köbök* to which we referred above, the hero is represented as reciting a poem of four strophes in praise of his horse, and another of eight strophes in praise of his falcon, his spear, his sword, and his whip.[6]

Elegiac poetry is commonly composed by women in celebration of the dead. When Prof. Bateson was in the neighbourhood of Lake Balkash he heard "a number of girls assembled to mourn with his mother for a man who was supposed to have died. They sat in a ring and covered the heads with coats and sang a monotonous dirge with a refrain. I couldn't exactly make out how much was extempore, but I fancy that it was extemporised upon some probably stock form."[7] In the narrative poem of *Sain Batyr*, also from the Kazaks, the hero's wife, on hearing of his downfall at the hands of the Kalmucks, tears her cheeks, loosens her black hair, enters her house, and sits down to celebrate him in an elegy.[8] Similarly in the Kara-Kirghiz poem on *Semätäi's Birth*, after the death of the hero Manas his wife Kanykäi tears her face and unbinds her hair and 'lamented him in song'.[9]

Radlov tells us that among the Kara-Kirghiz the wife sings elegies in

---

[1] Chodzko, p. 286 ff.   [2] *Ib.* p. 87.

[3] For the attention paid by the Turkomans to their horses we may refer to the poem attributed to the hero Kurroglou in which the points of a good horse are enumerated. See Chapter VII below.

[4] Burnes II, p. 58.   [5] *Proben* III, p. 80 f.

[6] *Ib.* I, p. 227 f.   [7] Bateson, p. 165 f.

[8] *Proben* III, p. 246 f.

[9] *Ib.* V, p. 283 f. Cf. also the references to the same custom in the Kazak elegy in *ib.* III, p. 27.

the *yurt* for a whole week beside the clothes of her dead husband, and a dead man is always celebrated in poetry by the woman most closely related to him. Such laments are never sung by men except by professional minstrels who will sing in public assemblies in honour of a famous man.[1]

Three independent examples of heroic elegies are published by Radlov from the Kara-Kirghiz. The first is composed on a hero Jantai.[2] It consists of one hundred and thirty-two lines, in which the hero's personal beauty, and the excellence of his character as a generous and heroic prince, are set forth, together with allusions to his relations with other princes.

The second is a lament on a prince Chokcholoi[3] by his daughter.[4] In it reference is made to the hero's conquests over the Kazaks, and to his journeys over desolate mountains, while he himself is compared to the heroes Koshoi, Manas, Joloi and others. Both these poems are composed in the continuous metre, and the style characteristic of heroic narrative poetry. Radlov tells us that they were dictated to him by people who were unfamiliar with epic songs; yet he himself observes that they conform so completely to the character of such songs that they look like extracts, and he compares them with the prelude to the third episode in *Manas*.[5]

Among the Kazaks the singing of lamentations and elegies for the dead is said to be kept up for a whole year. From these tribes we have several examples of such elegies. All the independent poems of this kind are, however, in strophic form. One of them is an elegy on Balgyn, daughter of Sultan Batyr Bek, by her mother.[6] Another example of a Kazak elegy is that sung by the sister of Sultan Bopo for her dead bridegroom.[7] They are full of tender reminiscence and sorrowful, hopeless reflection, and are more emotional in tone than the laments of the Kara-Kirghiz. The impersonal character and concrete allusions of general interest characteristic of the latter are here wholly absent.

On the other hand in the heroic narrative poem *Sain Batyr*, recorded by Radlov from the Kazaks of the Little Horde, which is composed entirely in the run-on non-strophic metre characteristic of the narrative poetry of the Kara-Kirghiz and the Abakan Tatars, a series of elegies occur in the text which are typically heroic in character. They are

---

[1] *A.S.* I, p. 486. [2] *Proben* v, p. 594 ff.
[3] The second half of this name is only a scribal variation of the name *Joloi*.
[4] *Proben* v, p. 598 ff. [5] *Ib.* p. xxvii.
[6] *Ib.* III, p. 25 f.; *A.S.* I, p. 486f. [7] *Proben* III, p. 26 ff.

recited for the hero who is believed to be dead, and are attributed to the hero's wife, his child, and his mother. Reference has already been made to the singing of elegiac poetry by the hero's wife in this poem. These elegies remind us of the elegies for the dead Hector in Homer, and are exactly what we might expect to find in *Manas* or *Joloi*. The reflective emotional tone of the preceding examples is foreign to these inset elegies in *Sain Batyr*. In the Kazak saga of *Dshelkildäk* a brief elegy of a similar character is also recited by Ös Temir, the son of Nörmön Bet, who returns home to find his elder brother and his nephew murdered, and his nieces carried into captivity.[1]

The Turkomans have preserved an elegy which is said to have been composed by Kurroglou on his horse Kyrat.

"O inconstant Fate! shall I proclaim to the world all thy wickedness? Thou hast befriended nobody faithfully to the end. Death was always thy last reward. How many potentates thou hast put on a level with the thorn, creeping on the earth?...Where is that Soleiman commanding the *divs* and the *peris*? Did not the king of kings, Kaykaus, that second Rustem, lose in play at dice with death?"[2]

A *tolgaw* or lament for the fate of the Tatars settled in Europe is preserved among the oral literature of the Astrakhan Tatars. It is said to have been composed by a poor Volga Tatar settled at the court of one of the Ghireis in the Crimea. The Tatar chiefs are referred to under the names of birds, and the whole is composed in purely figurative language, which to Chodzko suggested comparison with the poetry of the Norse 'skalds', though a closer parallel is to be found in the medieval Russian work, the *Slovo o Polky Igorevê*.[3] Though obscure to us without commentary, it was perfectly understood by the Ghirei to whom it was recited.

"When a startled doe runs away with her kids, it leaves a track on the swampy morasses.

"On the mountain of Caucasus the falcon Terlan will raise his voice.

"A solitary white-beaked vulture, perched on the top of a rock, screamed, and spread terror on the vast lake.

"Two eagles are shedding their feathers on the borders of *Ytill* (viz. the Volga), and fear arises in the hearts of the enemy."[4]

Addresses to individuals in the form of a request or prayer are not rare, and the Turkoman minstrels are in the habit of concluding

[1] *Proben* III, p. 134f.   [2] Chodzko, p. 341.
[3] See Vol. II, p. 65 of the present work.
[4] Chodzko, p. 372.

their recitations in such terms. Several examples occur also in the Kurroglou Cycle. Among the most interesting is that in which Kurroglou implores his horse Kyrat to leap a ravine, carrying Kurroglou himself and his adopted son Ayvaz. The poem opens with the words:

"O my steed, thy father was *Bedow*, thy mother *Kohlan*. On! on! my worthy Kyrat, carry me to Chamly-bill!"

And concludes as follows:

"Art thou not of the race of Kohlan? Art thou not the great grandson of Duldul? O Kyrat, carry me to Chamly-bill, to my brave ones! I will have satin housings cut out and sewed purposely for thee. We will enjoy ourselves, and the red wine shall gush out in a stream. O my Kyrat, my chosen one of five hundred horses. On! on! carry me to Chamly-bill!"[1]

Among the Turkomans it is the custom to sing war songs when entering into battle or when setting out on a foray, and Chodzko tells us that during the struggles for independence of the Turkoman tribes with their Persian masters, "when the two hostile armies are going to meet, before they engage in battle, they animate each other, and scoff at their opponents; the Persians, by singing passages from the Shahnama; the Iliats,[2] by shouting the war songs of Kurroglou".[3] Chodzko gives a specimen of these songs which was composed in memory of a successful battle against the Kurds, and points out the striking resemblance to two specimens published by Sir Alexander Burnes.[4]

"On Aghas. Onward", cries the poet, "Let Aly Shiraslan go. Barcha, skilful in curing pains, wise as Lockman, will go. From the desert of Moghan will come Mullah Baghanj...the descendant of the Aghas of Tuka. Next Zemen will follow. O Aghas, you should see his valour in the day of battle, his two-edged sword, his Arabian steed. Liberal like Hautem, he falls upon the enemy like a famished wolf upon a herd, mounted upon a prancing horse, spear in hand,..." and he concludes with the words: "Khan Mohammed, the wild boar; the father and the chief of the numerous tribes of Ozenlu; with a wolf's claws, he tears his enemies asunder in the day of battle."[5]

---

[1] Chodzko, p. 79f.   [2] I.e. the Turkoman nomads.
[3] Chodzko, p. 4.
[4] The reference which Chodzko gives is to Vol. III, p. 92 of Burnes's *Travels into Bokhara*, but in the edition of the latter work published in 1834 the poems in question occur in Vol. II, p. 114ff.
[5] Chodzko, p. 381.

Chodzko also gives the song which is said to have been composed in 1796 on Agha Mohammed Khan when going to battle against a Kurdish chief. The song is a combination of a panegyric on the khan and a call to battle.

"He has forty thousand horses tied up in stables; their saddles are set with precious stones; on their necks hang talismans; on their ruby tails sparkle diamond knots. He has forty thousand gunners to fire his guns. He has forty thousand men in ambush, posted along the passages in the mountains.... The shah has ordered it, and everybody must go. He has forty thousand dishes full of fat meat; and forty thousand swift horses in the stables. He took Kurdistan, and what is it to him to conquer you (Memish Khan)? The shah ordered, and you must follow him."[1]

The evidence of the poems and sagas makes it clear that heroes are in the habit of improvising personal and occasional poetry to the *chatigan*,[2] a kind of native zither. In the Küarik saga of *Taska Mattyr* (see p. 55 above) the hero makes himself known to Üdsäng Päg, his former master, by taking his 'forty-stringed chatigan' and singing the following song:

"Taska Mattyr took his departure from here three years ago. He has seen another sphere. Even now the hero, the strong one, Taska Mattyr is not yet dead."[3]

Our fullest evidence for the composition and recitation of personal poetry, however, comes from the Turkomans, where, as we have seen, extempore composition seems to be very widely practised. The largest collection of these personal poems is that which is scattered throughout the sagas of the Kurroglou Cycle. Chodzko tells us of the hero that

"his Improvisations were made without forethought, and, as it were, sprang forth by themselves, without the author's previous reflection.... On every principal event of his life, he left some improvisations in the Perso-Turkish language, which are used to the present day by the trans-Caucasian Mussulmans, as well as by those of Aderbaidjan and by the nomades of Tatar descent in Northern Persia."[4]

The question of the authenticity of the tradition of the poems has already been discussed. It may be remarked here, however, that whatever conclusion the reader may come to on this matter does not affect

---

[1] Chodzko, p. 387f.
[2] For a note on the *chatigan*, see p. 22 above.
[3] *Proben* II, p. 719.
[4] Chodzko, pp. 6, 12.

the fact that they offer indubitable testimony to the widespread and highly cultivated habit of the extempore composition of personal and occasional poetry.

It has already been mentioned that Kurroglou on any formal occasion, or whenever his emotions were stirred, is traditionally stated to have spoken in verse more naturally than in prose, and it is important to remember that the same custom appears to have been followed to a large extent by the people with whom he was in contact. Even most casual conversations are carried on in poetry. In the early part of the Cycle, when Kurroglou departs to seek and adopt Ayvaz, the son of a butcher, as his own son, he announces his intention to his followers in a song.[1] Ayvaz informs his father, the butcher, of the identity of Kurroglou, and implores him to send him away, in a series of short poems in which bare facts are expressed quite literally.[2] When Kurroglou is carrying Ayvaz away, a whole conversation is carried on between them in verse,[3] and a series of casual comments are made in verse by Kurroglou in the tent of a 'Turkish' merchant.[4] It would be superfluous to multiply instances which abound throughout the collection.

It will be seen that all forms of heroic poetry are found among the Tatars, though Type C appears to be only slightly represented in our collections. Authentic examples of personal poetry are also not common, but this is manifestly due to the ephemeral character of such poetry among a people who practise extempore composition more widely than verbal tradition. This facility in extempore composition is especially characteristic of the Kara-Kirghiz and the Yakut, but is by no means confined to them. It is not surprising that among such people personal utterances in poetical form pass unrecorded.

Before leaving the heroic poetry of the Tatars, we would call attention to a collection of fragmentary quotations from Tatar poetry contained in a MS. written by a native of Kashgar in 1073, probably from an earlier copy.[5] These quotations are therefore probably the earliest specimens of Turkish poetry which have come down to us,[6] and represent popular oral compositions of a period prior to the latter half of the eleventh century. They consist of quotations from elegies, love

---

[1] Chodzko, p. 45.   [2] *Ib.* p. 64f.
[3] *Ib.* p. 72f.   [4] *Ib.* p. 187.
[5] See Brockelmann, 'Altturkestanische Volkspoesie', *A.M.* 1923, p. 1 ff.; 1924, p. 24 ff.
[6] The *Kudatku Bilik*, to which reference is made on p. 193 below, was apparently written down a few years earlier (in 1069).

poems, drinking and hunting songs, boasting and gibing poems, and others. The poems from which these fragments are taken have been reconstructed to some extent by the editors, and enough remains to show the unmistakably heroic character of the originals. Like the *tolgaws* referred to above, however, they are not easy to classify. The first elegy is composed for a hero Alp Är Tonga, who is possibly to be identified with a well-known character who lived in the Eighth Century. The second is for an unnamed hero. A fragmentary panegyric on a princess also occurs. The poems which follow purport to be personal poems relating to the poet's experiences in warfare, and closely resemble the *tolgaws* (pp. 56, 62 above).

Note. Since the above was printed, I have, by the kindness of Professor Konovalov, been enabled to obtain a Russian translation of a collection of Yakut oral literature.[1] This contains, among other items, a number of narratives described by the translator as *byliny.* The translations are printed as prose, but the term *byliny* suggests that in the Yakut the form is that of rhythmical narrative, which was doubtless chanted by the narrator (cf. p. 158 f. below).

It should be added that among the Oirot of north-western Mongolia and among the Buryat heroic narrative poetry is still highly developed and still flourishes. Among the Oirot there are still to be found many professional singers who can recite poems of several thousand lines, and who can compose new poems on contemporary events in the traditional style. Among the Khalkha Mongols similar poetry is also to be found, but in a less flourishing condition. Among the Mongols everywhere such poems are not recited, but always sung. In the open steppe, when the people meet for horse-racing, wrestling, and shooting with the bow, the minstrel honours the victor with an 'ode', and the victorious race-horse with a 'panegyric', while heroic narrative poems are chanted by professional minstrels. In the evenings also the people love to listen to heroic songs in their *yurts* at the feast. From Poppe's account of the narrative poems of the Khalkha Mongols these would seem to resemble the non-heroic poetry of the 'Abakan' Tatars; but it is probable that the poetry of the Oirot, and perhaps also the Buryat, will approximate more closely to that of the Kirghiz. For Poppe's note, and a German translation of a Khalkha Mongol narrative poem, see *A.M.* v (1930), p. 183 ff.

[1] S. V. Yastremski, *Obraztsy Narodnoy Literatury Yakutov*, Leningrad, 1929.

CHAPTER III

THE HEROIC MILIEU

INDIVIDUALISM IN THE HEROIC POEMS

AS in the Yugoslav and the Russian Sections, we shall discuss the milieu of the Tatar heroic poetry and saga under the following headings: (1) the social standing of the personnel; (2) the scenes of the stories; (3) the accessories of heroic life; (4) the social standards and conventions observed in heroic poetry and saga. The great majority of our evidence will be drawn from the poetry of the Kara-Kirghiz, since this is the largest and most important body of heroic literature which we possess from the Tatars, though the heroic poetry and saga of the Kazaks and the northern Tatars also offer much for our purpose.

As in heroic poetry elsewhere, the personnel of the poems is aristocratic. All the heroes are princes, or at least aristocrats, and the heroines are the daughters of princes or people of noble rank. We have seen that the Turkoman hero Kurroglou and his retinue are of the middle class, or even of plebeian rank; but this is exceptional. In Tatar heroic literature as a whole we hear very little of the lower ranks of society, and the only glimpses which we get of their way of life are, in general, the pictures given of high-born people in captivity, such as Ak Saikal, Joloi's wife, tending the Kalmuck sheep. The lower classes take no part in the fighting. They are twice mentioned as expressly excluded from taking part in the games at Bok Murun's feast:

> The lower classes must stand back,
> Only the princes may take their places.[1]

And again:

> The lower classes must stand back,
> Only the princes may take their places,
> Take their places to tilt with lances.[2]

Manas has a retinue of forty followers, most of whom are named, and a brief description of their functions generally follows their names as an epithet: 'Kaman, Jaipur, two youths who never lost a horse's track

---

[1] *Proben* v, p. 171, l. 982f.   [2] *Ib.* p. 179, l. 1264f.

by night; Tas Baimat who brews tea in the cauldron.' They always accompany Manas on his expeditions, and it is even implied that they take an active part themselves. It is to be noted, however, that they are always referred to as 'heroes' rather than as retainers or servants. Some of the heroes of the comitatus, and those with whom they are brought into contact, play an important part in heroic story and recur constantly, like Vladimir's heroes of Kiev. Alaman Bet is the hero of several independent adventures. Other well-known names are Jamgyrchi 'the mighty wrestler'; Er Koshoi 'who opened the gate of Paradise'; Bok Murun at whose feast all the heroic world contended in the races; Kös Kaman, who comes—or pretends to come—from a long captivity among the Kalmucks, clad in Chinese armour, and wearing a pigtail; Er Töshtük, who is himself the hero of a long poem which relates his adventures in the Underworld, and who represents the spiritual, as opposed to the military point of view. The traditional enemies are an even more picturesque group. All are heathens. Er Kökchö, whose luxurious Uigur tent with its silk and satin hangings affords a striking contrast to the black horse-hair tents of the Kirghiz; Karacha, the Kalmuck prince who meets Joloi's sister as she is hawking and gathering wild cherries on the mountains, and who brings about Joloi's downfall; and most picturesque of all, Kongyr Bai, the 'snub-nosed, oblique-eyed Chinese', 'clothed in cold iron', and, 'girt with a sharp sword', who 'babbled in a language which no one could under-stand'—

> Lord of Kashgar and of Kokand,
> Ruler of a thousand Chinese,
> Snub-nosed, red-eyed,
> Kongyr Bai from China,
> Kongyr Bai with bald pate,
> Whose habits are outlandish.[1]

The most outstanding hero of the poems is Manas himself, a typical heroic prince, whose ancestors have ruled the Sary-Nogai for several generations. He is essentially a soldier. When he decides to raid the Uigurs, Er Kökchö seeks to buy him off by suggesting that they should divide between them the herds which Manas seeks to carry off; but Manas will not hear of it, and declares that one of them must die:

> I will have no agreement with you,
> I will have no reconciliation,

[1] *Proben* v, p. 146, l. 150ff.

I will have no equal division,
Nothing will I give back to you.
Come and take them—well and good!
If you cannot—then howl for them like a dog![1]

A complete contrast to Manas is Er Kökchö himself, who is at the head of the powerful Uigur confederacy, and represents the more diplomatic and enlightened elements in the poems. He is the furthest removed from the heroic ideal of any of the Tatar heroes. He lives in Chinese luxury, and entertains his guests to tea, the drink of China. Hemmed in on one side by the restless Manas, on the other by Jamgyrchi, Er Kökchö, no longer young, at least in the Kirghiz version of the story,[2] induces the Kalmuck prince 'Alaman Bet the Tiger-like' to abandon his own people, and accept the chief place in his comitatus. It is clear that he has no longer any love of combat himself, although we see from remarks dropped by his wife[3] that he has been a valorous hero. It is characteristic of him that when his suspicions have been aroused as to the infidelity of his wife Ak Erkäch with Alaman Bet, he induces that hero to leave his service unrewarded, yet without open warfare. When forced to encounter Manas he first tries, as we have just seen, to come to an agreement by negotiation. While Manas fights in his famous cuirass, Er Kökchö wears only a cloth coat. In the most up-to-date form of single combat—the duel fought with gunpowder—Er Kökchö is victorious over Manas.

Among the Kara-Kirghiz the women are at least as heroic and militant as the men, and apparently more savage. It is Joloi's sister 'Kardygach, the wicked witch', rather than her paramour Karacha who takes the initiative in seeking to destroy Joloi. Joloi himself cuts a very poor figure in the poem which bears his name, and would have perished over and over again, despite his gigantic strength and valour, had it not been for the heroic prowess of his two wives. Kanykäi, Manas' wife, is represented as the ideal woman of the steppe—loyal, gracious, hospitable, a skilled cook and doctor, a woman of the highest honour and culture according to the standards of the milieu in which she figures. Yet we have seen her showing great savagery in the treatment of her enemy (cf. p. 34 above)—a savagery which is shared also by Joloi's wives, and by other high-born Tatar women and maidens.[4]

---

[1] *Proben* v, p. 67, l. 162 ff.
[2] We have seen (p. 47 above) that in the Kazak version of the story Er Kökshü is represented as a young man.
[3] *Proben* v, p. 24, l. 595 ff. [4] Cf. e.g. *ib.* p. 443.

Very frequently the scene is laid in a prince's tent, and tent life is presented to us under all its aspects. One of the commonest of these is the feast, which is mentioned very frequently, though it rarely forms the background or chief incident of a poem, or serves as a static opening to the theme, as it does in so many of the Russian *byliny*. In the literature of the Tatars the feast is conducted on a large scale, and with considerable ceremonial and formality. We may refer to the description of the religious festival given by Manas on the arrival of the Kalmuck cortège in *Kös Kaman*.[1] At this feast the Kalmucks undergo conversion to the Mohammedan faith and have their pigtails shaved, and horses and sheep are slaughtered and much feasting takes place, together with horse races. During the banquet we see Kanykäi busying herself with the welfare of her guests, like the royal ladies in *Beowulf*:

> She inclined her head,
> And bowed from the waist...
> She took the wine-bag under her arm,
> Seized the porcelain cup in her hand,
> Handsomely she entertained the forty heroes;[2]
> They drank their fill of brandy and sherbet,
> And then began to raise their song.[3]

It is interesting to note that songs are mentioned as an accompaniment to the feast; and again in the same poem the Kalmucks are referred to as singing and carousing in their tents.[4] But we hear little in the poems of stringed instruments, unless one is referred to as an accompaniment of the prayer of Bek Toro in *Er Töshtük*.[5]

The Sary-Nogai, or people of Manas' retinue, and the Uigurs also are very fond of tea-parties and tea-making, which takes place on all sorts of occasions, though brandy is also sometimes drunk by the Sary Nogai, in spite of their Mohammedan faith. The tea is always drunk with sugar and cream. Milk appears never to be used for this purpose. Er Kökchö, on his first acquaintance with Alaman Bet, entertains him to tea in his tent, and the process of the tea-making is set before us minutely:

> Kökchö called his followers to him,
> Set up the white tent,
> Spread out silk-brocade and velvet,
> Spread thick coverlets,
> Stood the samovar by the fire,

---

[1] *Proben* v, p. 236f.   [2] I.e. Manas' retinue.
[3] *Proben* v, p. 237, l. 1007ff.   [4] *Ib.* p. 257.   [5] *Ib.* p. 539, l. 306ff.

> Put in tea, frothing white,
> Added to it clotted cream,
> Then added sugar to it,
> Added also a ripe apple,
> Poured in the sugar,
> Then prepared the tea,
> And handed it to Alaman Bet.[1]

Both at the feast and at other times the heroes boast proudly of their courage and strength and their deeds of valour, both past and future. As in *Beowulf* and among the ancient Gauls, such boasting seems to be part of the social ritual of the feast. We may cite the series of vows made by Ägrä Kara when feasting with a party of seventy heroes in the house of Tas Chüräk, as to the insults he intends to heap on the hero Puga-Däkä[2] in the second of the Sagai poems quoted by Radlov. The advantage to the community of such boasting when combined with a high sense of honour in carrying out the pledges is manifest from a passage in the Kachin poem of *Kara Tygan Khan and Suksagal Khan*. Here the hero is said to make a boast at his wedding feast, and on the following morning his wife tells him that in his drunkenness he boasted that he would restore two dead men to life. The hero turns for verification to his brother-in-law:

> "Did I say this?" he asked.
> "You said you would revive the dead", he replied.
> "If I actually said so,
> Have my heroic steed saddled";

and the hero, with his brother-in-law as his companion, rides away forthwith to fulfil his vow.[3]

It would seem as if the boasting had a stimulating effect, inducing an exalted impetus to do great deeds. It is with such a boast that the Kazak hero Sain sets off on the tracks of his ninety slaves, buoyed up by his own vow:

> You ninety slaves...
> Your steps will I trace...
> To the waterless steppe.
> Kudai[4] will cause you to come in my way.
> I will ride to bring this about
> All alone against a thousand foes.[5]

---

[1] *Proben* v, p. 10, l. 126ff.; cf. also *ib.* p. 50, l. 1460ff.
[2] *Ib.* ii, p. 25, l. 169ff.   [3] *Ib.* p. 587, l. 115ff.
[4] Kudai, 'God', lit. 'the strong one'. See p. 83 below.
[5] *Proben* iii, p. 219, l. 481ff.; cf. also p. 238, l. 1098f.

Even in the more trivial events of life great attention is paid to details of etiquette and procedure. These formalities are especially noted in the poems with regard to the reception and entertainment of guests, the welcome and housing of strangers, the preparations for a feast, sports, hunting, the farewell to those setting out on a journey. It is clear that the minstrel regards these details as significant, and of interest to his audience, and they enable us to form a clear notion of the routine and etiquette of steppe life. The insistence of the poems on matters of deportment is very striking. One gets the impression, even making due allowance for static poetic formulae, that life in the steppe is the most conventional in the world. The sense of decorum is most clearly seen in the almost total absence of impropriety throughout these heroic poems and sagas.

The horse plays an even more important part here than in the stories of the heroes of Kiev. All the horses are individualised and mentioned by name. It has already been mentioned that every hero's name has his horse's name appended, as we use a surname—Alaman Bet of the Yellow Piebald, Seräk of the blue steed. But the words employed for 'horse' are numerous, a separate word being used to denote each class according to its exact age and condition. The catalogue of horses which come to the races at Bok Murun's feast contains a detailed description of every horse famous in the heroic traditions of the Kara-Kirghiz. In this catalogue the description of Manas' horse Manykär occupies fifty-three lines. We have already referred to the poem which contains a detailed description of the 'points' of Kurroglou's famous steed Kyrat, and which is quoted as authoritative by horse breeders among the Turkomans to-day. Dogs are very rarely mentioned,[1] but after the death and burial of Manas his horse, hawk, and hound remain behind beside the tomb of their dead master to mourn his loss, and their grief is represented as so great that God sends His angels down from Heaven to enquire the cause of their sorrow. By this means they are instrumental in bringing about the hero's resuscitation.

The apparel, and more especially the weapons of the heroes are sometimes described with great care and minuteness. We have already seen Kanykäi shaking out her leather sacks containing the wardrobe with which she equips her guests, Manas and his 'forty friends', and which is said to consist of white corslets brought from Kashgar on a wagon, richly studded with bosses, and having a golden gorget and copper epaulettes. In addition she furnishes them with fine shirts,

This may be due to Mohammedan influence.

strong hose, and high boots reaching to the saddle.[1] We see Manas contending with Er Kökchö in his famous mail-coat, while Er Kökchö himself wears only a cloth coat. The admirable outfit of Kongyr Bai, Prince of China, is also described—his woven steel corslet, his sharp sword, his fir-shafted lances. In sharp contrast to these are the horse-hair jerkin and high black lambs'-wool cap of Alaman Bet of the Kara-Nogai. Manas' famous mail-coat and sword are mentioned constantly in the poems, and the passage which tells us how they were forged affords an admirable example of the skilful method by which the Kirghiz minstrel conveys description by means of narrative:

> That which the craftsman of the Chinese
> Painfully fashioned;
> Which the craftsman of the Russians
> Skilfully fashioned;
> Which the craftsman of the Kalmucks
> Fashioned as he muttered songs;[2]
> Which the musket never pierced,
> Nor the bullet ever bored,
> This, his outer white mail-coat,
> This white mail-coat he drew on.
> Where the charcoal was insufficient,[3]
> A patch of dense forest was stripped;
> When the water was insufficient,[4]
> The river Boschat was emptied.
> When the file was insufficient,
> Thirty files were brought into play.
> When the winter set in,
> Maw- and paunch-fat
> He portioned with it;
> When the spring set in,
> It was laid on the grass,
> And, that it might strike home,
> It was tempered in the blood of heroes,
> And plunged in poplar juice.
> This sword he bound to his belt.[5]

The life of the heroes is that of a typical barbaric community. Landed possessions appear to be unknown, and wealth consists wholly of flocks and herds. Life is sustained chiefly by hunting and plunder.

---

[1] *Proben* v, p. 210, l. 121 ff.

[2] So the text; but the reference is doubtless to charms.

[3] I.e. for smelting the steel. This line and all that follows refer, not to his mail-coat, but to his sword.   [4] I.e. for tempering the steel.

[5] *Proben* v, p. 43, l. 1227; cf. *ib.* p. 44, l. 1275 ff.

Agriculture also is unknown, and we hear nothing of artisans or of handicrafts, save in the instance just quoted. There is, of course, nothing resembling economic organisation, and references to trade are practically confined to the static epithet of Er Kökchö, 'who opened the shut bazaars'. The attitude of the hero to others of his own class is wholly irresponsible, the usual custom being that the young and strong plunder the old and weak, as soon as they feel themselves in a strong enough position to do so, and quite irrespective of any previous relationship which may have existed between them.

As in the heroic literatures discussed already, it is only rarely that social standards or moral judgments are expressed explicitly. Occasionally it happens that a character is singled out for an opprobrious epithet. Kardygach, Joloi's sister, is referred to as 'the wicked witch',[1] and Jakyp Bai, the father of Manas, as the 'evil slave'.[2] More often the poet makes clear only by implication that certain characters are to be deprecated, while others are approved. It is to be doubted whether courage is highly valued for its own sake, for many of the heroes show little enough, while their sisters and their horses—often their wives also—are surpassingly brave without gaining the slightest commendation from the poet. Joloi shows no courage or resolution, and Manas himself is less courageous than his enemy Er Kökchö, though the latter is naturally averse to fighting. The cowardice of old Sadai Khan on the approach of his enemy, the dreaded Kuskun Alyp, in the Koibal poem *Sugdjul Mergän* is made the subject of humour rather than censure, and he cuts a comic figure as he hides under the feather bed on the approach of his enemy, who pulls him out ignominiously by the legs.[3] Such absence of decorum is never found in the heroic poems, however. And all the heroes are credited with a naïve recklessness, and will at times go forth alone against a whole army.

The duty of loyalty is less emphasised perhaps in Tatar poetry than in other heroic literatures, owing to the individualistic character of the poems, especially among the peoples of the Abakan steppe. References to the practice of making a compact of brotherhood together, however, suggest that the virtue of personal loyalty is a recognised standard of behaviour. It is moreover generally implied throughout the poems that gratitude to a deliverer ought to bring loyalty in its train, and though we infer this more often from the breach than from the observance, disloyalty always meets with due punishment. In the poem

[1] *Proben* v, p. 432, and *passim*.
[2] *Ib.* p. 284.   [3] *Ib.* II, p. 317.

on the death of Manas the desertion of Manas' retinue from the tomb of their dead lord is brought into sharp contrast to the faithful watch kept at the tomb by his horse, hawk, and hound. It is moreover clear throughout the poems that the loyalty of a wife to her husband, of a sister to her brother, of a horse to its master, are the standards of conduct recognised by all. The sisters who betray their brothers are regarded by the poet as the worst characters in the poems, and all meet with their punishment before the conclusion is reached. Disloyalty of a wife is more venial, and is often forgiven by the hero. Disloyalty of a horse to its master is absolutely unknown.

But the hero is a law to himself. He may be gluttonous, slothful, worthless, like Joloi; or callous of wife and home, and negligent of parents and dependants, as many of the heroes are; he may spill innocent blood, or be guilty of cruelty. All these things are condoned, even approved, provided that he is successful in battle, and can carry off much booty. It matters little by what means his success is gained, whether by incredible strength, or skill, or cunning, or by supernatural aid—though this is rare in the poems of the Kara-Kirghiz. It may be by the courage or skill and endurance of his wife, or sister, or horse. It is all one, if only he achieves the end desired by all, and can drive home many flocks and herds, and the family and retainers of his enemy to augment the resources of his own establishment. All this is, of course, only what we should expect to find among a people who are singularly poorly provided with material wealth and comfort.

Yet it rarely happens that the actions of the hero, as distinct from his negligence, are of such a nature as wholly to disgust the reader, or to alienate his sympathy. This is partly due, no doubt, to the remoteness of the life and incident from those with which we are directly familiar. But this is not the only reason. The chief cause lies in the fact that the hero's standards of behaviour, as distinct from his way of life, are not, in general, remote from those of western heroic poetry. Vulgarity is wholly absent, and the home-life of the heroes, making allowance for the uncertainties of warfare, and the difficulties of subsistence, is an ordered and not ungenial one. The coarseness and boorishness incidental to a nomadic people are in striking contrast to the absence of obscenity, and the general air of decorum in the poems. The rarity of barbarities and of gratuitous cruelty makes us feel the Tatar nomad less remote from ourselves than the Assyrian conquerors, whose prowess and atrocities are portrayed on the wall slabs from Nineveh and Kuyunjik.

It is hardly necessary to say that the narrative poetry of the Tatars is wholly individualistic in its interest. Everyone who has any real existence or function in the poems is individualised and mentioned by name. It need cause no surprise that the poems show no sign of national interest, in view of the elementary stage of Tatar political institutions; but it is somewhat surprising that tribal feeling should hardly make itself felt in the poems. The words 'Turk', or 'Tatar', or 'Kirghiz' rarely occur, and we hear very little of tribal organisation. Even references to various branches of the Tatars are not common, apart from catalogues, though some few peoples are mentioned by name. We are told that Manas is a prince of the Sary-Nogai, Joloi of the Kara-Nogai, that Alaman Bet belongs to the Oirot, or Kalmucks, Er Kökchö to the Uigurs. We are told that

> The Kalmuck tribes who nomadise in the Altai
> Live at peace under the rule of Ai Khan;
> The Kalmuck tribes who nomadise in Künkai
> Live at peace under Kün Khan,
> Live at peace, ply their trade.[1]

But this is merely a means of identification employed by a people who have not the habit of referring to a fixed locality, and where no towns exist. There is no indication that any political distinctions are recognised, or any national unity felt, or animosity of one branch of the Tatars or Mongols, as such, towards another.

This absence of political consciousness is seen in the ease with which a hero will pass at will from one camp to another. The heroes are by no means necessarily of the same nationality as the people on whose side they fight. The most important example is Alaman Bet, who leaves his own people, the Kalmucks, to enter the service of Er Kökchö, the Uigur prince, and then again leaves him for Manas, a prince of the Sary-Nogai. Karacha, one of the heroes of Urum Khan, a Kalmuck prince, is himself of Russian origin.[2] Manas is in alliance with, and under the patronage of Russia. On one occasion Joloi is referred to as 'Joloi Khan, the Russian prince'.[3]

The Tatar poems are exceptional among heroic literatures in recognising the existence of a linguistic barrier. The Chinese are constantly referred to as 'babbling in a language which no-one can understand'. Alaman Bet[4] and others[5] are under the necessity of instructing the

---

[1] *Proben* v, p. 212, l. 160 ff.   [2] *Ib.* p. 17, l. 365 ff.
[3] *Ib.* p. 146.   [4] *Ib.* p. 8 f.   [5] *Ib.* p. 217.

Uigurs, the Sary Nogai, etc., in their language, and these lessons are quaintly given *verbatim* in the text. But as a general rule, in the ordinary intercourse of life no difficulty is experienced in communication. When Kös Kaman and his sons arrive at the camp of Jakyp Bai, they converse on easy terms with the Nogai, though, according to their own story, their whole life has been spent among the Kalmucks.

The poems give no hint of a clash of rival interests, or of difference of national ideals between the peoples who are at war with one another. In the geographical catalogues the neighbouring peoples are enumerated *seriatim*; but the interest of these is anthropological rather than political, and there is no hint of a consciousness of political feeling, whether of sympathy or animus, on the part of the reciter. The poems of the Abakan Tatars are even more individualistic in feeling, for here almost every chief appears to be independent. The only country which stands out from the rest as having a certain locale is China, which, unlike other territories in the poems, is referred to by name. But there is nothing which would lead one to suspect that the Chinese are a totally alien people. To the Kara-Kirghiz it is the country of their hated overlord to whom taxes are due; to the people of the Abakan poems it is indistinguishable from the world of spirits (cf. p. 90 below).

No such complete cleavage exists between the Mohammedans and the heathen in the *Manas* poems as the difference in religions would lead one to expect, though religious distinctions play some part in the actual stories, and have played their part also in the predilections and prejudices of the minstrels by whom they have been carried on. The Uigurs and the Sary-Nogai—the latter represented by Manas and his followers—are Mohammedans; the Kalmucks and the Kara-Nogai— the latter ruled by Joloi are heathen. The poems appear to portray the Mohammedan peoples just at the transition stage, and to reflect some of the religious antipathies governing the warfare and politics of eastern Central Asia during the eighteenth century.[1] Manas and his people are apparently newly converted, since Er Koshoi, who 'opened the gate of Paradise and the shut bazaars', is still alive. Religious controversy is raging among the Kalmucks, and Alaman Bet, the son of the ruling prince, is a convert to Mohammedanism; but his parents and their subjects resent his change of faith, and determine to remain heathen. Yet despite the fact that the period is one of transition, religious differences and religious controversy play little part in the poems, and religious bitterness may be said to be absent. The relations between the

[1] See Radlov, *Proben* v, p. xi.

Sary-Nogai and the heathen Kalmucks, who are generally identified in the poems with the Chinese, are in some respects not unlike those of the Christians and the Moors in medieval Spain, and do not exclude the possibility of friendly rivalry between individuals. Once more we may refer to the feast of Bok Murun to which all the heroes are invited, both Mohammedan and heathen, who figure in Kara-Kirghiz epic poetry. The religious bias of the poet undoubtedly makes itself felt in this story, for the Moslem tribes, led by Manas, on the one side, are pitted against the heathen on the other, and the former are represented as victorious in every trial of skill; but for the poet the personal interest and the incidents far outweigh the religious interest, and here, as elsewhere, strong religious emotion and religious animosity are very little in evidence.

It is characteristic of their freedom from national consciousness and national prejudice that the Tatar heroic stories, like the heroic stories of the Teutonic peoples, have to some extent an international currency. That is to say, stories and variants of stories which are current among the Kara-Kirghiz are found also among the Kazak and other Tatars. We may instance the story of *Er Töshtük*, one variant of which in prose form under the name *Jirtüshlük (Jär-Tüshtück)* is current also among the Tatars of the Tyumen and Yalutrowsk areas, while another version, also in prose, is found under the title *Kan Shentäi* among the Kazaks. Most of the important heroes mentioned in the *Manas* Cycle occur in the Kazak story of *Er Kökshü*, which is partly in prose, partly in verse. Other instances have already been mentioned and others again will be referred to later (p. 161 ff. below).

The individualism which is so salient a feature of the heroic poetry of the Tatars, as of other heroic poetry, is characteristic also of the methods of warfare, and of the motives for which it is carried on. Of generalship, or strategy, or the art of war the poems know absolutely nothing. All the fighting of which we have any details is of a personal character, and every battle described at any length resolves itself into a series of single combats, in which the heroes of noble birth alone take part. The war between the Sary-Nogai and the Uigurs consists of a series of duels between Manas and Alaman Bet and their immediate relatives on the one hand, and the Uigur and Kalmuck chiefs on the other. These duels are in every respect typical heroic encounters. We see the heroes deliberately discussing before the contest the various methods by which they are about to fight one another, and the weapons which they are about to employ. Each hero in vaunting terms threatens his opponent, and boasts of the death to which he will consign him. The actual encounter is generally described with spirit and freshness; but when the poet attempts to give an account of warfare on a larger scale, he at once falls into trite and meaningless formulae.

Despite the crudity of technique and the absence of refinement in the methods of warfare, the poems are in general remarkable for the rarity of brutality and butchery such as sometimes disfigures the heroic poetry of the Yugoslavs and the ancient Greeks. Head-hunting is unknown. It is also remarkable that it is only very exceptionally that the hero gains his advantage in battle either by supernatural means or by subterfuge. His colossal strength is, of course, exaggerated, but it is not in general different in kind from that of other men. The hero of Kara-Kirghiz poetry is no trickster, and no gods or angels lend him their aid in battle.

The Tatar heroes constantly undertake desperate, and, indeed, hopeless enterprises with reckless daring and total disregard of odds. In this they appear to be actuated rather by desire of gain and personal aggrandisement than by a desire of heroic honour or a thirst for fame. They are indeed more materialistic in their outlook than any other heroes with whom we have been in contact, owing, no doubt, to their poverty, and the absence of a settled mode of life. By far the most frequent cause of warfare and personal strife alike is desire for plunder, and no other pretext is felt to be necessary to start a raid. As in all heroic poetry, however, a very common cause of war is the unauthorised carrying off of women. Insults also are a fruitful source of strife.

Despite the fact that warfare plays so large a part in the poems the heroes do not appear to love fighting for its own sake, as the Yugoslav heroes do. The economic conditions of steppe life, rather than heroic sentiment, are the main incentives to heroism, and in such circumstances it is not surprising to find that the stronger prey upon the weaker. A young chief, growing up to find himself pauperised by a powerful neighbour, directs his whole attention to retrieving his lost patrimony. The jealousy of Guthrún, the polish and courtesy of Hrothgar, the self-conscious heroism of Hamðir and Sörli find no place in these poems. The poet himself is unfamiliar with these refinements of a more advanced state of society. The heroism of the Tatar poems is of a primitive character, and the conditions of life hardly permit of the subtler and wider motives which sometimes govern international relations and make for peace and war in more advanced communities.

But when due allowance has been made for these differences, which are, after all, differences of degree, it will be seen that the milieu and personnel of these poems correspond in their essential features with those of the other heroic literatures already considered. They are concerned with individuals of aristocratic rank, who lead a somewhat irresponsible existence, and live chiefly by plunder. Warfare is common, but it is chiefly of a personal character. Peaceful relations between one people and another are also chiefly personal. Agriculture and trade are practically unknown, though personal adornments and luxuries are highly prized, and intellectual accomplishments are not wholly lacking, especially among the women. In short the society depicted is a typical barbaric society in an unsettled phase of existence and with no clearly defined limits of territory.

CHAPTER IV

NON-HEROIC POETRY AND SAGA

POST-HEROIC poetry and saga of purely native origin appear to be wholly unknown among the Tatars, though post-heroic features are not wanting in the poetry of the Turkomans, as we have seen. Post-heroic prose of native origin, other than saga, is perhaps not wholly unknown, though examples are few and doubtful (cf. p. 52 ff. above). Prose saga composed under foreign influence contains a considerable proportion of post-heroic features. Poetry and saga, other than heroic, of purely native origin seem to correspond almost wholly to what we have elsewhere called non-heroic poetry and saga of the Heroic Age. This is, of course, what might be expected from the fact that among the Tatars the Heroic Age lasted until comparatively recent times.

The Tatars possess a great body of non-heroic literature. Much of this belongs to communities which also possess a rich store of heroic literature, especially of heroic narrative poetry. Indeed, non-heroic literature which is wholly divorced from heroic elements is not often found in Radlov's collections, except in the dramatic presentations of the shamans. It may perhaps be said that the great bulk of the material in Tatar literature which is manifestly unhistorical is also non-heroic in character. But in narrative poetry and saga unhistorical and non-heroic elements are almost invariably included in a heroic framework. Examples of narrative poetry and prose which are primarily concerned with non-heroic characters, such as professional shamans and shamankas,[1] are not common, though they are not unknown.

The range of stories contained in this non-heroic literature differs considerably from what is found in most of the literatures which we have hitherto considered, though it will be seen that it offers much which is closely akin to certain elements in ancient Greek literature and ritual, and to the ancient literature of Mesopotamia and of Japan. To this subject we shall return later. These non-heroic Tatar stories are of considerable interest, not only for their own sake, but also for the study of Tatar mythology and of religious and eschatological ideas. Owing

---

[1] I.e. female *shamans*. This form is a hybrid, the Russianised feminine of *shaman*, apparently itself a Tungus word. See p. 193 below.

to the great wealth of Tatar literature of this kind it will be necessary to confine our attention to a few examples of the more important branches, concentrating chiefly on the poetry of the Tatars of the Abakan and neighbouring steppes and of the Kara-Kirghiz. It must, however, be borne in mind that a large number of poems similar in character, though, in general, briefer and of less literary merit, are current also among other Tatar tribes, notably the Teleut and Chern Tatars, and the Tatars of the Altai.

In order to understand clearly the spiritual background of the poems it will be necessary to say a few words about the spiritual ideas and concepts of Tatar religion. For these our chief authorities are the pronouncements of the shamans, and the texts of the actual poems and sagas before us, more especially of the narrative poems of the Kara-Kirghiz and the Abakan Tatars, and the poetry recited by the shamans of the Altai during the performance of their religious ceremonies to which reference will be made below. Owing to lack of space it will not be possible for us to do more here than mention the most outstanding features of the personnel of the Tatar spiritual world. At the same time it is important for us to remember that in the form in which this non-heroic Tatar narrative poetry and saga has come to us it is composed and recited, not for religious purposes, but for purposes of entertainment. Here, just as also in other literatures in which mythology has passed similarly from a religious to a secular milieu, the spiritual beings have lost their austerity and remoteness, and tend to approximate to the figures of folk-tales. The evidence of oral literature for Tatar theology is not in agreement in all respects with Radlov's exposition, which was derived more directly from the teaching of the shamans themselves and from their hymns and prayers.[1]

The poems appear to recognise two spiritual environments which are mutually hostile. The personnel of the first are situated in the Heavens above, which are pictured as a series of superimposed planes. The highest of these is ruled by a supreme being, whose name is sometimes given as Kaira Khan,[2] sometimes as Bai Ülgen.[3] The personnel of the second live underground, and their ruler is Erlik Khan. His realm is the abode of the dead. The entrance to this gloomy region is through a hole or cave in the ground. The interests of the spiritual beings who

[1] See Radlov, *A.S.* II, p. 1 ff.   [2] So Radlov, *A.S.* II, p. 3.
[3] See Radlov, *Wörterbuch*, *s.v. Ülgen*. The difference may possibly be local. But complete consistency is not to be expected in a very elaborate theological system carried on by oral tradition.

dwell in the Heavens are opposed to those of Erlik and his followers; but these two classes of spirits never meet, or come into any direct contact with one another, at least in the narrative poems and sagas. The hero of these narratives is generally under the direct protection of the Heavenly beings, whose champion he is. His enemy, also a hero, but an unsympathetic character, is often the central figure of the beings who inhabit the underground realm, and frequently represents their interests on earth. Very often the hostile hero is said to be 'black', and he is sometimes referred to as an 'earth hero', i.e. one who lives underground.[1]

These spiritual beings constitute two communities of which the members stand in an implied relationship to one another which seems to be constant. The Heavens are occupied by the God Kaira Khan, Bai Ülgen[2] or Kydyr (who are also known as Kudai, 'the Strong Ones'), the nine *Jajan* or 'Creators',[3] and the Wise Maidens, who are generally three in number. The hero is under the protection of Kydyr, who takes an intimate personal interest in his affairs, but rarely comes in contact with him. The intermediaries are the nine *Jajan* or 'Creators', spiritual beings who are very commonly spoken of as acting and speaking in a body, though they have their own rivalries and their own differences, as we shall see. These spiritual beings dwell on the lower planes of Heaven, and protect a man throughout his life, perhaps as ancestral spirits. Higher than the *Jajan* in prestige are the three Wise Maidens, who seem to be identical with the three daughters of Kudai, and who are also sometimes referred to as the daughters of the *Jajan* themselves. They are the guardians of the herbs of healing and the water of life. In approaching them, the hero is sometimes spoken of as first encountering the *Jajan* who guide and direct him to them, and instruct him as to how he shall conduct himself in his relations with them.

[1] Among the Buryat, whose spiritual ideas and institutions resemble those of the Kara-Kirghiz closely, this schematisation appears to have been carried much further, and here a definite opposition of two hostile spiritual forces, working against one another, is officially recognised. There is a close resemblance to Zoroastrianism, which is emphasised also by the occurrence among the Buryat of certain loan words; see below. For accounts of Buryat theology, see Klementz, *s.v.* the article *Buryat*, in Hastings' *Encyclopædia of Religion and Ethics*, and the more recent work of Sandschejew. For the 'black hero' of Mongol epic see Poppe, *A. M.* v (1930), p. 185.

[2] Among the Buryat in certain localities Ülgen is significantly known as Khormusta-Tengri, i.e. Ormuzd (Klementz, *loc. cit.*).

[3] Radlov translates the word *jajan* throughout the *Proben* as 'Schöpfern'. In his *Wörterbuch der Türkischen Dialekte* he translates by the words *sozdatel*, *tvorets*, 'der Schöpfer', 'Gott'.

Erlik Khan, the prince or ruler of the Underworld, is pictured as an old man with a great black beard, and sometimes as black himself. He has a number of retainers, some of whom also act at times as the familiars of the 'earth-hero', who borrows them from Erlik and employs them to hunt human quarry. In addition he has a number of colleagues who also live under the earth. Among these we may refer to the earth-Aina, Jer Kara, who seems to represent the spirit of death or of the dead, and the swan-woman, Chekchäkäi, who is vividly portrayed as having leaden eyes and hempen plaits, and hands with yellow nails. He has also a respected colleague in Altyn Sibäldi, the 'Golden Witch', who is commonly referred to as 'leaden-eyed and copper-nosed'. She is the mother of nine sons, the *Jelbägän* (sing. *Jelmogus*, sometimes called *Dshalmaus, Jel Maja*, etc.), who are variously described as having seven, nine, etc. heads, and as living in a many-gabled house of stone, the entrance to which is guarded by great dogs with fiery breath. The exact nature of the *Jelmogus* is not wholly clear. The records frequently suggest that he is something in the nature of a dragon hero;[1] but Radlov was told among the Chern Tatars that he is a very strong demon with seven heads who has destroyed the moon, but is forced by Ülgen to restore it.[2] Sometimes *Jelmogus* appears to be used figuratively for the Uigur state.[3]

Among the Kara-Kirghiz, the only non-heroic poem recorded by Radlov is *Er Töshtük*. The poem is obscure in many particulars, and the poet has not remembered his story well, or through fatigue or some other cause has omitted much which would have made the narrative more intelligible. Some of these omissions can be supplied from the prose variant versions to be found elsewhere, and many of the obscure and difficult passages are also clearer or more specifically related in these versions. Summaries of these prose versions will be given in the section of the present chapter devoted to non-heroic saga, and a comparison of these texts will also be given in the chapter on 'The Texts'.

The poem is the biography of a man whose adventures and experiences appear to have been for the most part of a spiritual rather than of a material character, and whose life is largely spent underground in the spirit world. In spite of this fact, however, these adventures are similar in many respects to the ordinary heroic adventures of Manas and Joloi, and it is clear from references to the hero himself and to his famous steed Chal Kuiruk in the Cycles of *Manas* and *Joloi* that Er

---

[1] See e.g. *Proben* I, p. 28 ff.　　　　　[2] Radlov, *A.S.* I, p. 372.

[3] *Proben* v, p. 3, l. 53 where Radlov translates "Grimmig wird Manas"; but for a more literal translation see p. 28 above.

Töshtük is a well-known figure of heroic story. Reference has already been made to the poem of *Bok Murun* (p. 32 above), where Er Töshtük is brought into relation with Manas and Alaman Bet, and where he is represented as running a race with Joloi's wife; but even here his spiritual experiences underground are referred to, and there can be no doubt that he is the most outstanding spiritual figure in Tatar literature.

The central idea of the poem now before us is the visit of the hero to the Underworld and his safe return. The poem opens, like the *Manas* Cycle, with an account of the birth of the hero. Er Töshtük is born in answer to the prayer of his father Ilämän, whose youngest son he is, and we are tempted to believe that owing to this fact, and also to the fact that he is the ninth son, the hero is in some way specially endowed with spiritual gifts, and especially marked out by the inhabitants of the spirit world as their own. When the day comes to give the child a name, an old man with a white beard appears and names him 'Er Töshtük who finds favour with God', and then disappears as suddenly as he has come. From the many parallels to this incident in other stories it is clear that the old man is the god Kydyr.

One day, as Er Töshtük is away from home tracking his father's herds, which have been stolen, he comes upon a hut made of birch bark in charge of a black and hideous maiden called Bek Toro,[1] who promises him that his herds will be found, and insists on his spending the night in her hut. When he awakens at midnight all is bright within the hut, and the hideous maiden has become extremely beautiful, and he also finds food cooking on the spit beside the fire, which he takes and eats. Although it is not exactly stated, it is probable that by eating the food of Bek Toro the hero delivers himself into her hands, for it is spirit food. When he would embrace her, however, she forbids him, saying that she has prayed to God that he might be born. The passage is obscure, but the poet seems to suggest that Bek Toro claims Er Töshtük as her spiritual child. Her words are as follows:

> With golden frame and silver tongue
> My *komus*[2] have I played;
> I charmed the ear of God,
> You, Töshtük, for myself,
> I fitly formed, O hero.
> This false world is naught;
> Mine will you be hereafter, Töshtük.[3]

---

[1] Curiously enough this is also the name of one of Joloi's sons.
[2] For this musical instrument, see p. 23 above. [3] *Proben* v, p. 540.

The true significance of her words becomes clearer as the poem proceeds. Er Töshtük returns home, and his father sets out to look for a wife for him, and in his turn also encounters Bek Toro, and, being overtaken by night, is forced to accept her hospitality. He then proceeds on his way and obtains Kendshäkä, the youngest of Agai Khan's nine daughters, as a husband for the hero, though her father is very unwilling to marry her. But Bek Toro, who appears to regard Kendshäkä as a natural enemy and spiritual rival, meets her as she is on her way to the home of Er Töshtük, and tries to poison her. A strange dialogue takes place between the two women in which Bek Toro relinquishes Er Töshtük to Kendshäkä in this world, but lays claim to him in the next.[1]

When Kendshäkä overtakes Ilämän and his party they are obliged to encamp for the night at a spot against which her father has warned them, and Ilämän explains that this is due to her delay. Ilämän is forcibly seized by an evil spirit, *Jelmogus*,[2] and is obliged to promise Er Töshtük's soul to Jelmogus in order to save himself. Er Töshtük's soul is contained in a black steel file[3] hidden under the hearthstone, and on the arrival of the bridal party at the house of her future husband the bride at once asks for the file, doubtless with the intention of keeping it safe from Jelmogus. It is found, however, that Ilämän has left it behind at the evening bivouac, and Er Töshtük at once sets out to retrieve it. He finds it in the possession of Jelmogus, who is still in the same spot in the form of a hag, and after a prolonged struggle for the file, she sinks into the earth followed by the hero on his famous steed, Chal Kuiruk. From this point (l. 1100) the action takes place underground almost to the end of the poem, and relates a series of encounters, all more or less closely connected with one another, and all described as if they were ordinary heroic combats. In the course of his life underground the hero marries two wives and has a son, Bir Biläk.

At last the hero's horse grows weary of life underground, and begs his master to return to earth. The manner of Er Töshtük's return is

---

[1] This situation, and the dialogue between the two women—one a supernatural and the other a human being—bears a striking resemblance to the dialogue between Brynhildr and the *gýgr* in the *Helreið Brynhildar*, a poem contained in the early Norse collection known as the *Elder Edda*. See Vol. I, p. 27; cf. also p. 97 below.

[2] Cf. p. 84 above. The word *Jelmogus* seems to be merely a dialectal variety of *Dshalmaus*, which is defined by Radlov as lit. "'Snap-mouth', a monster which licks men up and swallows them" (*Proben* III, p. 154, footnote 1). This monster occurs very frequently in Tatar non-heroic literature.

[3] Some discussion of this is given by Chadwick, *J.R.A.I.* LXVI (1936), p. 311.

very striking. He comes to the middle of the earth and finds a lofty elm, its summit reaching to Heaven. A gigantic dragon is coiled around its trunk, while a pair of young eagles are perched on the top, lamenting loudly. Er Töshtük slays the dragon, and the grateful mother bird first renews the hero's youth by swallowing him and then spitting him out, and afterwards carries him up to earth on her back. From time to time she turns her head to be fed by him as she flies, and at last, having no more food to offer her, he is forced to give her one of his own eyes and a piece of his own shoulder. These are, however, restored to him by the eagle at their journey's end, and become whole again. The eagle flies back to the Underworld, and the hero places a turban on his head, and makes his way to his old home, disguised as a mullah, and then, on finding his family still hopefully awaiting his return, he reveals his identity to them, and all live happily together once more.

We have no doubt that the story of Er Töshtük is the biography of a person of shamanistic pretensions. The internal evidence of the story and its variants would seem to point to this, and the suggestion is supported by a comparison of the concluding portion of the poem with the practices of the shamans of the Altai district, as recorded by Radlov, as well as those of the Buryat and other east Siberian peoples. These practices will be considered more fully in connection with the shaman (cf. Chapter x). It may be mentioned here, however, that in the great annual sacrifice to Bai Ülgen, the god of the highest Heaven, the shaman first climbs a tree, and then mounts to Heaven on the back of a goose, after which he descends to the Underworld through a hole in the ground.

The Kara-Kirghiz have left us yet another story of the visit of a mortal to the Underworld, this time a man whom we have no clear reason for regarding as a professional shaman. The incident is related of Bolot, Joloi's son, who descends into the depths of the earth on his father's horse Ach Budan, following the tracks of his 'sister', the shamanka Kara Chach, just as Er Töshtük rides into the earth on his horse, following the tracks of Jelmogus. Previously to this incident Kara Chach has restored Bolot to his foster-father, Köchpös Bai, by her arts, and then, at the religious banquet at which the hero's external soul is sacrificed in the form of a sheep to Kydyr, Kara Chach herself disappears into the earth. When Bolot follows her on Ach Budan, he finds her riding on Jel Maja (i.e. Jelmogus; cf. p. 86, footnote 2 above), who warns him that he is compassed about by a heathen army. Bolot cuts down a fir tree and makes himself a mighty lance, and fights the heathen army till his strength is gone, and then he sees that Kara Chach is hovering over his head in the form of a grey hawk and routing his foes. The scene then changes to the upper world, where his brothers are also fighting the heathen host; but at last, again with the help of Kara Chach, they succeed in routing their enemy, and the wounded Bolot is restored to life and health by the further ministrations of Kara Chach, which she performs by tearing the lungs from Jel Maja, and striking Bolot on the head with them, and then gently stroking his side.[1]

The similarity of the narrative of Bolot's underground experience to the story of Er Töshtük are very striking, and this similarity is more evident in the original text, which is rich in detail and incident, than in this brief summary. The chief difference lies in the fact that in the story of Er Töshtük no friendly shamanka guides the hero's actions and protects him from his enemies. We may believe, however, that in the original form of the story Bek Toro played a more important part in the underground incidents, and this we shall see later is also suggested by the variants. She probably corresponds to Kara Chach, as Jelmogus corresponds to Jel Maja. It is also possible that the female eagle in the former story corresponds to the hawk in the latter, though this is less clear. It is far from clear in either story what is the exact relationship of either maiden to the hero. Kara Chach, under her name of Koitu Kung, is several times referred to by the hero as his 'sister'; but whether in a worldly or a spiritual sense is not clear, and it is doubtful if the relationship is to be pressed very closely. Neither woman appears to stand in the relationship of a lover, even of a spiritual lover. The nearest analogy seems to be the Norse *fylgjur*, the guardian spirits who follow a man throughout life and guide and direct both his soul and body for his welfare. The part played by *Kara* Chach, who hovers over the hero's head in battle in the form of a hawk and overcomes his enemies, is strikingly reminiscent of the part played by the maiden *Kara*, who in the form of a swan hovers over the head of the hero Helgi and fights his enemies in the Norse *Saga of Hrómundr Greipsson*.[2]

The epic poetry of the 'Abakan Group', that is to say of the Sagai

---

[1] *Proben* v, p. 524.

[2] For an English translation of this saga the reader may refer to Kershaw, *Stories and Ballads of the Far Past* (Cambridge, 1921), p. 62 ff. It is not impossible that the name *Helgi* has reference to this and other spiritual experiences of the hero, though the name is, of course, very common. It is interesting to note that the word *Kara* is unknown elsewhere in Norse.

tribes, and the Koibal, Katshin, and Kysyl Tatars (see p. 4 above), is contained in the second volume of Radlov's *Proben*. In spite of its somewhat restricted range of theme, it offers in many ways a more interesting field of study than any narrative poetry which we have found among barbaric peoples. The Sagai tribes, to whom the largest group belongs, are the most proficient in this form of poetry. They are said to be the least mixed with Finnish or Samoyedic peoples of all the Tatars of Siberia.[1] The subjects of the poems, so far as we can judge from the proper names and topographical details, are drawn from native sources, though we may suspect a certain amount of Mongolian influence, especially from the Buryat and Kalmucks. They are interesting, therefore, for their detailed pictures of steppe life, and still more for the information which they afford of the religious ideas and practices of the heathen Tatars. The people are still shamanists, and their poems are practically free from Christian or Mohammedan influence, though Buddhist and perhaps Manichaean ideas are not wholly absent.

The literary technique of the poems has attained to a remarkably high level. The average length of a poem is 770 lines, though the longest, the Sagai poem *Ai Mergän and Altyn Kus*, runs to nearly 4000 lines. Their narratives are the most complicated, and their structure the most ambitious which we have found outside Sanskrit literature, to which in this respect they bear some resemblance. The scene shifts constantly, and numerous characters are swept into the course of the narrative, each bearing a fresh set of complicated circumstances in his train. The handling of the material is astonishingly competent, and the poet never fails to resolve his discords, every villain being duly punished in his own turn, every hero provided with a wife, or refurnished with his own lost possessions before the end is reached. The climax of the Sagai poems comes, not at the end of the poem, but approximately in the middle. Already the poet begins gradually to unwind his clew, retracing his steps through the many localities where he has previously left only a tangled skein. The poems of the entire group which we have classed together as 'Abakan' are handled with a recognition of the relationship of incidents which is very rare in the heroic epic of oral tradition, and resemble a rich brocade. They are a triumph of structure and of memory.

These poems offer a totally different range of theme from those of the Kara-Kirghiz. The stories appear to form an independent group, and do not overlap to any great extent with those of the other Tatars, though identical incidents and motifs are sometimes found, as we shall

[1] Czaplicka, *Turks*, p. 19; cf. Vambéry, *Türkenvolk*, p. 96.

see (p. 95 ff. below). They are, in a sense, stories of adventure; but we are often in doubt as to whether these adventures are actual physical realities, or whether they are merely spiritual or intellectual adventures —adventures of the mind. At times they are clearly of the latter kind. Very often the main theme is a search. It may be that the hero is sought by a supernatural adversary, an emissary of Erlik. Sometimes the search is for an absent soul; for in these poems the soul is regarded as separable, and is sometimes contained in a lifeless object, though more often it has the form of a bird. At times the search is for stolen herds. A very common theme in the poems is a series of journeys, often of fantastic length and duration, and sometimes but slightly motivated, though generally culminating in the acquisition of a wife, and wealth of herds. Warlike encounters also play a certain part. In the latter the issue of events is generally governed by the cunning or knowledge of either a woman, or a horse, or of supernatural beings. But in all the poems supernatural elements play a large, even a preponderant part, and the personnel of the Heavens and the Underworld are rarely absent. It will not be possible in the limited space available here to do more than give brief summaries of a few of the poems which will serve to illustrate their unusual and interesting range of subject. In order to appreciate their technical merits it is necessary to read the actual texts of the poems.

The Sagai poem of *Ai Mökö* is a fair specimen of its class. It tells us that the orphan hero Ai Mökö and his sister are brought up by a certain Altyn Ärgäk, till one day, as Ai Mökö is out hunting, he encounters a certain Khan Kaigalai who says he does not honour Kudai. In the eyes of the shamanist Tatars, therefore, Khan Kaigalai is an atheist, and an encounter accordingly takes place between him and the hero, who at once champions Kudai. While they are contending, a dart is thrown by an unknown hand, whereupon Khan Kaigalai disappears into the earth. Ai Mökö picks up the dart and finds a piece of script attached, which purports to have been sent by a certain Chas Mökö in the land of Kudai.[1] The dart has been intended for a certain Akyrang Tas, with whom Chas Mökö has been at lifelong feud. He urges Ai Mökö to await the issue of the combat on the summit of the Altai, promising him that he will discover for him the whereabouts of his father, Altyn Airy. Before long Ai Mökö does actually find his father, a grey-haired old man, herding horses outside a princely dwelling.

The old man tells him that he has been overcome in battle by two

[1] In this poem the land of Kudai is identified with 'China', i.e., no doubt, Chinese Turkestan.

heroes known as Altyn Pyrgy and Kümüs Pyrgy, and advises him to
consult Chas Mökö, who 'has come from China', as to the advisability
of taking vengeance. Chas Mökö declares that Kůdai will not allow
Ai Mökö to be overcome, and the hero accordingly confidently undertakes to do battle with his father's enemies. In the single combats
which ensue, Ai Mökö slays the brothers, and then returns to Altyn
Argäk, accompanied by his father and Chas Mökö. Chas Mökö, however, soon leaves them to go in search of his old enemy, Akyrang Tas,
and Ai Mökö follows him, bidding his father continue on his course to
Altyn Argäk. Chas Mökö is slain, but Ai Mökö slays Akyrang Tas in
vengeance, and then goes to Altyn Argäk, who gives him in marriage
the noble lady Altyn Chüstük, the daughter of a certain Kisikai, and the
hero and his family return to their old home. Altyn Chüstük, it is to be
noted, is the name of one of the three 'Heavenly Maidens', daughters
of Kudai, who dwell in the Heavens, and possess the water of life and
the herb of healing.

The Sagai poem of *Puga-Däkä* also tells how a youthful hero sets
out to rescue his father who has been carried off by two brothers, Tas
Chüräk, and Pus Chüräk. He comes upon them as they are celebrating
the marriage feast of their sister, who is again Altyn Chüstük, and over-
hears a dialogue between the chief of the company, Ägrä Kara, a 'great
black man from the Underworld', and his aged opponent, Karyn Dara,
also from the nether regions, in which the former boasts that he will gain
possession of the youthful hero, while the latter denies his power.
Meanwhile Puga Däkä finds his father nailed to a lofty rock. He
returns to attack Ägrä Kara, and fighting together they sink down far
below the earth to Ägrä Kara's dwelling, where the hero slays him and
others, and then mounts to earth by climbing a tree which grows in the
Underworld, like that by which Er Töshtük mounts to the eagle's nest.
The rest of the story tells how the hero retrieves his lost horse-herds.

The Sagai poem of *Altyn Pyrkan* relates the prolonged search and
pursuit by a certain Saryg Khan of the young hero Altyn Pyrkan, who
is saved by the superior power of a foal who sucks the child up into
his nostrils and gallops away. In his efforts to capture his prey, Saryg
Khan calls to his aid a number of supernatural emissaries—his two royal
eagles, his two hounds, Kasar and Pasar, and Seven-headed Chalbägän[1]
—who seek their prey through air, earth, and underground. He also
sends the Swan-woman and Kär Palyk, the great royal carp which

---

[1] For the Chalbägän (Jelbägän), the Swan-woman, etc., cf. p. 84 above. All these
appear also in the epic poetry of the Khalka Mongols, where the hounds appear
as Assar and Bassar. See Poppe, *A. M.* VIII, p. 202 ff.

dwells on the bottom of the sea, and he himself makes enquiries of sun, moon, and stars, herbs, and all created things; but he cannot come up with his prey. Later in the story the child dies, but the foal secures the aid of Altyn Chüstük, who restores the dead to life, and to whom reference has already been made. She is here said to be the oldest of three maidens who possess this gift, and who live in 'the third Heaven'.[1] Actually it seems to be, not Altyn Chüstük herself, but her younger sister, Ai Aryg, who comes 'as a golden cuckoo' to the corpse, and sprinkles it with the water of life, and lays the yellow herb in its mouth, so that the child is restored to health and vigour, so much so that when he cracks his whip even the *jaj*, or tutelary spirit[2] who dwells in Heaven above, cannot remain seated. After this we learn without surprise that the hero returns and slays Saryg Khan and all his supernatural familiars.

The closing portion of this strange story is not the least interesting. The hero overcomes a certain Ottyg Chalyn and his brother, and then, instead of slaying them, he 'purifies their souls', and releases them. We next hear of the hero's journey to Heaven to woo for himself Altyn Chüstük, who is here said to be the youngest of the three sisters. As he passes through the first Heaven the nine *jajan* discourage him, but Ödürbä Jajan in the second Heaven befriends him on the ground that he has purified the souls of Ottyg Chalyn and his brother. It is to be observed that in these poems we frequently find the inculcation of mercy and gentleness, especially by divine beings, rather than of heroic virtue. Altyn Chüstük, however, has vowed only to marry the man who can overcome her in wrestling and archery, and a long and incredible struggle follows in which the earth is destroyed, despite the efforts of the *jajan*, who all assemble to hold it together. At last, after this Titanic combat, the hero succeeds in overpowering Altyn Chüstük, and, sticking her unceremoniously into his pocket, he rides home with her to his *yurt* and makes her his wife.[3]

The Sagai poem of *Kan Tögös*, like the majority of these poems, relates to a hero who has no parents, neither has he brother or sister; but he is wealthy, and his herds are cared for by nine 'bald-headed men', while he himself lies on a golden bed and eats delicate food. One day the 'bald-headed men' enter his *yurt* and tell him that most of his

---

[1] In shamanist theology the Heavens are represented as a series of superimposed planes.   [2] Pl. *jajan*; cf. above.

[3] The resemblance to the Russian *bylina* of Dobrynya and the *polenitsa* (see Vol. II, p. 37 above) is very striking, though in the Russian story the woman comes off victor, and pockets her vanquished wooer.

servants and herds have disappeared, they know not where. Khan Tögös at once strikes the earth asunder, and disappears underground in search of them. He soon comes upon Erlik Khan, the god of the Underworld, who directs him to Altyn Sibäldi, the golden witch, whom the hero slays, together with her nine sons, the nine *Jelbägän*, whom he finds playing at knuckle-bones.[1] He continues to overcome one hero after another, even calling down fire from Heaven to destroy their dwellings, till 'there is no peace for any between the Aina underground and the *Jajan* above'. At last, after incredible encounters and victories, he arouses by his arrogance the anger of the nine *Jajan* who have created all heroes, and they accordingly create a hero who forces him to flee underground once more. Here his final encounter takes place with a six-headed *Jelbägän* seated on a golden bed, and his unlovely wife, a leaden-eyed, copper-nosed witch, both of whom he slays. Finally he returns to earth, a white-haired old man, to find all his herds and people awaiting him. It is a particularly interesting feature of Khan Tögös that he is expressly stated never to have married or to have had any children. This statement would seem to be expressly made of other heroes in these poems (cf. p. 96 below), who, like Khan Tögös himself, are accomplished in the arts ascribed generally to shamans. The latter part of the poem of *Kan Tögös* has affinities with the poem of *Er Töshtük*, whom we have also seen to be gifted with shamanistic powers, and there can be no doubt that Khan Tögös is himself a person of this class.

The Sagai poem of *Kara Par* opens with an account of Russian kidnapping. The hero is stolen as a six-year-old boy by a Russian 'in a black coat', and sold to a childless old couple in exchange for nine deer-skins. When he is nine years of age a Russian conscription officer comes and 'writes him on his paper', giving him the name Kara Par; and three days later the boy rides forth to join the Russian army, but soon makes good his escape on a stolen horse, and rides away to his father's hunting ground. So far the poem is not remote from reality, and offers us a vivid picture of the relations between the Russians and Tatars viewed from a Tatar's personal standpoint.

The atmosphere of realism soon vanishes, however. Before long Kara Par finds his uncle, Khan Märgän, lying dead in his house, and, forbidding his retainers to bury the body till his return, Kara Par sets off to find the murderer. The murderer, somewhat to our surprise, is an old woman with nine ears, from which hang nine ear-rings, and she lives in a black house with nine gables. She confesses to Kara Par that

---

[1] The static formula used of a child in Tatar poetry.

she has cooked his father in a black kettle, and hidden his uncle's soul, in the form of a golden file, inside her black coffer. Her own soul, in the form of a seven-headed spotted snake, lies in the sole of her boot, and Kara Par forthwith dispatches it, cutting off the seven heads. He then enters the house, passing from room to room, each offering a spectacle more dreadful than the last, and we are not surprised when he exclaims on returning to the upper world—the horrors, it seems, are contained in subterranean caves—

> To such an Aina-*yurt*
> May my own child never come.[1]

At last the hero returns to his own *yurt* and restores his uncle's soul by means of the file; but he cannot restore his father—for has he not seen his head cooking in the cauldron in the cave of horror? The story is chiefly interesting for the detailed picture which it gives of the hero's experiences in the caves—experiences which are not rare in these poems, but which are not often related so fully.

An interesting parallel to the journey of Kara Par to the Underworld occurs, however, in a poem from the Sayan Steppe recorded by Castrén,[2] in which the picture of the Underworld is even more detailed, and which is especially interesting, since the visitor to the spirit world is in this case a woman. According to this story a certain hero, Komdei-Mirgän, is injured while hunting a fox, which is, in reality, the daughter of Erlik Khan in disguise. When the hero is disabled, the nine-headed Jelbägän rides up on a forty-horned ox and cuts off his head and carries it to the Underworld. The hero's sister, Kubai Ko, resolves to seek the head, and follows the track of Jelbägän to a hole in the ground through which she descends to the realm of Erlik Khan. Here she encounters many strange shapes and sights, among others, groups of people each suffering torment nicely adjusted to their evil deeds on earth. Hurrying by in fear, she at length comes to the bank of a river, on which stands the abode of Erlik, a stone house with forty gables. Before the entrance stand nine larch trees, all growing from one single root. Erlik's horses

---

[1] With this picture of the underground caverns of horror it is interesting to compare the account given by Waddell of the great chamber of horrors in Sam-Yäs monastery, about thirty miles from Lhasa, in which a man who enacts the part of the scapegoat is compelled annually to spend seven days, and from the horrors of which he has sometimes become demented and died (*Lamaism*[2], p. 512f.; cf. also *ib.* p. 267).

[2] Castrén III, p. 148ff.; IV, p. 239ff. A summary of the story is also given by Holmberg, p. 489ff.

are tied to the larches, and Kubai Ko also ties up her horse here and enters the house. She feels herself seized and tormented by invisible hands, while her clothes are torn to rags. When Erlik appears he ignores her, and refuses to speak to her, but Kubai Ko follows him through many rooms till at last she enters a room where eight princes of death are seated, and in their midst is their chief, Erlik Khan himself. Kubai Ko bows low and asks why their servant Jelbägän has cut off and carried away her brother's head. The princes reply that Jelbägän has acted under their orders, but promise to give her back the head if she can pull a goat out of the earth which is buried up to its horns. Kubai Ko accepts the ordeal, and is led through nine rooms filled with human heads, her brother's among them. She succeeds in exhuming the goat, and is escorted back to the larch, where she mounts her horse and then rides back to earth, carrying her brother's head, and accompanied by the princes of death, who expound to her the significance of all that she has seen. Kubai Ko now restores her brother's head to his body, and sits down beside him to lament; but Kudai has pity on her tears, and sends the water of life which she sprinkles three times on his lips, and the hero is restored to health and strength.

The Kachin poem of *Kara Tygan Khan and Suksagal Khan*, recorded by Radlov, opens with an account of the wooing and marriage of the daughter of a certain Ak Khan by the hero, Kara Tygan Khan, who is accompanied by his brother-in-law, named Olanger. The preliminary incidents of this poem have already been alluded to (p. 71 above). We have seen that the hero's wife and Olanger tell the hero that while he was drunk at his wedding feast on the previous night he boasted that he would restore to life two heroes, whose names are given as Altyn Ergäk and Kümüs Ergäk. In order to fulfil this vow Kara Tygan Khan and Olanger transform themselves into swallows, and their horses into swans. They then fly up to a certain tree on the Altai, on the summit of which grows the white herb which has the virtue of restoring the dead to life. The herb is guarded by two ravens who have built their nest in the topmost branches, and whose nestlings lie on the top of the herb; but the heroes in their bird-form secure it, and then, transforming themselves once more into men, fulfil their vow, and return with the bride to their own home.

One day, as Kara Tygan Khan is out hunting, his black horse stumbles, and breaks its neck. A white-haired old man appears suddenly, and supplies him with another horse, and with this he again goes hunting, and in due course reaches the dwelling of a certain Suksagal Khan, whom the hero clearly regards as having 'stolen' his black horse (i.e., presumably, 'stolen' its soul), though the story seems to be somewhat confused at this point. He is welcomed by his host, and by supernatural means he succeeds in finding his own black horse among Suksagal Khan's herds. The most interesting part of the story is what follows. Suksagal Khan, who is evidently possessed in a high degree of supernatural power or shamanism, and who has been much impressed by Kara Tygan Khan's display of similar power in regard to the horse, challenges him to a trial of skill. During the night he steals Kara Tygan Khan's eyes without his being aware of it. The following night, however, our hero steals Suksagal Khan's tongue, and the latter owns himself defeated. Suksagal Khan suggests to his rival that as neither of them will have any children they shall make a mutual compact that whichever of them dies first, the other will come to look at his bones— an office which we gather from these poems is observed by a man's son. The statement that neither hero will have children is interesting, and probably has reference to their shamanist faculties (cf. p. 93 above).[1]

The poem of *Südäi Märgän and Joltai Märgän* from the Kysyl Tatars offers a somewhat different range of theme from the preceding. It opens with an account of the efforts of a childless wife, Adshäng Ko, to rid herself of her husband, Südäi Märgän, and to marry a man by whom she may bear children. Südäi Märgän dresses himself in a bear's skin, and coming by chance to the court of a strange prince, Altyn Khan, is accepted by him as a son-in-law. He continues for some time to live in a house apart with his wife, Aidang Aryg, still wearing his bear's skin at home; but when he rides abroad his horse meets him, bringing to him fine clothing and weapons. With these he slays a predatory 'hero-bird' and a fierce tiger, but allows his two brothers-in-law to claim the credit of the deeds on condition that they give him a joint from their fingers and a strip of skin from their backs.

One day his wife reproaches him with his bear guise, and he leaves her, and, dispatching his horse home riderless with his bear's skin, as if he were dead, he builds himself a *yurt* in the forest. His brothers-in-law discover him and entrap him in a deep pit, but his wife finds him, and sends his horse to fetch Töng Asyn Aryg, the sister of Törömön Mökö who dwells on the border of Heaven, and who has extraordinarily long hair. By means of her hair the hero is drawn out of

---

[1] Can this be connected with the so-called 'Change of Sex' which is discussed at some length by M. A. Czaplicka, in *Aboriginal Siberia*, p. 243 ff.?

the pit, and he then marries Töng Asyn Aryg as his second wife. He returns to Altyn Khan and exposes the guilt of his two brothers-in-law, and afterwards returns to his home with his two wives. On his arrival he finds a daughter born to him after his departure, and shortly before her arrival Töng Asyn Aryg also bears him a son, who is named Joltai Märgän. The rest of the poem is occupied with the life of Joltai Märgän, and has some interesting affinities with early Norse literature.

Joltai soon discovers his uncle, Törömön Mökö, and after introducing him to his new home, he himself sets out to woo Pula Purkan, who is known as the 'maiden prince', and who seems to be a female 'hero' and ruler of the type corresponding to the second Hervör in the early Norse *Hervarar Saga*, and to the *polenitsy* in the Russian *byliny*. On his way he first encounters a cock which acts as sentinel and watchman, and he succeeds in tearing off its head before it has time to crow and arouse Pula Purkan's guards. He then slays the dog which is also on guard, and finally, having slain all Pula Purkan's heroes, he takes her home to be his bride. When they come to the spot where he has slain the dog, they find a maiden with three plaits[1] who sits there 'singing and warbling', and who, it is interesting to observe, taunts, not the hero, but Pula Purkan, the bride:

> When you were a prince,
> Had you any idea
> That you would marry and keep house?

Three times the maiden shouts her question, after which a cloud sinks down from Heaven, and dust rises from the earth, and when they clear, nothing is to be seen. Joltai Märgän cries angrily:

> Who is this Aina who stands in our way?

and would have struck at her with his sword; but his wife forbids him, and herself addresses the maiden:

> I am no longer a prince,
> I am no longer a lord,
> I am Joltai Märgän's wife.
> Sink below the golden earth.

The maiden with three plaits sinks below the earth, and the bridal pair pass on to the place where the cock was killed. Here two heroes

---

[1] Cf. p. 84 above. The plaits seem to be a characteristic mark of the 'Aina folk'.

attempt to detain Pula Purkan, but are slain by the hero, and he and his bride succeed in reaching his home safely.[1]

A group of poems recorded by Radlov from the Shor and Sojon Tatars resemble closely the poems of the Abakan group, and carry us in general into the same atmosphere. Here also the marriage of the hero forms the climax in almost every poem. In these texts, the themes are generally considerably weakened, and the brilliant narrative art of the Abakan poems is lacking. Two examples must suffice, though for purposes of comparative literature, and for the information which they afford of Tatar tradition and mythology, all these poems are full of interest.

The story of *Kara Khan* is interesting in that the chief figure in the story is a woman, as in the poem of *Kubai Ko* recorded by Castrén, of which some account has been given above. The heroine Altyn Aryg is the only child of an aged couple, who have grown too old to look after their own herds and possessions. Her father, Kara Khan, proposes to divide his possessions into two halves, bestowing only one half on his daughter, and as for the remaining half:

> My father under the earth
> May take half my herds,
> May take half my people.

Altyn Aryg, protesting her ability to manage the entire estate, goes forth after the manner of a hero, and slays a serpent prince, rescuing birds and beasts alive from its maw. On her return she is treated with well-deserved honour, and takes over the entire estate which she has proved her ability to defend. Her hand is sought in marriage by Katkandshula—a name which recurs more than once in the Abakan poems, where a character bearing this name is described as a noted horse thief, and closely connected with the beings of the Underworld. Altyn Aryg, by her prowess and force of character, cheats the dead of their share of her father's estate—whatever the precise meaning of the quotation given above; and it is clear, both from the quotation itself and from the reference to Katkandshula, that the atmosphere of the supernatural underlies this poem, despite its heroic framework.

---

[1] It will be seen that both the dialogue and the situation offer analogies to the early Norse poem the *Helreið Brynhildar* (cf. Vol. I, p. 27 of the present work). A similar situation occurs also in the Kara-Kirghiz poem of *Er Töshtük* and its variants (cf. p. 86 above, and the chapter on *The Texts*).

The next poem in Radlov's collection is entitled *A Youth*, but relates to the hero Ai Mangys, who, like so many of our heroes, begins life as a destitute orphan whose father has been robbed and killed by a powerful enemy. The outline of the story is only too familiar. The hero seeks out his enemy, and overcomes him with the help of a friend, and marries his daughter. Other heroes and their marriages are skilfully but conventionally interwoven in the narrative. One incident in the poem deserves more detailed notice. The youth hears a human voice addressing him from a birch tree, and looking up, he sees a white-haired old man sitting on the top.

> "Hold, youth," says he,
> "I will give you your name,
> Be Ai Mangys," says he. . .
> The youth. . . asked:
> "What man are you
> Who have given me my name?"
> The old man replied:
> "Who should I be
> But Kudai, the *jajuchi* (*chajuchi*)," says he;
> "To a man without a father
> I have at last given a name."[1]

The formal bestowal of a name on the hero when he reaches an age to own a horse is a very common feature in all our poems, and the name is often bestowed on him by an old man, often a stranger, who is sometimes said to be Kudai, and who generally disappears mysteriously when the ceremony is concluded. From the present passage it would seem that the old man is one of the *jajuchi*, and that he represents one of the hero's ancestral spirits. His position on the tree-top recalls the position of the shaman on the birch tree in certain ceremonies of the Altai Tatars and other peoples of northern Siberia, to which we shall refer later (p. 200 below).

The most outstanding poem from the Altai Tatars in respect of length and excellence of style bears the name *Kogutei*.[2] The real hero of the story, however, is not Kogutei himself, but a beaver, whom Kogutei finds as he is felling wood on the Altai, and who promises to serve him well if he will spare his life. Kogutei takes the beaver home

---

[1] *Proben* I, p. 358, l. 101 ff.
[2] This poem is not contained in Radlov's collection. It was published independently in a Russian translation in 1935. See the List of Abbreviations at the close of the present section, *s.v. Kogutei.*

to his wife, and the childless old couple adopt him as their son, and live in comfort by their fireside, the fuel of which is supplied by the beaver himself, who is, of course, exceptionally well qualified to collect it for them. By such touches of humour and realism the skill of the narrator clothes the fantastic narrative in homely human dress. In due course, the beaver begs Kogutei to go a-wooing on his behalf to a wealthy neighbour, Karatty Khan, and a further element of humour is introduced by the adroit manner with which the beaver stimulates the courage of the faltering Kogutei with strong spirits, and also in the uncomfortable reception which the presumptuous request receives from Karatty. It is only after the mission has been repeated several times that the beaver is duly married to Karatty's youngest daughter, Karatty Ko, and that he takes up his abode in the *aul* of his father-in-law, where the only creatures to whom his arrival brings pleasure are Karatty's dogs.

Karatty Ko's husband is treated with contempt by all on account of his beaver form, and he and his wife live alone in a distant part of the *aul*, apart from the rest of the family. He is not encouraged to take any part in their common enterprises. Yet while his brothers-in-law, the husbands of Karatty Ko's six elder sisters, are unsuccessful in every hunting expedition, the beaver never fails to bring down the quarry, allowing them to claim the credit, and only demanding their little fingers and toes in return. Their last great enterprise is undertaken to rescue Karatty Khan's colts which have been driven off by Khan Kerede,[1] the 'Bird Khan'. At this point the hero leaves his beaver coat at home in charge of his wife, and securing for himself a magnificent mount, he rides after his brothers-in-law under the name of 'Kuskun Kara Mattyr of the Raven Black Steed'. The brothers-in-law are only too glad to allow the hero to go on alone to attack the Bird Khan; but as he approaches the nest, he hears the fledglings lamenting their impending doom from a snake which devours their parents' fledglings every year. Forgetting that Khan Kerede is his enemy, Kuskun Kara Mattyr kills the snake, and rescues the fledglings, and the parent birds in gratitude give up the colts and make a bond of friendship with the hero.

Meanwhile his brothers-in-law plot his destruction. To this end they dig a deep pit into which they decoy him on his return, while they themselves drive home the colts to Karatty Khan, claiming full credit to themselves for retrieving them. Khan Kerede, however, learns of the

---

[1] The word is said to be identical with the Indian mythological bird Garuda. See *Kogutei*, Introduction, p. 36. See further the Mongol epic translated by Poppe, *A.M.* VIII, p. 202 ff., where the '*Garuda*' is prominent.

hero's plight, and rescues him, and Kuskun Kara Mattyr, after proving
the perfidy of his brothers-in-law by producing their fingers and toes,
lays the curse of death on the whole *aul*, and returns to Kogutei, whom
he enriches by his magical powers. Eventually he rides to a distant land
where he is joined by his wife Karatty Ko. The poem closes with a
vivid account of the feast and games which take place on the arrival
of a younger bride for the hero.

It will be seen that the story relates to incidents with which we are
already familiar from the Kara-Kirghiz and the Abakan poems. Still
further analogies will be found in some of the sagas which we are about
to consider. We shall examine the nature of their relationship more
closely in the chapter on the Texts. But it may be said here that
nowhere do these themes receive such competent handling from the
literary point of view as in *Kogutei*; for in point of style this is one of
the best of the Tatar poems or rhythmical stories. The story itself is
simpler, and the characters and incidents are, in general, fewer than we
generally find in the Abakan poems. As in the latter, the atmosphere is
that of folk-tale. The hero triumphs in every adventure, not by heroic
action, but by superior magic. Yet the supernatural elements which in
the Abakan poems generally constitute the most interesting part of the
narrative are here condensed into a few bare lines. The poet cares little
for the glamour of beaver magic. He loves to dwell on the heroic
incidents; to linger over the heroic details—the splendour of the
beaver's armour, the superb qualities of his steed. The story is magni-
ficently told. Boisterous humour, a vivid realistic treatment of the
incidents of daily life, a gift of presenting rapid contrasts, of seizing on
just the telling detail of description and of speech, betrays the artist
in every line, the artist versed in all the conventions, repetitions, and
formulae of heroic poetry at its best. The daring hyperboles, the
relevance and significance of the racy narrative, resemble the Russian
byliny. But *Kogutei* shows equally with the poems of the *Manas* Cycle
that even the Russian *skaçitely* must yield to the Tatar minstrel as an
artist in sustained narrative poetry.

Kogutei is described by Russian editors as a *chorchok*,[1] a 'rhythmical
skaçka', or 'folk-tale', rather than a strictly metrical poem, such as the
true epics (*koçhon*) of the Altai and the Kara-Kirghiz.[2] It belongs to a
particular literary (oral) genre of this region known as the 'heroic

---

[1] *Chorchok*, '*skaçka*', '*Das Märchen*', Radlov, *Wörterbuch*, s.v.
[2] *Kogutei*, Introduction, pp. 28, 31; but according to Dmitrêv (*Kogutei*, loc. cit.),
even the *koçhon* were already losing their strictly metrical form in Radlov's time.

skaƶka', in which themes and motifs commonly found in folk-tales are interspersed with heroic episodes, and related in the style of heroic poetry. We find the same type of hero as in the poems of the Abakan Group, and he performs much the same type of exploit; there is the same close connection between the hero and his horse; the same stress is laid on the colour of the horse, and here also there is the same convention of attaching the horse, specifying its colour, to the name of a hero as a surname. We have the same descriptions of battles, and the mighty races of heroes on their trusty steeds; the same feast with meat and vodka.[1] The style is similar to that of Yakut poetry, especially the liberal use of alliteration and parallelism, and the literary conventions are also similar. We have a similar presentation of the soul; and the same picture of the 'endless summer' enfolding the Altai, in which the hero ends his days at the close of his adventures; the same monster bird Kerede; the same love of the cuckoo, the welcome harbinger of spring alike on the Altai and the northern steppe. The action and the heroes, however, are in general the same as those found in Mongolian literature. *Kogutei* has little in common with the literature of the western Turks; but it has so much in common with the narrative poems and the *skaƶki* of the eastern Turks, the Yakut, and the Mongols, that it sometimes seems, as Dmitrêv observes, as if the oral traditions of all these peoples formed one big *skaƶka*.[2]

In the stories which we are studying, no insurmountable barrier exists between man's material environment and the spirit world.[3] Hero and heroine transport themselves from earth to the Heavens or the Underworld without apparent difficulty. For this purpose a certain technique must be observed. A hero must be conducted to the Underworld by a shamanka, or must follow on the tracks of Dshalmaus, or be conducted thither on a steed of special spiritual gifts—but what Tatar horse is not possessed of such gifts? A heroine must adopt the form of a bird and fly aloft singing; but few Tatar heroines have failed to acquire this accomplishment. In general the transitions from the natural to the supernatural take place simply and as a matter of course, with no elaborate preparation. And this is not surprising; for the Heavens and the Underworld are peopled by beings as material as the

---

[1] *Kogutei*, p. 35 f.   [2] *Loc. cit.*

[3] The spiritual character of the motifs which underlie these narratives of entertainment has been more fully demonstrated by N. K. Chadwick in a paper on 'The Spiritual Ideas and Experiences of the Tatars of Central Asia', in *J.R.A.I.* LXVI (1936), p. 291 ff.

heroes and the heroines who visit them, and subject to the same emotions as themselves. The realm of Erlik differs little from many of the lamaist monasteries, with their fearsome and materialistic representations of punishment and dissolution; the realm of Heaven, at least on its lower planes, offers much with which the men and women of the poems were perfectly familiar in the tents of their own khans.

Let us look for a moment at the *jajan* who form a community living on one of these lower Heavenly planes. This community is by no means always at unity. The *jajan* are addicted to gambling, and are prone to strive for precedence in a manner little calculated to inspire the respect of mortals, who, however, must treat them with formal deference. In the Sagai poem of *Tarba Kindshi*, a minor *jajuchi* lays a wager with a major *jajuchi* that the hero, Tarba Kindshi himself, who was created by the former, will overcome a hero created by the latter, and that Tarba Kindshi's horse will outleap the 'bird of God', i.e. doubtless the horse of the latter hero. The hero's victory ensures the exaltation of the minor *jajuchi* over his superior, a triumph which appears to be shared by his fellow *jajan*. We may interpret the incident as a humorous treatment of a revolt of the minor orders of Heaven against the deity, or of the subordinate orders of some kind of monastic or 'ecclesiastical' organisation against their superior. In the poem *Altyn Argäk* from the Shor Tatars, the *jajan* are again shown to us laying a wager that the horse created by the 'nine *jajan*' will outstrip the hero's horse, the creation of a single *jajuchi*. In this instance, however, the creation of the single *jajuchi* is successful, and his prestige strengthened. Sometimes such contests take place between the heroes themselves and the *jajan*. The Sagai poem *Ai Mergän and Altyn Kus* relates how a certain hero Kattan Khan challenges the *jajan* to a contest of power, but in this instance the hero is defeated.

The establishment of the *jajan* is kept up in some state, and certain ceremonial observances are required of those who seek audience with them, much like the great potentates of the steppe who were visited by Pian de Carpini and Friar Rubruck, in the thirteenth century, and by the Russian embassies in the seventeenth. When they desire to speak with Tarba Kindshi, they write a letter which falls down from Heaven through the smoke hole of his *yurt*, and which summons him to their presence. The hero's horse grows wings and transports him through three regions of Heaven till they reach the land of the 'nine *jajan*' which is said to be thickly populated. The hero opens the door and enters the dwelling of the *jajan*, bowing low, his cap under his arm; but the *jajan* are well versed in the behaviour traditionally associated with the great, and ignore his presence all day. In the evening they deign to notice him, and tell him of the wager which they have laid, and to which we have already referred. This scene, which humorously and realistically represents the *jajan* in the character of haughty tyrants, and undignified and emulous gamblers, is one of the most intimate pictures of Tatar 'high life' with which the poems present us. It is the more remarkable that when eventually they dismiss Tarba Kindshi with the reward which his services have deserved at their hands, their parting injunctions to him are that he shall

> Commit no sins, no cruelties,
> Slay no men.[1]

Cruelty and wanton destruction of life are no part of the standards of heroism on the Steppe.

Yet despite their realism and their concrete character—qualities which are inseparable from a literature of entertainment—it is impossible to doubt that the stories which we have been considering are in the main spiritual adventures. When Tarba Kindshi returns from a visit to the realm of Erlik Khan he must bathe himself in a 'golden lake' and fumigate himself with wild thyme[2] to remove the stench of mortality contracted in the realm of the dead, and at once

> The smell of the Aina disappeared,
> The smell of the world of daylight suffused him.

When the same hero returns to earth from the abode of the *jajan*, he descends through three regions of Heaven, and alights on the ridge of the Altai. The uncorporeal nature of his adventures is well illustrated by his own words when aroused from a deep sleep by the piping of an old woman:

> Ah, when you piped,
> Ere I had passed six mountain ridges, I awoke.

His soul, which has been absent from his body during sleep, is recalled to the empty form by the piping of the old woman and her assistants.

---

[1] We may compare the merciful injunctions given by the 'nine sons' of the old 'father shaman' to the young shaman at his consecration ceremony among the Buryat as recorded by Agapitov and Khangalov; see Chadwick, *J.R.A.I.* LXVI (1936), p. 88.

[2] We may compare the procedure of the early Japanese hero Izanagi, who bathes and cleanses himself after visiting his dead wife in the Underworld, *Kojiki*, p. 34 ff.

Among the adventures of the mind with which these stories are largely occupied perhaps the commonest are the long journeys. But these are not, in general, journeys on earth. More often they are journeys in any other element—in the air, in the water, under the earth. The last are far the commonest, though a considerable number of journeys are made through the air, and up to the various Heavens. The journeys are most commonly made by the heroes and heroines themselves, though sometimes they are made by their horses on their behalf. These journeys are sometimes undertaken by the wish of the hero or heroine, but are often forced on them by some enemy who is pursuing them, generally by supernatural means. When the journeys are undertaken voluntarily, it is frequently to seek something lost, it may be stolen herds, or runaway slaves, or parents or other relatives who have been carried off in a plundering raid by an enemy. Most often the journeys to the Heavens are undertaken, either to seek the water of life and the herbs of healing, or else a wife from among the maidens who are under the guardianship of the Heavenly beings, the *jajan*. The journeys underground are most commonly taken to rescue the soul, or the head, of a brother or sister, or it may be some other near relative who has been carried to Erlik's gloomy realm by some hag or monster, the demons of the Underworld, or their emissaries. These journeys to the Underworld to rescue the souls of the dead are perhaps the commonest of all the themes in our poems, as they are certainly among the most interesting. In such cases the hero is generally involved in a conflict with the demon or supernatural enemy who has carried off the soul which the hero is seeking to rescue. And here again it is perfectly clear that the conflict is a spiritual one, and takes place in the spirit, rather than the material world.

The poems, indeed, reflect the ideas and beliefs traditionally associated with shamanism. The hero and his pursuer take just such flights through the realms of nature and through the various elements as those taken by the Siberian shamans in their search for an absent soul. Like a shaman Saryg Khan calls to his aid the creatures supreme in the various kingdoms of nature; like a shaman he scrutinises the sun and moon in his mirror; and like a shaman he runs through the list of stars, herbs, and roots in his endeavour to find the lost tracks. The whole story of his pursuit of the hero Altyn Pyrkan relates the typical procedure of a shaman searching for an absent soul. The contest for superiority in the practice of magic, conjuring, or hypnotic power which takes place in the friendly rivalry between Kara Tygan Khan and Suksagal Khan is undoubtedly based on a shamanistic contest. The arrow shot from a distance by Chas Mökö is reminiscent of some such custom as that of shamans who are said to hurl missiles at one another from great distances, 'sometimes hundreds of miles'.[1] The journeys of heroes to Heaven and the Underworld to visit the spiritual beings who dwell there correspond in all particulars with the ceremonial visits of the shamans of the Altai Tatars and of the Yakut to the abode of the God Ülgen who dwells in the highest Heaven,[2] which will be discussed more fully in Chapter VII below.

Perhaps the most striking feature of the poems is their preoccupation with marriage. The marriage of the hero forms the climax in most cases. Even apart from this the feminine interest is very strongly represented throughout the poems. The dénouement is very frequently brought about by women, and they are undoubtedly more gifted, both intellectually and spiritually, than their husbands and brothers. One is led to suspect that the poems may have passed at some time through a feminine milieu, if they have not actually been composed by women. In this connection it is interesting to note that in the texts before us women are frequently spoken of as singing. Among the Yakut and the Tungus, the composition and recitation of poetry is still largely an accomplishment of the women.

Non-heroic sagas are numerous and widespread among the Tatars as a whole, though in general it will be found that their distribution is uneven. Where a large and flourishing body of narrative poetry exists, prose saga appears to be either lacking altogether, or at least very scarce. We have hardly any saga recorded from the Abakan Tatars,[3] while from the northern Tatars and the Kazak a varied and extensive body of saga has been recorded. These sagas fall naturally into a number of more or less clearly defined classes, some of which correspond closely in their subject-matter and style to the non-heroic poetry already considered, while others appear to be quite independent, and to have originated in a different milieu. Variant versions of a single theme are frequently found

[1] The expression is probably a figurative one. For a discussion as to its significance, see Chadwick, *J.R.A.I.* LXVI (1936), p. 89.

[2] For other names of the deity occupying the highest Heaven, see p. 83 above.

[3] Due allowance must, of course, be made for the fact that no collections have been accessible to us except Radlov's *Proben*. In Katanov's collection of oral literature from the Abakan Tatars a considerable number of prose texts are given, but they are very brief, and can hardly be classed as saga in the literary sense.

in more than one group of the Tatar peoples. It will therefore be convenient in this chapter to group the non-heroic sagas, not according to their geographical distribution, but according to their subject-matter.

The first group is very widespread, and constitutes the principal class of saga of entertainment among the Tatars. In these sagas the supernatural plays a large part, and the heroes excel in spiritual, especially magical and shamanistic gifts, rather than as military champions. The affinities of these sagas lie for the most part with the Abakan and the Altai poems, to some of which they offer variant prose versions. As in the latter, they relate to heroes who are not known from historical sources, at least from such sources as are known to us. In general they show in their style strong poetical influence, and a considerable proportion of poetry is generally interspersed in the narrative. Sometimes the poetry even predominates over the prose, though the actual thread of the narrative is still prose. Moral and didactic elements are wholly lacking. Intellectual gifts are highly prized, and cunning and wisdom and mantic and magical power are the qualities most admired in both men and women. In these gifts the women are generally regarded as superior to the men.

One of the most interesting types of non-heroic saga is that which consists of a contest between two heroes as to which possesses the greater knowledge and mantic power. The knowledge may be natural or supernatural, but the two are rarely clearly distinguished from one another or divorced from supernatural gifts or power. In the story of *The Two Princes*[1] from the Tatars of the Altai a certain prince named Altyn Chächän is represented as challenging a rival prince, Järän Chächän, to a contest:

"Let us not fight and slay one another, but let us propound riddles. If you can solve them all I will give myself up to you with all my people. If you cannot solve them all, I will take your people."

The challenge is accepted, the princes meet and feast and give themselves up to riddles:

> The stars of Heaven they enumerated,
> The fish of the sea they enumerated,
> The flowers of the earth they enumerated,
> The people of the earth they enumerated,
> The trees shone upon by the moon they enumerated,
> The stones shone upon by the sun they enumerated.

[1] *Proben* I, p. 197 ff.

Altyn Chächän knows three times more than Järän Chächän, and so gains the victory over him; but he is himself defeated in a subsequent riddle contest by the daughter-in-law of Järän Chächän, who knows seven times more than he, and the defeated Altyn Chächän is accordingly buried in a deep pit, and all his people are carried off by his victorious rivals.[1] We have seen that *chächän* (*jajan*) are divine beings who dwell in Heaven, and who are full of wisdom and supernatural knowledge. The word *Altyn*, 'golden', is commonly used of divine beings in these poems, while the word *Järän* seems to be connected with the word for 'earth'. The contest is, therefore, probably a shamanistic contest, between a human and a divine sage, or person of shamanistic character, in which the shamans, human and divine alike, are defeated by the supernatural gifts of a shamanka. The story may well be a humorous treatment of a serious theme, such as we have seen to be common in stories of the *jajan* among the Abakan Tatars.

Another story in which the shamanistic contest figures prominently is *Ak Köbök*. This extremely interesting story occurs in several versions, and has been recorded from the Teleut, the Baraba Tatars, and the Kurdak tribes. The form is that of mingled prose and verse, but in all versions the proportion of verse to prose is unusually high. In the Teleut version[2] the connecting thread of the narrative, which is in prose, relates the achievements of the hero Ak Köbök, both in magic and warfare, and his revenge and overthrow of the heroes Mangyt and Ködön Pi. Ak Köbök is represented as a brave champion, but his victories are all won by his supreme skill in magic, and although he is said to engage in warfare, his single combats are fought out, not on the field of battle, but in private, and by competitive efforts in destructive magic. His power over the weather is a salient feature of this magic, and his power of producing intense frost recalls Teutonic magical tradition.[3] He is also represented as engaging his companions and his enemies in riddle contests. The narrative element in this version is very slight, hardly more than a series of links to the songs. From the Baraba

---

[1] Capital punishment is sometimes the penalty of defeat in contests of wisdom between sages in Sanskrit literature. See Vol. II, pp. 504f. and 584 of the present work.

[2] *Proben* I, p. 224.

[3] We may refer to the snow-storm produced by Thorsteinn at the court of King Geirröðr in the Norse *Saga af Thorsteini Bœjarmagni*, and to the proficiency of the people of East Prussia in the art of producing artificial freezing as reported by Wulfstan in the account inserted by King Alfred the Great into his translation of Orosius' *History of the World*, though the reference here is not to a Teutonic people.

and Kurdak versions, however, it would seem that the narrative element has once been much greater, and has apparently been forgotten or curtailed, while the songs have remained; for in both those versions the prose narrative is much more fully developed than in the Teleut version, and one brief passage in the Baraba version consists of narrative poetry.[1]

An important group of non-heroic sagas is one in which the hero takes a journey to the Underworld. Some of these stories have points of resemblance with *Er Töshtük*, while some are actually variants of this story. Important examples of the latter are the Kazak saga of *Khan Shentäi*, and the saga of *Jirtüshlük* from the northern (Tyumen and Yalutrowsk) Tatars. A somewhat detailed account of both sagas is given here, partly because of the interest of the story for its own sake, and partly because we shall have occasion to refer to them again in some detail in the chapter on the Texts.

The saga of *Khan Shentäi*[2] opens with the theft of the herds of the wealthy and aged hero, Karys Kara, at the hands of the three Kara Bagys brothers. Karys Kara sets off in pursuit, but is soon overpowered by the robbers and buried alive in a deep pit. Meanwhile his aged wife bears him a son, who at an early age succeeds in rescuing his father, and then sets off to track his stolen cattle. Before long he comes upon an old woman in a deep cavern, the mother of the three robbers of whom he is in search, and by whom he is adopted as a son. He overcomes the robbers in wrestling, and then lives on friendly terms with them, taking the name Khan Shentäi. Presently he sets off to seek for himself as a wife the daughter of a distant prince named Aina Khan, who, like Brynhildr, lives behind a barrier of fire.

After various adventures, the hero, like Sigurðr, rides through the fire, and wins the maiden in a competition in horse-racing and wrestling, in which he takes part in the guise of a beggar. An interesting part is here played by a wise maiden, Synshy Sary Kus, who advises the heroine throughout, and ultimately succeeds in identifying the hero. In an interesting speech (p. 313) which makes it clear that she is speaking through clairvoyance, she recites the names of a catalogue of heroes, rejecting each in turn, till she comes upon that of Khan Shentäi. He, she declares, is the hero, and to prove her words and the authenticity of her right to pronounce, she bids him take the form of a blue dove, then of a hawk, and finally of a hero of surpassing beauty. The speech bears a close resemblance to the catalogue which enumerates the heroines

[1] *Proben* IV, p. 68. [2] *Ib.* III, p. 297 ff.

of the world visited by Kara Chach in seeking a wife suitable for the hero Bolot.[1] It is instructive to find the catalogue form associated constantly with mantic persons.

In due course Khan Shentäi's three adopted brothers come out to meet him and welcome his bride, and Khan Shentäi bids them conduct her to his home while he sets out on a fresh journey. He instructs them to pause for the night in the place which he indicates by drawing a circle; but where he draws a long line they must pass on, and he adds that he will know if they are faring well. This is the first clear indication that Khan Shentäi possesses supernatural powers. As the bridal party pursue their course they are seized and swallowed by a certain hero, Kara Tün, who is also called a *dshalmaus*, and who dwells below the earth. The narrative is not very clear at this point, but it suggests that Kara Tün has previously desired the daughter of Aina Khan for himself, but has been afraid to take her by force. Now in the absence of Khan Shentäi he seizes the whole party save the three brothers, and disappears with them into the earth. In their endeavour to save the maiden the three brothers lose their hands and feet, and in this condition they are found by Khan Shentäi, who returns in consequence of an evil dream.

The hero now descends under the earth by means of a rope, leaving his 'brothers' in charge of the upper end of the rope. Presently he comes to a great house in which lies the seven-headed *dshalmaus* fast asleep, while the hero's wife sits mourning at his side. A terrible fight ensues, and Khan Shentäi must inevitably have perished but for the timely help of Kydyr, who appears in the form of a white-bearded man, and slays the *dshalmaus* with his iron staff, and 'takes his soul', whereupon Khan Shentäi cuts open his body and releases all the people whom he has swallowed. He now shakes the rope, and would have returned to the upper air; but his brothers are unable to raise him and all the people whom he now has in his train, and the entire party are forced to remain beneath the earth.

Time passes, and one day the hero slays a dragon which has climbed a tree and is about to devour three nestlings. The nestlings help the hero to climb the tree, and the mother bird, whose name is Kara Kus,[2] promises out of gratitude that she will carry the hero, together with his wife and all his possessions, back to earth, if he will supply her with food on the journey. Accordingly they set out, and when the bird has devoured all the meat provided, and still requires food, Khan Shentäi cuts a piece from his own thigh, and on the strength of this the

[1] *Proben* v, p. 525, l. 5193 ff.   [2] Literally, 'Black bird'.

bird carries him and all his party safely to earth. She then spits out the piece of his thigh, which adheres; and she also swallows his three wounded 'brothers' and spits them out whole and sound. Khan Shentäi with all his following sets out towards his old home, and after various incidents, which are referred to only briefly, he is united once more to his aged parents, and rules as a prince till the day of his death.

The saga of *Jirtüshlük*[1] opens with an account of a wealthy prince and his seven sons who desire to marry. The prince eventually finds seven sisters, the youngest of whom is endowed with second sight or exceptional discernment. As his suit is pleasing to the girls' parents, the prince brings his six eldest sons to fetch their wives, leaving the youngest son at home in charge of his estate, and promising to bring his wife. The arrangement is not pleasing to the youngest maiden; but a 'childless'[2] old woman tells her that her destined bridegroom is superior to all his brothers, and advises her, as she is her father's favourite daughter, to beg from him at parting the steed Chal Kuiruk, who lives under seven regions of earth, and under whose liver lies a diamond sword. The maiden follows her advice, and the father grants her the steed and all his possessions, though he afterwards regrets his generosity, and follows the bridal party and begs back two-thirds of his herds from his daughter. The dialogue which takes place between them delays the bride, and the bridal party are obliged in consequence to spend the night at a spot against which her father has warned them. At night a dragon comes and threatens to swallow the prince, and in order to save themselves he and his six sons promise to deliver Jirtüshlük to him. On learning what has taken place the hero departs to find the dragon, and his bride at parting presents him appropriately with Chal Kuiruk.

The dragon takes him down through a hole in the earth, and here they pass through a host of dragons, and come to a town in the midst of which is the house of the princely master of his dragon convoy. When the hero enters he sees a little white snake coiled up in a corner, and presently many men enter and address him as 'bridegroom', and having prepared a bridal bed, and summoned a mullah who formally marries him to the snake, they all withdraw. He eats the food provided, and finally falls asleep. When he awakens the snake has become a lovely maiden. In the morning her father bids Jirtüshlük bring some precious bones from a lake, wherewith to build himself a house. On his way he comes upon a hideous woman in an earthen hut, who warns him on no account to look back when once the bones are in his possession, and by

---

[1] *Proben* IV, p. 443 ff.   [2] Cf. p. 96 above.

following her advice he succeeds in bringing home the bones and building a house in which to live with his bride. Numerous other heavy and dangerous tasks are laid upon him by his exacting father-in-law, all of which he discharges successfully with the old woman's helpful advice. In the course of these adventures he procures for himself a second wife.

When he comes to the end of his tasks, his father-in-law tells him that the reason why he sent the dragon to bring him to the Underworld is because they have been beset by many foes and unable to live in peace till the hero should overcome them. Now that they can be at peace he allows Jirtüshlük to return through a hole in the ground, or a cave, to his own home in the world above, taking his two wives with him. Before reaching home one of his two wives is twice stolen, but he is able to rescue her. Then as they are passing the night on the edge of a lake, a water spirit raises a great flood which separates her a third time from Jirtüshlük. She is washed up in a land belonging to a wealthy lord who makes her his wife; but she is ultimately restored to her true husband once more by the ministration of two doves. Finally the hero is reunited to his first wife Kendshäkä whom he has been forced to leave on the eve of their marriage, and he himself comes into possession of the khanate, and settles down happily with his three wives. The relationship of this story to that of *Khan Shentäi*, and of both to the Kara-Kirghiz poem of *Er Töshtük* will be discussed in the chapter on 'The Texts'.

The saga of *Mishäk Alyp*[1] from the northern Tatars relates how the hero, Mishäk Alyp himself, undertakes three different enterprises of a supernatural character at the command of Kara Khan. His second adventure is a slight variant of the Kara-Kirghiz story of *Er Töshtük*, and in the third adventure also the same story is continued. Here Mishäk Alyp seeks the hand of a princess for Kara Khan, and is carried to the spot by a grateful parent bird, exactly as Er Töshtük is carried to earth. Kara Khan omits to reward Mishäk Alyp, and comes to a sad end in consequence, and the story ends on a cautionary note. The motif of the second part—the killing of the snake, and the rescue of the nestlings—appears to be a common motif, since it appears again in the first part of a saga entitled *The Prince's Son*.[2]

We now come to a series of sagas whose affinities, both in style and content, lie with the Abakan poems. The Kazak saga of *Erkäm Aidar*[3]

[1] *Proben* IV, p. 26 ff.   [2] *Ib.* p. 115 ff.
[3] *Ib.* III, p. 321 ff.

relates the attempts of a sister, Naran Sulu, to rid herself of her brother, the hero Erkäm Aidar, who is opposed to her marriage with Usun Sary Alyp. To this end she feigns sickness, and sends her devoted brother on long and difficult journeys to obtain medicines for her. The brother fulfils all her requests with the help of three wise maidens; but each time, as he pauses on his homeward journey, the eldest of the sisters takes from his bag the 'medicine' which he has procured, and substitutes a counterfeit in its place. When he finally returns to Naran Sulu, he is slain by her lover; but his horse, true to Tatar ideals, saves his master by galloping for the three sisters, who restore him to life by means of the medicines which they have taken out of his bag. Ultimately the hero slays Naran Sulu and her lover, and marries the three wise sisters.

Owing to lack of space it will not be possible to do more than mention one or two more examples of the sagas of this kind. *Kadysh Märgän*[1] from the Baraba Tatars is a strange rambling tale of adventure. The first part relates how the hero slays three *Jelbägän* and carries off their wives to become wives to himself and to his brothers. The second incident in the story relates how Kadysh Märgän is wounded by his treacherous brothers, and how he is healed by eating a root which he has observed some mice using as a balsam. Then follows a weird episode in which the hero and two 'half men' are restored to youth and health by an old giantess. Finally the hero takes vengeance on his wicked brothers and rules happily ever after.

Altain Sain Sümä, *Jästäi Möngkö* and *Kara Kököl*, also from the Baraba Tatars, are again stories of marvellous adventures. The first[2] relates how the hero wins the daughter of a prince as a reward of prowess and of feats of supernatural skill. The second[3] is divided into two parts. The first part relates how Jästäi Möngkö wins a wife for himself in consequence of a service which he has once performed for an animal— a common theme in Tatar stories (see p. 99 above). The second part narrates how the hero on two different adventures slays Jelbägän and the hero Jär Kara Alyp,[4] and obtains a wife for a shepherd. He himself becomes a prince and the shepherd his vizier. *Kara Kököl*, of which we possess two versions,[5] is also the story of a hero who, by prowess and cunning, overcomes his enemies, the three Jelbägän brothers amongst others, and wins two princesses as his brides. As in the Abakan poems, he then returns home, avenges all his wrongs on his enemies, and

---

[1] *Proben* IV, p. 72 ff.   [2] *Ib.* p. 89 ff.   [3] *Ib.* p. 99 ff.
[4] The name doubtless indicates a 'black shaman'. *Jär*, 'earth'; *kara*, 'black'.
[5] *Proben* IV, pp. 81 ff., 109 ff.

finally becomes a prince. In this story, as in the other two, supernatural elements and shape-changing play a large part.

It will be seen that the resemblance between these sagas and the poems of the Abakan group is very close. The form is that of a disjunct series of adventures with a neat rounding off, generally effected by marriage. In both the supernatural plays a large part, and the intellectual rôle is generally filled by women, who figure prominently throughout. The diction resembles that of the Abakan poems in the love of static formulae and repetitions, many of which are indeed identical with those which occur in the latter.

The sagas of the next group present a striking contrast, both in form and style, to those which we have been discussing. They relate for the most part to well-known historical characters—the heroes of history in fact. They are told in a simple and direct style—what we may call the chronicle style—and appear to be wholly free from the influence of poetry. They are often so brief as to be mere anecdotes, such as *Kuchum Khan's Flight*,[1] or *Igi Seid Mirgän*;[2] others again are obviously summaries, such as the Kurdak version of the story of *Ermak*.[3]

The form of this group of sagas is generally that of mingled prose and verse, or of prose narrative interspersed with poetry, which we have seen to be characteristic of the Kazaks and the northern Tatars, though pure prose examples are common also. Post-heroic elements are prominent, and learned or foreign influence is to be suspected, though in general it is not very apparent. Very frequently a moral is inculcated, or some point of practical wisdom is emphasised, and it happens thus that stories of great and warlike heroes reach us sometimes through a non-heroic milieu. A striking example is the story of Timur the Lame (Tamerlane) from the Tobol Tatars,[4] which is a story of the triumph of brains over physical fitness. In this saga the great conqueror is represented as winning his chieftainship by a cunning trick, and as desisting from attacking the Tsar Ivan Vasilevich through fear. The reference to the great prestige of Russia at the conclusion suggests that the story may have reached us in a sophisticated form.

Abylai Khan is another figure around whose name non-heroic stories have collected. In a little Kazak anecdote, which appears to have been narrated to illustrate his love of candour, he is represented as rewarding with extravagant generosity a boy who has the courage to tell him an unpalatable truth.[5] Another story about the same hero, also from the

---

[1] *Proben* IV, p. 316f.   [2] *Ib.* p. 278f.   [3] *Ib.* p. 179f.
[4] *Ib.* p. 307ff.   [5] *Ib.* III, p. 89f.

Kazaks, relates how, in fleeing from his enemy, Kasy Bek, he effectively stops his pursuers by leaving behind him a kettle full of food. The ruse is said to have been suggested by his wife.[1] The traditions of Ermak which are so numerous in western Siberia, and are doubtless in part the result of antiquarian speculation, represent the great hero as conquering Siberia, not by prowess in arms, but by a trick. We shall refer to these traditions more fully in connection with 'Antiquarian Speculation'. It may be added here that many of the sagas relating to unknown individuals are markedly non-heroic in character.

In conclusion reference may be made to an interesting and unusual type of saga recorded from the Altai under the title of *The Iron Mountains*.[2] The story relates how the army of an Oirot prince is foiled in its efforts to conquer the land beyond the 'Iron Mountains', and is finally bought off with an offering of tribute and treasure by the peace-loving and wealthy inhabitants, and the narrative concludes with a clear confession from the Oirot khan that he feels himself unequal to a contest with people so rich in wealth, so advanced in culture, and so mighty.—"What manner of men will fight with such people? Who will make war on them without being afraid? Remain here; these are the only people whom the Oirot fear."[3] The saga contains no names of persons, but the people of the Altai are accustomed to refer to themselves as 'Oirot',[4] and it is most probable that the term here has reference to them, rather than to the Mongolian people usually designated 'Oirot' by ethnologists. The people 'beyond the Iron Mountains' are probably the inhabitants of Turkestan.

Non-heroic poetry other than narrative is chiefly represented by a number of poems recorded from the recitation of the shaman during the ceremonies in which he offers the annual tribal sacrifice to Bai Ülgen, and on other occasions. In some of these he recites poems mimetically which purport to be spoken by various beings, both natural and supernatural. The whole constitutes a kind of religious drama, or ballet, though, of course, practically the entire performance is executed by the shaman himself. Unfortunately we possess the actual text of only a few of the many poems or speeches in character recited by the shaman on these occasions, though our information is much fuller in regard to their tenor, and to the circumstances and manner of his

---

[1] *Proben* III, p. 90f.   [2] *Ib.* I, p. 194ff.   [3] *Ib.* p. 197.
[4] See Dmitrêv, Introduction to *Kogutei*, p. 14.

recitation. We shall therefore give a fuller account of poetry of this kind in later chapters.

In conclusion it may be mentioned that a large number of non-heroic speech-poems are also found in the sagas. Some of these have already been referred to from the Kazaks and from the western Tatars. In particular we may mention the poems contained in the sagas of *Ak Köbök* and *The Two Princes*. Some of these poems are clearly mantic in character, and will be discussed in Chapter VI below. Other poems attributed to the sages are gnomic and descriptive in character, and these also will be discussed later. There can be no doubt that in sagas like *Ak Köbök*, many of the poems have been composed by the author of the saga or others, and attributed to the sages, and it is at least doubtful if many of the poems were really composed by the people who are represented as reciting them, for among all the Tatars the art of extempore composition seems to be more highly developed than the art of memorisation.

One of the most interesting questions which arises from the non-heroic literature of the Tatars, and especially from the narratives recorded from the more eastern tribes, is the relationship of this literature to the ritual and tradition of the more civilised peoples of southern Asia. How, one wonders, does it come about that much of the *mise-en-scène* and the milieu depicted in these narratives recalls so vividly the caverns utilised for Buddhist symbolism in Tibet to-day, those of Korea and Turkestan dating from the Uigur period, of Gandhara and Ajanta from the same period and even earlier? How can we account for the reappearance of the themes and motifs of the Assyrian and Sumerian classics in the narratives of the shamanist Tatars? This is not the place in which to enter into difficult questions of origins; but in view of the close affinities which undoubtedly exist between the traditions of northern and southern Asia, there can be no doubt that the non-heroic literature of the eastern Tatars in particular is by no means independent of southern influence.

CHAPTER V

HISTORICAL AND UNHISTORICAL ELEMENTS IN HEROIC POETRY AND SAGA

UNFORTUNATELY we have not the means at our disposal of entering into a discussion of the historical value of the heroic poems of the Tatars. Nothing is known of the individual heroes of these Cycles from Western sources, and none of them has been identified from Oriental records. The events which form the background of the Manas poems, and the characters themselves, have been attributed to a period before the eighteenth century.[1] As the poems stand, the internal evidence suggests that they attained their present form at a period when Russian prestige was rapidly gaining ground, that is to say, during the latter half of the sixteenth and the early part of the seventeenth centuries; but this date may be somewhat early. Radlov regards the heroes themselves as mythical;[2] but he sees in the religious animosities reflected in the poems echoes of the warfare and religious animosities raging during the eighteenth century between the Moham-medan Kirghiz and their Kalmuck and Chinese overlords, whom they regard as heathen. Something has already been said on this subject (p. 77 above).

Though we cannot identify any of the personnel of the poems, a perusal of the Russian and other records relating for the most part to the seventeenth century, and published recently by Baddeley, leaves on the reader a general impression that the heroes of the Kara-Kirghiz epic poems belong to the Mongol world of this period. When we read in the *Manas* Cycle of Kongyr Bai, the Chinese or Mongol prince, we recall Khongor,[3] a Kalmuck prince of the sixteenth century, who is said to be directly descended from a brother of Jenghiz Khan; and the five sons of Khongor, known as the 'five tigers',[4] recall the static epithet of Alaman Bet, 'the tiger', who, as we have seen, left the Kalmucks to join himself to Manas and embrace Mohammedanism. Manas himself we have not been able to identify. The part which he plays resembles that of the great Bogatyr,[5] whose alternative name was

[1] Radlov, *Proben* v, p. xif.; cf. Michell, p. 100; cf. *ib.* p. 98.
[2] *Loc. cit.*   [3] Baddeley I, Genealogical Table D.
[4] *Ib. loc. cit.*   [5] *Ib.* II, p. 30ff.

Buni, the great Oirot prince who played an important part in the difficult politics of Central Asia at the beginning of the seventeenth century. So much for the 'Sary-Nogai' or the Oirot of the Manas poems.

Of the Kara-Nogai of the poem *Joloi* we are equally unable to make any reliable identification, and equally tempted to suggest certain possibilities. In particular it is tempting to see in the hero Bolot, Joloi's son, one of the seven Bolots,[1] sons of the great Dayan, who died in 1543, after having raised the Mongol power to a height which it had never attained since the days of Tamerlane.[2] The name of Bolot's grandson Seitäk recalls the Seidak, descendant of Ediger, who gave trouble to the Russians in the neighbourhood of Sibir, and was treacherously murdered by them towards the close of the same century,[3] while that of Er Töshtük's son Bir Biäk is identical with that of the son of the third of the Bolots mentioned above.[4] Such identifications have little value in themselves. The names in question, many of which have a definite meaning, may be common among the Mongols. But occurring as they do on the royal lines of the Oirot and other Mongol (Kalmuck) princes, and in the period to which our poems appear to have reference, they seem to suggest that our poems belong to the same milieu. But this is as far as we can go. Even this evidence, however, slight as it undoubtedly is, is important as seeming to suggest that the chief heroes of our poems are not of Turkish, but of Mongol origin—a conclusion to which, as we have seen, the internal evidence of the poems themselves also points. For an analogy to this celebration by the heroic poet of heroes of an alien stock, we may refer to the non-Greek names which occur in the line of Agamemnon.[5] It is possible that among the Tatar heroic poets, as among the Greek, the foreign origin of the heroes has come to be forgotten, though this is by no means certain.

One saga which we have seen (p. 52 ff. above) to be current among both the Kara-Kirghiz and the Altai tribes has preserved a detailed picture of the ruling family of Jungaria during the latter half of the seventeenth and the first half of the eighteenth centuries. The saga relates to the internal relations of this family among themselves, and also their relations with their overlords, to whom they are tributary. The outline of the saga, together with some variants, has been related

---

[1] Baddeley, I, Genealogical Table A.
[2] *Ib.* p. xlivf.
[3] *Ib.* p. lxxiff.
[4] *Ib.* Genealogical Table B, and p. xlivf.
[5] Cf. Vol. I, p. 194f. of the present work.

above in the chapter on 'Heroic Poetry and Saga'. There it was pointed out that motifs common to folk-tale, and to narrative heroic poetry, have been introduced into the sagas; but of the historical foundation of the stories there can be no doubt. A glance at the history of the Oirot, or the Kalmucks of Jungaria at this period, will make this clear.[1]

The *kongodoi*, *kongdaijy* or *kongtaichi* ('ruler') referred to in the first part of the Sagai Saga of *Sunu Mattyr* is Tse-wang Arabdan,[2] the great Kalmuck nomad prince and ruler of Jungaria, who was murdered in 1727[3] by his son Galdan Tseren—the Kaldan-Chärä mentioned in the Teleut saga. By his first wife, Tse-wang Arabdan had a son Sunu (Shünü); by his second wife, the daughter of the Torgut chief Ayuki (the Ajykku of the Teleut saga, though he is said there to be the uncle of Shünü), he had several sons, including Galdan Tseren (Kaldan-Chärä). One of his descendants was the Amyr Saran of our saga.[4] Considerable confusion exists with regard to the personal history of the historical Sunu or Shünü. Baddeley makes no reference to him. According to Howorth he distinguished himself in his father's wars against the Kazak-Kirghiz in 1723 and gained thereby the envy of his brother, from whose vengeance he escaped to the Volga. There he married, and died in 1732.[5] According to Radlov, however, a notice is said to have been received by the governor of Orenburg to the effect that Sunu had raised a rebellion, in consequence of which the *kongtaichi* had had him bound so tightly that one of his shoulder blades was broken

---

[1] For a brief outline of the events which form the background of these sagas and their variants, the reader is referred to Howorth, I, p. 640 ff.; Radlov, *A.S.* I, p. 161 ff.; Michell, p. 169 ff. The official Chinese version is translated by Parker, *C.R.* XXIII, p. 14 f. It appears to have been drawn up in 1763, and opens with the interesting notice: "In pursuance of the emperor's commands, the Great Officers of the Cabinet Council took in hand the Dzungar Genealogies, and submitted 'An imperially sanctioned sketch of the whole Dzungar nation.' It runs as follows: 'From ancient times some account has also been given of all outer barbarians. But the truth occurs as seldom as error happens frequently. Of course it is partly the difficulty of getting into their country and of verbally communicating with them which is responsible for the fact that we can only find out a percentage of what is to be learnt.... Remembering that they (i.e. the Jungarians) were once a great nation, and ought properly to be provided with a record, we have therefore availed ourselves of such facts as could be ascertained by personal investigation, and we now consign these to paper, as some slight contribution to Geographical History.'"

[2] For some further notices of this enlightened prince, see Baddeley I, p. clxxvii.
[3] See *Ib.* Genealogical Table G.
[4] The family relationships, and much of the family history, are given by Baddeley, *loc. cit.*
[5] Howorth I, p. 649.

and he could no longer draw the bow. Radlov adds that Shünü is said to have then fled to the Ayuki Khan. When the latter wished to deliver him up he fled to Petersburg. In 1740, under the title Karasakal, he raised a rebellion among the Bashkirs, and in 1745 he fled to the Kirghiz, where he took upon himself the title of Kara Khan.[1] It is beside the purpose of this book to sift the historical value of these variant accounts —manifestly based on discrepancies in tradition, whether written or oral. The name Sunu is not unknown elsewhere, and it is possible that mistaken identifications have taken place. It would seem, however, that at the time to which our saga refers a historical character of this name, the son of the *kongtaichi* of Jungaria, was living, and that his career had much in common with that which oral tradition attributes to him.

It is a curious fact, however, that Sunu should figure in a more distinguished rôle in saga than Amur-sana, though it must be confessed his saga is not a very convincing one. We have been struck by its similarity in several points to the actual history of his grandfather Senga or Senghé, the son and successor to the great Bogatyr (see above) and brother of Galdan,[2] the Jungarian chief who overran Central Asia towards the close of the seventeenth century. According to Kalmuck tradition[3] Senghé, during a war against the Kazaks, caused to be murdered one Onchon, who is identified with some probability by Howorth[4] with the youngest[5] of the five sons of Khana Noyon Khongor, known as the 'Five Tigers'. He also distinguished himself in war in Siberia, actually besieging the Russian town of Krasnoyarsk on the Yenisei in 1667. He extended and consolidated the Kalmuck power[6] which Bogatyr had established. His half-brothers, however, were jealous of him, and attacked him several times, and eventually murdered him in 1671.[7] It will be seen that the story has much in common with our saga, and it seems to us not improbable that in oral tradition Sunu has been confused with his grandfather Senghé, and that this confusion has not been altogether rectified by Western historians. If this is so, it is possible that in the story of Sunu's prowess against the tiger we have a reflection of the tradition which ascribes a similar feat to the great

[1] *A.S.* I, p. 169.
[2] For a brief notice of this chief, see Baddeley II, p. 139, note.
[3] See Howorth I, p. 621.   [4] *Ib.* I, p. 621.
[5] The name is given by Baddeley as Buyan Ochun Batur (I, Genealogical Table D).
[6] The Russians sent a mission to him under Kulvinski in 1667. See *Ib.* II, p. 180.
[7] *Ib.* II, p. 139, note. See also Parker, *C.R.* XXIII, p. 15.

Bogatyr,[1] and which may have been transferred already in oral tradition to his son Senga. We may compare the confusion which seems to exist between Galdan Tseren, Sunu's brother, and the great Galdan, brother of the Senga in question.[2] Such transference and confusion are not unfamiliar to us in heroic traditions elsewhere, and are similar to what have taken place in Teutonic heroic literature. At the same time the element of folk-tale is probably present. The whole story bears a suspicious resemblance to that related in the narrative poem of *Südai Märgän and Joltai Märgän* (see p. 96 f. above), and to the story of *Kogutei* (cf. p. 99 ff. above).

Amur-sana,[3] the Amyr Saran of our saga, is perhaps the most distinguished figure in the history of the Kalmucks. He succeeded Galdan Tseren, *kongtaichi* of Jungaria, who died in 1745, and extended the Kalmuck power over the whole of Mongolia. Ultimately, however, seeking to make himself independent of China, he was forced to flee northwards to Siberia, and died in the neighbourhood of Tobolsk in 1757. The Chinese emperor Kien-lung—the 'Mongol Khan' of the saga—demanded the corpse. The demand was refused by the Russians, but his remains were shown to the Chinese envoy that his death might be clearly ascertained.

It will be seen that the sagas which we have been considering relate to the Kalmuck princes who ruled the Jungars from the early years of the seventeenth century, from the death of the great Bogatyr, till the middle of the eighteenth century. Allowing for the possible telescoping of characters and events, notably of the two Galdans and of Senga and Sunu, our sagas may be said to cover, with sparse and somewhat disintegrated traditions, the period from the close of the second heroic period of the Kalmucks, which ended with the death of Dayan in 1543, to the destruction of the Jungarians by the Chinese in the middle of the eighteenth century. We have already seen reason to believe that the heroic poems themselves relate to the early part of this period, and to the ruling princes of the same stock. If we are right in our identification of the milieu of the poems—there can be no doubt as to the substantial historicity of the sagas—the oral literature of the Kara-Kirghiz in the neighbourhood of Lake Issyk-Kul recorded by Radlov has preserved for three centuries in a Turkish dialect the historical traditions of the Mongol (Kalmuck) rulers of Jungaria, whom they doubtless looked up to as their overlords at this period.

[1] See *Ib.* II, p. 30. [2] See e.g. Howorth I, p. 660.
[3] See Baddeley I, Genealogical Table G; Howorth, *loc. cit.* See further p. 130 below.

The historical existence of the Turkoman hero Kurroglou is vouched for by Chodzko[1] who lived for many years among the Turkomans in northern Persia, and was well acquainted with their history and traditions. The hero is said to have been a Turkoman Tuka and a native of Khorassan, and to have lived in the second half of the seventeenth century. He is further said to have built for himself a fort named Chamly-bill in the valley of Salmas in the province of Aderbaidjan, the ruins of which can still be seen. From this stronghold he was in the habit of plundering the caravans on the great commercial route from Persia to Turkey. The memory of his deeds and songs is said to be carefully preserved by the wandering Turkish tribes on the great steppe between the Euphrates and the Merve river.

It may be added that traditions of the hero Kurroglou are known also from other sources. According to Valikhanov[2] this 'classical robber' of the Turkomans figures also in Kazak 'rhapsodies'.

How far the incidents related in this cycle represent historical events we do not know. We are not able to test the historical foundation of the actual occurrences, and unfortunately Chodzko makes no pronouncement on this matter. It is a striking fact, however, that the cycle is singularly free from elements which are manifestly unhistorical. Supernatural elements and magic are almost wholly absent. Exaggeration is freely indulged in, but it is hardly for the most part of such a character that the audience would be expected to accept it in a literal sense. Not infrequently it is frankly humorous. It is also perhaps worth noting in regard to the fidelity of the traditions that the hero's failures are recorded as well as his triumphs. When he is defeated by a merchant[3] the incident is related with frankness, and no attempt is made to gloze it over. The hero is, however, neither censured nor criticised by the narrator, though he is represented as feeling ashamed of the incident himself.

In conclusion it may be mentioned that Yakut narrative poetry has apparently retained reliable traditions of a historical Yakut hero, the great Djennik, who headed a disastrous revolt of his people on the River Lena in the seventeenth century (cf. p. 43 above). Unfortunately none of this poetry has been accessible to us; but the preservation of traditions of this hero suggests that the historical element may be well preserved among these remoter Turkish peoples.

Of the vast amount of unhistorical elements in the poems there can be no doubt. These elements consist chiefly of exaggeration and super-

[1] Chodzko, p. 3 f.   [2] Michell, p. 100.   [3] Chodzko, p. 183 ff.

natural features. In regard to incidents and situations which are in conflict (*a*) with reliable historical evidence, or (*b*) with other heroic stories, it has already been stated that our knowledge of the history of the peoples in question is too limited to allow of our testing the events of the stories by the former, while our variants of heroic stories are hardly extensive enough to allow of our re-establishing the original form of a given tradition. Some indication of the unhistorical elements which have entered into the stories of Ermak and of Sunu Mattyr have already been given, however. It may be added here that in the narrative poetry of the Kara-Kirghiz it is probable that a similar telescoping of historical periods and events has taken place, and that there has been, in the course of oral transmission, a tendency to draw into the *Manas* Cycle heroes, incidents, and allusions which belong properly to other cycles, and perhaps to other periods.

The poems afford abundant examples of incidents and situations which are in themselves incredible. These may be said to consist of exaggeration, shape-changing, and supernatural elements of various kinds. These features are present in the narrative poetry of all the Tatars, and are very common in the sagas also. They are relatively less prominent in the poetry of the Kara-Kirghiz than in that of the Abakan Tatars and of the Altai and Teleut peoples.

The introduction of supernatural beings into the poems is very common, especially in the poems of the Abakan group. Among such incidents one which recurs very frequently is the sudden appearance of an old man, described as either grey-haired or bald, at the naming ceremony of a child (cf. p. 99 above). Sometimes he is identified with the god Kydyr; more frequently it is stated that no one knows who he is or whence he comes, and he disappears mysteriously immediately after bestowing a name on the child. One of the most frequent of the supernatural beings is a monster known as *Jelbägän* (*dshalmaus*; cf. p. 86 above), who possesses many heads and dwells underground, though he (she) frequently visits the world of mortals, sometimes under other forms, such as the lungs of an animal. This creature is generally represented as hostile to the hero's interests, though this is not always the case. We have seen that in the variant versions of the story of *Er Töshtük* Jelbägän is sometimes represented as hostile to the hero, sometimes as friendly.

Of other supernatural beings who figure in the stories something will be said in the chapter on 'Poetry and Saga relating to Gods and Spirits', to which the reader is here referred. A glance at this chapter and at the chapter on 'Non-heroic Poetry and Saga' will show at once that intercourse between human beings and the spirit world plays a very large and important part in the literature of the Tatars. We are not inclined to regard this intercourse as either fiction pure and simple, or yet as a mere literary convention. We shall see in the chapter on 'Recitation', etc. that direct personal intercourse between human beings and deities forms a part of the liturgy or libretto recited by the shaman at religious functions, and that such intercourse is actually believed by the Tatars to form a part of the spiritual experience of the professional *shaman* and *shamanka*. When such intercourse occurs as an incident in the narrative poems, therefore, we prefer to regard it, not as an unhistorical element in the poems, but as a constituent element in the spiritual life of the heroes. That is to say, among the Tatars intercourse between human beings and supernatural beings is to be understood as having reference primarily, not to actual, but to spiritual experience. We know that this spiritual experience is sometimes symbolised in dramatic action, both among the Tatars and other peoples (cf. p. 200 ff. below). It may be taken for granted also—and this is of the first importance—that this same spiritual experience has come to be commonly treated as a literary convention, a traditional motif in the poems. As a purely literary convention similar motifs are commonly to be found among other peoples also, notably among the Greeks and the ancient Irish. Where the Tatar evidence is of especial interest is in its closer relationship to the actual beliefs and practices of the peoples who recite the stories. This will be more clearly demonstrated in connection with the dramatic monologue recited by the shaman in the chapter on 'Recitation', etc.

The attribution of supernatural power to human beings and animals is very common. In comparison with Greek and Celtic heroic stories, much of the poetry of the Kara-Kirghiz is, on the whole, surprisingly sober in this respect; but in the Abakan poems it is normal and even usual for human beings to possess supernatural power. In the heroic poetry of the Kara-Kirghiz we cannot fail to be struck by the rarity of divine interference in human affairs. We never find the gods taking part in battle, or showing favour to individuals, or acting in their own persons, save in the instances of the appearance of Kydyr at the 'naming ceremony' just referred to, and the angels sent by God to the mourning creatures at Manas' tomb. The powers of Manas and Joloi are stupendous and exaggerated, but rarely supernatural. Exceptions occur however. An interesting passage in *Joloi*, to be discussed later, relates a contest between the Kalmuck prince Karacha and Joloi's wife Ak Saikal, both of whom are represented as transforming themselves into a series of animals, birds, etc.

Exaggeration is very common throughout Tatar literature. The hero Manas is represented as abnormally strong and invincible. He has a coat of mail which no lance can pierce. The hero Joloi possesses great strength and stature. He and his wife are capable of doing battle alone against whole troops of Kalmucks. When he is cast into a pit he is able to survive for fifteen years till he is finally rescued. This exaggeration assumes its most daring form in the indications of time and space in the Abakan poems. If a hero fights in single combat he is said to sink into the earth with the exertion, and may remain fixed there mourning for nine years. The combat may indeed last for forty years till all the mountains are overturned and all the trees are uprooted. Or a hero may ride in pursuit of an enemy through thrice nine worlds, and thrice nine heavens, over many seas. Manifestly such bold hyperbole is not intended to be interpreted literally.

Throughout Tatar literature, including that of the Kara-Kirghiz, human and superhuman faculties are attributed to horses. Not only are these generally gifted with human speech and reason, but they are, as we have seen, superior morally and intellectually to the heroes themselves. In the Kazak epic of *Sain Batyr* the hero's horse and breastplate are both represented as encouraging the hero to battle.[1] Birds also are sometimes gifted with speech and credited with much wisdom, and are represented as taking an active part in human affairs. In the Kara-Kirghiz poem *Er Töshtük* an eagle carries the hero to earth on her back from the Underworld, while in the Altai poem *Kogutei* an eagle delivers the hero from his imprisonment in a deep pit. In the Kachin poem *Kara Tygan Khan and Suksagal Khan* the herb which restores the dead to life is guarded by two ravens on a certain tree-top in the Altai. In the Kysyl poem *Kulatai and Kulun Taidshy* a cuckoo addresses the hero from a tree-top in human speech, telling him that his life will last just as long as that of the cuckoo himself and no longer. Such motifs are very numerous.

A curious supernatural feature commonly attributed to wild birds is that of being able to convey a letter safely and directly from the sender to the person to whom it is indited,[2] and we would call attention to the

---

[1] *Proben* III, p. 253, l. 1596 ff.

[2] G. Turner calls attention to the 'ocean postal service' on the Ellice Group in Micronesia, where the natives have trained frigate birds to act as carriers from island to island, sometimes as far as sixty miles distant (*Samoa A Hundred Years Ago*, London, 1884, p. 282 f.).

constant references to what appears to be a highly developed postal system on the steppe, in which birds act as letter-carriers. The women in the poems, who, as we have seen, are the most cultivated members of the community, appear to be mostly able to pen and read a letter. Thus in the Kysyl poem *Südäi Märgän and Joltai Märgän* the hero's wife calls a swallow to her, 'writes a letter on its wing', and sends it to her lover.[1] In the Sagai poem *Ai Mergän and Altyn Kus*, the maiden Altyn Aryg obtains a nest of young owls, and writes a message and sends it on a young owl (i.e. presumably on its wing). She then lets fly the two young owls, which alight on Ar Chotai's shoulder on the gable of a stone building. Ar Chotai reads what she had 'written on the two young owls'. The message runs: "Ai Mergän slew my father. Take me, O Ar Chotai!"[2]

Shape-changing is comparatively rare in the poetry of the Kara-Kirghiz, though interesting instances occur in *Joloi*, where the Kalmuck hero Karacha and Joloi's wife Ak Saikal are represented as transforming themselves into a series of birds and animals. The passage resembles the Russian *bylina* of Volga, and is even closer to the pursuit of Gwion Bach by Caridwen in the Welsh story of *Taliesin* (see Vol. I, p. 103). The passage in *Joloi* relates to the pursuit of Karacha and Joloi's sister by his wife Ak Saikal:

> But Karacha turned his steed,
> And escaped the hands of Saikal;
> Ere Saikal turned her horse
> That black-winged heroic steed
> Has become a blue dove,
> Soared aloft and flown away.
> But at once the brown horse
> Became a blue falcon,
> Struck it from the rear,
> Swooping from Heaven aloft.
> Prince Karacha now afresh....
> Became a red fox,
> And hid himself in a forest,
> And the horse became a black vulture,
> And swooped down from above,
> And so pierced the forest,
> His feathers fluttered in the air.
> Yet again the other escaped
> And became a white fish,
> And sped plunging through the water.
> The horse became a beaver,

[1] *Proben* II, p. 608. [2] *Ib.* II, p. 460, l. 2520.

Dived after him to the bottom of the water,
Seized him on the bottom of the water,
And so at last Ak Saikal
Seized Karacha the prince.[1]

Shape-changing frequently takes place in the Abakan poems also. In *Sugdjul Mergän* the three children pursued by Kuskun Alyp change themselves into bright falcons, and later in the poem resume their human form. In *Altyn Pyrkan* one of the three maidens who lives above Heaven comes to earth 'as a golden cuckoo'. In *Kulatai and Kulun Taidshy* the heroes' wives become two geese and fly up aloft. In *Kara Tygan Khan and Suksagal Khan* the heroes transform themselves into swallows and their horses into swans. Transformations of human beings into animals are much less common. The hero Puga-Däkä transforms himself into a fly, and the hero Altyn Taidshy changes himself into a mouse in order to spy secretly on his sister's behaviour. In *Ai Tolysy* the hero is assisted by three maidens, two of whom can assume swan forms at will, the third, that of an ermine. A variant of the shape-changing theme is seen in the stories of *Südäi Märgän*, in which the hero dresses himself in a bear's skin, and in *Kogutei*, in which the hero assumes beaver form. Even the horses can transform themselves apparently at will. In the poem of *Kartaga Mergän*, on the death of the hero's roan horse, his black horse transforms himself into a *jelbägän* (cf. p. 84 above), and flies through the air in pursuit of a bird, which proves to be the soul of the roan horse.

A curious feature among the supernatural elements in the Abakan poems is the 'naked' people who are said to take an active part in human affairs. Their assistance is sometimes given to the hero, sometimes to his enemy, according as they are the emissaries of Kudai or of Erlik. In *Altyn Pyrkan* the cruel and relentless Saryg Khan employs seven naked men who dwell beneath the earth to burn his own son to death. On the other hand in the poem *Kan Märgän* from the Sagai Tatars on the R. Se the three heroes whose drink has been poisoned are miraculously restored to health by a naked child sent from God. In the Kysyl poem *Kulatai and Kulun Taidshy* a naked little girl intervenes on behalf of the female 'hero', the 'maiden prince'. This little girl, as we have seen, ultimately becomes a 'maiden prince' herself, but the account of her origin is not clear.

Stories of the remarkable birth and childhood of heroes are common. Monster births appear to be rare in the literature of entertainment,

[1] *Proben* v, p. 431, l. 1996.

where they would doubtless be looked upon as indecorous, though the hero in the poem *Khan Märgän* from the Sagai Tatars on the R. Is is said to be the child of a mare. In antiquarian saga such monster births are quite common (cf. p. 143 below). The stories of the birth and childhood of heroes show on the whole surprising uniformity, and that in features which appear to us to be remarkable in themselves. Thus almost all the heroes are said to be either the children of their parents in extreme old age, often, like Manas, and Er Töshtük, the youngest of a series of brothers; or else orphans. In the latter case the hero and his sister are almost invariably alone, and, at least at the opening of the stories, the sole survivors of their family, their parents having generally been carried off or slain in a raid by a hostile chief. In the former case the hero may be sent in answer to a special prayer to God. Very commonly the hero is distinguished at birth by signs of beauty which, if we take the words at their face value, we should regard as supernatural features. Thus Manas is said to have had bones of copper, and flesh of exceptional whiteness. The hero Altyn Kiris, in *Khan Mergän and Ai Mergän*, is born with a head of gold and a body of silver. These are, however, to be regarded as hyperbolical expressions, figures of poetic diction, rather than as literal statements of supernatural characteristics.[1]

A similar uniformity governs the stories of the childhood of the heroes. All are said to grow and develop at an abnormal rate. When Manas is born we have an interesting account of his naming feast, to which come representatives from Yarkand, China, and elsewhere, and all prophesy good things for him. He himself boasts as he lies in his cradle of how he will lay waste the heathen, and 'open a path for the Moslems'. At ten years of age he shoots with bow and arrow; at fourteen he becomes a 'prince, a destroyer of princely dwellings'.[2] The hero Er Töshtük is said to have uttered the word 'Mother' on the second day of his life, 'Father' on the sixth, and while still an infant in the cradle he creeps out to his father who is herding sheep, and drives the flock home for him. In the poem of *Khan Märgän* from the R. Is, the new-born hero, who is the son of a mare, tears off the hand and foot of his enemy, Khan Kartaga. Practically all the orphan heroes go out into the world hunting or raiding long before, in the opinion of their wise elder sisters, they are of a suitable age to do so.

---

[1] For a similar poetical convention we may compare the description of an infant hero in a Norse fragment of heroic poetry quoted in the *Hervarar Saga*, Ch. XII, and the explanation given in the prose passage which follows.

[2] *Proben* v, p. 1 f.

Necromancy is commonly referred to. Many instances occur in the Abakan poems. In *Altyn Pyrkan* the young hero dies, but is restored to life by one of three maidens who dwell above Heaven. She comes 'as a golden cuckoo' to the corpse, and sprinkles it with the 'water of life' and lays a yellow herb in its mouth, which restores the hero to his full life and vigour (cf. p. 92 above). In the poem *Sugdjul Mergän*[1] the hero, with the help of his wife, restores a number of people to life. The poem is obscure in many points, but the tenor of the narrative suggests that the hero is chiefly responsible for the physical, or, as we might put it, the medical side of the necromantic process, the woman for the rescue of the soul from the hosts of enemies in the land of the dead, though even here she has to call the hero to her aid, so powerful are the hosts fighting against her.

It will be seen that the two forms of necromancy are quite different. In the first a supernatural being comes in the form of a bird and restores life by physical means. In the second two human beings, a man and a woman, enter the spirit world and fight against evil spirits as a part of the necromantic process. This second type of story is common in the Abakan poems. Nor is it confined to them. In the Kara-Kirghiz poem *Joloi* we have seen that the black *shamanka*, Kara Chach, restores Bolot to health by similar means, though here the hero himself accompanies her to the Underworld.

The account of Manas' death and revival is obscure, and the obscurity is increased rather than elucidated by a comparison of the various versions. We shall see (p. 170 f. below) that it is stated in one passage that the hero has made a journey underground, while elsewhere it is stated that he made no such journey. The obscurity is further increased by the ambiguity which exists, both here and also commonly elsewhere, as to whether a given hero is represented as, in actual fact, dead, or only as severely wounded. The versions of the *Manas* story differ on this point. When, therefore, we are told that his wife Kanykäi restores him with herbs and ointments, that is to say, by a natural process, we cannot be sure if her proceeding is merely curative, especially as she is assisted in her office by a Mohammedan mullah or pilgrim.[2] Finally the curious account of the angel from God transforming Manas' tomb into a fine house, and restoring the hero to a life of luxury within it is

---

[1] *Proben* II, p. 307 ff.
[2] To this incident we shall have to refer again in the chapter on 'The Texts', where it will be shown that at least two apparently incompatible versions of the story have been combined.

inexplicable as we have the story, and we suspect that connecting links have been forgotten which would have made the narrative clearer.

The chief cause of the obscurity, however, no doubt lies in the superimposition of Mohammedanism on the ancient heathen practices which in *Joloi, Er Töshtük*, and the Abakan poems appear in a clearer light. In these poems the restoration of the dead to life is described as a spiritual rather than a physical process, and is carried out by a shaman or a shamanka, or a man or woman acting in these capacities. Generally it involves a journey to the Heavens or to the Underworld, and carries us into a spiritual milieu, away from the material Universe. This subject has been treated more fully by one of us elsewhere,[1] and space will not permit of fuller treatment here; but it is hardly necessary to point out that a superstratum of Mohammedanism, little understood, being introduced by a heroic minstrel into the warp and woof of older heathen motifs, must necessarily leave much which is difficult to reconcile with either faith, and still more difficult to reconcile with known customs and authentic ritual. We have little doubt that many of our difficulties in the *Manas* stories in particular are to be accounted for by the two-fold religious traditions of the minstrel.[2]

[1] Chadwick, *J.R.A.I.* LXVI (1936), p. 291 ff.

[2] We understand from N. Poppe ('Russische Arbeiter auf dem Gebiet der Mongolistik,' *Asia Major* V, 1930, p. 217) that the story of Amursana referred to on p. 121 above (cf. also p. 52 ff. above) has been discussed in a short article by B. Vladimirtsov, 'Mongolskie Skazaniya ob Amursane', in a *Festschrift for Oldenburg*, Leningrad, 1927. Unfortunately this work has not been accessible to us.

CHAPTER VI

POETRY AND SAGA RELATING TO GODS AND SPIRITS, AND MANTIC POETRY

IN non-heroic sagas and poems gods and supernatural beings play a very large part, and they are frequently represented as visiting human beings on earth, while men and women are also very commonly shown as visiting the gods in the Heavens and the Underworld. Indeed such incidents form the greater part of the supernatural elements of these narratives. Some account of these spiritual beings has already been given at the opening of the chapter on 'Non-heroic Poetry and Saga'. But we have not found any stories relating primarily to the gods as a community,[1] like the stories of the gods in Norse and Greek literature, though we are not inclined to doubt that such stories may exist. The fact that they have not been recorded by Radlov and other collectors may be due to the persecution of shamanism under the tsarist régime.[2]

On the other hand a considerable amount of the poetry of celebration has survived, especially among the eastern Tatars. A large number of poems of this class are recited by the shamans of the Tatars of the Altai at the great annual sacrifice to Bai Ülgen, and consist of invocations, prayers, and kindred forms of poetry. These will be referred to more fully in the account of the performance of the shaman himself in the chapter on 'Recitation', etc. below. In this connection we may refer also to an invocation to the spirits recited by a *baksha*,[3] as the shamans of the western Tatars are called, in which the names of a number of gods and spirits occur. In spite of much that is obscure and corrupt in the poem, it is easy to recognise the names of a number of gods and spirits known to us from the Altai and Abakan poems, and the invocation

---

[1] Unless some of the material in Holmberg's work on *Siberian Mythology* is derived from such stories.

[2] What makes us suspect that such stories may exist is the fact that a very interesting story has actually been recorded from the Cheremis by E. Chirikov (translated by N. Kershaw in the *Cambridge Magazine* for February 23rd, and March 2nd, 1918, under the title of 'The Daughter of the Sky'). It is true that the Cheremis are a Finnish, not a Tatar people; but their religion would seem to be of a similar character to that of the shamanist Tatars.

[3] Radlov, *A.S.* II, p. 63 ff.

itself has close affinities with the invocation recited by the Altai shaman in the performance just referred to. It should, however, be clearly stated at the outset that in many cases it is impossible for us to draw any clear distinction between hymns and prayers on the one hand, and spells on the other. The invocation of the *baksha* might with equal propriety be classed among the latter.

Radlov cites an example of a hymn in fifteen lines of verse addressed to Erlik, the ruler of the Underworld, by a shaman of the Teleut.[1] This hymn was sung in recitative on two notes. He also gives a prayer of thanksgiving offered up by his host, a Teleut shaman on the R. Bachat, to the god Ülgen. It consists of twenty-seven lines,[2] and contains a personal request for the divine blessing and for well-being and prosperity. A refrain of two lines recurs four times. Vambéry cites[3] from Jadrintzew the hymn of a shaman to Ülgen's third son, Timur Khan ('Iron Prince'), the war god. The hymn consists of eight lines of panegyric, and closely resembles a heroic panegyric poem. Radlov gives examples of prayers from the Kazaks which contain references to sacrifice and to the god Kydyr, though they conclude with the Mohammedan formula *Allah ekbär*, 'God is great'.[4] An example of grace after meat from the Kara-Kirghiz which he gives elsewhere is almost identical with one of the prayers in this group.[5]

Prayers to the gods are quoted in heroic narrative poems and sagas. We may refer to a prayer made by the hero to the god Kudai to change his filthy hovel into a grand house, in the Kysyl poem of *Südäi Märgän and Joltai Märgän*.[6] In the Sagai poem of *Ai Mergän and Altyn Kus*, Ak Khan and his wife Agylang Ko are represented as praying to God to grant them a child, after which all their dependents unite in prayer that their wish may be granted.[7] All three prayers are quoted in full. The first two are very short. The public prayer consists of eleven lines.

An interesting instance of family prayer, combined with a solemn vow, occurs in the Kara-Kirghiz poem *Joloi*.[8] The object of the prayer is the return of the hero Bolot, the adopted son of Köchpös Bai. The entire family stands in a circle round Köchpös and each in turn drinks a ceremonial draught of *kumyss*. Thereupon Köchpös Bai orders his sons to bring him the *bosko*:

[1] Radlov, *A.S.* I, p. 341.
[2] *Proben* I, p. 238; cf. Radlov, *A.S.* II, p. 9.
[3] *Türkenvolk*, p. 117f.
[4] *Proben* III, p. 4ff.
[5] Radlov, *A.S.* I, p. 431.
[6] *Proben* II, p. 614, l. 234ff.
[7] *Ib.* p. 386, l. 26ff.
[8] *Ib.* v, p. 476.

His *bosko*, the welfare of the flocks,
His *bosko*, the welfare of the soul,
Bring now here to me.
I will send it up to Kudai.
Bolot, my dear offspring,
I will forthwith cause to fly to me.[1]

The poet did not know the meaning of the word *bosko*, but as Radlov observes, it must, from the nature of the context, be a bird which is regarded as a tutelary genius. When the *bosko* is brought, Köchpös Bai raises it on high and lets it fly away, and prays as follows:

"Give Bolot to me, O Kudai!" he cried;
"O my children, my children,
Until Bolot returns
I will not sleep under cover,
Or lay me down upon the earth,
I will not unloose my belt!
Kudai, my Lord, give Bolot to me!"[2]

References to spells are not uncommon, though actual examples of spells are rare. Radlov gives an example of a Teleut rain charm[3] of eighteen lines which was pronounced by one of his guides of the Tölös tribe (on the R. Cholyshman) near the source of the Abakan River in 1861, after a week of bad weather. The speaker was a *jadachi*, 'rain-maker'. After he had warmed his 'medicine' in a spoon over the fire, he raised both hands and the spoon to Heaven and pronounced his charm.[4] It is obscure to us, but the shaman seems to be apostrophising the Heavens and certain spirits in a conjuration or adjuration.

The most interesting example of a charm which we know is the formula quoted by the same author[5] which is said to be used by the shaman as an incantation to Erlik Khan. The charm is indistinguishable from a prayer to Erlik, and is valuable as giving a detailed picture of the god—a picture which is curiously reminiscent of the imagery and beliefs associated with the deities of the Bön of Tibet.

Thou, Erlik on the black horse,
Thou hast a bed of black beaver skins;
Thy hips are so mighty
That no girdle can span them;

---

[1] *Loc. cit.* l. 3540 ff.
[3] *Proben* I, p. 241.
[5] *Ib. A.S.* II, p. 10.

[2] *Ib.* p. 477, l. 3548 f.
[4] Radlov, *A.S.* II, p. 8.

Thy neck is so all-powerful
That no human being can clasp it;
A span broad are thy brows,
Black is thy beard,
Blood-flecked is thy fearful countenance.
O, thou mighty Erlik Khan,
Whose hair gives forth shining sparks,
Ever does the breast of a corpse
Serve thee as a bowl;
Men's skulls are thy beakers.
Thy sword is of green iron,
Of iron are thy epaulettes,
Sparkling is thy black countenance,
Thy hair floats in waves.
At the door of thy yurt
Stand many mighty thrones
An earthen cauldron hast thou,
And the roof of thy yurt is of iron.
Thou ridest a mighty ox.
For the purpose of thy saddle
A horse's skin is too small;
To overthrow heroes, thou stretchest forth thy hand,
To overthrow horses, when thou fearfully
Only drawest tight their belly-band.
O, Erlik, Erlik, my father,
Why persecutest thou the people thus?
Say, why dost thou destroy them?
Thy countenance is ever black as soot,
Glittering dark like coals,
O, Erlik, Erlik, my father,
From generation to generation
In the long course of time
We honour thee day and night;
From generation to generation
Thou art an honoured lord.

The poems of the Kara-Kirghiz afford a considerable amount of evidence for the widespread use of charms. At the birth of the hero Bolot a black shaman is called in, who is said to be a very excellent doctor and magician. He sits down at the head of the woman and calls all his spirits to her aid. The words which he utters, like the prayer to Erlik just quoted, are rather a prayer to the spirits than a spell, but the context makes it clear that magic rather than religion in the ordinary sense is operative.[1] We suspect that the opening lines of the Kara-

[1] *Proben* v, p. 471 f.

Kirghiz poem *How Alaman Bet becomes a Mussulman*, have been modelled on such a heathen conception:

> The son of Kara Khan,
> Alaman Bet, the tiger-like,
> When the saints assembled,
> Was born at their word;
> When the saints assembled,
> He was born by their spell.[1]

In these poems, charms are also said to be written down. In the Kara-Kirghiz poem *Joloi*, when Kara Chach desires to send a message to summon the hero Bolot to the house of his foster-father Köchpös Bai, she takes a piece of paper the size of a hand, spreads it out before her, writes a charm formula on it, and lets it fly to Heaven, whence it soon reaches Bolot.[2] With this passage it is interesting to compare the passage from the same poem quoted above, in which Köchpös Bai himself attempts to recall Bolot by praying for his return, at the same time releasing some spirit, perhaps in the form of a bird (cf. p. 133 above), which flies to Heaven.

It is often difficult to distinguish charms from blessings and curses. In the Kara-Kirghiz poem *Joloi*, Bolot's 'mothers,' Ak Saikal and Ak Kanysh, sacrifice a sheep and recite a blessing over him before he sets out to encounter his enemy Karacha.[3] It is clear in some cases, as in ancient Ireland, that a curse is immediately and practically operative. Again our evidence comes chiefly from the heroic stories. In the Kazak saga of *Khan Shentäi*, when the hero sets out on his travels, his mother bestows a name on him, and also bestows on him her blessing in a set formula, invoking the name of Kydyr.[4] Later in the same saga the hero is saved in a deadly combat against the seven-headed *Dshalmaus* by the intervention of a white-bearded man. 'This man was Kydyr, who had come through the blessing (*bata*) of his mother.'[5] In the Kazak saga of *Erkäm Aidar* it is clearly stated that the hero's only sister is an 'enchantress' (*duakär*), and that when he is setting out on his journey she makes a charm (*dua*).[6] The words of her charm are almost identical with those of the 'blessing' bestowed on Khan Shentäi by his mother. In the Kysyl epic of *Südäi Märgän and Joltai Märgän* from

---

[1] *Proben* v, p. 6, l. 9 ff. The word in the text is translated by Radlov *Segenswort*; but in his *Wörterbuch* the only meaning given is 'curse'.

[2] *Ib.* p. 498 f.; cf. p. 517.

[3] *Ib.* p. 485, l. 3841 ff.

[4] *Ib.* III, p. 303.

[5] *Ib.* p. 316 f.

[6] *Ib.* p. 321 f.

the Abakan group it is the uncle who bestows his blessing, combined with admonition and advice[1] (cf. p. 96 ff. above). In Tatar wedding ceremonial it is customary for the father-in-law or some relative to bestow blessings and advice on the bride. A long and elaborate example of such a blessing is given by Radlov in his account of the wedding songs and ceremonies of the Altai Tatars.[2] A similar custom seems to prevail among the Kazaks (see p. 157 below).

The evidence of the heroic poems makes it clear that the bestowal of a formal blessing is a recognised part of the 'naming ceremony'—that important function at which the hero is regarded as formally coming of age. One of the most interesting examples of such a blessing occurs in the Sagai poem *Ai Mergän and Altvn Kus*. The young hero Ai Mergän has not yet received a name. Riding one day in the mountains, he finds a letter tied to the top of a birch tree. It has been written by the seven *jajan* and left behind for him. It contains a message naming him Ai Mergän, bestowing blessings upon him, adjuring him to be brave and generous, and to avenge his parents. It also contains the assurance that if he practises the virtues inculcated, he will "live long, and stand higher than the *jajuchi*"[3].

Curses are sometimes very elaborate. We may refer to the curse which Ak Kanysh, Joloi's wife, threatens to hurl on him if he refuses to give his favourite horse to their son.[4] As an instance of the immediate effect of a curse we may refer to the Teleut story of *Ak Köbök*, in which the hero blesses his uncle in a verse of four lines for bestowing a horse upon him; but when his uncle refuses to grant him a second horse, Ak Köbök curses him, also in a verse of four lines. The prose narrative immediately relates the operation of the curse, and the uncle is glad to relent.[5] In this connection we must remember, however, that Ak Köbök is a sage as well as a warrior, and his curse would without doubt be especially potent. We have had no opportunity of studying the effect of the curse of an actual shaman among the Tatars. We may refer, however, to the account—too long to quote here—which Czaplicka gives of the actual operation of the curse of a Tungus shaman on a Tungus layman of her acquaintance who had incurred his enmity. The mesmeric effect on the victim as the shaman danced and called upon the powers of darkness is very striking, and its potency was such that the curse was believed to

[1] *Proben* II, p. 648, l. 1400 ff.
[2] Radlov, *A.S.* I, p. 319.
[3] *Proben* II, p. 410 f.
[4] *Ib.* v, p. 502.
[5] *Ib.* I, p. 226 f.

be operative not only on the victim, but on his family also, even after the death of the shaman himself.[1]

We know of no independent examples of vows which have attained to literary prestige, but mention may be made here of the vow of Alaman Bet when leaving the service of Er Kökchö[2] (cf. p. 30 above). The elaboration of this passage, and the set form in which Alaman Bet threatens revenge, the regular recurring refrain, and the categorical list of threats, all suggest that such vows follow a recognised formula which allows of considerable literary scope.

Prophecy is only very slightly represented in Tatar literature. Private or individual prophecy and political prophecy are alike wanting. In a saga recorded by Castrén which we have referred to more fully elsewhere (p. 198 below), a shaman claims knowledge of the future, and his claim is probably one which is commonly made by shamans; but their prophecies do not appear to have been recorded.

There is, however, one class of prophecy of which examples are apparently not very rare. We have from the Altai and Teleut Tatars two prophecies on the end of the world, both in poetical form. The first (Teleut) which consists of eighteen lines, contains a number of brief prophecies as to the destruction of natural objects and the subversion of natural values when the end comes. The second (Altai) is a more elaborate treatment of the same theme in eighty-seven lines. After the account of the dissolution of nature and the subversion of the elements and of the established order, the poet passes to a picture of mankind in this last extremity. Shal-Jime, who represents man, and who corresponds to Adam in the Altai story of the Creation, is represented as praying to Mandy-Shire, man's intercessor with the supreme Creator; but Mandy-Shire is silent. A second time Shal-Jime prays, this time to Mai-Tere, who is Ülgen's champion against Erlik and the spirits of darkness; but Mai-Tere is also silent. Then will Erlik arise with Karan and Kerei, and will come to earth to fight with heroes of Ülgen, Mandy-Shire and Mai-Tere, and the blood of Mai-Tere will burn the earth with fire, and that will be the end of the world. The conclusion of the poem indicates clearly the close connection between the literature of prophecy and that of cosmogony, as will be seen if it is compared with the conclusion of the Altai story of the Creation (p. 145 ff. below).

[1] Czaplicka, *S.Y.* pp. 210, 213 ff. [2] *Proben* v, p. 35.

The similarity of the last battle between the champion spirits of Ülgen and Erlik and his followers at the end of the world has something in common with the Norse conception of *Ragnarrök*. We quote the concluding lines of the poem:

> Then the black earth bursts into flame,
> Hosts of the people perish,
> The rivers arise from springs of blood,
> The mountains turn to dust.
> The rocks fall crashing down,
> The rainbow rocks trembling,
> The waves of the sea are heaped up
> So that the bottom of the sea is visible.
> Now on the bottom of the sea
> Nine great black stones are shattered,
> And from each of these stones
> Arises an iron hero;
> The mighty iron heroes
> Ride on nine iron horses.
> On the forefeet of the horses
> Shine brightly nine iron swords,
> And on their hind feet
> Gleam nine iron lances.
> When they come in contact with a leaf on a tree,
> All the trees fall prostrate.
> When they come in contact with living beings,
> They sink down destroyed.
> Kaira Khan,[1] the god, the father,
> He, the creator of this world,
> Then closes his ears,
> Does not give ear to the crying of the people.
> Shaljima[2] then calls in vain
> On Mandy-Shire[3] for help,
> For he gives no answer.
> On Mai-Tärä[4] he calls in vain,
> Mai-Tärä persists in silence.
> Then two heroes of Erlik,
> The hero Karan and the hero Kere,
> Come up out of the earth.
> On Mai-Tärä and Mandy-Shire

[1] For Kaira Khan, see p. 82 above.
[2] I.e. Man. For an account of this word see Holmberg, p. 367.
[3] A Buddhist *bodhisattva* (cf. p. ?;5 below).
[4] The Buryat also know Mai-Tärä under the name *Maidari-Burkhan*. The name is, of course, derived from the Buddhist Maitreya, the manifestation of the Buddha of the future (cf. p. 145 below).

These heroes rage and fight.
From the blood of Mai-Tärä
The earth now takes fire.
In this way the end of the world will some day come about.[1]

A number of other prophecies relating to the same subject are referred to by Holmberg in his chapter on 'The Destruction of the World'.[2]

It is, of course, self-evident that the prophetic literature just referred to has been composed under direct Buddhist teaching. There is reason for believing (cf. p. 203 below) that prophecy of purely native inspiration is not unknown, and may well be highly developed, though no considerable texts have come under our notice. There can, however, be no doubt that the doctrines of the shamanist Tatars have been affected, in some varying measure, by Buddhism, as well as by other civilised religions of the south, notably Manichaeism. The influence of Buddhism is still more marked in the beliefs and practices of the neighbouring Buryat. Indeed, it is probably in part through contact with the Buryat at various periods that this influence has spread among the Tatars, especially those Tatars who to-day occupy the mountains of Central Asia. We have already referred (p. 116 above) to other traces of the great civilisations of southern Asia which manifest themselves in certain branches of Tatar literature. The whole question of their transmission is of great interest, but here we can do no more than call attention to them. One of us hopes to demonstrate them in fuller detail in a future study.

On the whole the evidence of the texts of Tatar poetry and saga suggests that the Tatars are not so poor in mantic literature as might seem to be suggested by the paucity of actual recorded texts. Apart from prophecy most forms of mantic literature are represented in our texts, though often only incidentally in the narratives. The sparsity of references to elaborate literary magical and mantic formulae in the records made by travellers is doubtless to be ascribed largely to the proscription under which shamans have long laboured, and which must have operated especially against displays of mantic and magical art, and the recitation of the accompanying texts.

[1] Radlov, A.S. II, p. 13.
[2] For similar doctrines in India, Palestine, etc. cf. Vol. II, pp. 590 f., 622, 731.

CHAPTER VII

ANTIQUARIAN POETRY AND SAGA. GNOMIC AND DESCRIPTIVE LITERATURE. POETRY AND SAGA RELATING TO UNSPECIFIED INDIVIDUALS

IN general the literature of antiquarian speculation is not very highly developed among the Tatars, though certain genres are found in abundance. Such poetry as we possess which embodies traditional native learning consists for the most part of catalogues, which among the Kara-Kirghiz, as in Homer, form an important element in the narrative poetry. The greater part of antiquarian literature, however, is composed in the form of prose sagas and genealogies, and of cosmogonic myths and speculative matter. The former appear to be current chiefly among the western Tatars, the latter among the eastern, though this distribution is by no means exclusive.

Speaking of the antiquarian literature among these people, the Russian traveller Valikhanov wrote during the middle of last century:

"An abundance of traditions forms a marked and characteristic heritage of the nomadic races of Central Asia. These traditions are devoutly preserved by the elders of the tribes, either in the form of ancestral reminiscences and genealogical legends, or in ballads which are perpetuated by a special class of bards. Many words and locutions now obsolete prove their antiquity."[1]

In regard to the importance of genealogies the same writer continues:

"Genealogical traditions form a most important section of their legendary lore. The relation of one tribe to another depends on the degree of affinity which exists between the chiefs. The hereditary superiority of one branch over another is determined by the right of primogeniture. Traditions of this nature are in so far important as they represent the extraction of the people and the composition of society. It appears from the genealogical tables of the Kazaks, Uzbegs, and Nogais that they are a medley of different Turkish and Mongol tribes formed after the decline of the Golden and Jagatai Hordes."[2]

Genealogical lore is undoubtedly highly cultivated among the

[1] Michell, p. 95 f.   [2] *Ib.* p. 97.

Turkomans and the Kazaks, and among the Tatars generally. It was stated last century that every well brought up Kazak boy, even if he were only in his eighth year, could recite his ancestors for at least six generations.[1] Since written literature is rare, genealogies are of the utmost importance as the only guarantee of an individual's rights and titles, and it is not surprising to learn that these genealogies, and the ancestral and family traditions which accompany and doubtless form a commentary on them, are often clothed in a fixed literary form, which must have greatly assisted in their preservation.

In the actual texts before us genealogical material of this kind is generally found merely incidentally in historical sagas and narrative poetry, but is much commoner in the former. Brief genealogies occur occasionally in the opening lines of the heroic poems, such as *Er Töshtük*, but they seldom enumerate more than three or four generations. Among the Kazaks and the western Tatars antiquarian elements play a large part in many of the brief historical and semi-historical anecdotes characteristic of this region. Thus the Baraba version of the story of Ermak, the Russian conqueror of Siberia, contains some place-name speculation, and an explanatory passage which tells of the trick by which Ermak outwitted Kuchum Khan, and obtained land in Siberia, and, at the opening of the narrative, a brief chronicle of the rulers of the Tom, down to Kuchum Khan. These brief dynastic or genealogical introductions are characteristic also of the Kazaks. It may indeed be said in general that in Kazak saga antiquarian elements tend to be concentrated at the opening and conclusion of the narrative.

In the narrative poetry of the Kara-Kirghiz and the Kazaks learned elements are, as has been observed above, found chiefly in the form of catalogues. These are so long, and figure so frequently, that they doubtless have an independent existence apart from the poems and sagas in which they actually occur. This is supported by the fact that some catalogues, such as that of the heroes of Manas' retinue,[2] recur several times in different poems in almost identical form.

These heroic catalogues are introduced with great liberality by the Kara-Kirghiz minstrels. Much of our knowledge of heroic society is comprised in them, and they serve as mnemonic compendia of information to the heroic minstrels themselves, as well as to their audience. In the catalogue of heroes who are invited to take part in Bok Murun's games, we have a survey of the leading princes of the day, together with

---

[1] Vambéry, *Travels*, p. 368.
[2] *Proben* v, pp. 113 ff., 152 ff.

precise geographical indications as to their places of abode.[1] In the same poem the most famous horses mentioned in heroic stories are also enumerated at great length.[2] The catalogue of neighbouring princes whom Jakyp Bai tells Temir Khan he has visited in search of a wife for Manas has something in common with the Anglo-Saxon poem *Widsith*, but with a more systematic range. It is at once a survey of the political geography and of the ethnography of the world as known to the Kara-Kirghiz.[3] A closer parallel to *Widsith* is Kara Chach's catalogue of heroic princes whom she has visited, which occurs in the Kara-Kirghiz poem *Joloi*.[4] Here also geographical and ethnographical details are frequently added, and after the reference to each important hero visited, a summary mention is made of the principal heroic story with which he is associated, and of the kind of entertainment which she has received at his home. The catalogue in which this Tatar 'Widsith' relates her travels occupies three pages. An interesting prose catalogue of heroes occurs in the Kazak saga of *Khan Shentäi*, in which many heroes are enumerated by the *shamanka* Synshy Sary Kus in her endeavour to establish the identity of the hero.[5]

The tendency which we have found widespread in other literatures to speculate on the origin of place-names, and other forms of popular etymology, is common. The Kazak narrative poem *Kosy Körpösh* contains a large amount of popular etymology of place-names.[6] Instances have already been referred to as occurring in the Baraba version of the saga of Ermak the Cossack; and even among the Tatars farther east, where antiquarian elements as a whole are less fully developed than in the west, the same tendency is not wholly unknown. Further instances occur in the Altai saga of *Amyr Sanaga and Chagan Narattan* (cf. p. 54 above). As an example of popular etymology we may refer to the legend of the origin of the Kirghiz from forty maidens (*kirk kiz*) related below. The same tendency to etymologise place-names and other proper names is noticeable also elsewhere in sagas which are not otherwise distinguished by antiquarian features.

Speculation on the origin of places and of customs does not appear to be common, but the latter at least is probably not unknown. Holmberg[7] gives an interesting story of the first shaman, which is current among the Buryat in the region of Lake Baikal. The literature

---

[1] *Proben* v, p. 144 ff.   [2] *Ib.* p. 160 f.
[3] *Ib.* p. 83 ff.   [4] *Ib.* p. 511 ff.
[5] *Ib.* III, p. 313.   [6] *Ib.* III, pp. 272 ff., 297.
[7] Holmberg, p. 477 f.

of the Buryat is so closely akin to that of the Altai Tatars, especially in matters relating to religion, that we can hardly doubt the existence of such shaman traditions among the latter people also.

Antiquarian speculation on the origin of the race, or of special tribes, is very common. Most of the Tatars trace the origin of their tribe to the union of a human being and an animal, and such speculations are probably ancient, for they are said to contain many words now obsolete, and we are expressly told that they are considered indecent by the present generation.[1] In the story just cited the Kara-Kirghiz trace their origin, by a piece of popular etymology, to forty maidens (*kirk kiz*), the attendants of a daughter of a certain *khan*. According to one version of the story, they returned one day from a long walk to find their camp pillaged, only one living animal—a dog—remaining, which became the progenitor of the Kirghiz. Another version of the story relates that the princess and her maidens, having been miraculously fecundated by the foam of a certain lake, were expelled by their relatives. The princess was found by the progenitor of the Kirghiz, who installed her as one of his wives.[2] A satire composed by a mullah, and current among the Kara-Kirghiz, contains many allusions to the traditional origin of the Kara-Kirghiz and the Kazaks, the former being derived from a union of some thieves and a beggar-woman, the latter being related to a wolf.[3] Stories of this kind are not often found in poetry, though they are probably derived from native traditions. Similar speculations have evidently been current also among other steppe peoples, as can be seen from Chinese records.[4]

A considerable amount of material is available for studying the literature of antiquarian speculation on cosmogony and natural science generally. This material has been carefully collected and classified by Holmberg in his *Siberian Mythology*, to which the reader is referred for a large number of examples of the poetry and sagas relating to the subject. Among those Tatars who have been under Mohammedan, Buddhist, or Christian influence for several centuries, much of the material is naturally suspect, and generally speaking it is easy to see that the beliefs and traditions of such alien religious influence have banished or transformed the literature of native speculation. Among the Chern and the Altai Tatars the influence of alien tradition is not so easy to trace, and it is generally held that among these people the traditional

[1] Michell, p. 95 ff.
[2] *Ib.* p. 275; Vambéry, *Türkenvolk*, p. 262.
[3] Radlov, *A.S.* I, p. 407.   [4] Michell, p. 96.

beliefs of heathenism are preserved in the least adulterated form. To a great extent this is no doubt true. It must be remembered, however, that Nestorian and Manichaean influences, especially the latter, have undoubtedly affected native thought in the past; and that Buddhism (Lamaism) is a constant factor in the religious thought of the present day. Much of the mythology may be due to the influence of other faiths, whether this influence be direct or indirect. For obvious reasons it is much more difficult for us to trace foreign religious elements in the native mythology of these eastern Tatars than in that of their western neighbours, but we cannot doubt their permeating influence. We think it wiser therefore to touch only very lightly the literature of native speculation.

Native poetry on cosmogony and eschatology has certainly existed, and is no doubt still remembered to some extent by the shamans; but even such poetry as has survived is very little known. It is clear from the examples cited by Holmberg that an elaborate cosmogonic myth existed among the Tatars[1] which resembled closely the early Norse conceptions of Yggdrasil's Ash, the World Tree, *Miðgarðsormr*, and the Spring of Fate, with all of which we are familiar in Norse mythology from the elaborate account given in Ch. XVI of *Gylfaginning*.[2] Such a conception could hardly have prevailed in so picturesque a form and with so little inconsistency over thousands of miles of southern Siberia if it had not been transmitted in elaborate artistic form.[3] Holmberg has preserved a fragment from a poem of the Minnusinsk Tatars describing this world tree in terms which recall the Old Norse conception of *Glasir* in the *Prose Edda* (*Skaldskaparmál*, ch. 43).

> Piercing twelve heavens,
> On the summit of a mountain,
> A birch in the misty depths of air—
> Golden are the birch's leaves,
> Golden its bark,
> In the ground at its foot a basin
> Full of the water of life,
> In the basin a golden ladle....

Unfortunately the rest of the poem has not been accessible to us, but Holmberg tells us that it is further mentioned that this 'birch' is

---

[1] Holmberg, p. 349 ff.
[2] For some account of *Gylfaginning*, see Vol. I, p. 320 ff. of the present work.
[3] Cf. also the Tibetan conception of the World Tree, Francke, *T.H.* p. 14.

guarded by the 'old Tatar', the forefather of the Tatars, who was given this post by the Creator himself.[1]

Among the Tatars, as among other peoples who have come under the influence of a higher civilisation, such speculations have reached us for the most part in prose, and in a puerile form, on the level of folk-tale; and indeed in their present form such brief stories are indistinguishable from this class of literature. We may refer to a story which relates how Erlik, by a trick, succeeded in making mankind permanently impure, frustrating the efforts of Kudai who had sought to instil into them a pure soul.[2] A number of variants of this story are cited by Holmberg from different parts of Siberia.

Another story of this kind attributes the origin of fire to Ülgen himself, who is said to have struck together two stones, a black and a white, so that a spark flew down from Heaven and set the grass on fire.[3] One story from the Altai relating the creation of the Universe derives the earth and the rocks from earth which was brought in the beaks of two birds—one a white swan—which were sent by God. Equally puerile are the stories, current also among the Tatars of the Altai, of the origin of human life, of the sun and moon, and other heavenly bodies, and of living creatures, such as the mosquito.[4] These stories are extremely brief and perhaps represent only summaries of stories actually current.

More ambitious sagas on the same and kindred themes certainly exist however. Radlov gives an elaborate saga from the Altai on the Creation of the World,[5] which, in spite of its origin in a more civilised religion of ancient times, is full of significance for us on account of its highly developed saga form. It relates the Creation of the World by God, and his relations with Erlik, Mai-Tere,[6] Mandy-Shire,[7] and Jakpara; the creation and the fall of man; and the final withdrawal of God, after leaving the world to the guidance of Jakpara and Mandy-Shire. The story has much in common with the Biblical story of the Creation and the Fall, but has certainly been influenced largely by Buddhism, as the

---

[1] Holmberg, p. 350.

[2] Radlov, *A.S.* I, p. 373; *Proben* I, p. 285; Holmberg, p. 373.

[3] Holmberg, p. 449.

[4] *Ib.* pp. 377, 387, 421.

[5] *Proben* I, p. 175 ff. An abstract is given by Peisker in the *Cambridge Medieval History*, Vol. I, p. 344 ff.

[6] Mai-tere is the Buddhist Maitreya; cf. p. 138, footnote 3 above.

[7] Mandy-Shire, the Buddhist Manjussi, a *bodhisattva*; cf. p. 138, footnote 3 above.

names alone would show. This saga, which is more than nine pages in length, is narrated in the expanded narrative style which we associate primarily with literature of entertainment. The conversations are reported in full, and the effect is heightened by the addition of many picturesque details, such as the picture of Mandy-Shire, angling with his home-made net from a home-made boat, and shooting squirrels. The dialogues between God and Erlik are conducted with spirit:

"Now Erlik begged land from God. 'You have destroyed my Heaven, and now I have no land. Give me a little', said he. God said: 'No, I will not give you any land.' Erlik said: 'Do just give me one acre of land.' God said: 'No, I will give you no land at all.' Erlik said: 'Give me five lengths of land.' But God did not give him even five lengths of land. Thereupon Erlik stuck the stick which he had in his hand into the earth and said: 'O, my God, just give me as much land as the point of this stick covers.' God laughed and said: 'Take as much land as is under this staff.'"[1]

Although the ostensible purpose of this saga is to account for the existence of created things and of sin in the world, and to teach mankind his relations with God and with his representatives, the style has been so closely modelled on that of narrative saga as to make it probable that sagas of the gods are also told for purposes of entertainment, though, as we have seen, actual texts are wanting. A number of stories of creation similar to the one described above, but less fully related, will be found in the chapter on 'The Origin of the Earth' in Holmberg's *Siberian Mythology*.

More elaborate teaching has, however, been current in the past regarding cosmogony and the pantheon, as well as the physical Universe generally, than one would infer from the stories to which we have referred above. It is probable that genealogies of the gods were in existence. Sieroszewski heard a Yakut shaman invoking the gods and spirits by name, and he adds that each of these gods and spirits has his genealogical titles and his personal attributes, which must be cited.[2] The information obtained by Radlov from the Altai peoples reveals an organised pantheon and a conception of the spiritual Universe, for which we look in vain in the childish sagas and anecdotes just referred to.

According to Radlov,[3] the native teaching on these subjects was obtained by him chiefly from the shamans, and was contained in "allusions in a whole series of legends, sagas, folk-tales (*Märchen*),

---

[1] *Proben* I, p. 181f.
[2] *R.H.R.* (1902), p. 329.
[3] Radlov, *A.S.* II, p. 2f.

narratives (*Erzählungen*), songs". It is a noteworthy fact, however, that in the actual texts published by Radlov, hardly any poems are given which are composed primarily on cosmogony or mythology, and few sagas of which the contents cannot be traced with certainty to Buddhist, Manichaean, or Christian sources. This is hardly surprising in view of the rigorous measures taken by the Russians in the past to suppress shamanism, and the missionary activities of what we may term the civilised religions. Radlov's reconstruction[1] of Tatar religious and philosophical speculations, based as it is on literary (oral) allusions, probably comes nearer to representing the earlier religious beliefs than the more direct pronouncements of the shamans to-day, and enables us to see the great wealth of mythological and cosmogonic tradition which was current among the Tatars until recent times.

It will be seen that most of the subjects which we have found elsewhere as themes of antiquarian speculation or tradition are represented in Tatar oral tradition also, though for obvious reasons an exception is perhaps to be made, at any rate among the nomadic and semi-nomadic peoples, in regard to speculations on the origin of places and buildings. But though most of these subjects are represented, it cannot be claimed that Tatar literature as a whole is rich in antiquarian lore. In fact the reverse is the case. Moreover the forms of antiquarian lore which are most highly developed are not in general quite free from alien influence. The genealogical lore and the historical traditions of the Kazaks, the western and northern Tatars, and the Turkomans, are undoubtedly fostered to some extent by Mohammedan mullahs. The cosmogonic speculations and myths of the Altai and Teleut tribes are also undoubtedly indebted to some extent to Buddhist teaching, perhaps through the Baikal Buryat. How deeply the foreign influence goes, and how far it has displaced earlier 'native' speculations and traditions is not easy to determine. It is improbable in any case that a nomadic people will have a strong interest in local history and antiquities. But that the nomads have purely native methods of classifying their knowledge would seem to be shown by the wealth of heroic catalogues, while the non-heroic narrative poetry, which is a mine of information for the ancient heathen myths, seems to have been little affected by foreign religious teaching, at least in modern times.

Gnomic literature is common, in the form both of individual proverbs and of a consecutive series. The largest collection of proverbs with

[1] *Loc. cit.*

which we are acquainted was obtained by Radlov in the Altai,[1] though examples are cited also from the Kara-Kirghiz.[2] They are all or almost all composed in poetical form, and the greater number are composed of two lines of which the sense is parallel, and in which the second line is sometimes slightly more forcible than the first, e.g.

> He who has honoured a chief will himself be a chief,
> He who has honoured the rich will himself be rich.

It is the common practice of the Tatars and Turkomans to introduce these general observations couched in couplets conveying parallel statements into their ordinary conversation. An amusing anecdote is recorded by the Russian traveller Valikhanov who was evidently unaware of the custom, and who on one occasion, during his sojourn among the Tatars of the Altai, was led to conclude that his host was insane because his conversation was couched in cryptic couplets of general import (cf. p. 187 below). In reality it seems clear that the chief was merely entertaining his guest with the most formal and polite kind of conversation with which he was familiar. Such parallel couplets, sometimes expanded into quatrains, are frequently introduced into poems and sagas in formal speeches.[3] In the Abakan poems and elsewhere the usual formula in which to enquire a person's name is:

> Every wild beast has hair,
> Every person has a name,
> What are you called?[4]

The Turkoman hero Kurroglou is said to have been in the habit of carrying on his conversation by means of just such couplets of purely general import. Thus when Bolly-beg, a member of his retinue, appeals for his favour and that of his men, Kurroglou replies: "Some verses come to my mind; listen:

'Who has nothing to speak of, he had better be silent. It is better to refuse the bread and salt of a villain, than to eat it.'"

When Bolly-beg inquires in reply whether Kurroglou is averse to a reconciliation, he receives in reply the following stanza:

"I always repeat the same. The orchards cast off the withered leaves, which are unable to remain longer on the trees. It is better to be indifferent towards an inconstant flirt, than to love her."

---

[1] *Proben* I, p. 1 ff.
[2] See e.g. Radlov, *A.S.* I, p. 418.
[3] *Proben* II, p. 543, l. 94f.
[4] We may refer, e.g. to such passages as *ib.* p. 92, l. 92; p. 120, l. 1019; etc.

Further appeals from the unfortunate Bolly-beg only succeed in eliciting a further series of such improvisations.[1]

Such couplets are usually of a general character, but it is not to be supposed that all are proverbs. A large number of examples are given by Radlov to illustrate the metre in which extempore poetry is composed, and these examples, as well as those ascribed to Kurroglou, are indistinguishable in form and substance from many of the examples of proverbs cited by Radlov from the Altai. It is clear that the extempore poetry introduced into conversation among the Kirghiz and Turkomans consists largely of gnomic utterances, and these, when repeated singly, are to all intents and purposes proverbial utterances. It is interesting to observe that among the Tatars, and probably the Turkomans also, as among other peoples whose proverbs we have studied, a large proportion is concerned with observations of nature and physical science.

Two poems from the Kysyl Tatars of the Abakan group[2] consist of such couplets containing general observations, in which the second observation is a kind of moral drawn from the first, e.g.

> If the horns of the antelope did not fall off
> They would reach up to heaven;
> If men did not die
> The earth would not be made.

In the first of these poems the gnomes are inverted by being couched in the form of a question.

Very frequently these gnomic utterances are joined to form a sequence. We may quote a song from the Tobol Tatars[3] which consists of a series of nature gnomes.

> The cock knows when day breaks,
> The cuckoo knows when the sun rises,
> The traveller knows the near and the far away,
> He who has tasted knows the flavoured and the insipid,
> He who has lived there knows the people's excellence.

Several brief poems consisting of a sequence of gnomic utterances occur also among the Kazaks.[4] Some are concerned with observations on birds and animals and the world of nature generally, others with social conduct and behaviour. Among the Tatars of Astrakhan these gnomic sequences are very common, and are said to be current also among the Tatars from Ural to Kuma. The specimens which have come

---

[1] Chodzko, p. 275 ff.
[2] *Proben* II, p. 657f.
[3] *Ib.* IV, p. 331.
[4] *Ib.* III, p. 1 ff.

under our observation are all contained in Chodzko's Collection and are believed by him to be old. They are, as a rule, somewhat didactic in character, working up gradually from general observations to an implied moral. We may refer to nos. v, vII, IX, XIII of his collection.[1] As an example we quote no. IX:

"The hawk is the swiftest bird; it will not fly after the goose, after having passed the sparrow. Throw a slender rod with greater force than an arrow, it will not perforate a shield. There is no greater bird than the *berkut* (great eagle); but the luckiest of them will sometimes miss his prey. When a virtuous man gets into company with bad people, they will slander him, and plot against him. When such a man meets with misfortune, they will not overtake him, though they set out to pursue him."

Not infrequently these Astrakhan poems are frankly didactic.

"Hill, O grassy hill! did not you turn barren when upon your top the jackals and the foxes dug their holes and threw your sand up?

"Horse, high-legged horse! did not you die when you left your master on foot in the steppes?...

"Man, selfish man! did not you die when your robes of gold brocade became so heavy with the precious metals, that they folded no more upon you?

"Remain for ever with the name of an insatiable man; you would never help the poor!"[2]

And again:

"When you choose for yourself the means of conveyance, choose the camel. That animal will get over forty hills, and will not be tired.

"When you wish to be provided with milk, choose a mare. That animal never ceases to be in milk till the advanced frosts.

"When you are about to take a wife, choose a beautiful girl. Who will refuse to marry a fine widow when mourning your loss?"[3]

In some cases general observations are combined with advice or admonition, or with description. An interesting example from the Kazaks sets forth the disadvantages resulting from an unwise selection in taking a wife.[4] From the same tribes comes a poem of considerable length in which advice is given to a young bride.[5] This poem may be compared with similar 'advice' poems in Anglo-Saxon and Russian literature. It is interesting to compare also the Samoyed custom de-

---

[1] Chodzko, p. 347.
[2] *Ib.* p. 365.
[3] *Ib.* p. 370.
[4] *Proben* III, p. 2; Radlov, *A.S.* I, p. 506.
[5] *Proben* III, p. 15 ff.

scribed by Czaplicka, in which the mother-in-law is said to give advice in the form of gnomic utterances to her daughter-in-law.[1] Passages in the poems of the Abakan group also indicate advice poems as recited by older people and women to young heroes setting out on a journey. In a Kysyl poem, the hero's uncle at the naming ceremony (cf. p. 136 above) gives admonition and advice to his nephew, combined with his blessing.[2]

Gnomic and descriptive matter is frequently couched in catalogue form. A list of ten principal 'evils' to which man is subject occurs in a speech in a poem from the northern Tatars,[3] while in the Kazak saga of *Er Targyn* the characteristics of the hero at seven stages of his life are set forth in the form of a long panegyric addressed by a maiden to the aged Koshak.[4] The framework in which the characteristic features of a man at various stages of life are described in detail is parallel to that of Solon's poems on the *Seven Ages of Man*. The tendency to general descriptions is not confined to this passage. A Kazak poem on *How the Kalmuck laments for his Land*, though composed in the form of a lament, and in the first person, consists of a sustained description of the Kalmuck's mountain land and of the life lived there.[5] This composition may, however, be a conscious imitation of a foreign style; for it is quite in the fashion of Mongol lyrical poetry.[6]

Among the most elaborate of the descriptive poems which we have met are those which enumerate the points of an ideal horse, and which are ascribed to the Turkoman hero Kurroglou, and were possibly composed by him. They are actually general descriptions; but their purpose is certainly didactic, for they contain much information of a practical kind, and are full of shrewd observation and expert knowledge. "Listen to me," cries the hero of the first of this series, to Sultan Murad, "and learn by what signs a horse of noble breed may be known."

The hero then improvises his description, which is said to be so exact and authoritative that connoisseurs of horses in Persia appeal to it to-day in their disputes about the merits of their race-horses.[7] Several poems of a similar character are scattered throughout the Kurroglou Cycle.[8]

Among the Tatars and among the Yakut and the peoples of the Altai

[1] Czaplicka, *S.Y.* p. 110.   [2] *Proben* II, p. 648 f.   [3] *Ib.* IV, p. 168 ff.
[4] *Ib.* III, p. 165 ff.   [5] *Ib.* p. 66 f.   [6] Prejevalsky, p. 69.
[7] Chodzko, p. 23 f.   [8] *Ib.* pp. 169, 176.

region especially riddles are not uncommon. The examples which have come under our observation are chiefly, though not exclusively,[1] contained in riddle sequences. Indeed the literary convention which we have found to be common in Norse and elsewhere, by which two people ask one another a series of riddles—a riddle contest in fact—is a popular motif among the Altai Tatars and the Teleut. Such contests are generally of a serious nature, sometimes definitely hostile. They are, however, a favourite form of amusement also at social gatherings, especially among the Yakut (see p. 159 below). These contests are generally held between girls and youths. One party, consisting entirely of girls, seeks to overcome their opponents, a band of youths, or vice versa, with riddles or abusive extempore verses. He or she who cannot answer the riddle or 'cap' the abusive couplet or quatrain must pay a forfeit. The women are said to be especially proficient in this art.

In spite of the fact that such contests are essentially extempore, it is said that the better varieties of them remain in the memories of the public and pass from one end of the steppe to the other.[2] Radlov quotes[3] from the Kazak-Kirghiz an interesting example of such a famous poetical contest in which a man, caught in the act of stealing horses, is fettered and taken to the khan's tent and allowed to enter into a poetical contest with his daughter. The contest takes the form of an abusive dialogue, and apparently serves as a kind of neck-verse, or trial by ordeal, to discover if the man is a cultured person of good birth and social standing. In this case the man comes off victorious. Here and elsewhere it is clear that in these abusive dialogues neither party is prepared to spare the feelings of his opponent.[4]

Riddle contests are frequently held between two sages,[5] and also between a sage and an ordinary individual.[6] An account of such a contest, which occurs in the Altai saga of *The Two Princes*, has already been given (p. 107 above), and it has been pointed out that the story probably has reference to a contest between a heavenly and an earthly

---

[1] A collection of individual riddles is given from the Altai region in *Proben* I, p. 261 ff.   [2] Vambéry, *Türkenvolk*, p. 295.

[3] *Proben* III, p. 48; Radlov, *A.S.* I, p. 493 f.

[4] It will be remembered that in the Norse *Hervarar Saga*, Gestumblindi (i.e. *Gestr hinn blindi*, 'Guest the Blind', or Othinn) chooses to undergo a riddle ordeal rather than to abide a trial by the 'Judges' when summoned to appear before King Heiðrekr. See the translation of this saga by Kershaw, *Stories and Ballads of the Far Past*, p. 114 f.

[5] We may compare the contest between Väinämöinen and Joukahainen in the *Kalevala*.   [6] See e.g. Vambéry, *Türkenvolk*, p. 296.

sage, though the treatment is probably humorous. Reference has also been made (p. 108 above) to the saga of *Ak Köbök* which occurs in several versions, and which also refers to various contests of intellectual power and practical magic between the hero himself and others of similar intellectual and mantic pretensions, including his own brother. Riddle contests form an important part of these competitions. In the saga of *The Two Princes* and the Teleut saga of *Ak Köbök* the riddles are all propounded consecutively. Thus the answers, also given in a series, closely resemble the Anglo-Saxon gnomic verses, as we have found to be the case also in some of the early Norse and Russian riddles (cf. Vol. II, p. 212 f. of the present work). In the Kurdak version of *Ak Köbök*,[1] however, each riddle is answered before the next is asked, though several of the riddles in this series bear a close resemblance to those in the Teleut version.

In Tatar stories the ability to answer riddles is a test frequently applied to a suitor who asks for the hand of a lady in marriage. An instance of such an 'intelligence test' occurs in the brief Altai story of *The Riddle of the Bride's father*.[2] We may mention also a short story from the Kazak Tatars in which a princess is represented as having refused many suitors, only agreeing to marry the hero when he has successfully answered a riddle sequence.[3] In this series, as in the examples from the Altai, the riddles are all asked consecutively, and the answers are also consecutive. Almost all belong to that class of riddle which consists of the elucidation of the figurative speech of poetic diction, and almost all these figures or riddles are concerned with the animals or the natural features of the steppe.

It will be seen from the examples cited that the riddle contests form a kind of ordeal, whether an alternative to military combat, or to legal trial by judges, or a test of wit and culture. It is not impossible that the stories of such contests may in some measure reflect actual custom which at some period has been current on the steppe. Radlov was interrogated about the stars and the Heavens by an official among the Chern Tatars[4] in a series of questions, much as Ak Köbök is interrogated by Kidän Khan's envoy when Kidän Khan seeks to avoid battle with his strong rival, and to substitute for it a contest in wisdom and knowledge. The resemblance cannot be pressed, of course, as such questions are natural from an intelligent native official to an enlightened member of a higher civilisation.

[1] *Proben* IV, p. 181 ff.   [2] *Ib.* I, p. 60 f.   [3] *Ib.* III, p. 387 ff.
[4] Radlov, *A.S.* I, p. 371 f.

Apart from the similarity of form, however, which may be accidental, the similarity of the actual questions put by the official to the riddles which we have cited is interesting. The riddle sequences, like those of other countries, are principally preoccupied with natural science, more especially with those phenomena which are connected with the sky and the weather. On the whole, therefore, the testimony of the Tatar riddles supports the belief to which we are led by our examination of the riddles of other countries, that the asking and answering of riddles is traditionally regarded as an ordeal applied to people of intellectual pretensions as a test of culture in general, and of proficiency in natural science and the language of poetry in particular, though in modern times it has come to be largely a matter of social entertainment. We shall find further evidence of a similar character among other peoples to be considered later.

It is important to remember, however, that the prevalence of stories of riddle contests among the Tatars and the Yakut does not necessarily imply that the custom is native to this part of the world. The evidence for such contests is very widespread and ancient.[1] We have seen that in early Norse and modern Russia riddle sequences occur which resemble closely those which we have just considered, both in form and in the subjects treated, and that in Russia they are associated with marriage customs. It may be mentioned here that in modern Ladakh, on the western border of Tibet, riddle sequences are said to form an invariable part of the social ritual at marriage ceremonies, and consist largely of a recital of the names of the gods and of data relating to geography and primitive natural science. Such riddles are propounded to the bride-groom's party on their arrival at the bride's home in order to discover if they are cultivated persons and of good family. Both questions and answers are recited in the form of poetry, and constitute what is in reality a combination of a poetical and a riddle contest.[2]

Narrative poetry and saga, and poetry embodying speeches in character relating to people not known otherwise seem to have much in common with Yugoslav poetry. Almost all the narrative poems possess

[1] An Indian tradition represents King Kanishka as listening to the story of King Kriki who has had ten dreams which the brahmans interpret as evil portents, but which the sage Kasyapa explains otherwise. (See *J.B.T.S.* Vol. I, Pt. III, 1893, p. 19.) The list of the dreams and their interpretations is much like a riddle sequence or contest. But both conventions were doubtless already ancient in the time from which our record dates.

[2] See Francke, *I.A.* xxx (1901), p. 131.

the characteristics of style which we have seen to belong to heroic narrative poetry, and almost all are stories of adventure. Sometimes they resemble those of the Kara-Kirghiz, sometimes those of the Abakan Tatars. In particular a number of poems are recorded from the Altai which resemble closely those of the Abakan Tatars except that they are briefer and simpler. It will be remembered that the Abakan poems all relate to heroes who figure only in a single poem. Many of their heroes are either poor, or friendless orphans, or appear to be without anything resembling a staff of followers or an organised household. In this respect their resemblance to folk-tales is very close.

In illustration of poems of this class we may refer to two texts, recorded by Chodzko from the Tatars of Astrakhan, in which a dying warrior is represented as lamenting his fate.[1] These poems resemble very closely the heroic *tolgaws* or laments to which we have already referred (pp. 56, 62 above). We have no doubt that either they were composed by someone else after the hero's death, or else that they are merely exercises in compositions of this class. No names are mentioned. The first line of the second song:

My bay horse was fond of my singing a *tolgaw* while I was riding,

suggests that this class of composition is widely practised.

Poetry of this class is not very intimate or personal in character. Radlov cites four examples consisting of from two to four strophes each from the Northern Tatars,[2] one of which purports to be spoken by an exile in a strange land, longing for home. The theme is not uncommon. Dmitrêv quotes three examples from the Volga Tatars. He tells us that among these people it is one of the favourite forms, being composed for the most part to express the sorrows of the conscripts impressed into the Russian army.[3] From the Kazaks we have the poem of thirty-five lines referred to above (p. 151) in which a nameless Kalmuck describes his native mountains and bemoans his exile in a far land.[4] The type is probably of Mongol origin (cf. p. 62 above).

The greater part of the occasional poetry in Radlov's collections consists of improvised couplets and quatrains. These are especially common among the Tatars of the Altai.[5] They are general and reflective in character, and consist largely of parallel utterances, the first statement containing figurative speech, very often relating to physical nature, the

---

[1] Chodzko, pp. 368, 369 (nos. XI, XV).
[2] *Proben* IV, p. 391 ff.   [3] *J.A.* 1926, p. 317f.
[4] *Proben* III, p. 66f.   [5] *Ib.* I, pp. 246ff., 434.

second the literal interpretation.[1] Frequently poems of this kind, though recited in the first person, are almost wholly gnomic in character.

Love poetry is doubtless universal, and forms among the Tatars a large item in the poetry of social ritual. Vambéry tells us that among the Kara-Kirghiz it is a common pastime among the young people for the men and girls to stand in two semi-circles facing one another and improvise love poems.[2] Radlov records a number of love poems from the northern Tatars,[3] but in these particular examples foreign influence is to be suspected.

Poetry of celebration is chiefly represented by elegiac poetry, which, like narrative poetry, is heroic in style, at least in the few examples which have come before us. Such poetry is generally composed by women, except when a professional minstrel is hired. As an example we may refer to a widow's lament from the Tatars of the Altai cited by Radlov.[4] Radlov also records a hunting song from the Tobol Tatars.[5] Oddly enough the heroic manner is not prominent in this poem, which resembles rather the antithetical gnomic style of the strophic 'contest' poems.

Wedding songs are very widespread. Radlov gives us a bridegroom's song from the northern Tatars,[6] and another song from the same tribe,[7] composed to be sung at a wedding. In all such literature the emotion is traditional and conventional.

The formal part of the wedding celebrations everywhere seems to be conducted wholly in improvised poetry. Vambéry tells us[8] that among the Siberian Tatars generally on the first day of the wedding, the young people dance in circles and sing in chorus. On the second day, as the

---

[1] A similar form of composition seems to be current also among the Malays. Dr Reinhold Rost speaks of "improvised poems, generally (though not necessarily) of four lines, in which the first and third, and the second and fourth rhyme. They are mostly love poems; and their chief peculiarity is that the meaning intended to be conveyed is expressed in the second couplet, whereas the first contains a simile or distant allusion to the second, or often has, beyond the rhyme, no connection with the second at all. The Malays are fond of reciting such rhymes 'in alternate contest for several hours, the preceding *pantun* furnishing the catchword to that which follows, until one of the parties be silenced or vanquished'." *J.R.A.S.* xv (1885), p. 99.

[2] *Türkenvolk*, p. 271.   [3] *Proben* IV, pp. 98, 277, 331.
[4] *A.S.* I, p. 320.   [5] *Proben* IV, p. 335.
[6] *Ib.* IV, p. 384.   [7] *Loc. cit.*
[8] *Türkenvolk*, p. 111 f.

bride and bridegroom are conducted to their relatives, their intimate
friends advance before them, dancing and celebrating the bridegroom's
future happiness, while to the bride they sing:

"You marry a man whom your father has selected for you, you
are going with him now on a fine sledge. Be not homesick, conduct
yourself well in the house of your husband's family, and live in
prosperity and peace yourself."

Vambéry cites three strophes of a conversation, carried on in poetry,
from the commencement of the ceremony which takes place when a
young suitor comes of age and first makes a formal proposal on his own
behalf.[1]

These and other wedding songs recited by the bride and bridegroom
and by their friends appear to constitute a ritual which forms a fixed
ceremonial at Tatar weddings just as among Russian peasants. The
Abakan[2] and the Kazak[3] wedding songs, and perhaps also the wedding
ceremonial, differ from one another considerably, however, and our
information as to the order and method of the recitations is not explicit.
Among the Tatars of the Altai also songs are sung at recognised stages
in the wooing and wedding ceremonies. An interesting sketch of the
whole proceeding is given by Radlov, who also cites examples of the
song sung by the match-maker on first arriving at the house of the
prospective bride, the song sung by the bridegroom as he approaches
the house at a later stage in the proceedings, and an elaborate example
of the blessing pronounced on the bride by her father-in-law.[4]

Similar customs prevail among the Kazaks, where an elaborate
ceremonial takes place. This ceremonial resembles the Russian very
closely in its formality and in the similarity of the whole to a ritual
drama, and the two are probably not independent of one another. An
interesting account and several texts of actual wedding songs are given
by Radlov.[5] On such occasions a professional minstrel is often engaged
to compose extempore panegyric poetry. This, however, by no means
excludes the singing contest, which, as we have seen, is a favourite
accompaniment of Tatar weddings. At a later stage in the proceedings
the guests collect inside the *yurt*, the maidens and young women on one
side, and the young wooers on the other. The latter now compete
with the maidens in improvisation, and any who refuses to do so, or
is unable to respond is mercilessly mocked and maltreated by the

[1] *Ib.* p. 235 f.
[2] *Proben* II, p. 658 ff.
[3] *Ib.* III, p. 8 ff.
[4] Radlov, *A.S.* I, p. 316 ff.
[5] *Ib.* p. 476 ff.

women.[1] On the arrival of the young wife at the tent of her father-in-law she sits down on the left of the door, and her relatives sing to her as follows:

"Honour your father-in-law
—he is your father.
Honour your mother-in-law
—she is your mother.
Be not irritable," etc.[2]

It has already been mentioned that riddles form an important part of the social ritual of Tatar weddings, and that the riddle contest is closely associated with the singing match, which is also popular at weddings and other festivals. In this form of poetry the Kara-Kirghiz are said to excel.

"The singing fraternity generally take up their stand in two semi-circles of youths and maidens, and after one of the former has chosen his rival from the latter he begins to give expression in a single or double verse to his feelings of tenderness or admiration in a rhythmical speech, frequently adorned with metaphors drawn from external nature. This is answered by the maiden in a similar vein."[3]

In just such a way the hero of the Kazak saga of *Erkäm Aidar* is represented as holding a singing match with two maidens.[4]

It is interesting to compare with these wedding ceremonies of the southern Turks the account of a Yakut wedding given by Shklovsky. Here, although the young people indulge in a singing contest, like the southern Tatars and the Russian settlers in the west, it is clear that the old women are the best minstrels.

"The young people... went out into the meadow and formed themselves into two separate ranks, men in one, and girls in the other. With decorous and mincing steps these two living walls slowly approached each other.

'Ho, boys, ho! Let us enjoy ourselves while we are young!' chanted one of the men.

'Sing aloud, my throat!' sang a girl.

'Boys, let us dance and laugh while we are still unwed; ere yet the sinews of our strength are drawn out by a woman's little tongue!'

'Girls, let us play while we are still unwed, while we are still uncaught by the coarse hands of men!'

[1] Vambéry, *Türkenvolk*, p. 242f.   [2] *Ib.* p. 249.
[3] *Ib.* p. 271.   [4] *Proben* III, p. 330.

"This was all improvised. Jests, at times coarse, were freely bandied about. On hearing the merry voices some old women, mostly blind, came out of the hut. Their extreme thinness, their unkempt grey hair, their blind eyes and strange dress, gave them a most fantastic appearance, reminding one of the terrible Druid priestesses. . . . The old women listened attentively to the young people's jokes, and they also improvised songs in which they made mention of lost youth, the sweetness of man's embrace, and the sorrow of infirmity. I quote one of these improvisations which I noted down at the time, as a specimen of the wild poetry breathed by these untutored songs.

'How welcome is the warmth of the sun to my aged bones! How joyful to dance with you, my children! This may be the last time I shall sing. Soon will the earth cover my sightless eyes. Next year again you will come here to play, but on my grave the young grass will be green. Cold shall I be there, nor can the hearth fire warm my old body. Dance and sing then, O youth!'

"She sang with wild energy: 'And I too will dance with you for the last time. For the last time I shall drink the koumiss, and next spring you will gather here again in the sunlight. Then you will remember the old woman, and she will rejoice in her cold grave. She will hear your songs, and from the grave her darkened eyes will see you drink the koumiss. And her happy bones will dance to your merry songs.'"

Besides improvisations, they sang the customary songs, some of which expressed unbridled licentiousness and sensuality, the utmost plainness of language being employed. Others, on the contrary, were delicate and sad.[1]

Shklovsky tells us[2] that the party then proceed, at the suggestion of the old woman, to ask riddles.

It will be seen that the similarity between the poetry of social ritual in Russia and Siberia is very striking, more especially in that which is

[1] Shklovsky, p. 55 f. The custom of associating singing matches with marriage prevails also in the Himalayas north of Darjeeling. According to the Indian traveller Sarat Chandra Das, among the Limbus:

"When a man and a girl think of marrying, they meet, without consulting their parents, at some place—a market, if there be one near—in order to sing witty songs, in which test the man is required to excel his fair rival. If he is beaten in this contest by the maiden whose hand he covets, he runs away in deep shame at his defeat; but if he wins, he seizes her by the hand and takes her to his home without further ceremony, but usually accompanied by a female companion. If the man has had some previous knowledge of the girl's superior attainment in singing, he sometimes bribes the maiden's companion to declare him the winner in the singing competition." Sarat Chandra Das, p. 13.   [2] *Loc. cit.*

associated with weddings. In both we have singing matches and riddle contests, and in both improvisation on traditional lines is widely practised. Indeed the formal part of the proceedings would seem to be wholly conducted in traditional form, and constitute something very like a poetical ritual drama. Old people as well as young take part in the composition and recitation of extempore poetry on these occasions.

CHAPTER VIII

THE TEXTS

THE material offered by the Tatar poems in Radlov's collection for a treatment of the texts and of variant versions is unfortunately not nearly so full or satisfactory as that which is available for Russian and Yugoslav. In no case can we be certain that we possess more than a single text of a given narrative poem, whereas in Russian the great wealth of variant texts gives ample opportunity for comparative work, and for tracing the history of various oral traditions and forms. We do not doubt that if the same amount of work in collecting Tatar texts had been done by European scholars the discrepancy would have been much less; but as it is, we are wholly dependent on Radlov's single texts. Our study must therefore of necessity be confined to a comparison of the variant traditions occurring in different poems and sagas, and of variant passages within a single poem. It is hoped, however, that the material available will be enough to show both that Tatar oral tradition develops on similar lines to those of the literatures already considered, and also that at the time when Radlov recorded the poems this oral tradition was still a living and vigorous growth.

In Chapter II we have related at length the variant versions of the saga of *Sunu Mattyr* derived from the Sagai, Altai, and Teleut Tatars. We have seen that these versions represent what appears to be, in some measure at least, a genuine historical tradition relating to the Jungarian princes of the close of the seventeenth and the early part of the eighteenth centuries. The tradition is somewhat disintegrated, and we suspect that motifs have been incorporated from folk-tale or epic poetry. Indeed a comparison of these texts is instructive as showing the varied aspects which a series of genuine historical traditions can assume when carried on orally in prose form for a century and a half. This series of traditions has already been discussed in detail. They, together with the two versions of *Khan Shentäi* and *Jirtüshlük*, to be discussed later, afford the best material we have found for the study of Tatar prose variants.

Before leaving the subject of the variants of the saga of *Sunu Mattyr*, we may mention the similarity of one incident contained in the Kysyl poem of *Südäi Märgän and Joltai Märgän*, which has been related more fully in the chapter on 'Non-heroic Poetry and Saga'. The hero, it will be remembered, is represented as killing a tiger which has long troubled the people of his father-in-law.[1] His two brothers-in-law, who have also gone to hunt the tiger, persuade him to allow them to claim credit for the deed, giving him in exchange a strip of skin from their backs. Fearing exposure, they subsequently cast him into a deep pit, whence he is ultimately rescued by his wife. It will be seen that the story in its general outline bears a close resemblance to the incident in the Sagai saga of *Sunu Mattyr* in which the *kongdaijy* summons his men to go to hunt a tiger which is harassing his dominions. The young hero Sunu kills the tiger, but conceals the fact. When it is disclosed by a maiden, his elder half-brothers, moved by jealousy, conspire against him, and have him cast into a deep pit, from which he is freed at the end of three years. It is possible that this incident in the saga is derived from heroic poetry or folk-tale. The same motif occurs also in *Kogutei*; but it is interesting to find it associated with well-known characters of the close of the seventeenth or the beginning of the eighteenth century.

We will now consider as briefly as possible three versions of what is undoubtedly a single story. We will take as an example the story which is recited among the Kara-Kirghiz as the poem *Er Töshtük*.[2] We will call this version, for convenience, A. It has already been mentioned that one version of the story is current among the Kazaks as a saga, with the title *Khan Shentäi*,[3] which we will call B, and another version is also found in prose with the title *Jirtüshlük*,[4] which we will call C. A brief summary of each of these versions has already been given (pp. 109 f., 111 f. above). We will therefore refer the reader to these passages for the actual versions, and merely enumerate here very briefly the chief similarities and differences between the variants, and the characteristic features of each version.

In all these versions a hero, who is the youngest of several brothers, is about to marry a lady, but is prevented from accompanying her to her new home. In all versions the bridal party is attacked by a dragon in the bridegroom's absence as they are camping for the night, and in all the hero follows the dragon underground. In all he is forced to undertake a series of adventures before he is enabled to return to his own home. In all he is eventually able to return to his wife by the help of a bird or birds. Such, briefly stated, are the main points of similarity

---

[1] *Proben* II, p. 619 f., l. 424 ff. [2] *Ib.* V, p. 530 ff.
[3] *Ib.* III, p. 297 ff.
[4] *Ib.* IV, p. 443.

between the outlines of the three versions. A closer comparison would bring out much more fully the numerous points of agreement in the course of the narratives.

The differences between the various versions consist for the most part of omissions and transpositions. Thus in A and B the hero is claimed as a son or foster-son by a supernatural woman dwelling in a hut or cave. In A no sons of hers are mentioned, but in B the hero's father is raided at the opening of the story by her sons. No reason is offered. In C the woman is not mentioned in this part of the story, but a certain dragon hero shows himself inimical to the bridegroom, and carries off the bride because he has previously desired to marry her himself. It is clear that the 'old woman' and Bek Toro (A) are the same person, and it would seem likely, therefore, that in the original version of the story Bek Toro's opposition to the marriage between Er Töshtük and the maiden Kendshäkä was not wholly unmotivated. The female dragon of the Underworld claims the soul of Er Töshtük which has been promised to her. Her son, the dragon hero of the Underworld, claims the soul of Kendshäkä. Perhaps the reason why the souls of Er Töshtük and Kendshäkä are especially coveted by the dragons of the Underworld is that they are the youngest of their families, the children of their parents' old age, and, as such, are gifted with supernatural powers. Er Töshtük is said to have been given by God, and in B he is assisted in his encounter with the dragon in the Underworld by the god Kydyr himself.

In many of the points of difference the versions serve to supplement one another. Thus in C alone we are told how the famous horse Chal Kuiruk comes into the hero's possession. In A and C it is not clear why the hero voluntarily follows the Jelmogus or female monster below the earth, but B suggests that it is in order to rescue his wife who has already been stolen. In B there is no sufficient reason given why the hero should leave the bridal party on their homeward journey; but in A and C it is clear that he never accompanied them. In A neither he nor his brothers go to woo, while the journey to the bride's home is made twice by the father. It would seem that in A two variant traditions have been reconciled, in one of which the hero's father goes alone to fetch a bride for his youngest son—his eldest sons being hostile to him (B); in the other he and the six eldest sons go together (cf. C).

In C the hero's adventures in the Underworld differ from those in A. In A the hero carries out his underground tasks by his own efforts; but throughout C his successes are ascribed to the advice which he receives from an old woman who lives in an earthen hut, and who, as we have said, can be no other than Bek Toro (A) and his adopted mother (B). In B the only adventure mentioned in the Underworld is the slaying of the dragon prince, which is performed by Kydyr on his behalf. In B and C, however, the hero and his party have a number of adventures after leaving the Underworld, of which A knows nothing. This dragon prince of B is no doubt to be identified with the dragon which attacks the young eagles in A and C, and his previous crime against the hero is doubtless the reason why the hero slays him—an action which in A and C is left unmotivated.

It may be noted further that in B the hero, on his descent to the Underworld, finds his wife sitting weeping beside the dragon prince, who is known in this version as Kara Tün. In C, however, the hero finds, not his own wife, but a snake, to whom he is forthwith married by a mullah. The snake, therefore, may be presumed to be, in the original version, not a new wife, but the soul of his own wife who has been carried off by the dragon prince and transformed, but who regains her own human form on being reunited to her human husband.

Finally some minor transferences may be noted. In A and C the heroine precipitates the catastrophe by turning back to meet her father, who rides after her, and again in A by turning back when Bek Toro calls after her. In C it is also added that the hero is warned by the old woman in the earthen hut not to look back when he has performed his first task. In A the hero returns to earth in the guise of a mullah. The other versions know nothing of this, but in B a mullah marries the bridegroom to the snake-maiden. In A and B the hero returns to earth on the back of an eagle, who subsequently restores him to his wife. C knows nothing of the eagle, but a reminiscence of the part played by a bird at the close of the poem would seem to lie behind the incident of the two doves who help to unite the husband and wife towards the close of the story.

It is interesting to note that in its earlier portions A is fuller than B or C; but the closing portion would seem to be curtailed if we may judge from the other two versions. This is quite in accord with what we have noted elsewhere of the habit of the Kara-Kirghiz minstrel, who expends a wealth of art on the earlier and middle portions of a poem, and is apt to grow fatigued, and either mar or curtail his conclusion. B and C are, on the whole, freer from obscurities, and more complete in the concluding portions; but the poet's art is expended in A with a wealth of detail and poetical imagination which lifts it, despite its faults, to a higher level of art than either of the prose versions. A comparison of the three versions makes it clear that in the original version or versions of the tradition the story was a long and very elaborate one, rich in detail and incident, a masterpiece of narrative relating to the worldly and spiritual experiences of a person of shamanistic character, and his 'wise' wife.

There are many variant versions of the story of *Kogutei*,[1] but we have only had access to one of these. The story relates almost exclusively to incidents with which we are already familiar from other poems and sagas. In particular the story of the horses stolen by a monster bird, the hero's departure in search of them, his rescue of the fledglings from the snake, his treacherous brothers waiting around the pit which contains the hero, the hero's descent below the earth, his rescue by the grateful parent bird, and the previous departure of his brothers, are all incidents which recur in the various versions of the story of *Er Töshtük* (cf. pp. 84 ff., 162 ff. above), though the order of the events differs slightly. In its general outline the whole story offers a still closer parallel to the first part of the poem of *Südäi Märgän and Joltai Märgän* from the Kysyl Tatars (cf. p. 96 ff. above). We may refer to the beast disguise assumed by the hero, his solitary life with his wife, the enmity of his brothers-in-law, his superiority in hunting, including his courage in venturing alone against the predatory bird khan, the finger joints given him by his brothers-in-law in exchange for being allowed to claim credit for having brought down the quarry, the pit into which they entrap him, his subsequent reappearance with the incriminating finger joints, and his ultimate happy married life. All these constitute a story very close to the Kysyl poem, and there can be little doubt that some kind of relationship exists between them. We have already seen that a chain of incidents similar in many respects recurs in the prose narrative of *Sunu Mattyr*, and in stories allied to this which have laid claim to be regarded as historical tradition. It is interesting to see how wide a circulation such stories have achieved in Central Asia. *Kogutei* is, however, not so much a version of stories known to us from other poems and sagas as a mosaic of themes and motifs which have a wide currency among the eastern Tatars, the Yakut, and the Mongols. It has, in fact, been mentioned already (p. 102 above) that in the poems and *skazki* of all these peoples there is so much in common in motif, phraseology, and diction with the details of *Kogutei* that it sometimes seems as if it were 'one big *skazka*'.

[1] See *Kogutei*, p. 9.

7

Although we have no certain variants of a given poem as such, we have two poems, *Altyn Pyrkan*[1] and *Ai Mergän and Altyn Kus*,[2] which appear to be, in part at least, derived from a common original. These variants are valuable as giving some idea of the kind of differentiation which takes place in Tatar oral traditions. They are printed in Radlov's collection as two totally different poems, and were recorded in different areas. Yet despite these facts, and despite the considerable differences which the poems show, the points of similarity in the early parts of both poems are so striking that it is difficult to doubt that they are in reality variants of a single theme.

Some account has already been given of the story of *Altyn Pyrkan*. A comparison of this story with the text of *Ai Mergän and Altyn Kus* shows that in both the hero is the son of an aged couple, born after they have received a message from a powerful enemy that he is coming to carry them off with all their possessions. In both the old man promises compliance, and then seeks in vain to evade the fulfilment. In both the enemy comes in due course and carries off the child and all the possessions, and the old couple perish while in his power. In both the youthful hero is saved by a foal who sucks him up into his nostrils and carries him away. In both the enemy pursues him for a long period of time through earth, air, water, and even underground, employing as emissaries in the chase two dogs, birds, animals, etc. In both the foal eventually succeeds in delivering the infant hero into the safe-keeping of a maiden for his up-bringing—in one case his elder married sister, in the other a 'swan-maiden'.

From this point onwards the resemblances between the two poems are less close. In *Altyn Pyrkan* the hero dies in youth, but is restored to life by one of the three maidens who live in the third Heaven. In *Ai Mergän and Altyn Kus* it is the hero's benefactress, the swan-woman Ala Mangnyk, who is slain, and the hero himself restores her to life. In both the hero slays his enemy, but in the former he swears brotherhood with his enemy's son who has befriended him in his infancy; in the latter he slays him. In both poems, however, he marries a supernatural maiden who has assisted him—in the former, one of the three maidens who live in the third Heaven; in the latter, the swan-woman Ala Mangnyk. In the latter poem the hero has a son who marries a swan-maiden who appears to be a 'ward' of the nine *jajan*. It would seem, therefore, that the marriage which in *Altyn Pyrkan* is ascribed to the hero, is here ascribed to the hero's son—unless, indeed,

[1] *Proben* II, p. 89 ff.   [2] *Ib.* p. 385 ff.

Ala Mangnyk, herself a swan-maiden, is in reality a ward of the nine *jajan* also.

It will be seen that the first portions of the two poems resemble one another closely. We must suppose one of two things: either that the same traditional story lies behind both poems, or that the poet in each case has utilised a common motif. The latter is not very likely, partly because the similarities are found, not only in the outline of the stories, but also in a considerable amount of the details and circumstances. It is important to note also that although in the second part of the story the resemblance is not so close as in the first, nevertheless these points of similarity, taken in connection with the early part of the stories, are by no means inconsiderable. Such differences as exist are doubtless largely due to the fact that the poem of *Ai Mergän and Altyn Kus* is much longer than *Altyn Pyrkan*, thus allowing considerable room for the introduction of more incidents, and consequently more variation. We have no doubt that the two poems are derived from a single original story.

We have just examined two distinct poems which appear to have been derived from a common origin and carried on by independent tradition. Again, in our brief study of the versions of the story of *Er Töshtük* we have not only noted the existence of several variant versions, more or less complete, but we have also pointed out that there are reasons for suspecting that in several cases more than one variant tradition of an individual incident has been incorporated in one of these complete versions of the story. In the *Manas* Cycle the existence of unreconciled variants of individual incidents is common as between one poem and another, and even occurs from time to time within a single poem. Again in *Joloi* also we find incidents which are at variance with the parallel versions in the *Manas* Cycle. We will now consider some of the variant versions of an identical incident as it appears in different poems, and then pass on to consider some unreconciled variants of the same tradition occurring in a single poem.

We will pass over the discrepancy in the accounts of the death of Bolot as we have them in the poems *Joloi* and *Bok Murun*. In the latter Bolot is killed in battle by Alaman Bet immediately after the death of Joloi at the hand of Manas, whereas in the former Bolot is apparently slain by a spirit army in the Underworld. The account is far from clear, and the conclusion suggests that while the spirit battle is in progress, a real battle is taking place in the world between a heather army and the

sons of Köchpös Bai. Bolot is slain, but is revived by the black
shamanka, Kara Chach, and as he has only recently left Joloi alive and
well, we may perhaps assume that the tradition of his death recorded in
Bok Murun relates to a later period of his life.

The most striking variants in the poetry of the Kara-Kirghiz are
those which relate to Manas' wooing, and his marriage with Kanykäi,
his raid on the Kalmucks, and his death at their hands. These three
incidents are told in two distinct poems, which we will refer to for the
sake of convenience as A and B. The first (A) is the third poem in
Radlov's collection, and is entitled: *The Battle between Manas and
Kökchö. Manas marries Kanykäi. Manas' Death and Resurrection.* The
second (B) is Radlov's fifth poem, and is entitled *Kös Kaman.* The order
of events is not the same in the two poems. In the first, Manas' war
against the Kalmucks and their allies, the Uigurs, occurs before his
marriage with Kanykäi; in the second the war with the Kalmucks occurs
after the marriage.

A comparison of the brief summaries of these two poems given above
(pp. 30–34) will show that they represent two traditions which differ
considerably from one another, not only in the order of events narrated,
but also in the substance of the stories themselves. Some of these
differences are due to omissions, but others appear to be due to quite
contradictory traditions. Others again are due to the introduction of
important characters and episodes in one version of which the other
knows nothing. It is, indeed, surprising and instructive to see how
widely two poems recorded from oral tradition in the same community
can come to differ from one another while relating what are practically
the same events.

Both poems relate the marriage of Manas to Kanykäi. Both relate a
raid by Manas against the neighbouring peoples. Both relate that Manas
is wounded by a prominent member of the raided peoples, though in A
this is the Uigur prince Er Kökchö, in B a member of the Kalmuck
cortège whose name is not given. In both versions Manas makes his
escape and returns home. In both he is poisoned by the Kalmuck prince
Kökshögös as he is spending the night in a certain house on his homeward journey, and dies as a result, though in B Kökshögös despatches
him with a wound after poisoning him. In both versions Kanykäi
realises what has occurred—in A by means of a dream, in B by second
sight—and goes to find her husband. In both the hero is restored to
life and returns to his family.

Despite the general identity of the events narrated, however, it is certain that no close relationship exists between the actual texts of the two poems. The order of events is quite different. The account of Manas' wooing is also quite different, and, indeed, contradictory in the two versions. Further, whereas in B the story of Kös Kaman and his sons occupies the greater part of the picture, in A it is omitted, save for the brief reference to the poisoning of Manas in the house of 'two thieves' as he is on his homeward journey (in B after his marriage with Kanykäi). In A the names of the 'thieves' are given as Kökchö Kös and Kamang Kös,[1] which are manifestly identical with the names of Kös Kaman and his son Kökshögös, the latter of whom poisons Manas in A. Mengdi Bai himself, who plays so prominent a part in A, is not mentioned in B, and neither Temir Khan himself nor his wife appear in the latter poem. Indeed the wooing of Kanykäi is reported much more briefly in B, and there is no reference to the preliminary mission by Jakyp Bai. On the other hand the raid on the Kalmucks is much more fully told in B.

The poems differ also in regard to other details, and in some of these a comparison of the two texts may serve to re-establish the original version. Thus in A Manas is said to be restored to life by angels; but immediately afterwards we are told that it is Bakai Khan who arouses him; and again immediately afterwards, that he is restored to life by the Forty Friends. The first two are not irreconcilable, for we know that Bakai acts as (Mussulman) priest to Jakyp and Manas,[2] and he doubtless corresponds to Khan Kosha (Khan hodja, 'pilgrim'?), 'Prince of Mecca', who in B accompanies Kanykäi to heal and restore Manas.[3] The angels, therefore, are merely supplementary. In B, however, it is Manas himself who restores the Forty Friends, and this is probably the original version.

In A the raid on the Kalmucks precedes the wooing of Kanykäi, and if this were the correct position it would better account for Temir's conditional consent to the marriage. It is clear that the hero was severely wounded in the raid which, in spite of initial success, appears to have ended disastrously. It is perhaps because of this defeat that Manas undertakes his mission to the tsar in A, in order to beg his support. Hence also, perhaps, the tsar's severe injunctions to Manas to

[1] Proben v, p. 112, l. 1683.
[2] Cf. Ib. p. 241, l. 1156 ff.
[3] A detailed examination of both texts suggests that the version which we have called A was clearly composed under much stronger Mohammedan influence than the other.

observe the peace. It is not unlikely that the Russian tsar would disapprove of any unsuccessful attack on the 'Mongols' which would be likely to arouse them to reprisals against the Kara-Kirghiz, who are represented here as the eastern bulwark of Russia.

We have seen that in the poetry of the Kara-Kirghiz the Uigurs and the Kalmucks are not differentiated, and are sometimes actually identified. Now the name of the Uigur prince who wounds Manas in single combat during Manas' raid on his neighbours in A is Kökchö. But the name of the Kalmuck prince who poisons and stabs Manas in B is also Kökchö (Kökchö Kös or Kökshögös; cf. Kös Kaman). In A also Manas is poisoned by Kökchö. There can be no doubt, therefore, that the Uigur prince and the eldest son of Kös Kaman are identical. The name may, of course, be a common one; but it is most unlikely that Manas should be wounded in both versions by a man of the same name and the same people if they are not identical persons. And such an identification would help to account for the single combat between Manas and Er Kökchö in A, which otherwise is somewhat vaguely motivated.

The great problem which the comparison of the two versions fails to solve is whether Manas twice raids the Kalmucks or only once, whether he is twice wounded by Kökchö or only once. In A the order of events is (1) Manas raids and is wounded by Kökchö; (2) marries Kanykäi by force; (3) is again mortally wounded by Kökchö and Kös Kaman in their house on his homeward journey. Here we have only one raid and the hero is twice wounded. In B the order of events is: (1) Honourable marriage with Kanykäi; (2) Raid intercepted; (3) Manas wounded in Kös Kaman's house, probably by Kökchö; (4) Raid on the Kalmucks; (5) Manas and his followers poisoned by Kökchö. It is very tempting to suppose that (4) and (5) in B are a duplicate version of (2) and (3) in the same poem, especially as the second raid is introduced in words which are identical with those which introduce the first (cf. l. 1539 ff. with l. 156 ff.), and both are followed by the stabbing of Manas as he is feasting in Kös Kaman's house. If this is so, we must suppose that the duplication has taken place in an earlier version to which A also is indebted, for although only one raid is mentioned in A, Manas is twice attacked here also by Kökchö.

Occasionally we meet with variants in matters of detail which have considerable significance. Thus in A Manas declares (l. 315 f.) that he has spent 'twenty days and twenty nights under the earth'. In B, however, it is definitely stated (l. 2455) that Manas

Never descended into the earth,
He was a man of heroic soul,
He was a hero created by God.

The two passages seem to be flatly contradictory, and the second suggests, both in the text quoted above, and still more in the context, that a good Mussulman does not go underground. The first passage, then, would seem to attribute to Manas a heathen observance, viz. a journey underground in order to rescue the souls of his poisoned retinue. The second passage denies this, and declares that Manas recovered the lives of his retinue by pilgrimage and prayer.

The *Manas* Cycle is evidently known also to the Kazaks, as we have already seen (p. 47 above). Here Er Kökshü (Er Kökchö) is said to be still a young man, in contradistinction to the Kara-Kirghiz version, which represents him as aged. In the Kazak version the Uigurs are not specifically mentioned, Er Kökshü being described as the head of the tribes of the Nogai, and the ally of Manas. Here also his enemy is the powerful Dshangbyrshy (Jamgyrchi). Alaman Bet appears as Örmön Bet, but the events are represented as occurring after his death—a variant of his departure from the court of Er Kökchö, as the latter event is related in the Kara-Kirghiz version. The Kazak version treats of only a brief portion of the *Manas* Cycle. It narrates the story of the battle in which Er Kökshü meets his death, and adds an account, which is only found in this version, of the death of Dshangbyrshy's son, Temir Bai, at the hands of Er Kökshü's son Kosai in vengeance for his father. Unfortunately the account of the wounding of Manas and the death of Er Kökshü are hardly more lucid here than among the Kara-Kirghiz, but there is more than a suspicion, as in the latter version, that Manas behaves treacherously to his 'spiritual kinsman', and that he cheats Er Kökshü's heir of his father's share of the spoil which he has shared with Dshangbyrshy after the battle.

It is probable that a fuller comparison of the numerous variant traditions relating to Manas which occur in this Cycle, both with one another, and also with traditions relating to the same hero but occurring in other Cycles, such as in that of *Joloi*, and again with those of the Kazaks, would do much to bring into a clear and ordered scheme the persons and events of this great period of Kirghiz history. We have seen from the evidence of other Kazak stories (cf. p. 47 above) that not only the heroes with whom we are familiar from the Kara-Kirghiz narrative poems, but other Kazak heroes, such as Er Targyn, and possibly Dshelkildäk, are referred to the same epoch. If, therefore, by a fuller study of the variants, we were able to reconstruct the course of events with greater exactness, and to equate these events with others, contemporary but not necessarily connected, we should be in a position to establish in some measure the historical events to which they have reference, and the exact period when the chief persons who figure in the poems were flourishing.

Apart from the interest attaching to variant traditions, Tatar variant versions offer much that is of interest for the study of form and the history of the development of literary features. The non-heroic saga of *Ak Köbök* is especially interesting from the point of view of form. We have seen that this saga exists in three versions from the Teleut, the Baraba, and the Kurdak tribes. The first consists mostly of songs, with brief narrative passages forming connecting links. In the other two versions the proportion of prose to verse is much greater. It is clear that in the Teleut version the narrative element has shrunk, while the tradition of the verse element has been better preserved, whereas among the Tatars of the west and north the saga element is more fully retained.

The most interesting feature of the three variants of the story, however, is the fact that in all three, generally speaking, the poems follow a uniform scheme, and where the story seems to be well remembered they are introduced at corresponding points in the saga, though these poems are in no cases themselves identical. Thus in the Kurdak version we find a riddle contest between Ak Kübäk and the messenger who is sent by his enemy, Kidän Khan.[1] Two of these riddles occur in the Baraba version,[2] where they are propounded to Mangush, the son of Kidän Khan, by his servant. In the Teleut version, a similar riddle contest takes place between Ak Köbök and his brother.[3] But these riddle poems are quite different in each case. Again, all three contain panegyric poems by the hero on his horse, his hawk, and his general equipment, but these poems have nothing in common. Even the form employed is quite different in each case. The Teleut and the Baraba versions each attribute a poem to Ak Köbök's sister. But the poems are not the same. In the former[4] she offers food to her brother, in the latter,[5] in a shorter poem, to her lover. It is clear that the outline of the story was remembered and handed down by oral tradition, but the poems would seem to have been either composed extempore, or selected arbitrarily from the current traditional répertoire. In either case the

---

[1] *Proben* IV, p. 188 ff.   [2] *Ib.* IV, p. 62.
[3] *Ib.* I, p. 228 ff.   [4] *Ib.* I, p. 232.   [5] *Ib.* IV, p. 65.

cues at which poems were to be introduced seem to be the most rigidly fixed and faithfully reproduced features in the plan; and the prose passages in the version from the Tatars of the Altai seem to be in fact hardly more than such cues.

We will close this chapter with a brief consideration of the relationship between the poetry of the two versions of *Idägä Pi*, which, as we have seen (p. 49 above), are recorded from the Baraba Tatars and the Kurdak tribes. The version from the former consists for the most part of prose, though a considerable amount of verse is introduced, chiefly in the speeches. In the Kurdak version the prose is confined to a brief introduction in summary form. This version consists, for the most part, of a dialogue poem to which, it is clear, the prose at the beginning serves merely as an introduction. A certain amount of variation exists between the two versions regarding the actual narrative of events; but apart from omissions and additions these are not important.

A comparison of the poems in the two versions is more interesting. These are sprinkled throughout the Baraba version, whereas in the Kurdak version they follow one another continuously after the conclusion of the introductory prose narrative. The Baraba version gives only two poems in the portion of the saga covered by the poems in the Kurdak version. The Baraba poems consist of eleven lines of narrative and fourteen lines of dialogue.[1] These poems do not occur in identical form in the Kurdak version, but the contents of the Baraba narrative poem and a close paraphrase of the Baraba dialogue poem are included in *oratio recta* in the long dialogue poem at the conclusion of the Kurdak version, and it cannot be doubted that both versions—in this part of the saga at least—are derived from a common poetical prototype. This does not, of course, necessarily mean that the story did not exist in an original prose form, but it makes it probable that if this was the case it was interspersed with poems.

[1] *Proben* IV, p. 52 ff.

CHAPTER IX

RECITATION AND COMPOSITION

THE composition and recitation of poetry and saga is highly cultivated among the Tatars. Among the Tatars of Central and eastern Asia we have seen that formal narrative is carried on chiefly in the form of poetry, and rhythmical prose, and that both forms are recited, not in a speaking voice, but in recitative. It is probably largely for this reason that we know hardly anything of the art of the saga-teller among these people. Among the Tatars of the western and north-western steppe, however, where narrative is carried on chiefly in the form of saga, the art of the saga-teller seems to be fully developed. Levchine speaks of the elaborate mimetic art of the Kazak raconteur;[1] and among the Turkomans prose traditions appear to have been preserved for the past three hundred years, and are now cultivated and transmitted, by a professional class who are also responsible for the recitation of poetry. Unfortunately, however, our information about the art of the saga-teller is very slight even here.

For the composition and recitation of poetry our information is much fuller. The art of extempore composition is widely practised by both men and women all over northern and Central Asia. Among the Turkomans and the Kara-Kirghiz heroic poetry is largely recited by a professional class of men; but further east, notably among the Yakut, as also among the Mongols and the Tungus, such poetry is cultivated by women who do not seem to belong to a professional class. For the poetry of the Abakan steppe our information is less clear. There can be no doubt that narrative poetry is cultivated by men to some extent. But there is reason to suspect that here also the art is practised by women also. Our most interesting information for the poetry of the Altai relates to the dramatic recitations of religious poetry by the shamans. For all these peoples except the Turkomans our chief source of information is Radlov's collection of texts, though much can be learnt also from the casual observations of other travellers who have been present at recitations. On the whole it must be confessed that the information available to us is fragmentary and, to some extent, of unequal value. While it is comparatively full for the heroic poetry of the Kara-Kirghiz

[1] Levchine, p. 384.

and the Turkomans, we are very much in the dark about the composition of the non-heroic poems of the Abakan Tatars. We will take a brief survey of the conditions under which poetry is cultivated among each of these peoples, so far as the available material and the space at our disposal permit, beginning with the Turkomans, and passing eastwards till we come to the Yakut.

The Kirghiz and the Turkomans are said to esteem music and poetry as their highest pleasure. After a fortunate exploit, says Vambéry, the marauder, however tired and hungry he may be, will listen in the open street with real delight to the *baksha* who comes to meet him. Returning home from a foray, the young warriors are in the habit of amusing themselves throughout the night with poetry and music.[1] The *bakshas* are said to be very numerous,[2] and even in the desert, where luxuries are practically unknown, they are seldom absent. They are sometimes regarded as the representatives of the ancient shamans, who have disappeared in the west since the introduction of Mohammedanism (see p. 192 below); but Vambéry and others[3] use the term of any minstrel, especially those in the former Khanate of Khiva.

In a striking passage the same writer describes the effect of heroic recitation on the Turkomans:

"On festal occasions, or during the evening entertainments, some *Bakhshi* used to recite the verses of Makhdumkuli! When I was in Etrek, one of these troubadours had his tent close to our own; and as he paid us a visit of an evening, bringing his instrument with him, there flocked around him the young men of the vicinity, whom he was constrained to treat with some of his heroic lays. His singing consisted of certain forced guttural sounds, which we might rather take for a rattle than a song, and which he accompanied at first with gentle touches of the strings, but afterwards, as he became excited, with wilder strokes upon the instrument. The hotter the battle, the fiercer grew the ardour of the singer and the enthusiasm of his youthful listeners; and really the scene assumed the appearance of a romance, when the young nomads, uttering deep groans, hurled their caps to the ground, and dashed their hands in a passion through the curls of their hair, just as if they were furious to combat with themselves."[4]

---

[1] *Sketches*, p. 342. [2] *Ib.* p. 341.

[3] E.g. Fraser II, p. 342; Sir A. Burnes II, p. 114ff.

[4] Vambéry, *Travels*, p. 322. With this passage we may compare the account given by Priscus of a banquet at the court of Attila, and the performance of minstrels which followed the feast. See K. Müller, *Fragmenta Historicorum Graecorum* IV, p. 92 (quoted in Vol. I, p. 575 f. of the present work).

Both the poet and the saga-teller among the Turkomans recite chiefly during the evenings.

"It is only during the evening hours, particularly in the winter time, that they love to listen to fairy tales and stories; it is regarded as an enjoyment of a still higher and more elevated nature when a *bakshi* (troubadour) comes forward, and to the accompaniment of his *Dütara* (a two-stringed instrument) sings a few songs of Koroglu."[1]

Here, as elsewhere, the feast is a favourite occasion for the recitation of poetry.[2] Sometimes the minstrels are blind.[3]

Among the Turkomans, the professional minstrel is often also a saga-teller. In regard to the songs the tradition seems to be one of verbal memorisation rather than of improvisation, and even in regard to the prose stories the form seems to be strictly memorised. The minstrels and story-tellers are known as *ausheks*[4] or *khans*. Speaking of the transmission of the stories and poem of the hero Kurroglou, Chodzko tells us:

"The Kurroglian rhapsodes are called *Kurroglou-Khans*, from *khandan*, 'to sing'. Their duty is to know by heart all the mejjlisses of Kurroglou, narrate them, or sing them with the accompaniment of the favourite instrument of Kurroglou, the *chungur* or *sitar*, that is to say, a three-stringed guitar. Ferdausy has also his Shahnama-Khans, and the Prophet Mohammed, his Koran-Khans. The memory of those singers is really astonishing. At every request they recite in one breath[5] for some hours, without stammering, beginning the tale at the passage or verse pointed out by the hearers."[6]

The same writer tells us that in regard to the recitation of the songs attributed to Kurroglou:

"It is the duty of the *Ausheks*, the privileged rhapsodes of Kurroglou, to fill up the picture by a narrative in prose, explaining where, when, and on what occasion he improvised such and such a stanza.... Such narrators can be found in every Persian village and town."[7]

The authenticity of the traditions would seem to have been preserved with unusual care, to judge from Chodzko's report:

"I insisted upon their writing...every line, word by word, of the narrative dictated by the Kurroglou-Khans. After long and tiring

---

[1] Vambéry, *Travels*, p. 321.
[2] Cf. Fraser II, p. 342.   [3] *Loc. cit.*
[4] Professional singers who perambulate the towns and camps of northern Persia and attend at wedding ceremonies, festivals, etc. (Chodzko).
[5] Chodzko means, presumably, that they sing without pausing to rest.
[6] Chodzko, p. 13f., note.   [7] *Ib.* p. 12f.

inquiries, it appeared that, notwithstanding some differences in the narratives of various Ausheks and Kurroglou-Khans, they all agreed in their substance; and that the improvisations of Kurroglou especially were everywhere the same."[1]

Finally it may be mentioned that Chodzko collected his 'Specimens of unwritten poetry' from oral communications from people—generally the lower classes—who did not know how to read or write.[2]

It is obvious, therefore, that we are here dealing with a tradition which is both oral and verbal, and that this tradition appears to have been preserved with exceptional fidelity for three hundred years. Distinct cycles are kept strictly apart, and form the exclusive répertoires of professional reciters, whose memories are checked by those of their audiences, who are apparently by no means ignorant of the stories and songs to which they are listening.

Radlov tells us that the Abakan Tatars excel all the other groups in the wealth of their poetry. Nowhere else are so many 'singers' to be found. Here, as among the Tatars of the Altai, the poems are recited in a low guttural voice ('*brummend*'). The recitations take place in the evenings or at night. As the minstrel recites by the light of the fire, surrounded by the listening multitude, he is, says Radlov, a picture worthy of an artist's study.[3]

Speaking of the milieu and atmosphere of the Abakan poems Radlov observes:

"One can only fully understand this kind of poetry if one pictures to oneself the circumstances under which it is cultivated, and experiences the full effect which it has on the listener. This takes place chiefly in the Autumn and Winter evenings, when for weeks together in the wooded mountains the nomadic hunting peoples prepare for their night's rest in their huts constructed of branches. When the hunters, weary with the chase, sit covered in their furs round the fire, and have just refreshed themselves at their meal, and are rejoicing in the warmth of the fire, the singer takes his instrument in his hand and begins in a deep guttural voice the monotonous melody of a heroic lay. The dark night which envelops the whole scene, the magic of the fire-light, the roar of the storm which howls around the hut, and accompanies the guttural tones of the singer, all these form the necessary framework for the highly coloured shifting pictures of the songs."[4]

[1] Chodzko, p. 13f.
[2] *Ib.* p. vii.
[3] *A.S.* I, p. 384.
[4] *Proben* v, p. viif.

Czaplicka speaks of the opposition which she everywhere encountered among these people in her efforts to buy a *chatigan*.[1]

"I found it very difficult to persuade anyone to part with a *chatigan*.... One old woman who refused to part with a venerable dirt-caked instrument she showed me asked me whether I thought it likely she would sell her *chatigan* now that it had 'become musical' from the touch of so many hands."[2]

The incident is interesting as lending some colour to a suspicion which we feel that the poetry of this group is largely of feminine provenance, though Radlov gives us no hint of this. It may be mentioned in this connection that among the Yakut and the Tungus poetry is chiefly cultivated by old women.

It is said that the art of poetry is prized by the Kara-Kirghiz more than by any other of the peoples of Central Asia. No other accomplishment is held in such high esteem. Improvisation is widely practised, and practically everyone is ready to perform to a small circle of listeners, though only specialists and professionals are willing to perform to a large audience. Such specialisation is widespread, however, as the feasts which are of very frequent occurrence among the Kara-Kirghiz, especially at funerals, have given rise to a set of typical heroic minstrels known as *akin*, who make their living by passing from feast to feast, singing in honour of the host and for the entertainment of the guests. The Sultans consider it very necessary for their prestige to have one of these men attached to them, who will honour them by singing on all public occasions.[3]

Atkinson was entertained by one of these minstrels during his journey through western Jungaria, in the neighbourhood of the Alatau Mountains. He was visited in his camp by the most powerful Kirghiz sultan in the district, who brought his minstrel with him, and while supper was preparing he ordered the man to sing. The minstrel chanted forth songs describing the prowess and successful plundering expeditions of the sultan and his ancestors, which called forth thunders of applause from the tribe.[4]

Venyukov describes the performances of one of these minstrels of the Sary-Bagish tribe of the Kara-Kirghiz, who was attached to the Russian expeditionary column in 1860, and who was evidently equally proficient as a reciter of narrative poetry and of extempore panegyric.

[1] For the *chatigan* see p. 22 above.   [2] Czaplicka, *S.Y.* p. 237f.
[3] Radlov, *Proben* v, p. iv.   [4] Atkinson, p. 563.

"He every evening attracted round him a crowd of gaping admirers, who greedily listened to his stories and songs. His imagination was remarkably fertile in creating feats for his hero—the son of some Khan —and took most daring flights into the regions of marvel. The greater part of the rapturous recitation was improvised by him as he proceeded, the subject alone being borrowed usually from some tradition. His wonderfully correct intonation, which enabled everyone who even did not understand the words to guess their meaning,[1] and the pathos and fire which he skilfully imparted to his strain, showed that he was justly entitled to the admiration of the Kirghizes as their chief bard!"[2]

It is clear that the Russians were listening to the recitation of a heroic narrative poem such as *Manas* or *Joloi*. The same poet, it appears, was equally proficient in the art of extempore panegyric, for Venyukov goes on to tell us that when the chief of the expedition gave an entertainment to the Kirghiz, the same poet extemporised a panegyric on the virtues of the giver of the feast—"probably with a view to a noble largesse" (cf. p. 58 above). Passages such as these, which testify to the popularity of panegyric poetry among these people, are important because few texts of poetry of this type appear to have been recorded.

Radlov gives an interesting picture of one of these gatherings:

"One sees from a Kirghiz reciter that he loves to speak, and essays to make an impression on the circle of his hearers by elaborate strophes and well-turned expressions. It is obvious, too, on all sides that the listeners derive pleasure from well-ordered expressions, and can judge if a turn of phrase is well rounded off. Deep silence greets the reciter who knows how to arrest his audience. They sit with their head and shoulders bent forward and with eyes shining, and they drink in the words of the speaker; and every adroit expression, every witty play on words calls forth lively demonstrations of applause."[3]

In reading Radlov's texts one is constantly struck by the many weak places in the narrative, the many repetitions, and unreconciled contradictions. These flaws are especially noticeable in the more ambitious texts, especially in the lengthy narrative poems of the Kara-Kirghiz. His account of the manner in which the poems were recorded makes it abundantly clear how these flaws in the narrative have come about, and may perhaps serve to throw light on similar repetitions and discrepancies in other lengthy narrative poems.

"The noting down of the songs according to dictation was attended

[1] Cf. p. 186 below.
[2] Michell, p. 290; cf. also *ib.* p. 81.　　　[3] *Ib.* p. iii.

with great difficulty. The singer is not accustomed to dictate slowly enough for one to follow with the pen, and when this method is adopted he frequently loses the thread of the narrative, and by omissions falls into contradictions which are not easily resolved by questions, which only confusé the singer more. There remained for me in these circumstances nothing to do except first to let him sing for me some episodes, and then to make some notes during the course of the exposition, and to abstain from recording until I had been entrusted with the content of the episode. Then if the singer allowed omissions to creep in through lengthy dictation I could easily bring them to his notice. It will be seen that in spite of this course, very many omissions have occurred."[1]

A further difficulty was felt to lie in the absence of stimulus afforded by an applauding crowd.

"In spite of all my efforts I have not succeeded in reproducing the poetry of the minstrels completely. The repeated singing of one and the same song, the slow dictation, and my frequent interruptions often dispersed the excitement which is necessary to the minstrel for good singing. He was only able to dictate in a tired and negligent way what he had produced for me a little before with fire. I did not allow encouragements and presents to be wanting, of course, in order to put the minstrel in good heart; but this, of course, could not take the place of natural stimulus. The verses written down have therefore lost in freshness."[2]

There can be no doubt that Radlov's explanation of the omissions and discrepancies in the recitations of the heroic minstrels is correct. Zazubrin, the editor of the Altai poem *Kogutei*, writing in 1934, tells us that the standard of artistic composition among these people is very high. Their native oral narratives are faultlessly composed and recited among themselves. The minstrel is accustomed to recite in the *yurt* before a very large audience. Such discrepancies as have crept into recorded texts are due to two causes: (1) the lack of the stimulus and excitement of a critical and appreciative public; and (2) the fact that the slow process of writing or dictating causes him to lose his thread and diverge into some different variant of the story, of which in all probability he knows several. He is apt to begin with one version, and to end with another. But such so-called 'typical discrepancies' of popular poetry are quite foreign to his performance when he is at 'concert pitch'. Were a minstrel-reciter of the Altai to lapse into contradictions

---

[1] *Proben* v, p. xv.
[2] *Loc. cit.*

or confusion of his episodes before a native audience he would be held up to mockery, and never listened to again.[1]

In regard to the manner of reciting, Radlov tells us that the minstrel invariably employs two melodies, one.executed in quick tempo, for the course of the action, the other in slow tempo and as a solemn recitative for the speeches. He had the opportunity of observing these changes of melody among all minstrels who had any experience at all. Otherwise the melodies of the different minstrels are said to be almost exactly identical.[2] Radlov also tells us that in their clarity of enunciation the minstrels excel those of all other peoples, 'even the Kazaks', and he adds that their melodious recitation of the poetry interferes so little with the significance of the words that it is easy even for a non-Kirghiz to follow the song. Vambéry adds that the Kara-Kirghiz minstrel accompanies his singing of heroic narrative poetry on the two-stringed *köböʒ*.[3]

The form in which oral tradition is carried on by the poets of the Kara-Kirghiz is singularly fluid. If we understand Radlov aright, not only is there an absence of rigid verbal memorisation in the heroic narrative poems, but even the stories themselves consist of a mass of material, a number of episodes, which can be arranged and selected from at will, and which are subject to infinite new combinations and groupings. Thus it is that not only the words but the form of the narrative may be regarded as extempore, as is the case also in the Russian *byliny*. Radlov points out that it would be impossible to make an exhaustive collection of the epic poetry of the Kara-Kirghiz. Not only do the same motifs recur in an infinite number of combinations, but it is to be added that they will always recur in a different connection, producing a new form of story with every subsequent recitation.

"Every minstrel who has any skill at all always improvises his songs according to the inspiration of the moment, so that he is not in a position to recite a song twice in exactly the same form; but one must

---

[1] See Zazubrin, *Kogutei*, p. 7 ff.

[2] It would, in our opinion, be a mistake to attach much importance to Radlov's statement about the number of tunes known to the minstrel. We have seen (Vol. II, p. 243 f.) that similar statements were made in the past as to the paucity of tunes of the Russian *skaʒitely*, whereas it is now recognised that some at least of these men know a different tune to almost every *bylina*. The truth seems to be that the Western scholar and recorder, whose ear was attuned in a different musical tradition, was incapable of appreciating the distinctions of native tunes. We have heard of similar statements having been made in the past in regard to the paucity of tunes to which the Spanish ballads were sung, whereas there is reason to believe that these tunes were numerous. [3] *Türkenvolk*, p. 272.

not suppose that this process of improvisation involves composing a new poem every time. The procedure of the improvising minstrel is exactly like that of the pianist. As the latter puts together into a harmonious form different runs which are known to him, transitions and motifs according to the inspiration of the moment, and thus makes up the new from the old which is familiar to him, so also does the minstrel of epic poems. Through an extensive practice in production, he has whole series of 'elements of production',[1] if I may so express it, in readiness, which he puts together in suitable manner according to the course of the narrative. Such 'elements of production' consist of pictures of certain occurrences and situations, such as the birth of a hero, the growing up of the hero, the glories of weapons, preparations for battle, the storm of battle, the conversations of a hero before battle, the depicting of characteristics of persons and of horses, the characterisation of the well-known heroes, the praise of the beauty of the bride.... The art of the singer consists only in arranging all these static component parts of pictures with one another as circumstances require, and in connecting them with lines invented for the occasion.

"Now the minstrel can utilise in his singing all the formative elements specified above in very different ways. He knows how to represent one and the same picture in a few short strokes. He can depict it more fully, or he can go into a very detailed description with epic fulness. The greater the number of different formative elements at the disposal of the minstrel, the more diversified will be his performance, and the longer will he be able to sing without tiring his listeners by the monotony of his descriptions. The amount of the formative elements and the skill in putting them together is the measure of the skill of the minstrel. A skilled minstrel can recite any theme he wants, any story that is desired, extempore, provided that the course of events is clear to him. When I asked one of the most accomplished minstrels whom I had learnt to know if he could sing this or that song, he answered me: 'I can sing any song whatever; for God has implanted this gift of song in my heart. He gives me the word on my tongue, without my having to seek it. I have learnt none of my songs. All springs from my inner self.' And the man was right. The improvising minstrel sings without reflection, simply from his inner being, that which is known to him, as soon as the incentive to singing comes to him from without, just as the words flow from the tongue of a speaker without his producing

[1] We may compare the closely analogous method of the Russian *skazitel* described in Vol. II, p. 246 f.

intentionally and consciously the articulations necessary to produce them, as soon as the course of his thoughts requires this or that word. The accomplished minstrel can sing a day, or a week, or a month, just as he can speak, and narrate all the time. As, however, the man of many words talks himself out and becomes wearisome, because he repeats himself in the grouping of his thoughts, so also is it with the minstrel. If you let him sing too long his store of descriptions comes to an end, and he repeats himself and becomes wearisome. This is shown by the song *Töshtük*, which was repeated to me by the same minstrel who had dictated to me the song of *Joloi*. The minstrel wanted to recite to me also the song of *Jügörü*, but I had to break off in the middle of the latter song, and I have not included this fragment in my literary specimens, because it was merely a tiresome repetition of previous descriptions, devoid of any interest."[1]

The words in which the Kirghiz minstrel describes to Radlov the divine inspiration of his art carry us back to the Anglo-Saxon poet Cædmon and the angel visitant who put music and poetry into his heart;[2] and to Hesiod, who claims to have obtained his poetic art by inspiration from the Muses, who taught him poetry as he was keeping sheep on the slopes of holy Helicon;[3] to Phemios, the minstrel of Ithaca, who claims that he is self-taught, and that poems of all kinds have been implanted in his heart by a deity;[4] and to Demodocos, of whom the same is implied.[5] And what follows in Radlov's text is also very true. The weariness of the singer, and the consequent lapses of memory and flagging narrative are constantly brought home to us as we draw towards the close of Radlov's poems, which offer a striking contrast to their brilliant opening scenes. Nevertheless we grudge the loss of *Jügörü*.

The evidence suggests that among these people verbal tradition (i.e. exact verbal memorisation) is on an exceptionally low level, while the standard of extempore composition is very high, making the double demand of extempore narrative and extempore verbal composition on the reciter. As an illustration of the practice we may refer to the second episode of the *Manas* Cycle, which shows Manas as victorious over all

---

[1] *Proben* v, p. xviff.
[2] The story is told by Bede, *Ecclesiastical History*, Book IV, cap. XXV (cf. Vol. I, p. 572 of the present work).
[3] *Theogony*, l. 22ff.   [4] *Odyssey* XXII, l. 347f.
[5] *Ib.* VIII, l. 487ff. All these have been referred to more fully in Vol. I of the present work.

the surrounding peoples save only 'the Russians and the White Tsar', with whom he is represented as in close touch. It was Radlov's opinion that the Russian liaison formed no part of the original story, but had been introduced for the occasion by the reciter to show respect to the Russian official, Radlov himself, who was, of course, present at the recitation. Radlov also believed that the minstrel composed not only the poem, but also the actual story of Manas' birth and early years on the spur of the moment. He felt convinced that the story had no previous existence, the poet being stimulated to instant composition of a poem on the subject by a chance question from Radlov with regard to the birth of the hero.[1] But if Radlov is right, we may safely assume that the minstrel composed his poem along traditional lines. It will be seen that in the high development of extempore composition, as opposed to memorisation, the Kirghiz differ markedly from the Turkomans, among whom exact verbal memorisation is very highly developed.

Radlov has shown that the rank and temper of the audience have a very material influence on the content of a poem. In connection with his account of the effect of stimulus and excitement on the Kirghiz minstrel which has been quoted above he adds further:

"The external stimulus comes, of course, also from the crowd of listeners surrounding the minstrels. Since the minstrel wants to obtain the sympathy of the crowd, by which he is to gain not only fame, but also other advantages, he tries to colour his song according to the listeners who are surrounding him. If he is not directly asked to sing a definite episode, he begins his song with a prelude which will direct his audience into the sphere of his thoughts. By a most subtle art, and allusions to the most distinguished persons in the circle of listeners, he knows how to enlist the sympathy of his audience before he passes on to the song proper. If he sees by the cheers of his listeners that he has obtained full attention, he either proceeds straight to the business, or produces a brief picture of certain events leading up to the episode which is to be sung, and then passes on to the business. The song does not proceed at a level pace. The sympathy of the hearers always spurs the minstrel to new efforts of strength, and it is by this sympathy that he knows how to adapt the song exactly to the temper of his circle of listeners. If rich and distinguished Kirghiz are present, he knows how to introduce panegyrics very skilfully on their families, and to sing of such episodes as he thinks will arouse the sympathy of distinguished people. If his listeners are only poor people, he is not ashamed to

[1] *Proben* v, p. xiiff.

introduce venomous remarks regarding the pretensions of the distinguished and the rich, and actually in the greater abundance according as he is gaining the assent of his listeners. One may refer to the third episode in *Manas* which is intended to appeal to my taste solely.

"The minstrel, however, understands very well when he is to desist from his song. If the slightest signs of weariness show themselves, he tries once more to arouse attention by a struggle after the loftiest effects, and then, after calling forth a storm of applause, suddenly to break off his poem. It is marvellous how the minstrel knows his public. I have myself witnessed how one of the sultans, during a song, sprang up suddenly and tore his silk overcoat from his shoulders, and flung it, cheering as he did so, as a present to the minstrel."[1]

It is very curious what passages in the poems call forth most applause on the part of the audience. Radlov remarks that often most appreciation was shown for passages which made not the slightest impression on him, and which seemed to him merely a jingle of words and intricate interweaving of rhyme. One of the favourites in the *Manas* song was that of the catalogue of the 'forty heroes',[2] a fact which explains why this list is introduced so frequently in the poems. It will be remembered that among the Turkomans also the poem in which the points of an ideal horse are enumerated *seriatim* is among the most popular.

We would gladly have known more of the procedure of the Kirghiz minstrel, his preparation for his task, and his répertoire. But we have no detailed information on these points. We know (cf. above) that the same minstrel recited *Joloi* and *Er Töshtük*, and that his répertoire was not then exhausted. But we do not know how far his range and scope actually extended, or how far they were typical of other minstrels; nor have we exact information, such as we possess for the Russians and the Yugoslavs, regarding the speed of the reciter, or the length of time during which he is able to give a continuous performance. Valikhanov tells us that the Kirghiz say that three nights are insufficient for the relation of *Manas*, and that as much time is required for *Semätäi*;[3] and indeed if the whole of the *Manas* in Radlov's collection is recited, three nights would, one would think, be far short of the time required.

[1] *Proben* v, p. xviii f. With this and the preceding passages in which Radlov describes the effect of the minstrel's art on the audience we may compare Layard's descriptions of similar scenes among the Bedouin and other desert nomads. See Layard, *Early Adventures in Persia, Susiana and Babylonia* (London, 1887), p. 487; *ib. Nineveh and Babylon*, 2nd Series, p. 153 f.; and London, 1853, p. 319. Cf. also p. 58 above.

[2] *Proben* v, p. xix. [3] Michell, p. 101.

We have dwelt somewhat at length on the evidence afforded by Radlov relating to the recitation and composition of heroic poetry among the Kara-Kirghiz, partly because it is peculiarly full and valuable in regard to matters for which we have comparatively little information from other sources, and partly because Radlov is an exceptionally close and sympathetic observer, and a very reliable authority. Moreover much which he has told us of these people is manifestly true of heroic minstrels among other peoples. Indeed this is demonstrable in the case of some ancient literatures, as has been indicated above; and such evidence as we have for modern Russian and Yugoslav, as well as for other Tatar peoples, corresponds closely to Radlov's account. In particular we may refer to Levchine's account of recitation among the Kazaks, in which he tells us that the words of the songs, far from being learnt by heart, are never transmitted from one Kirghiz (i.e. Kazak) to another without variation, "for every Kirghiz is an improviser, and narrates events after his own fashion".[1]

Among the Yakut of the north heroic poetry appears to be especially cultivated by women. On the R. Kolyma it seems to be more particularly an accomplishment of old women, many of whom are blind.

"To this day," writes Shklovsky, "in the farthest north-east of Siberia, you will still hear in some dark hut, lighted only by the fire, the story of the dreadful Djennik told in monotonous recitative by an old blind woman." Djennik, it will be remembered, was the Yakut leader of a disastrous revolt against the Russians in the seventeenth century (cf. p. 43 above). Shklovsky also tells us that the Yakut epics are remarkable for their wonderful richness of imagery and wealth of description. "The old woman", he adds, "describes in minute detail the terrible operation of flaying, and what kind of knives were used; and on the seats by the wall are the listening Yakuts, with pale terrified faces, too frightened to utter a word."[2]

The minstrel's task of extempore recitation and composition is made lighter, and the standard of his art is no doubt higher, owing to the wide practice of amateur poetical composition among the Tatars, and to the general use of polished diction in ordinary conversation. It has been made clear in the preceding chapters that the art of extempore composition is widely practised by all classes of the population among the peoples of the Steppe. We are told that in these arts the Kirghiz excel all neighbouring peoples.

[1] Levchine, p. 380.   [2] Shklovsky, p. 209.

"The words of every Kirghiz", writes Radlov, "roll tripping from his tongue. Not only has he such a command of language that he can improvise long poems, but even his ordinary conversation shows traces of rhythm, and artificial arrangement. His language is figurative, his expressions are sharp and clear-cut. It need cause no surprise that among such a people a particularly rich oral literature has arisen."[1]

It would seem that extempore composition is regarded as one of the polite accomplishments of a well-bred nomad. An amusing incident is related by Valikhanov which illustrates very well the facile use of poetry for ordinary conversational purposes among these people. When the writer was in the neighbourhood of the Alatau Mountains, the caravan was visited by the sultan of the Jalair tribe of the Kazaks:

"Suddenly lifting his head, and casting a penetrating glance around, he exclaimed in rhyme: 'The Djalairs have many sheep, Jangazy has many thoughts.'... The Sultan meanwhile rolled his eyes about in a curious manner, giving occasional utterances to rhymes in couplets."[2]

Valikhanov, and the Russian authorities, regarded the Sultan as 'imbecile';[3] but this practice of giving expression to one's ordinary thoughts in brief poems is very widespread on the Steppe (see p. 64 f. above), and the Sultan was, in all probability, merely making polite conversation according to native standards. Erman tells us of the Yakut that

"The songs of these people... pass away, for the most part, just as they arise, for whether on a journey, or in cheerful humour at home, every one sings the new impressions made on him at the moment by the objects around him."[4]

The same writer tells us that their poems often contain remarkable passages, for "they assume that the trees of the forest hold intercourse with one another, and other inanimate things with men".[5]

From this it would appear that the poetry of the Yakut is composed in an elaborate and figurative diction. Their manner of reciting is equally remarkable:

"They have for that purpose a kind of song consisting of only two notes; these are reproduced in such a way that the higher note follows the lower till towards the end of each part or verse, when their order is reversed. The whole air sounds so melancholy that I often thought that I heard someone wailing aloud, when, in fact, it was only the extemporaneous song of the Yakuts."[6]

[1] *A.S.* I, p. 507. [2] Michell, p. 73. [3] *Loc. cit.*
[4] Erman II, p. 401 ff. [5] *Loc. cit.* [6] *Loc. cit.*

Cochrane also refers to the prevalence of the habit of extempore composition among the Yakut, apparently even when no audience is present. He overheard a Yakut 'prince' walking his horse and singing a song:

"There is", he observes, "no regular meaning in what they sing, being made up of any incidental allusions to the weather, trees, rivers, fatigues, horses, and the like, according to the immediate impulse of the moment."[1]

The widespread practice of extempore poetical composition among the Tatars, and the general use of polished, even poetical diction in ordinary conversation, must owe much to the contests in poetical improvisation which are popular everywhere, from the R. Kolyma on the extreme confines of north-eastern Siberia, to the Turkomans in the west. These contests or poetical competitions are held, as we have seen, both between professional singers, and also between all young people of both sexes. Sometimes two youths, sometimes a youth and a maiden, strive which can outlast his rival in improvising witty or scathing verses, or in asking and answering riddles. Among the Tatars of the Altai such poetical contests must have a particularly stimulating effect, for they are said to take place between famous singers of different tribes or groups.[2] The practice appears to be an ancient one among the Tatars, for already in the seventh century A.D. the celebrated Chinese pilgrim, Hüan Chwang, describes them as much given to singing songs in repartee;[3] and in China and India the custom of holding disputations in poetry appears to have been widespread at an early date.[4]

It will be seen that while amateur recitation is practised by both sexes alike, the professional minstrel and reciter of heroic poetry is generally a man, at least among the western Turks and the Turks of Central Asia. Among the Yakut (cf. p. 186 above), and probably among the Tungus also, narrative poetry is chiefly recited by women. We have already

[1] Cochrane I, p. 342. This type of casual extempore conversational poetry is by no means confined to peoples of Tatar stock. We have seen (Vol. II, p. 284f. of the present work) that it is common also among the Russian peasantry; and the Tungus seem to recite similar extempore poems relating to unnatural natural history. See Erman II, p. 490; cf. p. 458, and, for the manner of singing, pp. 440, 474.

[2] Radlov, A.S. I, p. 493.   [3] Parker, T.Y. p. 136.

[4] See Waley, C.P. p. 221, Thomas, p. 111. In the instance given by Thomas it is not actually stated that the contest takes place in poetry, but there is a considerable body of evidence which seems to indicate that both teaching and controversy among the early Indian Buddhists and Jains was not uncommonly carried on in the form of verse. See Thomas, *passim*.

seen reason to suspect that the poetry of the Abakan Tatars and the Kara-Kirghiz poem *Joloi* have formed a part of a feminine répertoire. This is, of course, mere conjecture. It is interesting to note in this connection, however, that among the Mongols the recitation of 'songs of love and war, of fabulous adventure, or heroic achievements' are said to be recited by women in public at the great Mongol feasts.[1]

In regard to the widespread practice of extempore composition and recitation of poetry which we have been considering it is interesting to turn to the evidence afforded by the texts. This is of a rather remarkable character; for we do not recall a single clear reference to the professional poet or minstrel in either poetry or saga. Indeed so far as we are aware the narrative poetry, whether heroic or non-heroic, gives no ground for supposing the existence of any professional class except that of the smith. Saga is equally silent on the subject.

On the other hand references to the recitation of poetry by private individuals are exceedingly common, both in prose and poetry, and extempore poetical composition appears to be an art universally practised by all classes. Not only in formal composition, but also in casual conversation the characters of the sagas are constantly represented as falling into metre. Some of the heroes, such as Ak Köbök (cf. p. 108 above), appear to be good musicians also. Ak Köbök could play both the *chatigan* and an instrument resembling a fiddle, and he is also represented as an intellectual poet. But he is a warrior and a prince, and not, apparently, a professional poet or minstrel.

In the oral traditions of the Tatars, therefore, the part which is played in modern times by the professional poet is played by the cultivated amateur, both on formal occasions, and in casual daily life. When Manas feasts with his 'forty heroes' they are said to sing songs.[2] Songs are also sung at the feast given by the Kuärik hero, Üdsäng Päg. When the company begin to eat, Üdsäng Päg is said to go about among them crying: "Sing!" and we are told that they 'sang and praised Üdsäng Päg'.[3] Heroes and heroines are also sometimes represented as singing as they ride on long journeys together. Üdsäng Päg himself is represented as laughing and singing with his companion Kara Mattyr as they ride up the hills.[4]

The most accomplished minstrel poet to whom reference is made in

[1] Clarke, *Travels* I, p. 319.   [2] *Proben* V, p. 237, l. 1019.
[3] *Ib.* II, p. 703.   [4] *Ib.* p. 704.

the literature however, is Üdsäng Päg's champion, Taska Mattyr. He is the only man in the retinue who can play forty different melodies on the forty-stringed *chatigan*. He plays so that the old folks marvel, and the birds turn in their flight and wheel three times round him listening! When he returns in disguise after a long absence he reveals his identity to Üdsäng Päg in extempore song:

"The forty-stringed chatigan lies on the black chest. The youth took the chatigan and placed the bridge under the strings, and began to play; he played the melodies which he had played in the past...but he did not play them well. Üdsäng Päg set brandy before him. When the youth had drunk he played better. Again he poured out brandy and he played still better. When he had drunk brandy for the third time, he played admirably, and sang in accompaniment: 'Taska Mattyr has gone away from here. It is three years ago. He has seen another land. Even now the hero, Taska Mattyr the Strong, is still not dead'."[1]

In the past minstrelsy appears to have been highly cultivated among the Tatars and the Mongols. Pian de Carpini, writing of his sojourn with Batu Khan while on his way to Karakoram in northern Mongolia to visit the court of Kujuk Khan during the years 1245–7, tells us that the former never drank in public, save to the accompaniment of singing and guitar playing,[2] and that whenever the latter came out of his tent the people sang to him.[3] Speaking of the Kipchak Turks, the same writer tells us that a great vat of *kumyss*[4] stood permanently before the door of his tent, and beside it a 'guitar player' with his 'guitar'; and whenever the 'master' began to drink, then, one of the attendants would cry with a loud voice, "Ha!" and the 'guitarist' would strike his 'guitar'.[5]

Ibn Batuta also speaks of the custom among the Kipchak Turks of drinking to the accompaniment of songs. When the sultan desired to drink, his daughter is said to have taken the cup in her hand and saluted her father on bended knee; then she offered the cup to him, after which she offered it to the great *Khatun*, and then to the other *khatuns* in turn according to their rank.—"Finally the inferior emirs rise and serve drink to the sons of the sultan, and during all the time they sing

[1] *Proben* II, p. 717f.
[2] Pian de Carpini, p. 11.
[3] *Ib.* p. 21.
[4] A drink of fermented mares' milk, much prized by the Tatars, and said to be very beneficial to health.
[5] Pian de Carpini, p. 62.

nawaliyah (short songs)."[1] The passage calls to mind the Anglo-Saxon poet's description in *Beowulf* of the young daughter of Hrothgar, king of the Danes, handing round mead at the feast of Heorot; here also a minstrel sang 'with clear voice'. Friar William of Rubruck, who sojourned at the court of the Mongol prince Mangu Khan in 1254, observed similar formalities in vogue, and a similar love of music for ceremonial purposes.[2]

[1] Quoted by Rockhill in his edition of William of Rubruck, p. 62, footnote 1.
[2] Rubruck, pp. 138, 247.

CHAPTER X

THE SHAMAN

HITHERTO we have considered only the poet who composes and recites for the purpose of entertainment and celebration, and the non-professional poet who composes occasional poetry and poetry of social ritual. There remains an important class of poets who are chiefly responsible for spiritual and intellectual poetry. These are the shamans, and the *bakshas*. The former are found chiefly in the mountains of Central Asia and in the eastern and northern steppes; the latter belong chiefly to the west. Generally speaking the shamans are found among the Tatars and other Siberian peoples who do not belong to any of the great religions such as Buddhism, Mohammedanism, or Christianity. The *bakshas* belong to the countries which have adopted Mohammedanism, such as the Kazaks and the Turkomans. They are described by a recent investigator as "singers, poets, musicians, diviners, priests and doctors, the guardians of popular religious traditions, and the preservers of ancient legend".[1] Radlov[2] and others have held that the *bakshas* are the modern representatives of the earlier shamans of the west, and that the ancient religious functions of the latter have been taken over by the Mohammedan mullahs, leaving to the *bakshas* only the less spiritual and intellectual of their functions. However this may be, there is no doubt that some of the *baksha* recitations show a clear connection with shamanism (cf. p. 210), and the studies of the *bakshas* published by Castagné[3] in 1930, and by Köprülüzade in 1931,[4] show that this connection is even closer than has been supposed.

In this brief study we shall concentrate chiefly, though not exclusively, on the shamans and female shamans or *shamankas*, of the heathen Tatars

---

[1] Castagné, p. 59.

[2] *A.S.* II, p. 59 ff.; Levchine, p. 334 f. See further Köprülüzade, p. 19, and *passim*, where the original connection between shaman and *baksha* is more fully worked out. See below.

[3] Castagné's work is the result of eighteen years' sojourn among the 'Turko-Mongol peoples' of Central and Western Asia, as well as in the libraries of Russia and Turkestan.

[4] The conclusions of Köprülüzade are based mainly on literary and historical evidence, much of which is extremely full and interesting.

of eastern and Central Asia. The terms *shaman* and the Russianised feminine form *shamanka*, 'shamaness', 'seeress', are in general use to denote any persons of the native professional class among the heathen Siberians and Tatars generally, and there can be no doubt that they have come to be applied to a large number of different classes of people. The word *shaman* is said to be found in actual current use only among the Tungus, the Buryat, and Yakut,[1] and to be native only to the Tungus.[2] The word in use among the Tatars of the Altai is *kam*. The Mongols, Buryat, Yakut, Altaians, Kirghiz, etc. all use the same word for a female shaman, whereas the term used of a male shaman is different in each of these groups.[3]

The word *kam* occurs first in the Uigur text *Kudatku Bilik*, written in the year 1069, where it is used several times.[4] It occurs also in a glossary of the language of the Kumans, compiled in 1303 by an Italian.[5] Shamanism is said to have been specially developed in the past near Lake Baikal and in the Altai Mountains, and to have reached the height of its power in the time of Jenghiz Khan and his immediate successors.[6] We shall see that the shamans of this region today are especially proficient in the art of extempore poetry and of dramatic presentation. In the following brief observations, therefore, we shall concentrate primarily on the natives of the Altai and the neighbouring regions, taking into account the closely allied shamanism of the Yakut, and of the neighbouring (Mongol) Buryat,[7] and, to a lesser extent, the practices of the *bakshas* of the west. In doing so we shall confine our attention as far as possible to those shamans whose functions are priestly and prophetic, and who are in the habit of embodying their intellectual and spiritual concepts in literary and artistic form. It is greatly to be regretted that the *shamanka* is almost entirely omitted from this study owing to the extreme scarcity of texts recorded from their recitation.

[1] Among the Mongols and the Buryat, however, the words chiefly used are *bö*, *buge*; among the Yakut, *ojun* (Stadling, p. 87).

[2] Mikhailovsky, p. 63. For a discussion of the current use of the terms shaman and shamanism, see an article by van Gennep in *R.H.R.* XLVII (1903), p. 51 ff.; and for a study of its etymology, see Laufer, *A.A.* (N.S.), XIX (1917), p. 361 ff.; cf. further Stadling, p. 86; Donner, p. 224.

[3] Stadling, *loc. cit.*

[4] Radlov, *K.B.* pp. 371, 442; Vambéry, *U.S.* p. 136; cf. also Radlov, *A.S.* II, p. 67.

[5] Radlov, *A.S.* II, p. 67.

[6] Mikhailovsky, p. 69; Czaplicka, *A.S.* p. 191.

[7] For a fuller treatment of the subject the reader may consult two papers by Chadwick, *J.R.A.I.* LXVI (1936).

It should always be borne in mind, however, that apart from the professional shaman the intellectual life of the steppe is largely feminine.[1]

The shaman's function is not easy to define. He is the intermediary between his fellow tribesmen and the spirit world. He offers up the prayers of the tribe to the spirits, whether to the spirits dwelling in the sixteen Heavens, or to Erlik Khan, the black ruler of the dead who dwells in the Underworld. He conducts the tribal sacrifice, to Bai Ülgen, the highest god, who dwells in the uppermost Heaven; and he conducts the souls of the dead to their final abode in Erlik's realm. In both these capacities he acts as a *psychopompos*, and seems to represent in his official capacity the communal soul of his tribe, which is commonly symbolised in the form of a bird. In his spiritual journeys he is frequently either mounted on a bird, or transformed into a bird himself; but in these respects usage varies locally in details. But it is safe to say that whatever the spiritual aspirations of the Tatars, and whatever the precise form of their religious beliefs, all these are focussed and concentrated in the shaman as the chief executive spiritual force of the community. He may be said to represent the tribe made spiritually articulate.

The manner in which the shaman gives expression to his function of spiritual representative of his tribe is both interesting and spectacular. So far as his manifestations have been recorded, they consist of a combined extempore performance of music—generally of the drum—song, dancing, and a certain amount of mimesis. The dramatic element varies perhaps more than any other, ranging from ventriloquial and voice-throwing feats, representing the voices of animals and birds coming naturally from various quarters, and the speech of dead relatives and friends of those present, to elaborate scenic performances bordering on genuine drama. The dance is generally rapid and exhausting, though often sustained for a long period, and—it is important to remark—perfectly controlled. The movements of the shaman appear abandoned and wild, partly because of the extreme rapidity of the dance, partly because of the unfamiliarity of this type of dance to European and native alike. It seems to have a close resemblance to the dances of the *bodhisattvas* depicted in Buddhist paintings; but it undoubtedly bears

[1] Stadling observes (*S.N.A.* p. 89) that among the Palaeo-Siberians shamanistic gifts are more frequently found among women than among men: "'A woman is a shaman by nature, and requires no special preparation', declare the Chuckchee shamans." According to Donner (p. 232) women shamans are common to the east of the Yenisei, especially among the Tungus.

some relation to the fire. It is an important fact that the shaman never hits any of his audience, though the dance generally takes place in the restricted space between the fire and the audience in the crowded *yurt*.

The shaman's powers are called into requisition both in public and in private. The greatest occasion when the shaman of the Altai and Lebed Tatars is called upon to officiate is the annual tribal horse sacrifice to Bai Ülgen, the greatest of the gods, who dwells in the highest Heaven.[1] On this occasion the shaman of the Lebed Tatar is assisted by nine men stationed round the horse.[2] A ceremony resembling that of the Altai Tatars in many respects takes place also among the (Mongol) Buryat. On these public occasions the audience are sometimes to a very limited extent also participators. Another public occasion on which the services of the shaman are called for is the autumn festival of the Yakut, which takes place at night, and is dedicated to the 'black' spirits. This festival is under the direction of nine shamans and nine shamankas.[3] In private the shaman is often called in when anyone is ill, or when anyone dies. The audience on these occasions consists only of the family of the deceased or sick person, and a few friends and neighbours. They are simply spectators, though the husband of the shamanka whose *kamlanie* Potanin witnessed rendered her some slight help at the beginning and end of her performance.[4]

The shamans may be said to constitute the professional class of the heathen Tatars. Apart from the smith, of whom we hear little, and an occasional mullah or trader, generally foreign, who is found now and then in the following of the more important of the chiefs, the professional, and more especially the intellectual life, is almost wholly vested in the shamans. Yet these men and women—the latter comparatively rare among the Tatars and the Tungus, though commoner among the Yakut—do not differ to any marked degree in their way of life from other people. They do not constitute any separate class in the community, but live among their fellows, carrying on the ordinary avocations, and working like them with their hands. They are in general more given to solitude, to spending periods alone in the steppe, and they are said to have a strange look in their eyes—a feature which often comes out clearly in their photographs[5]. But apart from those slight details there is nothing to distinguish a Tatar shaman from the rest of the community.

[1] See p. 200 below.   [2] Hildén, p. 139.   [3] Czaplicka, *A.S.* p. 298.
[4] Mikhailovsky, p. 72.   [5] See e.g. Donner, plate 30.

One of the most distinctive features of shamanism, not only among the Tatars, but among the peoples of northern Asia generally, is the absence of organisation. It is perhaps in this respect that the difference between the shaman, or 'seer', on the one hand, and the priest of communities more advanced politically, on the other, comes out most clearly. The latter holds office, either inherited or derived, from a central authority; but the Tatars have no priests in this sense, though the shaman's function of conducting the sacrifices may be regarded as sacerdotal. The shaman claims the respectful hearing of his community by virtue of his claim to divine inspiration. He maintains this claim by his ability to convince both himself and his fellows of his superior gifts —spiritual, intellectual, artistic. We are sometimes told that the office of shaman is hereditary, though not necessarily from father to son;[1] but it is not clear that among the Tatars this means more than that the tendency to a contemplative life is commonly found in the same family, and that such a tendency is commonly noted in childhood and fostered from an early stage. Very often, however, it happens that the 'call' to shamanism comes during adolescence or early manhood, whether from some dead ancestor in the form of a vision or dream, or as the result of an illness. Once a shaman, always a shaman. One never hears of a shaman who abandons his calling, or allows it to lapse permanently.

In the absence of organisation, the shaman must maintain a certain standard in the execution of his calling, otherwise he would lose the respectful attention of his tribe. Public opinion raises the standard of his performance, and the absence of a written text keeps his effort ever on the alert. He must be ready with a fresh mind and a well-stored memory to extemporise the libretto of a performance as the occasion may require, on traditional lines, already familiar in their general outline to his audience, but composed afresh at every recitation. For verbal memorisation has never crystallised the texts of the Tatar poets, whether heroic poet or shaman. We may presume that the standard is further maintained by competition. In a Tungus tribe, when a new shaman is needed, the choice is sometimes made by a kind of public examination of the rival claimants,[2] and among other peoples also, both in Europe and in Asia, some kind of competitive system is often referred to in both ancient and modern literature. We have seen that Tatar oral literature recognises the practice in the *Saga of the Two Princes* (pp. 107 f. above). Moreover, the recognition of a standard of

---

[1] On this subject, however, see Hildén, p. 132.
[2] Shirokogoroff, *Shamanism*.

performance is universally referred to among the Tatars, who speak of one shaman as 'a little shaman', of another as 'a very great shaman', mentioning the extent of their spiritual and intellectual achievements. Thus we are told[1] that although all shamans can mount to Heaven, only very few of the greatest shamans can mount to the sixteenth Heaven.

Unfortunately the evidence for the education of the shaman and his preparation for his calling is very limited. It would seem that in general the outlines or principles of *kamlanie*, or shamanism, are traditional, and learnt partly by observation of other older shamans, partly by a period of special instruction from them. The training is said to include singing, dancing, drum-beating, ventriloquism, and other 'tricks'. But these are merely matters of external technique. According to the shamans themselves, their principal teachers are the spirits, in some cases the spirits of their forefathers.[2] We have seen that among the Lebed Tatars, the Yakut, and the Buryat, an old shaman is assisted in certain ceremonies by young men, sometimes nine in number. At the inauguration ceremony of a young shaman among the Yakut, an old shaman furnishes him for the occasion with a number of attendants, who may perhaps be regarded as his assistants,[3] while the old shaman himself delivers an address to him consisting partly of mythological and mantic information, partly of precepts as to how he is to conduct himself in his new calling.[4] A similar ceremony takes place at the investiture of a Buryat shaman,[5] when the young shaman receives detailed injunctions from an older shaman as to how he is to comport himself, especially in his professional relations with his fellow men. Miss Lindgren mentions[6] the interesting fact that a Tungus shamanka of her acquaintance, named Olga, after hearing the call of the spirits, had studied her profession thoroughly under an old shaman, whereas some untrained members of her tribe, also claiming shamanistic powers, only exercised them, so the shamanka said, when intoxicated. Professional jealousy might account in part for Olga's attitude. But there is reason to believe that a certain amount of special training is regarded as an indispensable qualification among the Tungus, and this is probably general among the Tatars also.

For the most part, however, the shaman claims to receive his knowledge and his power, not by his own efforts, or from his fellow men, but

[1] Radlov, *A.S.* II, p. 49 f.   [2] See Hildén, p. 132.

[3] The possibility of a different explanation suggests itself from early usage among the *bakshas*. See Castagné, p. 15.   [4] See Czaplicka, *A.S.* p. 184 f.

[5] *Ib.* p. 185 ff.   [6] *J.R.C.A.S.* XXII (1935), p. 221 ff.

by inspiration. His knowledge is not learned, but 'revealed', and covers the whole field of human experience and consciousness. It includes knowledge of the past, and the hidden present, as well as the future, and embraces historical and scientific matter, according to the standards of native 'learning', as well as all knowledge of the hidden present, all 'occult' knowledge. Perhaps the shaman's functions and powers are best described by himself, as we find them in one of the stories given by Castrén:

"'God has appointed that I must wander both beneath and upon the earth, and has bestowed on me such power that I can comfort and cheer the afflicted, and on the other hand I can cast down those who are too happy. The mind of those who are too much given to striving can I likewise change, so that they will love cheerful amusement. I am called Kögel-Khan and I am a shaman, who knows the future, the past, and everything which is taking place in the present, both above and below the earth.' 'Let us know', said Kanna Kalas, 'what our people are doing, far away in our own home; but if you do not tell the truth we will cut your head off.' The old man put on his shaman's dress, and began to shamanise. He shamanised and told all of them the whole and simple truth."[1]

It is not easy to illustrate from Tatar texts the shaman's claim to knowledge of the past through revelation, though in Polynesia we shall see that the seers are the chief repositories of historical and genealogical matter. In Siberia the elaborate and spectacular nature of the shaman's performance of dance, music and mimesis, coupled with the unfamiliarity of their language to most Western observers, has overshadowed the intellectual aspects of the seer's functions. These are nevertheless important, as we gather from the native oral texts of the poems and sagas in which they figure, or which are attributed to them. We have already referred (p. 146 above) to Radlov's statement that poetry and saga relating to the Heavens and to cosmogony and supernatural matters were largely obtained by him from the recitation of the shamans. And we have seen that precepts and didactic matter are recited at the inauguration of a new shaman among the Yakut and Buryat. Among the latter[2] the shamans are also said to be the chief preservers of narrative poetry, as well as of other songs. Tatar non-heroic sagas such as that of *The Two Princes*, and poems such as *Kara Tygan Khan and Suksagal Khan*, represent the seer as maintaining his prestige by his

[1] Castrén, IV, p. 256.
[2] Sandschejew, *Anthropos* (1927), p. 306.

ability to excel in knowledge of elementary (native) natural science or natural philosophy, and the skilled use of poetic diction. The use of a traditional poetical diction fills a large place in the equipment of a Yakut shaman, whose poetical vocabulary is said to comprise some 12,000 words, as compared with 4000 words only in daily usage.[1] The free introduction of the mantic catalogue in the recitations of the black shamanka in the poem *Joloi* indicates the importance attached to ordered knowledge, both geographical and ethnographical, by men and women who, whatever the limitations of their knowledge, must certainly be regarded as the intellectual leaders of their community.

There remains to be considered another form of literature which appears to be practised exclusively by shamans—in modern life by professional shamans. The Tatars of the Altai and elsewhere possess something in the nature of dramatic literature, or rather dramatic monologue. This genre includes to a limited extent some of the literary forms already considered, such as hymns and prayers, blessings, precepts, and other forms already associated with the shaman. In the dramatic monologue, however, these are associated or connected together by the shaman in an ordered sequence of an ambitious artistic character and considerable dramatic skill.

The subjects are religious in all cases, and represent the journey of the shaman, sometimes to the realm of Erlik Khan, the god of the Underworld and of the dead, sometimes to the upper regions, the several superimposed planes of Heaven, even to Ülgen himself, the god of one of the highest Heavens.[2] On these journeys the shaman represents himself in his recital as riding variously on the back of a goose, or a horse, and as generally accompanied, at least for a part of his journey, by one or more companions. The journey is frequently represented as long and difficult, and the companions feel tired and flag by the way, but the shaman helps and encourages them till they finally reach their goal. He then returns alone, rejoiced to be once more in the world. It would seem that the true emphasis of the dramatic monologue lies on the safe conveyance of the shaman's companions to their goal. The shaman himself is but the guide or emissary, like Hermes Psychopompos.

The texts of these religious dramas consist wholly of songs and exclamations. They are sung exclusively by one shaman, who, however, changes his voice mimetically to represent different persons and even animals. The songs are accompanied by dramatic action and much

[1] Stadling, p. 130.
[2] On Ülgen's claim to supremacy, see p. 82 above, and footnotes.

dancing, and the whole is performed to a highly developed and sympathetic accompaniment of the large shaman tambourine. The performance is long and elaborate, and the songs are at least partially extempore, the shaman being the composer as well as the reciter of his score, and also minstrel, actor, and dancer in one.

To this end he makes use of certain stimulants, such as intoxicating drink, and tobacco. He indulges in a long period of silence before beginning a performance, during which the audience assist him by their silence in his task of thinking away his material surroundings, and of concentrating on spiritual matters. All shamans wear a special costume when performing, which is generally made in the semblance of a bird, or less commonly of some animal. The form varies considerably, but generally consists of special boots, hat, and coat, all decorated with or resembling birds' feathers. Other accessories are also common. Almost invariably the shaman carries a drum or tambourine and a drum stick, which play an all important part in his performance. Often the costume is hung about with little iron pendants, or with coloured handkerchiefs, which swing freely as he dances. The tribal sacrifice performed annually by the shaman of the Altai Tatars requires a large number of other accessories amounting almost to a scenario. In general the principal part of a shaman's performance takes place in the *yurt* and at night. Sometimes, however, it takes place out of doors in summer.

One of the fullest and most important accounts of a great *kamlanie*, as a shaman performance is called in the Altai, is the abridged version given by Radlov from that published by the missionary Verbitski in the *Tomsk Journal* of 1870, consisting of material obtained in 1840.[1] This is a great religious drama which forms a part of the greatest of all the tribal sacrifices among the Tatars of the Altai, that to Bai Ülgen, who is here said to dwell on the Golden Mountain in the sixteenth Heaven. The performance takes place in the evenings of two or three days, and large numbers of people are present. On the first evening the *kam*, as the shaman of the Altai is called, places a new *yurt* in a birch-thicket, and surrounds it by a fence as if to pen cattle. Inside the *yurt* stands a young birch-tree, the lower branches of which have been stripped off,

---

[1] Radlov has given a German translation of the greater part of Verbitski's text in the second volume of *Aus Siberien*, II, pp. 19–51. A summary of Radlov's version, including many of the songs, was published by Prof. Mikhailovsky of Moscow, and translated into English by O. Wardrop in the *Journal of the Anthropological Institute*, XXIV (1894), p. 74 ff., and an abridged version is also given by Czaplicka in *A.S.* p. 298 ff.

and in the trunk of which nine notches (*tapty*) have been cut, to serve as foothold for the *kam* when he must climb the tree during the ceremony. A light-coloured horse, such as will be acceptable to Ülgen, is selected for the sacrifice, and a certain man is also selected by the *kam* to act as groom throughout the sacrifice. He is known as *bash-tutkan kiski* ('he who holds the head', i.e. of the horse), and the Altaians believe that his soul accompanies that of the horse into the presence of Bai Ülgen. Except the *kam* himself he is the only actor in this strange drama. The whole of the libretto, except the imitative or ventriloquial passages, is chanted in poetry.

The *kam* now enters the *yurt*, and, seating himself by the fire which has been kindled beside the birch-tree, he allows the smoke to envelop his tambourine. He then proceeds to summon the spirits individually, collecting them as they assemble in his tambourine. The words of the conjurations are quoted by Radlov, and constitute a series of songs; and as each spirit is caught in the tambourine the *kam* replies in a hollow stage voice, speaking as for the spirit: "*A kam ai*" ("Hail kam, here I am"). The *kam* now goes out of the *yurt* to a place where a goose has been made of cloth and stuffed with hay, and on this scarecrow he takes his seat, flapping both arms like wings,[1] as if he were flying through the air, and chanting as he flies:

> Below the white Heaven,
> Above the white clouds,
> Below the blue Heaven,
> Above the blue clouds,
> Rise up to Heaven, O bird.

Whereupon the *kam* replies, imitating the cackle of a goose:

> Ungai gak gak, ungai gak,
> Kaigai gak gak, kaigai gak.

And a considerable dialogue takes place between the goose and its rider, in which the shaman is the speaker throughout, though talking 'goose talk' in a 'goose voice'.

The object of the ride is to pursue and capture the soul of the *pura*, or sacrificial horse, which neighs "Myjak, myjak, myjak" on hearing the shaman's call, and the neighing is also done by the shaman. When at last the *pura* is captured and secured to a post in the pen, the shaman neighs, kicks, and plunges like a horse till the *pura* is quieted and

---

[1] One is instinctively reminded of the apparition of Indra riding on the eagle at the close of the Sanskrit play *Çakuntalā*.

fumigated with juniper ready for the sacrifice. The *kam* now dismisses his goose with the words:

> Take food from Sürö-Berg,
> Take drink from the White Milk Sea,
> Mother Goose, thou my cackler,
> Mother Bird, Kurgai Khan,
> Mother Bird, Engkai Khan;
> Press close upon the people,
> Call upon them, crying "Au, Au",
> Call them to you, crying "Jä, Jä".

After this the shaman proceeds in his own person to sacrifice the horse. The first part of the ceremony is at an end.

The most important part of the performance takes place on the second day, after sunset, when the *kam* enacts in his own person an entire religious drama, or ballet, representing his pilgrimage to conduct the *pura* to Bai Ülgen. As the fire burns brightly the *kam* first chants a blessing to the *bash-tutkan*, and then offers food and drink to the spirits, the 'lords of the tambourine', on behalf of the assembled household, chanting addresses to them as he does so. He also offers a rich present of clothing to Ülgen himself on behalf of the master of the household. It is interesting to note that the lord of the fire is regarded as the personified power of the family of the *yurt* providing the sacrifice.

> Take it, O Kaira Kan,[1]
> Three-headed Fire Mother,
> Four-headed Maiden Mother,
> When I call "Chok"[2]—bow.
> When I call "Mä"[3]—receive it.

The diction in which the *kam's* songs are couched is identical with that with which we are familiar from the narrative poems, the clothing being referred to as

> Gifts which no horse can carry,
> Which no man can lift,
> Garments with three-fold collars, etc.

The *kam* next proceeds to fumigate his drum, and now for the first time he puts on his shaman's dress and remains quietly beside the fire,

---

[1] See p. 82, footnote 2 above. He is said to be the originator of all existing things. See Hildén, p. 126.

[2] Among the Altai Tatars the word *chok* is the name of the libation, and is called out by the shaman during the sacrifice. See Radlov, *Wörterbuch*, *s.v.*

[3] The exclamation *mä* in Tatar means 'there!' 'take', 'accept'; *loc. cit.*

enveloped in smoke, after which he begins to beat his drum with measured strokes, summoning to him many spirits, reciting a separate invocation to each, and including an invocation to Bai Ülgen and his family. Towards the close of the invocation the *kam* invokes Merkyut, the bird of Heaven, concluding significantly with the words:

> Come to me singing,
> Come sporting to my right eye,
> Settle on my right shoulder.[1]

Various other ritual acts are performed by the *kam*, and at last begins the climax of his *kamlanie*, namely, his ascent to Heaven. This is a gradual process, for he mounts his *tapty* slowly, and indicates by recitation and pantomime that each step represents one of the superimposed horizontal planes of Heaven, each with its separate scenery, personnel, and experiences—all of which are described. To give verisimilitude and variety to his performance various episodes are introduced as the *kam* passes through the various superimposed Heavens. The *kara-kush*, a 'black bird' in the service of the *kam*,[2] is treated to a pipe of tobacco; the *kam* waters the *pura*, and imitates the horse drinking; he also sends his servant to course a hare; he interviews the great *jajuchi*, who foretells to him the future. It is interesting to note that the latter incident takes place in the fifth Heaven, while in the sixth the *kam* does honour to the moon; in the seventh, to the sun. In the eighth and ninth Heavens we have scenes enacted, prayers, prophecies, narratives, and blessings, etc. recited. The greater the power of the *kam*, the greater the number of Heavens through which he can penetrate—eleven, twelve, or even more —in some cases as many as sixteen. At last, when he has reached the limit of his power and knowledge, he calls upon Bai Ülgen himself, and, lowering his drum, and bowing humbly before him, he addresses him in a prayer. From Bai Ülgen the *kam* learns whether the sacrifice has been accepted, and receives prophecies relating to the weather and the harvest, and injunctions regarding sacrifice. The *kam's* ecstasy culminates in this last great scene, and he sinks down exhausted, while the *bash-tutkan* gently withdraws his drum and stick. For a time he is motionless, and silence reigns in the *yurt*, after which the *kam* seems to awaken as if from sleep. He rubs his eyes, smoothes his hair, spreads out his hands, wrings the perspiration from his shirt, and looks around

---

[1] Cf. pp. 87, 110 above.
[2] Cf. the gigantic black bird which helps Kogutei, p. 100 f. above.

him and greets those who are present, as after a long journey. The *kamlanie* is over.[1]

A comparison of this account with the narrative poems of the Abakan Tatars shows that the visits of heroes and heroines to the Heavens resemble closely these journeys of actual shamans to the abode of Bai Ülgen.[2] The closest parallels are, however, to be found among the Yakut[3] and the neighbouring non-Turkish peoples, such as the Yenisei Ostyak, and the Yurak.[4] These ceremonies are so close to those of the Tatar shaman that though space will not permit of more than the briefest reference here, it will be obvious from the most cursory glance that they are valuable as supplementing our knowledge of the Tatar ceremonies.

In the old days, say the Yakut, there were shamans who really did ascend to the sky, and the crowd of spectators were able to see the sacrificial animal floating on the clouds, while the shaman's drum sped after it, followed by the shaman in his mantic coat.[5] In the same way the feat of mounting to Heaven on horseback is attributed to a great Mongol shaman of the time of Jenghiz Khan.[6]

A reference to the visit of the Yenisei Ostyak to the sky may give us some idea of the concluding portion of the Altai shaman's visit to Bai Ülgen, though in Radlov's account this part of the latter ceremony is only briefly touched on. The Ostyak shaman sings that he is climbing to Heaven by means of a rope[7] let down to him, pushing aside the stars which block his way. He sails in the sky in a boat, and finally descends to earth with such rapidity that the wind blows through him. After this he makes a journey to the Underworld, assisted on his course by the aid of 'winged devils'.[8] Again we are told that among the Ostyak and the

---

[1] For recent though far less detailed accounts of shaman ceremonies among the Altai Tatars, and the sacrifice of the horse among the Lebed Tatars, who are their near neighbours, see Hildén, p. 138 ff.

[2] For a fuller treatment of this subject the reader may refer to Chadwick, *J.R.A.I.* LXVI (1936), p. 291 ff.

[3] Sieroszewski, *R.H.R.* (1902), p. 331 f.

[4] There appears to be a certain dramatic appeal in the performances of Tungus Shamans also. See Lindgren, *N.R.T.* p. 19 f.; cf. also Shirokogoroff, *Shamanism*.

[5] See Czaplicka, *A.S.* p. 238.   [6] See Köprülüzade, p. 17.

[7] We may compare the means by which the Polynesian heroes rise to Heaven (see Part II below).

[8] Mikhailovsky, *J.A.I.* XXIV, p. 67. Mikhailovsky was a professor in the University of Moscow. His two articles on shamanism, to which we make constant reference, are based on information derived from Russian travellers, and are very useful as affording information not otherwise easily accessible.

Yurak the shaman rises to the sky and sings of his sojourn in varying types of country, among roses, and again among larches on the tundra, where his grandsire formerly made his tambourine—an interesting reference to the belief in the inheritance of the mantic gift from an ancestor in the second generation. He falls asleep among purple clouds, and finally descends to earth by means of a river,[1] and then, after doing honour to the heavenly deity, the sun, moon, trees, and beasts of the earth—in this order—he prays for long life, happiness, etc.

With these accounts of the journeys of shamans to the Heavens we may compare the accounts of the Buryat investiture of a new shaman and the ceremonial at the great sacrifice of the horse. The latter takes place under circumstances closely resembling those of the Altai ceremony, except that from Curtin's account of the Buryat ceremony it appears that the shaman does not himself deal the death-blow to the horse, but delegates this task to another. For the Buryat sacrificial ceremonial a large tree is planted in the middle of the *yurt*, its top projecting through the smoke hole. To this top are fastened silk strings representing the colours of the rainbow. The strings are carried to a tree called 'the pillar',[2] at a little distance, and tied to its highest branch. Some of the shamans go to the tops of the trees and make offerings to the gods from there. "In old times", adds our informant, "there were such mighty shamans that they could walk on the silk strings connecting the top of the tree which comes up through the smoke-hole of the *yurt* with the great birch-tree outside; this was called 'walking on the rainbow'."[3] In a similar procedure, which takes place at the investiture of a Buryat shaman, we are further told that the large tree planted in the *yurt* represents the porter god who allows the shaman ingress into Heaven. Red and blue ribbons are stretched from its summit to a row of other birches outside: "This is a symbolical representation of the path of the shaman to the spirit world."[4] The shaman climbs the birch-tree inside the *yurt*, and also at least one of those outside, sometimes leaping

---

[1] We may compare the procedure of the seeress of the Sea Dyaks, who conducts her party of souls to the Underworld in a boat along a river (cf. p. 490 below).

[2] One instinctively thinks of the Irminsul, the sacred pillar of the Old Saxons, which is described as *universalis columna quasi sustinens omnia* (*Translatio S. Alexandri*, cap. 3. *Mon. Germ.* II, p. 676).

[3] Curtin, p. 108. With this account of Siberian ritual it is interesting to compare the Polynesian sagas and poetry connected with such heroes as Tawhaki. See e.g. p. 298 f. below, and see also p. 338.

[4] See Czaplicka, *A.S.* p. 188.

from summit to summit along the entire row, claiming thus to pass from one Heaven to the next, till from the top of the last he claims to reach the highest Heaven to which he can attain. It is easy to see how this symbolism has given rise to the statements that in the past the shaman could be seen in the sky.

We are inclined to suspect a reminiscence of some such ceremony as the Altai shaman's journey to the presence of Bai Ülgen in a passage in the Uigur poem *Kudatku Bilik*, which was written in the eleventh century in eastern Turkestan. The passage to which we refer is the dream related by a certain Otkürmish to the prince Kün-Tokty-Elik.[1] Otkürmish relates how in a dream he saw before him a high ladder with fifty steps.[2] He climbed up these steps to the top of the ladder, which, according to the version given by Vambéry, amounted to seven stages. At the top of the ladder a female attendant or guardian gave him a drink of water, and, refreshed by the draught, he was able to make his way up to Heaven, though he was unconscious, "perhaps from the effort".

This interesting passage seems to have given some difficulty to the translators, and several points still remain obscure. One naturally thinks of the vision of Jacob's Ladder seen also in a dream.[3] But the closest affinities of the passage seem to lie with the practices and beliefs of the Altai shamans, and we think it likely that a closer study of these might throw light on the obscure passages in the Uigur text.

The second class of religious drama of the Altai represents a journey of the shaman to the abode of the dead, the realm of Erlik Khan. Among the Yenisei Ostyak we have seen (p. 204) that this second performance sometimes follows immediately on the visit to Heaven.

Potanin[4] has preserved a summary narrative of one of these dramas which he obtained from the Russian missionary Chivalkov. It represents the journey of a shaman of the Altai Tatars, who is convoying a number of dead souls to the Underworld, to the region of Erlik Khan, the god of Darkness. This work has not been accessible to us, and we are only able to give an account of the performance from the summaries pub-

---

[1] Vambéry, *U.S.* p. 158; Radlov, *K.B.* p. 501.

[2] The type of ladder referred to is no doubt that still in general use in Siberia to-day, which consists of a single pole with steps projecting alternately up each side, like a fir-tree stripped and trimmed, with the stumps of a few branches left on—somewhat like the steps on our own telegraph poles.

[3] Genesis xxviii. 12.

[4] Potanin IV, p. 64 ff.

lished by M. A. Czaplicka[1] and Mikhailovsky.[2] Unfortunately none of the songs are quoted, and very few of the actual words of the shaman. Enough is given, however, to show that the performance is an elaborate one, the vivid details of which show a close analogy to many passages in the narrative poems of the Abakan Tatars relating the supernatural journeys of heroes.

In his monologue the shaman describes his travels, beginning from the place where he is performing. The road runs southward over the Altai, and then over the Chinese land with its yellow sand, over a yellow steppe "across which a magpie cannot fly". The functional nature of the shaman's aesthetic performance is made clear by his own words: "With songs we shall traverse them", he cries, and the company mount cheerfully, and accompany him in song. A wan-coloured steppe follows, "over which no raven has ever flown", and again the *kam* encourages his followers by his songs. After the steppe comes a mountain so high that the *kam* breathes heavily as he reaches the summit. He does not fail to point out to his followers the bones of many unfortunate *kams* who have failed to make the ascent successfully: "On the mountains men's bones lie heaped up in rows; the mountains are piebald with the bones of horses." It is in such passages as these that we see the traditional geography and general setting of the poems. The difficulties and hardships encountered by the shaman and his cortège remind us forcibly of those encountered by all travellers over the deserts and mountains of eastern Central Asia, from Fa-hien to von le Coq, Fleming and Maillart.[3]

Having ascended the mountain, the cortège rides through a hole in the ground which leads to the Underworld, "the jaws of the earth". A sea must be crossed by a hair, and again the shaman gains credit to himself by pointing out the bones of many fallen shamans at the bottom of the sea. Once across, the *kam* makes his way to the abode of Erlik Khan, which bears a close resemblance to a Buddhist monastic

---

[1] Czaplicka, *A.S.* p. 240f.   [2] *J.A.I.* xxiv, p. 72f.

[3] The Chinese Buddhist pilgrim Fa-hien, writing of the Taklamakan Desert c. A.D. 400, describes it as containing many evil demons, and adds that there are "no flying birds above, no roaming beasts below....It would be impossible to know the way but for dead men's decaying bones, which show the direction." (See *Travels of Fa-hien*, in Beal's *Buddhist Records of the Western World*, London, 1884, I, p. xxiv.) Three centuries later another Chinese pilgrim, Huien-Tsiang, also mentions that the passes of the Hindu Kush were so high that the birds could not fly over the summits. (See Beal, *Budd. Records*, etc. II, p. 285 f., and see further le Coq, *Buried Treasures*, p. 154 ff.)

settlement, with its great dogs, its porter, by no means averse to presents, and finally the great khan himself. The *kam* with admirable dramatic instinct goes through the ceremonial of an audience with the great potentate, who is depicted as a typical oriental, haughty, despotic, but easily overcome with wine and presents. Comic relief is afforded by a telling representation by the shaman of the drunken god, who is finally induced to give his blessing, and even imparts knowledge of the future to the *kam*, who returns home joyfully, glad to be safely away from the abodes of the dead. He returns to earth, not on the horse which had carried him to the Underworld, but riding on a goose— doubtless symbolical of a dead soul[1]—and he walks about the *yurt* on tiptoe as if he were flying, imitating a goose's cackle. The *kamlanie* comes to an end, the tambourine is taken out of his hands by one of those present, and the *kam* rubs his eyes as if awakening from sleep. He is asked what kind of a ride he has had, and how he got on. And he replies: "I have had a successful journey; I was well received."

Sieroszewski has recorded much of the libretto of a Yakut shaman called in to heal the sick,[2] which resembles in its general features the preceding account of the Altai shaman's journey to the Underworld. Moreover, there can be no doubt that many of the *kamlanie* which have been briefly described by European eye-witnesses are similar, sometimes less elaborate, dramatic performances. Potanin witnessed a representation of a visit to the Underworld given by a young Altai shaman named Enchu,[3] and also a performance by a shamanka[4] which resembled that of Enchu in some important particulars which we cannot enter into here. Radlov witnessed a dramatic representation of a shaman's visit to the underworld which formed a part of a purification ceremony performed in a house on the fortieth day after the death of one of its inmates. In Radlov's account the *kam* represents himself as conducting the soul of the dead person to its last abode in the realm of Erlik, and mimics the voice of the dead person—in this case a woman—in a falsetto squeak. He also holds converse with the dead relatives of the deceased who are already in the abode of Erlik. Radlov tells us that the wild scene, with the magic illumination of the fire and the shaman's dance, made such a strong impression on him that for a long time he followed the shaman with his eyes, and wholly and completely forgot his surroundings. Even the Altaians, he adds, "were moved by the wild scene; their pipes

[1] See *J.A.I.* xxiv, p. 72 f.   [2] *R.H.R.* (1902), p. 331 f.
[3] Mikhailovsky, p. 71 f.; Czaplicka, *A.S.* p. 240.
[4] Mikhailovsky, p. 72.

sank to the ground, and perfect silence reigned for a quarter of an hour ".[1] Stadling[2] and Sieroszewski were equally impressed by the art which the Yakut shaman put into his performance. The latter in particular calls attention to the literary excellence of the performances of the most proficient among them, the skill with which they make silence alternate with strange cries, the telling vibrations of the voice, now imploring, now menacing, by turns harmonious and terrifying; the thundering of the tambourine, which is made to correspond exactly with the mood of the moment; the startling and skilled use of poetic diction, and figurative language, the expressive turns of phrase, the bold metaphors, which would render translation impossible.[3]

Visits to the realm of Erlik closely resembling those of the Yakut shaman in his capacity of physician are also made by the shamans of the Buryat, where again one of our best accounts is of a shaman called in to heal a sick person. The shaman seeks the soul of the patient, which is believed to have left the body. He searches in every part of the world— in the deep woods, on the steppes, at the bottom of the sea; and having found it, he restores it to its body.[4] If it cannot be found in the world, the shaman must seek it in the Underworld, making a long and toilsome journey thither, and offering costly presents to Erlik. Sometimes the shaman informs the patient that Erlik demands another soul in exchange for his, and ensnares the soul of a friend of the patient while the owner is asleep. The soul turns into a lark; the shaman in his *kamlanie* takes the form of a hawk, catches the soul, and hands it over to Erlik, who frees the soul of the sick man.[5] The ceremony cannot fail to recall many poems of the Abakan Tatars in which the soul of a hero is similarly pursued throughout every region of the Universe, and in every element by an 'earth hero', a black man from the Underworld, who acts as an emissary of Erlik.

Visits to the abodes of Erlik and Ülgen such as we have just described by no means exhaust the dramatic presentations of the Tatar shamans. Among the Yakut sacrifices are offered to the guardian spirit of huntsmen and fishermen, and these are said to be accompanied by dramatic performances given by the shaman who, in acting the part of Baryllakh,

---

[1] Radlov, *A.S.* II, p. 53 f.　　　　　　　　　　[2] Stadling, p. 134.

[3] *R.H.R.* (1902), p. 325.

[4] We may compare Shirokogoroff's statement (*Shamanism*) of the Tungus shaman, whose soul is said to be able to "go away to visit the Heavens, or distant places on the earth, in order to find the spirits who caused the malady or misfortune".

[5] So Potanin; see Mikhailovsky, p. 69 f.

the spirit of the chase, is said to laugh and smirk.[1] The Yakut, we are told, represent this spirit as always giggling and fond of laughter.[2]

Performances which resemble in their main features those of the shaman are commonly given also by the *bakshas* of the western Turks. The important work of Castagné, published in 1930, who spent eighteen years among the Turko-Mongol peoples of Central and western Asia, has added much to our knowledge of the *bakshas*, and enabled us to see more clearly than was possible from the works of earlier scholars[3] the close connection which exists between their mental equipment and that of the shamans of the eastern Turks and of the peoples of northern Siberia. In particular we would emphasise here the important part which poetry and the music of the *kobuz*, the *baksha's* stringed instrument, play in the performance. The *baksha* has no drum, but the articulate part of his performance, which forms the greater part of it, is chanted throughout in poetry, and is largely accompanied by the *kobuz*, and it appears to be exclusively, or almost exclusively, by the music of this instrument in the hands of the *baksha* himself that the latter brings himself into a state of ecstasy. It is interesting to note that in Castagné's accounts of the performances of a number of men of this class there is no mention of the use of stimulants, such as tobacco or other stimulating fumes, or of intoxicating drinks. The latter is, of course, only what we should expect from Mohammedans. The stimulus and excitement appears to be produced wholly by the use of the musical instrument,[4] which is said to be endowed with magic power,[5] and much time and pains are devoted to the art of performing on its strings.[6]

In the elaborate *baksha* performance about to be described it is interesting to note that in some cases the *jinns* themselves are addressed as carrying musical instruments—one his *kobuz*,[7] another his *musette*,[8] covered with fine velvet. The importance in which music is held by these mantic persons is aptly illustrated by the story of a famous *baksha*

---

[1] Mikhailovsky, p. 96. We may compare the portion of the ecstasy of the *baksha* recorded by Koustanaiev, Castagné, p. 103.

[2] Mikhailovsky, *loc. cit.*

[3] Much material has long been available for the study of the *bakshas* in Russian libraries, but this has, unfortunately, been inaccessible to most of us. Many valuable references to publications on this subject in Russian and Asiatic periodicals will be found in Castagné's work.

[4] Cf. Shirokogoroff, *Shamanism*, where the same effect is attributed to the drum of the Tungus shaman.

[5] Castagné, p. 67.   [6] *Ib.* p. 68.   [7] *Ib.* p. 83.

[8] *Ib.* p. 88. The *musette* is a kind of bagpipe. Musical proficiency is also ascribed in Tatar oral literature to Jelbägän. See Radlov, *Proben* I, p. 298, l. 103 ff.

of the past, named Khorkouth, who was regarded as the founder of all the *bakshas*. He is said to have been at once a sorcerer, diviner, and musician, and to have taught his people the art of singing and playing to the *kobuz*. He was also the originator of a particular kind of epic poetry. When he realised that his death was near, his first act was to make a new *kobuz* for himself, after which he divided his time between reciting prayers and verses from the Koran, and singing to the accompaniment of his *kobuz*. After his death, his *kobuz* was laid on his grave, and tradition asserts that for many years it played plaintive music every Friday in memory of its master.[1]

From the point of view of oral literature, the most interesting accounts of *baksha* performances given by Castagné are those which relate to the healing of the sick. Castagné has published,[2] with French translations, a number of the invocations and songs chanted by the *bakshas* on such occasions, and one series which he gives in extenso, and which were recorded from the recitals of native Kazaks, enable us to see both the general character of such performances, and also their similarity to, and integral connection with, those of the Tatars of the Altai.

These performances open with the sacrifice of an animal, after which the *baksha* takes his *kobuz*, or sometimes a *domra*, or even a tambourine, in his hand, and entones a chant of great sadness.[3] The chant opens, as is to be expected, with a reference to the Koran, and proceeds to a series of invocations to God, to Adam and the Patriarchs, and finally passes to a series of invocations to Saitan and the *jinns*. It is in the latter that the close connection between the *bakshas* and the shamans is most clearly seen, for many of the *jinns* are the spirits whose acquaintance we have already made as belonging to the realm of Erlik Khan, and as spiritual beings hostile to the heroes and heroines of the narrative poems. Here again we meet with the great black bird Kara Kus, and with the 'yellow maiden', Sary Kus, and a number of other spirits, who are addressed under the guise of horses, dromedaries, serpents, and even tigers, and sometimes as spirits mounted on such creatures, as we have seen Kara Chach mounted on *Jelmogus* in *Joloi* (cf. p. 87 above). The recital is broken from time to time by the voices of the audience and the *baksha's* assistants, who, by his invitation, add their own interjections by way of corroborating the *baksha's* invitations to the various spirits.

It is clear that throughout the invocation the potent factor in assembling the spirits to the assistance of the *baksha* is his music.

[1] Castagné, p. 67. [2] *Ib.* p. 70 ff.
[3] The text and musical score of this chant are given by Castagné, *loc. cit.*

"Voilà", he cries, "la manière que j'emploie pour appeler les djinns...
Qu'est-il advenu de ma voix,
Qu'elle ne puisse accompagner mon kobouz?
J'ai pris en main mon kobouz en bois de sapin,
Et me replie comme un serpent d'eau.
Mon kobouz ne se casse point,
Mon âme malheureuse ne connaît pas de repos."

And he goes on to sing of how the *jinn* took possession of him at the age
of fifteen, and became his friend at the age of twenty—the intervening
period evidently the length of time required for the training and
education of the *baksha*. He also makes it clear to us that his 'call' to be
a *baksha* was not of his own seeking, but even against his own will; and
further that the 'call' was integrally connected with the art of minstrelsy.

Il (i.e. the *djinn*) m'a décidé, malgré moi, à m'occuper d'une affaire;
Il m'a rivé à cet arbre déjà sec (i.e. the *kobuz*).

These autobiographical details again remind us of the recital of the
black *shamanka*, Kara Chach, and are especially interesting as coming
immediately before the height of his frenzy, when the *jinns* are believed
to take possession of him.

At this point the *baksha* begins to demonstrate the supernatural
condition to which he has attained, by walking on red hot tools, placing
lighted tapers in his mouth, beating himself, or the patient, with clubs
or other heavy objects, without apparently feeling or inflicting pain.
This is held to be a certain test of shamanistic 'virtue', the lesser *bakshas*
feeling pain in proportion to their lack of supernatural achievement.[1]
Once more he takes his *kobuz*, and invokes a further series of destructive
jinns, mostly having animal forms, after which he waves his hands in all
directions, making it appear to the onlookers that everything towards
which he waves his hands, or points, breaks or is destroyed. Working
himself up into a frenzy of excitement, the *baksha* rushes around the
tent, imitating 'with remarkable precision' the movements and the cries
of various animals and birds, in whose guise the spirits evoked by the
baksha have come to the assembly. Taking his *kobuz* he again begins to
play. Music and song become more and more rapid, the more rapid his

---

[1] Castagné, p. 94. We may compare the interesting statement made by Shirokogoroff of the Tungus shaman. "They can...jump as high as four or five feet,
in spite of age and their very heavy costume (sometimes about eighty pounds);
they can cut their hands and faces in such a way that recovery takes a very short
time; they can burn their hands and faces almost without leaving traces the following
day....All these experiments have no serious consequences so long as they are
made during ecstasy." (*Shamanism.*)

movements. He foams at the mouth, and his face assumes a savage expression, while he slashes his face with a knife without leaving any apparent trace of cuts. A final chant in which the assembled spirits are dismissed to their own sphere closes this remarkable scene.

Castagné lays stress on the elaborate technique of the *baksha's* performance, both in regard to his mimetic gifts, and his musical skill. The *baksha* himself evidently regards his *kobuz* as his most important accessory.

De la baguette d'une ulmaire
Est fait l'archet de mon kobouz;
De la peau fine d'un "djelmaïa"[1]
Est orné mon kobouz, tout comme un petit miroir.
Des crins d'un bon coursier
Est fait l'archet de mon kobouz.[2]

It will be seen that the shaman and the *baksha* combine within their own persons the functions of priest and prophet. Their prophetic vision is presented in an artistic production which combines music, poetry, the dance, and mimetic performance—in fact a synthesis of all the arts, resembling a ballet. The shaman or the *baksha*, as the case may be, is the sole or almost the sole performer in this ballet, which is of a most exacting character, and makes the heaviest possible demands simultaneously on all his intellectual and artistic faculties. The entire performance, while following a traditional outline, or a traditional channel of thought and traditional artistic style, is nevertheless extempore. It seems clear that just as the heroic poet extemporises not only the actual words, but even to some extent the form of his narrative during the actual recitation, so the shaman, within a framework prescribed by traditional theology, extemporises his dramatic songs, varying his motifs, and drawing from experience, personal or borrowed. His diction is identical with that of the heroic poems. Phrases and descriptions and groups of lines, and much of the imagery, are familiar to us from the narrative poems. But the actual process of composition takes place during the recital.[3] It is easy to see, therefore, why, when once the performance is over, the shaman is unable to recall the words which he has spoken.

[1] According to Castagné's note the *djelmaïa* would seem to be some kind of camel or dromedary. See, however, p. 84 above.   [2] Castagné, p. 92.

[3] According to Sandschejew, himself a Buryat of famous shaman stock, and trained in early life for the profession of shaman, the question has already been mooted in the Buryat press of adopting the shaman 'with his aesthetic gifts, and his power of improvisation', into the state theatre. See *Anthropos* (1927), p. 576.

The extent to which the seer acts and speaks as a voluntary agent during the manifestations of his divine inspiration is an important question which cannot be regarded as settled. The question is one of very wide bearings, and affects a large part of the world. Ultimately it is a matter of psychology. But even from literary evidence it seems clear that at certain times, and in certain communities, the seer speaks and perhaps 'composes' a coherent libretto in a state of mind in which there appears to be little or no consciousness of his material surroundings. This we shall see to be the case in certain communities of Polynesia and Africa, and the ancient literatures of Europe know of similar phenomena. In northern Siberia the evidence for this dissociated condition of the seer is particularly strong.[1] Among the Tatars also it is undoubtedly found. Radlov tells us[2] that it is on record that even the *knout* of the Cossack has failed to arouse the Tatar shaman from his trance.[3]

On the other hand, in the great public performances at least, and probably to a great extent in Tatar performances generally, the procedure characteristic of the dissociated condition has crystallised into a ritual. This would be difficult to prove, and space hardly allows of discussion of the matter here, especially as the question does not directly concern literature. One of us has, however, discussed the matter more fully elsewhere.[4] It is difficult for us to believe that the extremely elaborate nature of the shaman's performance, especially at the great tribal gatherings, could be achieved save by a mind in full possession of all its faculties, and with those faculties heightened and sharpened to their fullest pitch. While the traditional manner of ecstasy still governs the Altai shaman's manifestation of inspiration, his actual performance would seem to be largely artificially regulated, and intellectually controlled.[5]

Many of the motifs in the literary traditions of the Tatars which have come to light in the preceding survey, and many of the corresponding

---

[1] See Czaplicka, *A.S. passim*.   [2] *A.S.* II, p. 57.

[3] An excellent parallel is furnished in *The Veddas* (p. 209 ff.) by the Seligmans, in which an elaborate mimetic ceremonial is performed by a seer who is undoubtedly in a condition of almost complete dissociation. If we have understood the text aright, however, it does not appear that the 'shaman' composes or recites elaborate invocations during his actual possession. The recital appears to precede the fits of possession in every case where they are given by the 'shaman' himself.

[4] *J.R.A.I.* LXVI (1936), p. 101.

[5] In this connection I must refer to a remarkably interesting observation made by Miss Lindgren, who has witnessed a number of performances by Tungus

elements in the religious beliefs and practices of their shamans, as the latter have been briefly indicated in the present chapter, are to be found widespread also in the literary traditions of other peoples of Central Asia. Mention has already been made of certain traces of these beliefs and themes among the ancient Uigurs, nor would it be difficult to multiply these instances if space permitted; and we hope to do so more fully at a future date. We may, however, call attention here to an important parallel, both in form and content, to the poems and sagas, and the religious observances of the Tatars and neighbouring peoples, which is to be found in the narratives and sagas of a certain Kesar, or Gesar, King of Ling. These are current today in both oral and written form throughout Mongolia, Tibet, and Ladakh.[1] The Cycle, in its present form, has been thickly overlaid with Buddhist ideas and motifs, and we are not in a position to say at present how far some at least of these may have formed an original element of the whole. But the main outlines of the life-story of Kesar in the most widely known versions are undoubtedly heroic. It is especially interesting, therefore, to find that, like the Kara-Kirghiz hero Bolot, Kesar goes to the Underworld in boyhood as a part of his initiation, and here also the entrance to the Underworld is through a hole or cave in the rocks on the summit of a mountain. Like Bolot he is guided on his way by his tutelary spirit, a woman (*Manene*, lit. 'grandmother'), who rides, like Kara Chach (cf. p. 87 above), on an animal. And, like Kara Chach also, this tutelary spirit appears to Kesar in the Underworld, and lends him assistance against a host of monster foes. Like Bolot, Kesar returns triumphant to the

and Mongol shamans. During the dance one of these *shamankas* wore a costume to which forty pounds of metal were attached, largely in the form of bronze mirrors and bells attached to the dress. The dance takes place within the constricted space between the fire and the members of the audience, squatting round the inside of the walls of the hut, and the shamanka's movements appear abandoned and 'wild'. Yet although the pendants swing freely within an inch or two of the faces of the audience, Miss Lindgren assures us that she never once saw anyone struck during the dances. It is difficult to believe that such skill has not been acquired by long practice in a normal condition of mind, or that it can be mechanically applied by a virtual automaton in a condition of dissociation. Shirokogoroff insists that the Tungus shaman 'cannot let himself fall into a nervous fit' while shamanising, and also that the shaman must be a healthy person (*Shamanism*); and Castagné points out (p. 99) that during the ecstasy of the Kazak *baksha*, while he is flinging himself about with closed eyes, he can nevertheless lay his hands on anything he may happen to require.

[1] A general account of the Cycle as it is current in Tibet will be found in David-Neel and Yongden, *Gesar*. For details of the various forms and their distribution the reader is referred to the works of Francke cited on p. 48, footnote above, and p. 220 below. Cp. also p. 218, footnote 2 below.

world of men, bearing with him, like many of the heroes of the Abakan poems, the food of immortality and the water of life. Like the shamans of the Altai, he mounts to Heaven on the back of a bird, in order to secure healing herbs for his people. Many other features might be cited, and in particular we would call attention to the autobiographical character of the narrative, so characteristic of Tatar narrative poetry and of the Russian *byliny*, and so alien to early Teutonic and Greek heroic poetry in general. The circumstances in which the narrative poems of Kesar are recited also seem to resemble closely those of the recitation of the Tatar nomads of the mountains and steppes of east Central Asia. The wide popularity of the story and its distribution throughout a large part of eastern Central Asia suggest, of course, that it may have a long history behind it. The hero is claimed both by Mongols and by Tibetans as a native of their districts, and it is fair to suppose that the stories now associated with Kesar were probably well known in eastern Turkestan before the downfall of the Uigurs.

It may be pointed out further that certain features of the shaman's ceremonies have manifest affinities with customs and traditions current today among the civilisations of Central and southern Asia. In particular we may mention that the aerial adventures of Tatar, Yakut, Tungus, and Buryat shamans can hardly be wholly independent of such forms of oriental dramatic art as we see in the aerial puppet shows witnessed by Rock at the great annual Butter Festival in the lamasery of Choni in the province of Kansu on the eastern border of Tibet, where Buddhist deities were made to play their part in a realistic representation of the various regions of the Heavens, the whole being worked by means of wires stretched across the courtyard overhead.[1] Even closer analogies are to be found in the New Year and other important ceremonies held in the neighbourhood of the Potala Palace at Lhasa, such, for example, as the ceremony of the 'Flying Spirits', in which a man slides with the speed of lightning down a rope stretched from a pinnacle of the lofty palace to a *stupa* in the courtyard, bringing with him blessings from Heaven to the people below.[2] The dramatic form of the

[1] J. Rock, *N.G.M.* (Nov. 1928), p. 612; *I.L.N.* (Oct. 12th, 1929), p. 639. Rock's account may help to explain certain obscure statements made by native informants about their shamans of the past, such as that of the Yakut, who say that in the past their shamans really did ascend to the sky, and could be seen floating on the clouds. (See p. 204 above.)

[2] For some account of these ceremonies see Waddell, *Lhasa*, p. 397f.; Macdonald, p. 202ff. For a similar ceremony at the lamasery of Tashilhunpo, see Sarat Chandra Das, p. 77, and for one in Nepal, see Moorcroft, I, p. 17.

shaman's monologue can hardly be independent of dramas of the adventures of the human soul such as the play of Langdarma, held annually
at the same time in Lhasa, in which, among many other incidents, good
and evil spirits are represented as waging battle for the soul of man.[1]

Moreover, it is strange that the journey of the shaman and his caravan
of souls should take them south over the deserts of Chinese Turkestan,
over the lofty mountains which border it on the southern frontier, and
finally that they should enter the Underworld by a hole in the ground
after making the ascent. In detail the regions which are reached through
this hole or cave bear a striking resemblance to the Buddhist cave temples
of Turkestan, Korea, and Tibet, which in their turn are, of course, later
forms of the types of caves familiar to us from India, especially those of
Gandhara in Kashmir and of Ajanta on the Deccan. It may be pointed
out further that the subterranean sojourn of the shaman in Erlik's
realm, as well as of many heroes and heroines of the non-heroic poems,
calls to mind the ceremony of the 'Scapegoat', held annually in more
than one place in Tibet today,[2] and referred to in Chinese sources
already in the eighteenth century.[3] Here we see a man bearing the sins
of the people chased into a cave or chamber of horrors, where he must
sojourn for a time, and where the entire mise-en-scène, the entire
concrete paraphernalia, and the horrors which he must encounter,
remind us forcibly of those depicted in Erlik's realm in the recitations
of the shamans, and in the narrative poems, such as those of *Kara Par*
(p. 94 above). In general, in fact, Erlik's realm may be seen on the
walls of many a cave temple explored by Stein, Grünvedel, and Le Coq,
as well as in those farther afield, such as Korea.

The literary themes and religious observances which we are studying
are by no means new, nor are they confined to the Continent of Asia.
We have seen that among the Tatars visits of men and women to the
Heavens and the Underworld can be traced back to the time of Jenghiz
Khan, and perhaps to the ancient Uigurs. Such visits were already well
known in literary circles in Japan early in the eighth century in connection with the native (*not* Chinese) mythology, and with the ancient
religious shrines of Izumo and Yamato.[4] Assyrian narrative poetry

---

[1] Waddell, *Lamaism*[2], p. 516; Gompertz, p. 202f.; Macdonald, p. 214; Knight,
p. 201ff.; cf. further Rock, *N.G.M.* (Nov. 1928), p. 606.
[2] Waddell, *Lhasa*, p. 512f.; Macdonald, p. 213; Sarat Chandra Das, p. 252.
[3] Rockhill, *J.R.A.S.* (1891), p. 221.
[4] We may refer to the stories given in the Japanese chronicle known as the
Kojiki, compiled in Japan from native sources in the early years of the eighth

relates the journey of the goddess Ishtar to the Underworld to rescue the soul of her son or husband Tammuz,[1] and similar motifs occur in Homer and in Greek mythology. The theme is therefore very ancient on the Eurasian Continent. On the other hand it is current today in a much wider area than this. We shall find it widespread in the oral literature of the Sea Dyaks of north Borneo and throughout Polynesia. Moreover, a modified cult of the sky-god is also known to Polynesian mythology, and to that of the Sea Dyaks of north Borneo, while among the latter the seeress still conducts parties of the dead to the Underworld in chanted song resembling that of the shamans of the Tatars and neighbouring peoples. It may be reasonable to hope, therefore, that future research will bring to light the centre of distribution of the themes and motifs which we can still trace at different points on the periphery and in the inner rings of a great circle. One naturally thinks of India. But we must postpone discussion of this matter till the Polynesian evidence has been considered.[2]

century. This work has been translated into English by B. H. Chamberlain as a supplement to Vol. x of *T.A.S.J.* (1883); and Book I, which contains the story in question, has also been translated by Florenz into German. See List of Abbreviations below. For further references, see Chadwick, *J.R.A.I.* LX (1930), p. 428 ff.

[1] See the metrical fragment of the story inscribed on the clay tablet from Nineveh, *British Museum Guide to the Babylonian and Assyrian Antiquities* (1908), p. 44.

[2] In addition to the works relating to Kesar or Gesar cited on p. 215, see also an article by N. Poppe, 'O Nekoterykh Novykh Glavakh "Gesar Khana"', in the *Festschrift for Oldenburg* published at Leningrad, 1927. We regret that this work has not been accessible to us.

LIST OF ABBREVIATIONS[1]

NOTE. In this list, and in all those which follow, books and periodicals are referred to under the names of the authors, as these are printed in the right-hand column. In the text above, the author's name is followed by one or more prominent words of the title of the book, or the initial letters of the most prominent words forming the title of the book or periodical referred to. Where one work of an author is referred to exclusively, or almost exclusively, the author's name alone is given, unless it is otherwise indicated. Abbreviations are used throughout in referring to titles of periodicals, for the sake of convenience. Titles of articles are, in general, merely indicated by reference to the number of the volume and year of the periodical in which they occur, though occasionally the title of an important article is given in full. Letters following the title of the article, or the name of an author, and standing in place of the title of a book, refer to periodicals. The full titles of these periodicals will be found in a separate list following immediately upon the list of abbreviations of titles of books.

AUTHOR AND TITLE OF BOOK	ABBREVIATION
ASHTON, A. L. B. *An Introduction to the Study of Chinese Sculpture.* London, 1924.	Leigh Ashton.
ATKINSON, T. W. *Oriental and Western Siberia.* London, 1858.	Atkinson.
BADDELEY, J. F. *Russia, Mongolia and China.* 2 vols. London, 1919.	Baddeley.
BARTHOLD. See Radlov, *A.I.M.*	Barthold.
BATESON, W. *Letters from the Steppe written in the Years* 1886–1887. . . . Edited, with an introduction, by Beatrice Bateson. London, 1928.	Bateson.
BEAL. 'Travels of Fa-hien.' In Beal's *Buddhist Records of the Western World.* Vol. I. London, 1884.	Beal, *Bud. Records.*
—— 'Huien-Tsiang's Si-yu-Ki.' In Beal's *Buddhist Records of the Western World.* Vol. II. London, 1884.	Beal, *Bud. Records.*
BELL, C. *The People of Tibet.* Oxford, 1928.	Bell.
BINYON. See Stein and Binyon.	Binyon.
BOSWELL, A. B. 'The Kipchak Turks.' In *S.R.* VI (1927–8), p. 68 ff.	Boswell, *S.R.*
BROCKELMANN, K. Articles in *Asia Major.*	Brockelmann, *A.M.*
BURKITT, F. C. *The Religion of the Manichees.* Donnellan Lectures for 1924. Cambridge, 1925.	Burkitt.
BURNES, Sir ALEXANDER. *Travels into Bokhara; being the account of a journey from India to Cabool, Tartary and Persia, etc.* 3 vols. London, 1834.	Burnes.
CARPINI. See Pian de Carpini.	Carpini.
CASTAGNÉ, J. *Magie et Exorcisme chez les Kazak-Kirghizes et Autres Peuples Turks Orientaux.* Paris, 1930.	Castagné.

[1] This list of books, and the lists which follow later in this volume, as well as the list already given in Vol. II, are not intended as Bibliographies. Their purpose is explained more fully in the Preface.

AUTHOR AND TITLE OF BOOK	ABBREVIATION
CASTRÉN, M. A. *Nordische Reisen und Forschungen.* Vols. I–XII. Edited and translated from the Swedish by A. Schiefner. St Petersburg, 1853–58.	Castrén.
CHADWICK, N. K. *Russian Heroic Poetry.* Cambridge, 1932.	Chadwick, *R.H.P.*
CHAMBERLAIN, B. H. *The Kojiki.* Translated into English as a supplement to Vol. x of the *T.A.S.J.* (1883).	*Kojiki.*
CHAVANNES, É. and PELLIOT, P. 'Un Traité Manichéen retrouvé en Chine.' In *J.A.*, 11th Series, 1 (1913).	Chavannes and Pelliot, *J.A.*
CHODZKO, A. *Specimens of the Popular Poetry of Persia*..., translated with...notes by A. Chodzko. London, 1842.	Chodzko.
CLARKE, E. D. *Travels in various countries of Europe, Asia and Africa.* 4th ed. 8 vols. London, 1816–18.	Clarke.
COCHRANE, J. D. *A narrative of a pedestrian journey through Russia and Siberian Tartary...performed during the years 1820–23.* 2nd ed. (with an appendix). 2 vols. London, 1824.	Cochrane.
CURTIN, J. *A Journey in Southern Siberia.* Boston [Mass.], 1909.	Curtin.
CZAPLICKA, M. A. *Aboriginal Siberia.* Oxford, 1914.	Czaplicka, *A.S.*
—— *My Siberian Year.* London, 1916.	Czaplicka, *S.Y.*
—— *The Turks of Central Asia in history and at the present day.* Oxford, 1918.	Czaplicka, *Turks.*
DAVID-NEEL, A. and YONGDEN. *The Superhuman Life of Gesar of Ling.* London, 1933.	David-Neel and Yongden, *Gesar.*
DMITRÊV, N. K. 'Les Chansons populaires tatares.' In *J.A.* CCVIII (1926).	Dmitrêv.
DONNER, K. *Sibirien: Folk och Forntid.* Helsingfors, 1933.	Donner.
ERMAN, G. A. *Travels in Siberia.* Translated from the German by W. D. Cooley. 2 vols. 1845, etc.	Erman.
FLORENZ, K. *Die Historischen Quellen der Shinto-Religion.* Göttingen, 1919.	Florenz.
FRANCKE, A. H. 'Der Frühlingsmythus.' In *M.S.F.* No. xv. Helsingfors, 1900.	Francke, *Frühlingsmythus.*
—— 'The Ladakhi Pre-Buddhist Marriage Ritual.' In *I.A.* XXX (1901).	Francke, *I.A.* 1901.
—— 'The Spring Myth of the Kesar Saga.' In *I.A.* (1902).	Francke, *I.A.* 1902.
—— *A History of Western Tibet.* London, 1907.	Francke, *Tibet.*
—— *Tibetische Hochzeitslieder.* Übersetzt nach Handschriften von Tag-ma-cig, mit einer Einleitung über die Mythologie der Tibetischen Sagenwelt und Bildern, etc. Hagen and Darmstadt, 1923.	Francke, *T.H.*

Author and Title of Book	Abbreviation
Fraser, J. B. *A Winter's Journey (Tártar) from Constantinople to Teheran, with travels through various parts of Persia, etc.* 2 vols. London, 1838.	Fraser.
Gompertz, M. L. A. *Magic Ladakh.* . . . With illustrations and map. London, 1928.	Gompertz.
Handbook of Siberia and Arctic Russia. Vol. 1. General. Compiled by the Geographical Section of the Naval Intelligence Division, Naval Staff, Admiralty. Published by His Majesty's Stationery Office. London, 1920.	*H.S.A.R.*
Hildén, K. 'Om Shamanismen i Altai.' In *T.G.F.T.* XXVIII (1916), p. 123 ff.	Hildén.
Holmberg, U. *Finno-Ugric, Siberian (Mythology).* Boston, 1927. [Mythology of all Races, Vol. IV.]	Holmberg.
Howorth, H. H. *History of the Mongols, from the Ninth to the Nineteenth Century.* 4 parts. London, 1876–1927.	Howorth.
Karamzin, N. *Histoire de l'Empire de Russie...* traduite par MM. St Thomas et Jauffret. 11 tomes. Paris, 1819–26.	Karamzin.
Katanov. See Radlov, *Proben.* (Katanov's collection of poetry from the Abakan Steppe and the neighbouring district forms Vol. IX of Radlov's *Proben.* No translation of this volume appears to have been published.)	Katanov.
Kennan, G. *Tent Life in Siberia.* New York and London, 1910.	Kennan.
Klaproth, M. J. v. *Mémoires relatifs à l'Asie, contenant des recherches historiques, géographiques et philologiques sur les peuples de l'Orient.* 3 vols. Paris, 1824–8.	Klaproth.
Klementz. Article 'Buryat' in Hastings' *Encyclopedia of Religion and Ethics.*	Klementz.
Knight, E. F. *Where Three Empires Meet: a narrative of recent travel in Kashmir, Western Tibet, Gilgit, and the adjoining countries.* London, 1893.	Knight.
Kogutei: Altaiski Epos. Composed by M. Yutkanov; translated into Russian by S. Tokmashov; edited by V. Zazubrin and N. Dmitrêv. Academia, Moscow-Leningrad, 1935.	*Kogutei.*
Köprülüzade Mehmed Fuad. *Influence du Chamanisme Turco-Mongol sur les Ordres Mystiques Musulmans.* (Mémoires de l'Institut de Turcologie de l'Université de Stamboul. Nouvelle Série, 1.) Istanbul, 1929.	Köprülüzade.

AUTHOR AND TITLE OF BOOK	ABBREVIATION

Kyz-Zhibek. Narodnaya Kazakhskaya Poema. Ka-   *Kyz-Zhibek.*
zakhstanskoe Kraevoe Izdatelstvo. Alma-Ata,
1936. Moscow.

LAUFER, B. 'Origin of the Word Shaman.' In *A.A.*   Laufer.
(N.S.), XIX, No. 3 (1917), p. 361 ff.

LAVIGNAC. *Encyclopédie de la Musique.* Edited by   Lavignac.
Lavignac. Our references are to the article
'Russie', by René Delange and Henri Malherbe.
Partie I, Vol. v.

LE COQ, A. v. *Buried Treasures of Chinese Turkestan.*   Le Coq.
An account of the Activities and Adventures of
the second and third German Turfan expeditions.
Translated by Anna Barwell. London, 1928.

LEVCHINE, A. DE. *Description des Hordes et des Steppes*   Levchine.
des Kirghiz-Kazaks, ou Kirghiz-Kaïssaks...
traduite du Russe par Ferry de Pigny. Paris, 1840.

LINDGREN, E. J. 'Notes on the Reindeer Tungus of   Lindgren, *N.R.T.*
Manchuria.' (Published in Abstracts approved
for the Ph.D., M.Sc. and M.Litt. Degrees in the
University of Cambridge, 1935–6, p. 19 f.)

—— 'The Shaman Dress of the Dagurs, Solons, and   Lindgren, *G.A.*
Numinchens in N.W. Manchuria.' In *G.A.*
(1935), p. 365 ff.

—— 'The Reindeer Tungus of Manchuria.' In   Lindgren,
J.R.C.A.S. XXII (1935), p. 221 ff.   *J.R.C.A.S.*

—— 'Field Work in Social Anthropology.' In   Lindgren,
B.J.P. (General Section), XXVI (1935), p. 174 ff.   *B.J.P.*

LUBINSKI, KURT. 'Bei den Schamanen der Ursibirier.'   Lubinski.
In *B.I.Z.* No. 48 (Nov. 25th, 1928).

MACDONALD, D. *The Land of the Lama....* With   Macdonald.
illustrations and a map. London, 1929.

MICHELL, J. and R. *The Russians in Central Asia...* by   Michell.
Valikhanov, Venyukov and other Russian travel-
lers. Translated from the Russian by J. and
R. Michell. London, 1865.

MIKHAILOVSKY, V. M. 'Shamanism in Siberia and   Mikhailovsky.
European Russia.' In *J.A.I.* XXIV (1894). Translated by O. Wardrop.

MOORCROFT, W. *Travels in the Himalayan Provinces of*   Moorcroft.
*Hindustan and the Panjab; in Ladakh and Kash-
mir; in Peshawar, Kabul, Kunduz and Bokhara,...from 1819 to 1825.* Prepared for the
press from original journals and correspondence
by H. H. Wilson. 2 vols. London, 1841.

ASTON, W. G. *The Nihongi.* Translated into English   *Nihongi.*
as a supplement to the *T.P.J.S* (1896).

Author and Title of Book	Abbreviation
Noel, J. B. L. *Through Tibet to Everest.* London, 1927.	Noel.
O'Donovan, E. *The Merv Oasis.* 2 vols. London, 1883.	O'Donovan.
Parker, E. H. *A Thousand Years of the Tartars.* 2nd ed. London and New York, 1924.	Parker, *T.Y.*
—— *C.R.* xxiii, p. 14 f.	Parker, *C.R.*
Pelliot. See Chavannes and Pelliot.	Chavannes and Pelliot.
Pian de Carpini, John of. *The Journey of Friar John of Pian de Carpini to the Court of Kujuk Khan, 1245–1247.* Ed. by W. W. Rockhill, London, 1903.	Pian de Carpini.
Poppe, N. 'Zum Khalkhamongolischen Heldenepos,' in *A.M.* v (1930).	Poppe.
Potanin. *Sketches of North-Western Mongolia.* (Imperial Royal Geographical Society, St Petersburg, 1881–5. In Russian.) Vol. iv.	Potanin.
Prejevalsky. *Mongolia and the country of the Tangut. Three years' travels in Eastern High Asia.* Translated by E. D. Morgan. London, 1876.	Prejevalsky.
Radlov, V. V. *Proben der Volkslitteratur der Türkischen Stämme und der Dsungarischen Steppe.* Edited by V. V. Radlov. 1866–1904. The collection comprises ten volumes. The material consists of Radlov's own collections, with the exception of Vol. ix, which is the collection of N. T. Katanov (not translated), and Vol. x, which contains the collection of V. Moschkov (with translation into Russian). Vols. i–vi have companion volumes translated into German by Radlov himself. Vol. vii is not translated. Vol. viii has a Russian translation.	Radlov, *Proben.*
—— 'Ueber die Formen der gebundenen Rede bei den Altaischen Tataren.' In *Z.V.-P.* iv (1866).	Radlov, *Z.V.-P.*
—— *Aus Sibirien. Lose Blätter aus dem Tagebuche eines reisenden Linguisten.* 2 Bde. Leipzig, 1884.	Radlov, *A.S.*
—— *Das Kudatku Bilik des Jusuf Chass-Hadschib.* .... Herausgegeben von W. Radloff. 1891, etc.	Radlov, *K.B.*
—— *Die Alttürkischen Inschriften der Mongolei.* 3 parts. St Petersburg, 1895–9. *Anhang* by Barthold.	Radlov, *A.I.M.*
—— *Versuch eines Wörterbuch der Türkischen Dialekte.* (Turkish-Russian-German.) St Petersburg, 1893–1911.	Radlov, *Wörterbuch.*
Rock, J. F. 'Life among the Lamas of Choni.' In *N.G.M.* (Nov. 1928), p. 569 ff. Abridged as 'A Demon Dance by Tibetan Lamas' in the *I.L.N.* (Sept. 28th, 1929).	Rock.

Author and Title of Book	Abbreviation
ROCKHILL. 'Tibet from Chinese Sources.' In *J.R.A.S.* (1891).	Rockhill.
RUBRUCK, William of. See below.	
SANDSCHEJEW, S. 'Welt-Anschauung und Schamanismus der Alaren-Burjaten.' Translated into German from Russian by R. Augustin. In *Anthropos* (1927).	Sandschejew, *Anthropos.*
SARAT CHANDRA DAS. *A Journey to Lhasa and Central Tibet.* . . . Edited by the Hon. W. W. Rockhill. London, 1902.	Sarat Chandra Das.
SCHUYLER, EUGENE. *Turkistan. Notes of a journey in Russian Turkistan, Khokand, Bukhara, and Kuldja.* 2 vols. London, 1876.	Schuyler.
SHAW, R. B. *Visits to High Tartary, Yârkand, and Kâshghar.* London, 1871.	Shaw.
—— *A Sketch of the Turki Language as spoken in Eastern Turkistan* Part I. Lahore, 1875.	Shaw, *T.L.*
—— 'Grammar of the Language of Eastern Turkistán.' In *J.A.S.B.* XLVI (1877), p. 242 ff.	Shaw, *J.A.S.B.*, etc.
SHIROKOGOROFF, S. M. 'What is Shamanism?'[1] In *C.J.S.A.*	Shirokogoroff, *Shamanism.*
—— *Psychomental Complex of the Tungus.* London, 1935.	Shirokogoroff, *P.C.T.*
SHKLOVSKY, I. V. *In Far North-East Siberia.* . . . Translated by L. Edwards and Z. Shklovsky. London, 1916.	Shklovsky.
SIEROSZEWSKI. 'Du Chamanisme d'après les Croyances des Yakoutes.' In *R.H.R.* (1902).	Sieroszewski.
STADLING, J. *Shamanismen i Norra Asien.* Stockholm, 1912.	Stadling.
STEIN, Sir A. *The Thousand Buddhas. Ancient Buddhist paintings from the cave-temples of Tun-Huang on the Western frontier of China.* Recovered and described by A. Stein. . . . With an introductory essay by Laurence Binyon. London, 1921.	Stein and Binyon.
THOMAS, E. J. *The Life of Buddha as Legend and History.* London, 1927.	Thomas.
VALIKHANOV. See Michell.	Valikhanov.
VAMBÉRY, A. *Travels in Central Asia.* London, 1864.	Vambéry, *Travels.*
—— *Sketches of Central Asia.* London, 1868.	Vambéry, *Sketches.*

[1] This paper was read before the Quest Society in 1924, and printed in the *C.J.S.A.* An offprint was kindly lent to me by Miss Lindgren. The year of publication, number of volume, and page references were not clearly indicated on the offprint.

AUTHOR AND TITLE OF BOOK	ABBREVIATION
VAMBÉRY, A. *Das Türkenvolk in seinen ethnologischen und ethnographischen Beziehungen geschildert.* Leipzig, 1885.	Vambéry, *Türkenvolk.*
—— *Uigurische Sprachemonumente und das Kudatku Bilik* [a didactic poem in the Uigur Dialect by Yúsuf Kháss Hájib]. Uigurischer Text mit Transscription und Übersetzung nebst einem... Wörterbuch und...Facsimile aus dem Original-texte...von H. Vambéry. Innsbruck, 1870.	Vambéry, *U.S.*
VAN GENNEP. 'De l'emploi du Mot Chamanisme.' *R.H.R.* XLVII, 1903.	Van Gennep, *R.H.R.*
VERBITSKI, V. *Altajskije Inororodtsyj.* (*Sbornik etno-grafičeskix Statej i izsledovanij.*) Moscow, 1893.	Verbitski.
WADDELL, L. A. *Lhasa and its Mysteries. With a Record of the Expedition of 1903–1904.* 4th ed. London, 1929.	Waddell, *Lhasa.*
—— *The Buddhism of Tibet or Lamaism.* 2nd ed. Cambridge, 1934.	Waddell, *Lamaism*[2].
WALEY, A. *An Introduction to the Study of Chinese Painting.* London, 1923.	Waley, *C.P.*
WILLIAM OF RUBRUCK. *Journey of Friar William of Rubruck.* Ed. by W. W. Rockhill, London, 1903.	William of Rubruck.
WILLIAMS, E. T. *A Short History of China.* New York and London, 1928.	Williams.

PERIODICALS

American Anthropologist. New York, 1888, etc.	*A.A.*
Archaeological Journal, 1844, etc.	*A.J.*
Anthropos. Salzburg, 1906, etc.	*Anthropos.*
Asia Major. Leipzig, London, 1924, etc. Hirth Anniversary Volume, 1923.	*A.M.*
Berliner Illustrirte Zeitung. Berlin.	*B.I.Z.*
The China Journal of Science and Arts.	*C.J.S.A.*
The Classical Quarterly. London, 1907, etc.	*C.Q.*
The China Review, or Notes and Queries on the far East. Vols. i–xxv. Hong Kong, 1872–1901.	*C.R.*
The Contemporary Review. London, 1866, etc.	*Contemp. Rev.*
Geografiska Annaler, 1935, etc.	*G.A.*
The Indian Antiquary. Bombay, 1872, etc.	*I.A.*
The Illustrated London News. London, 1843, etc.	*I.L.N.*
Journal Asiatique. Paris, 1822, etc.	*J.A.*
See *J.R.A.I.*	*J.A.I.*

Author and Title of Book	Abbreviation
The Journal of the Asiatic Society of Bengal. Calcutta, 1832, etc.	*J.A.S.B.*
The Journal of the Buddhist Text Society.	*J.B.T.S.*
Royal Anthropological Society. *The Journal of the Royal Anthropological Institute of Great Britain and Ireland.* London, [1871, etc.]	*J.R.A.I.*
Royal Asiatic Society. *The Journal of the Society.* London, 1834, etc.	*J.R.A.S.*
Asiatic Society of Bengal. *Journal and Proceedings.* Calcutta, 1832, etc.	*J.R.A.S. Bengal.*
The Journal of the Royal Central Asian Society.	*J.R.C.A.S.*
Royal Asiatic Society, Straits Branch. *The Journal of the Straits Branch of the Royal Asiatic Society.* Published half-yearly. Singapore, 1898, etc.	*J.S.B.*
Mémoires de la Société Finno-Ougrienne.	*M.S.F.*
National Geographic Society. *The National Geographic Magazine.* Washington, 1923, etc.	*N.G.M.*
Revue de l'Histoire des Religions. Paris, 1880, etc.	*R.H.R.*
La Revue du Mois. Paris, 1906–20.	*R.M.*
The Russian Review.	*R.R.*
The Slavonic Review, 1922, etc.	*S.R.*
Transactions of the Asiatic Society of Japan. Yokohama, 1872, etc.	*T.A.S.J.*
Terra, Geografiska Föreninges Tidskrift. Helsinki, 1930, etc.	*T.G.F.T.*
Transactions and Proceedings of the Japan Society of London, 1896.	*T.P.J.S.*
Zeitschrift für Völkerpsychologie. Berlin, 1860, etc.	*Z.V.-P.*

PART II

THE ORAL LITERATURE OF POLYNESIA

CHAPTER I

INTRODUCTION

HITHERTO our surveys have been of continental areas, more or less extensive, and subject to influence from surrounding peoples. The area next to be considered is a maritime area, much more extensive than any of the areas previously examined, extending over a large part of the Pacific Ocean, from the Hawaiian Group in the north-east to New Zealand in the south-west—some 4,000 miles; and from Easter Island in the south-east to Fiji in the north-west—some 4500 miles. Comparatively little of this area is composed of land, and the real unit is the sea; the people are a seaboard population. But the ocean is the least effective of barriers, and in spite of the vast size of our area, the language and literature present on the whole great uniformity. Though there are, of course, variations of dialect and culture, these are, comparatively speaking, unimportant. On the other hand, it is generally believed that for many centuries these islands have been subjected to little outside influence. The peoples of the continents which enclose the Pacific have not in general been maritime peoples in recent times.

As an island people, however, the Polynesians themselves are essentially seafarers. They are free from the difficulties of communication or transport presented by lack of roads, or mountain ranges. As an island people also they enjoy a universal intellectual democracy. There are no backward peoples—up-country or remote populations, or dwellers among the mountains or remote valleys. Generally speaking such knowledge and enlightenment as is accessible to the chiefs is accessible also to the lower classes. The sea, with its wide horizon and its intellectual stimulus of arrival and departure, is accessible to all, the native element of all.

All evidence goes to prove that in the past the Polynesians have been among the great navigators and explorers of the world. In their double canoes and outriggers they made repeated voyages from Tahiti to Hawaii—the latter the most isolated archipelago in the world. From Tahiti in the Central Pacific several migrations reached New Zealand— a distance of over 2000 miles. The journey was broken at Rarotonga;

9

but Rarotonga is about 1600 miles from New Zealand.[1] Tradition suggests that some may even have reached the Antarctic, and returned safely to hand on the traditions of the bull-kelp, icebergs, and walruses which they had seen there.[2]

The causes of this activity are a matter for speculation. As it took the form of colonisation and conquest as much as of discovery,[3] we may assume the principal incentive to have been economic; but other motives undoubtedly entered in. In many cases these voyages can be traced directly, as in our own Viking Age, and as in Greece in the seventh century B.C., to the disappointed ambition of discontented chiefs.[4] These long voyages were made in double canoes, sometimes as much as 150 feet long, and capable of holding a large number of people, and it appears that not only the men made the voyages, but the wives and families of at least the more important of the chiefs also.[5] In more recent times the islanders have not been able to make these great voyages, and the period known as the 'Migration Period', or the 'Period of the Long Voyages', is believed to have come to an end with the colonisation of New Zealand about the middle of the fourteenth century. But the double canoes have not long been out of use,[6] and there is abundant evidence that in modern times voluntary and involuntary exile of canoe crews has taken place from time to time; and both predatory and peaceful colonising parties have at all times left various islands in search of fresh homes.[7]

There can be little doubt that the intellectual level, and even the material culture, were on a higher level in Polynesia between the tenth

---

[1] Occasionally, we are told (Best, *Maori* I, p. 31), a vessel in its course from Rarotonga to New Zealand sighted and sojourned a while at Rangitahua, Sunday Island, one of the Kermadecs; but this does not appear to have been usual.

[2] Smith, *J.P.S.* XXVIII, p. 142 f.

[3] See Best, *P.V.*; Smith, *J.P.S.* XXII, p. 60.

[4] See e.g. C. F. Wood, p. 25, and cf. *Fornander Collection*, First Series, Pt. I, p. 44 f.

[5] For an account of the canoes used in the past by the islanders for deep-sea navigation, and other matters relative to their seamanship, see Best, *P.V.* p. 35 ff.; *ib. Maori* I, p. 30.

[6] An excellent photograph of a double canoe of Samoa, taken before it fell to pieces, is published by Krämer II, p. 262, and a number of pictures of models are published in the same volume. Pictures of double canoes of Samoa, also from photographs of the actual canoes, are published by Best, *Maori* I, p. 123, and by Smith, *Hawaiki*, opposite p. 264. A picture of a double canoe of Ra'iatea in 1769 is reproduced from a plate in Cook's *Voyages* in *ib.* opposite p. 89.

[7] Best, *P.V.* p. 13 ff.; but the instances here cited might be multiplied many times, as our own notes testify.

and fourteenth centuries A.D. than at any subsequent period. The long voyages over thousands of miles of sea could only have been accomplished by people with a knowledge of astronomy, of winds and currents and the general geography of the ocean and of meteorology, far superior to that which they possess today. The double canoes in which the voyages were made, and of which a few relics have survived to modern times,[1] show a higher level of craftsmanship than the single canoes, built only for shorter voyages, now in general use. Moreover we hear of religious innovations and building traditions, periods of busy legal enactment and social reorganisation resulting from the long voyages. Indeed the constant contact with communities and cultures hundreds and thousands of miles away must have acted as a cultural stimulus difficult to overestimate.

In studying the civilisation of the Pacific in modern times, one is struck by the curious discrepancy between the material and the intellectual culture. Indeed at the beginning of last century the state of material culture among the islanders was analogous in many respects to that of the palaeolithic period in the Northern Hemisphere. Generally speaking, the Polynesians were without pottery, metal, or grain, without the loom, and almost without domestic animals. The ceremonial dress of their aristocracy was composed of grass and feathers. Their little cultivation was that of nuts, fruits and roots, while they lived largely by fishing. The mildness of the climate in general and the genial aspect of nature enabled a strictly limited population to live in ease and plenty with the minimum of exertion or enterprise, while the limited area and resources of their islands did not call for special initiative.

The intellectual development of the Polynesians, however, is far in advance of their material culture. In natural intelligence and artistic capacity, even in capacity for any kind of sustained thinking, they are in no way inferior to the civilised nations of Europe. The intermarriage of Europeans or Americans with the Polynesians arouses no misgivings, and where the latter have had opportunities of education and culture similar to ourselves, we mix with them as equals. Even at a period before the natives had enjoyed such opportunities, the more enlightened of the early voyagers and missionaries were awake to the high level of their minds.[2]

The islands have been, in general, more or less politically independent of one another, though in the larger groups, such as Samoa, Tonga,

---

[1] See p. 230, footnote 6 above.
[2] See e.g. Stewart, *Visit* II, p. 127ff.; *Residence*, pp. 101f., 103, 105, etc.

Tahiti, and Hawaii, great monarchies have arisen which have at times extended their sway over the surrounding and neighbouring islands. In the Central Pacific at least this growth of monarchies has only been possible at the cost of much bloodshed, and has tended to develop a fierce and warlike people. In Tahiti in particular the savagery of native warfare is proverbial. But other influences even more potent have tended to make the islanders a fierce race. Among the Maori, where the government remained tribal to the end, warfare was a passion, and the Marquesans, who probably represent the tribal organisation in its most perfect form, have been among the fiercest warriors and cannibals in the Pacific. In the little island of Mangaia in the Cook Group, which can never at any time have numbered more than a few hundred souls, which was at all times independent, and was for many centuries probably the most literary community of its size in the world, every page of early history, and almost every poem composed was wet with blood.

The cause of this love of warfare and prevalence of bloodshed is undoubtedly economic. Nothing could be further from the truth than the idea which formerly prevailed in Europe that Polynesia consists of the islands of the blest. The governing factor in the history of the race has always been the food problem. In a large proportion of the islands the interior is mountainous and virtually uninhabitable. The population fringe the foothills and the seashore. It is true that the climate makes it possible to live here in conditions which would scarcely support life elsewhere; but where agriculture was hardly known, where no animal food existed, and where the population increased with exceptional rapidity, the islanders were constrained before the advent of Europeans to restrict the population artificially and continuously. This they did by various means. To a certain very limited extent, notably in the Tahiti Group, the destruction of offspring was practised; compulsory expatriation and 'casting adrift' were also resorted to from time to time throughout the Pacific; in Mangaia unwanted clans who had settled on the islands were either exterminated or devoted as human sacrifices to the god. But by far the commonest method of relieving the economic pressure was warfare. The population must be kept down. The food must be made to go round.

Among a people so much addicted to bloodshed the strongest bond of unity was religion. The power of the priesthood was much stronger and more all-pervading in the Polynesian Islands than in any other region with which we have been concerned. This power was greatly supported in the central and northern Pacific by the existence of great local sanctuaries of high antiquity, to which people repaired from distant islands. The person of the priest was not only sacred, but in some cases was believed to be, at times, the dwelling-place of the particular god whose minister he was. The worship of the gods had lost none of its vitality when the missionaries first began their work in the Pacific. The Polynesians were essentially a religious and devoted people.

A general similarity prevailed throughout Polynesia in pre-European days in regard to social organisation. This organisation was everywhere tribal. Rank was based primarily on primogeniture, descent being normally through the male line. The highest rank was that of the *ariki*, a term denoting the first-born male or female of a leading family or tribe. The leading *ariki* chiefs were themselves descended from lines tracing descent through an unbroken first-born line, at least theoretically. A female of corresponding rank was also known as an *ariki*, or *ariki tapairu*, or sometimes simply *tapairu*. All men and women alike who were of good family were known as *rangatira*, a term denoting 'chief'; but as the term *ariki* was habitually applied to the descendants in the first-born line, the term *rangatira* commonly signifies in practice the men and women of the rank of chief, but not the highest chiefs, though theoretically the *ariki* may be said to be a *rangatira* also. In English idiom we should call the *ariki* 'nobility', the *rangatira* 'gentlefolk'. The professional class were all known as *tohunga*, though there were many types of *tohunga*, of very varying social grades, as we shall see. The commonest were the priests. A male *ariki* was often a *tohunga*, and the principal families of *tohunga* often traced their descent to a collateral branch of an *ariki* line. Among the classes of *tohungas* met with most commonly are the *taura*, or *taura atua* (Marquesan *kaula*, Hawaiian *kaua*), the seers or mediums of the gods.

In general the different island groups of the Pacific formed cultural and economic units, such as the Hawaiian Archipelago; the Tongan Islands; the Samoan group; the Cook Group—a very important group for literary purposes, despite its small size; the islands of the Tahiti Group, generally known as the Society Islands; the Marquesas, also extremely important for literary purposes because of their remote position and consequent conservatism in artistic matters; the Paumotu Archipelago; New Zealand, also virtually isolated; and perhaps most interesting of all, the Chathams about 400 miles to the east of South Island, with their Moriori, or pre-Maori population; and Easter Island, remote from all others in the extreme east. All these groups have enjoyed an active literary life for many centuries, and yield an astonishingly rich store of tradition for the student of oral literature. The two groups last mentioned have naturally few literary compositions to give us, partly because of their small size, partly because their populations were already greatly depleted before the advent of Europeans; but the few Moriori texts (oral) which remain are of great interest, and the fragmentary traditions from Easter Island are valuable as throwing light on the literary remains and customs of other more progressive island groups.

Writing was unknown throughout the Pacific Islands before the advent of Europeans.[1] The literature and the knowledge of the past were preserved only in oral tradition. It is all the more remarkable, therefore, that the standard and range of their oral literature shows a greater intellectual activity than that of any other people with whom we have been concerned. In both prose and verse, aristocratic, priestly, and popular, a wealth of compositions has been recorded from all parts of the Pacific. Oral literature is everywhere a living art, and both extempore composition and exact verbal memorisation are everywhere highly cultivated. Every event of importance, whether in the life of the individual or of the community, finds suitable celebration in song.

Perhaps the most remarkable feature of this intellectual activity is the vitality and longevity of the oral traditions, which have been the subject of wondering comment by almost everyone who has known and written about the islanders. In Hawaii until quite modern times there are said to have been 'bards or story-tellers' attached to the courts of chiefs who were trained in the art of *apo*, or 'catching literature', that is to say of memorising instantly at the first hearing. Mr Rice, who has preserved for us a valuable collection of Hawaiian traditions, several times heard these men reciting for two or three hours at a time, and we are told that when one had finished his auditor would begin at the beginning of the chant or story, and go through the whole without omission or alteration.[2] The same faculty is ascribed by other writers to the Maori.[3] Ellis tells us that in Tahiti the songs were a kind of 'standard or classic authority, to which they referred for the purpose of determining any disputed fact in their history', and he adds that the variant versions of their traditions were adduced in any discussions which arose, and served as a means of

---

[1] With the possible exception of the script (if such it be) of Easter Island, which has not yet been deciphered, and of which the affinities are unknown. This script has been the subject of many articles recently in learned journals, such as *Man* and *Antiquity*.

[2] Rice, p. 4.

[3] See Johnstone, p. 39 f.; cf. Dieffenbach II, p. 84 ff.

checking the facts, and preserving the standard of accuracy.[1] In precisely the same way Kotzebue found the natives in Micronesia referring to their songs in settlement of disputed points in matters of native history,[2] while Gill states that in the same way all record of the past has been handed down in Mangaia.[3]

Sir Basil Thomson has preserved some interesting details relating to oral tradition in the Tonga Islands. From ancient sagas he has succeeded in obtaining much information relating to the line of the Tui-Tongas, the ancient sacred kings.[4] Others relate to the long voyages made by the Tongans themselves. He refers to sagas which relate to their visits to the Niuas, to Uvea and to Futuna, as early as the sixteenth century, and to 'a very ancient saga' which relates to their visit to the Line Islands at 'a very remote date'.[5] Historical events were recorded in song and handed down for centuries in oral tradition. Thomson refers again to a tradition, preserved in poetical form, which relates to Kau-ulu-fonua, who lived in the early part of the sixteenth century.[6] The visits of Schouten in 1616, and of Tasman in 1643, were both recorded in native songs, the latter heard in 1767 when Wallis visited the islands.[7] Mariner knew of poetry recording the visits of Captain Cook and D'Entrecasteaux.[8]

The memorising powers of the Maoris are no less remarkable. In 1896 Best recorded from an old native of the Ruatahuma district the words of no less than 406 songs, together with much information of an explanatory nature about them. All these songs were recited from memory.[9] Even more striking is the preservation of their historical and genealogical lore. Traditions which relate to the arrival and settlement of the Great Fleet of seven canoes in New Zealand some twenty generations ago are still preserved in the traditions of Tahiti and Rarotonga, together with the names of six of the canoes and their leaders.[10] When the Maori chief Tamarau Waiari appeared before the Land Commission at Ruatoki, 'in order to explain the claim of his clan to certain

---

[1] Ellis[1] I, p. 286 f.
[2] Kotzebue III, p. 102. [3] S.L.P. p. 179.
[4] Thomson, *Diversions*, p. 291 ff.
[5] *Ib.* p. 307. [6] *Ib.* p. 293.
[7] *Ib.* p. 310. [8] Mariner,[3] II, p. 217.
[9] Best, *M.S.L.* p. 5; cf. further Smith, *Hawaiki*, p. 16 f.
[10] Best, *P.V.* p. 10; and cf. Smith, *Hawaiki*, p. 265 ff.; cf. *ib.* p. 185. The reason why Rarotongan tradition knew only six canoes appears to be that while all these canoes sailed from Rarotonga the seventh, the Aotea, sailed from Ra'iatea shortly before the others. See Smith, *Hawaiki*, p. 271.

lands, he traced the descent of his people from an ancestor who flourished thirty-four generations ago. The result was a long table of innumerable branch lines, of a multitude of affinitive ramifications. This marvellous recital occupied the attention of the Commission for three days. The old man gave much evidence as to occupation, extra-tribal marriages, etc., and the genealogical table contained well over fourteen hundred names of persons'.[1] It was a part of the education of every Polynesian of aristocratic rank to know his pedigree for at least twenty generations, and the family alliances to remote degrees.[2]

The cultivation of oral tradition has been carried on with great verbal exactitude, apparently for centuries. Poems and charms are very common which contain obsolete words, the meaning of which has been forgotten by the reciters, though the words themselves have come down by tradition from the past. S. P. Smith professed himself unable to translate correctly much of the Rarotongan poetry contained in the native traditions, since both this poetry and that of the Maori, which it closely resembles, is 'extremely ancient, and full of obsolete words'.[3] The same is true also of the poetry of Hawaii,[4] Mangaia,[5] and other groups. When Smith visited Rarotonga he was told of a ship in command of one *Makore* which had called at the island many years before. This can be no other than the name of McCoy,[6] one of the ring-leaders of the mutiny of the *Bounty*—a fact which shows that the vessel reached Rarotonga after the actual mutiny, or in May 1788, for the ship had previously been under the command of Bligh.[7]

The most remarkable evidence of exact verbal tradition in the Pacific, however, is afforded by a comparison of the pedigrees of noble families. It has been justly remarked that probably no race has more highly valued their pedigrees or possessed so many.[8] Pedigrees which have been carried on wholly by oral tradition, and which extend back

---

[1] Best, *M.S.L.* p. 5. Doubt has recently been cast on the value of much of the Land Court evidence for Maori genealogical data (see Fletcher, *J.P.S.* XXXIX, p. 316); but while this should serve as a warning against uncritical acceptance of all such evidence, there can be no doubt as to the value of many of the genealogies adduced in support of land claims, such as the one cited above.

[2] Smith, *Hawaiki*, p. 18; Arii Taimai, p. 17.

[3] *J.P.S.* VIII, p. 62; cf. Best, *Maori* II, p. 136.

[4] See *Fornander Collection*, First Series, Pt. I, p. 1.

[5] Gill, *Myths*, p. xix f.

[6] *Makore* is the Rarotongan pronunciation of *McCoy*.

[7] Smith, *Hawaiki*, p. 264.

[8] *Ib.* p. 17.

for many centuries, have been collected in modern times from Hawaii,[1] Samoa,[2] Rarotonga,[3] New Zealand,[4] and elsewhere.[5] A comparison of the various branches on these lines with one another within the same island Group is of the utmost value in helping us to establish the chronology of the group, and will sometimes yield data which can be relied on to establish a definite chronology for several centuries. As, however, there are no dates in Pacific history, and we are dependent on a computation of generations,[6] the chronology of the early periods will necessarily be more often relative than absolute. Maori scholars are generally agreed that Maori chronology may be regarded as settled for the period since 1300, for a comparison of the principal Maori lines back to the chiefs who migrated thither in the Great Fleet twenty-one to twenty-two generations before 1900 establishes a date, counting twenty-five years to a generation, at about 1300. In general, however, it would be unwise to place reliance on an exact chronology much earlier than the fifteenth century, though we can perhaps postulate the relative sequence of events considerably further back.[7]

A still more severe test of the validity of the oral traditions was made by Fornander in Hawaii[8] during the 'eighties of last century, and later by S. P. Smith in New Zealand,[9] in their comparisons of the genealogies, not only of different families within a given island group, but also of the different branches of the race, notably of the Hawaiians, the Tahitians, the Rarotongans, and the Maori. It has generally been held that the greater island groups had been wholly out of touch with one another since the fourteenth century. When, therefore, Fornander and Smith were able to show an appreciable amount of agreement between the genealogies of the *arikis* of these groups, and when, moreover, it was shown that these agreements were closer for the earlier periods than for the later, the same names of well-known heroes often occurring in

---

[1] See Fornander, *P.R.* I, p. 181 ff.   [2] See Krämer I, *passim*.

[3] S. P. Smith, *J.P.S.* II. See also W. W. Gill, *A.A.A.S.* (1890), p. 628f.

[4] The Maori genealogies are published in numerous volumes of *J.P.S.*

[5] See e.g. for Tonga, West, p. 54.

[6] Fornander adopted the standard of thirty years to a generation (see *Polynesian Race*, II, p. 108); but the majority of Polynesian scholars hold that twenty-five years is a nearer estimate, and this is the standard adopted by S. P. Smith and most modern writers. We have, therefore, thought it best to adopt it in the present survey, though even this may possibly be too long. See Stokes's calculations, *J.P.S.* XXXIX, p. 1 ff., and cf. Fletcher, *ib.* p. 189; cf. further Stokes, *ib.* XLIII, p. 30.

[7] See Buck, *J.P.S.* XLII, p. 330.   [8] See Fornander, *P.R.* I, p. 180ff.

[9] See Smith, *Hawaiki*, p. 20. And cf. also *J.P.S.* XXXI, p. 85f.

groups thousands of miles apart, it was claimed that the common ancestry of these groups had been demonstrated, and that a corresponding chronology could be established. It was long before any serious attempt was made to disprove this conclusion, though occasionally a voice of protest was raised.[1] But there is arising a feeling in our own day[2] that the conclusions drawn by Fornander and Smith from their valuable and most interesting comparative work on pedigrees has met with a too uncritical acceptance, at least in relation to the earlier periods. We ourselves suggest further that the negative evidence of the traditions does not prove the absence of inter-island intercourse, and that both the names of chiefs and stories which are known to the widest area in the Pacific do not therefore necessarily belong to the oldest stratum of tradition, but may, on the contrary, be comparatively recent. Moreover the recent publication of much cosmogonic matter has tended to show that a certain amount of cosmogonic genealogical material has been incorporated into the genealogical tables of the *arikis*, which in this respect naturally show considerable similarities among themselves. The love of the *tohungas* for introducing lists of all kinds into their chants makes it peculiarly difficult to gauge how much of the genealogical material is intended to be regarded as even having reference to human beings, especially in the earlier portions of the genealogical chants. The difficulty is still further complicated by the habit of the Polynesians of changing their names during their lifetime, and, in some Groups after death, as well as of adopting names which, when translated, do not necessarily suggest a human being.[3] Yet when this has been said, enough remains to enable us to feel on fairly safe grounds with Polynesian genealogical computations for some four centuries or more, and the sceptics have not as yet succeeded in destroying our faith in many genealogical lines which have reference to earlier periods.

These genealogies served as laws and charters alike to the Polynesians. According to the Arii Taimai, the social ranks of chiefs in the South Seas were so well known, or so easily learned, that few serious mistakes could be possible.

"Chiefs might wander off to far-distant islands, and be lost for generations; but if their descendant came back, and if he could prove

---

[1] See Basil Thomson, *J.R.A.I.* xxxii, p. 83.

[2] See Stokes, *J.P.S. loc. cit.*; Buck, *J.P.S. loc. cit.* See also Williamson, *S.P.S.* i, p. 17.

[3] W. W. Gill warns us (*D.L.P.* p. 317) of the danger of attaching importance to the meanings of proper names.

his right to a seat in the family Marae, he was admitted to all the privileges and property which belonged to him by inheritance. On the other hand, if he failed in his proof, and turned out to be an impostor, he was put to death without mercy. Relationships were asserted and contested with the seriousness of legal titles, and were often matters of life and death. Every family kept its genealogy secret (cf. p. 392 below) to protect itself from impostors, and every member of the family united to keep it pure."[1]

It will be seen later (p. 271 ff.) that in addition to the genealogies there are many stories attached to heroes mentioned in the genealogies which appear to be the common property of various Polynesian peoples, and to have been preserved independently for several centuries.

The preservation of the oral traditions of the islanders was not entrusted to chance transmission. In the principal groups, such as Samoa, Hawaii, New Zealand, Rarotonga, and in important island sanctuaries, such as Ra'iatea, institutions existed in which all the learning of the people, both the traditional learning and the newly acquired knowledge, was carefully preserved by the *tohungas* of high grade, specially trained for the purpose. These institutions were generally known by a special name. That of the Maori was known as the *whare wananga*, which means literally 'house of occult knowledge'; but all knowledge was regarded as sacred, or worthy of veneration by the Maori, and the broad meaning of the term is simply 'institution for the preservation and transmission of knowledge'. Similarly in Hawaii, and in Samoa also, institutions existed for the preservation of the pedigrees of the chiefs, which, though subject to modification and deliberate falsification to a strictly limited extent, were nevertheless stringently controlled and censored by a jealous hierarchy of priests in the interests of the chiefs who were their principal supporters, and in many cases their near relatives. In Hawaii this institution was known as the *aha alii* ('the congregation of chiefs').[2] These institutions were of the utmost importance in the intellectual life of the islanders, and are evidently of great antiquity, and we shall have occasion to refer to them constantly in the following pages.

There does not appear to be any hard and fast line as regards form between Polynesian prose and poetry. Prose was spoken—poetry

[1] *Arii Taimai E*, p. 17. The Arii Taimai (Mrs Salmon) was a native female chief of the highest rank in Tahiti. Her book is one of our best authorities for this Group.   [2] Fornander, *P.R.* II, p. 28f.

sung, and the chanting of the words seems to constitute the principal essential difference between the two forms of utterance. But the 'songs' are described as rhythmical, which implies a certain artificial limitation of the length of the line, though it is clear from reference to the texts before us that great elasticity prevailed in regard to the actual length of the lines, and that no uniformity in this respect was either observed or aimed at by the reciters, even within the limits of a single poem, or in lines recited in juxtaposition. The rhythm, therefore, must be supplied partly by the music, and partly by the *hianga*, which consists of the dying away of the voice at the end of a musical phrase, 'line', or sentence. But the relation of the *hianga* to the 'line' seems to be rather like that of the hen to the egg. That is to say, the *hianga* marks the length of a line; but the arrival at the end of a line is a signal for the chanting of the *hianga*. The *hianga* is often represented by a single vowel-sound, artificially lengthened by the voice *e-e-i, ai-i*. These sounds form a marked feature in the elegiac poems and mythological dramatic texts recorded by Gill from Mangaia. Sometimes these vowel-sounds are preceded by a consonant, as *na-i-i*. Rhyme is unknown, and the *hianga* precludes its use; but as every Polynesian word ends in a vowel, the effect is one of universal assonance.

The point at which the singer stops to take breath is marked for the most part by the *hianga*, though it is said that the singer will recite for a surprising length of time without pausing for breath. Possibly the *hianga* represents sometimes, therefore, a pause for thought. It occurs at times in the middle of a sentence, and appears to bear a direct relationship to the musical cadence even more than to the words.

The strophic form is unknown except in western Polynesia, and, to a slight extent, in Hawaii. To these instances fuller reference will be made later. Verse paragraphing, as we understand it, appears to be in common use, however. The word *rangi* means not only the air or tune to which a song is chanted, but also a 'stanza', 'verse', or division of a song. The words *whiti* and *upoko* are also used of such a 'verse' or 'division'. Best refers[1] to a lament for a dead child which covers seven foolscap pages when written down, and which is divided into nine *whiti*.

Of the music itself we are unfortunately not in a position to speak; and indeed hardly anything appears to be known of the technical side of this subject, even among Polynesian scholars.[2] But all authorities are

[1] *Maori* II, p. 140.
[2] Best, *Maori* II, pp. 136, 137. Fortunately work is being done on this most

agreed that poetry was habitually 'chanted', and that a speaker passed almost involuntarily from speech to song, i.e. from prose to poetry, in moments of emotion, and on occasions of formality. Formal speeches and public addresses were very frequently chanted, and a Polynesian orator would pass alternately from spoken to chanted speech in a single delivery, according to the strength of his convictions, or of his emotion. Best tells us that the Maori have a strong tendency to intone many expressions which by us would be delivered in an ordinary conversational tone of voice. Even an enquiry as to the name of a stranger would be 'intoned' by an old-time Maori, while the reply would be given in the same manner. The same forms of expression are observed even in connection with the most prosaic occurrences. It is said that even a child will deliver the simplest recital with musical modulations of the voice.[1]

In addition to the musical cadence of the delivery, and the *hianga*, Polynesian poetry is also distinguished by a highly artificial 'poetic diction'. Much of this diction is very archaic, and is full of metaphorical and figurative expressions, veiled and allusive phraseology, and aphoristic matter, which is the despair of the translator.[2] Very frequently the poet makes use of words of which the meaning is no longer remembered. This is naturally to be looked for in the old traditional compositions more commonly than in those of modern times; but the diction and phraseology in general are so conventional and archaic, that it is not always easy in the shorter lyrical poetry to distinguish the older from the more recent compositions. In fact it would seem that here, as in other literatures which we have been considering, no hard and fast line exists between extempore poetry and poetry orally transmitted. The occasions suited to poetic celebration or expression had been stereotyped in the past, and the form which such expression should take, and the manner in which it could be fittingly expressed, were hallowed by tradition. The diction and formulae of the past served as a rich storehouse on which the poets of later times could draw abundantly, and those well versed in ancient lore could always be sure of finding plenty for their needs as these might arise.

interesting subject in some areas. See the article by E. G. Burrows on certain Paumotu chants, some of which have been transcribed by Burrows himself, in Stimson, *L.M.T.* p. 78 ff. After the present work had been completed for Press we received notice of the first considerable general study of Maori music, by J. C. Andersen (in *M.M.P.B.*).   [1] Best, *Maori* II, p. 136.

[2] *Ib. loc. cit.* Cf. also p. 236 above.

CHAPTER II

SAGA AND POETRY RELATING TO THE
MIGRATION PERIOD AND TO LATER PERIODS

THE Pacific is rich in the possession of a vast body of oral prose saga, which is distributed throughout the entire area, every considerable group of islands having its share of oral prose texts. Almost every kind of prose narrative is represented in all stages of development—local legends, stories of the gods, of heroes, of priests, of private individuals, stories of adventure, of domestic life, explanatory stories, Creation myths. Sometimes the versions reach us in a rudimentary form. Very often they are highly elaborate specimens of narrative prose, couched in ambitious artistic diction, and containing many speeches and a great variety of characters. These elaborate stories introduce us to many changes of scene, and the more ambitious specimens carry their narrative through several generations. Sometimes the same story comes to us in variant versions from different parts of the Pacific, and in very different stages of development and art. But always and everywhere we meet with a great wealth of saga, delight in narrative, well-stored and retentive memories among the natives, and a high standard of art and technique.

The Polynesian sagas cover a long period of time. No absolute chronology is indicated in the texts (oral) for the events which they record,[1] any more than in the Norse or Irish sagas; and in consequence we have no absolute chronology for the Pacific. The distance in time from the speaker is suggested by vague expressions such as 'long ago', or 'I learnt what I have told you from my father and grandfather, and they learnt it from their *tupunas* (ancestors)', or 'This history was handed down by the generations of our ancestors of ancient times, and we continue to rehearse it to our children, with our incantations and genealogies, and all other matters relating to our race'.[2] In spite of the absence of absolute chronology, however, we are often able to identify

---

[1] On the subject of Polynesian chronology, see Smith, *J.P.S.* XXII, p. 1. Speaking of one of his informants, W. W. Gill says (*ib.* XX, p. 146): "Maretu, like most Maori writers, is very sparing in his quotation of the years, though months and days are frequently mentioned—this is a characteristic feature of Polynesian narratives." Cf. further, p. 237 above.   [2] Westervelt, *L.M.* p. 137.

the heroes, and to synchronise them with others whose names have acquired an established place in the pedigrees, thus suggesting a relative chronology for the periods of which the sagas treat. Computing the periods by these genealogies, many of which have been preserved with remarkable consistency and accuracy, it has been generally held that the subjects of the sagas range from the eighth century down to the present day. In this matter there is, of course, great variation between one group and another. In general, however, the finest sagas, and the longest, relate approximately to the period which has been computed as ranging from the eighth to the fourteenth centuries.[1] To the question of the chronology of the 'historical' sagas we shall return later.

Many sagas have reference to individuals whose names are found with a considerable amount of consistency in the pedigrees of the ruling lines in most of the principal island groups. The names occur relatively early on the pedigrees, and in a fairly constant family relationship. From their early position and their wide distribution it has been, and still is, generally held that these heroes date from the period before the Polynesian race—or at least the last wave of immigration of the race—dispersed to their present island homes in the various Groups. Consistently with this view it is also generally held that these stories date from the oldest stratum of Polynesian tradition, the period generally referred to by students of Polynesian history as the 'Mythical Period'.[2] We ourselves are very much inclined to suspect that the consistency of the names and the wide distribution of the stories point to the opposite conclusion, and that the names and stories, by their very consistency, suggest a relatively late tradition. This is not the place in which to embark on a discussion which would require much space and minute detail, and the question must be regarded at present as still unsettled. But whatever view we take as to the relationship of these stories to genealogical tradition and to the early Migrations of the race, and however we account for their distribution with only slight variations from Hawaii to New Zealand, there can be no doubt as to the consistency with which persistent Polynesian tradition ascribes the heroes in question and their adventures to the earliest stratum of valid tradition, as distinct from antiquarian speculation.

The chief preoccupations of the heroes of these early sagas are with the dead. Their most important adventures are undertaken to avenge the death of a relative, or to rescue his or her bones, even to rescue the

---

[1] So the older scholars; but we are inclined to suspect that the upper limit is too early.   [2] See Buck, *E.T.* p. 15 f.

dead relative himself or herself from the home of the dead. It naturally follows that a large part of their adventures take place in the Heavens or the Underworld, or in other supernatural spheres. Moreover, supernatural features form a very large—perhaps the predominant—proportion of the material of these sagas. These supernatural features have generally been regarded as due to the early period to which the sagas themselves have reference, and the growth of the marvellous to their long period in oral transmission. But it is to be doubted if this is the most important factor in the relationship of natural and supernatural features, of historical and unhistorical elements, in these stories. To these subjects we shall return later.

Among the most important of the sagas of this early family we may mention those relating to Tawhaki, and his son or grandson Rata. These heroes are generally represented as human beings, though possessed of supernatural powers. In this respect, however, the evidence is somewhat inconsistent, Rata being known in Mangaia (in the form Raka) only as a god of the winds, while in Hawaii Rata (in the form Laka) is a goddess. As heroes, their place in the pedigrees has been held to entitle them to a date about the late seventh or early eighth century,[1] and adopting Smith's chronology as a working principle for the present, this date may be accepted provisionally.

As we leave the early period behind, the character of these narratives of adventure changes. The subjects become more familiar, less bizarre. They begin to assume at least a semblance of history. The sagas relating to the period of the Great Migrations, from the time of Kupe,[2] who, it is believed, was the first Polynesian to arrive in New Zealand c. 925, down to about 1350, bear a striking resemblance to the sagas of the Viking Age in Norway and Iceland, both in the nature of their subjects, and in the naturalism and realism of treatment. In the majority of cases this verisimilitude is greatly enhanced by the simplicity and directness of their style. Like some sagas of the Viking Age they relate to great heroes, whose fame was widespread throughout many island groups, who ventured abroad on voyages of discovery, and led migrations on a large scale to other lands. As in the sagas of the Viking Age, however,

---

[1] On the period of the heroes in question, see *J.P.S.* xix, p. 195. Cf. Andersen, p. 190. Cf. further, p. 271 ff. below.

[2] There appear to have been two great navigators and explorers of this name. The first lived c. 39 generations ago, or computing, according to the general system of chronology, by 25 years to a generation, c. A.D. 925; the second c. 24 generations ago, or c. 1300. According to S. P. Smith (*Hawaiki*, p. 216), there can be little doubt that the first Kupe was the real discoverer.

the heroes and their deeds are depicted with the reserve and moderation of sound historical narrative. They are not exalted to the heroic level of the Homeric heroes, nor yet viewed through the glamour of things unfamiliar alike to reciter and audience, as in the early Cycle of Tawhaki. On the other hand we miss in many of the Polynesian sagas of the Migration Period the individuality and the study of personality and emotional situation which give their unique human appeal to the Norse sagas. The Polynesian sagas of this phase, at least in the central and southern Pacific, are heroic rather than realistic; but it is a heroic tempered by the enlightenment which comes of travel and wide experience of men and of the contacts of peoples, both peaceful and hostile. We have no doubt that the difference between the heroic sagas of Polynesia on the one hand, and the sagas of ancient Ireland and the Homeric poems on the other, is due, in part at least, to the influence of their oceanic environment. It is a maritime 'heroic'.

After the period of the Great Migrations, say after about 1350, another change takes place in the character of the narratives. The subjects become more local and circumscribed in their interests and the sphere of action is correspondingly narrowed. The great navigators give place to the heroes of inter-tribal warfare, or even of family feud. The attitude of the saga-teller to his hero and subject undergoes a corresponding change. The central figure of the narrative is not necessarily in his eyes a great man, and he views the events as interesting rather than important. His attitude to his subject has become critical. The glamour of distance and the unfamiliarity of the milieu of the early sagas, and the true greatness of the men and events of the sagas of the later Migration Period, give place in the sagas of modern times to the verisimilitude of what is seen familiarly and known intimately.

It will be seen that the sagas of the Migration Period correspond in their main characteristics with those of Scandinavia of the Viking Age and earlier. The sagas relating to the period of Tawhaki and his descendants, that is to say of the earliest period of which consistent genealogical evidence has been preserved, correspond to the *Fornaldar Sögur* of Iceland; those of the period from the tenth to the fourteenth centuries to the *Íslendinga Sögur*, referred to more fully in Vol. I, p. 332f. of the present work. We will leave the earlier sagas, with their mythical or supernatural features, to be discussed in a later chapter, and confine our attention here to stories of chiefs and priests which have the appearance of valid historical tradition. No attempt will be made to distinguish between heroic and non-heroic elements; for here, as in the

Russian *byliny*, the preponderance of one or other of these elements often depends on the version which we happen to be following. The *ariki* ('chief') and the *tohunga* ('priest') were often united by ties of the closest family relationship, and no event of importance was undertaken by the former without the full co-operation of the latter. From this it naturally follows that in any unbiassed traditional account of such enterprises, heroic and priestly or mantic elements will be represented in more or less equal proportions. On the other hand it very often happens that we have variant traditions, in one of which the heroic, in the other the priestly interests are largely, or even exclusively present. At times we have traditions which have been preserved exclusively in either a heroic or a priestly milieu. And again in one and the same story we very frequently find both elements preponderating in different parts of the story. We have therefore treated these historical sagas all together in this section, whether the hero be *ariki* or *tohunga*, and whether the preponderant interest be secular or sacerdotal, only reserving for later treatment such non-heroic stories as are definitely outside the chronological scheme of the present chapter, or such as are mainly occupied with supernatural elements.

The earliest saga relating to New Zealand which appears to consist principally of historical material is the story of the discovery of the islands by Kupe,[1] to whom reference has been made above, together with his companion Ngahue. These two chiefs are reported to have sailed in two canoes from the Island of Ra'iatea in the Society Group. Our information on this subject is preserved in the Maori 'school' of oral learning, to which reference has already been made, and which will be discussed more fully on p. 458 ff. below. According to this account, Kupe and his companion arrived at the North Cape, and then circumnavigated both North and South Islands, taking in supplies as need arose, and afterwards returning to Ra'iatea. On their return voyage they called at Rarotonga, and on arriving in the Society Group, they reported what they had seen and done. A record of their adventures, and of the sailing directions to be followed by any subsequent voyagers sailing to New Zealand, was handed down in oral tradition by the local *tohungas* of Ra'iatea also, and affords one of the texts of the saga of Kupe. Among the more interesting of Kupe's reports was that of the *moa*, the gigantic wingless bird, of which many remains have been found in New Zealand, and which, according to tradition, was not yet extinct at that time. They also found and reported the jadeite which was later

[1] *Mem. P.S.* IV, p. 53 ff.; cf. also Smith, *Hawaiki*, p. 216 f.; Best, *Maori* I, p. 40 ff.

to become so important a commodity among the Maori. The most important of Kupe's statements, however, and one which is consistently repeated in all versions of the saga, is to the effect that the islands were uninhabited.[1] None of Kupe's party appears to have remained behind in New Zealand. He belonged to what has been called the 'Exploratory Period', as distinct from the 'Settlement Period', which did not begin till some two centuries later.[2]

Both the North and the South Islands of New Zealand preserve traditions of the *tangata whenua*,[3] or *Mouriuri* (Moriori),[4] the first occupants of New Zealand, who appear to have arrived and occupied the islands subsequently to the visit of Kupe,[5] and whose descendants must have been in their homes for at least two hundred years when next we hear of the arrival of canoes from Polynesia some twenty-eight or twenty-nine generations ago. These *tangata whenua* have been identified with the Moriori[6] who appear at a later date in occupation of the South Island, and who still later migrated to the Chathams, where the last remnants of their descendants survived down to our own time. The stories relating to them are fragmentary, and resemble the brief notes of the Norse *Landnámabók*, 'the Book of the Settlement of Iceland',[7] whereas the sagas of the Maori are far superior as pure narratives. We will pass on therefore to tell of the first occupation of the islands by the Maori.

One of the best of the sagas of the Migration Period, and one of the best authenticated in tradition, is the story of the voyages of Toi and Whatonga, and of their settlement in New Zealand.[8] The date of this

[1] See especially *Mem. P.S.* IV, pp. 63, 64. See, however, Best, *Maori* I p. 41.

[2] For the three periods—the 'Mythical', the 'Exploratory' and the 'Settlement'—into which the early history of a Polynesian community is commonly divided, see Buck, *E.T.* p. 15 f.

[3] Smith, *Hawaiki*, p. 218 ff.; Best, *Maori* I, p. 42 ff.

[4] Alternative names also used are *Pakiwhara*, *Maruiwi*. See Best, *Mem. P.S.* IV, p. 71 ff.; cf. *ib. Maori* I, p. 44, and cf. Downes, *J.P.S.* XLII, p. 156.

[5] The evidence lies partly in the traditional statements that at the time of Kupe's visit the islands were unoccupied; partly in the Moriori traditions of their arrival on the islands, and the genealogies of some leading Moriori families, supported to some extent by comparison with Maori genealogies. See Best, *Maori* I, p. 41; Smith, *Hawaiki*, p. 218, and the papers on this subject contributed by Shand and Beattie to the *J.P.S.*

[6] For the Moriori and their traditions, see Shand, *J.P.S.* II, 74 ff.; Smith, *Mem. P.S.* IV, p. 149 ff.

[7] For an account of this work, see Vol. I, p. 287 of the present work.

[8] Smith, *Mem. P.S.* IV, p. 97 ff.; *J.P.S.* XIX, p. 207; cf. also *Hawaiki*, p. 229 ff.; Best, *Maori* I, p. 48 ff.

occurrence is said to be one of the most reliable in the history of this period, and to be thirty-one generations back from 1900, or c. 1125. Toi is said to have been a great navigator. His home was in Hawaiki, which is generally thought to refer in this story to Tahiti. The saga opens with a canoe race in Hawaiki, which was held for the most part in the shallow waters of the lagoon; but a number of canoes decided to race in the open sea, and during their competition a gale sprang up, and scattered the canoes far and wide over the ocean. Among the heroes thus lost to their relatives was Whatonga, who was driven ashore in the island of Ra'iatea, where he settled down among the inhabitants. His grandfather Toi, hearing no news of him, resolved to set out in search of him. Having obtained the sailing directions left by Kupe with the record-keepers of Ra'iatea (cf. p. 457 below), he set sail for the Cook Group, and eventually reached New Zealand. "I am departing", he said to the chief of Rarotonga, "to search for my grandchildren. If anyone arrives here in search of me, tell them my canoe is directed toward New Zealand.... Perhaps I shall stay there, perhaps I shall return. If I do not reach there, I shall have descended to the bottom of the great belly of Lady-Ocean."[1] He sailed actually too far east, and seems to have discovered the Chathams, at that time unoccupied; but it did not take him long to redirect his course to the east coast of North Island, where he eventually settled down among the Moriori, whom he found in possession of the land.

Meanwhile the story tells us that Whatonga's trained bird,[2] carrying messages formed by knotted cords,[3] succeeded in bringing news to his master from his relatives in Hawaiki, and by watching the direction taken by the bird on its return flight, Whatonga succeeded in finding his way home. On learning of his grandfather's long quest, Whatonga resolved to seek him in New Zealand. The preparations for the voyage

[1] *Mem. P.S.* IV, p. 150. The dates are Smith's, *Hawaiki*, p. 229.

[2] For an interesting note on the use of trained birds as message-carriers, see *Mem. P.S.* IV, p. 104, footnote. An instance of the practice occurs in a saga from the Paumotu Archipelago. See *J.P.S.* XXVII, p. 30f. See also Turner, p. 282.

[3] This is generally identified with the *qipu* of the Mexicans; but is it not more probably some form of cat's cradles such as we know to have been highly cultivated in Polynesia? Is it possible that the latter form of pastime originated in some form of code? In the localities where it is most in vogue the figures represent well-known stories; i.e. the figures can be used to communicate or suggest narratives. Some kind of code therefore seems to be possible. It is perhaps worth remarking in this connection that Chinese historians tell us in connection with the new form of writing introduced by Confucius that before his time people communicated by means of knotted cords.

are related in great detail and the course of the voyage also. At length Whatonga and his party were ready to start, and calling in the Cook Group, as Toi had done, and learning that his grandfather had left for New Zealand, he set sail, and eventually landed on the North Cape. He succeeded in locating his grandfather, and settled down with his followers in the new land.

After the settlement of Toi and Whatonga a number of other parties made their way to the new land, some of whom made the return journey to Rarotonga.[1] The most important of these expeditions is that of the seven canoes, known as the 'Great Fleet', which sailed from the Society Group, via Rarotonga, about 1350.[2] This was a carefully organised migration on a large scale, and it is clear that the expedition had been planned for some years before the final departure of the Fleet took place. There was no thought of return. The emigrants had come to stay, and the North Island of New Zealand was settled and allocated to the various arrivals, more or less according to districts named after the canoes in which they are supposed to have sailed. The new arrivals did not effect their settlement without many feuds and much bloodshed, and sub-sequent tradition is full of the battles fought, the stratagems invented, and the feuds carried on for many generations, both among the new settlers, and between them and the earlier population, the latter partly Moriori, partly a mixed race, the result of intermarriage between the pure Moriori and the earlier settlers under Toi and his successors.

The events which led to this migration from the Central Pacific are not clearly known, and vary greatly in detail according to the version which we happen to be following; but it is clear that it was in some way owing to disturbed conditions in the home area, and that the chief object of the emigrants was to escape from the destructive wars which were being waged in the Society and neighbouring groups. In Sir George Grey's version of the story of the burning of the Arawa canoe,[3] the leader of the Great Fleet, by the crew of the Tainui canoe after their arrival in New Zealand, we learn of the reluctance of the Arawa crew to take vengeance for the insult, on the ground that it was chiefly in order to avoid these destructive wars that they had left their old home in 'Hawaiki'; and they remind themselves of the parting words of their father in which peace was inculcated at all costs. Never-theless this did not prevail to prevent the Arawa people from eventually deciding unanimously in favour of vengeance.

[1] *Mem. P.S.* IV. For a summary, see Best, *Maori* I, p. 56; cf. Smith, *Hawaiki*, p. 275.   [2] *Mem. P.S.* IV, p. 205 ff.   [3] Grey, p. 102 ff.

The events which we have been describing are preserved in oral sagas of considerable length and detail both in New Zealand[1] and in the Central Pacific, notably in Rarotonga.[2] An immense number of versions have been recorded, which differ greatly in details, but are in almost complete accord in regard to the main points of history. The Pacific, like a great lake, was the scene of ambitious enterprises, and was peopled with men and women whose likeness to those of the Viking Age in the north of Europe is truly astonishing. In the more detailed of the sagas even the personalities are developed in some measure like the men and women of the *Íslendinga Sögur*, and events and actions are described down to the minutest detail, and with the most complete realism. These characteristics will become more apparent as we proceed, and are perhaps even more developed in the sagas of the Central and northern Pacific. In the Maori sagas there has perhaps been a tendency for the intertribal feuds of later days to bias the narrative of earlier times, and set undue stress on boundary quarrels and hereditary feuds, on disputes as to rights of ownership and of precedence. These somewhat jejune and impersonal themes at times tend to outweigh the human elements in the sagas—which nevertheless are rarely absent. But is not this also true of the *Íslendinga Sögur* themselves? In the briefer compass in which the Maori sagas have been transmitted, the proportions of the impersonal, and what we may term the family or tribal elements, to the personal are probably not dissimilar on the whole to those in the sagas of Icelanders, and the general resemblance between the sagas of Iceland and those of the Antipodes has made a lasting impression on everyone who is at all familiar with both literatures.

Among the best known of the saga cycles of the Central Pacific relating to the Migration Period are those of the great voyages of the hero and navigator Tangiia[3] of Tahiti, whose position in the pedigrees seems to entitle him to a date somewhere in the thirteenth century. It is computed that his voyages must have covered well over twenty

[1] The most easily accessible popular account of these will be found in Sir George Grey's *Polynesian Mythology*; but almost any good book on New Zealand records a number of sagas of the Settlement.

[2] See Smith, *Hawaiki*, p. 263 ff. and the references there cited. See also *Mem. P.S.* IV.

[3] It is important to bear in mind that neither Tangiia nor Tu-tapu are proper names. The former is one of the titles borne by the high chiefs of Tautira, the inland district of Tahiti to which Honoura belonged (cf. p. 278 ff. below), while Tu-tapu was formerly the regal name of the high chiefs of Vai'anae, Mo'orea, and Papa-tea, a title inherited from their Tahitian ancestry. See Henry, *A.T.* p. 522 (footnote 16).

thousand miles, and ranged from Samoa and probably Fiji to Easter Island. On the death of his father, or foster-father, Tangiia usurped the chieftainship of Tahiti and earned the lasting jealousy and hatred of his cousin Tu-tapu. A series of wars followed in which Tu-tapu over and over again pursued his cousin and attempted to destroy him. Tangiia also carried on hostilities for a long time with another chief Karika, but eventually cemented a peace by marrying his daughter. After a number of long voyages, he eventually concluded his stormy career by a quiet old age devoted to the interests of peace and to the building of *maraes*, as the native temples are called, and to the promulgation of something like a code of laws in Rarotonga.[1]

Among the most fully reported and elaborate of the sagas of the Central Pacific relating to this period are the stories of Uenuku and of his son Rua-tapu.[2] The stories have been preserved in many sources, including that of the Rarotongan *Whare Wananga*, and also among the Maoris. Uenuku and his son Rua-tapu are believed to have lived in the generation in which the Great Fleet left for New Zealand,[3] and to have been deeply involved in the feuds which were raging in the Central Pacific at that time. According to one Maori version, Uenuku slew his wife Taka-rita in punishment for an act of infidelity and cooked her heart and gave it to his son to eat. Her brothers, chief of whom was Tawheta, in vengeance slew four of Uenuku's sons and a number of his people; but a fifth son of Uenuku escaped without the knowledge of Tawheta and his followers, and reported the deed to Uenuku. Tawheta and his party were actually feasting with Uenuku at the time when the news reached him; but being of a chivalrous disposition he allowed his guests to depart in peace, promising that his full vengeance should fall upon them later for their barbarous deed—a promise which he did not fail to fulfil, sparing only Pai-mahutanga, the daughter of Tawheta. But by doing so Uenuku had only sown the seeds of dissension in his own home. His son by Pai-mahutanga, named Rua-tapu, who was held in lower estimation by his father than his other surviving brothers on account of his mother, desiring to avenge the insult both to her

---

[1] See Smith, 'History and Traditions of Rarotonga', in *J.P.S.* Vols. XXVIII, XXIX. Many versions of this story are extant. See Smith, *Hawaiki*, pp. 233 ff., 246. See also Emerson, *L.V.* p. 2 ff. Another version from Rarotonga is recorded by Williams, *M.E.* ch. XIII, who also mentions a Tahiti version (p. 196).

[2] We have followed the outline of the story in general as given in summary form from the Maori version by Andersen, p. 93 ff. For variant versions of this story, see Grey, p. 92 ff. (also Maori); D. Low, *J.P.S.* XLIII, p. 73 ff.; cf. *ib.* p. 171 ff. (Aitutaki, Cook Group).   [3] Smith, *Hawaiki*, p. 249.

and to himself, knocked a hole in the bottom of the canoe in which he and his brothers were sailing far out at sea. When she foundered, he held his brothers' heads under water, each in turn, till all were drowned, sparing only one to return home and tell the sorrowful news to Uenuku. Rua-tapu himself was drowned with his brothers.

The Hawaiian sagas of the Migration Period are, in general, less warlike and more domestic in character than those of the Central and Southern Pacific. The difference is generally attributed to the fact that Hawaii, owing to its remote position, was isolated from the storm centre. But the heroes of the early period frequently cover the 2300 miles of open sea between Hawaii and Tahiti, and journeys from Samoa to Hawaii are also reported. During this period it is clear that Hawaii shared the culture of the Central Pacific. Innovations in religious practices are traditionally stated to have been introduced from Samoa or Tahiti by the great *tohunga* Paao,[1] in tattooing and dress from Tahiti by Olopana and Lu'ukia,[2] in poetry and music by La'a-ma-i-kahiki, also from Tahiti.[3] All these people play a prominent part in the Hawaiian sagas of the period, as we shall see. After about 1325, however, the long voyages apparently cease here also,[4] for we hear no more of them.

Among the saga Cycles of the great chiefs who constantly made the voyage between Hawaii and Tahiti during the twelfth and thirteenth centuries, the Hawaiian Cycle of Moikeha and his descendants is one of the most interesting.[5] The Cycle follows in intimate and elaborate detail the fortunes and adventures of various members of this great family through three generations. The names of another hero Olopana and his wife Lu'ukia, who play an intimate part in the Cycle, appear on both Hawaiian and Maori lines, their probable place being twenty-six or twenty-eight generations ago, or about 1200 or 1250.[6] Olopana himself is a chief of southern extraction, though his father's home was in Hawaii. His grandfather Maweke is said[7] to have made the voyage frequently between Hawaii and Tahiti.

In the Hawaiian version of his family saga, the first hero of whom we have full record is Moikeha, who is here a contemporary of Olopana, though in general there is no consensus among Hawaiian records as to

[1] Emerson, *L.V.* p. 12.   [2] *Fornander Collection*, Vol. iv, p. 156 ff.
[3] See p. 388 below.   [4] See Smith, *Hawaiki*, p. 227.
[5] See *Fornander Collection*, First Series, Vol. iv, p. 112 ff.
[6] Smith, *Hawaiki*, p. 22 f. Their probable connection with the Tahiti line has also been shown. See Smith, *loc. cit.*
[7] *Ib.* p. 24.

Olopana's pedigree.[1] Moikeha, who is said to have been paramount chief in Tahiti, was the father of La'a-ma-i-kahiki, who is traditionally stated to have introduced the *hula*, 'dance', and the big drum into Hawaii. The occasion of Moikeha's leaving Tahiti was as follows. When Olopana and his wife Lu'ukia came to Tahiti from Hawaii, Olopana obtained a high administrative post under Moikeha, and the latter took Lu'ukia as his paramour, with the willing connivance of her husband. A certain Mua, jealous of Moikeha, slandered him to Lu'ukia, who thereupon debarred her lover from approaching her. Distracted with grief, Moikeha set out for Hawaii with his two sisters, his two younger brothers, and his priest. The daughters of the king of the Island of Kauai in the Hawaiian Group fell in love with the handsome youth as he was surf bathing, and thus Moikeha became king of Kauai after their father's death. The story of his son Kila is no less fully told. After following the hero through the training of his boyhood and his childish games, it relates how he made the voyage to Tahiti to seek Moikeha's son Loa, who had been left behind there. Kila's adventures, both on the voyage and in Tahiti, are fully set before us—how the crew almost died of starvation on the voyage, how they searched in vain for Loa who was hiding in the mountains, how they eventually found him as he was attending a religious service, and bore him back with them to Hawaii. The later adventures of all these characters are related in the same circumstantial manner.

Stories of domestic life often exist side by side with the stories of adventure. The Hawaiian story of Liloa's amours with the woman in the Hilo district, and of the subsequent birth and recognition of his son Umi, afterwards supreme hereditary chief of Hawaii, belong rather to the domestic journal of the Hawaiian royal family than to heroic saga, and Fornander mentions that "The legends make no mention of any wars or contentions having occurred during Liloa's long reign to disturb the tranquillity of Hawaii".[2] The travels incognito of Lono, an earlier supreme chief of Hawaii, in search of a certain kind of wood, his sojourn and entertainment whilst weather-bound on the island of Molokai, his jealousy of his wife and their ultimate reconciliation, form the subject of a saga which has much in common with the sagas of the Viking Age in Iceland.[3] The preoccupations of the latter saga in particular are with private and domestic life, though the characters belong to

---

[1] *Fornander Collection*, First Series, Vol. IV, p. 154.
[2] Fornander, *P.R.* II, p. 75.
[3] *Ib.* p. 117 ff.

the royal families of the Hawaiian Islands, and we are conscious that momentous events are taking place around them.

The sagas which we have been discussing form a great contrast both to the sagas relating to earlier times, which we shall discuss more fully in the next chapter, and to the Maori traditions already referred to. The supernatural features and the preoccupation with dead ancestors characteristic of the earlier Cycles, both in Hawaii and elsewhere, are either wholly absent, or confined to the mundane magical practices of normal human beings, who show no tendency to fly skywards, or to descend to the depths of the earth. On the other hand the tribal and topographical preoccupations, and the predominance of warfare and bloodshed which characterise Maori sagas, are equally absent. In the Hawaiian sagas of the Migration Period we have an intense preoccupation with the affairs of the world of the living—its loves and domestic quarrels, its adventures and its dangers, its recreations and its artistic life, its great scope for human activity on the grand scale. These activities are narrated with a combination of realism and romance which is at once rare and delightful; for it is also convincing. We are the privileged intimates of the domestic and public life of the leading families of two great island groups in an age of high adventure and romantic incident. Our introduction is effected through oral prose narratives, which have been preserved by narrators whose standard is that of preserving and relating a record of the past as accurately and as fully as human memory is capable of doing.

In addition to the sagas which we have been considering, and which may be said to relate to the great secular characters of the historic past, the Pacific is also rich in sagas relating to the lives and characters of priests, and to the religious life of the islanders. It has already been mentioned that in many of the stories of maritime adventure—stories which we may term the maritime heroic—the priests figure as prominently as the *ariki*, and are often of the same rank, and belong to the same families. Among the most interesting of these essentially non-heroic sagas is that of the priest Paao already referred to, who is believed to have migrated during the early period (c. 1200) from Samoa to Hawaii, where he succeeded in changing the native dynasty, introducing a new line from Tahiti.[1] To Paao also is ascribed the introduction of the cult of the volcano goddess Pele; but whether direct from Vavao or Upolu—by which name Samoa seems to be designated[2]—or by way of

[1] See Fornander, *P.R.* II, p. 33 ff.; Malo, p. 24 ff.; Emerson, *L.V.* p. 5 ff.

[2] So Fornander, *P.R.* II, p. 33 f.; cf. Emerson, *L.V.* p. 5.

Tahiti, is stated variously according to the version which we are following (cf. p. 324 below).

One of the most striking of these non-heroic sagas is that of Umi,[1] who is believed to have lived during the sixteenth century. He is said to have been a younger son of Liloa, the hereditary paramount chief of the district of Waipio in Hawaii. We are told that before his death Liloa willed all the lands of Hawaii to his first son, Hakau; but left the temples and the gods to his younger son, Umi[2]—a disposition which is interesting as illustrating the typical relationship of the *tohunga* to the *ariki* at this period. Umi managed at an early age to secure the throne for himself by guile, and by the help of the priesthood, who utilised him for their own ends, and were in turn used by him for his own purposes. By his mild rule, and his political sagacity, he managed to extend his kingdom until it included many other islands in the Group. He is a typical Polynesian priest-king, wily, unscrupulous, able and naturally peace-loving. In many respects the stories relating to him call for comparison with the traditions of the great priest-king Mautara, who during the first half of the eighteenth century abrogated to himself supreme power in the little island of Mangaia in the Cook Group in the Central Pacific, and whose clan swayed the destinies of the island for c. 150 years.[3]

After the middle of the fourteenth century we hear no more of the long voyages, such as those which have made the great names of the Migration Period famous over almost the whole Pacific Ocean, and throughout a period of some seven hundred years. After this period the traditions of the various groups developed each on their own lines. But the vitality of these traditions seems to have been in no way impaired by this. Samoa, Hawaii and New Zealand have kept their island records by means of carefully transmitted traditions down to the arrival of Europeans, and there can be little doubt that the same is true of most of the groups, whether these traditions have been recorded subsequently or not. But their history is henceforth local history.

Among the most remarkable of these later traditional histories is that of the island of Mangaia just referred to. Gill has recorded traditions[4] relating to the early settlement of the island by the Ngariki clan, apparently from Samoa, and continuing through the sixteenth century down to the present day. Even in traditions believed to date from the sixteenth century the element of the marvellous is restrained, while for

[1] *Fornander Collection*, First Series, Vol. IV, p. 178.
[2] *Ib.* p. 186.   [3] Gill, *Myths*, p. 87.
[4] *S.L.P. passim.*

the seventeenth and eighteenth centuries we have a series of brief personal and tribal sagas which enable us to reconstruct with a fair amount of coherence the history of the entire island, with its warring clans, its ruthless priests, its strange double or triple 'kingship',[1] and its complicated ecclesiastical intrigues. Like the majority of Polynesian sagas elsewhere, the Mangaian sagas are a record of events rather than a portrait gallery of individuals. The struggle for existence and the fight for life was more calculated to develop heroic features than individualism; and in a community so torn by warfare, the tragedies and the heroism of the past have naturally made a more lasting impression on the story-tellers than the individual traits of the men and women who play their parts in the stories. It is even to be suspected that comparatively few lived long enough to develop the individuality which comes of leisure and a quiet mind.

The Mangaian heroes are often individuals of no particular rank or prestige. Such were the father (Temoaakaui) and son (Uriitepitokura) who lived for years as fugitives among the rocks of Te Vaenga, manu-facturing their beautiful feather garments and fish-nets till peace reigned and enabled them to bring their rich stores out of their retreat.[2] Such was Rori, the son of an immigrant craftsman from Tahiti, whose thirty years of seclusion as a cave-man on the same barren rocks form the subject of a long saga,[3] which is referred to more fully below (p. 366 ff.). Among the favourite subjects of such stories are those of cannibals and their horrid banquets, such as that of Vete and his companions,[4] and the notorious cannibal Tangaka.[5] But it is to be noted that the very fact of such stories having survived shows that such practices were deprecated and remembered with execration.[6]

An interesting saga relating to early times is that recorded by Gill under the title of 'The Twin Kites'.[7] The story relates to a kite-flying

---

[1] The secular rule of Mangaia was in the hands of a chief whom Gill calls the 'temporal lord', and this temporal power had to be contended for afresh every few years. In addition there were also two hereditary high priests, whose rule was chiefly spiritual, and who had their official residences, one in the 'interior' of the island, the other on the seashore on the west coast of the island. See Gill, *Myths*, *passim*; Buck, *M.S.* p. 112 f.

[2] Gill, *S.L.P.* p. 7 ff.   [3] *Ib.* p. 152 ff.
[4] *Ib.* p. 119 ff.   [5] *Ib.* p. 72 ff.

[6] From notices in a MS. note-book made by the Rev. W. W. Gill it would seem that in modern times at least cannibalism on Mangaia and Rarotonga was almost, if not wholly, restricted to times of famine. The MS. is in the possession of the London Missionary Society, by whose kindness we have been permitted to consult it. Cf. further Cook[1], I, p. 172.   [7] Gill, *S.L.P.* p. 18 f.; *D.L.P.* p. 39 ff.

competition, such as was formerly much in favour in the islands of the Cook Group and elsewhere. In these competitions not less than ten competitors took part. The kites, which were sometimes very large, were all known by individual names, and the object of the competitors was to see who could fly his kite highest. The sport is said to have been especially popular among elderly men. On one occasion a chief named Ake, of the island of Atiu, flew a beautiful pair of twin kites known as 'The Sorrowful Ones'; but unfortunately the string broke, and the kites were lost to view. The chief, knowing that the wind was favourable for Mangaia, remarked that in all probability the kites would come down there, and his son Akatere ariki accordingly manned a canoe and set sail. In two nights[1] he landed near the *marae* or temple platform of Rongo on the west coast, and enquired whether the twin kites of Ake had been seen. He was assured that a pair of foreign kites had recently come ashore on the eastern part of the island, which proved to be the pair of which Akatere ariki was in search. The story is interesting, not only as showing the importance of kite-flying, and the singularly intimate knowledge of winds and weather which is inseparable from this sport, and which, in an advanced form, develops it into a science,[2] but also for the manner in which the story itself has been recorded. The tradition has been preserved in the form of a dramatic song of the kind to be referred to in Ch. VI below, and when the Rev. W. W. Gill visited the island of Mauke in 1865 he and the natives who accompanied him were met by an aged man of Atiu, who asked them if they had ever heard of Akatere ariki. The deacon who accompanied Gill replied that he had heard of his visit to Mangaia, and forthwith chanted the song which has reference to the saga related above. The old Atiuan declared that though now naturalised in Mangaia, it was originally derived from Atiu, and referred to his ancestors.

Owing to the important part played by the priesthood in Mangaia, heroic and priestly elements are generally combined throughout their saga history. The island is, indeed, especially rich in non-heroic literature, which under the priest-king Mautara (cf. p. 352 ff.) had great chance of development. Many of their sagas are concerned with the *tabus*, the temple sacrifices, and the services of the god Rongo, and with the relations of the various clans with the immigrant Tongan clan, devoted by order of the god to furnish human sacrifices, as these

---

[1] The Polynesians usually sailed by the stars.
[2] For an account of the art of kite-flying in the Pacific, and the traditions associated with it, see Chadwick, *J.R.A.I.* LXI (1931), p. 455 ff.

might be required. The works of Gill abound in examples of these Mangaian historical sagas, which have been preserved mainly as the background and commentaries to the dramatic elegies to be considered later. Two interesting examples of stories in which the leading rôle is played by priests are the sagas and poems relating to 'The Expelled God', which are believed to date from the seventeenth century.[1] In the first, Ue, priest of Tane, expelled from Tahiti, seeks to establish a sanctuary for his god on Mangaia, but is at last forced by the hostility of earlier settlers from Tahiti to leave the island, in company with his friend Mataroi. In the second story, Ue (the priest mentioned above) and his friend Mataroi depart from Mangaia and go to Aitutaki to aid in the deliverance of the king from a war-band of Samoan invaders. Their enterprise is successful, and in the division of lands which follows, the enfranchised king bestowed great possessions upon Ue. Another story of this class, known as 'A Poisoned Bowl', relates how the chief Marere of the royal Akatauira clan in the south of Mangaia poisons the cannibal priest Tangiia, who has demanded his little son as a relish with his *kava*.[2]

It is of interest to enumerate the main points of resemblance between the Polynesian sagas and those of Iceland and Ireland. Like the latter the Polynesian sagas are primarily stories of adventure related for the purpose of entertainment, though the political and practical importance of keeping records of past events must have acted as a strong incentive to their preservation. This, as Te Arii Taimai points out (cf. p. 238 above), is of especial importance in conditions where a chief may live abroad for many years, and must prove his right to his property on his return without the aid of written records, charters, or wills. It is clear, however, that mere desire of scientific accuracy could never have produced the telling narratives of life in the Pacific in the Migration Period such as we have been discussing, which show artistic literary features of an exceptionally high standard.

As in the sagas of Iceland and of Ireland, the longest and best of these sagas relate in general to the early periods. The majority of the finest examples relate to a period before the close of the Great Migrations, that is to say before c. 1350. But this cannot be pressed too closely, especially for New Zealand or the Chathams,· where we have many ambitious sagas relating to later periods, while sagas from Mangaia

---

[1] Gill, *S.L.P.* p. 32 ff.
[2] *Ib.* p. 99 ff. *Kava* is the intoxicating drink of Polynesia, reserved for the high chiefs and the priests.

chiefly have reference, as we have seen, to a period not earlier than the sixteenth century. It is true that our texts of these latter are in general much shorter than those relating to the earlier periods from Hawaii, Tahiti, and New Zealand; but we have to bear in mind the circumstances under which the sagas of the various groups have been recorded, and also published. It is natural to suppose that only comparatively wealthy communities such as Hawaii and New Zealand can afford to publish the texts of their longer sagas and Cycles *in extenso*; whereas for a small island like Mangaia such an enterprise would be out of the question, even if there had been many ready to record them instead of a single missionary. The genius of the Rev. Wyatt Gill, on whom we are dependent for almost all our knowledge of the sagas of the Cook Group, has preserved in his brief summaries enough of the character of the texts to enable us to see that in their main characteristics they follow the same lines as the more ambitious texts of the Groups mentioned above.

Like the Norse and Irish sagas, those of Polynesia are all anonymous. In no case, so far as we are aware, do we know the author of any saga. This is in striking contrast to the Polynesian poems. In regard to these we are very frequently told who composed them, and under what circumstances.

Finally, a word may be said as to the wealth of detail which characterises the narratives everywhere. In this respect Polynesian 'historical' saga offers a close parallel to the sagas of Iceland. We are told the motives which cause the chiefs to set out on their long voyages, and something of their home life before they come to a final decision to change their place of abode; the misfortunes which overtake them on their voyage, their sojourn in foreign lands. In stories such as that of the migration of Paao to Hawaii (cf. p. 254 above), or of the launching of the Takitumu canoe, and its migration to New Zealand,[1] we enter into the discussion as to who should be included in the expedition and who should be left behind, and why; the exact placing of the crew; the dispute as to precedence and responsibilities; considerations as to the most suitable weather for sailing; the provisioning of the boats; the embarking of the gods. Conversations are related in full, and all with great vivacity and variety.

All the sagas of the Migration Period, and practically all those of the later periods also, are individual in their interest, and are in the nature of personal anecdotes or biographies. The idea of a state, or of public

[1] *J.P.S.* XXIII, p. 28 ff.

responsibility, never develops, and we hear nothing of the people as a whole, save only of the individuals who play a part in the stories. The interest is wholly centred in people of the upper class. The priests are no exception, for they seem generally to belong to royal or chiefly families. In these features the stories of the Migration afford a contrast to those of the later periods, especially in Mangaia and New Zealand, in which, as we have seen, we often have sagas relating to people of relatively humble rank, and in which tribal interest is represented to a considerable extent.

Probably no race has ever held its history in higher esteem than the Polynesians. In their devotion to their early records they are comparable to the Chinese. The proportion of attention devoted to events of centuries long past, and personalities long dead, is the more remarkable since these records have always been carried on without the aid of writing. Such a task could only have been accomplished by generations of specialists, saga-tellers highly trained in the art of memorising as well as in their critical faculty. And such a class of men could only exist where their art was held in high esteem and supported on generous lines. We have seen that the very absence of written records has afforded one of the main incentives among Polynesian chiefs towards the support of their oral record keepers. The result of this happy circumstance has been the production in Polynesia of one of the two finest oral historical literatures in the world.

In the Pacific as a whole, narrative poetry appears to be almost unknown. From Samoa and Tonga we have a fairly extensive collection of narrative poems; but the examples which have come under our notice do not relate to historical persons, but only to non-heroic stories and to individuals unknown from other sources. In saying this, however, we must mention the fact that the prose sagas are hardly distinct from poetry; for as told by the old narrators they were chanted in a kind of recitative rather than recited in a speaking voice. To the manner of recitation we shall return later.

It is important to emphasise the poetical (recitative) form of the recitation of narrative, and indeed of all formal speech, as well as the undefined character of Polynesian 'poetry' as such, because Sir Basil Thomson speaks of an 'epic' of Kau-ulu-fonua, who is believed to have lived in the early part of the sixteenth century, and from whom Tongan history is said to date.[1] He also refers to other historical poems which

[1] Thomson, *Diversions*, p. 293.

celebrate and record one of the earliest visits of a European ship with a cat ('*pusi*') sitting on the fo'c'sle.[1] The coming of Tasman in 1643 is also recorded in poetry, even to the minutest details, including the iron tools which he had presented to the natives.[2] Thomson refers to Tongan traditions relating to the visit of the Dutch ships of Schouten and Lemaire in 1616, and he adds: "the fame of Schouten's prowess, recorded in a rough poem, may have served to protect his great countryman Tasman".[3] The importance of these historical traditions, whatever their precise form, would be difficult to overestimate; but is it really true that they are couched in 'epic' form, in the strict sense of the term? Ellis also speaks of 'ballads' in Tahiti which record historical matter.[4] It is possible that these resemble the 'ballads' of Tonga and Samoa relating to legendary subjects; but we have not seen such poetry from Tahiti, and it is more likely that Ellis is referring to dramatic recitations on historical subjects, such as those which have been recorded in Mangaia, to which we shall refer later.

Speech poems are exceedingly common in all parts of the Pacific, and in the sagas relating to all periods. Many of these poems purport to be spoken by characters in the sagas, and thus, in the case of such sagas as are historical, claim to have been composed by the men and women who are represented as reciting them. How far the poetry of the past has been verbally remembered, and how far it has been modified in the course of transmission, it is difficult to say; there can be no doubt that in some degree the exact verbal tradition has been preserved (cf. p. 236). On the other hand, we shall see that old forms and formulae are re-utilised by modern singers in the composition of new poems, and the extent to which this is done will, of course, vary with every singer and every composition. It is probable, therefore, that while many of the poems in the sagas were really composed—in nucleus—by the characters who speak them, others have actually been composed in more modern times for the place which they now occupy. Examples of such poems are innumerable, and do not, in general, call for special mention. A specially interesting form of speech poetry is the dramatic poetry, and the elegiac poetry composed in dialogue and semi-dramatic form. This class of poetry, however, is a more ambitious form of composition than the speech poems or elegies commonly found in sagas. We have reserved further discussion of it to a separate chapter.

[1] Thomson, *Diversions*, p. 386f.   [2] *Ib.* p. 312.
[3] *Ib.* p. 311; cf. further Mariner[3] II, p. 217.   [4] Ellis[1] I, p. 530f.

Poetry embodying formal speeches appears to have been widespread at all periods in the Pacific, and is found in all its principal varieties—panegyrics, elegies, addresses, and poems of celebration. Many panegyrics are attributed to the Migration Period, and though it is, of course, uncertain how far we have before us the text of a poem as it was composed at that period, the evidence here again points to the conclusion that tradition has often preserved the nucleus of the original, and that the original would not have differed very materially from its modern representative. In many such cases, no doubt, transference has taken place. Only a few instances of panegyrics can be referred to here. One poem which is recorded from the island of Aitutaki in the Cook Group claims to have been recited by Moe-terauri, the father of a hero Iro, for Iro himself.[1] We also possess the text of a poem which purports to have been sung at the anointing of one of the ancient kings of the island of Niue.[2] Fornander records from the early period (about the twelfth century) an instance of the recitation of a panegyric poem for a female chief from Kauai as she was on a visit to Hawaii.[3] A panegyric which appears to have been composed originally for Umi (cf. p. 255 above) is said to be still sung as a sort of harvest home by the priests and people as they bring the *koa* tree[4] down from the mountains.[5]

One of the commonest forms of panegyric poetry in Hawaii to which we have reference in the sagas of the Migration Period and later times is the *mele inoa* (lit. 'name poem'). Emerson defines a poem of this type as 'a eulogy or panegyric of the ancestral and personal virtues, real or fictitious, of a king or princeling', and there is no doubt that in such poems the chiefs recited their claims to be admitted as members of the Hawaiian aristocracy. But the instances seem to show that the *mele inoa* had also a wider significance than this, and the phrase appears to have been used, at least sometimes, of any poem by which a chief was able to distinguish himself, whether by the personal nature of its contents, or by the novelty of its theme (cf. p. 414 below). The *mele inoa* was not confined to men, and an interesting instance in the saga of Lono-i-ka-makahiki, grandson of Umi and king of Hawaii, refers to the filching by the hero of the *mele inoa* belonging to the female chief referred to above. He is led to steal the poem by the attraction of

---

[1] *J.P.S.* XII, p. 139; cf. also p. 365 f. below.   [2] *Ib.* p. 118.
[3] Fornander, *P.R.* II, p. 118; *Fornander Collection*, Vol. IV, p. 276ff.; cf. also p. 414 below.
[4] The *koa* tree supplies the wood of which a certain temple was built (Ed.).
[5] Malo, p. 246f.

its extreme novelty. The lady declares that it is 'a very late one, not heard in the country districts'. Later in the same saga we have another long *mele inoa* chanted by a female chief Kaikilani in honour of the same hero as she approaches the house in which he is staying.[1]

Heroic panegyric poetry has been frequently recorded in modern times from the recitation of the natives on important occasions. In Mangaia it was a part of the wedding ceremonies at the marriage of the first-born in important families that the bridegroom should walk along a pathway composed of the prostrate bodies of the bride's tribe from his own dwelling to that of the bride, while his near relatives accompany him, walking on the ground, clapping their hands and 'chanting songs in his praise, or reciting the deeds of his ancestors'. On a later occasion the bridegroom's family did honour to the bride in a similar manner, permitting her to walk over their prostrate bodies to the house of her father-in-law, where she ate her meal seated on a couch formed of living bodies, to the accompaniment of songs which were chanted in praise of her beauty and accomplishments.[2]

The chanting of panegyric poetry was often accompanied by the dramatic dance known as the *hula* (lit. 'dance'). Stewart witnessed the performance of a '*hura-hura*' in Hawaii at the beginning of last century, in honour of the arrival of the queen and princess.

"The theme of the whole was the character and praises of the queen and princess, who were compared to everything sublime in nature, and exalted as gods."[3]

In the Marquesas we hear of a special kind of poetry known as *i'i*, which is said to have been composed by guests who come from a distance in honour of a female chief who gives a feast.[4] We may refer also to the panegyrics composed in the same islands on the sons of chiefs and others, which are said to be frequently mimetic and choral in character.[5]

An interesting analogy to the panegyrics and elegies on favourite horses, hawks, etc. among the Tatars is furnished by the panegyrics on fighting cocks, which are said to have been common in Tahiti. These birds were kept for purposes of competitive sport, and appear to have been treasured and cared for much as a race-horse is valued by its owner in our own country. The prowess of these birds was celebrated in poetry like the great deeds of mighty champions, and the traditions of

---

[1] *Fornander Collection*, Vol. IV, p. 302.
[2] Gill, *L.S.I.* p. 60f.   [3] Stewart, *Residence*, p. 190.
[4] Handy, *N.C.M.* p. 338.   [5] *Ib.* p. 336ff.

combats between districts were preserved like those of their greatest battles.[1]

In Polynesia, as frequently also elsewhere, panegyric and elegiac poetry are often indistinguishable in form. Ellis calls attention to the elegiac poetry of Tahiti, which seems to have been composed by professional poets, and to have been highly figurative in diction, while 'recounting, under all the imagery of song, the leading events in the life of the individual'. These poems, we are told, were remarkably interesting when the life had been one of enterprise and adventure, and Ellis rightly emphasises the importance of poems of this class for the preservation of saga and legend. "Many of their legends", he tells us, "were originally funeral and elegiac songs, in honour of departed kings or heroes";[2] and he adds that he is disposed to ascribe the highest antiquity to poems of this class. In Mangaia also elegiac poetry appears to have been preserved for several centuries, and to be among the oldest literary records of the island. Gill has recorded innumerable examples,[3] some of which will be referred to later (p. 354 ff. below). From the island of Aitutaki in the same Group we have the lament which purports to have been composed by the son of the hero Iro (cf. above) for his murdered mother.[4]

Among the most formal and ambitious of the elegies of modern times are those of the Maoris. Mention has already been made (p. 240 above) of an elaborate Maori elegy on a dead child, which covers seven foolscap pages when written down. A rich harvest has been reaped of Maori elegies which were composed on chiefs slain during the Maori wars of the early part of last century.[5] Some of them have reference to even earlier times. As an example we may refer to a lament composed by an old Maori for his son who died about 1700, which, like all the older Maori poetry, is rich in mythological allusion.[6] These elegies were recited with the greatest ceremony, both on the occasion of the death of a person of rank, and also on later occasions in his honour.[7]

Maning describes a funeral chant known as a *pihe*, which seems to correspond to the Mangaian *pe'e*, and which is evidently a very ancient and formal type of liturgical elegy, full of obsolete diction and allusion to ancient traditions.[8] The *pihe* was sung standing before the corpse,

[1] Moerenhout II, p. 147 f.   [2] Ellis[1] I, p. 530.
[3] See Gill, *S.L.P. passim*.   [4] *J.P.S.* XII, p. 136.
[5] As examples we may cite *J.P.S.* XIX, p. 35; IX, pp. 97, 148.
[6] *J.P.S.* XXIX, p. 29.
[7] For detailed accounts of some of these Maori funeral scenes, see Reeves, p. 73.
[8] Maning, p. 223, footnote.

and was followed by a series of panegyrics recited by the near relatives, and possibly also the friends of the dead. Maning has left us a singularly striking description of the celebrations which took place after the death of the chief Hauraki, who was slain in the war in the north of New Zealand against the chief Heke.

"When Hauraki died, and his body lay at Wirinake to be seen for the last time by his relations, there was a great gathering of the Rarawa and Ngapuhi, to fulfil the last rites due to a chief. And when the *pihe* had been sung, then the chiefs arose one after another to speak in praise of the dead. This was the speech of Te Anu, he who is known as having been in his youth the best spearman of all the Ngapuhi tribes. Bounding to and fro before the corpse, with his famous spear in his hand, he spoke as follows: 'Farewell, Hauraki! go, taking with you your kindness and hospitality, your generosity and valour, and leave none behind who can fill your place. Your death was noble; you revenged yourself with your own hand; you saved yourself without the help of any man. Your life was short; but so it is with heroes. Farewell, O Hauraki, farewell.' At this time it was night, and the sister and also the young wife of Hauraki went in the dark and sat beside the river. They sat weeping silently, and spinning a cord wherewith to strangle themselves. The flax was wet with their tears. And as they did this the moon arose. So when the sister of Hauraki saw the rising moon, she broke silence, and lamented aloud, and this was her lament—the part I remember of it:

> It is well with thee, O moon! You return from death,
> Spreading your light on the little waves. Men say,
>> 'Behold the moon reappears';
> But the dead of this world return no more.
> Grief and pain spring up in my heart as from a fountain.
> I hasten to death for relief.
> Oh, that I might eat those numerous soothsayers
> Who could not foretell his death.
> Oh, that I might eat the Governor,
> For his was the war!

"At this time men came who were in search of these women, and prevented the sister of Hauraki from killing herself at that time. They watched her for several days, but she died of grief. But the wife of Hauraki consented to live that she might rear her son, so that he might fight with the Kapotai, on a future day.... The lament of the sister of Hauraki was sung by all the divisions of all the Ngapuhi, from the west coast to Tokerau."[1]

[1] Maning, p. 222 ff.

Poems embodying formal speeches or addresses are very common, especially among the Maori, from whom a large number of technical terms has been recorded which denote different types of poetry of this class, such as the *ngeri*, or derisive song, the *puha*, or song of defiance, and many others.[1] A large number of so-called 'cursing songs' have been recorded, also from the Maori; but they are more preoccupied with the celebration of the dead than with the cursing of the living.[2] Poems composed in the spirit of Tyrtaios urging warriors to battle are especially numerous. These may be addressed to a single warrior, or to a whole band. But in the latter case it is usual for a number of individuals to be singled out by name. Many poems have been recorded which celebrate victories, or taunt the returning warriors after a defeat. The former generally develops into a boasting poem,[3] the latter into a threat of vengeance.[4] One example of the latter was composed as a part of the ceremony of dedicating a Maori child to revenge, and was sung as a lullaby to the child.[5] In contrast to this we have from Mo'orea island, Rarotonga, a poem recited by a mother to her son to dissuade him from going to avenge his father—"She repeated an ancient *ayory* ('song') in favour of peace." This remarkable appeal, which is apparently preserved in full, concludes as follows:

> Let there not be war; for a man of war can ne'er be satiated;
> But let my son be instead a man of wisdom and learning—
> A keeper of the traditions of his house.
> Let there be no war.
> Plant deeply the spirit of peace,
> That your rule may be known—the land of enforced peace.[6]

It is characteristic of Hawaii that the more interesting examples of the formal addresses generally have reference to civil life, and conditions of peace. This is especially true of those which relate to the early period of the history of the Group. We may refer to the invitation chanted by Paao to Lonokaeho of Tahiti, when the former sailed to that island to invite Lono to become king of Hawaii.

[1] An excellent account of the various types of Maori songs, with their native names, is given by Best, *Maori* II, p. 135 ff. Here (p. 144) the *ngeri* is defined as a 'derisive song', and the *puha* as a 'war song'. See further Tregear, Williams, *Dictionaries*, s.v. The *ngeri* is not always of a bitter character, being sometimes addressed to friends and relatives; see e.g. *J.P.S.* XI, p. 142 ff.

[2] Examples will be found in *J.P.S.* I, p. 92 ff.; IX, p. 138 ff.

[3] See e.g. *J.P.S.* VI, p. 119; cf. also VII, p. 24 ff.

[4] See e.g. *J.P.S.* XI, pp. 143, 146.   [5] *Ib.* XI, p. 139.

[6] *Ib.* XXI, p. 59.

O, Lono, Lono, Lonokaeho...
Here are the canoes, come aboard,
Return (with us) and dwell in green-clad Hawaii...
When the canoes land, come aboard,
Sail away, and possess the island Hawaii.
Hawaii is the island for Lonokaeho to dwell in.[1]

In the sagas of this Group the arrival at a strange island after a long voyage is invariably celebrated in song. On such occasions the island is usually apostrophised as if it were a man (*kanaka*). These poems were chanted by the *tohunga*,[2] who, as we have seen, always accompanied such expeditions, and occupied the position of highest honour after the *ariki*. One of these poems purports to have been composed by Kama-hualele, who accompanied Moikeha from Tahiti to Hawaii (cf. p. 253 above), and who, on catching sight of the island of Hawaii, broke into a chant:

Here is Hawaii, the island, the man,
A man is Hawaii, —E[3]
A man is Hawaii,
A child of Kahiki,[4]
A royal flower from Kapaahu, etc.[5]

Before leaving the subject of formal speeches a word must be said about oratory. This art is very highly developed in Polynesia, and had the speeches of the orators been preserved we should have possessed a fine body of prose of this class. Much of the oratory was chanted, however, and therefore poetical or rhythmical in form. The high artistic development to which formal speech attained is best studied from the accounts of travellers who have heard the orators, and we have therefore reserved fuller mention of this subject to the chapter on 'The Tohunga and the Kaula.'

A considerable number of personal poems are ascribed in the sagas of the Migration Period to the great heroes of early times. It has already been mentioned that owing to the large amount of genuine traditional poetry which has been preserved from the past, and the conservative character of the style and diction of modern poetry, it is often impossible

[1] Emerson, *L.V.* p. 10.
[2] The Hawaiian form is *kahuna*. *Tohunga* is the Maori form.
[3] This represents the long drawn sound (*hianga*) made at intervals by the singer, and one of the chief characteristics of Polynesian chants; cf. p. 240 above.
[4] I.e. Tahiti.
[5] Fornander, *P.R.* II, p. 10f.; cf. Emerson, *L.V.* p. 16f.

to distinguish poetry which was actually composed by the heroes of early times from poetry composed in the traditional style and ascribed to them in later times. The great navigator Tangiia, who is believed to have lived about the first half of the thirteenth century,[1] is said to have composed a love-song to two girls on Mauke Island, in the Cook Group,[2] and also a song of farewell to Tahiti,[3] both of which are still preserved. The latter is practically a catalogue poem enumerating the natural features and places dear to his recollection around his old home.

> Great is my love for my own dear land—
> For Tahiti that I'm leaving.
> Great is my love for my sacred temple—
> For Pure-ora that I'm leaving.
> Great is my love for my drinking spring...
> For my own old homes, for Puna-auia,
> For Papa-ete, that I'm leaving, etc.

Poems of this class are very common, and Mariner tells us that they are more widely current than any other in Tonga.[4] He quotes the words of a poem expressive of regret at leaving the Island of Vavao 'with its beautiful prospects', for the islands of Toofooa and Kao, noted for making coarse mats.[5] The words of the poem are singularly close to those of Tangiia's.

Gill records a poem from Mangaia which we may call 'A Wife's Complaint', and which is undoubtedly a personal poem, dating probably from the famine in the early part of last century.[6] It is said to have been composed by an unfortunate woman called Rao as a dirge for herself before she was eaten by her cannibal husband.[7]

"As with the marvellous stoicism of heathenism she watched the preparations for the horrid banquet, she vented her feelings in a dirge, which was carefully treasured up by her afflicted sister-in-law, and thus transmitted to Christian times. It is now for the first time written. This pathetic death-lament is well-known to the natives of the Hervey Group."[8]

[1] See Emerson, *L.V.* p. 2; cf. Smith, *Hawaiki*, p. 233.

[2] Smith, *Hawaiki*, p. 236; *J.P.S.* xxviii, p. 186.

[3] Smith, *Hawaiki*, p. 238; *J.P.S.*xxviii, p. 189. The poem is strangely reminiscent of the Irish poem of Deirdre's lament for Alba, referred to in Vol. 1, p. 550 of the present work.　　　　　　　　　　　　　　　[4] Mariner[3] 1, p. 244.

[5] Mariner[3] ii, p. 218; cf. other poems of this class in *J.P.S.* xix, pp. 51, 136.

[6] See the MS. note-book of the Rev. W. W. Gill referred to on p. 256 above.

[7] Other similar cases of cannibalism are recorded from this Group, but all, seemingly, occasioned by famine conditions. See p. 256 above.

[8] W. W. Gill, *L.S.I.* p. 165 ff.

The poem is interesting as showing with what care these personal poems were sometimes preserved and handed down.

Occasional poetry is very common, no event being too trivial for poetical treatment, which seems to depend rather on the mood of the reciter than on the nature of the subject. As soon as the mood of the speaker gains in emotional intensity, there is a tendency for the words to assume a poetical form and for the voice to be raised in a chant. Thus it comes about that Polynesian sagas, like the sagas of Iceland, contain a considerable proportion of conversation in poetical form. Gill refers to this practice on the island of Atiu in his account of the visit of the missionary Williams in 1823. The people resolved to take the little mission vessel, but Romatane, the leading chief of the day, was so astonished at the big canoe, moving without paddles over the ocean, that he forbade his followers to offer any violence to the strangers, "uttering the following poetical words":

> By whose command shall an attack be made
> On a race of gods from nether-world?
> Shall a race of weaklings
> Dare to molest so wise a people?
> Look at yon vessel;
> Gaze at its masts;
> At its multitudinous, innumerable ropes.[1]

News is often passed on in the form of song, and the tendency for speeches made in moments of emotional intensity to be chanted may be illustrated by the fact that when Governor King returned two natives of New Zealand to their homes in 1793 he mentions that their friends related to them the tribal news in song.[2] The practice had not died out by last century, and occasional poetry was still extremely common. It was composed even on trivial subjects, apparently by all members of the community. Dieffenbach quotes a poem composed by the natives of the Awaroa Valley, in which they relate the want and hardships which they have undergone in cutting a bridle path for thirty-four miles through the forest:

"The tobacco is gone: we have no food cooked in a pot: Etiki is hungry: Taewa is sick: Te Paki is hungry: all our good cheer is

---

[1] Gill, *Jottings*, p. 45.
[2] Best, *Maori* II, p. 142. The reference is doubtless to the *tangi*. Cf. further p. 466 below.

exhausted: we turn back towards the Reinga:[1] we are sick for some food."[2]

It is impossible to do justice to Polynesian poetry, either by a general account, or by attempting to translate it.[3] The unfamiliarity of the form of the verse and its metrical freedom, the traditional and difficult diction, the highly allusive and figurative phraseology, all make the task of translation peculiarly difficult. Those who have spent a lifetime on the study of Maori poetry are the most pessimistic in regard to the possibility of doing anything like justice to the art in any other language than its own, and the most reluctant to undertake the task of translation. On the other hand, the facility with which men and women of all types compose extempore poetry on all occasions in Polynesia may well mislead us into the supposition that the poetry is itself generally of a trivial nature. This is belied by its extremely conservative character, as well as by the testimony of those most familiar with Polynesian literature. The great wealth of short occasional poetry and the universal practice of composition are to be viewed in the light of the high development of Polynesian intellectual life, and the widespread cultivation of oral literature everywhere throughout the Pacific. Facility of composition, so far from indicating a low standard of art, is a part of the equipment of every cultivated Polynesian, among whom literary art is probably held in higher esteem and more sedulously cultivated than among any other people in the world.

[1] The path to the spirit world, which was reached, according to Maori belief, by descending the sheer face of the cliff off the North Cape, North Island. See p. 315 below, and cf. p. 290.   [2] Dieffenbach I, p. 220.
[3] On this subject, see Best, _Maori_ II, p. 135 f.

CHAPTER III

NON-HEROIC SAGA AND POETRY RELATING TO LEGENDARY CHARACTERS OF THE PRE-HISTORIC AND LATER PERIODS

IT has already been mentioned that we have in Polynesia extensive Cycles of stories relating to persons whose names appear in the pedigrees of the leading families of the various Groups in an earlier position than those of the heroes considered in the preceding chapter. These Cycles have been recorded—sometimes, it is true, in a fragmentary form—in Groups as far apart as Samoa, Hawaii, Tahiti and Rarotonga, in New Zealand, and even among the Moriori of the Chathams. They relate to heroes whose names are found in the pedigrees of the ruling families of Rarotonga and New Zealand, as well as those of Hawaii. In the latter case it was held by Fornander[1] and Smith[2] that the southern pedigree had been grafted on to the Hawaiian line in the twelfth and thirteenth centuries, though Smith[3] and others[4] nevertheless emphasise rightly the full and circumstantial nature of the Hawaiian saga tradition relating to Tawhaki and his descendants. Even if the Hawaiian evidence is comparatively late and not independent of southern tradition, the consistency with which the legends and genealogical data have been preserved—more or less independently, according to general belief—for at least five centuries over the entire Polynesian area is sufficiently remarkable.

The earliest series of names which appear with reasonable consistency in the more important of the pedigrees, and to which an ambitious saga Cycle is attached, are those of Hema (Ema) and his sons Kariki (Karii) and Tawhaki (Taaki), and their descendants.[5] The Rarotongan pedigrees derive their ancestry from Karii, who, according to their claim, was the elder brother and the more important *ariki* of the two. The Maori, on the other hand, claim descent from Tawhaki, to whom they ascribe

---

[1] Fornander, *P.R.* I, p. 198 ff.   [2] *Hawaiki*, p. 196.
[3] *Loc. cit.*   [4] See e.g. Stokes, *J.P.S.* xxxix, p. 33.
[5] The home of the Tawhaki Cycle has been located in Samoa. For some references and remarks on the subject, see Krämer I, p. 455 ff. Perhaps the most ambitious literary records of Tawhaki himself are the sagas and chants recorded from the Paumotu Archipelago by Stimson, *L.M.T.* See also p. 383 below.

seniority over Kariki. The most widely known and highly developed Cycle of these early sagas is that which relates to Tawhaki and his immediate descendants. Not only Tawhaki himself, but his son or grandson Rata—the versions differ as to the exact relationship—and their descendant Apakura, are known throughout the Pacific. A comparison of Maori and Rarotongan pedigrees with one another, and with those of other groups, brought S. P. Smith to the conclusion that the stories of Tawhaki and Rata relate to a period c. A.D. 700; and a comparison of the distribution of the stories and the position of the names in the pedigrees of the leading lines of the chief island groups has led to the general belief among Polynesian scholars that the heroes in question had an historical existence about this period. These dates have recently been called in question by more than one scholar (cf. p. 238 above), and there can be no doubt that the whole question of the historicity of these early heroes requires revision in the light of modern critical standards in regard to the evaluation of oral tradition.[1] But this is not the place in which to discuss the question with the fulness which it deserves.

According to Maori tradition[2] Tawhaki is a man of great beauty and a skilled builder of beautiful houses. Among his chief exploits are his journeys, first to rescue the bones of his father who has been killed by a strange ocean race known as the Ponaturi, and then to the Underworld and the Heavens. In most versions the journeys to the Underworld and the Heavens are undertaken to rescue the soul of his wife, a 'fairy' from Heaven, who visits him in his home and remains with him till the birth of their first child. But one day after this, feeling herself insulted by some casual remark made by her husband, she flies up to the roof-tree of their house, and chants a farewell,[3] and then returns to her home in the skies, taking the child with her. Tawhaki determines to follow her in company with his younger brother Kariki. The two brothers pay a

[1] It is not for a moment the intention of the present authors to imply the slightest doubt as to the value of Polynesian oral tradition for the purpose of reconstructing history. They are of the opinion, however, that the traditions have been accepted too literally and uncritically in some circumstances.

[2] See e.g. Grey, p. 42ff.; Andersen, p. 160ff.

[3] In Polynesian tradition it is common for supernatural wives to fly up to the roof-tree, and from there to chant a farewell before taking their final departure to their old home. It is interesting to compare the first strophe of the Sea Dyak dirge recorded by Howell (cf. p. 489 ff. below), in which the land of the dead is referred to as 'the land of those who were cut off and took refuge on the roof-tree'. The spirit of the dead person is clearly thought of in the form of a bird.

preliminary visit to their old blind ancestress in the Underworld. Tawhaki succeeds in curing her blindness,[1] and in return she directs them as to how they may reach the Heavens by climbing a vine, the roots of which are in her own realm.[2] Tawhaki succeeds in making the ascent, but Kariki fails, and is obliged to return home. Tawhaki, however, succeeds in reaching the Heavens, where he is ultimately reunited to his wife and child.

The versions of Tawhaki's journeys offer considerable variation, as is, of course, natural in a widespread story preserved by oral tradition. Thus the Ponaturi are sometimes represented as in Po, which in the Paumotu version of the story[3] is the realm of Kiho, the supreme god (cf. p. 307 ff. below). The approach is variously described as up a high rock,[4] down a deep chasm, and across the sea.[5] His ascent to the Heavens is described in a variety of ways. According to one Rarotongan version he reaches his goal by climbing up a tall cocoa-nut tree.[6] In New Zealand he is variously described as ascending by means of a rope, a spider's thread, a kite.[7] One of the most interesting of these Maori versions has it that when he tries to ascend by means of a kite made by the hands of man, he fails, and only succeeds when he mounts on a hawk.[8] Moriori chants also speak of him as battling with the winds, manifestly in the form of a kite.[9] Hawaiian versions speak of him as climbing painfully up the path of the rainbow.[10] In one version from Tahiti the hero merely journeys up a high mountain, and overtakes his wife on the path of death.[11] The hero's experiences are often duplicated in the accounts of his different journeys. During the course of these journeys he frequently encounters women—his female ancestors—who direct him on his path. He also meets and converses with people who are returning to earth by the same path as that on which he is travelling. Evidently he is following a much used thoroughfare.

[1] This motif is a very common one in Polynesian saga, and is attributed elsewhere to the god Tane, and to a number of other heroes; see pp. 319, 344 below. In the version of the story of Tawhaki—also Maori—recorded by Taylor (p. 141) the curing of the old woman's blindness is said to take place in the Heavens, in the house of the Ponaturi; but the words 'Heaven' and 'Underworld' are misleading in reference to Polynesian eschatology and mythology, and are only used as a matter of convenience. For a discussion of the localities of the supernatural regions, see p. 313 f. below.
[2] So Reeves, p. 67; Grey, p. 51.   [3] Stimson, L.M.T. p. 66.
[4] J.P.S. xxi, p. 11; cf. also Smith, Hawaiki, p. 194.
[5] Gill, Myths, p. 250 ff.   [6] Smith, J.P.S. xxx, p. 4.
[7] Taylor, p. 141; see further Andersen, p. 432.   [8] J.P.S. xxxvii, p. 362.
[9] Ib. vii, p. 78.   [10] See p. 298 below.   [11] Henry, A.T. p. 563 ff.

In the versions which represent Tawhaki as ascending through several Heavens, as also elsewhere in Polynesian mythological and theological tradition,[1] the Heavens are represented as a series of regions one above another, access being given to each Heaven from the one immediately below. The resemblance to the Tatar conception of the Heavens will be observed at once. Tawhaki's journey through each successive Heaven to the highest Heaven also resembles in many respects the journey of the Tatar shaman to the abode of Bai Ülgen (cf. p. 200 above). Like the latter it is full of incident, and, as the hero pauses in each successive Heaven of his upward course, he encounters many adventures.

Tawhaki's son by his first wife is Wahie-roa, who is murdered by a certain Matuku, the *tohunga* of the Ponaturi. One of the most widespread sagas of the Pacific is the story of the vengeance of Wahie-roa's son Rata[2] for his father's death. The variant versions of this saga differ even more than those of Tawhaki; but all agree in attaching great importance to a certain canoe, by means of which the voyage of the avenging party is made, and in attributing special circumstances to its fabrication. According to a version of the story current among the Maori[3] Rata goes to the forest to cut down a tree in order to build the canoe immediately on hearing from his mother of his father's death; but as often as he cuts the tree down it is again found standing in its place on the following day. At last Rata catches some wood spirits, and learns from them that he must perform certain ceremonies before cutting the tree, and when these have been duly carried out, Rata, on returning to the spot, finds, not the tree, but the canoe already shaped, and ready to be launched. He sails away till he comes to the island where Matuku dwells in a deep cavern at the top of a high mountain, and by means of the magic of Rata, which is more powerful than that of Matuku, the latter is lured out of his cavern and slain. It is also by the superior magic of Rata that his followers are enabled later to destroy a great host of the Ponaturi who attack them after their return home in vengeance for the death of their *tohunga*. A consensus of tradition,

---

[1] E.g. Reeves, p. 65 ff.; Taylor, pp. 114, 141, 220; Grey, p. 60. See also Gill, *Myths*, p. 2, where a similar conception of the Heavens is given. There are said to be at least ten separate Heavens, one above another; but in certain diagrams they envelop the upper half of the egg-shaped Universe, and seem, therefore, to be concentric rather than parallel. Cf. p. 313 below. In New Zealand the usual number of Heavens is twelve. See Best, *Maori* 1, p. 88; Andersen, p. 352.

[2] It has already been mentioned (p. 272 above) that Rata is sometimes represented as Tawhaki's son, sometimes as his grandson. Cf. also pp. 313, 374 below.

[3] Grey, p. 79 ff.; Andersen, p. 174 ff.

therefore, represents Rata as a great navigator and a great magician—in fact, a great *tohunga*.

The story of Rata is very widespread and is found in all the principal Groups, e.g. New Zealand, Rarotonga, Aitutaki and Paumotu (in the dialect of Tahiti), and traces of the story are found also in Samoa.[1] In Hawaii Rata (Lata) is the goddess of nature and especially of the rain-storm;[2] but elsewhere he figures, in general, like Tawhaki, as a great controller of the weather, and a great navigator. The versions differ also in regard to other details. Thus in the Rarotongan account[3] the brothers of a certain Atonga attempt to escape from Atonga's harsh treatment by building a canoe for themselves from a tree belonging to Rata. In the Maori,[4] Aitutaki[5] and Paumotu[6] versions, it is Rata himself who attempts to cut down the tree to build a canoe, his object being, in some cases to avenge his father, in others the exploration of new lands. Thus while the story is the same in all cases, both the principal actors and the motives vary.

It often happens in regard to these non-heroic and legendary sagas, as in regard to the historical sagas considered in the last chapter, that the same story may be told with the chief emphasis laid, not on the *ariki*, but on his *tohunga*. In such cases it naturally happens that the story is related from a somewhat different point of view, or in a different literary style, which may at times give the effect of a totally different kind of narrative. For example, the Rarotongan version of the story of Rata actually relates the mythical adventures of a *tohunga* named Nganaoa, who accompanies Rata on his voyage to avenge the death of his parents. On the voyage the *tohunga* proves himself to be a man of supernatural powers, and by means of a magic calabash[7] is able to save the crew from many dangers. At the beginning of the voyage, however, when Rata asks him what his calling is, he replies: "I fly kites."

"Rata said, 'You fly kites; and what then?'

Nganaōa said, 'I leap up to the heavens and extol my mother with exalting songs.'[8]

Rata said, 'You extol your mother, and what then?'

Nganaōa replied, 'O, I exalt our mother, and that is all.'

[1] *J.P.S.* IV, p. 239.   [2] Emerson, *U.L. passim.*   [3] *J.P.S.* IV, p. 100.
[4] Grey, p. 81 ff.   [5] Gill, *Myths*, p. 142 ff.   [6] *J.P.S.* XIX, p. 176 ff.
[7] For the real nature of the 'magic calabash', and its actual scientific value in navigation, see Gill, *Myths*, p. 319 f.; cf. Andersen, pp. 42, 358 f. Cf. also p. 284 below.
[8] Perhaps a reference to the musical form of kite in use in certain parts of the Pacific.

Rata said, 'I do not want you, you cannot come', and it was with great difficulty that Nganaoa persuaded him to take him on the voyage."[1] Rata's son Tu-whakararo takes as his wife Apakura, by whom he has a large family. The youngest is a son named Whakatau, who is adopted by a sea ancestor and trained to be skilled in magic. He is especially skilled in the art of flying kites—an art in which all the members of Tawhaki's family excel, and Whakatau is so proficient that he is said to be able to fly kites even under water.[2] Tu-whakararo is murdered and eaten while on a visit to his sister, and Whakatau, who is an intrepid warrior as well as a magician, makes a long voyage in Rata's famous canoe to avenge him. The account of his arrival at the house where the tragedy has taken place, the disguise devised for him by his aunt who meets him secretly on his landing, and the scene in which he reveals himself to the murderers, extinguishes the fires, and under cover of darkness seizes his father's bones and makes good his escape, together with his aunt, are all vividly described in the Maori version of the saga which we are following.[3] The story of Apakura is widely known throughout the western and southern Pacific, notably in Samoa, Rarotonga, Maori, and Moriori traditions. In these traditions she figures as a famous mourner, and many tangis[4] or mournful chants are attributed to her.[5]

[1] *J.P.S.* XIX, p. 149 f. With this version we may compare the one from Aitutaki recorded by Gill, *Myths*, p. 142 ff. Cf. also versions from Tahiti and Paumotu recorded by Henry, *A.T.* p. 481 ff.; and from New Zealand by Grey, p. 79 ff. and by Shortland, p. 67 ff. In the Tahiti and Paumotu versions, the monsters of the deep are overcome by Rata himself; in the Maori, by his son. An obscure reference to the use of the kite by the *tohunga* in navigation doubtless lies behind the Mangaian tradition recorded by Gill, *Myths*, p. 287; cf. also *ib.* p. 123.

[2] A detailed account of the kite-flying activities of Tawhaki's family and a discussion of their significance has been published by Chadwick in the *J.R.A.I.* LXI (1931), p. 455 ff.; cf. also *ib.* LX (1930), p. 425 ff.

[3] Andersen, p. 180 ff.

[4] The *tangi* is often translated as 'lament', owing no doubt to the mournful tone in which the chant is sung; but it does not appear that the words recited necessarily bear any sorrowful interpretation, though the *tangi* is very commonly recited on solemn, and even mournful occasions, such as a death, or a parting. But it is equally readily recited at the reunion of friends or relatives after long absence, though on the latter occasions the impression made by the recital on the mind of a European is no less mournful, owing to the tones of the chant. The word *apakura* is also used in Maori to denote an 'elegy'.

[5] For a brief account of Apakura, and an enumeration of some of the variant versions of traditions relating to her, and her hardly less famous son Whakatau, see Smith, *Hawaiki*, p. 201 ff.; *J.P.S.* XVIII, p. 139 ff.

It will be seen that all the heroes of the line of Tawhaki are great navigators and formidable adversaries. Their canoes are the most famous in Polynesian legend, and all the members of this great family are ready to undertake journeys of the most difficult and dangerous kind in order to rescue—dead or alive—their relatives who have been carried off, or to exact vengeance for insults or injuries. Yet they are not warriors in the true sense of the word. Their ends are achieved by magic rather than by valour. It is by superior knowledge rather than by prowess that they succeed in overcoming their enemies, especially by knowledge of charms and of physical science. They are skilled in observations of the weather and in sailing directions, and especially in meteorics, and in the allied art or science of kite-flying, which, in its more highly skilled forms, implies a knowledge of both. They are accordingly said to be able to 'control' the winds. In Mangaian versions especially they are closely associated with the stars and the Heavenly bodies.

Apart from innumerable versions of the Cycle of Tawhaki and his descendants, we have also from different parts of the Pacific a number of stories which bear so close a general resemblance to this Cycle as almost to constitute another series of variants in themselves. Whether this is in reality the case, or whether these analogous stories are quite independent in literary origin, though similar in theme, could not be determined in a survey like the present. The question depends largely on historical and theological data, and on considerations as to the extent to which the customs and beliefs of the past are responsible for the myth and ritual reflected in the traditions of the various Groups in the Pacific today. This series of stories, and the interesting problem to which they give rise, may be illustrated by a brief account of two of the more outstanding examples, that of Aukele from the northern and of Ngaru from the Central Pacific.

The saga of Aukele immediately precedes that of Moikeha in the *Fornander Collection*[1] of Hawaiian sagas, and it may be assumed, therefore, that he is traditionally believed to have lived about 1100.[2] He is the youngest of his brothers, whose envy he arouses by his beauty and prowess, and by whom he is cast down a deep pit. Here, however, he finds his ancestress, who undertakes his education in all matters pertaining to a sage and mantic person; and when at a later date he emerges from the pit, and accompanies his brothers on a long voyage, he acts as the *tohunga*, and overcomes the perils of the sea by his mantic powers, while his brothers perish through neglect of his counsel. On

[1] Vol. IV, p. 32 ff. [2] See Smith, *Hawaiki*, p. 22 f.

coming ashore he marries a supernatural woman, the cousin of the goddesses Pele and Hiiaka, after which he undertakes various super-natural adventures. Among the chief of these are his encounters with supernatural birds, which resemble Tawhaki's adventures with the Ponaturi, and his journey to the Underworld to steal the water of Kane (Tane), which restores the dead to life. In the former adventure he is assisted by the god Lono whom he invariably carries with him in a box, and who acts as his tutelary genius throughout life; in the latter adventure he is advised by his supernatural wife, whose knowledge of the topography of the Heavens and the Underworld is evidently much greater than his own. Like many other heroes who make the journey to the supernatural regions, he is also assisted by dead ancestors whom he meets on his route.

In Mangaia the adventures of Ngaru[1] resemble those of Tawhaki and of Aukele in their main features. Like them, the hero is educated by an ancestor underground, and like theirs his adventures consist of an initial encounter with monsters in this world, followed by a journey, first to the Underworld, and then to the Heavens. Here also his destiny is governed by his wives, the four daughters of Miru, who are represented as binding and trussing their husband as the Mangaians treated a body for burial, and as carrying him to the underground oven of Miru, the blind ogress of the Underworld in Mangaian myth. The hero escapes, like Tawhaki, by catching hold of a fibrous plant growing in the Underworld, and making his way, first to a land known as Taumareva, 'where fruits and flowers grow profusely, and the inhabitants excel in flute-playing', and thence to earth. His last exploit consists in allowing himself to be drawn up to Heaven in the great basket of the sky demon Amai-te-rangi, whom he slays with the help of a number of little lizards dispatched by his grandfather for the purpose.

The adventures of the hero next to be considered are of a totally different type from those of Tawhaki, Aukele, or Ngaru. The story of Ono-kura is known only in the Central Pacific. Like many of the stories which we have been considering, it has been preserved in both heroic and non-heroic forms, according to the milieu from which it has been recorded. One version from Rarotonga is said to be among the longest and most elaborate Polynesian sagas which we possess, and to be interspersed with songs, many of which are couched in a form of diction so archaic as to render translation almost impossible.[2] Another

---

[1] Gill, *Myths*, p. 225 ff.
[2] See Smith, *Hawaiki*, p. 223 f., where a brief summary of this version is given.

version from Ra'iatea is also a very elaborate piece of narrative, consisting of an intermixture of prose and verse, even the prose being in a highly poetical and archaic diction.[1] Important versions have been recorded also from the Marquesas,[2] the Paumotu Archipelago,[3] and Mangaia.[4] It is curious, therefore, that no version of the story, and no occurrence of the name, seems to have been recorded from either Hawaii or New Zealand.[5] The position of the hero in the Rarotongan pedigrees would entitle him, on the usual computation (cf. p. 237, footnote 6 above), to a date about 1100; but his absence from the northern and southern Groups suggests that he was not known to the Central Pacific before the fourteenth century.

The version from Ra'iatea represents the hero as a sage and recluse possessed of supernatural powers, although a warrior of great prowess. The story relates the arrival of his ancestors in Tahiti, and there seems to be a general agreement that Ono was not a native (see p. 280 below). His childhood is such as is commonly ascribed to mantic persons in the Pacific, both in custom and legend. He is the youngest son of his parents, born under peculiar circumstances, and placed in a cave where he grows to manhood, like the last high priest of Rarotonga.[6] Here, like Aukele (see above), he acquires a familiar spirit, which becomes his constant companion through life. His relations with his mother are peculiar and obscure, but they seem to resemble those between Maui and his own mother (cf. p. 284 f. below), and like Maui he is reproached by his elder brothers for his disrespectful treatment of her, and perhaps for his too great intimacy with her.[7]

---

[1] This version was published by W. W. Gill in *J.P.S.* IV, p. 256ff., where a translation by Miss Teuira Henry is also given. See also Henry, *A.T.* p. 516, footnote.

[2] Handy, *M.L.* p. 104ff. [3] Henry, *A.T.* p. 516ff.

[4] Gill, *Myths*, p. 81ff.

[5] Smith suggests that the hero was perhaps known to these Groups under another name; but if this were so the stories connected with him would have been recorded, and this does not appear to be the case. There seems to be some evidence from Rarotonga that a certain Naea, a contemporary of Honoura, fled to Hawaii; see Henry, *A.T.* p. 536.

[6] See p. 452 below, and cf. the custom with regard to the youthful heir to the throne of the Gambier Islands, Smith, *J.P.S.* XXVII, p. 121; Caillot, *Mythes*, p. 150; Dumont d'Urville III, p. 428; Cuzent, p. 73ff.

[7] Cf. the Paumotu version at this point, Henry, *A.T.* p. 523. He is even addressed as *Maui* (see Henry, *A.T.* p. 520). According to Henry the word means 'backwoodsman', perhaps in relation to the seclusion in which he was brought up; cf. however, Gill, *J.P.S.* V, p. 126.

Honoura (Onokura) gives evidence of mantic powers already before his period of seclusion in the cave is completed,[1] and a series of youthful exploits follows, all of which partake of the marvellous. When King Tangiia[2] sails to the eastern islands on warlike expeditions, Honoura accompanies the ship, and by magic and single combat slays the monsters of the deep and the human enemies of the king. When the king is wounded Honoura cures him, sucking his wound, pouring medicine into it and tending the patient; but he is not a *tohunga*, for we are told that a *tohunga* accompanied the expedition, taking with him the conch shell trumpet of the god Oro, and the drum of Honoura.[3] The distinction is interesting, and is made even clearer when meat is apportioned, for we are told that while one portion only is given to the *tohunga*, Honoura has two portions, one for himself, and one for his familiar spirit, whom he is always careful to feed. His association with the god Oro is also interesting. His last chant concludes with the words:

> O god of the Arioi,
> Thou art my god.

The *areoi* are a corporation of men and women closely associated with the god Oro, who by their gaiety and public performances of dance and song made a great impression on travellers and missionaries early last century. They will be discussed more fully in a later chapter. In the résumé of the story of Ono recorded by Handy[4] from the Marquesas, Ono is associated with a band of *hoki*, a class of people having much in common with the *areoi* (cf. p. 434 f. below).

In the version from Mangaia,[5] Ono (Honoura, Ono-kura) figures, not as a warrior, nor yet as a magician, but as a foreigner possessed of superior implements and skill, and perhaps also superior intelligence, but hardly of a supernatural character. His chief exploit in this brief

---

[1] On this passage, see Chadwick, *J.R.A.I.* LXI, p. 472.

[2] For the title, see p. 250, footnote 3 above.

[3] In the island of Mangaia and elsewhere the conch shell trumpet was sacred to Oro or Rongo, the drum to Tane. In Hawaii, however, the priest of Tane (Kane) appears to have used a conch shell, the drum being introduced into the Group in relatively recent times from Tahiti (see p. 253 above).

[4] Handy, *M.L.* p. 104.

[5] According to Henry, *A.T.* p. 532, this version has been blended with the legend of Rata, to which it undoubtedly bears a very close resemblance; but corroborative evidence for its association with Ono is not wanting from the western Pacific (see above), and the songs relating to the hero are stated by Gill to be the oldest, and presumably the best preserved in the island. According to the same tradition Ono came from Tonga (see Gill, *Myths*, p. 84).

but sober version consists in cutting down a giant casuarina or iron-wood tree which had been imported from Tonga by the members of the immigrant Tonga clan, and which had previously been the dwelling-place of a demon who slew all who attempted to fell it. In this version Ono is represented as an immigrant from Tonga,[1] where, according to Gill, the story of Ono was also known. We have not ourselves been able to trace the Tongan version, but corroborative evidence may be seen in the fact that in Tonga the casuarina or iron-wood tree, which figures promimently in the Mangaian version, is specially sacred, and is spoken of in Tongan myth as under the guardianship of a man of priestly class, and as the means by which the gods descend to earth.[2] Moreover in Samoa a very similar myth relating to One (Ono?) and certain sacred trees was well known, and apparently here also con-nected with Tongans.[3] According to Gill the Tongan clan introduced the iron-wood tree into Mangaia.[4]

The heroes whom we have hitherto considered may be regarded as having a possible claim to a historical existence in the past, despite the fact that they figure as gods in certain versions of the stories with which they are associated, and also despite the large proportion of unhistorical and supernatural matter which appears in these stories. We do not think that any such claim can fairly be made for Maui, the hero of the Cycle next to be considered, or for Hina, who is closely associated with him, being sometimes represented as his wife, sometimes as his sister. It is true that both Maui and Hina appear on the genealogies. The Raro-tongan history represents Maui as a son of Tangaroa, and Hina as a daughter of Vai-takere, and also wife of Tangaroa. If the Vai-takere in question is identical with the person of this name who appears on the Rarotongan genealogies, this would place Maui and Hina, according to Smith's computation, as early as the first century A.D.[5] Without dis-cussing the probability of this chronology, it may be pointed out that the close connection of Hina with Tinirau cannot be overlooked, and that, according to Maori genealogies, Tinirau would have flourished about A.D. 500.[6] But it is greatly to be doubted if any reliance can be placed in their historicity, even in regard to the period to which they are traditionally ascribed.

It might indeed be argued with a considerable degree of justice that

[1] *Myths*, loc. cit.   [2] Gifford, *T.M.T.* p. 25 ff.
[3] Turner, pp. 63, 66.   [4] *Myths*, pp. 81, 274, footnote 3.
[5] See *Hawaiki*, p. 154, and the table of Rarotongan genealogies, *ib. ad fin.*
[6] Smith, *Hawaiki*, pp. 166, 283.

there is little more ground for the historicity of Tawhaki and his family than for that of Maui. Both heroes occur very early in the genealogies; both are chiefly associated with supernatural rather than with normal human adventures; in several cases their adventures are the same. Nevertheless there is a difference. In the first place there is great inconsistency in regard to Maui's place in the pedigrees, and in his relationship to other names, such as that of Hina, while collateral lines are not forthcoming. Moreover, none of the leading royal or noble lines of the Pacific stress any claim to be descended from him, as they do from Tawhaki. It will be seen that Maui's name generally occurs in a position which would place him many centuries before Tawhaki and his family. This would be much earlier than any period for which we have evidence for a stable relative chronology in the Pacific. Finally, it will be seen that the stories relating to Maui are very close in their general style to those of folk-tales; and though on a literal interpretation the stories of Tawhaki and Rata carry no conviction, and are fraught throughout with the marvellous, a careful comparison of the variant versions from different parts of the Pacific suggests that this is to be attributed in some measure to figurative diction, and traditional phraseology, while a further comparison with the stories contained in the early Japanese chronicle known as the *Kojiki*, and with the oral literature of the shamans of the Tatars and other tribes of Central and northern Asia, suggests that these motifs are ancient, and connected in some way with religious ritual. This subject has been discussed by one of us more fully elsewhere,[1] and we must not dwell longer on it here, but pass on to give a brief account of the Cycles of Maui and of Hina.

The stories relating to Maui are recorded from all over the Pacific. Perhaps the largest and most complete Cycle is found in New Zealand,[2] but extensive Cycles have also been recorded from Hawaii,[3] the Paumotu Archipelago,[4] and elsewhere. In general the versions of the stories are comparatively uniform, the chief variants being generally due, in all probability, to the extent and manner in which the highly figurative diction of the more ambitious versions of the stories has been interpreted already in many of the native records, and transformed into

---

[1] Chadwick, *J.R.A.I. loc. cit.*

[2] These Maori versions will be found scattered throughout the volumes of the *J.P.S.* See also Andersen, p. 192 ff.

[3] See Westervelt, *L.M.*; cf. further a review of this book by S. P. Smith in *J.P.S.* xx, p. 35 f.

[4] The most ambitious version, from a literary point of view, is embodied in the narrative and chants from the Paumotu Archipelago recorded by Stimson, *L.M.T.*

literal form. In the western Pacific the stories are preserved in a more fragmentary form than elsewhere. Taken as a whole, however, the stories of Maui are undoubtedly more numerous than those of any other hero. This is no doubt partly due to transference. Many stories which are told in some islands of unspecified or unknown heroes are told in others of Maui, who has thus become the hero of many stories of which the original hero has been forgotten. When this is said, however, there remain from a dozen[1] to twenty[2] stories of considerable length and distinctive form which belong properly to the Maui Cycle. No complete corpus of stories is, however, recorded in any single répertoire.[3]

Maui's ancestors are generally represented in the stories as supernatural beings. According to Maori tradition[4] he is in the sixth generation in descent from a certain Mata-ora and his 'fairy' wife Niwa-reka (cf. p. 294 below), and his mother is Taranga, a 'fairy' of the Underworld, while Rarotongan tradition represents his father as Tangaroa, but whether the god, or the human voyager of the same name, is not certain.[5] In the Paumotu version recorded by Stimson, Ataraga (Tangaroa) is the name of Maui's father,[6] his mother's name being Huahega. Maui himself is commonly stated to have been born prematurely on the seashore, which probably accounts for the small stature constantly attributed to him.[7] He is educated first by the sea-deities, then by his 'ancestor', Tama-nui-ki-te-rangi, after which he rejoins his mother and his brothers.

As he sleeps at night at his mother's side, he learns that she disappears every morning through a hole in the ground, and he determines to follow her. Transforming himself into a wood-pigeon, he descends through the same hole to the Underworld, where he finds his parents. His father purifies him at a running stream, and performs the naming ceremony over him;[8] but in reciting the *karakia* or chant, he omits one

---

[1] See *J.P.S.* xxxviii, p. 22. This estimate is based principally on Maori material. A useful list of versions and data relating to Maui as published in this Journal is also given here.   [2] See Westervelt, *loc. cit.*

[3] An interesting series of Maui stories occurring in a single répertoire is recorded in *J.P.S.* xxxviii (1930), p. 1 ff.   [4] Andersen, p. 192.

[5] See Smith, *Hawaiki*, p. 153; and cf. the Hawaiian legends of Maui's parents recorded by Westervelt, *L.M.* p. 1 ff.

[6] See Stimson, *L.M.T.* p. 5 ff.

[7] Polynesian tradition persistently associates premature birth and small stature with the 'fairies' (see p. 286 below).

[8] We may compare the performance of a similar rite by the *tohunga* in New Zealand over pupils in the *Whare Wananga*. See Best, *Maori* i, p. 75.

name, whence it comes about that Maui incurs the anger of the gods, which is the ultimate cause of his death. Meantime, however, he returns to earth, and teaches his brothers the arts of cultivation, and has many further adventures, all tinged with the marvellous. One of the most widespread of these relates how he snares the sun with a noose; another tells how he steals fire from a supernatural being in the Underworld. Other stories tell of his kite-flying, his long voyages, and his invention of the calabash of the winds—a native invention of combined sextant and compass (cf. p. 275 above); Maui's fishing exploits form a whole Cycle in themselves. They relate how he improves eel-spears by the addition of barbs; how he invents a new and superior fish-hook; how he steals his brothers' fish. Almost all the Pacific islands relate that they were fished up from the bottom of the sea by Maui. In all these stories he gains his ends by cunning and guile and superior knowledge. His sense of honour is very low, and he is the reverse of a heroic figure. He rarely fights, and he is chiefly represented in his relations with his own family. Only occasionally is he brought into contact with other human beings. His path hardly ever crosses with that of heroes of other Cycles.

The most remarkable of all Maui's adventures is that in which he enters the Underworld to destroy death.[1] According to a widespread version of the story[2] he attempts to enter the body of his great ancestress Hine-nui-te-Po, and to emerge through her mouth, passing through the very bowels of death. It is an attempt to be twice born, and thereby to achieve immortality, both for himself and for mankind as a whole. But the attempt fails, and Maui meets his own death just when success seems at hand. His failure is attributed by his father to the flaw in the *karakia* or invocation recited at the naming of the hero (p. 283 above).[3] It is interesting to compare with this story, however, that of the *ariki*

[1] See Westervelt, *L.M.* p. 128 ff.; but the myth is apparently best preserved and most widely current among the Maori. For a version differing widely from the usual form of the story, see the Paumotu text, Stimson, *L.M.T.* p. 46 ff.

[2] *Mem. P.S.* iv, p. 176 ff.; Grey, p. 39 ff.; Andersen, p. 212; *J.P.S.* xxxviii, p. 13 f.; Westervelt, *L.M.* p. 128 ff.

[3] There can be little doubt that the *karakia* in question is recited as an invocation, whether to the gods, or to Maui's own ancestors, and that the omission of the name brings down on the child the wrath of the ancestor or god whose name is omitted. It is interesting to compare the motif in the early Norse saga of Nornagestr, according to which, when the norns are invited to Nornagestr's naming ceremony, the youngest of them is inadvertently omitted, and in revenge pronounces a curse on him which ultimately proves his undoing. The motif is a common one. See Kershaw, *Stories and Ballads of the Far Past* (Cambridge, 1922), p. 36.

Ngata, son of Tangaroa, recorded from the recital of the last high-priest of Rarotonga,[1] in which a number of relatives of a dead man are said to attempt to pass through a corpse as it lies on a raised wooden platform, in the same manner as Maui. Here also they fail; but the feat is successfully accomplished by the *ariki*, and the corpse is restored to life.

This strange story contains many features which are also to be met with in other Polynesian traditions of supernatural and mantic persons —the premature birth; the fairy mother who disappears at dawn; the visit of a hero to the Underworld in search of his wife (for Taranga seems to be Maui's wife as well as his mother); the contact with water in the Underworld in circumstances which give it a peculiar power; the return to earth laden with knowledge and wisdom, especially knowledge of agriculture. Maui's purification and naming by his father in a cave or underground look like some kind of initiation ceremony through which his elder brothers are not called on to pass, though they gladly avail themselves of his knowledge. The entire series of experiences has the appearance of those undergone by mantic persons.

We do not know any very close parallel to the Maui stories in the Old World. He has some features in common with Brer Rabbit (or his equivalents) of the African folk-tales. He is like him in his smallness, his restless activity, his mischievous tendencies, above all in his cunning and resourcefulness. Brer Rabbit's habits, however, are all directed towards self-interest. Maui's, on the other hand, are by no means always dictated by such motives. Sometimes they are avowedly altruistic, as when he snares the sun on behalf of his mother and her industries.[2] Even when they appear to be almost motiveless, as when he steals fire, or sails about fishing up islands, mankind in general is benefited by his exploits. He is something of a culture hero.

The Cycle relating to Hina or Ina, who is commonly represented as Maui's sister, is also very widespread. Stories relating to her have been recorded from Groups as far apart as Hawaii and the Chatham Islands,[3]

---

[1] *J.P.S.* xxvii, p. 180.

[2] There is probably no Polynesian mythical story in which the supernatural features can be traced so directly and certainly to the literal interpretation of poetic figurative diction as this story of Maui's snaring the sun. For the rational explanation of Maui's real achievement, see below.

[3] According to Tregear (*Maori-Polynesian Comparative Dictionary*, Wellington, 1891), Hina is 'by far the best known of all Polynesian legendary personages'. A number of variant versions of the whole Cycle of stories relating to Hina, Tinirau, Koro, and a certain *tohunga* called Kae (see p. 288 f. below), etc., are given in an abridged form in an article by Chadwick, *J.R.A.I.* lx (1930), p. 425 ff.

but she appears to be best known in Samoa[1] and Tonga.[2] Her exact nature is by no means clear. In certain Maori traditions she is Maui's sister, apparently by the same parents.[3] According to a tradition from Atiu in the Cook Group, she lived in the sky with her mortal husband.[4] In Mangaia Ina is the name of one of the supernatural maidens inhabiting the sky, the eldest daughter of Kui-the-Blind, and here also one of her brothers is Rupe, 'the wood-pigeon';[5] but variant traditions of the same island ascribe human parentage to her.[6] In Paumotu tradition she is Maui's wife.[7] In the Tahiti Group she is the mother by the god Tangaroa of the first two *areoi* (cf. p. 318 below), the younger brothers of the god Rongo.[8] The word Hina (Samoan *Sina*) means literally 'moon', and it is commonly stated by scholars that Hina is a moon goddess; but it is doubtful if this view is correct.[9] In the great majority of versions her husband is Tinirau (see below).

A widespread tradition represents Hina as prematurely born, and cast into the sea by her mother, whence she is rescued and reared to maturity,[10] sometimes by her brother Rupe,[11] sometimes by strangers. In Mangaia her parents are said to be the wealthiest people in the land,[12]

---

[1] See e.g. Krämer II, p. 124 ff.   [2] See Gifford, *T.M.T.* p. 1 ff.

[3] Tregear, *loc. cit. s.v. Hina.*   [4] Andersen, p. 261.

[5] Gill, *Myths*, p. 95 ff. *Kui* simply means an elderly woman.

[6] *Ib.* p. 88 ff.; cf. Andersen, pp. 125, 260.

[7] See Caillot, *Mythes*, p. 105 ff.; Stimson, *L.M.T.* p. 28 ff.

[8] Andersen, p. 432.

[9] Maui is represented as snaring the sun with ropes made of Hina's hair, or according to a variant, with ropes made of twisted stalks of green flax. Vegetation of various kinds is often referred to as 'Hina's hair', however, and probably Maui's real achievement, literally stated, is the introduction of an improved form of artificial light, e.g. wicks formed from the twisted stalks of the flax plant. This would be quite in accordance with Polynesian figurative diction, and would tally well with Maui's achievement in introducing fire-sticks.

[10] We may compare the details of the early days of Maui's life (p. 283 above). This premature birth, and its completion, as it were, by the sea, is commonly found in stories of the offspring of parents of whom one is divine. We may compare the Maori story of the premature birth of the daughter of the god Uenuku and the human mother Iwi-pupu, recorded from the teaching of the Sage, *Mem. P.S.* IV, p. 176.

[11] *Rupe* is the name of a variety of wild pigeon. The word is said to be in widespread use in Paumotu poetry in a metaphorical sense, to denote the human soul. See Stimson, *T.R.* p. 125. It is also in common use as a proper name, at least in the Cook Group. Elsewhere in Polynesia 'Rupe's people' are synonymous with 'messengers of death', with reference to old women who in mythological tradition habitually performed the Caesarian operation on the supernatural wives of the early heroes.   [12] Gill, *Myths*, p. 88.

and a story is told of their entrusting their rich personal ornaments to her care; but owing to her indiscretion the treasures are stolen, and Ina is punished. She leaves the island, riding away on the back of a fish to the sacred island of Tinirau,[1] the lord of all fish, whom she marries. Maori[2] and Paumotu traditions[3] assign quite a different reason for Hina's departure from her own home.

The most widespread of all the stories associated with Hina is that which tells of her pursuit by the eel. The commonest form of the story relates that she is struck by the tail of the eel (Tuna-roa) while she is bathing. She tries to leave the place, but the eel follows her everywhere, till at last a certain chief succeeds in poisoning him. Before he dies he bids Hina bury his head and watch the spot. She obeys, and a cocoa-nut tree grows from the head.[4] The story has certain features which clearly originate in an antiquarian speculation on the 'eyes' in the cocoa-nut; but these features seem to be merely incidental. In the Paumotu narrative and chants of Hina and the eel,[5] which offer the most complete and elaborate statement of the story known to us, the erotic significance of the narrative is clearly brought out. On the other hand, in the Mangaian variant[6] this is somewhat disguised, though there can be no doubt as to its presence. Here Hina is brought up in seclusion, doubtless as a *puhi* (see p. 435 below), and her lover is represented as a human being, a 'thief' who comes during her parents' absence and beguiles the inexperienced girl by dressing up in the precious finery entrusted to her care, and dancing before her till she is off her guard, after which he steals her treasures. It should be added that in the Paumotu versions Tuna ('Eel') is slain by Maui.

Tinirau is himself a person of great interest. He is almost as widely known as Hina herself, and stories are found relating to him in Tonga,[7] Samoa,[8] Mangaia,[9] New Zealand,[10] and elsewhere. In Mangaia he is known as the lord of all fish, and is said to be a brother of Vatea,[11] and

---

[1] *Tinirau* is said to mean literally 'forty millions', and is used figuratively to denote a large number, doubtless with reference to the fish in the sea round the 'Sacred Isle'. See Gill, *Myths*, p. 95.   [2] See Grey, p. 35 ff.

[3] See Caillot, *Mythes*, p. 95; Stimson, *L.M.T.* p. 28 ff.

[4] Among many other references to this form of the story we may refer to Turner, p. 242 ff. (Samoa); Caillot, *Mythes*, p. 104 ff. (Paumotus); cf. also Westervelt, *L.M.* p. 96 f.; for Maori variants, see *ib.* p. 91 ff.

[5] Stimson, *L.M.T.*

[6] Gill, *Myths, loc. cit.*

[7] Gifford, *T.M.T.* p. 181 ff.

[8] Krämer I, p. 127 ff.

[9] Gill, *Myths*, p. 94.

[10] Grey, p. 58 ff.

[11] Gill, *A.A.A.S.* (1890), p. 633, footnote 3.

to have been himself partly of fish form.[1] He is possessed of several pools of clear water in which he is accustomed to admire his own reflection. He also possesses two pet whales. Although married to Hina, he also has other wives, for fear of whom he keeps Hina hidden until the time their child shall be born. Some stories relate that these other wives learn of this, and come to kill Hina, who saves herself by murmuring a *karakia*.[2] In Moriori tradition we learn that Rupe's people—the wood-pigeons—come and carry off Hina and her child as well.[3] Rupe's beak is red with her blood, and in this version it is clear that Hina belongs to the 'fairy' women who are forced to die on the birth of their first child (cf. p. 286 above). The matter is set forth in plainer terms in a Marquesan variant,[4] according to which Hina belongs to a community consisting wholly of females, among whom old age and natural birth are alike unknown, the child being taken from the mother by two priests (*tuhuna*), also known as *atua*, who use knives formed of sharks' teeth. The death of the mother invariably follows. In this story Kae, the husband of Hina, is the first to teach how a child may be born naturally, thus saving Hina's life. A very similar version of the story was current also in ancient Japan.[5]

The son of Hina and Tinirau is Koro. Koro's naming ceremony is performed by the *tohunga* Kae, who is summoned from Tonga by Tinirau for the purpose. Kae has already been referred to as the husband of Hina in Marquesan tradition and his story is related below. Koro sometimes lives with his father in the north of Mangaia, though the real home of both is on Motu-tapu, 'the sacred isle'.[6] One story relates how he secretly follows his father to the seashore, and watches him summon all the fish by means of a *karakia*, and of cocoa-nuts ritually gathered. First the little fish of the reefs, then the deep sea fish, and finally the island Motu-tapu itself, with its ponds and tame fish, come to his call. All assemble on Motu-tapu, and the fish proceed to change into a partial semblance of human beings, and dance together with Tinirau the famous dance *tautiti*, a graceful dance much in favour in Mangaia and elsewhere, in which hands and feet move simultaneously.[7] The origin of this dance is

---

[1] Gill, *Myths*, p. 4f.   [2] *J.P.S.* v, p. 133.   [3] *Ibid.*

[4] Handy, *M.L.* p. 56ff.   [5] See *J.R.A.I.* LX, p. 437.

[6] At Ngatangiia, Rarotonga, there is an islet overgrown with cocoa-nut trees so named; but according to Gill this is a modern identification, the true Motu-tapu being in 'the shades'; *Myths*, p. 5, footnote 1.

[7] Gill, *Myths*, p. 100ff.

ascribed to Tautiti, the son of the blind old woman of the Under-world.[1]

Before leaving the Cycle of Tinirau, a word may be said of the hero and *tohunga* Kae, who is closely associated with him, and who is himself a very interesting figure for various reasons. The story of Kae and his relations with Sinilau (Tinirau) is current in Tonga both in prose and in poetry. According to the prose version,[2] a certain king Loau takes two *tohungas* with him on a voyage, one of whom is Kae. When the canoe is in danger of being cast on a reef, Kae swims ashore, and reaches the court of Sinilau, who is here represented as the ruler of Samoa, though he is more often represented in the Pacific as a sea-god. When Kae desires to be sent back to Tonga, Sinilau has him conveyed on two pet whales on condition that the whales shall be sent back loaded with tribute; but Kae deals treacherously, and, on arriving in Tonga, he instigates the islanders to kill and eat the pets. One of the whales escapes to Samoa, however, with spears and axes sticking in its back, and Sinilau, naturally enraged, has Kae captured in his sleep, and eventually killed and eaten. Many supplementary details might be added to this story, both from the Tongan poem, and from the many variants current in Samoa,[3] Rarotonga,[4] New Zealand,[5] the Marquesas,[6] and elsewhere, and a fuller discussion of the whole story and its ramifications and variants has been published elsewhere.[7] The story is told with rich humour, especially in Tonga, and is one of the best pieces of Polynesian story-telling known to us.

We would, however, call the reader's attention once more to the very interesting and close parallel to our story afforded by a portion of the Japanese chronicle known as the *Kojiki*, to which reference has already been made, as well as to a story which occurs in the modern mythology of Ongtong Java. A story resembling our story of Kae and his relations with Sinilau, even down to minute particulars, is related in the former in connection with the hero 'Fire-fade'. In this narrative many other incidents closely resembling the stories of Sinilau and Hina also occur in close juxtaposition, including a close parallel to that of the birth of Hina's child, and of the origin of the dance *tautiti*, and there can be no doubt that the Japanese and the Polynesian traditions are merely variant versions of a single story or Cycle. Space will not permit us to discuss

[1] *Ib.* p. 186, footnote 1; cf. *ib.* p. 256.   [2] Gifford, *T.M.T.* p. 40f.
[3] Turner, p. 110; Krämer I, p. 128.   [4] *J.P.S.* VIII, p. 172.
[5] *Ib. loc. cit.* footnote 1; Grey, p. 65 ff.; Shortland, p. 64 ff.
[6] Handy, *M.L.* p. 56 ff.   [7] Chadwick, *J.R.A.I.* LX (1930), p. 433 f.

these variants and their relations to the Polynesian tradition more fully here. These have been discussed in some detail elsewhere,[1] and here we must content ourselves with merely emphasising once more the importance of the study of early Japanese texts—both the *Kojiki* and others—in connection with Polynesian oral literature. It is to be doubted if the isolation of Polynesia has been as great in the past as has been generally supposed, and there can be no doubt that a comparative study of early Japanese and modern Polynesian literature would be illuminating to both.

The heroes whom we have hitherto considered in this chapter may be described, with the exception of Aukele of Hawaii, and Ngaru of Mangaia, as international. That is to say, they are widespread over the Pacific. We will conclude with some references to heroes whose traditions we have not met outside a single Group, or a restricted area. In general their adventures will not differ materially from those already discussed, though they are for the most part more restricted in scope. The majority consist of adventures in the Heavens or the Underworld. Journeys to the Underworld are undertaken in order to rescue the soul of a dead person. Stories are not uncommon, however, in which a person makes the journey to the land of the dead and returns to earth without the help of a living person. A story is recorded by Shortland from the Maoris near Lake Rotorua of a woman who entered the abode of spirits and then returned to her relatives and related her experiences. The story is of especial interest as relating to the aunt of Shortland's own servant.

An aunt of this man (Te Wharewera) died in a solitary hut near the banks of Lake Rotorua. Being a lady of rank she was left in her hut, the door and windows were made fast, and the dwelling was abandoned, as her death had made it tapu. But a day or two after, Te Wharewera with some others paddling in a canoe near the place at early morning saw a figure on the shore beckoning to them. It was the aunt come to life again, but weak and cold and famished. When sufficiently restored by their timely help, she told her story. Leaving her body, her spirit had taken flight toward the North Cape, and arrived at the entrance of Reinga. There, holding on by the stem of the creeping akeake-plant, she descended the precipice, and found herself on the sandy beach of a river. Looking round, she espied in the distance an enormous bird, taller than a man, coming towards her with rapid strides. This terrible object so frightened her, that her first thought was to try to return up the steep

[1] See the references on p. 289, footnote 7 above.

cliff; but seeing an old man paddling a small canoe towards her she ran to meet him, and so escaped the bird. When she had been safely ferried across, she asked the old Charon, mentioning the name of her family, where the spirits of her kindred dwelt. Following the path the old man pointed out, she was surprised to find it just such a path as she had been used to on earth; the aspect of the country, the trees, shrubs, and plants were all familiar to her. She reached the village, and among the crowd assembled there she found her father and many near relations; they saluted her, and welcomed her with the wailing chant which Maoris always address to people met after long absence. But when her father had asked about his living relatives, and especially about her own child, he told her she must go back to earth, for no one was left to take care of his grandchild. By his orders she refused to touch the food that the dead people offered her, and in spite of their efforts to detain her, her father got her safely into the canoe, crossed with her, and parting gave her from under his cloak two enormous sweet potatoes to plant at home for his grandchild's special eating. But as she began to climb the precipice again, two pursuing infant spirits pulled her back, and she only escaped by flinging the roots at them, which they stopped to eat, while she scaled the rock by help of the akeake-stem, till she reached the earth and flew back to where she had left her body.[1]

Stories are common in the Marquesas also which relate the journeys of heroes to the realms of the dead to rescue the souls of their wives. The hero Kena makes the journey twice, bringing his wife back to earth in a basket. In order to reach the spirits of the dead which 'dwell' in the fourth Hawaiki, Kena has to make a long journey with a companion through three previous Hawaikis in a canoe. Here he meets with many adventures, being detained by strange women. On one occasion his mother descends as far as the second Hawaiki to rescue him and his companion from the female chief of this region who is about to strangle and roast them. He narrowly escapes death at the entrance to the fourth Hawaiki from "two great rocks which continually clash together and swing apart, so that anyone trying to pass is in danger of being crushed." Kena escapes, but his companion is crushed to death.[2] The atmosphere of this Polynesian canoe voyage is strangely similar to that of the adventures of Odysseus. Haha-Poa is another hero who journeys to Hawaiki to rescue his wife, but this time the journey is made downwards, through the ground. The stages of the journey are described with a

[1] Shortland, p. 150.
[2] Handy, *M.L.* p. 117 ff.

similar wealth of incident.[1] All these journeys of mortals to the abode of the dead bear a striking resemblance to stories of the visits of mortals to the Underworld in the oral literature and ritual of the Tatars (cf. pp. 81 ff. and 206 ff. above), and to the stories related in the Japanese Chronicle, the *Kojiki*.

Bastian relates a story of a certain Hawaiian chief who journeys to Miru's realm to rescue the soul of his wife.[2] In order to do this he enlists the help of a priest who furnishes him with a god called Kane-i-kon-alii to guide him. The god rubs him all over with stinking oil so that he may pass unobserved as a corpse in Miru's realm. The chief finds the dead engaged in noisy and tumultuous sports in which he joins, and by a ruse succeeds in temporarily blinding them and rescuing his wife from the realm of Akea or Wakea. In this story the realm of Akea appears to lie beyond Miru's realm, through which however it is necessary to pass.

Samoa, on the other hand, abounds in stories of the visits of mortals to the Heavens. In these the object of the visit is different from that of the visits of mortals to the Underworld, for the heroes generally return to earth, not with a rescued wife, but loaded with useful fruits and vegetables. A local legend of Lefanga[3] recalls one of these visits, relating how nine men journey to the Heavens, and are challenged by the gods to a series of ordeals, in which they themselves are to compete as rivals. In all of these ordeals the men are successful, and the gods have to pay the forfeit. The story has points of close resemblance with the Dyak account of 'Klieng's War Raid to the Skies' (see p. 480 ff. below), and with many Tatar stories in which the hero enters into competitive sports with divine or supernatural beings dwelling in the various spheres of the Heavens. Strictly speaking this story should be treated among those which relate to unknown heroes; but its affinities clearly lie with the present series, and more especially with the next story to be considered.

This legend[4] relates how two of the Tangaloans, or gods dwelling in the skies, steal some birds belonging to a chief named Lu, who pursues them through nine Heavens; but when they reach the tenth Heaven Tangaloa (Tangaroa) appears, and warns them that the place which they have reached is a great sanctuary, where no strife is permitted. Lu tells him of the theft, and in compensation Tangaloa grants him his daughter in marriage on condition that he will return with her peaceably to earth. The picture of the successive Heavens, with the sanctuary ruled by the highest god, and his bestowal of his 'daughter',

[1] Handy, *M.L.* p. 121 ff.   [2] Bastian, p. 265 f.; cf. Frazer, *Belief*, p. 430.
[3] Turner, p. 249 ff.   [4] *Ib.* p. 12 f.

is again strikingly similar to motifs which recur frequently in Tatar poetry, and to the Tatar conceptions of the Heavens.[1] Another Samoan story,[2] perhaps a variant of the last, relates a war raid to the skies made by a chief named Losi, who returns to earth victorious, bringing with him *taro*, cocoa-nuts, and *'ava*.[3] In this story, however, as in all Samoan stories of this class, the heroes are successful by guile and not by violence. The Tangaloans are able to keep warfare at least out of the tenth or uppermost Heaven. We may compare the Maori conception of the tenth Heaven as the place where lived Rehua, the 'Lord of Loving-kindness', with a large host of attendant deities.[4]

A large class of non-heroic stories treats of the relations of mortals with supernatural beings known by various names—e.g. in New Zealand *turehu*, *patu-paiarehe*, etc., in Mangaia *tapairu*. The word *turehu*[5] is often translated by English writers as 'fairies',[6] but it seems to be used in a wide sense of supernatural beings, generally, though not invariably, distinct from gods or divine beings. These 'fairies' are often small and fair, and are said to haunt the hills,[7] even when their home is underground. In Mangaia the *tapairu* are sometimes spoken of as the daughters of Miru, the mistress of the Underworld, and their dwellings are sometimes underground, sometimes in Heaven.[8] The habits of all these supernatural beings are nocturnal, and they themselves are generally ignorant of cooked food. The two last features are very prominent in both Maori and Marquesan stories. In these Groups also the 'fairies' are commonly said to be ignorant of the natural means of birth, having always been subjected to the Caesarian operation, which is said to have involved the death of the mother with the birth of the first child. In the Marquesas tradition relates that a god teaches them how the life of a mother may be saved by natural birth.[9] The Mangaian and Marquesan 'fairies' are cave-dwellers; but the Maori 'fairies' are a very varied class of beings, and are sometimes represented as minute in size, and as living in the trees like birds. It is clear therefore that there are many distinctive features associated with these strange beings, which require explanation, but we must reserve further discussion to a later chapter.

[1] See the study of 'The Religious Beliefs and Experiences of the Tatars of Central Asia', by Chadwick in *J.R.A.I.* LXVI (1936), p. 320 ff.   [2] Turner, p. 105.
[3] *'Ava* is the Samoan form of *kava*, for which see p. 258, footnote 2 above.
[4] Reeves, p. 65.   [5] See p. 328 f. below.
[6] See Tregear, *Dictionary*, *s.v.*; Williams, *Dictionary*, 'Ghost', 'fairy'. See also p. 328 f. below.
[7] See Cowan, *P.H.* and *F.F.T. passim*; Gill, *Myths*, p. 256 ff.
[8] Gill, *loc. cit.*   [9] See Handy, *M.L.* p. 56 ff.

The most interesting and the most numerous class of stories of this kind relate to the rescue of a fairy wife by her husband. Such is the Maori story of Mata-ora, who is held to be the ancestor of the Taranaki tribe in the sixth generation from Maui, and whose wife, the beautiful Niwa-reka, like Maui's mother, belongs to the *turehu*, or 'fairies'. One day, Mata-ora strikes her in anger, and she flees to her father in the Underworld. As her husband follows her, he is met on his route by the fan-tailed bird, who tells him that a woman has passed by, downcast and sobbing. Later he is met by his father-in-law, who, in punishment, has him tattooed in a peculiarly painful manner; but Niwa-reka hears his cries, and nurses him back to health, and the two return to earth together.[1]

In the story of Tura,[2] also from New Zealand, the situation is reversed, the hero going to live with his fairy wife. Tura is a friend and companion of the voyager Whiro, who is believed to have lived about the thirteenth century, and the hero therefore belongs to the period of the Great Migrations. He lands alone on an island called Otea, where he meets the blind woman, Ruahine-mata-morari, who seems to be acting in the capacity of chaperon to the fairies, and who grants him permission to marry one of them, her own daughter. These fairies are described as *atua*, 'spirits', and are said to be very small and kindly, and to dwell in the trees like birds. In their land both natural birth and natural death are unknown. When a child is to be born, it is cut from its mother's side by old women; and old men are never seen in that land, nor grey hairs on anyone. And when Tura's hairs begin to go grey he is forced to depart to the coast and live in seclusion. We may compare the Marquesan version of the story of Kae (see p. 289 above), in which it is related that when grey hairs appear, Kae leaves his wife Hina, and the community of women—evidently 'fairies'—among whom he is living, and returns to his own land. It is clear that in spirit land there is no old age.

In the Rarotongan story of Ati and Tapairu,[3] as in Mangaian traditions,[4] the land of spirits is separated from that of mortals by water, the fairy in this case coming from the Underworld through a spring. Here also the 'fairy' wife, the *tapairu*,[5] who is a daughter of Miru, tells her husband that in her own land children can only be born by means of the Caesarian operation, causing the death of the mother. In certain

[1] *Mem. P.S.* III, p. 182 ff.; cf. Reeves, p. 66 f.; Andersen, p. 288 f.
[2] Andersen, *op. cit.* p. 115 f.
[3] Gill, *Myths*, p. 265 ff.; cf. Andersen, p. 119 ff.   [4] Gill, *Myths*, p. 256 f.
[5] For the word *tapairu*, see p. 293 above, and p. 328 f. below.

Maori traditions a fairy husband marries a mortal wife, and lives with her on earth. Thus in certain stories,[1] Hina is the mortal wife of Miru, who is here represented, not as a woman, but a man, a chief in the Underworld, the principal teacher in the supernatural counterpart of the Maori *whare kura*, or house of learning, to which fuller reference will be made later. Strangely enough, however, Miru returns to his own supernatural sphere after the birth of the second son; and he takes with him as his permanent wife, not the mother of his sons, who is left behind on earth with her two boys, but her younger sister. This is to some extent in accordance with the original design of the parents of the girls; for we are told that the elder sister had been set apart by her parents as a *puhi*, a virgin, and had lived in a separate house by herself before Miru discovered and fell in love with her. Possibly her union with him and the birth of their children did not entirely release her from this restriction.

It will be seen that the personnel of this chapter falls in the main into two classes. The first consists of heroes known throughout an extensive area, the second of heroes whose fame is more or less restricted to a single group. All the heroes of whichever group acquire their fame in virtue of supernatural achievements, or at least of marriage with a supernatural being. Of these achievements the most frequent and the most striking are the journeys to the Heavens and to the realm of Miru, or some other region often located below ground; but sometimes journeys to the land of supernatural beings are said to be taken under water, or across the sea, and in some of these the spirits are represented as living on the same plane as ourselves. In general the journeys possess many striking features in common. In fact a marked similarity characterises the stories of this class as a whole. For the most part, however, the achievements of the heroes known throughout a wide area are more grandiose and varied than those known only to their own Group. It is from these more resplendent characters that the ruling lines of chiefs are proud to trace their descent.

The heroes themselves are closely associated with the gods, or the 'fairies', either by parentage, or marriage, or both. Marriage within the first degree is not infrequently stated or implied. The heroes are not as

[1] Cowan, *F.F.T.* p. 24ff.; cf. Best, *Maori* I, p. 323 ff. It is interesting that among the Dyaks we hear of 'fairy goddesses' who live among the waterfalls, and who, like the *tapairu* (cf. Gill, *Myths*, p. 256), are noted for their long hair; see Howell, *Sarawak M.J.* I, p. 25 and footnote 31, where they are referred to among the occupants of the land of the dead.

a rule stated to be gods themselves, at any rate during their lifetime; but this is not an invariable rule by any means, and on this point the evidence is obscure and inconsistent. Their birth and earliest appearance among mankind is often abnormal and premature, and they are never described as dying—never, that is to say, save in the case of Maui. Maui's greatest adventure is a failure; for he dies in seeking rebirth. Death amid normal surroundings appears to be unknown.

It has been said that the names of heroes and heroines of these stories are frequently found in the genealogies of the chiefs, even when they are said to be of divine parentage. Such names generally occur early in the lines—earlier than those of the chiefs of the Migration Period. But such heroes are never primarily warriors or leaders of men. They rarely fight with weapons. They achieve their ends by supernatural means. They possess knowledge in a greater degree than their fellows, and use it in general for the public good. They do not, however, figure to any considerable extent in relation to the community, or to large bodies of people. The stories are purely individual in their interest, and the personal interest rarely extends beyond the family.

The knowledge acquired by the heroes is not attained by application or experience, but by revelation, generally in the Heavens or the Underworld. A period of seclusion often takes place, either in a cave or in the 'Underworld' in early life, sometimes accompanied by ritual observances. The Maui stories make it clear that these initial ceremonies are analogous in some essential features to those which were undergone by the last high priest of Rarotonga, and by certain rulers in the Paumotu Archipelago, as well as to those undergone by the pupils of the Maori *Whare Wananga*, or school of sacred learning, to which fuller reference will be made below. Our stories make it clear that this early period of seclusion and special 'education' is not allotted to all, and that only a small proportion of men undergo it, though the basis of selection is not actually stated. It seems to be most commonly associated with the youngest son, and very frequently with abnormal birth.

The knowledge in which these heroes excel consists largely of physical science. Tawhaki, Rata, Maui are all experts in meteorics, and are all good kite-fliers. Tawhaki has power over the rain-storm, and the winds. To Maui is attributed the innovation of the calabash of the winds, which is now known to possess an actual scientific value in navigation. Rata also succeeds on his voyages by means of a magic calabash. He also has control over the winds and is associated with a sacred tree or grove over which also he possesses supernatural control, and we cannot doubt that he was originally conceived of as the guardian of a sacred forest, such as we know to have existed in Samoa. In Mangaian myths especially the stars and heavenly bodies are very prominent, and heroes are commonly associated with them in various ways. Aukelenuiaiku easily finds his way from one heavenly body to another. Many heroes make use of the path of the rainbow.

In addition to their knowledge of the Universe, and command over the elements, the heroes also frequently bring back with them from their sojourn in the Heavens or the Underworld knowledge of a more practical, or at least a more concrete kind, such as knowledge of new food plants, new kinds of timber, improved methods of agriculture, new methods of tattooing. They also bring back knowledge of times and seasons and the calendar. While in Heaven they frequently engage in contests against the gods in games of skill and in warfare—these, how-ever, only on the lower planes of the Heavens. The heroes are often victorious; and sometimes they bring a divine wife back to earth to dwell with them among mortals; but whatever their object, they always return to earth wiser in natural science than they were before.

It will be seen that the arts which these heroes are represented as acquiring with such difficulty and danger, and which they use for the benefit of society, are the arts of peace and prosperity. No benefits could be greater to islanders living without metal in scattered islands than improved food supplies, improved timber, and knowledge of forestry, and improved knowledge of the elements and the sea. The evidence therefore suggests that these heroes owe their prominence to intellectual and spiritual pre-eminence, their power over the visible and invisible Universe. They are great seers and sages.

And what of their wives, the 'fairies', supernatural beings who come from their homes in the Heavens and the Underworld, the caves, the forests, and the springs, and who return mysteriously to their own homes, generally on the birth of their first child? It is very often stated or suggested that these 'fairies'—whether men or women, for both are found—represent various ethnic population groups with whom the Polynesians have come into contact at various times and in various places. It is, however, extremely doubtful if the 'extinct aboriginal race' theory meets the case in New Zealand at least. We shall see presently that many of the features associated with them have affinities in certain Polynesian institutions which were perhaps already dying out when the islands were first opened up to European influences during the latter part of the eighteenth century, and which have therefore been only sporadically and partially recorded. In the meantime, however, in view of the fact that these 'fairy' men and women, whatever their origin, are clearly regarded as supernatural beings in the oral traditions of the islanders, we shall postpone further discussion of them to the following chapter, where their characteristics will be more fully detailed.

Except in the western Pacific, traces of narrative poetry are extremely rare, and only one or two from Hawaii have come to our notice. These are connected with the Tawhaki Cycle. One fragment relates to Tawhaki's father Hema; but it is unfortunately very short. According to Malo's translation[1] the passage is as follows:

> Hema voyaged to Kahiki to fetch the red coronet,[2]
> Hema secured it, but he was captured by the Aaia,
> He fell in Kahiki, in Kapakapakaua,
> His body was deposited at Ulu-pa'upa'u.

Another brief fragment of narrative poetry from Hawaii[3] is of exceptional interest, resembling in style the narrative poetry of the Sea Dyaks. It relates to Tawhaki's journey to the Heavens, and the style is so close to that of the Dyak narrative poetry of 'Klieng's War Raid to the Skies' (cf. p. 480 f. below) that some kind of historical connection between these two types of poetry must have existed. We have the same abrupt transition from narrative to speech, the same use of heroic adjectives, of figurative diction, the same grandiloquent manner. The passage is so brief, and so exceptional that we give the text in full. In the version which it represents, Tawhaki's journey to Heaven was undertaken for the purpose of seeking, not his wife, but his father Hema, and his ascent is by means of the rainbow.

> The rainbow was the path of Kaha'i (Tawhaki),
> Kaha'i climbed, Kaha'i strove,
> He was girded with the mystic enchantment of Kane (Tane),[4]
> He was fascinated by the eyes of Alihi.
> Kaha'i mounted on the flashing rays of light,
> Flashing on men and canoes.
> Above was Hana-ia-kamalama,
> That was the road by which Kaha'i sought his father.

[1] Malo, p. 325.

[2] Emerson is doubtless right in suggesting that the word here translated 'coronet' should be 'girdle', with reference to the red girdle worn by the Hawaiian rulers.

[3] Malo, p. 326; cf. Fornander, *P.R.* II, p. 16 f.

[4] We may compare the description of himself given by Ru, the traditional discoverer of Aitutaki, *J.P.S.* XXXII (1934), p. 17.

Pass over the dark-blue ocean,
And shake the foundation of heaven.
The multitudes of the gods keep asking,
Kane and Kanaloa (Tangaroa) enquire,
What is your large travelling party seeking,
O Kaha'i, that you have come hither?
I come looking for Hema.
Over yonder in Kahiki, over yonder in Ulupa'upa'u,
Yonder by the Aaia constantly fondled by Kane,
I have travelled to the pillars of Tahiti.[1]

It has already been said that almost all the narrative poetry known to us is found in Tonga and Samoa. In these two Groups we have considerable fragments of narrative poetry relating to the Cycles of Maui, Hina, Sinilau and Kae. It would seem that these Cycles are more fully developed in these Groups than anywhere else, though found throughout the Pacific. On the other hand, stories of Tawhaki and Rata, though known in Samoa, are obviously not so much in vogue in these Groups, and accordingly little or no narrative poetry relating to them appears to have been recorded here. In regard to these two great groups of stories, therefore, the eastern and western Pacific may be said to be roughly divided into two literary areas, in regard to both their prose and their poetical traditions. An exception must, however, be made for the stories of Maui, which are found everywhere. The latter are rarely found in the form of narrative poetry, but a brief poem of eight strophes from Tonga enumerates some of Maui's exploits.[2]

A brief poem from Tonga[3] relates the story of Hina and the eel, to which we have already referred (p. 287 above). We have seen that the saga is sometimes related as accounting for the origin of the cocoa-nut palm, and it is interesting to note that this motif is preserved in the poem also. Another narrative poem, recorded from Samoa as the *Song of Pili*,[4] relates to the same subject. In this version, however, the lizard has taken the place of the eel. A further example of narrative poetry from Tonga relates to the *Adventures of Kae*,[5] whose death at the hands of Tinirau has already been mentioned (p. 289 above). The poem relates in about 150 lines the whole series of Kae's adventures—his first voyage and return to Samoa, his cordial reception by Sinilau (Tinirau) and further voyage to Tonga, his treachery and ultimate death at the hands of Sinilau. The form of the poem appears to be that of strophes of irregular length.

[1] Malo, p. 326. [2] Gifford, *T.M.T.* p. 21. [3] *Ib.* p. 181.
[4] Krämer I, p. 439. [5] Gifford, *T.M.T.* p. 145.

Poetry other than narrative is abundant, and occurs both independently and also incorporated in the sagas. In general it resembles that which we have already considered in the preceding chapter. Here also the most interesting development is the poetry composed to be recited with dramatic action, and this will be discussed later in a separate chapter. In addition to poetry of this type, speech poems abound throughout the non-heroic sagas, though these do not call for any special comment. Poetry of celebration is also common in sagas such as those which we have discussed in this chapter. As an example of elegiac poetry we may refer to a lament recorded from the Chatham Islands in which Apakura, who, it will be remembered, is known in Polynesian tradition as 'the famous mourner' (see p. 276 above), laments the death of her eldest son.[1] Boasting poems and challenges are perhaps more in place in reference to essentially heroic characters than to the people we have been considering; but we have seen that the hero Ono-kura (Honoura) is at times engaged in heroic enterprises, and in the version of his saga from Ra'iatea he boasts in poems of great formality, both before slaying the man-devouring beast, and before and after attacking the men of Hiva.[2] His challenge to the boars of Ra'iatea[3] in the same saga is also a poem of great formality.

In reviewing the stories and Cycles which have come in for consideration in this chapter, certain features call for special comment. Among these are the wide distribution, the comparative consistency, and the general independence of the stories of Tawhaki and of Maui. Maui is placed earlier in the pedigrees than Tawhaki and his line, and, despite the inconsistencies in his position, this relative position may be regarded as constant. It is admitted in all the traditions that Maui's achievements are primarily intellectual. He is credited with having introduced a large number of improvements into the material condition of the islanders, and with having been also a pioneer navigator, a 'fisher up of islands'. His achievements are those of a *tohunga*; but he lacked spiritual power. He never went to Heaven to visit the gods; he never rescued any soul from Miru's realm. He failed to achieve immortality, even for himself. Maui died.

After Maui's death another Cycle of men enter into the traditions and appear on the genealogies, whose achievements, like his, are to a great extent intellectual; but their spiritual achievements are even greater.

[1] *J.P.S.* IV, p. 162.
[2] *Ib.* pp. 275 f., 281, 283, 289.   [3] *Ib.* p. 279.

They can rise to the highest Heaven, even to the tenth or twelfth, the abode of Rehua, the supreme god of peace. They can pass with impunity through Miru's realm, they can rescue the souls of the dead. They themselves do not die. They achieve immortality, both for themselves and for those whom they choose to rescue. Tawhaki, Aukele, Ngaru, all pass through Hine-nui-te-Po, or the Underworld, and triumph over death. And like the god Tane they bring light to Miru's dark realm, restoring sight to her blind eyes.

We are inclined to suspect that the great prominence of both Maui and Tawhaki is due in a large measure to the intellectual or priestly class in the Pacific, though their Cycles have, of course, been widely cultivated as literature of entertainment in a secular milieu. The prominence which is everywhere given to intellectual and spiritual achievements, and the absence of heroic elements, such as we should expect to find in the ancestors of the *ariki* class, cannot be overlooked. The opposition which these two great Cycles show in regard to the supreme question of all, namely the immortality of the soul, would seem to reflect a spiritual clash. There can be little doubt that Tawhaki is the hero favoured by the *tohungas*. And this is in accordance with the direct utterance of the Maori sage, who contemptuously declared the stories of Maui to be 'ovenside (i.e. fireside) stories'.[1]

It is clear, therefore, that the *ariki* class, in deriving their descent through Tawhaki's line, are claiming a share in his spiritual honours. The diction of the Pomares of Tahiti leaves no room for doubt. Pomare is not a mortal dwelling on earth, but an *atua*, a spiritual being dwelling in Heaven. Ellis, writing of Tahiti during the twenties of last century, tells us that:

"It was not only declared that Oro[2] was the father of the king, as was implied by the address of the priest when arraying him in the sacred girdle, and the station occupied by his throne, when placed in the temple by the side of the deities, but it pervaded the terms used in reference to his whole establishment. His houses were called the *aorai*, the clouds of heaven; *anuanua*, the rainbow, was the name of the canoe in which he voyaged;[3] his voice was called thunder; the glare of the torches in his dwelling was denominated lightning; and when people

---

[1] *Mem. P.S.* III, p. 182.

[2] Oro is the supreme god of the Tahiti Group.

[3] This was also the name of the canoe in which Tawhaki voyaged according to Tahiti tradition (Henry, *A.T.* p. 558), and the name of the sacred canoe of the *areoi* (*ib.* p. 190).

saw them in the evening, as they passed near his abode, instead of saying the torches were burning in the palace, they would observe that the lightning was flashing in the clouds of heaven. When he passed from one district to another on the shoulders of his bearers, instead of speaking of his travelling from one place to another, they always used the word *mahuta*, which signifies to fly, and hence described his journey by saying that the king was flying from one district of the island to another."[1]

At exactly what period the phase of religious thought represented by the traditions discussed in this chapter spread over the Pacific we are not prepared to say. But the similarity with which they appear over many thousands of square miles suggests that they entered our area, not with the earliest Polynesian invaders, but in comparatively recent times— probably not much earlier than the fourteenth century, and possibly even later. Moreover the character of these traditions, with their sacerdotal bias and absence of heroic features, their stress on spiritual and cultural innovations, suggests that they reflect a cultural movement, a wave of fresh intellectual and spiritual stimulus superimposed on an earlier culture, rather than a great conquest or movement of whole populations. There can be no doubt that the origin of these innovations is to be sought in the West.

In the oral literature of the Sea Dyaks of North Borneo, to be discussed presently, we shall find ancient traditions of a great Dyak hero Klieng, who makes a journey to the Heavens very similar to that of Tawhaki, and for a similar purpose; but we have not found among these people any traditions resembling those of Maui—a fact which may possibly be due to the very scanty material available for the study of Dyak oral literature. On the other hand certain Hindu customs still surviving on the island of Bali are strikingly reminiscent of the adventures of both Maui and Tawhaki. When a Balinese prince dies, his corpse is cremated in a high tower[2] temporarily constructed of light materials. The tower resembles a pagoda in appearance, and consists of a number of storeys, eight or more, sometimes rising to a great height.[3] The idea would seem to be that of elevating the soul of the deceased as high as possible, and one is reminded of Tawhaki painfully making his way through Heaven upon Heaven, till at last the highest Heaven of all is reached. We have

---

[1] Ellis[1] II, p. 359 f.

[2] For a detailed account of this practice, see Friederich, *J.R.A.S.* IX (1877), p. 93 ff.

[3] We may compare the structures in Hawaii described by Cook and others, and cf. Friederich, *loc. cit.*

already seen the Tatar shamans performing a ritual based on the same conception (p. 203 above).

This form of funeral, however, is said to be reserved for men of princely rank. In the case of wealthy men whose rank is high, but inferior to that of the princes, the corpse is cremated in the interior of a wooden bull, or more rarely that of some other animal, being inserted through the mouth.[1] Like Maui, they enter never to emerge. There is, however, another Balinese ceremony in which the cow figures prominently, and which seems to symbolise the successful performance of the feat which Maui failed to achieve. We have seen photographs taken on the same island of temple ceremonies in which men are seen crawling on all fours under wooden cows, passing beneath the animal between the hind legs, and emerging between the fore legs. The photographs show this ceremony being performed by a number of people in a series. The symbolism seems to be that of rebirth. Those who perform it successfully may be said to be 'twice born', like the upper castes of India,[2] and like them to become gods.

Customs formerly practised in the native state of Travancore in southwest India may help to throw further light on the matter. Here the rulers are drawn from the Kshatriya caste, and descent is through the female line. The administration of the country, and the temples, however, as well as all the chief offices of state, are in the hands of Brahmins, who are regarded as 'gods' and referred to as the 'god-people'. Before the rajah can mount the throne he is conducted by Brahmins to a special temple in Trevandrum.[3] In the temple there was a large golden cow. The rajah entered the golden cow, and when he emerged he was blessed and accepted as a Brahmin. The ceremony is said to symbolise the double birth of the Brahmin, as man and as god, the cow being the sacred animal. The ceremony was carried out at night, and when it was over, the rajah had to bathe in the enclosed tank in the temple.[4]

[1] We may refer to the ceremony performed in relation to the corpse in the Rarotongan tradition referred to on p. 285 above. In this case also the corpse is elevated on a wooden platform, and the *ariki* is said to pass through the body of the corpse. The Balinese custom looks like a ritual performance of the same ceremony.

[2] These are known in India as the *dvija*, "born twice". See Friederich, *J.R.A.S.* IX (1877), p. 83, where the traditional explanation of the origin of the term is given.　　　　　[3] Trevandrum is the chief town in Travancore.

[4] We are indebted for this information to a letter from Dr A. D. M. Hoare, dated September 11th, 1936. Miss Hoare obtained the information from Mr Alastair McTavish, late of Travancore. The letter further states that

"As soon as the rajah has passed through the cow, he steps on to a weighing

There can be little doubt that these ceremonies, and those already referred to in the island of Bali, are in some way related to the Dyak poems of Klieng, and the Polynesian tradition of Maui and Tawhaki. The passing of the *Kshatriya* through the cow in order to become a god is strangely like Maui's attempt to pass through Hine-nui-te-Po in order to attain to immortality. And it seems likely that the people in Bali creeping beneath the cows, passing beneath through the hind legs, and out through the fore legs, are performing a symbolic act of a similar kind, and perhaps of a similar significance. The curious thing about the Pacific traditions is that the popular hero Maui should fail to pass the ordeal. We have seen (p. 285) that in Rarotongan tradition the *ariki* succeeds exactly where Maui fails. In this tradition also the feat is attempted by four other people, not of *ariki* blood, who fail likewise. On the other hand Tawhaki passes the necessary ordeals, and attains to the Heavens, as the Hindu *Kshatriya* attains to Brahminic divinity.

At exactly what period this Hindu influence entered Polynesia is uncertain. It must, of course, have been before the great Hindu empire of Indonesia, with its centre in Java, gave way under the Mohammedan conquest of the early fifteenth century, and it may probably be assumed to have been before the colonisation of New Zealand. Doubtless it was indirect, possibly through Samoa. It is unlikely, to say the least, that any Hinduised Indonesians made their way to the outer islands of their world. But the great political and religious changes which took place in Indonesia during the period from the sixth century, and even earlier, to the fifteenth century cannot have taken place without considerable disturbances to the vested interests of the priesthood of the islands immediately to the east of them, and these in their turn must have played their part in spreading the ripple to islands even more remote.

In making these few suggestions regarding the significance of the Maui and Tawhaki Cycles for the history of Polynesian thought, we have said nothing about the 'fairies' who, according to the traditions, are closely connected with both. We have rejected the view generally held that they represent in any immediate sense the aboriginal inhabitants of the islands in which they are found. On the other hand we are

scale, his weight in gold is put into the opposite pan, and the money afterwards given to the Brahmins. On the day of the ceremony, all the Brahmins throughout the entire state of Travancore are fed at government expense."

The reader will find a more detailed account of the ceremony, and some variations in custom, on p. 169 ff. of *The Land of Charity* by S. Mateer (London, 1871).

disinclined to dismiss them as mere traditions introduced into the islands from some outside source in the form of stories of mythical beings. The picture which we have of them is, we think, too consistent, and too closely interwoven with the traditions of the famous characters of other Cycles to make such a view probable. We are inclined to believe that the 'fairies', like the heroes already discussed in this chapter, represent a traditional picture of some class of people who have played their part in the religious thought and intellectual life of the islanders but of whom little direct knowledge has survived. But we think it better to postpone further discussion regarding their origin to a later chapter.

SAGA AND POETRY RELATING TO DIVINE BEINGS, AND MANTIC POETRY

STORIES and poems relating to the gods and other supernatural beings are found widespread throughout the Pacific. These are exceptionally varied, not only in form, but also in their character and tone, in their origin, in their milieu and in their geographical distribution. Prose stories are especially numerous; but *karakias*, or 'chants', are often religious in character, and include hymns and spells, invocations to the gods, and other forms of religious and mantic literature. In addition we are especially fortunate in possessing a considerable body of dramatic poetry of this class. This, however, together with the other dramatic literature of the Pacific, has been reserved for treatment in a separate chapter. We will consider here the prose stories and the poems which relate to the gods, whether of secular or religious origin, and the mantic lore, which is often indistinguishable from the religious poetry.

Prose stories of the gods are found everywhere in the Pacific. The literature of pure entertainment relating to divine beings is, however, extremely limited, owing to the fact that at the time when the stories were recorded, that is to say soon after the opening up of the Pacific to European influences, and before the advent of Christianity had weakened the native religion, this religion was one of the most powerful factors in the native life and thought—in some island Groups it may be said to be the most powerful factor of all. In Hawaii the influence of the priests is manifest throughout their history, and here, as well as in Tahiti, the Marquesas, and the Paumotus, the kings and great chiefs claimed to rule in virtue of their divinity. In Mangaia the double 'kingship' consisted of two priest-rulers, while the secular ruler was suffered to rule only temporarily, by virtue of his military prowess and only by sacerdotal sanction and investiture. Among the Maori the influence of the *tohungas* was still paramount. The religion nowhere showed signs of weakening; and a powerful hierarchy of *tohungas* ensured its continuance by jealously controlling the pedigrees of the *arikis*, and by emphasising everywhere throughout the traditions the important part which the *tohungas* had played in the past and their close relationship to the *ariki* class.

As a natural consequence cultured stories of entertainment relating to the divinities are comparatively few. We have only occasional examples of stories in which a highly developed narrative art has expended itself on the unedifying exploits of the gods for the amusement of a cultivated and cynical audience, such as we find in Greek and early Norse literature, and in the early prose stories in the Japanese chronicles (cf. p. 282 above), which closely resemble them. But for the most part the Polynesian stories are either grave or puerile. They bear the impress of, alternatively, a sacerdotal or a popular milieu. The scarcity of court literature of this kind is nowhere more marked than in the rarity of a refined and discriminating sense of humour, and of the heroic style in the treatment of the gods. In this respect Polynesian literature offers a marked contrast to the literature of the Tatars, and resembles that of ancient Ireland.

In accordance with the vitality of the native religion, and the paramount influence of the intellectual class, as represented by the *tohungas*, a very large proportion of Polynesian mythology has assumed the form of antiquarian speculation. This type of literature is extremely voluminous in the Pacific, and will be treated in a separate chapter later. But apart from purely antiquarian literature, antiquarian speculation has touched a large proportion of stories primarily relating to divine beings, and therefore presumably ultimately of religious origin. These stories are commonly preserved in two principal versions,[1] the one recorded from the higher class of *tohungas*, which is often esoteric and dignified, but has in general nothing to do with the literature of entertainment; the other, which consists of what the natives call 'oven-side stories', represents the popular versions of myths. The cult of the supreme god Kiho contains examples of the former class; the stories of Maui fishing up islands, regarded by the *tohungas* as a 'winter night's tale', belongs to the latter.[2] It is sometimes the case, e.g. among the Maori, that Maui is regarded as a god.[3] Intermediate between these two classes of myth we have a number of others relating to an anthropomorphic pantheon, less elevated than the conception of Kiho, more dignified in general than those of Maui. The gods of this pantheon are all male. The Cycle of myths of which they are the subject is the most widely known and the most universally accepted in Polynesia.

In addition to this widely known and accepted pantheon, we also

[1] Best, *M.S.L.* p. 5.   [2] *Mem. P.S.* III, p. 182.
[3] See e.g. Taylor, p. 133.

have a number of groups of divine beings whose cult or mythology is confined to a more restricted area. The cult of the volcano goddess Pele and her family is restricted, at least in modern times,[1] to Hawaii, the Marquesas, Paumotu, and the Cook Group (cf. further p. 326 below). We also have gods which are not anthropomorphic in form, and which form local groups. The fish gods are most prominent in Central Polynesia, e.g. in Tonga and Mangaia; but they are known elsewhere, e.g. in New Zealand.[2] Sometimes a god who is widely known, but not prominent, will be raised to special prominence in a special area. We have already seen (p. 258 above) how the priest Ue, having failed to establish the cult of his god Tane, first in Tahiti, then in Mangaia, succeeded finally in establishing a flourishing and permanent cult in Aitutaki. Among the Maori, tribal gods are sometimes given a temporary prominence owing to the prestige of one of their *tohungas*. We shall see an interesting instance of the creation of a cult among the Maori (cf. p. 454 below).

Though the cult of the supreme god Io, or Kiho,[3] with its superior monotheism, has been actually recorded only in Tahiti, Paumotu, the Cook Islands, and New Zealand, it has been shown by Stimson to have been widespread at an early date.[4] This cult is known only to the higher grades of priests and *ariki*,[5] and the name is rarely mentioned. Even the lower grades of *tohungas* are unfamiliar with the cult of this supreme being, and the common people are said to be ignorant even of his existence. A Maori *tohunga* once observed in the course of a discussion on this subject: "All gods are one, but the people must not be told so. All gods are one, but he has many names."[6] This great and supreme god is the creator of the Universe and of everything within it. In a number of poems he is represented as chanting hymns in praise of his own sublimity. He has existed for all time. He was never born. The ritual relating to him bears the impress of a lofty speculative philosophy, concerned with metaphysical abstractions. Even here, however, at least

---

[1] The name is said to be identical in form with Samoan *Fe'e*, and certain Hawaiian traditions represent Pele as migrating to Hawaii from Samoa. Fe'e, however, appears in Samoa today as a cuttle-fish deity.   [2] Taylor, p. 134.

[3] The name is known to the Maori and Cook Islanders as *Io*; to the Paumotuans as *Kiho, Kio, Iho, Io*; but the correct form seems to be *Kiho*. The name is commonly found in the form *Kiho-tumu*, 'Kiho the First Cause', or 'the Primal Source'. See Stimson, *Kiho-tumu*, p. 4.

[4] Stimson, *T.R.* p. 105 ff.; cf. Best, *M.M.R.* p. 19.

[5] Stimson, *loc. cit.*   [6] Best, *M.M.R.* p. 21.

in the Paumotu version recorded by Stimson, a certain concrete element of realism is introduced in the form of dialogues between Kiho and the god Tane, who is represented as delegated by Kiho to rule the Heavens as his vice-regent, while Kiho himself withdraws into a sublime and permanent retreat beyond human ken. In the Maori teaching relating to Io, also, it is Tane who brings knowledge of this supreme being to mankind.[1]

Few myths relating to the gods belong to the lofty class of Kiho. As Best has pointed out, the lower grades and lower levels of religious thought are those with which an alien observer comes most readily into contact, and the majority of stories of the gods recorded by Europeans are not in general the loftiest known to native cultivated thought, even what we might call the secular thought of the *ariki* class, as distinct from that of the more spiritual conceptions of the *tohungas*. Moreover the higher type of myth which has been recorded from the *tohungas* themselves is rarely couched in narrative form. It is generally given as their direct teaching, as it would be delivered to their own pupils or adherents, and is contained in brief statements and allusions incorporated in their religious chants. We may refer to the teaching of the *are vananga* recorded from Rarotonga;[2] to that of the *whare wananga* recorded from the Maoris;[3] and to the *fagu* or 'religious chants' of the Paumotuans[4] and the chants of the Marquesas.

According to the teaching of these institutions, and the oral texts (*fagu*) of the Paumotuans, it would seem, as we mentioned above, that, owing to the remote retirement in which Kiho is secluded, it is necessary for him to have agents or 'regents' who act as his representatives and intermediaries, and who are the highest type of supernatural beings of whom the common people have any knowledge.[5] These are the Polynesian gods of the hierarchy with whom we are familiar from oral literature and cults throughout Polynesia, and who are represented in Maori myth as occupying the various spheres of the Heavens.[6] These gods are anthropomorphic, and form a community, or an ordered

---

[1] *Mem. P.S.* III, p. 108.   [2] *J.P.S.* XII, p. 219 ff.
[3] See p. 458 ff. below.   [4] See Stimson, *loc. cit.*

[5] This at least is the explanation of the relationship of the esoteric cult of Kiho to the exoteric cult of the Polynesian pantheon offered by Stimson (*T.R.* p. 104 f.). The parallel which it offers to the Buddhist conception of the Buddha and his relation to the *Bodhisattvas* is very striking, though this is not remarked by Stimson himself. The analogy of the Tatar pantheon (see p. 83 above) is equally striking.

[6] Stimson regards this myth as to some extent contaminated with alien ideas. See *T.R.* p. 89.

scheme, and the most widely known form a family or tribe. But as a matter of fact their relationship to one another varies very greatly, not only in various parts of the Pacific, but even in a single Group. This is, of course, what we should expect among a people whose traditions and theological teaching are carried on exclusively by oral tradition. But in general it may be said that, subject to such local variation, this divine community and family are known throughout the entire Pacific, and form the subject of a very large proportion of Polynesian mythology and religious chants. The cult of Kiho, however, belongs to the sphere of religion rather than of mythology, and as such lies for the most part outside our sphere.

The family which figures almost universally in Polynesian stories of the gods is that of Rangi, the personified form of the sky, or atmosphere,[1] and Papa, the personification of the solid rock, and their offspring, Tane, Tawhirimatea, Tangaroa, Rongo, Whiro, Tu and the rest. According to a widespread myth, Rangi originally rested on his wife Papa in a perpetual embrace. This rendered the earth fruitless, as only a few plants could grow in such a confined space. Moreover their children, who were many, grew tired of groping about in darkness. They decided, accordingly, to separate their parents, and the feat was accomplished by Tane Mahuta, who succeeded in pushing Rangi up to his present position in the sky. But one member of the family was angry at the decision of the rest to separate the parents. This was Tawhirimatea, the god of the winds. He strongly opposed the decision, and when Tane prevailed, he rushed up to Heaven to join Rangi his father, and from there waged fierce warfare on his brothers. He destroyed the trees, in which resided Tane Mahuta himself. He 'assaulted the waters', causing strife between Tangaroa and Tane, and wrought havoc on all sides.[2] The only one of the offspring of Rangi and Papa able to withstand the force of the wind god was Tu, 'man'. The strife between them still continues.[3]

[1] According to Stimson, the word *rangi, ragi,* means, not Heaven, or the sky, but lit. 'the region of the not-earth world'. For a discussion of the term and its bearings on the interpretation of Polynesian mythology and eschatology, see Stimson, *T.R.* p. 89 ff.

[2] With this account of the behaviour of the tornado or wind-storm god we may compare the story of Susa-no-wo the wind god in Japanese mythology and that of Salulut Antu Ribut the wind spirit in the poetry of the Sea Dyaks of Borneo (see p. 486 below).

[3] Perhaps the *locus classicus* for the orthodox Maori version is that recorded from the sages, and published in *Mem. P.S.* III, p. 115 ff. Valuable accounts are also

Although the story bears the impress of schematisation in the hands of the learned class, and shows clear signs of an attempt to reconcile conflicting religious ideas and mythological traditions, this has not been its last stage. As we have it the narrative has passed through an artistic medium which has welded the whole into a consistent story of incident in the family-life of the gods. The family itself, though composed of heterogeneous elements, is conceived after a model with which we are not entirely unfamiliar in European literature; but its members are less humanised, less truly anthropomorphic, and the absence of any feminine element[1] except that of Papa, the earth mother, strikes us as alien and strange. Humour and detail are wholly absent.

The father of this divine family is sometimes said to be, not Rangi, but Vatea. Vatea is the father of Rongo and Tangaroa in Mangaia.[2] The gods of this divine family are known individually in the various Groups, and figure quite independently of one another in many of their adventures. Tane and Rongo are often associated together. Tane is commonly represented as the elder of the two, as for example, in certain New Zealand versions already referred to; but in Taylor's list, also from New Zealand,[3] the eldest son of Rangi and Papa is Rongomatane, i.e. 'Rongo and Tane', who seems to be a combination of the two gods,[4] and this is thought to be the same as the god of the *areoi* Heaven (cf. p. 426 below); but in Taylor's lists, and other lists from New Zealand, Tane also figures independently as another son. Rongo does not appear in this list independently, but in Mangaia he is the eldest son,[5] and of the greatest possible importance. In Rarotonga also he holds an independent place.[6] Tangaroa is commonly represented as the youngest of the family, Tu, Whiro (Hiro, Iro), and other gods being intermediate in age. Among the Maori, Uenuku, the rainbow god, who is also known as a war god, is sometimes included in this divine family. More often, however, he is regarded as a minor deity, the personified spirit of the

recorded by Taylor, p. 115 ff.; Best, *M.M.R.* p. 10f.; Grey, p. 1 ff. A valuable comparative account of the stories relating to Rangi and Papa and their offspring is given in Andersen, p. 349 ff., together with much relevant antiquarian matter.

[1] There are, consequently, no children or very young members of the divine pantheon.

[2] Gill, *Myths*, p. 10.   [3] Taylor, p. 116.

[4] This is the usual explanation of the name. A different explanation has recently been suggested by Stimson, *T.R.* p. 123. This name, contracted to *Romatane*, was the name of a chief of Atiu when John Williams visited the island last century. See p. 269 above.

[5] Gill, *Myths*, p. 123.   [6] Buck, *M.S.* p. 31.

rainbow.[1] An elaborate story is current among the Maori[2] of his relations with his divine wife, which resembles closely those of Tawhaki
and other heroes who marry divine or 'fairy' wives.

The gods Iro (Whiro) and Uenuku are commonly confused with
heroes of the same names who are traditionally believed to have lived
in the Migration Period, and indeed it is not clear how far the distinction
is to be pressed. Tangaroa figures very widely as the god of the ocean,
Whiro as the god of disease and all evil, and as the patron of thieves.
But in Easter Island Whiro is the god of the sky, and apparently of the
rain-storm, and he seems to be a volcano god also.[3] He is rarely a
'sympathetic' character. Tane (Kane—the name means 'man', 'husband')
has all the attributes of a jungle god. He is a god of nature, whose
dwelling is in the trees, and he is the 'father' of the trees ànd the birds.
He seems indeed to bear a close resemblance to the Sea Dyak war god,
Singalang Burong (cf. p. 478 below). In Mangaia he is also the patron
of poetry and the dance. In the Paumotu Archipelago and in certain
other groups he is the highest of the gods.[4] Throughout the Central
Pacific Rongo is the god of agriculture, but in Mangaia he is the god of
war, and of the ocean.[5] His name means 'the Resounder'. In New
Zealand Tu is the god of war.[6] Almost everywhere Tangaroa figures
as an ocean god, and the god of arts and crafts. These are only a few of
the attributes of the gods of this divine family as they are found here
and there in the various Groups. But their attributes are many and
varied, and the number and relative importance of the gods varies
similarly.[7]

It is not to be supposed that the departmental character of these gods
is consistently preserved or distributed in the various Groups. In some
Groups one or two of the gods only are prominent, the rest being of
little account or unknown. Thus in Hawaii the principal gods are Tu,
Rongo and Tane. The two last named are perhaps not clearly dissociated even here. In Tahiti and elsewhere[8] until recently Tane was the
chief god of the pantheon, but he has recently been superseded by
Tangaroa, though early last century Tane still retained his supremacy

[1] Best, *Maori* I, p. 237 f.   [2] *Ib.* p. 156 ff.
[3] Routledge, p. 242; cf. also Taylor, p. 146.
[4] See Stimson, *Kiho-tumu*, p. 25 ff.
[5] Gill, *Myths*, p. 14, and *passim*; Buck, *M.S.* p. 162.
[6] Best, *Maori* I, p. 236.
[7] The above remarks are intended merely to be illustrative. For fuller details
the reader is referred to Williamson, *R.C.B. passim.*
[8] See Stimson, *T.R.* p. 119.

in Borabora and Eimeo. In the Cook Group Rongo and Motoro[1] are the most important gods, and during times of war Rongo is in the ascendant; but in times of peace Tane, third in importance,[2] is said to hold sway, though generally of less account than Rongo and Motoro. In New Zealand the name sometimes given to the supreme god of the pantheon is Rehua, the god of peace and 'loving-kindness', who is sometimes represented as the god of the highest (tenth) Heaven, 'attended by an innumerable host',[3] the other gods dwelling on the lower planes of the Heavens. A similar conception of the relative dwellings of the gods is found also in other Groups. There is a general tendency in modern times for Tangaroa to take the place of supremacy throughout the Pacific.

The same god does not always retain the same characteristics in different Groups. In Hawaii the echoing of the conch shell of Kane (Tane) suggests that the god is demanding a human sacrifice (cf. p. 349 below), while the first *marae*, or temple-platform of Tane in Mangaia, founded by a colony from Tahiti, was largely built of the skulls of their enemies slain in battle, though among the natives of this island he is the patron of the arts, of peace, and especially of poetry and the dance. The arts themselves are not uniformly under the patronage of the same god or goddess. In Hawaii the *hula* ('dance') is under the patronage of Lata (Rata), who is here represented as the goddess of nature and vegetation, and seems to have the functions attributed in Mangaia to Tane. In Mangaia Raka (Rata) is known as the god of the winds.[4] The god to whom the *areoi* sacrifice is Rongo.

It has already been mentioned (p. 274 above) that the Heavens are sometimes pictured as a series of parallel planes, or concentric arcs, one above another. This conception is fully developed in Mangaia,[5] Paumotu,[6] and New Zealand,[7] and doubtless elsewhere also. In these upper spheres the gods are pictured as dwelling each on his appropriate plane or floor, and in Mangaia the warriors' 'Paradise' also is said to be situated somewhere above in the skies.[8] On the other hand another and rival abode of spirits exists, which appears to have little in common with

---

[1] Motoro was the god of the Ngariki, for centuries the dominant clan in Mangaia. He is said to have been introduced from Rarotonga at an early date.

[2] Gill, *Myths*, p. 107.　　　　　　　　　　　[3] Reeves, p. 60.

[4] Gill, *L.S.I.* p. 80.　　　　　　　　　　　[5] Gill, *Myths*, pp. 2, 153.

[6] Stimson, *T.R.* p. 62 ff. Stimson denies, however, that these divisions of the Heavens are above the earth; cf. p. 316 below.

[7] See p. 274 above, and the references there cited.

[8] Gill, *Myths*, pp. 18, 162 ff.

this schematised view of the Heavens. This region is generally pictured as underground, and more or less dark, and is known as *te Po* 'night', or 'the shades'. Here, according to Mangaian belief, dwells Miru, a cannibal ogress who cooks and eats all who come to her realm. Here also dwell her son Tautiti; her daughters, the *tapairu*, or 'fairies'. Miru seems to be identical with an elderly woman commonly mentioned in the stories as Kui-the-Blind, whom the hero often visits, and whose blindness he cures by means of cocoa-nuts. According to the belief of the Cook Islanders,[1] those who die a natural death all eventually end in Miru's oven. But in both Hawaii and New Zealand Milu (Miru) is a man. Not infrequently the same story is told of the Heavens and the Underworld, as we have seen, and the same gods and supernatural beings are pictured as occupying both regions. It would seem that the eschatology of the Pacific has not been completely brought into a consistent scheme in native thought.

Among the fullest and most interesting accounts of the fate of those who die a natural death are those which are given by Gill[2] from Mangaia. These are not always consistent in regard to details, but they are all the more valuable as representing the actual pronouncements of the natives, which in matters of this kind are rarely uniform. According to the fullest of these accounts, which Gill tells us represents the standard and esoteric teaching of the priests, the souls leave the body before life is quite extinct, and travel to the edge of the cliff on the west of the island,[3] near the *marae* ('temple-platform') of Rongo, where a gigantic wave approaches, and simultaneously a gigantic *bua* tree springs up from Avaiki.[4] Up this tree the spirits climb, and creep along its branches, each branch being reserved for the worshippers of each of the principal gods of Mangaia. The tree then disappears with its human burden to the nether world, where the human spirit is dropped into a lake at the foot of the tree and caught in the great net of Miru. The secret of Miru's power over her victims is said to be the great *kava* root which grows in Avaiki, and from this root Miru's four lovely daughters are directed to prepare bowls of strong *kava* for her unwilling visitors, who, stupefied by the draught, pass unresisting into her oven. Never have priests devised a more effective incentive to the warrior class than in these doctrines of the fate awaiting those who died naturally.

According to popular belief in Mangaia, as opposed to the religious

[1] Gill, *Myths*, p. 160ff.   [2] *Loc. cit.*
[3] The western point of the spirit's leap has been constantly emphasised by European writers; but see below.   [4] For *Avaiki* (Maori *Hawaiki*) see below.

teaching, the spirits of the departed are pictured as wandering along the shore of the island, their bodies 'arrayed in ghostly net-work', and in a fantastic mourning of weeds, while a red creeper, resembling dyed twine, was wound round and round the head like a turban. They are also said —somewhat inconsistently, as Gill remarks—to blanch their new-made garments on the shore hard by. When a considerable number have gathered together, and a youth of renown has died, who is fitted by rank and experience to act as their leader, the sorrowful band of ghosts take their departure from a point on the western side of the island, following the path made by the last rays of the setting sun.[1] In all the islands of this Group,[2] as well as in the Samoan islands,[3] a favourite point of departure of the spirits is at a point on the western side of the island; but this is not always so in other Groups. In New Zealand, where it is also held that the spirits of the dead depart over the sea, *Te Reinga*, or the 'Spirits' Leap', is at the North Cape, on the northern part of the island.[4] In Hawaii the Hidden Islands of Kane (Tane), the abode of the gods, whither depart "the spirits of all those who are religious...who have kept the *tapu*", are situated in the sea, and we are told that "this land... appears at dawn at the *eastern* points of the various islands".[5]

We have emphasised this variation in regard to the points of the compass where the land of the departed is situated, because it has commonly been remarked by European scholars that Hawaiki (Avaiki), the ancient home of the race, and the destination, according to many traditions, of the soul after death, is consistently situated in the west. The evidence on this point, it will be seen, is by no means consistent. Stimson has pointed out[6] that the error has arisen largely owing to the practice of translating the word *raro* by 'west', whereas in reality the word means 'down', and has only come to be used especially frequently of the west because the west is the point of sunset. As regards Mangaia, however, it should be pointed out that the point on the west, whence the spirits departed, would be the natural place for them to select, seeing that here is the only break in the coral reef, and the only place where 'Landing' is marked on the Admiralty Chart (298. 35). The spirits in fact left Mangaia by the route followed by all departing voyagers.

[1] Gill, *Myths*, p. 157 ff.
[2] See p. 397 below. In Mangaia, however, spirits are sometimes referred to as departing from the east of the island. [4] See e.g. Reeves, p. 61 ff.
[3] See Williamson, *R.C.B.* I, p. 323 ff., and the references there cited.
[5] Kepelino, p. 189. Turner (p. 330) mentions that in Eromanga also, in the New Hebrides, the spirits of the dead went westwards. See further Henry, *A.T.* pp. 201, 563. [6] *T.R.* p. 92; Dieffenbach II, p. 66.

It will be seen that according to the traditions as we have them, at least two quite different views prevailed in Mangaia in regard to the destination of the souls of those who die a natural death, though the teaching of the priests recognises only that of Miru's oven. Yet a third view recognises a warriors' Paradise in the skies above.[1] But, as Stimson points out, we hear little of the latter. It is clear that these alternative views require explanation. We shall discuss them further in a later chapter (p. 369 ff. below), but we cannot leave the subject here without at least a passing reference to an important criticism which has recently been made on the commonly accepted view of the geography of the regions to which the soul passes after death. This criticism has been made by Stimson in one of the most important recent contributions to the study of Polynesian religion and mythology. In discussing the conception of the Heavens, recorded from the Maori and other islanders, Stimson suggests that the view that the Heavens are situated in the upper skies, and that the gods dwell up above in the skies, is due to Christianity, whether to its influence on native thought, or to its influence on the records of missionaries, etc., and he holds that the conception of a warriors' Paradise in the skies is spurious.

"The destination of the Polynesian after death in pre-Christian times, with very few if any real exceptions, was the nether world."[2]

It is only with great diffidence that we venture to question the view of a scholar of the learning and critical acumen of Stimson. But we are nevertheless inclined to doubt the uniformity of the Polynesian views in regard to the destination of the soul. Such uniformity would be quite contrary to what we generally find among other peoples in regard to this matter. Moreover it seems to us that even from the internal evidence of the Polynesian records, the discrepancy to which Stimson rightly calls attention is due, not to errors of record, but to contradictory ideas current among the natives themselves.[3] These views have, perhaps, entered the Pacific at different times, and perhaps from different sources. But our study of the traditions referred to in the preceding chapter, and of others to follow in Chapter v, makes it clear that the approach to the land of the dead must, according to certain phases of Polynesian thought,

---

[1] Apparently this warriors' Paradise above the clouds is not known in Rarotongan myth (Buck, *M.S.* p. 206). Can it possibly be a recent introduction, due to influence from Melanesia? For a somewhat similar idea, see Thurnwald, p. 8.

[2] Stimson, *T.R.* p. 93.

[3] An interesting passage which illustrates both the belief in the ascent of the soul through a series of Heavens, and the contradictory and inconsistent ideas held on this subject will be found in Taylor, p. 220.

be by *climbing up*. This conception is particularly strong in Moriori chants and is conserved throughout the Pacific. Moreover, in order to reach the Heavens or the abode of the gods, the hero must climb through a number of successive Heavens. It is true that he must also frequently go down to Po. This is another matter. The one idea is as important as the other, and the inconsistency—if such it is—is consistent everywhere. But the idea of climbing is too much a part of the warp and woof of Polynesian thought to be due to European influence. Moreover we have seen that an identical conception is found in a fully developed form among the shamanistic Tatars, where—and this is of the utmost importance—the climbing and the dramatic representation of the superimposed Heavens form a part of their most fundamental and sacred ritual (cf. p. 200 ff. above).[1] In our opinion the real hope of the solution of the problem lies, not in trying to explain away the Polynesian conceptions of the upper Heavens, but in determining its relationship to that of the Tatars. To apply Stimson's own excellent principle of peripheral distribution, we must surely look for some common centre of distribution at some period in the past.

A number of stories are related in which the scene is laid in Heaven or the Underworld, and in which the gods alone take part, without the participation of human beings. In these stories the gods are represented as engaged in adventures similar to those of human beings, and it is significant how largely sports figure among their occupations. Thus we have a story from Mangaia[2] which relates that Tane in the 'Shades' once challenged his brother Rongo to a kite-flying match; but Tane was hopelessly beaten because Rongo had secretly provided himself with an enormous quantity of string. The chiefs of Mangaia were similarly accustomed to amuse themselves with kite-flying competitions.[3] In the Tongan story of Tui Tofua, the shark god, Tui Tofua himself is shown to us engaged in playing at a game called *sika*[4] with a number of companions before they assume their shark form, and while they are still in the form of men.[5] In another story from Mangaia the god Tangaroa also takes an active interest in a reed-throwing match in which his son (by Hina) engages against the seven dwarf sons of a certain Pinga.[6] We

---

[1] In the passage cited in the preceding footnote the Maori *tohunga* also by his ritual assists the soul in its ascent through the Heavens: "Every prayer uttered over the bones was supposed to aid the soul in its ascent."

[2] Gill, *Myths*, p. 123.   [3] *Ib. S.L.P.* p. 18 ff.

[4] *Sika* is a game in which peeled sticks resembling spears are slid along the ground, in some kind of competition.

[5] Gifford, *T.M.T.* p. 77 ff.   [6] Gill, *Myths*, p. 118 ff.

have already seen (p. 292 f. above) that the gods of the Heavens are commonly represented in Tongan and Samoan myths as engaged in competitive sports and contests with their visitors from earth or from Bulotu.

One of the most striking of the stories of the gods is that of the origin of the *areoi* society, to whom reference has already been made (p. 311 above), and who will be discussed more fully in a later chapter. In a version recorded by T. Henry[1] from Tahiti, where this society has been observed in its most elaborate form, the god Rongo is said to dwell in the sky with many other gods, and to have had originally a wife by whom he had a son and three daughters. Rongo grew tired of his wife and cast her out of Heaven; but as he grew lonely for lack of her, his two sisters—or, commonly, his two brothers—volunteered to go down to earth to seek a wife for him. Passing down by the usual divine path of the rainbow, they sought throughout all the islands of the Tahiti Group and at last on the island of Borabora they found a maiden of beauty worthy of the god. Rongo accordingly descended to earth and married the maiden, but having no presents suitable to offer in accordance with earthly custom, he returned to Heaven and transformed two serving lads, his sisters' attendants—or according to other versions of the story, his own brothers—into two pigs, one a male, the other a female, and presented them to his wife. The incarnation of the god, according to this version, was King Tamatoa I of Ra'iatea, where at Opoa the principal sanctuary of the god was situated down to modern times. This Tamatoa was instituted by Rongo as the first *areoi*, and, through his friend Mahi,[2] who in his turn impersonated Tamatoa himself, the institution of the *areoi* was established on the neighbouring islands also. It is probable that certain features in this story connected with the pigs have been modified in modern years in conformity with

[1] *A.T.* p. 230 ff.
[2] The name *Mahi*, lit. 'fermented bread-fruit', has always been a great puzzle. For a description of the preparation of *mahi* in the island of Aitutaki, Cook Group, by storing bread-fruit in underground pits, see Buck, *M.C.C.I.* p. 62. It should be mentioned that when the Mangaian hero Ngaru wished to blanch his complexion, his grandfather advised him to follow the recipe for ripening bananas, and bury himself in an underground pit lined with banana leaves for eight days. This he did and emerged with a complexion of dazzling fairness (Gill, *Myths*, p. 227). It will be seen later that high-born youths and maidens, and those who were preparing to take part in ritual and dramatic dances, underwent a period of seclusion in darkened huts, and there is reason to believe that the practice was followed by the *areoi* and similar people. We suggest, therefore, that *Mahi* is a nick-name having reference to this period of seclusion, and the characteristic fair complexion of the first *areoi*.

modern standards of taste. The pig has always been sacred to Rongo, and the *areoi* always carried one on their canoes, and began their performances with the sacrifice of one of these animals.

Gill records from Mangaia [1] a remarkable story of the adventures of Tane in search of a wife. The story opens with an account of how the god and a chief named Aki journey together to Ukupolu, which is identified by Gill with Upolu in Samoa, to woo a maiden of great beauty. The maiden rejects the advances of the god in favour of Aki, and Tane retires discomfited to the seashore. Being unable to return to his home in Avaiki, [2] he climbs a gigantic *bua* tree, [3] and clambering to the extremity of one of its branches, he jerks himself into Enuakura, 'the Land of the Red Parrot Feathers'. [4] Here he meets his grandmother, Kui-the-Blind, who catches him with the hook by which she secures human victims. Tane, however, climbs her cocoa-nut tree, and after destroying its guardians, a lizard, a centipede, and a mantis, all the familiars of Kui, he steals all the nuts save two, and with these he cures her blindness. In gratitude she gives him the choice of her four daughters, here all called Ina, and the god marries the fourth daughter; but after a time his wife grows jealous of him, and the god, weary of her chiding tongue, makes wings for himself and flies back to Avaiki.

It will be seen that this journey of Tane to the Underworld bears a close resemblance to that of Tawhaki and a number of other heroes already related, not only in the adventure with Kui-the-Blind, but also in the object of the journey—that of procuring a wife, though, as we have seen, the god is obliged after all to leave her behind in the land of the 'Shades'. The resemblance to the adventures of Tawhaki does not end here, however, for Tane also journeys to the highest Heaven, his object being to visit the supreme god Io, in order to procure the baskets of knowledge. [5] The means which he utilises in order to make these

---

[1] *Myths*, p. 107 ff.; a Rarotongan version of this story recorded from the recital of the last high priest of the island is given in *J.P.S.* xxx, p. 201 ff.

[2] This name (*Hawaiki*) is generally regarded either as having reference to the original home of the Polynesian race, or as an alternative home of the dead, or spirit world. But, as Gill points out (*Myths*, p. 114), the word is the same as the Samoan Savai'i, an island of the Samoan Group; and it is very probable that this is the locality referred to in our story.

[3] The tree which mortals ascend in order to lower themselves down to the spirit world (see p. 314 above).

[4] I.e. the land of the gods, red being the divine colour.

[5] Best, *M.M.R.* p. 13. In Maori tradition knowledge is stored in baskets, and in the Maori School of Learning, each form of knowledge is said to be represented by pebbles which are stored in baskets, and placed by the *tohunga* in the mouths of his pupils during certain phases of the teaching.

journeys also correspond in some features with certain versions of the Tawhaki story, e.g. the kite form under which Tane sometimes mounts aloft.[1] These stories are doubtless religious in origin, and not infrequently tendencious. Thus we can trace the controversial interests of the *tohungas* in the story of the kite-flying competition between Rongo and Tane. Gill tells us that the story just related of Tane's adventures in search of a wife formed a part of the esoteric teaching of the Mangaian priests.[2]

A considerable amount of similarity exists between the exploits of the divine family of Rangi (or Whatea) and Papa, and those of the divine family of early Japanese records. The belief that Heaven was formerly much nearer to earth, is referred to in both the *Nihongi*[3] and the early anthology known as the *Manyoshiu*, 'The Myriad Leaves',[4] and here and in the *Kojiki* already referred to the Japanese divine family dwells on the 'plain of high Heaven', very much as the Polynesian gods dwell in the regions of the upper Heavens, above the sky. The rainbow path by which the Polynesian gods and *arikis* commonly pass between earth and Heaven is represented in Japanese by the *ama no ukihashi*, the 'floating bridge of Heaven', which is generally identified with the rainbow.[5] An important person in the divine family of both peoples is the rain-storm god known to Japanese tradition as Susa-no-wo. The rough and boisterous behaviour of the latter in the household of his sister Amaterasu, whom he visits on the plain of High Heaven,[6] has much in common with the account of Tawhirimatea, the Maori wind-storm god,[7] and with the wind spirit, Salulut Antu Ribut, among the Sea Dyaks (see p. 310 above, and 486 below).

The majority of stories of the Polynesian anthropomorphic gods resemble in tone the stories which we have been considering. The mythical adventures tend to be of the nature of 'pranks', and an absence of dignity, combined at times with crude humour, pervades the narratives. In most stories of this kind the gods are associated with human beings, sometimes as rivals, sometimes as enemies. Several examples of stories of this class have already been referred to (cf. p. 292

[1] See *J.R.A.I.* LXI (1931), p. 455 ff., and references there cited.
[2] *Myths*, p. 114.
[3] *Nihongi*, p. 18.
[4] Transl. by Dickins, p. 28; cf. *ib.* p. 30, note 6.
[5] See Aston[1], p. 87. Cf. *ibid. Shinto*[2], p. 21. Florenz, *H.Q.* p. 12, footnote 3. The same conception is found also among the Cheremissi on the R. Volga.
[6] *Kojiki*, p. 45 ff.   [7] Taylor, p. 115 ff.

above), in which a group of mortals go up to Heaven, or a group of gods come down to earth, in order to acquire some advantage for themselves by fair means or foul. Sometimes the gods of the Heavens, or of Bulotu, are opposed to the gods of earth. We have seen that stories of this kind are especially common in Tonga and Samoa. An example of a story of strife between the gods of earth and of Pulotu (Bulotu) has been recorded from Tonga both in the form of prose and of narrative poetry. The prose story[1] relates that four gods of earth visit the island of Bulotu, the Tongan Heaven, in company with an old woman named Faimalie. In this Tongan story, however, the journey is made by boat. The gods of Bulotu regard their visitors with great contempt as merely 'gods dwelling in the world', and resent their intrusion; but they are reluctant to shed blood or take violent action, and instead insist on the gods of earth undergoing a series of ordeals, threatening them with death only in case of failure. Thanks to the help of Faimalie, the gods of earth prove more than equal to every test, and the gods of earth return in their boat—not, however, before Faimalie has possessed herself of some of their most useful vegetables with which to enrich mankind. The fact that the journey is made by boat rather than in the way generally referred to elsewhere in the Pacific is very characteristic of Tongan mythology, where the Heavenly journey is generally either rationalised into a canoe voyage, or transformed into a journey on the back of a shark, or whale. In this story it is interesting to observe that the old woman Faimalie plays the rôle commonly ascribed to the *tohunga* in stories of voyages. For when the gods decide to make their cruise, she only succeeds in inducing them to take her with them by her importunity, though actually she proves to be of the greatest service to them. We may compare the part played by Nganaoa in the story of Rata's voyage, and that of Kae in similar stories (cf. pp. 275, 289 above, and the references there cited).

It will be seen that the majority of the narratives relating to the gods in Polynesia which have come under our observation have developed from or been adapted to various kinds of antiquarian speculation. That is to say they have passed through an intellectual medium—the influence of the *tohunga*—at some stage of their history. Thus the humorous account of the Council of the gods in Upolu,[2] which meets to deliberate on what should be the end of the life of man, appears to have originated from a contemplation of the various forms of death and rejuvenation to which all forms of life are subject. The story of the origin of the *areoi*

[1] Gifford, *T.M.T.* p. 155 ff.   [2] Turner, p. 8 f.

referred to above (p. 318) has many antiquarian features. The Samoan story of Lu's search through the heavens for his lost fowls, and his marriage with the daughter of Tangaloa is ostensibly built round a philological speculation on the word Samoa.[1] The Samoan story of how Tiitii, the son of Taloga (Tangaloa), obtained fire from Mafui is a variant of the account of the discovery of fire which is found all over the Pacific (cf. pp. 284, 343). In Hawaii, Westervelt has collected a large number of stories which relate to antiquarian subjects, such as Creation myths, and the introduction of useful arts. These have frequently been adopted as local legends and have developed as stories of entertainment. We may instance the story of *The gods who found water*, which is associated with many local features in the neighbourhood of Honolulu.[2] Gill records a story which he heard from Te Ariki-tare-are, the last high priest of Rarotonga, and which relates a contest between rival gods in Rarotonga for possession of a spring on the summit of the mountain known as 'The Mist'.[3]

Two star myths related by W. W. Gill from Mangaia[4] may also be mentioned here. The first relates how a girl ('Inseparable') and her brother run away from a cruel mother and leap up to the sky, Inseparable holding on to her brother's girdle. The second, the saga of the origin of the Pleiades, relates how this constellation, originally one star, was shattered by Tane in jealousy of their brightness. Though the stories are explanatory in origin, and are included below under 'Antiquarian', the first at least is elaborated into the pure narrative style of a saga of entertainment, and we suspect that the second is a greatly condensed version of a more elaborate saga. One would like to have known something of the circumstances of the composition and recitation of these sagas, with both of which 'dramatic' poems are associated.

Gill has an interesting note on a myth of the sun and moon which adds something to our information about the political value attached to myths by people who pretend to take them quite seriously. He tells us that this particular myth was obtained from the 'now almost extinct Tongan tribe' of Mangaia. It was, however, "rejected by the victorious tribes; *not* on the ground of its excessive absurdity, but on the ground of its representing Tonga-iti as a *husband* of Papa, instead of being her third *son*. By this account the almost extinct tribe of Tongans should take the precedence of their hereditary foes, the descendants of Rongo."[5]

[1] Turner, p. 11.   [2] Westervelt, *L.O.H.* p. 32 ff.
[3] *A.A.A.S.* (1890), p. 616 ff.
[4] Gill, *Myths*, p. 40 ff. Cf. also Andersen, p. 398 f.   [5] *Myths*, p. 44 f.

From this it is clear, not only that some myths are purely tribal, but also that they are used to play their part in tribal politics.

It will be seen that in the stories which relate to the family of Rangi and Papa, and the rest of the gods of Heaven, the feminine interest is hardly represented. Papa exists merely in order to be the mother of a large family of sons. There are no daughters. Faimalie is an interesting figure, for she occupies the place of a *tohunga* in the stories where she occurs. But there are no young or unmarried women. Miru, who is feminine in Central Polynesia, where she is very prominent, is hardly more than a personification of the destructive force of death and the Underworld. Her daughters are *tapairu* (cf. p. 293 above), and whatever the exact significance of the word, they are certainly not divinities. The orthodox religion of Central Polynesia, with its warriors' Paradise, its annihilation of those who die naturally, and its male gods, has no feminine interest, and no feminine hope.

From Hawaii, however, we have a great Cycle[1] of volcano divinities, in which the interest is wholly feminine. This Cycle appears to be more or less confined to the Hawaiian islands, at any rate in modern times, though one tradition represents Pele and her family as immigrants from Samoa (p. 254 above). This Cycle is very extensive, and especially interesting from the fact that its literary development is unusually high. Innumerable songs are associated with the stories, and are sometimes incorporated in the sagas, but more often recited independently of them. We shall have occasion to refer to the poems later. They are, however, entirely lyrical in character. The narrative is confined to prose, though from allusions in the poems the stories implied as a background can often be discerned fairly clearly.

The most important characters in this Cycle are always women. We meet here for the first time, therefore, a group of sagas of the gods of almost exclusively feminine interest, and we move in an atmosphere of matriarchy. How far they treat exclusively of supernatural beings we cannot say, as we have clear record that the priestesses of the goddess Pele identified themselves with the divinity whom they served. There can, however, be no doubt that these stories of Pele and her family are regarded by the Hawaiians themselves as stories of the gods in the same way as those of Rangi and Papa and the divine pantheon.

The stories of the Pele Cycle are generally of a more ambitious character than the other sagas of the gods in Polynesia. The more expanded examples are related with a great wealth of detail, and variety

[1] Westervelt, *H.L.V. passim.*

of incident, and of personnel, and are full of songs in the form of speeches. Some of the more elaborate examples contain sagas within sagas. Others are themselves contained in longer sagas relating primarily to human heroes.

An example of the latter type, and one of the most important of the sagas of Pele, is that which relates to her first arrival in the Hawaiian Islands. This story is contained in the saga of Aukele, to which reference has already been made (p. 277 f. above), and relates how the hero meets his wife's cousins, Pele and Hiiaka, as he is out fishing during his residence in Tahiti. From his frequent and prolonged absences his wife begins to suspect that he is spending his time with other women, and, on discovering the truth, drives her cousins away from the island. They take refuge in the Hawaiian Group, but their relentless cousin drives them from island to island till at last they settle in Hawaii itself, creating the active volcano of Mount Kilauea to be their permanent home. Their cousin is at last defeated; she cannot drive them away from there.

There are many versions of the arrival of Pele in Hawaii, but all represent her as an immigrant. On the other hand there were already native gods on the islands before her arrival. Among these is Kama-pua'a, who is sometimes represented as a man, sometimes as a hog; and again as able to change his form from the one to the other. On hearing of Pele's arrival, Kama-pua'a crosses over from his home in the island of Oahu to Hawaii, and unobserved watches the fire dance of Pele and her sisters in the crater of Mauna Loa. At last one of Pele's sisters sees him in the form of a handsome man dancing to the sound of a small hand-drum high up on the lip of the crater, and Pele in indignation spouts fire from the volcano at him, and taunts him in abusive terms. A great battle takes place between them, but eventually Pele becomes reconciled to her lover, and even consents to be his wife; but the union is not destined to last. Pele seeks to overcome her lover with fire from her depths; Kama-pua'a seeks to quench her fires with torrential rains. At last with a mighty eruption of liquid fire Pele drives her lover into the sea, and the parting is complete.[1] In some versions of the story, however, the result of the battle is represented as a compromise, both sides claiming the victory. But Kama-pua'a is the hero of many stories quite independent of the Pele Cycle. One suspects in these stories of Pele and Kama-pua'a a political motive, a hidden religious controversy between the priests of rival divinities; but in modern times the narratives are current as stories of entertainment.

[1] Westervelt, *H.L.V.* p. 45 ff.; cf. Fornander, *P.R.* I, p. 51; Emerson, *U.L.* p. 228; Rice, p. 51 f.

Many other sagas relate to the relations of the goddess with her enemies and rivals, her love and courtship with mortals, her contests with them in games of skill, her domestic relations with her many husbands, and her sudden outbursts of devastating anger. These subjects form a vast Cycle of legends in the Hawaiian Islands, very frequently attached to definite localities and natural features. She has many lovers, but the most romantic story is that of her relations, and those of her sister Hiiaka, with a certain Lohiau, a chief of the island of Kauai. The story relates that during a long sleep the spirit of Pele hears the sound of a *hula* drum, and a voice chanting very beautifully. Her spirit leaves her body sleeping in the crater in the care of her sister Hiiaka, and follows the sound of the music till she comes to the long dancing house of Lohiau on Kauai, where she finds that the singing is that of Lohiau himself. Pele is welcomed, and proceeds to take part in the dances. She gives a magnificent exhibition of a wind dance, invoking all the winds to come to her aid, and she and Lohiau become man and wife. But there are three supernatural female beings present—Westervelt calls them dragons—who are full of jealousy of Pele, and when the time comes for her spirit to return to her body in the crater of Kilauea, they carry off the dead body of Lohiau to a cave, and hide his spirit in a cocoa-nut shell.

When Pele awakes from her long sleep, her spirit longs for her lover, and she sends her youngest sister Hiiaka to seek Lohiau and bring him to her, promising that during Hiiaka's absence she will protect her forests and her friend Hopoe who has taught her the *hula*. Hiiaka's adventures on this journey themselves form a whole Cycle of traditions; for she is assailed in her travels through the forest by many demons and spirits, till all the forces of nature seem banded against her to prevent her progress, and at times it seems that she must be overcome; but by means of the lightning in her *pau*, or grass skirt, Hiiaka is enabled to overcome all adversaries, and at last to rescue the body and spirit of Lohiau, and to restore him to life. But as they travel together to Kilauea, Hiiaka becomes aware that Pele in her impatience and jealousy at the long delay has broken all her promises, and destroyed her sister's forests and her playground, and even killed her friend Hopoe. Now for the first time Hiiaka turns and gives response to the love which Lohiau has often proffered to her on their long journey. Pele has lost the lover of her dreams.[1]

---

[1] This narrative will be found in a series of separate stories recorded by Westervelt, *H.L.V.* pp. 72 ff., 126 ff., and in a consecutive form by Rice, p. 7 ff.

Unfortunately in Westervelt's collection the sagas of Pele are only related to us in summary form. In Emerson's collection of 250 pages of legends of Pele and Hiiaka, the story of Hiiaka's journey is given in fuller form. This has unfortunately not been accessible to us. In S. P. Smith's review,[1] however, we are told that "it is in the form of a series of poems with recitative interludes, very much, in that respect, like the Rarotongan story of Ono-kura, which is equally long, and of the same type of song and recitative". Now Smith has elsewhere[2] described the Rarotongan version of Ono-kura as 'a complete South Sea Opera' of mingled songs and recitative which would take many hours in delivery. The Hawaiian parallel is especially interesting, therefore, as suggesting that elaborate dramatic ritual poetry of the gods, of the kind which we are about to study in Mangaia, was probably in existence formerly in Hawaii also. It is also interesting as affording further illustration of the curious fact to be noted again in Mangaia that most of the saga there appears to be a prose paraphrase of, or commentary on, older poems, especially dramatic poems. We shall see later (p. 387 below) that the *Hula Pele*, or dance with action songs in honour or commemoration of Pele, which was popular in Hawaii, has much in common with this dramatic poetry of the Central Pacific.

The Cycle of Pele is not wholly confined to the Hawaiian Group, and traces occur in the Marquesas and the Paumotu Archipelago[3] as well as in Rarotonga. In the last-named island Mahuike, the great goddess of fire, has a daughter, also a fire goddess, whose name, Pere, is identical with Pele, and who is credited with having blown off the top of the island Fakareva in a fit of anger. "Earthquakes and explosions terrified the people. Mahuike tried to make Pere quiet down, and finally drove her away. Pere leaped into the sea and fled to Va-ihi (Hawaii)."[4] A somewhat similar story is told in Samoa of Mahuike, who is there the god of fire. According to this tradition the banished daughter passed under the ocean, first to the Marquesas, and then to Hawaii. It has already been mentioned (p. 308 above) that the name has been equated with that of the Samoan Fe'e, who is described as a cuttle-fish with supernatural powers.[5]

Stories of deified heroes are very widespread throughout the Pacific. A large number of Polynesian heroes bear the same names as gods, with whom there can be no doubt they are in many cases identified.

[1] *J.P.S.* XXIV, p. 113.　　　[2] Smith, *Hawaiki*, p. 222.
[3] See *J.P.S.* VII, p. 109.　　　[4] Westervelt, *H.L.V.* p. 67.
[5] *Loc. cit.*

A notable case is that of Whiro or Iro, a chief of comparatively modern times—perhaps about the thirteenth century—who is frequently confused or identified with Iro, the divine enemy of the god Tane.[1] In many instances the great heroes of the past have undoubtedly been deified. A reflection of this custom may be seen in the Rarotongan story of the apotheosis of the great voyager Tangiia whose spirit is said to have flown up above to the 'wandering spirits' after his death, and there bewailed his dead body lying below near the sea.[2] The picture of the assembly of the gods drinking *kava* in the house of Rongo-ma-Tane, the menial part played by the god Tangaroa, the efficiency of Tonga-iti, and the lordly airs of Rongo, the speeches introduced, and the general air of naturalism are curiously parallel to Norse stories of the gods, and admirably illustrate this type of literature at its best, when developed for purposes of entertainment.

Closely related to the stories of deified heroes are stories relating to deified ancestors. W. W. Gill tells us that the Mangaian king, Tiaio, who was clubbed to death, "was afterwards deified, and associated with Motoro in worship".[3] Elsewhere in speaking of the inhabitants of the island of Nanomanga he tells us that they spoke of their deified ancestors as 'the good gods', and that "the principal objects of adoration are *the skulls and jaw-bones of the dead*".[4] Turner tells us of a lady called Taisumalie who lived in Upolu in Samoa, and who, when she "went away among the gods, was worshipped first by her family and then by all the people of the land where she resided. She spoke through one of the heads of the family."[5]

Stories of fish gods have been recorded from various Groups, notably Tonga, Hawaii, and New Zealand. As a rule they are brief and bear a close resemblance to folk-tales. We may refer to the story of the shark god, Tui Tofua, of which several variants have been recorded from Tonga, both in the form of prose saga and of narrative poetry.[6] Tui Tofua himself is the son of the lord of Tofua island, who is banished by his father for some trivial offence. He and his followers sail away, and when they reach mid-ocean Tui Tofua tells all his followers to throw themselves into the sea. This they do, and he turns them all into sharks, all save one Samoan, who refuses to be transformed. Last of all he turns into a shark himself. But the Samoan returns to the ship, and

[1] See e.g. the Rarotongan traditions, *J.P.S.* xxix, p. 120; cf. also Smith's note, *ib.* p. 113.   [2] *Ib.* p. 63.
[3] Gill, *S.L.P.* p. 21.   [4] Gill, *Jottings*, p. 21.
[5] Turner, p. 56.   [6] Gifford, *T.M.T.* p. 76 ff.

sails to land, bearing with him a message from Tui Tofua to the people of Tofua that they shall meet the sharks on the seashore two days later, and hold a festival. When the appointed time arrives the people all meet on the shore with garlands of flowers, and festal array, and the parents all recognise their own sons. Tui Tofua does not forgive his own parents, however, and refuses to come near them. The story concludes with a battle which Tui Tofua wages successfully against another fish god Seketoa who is doing mischief to the islanders.

In addition to the supernatural beings whom we have been considering, there are also a number of others less easy to define, and differing to some extent in each island group. All these beings, of whatever type, are commonly referred to by Europeans as 'fairies', and though the term has a connotation which has no equivalent in the Polynesian conceptions, it is not easy to find any other handy term which includes all these extremely elusive beings. We have already made some reference to them in the preceding chapter (p. 293 ff. above), and some account has been given of those 'fairies' who in the past have been in the habit of marrying mortals. This is the type of 'fairy' who plays the largest part in Polynesian tradition, and we shall see in the following chapter that such intermarriage is by no means confined to stories of famous heroes which have an inter-island currency, but is commonly attributed to local heroes. There are, however, a number of other types of 'fairy' beings, who are found in the stories, and who in some cases differ considerably from those who become the wives of heroes. All these supernatural beings are known under a number of different terms, and have in general different characteristics.

It has already been mentioned (p. 297 above) that the specific ethnological characteristics of these supernatural beings are in general so consistently insisted on in the traditions that the suggestion has often been made that they represent the earlier occupants of some of the Pacific islands. This supposition is particularly insistent in regard to the *menehune*, who appear in Hawaiian traditions as a dwarf race, of great strength and skill, whose habits are nocturnal.[1] In Tahiti the name occurs in the form *manahune* with reference to a class of the population, while in the Cook Group the name *Manaune* is found also in connection with human beings—in Mangaia as the eponymous ancestor of a tribe still bearing this name.[2] In New Zealand the 'fairy' people are known as the *turehu*, the *patu-paiarehe*, etc. The latter are represented as very small,

---

[1] Rice, p. 33 ff.; Thrum, *J.P.S.* xxix, p. 70 ff.
[2] See note by S. P. Smith, *J.P.S.* xxix, p. 72; cf. Buck, *M.S.* p. 76f.

but according to the most authentic tradition[1] the *turehu* are the size of normal human beings, but having flaxen hair, fair skins, beautiful faces, and wearing aprons like sea-weed. They are said to be excellent dancers, especially of the *haka*, to which we shall refer more fully later. All these beings are described as nocturnal in their habits, as generally living apart from human beings, and as hating cooked food (see p. 293 above). Tregear identified the *turehu* with the Moriori;[2] but Cowan's collection of local legends and traditions generally from among the Maori[3] suggests a more mixed and complicated origin for them, and Best is strongly opposed to the view that they represent any race that was ever in occupation of New Zealand.[4]

The class of beings known as *tapairu* is very baffling. The term is applied by the Polynesians themselves to both human and supernatural beings. Prof. Buck[5] informs us that the word is in common use today in the Cook Group, and that it denotes a first-born daughter, and also a woman of high rank.[6] S. P. Smith defined the term as the eldest-born daughter who has functions of a peculiar and semi-sacerdotal character, and he records an interesting Maori tradition of a *tapairu* wife of Tamatea, the high chief who migrated to New Zealand in the great fleet.[7] Low gives us the additional information that a *tapairu* is also a virgin and good looking.[8] Gill tells us that the word was a favourite name in the eastern Pacific for a girl, and that in this usage the meaning was 'fairest of the fair';[9] and the missionary John Williams took back with him to Rarotonga from Aitutaki a woman who is said to have borne the name *Tapairu*. This woman, however, was a near relative of Makea, the head of one of the two ruling lines of Rarotonga. She was therefore an *ariki*.[10] It does not appear that she ever married, and it is probable that in this case, and in that of some of the girls referred to by

---

[1] Recorded from the teaching of Te Matorohanga, *Mem. P.S.* III, p. 183.
[2] *Dictionary, s.v.*   [3] Cowan, *P.H.; ib. F.F.T. passim.*
[4] Best, *Maori* I, p. 220. With the views here expressed, cf. a recent pronouncement by Skinner, a summary of which will be found in *Man* XXXVI (May, 1936), p. 81. Skinner points out that archaeological evidence is entirely opposed to the theory of an ancient non-Polynesian population in New Zealand, and that the whole of the material culture hitherto revealed is East Polynesian.
[5] Prof. Buck resided on the island of Mangaia from December 1929 to April 1930. See *Mangaian Society*, p. 3. This book is therefore based on first-hand knowledge, as well as on the results of previous investigators, notably on those of W. W. Gill.   [6] In a letter to ourselves; cf. also *M.S.* p. 201.
[7] *Mem. P.S.* IV, p. 175; cf. also Williams, *Dictionary, s.v. tapairu.*
[8] *J.P.S.* XLIII (1934), p. 18.
[9] *Myths*, p. 257.   [10] Gill, *Jottings*, p. 237.

Gill, the word is used as a common noun rather than as a proper name. In the traditions of Aitutaki recorded by Buck, and by Low, Ru-enua, the legendary discoverer of the island, brought with him his four brothers, his four wives, and 'twenty unmarried *tapairu* women of high rank',[1] in order to introduce high rank into his new colony; for Ru was not himself of *ariki* blood. The implication of all this seems to be that the form *tapairu* refers to groups—to some extent organised groups— of good-looking girls of the highest rank and prestige (? the feminine counterpart of the male *ariki*), for the most part the eldest unmarried daughters of the *ariki* class, and that tradition ascribes great antiquity to the institution—as great, indeed, as that of the *ariki* themselves, if not greater.

The term is also applied by the Polynesians to supernatural women of great beauty and prestige. In this sense Gill generally translates the word 'fairies', and, as we have seen, records traditions from the Cook Group, especially from Mangaia, in which one set of *tapairu* figure as the daughters of Miru, the female guardian of the Underworld, another as the inhabitants of the sky. The *tapairu* of the Underworld come to the world of men at the sound of the 'great drum'[2] through crevices in the rocks, and through springs. The two sets overlap to some extent, and there are also said to be male 'fairies'. All the supernatural *tapairu* are remarkable for their 'peerless beauty', and are spoken of as extremely fair in complexion. We shall find them closely associated with the god Tane, and the dances sacred to him. At times they are said to lodge with the 'shore king',[3] as his guests,[4] but whether this refers to the super- natural beings, or to the human ladies who sometimes impersonated them in dramatic presentations held in the 'shore king's' precincts at Kaputai, close by the altar of Rongo[5] (see pp. 369, 374 below), is un- certain. The exact relationship of the supernatural *tapairu* to their human counterparts is a question of great interest and considerable importance for Polynesian literature, and we shall have occasion to refer to it again in a later chapter.

None of the supernatural beings whom we have been considering can be regarded as hostile to human beings. Most of them are fond of robbing human beings, and still more of kidnapping and intermarrying with them, but they rarely harm them. There are, however, other classes

---

[1] Buck, *M.C.C.I.* p. xix; Low, *loc. cit.*

[2] Gill, *Myths*, p. 260. The big drum was known as 'the voice of Tane' (see p. 380 footnote 9 below).   [3] For this title, see p. 256, footnote 1 above.

[4] Gill, *Myths*, p. 264.   [5] *Ib.* p. 245, and footnote 2.

of supernatural beings who are definitely hostile to heroes and heroines alike. Of these by far the most prominent and widely known are a gigantic race known to Maori tradition[1] as the Ponaturi, and to other Groups under a variety of names. They are especially important in Hawaiian traditions, but they are also known in the Central Pacific. They are generally represented as a maritime race of exclusively nocturnal habits and mischievous propensities, whose extinction is only finally brought about by the rays of the sun. Sometimes they are represented as monstrous birds, sometimes as having the form of gigantic human beings of cannibal propensities, and as devouring the human beings whom they steal (cf. p. 272 above). They are probably to be identified with the gigantic birds of the Hawaiian story of Aukele, and seem to bear some relationship to the unsympathetic 'heaven dwellers' of Tongan and Samoan myth, and learned speculation has again been busy in attempting to equate them with some other race. Many other supernatural beings figure in the stories, but these are in general less widely recognised throughout the Pacific, and are therefore referred to only incidentally in our pages.

Narrative poetry relating to the gods is not unknown in Tonga, though we have not found instances relating to the gods of the divine family of Rangi and Papa, such as Rongo, Tane, or Tangaroa. The gods of Tongan poetry, like those of the prose stories, resemble the heroes of folk-tales, and are generally of more or less local fame. The longest example of a narrative poem of this class known to us is that which relates the story of the voyage of two gods of earth and the old woman Faimalie to visit the gods of Bulotu,[2] and is a variant version of the prose saga to which reference has already been made (p. 321 above). We may perhaps mention here also a narrative poem,[3] also from Tonga, relating to a man from Samoa dwelling in Tonga, and his endeavours to escape from two goddesses who have fallen in love with him on account of his fair complexion. Finally he succeeds in sinking his unwelcome admirers in the sea, whence they are, however, eventually rescued by the agency of the god Tangaloa (Tangaroa). In a prose variant of this story[4] the initiative is transferred from the mortal to the deities, though no hint is given as to their sex, or of their infatuation for the Samoan. It is clear from even the few examples before us that both the antiquarian

---

[1] For a brief general account the reader may consult Andersen, p. 138 ff.
[2] Gifford, *T.M.T.* p. 164 ff.
[3] *Ib.* p. 196.   [4] *Ib.* p. 199.

element, and the undignified prank characteristic of·folk-tale, are as
prominent in the narrative poetry of this class as in the prose sagas.

One instance of narrative poetry has been recorded from Tonga
relating to the fish god, Tui Tofua.[1] The poem, which is said to be
ancient, is called a *taanga*, and consists of only 83 lines; but it is incomplete. It relates the same story as the one already referred to (p. 327
above), which occurs in a number of prose versions, but our fragment of
narrative poetry concludes at the point at which the Samoan expresses
his reluctance to be turned into a shark. This passage is the most
expanded part of the poem, the remaining narrative being given for the
most part in a series of short bare statements:

> And they steered their vessel
> And Tui Tofua spoke thus,
> "Stop here and we jump one after the other,
> And if lucky turn into a shark,
> If unlucky turn into a stone".
>
> The Samoan alone
> Cried, not wishing to be a shark.
> Faia cried tear drops,
> Cried not wishing to be a shark,
> Lest (he be) noosed by a fishing canoe,
> And taken on shore to the people,
> And then apportioned and rejoiced over.[2]

The god who figures in this poem appears to be a local deity, though
a shark god was undoubtedly worshipped in Mangaia,[3] and perhaps
elsewhere. No shark god, however, figures among the more familiar
beings of the pantheon of the prose sagas or of the ritual poetry. The
affinities of the poem of Tui Tofua lie with the timeless-nameless prose
stories relating to fish and trees which have been recorded from Tonga
and Samoa, and to which fuller reference will be made in the following
chapter.

Speech poems and poetry of a dramatic character relating to the gods
are abundant. Perhaps the most important class of poetry of this kind is
that which is recited in dramatic form at religious festivals, or in 'action
songs' sung on occasions which still retain something of their original
religious significance, though in many cases this religious association is

---

[1] Gifford, *T.M.T.* p. 80f.   [2] *Ib.* p. 80f.
    In Mangaia Tereavai, the last high priest of Tiaio, the shark god, survived to
embrace Christianity. See Gill, *D.L.P.* p. 335.

now hardly more than a tradition. In addition to the ample texts which have been recorded of poetry of this kind, especially from Mangaia and Hawaii, we have numerous fragments of poetry resembling these texts, of which the exact milieu has not been recorded, but which from the nature of their contents and form we believe to belong to the same class of poetry. If this is correct it would seem probable that dramatic poetry relating to the gods was widespread throughout the Pacific in pre-Christian times. We shall return to this subject in a later chapter (p. 352 ff. below), and confine ourselves here to a brief discussion of poetry of this class relating to the gods, as this is found incorporated in the texts of sagas, and in isolated fragments.

Speech poems are frequently attributed to the gods in the sagas, especially in the Cycle relating to Pele and Hiiaka from Hawaii. These poems are practically all lyrical in quality, and the recorded specimens refer almost without exception to the phenomena of external nature and the elements. It is believed that they are, in fact, allegorical, and symbolise human passions under every form; but it is a notable fact that they resemble very closely the descriptive and lyrical poetry which has been recorded from Tonga, and to which we shall refer more fully later (p. 405 ff. below). But the speech poems attributed to supernatural beings are not confined elsewhere to poetry of this class, and the sagas are interspersed throughout, like Irish saga, with speech poems of all kinds. As examples we may refer to two poems attributed to the god Tangaroa in a Rarotongan saga,[1] of which the first celebrates his union with a mortal called Vaine-uenga, the wife of Ataranga, while the second embodies an appeal to the gods Rongo and Tane that his child may be duly named and honoured at its birth. Poems of this class from Mangaia, such as that in which the god Tane laments his inability to return to Avaiki because a hole has been made in his canoe,[2] may possibly be quotations from longer dramatic poems.

Elegiac poems, and also poems composed as hymns and spells, are commonly attributed to the gods, and these also are frequently embodied in sagas, though independent examples are not rare. In Rarotonga the *atua-tini*, 'the many gods', are represented as singing a lament for the sacred bird of Tane, which has been maltreated by the crew of Iro's canoe on his voyage to Kupolu.[3] The prayers and spells attributed to the gods are often indistinguishable. In the great contest between Pele and the supernatural monster Kama-pua'a (cf. p. 324 above), Kama-

---

[1] *J.P.S.* VIII, p. 67 ff.   [2] Gill, *Myths*, p. 109.
[3] *J.P.S.* XXIX, p. 121.

pua'a chants a prayer invoking rain.[1] Spells are commonly chanted by Hiiaka, the sister of Pele. She chants a spell in her efforts to gain time to climb a precipice in order to catch the ghost of her lover Lohiau.[2] By means of her incantations she restores his dead body to life when she finds it in a cave.[3]

Poetry containing addresses to the gods, such as hymns, prayers, songs of celebration, and invocations, are exceedingly numerous and widespread. In their more popular form poems of this class are often indistinguishable from charms, which are equally numerous. But there is also a higher class of religious poetry, associated with the cult of Kiho (Io)[4], which is quite unlike these. Its affinities lie rather with antiquarian poetry. Owing to its esoteric and aristocratic character the amount of this poetry of Kiho which has been preserved is limited, but five examples have been recorded from the Paumotu Archipelago[5] and New Zealand.[6] The Paumotu examples are exceptionally well preserved and pure, owing to the jealous care with which the texts (oral) were transmitted, and to the superior intellectual attainments and religious and spiritual responsibility of the *tohungas* whose duty it was to preserve and transmit them.

Apart from these prayers and addresses to Kiho, which were never recited in public, we hear constantly of elaborate addresses made to the gods on occasions of public ceremony, such as the great annual festival of the *areoi* (cf. p. 426 f. below), or the investiture of a new king or chief. An impressive and dignified hymn of nearly seventy lines has been preserved which was addressed to the god Oro on the investiture of a new king of Ra'iatea.[7] This hymn was chanted by the high priest at the ceremonial purification of the king in the sea. A fragment of the hymn recited when divine honours were conferred on Captain Cook in Hawaii has been preserved by Kamakua.[8] Hymns recited by the 'praying chief' (*te ariki karakia*) over the human sacrifices to Rongo from Mangaia have also been preserved.[9] The first is a thanksgiving, the second a prayer for peace. The language of these hymns is lofty and poetical in tone and full of allusions to history and mythology. All poems of this class, whatever their date, are said to be a mosaic of

---

[1] Westervelt, *H.L.V.* p. 51.   [2] *Ib.* p. 131.   [3] *Ib.* p. 133.
[4] *Mem. P.S.* III, p. vi.
[5] See e.g. Stimson, *T.R. passim*; *ib. Kiho-tumu, passim*.
[6] See *Mem. P.S.* III, p. 92 ff.   [7] Henry, *A.T.* p. 191.
[8] Fornander, *P.R.* II, p. 178.   [9] Gill, *Myths*, pp. 295, 299.

ancient fragments or motifs, and to contain many allusions to the oral literature of the islanders.

Intermediate between these formal prayers offered by the priests on public occasions and those of private individuals are the prayers offered by groups of people before undertaking any enterprise. These appear to have been universal, however trivial the occasion, and are often indistinguishable from charms. They were offered to spirits as well as to the gods. Gill quotes an 'old song' which appears to be an invocation to Uti, a 'female fairy', who rules a district in the Underworld. It is apparently sung by a party of people starting on a fishing expedition:

> Light thy torch, O Uti,
> That illuminates spirit-world [literally, Manomano].
> Rurapo has been consumed;
> Te Vakaroa is all bare.   ·
> Up! ye children of Vatea:[1]
> Keep watch through the night—
> The gloomiest, wettest night—
> When Iro[2] comes up by devious ways
>> From the depths inhabited by Tu.[3]

An interesting example of a communal prayer of this kind from Rarotonga has been preserved for us by Williams as it was given to him by an old priest. Its occasion was the arrival of Captain Cook off the shores of their island:

"O, great Tangaroa, send your large ship to our land; let us see the Cookees. Great Tangiia, send us a dead sea, send us a propitious gale, to bring the far-famed Cookees to our island, to give us nails, and iron, and axes; let us see these outriggerless canoes."

Williams adds that after reciting this prayer, the islanders vociferated the names of all their gods, invoking them to unite their energies in the accomplishment of this greatly desired object.[4]

Family prayers were commonly offered on the same occasions as among ourselves, as well as on other occasions of importance in the private life of the individuals. We may refer to two prayers from Samoa recorded by Turner, the first recited by the head of the family as he

---

[1] For Vatea, see p. 311 above.

[2] In the Cook Group and elsewhere Iro (Whiro) is the patron god of thieves. See Gill, *Myths*, p. 126. Cf., however, p. 312 above.

[3] Gill, *ib.* p. 125. Tu, as explained by Gill, is a supernatural being who, according to Mangaian myth, lives in the lowest department of Avaiki. Here the phrase is used to indicate great depth below the earth. Cf., however, p. 310 ff. above.

[4] Williams, *M.E.* p. 199.

poured out the drink offering to the gods at the commencement of the evening meal, the second recited on similar occasions with an offering of flaming fire.[1] From Hawaii we have a woman's prayer to the goddess of lactation on weaning her child.[2] Very often the prayer is offered by the *tohunga*, even though the occasion is a private one, such as the prayers for the sick, for the consecration of a canoe, for the temporary dispensation from *tapu* for a *tapu* chief.[3] Prayers such as these are too numerous to cite, and do not in general call for any special comment, though they are sometimes surprisingly elaborate, such as a Hawaiian prayer to Lono (Rongo) recited by the father of a boy when he becomes of age to eat with the men.[4]

Many of the examples cited above are stated to be very old, but we do not know to what extent they were handed down unchanged. Certainly traditional forms and formulae were handed down, and there can be no doubt that these prayers have incorporated much of this ancient diction and style. Forster noted long ago[5] that in such prayers the language differs from that used on ordinary occasions, and the formal and stereotyped nature of much of the devotional literature is beyond doubt. In illustration of this we may point to the *kanaenae*, a kind of complimentary address to the god, which stands as a prelude to the more serious matter of a prayer or *mele* (chant) in Hawaii,[6] and to the prologue to the prayers to Kiho and those to other gods in the Paumotus.[7] There can be no doubt as to the antiquity of the texts (oral) of the chants (*fagu*) and invocations (*pure*) which formed a part of the cult of Kiho in the last-mentioned Group. They were regarded as 'semi-sacred' and it was considered sacrilegious to alter or tamper with them in any way.[8]

Charms and spells are very common throughout our area. Almost every important event in the life of an individual or of the community is inaugurated or carried on to the accompaniment of the recitation of spells. These are sometimes brief and highly specialised, sometimes long and elaborate compositions. The word used of a mantic chant is *karakia*. But this word also appears to be used with no magical significance, e.g. of a hymn to the gods, and in such cases it would seem that the radical sense of the word is the chanting, that is to say, the musical (vocal)

[1] Turner, p. 116.   [2] Malo, p. 123 f.
[3] *Ib.* p. 46.   [4] *Ib.* p. 121 f.
[5] J. R. Forster, p. 470.   [6] Malo, p. 143.
[7] Stimson, *T.R.* p. 55.   [8] *Ib.* p. 29; *Kiho-tumu*, p. 3.

accompaniment of the words. It is, however, very difficult to draw a clear distinction between Polynesian prayers and charms, even when the prayers are addressed to the gods; and more often than not when these prayers are addressed by a private individual they seem in themselves to have the power of carrying their own fulfilment.[1] Thus it is by the utterance of powerful *karakias* to their gods, taught them by their ancestors, that heroes are enabled to climb up to Heaven, despite the difficulties which beset them on the way.

The magical power of the *karakia* seems to rest, not so much on the nature of the words as on the form and manner of recitation. A *karakia* appears to be always poetry and always sung. The power lies, not in the words alone, but in the combination of words with vocal music. We have seen that among the Tatars music is believed to have a magical effect, chiefly that of summoning spirits.[2] The Polynesians, among whom musical instruments are rare, produced their magic by means of vocal music. Poetry is in itself magical because sung. It is not surprising, therefore, that many poems recited with a magical significance were originally composed for quite a different purpose. We shall see (p. 393 below) that genealogies were frequently sung as lullabies to children, and these lullabies were themselves regarded as charms for the well-being of the child. We have also seen (p. 283 f. above) that the recitation of the *karakia* over Maui in the Underworld by his father was virtually a mantic performance, and that the omission of a name from the chant proved Maui's undoing. On the other hand although all concerted actions, such as marching and hauling, were accompanied by songs or *karakias*, it seems to us very doubtful in many cases if these were really believed to possess any power beyond that of the assistance rendered to the workers by the rhythm, and perhaps a suggestion—conveyed at times by the words—of the great occasions in the past when such actions had been successfully performed.

This brings us to another question. Certain poems believed to date from very early times, and having reference to the heroes of the past, especially to the Tawhaki Cycle, are remembered and recited in modern times in circumstances analogous to those which they celebrate. For example, in the Aitutaki version of the saga of Rata, the birds are represented as carrying Rata's newly-built canoe through the air, and

---

[1] See Maning, p. 234.
[2] We may compare also the interesting passage from *Thorfinns Saga Karlsefnis* referred to in Vol. 1, p. 474, in which Guðríðr is persuaded to sing the *varðlokkur* to summon the spirits because she has learnt the tunes from her grandmother.

singing each with a different note, and Gill tells us that the song which occurs in this passage in the (oral) text in question has always been in use in Aitutakı and Rarotonga as one of those chanted in hauling heavy timber.[1] Similarly in Mangaia a reference occurs to the same hero in the canoe-making song:

> Commence cutting, O Una;
> It is the mottled adze of another land,
> That hewed in the forest with Rata.[2]

The Maori also while building their canoes sing the song traditionally chanted by Rata.[3] We shall see presently (p. 477 ff. below) that ancient heroic poems, and poems relating to gods and spirits, are chanted by the Sea Dyaks of modern times under similar circumstances to those which form the subjects of these poems, and we are told that these Dyak recitals are believed to be potent in regard to the occasions and situations for which they are recited nowadays. But both here and in Polynesia it is difficult to say exactly how far the recitations are really believed by the Dyaks to possess inherent power, and how far their recitation is due to a sense of their artistic relevance.

The question is one of some importance for mantic studies. And here we may refer to a particularly interesting series of charms collected from the Moriori of the Chatham Islands,[4] which celebrate in the form of monologue and dialogue Tawhaki's ascent to the Heavens. The Moriori recite these poems when in difficulties at sea, or in any undertaking requiring favourable winds. These *karakias* are addressed by the reciters to Tawhaki as the father of the winds, and are themselves called 'Tawhakis'. Some of them enumerate by name all the winds known, and their veering points. The form of the poems would suggest, however, that they were originally composed, not as charms, but as speeches forming a part of a long recitation on the deeds of Tawhaki, perhaps like the Mangaian *kapas*, perhaps like the Dyak recitals just referred to; but this is merely conjecture.[5]

On the other hand the charm sung by Tawhaki in the Maori version

---

[1] Gill, *Myths*, p. 142 ff.

[2] Translated by Buck, *M.S.* p. 134, where twenty lines of the song are recorded; cf. Gill, *Myths*, p. 149, where only the beginning is given.

[3] Shortland, p. 7, footnote.   [4] Shand, *J.P.S.* VII, p. 75 ff.

[5] The custom of calling certain classes of poems by the name of a famous character of the past with whom such poems are especially associated appears to be common among the Maori. We may refer to laments which are generally known as *apakuras*. See Best, *Maori* II, p. 144.

of his saga given by Taylor can only have been composed as a definitely mantic utterance. The poem represents Tawhaki as ascending through ten successive heavens, and exclaiming at each stage of his upward course:

Ascend, Tawhaki, to the first (second, third, etc.) heaven,

and concluding:

Cling, cling, like the lizard, to the ceiling.
Stick, stick close to the side of heaven.[1]

We conjecture that this charm belongs to the class of *karakias* known as 'kite-songs', which were sung in Rarotonga, Mangaia, and New Zealand at the beginning of a kite-flying competition. We have shown elsewhere[2] that these competitions were religious in origin, and held in honour of the gods.

The sagas frequently refer to the recitation of genuine spells. In the account of the departure of the Takitumu canoe from the Central Pacific to New Zealand recited by the old chief Whatahoro to Downes, it is stated that when the canoe was well out to sea, two *tohungas* stood up and recited a *karakia*, calling upon the whole of the whale family to act as an escort to the vessel on her voyage.[3] A medical charm from Mangaia is especially interesting on account of its traditional usage by the first king Rangi to save those wounded in the first battle ever fought on Mangaia. It was believed by Gill to be of great antiquity.[4] In this poem the injunction is delivered direct to the wound, and this would seem to be the form of most medical charms, of which we have extensive collections from the Maori,[5] the Moriori,[6] the Marquesans,[7] and others. Such practical charms were in general use down to quite modern times. In warfare especially they were habitually recited, both before and during a battle, especially by the Maori[8] and the Marquesans,[9] who were perhaps the most warlike people of modern times.

Poetry embodying blessings and curses has not been recorded in great quantities, and has already been referred to (p. 266 above); but

---

[1] Taylor, pp. 114, 141.
[2] *J.R.A.I.* LXI (1931), p. 455 ff.; cf. also p. 317 above.
[3] *J.P.S.* XXIII, p. 30.
[4] Gill, *L.S.I.* p. 68 ff.   [5] See Best, *Maori* I, p. 263 ff.
[6] Shand, *J.P.S.* IV, p. 92.   [7] Handy, *N.C.M.* p. 340.
[8] *J.P.S.* XII, p. 147 ff.
[9] Handy, *N.C.M.* p. 339 f.

we may refer here to an interesting example of a curse to kill a sorcerer and his accomplice as recorded from Hawaii.[1] It consists of a chant in which the various processes of the body's annihilation ('burning', 'rotting', 'maggots', etc.) are enumerated in an imprecation, which is addressed to the god Tane. Prophecies, and other forms of mantic utterance, such as oracles, are also highly developed in poetical form. In this connection we may also mention an invocation recorded from Samoa which was sung to awaken a prophetess.[2] The prophecies and the oracles were commonly indistinguishable from one another, and both were known as *wanana*,[3] and were sought from the Hawaiian seers (cf. p. 446 ff. below) by the kings before undertaking great enterprises. These oracles, when short, resemble the cryptic oracles of the Pythia. The following example from Hawaii was spoken by Kapihe, the noted seer of last century:

> That which is above shall be brought down;
> That which is below shall be lifted up;
> The islands shall be united;
> The walls shall stand upright.[4]

A number of other examples have been preserved, including two variants of a prophecy from the time of Kahahana,[5] and a brief prose prophecy by Kama, a medicine man of the time of Kamehameha II.[6]

Many Hawaiian *wanana* are long and elaborate. A famous chant by the great poet and prophet Keaulumoku describes the horrors of contemporary civil war, and prophesies the success and glory of Kamehameha I. Keaulumoku was the son of Kauakahia, a cousin of Kekaulike, king of the island of Maui in the Hawaiian Group.[7] His great prophecy[8] runs to 809 lines, and is one of the most ambitious efforts of Polynesian poetry. Like the Galla and Hebrew prophecies it is highly allusive, rhetorical, and exclamatory, passing with bewildering rapidity from history to dialogue, from dialogue to monologue, and back to history. The foretelling of the future forms a very slight element in this

---

[1] F. G. Stokes, *J.P.S.* xxxix, p. 13.

[2] *J.P.S.* vii, p. 16.

[3] The word is often translated 'prophecy', but in reality it denotes occult knowledge; see Best, *Maori* i, p. 67.

[4] Malo, p. 154. With this example we may compare Fornander, *P.R.* ii, p. 123.

[5] Malo, *loc. cit.*   [6] *Ib.* p. 321.

[7] Fornander, *P.R.* ii, p. 156.

[8] The text has been published in the *Fornander Collection*, Third Series, Vol. vi, p. 368 ff.

composition, but the metaphors and veiled sayings are couched in a series of vivid images. Indeed the poem is a riot of brilliant metaphors, though the emotional element is strictly subordinated to the artistic and intellectual qualities. The sustained image of the Hawaiian battle-chiefs as fighting cocks[1] occupies the whole of the first half, the eager impetuosity of the fighting birds being forcibly contrasted with the quiet house of sleep in the second half.

[1] Fighting cocks are highly prized possessions in many of the Pacific Groups; see Moerenhout II, p. 147f. Cf. also p. 494 below.

CHAPTER V

SAGA AND POETRY RELATING TO
UNSPECIFIED INDIVIDUALS

SAGAS relating to unnamed or unknown individuals are very numerous, and range from brief anecdotes to ambitious narratives. In general, however, stories of this class are on a lower level of art than those relating to well-known historical or legendary characters. Among the natives they are commonly classed as 'oven-side stories', or, as we should say, 'old wives' tales'[1] (cf. p. 307 above). There is no satisfactory evidence, so far as we are aware, for the cultivation of deliberate fiction,[2] and folk-tales and folk-motifs which can be recognised from other (e.g. European) parallels are rare.

On the other hand certain Asiatic motifs recur frequently in the Pacific stories. As an example we may refer to the common situation in which a person who has behaved treacherously boasts to his companions in the common sleeping-house of his evil deeds, abusing and ridiculing his victim, while the victim himself listens outside and then transports the boaster in his sleep back to the scene of his crime, and there takes vengeance.[3] Another instance is the burial of a murdered person under the chips of a newly built canoe, when the murder is discovered by the swarm of flies which collects over the spot.[4] The motif of the 'water of life' is widespread throughout the Pacific, its successful discovery being attributed to various gods (cf. p. 388 below), heroes (cf. p. 278 above), and others. This last motif is widespread also throughout the literature of the Tatars, as we have already seen. It is not unknown in European folk-tales and occurs also in one Russian *bylina*.[5] It would seem, therefore, that there are certain folk-motifs which are distributed throughout Polynesia, some being purely local within this area, others being current in Asia, and even farther afield.

---

[1] See *Mem. P.S.* III, p. 182.

[2] On this subject we may refer to Mariner[3], Vol. II, p. 333.

[3] See the story of Kae, Gifford, *T.M.T.* p. 146ff., and elsewhere, and compare that of Huuti, Handy, *M.L.* p. 24f.

[4] See the incident as it occurs in a historical saga, Emerson, *L.V.* p. 7. The motif is not rare.

[5] In a number of versions of the *bylina* of Mikhailo Potyk. See Vol. II, p. 42 of the present work.

The range of folk-tales with which we are familiar as common to Africa, Europe, and, to a limited extent, western Asia, appears to be practically unknown to the Pacific as a whole.

Explanatory folk-tales are common. Sometimes they are found attached to the Cycles of well-known heroes or gods. We have a story in Tonga which professes to explain 'Why Moungaone people are immune from Sharks',[1] where the hero of the story is a god. A Mangaian story relates how the tern acquires the black marks over its eyes from Maui's fire-stick, while the hero is learning fire-making from Tangaroa.[2] Among the Maori we have a number of such stories relating to animals, birds, etc. Thus one story relates how the god Tangaroa assembles all the fish of the ocean to fight against man— apparently on behalf of deserted women—and when they have obtained the victory, he ordains that each fish shall have the reward of the spoils which he has obtained. Accordingly the garfish, which has found a long spear, asks that his nose may be such a spear, the flounder sees a fly-flap, and asks that he may be like it in form. In this way the forms of the various fish are accounted for.[3] A variation of this kind of story occurs in the account of the battle between the dogs and the lizards, which claims to account for the reduction in the number of dogs among the Maori by the fact that after a battle between the dogs and the lizards, the dogs ate the lizards, and so lost much of their fertility.[4] This event is said to have taken place 'in olden times'.

Anecdotes relating to unknown people are common everywhere, and rich collections have been recorded by Turner from Samoa, by the Gills from Mangaia and Atiu,[5] by Westervelt from Hawaii,[6] and by many other writers from New Zealand and elsewhere. The more ambitious timeless-nameless sagas cover for the most part the same range of theme as the prose sagas already discussed, and like the non-heroic sagas, they follow a limited range of stereotyped subjects. It is clear that in many cases they are identical with stories of this class and stories of divine beings. In some cases no doubt the proper names have been forgotten, but we doubt if the identity is due in general to this cause. It seems more probable on the whole that stories of this class had their origin in early ritual, which has ceased to be practised, and survives only as tradition. Something has already been said on this subject above (p. 300 ff.). On the other hand, many of the stories which

[1] Gifford, *T.M.T.* p. 82 f.   [2] Gill, *Myths*, p. 67.
[3] Best, *Maori* I, p. 181 ff.   [4] *Ib.* p. 185 f.
[5] See especially *S.L.P.* and *Gems*.   [6] *L.O.H.*

seem to us to be timeless-nameless may in reality refer to heroes who are well known to the islanders themselves. In giving examples of stories of this class, therefore, it is to be understood that their inclusion here is merely tentative. The heroes are unknown to ourselves from other sources, and do not carry any obvious marks of historicity, or of belonging to well-known Cycles.

A favourite theme of such stories relates to visits of mortals to the Heavens and the Underworld. We may refer as an example to the Maori story of Hutu and Pare, in which Hutu descends to the abode of spirits to seek the soul of Pare, who has taken her own life in her grief at his rejection of her advances. He succeeds in finding Pare and in inducing her to entrust herself to him on the Maori swing, and in this way they are able to swing up to the roots of the trees growing in this upper world, and so scramble up to earth.[1] The Hawaiian story of Hiku and Kawelu is very similar.[2] A story from the Cook Group relates how a certain woman falls from the branch of the sacred *bua* tree (cf. pp. 314, 319 above), down a fearful chasm into the Underworld. Her husband follows her, and after a careful search, discovers her and brings her back to earth.[3] An interesting Maori story is that of the ancient magician, Pou-rangahua, who journeyed to Hawaiki for the *kumara*[4] plant, hitherto unknown in New Zealand, and returned across the ocean on the back of the great bird of Tane, Rua-kapanga.[5] A Rarotongan version of this story has also been recorded (cf. p. 333 above). Stories of a similar kind are found widespread throughout the Pacific, and have already been discussed in Chapter III.

A large number of stories of timeless-nameless heroes relate their adventures with supernatural beings. Reference has already been made (pp. 273, 319 above) to the healing of the blindness of Kui, the cannibal ogress of the land of the dead, whose sight is restored by many a hero and even by the god Tane himself. Stories of adventures of mortals with 'fairies' are equally widespread, and are by no means confined to stories of fairy wives. We may refer to the Maori story of Te Kanawa, who is surprised in his sleep by the fairies, and offers them his jewels; but they retain only the shadows, returning the jewels to the hero.[6] Another Maori story relates the pursuit of a mortal woman by the fairies, who are forced to relinquish the chase when her mortal husband rubs her with pungent red ochre, and fills the air with the steam of

---

[1] Andersen, p. 298 ff.
[3] Gill, *Myths*, p. 221 ff.
[5] Best, *Maori* I, p. 207 f.

[2] *Ib.* p. 302 ff.
[4] The *kumara* is the sweet potato.
[6] Grey, p. 212 ff.

cooked food. The fairies invariably eat their food uncooked, and are unable to endure the smoke of the oven.[1] One of the most interesting of these stories of the fairies is that of the Maori hero Punga-rehu and his companion, who are adopted by the fairies of the forest, and learn from them of a monstrous bird who preys upon them. The men make a house with only one opening, and, when the bird flies near, they kill it, first lopping off the wings. They then return home to their wives.[2] The story may perhaps retain some echoes of the cult of Tane—the house with only one opening recalling 'Tane's house' seen by Tyerman and Bennet in the Tahiti and neighbouring Groups.[3]

Many other stories are current relating to gigantic birds of prey[4] and to other monsters. A common theme in Maori stories of local heroes relates to lizard-like monsters which are said to have lived in caves in mountains and cliffs in old times, and in the waters underground, and to have harassed those who incurred their displeasure, often killing the women, or carrying them off to be their wives.[5] Similar stories, in some cases actual variants, have also been recorded from Tahiti.[6]

It has frequently been remarked as strange that the Polynesians should have stories of monsters which seem to resemble crocodiles. The explanation generally believed is that the stories were brought into the Pacific by the early Polynesian immigrants. We see no ground for such a belief. Stories travel faster than movements of population, and quite independently of migrations. There is no reason to assume that these 'lizard' or 'crocodile' stories entered Polynesia at an early date. It is interesting to observe, however, that a story which has affinities with both *Pitaka and the taniwha*[7] and *Hina and the eel (Tuna)* (p. 287 above) is found also in Madagascar in the story of the *Three Sisters and Itrimobe*,[8] in which the cannibal monster, 'whose upper part was in the form of a man, but the lower like an animal, and who had an exceedingly sharp tail', follows the heroine from district to district and over every obstacle till she finally succeeds in killing it.

Stories are also very common in which the heroes are birds, and fish, and inanimate objects, and in which human beings play no part. The Samoan Group and the neighbouring islands abound in stories of

[1] Cowan, *F.F.T.* p. 55 ff.
[2] Andersen, p. 126 ff.
[3] Tyerman I, p. 282.
[4] See e.g. Andersen, p. 129 f.
[5] Best, *Maori* I, p. 186 ff.; Cowan, *F.F.T.* p. 77 ff.
[6] Best, *Maori* I, p. 191.
[7] Andersen, p. 139 f.
[8] *Antananarivo Annual*, No. III (1877), p. 107.

battles between the various kinds of fish, naval expeditions by one set of trees against another,[1] disputes between birds and reptiles,[2] shell-fish, etc. We may refer e.g. to the Samoan story of the expedition of the army of fish, headed by the shark, against the great fish Manu'a,[3] and the piscatorial combat from Nui Island in the Ellice Group.[4] The Maori have a story of a great invasion of the land by sea birds, and of the great battle between the sea and the land birds which followed, in which the latter succeed in driving off the invaders.[5] Some of these stories have all the characteristics of heroic narratives. Others partake largely of the supernatural, even in their details. Others again suggest a moral —to our minds at least; though it must be confessed that this is not emphasised in the form of the stories which we possess. The majority in any case are told purely for entertainment.

It is very probable that accounts originally historical, though couched in figurative terms, may lie behind many of these narratives. Turner himself is clearly of this opinion. His note is significant for the study of the growth of fiction: "As many of the towns and districts are spoken of figuratively by the names of trees noted for strength or beauty, the inference as to the real actors in these tree fights is obvious. The present generation however will hardly admit that they may describe the wars of *men*."[6] We are of opinion that Turner's remarks hold good for other parts of the Pacific also. We may refer to the Hawaiian legend of '*The shark punished at Waikiki*',[7] in which a man-eating shark from the island of Maui plots with the sharks of Oahu to catch surf-riders, but is outwitted and destroyed by his intended victims. It is interesting to compare this story of the 'sharks' with the Maori story of the 'Battle of the Birds' just referred to. When these stories are taken in conjunction with the stories of Tinirau and his pet whales, the genesis and history of such tales become at least a little clearer. They are doubtless of a totally different origin and milieu from African animal folk-tales.

Narrative poetry relating to individuals who are not known to us from other sources, like other forms of narrative poetry, is practically confined in the Pacific to the western islands, and here again our examples come almost exclusively from Tonga and Samoa. Here, however, poetry of this kind seems to be not uncommon. The examples

[1] Turner, p. 213.
[2] *Ib.* p. 218.
[3] *Ib.* p. 214.
[4] *Ib.* p. 301.
[5] Best, *Maori* i, p. 178 ff.
[6] Turner, p. 213 f.
[7] Westervelt, *L.O.H.* p. 55 ff.

from Tonga which have come under our notice[1] vary greatly in regard to length. The flow of the verse is broken at irregular intervals by the interjection of the expression *Ala*,[2] which gives the impression of a refrain. The opening lines are frequently a favourite Tongan formula, such as:

> Listen to me, O poet,
> While I sing about Muni the conqueror.

Or

> Listen, you of enlightened minds,
> While I tell you a tale of the shore.

The diction is simple and direct, and the whole narrative resembles in all respects that of the narrative poetry treating of the gods which we have already described (p. 331 f. above).

The heroes do not appear in general to be people of historical importance, and the subject and manner of treatment resemble the romance and the ballad rather than heroic poetry. The *Chant of Metevae*[3] from Tonga relates how two wives, Ila and Hava, go fishing, how the favourite wife Ila discovers that her companion Hava has a secret fish-pond, and how she pulls away the enclosing stone of the pond and lets the fish escape. The climax of the story is the description of the fruitless efforts of Hava to prevent the fish from escaping. Finally the two women, together with their husband, are transformed into stone, and may, we are gravely assured, still be seen at the entrance to the harbour. Another of the Tongan narrative poems of this class is the story of *Muni-of-the-torn-eye*,[4] which relates the birth and early life of the hero Muni, and concludes with an account of a wrestling-match in which he is victorious over a cave-dweller, Motuku.

Narrative poems are also recorded from Samoa. They are of no great length, the longest recorded by Turner consisting of twenty-six verses.[5] They are very limited in range, the subjects being in all the instances cited by Turner what we should popularly call 'folk-tales', though this term cannot strictly be applied to stories of the range of which we are wholly ignorant. The supernatural plays a large part in all these poems.

The first poem which Turner quotes in full[6] relates how two children

[1] Gifford, *T.M.T.* p. 91 ff.　　　　[2] Gifford translates "Dear!"
[3] *Loc. cit.*　　　　[4] *Ib.* p. 130 f.
[5] The 'verses' as indicated by Turner seem to vary between two and three lines each.
[6] Turner, p. 85 ff. For what appears to be a Mangaian version of this story, see p. 375 below and cf. p. 322 above.

leave their cruel parents and wander to the house of Tangaloa[1] of the heavens. Here Tangaloa marries the girl, but the boy is murdered by the jealous god on account of his beauty. He is, however, miraculously restored to life and flees with his sister. A recognition and reconciliation with the now repentant and affectionate parents concludes the poem. Another poem relates a singing contest between 'A youth called Saiti, noted for his singing', and 'a serenading god', in which the former is victorious and wins the god's daughter in marriage. A series of episodes follows in which his divine wife successfully performs all the Herculean labours set for her husband by the ill-natured god.

The next poem quoted by Turner has a more ambitious 'plot'.[2] Two sisters, Sinaleuuna and Sinaeteva, long for a brother. At last one is born, but they, living at a distance, do not see him for a long time. When one day he brings food to them they rejoice that they have a brother:

> Then the sisters sat down and filled into a bamboo bottle
> The liquid shadow of their brother.

Forthwith they set out to Fiji, taking with them the shadow. Here, being ill-treated by a lady Sina, they pour the liquid shadow of their brother into the water where she is bathing. Sina is enraptured with it, and holds a *suayamvara* of all the young men of the village, but no one corresponds to the shadow. In the meantime:

> When Maluafiti [the brother] turned about in his own land,
> The shadow wheeled round and round in the water.

At last Maluafiti arrives in his canoe to marry the lady Sina and fetch his sisters. On hearing of their ill-treatment at her hands, however, he leaves her behind, and in attempting to follow them Sina is drowned in the ocean. This 'cautionary' element is rarely found in Polynesian narrative, where poetic justice is almost unknown.

In spite of the elaborate story, the poem consists of only twenty-four 'verses' in the translation, and its brevity, combined with the abruptness of the transitions, and the summary character of the narrative, give the appearance of a ballad to what, in the scope of the subject, might well be expanded into an epic or long poetical 'romance'. The subjects, both of this and of the other Samoan poems cited by Turner, resemble the episodes from the *Rāmāyana* and the *Mahābhārata* which form the subject of many Malay epics, and which one would not be·surprised to find in the *Arabian Nights*. We are on the whole inclined to regard

---

[1] I.e. Tangaroa.   [2] Turner, p. 98 ff.

these timeless-nameless narrative poems from Samoa as ballads based on foreign epic themes.

Speech poems are found frequently in the sagas of individuals who are otherwise unknown. Like many of the sagas themselves, these do not differ essentially from the poetry already discussed in the preceding chapters, where, as we have seen, compositions attributed to illustrious characters of the past, whether historical or legendary, form the prototype or pattern for later poems of the same type. Especially in regard to all personal and occasional poetry, and to all poetry of social ritual, new compositions tend to follow traditional forms, and to fall into clearly defined classes. We may refer, for example, to the songs chanted at the ceremonial *kava* drinking, which are common in both Samoa and Hawaii, and doubtless elsewhere also. It is interesting to note that in examples of these 'ritual' chants, from Samoa, the *kava* is personified, like the Sanskrit *soma*,[1] the Samoan chants being composed in the form of an invocation or address to *kava*.[2]

In Hawaii the *'ava* (*kava*) songs frequently form a part of the répertoire of the *hula* ('dance') to be discussed later. The following are the opening lines of an *'ava* song which was sung by the *hula* with expressive gesture at an *'ava* drinking bout on the island of Oahu, Hawaiian Group, in 1849, during a circuit of the island by King Kamehameha II:

> Kane is drunk with awa (kava);
> His head is laid on the pillow;
> His body stretched on the mat.
> A trumpet sounds through the fog,
> Dimmed are the stars in the sky. . . .

Here, as frequently, the priest is identified with the god, whose impersonation he is, and is spoken of as if he were the god himself. The poet goes on to describe the gloomy sound of Tane's conch-shell trumpet from the temple, which probably bodes a demand for a human sacrifice, and the king is inconsolable at the sound:

> The king's awa fails to console him. . .
> 'Tis the all-night conching of Kiha-pú.
> Broken his sleep the whole winter. . . .[3]

Even elegiac poetry tends to follow a stereotyped form, for we hear both from Tahiti and Mangaia of the wailing for the dead in formal

---

[1] See Vol. II, p. 530, of the present work.
[2] Krämer I, p. 410ff.   [3] Emerson, *U.L.* p. 130.

speech. In describing the funeral customs of the latter island Gill observes:

"Wailing for the dead is long and loud.... The most affecting things are said on such occasions, but always in a set form. Many persons have the reputation of being clever wailers."[1]

In the Marquesas the dirges for the dead, even for private individuals, were commonly composed by the *tohungas*, and chanted at the death of a relative and at memorial festivals.[2] Strangely enough the words are said to have been erotic; but this is quite consistent with the account given by Clavel from the same island Group of a scene of mourning for a person of consequence. Among other mimetic representations of scenes from the life of the deceased, his most private actions were re-enacted by the mourners beside the corpse.[3] The Marquesan dirges are said to have been handed down in families from generation to generation, the names being changed to suit the persons concerned.[4] In these islands also love poetry appears to have been equally stereotyped, and to have consisted of two kinds, known as *uta* and *rari*. These were usually simple love lyrics of an informal character recited by the youths and maids to one another,[5] and were composed by the *tohungas* to be recited by groups of youths and maidens on formal occasions. To these chants we shall refer again (p. 462 below).

Poetry recited to the accompaniment of rhythmical action is very common in the Pacific everywhere. We may refer, among innumerable examples which might be cited, to the chanteys of the Paumotu Archipelago recorded by Stimson,[6] the paddling songs of the Maori boatmen, referred to by Angas,[7] and by Shortland,[8] and those of Tonga described by Mariner,[9] the hauling songs of the Maori boatmen referred to by Shortland,[10] and those of Tahiti mentioned by Ellis.[11] Similar poetry is commonly referred to in the sagas. A hauling song is said to have been recited at the hauling of a draft of fish by the crew of the Takitumu canoe sailing to New Zealand to colonise the islands.[12]

---

[1] *L.S.I.* p. 78. We may compare the recitations of the professional mourner who is sometimes engaged to compose and recite the formal dirges among the peasants of north Russia; see Vol. II, p. 286 ff. of the present work.

[2] Handy, *N.C.M.* pp. 104, 331 f.   [3] Clavel, p. 43.

[4] Handy, *op. cit.* p. 331 f.   [5] *Ibid.*

[6] See Stimson, *J.P.S.* XLI, p. 181 ff.   [7] Angas II, pp. 19, 27.

[8] Shortland, p. 167 f.   [9] Mariner[3] II, p. 217 f.

[10] Shortland, p. 162 f.   [11] Ellis[1] I, p. 285.

[12] *J.P.S.* XVI, p. 223.

Other canoe hauling and launching songs are also quoted in the same saga.[1]

In Hawaii a whole series of poems were recited by the people at various stages of the building of a new *heihau*[2] by the king. Many such poems are quoted by Malo.[3] Some of them embody prayers addressed to the gods Kane and Lono, and the priest generally recites or takes part in them. Most of these are probably very old and traditional. The song sung when the branches of the *koa* tree were brought down from the mountains[4] ('a scene of riot and tumultuous joy, like the procession of a Bacchic chorus, or shouting the harvest home') probably dates from the time of Umi (cf. p. 255 above).

In general the poetry of social ritual, and poetry associated with individuals not widely known, partakes of the characteristics of the particular island Group from which it is recorded and shows few individual features, whatever its type, or the nature of the person by whom it purports to be recited. Thus we commonly find that poems of this class from Hawaii or Tonga have reference to natural scenery, or the weather, or wild nature in some form. As an example we may refer to a little poem from Hawaii which purports to be chanted by a little yellow shark of Pearl Harbour on that island, when homesick for the beauty of the coast of Puna where it has been reared.

> O my land of rustling *lehua* trees![5]
> Rain is treading on your budding flowers,
> It carries them to the sea.
> They meet the fish in the sea.
> This is the day when love meets love,
> My longings are stirred within me
> For the spirit-friends of my land.[6]

In form this poem is indistinguishable from the *hula* ('dance') poetry of Hawaii (see below), which is largely occupied with natural descriptions. Innumerable examples of a similar character might be cited, and it is probable that many poems of this class have found their way into the *hula* répertoire, though in communities where extempore composition on traditional lines is so widely practised the origin of any given poem must always be to some extent problematical. We shall have more to say about poetry of this kind in the fuller discussion of the *hula* in Ch. vi.

---

[1] *J.P.S.* xvii, p. 99 ff.   [2] A *heihau* is the Hawaiian name for a temple.
[3] Malo, p. 210 ff.   [4] *Ib.* p. 247.
[5] For the *lehua*, see Emerson, *U.L.*, Plate xiii.
[6] Westervelt, *L.O.H.* p. 55.

CHAPTER VI

DRAMATIC AND RITUAL POETRY

PERHAPS the most interesting, and certainly the most unique development in the native literature of Polynesia is its dramatic poetry. It is found in varying degrees all over the northern and Central Pacific, and we have traces of it in other quarters. Its history is bound up in some areas with that of certain institutions, such as those of the *areoi*, the *hoki*, the *hula* and the *siva* dancers, to whom we shall refer more fully later (p. 423 ff. below); but in some islands, such as Mangaia, whence our fullest collections of texts of poetry of this kind have been recorded, the performers, men and women alike, were not attached to any such society, though the composers of the dramatic poems were generally well-known poets. There is reason to believe, however, that wherever these dramatic poems were recited and acted, the authors and performers underwent some kind of special preparation, and generally lived in seclusion for some time before a performance took place. Temporarily at least they were regarded as a class apart.

Our most ambitious literary (oral) texts, and those which approach most nearly to drama, come from Mangaia, and were recorded by the Rev. W. W. Gill,[1] who has also left us extremely interesting and valuable notes regarding the circumstances of authorship and production, and also the subjects of the dramas and the historical and mythological events which form their background. Some of the dramas are believed to relate to events which are at least as old as the fifteenth century, and some few of the actual texts are believed to be not much later; but the majority of historical texts relate to the seventeenth and eighteenth centuries. During this period, under the Mautara family, which was supreme in Mangaia for about 150 years, peace reigned throughout the island. It was probably the first time in the troubled history of Mangaia that settled conditions prevailed for any length of time. Song making became a national passion,[2] and a highly developed school of oral poetry, most of which was composed by men of the highest rank, has come down to us by a singularly well-preserved oral tradition as a rich heritage from the past.

[1] Gill, *Myths*; *S.L.P. passim.*   [2] Gill, *Myths*, p. 87.

These Mangaian dramatic poems show a standard of composition which would do credit to a civilised people in their delicacy of thought and expression, their total absence of coarseness, their tensity, their wistful suggestiveness. Their range is very wide, and comprises dramas composed in celebration of the gods, or the inhabitants of the spirit world, of departed chiefs, and of members of priestly families, of historical events of general importance. Invocations are also addressed in liturgical or dramatic dialogue to the stars and the heavenly bodies; and the myths to which they have given rise, as well as those relating to spirits and the inhabitants of the realm of the dead, also form the subjects of these compositions. These poems are, however, essentially lyrical, and the events which form the background or the inspiration of the theme are rarely related or reproduced directly, but by allusion. They may be described as the expression of the intellectual and emotional attitude of a group of people to a given theme. They are of varying length, not as a rule very long, but consisting of several parts, sung at different periods of the festivities or celebrations. The verses are sung alternately in chorus and solos, the whole being consistently lyrical. The resemblance to the Greek dramas of Aischylos has been noted by many. A still closer analogy is that of the *No* plays of Japan, which resemble them not only in form, but also in their religious associations, and in their close connection with the commemoration of the dead.

The action which accompanies these poetical dramas is rather in the nature of a dramatic dance than of true mimesis. The graceful movements of groups of men and women in concert have much in common with the ballet. Dramatic action is used, but generally sparingly. On the other hand it is at times extended with a freedom which steps beyond the limits of drama, as in the 'Drama of Ngaru',[1] to which we shall refer more fully later, and in which the women, who are the sole performers in this 'play', carry the corpse of their husband Ngaru over the hills. The greater part of the dramatic performances, however, consists generally of what the Greeks called 'dancing with the hands'. As in a ballet, poetry, music, and the dance, together with restrained dramatic action, combine to form a harmonious artistic whole.

The dialogue is carried on for the most part by two groups rather than by individuals, though brief chants or strophes are sung by the leaders of the groups, especially at the beginning of the performance in order to introduce the theme; and in some cases the opening line is spoken by a near relative of a person whose death is being commemo-

[1] Gill, *Myths*, p. 238 ff.

rated. But in general dialogue between individuals such as we are accustomed to in our own dramatic compositions is unknown. Very little sustained impersonation takes place. Realism is, indeed, almost wholly eschewed, the ideal aimed at being a wistful and remote reflective attitude in regard to events well known to all. There is only rarely an attempt at illusion. Detachment, even in regard to dire tragedy, is usually achieved. We shall see as we proceed the means which the poet employs in order to attain this effect of 'emotion recollected in tranquillity'. The effect is not stimulative, but cathartic.

An English reader who approaches these poems for the first time in translation is often bewildered by what appears to be a perpetual shift from the dramatic to the narrative. At one moment the reciter seems to be speaking in his own person, as if he were himself the person of long ago whose actions and words are reproduced. In other words he appears to be impersonating a person of the past. But a moment later the events of the past are presented to us in the form of narrative. This shift of presentation, while incidental in part to the lyrical and ritual character of the recitations, is largely due to the fact that in the Polynesian languages there is no tense system, as in the Indo-European languages. Instead there are aspects, and in poetry more or less dramatic these are very difficult to reproduce in English with anything like what we may call a consistent 'tense atmosphere'. The reader must, like the reciter, endeavour to project himself into a kind of intermediate position between the immediate action and the present time—a timeless attitude, like that of the Greek chorus.

The chief occasions of the performance of drama in Mangaia were associated with death ceremonies,[1] whether the deaths of private individuals, or of the human sacrifice which was usually offered to put an end to warfare and to placate Rongo. The former are commonly referred to by Gill as 'death-talks' (e tara kakai, lit. 'talk about the devouring'),[2] the latter as 'fêtes' (kapa, lit. 'dance'); but the distinction does not appear to be rigidly kept. Indeed, it would be difficult to see how this could be the case, seeing that almost every kapa was a funeral celebration to the human victim, as well as a public tribal festival. In a general sense these fêtes may be said to have been held to honour Rongo; but the number of people taking part was usually very considerable, and the ensuing period of peace was naturally of more importance to the islanders as a whole than the immediate occasion. The

---

[1] Gill, Myths, p. 268 ff.
[2] Ib. p. 269. When anyone died, he was said to be 'eaten up by the gods'.

importance of the elegiac element was subordinate to the inauguration of peace and the arts of music and poetry and the dance which accompanied it, and which were associated with Tane. In this way the two gods combined in a kind of double conception to foster the national arts, and it is possible that in some such way as this a double godhead known as Rongomatane, who is found in Taylor's list of gods recorded in New Zealand (cf. p. 311 above), came into being.

Whenever anyone died in Mangaia, a curious series of mimic battles, known as *ta i te mauri* ('ghost killing'), was fought on the following day between the young men of the district where the corpse lay, and those of the surrounding villages. In these battles, the first group, clad in mourning garments, represent *mauri*, 'ghosts', the leader representing the deceased. Their opponents represented malignant spirits, who were, of course, defeated by the deceased and his companions.[1] A similar rite prevailed in Tahiti,[2] and also in Easter Island,[3] and no doubt elsewhere also. The 'ghost fighting', as the ceremony was called in Mangaia, appears to have been carried on in pantomime, and no literary texts are recorded as having accompanied them. But, as we shall see, mock battles commonly formed a part of the *eva*, or pageantry of the funeral celebrations, and we suspect that these are not wholly distinct from the 'ghost fighting', though the point is not clear from Gill's texts.

Some months after the death of a person of distinction, the 'dirge proper' was sung, as among the Sea Dyaks (see p. 488 ff. below), and funeral games (*eva*) took place. Sometimes the friends of a distinguished dead person chose to have a *kakai*, a grand tribal gathering, at which songs were recited in honour of the dead person by each of the adult male relatives, who were generally responsible for the composition also. *E tara kakai*, 'the death-talk', generally took place at night, in large houses built specially for this purpose. As many as thirty songs,

---

[1] Gill, *Myths*, p. 268 f. According to Gill, the object of the 'ghosts' in these conflicts was to prevent the malignant spirits from doing further harm to mortals. Is it not more probable, however, that here, as elsewhere, the ghostly companions of the newly dead were concerned rather to protect the soul of the latter till the *tangi* and the *eva* should take place, so that the soul might be consigned to its own sphere in the spirit world? We may compare the custom at Balinese cremation ceremonies, where before the corpse is placed in the interior of a model bull preparatory to cremation, the men who have carried it to the spot divide themselves into two parties representing good and evil spirits, and proceed to fight for possession of the corpse; see Gorer, p. 259; Krause, p. 59 and Plates 164 ff. A different explanation of the Mangaian custom is suggested by Prof. Buck (*M.S.* p. 189).

[2] Ellis[1] I, p. 533.   [3] Routledge, p. 234.

called *tangi* ('emotional chants'), were often composed for one *kakai*. These were the laments, 'weeping songs', that is to say, the dirges proper. Each *tangi* was followed by a *tiau* ('partial weeping'), or *pe'e* ('mourning chant'). Thus as many as sixty songs might be composed in all, each male relative reciting a song. A near relative started the first *tangi*, the chorus taking up the words at the proper pauses, and carrying on the theme. The *tangi* regularly opened with the words: "Sing we —", followed by the name of the dead person. Much of the history of the island has been preserved in the allusions contained in the *kakai*. The *pe'e* in particular consisted of songs referring to events of the past history of the islanders, the authenticity of which is vouched for by the substantial agreement of the parallel sets of traditions preserved by hostile clans.[1]

Each song consisted of a number of divisions or stanzas, and each division was designated by a technical name. Thus the opening stanza, spoken, of course, as a solo, was called the *tumu*, which was followed by another called the *papa*, also spoken as a solo, and sometimes separated from the *tumu* and from what followed by a refrain, spoken by the chorus. Several stanzas known as *inuinu* (*unuunu*) followed (*inuinu tai*, 'first *inuinu*'; '*inuinu rua*', 'second *inuinu*', etc.), sometimes as many as five in number, and each of these consisted of one or more pairs of alternating recitals by solo and chorus. The exact meaning of these terms seems to be somewhat indeterminate. Gill translated *tumu*, 'introduction' (Buck, 'introduction, cause'), and *papa*, 'foundation'— which are, of course, the literal meanings of the words. Both writers translate *inuinu*, 'offshoot'.[2] As they stand these terms are not very lucid, and it is tempting to call attention to the performances of the *hula* of Hawaii, which resemble those of Mangaia in many essential particulars.

Here we find[3] the performers divided into two parties, as in Mangaia, the leader of the whole troupe being known as the *kumu* (Mangaian *tumu*). More particularly the *kumu* personally leads one party of the performers in song, while the leader of the other party is known as the *poo-pua'a*. A performance opened, at least in some of the *hula*, with two short chants or stanzas, spoken one by the *kumu*, the other by the *poo-pua'a*, after which a number of others followed in the order previously determined by the *kumu*. It is not improbable that the terms

---

[1] See Gill, *S.L.P.* p. v.   [2] Buck, *M.S.* p. 193.
[3] For the arrangement of the chants in the *hula*, and the singers to whom they are assigned, see Emerson, *U.L.* p. 58; and cf. *ib.* p. 28.

used in the Cook Group are in some way related to those in Hawaii, as the procedure appears to be similar, and it is tempting, therefore, to suppose that the Mangaian terms *tumu* and *papa* originally referred to the reciters of the opening and answering chant by the two leaders of the opposite groups or lines of the chorus.[1]

In Mangaia each male relative of the deceased must chant a song in these performances, and it is probable, therefore, that the term *inuinu*, 'offshoot' (first, second, etc.), has reference to these 'offshoots' or scions of the stock to which the dead man belonged, as each relative in turn steps forward and recites his solo. In support of this we may refer to the 'Dirge for Vera' (cf. p. 369 f. below), where we find the words 'Tueva (i.e. the father of the dead man)...is mourning', in the 'first offshoot', and 'Mautara (i.e. the grandfather of the dead man) weeps for thee' in the 'second offshoot'.[2] If we are right in this, and in the Hawaiian analogy, the Mangaian terminology seems to have reference to the personnel of the reciters, rather than to the technical literary character of the divisions; and this is perhaps more natural in poetry composed wholly for oral recitation, especially as it was recited according to an artificial and elaborate scheme. It may be added that the general unity which commonly prevails among the *inuinu* may be partly due to the fact that those who could not compose themselves must pay someone to compose one for them; and thus it naturally comes about that an accomplished poet often composed the majority of the songs for a given *kakai* (cf. p. 417 below). This would naturally tend to develop a unity among the songs.

Gill uses the word *eva* to denote 'dirge proper';[3] but this seems to include not only the funeral ceremonies in which the people as a whole took part, and which were generally held by day, usually in the early morning, but also the *kakai* ('death-talk'), which took place at night, and, in addition, the reed-matches, dancing festivals, etc.[4] The funeral games about to be described may perhaps have taken place in addition to the 'death-talk'. The *eva* proper consisted of the following:

[1] This suggestion would seem to be in accordance with the terminology and arrangement adopted by Stimson in the Paumotu texts of the dramatic chants of Maui and Tawhaki. See Stimson, *L.M.T. passim*. In Tongareva the term *tumu* is applied to a kind of circular dance; see Buck, *E.T.* p. 79. It is a curious and interesting fact that in Rarotongan tradition, which would naturally be closely related to the Mangaian, the original ancestors of the priests and of the minor chiefs are spoken of as *te tumu* and *papa*. See *J.P.S.* VIII, p. 62.

[2] Gill, *Myths*, p. 190f.

[3] *Myths*, p. 271; cf. pp. 269, 273.

[4] *Ib.* p. 273.

(1) An interesting performance known as the *eva tapara*, or funeral dirge, in which the performers blackened their faces, and disfigured themselves in a manner suggestive of the inhabitants of Miru's realm. An example of the *eva tapara* is the 'Dirge for Atiroa',[1] an atheistic dirge composed about 1820 by Koroneu, the father of the dead man, in which the gods are abused for 'eating up' (i.e. causing the death of) Atiroa. The following lines will serve to illustrate the general tenor of this recitation:

Solo

O, Pangeivi,[2] who treated my son,[3]
The canoe has sunk.[4]

Chorus

Ah, you are no help, my god (Tane).
Through you he should have returned,
(For we are) a forest protected by you,
Not one was to be allowed to die on the evil-smelling pillow . . .[5]

(2) The *eva puruki*, or 'war dirge', in which long spears were used, and a series of short chants on the heroic deeds of the tribe was recited by the person most nearly related to the deceased, and by a chorus composed of two opposing armies facing one another. These war dirges were most carefully elaborated, and embodied the whole history of the past known to the islanders. Here, as elsewhere, however, the historical matter is allusive rather than narrative. Perhaps the most famous example which has survived is the 'War Dirge for Tuopapa',[6] composed by Teinaakia about 1790, in commemoration of a chief of the Teipe branch of the Tongaiti clan, which was dominant in Mangaia for a short period in the latter half of the seventeenth century. The hero for whom the war dirge was composed seems to have been slain in battle about 1666,[7] and the circumstances are recalled in a series of brief ejaculations characteristic of Mangaian dramatic poetry:

There are the first fruits of Tutavake.
Move on, O my friends, make way;
Move right! Move on!
Recite a spell over your weapons to get a warlike spirit,

[1] Gill, *Myths*, p. 281.
[2] Pangeivi was the priest of Tane at this time.
[3] So Buck; Gill translates 'the case is hopeless', which is very free.
[4] I.e. 'the child is dead'.   [5] Buck's translation, *M.S.* p. 194.
[6] Gill, *S.L.P.* p. 64; *D.L.P.* p. 97f.
[7] See the list of battles fought in Mangaia, Gill, *D.L.P.* p. 310; Buck, *M.S.* p. 35.

To break the backbone of the Tongaiti tribe.[1]
Crash! Crash!! Crash!!!
Scatter them, O Rongo,
That they appear as a flock of tropic birds in the west,
In the daylight; some die, some live![2]

(3) The *eva toki*, or 'axe dirge', said to be used by artisans, in which the performers carried wooden axes, and symbolised by their actions a desire to split open the earth, and so release the spirit of the dead. An example of an *eva toki* is the dirge for Ruru,[3] composed by Karapanga about 1816 in commemoration of Ruru. In this poem, though Ruru died a natural death, an appeal is made for vengeance on behalf of the tribe against the Tongaiti clan who had slain one of his ancestors in his sleep:

> This axe is to slay the brave
> When buried in sleep.
> E'en as Kaukare perished in the night.
> The fiat went forth.
> The axe from spirit-land did the deed.[4]

In this way the chanters conjure up the deed done long ago, and they continue their theme, recalling that ancient slaughter:

> Prostrate they all lay on the ground.
> Alas my son! Alas my offspring!
> They come rushing on...
> Their axes enter the skulls...
> Tongaiti[4] struck the blow.
> Tongaiti shed thy blood.
> Rongo is delighted....

The recitation, which, with the exception of the first two lines, was chanted by the entire chorus, concludes with a war-dance twice performed.

(4) The *eva ta*, or 'crashing dirge', another mock war dirge, in which two opposing mimic armies took part, each armed with a wooden spear or sword. An example of this type was also composed for Ruru by Arokapiti about 1816,[5] which differs somewhat in style from the last

---

[1] The Teipe branch had quarrelled with the rest of the Tongaiti about this time.
[2] Translation by Buck, *M.S.* p. 195.
[3] Gill, *Myths*, p. 273 ff.
[4] This line and the one preceding it are somewhat freely translated.
[5] Gill, *Myths*, p. 276 ff.; Buck, *M.S.* p. 195 f.

mentioned, being highly figurative in diction and allusion. The *eva* opens with a remark by the solo:

> Ruru was the prop of the sun.[1]

After which the rest of the chant is carried on wholly by the chorus:

> There, O Ruru, is the lightning flash to loosen thy spirit;[2]
> O Ruru, broken, alas!
> The thunder crashes in the Heavens in salutation.

> (*War dance*)
> Cleave, great Rongo, a space between the winds
> Through which flashes may penetrate from Avaiki, etc.[3]

Most of this *eva* is so full of allusion to legend and mythology as to be unintelligible without a full commentary. The serious part of the performance closes with the announcement that the dancing ground is sacred to Ina and the other 'fairies':

> This place is henceforth sacred...
> Only the 'fairies' may come, Teiiri and Terama,
> Rongo himself has been here.[4]

Like many of the performances of this class, the *eva* in honour of Ruru concludes with a kind of comedy, which is introduced by an announcement from the soloist that Ina's nuts are being stolen. The nuts are evidently growing on a pandanus-tree overhanging the dancing ground, and the chorus, divided into two parties, alternately urge the land crabs to climb the trees and catch the thieves:

> *Solo*
> Hail Ina, hail Ina,[5]
> Thy fruits are being stolen. Alas, Ina! Alas, Ina!

> *Chorus*
> Catch! The sky is threatening.

---

[1] So Buck, who understands the expression to mean that Ruru was a high chief (Gill also translates 'predestined chief').

[2] According to Gill (*Myths*, p. 280), there was a thunderstorm on the day of Ruru's death, which was interpreted as a compliment to the dying chief; but in the old 'royal language' of Tahiti and elsewhere, diction such as that of our text was used habitually of the most casual and mundane movements of the high chiefs; see Ellis[1] II, p. 359f.

[3] Gill translates: 'through which may be heard the whispers of spirit-land', hich does not seem to be very literal, or to agree so well with the context.

[4] Gill, *Myths*, p. 278.

[5] For the myth of Ina, see p. 285 f. above.

One half
Climb and catch them, O robber-crab.

Other half
I will not climb: let the *irave*[1] crab climb, etc., etc.

This dialogue continues for some time.[2] Meanwhile two of the men taking part in the performance, calling themselves 'rats', actually climb a pandanus-tree well laden with berries hard by the dancers, and squeak, showering the nuts down on the performers, who sing words imitative of rats crunching nuts and squeaking and fighting. The theme is perhaps based on the myth of Ina and her son Koro alluded to in Ch. iii above; but the treatment is, of course, purely humorous.

Gill gives several examples of 'dramas' performed at reed-throwing matches. According to Prof. Buck, these reed-throwing matches also formed a part of the commemoration of the dead,[3] and the evidence of the traditions[4] suggests that they were performed on more cheerful occasions also. Buck tells us that the 'death dramas' performed at these matches were "extensions of the *eva ta* ('crashing *eva*'), with more acting". Examples of dramas of this kind will be discussed later (p. 378 f. below).

Not infrequently it happens that more than one of these dramatic performances are combined in a single *kakai* ('death-talk'), and form sections of the entire celebration. We have a large number of these individual songs in Gill's collection, which are often, though not invariably, distinguished by descriptive titles, so that we may know exactly which part of the 'death-talk' the words in our text are intended for, and the manner of performance. We will give a few details of one or two of the dramatic poems of an elegiac character from Gill's collection of historical songs before proceeding to the mythological collection. Where we do not distinguish the technical character of the performance, it is to be understood that no such distinction is made by Gill himself. In general it is probable that little or no action accompanied the *tangi* and the *tiau*. In any case such action as accompanied

---

[1] The *irave* is a variety of land crab (Gill, *Myths*, p. 279, footnote).
[2] For the literary convention by which a number of creatures of the animal world are in turn asked to take a message, and refuse, we may compare the Sea Dyak dirges and other poems, p. 491 below.   [3] Buck, *M.S.* p. 196.
[4] We may refer to the reed-throwing match organised by Tongatea in the legend of Ngaru (Gill, *Myths*, p. 228), and to that of Tarauri and the sons of Pinga (*ib.* p. 118 ff.).

these ritual elegies would be restrained and conventional, unlike the dramatic element in the closing 'act' of the *eva* just cited.

As an example of the *tangi* we may refer to the dramatic dialogue composed c. 1810 as a part of the *kakai* for Ngutukū, slain as a human sacrifice to Rongo.[1] No details are given of the *mise-en-scène*, or of the manner of performance, but the character of the poem suggests that a certain amount of action accompanied the recitation.

> Let us attack the guardian of the cave.
> > His hour has come,
> > He vainly dreams of safety.
> Up, attack the stronghold of the Tongaiti.
> Vaarire[2] is the offering for the altar
> > —the price of peace.
>
> Yonder! Ngutukū, Ngutukū,
> > Ngutukū has fallen.
> Ngutukū is destined for the altar,
> A 'fish' for the altar of Rongo.
> Secure the victim well to the litter.
> Vaarire is slain, Vaarire is slain,
> > Ngutukū is slain!
> Yes, Ngutukū, Ngutukū is hurled down.[3]

The second half is elegiac in tone, though, unlike the elegies for men who have died a natural death, it is characterised by reminiscences and allusions to details of the past life and daily avocations of the victim:

> Once thou didst despatch thy hurried meal;
> > The well-secured basket of tackle
> > Slung to thy shoulder—
> Thou madest thy way to the sea for sport.[4]

In the penultimate strophe, the appearance of the sacrifice is dwelt upon. In the last, by a refinement of cruelty, the weeping children of the victim are informed:

> *Your father is being borne to the altar.*[5]

A *pe'e* and a *tiau* 'for Vivi and Tito'[6] were composed about 1795 by

[1] Gill, *Myths*, p. 309 ff.
[2] Vaarire was the original name of Ngutukū. See Gill, *Myths*, p. 310, footnote 1.
[3] Gill, *Myths*, p. 310.
[4] *Ib.* p. 311. [5] *Ib.* p. 312 (the italics are Gill's).
[6] Gill, *S.L.P.* p. 77 ff.; *D.L.P.* p. 119 ff.

the poet Koroa for the *kakai* ('death-talk') of Puvai, a member of the
Teipe (Tongaiti) clan, who died about a century after the event which
it celebrates. The song commemorates the murder of two members of
this clan, Vivi and Tito, at the close of the seventeenth century. The
Teipe clan of Tongaiti were 'devoted' to furnish human victims to the
god Rongo, and the *pe'e* and the *tiau*[1] allude to the unhappy fate of two
of the members of the doomed clan who had vainly sought refuge from
their pursuers in a secluded valley. The form of this composition is
typical of the more elaborate compositions of this class. In the first
four lines, the theme is given out, as it were:

> Helpless, entirely helpless, were the sons of Tokoano;
> Hence the flight of Vivi
> From the deep valley
> To the steep hill, alas for both of you.

Then follows the *papa*, consisting of four lines:

> Ye were sought in Tepikoiti and in the makatea[2]
> To become vassals to Mautara.
> Even there the evil foe ensnared
> And slew the well-beloved Tito.

After this follow five short verses of eight or nine lines, each of which
is headed by Gill in the Mangaian text, *Unuunu*,[3] and in English 'First
Offshoot', 'Second Offshoot', etc. These terms also probably have

---

[1] Gill translates the word *tiau* as 'a slight shower', 'a partial weeping' (*Myths*,
p. 270). Buck defines the *tiau* as 'a slight shower of rain', and says that it was so
named in contrast to the heavy shower of weeping that accompanied the *tangi*
which preceded it (*M.S.* p. 193). According to Gill, however (*loc. cit.*), the *tiau* is
an alternative to the *pe'e*, the *tangi* being followed by either the *tiau* or the *pe'e*.
Nevertheless, the only chants to which Gill specifically applies the term *tiau* appear
to have been composed for children or very young people, viz. two for Vera
(*Myths*, pp. 189, 194), one for Puvai (*ib.* p. 199), one for Kourapapa (*ib.* p. 202),
and yet another for Vivi and Tito (*S.L.P.* p. 81). All except the last mentioned
occur in juxtaposition in *Myths*, and are immediately followed by two 'Laments'
for Kourapapa who died at the age of four or five, and a 'Death-lament' for a
'damsel' Varenga, who was also clearly quite a young girl. Gill is evidently recording
a series of dirges for those who died very young. It seems possible, therefore, that
the '*tiau*', the 'partial weeping', may be the technical name of the mourning chant
looked upon as especially fitting for children, the more ambitious *pe'e* being
reserved for adults. But Gill never, so far as we are aware, actually applies the
term *pe'e* to any specific chant.

[2] The *makatea* is a raised coral platform about 230 feet high, which surrounds the
island of Mangaia.

[3] Gill generally writes *unuunu*, but occasionally *inuinu*; Buck *inuinu* (*M.S.*
p. 193).

reference to the manner of reciting, or to the people responsible for their recitation. The first of these will give an idea of their style:

> *Unuunu Tai* ('First Offshoot')
> Utterly friendless, they first hid near the ocean—
>   Near the ocean.
> They subsisted on wild berries and fruits,
>   Found in the depths of the rocks.
> Favoured by Rongo and the forest gods.
>   Did they not worship the centipede?[1]
> (They ran) from the deep valley
>   To the steep hill where both perished.[2]

The chanting concluded with a farewell, which, like similar expressions in Maori poetry (cf. p. 240 above), consists of sounds rather than articulate speech:

> Ai e ruaoo e. E rangai e.

The 'Song of Inangaro'[3] is also sung in modern times in commemoration of one of these altar victims of the Teipe clan. A number of these poor wretches had taken refuge in a cave, where they contrived to subsist for a time on the kernel of the pandanus berry, eked out with a little surreptitious fishing. One day their leader Inangaro discovered himself to a woman named Inaango in order to pretend love to her in exchange for food with which she supplied them. But shortly afterwards his brother Ngaae fell in love with a maiden named Kurauri, who also brought them supplies of food in secret. Now Inangaro did not really care for Inaango, and likewise fell in love with Kurauri, and his younger brother generously gave way to him, so that Inangaro became the lover of Kurauri himself. When Inaango discovered that she had a rival, she betrayed the fugitives in their hiding place, and they suffered the fate of the rest of their clan at the hands of the Ngariki or dominant tribe. Inangaro himself was slain and laid as a sacrifice on the altar of Rongo.

---

[1] The god of the Teipe clan was the centipede.

[2] Gill's translation is far from literal; but it conveys the true sense better than a more literal translation would do. It is impossible in any translation to convey the impression of grief and lamentation attained in the original by the skilled use of repetition of word and phrase, which gives a strange and wistful effect when carried through line after line, as if the voices were echoing up the hills. The device is, however, a common one in Polynesian poetry everywhere, and the effect of sadness which it conveys to a European ear may be, in part at least, accidental.

[3] Gill, *S.L.P.* p. 57; *D.L.P.* p. 96.

The song in which this tragedy is commemorated is believed to have been composed originally by Inangaro himself for his sweetheart. It was recited, according to the saga in which it is incorporated, by the girl herself before the entire assembly over the body of her lover as it lay on the altar, and was so much admired by all who heard it that it has been remembered and recited for two centuries. In diction and style the poem is said to show evidence of considerable antiquity, and it has probably been preserved in what is substantially its original form. Even among the islanders themselves it is regarded as a literary curiosity.[1] The literary history of the poem is especially interesting, for among those present while the poor girl was chanting over the body of her lover was a certain Iro. This same Iro, together with a number of his clansmen, was expelled from the island and afterwards reached Rarotonga in safety, where he became the head of a little Mangaian colony. Here the song was remembered and handed down, and is recited among them to this day in all times of scarcity. When Christianity was introduced, bringing into communication islands long separated, the Mangaians of Mangaia were naturally much surprised to find that this song was well known to their neighbours. As the song is included by Gill among these ritual 'historical' songs, and as it illustrates their formal structure well, we give it below in full.

Tumu[2]

Under yon ancient banyan tree
Was I first seen by my lover,
Covered with sweet-scented flowers.

Papa

Who now shall gather food
For these starving wretched exiles?

Unuunu Tai

Long has Kurauri waited;
Wearied out was Kurauri,
Hoping again to meet Inangaro.

Unuunu Rua

He was searching, searching for wild berries,
Such as grow on the red cliffs—on the red cliffs;
Sweet-tasted pandanus kernels his only food.

[1] See the remarks by Gill, *S.L.P.* p. 63; *D.L.P.* p. 96.
[2] For the technical terms which mark the different divisions of the song, see p. 356 above, and footnote.

Unuunu Toru
Who now shall gather food
By torchlight fishing,
When Kurauri gave the spoil to Ngaae?

Unuunu A
Sometimes thou didst venture, didst venture
Into the *tabu* district of the Ngariki;—
I following thee with my basket;—
Sweet-scented pandanus kernels thy only food.

Interesting examples of ritual elegies on historical subjects are two 'Laments for Iro',[1] composed about 1791 in commemoration of the exile of Iro referred to above, and a number of other members of the Tongaiti clan from Mangaia, towards the close of the seventeenth century, in consequence of an unsuccessful attempt to displace the Ngariki, the dominant clan, from the pre-eminent position which they held. These *pe'e* were both composed by the poet Koroa to be recited at the 'death-talk' of a certain Vaiaa, about 1791. They refer to the departure of the two great double canoes, carrying the exiles away to an unknown destiny, and repeat, in a refrain, the last words of Iro to his nephew, urging him to take vengeance. The story of their subsequent fate has already been referred to.

The importance of these songs in helping to preserve the history of the islanders is illustrated by the story of Rori,[2] who lived for thirty years as a fugitive among the barren rocks known as Te Vaenga on the north of Mangaia. He was the son of an immigrant from Tahiti, and both father and son were exceedingly skilled craftsmen, especially in the art of wood-carving. The carved wooden gods which before the advent of Christianity were preserved in the idol house in Mangaia were all (with two exceptions)[3] the work of Rori. On Rori's death his surviving sons planned a 'death-talk' (*e tara kakai*). 'The food was planted for the feast, and most of the songs got ready'; but war broke out, and the sons were slain, and the intended 'death-talk' never came off. But Rori's fate is commemorated in saga, and his history is one of the best known on the island. Probably the songs intended for the 'death-talk' have served to perpetuate his tradition, for two of these songs still survived and were sung in modern times.[4]

[1] Gill, *S.L.P.* p. 91 ff.; *D.L.P.* p. 130 ff.
[2] *Ib. S.L.P.* p. 152 ff.; *D.L.P.* p. 214 ff.
[3] *Ib. D.L.P.* p. 331; cf. p. 333, footnote 1.
[4] *Ib.* p. 236. See especially footnote 1.

Many of the Mangaian chants forming a part of these 'death-talks' have reference to priests. One of the most interesting is a dialogue entitled 'The Expelled God', which was composed by a poet named Tuka to be sung as an interlude to celebrations in honour of Parina about 1816. The poem recalls the past sufferings in the island of Mangaia of the tribe of Tane—refugees from Tahiti—and ends on a note of triumph for their descendants, as well as for the dominant tribe of the Ngariki. The final strophe is a tactful compliment to Pangemiro, himself one of the Ngariki, who was the warrior chief of Mangaia at the time:

> Mighty is the tribe of Ngariki.
> A mountain touching the sun.[1]

The song is said to have been recited, stanza by stanza, alternately by two bands of performers until the final verse, when both parties met and recited this final verse with tremendous emphasis. Then 'the drum was again beaten, and the *kapa* or semi-drama proceeded'. The close association of this ritual elegy with the saga which has been preserved on the same subject (cf. p. 258 above) is important. The poem is clearly reminiscent, as its title and context in Gill's collection implies, of the priest Ue, who suffered many vicissitudes in his loyalty to Tane, the 'expelled god' from Tahiti.

A second song, also composed by Tuka, celebrates the finding of Tane by Ue.[2] It was composed about 1817 for the 'death-talk' of a famous chief of the Tane tribe. Its political bias is therefore definitely pro-Tane. The poem traces in a series of allusions and apostrophes, the fate of the god Tane after his expulsion from Tahiti. Each section of the song ends with a refrain—a common feature in these poems:

> Behold the guide of [the tribe of] Tane,
> How he gazes on its rising.

The last line is an allusion to the morning star. Star worship is closely associated with the Tane tribe in Mangaia,[3] and Ue was careful to set up the altar of Tane where the morning star rose directly over it. This song, with its allusions to the day star, would be appropriate as the last song of the 'death-talk', and was doubtless composed to be sung at dawn (cf. p. 375 below).

---

[1] Gill, *S.L.P.* p. 35; *D.L.P.* p. 56ff.
[2] *Ib. S.L.P.* p. 39f.; *D.L.P.* p. 65f.
[3] *Ib. S.L.P.* p. 34, footnote 2; *D.L.P.* p. 60, footnote 1.

In commemorating the individuals for whom the 'death-talks' were held, other heroes, generally of the earlier generations of the same family, are also celebrated, and much historical matter pertaining to the history of the tribe is thus preserved by allusions in the poems. We have a whole series of songs preserved from the 'Death-talk of Aro-kapiti ',[1] held in 1817. But these poems tell us very little of Arokapiti himself. They are wholly occupied with the deaths of two chiefs named Tukua and Ata-toa, two members of the Ngariki clan,[2] by this time rapidly becoming extinct. One of the most interesting of these poems[3] is the *tangi* or dirge recited by the son of one of the slain men. This poem opens with a muster of a section of the victorious Mautara clan for the onset, and descants on the murder of a number of members of the clan to which Tukua and Ata-toa belonged,[4] but purports to be spoken by a member of the victorious party. The tragic irony to which this device lends itself is heightened both by the fact that the actual speaker is a son of one of the murdered men, and also by the concentration and economy of the literary treatment. The bitterness of this *tangi* is, of course, absent from the *pe'e*, which are full of the wistful gentleness characteristic of such poems. One such *pe'e*, by recording the arrival and settlement of the tribal god, lifts the tragic event on to a plane of general significance. The *pe'e* preserve the cathartic quality of tragedy in perfection.

Among the most interesting of the *kakai* ('death-talks') are a series of poems which Gill groups together under the title of the 'Immortality of the Soul'.[5] They belong to the class of composition known as *tiau* (cf. p. 356 above), and with one or two exceptions, which are really outside the series, they are composed for very young people, both boys and girls, who have died a natural death, and therefore are presumably debarred[6] from the warriors' paradise (cf. p. 316 above). In a number of these poems the spirits of the departed are spoken of as wandering round the shore of the island, and resting in the caves[7] which on south,

[1] Gill, *S.L.P.* p. 214ff.; *D.L.P.* p. 296ff.
[2] For this family, see Buck, *M.S.* p. 66 f.
[3] Gill, *S.L.P.* p. 221; *D.L.P.* p. 305.
[4] The quarrel appears to have been between two branches of one family of the Ngati-Vara—the clan to which the Mautara family belonged; but the intermarriage which took place between the various clans, and the intricate relations which these involved, render this period of Mangaian history peculiarly complicated. For details, see Buck, *M.S.* pp. 57, 79f.
[5] *Myths*, p. 181ff.   [6] Cf. however, *ib.* p. 191, footnote 1.
[7] It is much to be regretted that no maps of Mangaia appear to mark the caves, though several of these are large, and have played an important part in the history of the islands.

east, and west are found on the shore of Mangaia, and which served as natural mausolea. It is natural, therefore, that the spirits of the dead should be figuratively spoken of in the poems as wandering about the precincts of these caves where their bodies, or those of their relatives and friends, already rested. Thus in Koroa's lament[1] for Varenga,[2] a girl of the tribe of immigrants from Tahiti (see above), who was actually buried in the family *marae* facing east—the direction from which the tribe had originally come—the spirit is referred to as hovering round the entrance to the cavern Auraka, the great cemetery of the Ngariki or ruling tribe, situated on the western shore of the island, in the precincts sacred to the god Rongo. Again in another lament composed by the same chief for his own children[3] we read of their spirits wandering about the rocks before setting off on a voyage to 'Iva'.[4]

The most interesting of these poems, however, are two composed by Uanuku for Vera, the nephew of Ngarā, priest of Motoro, who was paramount chief of Mangaia at the time of Vera's death c. 1770.[5] Vera's remains were conveyed to Tamarua on the south of the island, and flung down the terrible cavern Raupo, the tribal burial-place of the Tongaiti clan; but his spirit is pictured as wandering along the shore preparatory to taking its departure at sunset over the ocean. This is not necessarily a personal touch, however; for by a beautiful poetical device Vera is identified with Veêtini, a mythical being who is traditionally stated to have been the first to die a natural death in Mangaia, and whose death is celebrated in a *kapa* or tribal fête to be described later (p. 374 below). Vera's parents are referred to in his dirge, not only under their own names, but also under those of Veêtini's parents,[6] and are pictured, like the parents of the mythical hero, as making a circuit of the island, scanning the ocean in the hope of seeing their son return to them, as Veêtini is said to have done for the brief space of a few hours. It is in the person of Veêtini that Vera is said to depart at last far away over the ocean 'by a perilous path to Iva', accompanied by a little band of followers, who, like himself, have assembled at the western point, and await a favouring breeze. The little band is pictured like any other band of voyagers,

---

[1] Koroa was a high chief at the time of Captain Cook's visit, and was one of the best poets of Mangaia in the latter half of the eighteenth century, and at the beginning of the nineteenth. [2] Gill, *Myths*, p. 208 ff.
[3] *Ib.* p. 215 ff. Cf. further *S.L.P.* p. 217. [4] For 'Iva' see p. 436 below.
[5] Gill, *Myths*, p. 189 ff. [6] *Ib.* p. 193.

leaving the island at the most convenient 'landing' place,[1] and setting sail at sunset, like true Polynesian voyagers, who use the stars as their compass. The only dirge for Veêtini which has been recorded *in extenso* is much later (1794) than the dirge for Vera; but a fragment has also been recorded which dates from about 1760[2]; and if, as very commonly happens, the dirge for Vera is based on an earlier original, it may be *e veru*, 'second-hand', and merely an adaptation of an earlier dirge for Veêtini.

With the picture of the departure of the spirits of Vera and his companions in this dirge, it is interesting to compare the account of the enforced exile of Iro and his companions from Mangaia in the seventeenth century (p. 366 above). In both the period before the final departure is spent in making preparations for the long voyage. In both the crews finally assemble their full numbers and pass to the western side of the island, where the best 'landing' is situated. In both the last sad hours are spent in feasting and talking with their relatives and friends. Both the actual and the spiritual migrations are represented as setting out from the westernmost point of the island. In both the canoes with their unwilling burdens take their reluctant departure amid the tears and lamentations of those who remain behind. It is obvious that the conception of the departure of the spirits of the dead over the ocean is based on the procedure of a party of emigrants.

One more of these laments must be mentioned. This is a *tiau* composed by a certain Iikura for Puvai, nephew to Potiki, supreme temporal lord of Mangaia c. 1795.[3] Puvai, like Vera, died young, and his high birth qualified him to lead a band of spirits to their final home. Now Puvai was a native of the district of Tamarua, on the southern side of the island, and belonged to the Ngati-Vara clan. We should have expected his body to be flung, like Vera's, down Raupo, a deep cavern on the southern shore;[4] but no reference is made in the poem to Raupo. Instead the band are spoken of as occupying the Red Cavern Anakura on the east coast,[5] and as awaiting favourable breezes from the north-west and the south-west to waft them clear of the island to Iva.

[1] The breaks in the coral reef are at Oneroa and Avarua on the west coast not far from the ancient site of the *marae* of Rongo.

[2] Gill, *Myths*, p. 187.   [3] *Ib.* p. 199 ff.

[4] For an account of these caves, and the burial customs associated with them, the reader is referred to Gill, *L.S.I.* p. 71 ff.

[5] So Gill, *Myths*, p. 183. According to Buck (*M.S.* p. 197) Anakura is on the west coast. The maps do not help us, but the context suggests that Gill is right.

Solo

The canoe! the canoe!

Chorus

The canoe of Puvai.
Sorrowfully he bends over it.

Solo

Aye, very sorrowfully does he bend over it.
Take thy seat, son, in front,
Clothed in ghostly network;[1]
And turn thy face to yonder land.
He is about to depart.

Chorus

Lightly he skims o'er the crest of the billows, etc.

It will be seen that in the poems of Uanuku and Iikura the heroes
Vera and Puvai are represented as leading a band of followers over the
sea in a canoe to Iva, and as lingering for a while around the burial
caves and the rocks of the shore before their departure, awaiting the
full muster of their crews, and also favourable winds, and the suitable
time of day for departure. The imagery in these laments is highly
figurative, and we must be on our guard against interpreting them too
literally. The poets who composed these laments, and the others to
which we have just referred, belonged to a highly polished school of
poets; Koroa in particular was steeped in the mythology of Mangaia,
and his poetry, both here and elsewhere (cf. p. 369 above), is redolent of
imagery and metaphor drawn from a great body of legend and myth—
itself preserved in a highly figurative and picturesque style. In particular
he loves to dwell (cf. p. 379 below) on the mythology associated with
Hina and the fairies, and their association with the realm of Miru, the
land of the dead. Under the images drawn from such myths Koroa and
his fellow poets symbolise their theme, seeking for the closest analogies
in past legend to the tragedy which it is their sorrowful task to celebrate.
And by this means they succeed in infusing a spirit of withdrawal into
their work. Vera and his sorrowful parents have become Veêtini and
the family who sought sorrowing for their beloved son until they
brought him back from somewhere over the ocean to instruct them in
the ritual proper for the dead—the last office which the living can

---

[1] For the network worn by departed spirits, and wrapped round corpses, see
p. 420 below, footnote 6.

perform. It would be a mistake to interpret this voyage of the dead as an article of faith in Mangaia. It is the poetical imagery current among a polished circle of poets at a given period, and derived directly from traditional versions based ultimately on a realistic presentation of the departure of crews of exiles or emigrants.

It will be seen that these *kakai* ('death-talks') are solemn recitals of a dignified character and lofty tone. Humour is entirely absent, or confined to the closing scene of the *eva*. The purpose is not entertainment, but commemoration—the commemoration of the illustrious dead ancestors of the various families, and characters famous in the history of the island. The most perfect decorum prevails throughout all the poems, and a sense of propriety and good taste, combined with the utmost refinement and delicacy of feeling. The large place occupied by details of the loss of human life and of the subsequent fate of the dead bodies, even of cannibalism, are naturally strange and repulsive to a European. But they are incidental to a literature devoted to the commemoration, with exact historical details, of a people to whom famine was no stranger, and of whom so many died violent deaths. Otherwise coarseness and indecency of any kind, or outspoken references to subjects not mentioned in polite society are absolutely absent from the literature of the polished Mangaians.

In addition to the 'ghost fighting', which seems to have consisted of pure pantomime, with no considerable libretto, and the *kakai* ('death-talk'), which is a more poetical performance—though both of these were held primarily in honour of a dead person—there was also a third type of dramatic performance. This also was literary, known as a *kapa* ('fête', lit. 'dance'), held primarily in honour of the gods. The *kapa*, like the *kakai*, or 'death-talk', took place at night, and was held in long booths, or under trees, on a specially prepared dancing floor. Gill tells us that the natives carefully distinguished the type of traditions which formed the subjects of the *pe'e* (cf. p. 356 above) from those of the *kapa*, the former relating to 'veritable history', the latter most commonly to the gods and 'the supposed experiences of men after death'[1]—in short, to supernatural beings. The *kapa* was usually divided into three parts, and its dramatic and pantomimic character will be readily apprehended from the examples recorded by Gill.[2] It will be seen that here humour is by no means absent, in spite of the religious associations.

The *kapa*, as already stated, differs from the *kakai* ('death-talk') both

[1] Gill, *S.L.P.* p. v; cf. *ib. Myths*, p. 262.
[2] *Myths, passim.*

in the manner of its performance, and also in the form and in the subjects treated. Unfortunately we have no detailed record of the songs of a complete performance, and no complete account of a single *kapa* from Mangaia. On the other hand we have detailed accounts of similar performances from the Island of Penrhyn or Tongareva, and from Mangaia we have a large number of the songs sung at various points in different *kapas*, so that it is possible to obtain a fairly coherent idea of a whole performance. Thus we are fortunate in having the texts of two of the 'Prologues' of these Mangaian *kapas*, or 'fêtes' as Gill calls them, and in these we see Tane and the *tapairu*, or, as Gill translates the term, 'fairies', invited to come up out of the Underworld to grace the dance with their presence.[1] We also possess more than one song composed to be sung at the close of the ceremony, on the appearance of the day-star. The majority of the songs belong to the main series in the various *kapas*, and again we are fortunate in possessing a number of songs from more than one *kapa*. From these we may deduce the important fact that the majority, if not all the songs of any given *kapa*, have reference to a particular group of supernatural beings. A homogeneous atmosphere must thus have prevailed throughout the fête.

Gill has preserved for us a dramatic song of Miru, who, it will be remembered, is known in Mangaia as the mistress of the Underworld home of the dead. The song was composed for Tereavai's 'fête' in 1824. It is very short, and appears to be incomplete, but it is interesting as showing the close association of the 'fêtes' with the god Tane, and their incompatibility with warfare, as typified in the person of Rongo; for here the poet sings of an occasion when

> An end was put to the dance...
> By the war-like behest of Rongo.[2]
> Alas, Tane, author of all our amusements,
> Those pleasures all came to an end.[3]

Not infrequently these dramas relating to supernatural beings are composed in illustration of antiquarian speculations. An example is the 'Dramatic Song of the Creation'[4] composed about 1790 for the fête of Potiki. This dramatic chant relates to the beings dwelling in the lowest spaces of the Underworld; to the creation of Vatea by Vari, a woman dwelling alone in the lowest depth of all; and to Vatea's journey to the lowest planes of the Underworld to woo Papa (cf. p. 311 above), by

---

[1] Gill, *Myths*, pp. 217, 259. For the *tapairu* see p. 293 above.
[2] For the attributes of Rongo and Tane, cf. p. 312 f. above.
[3] Gill, *Myths*, p. 176.   [4] *Ib.* p. 8 ff.

whom he becomes the father of the twin gods Tangaroa and Rongo. The subject of these antiquarian dramatic compositions is of special interest because we are told that the dramatic performances of the *areoi* in Tahiti usually began with the dramatic representation of the Creation myth[1]. A fragment of another 'fête' song composed by the famous poet Koroa about 1818 in memory of Tekaire[2] refers to an antiquarian 'Deluge' myth, according to which a contest for power once took place between Aokeu, a son of Echo,[3] and Ake, whose home is the ocean. Ake was assisted by Raka (Rata), who is here a god of the winds (cf. p. 313 above), but Rongo saved the island from destruction at the prayer of his son Rangi, the first king of the island.

A dirge was performed c. 1794, and again in 1819, for Veêtini,[4] who, as we have mentioned already (p. 369 above), was traditionally regarded as the first man to die a natural death in Mangaia. The myth is therefore a piece of antiquarian speculation on the origin of funeral practices. According to this legend, Veêtini's parents instituted in his honour the signs of mourning and all the funeral games and other practices which were ever afterwards observed in Mangaia on such occasions. Hence arose the *eva* or dirge 'in its four varieties' (cf. p. 357 ff. above), and the 'mourning dance'. On the evening after his burial, close to the sacred dwelling of the Shore King on the west coast, the dirges and dances which had been composed in his honour were performed on the shores of the island towards all the points of the compass, and at last Veêtini was seen lightly skimming over the ocean from the east. He had been allowed to return for the brief space of a day to comfort his parents, and to show mortals how to make offerings of food to gratify the dead. As the sun set, Veêtini departed from the western shore, near the Shore King's dwelling, his shadowy form lightly evading, like that of the father of Aeneas, the hands that would have clasped and detained him. The myth calls to mind the 'voyaging spirits' (*folaunga-aitu*) who in Samoan belief were accustomed to visit the islands, and for whose gratification the people were accustomed to place food offerings on the beach and leave them there. It was in accordance with this belief that offerings of food were taken with much ceremony to the beach and solemnly offered to the 'mysterious visitors' on the arrival of the first European ships, which were supposed to contain parties of such *folaunga-aitu*.[5]

---

[1] Handy, *H.C.S.I.* p. 65.   [2] Gill, *L.S.I.* p. 82.

[3] In the Marquesas, divine honours were paid to Echo even in modern times (Gill, *Myths*, p. 117).

[4] Gill, *Myths*, p. 181 ff.   [5] Stair, *J.P.S.* v, p. 47.

A number of fête songs have reference to the stars. A song was composed by a poet named Reinga for a fête held about 1815 relating to *Scorpii*, who are represented in myth as a boy and girl who fled to Heaven in consequence of the ill-usage of their parents.[1] The same poet refers to the wars of the star-gods:

> Vena was angry with Aumea [Aldebaran],
> On account of the brilliance of his rising.
> She demanded if he recollected the fate of the Pleiades,
> Shivered by Sirius and his friends, etc.[2]

The Pleiades are the constellation most frequently alluded to in these stories, on account of their forming a part of the worship of Tane, the god to whom the *kapas* were sacred. The day-songs, which were chanted on the appearance of the morning stars as a signal that the *kapas* were over,[3] make constant mention of the stars and their association with the god.

In a 'Day-song for Maaki's Fête',[4] composed by Tangataroa and Tiki about 1820, we have a remarkable liturgical drama of 'Birds'. In this dramatic poem six men in masks representing the 'warning birds', the incarnations of the god Tane, come as messengers to warn the assembled guests that night is over, and they must disperse with the first streak of dawn. The day-song is in essence a graceful dismissal of the assembly— a poetical announcement, as by the master of ceremonies, that the revels now are over. Our text is merely the concluding portion of a dramatic evening. It is interesting to compare the 'warning birds' of Tane with the 'omen birds' of Singalang Burong in Dyak mythology (see pp. 478, 486 below) to whom they bear a very close resemblance.

We have a number of songs relating to the dramatic fête of Potiki, about 1790. The 'Dramatic Song of Creation', already alluded to, belongs to this series, and was probably recited at an early stage in the proceedings. The 'Prologue'[5] to this fête is a long and elaborate invocation to the 'fairies', in which the 'fairies', both male and female, are represented as coming up from the Underworld to take part in the dance. The part of the fairies was actually acted by human beings.[6] The prevailing sentiment of the poem is one of relief that the peace drum has sounded and a time of security is at hand; for in time of peace the 'fairies' are said to creep up through the crevices in the rocks to join in the dance of mortals. The note thus delicately struck in the 'Prologue' is evidently characteristic of the fête, for in the same series we

---

[1] Gill, *Myths*, p. 42. [2] *Ib.* p. 43.
[3] For a curious parallel, cf. p. 524 below. [4] Gill, *Myths*, p. 49 f.
[5] *Ib.* p. 259. [6] *Loc. cit.* footnote.

have a dramatic song[1] in which the hero competes successfully against
the female fairies of both the Heavens and the Underworld in a game
which consists in keeping a number of balls in motion simultaneously.
In this game the 'fairies' of both the Heavens and the Underworld are
believed to have been especially proficient; but they are said to be
beaten by the hero. His name is not mentioned, but he is probably to
be identified with Ngaru, a mythical hero (cf. p. 278 above) who is
traditionally stated to have learnt the art from them.[2]

One type of drama performed at the fêtes or *kapas* was known as
'visitors' songs'.[3] These have reference to the arrival of strangers in
Mangaia, such as Ono from Tonga,[4] in ancient times, and that of
Captain Cook in 1777. The dramas relating to Ono are believed to be
among the oldest songs extant, and to have been composed several
centuries ago. Ono is identical with the hero of this name already
referred to (p. 278 ff. above); but our dramatic poems know nothing of his
warlike exploits, and it is clear from the constant allusions to the sin of
sacrilege and punishment that the Mangaian songs and saga were composed in a milieu where sanctuary influence was very strong.

In modern times these 'visitors' songs' were often treated humorously and with more realism than the other *kapas*. The drama which
relates to the visit of Captain Cook to the shores of Mangaia in 1777
is an excellent example.[5] It will be remembered that Cook was unable
to land on the island, owing to the hostile aspect of the Mangaians; but
he sailed close in to the shore, and addressed them through his interpreter Omai, or Mai.[6] The play represents the arrival of the 'big canoe',
and describes the excitement of the natives, mimicking humorously and
realistically the contrary directions given to Cook by the natives as to
where he should land:

> "This way, this way."
> "No; that way, that way"—

and the gibberish talk of the foreigners with their 'white faces'. More
serious is the hostile bearing of the warriors on the shore:

> We come, by hundreds and hundreds,
> Warriors, warriors to fight, to fight,
> Mangaians to fight, to fight the canoe.

---

[1] Gill, *Myths*, p. 244 ff.   [2] *Ib.* p. 232.   [3] *Ib.* p. 85 f.
[4] So Gill; but see Buck, *M.S.* p. 37.
[5] Gill, *S.L.P.* p. 182 ff.; *D.L.P.* p. 254 ff.
[6] The *O* is the article, commonly used with proper names in Polynesian languages.

The song is accompanied with realistic pantomime. Coming as it does among the more serious chants of the *kapa*, with its solemn ritual and religious associations, drama of this kind has much the effect of the medieval interlude in relation to the miracle plays of our own country, and the play of Langdarma amid the solemn New Year festivities among the lamas of Tibet. We shall see later that plays closely resembling this of Cook are by no means rare in other parts of the Pacific.

Dramas and dramatic dances resembling those of Mangaia were, and still are, performed throughout the islands of the Cook Group. An interesting account of the dramas and funeral dances (*evas*) and mimic battles traditionally held to have been appointed by the early voyager Tangiia in Rarotonga in memory of his father is recorded from the recital of the last high priest of the island.[1] Writing of Ru-enua, the traditional 'discoverer'[2] of the island of Aitutaki, and of Te Erui and Rua-tapu, who came to the island on two later voyages, Prof. Buck makes the following important statement:

"Incidents in the history of the first three were represented dramatically to the author, with the accompaniment of song and dance. Thus the village of Amuri played 'The coming of Ru' and 'The fishing quarrel between Rua-tapu and his son',[3] whilst the village of Reureu danced 'The song of Te Erui's adze'.[4] Such dramatic representations help to preserve the history of the past."[5]

In a letter to the authors he makes the following interesting statement:

"Dramatic dances were known and acted on every island in the Cook Group, and it is only in recent years that they are being discarded. The Mangaians continued to dance them long after Gill's time, but probably the full form of the funeral celebration (*kakai*) was modified."[6]

In Mangaia the *kapas* 'in honour of the gods' appear to have been composed to celebrate the assumption of each new 'temporal lord', who won his office by force of arms, and held it only until such time as a stronger chief should arise and wrest it from him. Each new temporal lord celebrated his assumption of office by a dance in honour of Tane and the 'fairies', and by offering a human sacrifice to appease Rongo,

---

[1] *J.P.S.* xxx, p. 129f.

[2] It is interesting to note that according to Aitutaki tradition, before Ru left Havaiki, he noted that the valleys and hills of Aitutaki were thickly populated. Instances of tradition relating to a definite human population of the islands before the period of the great voyagers are not very common. See Buck, *M.C.C.I.* p. xix.

[3] Buck, *ibid.* p. 296.   [4] *Ib.* p. 245.   [5] *Ib.* p. xxi.

[6] Letter dated November 14th, 1936.

378 ORAL LITERATURE OF POLYNESIA

the god of war, who might be supposed otherwise to have resented the ensuing peace time, which deprived him of his prey. Such festivals may therefore be said to have been in honour of both gods jointly, i.e. of Rongo with Tane (Rongo *ma* Tane). In this respect we are reminded of the god of the *areoi* paradise who was known as Romatane, and who is perhaps a combination of the two gods.[1] In Mangaia at least he may have been something like the Latin Janus. On rare occasions it happened that the temporal sovereignty was transferred without a battle. On such occasions a mock battle or reed-throwing match[2] may have been substituted, the reeds representing spears. The song entitled 'Makitaka's Lament on the Loss of the Temporal Sovereignty'[3] was composed by the poet Tuka c. 1815 to be recited at a reed-throwing match which must have taken place after the temporal lordship was peaceably transferred to Pangemiro in 1814, the necessary human sacrifice having been offered.[4] The poem appears to have been recited by the defeated party while the human sacrifice was lying on the altar. The occasion was one of great importance for the islanders, since it signalised the downfall of the Mautara clan which for 150 years had maintained the peace of Mangaia, and fostered its wonderful development of song and dance.

The tact and delicacy of thought in the poetry of this island is aptly illustrated in another dramatic poem composed by the same poet for a reed-throwing match for women in honour of Patikiporo,[5] which was recited on the same occasion. This song is founded on the legend of Ngaru, to which reference has been made above (p. 278). The mythical hero Ngaru is sought by Miru in marriage for her two *tapairu* daughters, by whom he is carried off, corded and wrapped like a corpse, to the Underworld. We have already seen how the hero succeeds in escaping from Miru. The parts of Ngaru and the *tapairu* were actually acted by women, who carried a bundle, representing the corpse, over the hill to be thrown down the cavern Auraka. Only women were allowed to take part in this play. At a later stage in the story Ngaru also goes to Heaven, where he succeeds in overcoming a still more dangerous foe.

[1] The god Rongomatane is also known in Hawaii and New Zealand. For a fuller discussion of the name see p. 311 above.

[2] For a detailed account of a mythical reed-throwing match, and a note on the modern practice, see Gill, *Myths*, p. 118f.; Buck, *M.S.* p. 196. See further p. 361 above.

[3] Gill, *Myths*, p. 312.

[4] Gill, *D.L.P.* p. 311.

[5] Gill, *Myths*, p. 238.

The second journey is not referred to in this song, but another fête song has already been discussed (p. 376 above) which represents Ngaru as overcoming the *tapairu* of both the Heavens and the Underworld in ball-playing. Ngaru, in fact, triumphs over death—whether natural death, as represented by Miru, or violent death (i.e. in battle), as a result of further achievements during his journey to the skies. The subject is thus chosen here as suggesting a ray of hope for the victim lying slain on the altar of Rongo, and however alien the whole thought and scene are to our own ideas, Tuka must have brought some comfort to the mourning relatives by the allusion to the attainment of immortality by those who die violently.

The chant on the Voyage of Ina (cf. p. 360f. above) composed by the poet Koroa for a female reed-throwing match about 1814[1] was possibly intended to be recited on the same occasion, for the milieu represented in the poems is the same, Ina being one of the sky *tapairu*. The prominence given to the reed-throwing match for women on this occasion was doubtless due to the fact that in the prose version of the story of Ngaru, the hero's wife, Tongatea, is represented as organising a reed-throwing match for women. This likewise is represented as a festive occasion, for the women are in gala dress, and the men are only present by invitation, in the capacity of umpires and audience.[2]

It has been mentioned that each *kapa* (fête) is held in celebration of some particular supernatural or mythical being or group, and the spiritual milieu of all the songs in any given *kapa* is therefore identical. The songs in Gill's collection are therefore not single examples of a discrete series, but elements in an organic artistic creation, which seeks by suggestion and reference, invocation and dramatic representation, to create a spiritual illusion, complete, and remote from realism, yet relevant to the occasion which it commemorates. The unity of idea and subject is preserved even though the songs of several poets are sung at one *kapa* or fête. For example, several songs have been recorded which were composed for a fête held about 1814. These songs were composed by at least three different poets—Koroa, Tuka, and Vaarua; and either the fête must have been held in honour of more than one person, or else several fêtes were held within the space of about a year, though either procedure would have been unusual. Despite these circumstances all the songs are directly based on the myth of Ina and the *tapairu*, and Ina's journey over the sea to join her husband Tinirau—a Cycle of stories already referred to in Ch. III above.

[1] Gill, *Myths*, p. 97.　　[2] *Ib.* p. 228.

This will become clearer if we pause to look more closely at this series, which also gives a fair idea of the scope of a single fête, though it dates from a time when the best period of Mangaian poetry was past. The little song of Ina composed by Tuka for Akatonu's fête[1] represents Ina as actually making the journey to the Sacred Isle, the home of Tinirau, on the backs of fish.[2] The song for Tenio's fête composed by Vaarua[3] appears to be an invocation to Ina's brother Tautiti[4] (cf. p. 288 f. above) to rise from the Underworld and lead off the dance, and the same poem contains references to her son Koro and the famous pandanus tree which he planted. The song composed by Koroa for the female reed-throwing match already referred to[5] also represents Ina making the voyage to her husband Tinirau, and landing on the sacred isle. In the little 'Kite-song' by Koroa[6] Tautiti seems to be competing with Rongo and Tane in kite-flying. Finally, the 'day-song', or dawn song, composed by Koroa for Tenio's fête[7] draws a curtain over the festivities with the safe arrival of Ina at the Sacred Isle, and the departure of Tautiti:

> Ina invoked the aid of many fish
> To bear her gaily on their backs. . .
> To her royal spouse,
> To Tinirau in the ocean. . .
> On her voyage to the Sacred Isle.
> Softly she beats the drum.
> Tinirau is enchanted
> By the music of the lovely one.
> Our sport is over: the visit of Tautiti is ended,
> The guests from spirit-world are gone.[8]

This Cycle offered a happy choice of subjects for such dances, since Ina's son Koro and her husband Tinirau were both famous in myth for having danced the *tautiti*, a favourite dance at these *kapas*, and Ina herself makes known her presence on the Sacred Isle by beating the drum, which always accompanied the *kapa*, and the sound of which heralded the period of dance and song—the period when Tane was in the ascendant,[9] and warfare was at an end.

[1] Gill, *Myths*, p. 95.
[2] Ina is generally said to have made the journey on the backs of two fish, which is probably a poetical reference to the double canoe.   [3] Gill, *Myths*, p. 104.
[4] Tautiti is sometimes said to be a son of Miru.   [5] Gill, *Myths*, p. 97.
[6] *Ib.* p. 123.   [7] *Ib.* pp. 96, 186.   [8] *Ib.* p. 96 f.
[9] The big drum, a kind of national instrument, was known as the 'voice of Tane', and was beaten to inaugurate a period of peace. A smaller drum accompanied the dance of the *kapa*.

Poetical forms resembling those which we have been discussing are widespread throughout the Pacific. Poems known as *pihe* are found among the Maori, though our information about them is insufficient to give us much guidance as to their form.[1] On the other hand the *pehu* and the *kapa* as performed on the island of Tongareva or Penrhyn, north-east of Samoa, undoubtedly bore a considerable resemblance to the *pe'e* and the *kapa* of Mangaia.[2] Here also they signify dances more or less ritual in character, which were—and still are[3]—performed ceremonially on all important occasions by groups or rows of men or women separately. They are, however, by no means restricted to mourning for the dead, but were just as readily performed to welcome the living on all occasions of public rejoicing. One performance of a *kapa* described by Lamont is particularly interesting, for after the performance in the evening of a ceremonial 'dance' (*pehu*), a dramatic presentation was given on the following morning 'in several scenes' of the wreck of Lamont's own ship, which had taken place some months previously.[4] It would seem, therefore, that the visits of the ships of white men formed a favourite subject of the *kapa* everywhere. In both the performance witnessed by Lamont, and in the 'Drama of Cook' from Mangaia referred to above (p. 376), the subject is treated humorously. In Samoa also the representation of a crew of bluejackets rowing a ship forms a favourite subject of the action dance known as the *siva*.[5] Churchill describes the *taupou* or village belle assuming the rôle of a naval officer, and putting her party of girls through a mock drill with cocoa-nut stalks for muskets, while she gives orders in gibberish which are intended to reproduce the words of command.[6]

Dramas are also still popular on the island of Rakahanga, a little to the south-west of Tongareva. They are known as *nuku*, and relate to

---

[1] Best, *Maori* II, p. 144.

[2] Our information on this subject is derived chiefly from Lamont, who was shipwrecked on the island in 1853 and resided for several months among the natives. He saw several performances of the dances in question. In this connection it is interesting to note that Mangaia was aware of the existence of Tongareva long before Europeans were aware of its existence; and when Tongareva was discovered by Europeans, the inhabitants of this island also knew already of the existence of Mangaia. See Gill, *S.L.P.* p. 49. The similarity of the literary forms of the two islands is therefore probably not accidental. A brief, but more recent account of the Tongarevan *pehu* and *kapa* is given by Buck, *E.T.* p. 77f.

[3] See Buck, *E.T.* p. 77f.   [4] Lamont, p. 314ff.

[5] Almost all writers on Samoa give a description of the *siva*, and we have therefore not made a detailed study here. The reader may refer to Churchward, p. 226; Churchill, p. 71 ff.; Pritchard, p. 78; Turner, p. 124 f.; Wilkes, II, p. 133; and more recent authors. See also p. 384 below.   [6] Churchill, p. 76.

the mythical ancestors of the islanders. An interesting account of a four-act play, acted in the village street, has been published recently by Prof. Buck.[1] The first act represents the first voyage of discovery by the mythical ancestor Huku from Rarotonga. The second represents the journey of Maui to visit Hina, who is represented as an old woman living at the bottom of the sea. The third act represents a fishing expedition of Maui and his brothers, in which Maui, with the help of Hina, fishes up the island of Manihiki, while the defeated brothers plunge overboard and are lost in the ocean. In the fourth act Huku takes possession of the island; but a mischievous and humorous character named Wheatu, who has managed to forestall him, has first to be dispossessed and summarily dismissed. The character of Wheatu is purely comic, and the islanders derive much mirth from the crudely amusing by-play of this part of the drama.

An interesting feature of the play is the disguise worn by the characters. They are smeared all over with grey mud, no doubt to represent corpses. Huku himself is naked, save for a loin-cloth and a turban made of fish-net, a false beard and moustaches of cocoa-nut husk; otherwise he also is covered with grey mud.[2] Another interesting feature is the mention of the 'reciting' of a *kapa* 'with appropriate hand and foot action', by both Maui and Hina at the close of the second act. Elsewhere[3] Buck tells us that the Tongarevan *kapa* resembles the Samoan *siva*, though the more elaborate examples resemble historical pageants.

Another *nuku* referred to by Buck as performed at Rakahanga represents the visit of two heroes to Hawaiki, and an encounter with Kui-the-Blind. A third represents the departure of the people to Manihiki, presumably from Rarotonga, leaving behind a woman of high rank who is troubled in their absence by spirits. These parts are acted by about twenty children, 'naked, like Huku, save for their loin-cloths, and like him liberally sprinkled with grey mud'. Yet another *nuku* represents the voyage of an ancestor to Aitutaki to see a *hala* tree, which was planted there by his ancestor. Buck tells us that the *nuku* are 'old', and are acted throughout the Cook Group,[4] the

[1] Buck, *E.M.R.* p. 198 ff. For the various versions of the myth on which this play is based, see Williamson, *R.C.B.* I, p. 38, and the references there cited.

[2] An interesting photograph of Huku performing his part as he paddles his canoe, improvised of cocoa-nut leaves, down the village street, is reproduced by Buck, *E.M.R.* Plate XII.　　　　　　　　　[3] *E.T.* p. 78 f.

[4] Buck presumably regards them, therefore, as closely related to the *kapas* of Mangaia, though he makes no reference to the latter in this connection.

Society Islands, and the Paumotus. All seem to be preoccupied with the traditional history of the islands, and have doubtless assisted, as Buck observes, in memorising the events of the past.

Two series of ritual chants relating to the heroes Maui and Tawhaki have been recorded from the Paumotu Archipelago.[1] These chants and certain others from the same area[2] closely resemble those of Mangaia in form, and are probably archaic. We are also fortunate in possessing the complete text of a 'play' from the same area relating to Tutepoganui, the 'king', or, as some say, the god of the sea.[3] A picture of his great wooden mask is also given,[4] and a strange object it is, carved of cocoa-nut wood, stuck over with imitation shells, and having holes for eyes, and, like Huku, a great beard and moustache of cocoa-nut fibre. The whole is the most elaborate stage property we have met with, and reminds one of the devices used in an Elizabethan masque.

The drama opens with a dialogue between Rogomatane, or Rongo-matane,[5] who is here represented as a human being dwelling on the land, and a certain Tohoropuga, who is described as a sea-lord, and governor of the products of the ocean, and who is represented as paying a surreptitious visit to land. Suddenly his own overlord Tutepoganui, the king who dwells in the depths of the ocean, is seen approaching land. Tohoropuga is terrified at being thus caught 'off duty', as it were; but Tutepoganui assures him that he has come primarily to look for two of his subjects who have been taken captive by the landsmen, and promises him forgiveness if he will find them. While Tohoropuga and his companions are absent, the king of the sea converses with an old woman, who proves to be Hina, and who tells him the sad and somewhat shocking story of her life. The return of the searchers with the captives, and the forgiveness and departure of the ocean 'king' conclude the play. Hina's story, inserted as a relatively lengthy and irrelevant narrative in the body of the play, is evidently intended to fulfil the function of an interlude, such as that of the visit of Captain Cook in the Mangaian *kapa*; but the humour is crude, and the whole play more childish and perhaps more sophisticated than the Mangaian dramas. On the other hand the *dramatis personae* are extremely interesting. The office of Tohoropuga bears a suspicious likeness to that of the Mangaian 'Shore King', or 'seaside king', while the inland-dwelling Rongomatane

[1] Stimson, *L.M.T.*; see also p. 282, footnote 4 above.
[2] See e.g. the ancient chant or *fagu*, 'The Return of the *Marama* from Hiti', Stimson, *J.P.S.* XLI, p. 190.   [3] Caillot, *Mythes*, p. 95 ff.
[4] *Ib.* p. 93.   [5] For this deity see p. 311 above.

also has his counterpart in Mangaia, as well as among the *areoi*. We have no reason to doubt that this Paumotu play is at least based on genuine tradition.

Traces of poetry which possibly has a dramatic origin have been recorded from the Maori and the Moriori peoples. From the former we have fragments of a dramatic dialogue relating to Rata,[1] which seems to have a certain resemblance to the arrangement of the speeches in the Mangaian texts; but the remains are too fragmentary to permit of any certainty on this matter. From the Moriori a number of chants have been recorded to which we have already referred (p. 338 above), and which are known as *tawhakis*, having reference to Tawhaki's journey to Heaven.[2] These poems are said to have been recited in modern times as charms; but their form is that of monologue and dialogue, and they appear to have direct reference to the Tawhaki saga, of which these islanders possessed important versions. It is true that we possess only a few single poems; but this would be easily accounted for by the fact that most of the Moriori *tohungas*, who were the chief repositories of the traditions, were already dead at the time when the record was made. But we have no certain evidence that dramatic poetry has ever been highly developed in the extreme south of the Pacific in modern times (see, however, p. 439 below).

Songs accompanied by dances of a more or less pantomimic character and a limited amount of action are recorded from many other parts of the Pacific. Perhaps the best known of these are the *siva* of Samoa and the *hula* of Hawaii. Both are accompanied by poetry which is almost wholly lyrical, and both by the dance, in which sometimes men take part, sometimes women, as in Mangaia. This is commonly[3] a rhythmical seated dance in Samoa, whereas in Hawaii the dancers are generally on their feet. The relationship of the Hawaiian *hula* to dramatic representation is perhaps comparable to that of European ballet, but it differs from any European musical drama in that it is religious in origin, and still retains many of the religious conventions and much of its traditional ritual. We do not know of any comprehensive collections of the *siva* répertoire, but a large number of songs of the kind which are sung to the accompaniment of this dance are published by Krämer, and consist for the most part of ordinary lyrics, much like the poetry of Tonga (cf. p. 405 f. below).

---

[1] Shortland, p. 165 f.   [2] Shand, *J.P.S.* VII, p. 73 ff.
[3] Not always, however. See Wilkes, III, p. 133.

For Hawaii we are fortunate in having Emerson's invaluable collection[1] of texts and descriptions of the various *hulas*, and their accompanying words. Here also the songs are mainly lyrical, and dialogue may be said hardly to exist; but the action which accompanies the songs at times becomes pantomimic, and the répertoire of the *hula* dancers even included puppet plays. We have made a very brief study of the *hula* in this chapter, therefore, though it must be borne in mind that we are much farther removed from drama here than in the Central Pacific. In Hawaii, drama such as we find in Mangaia, with its coherent and relevant theme, and organic structure, appears to be unknown in modern times.[2]

Close similarities undoubtedly exist between the *hula* organisation and ideals, and their manner of performance on the one hand, and those of the Groups previously considered on the other. In the *hula*, however, historical and legendary elements are chiefly concerned with allusions to the early sagas of the Migration Period, more particularly to those which relate to heroes traditionally regarded as famous poets and patrons of the *hula*, such as Lono-i-ka-makahiki,[3] and Liloa.[4] On the other hand a large number of poems make reference to the characters connected by ties of family relationship with the volcano goddess Pele, and allusions to the Cycle of stories in which they figure are very common. The affinities of the Hawaiian *hula* lie, therefore, with the Mangaian tribal songs, which are commonly called *kapas*, rather than with the family mourning songs, or *pe'e*.

Like the *kapa* also, the *hula* is a religious function, as well as a source of artistic and social pleasure. It was sacred to Laka (Rata)[5]— who in Hawaii, as we have seen, is a female deity—and also apparently[6]

---

[1] *The Unwritten Literature of Hawaii.*

[2] It is nevertheless possible that something of this kind has existed in the past, for Emerson heard a joint performance between a man and his wife, in which the man was the reciter, while the woman took the leading part and performed the dance; but Emerson tells us that "to this rôle she added that of prompter, repeating to him in advance the words of the next verse, which he then took up" (*U.L.* p. 159). This evidently struck Emerson as an unfamiliar, or a fumbling performance; for he explains it by supposing her verbal memory to have been better than her husband's. In the Paumotu dramatic chants, however, it is a regular convention for the first solo thus to suggest the opening words of a phrase or theme, which was immediately caught up and carried forward by the second solo and again by the chorus (see Stimson, *L.M.T. passim*). Similarly in the Mangaian chants the chorus commonly complete the sentence begun by the solo and left unfinished.

[3] For traditions relating to this hero, see *Fornander Collection*, First Series, Vol. IV, p. 256 ff.

[4] See Emerson, *U.L.* p. 14.

[5] Malo, p. 113; Emerson, *U.L.* p. 14 ff.   [6] Emerson, *U.L.* pp. 14, 24 f.

to her mother Kapo, sister of Pele,[1] though Laka is far more prominent than Kapo, and is undoubtedly regarded as the patron of *hula* dancers, at least in modern times. A large number of hymns and prayers to Laka have been recorded from the *hula* répertoire, and these were recited on all formal and ceremonial occasions by the members of the society.[2] Despite their association with Laka, however, the *hula* subjects, in so far as they contain personal names, relate to the Cycle, not of Tawhaki and his descendants, but to the great family of the Volcano goddess Pele, and her sisters, her lover, Lohiau, the great swine deity Kama-pua'a, and other local deities of Hawaii. In addition to one special *hula* which is devoted to Pele, we have constant references to the great Cycle of stories with which she is associated, and a number of songs incorporated in other *hulas* purport to be spoken by Hiiaka, Pele's youngest sister. These chants celebrate Pele's many husbands, and her enemies, and also the travels and adventures of Hiiaka, and her relations with Lohiau. With the help of allusions in the poems and the prose sagas of the Cycle, it is possible to trace and correlate the incidents of a great family history of the volcano deities.

The majority of the *hula* songs of Hawaii are almost exclusively occupied with two themes, the passion of love, and description, or rather allusions and addresses to wild nature—the rain storm, the lightning, the flowers, and ferns, and trees of the forest. This is in accordance with the dedication of the *hula* to Laka, the goddess of wild nature. But the natural landscape is not described statically, but dynamically, and generally with reference to the emotions of the speaker. The nature poems, in fact, bear a close resemblance to those of the western Pacific, notably Tonga and Samoa. Emerson emphasises this personal reference of the Hawaiian nature poetry as its most essential feature, and insists that all such poetry is figurative in intention. The whole *hula* répertoire, in fact, symbolises the passion of love under all its aspects.

The *hula* répertoire, nevertheless, contains a number of varied performances, more or less crystallised by tradition. Each of these performances is itself known as a *hula*, and has its own individual name. It would seem that each actual *hula* forms a distinct *unity*, like a ballet; but the unity consists rather in the manner of performance, and perhaps the diction and the music, than in the actual contents of the poems,

---

[1] Nevertheless, as Emerson observes (*U.L.* p. 24), Laka seems to have been a friend, not a relative of Pele. This is the general testimony of Hawaiian tradition.

[2] Emerson, *passim.*

which are said to be selected without any intention of strict relevance, and certainly without any direct connection with one another. The choice of these songs rested with the *kumu*, who is at once the leader, trainer, and 'business manager' of the troupe,[1] and who selected or composed the songs for each *hula* with an eye to their general fitness, taking care that they should not clash with the general unity which characterised each performance. Another important official was the *kahuna* (*tohunga*), who acted as the leader in the religious exercises, and interpreted the will of the gods, whose favour determined the failure or success of the performances.

From our point of view, perhaps the most interesting of the *hulas* is that devoted to the celebration of Pele.[2] This *hula* was regarded with special reverence, and only performed on the most solemn occasions in honour of kings and other august persons, and prefaced with prayer and sacrifice—not in this case, to Laka, as in most *hula* performances, but to Pele herself, the patron of this particular *hula*. The songs celebrate various situations in the great Pele Cycle. Of these the most interesting is the one which was chanted at the opening of the *hula*, and which celebrates in five stanzas of narrative the voyage of Pele from Kahiki (Tahiti), and her first arrival in the Hawaiian Group.

Space will not permit us to do more than mention one or two of the most ancient and striking of the *hulas*; but the number of *hulas* on record is very considerable, and for fuller information on the subject, and a large number of texts, the reader is referred to Emerson's *Unwritten Literature of Hawaii*. One of the most ancient, and one held in very high honour among the *hula* dancers themselves, is the *Hula Ala'a-papa*, which, like the *hula* just described, has reference to the Pele Cycle, especially to Pele's younger sister Hiiaka and to Hiiaka's friend Hopoe, who taught her the *hula* dance. In its best days this *hula* is said to have been a stately and dignified performance, comparable to the old-fashioned courtly minuet.[3] Another early example, the *Hula Pa-ipu*, or *Kuolo*,[4] refers apparently to an incident which took place in the Migration Period, as we see by allusions to the Cycle of Olopana (cf. p. 252 f. above). The vigour of its literary style is said to stamp it as belonging to the archaic period which closed in the early part of the eighteenth century, though here, as in the *hula* last mentioned, some of the songs included have obviously been composed or recast at a later period.

---

[1] Emerson, *U.L.* p. 29.　　[2] *Ib.* p. 186 ff.　　[3] *Ib.* p. 57 ff.　　[4] *Ib.* p. 73 ff.

The ancient *hula* répertoire included a *Hula Ki'i*,[1] a *hula* to be danced with marionettes, some interesting sketches of which are reproduced by Emerson.[2] This *hula* is said to have approached more closely to drama than anything else which we have from Hawaii. It lacks the dignity and classic touch of the preceding, and introduces elements of crude humour and social allusion. In this it appears to have elements in common with the 'interlude', of the Central Pacific dramas, such as that of the arrival of Cook off Mangaia (p. 376 above).

In illustration of the lyrical character of the songs of the *hulas*, we may quote the following little dialogue poem from the *hula* répertoire, which has reference to an oft-recurring theme of these songs, namely the 'water of Life', also known as the 'water of Kane',[3] that favourite quest of Polynesian gods and heroes alike. Each strophe begins with a query:

> A question I ask of you:
> Where is the water of Kane?

And the answer follows:

> Out there with the floating sun,
> Where cloud forms rest on Ocean's breast,
> Uplifting their forms at Nihoa,
> This side the base of Lehua;
> There is the water of Kane.

And so on:

> One question I put to you:
> Where, where is the water of Kane?

In conclusion it may be mentioned that a number of *hulas* take their name from the musical instrument which accompanied them, such as the *Hula Pahu*, or drum, a performance of formal and dignified character, reserved for distinguished guests and the most important occasions.[4] The introduction of this big drum is traditionally ascribed to La'a-ma-i-kahiki, who is said to have brought it to Hawaii from the south.[5] La'a was himself a keen patron of the *hula*, and is said to have toured the islands of the Hawaiian Group, teaching the natives new *hula* forms. The drum is thought to have been restricted originally to the temple services. It will be remembered that in Mangaia the beating of the drum betokens the inauguration of a period of peace, and the big drum

---

[1] Emerson, *U.L.* p. 91.   [2] *Loc. cit.*
[3] *Ib.* p. 258.   [4] *Ib.* p. 103 ff.
[5] *Fornander Collection*, First Series, Vol. IV, p. 154.

was sacred to Tane (see p. 380 above), and in the texts which we have quoted above (p. 380) Hina is also represented as beating the drum on her arrival at the Sacred Isle of Tinirau. It is clear, therefore, that the drum is the instrument primarily associated with the arts of poetry and the dance, and with the 'fairies', of whom Ina was the most illustrious.

The *hula* is not confined to Hawaii, though as the word means simply 'dance', it is by no means easy to gauge how far notices of its occurrence elsewhere imply the existence of a similar performance. Melville speaks of *hula* 'plays', however, as performed in the Marquesas,[1] and Caillot tells us that in the Paumotu Archipelago performances were given which consisted of dancing, pantomime, gymnastics, melodrama, and mythology, and that the leading rôle in these was played by the volcano god Pere (Pele).[2] As Caillot himself points out,[3] the name must be intrusive in Paumotu, for no volcanoes exist in this archipelago.

[1] Melville, p. 174.   [2] Caillot, *P.O.* p. 41.
[3] *Ib., Religions*, p. 65. See further Williamson, *R.C.B.* ii, p. 215.

CHAPTER VII

ANTIQUARIAN, GNOMIC AND DESCRIPTIVE LITERATURE

POETRY and prose embodying native learning are cultivated everywhere in the Pacific. Indeed the astonishing amount of native literature from all parts, containing not only antiquarian speculation, historical and genealogical knowledge, but also geographical, astronomical, and meteorological information, is one of the features which shows most unmistakably the high level of intellectual life in the South Seas. Much of this information was common knowledge to people of all parts, but the class mainly responsible for its preservation and dissemination were the priests or *tohungas*. In many parts of the Pacific definite courses of instruction, carefully graded and lasting over a period of several years, were devoted to the teaching of native knowledge, and a special building was, in many instances, set aside for the purpose. To this subject we shall return later.

Most of this literature is not embodied in a form which we are accustomed to regard as appropriate to scientific knowledge. The tendency to narrate encroaches everywhere on classification. This is, of course, commoner in popular learning than in that of the *tohungas*, and is doubtless to be accounted for in part by the high development of Polynesian saga. In consequence of this tendency, phenomena are represented as occurring in succession when in actual fact they are static, and would be more properly set out in tabular form. Thus the different winds and various types of waves are frequently enumerated in catalogue form and in great detail; but instead of being classified, they are reported as impeding the course of a hero's voyage, or the migration of a people. From Hawaii we have a chant of more than four hundred lines which relates to the voyage of one of the ancient Hawaiian chiefs, and which enumerates by name "all the winds that ever blew on the coasts and the mountains of the group".[1] A similar catalogue of winds is conjured up by the goddess Pele as she dances the *hula*.[2] Even hymns embodying cosmogonic information often assume the form of narratives.

The literature of antiquarian record and speculation is particularly

[1] Fornander, *P.R.* II, p. 112.   [2] See e.g. Westervelt, *H.L.V.* p. 79f.

rich throughout our area. It is necessary here, as in regard to the religious teaching and stories of divine beings referred to above (p. 308 ff.), to distinguish various distinct strata of oral learning. The highest class represents the standard and esoteric teaching of the priests, the second the traditions of the chiefs, and the third the popular traditions handed on by the lower classes, unchecked by special training in memorising or critical faculty. Here also it often happens that different, and sometimes contradictory types of tradition exist in the same area in a different social milieu. These variant traditions are especially valuable because of the wealth of information which has been preserved for us as to the exact source from which they have been recorded. From the earliest period of work in the Pacific, missionaries such as W. W. Gill and J. Williams were awake to the distinction in kind between these different types of tradition, the relative value to be attached to them, and the importance of variant versions, and of the necessity of keeping a record of the exact source from which they were obtained.

(1) Perhaps the most remarkable monuments of antiquarian learning, and indeed of oral learning generally in the Pacific, are the genealogies. The astonishing length and substantial agreement of the genealogical lines of the chiefs from various groups of islands have already been commented on (p. 336 ff. above), and in general these serve as an admirable basis for the reconstruction of Polynesian history. At the same time these genealogies serve as charters, letters patent, and general data of reference in both practical and legal matters to the Polynesians themselves,[1] and often proved a formidable political weapon in the hands of those who knew how to preserve and how to make use of them. In accordance with this the *tohungas*, who were the chief custodians of the genealogies, were not incapable of forging and tampering with the genealogies of the chiefs, more especially those whose line would not bear too close a scrutiny. In Hawaii in particular the habit of inflating the genealogies by the insertion of genuine *ariki* lines which did not originally belong to them is abundantly clear,[2] while a modified form of the same practice prevailed in Samoa. The *tohunga*, the custodian of these genealogical traditions, we are told, is well aware of these weak points in the genealogy of the chief, and the knowledge is used by him at times "almost to the extent of blackmail".[3]

[1] Arii Taimai, p. 17; cf. Salmon, *J.P.S.* XIX, p. 43.
[2] See Fornander, *P.R.* II, p. 27; cf. p. 26. See also *ib.* I, p. 199 and cf. II, p. 22.
[3] O. F. Nelson, *J.P.S.* XXXIV, p. 124f.

It must not be supposed, however, that this falsifying of the genealogies was an arbitrary or excessive aberration. We have already seen that considerable reliance can be placed with safety on much of the genealogical tradition of the Pacific. Indeed both the conservation and the modification of the genealogies were guarded with the strictest jealousy, and often secrecy, by the most intellectual members of the community. In Hawaii we have the opportunity of watching the whole process crystallise into an institution known as the *aha alii* which is described as a kind of heralds' college, and which had as its chief function the preservation of the aristocratic tradition and prerogatives. Side by side with the spurious genealogies, therefore, we have also from Hawaii lines like those of the powerful Kalona families on the island of Oahu, which had been preserved for twelve generations inviolate, and served as a useful check on others less genuine.[1] Such genealogies were sometimes preserved in the Hawaiian islands in poems, often panegyric in character, known as *mele inoa* ('name poems'), to which reference has already been made (p. 262 above). Precautions against the 'stealing' of someone else's *mele inoa* are to be seen in the fact that there were two kinds of such *meles*, one in which an account of one's ancestry could be given out in public, and another which was received by a man from his ancestors and recited only in private in the presence of his peers.[2] A fragment of a *mele inoa* of the latter kind belonging to Kakuhihewa, an ancient king of Oahu, or rather to one of his descendants, is quoted by Malo, and opens with the line:

I am not one to give my name to every challenger.[3]

A fuller version of the poem is given in the Fornander Collection,[4] where it occurs in its proper context in the saga of Lono (cf. p. 262 above), and other examples are to be found in the same saga. These genealogies are looked upon in some measure as sacred, and are recited at religious ceremonies, preceded by *karakias*, or invocations. In the Marquesas mothers teach genealogies to their children as singing games,[5]

---

[1] Fornander, *P.R.* II, p. 26 f.
[2] Malo, p. 263. Gill refers to the anxiety and care with which the secrecy of the Rarotongan and Mangaian royal pedigrees was preserved, *A.A.A.S.* (1890), pp. 627, 635.   [3] *Loc. cit.*
[4] *Fornander Collection*, First Series, vol. IV, p. 282 ff.
[5] Handy, *N.C.M.* pp. 302, 342 ff.

while among the Maori genealogies are sung to children as lullabies, and often include references to old myths, and historical incidents.[1]

(2) The catalogue form is universal throughout our area. This is naturally chiefly to be found in the form of poetry. The subjects enumerated in these poetical catalogues are rarely described fully. There is little or no tendency to enlarge on any given theme. The catalogue, in fact, supplies merely the verbal mnemonic, fuller information being supplied by prose, chiefly in the form of saga. Such catalogues are used to enumerate the names of chiefs and heroes of the Migration Period and later times, and other matters of scientific and educational significance, such as the names of the gods and their attributes. An interesting example of a poetical catalogue of this type has been recorded from the Moriori of the Chatham Islands, in which a list of the gods is invoked in order 'to give effect to the *karakia*', which is traditionally stated to have been recited by the original Polynesian migrants as they voyaged from Hawaiki to the Pacific Islands.[2] Among the commonest forms of classification are geographical catalogues, which are generally chanted as poetry or songs, and most commonly embody the names of islands. Stewart noted in the songs of the Marquesans the names of forty-four islands besides their own.[3] Such geographical lists follow in general a definite order, and are in no way fortuitous, though it is not always easy for a European to recognise the individual islands. De Torres learned from the Micronesians of the Carolines that the route from the island of Ulle in the latter Group to that of Guahon in the Marshall Group was recorded in their songs, and that by following this route, they were able to find their way between these two islands, which are more than three hundred miles apart.[4] One of the *hula* songs of Hawaii, though composed in the form of a lyric, is simply a poetical itinerary, and follows a recognised route.[5]

These poetical catalogues frequently take the form of what claim to be the logs of the islanders when on their migrations to their present homes. Examples have been recorded from Rarotonga,[6] and in one of these, which is incorporated in the saga of the migration from Hawaiki

---

[1] Best, *Maori* II, p. 139; cf. p. 147; Smith, *Hawaiki*, p. 18.

[2] *J.P.S.* v, p. 22 (cf. p. 24).   [3] Stewart, *Visit* I, p. 246; cf. p. 250.

[4] Kotzebue II, p. 240 f.

[5] Emerson, *U.L.* p. 203. Passages such as these offer a close parallel to some of the shorter of the Irish 'itineraries' akin to the *Dinnšenchas* collections referred to in Vol. I, p. 283 ff.

[6] See e.g. Gill, *L.S.I.* p. 27; Smith, *Hawaiki*, p. 94.

in the time of Tamarua-metua, some eighty islands are mentioned by name. A number of chants are recorded from the Marquesas which purport to record the migrations of the Marquesans to their present islands,[1] and similar chants have been recorded from the Paumotu Archipelago.[2] Many of these chants record details of the various islands, such as the names of the rulers, and even mention incidents which have taken place during the supposed residence of the people on their migrations. An ancient chant from Hawaii refers to a number of islands visited by Kaulu-a-kalana, a famous Hawaiian navigator of the early period.[3]

The antiquarian information represented by such chants is not always readily distinguishable from genuine historical tradition, and it has been the fashion among Polynesian scholars to regard these 'logs' and lists as embodying valid records of the early migrations of the islanders. It is to be suspected, however, that at least the catalogues of islands which the Marquesans claim to have touched on their way to their present homes may be traditional trade routes cast in poetical form, and applied by the *tohungas* to their present position in the chants as more or less static geographical itineraries. The form may well have been invented in the first place to embody traditional records of voyages; but its convenience as a mnemonic for geographical teaching must have been recognised at an early date by the *tohungas* responsible for the instruction of the islanders in such matters, and has no doubt been utilised as a literary convention, much as we have found a similar literary convention used by the Anglo-Saxon poet of *Widsith*,[4] or by Kara Chach in the Kara-Kirghiz poem *Joloi*.[5] The fact that the Polynesian chants of this kind were sometimes addressed to the gods, and are recited under religious auspices, is no criterion of their authenticity as records of fact, or even that the form was understood literally, for to a great extent all knowledge was regarded by the islanders as 'sacred'.

(3) Stories which purport to account for the origin of personal and place-names are common. A striking instance of the former occurs in the version of Kupe's visit to New Zealand preserved in the Maori *Whare Wananga*, or native 'course' of learning. Here in the account of the circumnavigation of the islands by Kupe himself and his

---

[1] Handy, *M.L.* p. 84 ff.; Smith, *Hawaiki*, p. 96 ff.
[2] Smith, *Hawaiki*, p. 99.
[3] Fornander, *P.R.* II, p. 13 f.; cf. also Emerson, *L.V.* p. 14.
[4] See Vol. I, p. 25 f.   [5] See p. 142 above.

family, and of their various landings, a large number of names of localities and natural features are enumerated and explained as commemorating their actions and remarks on these occasions.[1] Thus the Cape Te Kawakawa is said to have been so named from the circumstance that one of Kupe's daughters here made a wreath of *kawakawa* leaves. The origin of the name of the eldest son of Kupe's friend Turi, Turanga-i-mua, is stated in the same source[2] to have been given to him by Kupe himself in commemoration of his own pioneer visit to New Zealand—*Turanga-i-mua*, 'Standing at first', i.e. the first to land. The similarity of these and numerous similar speculations to those of the Norse *Landnámabók*[3] is very striking. Instances might be multiplied from other parts of the Pacific.

(4) A large number of stories have been recorded from all parts of the Pacific which embody speculations, both learned and popular, attempting to account for the origin of places and natural features. These speculations are generally of no historical value, and the supernatural element is prominent. Instances are too numerous to mention, but we may refer as an example to the Samoan story of the introduction of the cocoa-nut, and the origin of the name of the village Laloata, which is explained[4] as meaning 'under the shade', from the cocoa-nut tree which grew from the buried head of an eel which figures in the story of Sina (see p. 287 above). Akin to these place-name speculations is the traditional explanation of the name *Rarotonga*, given by a representative of the Tui-tonga, the sacred king of Tonga in former times.[5] This explanation, which differs from that current in Rarotonga, of course, is that the people gave the name *Tonga* to some hill, or mountain under which they lived—a wholly unscientific explanation.

Local legends abound everywhere, and in many cases these undoubtedly record historical fact. We may refer especially to those associated with the Maori or pre-European native forts. Excellent examples of this type of tradition at its best are to be found throughout the works of W. W. Gill, where its relation to solid history is clearly demonstrated. Such local legends are, however, to be sharply differentiated from legends on the origins of place-names. The latter are generally wholly speculative and often puerile in character. Equally childish are the

---

[1] *Mem. P.S.* IV, p. 59 ff.   [2] *Ib.* p. 67.
[3] See Vol. I, p. 287 of the present work.
[4] Turner, p. 242 f. For other instances see *ib.* p. 222 ff.
[5] *J.P.S.* xx, p. 165.

stories of the origin of islands, which abound everywhere, and generally resolve themselves into a statement that such and such an island was fished up from the bottom of the sea by Maui, Vatea,[1] Rangi,[2] or the god Tangaroa during a fishing expedition.[3] It should be noted, however, that what appears to the European as particularly futile in such stories is, in reality, due to our own tendency, and perhaps that of the modern Polynesian also, to interpret literally the ancient traditional figurative diction in which such speculations and traditions are often couched. The significance of these legends is, not a miracle, or supernatural feat, but the simple statement that some early hero or navigator first discovered or led a colony of immigrants to the island in question.

Legends have sprung up in connection with the megalithic and other stone monuments which are found in many of the island Groups. A number of such legends have been recorded relating to the stone pillars which appear to have formed the base of a building in Samoa, known as the *fale o le fe'e*, 'the house of *o le Fe'e*'. Some of these may actually preserve genuine tradition, or at least reasonable speculation. One recorded by Pritchard[4] states that the 'house' (*fale*) was built by the forced labour of a number of subject gods, working in obedience to the tyranny of a greater god called Le Fe'e. Divorced of its figurative diction, in which the *ariki* are referred to as divine, the story is not improbable. The word *Fe'e* means the 'cuttle-fish', and is the name of an important deity of the Samoans, and the stone structure may preserve the remnants of an ancient temple of this or some other divinity, built to the order of the priests of *o le Fe'e*. The innumerable stories accounting for the origin of the *Hamonga*, the famous stone trilithon of Tongatabu, are generally less convincing, and often contradictory. In Hawaii the most interesting legends account for the existence of the stone-built fish-ponds, and of many of the *heihaus*, or 'temples', by the efforts of the *menehune*,[5] the vanished dwarf race to whom we have referred already (p. 328 above). Much legendary lore is also associated with the building of the *maraes* or temple-platforms of Tahiti,[6] and of the Marquesas.[7]

Throughout the Pacific local legend has been active in identifying

---

[1] Gill, *Myths*, p. 48.   [2] Gill, *ib.* p. 14.

[3] See e.g. Mariner[3] I, p. 271f. Contrast Gifford, *T.M.T.* p. 19f.

[4] Pritchard, p. 117ff. For other stories told of the same monument, see *J.P.S.* XXIV, p. 118f.; Churchward, p. 181.

[5] See Fornander, *P.R.* II, p. 6; Thrum, *J.P.S.* XXIX, p. 70f.; Smith, *Hawaiki*, p. 150.   [6] See *J.P.S.* XXII, p. 25f.   [7] Melville, p. 174.

the place whence the spirits departed to Heaven and the abode of the dead. This is generally located on the seashore, or out at sea. In Rarotonga,[1] Mangaia,[2] and Samoa,[3] the point of departure of spirits is generally on the west coast of the islands, but, in New Zealand,[4] usually on the north. The route followed by the spirits is specified with astonishing minuteness, especially in Samoa and Tahiti. In the former it consists of a journey from island to island throughout the entire group, the point of departure being always from the most westerly point. In Tahiti the whole course is clearly visualised,[5] and even the topography of Heaven is minutely set forth.[6] Legend is not always consistent in this respect, and in Mangaian oral poetry the spirits of the dead are sometimes represented as leaving the island from the east coast (cf. p. 370 above). It has often been suggested that the place of the departure of spirits, and the course which they take, correspond with those of the ancient migrations of the race. Space will not permit of a full discussion here,[7] but we do not think that this theory can safely be pressed, in view of the inconsistency of tradition in regard to the spirits' course, and in view of certain known facts regarding some of the migrations of comparatively recent times, e.g. into Mangaia. But there can be no doubt that the spirits' route bears a definite relationship to actual maritime routes, and in the Cook Group it is certain that the dead habitually chose the points near where the best landing was to be found, e.g. near Oneroa in Mangaia, and near Avarua in Rarotonga.

(5) Legends which attempt to account for the invention of useful arts are common, and legends of the introduction of useful vegetables, whether by gods or 'culture heroes', are almost universal. These benefits are very often derived from the Heavens, sometimes from 'Hawaiki', the mythical home of the race. Such legends are generally of a somewhat elementary character, often puerile. Stories of this kind belong, of course, to a popular milieu. More ambitious examples occur, however, especially in Tonga and Samoa. Reference has already been

---

[1] Gill, *Myths*, pp. 154, 159; cf. Andersen, p. 230.   [2] *Ibid.*

[3] Stair, *J.P.S.* v, p. 39; cf. also p. 315 above.

[4] Reeves, p. 65 f.; Dieffenbach II, p. 66.

[5] See e.g. Henry, *A.T.* p. 200 ff.; cf. *ib.* p. 563 f.

[6] This seems to be the case in certain Maori chants also. See Best, *Maori* I, p. 88 f.; II, p. 140.

[7] For a discussion of the theory, and a great wealth of allusion and reference to the 'spirits' route' throughout the Central Pacific, see Williamson, *R.C.B.* Chapters XII–XXII inclusive. See further Handy, *P.R.* p. 69 ff.

made (pp. 292 f., 321 above) to the stories of the human beings who visit the Heavens and, with the help of an old woman, succeed in overcoming the hostility of the gods and in securing *kava*, cocoa-nuts, or yams which they bring down to earth, and introduce among mortals. Numbers of variants of this motif are current, and from other parts of the Pacific similar antiquarian speculations on the introduction of useful foodstuffs are so numerous that it is unnecessary to adduce examples. At times these themes are introduced merely incidentally, at others they form the basis of elaborate stories of entertainment.[1]

Sagas accounting for the origin of institutions are also widespread. Fornander tells us of a number of Hawaiian legends from various periods accounting for the origin of social classes, which are generally stated to have sprung from the sons (variously given as two and three) of a famous Hawaiian ancestor.[2] From the same island Group Malo records an antiquarian speculation on the origin of a religious ceremony, together with a liturgical hymn which accompanies it.[3] Legends occur in most Groups accounting for the origin of the practice of tattooing, and generally deriving it from the *tapu* house of learning in Hawaiki (cf. below, and pp. 294, 297 above). From Tonga we have legends of the origin of the institution of the Tui-tonga, the sacred king of the islands.[4] A tradition from Rarotonga records in narrative form the introduction of cannibalism into the island.[5] The traditions relating to the origin of the *areoi* have already been referred to (p. 318 above). Among the most interesting and significant of such speculations are those which relate to the origin of the *whare wananga*,[6] the 'house of learning', and of the *whare runanga* or 'council chamber' among the Maori.[7]

(6) The Polynesians have practically all preserved traditions of the colonisation of their various island Groups. Many of these stories are connected with stories of the origin of mankind and of the race, and with creation myths. Their value, as will readily be supposed, is very uneven. Here again, however, it is necessary to remind ourselves that the highly figurative diction in which the oral literature of Polynesia is couched is apt to lead us into a too facile dismissal of the stories as

[1] See e.g. Turner, p. 242 f.
[2] Fornander, *P.R.* I, p. 112.
[3] Malo, p. 204 f.
[4] Gifford, *T.M.T.* p. 25 ff.
[5] *J.P.S.* xx, p. 205.
[6] Best, *M.S.L.* p. 8 f.; cf. also *J.P.S.* xxix, pp. 30, 32.
[7] Johnstone, p. 47 ff.

fanciful or mythical, when in fact they are neither intended nor understood as a literal statement of fact by the people themselves. This figurative phraseology is said to be deliberately cultivated by the *tohungas*, who are, of course, chiefly responsible for the transmission of historical traditions. Many of the traditions are sober enough, and may well be historical. We may refer to those which derive the origin of the people of Manihiki from Rarotonga[1] and those deriving early migrations into Tongareva from Aitutaki and Rakahanga,[2] as well as certain traditions of the settlement of the Marquesas.[3] Mangaian tradition is both serious and circumstantial in regard to the early occupation and invasions, despite the mythical origin.[4] The great majority of the traditions trace the migration both of the race and of the occupants of their own islands from the west. Samoa and Tonga[5] are exceptional in deriving the creation of man and the invasion of their islands from a locality eastward of their group. These islands have also preserved an interesting tradition of a time when war was unknown, and when the population was greater and the people lived peaceably together.[6] From the same islands also come traditions relating to a later time, which tell of the invasion of Samoa by the Tongans, and of the warfare between them.[7]

Side by side with these traditions of the migrations of the islanders to their present homes we sometimes find contradictory traditions which declare the first man to have been created actually on the island which they still occupy. In the island of Atiu in the Cook Group the creation of the first man is said to be due to the union of the pigeon of the god Tangaroa with a female shadow in the water,[8] while the creation of the first man and woman of Rarotonga is ascribed to Tiki.[9] In Aitutaki[10] and New Zealand[11] tradition allows an earlier population

[1] Gill, *J.P.S.* XXIV, p. 144ff.; Buck, *E.M.R.* p. 14ff.
[2] Buck, *E.T.* p. 17f.
[3] *J.P.S.* IV, p. 197f.; see also Fornander, *P.R.* I, p. 20.
[4] Gill, *Myths*, p. 16ff.; *S.L.P.*, *D.L.P.* p. 1ff. The Mangaian evidence is summarised by Buck, *M.S.* p. 18ff.   [5] Pritchard, p. 396.
[6] Pritchard, p. 383. The same writer observes that according to priestly tradition in Fiji there was formerly no warfare in these islands, either among themselves, or against strangers who might land there. Cannibalism also was unknown.
[7] Turner, p. 64 f.   [8] Gill, *S.L.P.* p. 188.
[9] Williams, *M.E.* p. 103. Tiki is sometimes regarded as the first man, sometimes as the creator of the first man. See Andersen, p. 413.   [10] Buck, *M.C.C.I.* p. xix.
[11] Traditions relating to the Moriori need not detain us here. See p. 247 above. A concise collection of traditions relating to the supernatural occupants of New Zealand will be found in Cowan, *F.F.T. passim*; cf. also p. 293 ff. above.

than that from which the present people derive their ancestral lines. The Maori in particular have preserved many traditions of the *tangata whenua*, or pre-Maori inhabitants of New Zealand. In addition to such definite recognition of earlier ethnic groups in their midst as this, traditions are also current in various parts of the Pacific of the survival, or at least the existence, of an alien population in the islands. This alien element is often regarded as supernatural, but always of material existence. Reference has already been made (p. 293 ff. above) to the small dwarfish race referred to in the traditions of many islands, notably Hawaii, Tahiti, the Cook Islands, and New Zealand. The most tempting of these traditions are those of Hawaii. The *menehune* of the latter group in particular can hardly be anything else but the remains of a dwarf race.

Traditions or speculations about the original home of the race are also widespread. These are commonly descriptive rather than narrative in character—a fact which is probably due to their currency in an intellectual milieu among the *tohungas*, who are our chief source of information on this subject. The classic example of a picture of this homeland is that of the Maori, among whom it is known as Hawaiki, and by whom traditions of its greatness, its high culture, and its occupants are cherished with a great love, and much learning. From this original homeland, which contained the prototypes of all the fruits and foodstuffs, all the arts and crafts most valued by the Maori, and the great *marae* of the god Rongo,[1] the Polynesians migrated 'to the islands of the great ocean'. A legendary 'first home' like that of the Maori is widely known throughout the Pacific, and may be regarded as one of the most universally accepted beliefs of Polynesian tradition. An example resembling that of the Maori is known also in Hawaii.[2] We may refer also to the Pulotu, the future Paradise of the Samoans, and Bulotu of the Tongans, "at once the paradise whence sprang the race of chiefs, and to which the souls of their departed chiefs and heroes return".[3] It is referred to as the scene of all the pleasures which a Tongan can imagine.[4]

(7) Polynesia offers a richer store of traditional learning and speculation regarding cosmogony and the creation of mankind and the Universe than any other area known to us. These traditions vary, like antiquarian and other learned matters, according to the milieu in which they

[1] S. P. Smith, *Hawaiki*, p. 106.
[2] Fornander, *P.R.* I, p. 78.
[3] Pritchard, p. 401; cf. Mariner[3] II, p. 217.
[4] Pritchard, *loc. cit.*

circulate. In the highest cosmogonic systems we have a process which resembles in many respects the act of Creation by the simple effort of divine will which is found in the Book of Genesis. This type of thought is seen at its best in the cosmogonic chants of the Paumotu Archipelago recently recorded by Stimson;[1] but similar and almost equally lofty systems of thought have been recorded also from New Zealand[2] and the Marquesas.[3] In the Paumotu chants, and the esoteric or 'superior' Maori teaching, the whole of Creation owes its inception to the will of the supreme god Kiho (Io)[4]—the great spirit dwelling in space, without parents, wife, or offspring, He who first separated light from darkness, and then formed the Heavens and the earth, and appointed Tane and others as his vice-regents, his representatives in relation to mankind.

The act of Creation is more usually narrated as a generic process, the whole of the Heavens, the gods, and the material universe being described in terms of human birth.[5] In accordance with this we have a great development of inanimate genealogical material. In the Marquesas the plants, stones, and living things are enumerated in the form of genealogies, each class being derived from Atea (Vatea) by its particular mother.[6] From the same islands we also have a genealogy of twelve moons (months) from the same father (Atea, Vatea) by three different mothers, one of whom is a star.[7] The great development of cosmic genealogies in New Zealand[8] and Samoa[9] recalls those of Hesiod. In the Samoan account the earth is spoken of as the progeny of a union of the high rocks (male) and the earth rocks (female), and such unions are repeated twenty-two times down to the birth of Savea, the first Malietoa, from whom in twenty-three generations is descended Malietoa Talavou, who was proclaimed king in 1878. A chant from Hawaii attributes the creation of each of the Hawaiian islands individually to the union of Wakea (Atea, Vatea) and Papa, 'begetter-of-islands',[10] and from the former fifty-nine generations are traced through mythical heroes, gods, etc. down to Liloa, who is

[1] T.R. p. 75 ff.; Kiho-tumu, passim.
[2] Mem. P.S. III, ch. III; Best, M.M.R. p. 20; Maori I, p. 89; Andersen, p. 353 ff.
[3] Handy, N.C.M. p. 322 ff.   [4] Cf. p. 308 f. above.
[5] The most complete systems of cosmogenesis known to us have been recorded in the Paumotu Archipelago. See Stimson, T.R. p. 75 ff.; Handy, N.C.M. p. 322 ff.
[6] Handy, N.C.M. p. 345.   [7] Ib. p. 346.
[8] An account of these will be found from various sources in Andersen, p. 354 ff.
[9] Turner, p. 4 f.
[10] Malo, pp. 311 ff., 318. See also the references cited in footnote 5 above.

generally regarded as the first king of whom the oral records preserve a considerable amount of fairly historical tradition.

Often it happens, however, that the teaching of the priests takes a popular form, due again partly to the figurative character of their diction, partly to a desire to adapt their more serious esoteric lore to the simpler comprehension of their audience. For example we may refer to a Hawaiian statement of the principle of evolution, according to which when man was first created he had no joints, and his arms and legs were attached to his trunk by a web of skin, till Maui broke the limbs at the joints and released them from their enclosing skin. The narrative goes on to relate that when hunger impelled man to search for food his toes were cut from the solid foot by the brambles, and his fingers by sharp splinters of the bamboo plant.[1] It will be seen that the only really extravagant element in this account is the personal part attributed to Maui. In a chant recorded from the lips of two old Samoan chiefs[2] the separation of land and water, and the evolution of man from a primeval grub or worm are set forth. It is characteristic of such poetry that the account of the primeval flood contains a catalogue of the technical terms by which the various kinds of waves are known to these great seamen.

To a race of born navigators, who spent much of their life on un-charted seas, scientific knowledge of the stars and the various aspects of the Heavens was of the first importance, and records (oral) were kept by the *tohungas* in the traditional accounts of the long voyages of the great explorers, in which the aspect of the starry Heavens at night formed the principal sailing directions by which their successors were able to reach the same spot in after times. We may refer to the oft-quoted sailing directions which are traditionally stated to have been left at Ra'iatea by the great explorer Kupe I, the discoverer of New Zealand, and preserved by the *tohungas* in the Maori school of learning about to be discussed:

"In sailing from Rarotonga to New Zealand, let the course be to the right hand of the setting sun, moon, or Venus, in the summer, in the month of November."[3]

[1] Westervelt, *L.M.* p. 132.

[2] *J.P.S.* VI, p. 19 ff.; cf. also Krämer I, p. 395.

[3] *Mem. P.S.* IV, p. 65; cf. Smith, *Hawaiki*, p. 216. An excellent impression of the hopeless feeling experienced by those without knowledge of the technicalities of navigation when seeking some of the smaller islands of the Pacific will be gained by reading the account of the voyage of John Williams to the island of Rarotonga. See Williams, *M.E.* p. 98 f. A more recent description of a similar personal experience is given by Lenwood, p. 20f.

Even if we doubt the extreme antiquity of the directions asserted by the *tohungas*, their accuracy and relevance to their present place in the saga of Kupe's great voyage are sufficiently remarkable, especially as their antiquity must at least be very considerable (cf. p. 246 above).

Knowledge of the skies is often couched in poetical form, and here again scientific knowledge is often combined with mythological tradition—not necessarily in such a manner as to suggest that the latter is anything more than a poetical ornament. One of the most interesting of these chants is one recorded by Gifford from Tonga, in which the poet attempts to set forth the different strata into which the Heavens above are divided.

"Listen, O poet", the reciter begins, "while I tell of the skies", and he proceeds to enumerate the characteristics of the atmosphere above us at different altitudes:

> Our lands are two—
> The sky and the underworld.
> Third sky and fourth sky,
> Dwell there the covered and the inclouded,
> The different sky, the sky that rains
> And that hides the cloudless sky.
> Fifth sky and sixth sky,
> Dwells there the sun who dies in crimson, etc.[1]

The descriptions of the Heavens and the appearance of the stars are often cast in narrative form which to a European mind appears highly unscientific; but it is merely a literary convention, not to be taken seriously. Thus an old woman of Borabora recited how "Fetua-tea (the Pole-star) was the king, he took to wife the dome of the sky and begat the stars that shine and obscure, the host of twinkling stars, the smallest stars..." and she proceeded to enumerate the stars 'born' later—"the star-fishes, and two trigger-fishes that eat mist and dwell in holes, vacant spots, in the Living Water of Tane (the Milky Way). The handsome shark is there", she added, "in his pool", etc.[2] It would be an injustice to these intelligent islanders to suppose that they really peopled the skies with living fish. They give the names of living things with which they are most familiar to the constellations, as other peoples have always done; and in concluding this section we may perhaps be allowed to quote a passage referring to the treatment of similar material by the natives of the New Hebrides which illustrates well the mixture of scientific and practical knowledge and traditional popular 'lore'.

[1] Gifford, *T.M.T.* p. 18.　　　　　[2] *J.P.S.* xvi, p. 101 f.

"They seemed to have the heavens portioned out into constellations. They had the canoe with its outrigger, the duck and a man near it with his bow drawn and taking aim, the cooking-house tongs, the company of little children all sitting eating, and many other objects. These constellations formed their astronomical clock, and by looking up they could tell you whether it was near morning or midnight. Then they have their traditions as to how these canoes and ducks and children got up to the heavens; I was told by an old man that the stars were the eyes of their forefathers looking down on them; but the minutiae as to their sidereal notions and nomenclature can only be ascertained by a lengthened residence on the island."[1]

Gnomic and didactic literature is rare in Polynesia. Examples are, however, occasionally incorporated in early traditions, and an interesting series of moral injunctions is incorporated in the saga of the hero Tangiia, where they are stated to have been delivered by Tangiia himself to his people when his warfare was over (cf. p. 251 above).

"Let man be sacred; let man-slaying cease; the land must be divided out among the chiefs, from end to end; let the people increase and fill the land.... Any expedition that arrives here in peace, let them land. Any that come with uplifted weapons, strike off their heads with the clubs."[2]

It will be noticed that these injunctions bear some resemblance to a code of laws. The laws of Hawaii are known to have been carried on by oral tradition after having been established by usage, or by royal edict, and to have been proclaimed throughout the country by heralds.[3] According to legends from Oahu, in the same Group, the name of Mailikukahi, an early Oahu king, is associated with the enactment of at least one code of laws,[4] which must, of course, have been promulgated and transmitted orally.

Perhaps the most interesting and important example of an ancient composition embodying didactic and instructive matter is a Maori poem[5] composed in the form of an elaborate address delivered to a newly-born child by his grand-uncle, who is believed to have lived

---

[1] Turner, p. 319 f.   [2] Smith, *Hawaiki*, p. 246.
[3] W. F. Frear, *Early Hawaiian Jurisprudence*, p. 5.
[4] Fornander, *P.R.* II, p. 89. Cf. further p. 700 below.
[5] The poem is published, together with a verse paraphrase by Pope and Davies, in *J.P.S.* XVI (1907), p. 47 ff. It is stated to be contained in a MS., but to be full of obscurities.

three generations after the colonisation of New Zealand. The poem is divided into a number of sections by the recurrent phrase "Hara mai E tama", "Come here, O son", which is evidently intended to rivet the attention of the child. The opening section consists of a scientific account of the prenatal physical development of the child, and then the speaker greets the newly-born with a brief statement of the privileges and responsibilities of man, who must be just, intelligent, and devoted to agriculture—a true Maori touch. The importance of acquired anti-quarian knowledge is stressed, especially the traditional sagas and chants (*wananga*)[1] which it is claimed have been received from the dead, and which are divided into three classes: (1) *wananga* relating to evil, regarded as the lowest form of knowledge; (2) *wananga* relating to good; (3) true wisdom, which seems to be spiritual contemplation or esoteric religious thought of a lofty philosophical type relating to Io (cf. p. 308 above). The myth of Rangi and Papa, and the introduction of strife into the world are next touched on, and an account of *Te Reinga*, the abode of the dead. The rest of the poem bears a close resemblance to the work of Hesiod. The form is that of alternating precepts and gnomes of observation, and instruction is given in right social conduct, mythological matter, agriculture, and other practical observations of the workings of nature.

In this connection we may refer also to the menologia, and native oral calendars, which have been recorded from the Marquesas[2] and from Samoa,[3] as well as from the Moriori of the Chatham Islands.[4] In these calendars the mention of the month or season is generally followed by a brief statement of its salient characteristics, or of the particular useful foodstuffs then in season. Thus in the Marquesas we learn that in July: 'Breadfruit grows large; it is warm; the sea runs high.'[5]

The western and northern Pacific is rich in descriptive poetry, especially descriptions of nature. Both Mariner[6] and Gifford[7] have been impressed by this special feature of Tongan poetry, which, as Mariner observed, is often combined with moral reflections. The *hula* songs of Hawaii, as we have already noted (p. 386), consist very largely of descriptions of nature, though according to Emerson[8] the majority have a metaphorical sense. Poems embodying topographical surveys

---

[1] *Wananga*, 'occult knowledge', i.e. 'the knowledge of hidden mysteries'. ED.
[2] Handy, *N.C.M.* p. 351.
[3] Turner, p. 203f.
[4] *J.P.S.* VII, p. 84f.
[5] Handy, *loc. cit.*
[6] Mariner[3] I, p. 244.
[7] Gifford, *T.P.N.* p. 5.
[8] Emerson, *U.L.* p. 123f.

are also much in vogue in this Group, and into this framework much matter is interwoven descriptive of natural scenery, and the appearance of natural features under every aspect of varying weather conditions. These topographical poems are sometimes expressed in the form of catalogues. Their opening lines suggest that they formed a part of the choral répertoire, and were addressed by the solo singer to one of the two main groups of singers (cf. p. 439 below):

> Listen, you who sing bass,
> While I chant to you about the weather-shore of Tonga;

or

> Listen, you with intelligent minds,
> While I sing of the sea-shore,
> Of our weather-shore that entices,
> Lest someone else should praise it first.

A poem which begins:

> Listen, oh, alto singers,
> I will sing of the islands and see if you know them,

then passes to a catalogue of the islands of Tonga-tabu, many with a brief description attached, or a mythological account of its origin. The conclusion is particularly interesting, as suggesting that the poem may have been recited as part of a poetic contest.[1] And again,

> Listen to me, you,
> These are all the islands.
> If not contested, then sue for pardon—

which latter expression means, as Gifford tells us:[2] "If another poet cannot outdo this composition, then let him sue for pardon."

The *hula* poetry of Hawaii is especially rich in descriptions of nature. These *hula* songs love to dwell, like the poetry and art of Japan, on the country-side, the skies and the sea under various aspects—the wet swamp in mist, the tropical forest in torrential rain. The following is a telling description of a tropical rain-storm, which purports to be recited by Hiiaka, the sister of the Hawaiian goddess Pele (see p. 324 f. above):

> 'Twas in Koolau I met with the rain:
> It comes with lifting and tossing of dust,
> Advancing in columns, dashing along.

---

[1] For fuller details of poetic contests in Polynesia, see p. 462 ff. below.
[2] *T.P.N.* p. 11, note 11.

> The rain, it sighs in the forest;
> The rain, it beats and whelms, like surf;
> It smites, it smites now the land.
> Pasty the earth from the stamping rain;
> Full run the streams, a rushing flood;
> The mountain walls leap with the rain.
> See the water chafing its bounds like a dog,
> A raging dog, gnawing its way to pass out.[1]

Poetry which is concerned with natural descriptions is by no means confined to the northern and western Pacific, however, as the following song from the Paumotus will show:

"This is the land of Niuhi,[2] where blows the gale so strongly that when a canoe sails in the offing it is driven out to sea, and also when sailing homewards it is driven out to sea.

"Would you mark the form of Niuhi, you will see that it is like a roll of *raufara*[3] at the hour when daylight dies, and a great calm fills the broad horizon, a calm broken from time to time by light breathings of wind from the north-east. But I can sing no more; my breath is failing.

"O fair land of Niuhi."[4]

Riddles are much cultivated in the northern and western Groups, and the evidence offers interesting analogies to the riddles of other literatures. The Samoan riddles recorded by Turner[5] are brief and simple in form, and, like most other riddles already considered, they are concerned primarily with natural objects, such as finger- and toe-nails, tongue, nose, banana, surf on the reef, smoke, bark of the paper mulberry, etc. These replies, then, depend on observation and reflection on anatomy or natural objects. None of the riddles are couched in the antithetical form common to Europe, but consist of a simple statement. The language, however, is figurative, and the intellectual exercise consists in interpreting the metaphor correctly. The riddles are, in fact, a series of current *kennings*. The answers consist in the translation of the *kennings* into literal speech. A riddle contest in Samoa, therefore, would consist of a competition in the knowledge and correct use of poetic diction, or the figurative language which is universal in Polynesian poetry. Traces of riddle contests are indeed not rare in

---

[1] Emerson, *U.L.* p. 59.
[2] I.e. Fakahina in the Paumotu Archipelago.
[3] This is explained by the translator as pandanus leaves rolled on a stake.
[4] *J.P.S.* XXVIII, p. 163.   [5] Turner, p. 129.

Polynesian sagas. A contest of this kind takes place in the Rarotongan version of the story of Rata.[1] In a story recorded from Hawaii the hero wins a female chief for his bride by successfully answering a series of riddles.[2]

Before leaving the subject of Polynesian riddles it is perhaps permissible to call attention to two brief notices of Malagasy riddles[3] which have appeared in the *Antananarivo Annual*. The articles in question were written by the editor, Mr James Sibree, in Vols. XIII, XIV, and are entitled 'The Oratory, Songs, Legends and Folk-Tales of the Malagasy'. In these articles Sibree gives a brief abstract of a book published at Antananarivo in the Malagasy language by a Mr Doble, entitled *Malagasy Folk-Lore*, and in a note on the collection the writer of the article discusses the manner in which the riddles are asked:

"In the appendix to the book three specimens of the Conundrum Games are given, the custom being for the proposer to mention first a number of things, from a dozen to thirty, calling upon the rest of the party to guess what they are when he has done. In the first of these a number of insects, birds, and household objects are mentioned by some more or less vague description of them, such as: 'Adornment of the Sovereign? *The people*.' 'Horns (i.e. protection) of the people? *Guns*.' 'Top-knot of the town? *A big house*.' 'Two-thirds of his sense gone before he gets arms and legs? *A tadpole*, when it changes to a frog', etc."

In the second game, all the different parts of an ox are described in an enigmatical way, thus: "God's pavement? *Its teeth*." "Two lakes at the foot of a tree? *Its eyes*." "Continually fighting but not separating? *Its lips*." "Blanket worn day and night and not wearing out? *Its skin*"; etc.

In the third game occur the following: "Fragrance of the forest? *Ginger*." "Fat of the trees? *Honey*." "The lofty place, good refuge from the flood? *Antananarivo*." "The lofty place good for sheltering? *Ambohimanga*."[4]

It will be seen that the general tendency of these riddles is educational. Observation of nature, the catalogue form, and a tendency to classification all suggest that the riddles are composed with a view to imparting instruction. They suggest an oral examination in general

[1] *J.P.S.* XIX, p. 153.   [2] Westervelt, *L.O.H.* p. 75 ff.
[3] It is hardly necessary to remind the reader that the Malagasy are closely related, both by language and by race, to the Polynesians.
[4] *A.A.* No. XIV, p. 175.

useful information, and are calculated to encourage the training of the powers of observation and orderly thinking. They remind us in some respects of the Galla nature riddles, and in their series form recall the Russian riddles, and the Norse riddles of Gestumblindi. Here, however, as in the Samoan riddles, there is an absence of references to the elements and the sky and heavenly bodies, which is surprising in a people who, like the Polynesians, must formerly have been great navigators. It would be interesting to know from what class of the population they were collected.

In concluding this chapter we would once more call attention to the close similarity which exists between Polynesian literature and the literature of early Japan. The antiquarian traditions and speculations of which we have given a brief account in the preceding pages are in general very much like the antiquarian elements which abound in the pages of the *Kojiki* and the *Nihongi*.[1] This is especially marked in regard to Cosmogony. In both systems the act of creation is chiefly narrated with reference to gods, and to islands and natural features, for all of which elaborate pedigrees are furnished—in the latter case often inanimate. In both systems the catalogue is a favourite device. We notice in both systems a marked absence of interest in the animal and vegetable kingdoms, and a preoccupation with the elements.

The affinities between the Polynesian descriptive and kindred poetry, briefly referred to in the latter part of this chapter, and early Japanese poetry and art are equally striking. This is especially marked in the lyrical poetry of Tonga and Samoa and the *hula* poetry of Hawaii, on the one hand, and the brief Japanese poems known as *uta*[2] on the other. In both the poet's preoccupation is with land- and sea-scape as these appear under every aspect of changing light and atmosphere—morning mist, baffling wind, driving rain, evening calm. In both the poet is minutely aware of the effect of atmosphere and weather on the trees and flowers around him. In both, as in the art of the T'ang artists of China, the animal kingdom is of interest chiefly as a feature of the landscape—a marked contrast[3] to the attitude of the Sung artists of China. In both Japanese and Polynesian poetry the personal element

[1] For these chronicles, see p. 217, footnote above; and see also the List of Abbreviations to Part I.

[2] The Japanese poems in question can best be studied by English readers in the translations of Waley and Dickins (see List of Abbreviations at the close of the present Part) and in the translations of the early chronicles (see above).

[3] There are, of course, many exceptions, e.g. the *uta* of the frogs, Waley, p. 75, and of the deer, *ib.* p. 77.

stands in a humbler and more proportionate relationship to the world of nature than is usual in Western poetry. This is not the place in which to enlarge on the points of similarity between the two literatures, but there can be no doubt that a fuller comparison of the mythology, the antiquarianism, and the literature and art of the two peoples—the early Japanese and the modern Polynesians—would bring out clearly the essential unity of many aspects of their culture.

CHAPTER VIII

RECITATION AND COMPOSITION

OUR information relating to saga-telling in the Pacific is not very extensive, considering the wealth of saga texts. The most important of the historical and antiquarian sagas were recorded from the recitation of the *tohungas*, who were undoubtedly the chief specialists in this class of literature. It was from the last high priest of Rarotonga that some of the most interesting of the Rarotongan records have been obtained, and we shall see in the institutions to be referred to at the close of the present chapter the important part which the *tohungas* played elsewhere also in preserving the native records everywhere. But saga-telling was by no means confined to the priesthood. It was a very general accomplishment among men and women of all ranks, and in Hawaii seems to have been something of a profession in itself.[1] The prominence of saga-telling in the intellectual life of the Cook Islanders will have been observed from what has been said already, and a glance through the pages of W. W. Gill's books, almost anywhere at random, will serve to show the great wealth of saga in the répertoire of the people of this Group as a whole.

Among the Maori also saga-telling was a favourite form of intellectual entertainment, particularly among the women. Graham refers to the sagas which he heard in particular from an old lady, a certain 'old Mereri', who, he tells us, was well versed in ancient lore.[2] Not infrequently the wife of a chief enjoyed a reputation as a saga-teller. Among the Rotumans was an old lady, the wife of a chief, who entertained the Rev. C. F. Wood for whole evenings together, and would have gone on all night, relating the 'old stock stories of the islands'.[3] Cowan gives a number of vivid accounts of Maori saga-tellers, and of the circumstances in which they recited their stories to him—very often, like Gill's stories from Mangaia, suggested by some historical spot or natural feature rich in ancient historical and antiquarian associations.[4] Parallels might be multiplied from the narratives of most European sojourners in the South Seas.[5]

The best of the Polynesian saga-tellers—those who have retained

---

[1] See p. 234 above, and the references there cited.
[2] *J.P.S.* XXVIII, p. 107; cf. also *ib.* XVII, p. 224.   [3] Wood, p. 29.
[4] Cowan, *F.F.T. passim.*   [5] See e.g. Pritchard, p. 125.

the traditional manner of recital—do not speak their stories, as we do, but chant them in a kind of droning recitative. This is often spoken of as chanting or 'intoning' the stories; but again it differed totally from their manner of actually singing, even from the native style of singing. The latter was reserved for lyrical poetry, pure and simple; but this again differed from the European style of singing, which in the native mind is associated exclusively with Christianity, or was until recently.[1] Churchill tells us that in Samoa the reciter droned a large part of the poetry of his stories on a low note, then passed suddenly to a higher pitch, and chanted a short passage, after which the listeners broke out into a lyric chorus, and then the reciter returned to the droning recitative.[2] We have seen that many sagas contain much poetry, and that in some cases the poetry almost predominates over the prose, which is hardly more than a liaison between the songs. Smith has called attention to this form of saga as characteristic of eastern Polynesia; but it is found also among the Maori and the Moriori. It is probable that in earlier times the form of rhythmical, accentual, chanted prose was much more widespread than in modern times, and extended beyond our area to the Sea Dyaks of Borneo and elsewhere.

The composition of extempore poetry was widespread among all classes throughout the Pacific, and such poetry was always chanted. The early voyagers refer constantly to this feature in the poetry of the islanders, and also to the topical nature of many of their songs. J. R. Forster noted of the poetry of Tahiti that many of their songs had relation to persons on board his ship, or to transactions which took place during his stay. At the same time he emphasises the traditional character of the diction used in such poetry, which he says is different from that used in ordinary conversation. He also observes that the rhythm of the poetry—or, as he expresses it, the regular division into feet—is reflected in the manner in which the verses are sung.[3] Moerenhout also stresses the love of the people of Tahiti for poetry, and emphasises the elaboration of their diction and their proficiency in extempore composition; but he adds that their skill was incomparably greater in the past.[4] It has already been pointed out (p. 270 above) that this traditional and highly elaborate and figurative character of the diction is also a characteristic feature of Maori poetry.

Poems are very often attributed to men and women of the rank of

---

[1] Gill, *S.L.P.* p. 35.
[3] J. R. Forster, p. 468 f.
[2] Churchill, p. 70.
[4] Moerenhout I, p. 412.

chiefs, and even, in those islands which had developed a monarchy, to members of the royal family. An extempore poem has been quoted above which was chanted by Romatane, the ruler of the island of Atiu, on the arrival of Captain Cook's ship.[1] Poems recorded in the works of Emerson and Malo show that several members of the royal family of Hawaii were credited with the composition of poetry. Emerson quotes a poem said to have been composed by Kamehameha II himself,[2] and another which is said to have been the product of Prince William Lunalilo, afterwards king of the Hawaiian islands.[3] This was addressed to the Princess Victoria Kamamahu, whom he sought in marriage. We may refer also to the Hawaiian love song which is attributed to Kalola, a widow of Kamehameha I, at a time when she was an old woman.[4] In Mangaia we have seen that a large number of the dramatic compositions are attributed to the temporal rulers, while other poems are attributed to the 'priest-king' Mautara, and others of his family.

The composers are frequently women. In Hawaii, to judge from the répertoire of the *hula* dancers, and the evidence of the sagas of the Pele Cycle, the composition of poetry by women was especially common in the past. As an example we may refer to a little *mele* or poem of the *Hula Pua'a*, the *hula* which is concerned with Kama-pua'a (see p. 386 above). The poem in question is said to have been the joint production of two women, themselves the daughters of a famous bard;[5] but examples are really too numerous to instance. One of the most striking productions from Mangaia is the poem already referred to (p. 268 above) which is said to have been composed by a woman as she prepared the oven in which her cannibal husband was about to roast her. The poem is full of wistful regret for the happier days of the past which they had spent together, and it was preserved by the sister of the woman.[6] Among the Maori the composition of poetry was especially common among women, and in Samoa the songs of the *siva* (cf. p. 384 above) are said to have been frequently composed by women.[7]

Apart from the literature of learning and of social and religious ritual, which is mainly the prerogative of the *tohungas*, our information is fullest for the composition and recitation of poetry embodying an

[1] Gill, *Jottings*, p. 45; cf. p. 269 above.   [2] Emerson, *U.L.* p. 69.
[3] *Ib.* p. 109.   [4] *Ib.* p. 118.
[5] *Ib.* p. 228.
[6] It has already been mentioned (pp. 256, 268 above) that such atrocities were not a native 'custom', but due to exceptional famine conditions.
[7] Williams, *M.E.* p. 535.

address or celebration. Gill tells us that at Mangaian weddings the bride-groom's relatives accompanied him in his progress to the bride's home, chanting songs in his praise, or reciting the deeds of his ancestors, and songs were also chanted in praise of the bride's beauty and accomplishments.[1] Among the Maori, as one would expect, songs were sung by the women in praise of warriors returning from battle.[2] Among the Maori[3] also, as among the Polynesians generally, when people met after long absence, they chanted a *tangi*, a formal address of solemn character, and Dieffenbach tells us that when Mr Barrett returned to his old Maori friends in the neighbourhood of Mount Egmont, they welcomed him with tears, and "in a singing strain of lamentation they related their misfortunes and the continual inroads of the Waikato".[4] A similar instance of the chanting of a song (*tangi*) after long absence has been mentioned above (p. 269). Lamont gives many instances of the practice in the island of Tongareva,[5] where such *tangis* were cere-monially performed by large numbers of people.

The importance attached to rank in Hawaii, and the formality which required a new arrival to announce his pedigree and claim to nobility, have done much to foster an interesting class of poetry known as the *mele inoa* (cf. p. 262 above). In the early saga of Lono-i-ka-makahiki we have an opportunity of observing circumstances in which the *mele inoa* was recited. In this story Lono is represented as a jealous rival of a certain Kakuhihewa in a literary and intellectual contest known as *hoopapa*[6] (cf. p. 415 below). He accordingly begs a female chief from Kauai, one of the Hawaiian islands, to teach him the *mele inoa* which has just been composed in her honour, and which is therefore quite new—"not yet known in the country districts, and only chanted in the royal court up to the time of her departure". With this chant he is sure of silencing his opponent. Actually it happens that Kakuhihewa also 'borrows' the chant from the lady just as she is stepping into her canoe; and by making each of the crew commit one line to memory he is able to piece the poem together and get it by heart on his return to the

---

[1] Gill, *L.S.I.* p. 59.
[2] Johnstone, p. 49.
[3] An excellent account of the custom of the *tangi* of New Zealand, and the *pehu* of Tongareva which closely resembles it, and an intimate analysis of the emotions which inspire them are given by Prof. Buck, *E.T.* p. 75 f.
[4] Dieffenbach I, p. 138.
[5] Lamont, *passim*; Buck, *E.T.* p. 71 ff.
[6] *Hoopaapaa*, or *hoopapa*, means 'to dispute; wrangle; contend stubbornly; debate; to have a mental contest of language and wit' (Thrum, *Fornander Collection*, First Series, vol. IV, p. 266, footnote).

house. Naturally Kakuhihewa, sure of having acquired the very latest current poetical composition, is not a little surprised to find in the singing contest which follows between himself and Lono that the latter has already learnt the chant. The comment of his friends is equally interesting as showing the native method of publication. "We lived with him in Hawaii, but he had no chant of this kind. It is possible, however, that a canoe has gone to Hawaii without touching here, and the chant was carried to Hawaii in that way."[1]

Singing contests, such as the one to which we have just referred, have done much to foster the cultivation of poetry in the Pacific. Where no written texts exist, and where extempore composition is widely practised, such contests help to keep effort ever fresh, and the standard high. This is aptly illustrated by the account of two Maori poets, named Makere and Tu-raukauwa, who are said to have been in the habit of carrying on a poetic war, each trying to outdo the other in their efforts.[2] It is unnecessary to point out the stimulating effect of such an amicable permanent arrangement, by which both parties must have gained much intellectually. No one would lightly undertake to compete without at least a reasonable chance of success, for failure meant disgrace, perhaps in some cases even a heavier penalty (cf. p. 462 below), and in general a careful preparation and poetical education preceded any contest. Thus in the case of Lono we are told that when he proposed to take up the rôle of *hoopapa* (cf. above), he "was educated into the different things of the profession, pertaining to that part relating to language, and...after he had mastered it he became famous all over the islands".[3] It is interesting to find that here, as among the Tatar and the Sanskrit sages, and those of ancient Ireland, poetic diction is held in the highest importance, and is cultivated in an artificial and stereotyped form. Here also poetic contests are largely occupied with learned and 'scientific' material, as we have seen from the opening lines of one of the Tongan poems in which the names of a number of islands are enumerated in catalogue form (cf. p. 406 above and cf. further p. 462 below).

The composition of poetry is often attributed to the gods. One of the *hula* poems recorded by Emerson is said to have been taught to Hiiaka by her friend and *hula*-teacher Hopoe.[4] We are told that one of the old *karakias* used in the building of the ancient vessel *Uruao* has

---

[1] *Fornander Collection*, First Series, vol. IV, p. 274ff. [2] *J.P.S.* XVII, p. 171.
[3] *Fornander Collection*, First Series, vol. IV, p. 266.
[4] Emerson, *U.L.* p. 63f.

been preserved and has formed the type for similar ones in after-days down to late years. This *karakia* is supposed to have been recited by Tupai, the younger brother of Tane-nui-a-rangi, both gods, and off-spring of the sky-father and earth-mother.[1] Other examples have already been mentioned in the preceding pages.

The period of highest artistic activity in the east and north Pacific seems to have been the eighteenth and early nineteenth centuries—a period which coincided with the coming of the Europeans, or just preceded it. The eighteenth century would seem to have been the time when political development had reached its highest point in the forma-tion of an absolute monarchy in Mangaia under the great priest-king Mautara, and it was under the rule of his tribe that the poetic faculty of the Group was most highly cultivated.[2] In Hawaii under the great conqueror Kamehameha I, and in Tahiti under Pomare I poetry seems also to have reached its highest development, though in the latter Group we are not able to speak with the same knowledge of the earlier styles of composition. This period seems to have been the time when court patronage encouraged poetical specialisation, and gave us the names of some famous poets. It is the period too to which are attri-buted the best dramatic and lyrical productions of the *areoi*, and the *hula*[3]—groups of dramatic performers whom we are about to study—and the closely analogous compositions of the Marquesas and of Mangaia.

The Marquesas in particular offer a rich storehouse for the investi-gator of the oral poetry of the Pacific, and the customs connected with recitation and composition. The works of Handy are invaluable for the amount of native tradition which they record relating to the custom of the *tabu* in connection with the composition of poetry to be recited at what we may call the various types of musical festivals of the islands; the different classes of poetry proper to old people, such as the *uta*, and to young people, such as the *rari*; the occasions for which such singing festivals were given, some of which we have already mentioned; the manner of their private rehearsals and public performances.[4] Handy[5] and earlier writers, such as Clavel[6] and Porter,[7] also give us detailed descriptions of the astonishingly elaborate Marquesan funeral cere-monies, and the poetical and mimetic celebrations of the dead. Owing to lack of space we must content ourselves here with directing the reader

---

[1] *J.P.S.* XXII, p. 18. [2] Gill, *Myths*, p. 87.
[3] See Emerson, *U.L.* p. 73; cf. p. 82.
[4] See e.g. Handy, *N.C.M.* p. 331 ff. See also the writings of Stewart.
[5] *Loc. cit.* [6] Clavel, p. 43. [7] Porter II, p. 47.

to these authors and pass on to give a brief note on the manner of chanting the ritual and dramatic poems.

The manner of the performance of these dramatic songs differed considerably in different regions; but they were generally accompanied by dances, and they seem generally, though by no means invariably, to have taken place at night. We have seen that one of the most important types of lyrical drama in Mangaia is the so-called 'death-talk' (*te kakai*), which is performed as part of the funeral celebrations of departed chiefs and distinguished persons, and is held at night in a large house built specially for the purpose, and well-lighted with torches. The *tangi*, or keen proper, followed by the *tiau* or *pe'e*, which may be described as elegies, were chanted alternately in solo, and in chorus by the relatives of the deceased. A near relative of the deceased had to start the first solo of the *tangi*, and each adult male relative must chant a song, and if unable to compose one himself, he must pay someone to compose one for him. The warrior chief and poet Koroa composed ten different songs for different people for a single *kakai*.

In the *tiau* which usually followed the *tangi*, however, the chief mourner was the solo, chanting in a soft and plaintive voice. In the intervals of his chanting the chorus took up the strain while the solo wept loudly. The performance was accompanied by a great wooden drum[1] and the harmonicon. Sometimes a smaller drum[2] was also used, but the musical instruments are said to have been used *between* the songs, thus accompanying, not the songs, but the dances, though in the *tiau* and the *pe'e* the big drum accompanied the grand chorus. The most touching of the songs were long remembered, and sometimes used again on subsequent occasions, being termed *e veru*, 'second-hand'.[3] Several months were required for the preparation of a *kakai*, to allow time for the songs to be composed, special dresses to be provided, food to be stored in readiness for the large assembly, and the complexions of the performers to be prepared.[4] The poetical compositions recited on such occasions, and the *eva*, or memorial celebrations, have already been described.

In addition to the *kakai* and the *eva*, we have also discussed the poetical compositions proper to a different kind of performance known as the *kapa*, a combined entertainment of dance, song, and mimetic

[1] For the big drum, see pp. 330, 380, footnote 9 above.
[2] Usually associated with Tautiti, Miru's son, and also with a dance of the same name.　　　[3] Gill, *Myths*, p. 269 f.　　　　[4] *Ib.* p. 271.

action held in honour of one or more of the gods. The performers in this case were[1] no less than the entire body of worshippers of the god in whose honour the *kapa* was held. The *kapa* was thus something in the nature of a religious festival, and was accompanied by a grand feast. A brief description of this performance has already been given (p. 372 ff. above). It was held in long booths, or under a canopy of green leaves, and the dancing floor was spread with banana leaves.[2] These performances always took place at night. Both men and women took part in the dance and song, but not together. While one sex danced, the other held the torches. At a *kapa* given by a chief named Poito in honour of the shark god Tiaoi and Tane jointly, all the worshippers of these two gods took part, numbering nearly two hundred men, while the entire remaining population were present as torch-bearers and spectators.

Twenty songs were required for one *kapa*, or fête, and these were usually encored. Six artists were usually engaged to compose the songs and arrange the performance, which began at sunset, and continued till midnight, when refreshments were taken, after which the performance began again, and continued till the appearance of the day-star. This was the signal for the close. The last song[3] and the last dance were gone through, and the performance was over. The words of these day-songs were slowly chanted in a monotonous voice, sometimes by the master of ceremonies, who stood on an elevated platform;[4] sometimes by all the performers. Each fête had its own distinctive symbolic actions and properties. In 'Captain Cook's Visit' 'caulking' the seams of a canoe is represented. In the Prologue to the fête to Potiki the men carried bundles of bamboos for fishing-rods, while the cloth-beating mallet of the women could be heard, all these employments being symbolic of peace.[5] The dance, like those of the *areoi*, was something of a fertility rite.[6] A year was required for the preparation of one of these festivals, for again the songs had to be composed and rehearsed, the food to be grown and prepared, and the performers had to prepare themselves by

---

[1] For the ubiquity of dramatic dances throughout the islands of the Cook Group, see p. 377 above. Festivals which depict 'heathen' scenes are, however, dying out; but though we have referred to these latter in the past tense, we understand that even yet they are not wholly extinct.

[2] It was said that the 'fairies' sometimes took part in the dances, provided that one end of the floor was strewn with fresh-cut banana leaves. Gill, *Myths*, p. 257.

[3] For examples of these dawn songs, see Gill, *Myths*, pp. 50, 186.

[4] Cf. the leader of the *areoi* performances, p. 428 below.

[5] Gill, *Myths*, p. 258, footnote.

[6] See Gill, *S.L.P.* p. 181, footnote.

blanching their complexions in the shade, and fattening themselves as much as possible.[1]

Gill gives us some further interesting notes with regard to this fattening process. Speaking of a heroine of an incident[2] which occurred by his computation about A.D. 1500,[3] he tells us that as she was considered a great beauty, and her parents were very proud of her, they compelled her to live entirely inside a house *specially erected for the purpose*[4] (*noo are pana*) "in order to blanch her complexion and fatten her against the day when a certain grand dance should come off". The parents' object, we are told, was an eligible marriage with some young chief. Gill then adds a note to the effect that the great requisites of a Polynesian beauty are to be fat and fair, and to ensure this, the favourite children, whether boys or girls, were regularly fattened and imprisoned till nightfall. He adds that songs were made in honour of the fair one on occasion of her début.[5] We shall see that similar customs prevailed in the Marquesas and in Easter Island. In the Mangaian story of Ngaru referred to above (pp. 278, 378), the hero is at great pains to blanch his skin artificially, in order to render himself more pleasing to his wife.[6] At a later stage in the same story, after leaving Miru's abode, he goes to a land known as Tamuareva, where fruits and flowers grow profusely, and the inhabitants excel in flute-playing, and here he marries a girl "kept by her parents inside a house in order to whiten her skin".[7] In a story of *Hine-rangi* recorded by Cowan, the fairy wife of the hero Miru is described as secluded during her girlhood in a precisely similar manner by her parents (cf. p. 435 below). We shall see in the following pages that this period of special preparation, and the features which accompany it, are found widespread elsewhere among this people in association with the dramatic dances, and especially among the *areoi* of Tahiti.

Performances resembling those of Mangaia were known also in other Groups, notably in Tahiti, where they were known as *heiva* (Mangaian *eva*).[8] Cook witnessed such a *heiva*, in which the principal parts were played by three royal ladies.[9] Ellis describes one type of performance which seems to correspond to the Mangaian *kapa*, in which men and women danced separately, while 'songs and ballads' were sung

---

[1] Gill, *S.L.P.* p. 180f.   [2] *S.L.P.* p. 7ff.   [3] *Ib.* p. 4.
[4] The italics are ours; cf. p. 421 below.
[5] *S.L.P.* p. 10f.; *S.P.N.G.* p. 13.
[6] Gill, *Myths*, p. 227.   [7] *Ib.* p. 232f.
[8] Ellis[1] I, p. 298f.; *L.M.S. Trans.* I, pp. 231, 258.   [9] Cook[2], II, p. 48.

to the accompaniment of drum and flute. There were also other dances in which the numbers engaged were smaller. They were sometimes held in the open air, but more often in a spacious house erected for public entertainments. The *patau* or leader sat by the drum and regulated the performances. The gods were supposed to preside over their dances. Ellis mentions athletic exercises as taking place during the day, which doubtless correspond to the Mangaian *eva*, while the dances ensued in the evening, and were continued till dawn, like the Mangaian *kapa*. The dress of the women is worth noting, and consisted of a fillet of human hair on the heads, shells or network and feathers on the breasts and a skirt of white with a scarlet border. It will be seen that this costume bears a striking resemblance to that worn by the departing spirits in the 'Dirge for Vera' (p. 371 above). Their movements were slow, as became the elaborate character of their costume, and their dances were led by the music of drum and flute.[1] Two plates published in Cook's *Voyages*[2] give some interesting additional details of the dress of the women, most striking of which are two projections from the shoulders, resembling wings. Feathers were also worn on the forefingers, and feather pompoms were worn on the breasts, while feather tassels hung from the waist. It is clear that both in Tahiti and the Marquesas the women's dress represented birds.[3]

The London Missionaries mention that the *heiva* is sometimes 'theatrical'. Moreover, we also hear of performances which seem to resemble the ghost-fighting of Mangaia, but, unlike the latter, they took place some weeks after a person's death. The men and boys were naked save for a girdle, and for the red and white clay and charcoal which were laid on their heads and bodies partially, and in stripes,[4] resembling the *mauri*, or 'ghosts' of Mangaia, and recalling the grey clay with which Huku and the other actors are smeared to resemble the dead in Tongareva (p. 382 above). "These men and boys were armed with a club or cudgel, and proceeded through the district, seizing and beating every person they met with out of doors...and were supposed to be inspired by the spirit of the deceased."[5] Again, we hear of the curious dress of network with shells and feathers attached, which was worn by the leader.[6] Clearly, therefore, some connection must have existed, at

[1] Ellis[1], *loc. cit.*; cf. Cook[2] II, p. 48.
[2] Cook[2] II, Plates 28, 29. These plates are reproduced by Handy, *H.C.S.I.* Plate IV.   [3] Handy, *op. cit.* p. 60.
[4] *L.M.S. Trans.*, *loc. cit.*; see also *ib.* p. 56.   [5] Ellis[1] I, p. 533f.
[6] According to Gill (*Myths*, p. 201, footnote), network was held in Mangaia to

least in idea, between the ghost-fighters and the *kapa* dancers, as well as the *areoi*. All seem to have worn a spirit dress.

There are distinct traces on Easter Island of ceremonies similar to those which we have been discussing. A dance known as a *kaunga* is said to have been performed 'in honour of a mother' on paved strips,[1] also known as *kaunga*, over 200 feet long, by 2 feet wide, along which the dancers proceeded in single file, holding dancing paddles in both hands. Near each *kaunga* there was a small house where the dancers prepared themselves in seclusion 'to get their complexions good'—a touch which shows, as Mrs Routledge points out, that a white skin was admired. The islanders emphasise the fact that the dancers were 'fine men, fine women'[2] (cf. p. 419 above). In addition to the *kaunga*, there was also a *koro*, or festival held in honour of a father, living or dead.[3] The *koro* was held in a temporary thatched house set up on poles, said to have been some hundreds of feet in length, and 20 feet high.[4] These feasts were attended by large numbers. "The old people sang, the young people danced, and the host, who lived in a little house near, came and looked on."[5] It is said that these feasts were held in certain months only, "determined by the appearance of the heavens after nightfall."[6]

In addition we may mention also two customs of Easter Island which are distinctly reminiscent of the ghost-fighting of Tahiti and Mangaia. The first relates to some half-dozen youths who are called *toa-toa*, who lived in a cave, and who were in the habit of going about after dark with their faces painted red, white and black, claiming that they were 'gods',[7] and visiting houses and demanding food, which the inhabitants

be part of the clothing of departed spirits. Thus in the *tiau* for Puvai (c. 1795), the spirit of Puvai is said to be 'clothed in ghostly network'. See also pp. 315, 382 above. Similarly the human sacrifices offered to Rongo (spoken of as 'fish') were wrapped in network when placed on the altar, and the network was used for removing the body from the altar, and subsequently wrapped round the stone image of the god himself on the seashore; Gill, *Myths*, pp. 296, 305. The term frequently applied to human victims was *ikakaa*, 'fish caught in the net of Rongo'.

[1] We may compare the long houses in which the *areoi* are said to have performed (pp. 426, 433 below), and the Marquesan structures (p. 433 below).

[2] Routledge, p. 234.

[3] It is noteworthy that the name is the same as that of the son of Tinirau and Hina in Mangaia and elsewhere. Tinirau and Koro are closely associated together in some kind of exclusively male dance (cf. p. 288 above).

[4] We may compare the 'booths' and the 'dancing floor' under a canopy of green leaves where the Mangaian *kapas* were performed (p. 418 above).

[5] *Loc. cit.*   [6] Routledge, p. 235.

[7] The native word is doubtless *atua*, which is used of any supernatural or spiritual beings, including the gods, and also the spirits of the dead.

accordingly gave them.[1] Again in times of drought the head of the Miru clan sent his younger son and other of his clansmen to a hill-top to pray to the god Hiro[2] for rain. They were painted on one side red, on the other black, with a stripe down the centre.[3] There can be no doubt that in both cases the youths were coloured to resemble the spirits of the dead.[4] It is of interest to note that the men of the *areoi* society of Tahiti also coloured their bodies red and black when acting. The close connection between both the 'ghosts' and the dances of Mangaia, Tahiti, and Easter Island, is clear from the manner of performance, the period and technique of preparation, and the costumes worn. It is possible that the cave residence of the *toa-toa* is reminiscent of cave burial of the dead, such as was widely practised in Mangaia.

Tonga and Samoa also had dramatic or mimetic dances similar in many respects to those which we have been discussing. These are known by a variety of names. In Tonga the *hea*, a mimetic seated dance, is practised only by chiefs and people of rank;[5] the *oola* or night dance consists of two parts, the *hiva*, or recitative without dancing, and the *langi* which follows it, and is accompanied by dancing. From details supplied by Mariner it would seem that these dances resemble those which we have already found elsewhere, especially in Mangaia, both in the manner of performance, and in the character of the songs. Here also, during the period of preparation which preceded the dance, those who were skilled poets retired to a sequestered part of the island and composed a number of songs for the occasion. One poet, we are told, was very expert in the composition of humorous pieces; another, who seems to have been in the service of one of the minor Tongan divinities, was famous for a higher order of composition. He is also spoken of as the 'principal instructor' of one of the bodies of singers.[6]

Reference has already been made to the Samoan *siva*[7] (p. 381 above), which consists[8] of dramatic dance and action song. This was followed by a dance known as the *taulunga* performed by the *taupou*, who is leader of the dancers, with the help of a few girls. The *taulunga* is more

---

[1] Routledge, p. 224.
[2] For Hiro (Iro, Whiro), see p. 310 ff. above.   [3] Routledge, p. 242.
[4] Cf. also p. 420 above, and p. 427 below.
[5] Mariner[3] II, p. 214.   [6] *Ib.* p. 219.
[7] For a general account of the *siva*, see pp. 381, 384 above and the references there cited. See especially Churchill, p. 71 f.; Pritchard, p. 78 f.; Wilkes II, p. 133.
[8] It is permissible to use the present tense of the *siva*, since the institution is still flourishing in Samoa, though chiefly, it seems, as an exhibition given for the benefit of foreigners.

dramatic in character than the *siva*, which precedes it, and is often burlesque, as we have seen. These dances are usually performed in the *fale-tele* or public hall of entertainment in the village. The *taupou* is a maiden of great importance. She is the village belle, and generally the daughter of a chief, or selected for her high birth and good looks. She acts as hostess of the village, and it is her function to see to the entertainment of visitors. In the old days she was jealously guarded by an old woman, and the loss of her virtue was punishable by death. In modern times she is still guarded with great care, and kept apart from young men except in public, and is eventually destined to make an important political marriage.[1] Her position seems to correspond, therefore, to that of the *puhi* of New Zealand, and to the maidens brought up in seclusion in Mangaia mentioned by Gill, and referred to above (p. 419). Such maidens seem everywhere to have been closely associated with religious dances, which were apparently in some measure given in their honour, and of which they were in some degree the leaders, at least of the women. The evidence as a whole rather suggests that youths similarly chosen for their birth and beauty, and similarly privileged, formed the leaders of the men in such dances, though we have not seen this anywhere definitely stated.

Among the most interesting accounts of recitation in the Pacific are those which relate to the *areoi*, a society centred in the Tahiti Group, having its headquarters in the island of Ra'iatea. Among our chief authorities, many of whom were themselves acquainted with leading *areoi*, are Moerenhout, de Bovis, Tyerman and Bennet, Ellis, and Miss Teuira Henry.[2] Of these Moerenhout gives us in many respects the fullest and most unbiased information. Much valuable information is also afforded by others, especially from the early missionaries. Many of the facts recorded of the *areoi* could not fail to give great offence to the sense of propriety of the early recorders and investigators; for some of the *areoi* institutions violated the canons of civilised society, as the term is generally understood. Moreover, some of our most important records, such as those of Tyerman and Bennet, and of Ellis, were derived from information largely supplied by converted *areoi*, who would naturally place the society in an unfavourable light when discussing it with the

[1] We are indebted for some very interesting notes on the Samoan *taupou* to the Rev. A. Hough of the L.M.S., formerly in Samoa. See further S. P. Smith, *J.P.S.* XXIX (supplement), p. 4, where an excellent photograph is also given. Churchill, *loc. cit.* [2] For the works of these authors, see List of Abbreviations below.

missionaries; and this is seen not only in their manner of expression of the facts which they relate, but still more in their omission of anything which might place the *areoi* in a favourable light. More recent investigators, while suspecting that the 'licentiousness' and 'vicious practices' of the *areoi* may have been exaggerated, or at least confined to the lower classes, nevertheless still regard them as 'vagabonds', 'strolling comedians', 'popular entertainers'. Sir J. G. Frazer calls them 'a licentious fraternity of strolling players and mountebanks'.[1] It is not improbable that the word *areoi* is itself a native nickname, its cognates being found in various Polynesian dialects with the sense of 'to loiter', 'idle' (Maori); 'lust', 'lewdness' (Mangarevan); 'immodest', 'indecent' (Tuamotuan).[2]

There can be no doubt, however, that the *areoi* formed one of the most important artistic corporations in the Pacific. It will, unfortunately, only be possible in a work like the present to give a brief notice of the society. We wish to emphasise, however, the prominence of their artistic and intellectual activities, and the high prestige accorded to them by the islanders themselves. Our information may be taken in general as coming from Moerenhout or Ellis unless it is otherwise stated. Much of the information regarding the *areoi* is given by more than one author, and in such cases we have not in general multiplied references in the footnotes.

References to the *areoi* suggest that they were to be found everywhere throughout the Tahiti Group. Their organisation was extremely elaborate. They are said to have been originally divided into twelve lodges,[3] each with a grand master, stationed at various islands, the most important being on the sacred island of Ra'iatea. In addition to these twelve superior grades there were several inferior grades to which every initiated *areoi* might aspire, irrespective of rank. The grades were distinguished by their dress[4] and tattoo marks.[5] Chiefs (*ariki*) who aspired to be *areoi* might be initiated directly into the superior grades.

---

[1] Frazer, *Belief*, Vol. II, p. 259. Rivers similarly stresses the 'licentiousness' and the infanticide of the *areoi*. We think that he took a disproportionate view of the importance of both, even while attempting to extenuate them, and that he fails to distinguish the regulated 'licence' of certain *areoi* practices from libertinism, and to realise the widely accepted custom of infanticide throughout the Tahiti Group and elsewhere. See *Melanesian Society* II, pp. 242, 399.

[2] Tregear, Williams, *Dictionaries, s.v. karioi*. Similarly in his Mangaian Vocabulary, Christian glosses the word *karioi* as 'profligate'; 'debauched'.

[3] Moerenhout I, p. 489 ff.   [4] Henry, *A.T.* p. 234 f.

[5] Moerenhout I, p. 491; Ellis[1] I, p. 319 f.; Henry, *loc. cit.*

Auna, the principal *areoi* of Ra'iatea, was at once a priest of the god Hiro, a principal chief, and a leader among the *areoi*.[1] The society as a whole is said to have consisted of the cleverest and handsomest of both sexes. Each *areoi* is said to have had his own wife, also an *areoi*,[2] but inconsistently with this statement we are told that the proportion of men to women was as five to one.[3] All the members of the lower grades swore an oath to destroy their offspring; but the children of the chiefs were permitted to live.[4] Young girls of the highest rank were sometimes enlisted in the ranks of the *areoi*, and these were carefully guarded and chaperoned by the chief *areoi* women. Their persons were regarded as sacred, and respected by all members of the society.[5] When the *areoi* grew too old for active life they became farmers and workers for the society,[6] though this is doubtless true only of the lower grades, who must have formed the majority of the members.

Anyone of whatever rank might offer himself as a candidate for admission to the society, but his first qualification must be evidence of divine inspiration.[7] Then came a long and arduous training, followed by an exhibition of proficiency in poetical recitation and literary tradition, exact verbal memory being insisted on. On his admission he was introduced to the *areoi* society by a new name, by which he was ever afterwards known to its members.[8] Great ceremony accompanied the admission of a new member, and similar exhibitions took place as the candidate passed from grade to grade. Religious ceremonies were also held both on these occasions, and at the opening of their principal performances, when pigs were offered to the god Rongo.[9] The religious nature of the society is also emphasised by traditions regarding its origin,[10] and by many of their practices. The members of their society were sacrosanct, and regarded as the direct representatives of the gods on earth, if not actually as divine beings themselves.[11] In their prayers they refer to themselves as *maru*, 'shadows'.[12] An *areoi* told Tyerman

---

[1] Tyerman I, p. 353; Ellis[1] I, p. 315; cf. Williamson, *S.P.S.* III, p. 44.
[2] Ellis[2] I, p. 238.   [3] Tyerman I, p. 326.
[4] Henry, *A.T.* p. 235.
[5] *Ib.* p. 236.   [6] *Ib.* p. 237.
[7] Moerenhout I, p. 491 ff.; Ellis[1] I, p. 321; Henry, *A.T.* p. 235 f.
[8] Handy, *H.C.S.I.* p. 63.
[9] See e.g. *L.M.S. Trans.* I, p. 16 f.; Moerenhout I, p. 536; Tyerman I, p. 326 ff.; Ellis[2] I, p. 234; Henry, *A.T.* p. 241.
[10] Moerenhout I, p. 485 ff.; cf. Ellis[1] I, p. 312 ff.; Henry, *A.T.* p. 231 ff.
[11] Ellis[2] I, pp. 239, 241; Moerenhout I, p. 492; cf. Arbousset, p. 23.
[12] Henry, *A.T.* p. 237 f.

and Bennet that after death they enjoyed all manner of sensuous delights in the midst of an immense plain, round which stood the gods with joined hands and interlocked fingers, forming an impenetrable barrier.[1] According to some, the Heaven shared by the *ariki*[2] and the *areoi* was known as Rohutu-noa-noa, 'Sweet-scented Rohutu', and was ruled by the god Romatane.[3] It was situated on or above the summit of a high mountain in the island of Borabora[4] or Ra'iatea.[5]

All sources emphasise the mobility of the *areoi* organisation during their periods of activity. They are constantly pictured as moving in a grand flotilla of canoes from place to place in gala costume to the music of drum, flute, and song, their heads decorated with feathers and flowers.[6] Their performances are spoken of as practically continuous in Tahiti; but there can be no doubt that both here and in the Marquesas, where a similar society existed, their special fêtes were seasonal, at least in part, and associated with the compulsory peace which reigned during the seasons preceding and during the harvest.[7] During their feasts peace was maintained, and a general festival was held among the population, as during the celebration of a *kapa* in Mangaia. Like the latter also the performances of the *areoi* were frequently held at night in well-lighted houses, which are sometimes said to be more than 300 feet long.[8] The *areoi* generally slept by day. The provision of the entertainment at their feasts was the peculiar duty and privilege of the *areoi*, and more especially of the lower grades; for we are expressly told that the members of the senior grades were grave and dignified persons in whom were vested the higher religious tenets of the society, and who did not take any part in public performances,[9] but sat on high

[1] Tyerman I, p. 251; Moerenhout II, p. 135. Can there possibly be any connection between this strange conception and the stone images on their platforms partly ringing round the coast-line of Easter Island?

[2] In Mangaia, however, the warriors' Paradise is known as Tiairi; cf. Gill, *Myths*, p. 278.

[3] Handy, *H.C.S.I.* p. 64. We have already seen that this was also the name of the chief of the island of Atiu (cf. p. 269 above). It is said to be an abbreviated form of the name of the god Rongo-ma-Tane.

[4] Moerenhout I, p. 434 f.; Tyerman I, p. 273; Ellis[2] I, pp. 245, 397.

[5] Ellis[1] I, p. 327.

[6] Moerenhout II, p. 132; Ellis[1] I, p. 316 ff.; Tyerman I, p. 326; *L.M.S. Trans.* I, pp. 16 ff., 216; Handy, *H.C.S.I.* p. 65 f. See Cook's First Voyage, Plate LXI.

[7] Moerenhout II, p. 132; Wilson, p. 209; Henry, *A.T.* p. 239; *L.M.S. Trans.* I, p. 123 f.; II, p. 126 f.

[8] Henry, *A.T.* p. 230; cf. Tyerman I, p. 113.

[9] Moerenhout I, pp. 495, 498; II, p. 135; Ellis[2] I, pp. 238, 241.

stools on a high platform erected at one end of the house.[1] The lower classes performed games of skill, and dramatic dances and recitations. Songs were also given, and performances in which all three arts were combined. These seem to have resembled in many respects the performances already described in other Groups.

An important sign of rank among the *areoi* men was their tattooing. It is said that the particular grade to which a male *areoi* belonged was indicated by the amount and position of the tattoo patterns.[2] This feature was so striking a part of their equipment that a fully tattooed *areoi* appeared to an onlooker as if he were fully clad. This tattooing was one of the customs of the *areoi* which they cherished most proudly, and which died hardest.[3]

When giving their performances the *areoi* men dyed their faces red, and blackened their bodies, a custom which we have also seen elsewhere (p. 422; cf. also pp. 420, 440 below). Sometimes they wore a girdle of yellow leaves. At other times they wore a vest of ripe yellow plantain leaves, and ornamented their heads with wreaths of bright yellow and scarlet leaves.[4] Other decorations are also mentioned, the dress being apparently regulated according to the rank in the *areoi* society occupied by the member in question.[5]

Their répertoire was very varied. Moerenhout tells us that their greatest performances opened with chants on religious subjects, such as Tangaroa and his union with matter, the creation of the Universe and of the elements, and the great exploits and journeys of the gods, such as Hiro. These were followed by the 'lives of the demi-gods or heroes', such as Maui, their journeys and combats. The erotic dialogue and comic dramatic representation followed, and the performance invariably concluded with a dance. The whole offers a close analogy to Gill's texts of the Mangaian *kapas*, as will be seen at a glance by reference to the account given on p. 372 ff. above. The *areoi's* performances on

[1] Henry, *loc. cit.*

[2] See Handy, *H.C.S.I.* p. 62; Henry, *A.T.* p. 234f.

[3] The early journals of the London Missionaries are particularly interesting in this respect. The Journal of William Pascoe Crook relates (May 14th, 1824) that he upbraided the *areoi* for their distinctive costume and practices; but "one of them stood in a corner and muttered that they were resolved to go on and tattoo their bodies". On May 21st he wrote: "One of our school-boys has mixed with the *areoi* class, and learnt the art of tattooing." On July 1st: "The attendants of Pomare and his wife with one or two exceptions are all wild young men (*areoi*).... They carry on the operation of puncturing their bodies," etc.

[4] Ellis[1] 1, p. 317; cf. Handy, *H.C.S.I.* p. 62f.

[5] Henry, *A.T.* p. 234ff.

less exalted occasions began with mock combats,[1] which seem to correspond to certain of the *eva* of Mangaia (cf. p. 358 f. above), and may or may not have been connected with the 'ghost-fighting' (pp. 355 above). Their displays were known as *heiva, oopawpah (paupa, upa-upa)*,[2] etc.

In these performances the leader was generally seated in the middle, or on a high seat at the end. Tyerman and Bennet picture him as seated cross-legged on a stool seven feet high, with a fan in his hand,[3] in the midst of a circle of laughing and admiring auditors, whom he "delighted with his drollery or transported with his grimaces".[4] The reference is perhaps to the light comedy with which these entertainments often concluded, and which were performed by the lower orders of the society. Their sallies had doubtless something in common with those of the medieval fool, for Ellis tells us that "allusion was ludicrously made to public events", and that the priests were fearlessly ridiculed.[5] A curious feature mentioned by several writers is the continuous movement of all parts of the body during the dance, including the hands and feet, fingers and toes,[6] which somehow sounds as if it were connected with the dance *tautiti* (cf. p. 288 above). It is hardly necessary to remind the reader that the 'leader' in these performances corresponds to a coryphaeos, and is not to be confused with the members of the upper grades of the *areoi*, who took no part in such displays. The latter consisted of the highest nobility in the land, and even of certain of the priests. When on their journeys, one of their number even represented the god of the *areoi* Paradise, Romatane himself.[7]

All accounts of the *areoi* stress the happy and privileged position which they enjoyed. It appeared to spectators that their life was a continuous round of feasting and pleasure.[8] It is probable that both the *areoi* and the society which supported them realised that the high standard of artistic performance demanded of them could only be attained if the *areoi* were immune from need, and from worldly cares and anxieties. But it is probable also that the *areoi* themselves found life

---

[1] Moerenhout II, p. 130 ff. Cf. also p. 141 f., which possibly refers to the *hokis* (cf. p. 433 ff. below). Cf. also Tyerman and Bennet I, pp. 94, 327; J. R. Forster, p. 327; *L.M.S. Trans.* (1801), p. 214.

[2] For an interesting Hawaiian tradition relating to the *upa-upa*, see p. 414 above.

[3] The use of the fan is said to signify divinity.

[4] Tyerman I, p. 328.

[5] Ellis[1] I, p. 317; cf. also Henry, *A.T.* p. 240.

[6] See an interesting account in the *L.M.S. Trans.* I, p. 216 f.; cf. also Handy, *H.C.S.I.*   [7] Henry, *A.T.* p. 238.

[8] Moerenhout I, p. 535 ff.; II, p. 130 ff.

more strenuous than their audience supposed. They followed a pursuit which required of its members an exacting physical and mental discipline, and an arduous and severe mental training. They provided a high standard of aesthetic entertainment, combining the arts of music, dancing, and poetry. They practised extempore composition to some extent, and perfected the art of memorising to a remarkable degree. They made themselves responsible for the preservation of much of the traditional literature of their islands. We know that a long and arduous training preceded their performances and their preferment. How far, therefore, the *areoi* themselves shared the gaiety which it was their function to inspire it would be difficult to say. We shall probably be safe in assuming that their happiness was largely professional.

Almost all writers have laid stress on the 'immorality' practised by the *areoi*, whom they frequently represent as monsters of vice and cruelty. There can be no doubt that at certain seasonal festivals public fertility rites were practised with accompanying orgies.[1] But Moerenhout long ago pointed out the religious nature of the voluptuous and erotic scenes enacted by them, and emphasised the fact that their exercises always began with religious subjects—the description of the union of the god Tangaroa with matter and the consequent creation of the Universe.[2] The cruelty attributed to the *areoi* is due to the fact that all members except those of the highest orders had to undertake a vow to destroy their offspring.

It may indeed be safely said that ignorance of the laws and conventions governing a society very different from our own is chiefly responsible for the disrepute in which the *areoi* have generally been held by Europeans, and that this prejudice has obscured the real value and importance of the *areoi* and kindred institutions in the intellectual, and especially in the literary life of the islanders. It is important, therefore, to bear in mind the estimation in which the *areoi* were held by the Polynesians themselves—not so much by those members of the society who eventually became converts to Christianity, as by the population as a whole. Among these it is clear that they held a position of the greatest honour and importance, associated with the gods, with kings, with leading chiefs and *tohungas*, and welcomed everywhere, while their persons were held sacred both in peace and in war.

The origin and affinities of this strange corporation are still matter for speculation. We have seen (p. 318 above) that one tradition, preserved in the form of an elaborate saga, derived the first *areoi* from the

[1] Handy, *P.R.* p. 309.　　　　[2] Moerenhout II, pp. 131 f., 134.

union of the god Rongo with a very beautiful maiden dwelling on earth, and living in seclusion on the island of Borabora. According to the Orsmond-Henry tradition,[1] derived from a descendant of Tamatoa I, ruler of Ra'iatea, the issue of this union was Tamatoa I himself. He was therefore regarded as the incarnation of the god Rongo, and the first *areoi*. This Tamatoa lived in Ra'iatea about the early years of the sixteenth century,[2] and it is significant that in the eighteenth century the headquarters of the *areoi* of the Tahiti Group were still in Ra'iatea. There are versions of the story of the origin of the *areoi* which differ considerably from the story just referred to in regard to details; but the principal facts of the divine origin from Rongo and a maiden dwelling on earth are substantially constant.

When we consider the life-vows of the *areoi*, the religious associations of their performances, and of their origin, the intellectual nature of their répertoire, their religious dances, and the comic interludes of their dramatic presentations, we are reminded of a mobilised lamaserai, or a convent of mixed occupants, who, nevertheless, are kept ritually apart in much of their routine. The divinity to which the *areoi* lay claim, and their religious functions and accessories, the impersonation of the god Romatane in their midst, the professional happiness and gala atmosphere which surrounds them, suggest the enactment on earth of their own paradise, with its immunity from danger and want, its sensuous delights (cf. p. 426 above). The costume of the *areoi*, both men and women, suggests that of the dead (cf. p. 420 above), while they refer to themselves as *maru*, 'shadows'. Is it possible that the *areoi* of Tahiti are, like the brothers and sisters of European monasteries, 'dead' to the world? Are they impersonating spirits dwelling in Heaven, enacting a perpetual and seasonal pageant of immortality for the edification of their fellows? This would help to account for their life-vows, the divine inspiration to which every aspirant must prove his title, and the importance of infanticide.

Societies resembling the *areoi*, and even bearing the same name, are found outside the Tahiti Group. The Jesuit missionaries mention a privileged body of people in the Caroline and Ladrone Islands known as *uritoy*, whose practices are said to resemble those of the *areoi* in some respects.[3] It is, however, chiefly in the Marquesas that the closest analogies to the *areoi* are to be found. Stewart gives a detailed account[4]

[1] Henry, *A.T.* p. 232. 　　　　[2] Handy, *H.C.S.I.* p. 62.
[3] Cook[2] II, p. 158, footnote; Ellis[1] I, p. 312; cf. Tregear, *s.v. karioi*.
[4] Stewart, *Visit* I, p. 233 ff.

of an elaborate performance in a *tahua*, or combined theatre and temple, in the Marquesas in which the *kaioi* (*areoi*) played a leading part, if not the exclusive rôle. The performance opened with a slow posture dance, followed by songs from forty or fifty young girls who had learnt a new set of songs for the occasion, and who had been placed under restrictions of *tabu* for some months previously—a feature reminiscent of Mangaia and Easter Island. The performance appears to have been held to celebrate their reappearance, and was known as a *koika*. On such occasions we are told that the *kaioi* were the poets and composers, as well as the performers of the songs sung, and that a favourite subject was current events, or the arrival of a ship. Stewart tells us that the most important of these performances took place at the ingathering of the bread-fruit harvest, and at the ratification of a peace—the latter again reminiscent of Mangaia and Tahiti. The performances witnessed by Stewart were doubtless similar to those of the *hoolah-hoolah* referred to by Melville,[1] and to those described by Porter[2] and others. All writers are in agreement as to the important part played by the *tuhuna* (*tohunga*) as composer, teacher, and leader of the songs.

There appears to be no reasonable grounds for believing that in the Marquesas the *kaioi* were professional performers in any sense. According to Handy they constituted the younger members of the families of the tribe, both youths and maidens.[3] They took part in the great festivals held at the time of harvest, in which there can be no doubt fertility rites and orgiastic practices (strictly regulated, be it noted) played a considerable part. At these rites erotic songs, known as *uta*, were chanted in honour of the dead. The bodies of the performers were smeared with sweet-scented oil, as in Samoa, and stained yellow, like the *areoi* of Tahiti, and the *hula* dancers of Hawaii and elsewhere.[4] Handy has published some valuable notes on the part played by the *kaioi* in the tattooing of the *opou*, the eldest son of a wealthy man, who seems to correspond to the 'eldest or pet son' mentioned by Gill in the Cook Group (cf. p. 433 below). The *kaioi*, who consisted of a band of from forty to fifty young people, built a special *tapu* house for the tattooing of the *opou*, and looked after themselves, the *tuhuna* who performed the operation, and the *opou* while the period of seclusion lasted. In return they themselves received a partial tattooing.

[1] Melville, p. 185. *Hoolah-hoolah* is simply the word for 'dance' here, as in Hawaii. [2] Porter II, p. 47.
[3] Handy, *M.L.* p. 21; *ib. P.R.* p. 307; *T.M.* p. 1 ff.
[4] *Ib. P.R. loc. cit.*

The Marquesan sagas make special mention of the rite of the tattooing of the *kaioi*,[1] and represent them as occupied in playing at *teka*, or reed-throwing,[2] a favourite accompaniment of the dramatic dances of Mangaia, as we have seen (p. 361 above). The saga of Kena[3] gives an account of their daily routine as that of a pleasure-loving set of youths, quite consistent with the picture of the *areoi* of Tahiti, but in no way suggestive of a professional troupe. In this story Kena, a kind of Marquesan male Cinderella, goes to join a troop of *kaioi* in the capacity of servant. The *kaioi* are bent on ingratiating themselves with a female chief by their flute-playing, but are superseded in her affections by Kena, whose flute-playing excels their own.

The institution of the *areoi* was undoubtedly known on the Cook Group. The word figures in Christian's vocabulary,[4] where, as we have seen, it is glossed 'profligate', 'debauched', and compared with the Rarotongan *kariei*. We have no doubt that this meaning has only come to be attributed to the word in modern times, since the conversion of the people to Christianity, and that originally it bore a technical significance akin to that of the Marquesas. An unpublished story recorded by Gill[5] from Mangaia bears the title *Araiti's Oven; or 30 girls (are kareoi) deceived to death*. The story itself relates to Rarotonga, and opens as follows:

"At Avarua, Rarotonga, there was once a lovely daughter of Makea who lived with a large number of young female friends and dependants in a separate dwelling. In all, there were 30 young women. They were accustomed to go to the stream to bathe every morning and evening. So 'tapu' was Makea's daughter in the eyes of her friends that they were accustomed to spread clothes along the pathway to the stream, so that she never set her nude but dainty feet on the bare earth."

The rest of the story, which relates to the deception practised on the unsuspecting girls as they went to bathe, and their deaths at the hands of a band of cannibals, need not concern us; but the opening of the story points clearly to a community of young and high-born girls living in retreat on ritual grounds, and known as *kareoi*. It is important therefore that on a later page of the same MS. Gill refers again to the story, and states positively that it is quite true, and that the incident occurred during a time of famine. From other instances of cannibalism on

---

[1] Handy, *M.L.* p. 117f.   [2] *Ib.* p. 21.
[3] *Ib.* p. 117ff.; cf. also *ib.* p. 93.   [4] Christian, *M.V. s.v. karioi.*
[5] The MS. is in the possession of the London Missionary Society, to whose kindness I am indebted for permission to quote this passage.

Rarotonga referred to in the same MS. as taking place during the same famine, we gather that the story has reference to the early years of last century. It may perhaps be mentioned in passing that Gill's reference[1] to the eldest or 'pet son' as one specially privileged and immune from labour recalls the wide divergence of treatment of the *opou* and the *kaioi* of the Marquesas (cf. p. 431 above).

The evidence from Aitutaki is fuller. Here we are told[2] that there were in former times large houses for the entertainment of the villagers and visitors. They are said to have been built to the order of a high chief for the entertainment of his unmarried daughters, and were used for singing, dancing, and all indoor entertainments. These houses were called *hare karioi*,[3] and each village is said to have possessed one. The most famous *hare karioi* of Aitutaki is traditionally stated to have been built fourteen generations ago, and was largely the work of a priest. Remains of the structure are still in existence. It is 72 feet long, by 34 feet wide, and the floor space was paved with unworked stones not closely set, above which white coral gravel had been spread. The place where the doors stood was midway along the sides. It will be seen that the structure bears a close resemblance to similar *areoi* houses described by early travellers in the Marquesas and Tahiti. It is interesting to note that Buck records a story in which a deserted wife traced her husband to the *hare karioi*, where an entertainment was going on,[4] and made herself known to him by leaping into the dance, exactly as Pele discovered herself to Lohiau in the *hula* on the island of Kauai in the Hawaiian Group (cf. p. 325 above). A Rarotongan tradition assigns to an early ancestor of the Makea family[5] the building of a great assembly hall to be a meeting place for the gods, and the spirits of mankind, such as the high chiefs, and to serve his subjects as a public centre; but his most delightful institutions were the drums, the trumpet, the various kinds of dances (especially *evas* and *peu*) and the *karioi*.[6]

Performances are also recorded from the Marquesas as given by troupes of men and women known as *hoki*, who resemble the *areoi* of Tahiti in some respects, though they are believed to be native to the

[1] In the MS. referred to above.

[2] The evidence for Aitutaki will be found in Buck, *M.C.C.I.* p. 36f.

[3] The word *hare* is doubtless the same as the Mangaian word transcribed by Gill *are* in the passage quoted above. For the initial *h* see Buck, *M.C.C.I.* p. xxif.

[4] A somewhat similar scene takes place in a tradition recorded from Rarotonga. See *J.P.S.* xxvii, p. 183; cf. p. 192.

[5] One of the two royal families who divided the rule of Rarotonga.

[6] *J.P.S.* xxviii, p. 64f.

Marquesas. They went from valley to valley, and from island to island, in bands of about forty. Their performances consisted of singing and dancing, and we are told that the purpose of the songs was laudatory. The songs themselves were arranged so that the names of different persons could be inserted in them when sung in anyone's honour.[1]

The *hoki* are frequently referred to in the sagas. In the Marquesan story of Ono, the hero joins a troupe of *hoki*, and becomes a famous wrestler. These *hoki*, we are told, were making a tour of the island, performing their dances and sports, and enjoying the entertainment of the tribes inhabiting the different valleys.[2] In another saga[3] a certain maiden named Taa-po is carried off by two 'gods' to the abode of the dead, where she sees a group of young people performing a *kapa*, and on her return to earth she teaches her relatives the *kapa* which she has heard sung by the *atua* in the land of the dead, and which consists largely of a catalogue of islands, together with the chiefs who rule them —another indication of the serious educational character of these performances. The girl suggests to her relatives that they should set out as a 'singing troupe in her honour', carrying the *kapa* with them. They sail accordingly to Puamau in Hivaoa—a district which we are told was anciently famous for *hoki*. The saga goes on to speak of further performances of the *kapa*, part of which consists of a duet between the heroine and her father. In the saga of Tona-Hai-Eee we hear of a singing festival in honour of a female chief, in which various people are represented as singing *i'i* as eulogies on the chief herself, partly in the form of solos, and partly in chorus, by the whole assembly.[4]

These sagas are of great interest for the light which they throw on the literary life of the islands from many angles. In particular the story of Taa-po is full of significance. It connects the *kapa* with the *hoki*, deriving the former, like the dance *tautiti* (cf. p. 288 above), from the dead. It shows us that educational poetry, such as the catalogues which we have found widespread throughout the Pacific, were recited by the *hoki*. Incidentally we learn that the district Puamau in the island of Hivaoa was famous for its *hoki*, and Handy tells us elsewhere[5] that the ancient district of Vevau on the same island was recognised by all Marquesans as the great centre of lore. This association of the *hoki*

[1] Handy, *N.C.M.* p. 309. We may perhaps compare the 'Dirge for Vera' from Mangaia, in which the name of Vera has probably been substituted for that of Veētini (cf. p. 369 above).

[2] Handy, *M.L.* p. 104f.   [3] *Ib.* p. 82f.
[4] *Ib.* p. 54.   [5] *N.C.M.* p. 193.

with traditional learning and education should not be overlooked. It is in this same district that, according to the saga of Kena, the tattooing rites of the *kaioi* were performed.

The knowledge of catalogues of islands, together with their rulers, and the new dances and songs which Taa-po acquired in the land of the dead, and which qualified her to set out as leader of a band of *hoki*, call to mind a Maori saga recorded by Cowan.[1] This tale relates that a certain maiden named *Hine-rangi*, 'Sky maid', was set apart by her parents as a *puhi*, 'Virgin'. She was given a separate house some little distance from the others, and was not allowed to indulge in early love affairs like the other girls of the tribe. We have already seen that a similar class of maidens existed also in Mangaia, and in Samoa. Now Hine-rangi was secretly wooed by a man of the *patu-paiarehe* or 'fairy' people (see p. 293 above), whose name was Miru, and who visited his bride at night, disappearing always at the peep of dawn, like the Mangaian fairies.[2] This Miru, like the Miru of Mangaia, lived with the fairies in a land beyond this world; but in other respects he differed from the female Miru. He was the ruler of a supernatural house of learning, the original *whare kura* to which fuller reference will be made below, and in which we are expressly told that 'all the sacred wisdom of the people was taught'. But this was not all; for games such as cat's cradle were also taught, and 'the working of the wooden marionettes (cf. p. 439 below) that were caused to imitate *haka* dancers'. Clearly, therefore, Miru's *whare kura*, and the land where it was situated, is to be equated with the land of the dead visited by Taa-po. The songs and dances, like those of the *hoki* and similar troupes, are learnt from Miru and the fairies, men and women who occupy the land of the dead, and who are variously known in Mangaia as 'sky fairies' and fairies of the Underworld, according to the particular Paradise or land of the dead to which we are referring.

It is to be suspected that the leaders of the religious dances which we have been considering—whether these were *areoi*, *hoki*, or the temporary associations found on Mangaia, Samoa, and elsewhere—were drawn from the class of men and girls known as *puhi, taupou, tupu*, etc., of which we have found traces in New Zealand, Mangaia, Samoa, and other islands. These men and maidens were selected for their rank and beauty, and the latter had complexions artificially fair. In

---

[1] *F.F.T.* p. 23 ff.
[2] It will be remembered that the *areoi* of Tahiti also are said to have slept by day and danced by night.

their secluded and protected manner of life and in their appearance, therefore, they resembled the *tapairu* of Mangaia, the *patu-paiarehe* and the *turehu* of New Zealand. In their nocturnal dances, which must close, at least in Mangaia, with the appearance of the day-star, they also resembled the fairies. We have also seen reason to regard them as the living representatives of the dead on earth. There can be no doubt that in Mangaia the three-cornered relationship of the fairies, the dancers, and the spirits of the dead is especially clear, and is to be found in its frankest form in the Dirges for Vera and for Puvai; but this relationship is almost equally clear in the remaining songs in Gill's collections relating to the 'fairies' and the Underworld, especially in those relating to the myth of Ina, whose story has been treated at greater length in Ch. III above.

Let us glance once more at these dirges before we finally leave the subject. A band of young unmarried youths assemble to take a canoe voyage to Iva; they are clad like the dead, or those who mourn them, in garlands of red and yellow leaves and flowers, and in mourning garments, and in network in which the dead and the *areoi* alike are dressed. Before their departure they wander along the rocks of the shore—the only road of the island—dwelling in temporary booths,[1] or haunting the caves where the dead lie, and which are also the home of the 'fairies'. The maidens also haunt the rocks and the caves, similarly clad. The noblest occupy temporary houses or booths erected on the west coast[2] near the dwelling of the Shore-King with whom the 'fairies' were wont to take up their abode at times. The band depart at last, like all departing Polynesians, amid the tears and mournful strains of the *tangi*, sailing at evening over the ocean. The pageantry is that of the dead; but it can hardly have been suggested by the Mangaian corpse, trussed and corded, and dropped down Raupo, or laid on a ledge in the depths of Auraka. The imagery, despite the tears, is that of a troop of voyagers, such as the *areoi*, setting off in gala costume in their canoes, to perform their *kapa* in some neighbouring island. The name most commonly mentioned is *Iva*, which Gill here translates 'spirit land', but which elsewhere he invariably translates 'Nukuhiva', an important island in the Marquesas. The translation 'spirit land' seems arbitrary. If the Marquesas were not so far from Mangaia one would be tempted to suggest that the *Iva* and *Vavau* referred to in the poems are possibly to be identified with Hivaoa and Vevau, which we have just seen to be the district most famous in the Marquesan Group for its poetical school,

---

[1] Gill, *Myths*, p. 184. [2] *Ib.* p. 209, footnote 2.

its troop of *hoki*, and its general literary development. But the dirge also makes mention of Tahiti, of Tutuila, and of Tonga as places in which the spirits sojourn. It is just possible, therefore, that the poet merely wishes to enumerate the principal places known to him in the Pacific.

Perhaps the most important features common to the *areoi* and the 'fairies' are those connected with birth and death. We have seen (p. 294 above) that in the land of the latter no-one is allowed to remain once he has shown signs of grey hairs. Among the *areoi* also it is said that those who grow too old for active life must retire from active participation in the dances and public displays, and become farmers and artisans (cf. p. 425 above). An aged *areoi* is never heard of.

We have seen that throughout the Pacific, the 'fairies', by whatever names they are known, are said to die with the birth of their first child, till Hina, or in certain variants another, is taught by a man, generally a *tohunga* (sometimes called an *atua*), the means of natural birth. Hina, as we have seen, is the chief of the 'fairies' in Mangaia and elsewhere. Generally, though not invariably, the child perishes with the mother. We have also seen that the most important maidens of this class, often the daughters of the highest chiefs, are jealously chaperoned, and that it is a capital offence for these chosen maidens to lose their virtue. On the other hand the children of the high chiefs are said not to be destroyed (cf. p. 425 above). It seems likely, therefore, that the death of the 'fairy' mother is due to the fact that the 'fairies' must not, according to certain (e.g. *areoi*) vows, bear children, and that the way in which such a stringent rule was avoided was by means of the Caesarian operation (cf. p. 294 above). This would naturally be performed especially in the case where the husband was known to be an *ariki* such as Tawhaki, and where, consequently, it was not desirable that the offspring should be destroyed. It must, of course, happen as a natural result that the mother will generally perish, while the son may be said to be 'not born', or 'prematurely born'. And this is precisely what we have already observed to be the case in regard to many of the principal Polynesian heroes, such as Ono-kura, and Maui, whose mother, it will be remembered, belonged to the class known as 'fairies'. Hina herself is said to have been born prematurely, and thrown away by her mother. This procedure is not rare in the traditions, and can only be accounted for by the supposition that the women, like the *areoi*, were interdicted from bearing children.

The oral sagas of the Pacific commonly make mention of communities composed exclusively of one sex. These communities resemble those of the *areoi* and the *hoki* in many respects. We have seen the Mangaian hero Ngaru visiting a community of women wholly given up to pleasure and flute-playing in a land of plenty (p. 278 above). In the Marquesan saga of Kena the *kaioi* visit in large numbers a female chief whom they endeavour to please by their flute-playing (p. 432 above). In the version of Kae from the same island Group, a female community without husbands is drawn for us with Hina at its head.[1] This community shares the attributes elsewhere invariably associated with the 'fairies'. In particular these women are said to be ignorant of natural birth, till Kae, the *tuhuna* (*tohunga*) or *atua* husband of Hina, instructs her how, by natural birth, the life of the mother may be saved. But it is obvious from the whole conduct of this story that the community can only be temporarily withdrawn from male society, like the *hoki* groups of the Marquesas during their period of preparation before their public appearance (cf. p. 434 f. above). It seems clear that such pictures as these are based on societies of the kind which we have been studying, and there can be no doubt that a closer study of the oral traditional literature of the Pacific would greatly enlarge our knowledge of these strange and most interesting institutions.

The *hula* performances of Hawaii resemble those of the *areoi* in many respects. Like these the *hula* is religious in its associations, and combines poetry, music, pantomime, and the dance.[2] Like them too it was a very popular institution among all classes of the population, though usually under royal or chiefly patronage. The performance of a *hula* was a favourite way of conferring distinction on an *alii* (*ariki*) and on people of wealth, and much wealth was lavished on the dance.[3] Great care was bestowed on the training and education of the company, especially in refinements of elocution and singing. The preparation of the troupe and their life for some weeks before a performance was attended with great ceremonial, and passed in the strictest privacy. Their songs were often composed by the leader of the *hula*, known as the *kumu-hula*, who also imparted them to the *hula* dancers, to be committed to memory. It was the function of the *kumu* also to decide on the attitudes and gestures. The training and performance took place in a special house or *halau*, which is said to have been built specially for the purpose and to be sacred. It contained an altar. The leader was in some measure a priest as well as a business manager, and the whole

[1] Handy, *M.L.* p. 56 ff.
[2] Our chief source of information regarding the *hula* is Emerson's *Unwritten Literature of Hawaii*.   [3] Malo, p. 18.

conduct of the company was governed by the laws of the strictest *tapu* character.

The performances of the *hula* have often been described in detail, and a few words will therefore suffice here.[1] The *hula* dancers are divided into two parties, one party (the *olapa*) performing the most active part of the dance, sometimes accompanying their movements with song, the other party (*hoopa'a*) sitting or kneeling while performing with the heavier musical instruments, and taking an active part in the singing. At a signal from the *kumu*, who sits with the *hoopa'a*, the *poo-pua'a*, or leader of the *olapa*, calls the *mele*, that is to say begins the recitation in a sing-song quiet manner. The *kumu* then joins in in a grandiloquent manner, sometimes heightening the oratorical effect of his recitation by 'choking down his voice like a growl',[2] as the *areoi* and the Mangaian priests are sometimes said to do. The whole company then join in in the same style as the *kumu*. The similarity of the general arrangements to those recorded by Lamont from Tongareva and by Gill from Mangaia is very striking. Such performances have constantly reminded those who have witnessed them of the early drama of the Greeks, especially of tragedy before the introduction of dialogue. "We fancy", wrote Kotzebue, "that we see the antique starting into life."[3]

No class of performers comparable to those whom we have been considering is recorded from among the Maori, though the word *Karioi* occurs as a place-name,[4] and as a proper noun. Moreover, hardly any examples of dramatic poetry have come under our notice from New Zealand, though we have seen (p. 384 above) that a fragment of a dramatic dialogue relating to Rata was recorded by Shortland. On the other hand the famous Maori dance known as the *haka* is believed to be akin to the dramatic performances which we have been discussing,[5] and

---

[1] Emerson, *U.L.* p. 58.   [2] *Ib.* p. 90.   [3] Kotzebue III, p. 253.
[4] Smith, *Hawaiki*, p. 138, footnote. It is perhaps just worth noting that the British Museum possesses a wooden jointed doll or marionette worked by wires or strings which was brought from New Zealand, and which is said to have been used in some kind of dance, while songs were sung in accompaniment. We have already referred to a story, also from the Maori, in which 'the working of wooden marionettes that were caused to imitate *haka* dances, etc.', is said to have been taught in the home of Miru, who is here represented as a man of the land of the *patu-paiarehe*, or 'fairies', and the head of the supernatural 'House of Learning', of which there are many earthly counterparts. See Cowan, *F.F.T.* p. 28. Puppets are also used in similar amusements in the version of the saga of Kae recorded by Sir George Grey (p. 68) from the Maori. We may compare the puppets used in certain of the Hawaiian *hulas* (cf. p. 435 above).
[5] See Smith, *J.P.S.* XIX, p. 137. According to Handy (*N.C.M.* p. 305) the

is said to have been originally an evening dance accompanied with song and dramatic action.[1] Shortland describes the '*rurerue* or *haka*' as songs generally expressive of the sentiment of love, sung in the evenings in alternative chorus and solo by men and girls seated in a row, their hair dressed with feathers and their faces smeared with red ochre and charcoal.[2] In this dance the hands are used with a peculiar movement known as *kakapa*. The colour scheme of red and black suggests that the affinities of the *haka* lie with the 'ghost' performances of Mangaia and Tahiti.

In conclusion we should like to call attention once more to certain traditions regarding the origin of the *areoi* and kindred communities in the various Groups. We have seen that Maori and Rarotongan traditions speak[3] of an original house in the land of Hawaiki where the dance and the drum originated, and where the intellectual life of the people was focused. In Hawaiki also we hear of an original *whare kariei* which seems to correspond to the material *are kariei* of which traces still exist in Aitutaki. It has also been mentioned that the drum and the *hula* are traditionally stated to have been introduced into Hawaii from Tahiti by the hero Lono-i-ka-makahiki at a period generally computed to be about the twelfth century, but probably later. According to the same tradition the drum was at first restricted to use in the temple. It will be remembered that the Pele family, who excelled in the *hula*, are also stated, according to the best traditions, to have come to Hawaii from Tahiti, though they cannot have originally belonged to the eastern Pacific, and probably went there from Samoa. Persistent Hawaiian tradition, therefore, ascribes the origin of *hula* and drum to Tahiti, where we have found the *areoi* most highly developed, with their headquarters on the sacred island of Ra'iatea in the same Group.

Now Ra'iatean tradition derives the origin of the society from the god Rongo, to whose cult the island was sacred, and with whom the corporation of the *areoi* is closely bound up, though the name of the god whom they actually carried on their canoes was Romatane (see p. 428; cf. also p. 426). Rongo, as we have seen, descended from the sky and married a maiden of Borabora, an island of the Tahiti Group. What is the exact significance of this tradition? There is a tradition reported

---

commonest and most popular dance in the Marquesas was the *haka pohaka*, a dance for men only. The *saka* of Tongareva corresponds to the Maori *haka* in many respects (see Buck, *E.M.R.* p. 197; *E.T.* p. 79). The *saka* is also found on Futuna as a 'dance with movement of the feet and of the hands' (Burrows, p. 214).

[1] Angas I, pp. 239, 328; Shortland, p. 169.
[2] Shortland, *loc. cit.*
[3] Smith, *Hawaiki*, p. 138.

by the missionary John Williams, and, as he tells us, 'universally believed', that a certain Iouri, a chief of the Aitutaki islands in the Cook Group, obtained a quantity of *mahi*, or preserved bread-fruit, from Rarotonga in the same Group, and brought it to Ra'iatea and dedicated it to the god.[1] There would be nothing unusual in such a proceeding, but we have already seen that *Mahi*, 'preserved bread-fruit', is the name attributed by tradition to the man chosen by Tamatoa I to spread the cult of the *areoi* in the Tahiti Group, and it is to be suspected for reasons already given (p. 318, footnote 2) that the word is a nickname for the *areoi*. Moreover, from another tradition obtained by Williams, like the last, 'in conversation with an old priest' of Aitutaki, we learn that it was the custom in the past for the Rarotongans to take gifts to the same sanctuary, and that on one occasion 'in the exercise of their piety' they sent a large drum as a present to Oro, which was regarded by the gods as an exceptionally valuable present. After the dedication of the drum the Ra'iateans killed the priests. "The gods were so much enraged that persons who had brought them so valuable a present should be killed that they took up the island, with its population, and carried it completely away."[2] It is not improbable that the story reflects some sacerdotal quarrel of the past, ending in a cessation of intercourse between Rarotonga and Ra'iatea, and the beginning of the autonomy of the Rarotongan priesthood. The drum, to which so much value is attached, may well be connected with the *mahi* offered by the same people at the same temple, for the drum and the dramatic dances associated with the *areoi* are closely connected, as we have seen. Can the significance of all these traditions be that the *areoi* society reached the island of Ra'iatea from the Cook Group, whence it spread to Tahiti and Hawaii? We have seen that the leading chief of Atiu, one of the Cook Islands, was hereditarily known as Romatane,[3] implying descent from the god who accompanied the *areoi* on their excursions. The suggestion that the institution of the *areoi* reached Ra'iatea from the Cook Group would of course be fully in accord with the dramatic dances which we have seen to be highly developed in these islands, and the fact that we hear little in the Cook Islands of the actual institution may be easily explained from the facts of the history of Christianity in these islands.[4] But the suggested history of the spread of the institution

---

[1] Williams, *M.E.* p. 56 f. [2] *Loc. cit.*
[3] See the MS. of Gill referred to, p. 256 above.
[4] The conversion of the Cook Group was effected entirely by native missionaries, so that we have no early (pre-Christian) account of the institutions of these islands such as were made by the European missionaries for Tahiti, Ra'iatea, etc.

can be no more than a suggestion until the traditions of the islands are better known. And the next question would naturally be: whence did the institution reach the Cook Group?

It will be seen, however, that the recitation of poetry to the accompaniment of dramatic action and dancing was very widespread in Polynesia, and that the forms under which it is found in the various Groups are often historically connected. A long and careful preparation was made in solitude for the performances, which were generally held under religious auspices, and often in a special building. There are indications that this period of solitude is partly directed towards seeking divine inspiration. The performances were held on a variety of occasions—for tribal religious festivals in honour of the gods; on great secular occasions in honour of people of consequence; on occasions of mourning in commemoration of the dead. A high standard of diction and poetry was cultivated everywhere, and the results clearly indicate that these performances have been among the most important factors in the literary artistic life of the Pacific.

In conclusion it may be noticed as remarkable how frequently the arrival of a ship is referred to as forming a theme of these performances. We have already found it in the Marquesas, Mangaia, Easter Island, Samoa and Penrhyn; and there are doubtless other instances. There can be no doubt that the theme is a relic of a widespread and comparatively ancient tradition, and it seems to us, therefore, that in the instances where the representation is that of a European ship, this has been substituted for something earlier. We have seen that in the Tahiti Group, where the institution of the *areoi* is most fully developed, and where our evidence for such performances is full and early, the *areoi* themselves arrived in a magnificent flotilla to give their performances. We have also seen reason to suspect that the representation in poetical form of the departure of the dead from Mangaia in a fleet of canoes is not unconnected with such a practice, and traces seem to linger also in Samoan tradition, where the identification of the first European ships with the ancient 'voyaging spirits' is clearly demonstrated. It seems on the whole not improbable, therefore, that the dramatic performances in general, opening with the Creation, passing to the lives of the gods and heroes, and concluding with the arrival of a ship, are traditional representations of the last migration to the Pacific islands of a people known in Polynesian diction as 'gods' and represented dramatically by *areoi* and similar bodies of performers. The performances, are, in fact, historical pageants of the aristocracy (*ariki*).

CHAPTER IX

THE TOHUNGA, KAULA, ETC.

THE intellectual life of the Pacific as a whole is largely in the hands of a professional class of men known as the *tohunga*. The word is generally translated 'priests'; but the functions of the *tohunga* are really much wider than those of a professional religious person. The *tohunga* commonly combines the functions of scholar and physician with those of the priest, and in the widest sense the word seems to be used of any expert or specialist, even of an expert carpenter or craftsman of any kind.[1] This is to be accounted for by the fact that differentiation of function is not carried so far in the Pacific as among more highly civilised peoples, and the combination of functions is also frequently different. In general, however, the word *tohunga* is current in the sense of a priest, or of a person combining the functions of priest and prophet, and it is in this sense, more especially the former, that the word is used in the following pages.

The status and functions of the *tohunga* vary considerably from one area to another, and again at different periods in the same area. In some Groups, and at some periods, the functions of the *tohunga* are fulfilled in part by the chiefs. In some these functions are combined with those of the prophet and recluse, while in others they are sharply differentiated. It is therefore difficult to make general statements which will be equally true of the whole of our area. On the other hand exhaustive treatment is obviously out of the question in a work of this kind. It may be mentioned that the authors have made a somewhat detailed survey of the various Groups before venturing on the more or less general statements contained in the following pages. For fuller information the reader is referred to the recent works of Williamson on the Central Pacific, more especially to the chapters entitled 'The Sanctity of Chiefs', and 'Priests and Sorcerers', in Vol. II of *The Social and Political Systems of Central Polynesia*. In the following pages we shall confine ourselves to a brief account of the intellectual standards and acquirements of the *tohungas* in relation to the intellectual life of the society whose literature we are studying.

[1] See e.g. *Fornander Collection*, Third Series, vol. VI, p. 56f.

For evidence regarding the religious classes of Polynesia we are largely dependent on the records of missionaries and travellers. These records only comparatively rarely differentiate between one class of religious functionary and another. In some areas, however, the distinction between these classes has been sufficiently well marked to impress itself on European observers. In other instances the observation of such distinctions has no doubt been due to the more especial interest which the particular writer has taken in the customs of the people of whom he is writing. We are especially fortunate in regard to certain island Groups whose oral traditions and native customs have been recorded by a specially sympathetic and exact observer. As instances of the latter we may refer to the works of W. W. Gill on Mangaia, of Henry and Handy on Tahiti, of Stimson on the Marquesas, of Taylor and Dieffenbach and Best on the Maori; of Fornander on Hawaii; and there are many others.

It is clear, therefore, that accident may play a large part in the nice distinctions which we instinctively draw between the various religious classes in the northern Pacific, e.g. Hawaii and the Marquesas, as compared with New Zealand, where the evidence for such exact differentiation is less clearly marked. It has generally been held that the northern Groups developed these religious distinctions more fully than the southern Group. And this may be correct. On the other hand, it may well be that during the colonisation of New Zealand by the Maori such distinctions as may have existed in the past were to some extent obliterated. The absence or rarity of local sanctuaries among the Maori would favour such a view. Again, the history of New Zealand last century must account for the loss of many native customs, and still more of the record of such customs, before they were noted by the kind of Europeans who would be likely to make exact observations. In this and other matters, negative evidence can have little value in regard to the *tohungas*.

In Hawaii our records speak of three distinct classes, viz. *atua*, 'gods', or human beings who were actually themselves regarded as divine beings during their lifetime; *kaula* or 'prophets'; and *kahuna*, i.e. *tohungas*. The *kaula* or *makaula* are, in reality, a class of *tohunga*, from the rest of whom, however, in the northern and east-central Pacific they are sharply differentiated. It must be borne in mind, however, that the distinction is rarely observed by travellers, and confusion of the two classes is very common.

The first class, those who claim actual divinity for themselves, are represented in Hawaii by certain women, who lived in the craters of

Mount Kilauea and neighbouring volcanoes. Early missionaries speak of these women as the priestesses of the volcano goddess Pele; but it is claimed that these women regarded themselves as divine beings, the living and permanent incarnations of the goddess—a claim which was fully admitted by their adherents. An interesting account is given by Ellis of a meeting between a delegation of early missionaries to Hawaii in 1825, and a priestess of Pele named Oani, who claimed to be Pele herself. "Pele is my deity", she assured the missionaries, and proceeded in a song to give a long account of the deeds and honours of Pele, pronounced in a rapid and vociferous manner accompanied by 'extravagant gestures'. Towards the close she appeared to the missionaries to lose all command of herself. Nevertheless, she was able immediately afterwards to carry on a logical and balanced argument in discussion with them. Pele, she assured them, was a goddess who dwelt within her, and who through her would heal the sick chief who happened to be present. Assuming a haughty air, she said:

"'I am Pele, I shall never die; and those who follow me, when they die, if part of their bones be taken to Kilauea,[1] will live in the bright fire there.' Ellis said: 'Are you Pele?' She said, 'Yes, I am Pele,' then proceeded to state her powers."[2]

Elsewhere the same writer gives an account of an official visit of a priestess of Pele, arrayed in her prophetic robes, having the edges of her garments burnt with fire, and holding a short staff or spear in her hand, preceded by her daughter, who was also a candidate for the office of priestess. On this occasion the priestess claimed that 'in a trance or vision she had been with Pele' who had charged her to lodge certain complaints against the foreigners who had violated her sanctuary.[3]

The Rev. C. S. Stewart also, who visited the island in the same party, describes his meeting with an inferior member of her order:

"I unexpectedly met her in an evening walk, followed by a considerable company; some, evidently under the influence of a superstitious feeling in reference to her; and others as evidently disposed to deride her pretensions. She was dressed in a fantastic manner, with dishevelled hair—her eyes flashing in a half-frenzy, from the degree of excitement to which she had wrought herself—and appeared altogether like a maniac: such as I supposed her in reality to be, till undeceived by the exclamations of the crowd, '*it is a goddess—it is a goddess!*' As if to intimidate, she approached me with a fierce and daring look; and waving

---

[1] The name of the volcano.   [2] Ellis² IV, p. 308 ff.
[3] *Ib.* p. 275.

before her a small flag of tapa, appended to a light staff, supported the claim by the declaration, '*I am a goddess—a goddess indeed*'."[1]

Stewart has preserved some interesting details of the cult of Pele and her last chief 'priestess' or incarnation, who came to visit him at his request during his visit to Hawaii after her conversion to Christianity. She was attended by her household, consisting of eight or ten men and women. She was at that time about forty, or forty-five years of age, tall, well-built and majestic. At the time of sacrifice the priestess had been accustomed to descend into the depths of the volcano, and approaching the place most accessible and most active with fire, she had cast the gifts into the flames, with the exclamation: "Here, Pele, is food for you."[2] Her father was the hereditary *kahu*, or steward, as she was the priestess of Pele. His duty was to provide the materials for the general sacrifices—'the food and raiment of the supposititious deity' —and to have all things in readiness for the offerings at the appointed seasons. Two plantations were sacred for this use, one on the seashore, and another within the precincts of the crater, and the *kahu* and his family resided, part of the time on the coast, and part in the neighbourhood of the crater. One instinctively thinks of the 'seaside king' and the 'king of the interior', both with sacerdotal functions, in Mangaia;[3] but Pele's younger sister Hiiaka is closely associated with the tidal wave, and the residence and plantation on the seashore may have been connected with her cult.

Evidence of human *atua* in Hawaii appears to relate exclusively, or at least principally, to women. There was, however, a class of men known as *kaula* ('seers'), who laid claim to temporary fits of divine inspiration, during which they were believed to be possessed by the spirit of some deity, such as Kane-nui-akea, who forewarned them of future events, especially such as concerned the nation as a whole, or the royal family. Their utterances during their periods of ecstasy were known as *wanana*, the word by which the Hawaiian translators of the Bible translate our word 'prophecy' (cf. also p. 340 above), but which appears to have reference to any 'inspired' utterance of a sustained and formal character.

The *kaulas* do not appear to have been restricted to any particular routine; but in this respect again negative evidence may be deceptive, for it would seem that in the Central Pacific such men were closely connected with the *maraes*, or temple-platforms, and even with the

---

[1] *Visit* II, p. 101f. [2] *Ib.* I, p. 100f.

[3] See also the Paumotu play of *Tutepoganui*, p. 383 above, where possible traces of a similar institution may be found.

religious services of a particular god. In Hawaii we see the *kaulas* attached to a king or chief, apparently living in his following at court, and changing their allegiance at will. We may cite the great prophet and poet Keaulumoku, who, as we have seen (p. 340 above), belonged to the royal family of Maui. When we first hear of him he is in the following of Kahahana, King of Oahu; but he afterwards leaves him and goes to Hawaii, where he is received at the court of Kalaniopu. Like the Hebrew prophets whom they resemble in many respects, the *kaulas* are deeply interested in politics and state affairs.

The *kaula* might be either a man or a woman, if we may judge from the evidence of the sagas. A legend of Kalaunuiohua, a chief of the royal line of Hawaii about three generations after the Migration Period, associates a prophetess or *kaula* called Waahia with his expeditions, or with the negotiations for his release out of captivity.[1] Hawaiian tradition frequently mentions the existence of such a class in Tahiti also, as we shall see.

The *kaulas* of the Hawaiian Group are included by Malo[2] among the *kahunas* (*tohungas*), but they are said to possess more power than other *kahunas*, owing to their prophetic gifts. Pakui, the great bard and historian of the time of Kamehameha I, is said to have been both a priest and a prophet. When Kamalalawalu, the *moi*, or ruler of the island of Maui, invaded Hawaii, Lanikaula, a high priest from Molokai, implored him to desist in a *wanana*, or 'prophecy', which has been preserved.[3] The great majority of the Hawaiian *kahunas*, however, do not appear to have laid claim to divine inspiration, but to have been connected with some local sanctuary, where they officiated as its guardians, and as sacrificing priests. They were also in a high degree the teachers of the people and the custodians of the ancient traditions, the chief repositories of learning. They also acted as physicians—not generally as surgeons. Their persons were sacred and their political status was high. In general they belonged to the same class as the chiefs.[4] Their rights and functions were in some degree hereditary in certain families. In these respects the functions of the Hawaiian *kahunas* are in general identical with those of the *tohungas* everywhere.

The prestige of the Hawaiian *kahunas* has always been very great, and we may observe strong testimony to the importance in which they

[1] Fornander, *P.R.* II, p. 69.
[2] Malo, p. 152.
[3] Fornander, *P.R.* II, p. 122.
[4] *Fornander Collection*, Third Series, vol. VI, p. 279.

were held from the fact that so large a number of their names have been preserved by tradition—a distinction which they share with the *tohungas* of the Maori.[1] Fornander has preserved a legend of the terrible famine and drought which overtook Hua (an ancient ruler of Maui, Hawaii Group) and his people in consequence of his having slain a priest.[2] Malo tells us that an irreligious king, or one who neglected his religious responsibilities, was practically unknown in Hawaii.[3] Indeed the political power of the priests has always been great in modern times, and their ascendancy over the temporal chiefs is stressed by all writers.

Instances are not wanting in the sagas to show that their power has at times been even greater than that of the temporal rulers. An interesting case is that of the high priest Paao,[4] the brother of the Samoan chief, who, though not himself a king, succeeded in bringing about a revolution in Hawaii about the close of the twelfth or the beginning of the thirteenth century. At the same time he set on the throne a chief of Tahiti stock, himself remaining as his priest.[5] We may compare the important part played in politics by the high priest of Oahu in the same group of islands.[6] Other instances might be given of the political activity and influence of the high priests in Hawaii.

In the Marquesas[7] also the same distinction is recognised between the three classes of priestly and mantic persons—the *atua*, the *taua* (*kaula*), and the *tuhuna* (*tohunga*). According to Crook, who visited the islands towards the close of the eighteenth century, the *atua* claimed the title of divinity—"not through a professed inspiration, or possession by a supernatural influence or power, but in their right of godship as those who control the elements, impart fruitfulness to the productions of the earth, or smite with blasting and sterility; and who exercise the prerogatives of the deity in scattering disease and wielding the shafts of death." These *atua*, he adds, were few in number, not more than one or two on an island at most, and they lived in great seclusion. One who was still living on the island of Tahuata during Crook's residence there in 1797, is described as of great age, and as having lived from early life in a large house surrounded by an enclosure at Hanateiteina. In the

---

[1] For the latter see Gudgeon, *J.P.S.* XVI, p. 63 ff.
[2] Fornander, *P.R.* II, p. 41 f.　　　　　　　　　　[3] Malo, p. 252.
[4] For an account of Paao, see Fornander, *P.R.* II, p. 18. Cf. also p. 254 above.
[5] *Ib.* p. 22.
[6] *Fornander Collection*, Third Series, vol. VI, p. 282 ff.
[7] We are singularly rich in information regarding the religious classes of this Group. For further references, see Williamson, *S.P.S.* II, p. 428 ff.

house was an altar, and human carcasses, scalped, are described as hanging from the beams inside the house, and on the trees around. Only his servant was allowed to enter the premises except when human sacrifices were offered; but it is said that he was invoked, and offerings were sent to him from all parts of the island. The functions and prerogatives of the *atua* are said to be sometimes, though not invariably, hereditary.[1] It is probably to men of this class that Christian refers when, in his account of the *tohungas*, he tells us that

"At times one of them would turn *moke*, leaving his village for good and all, and would take up a solitary abode in some lonely nook of the hills, like one of the hermits of the Middle Ages. These," he adds, "are looked on as men of great sanctity".[2]

Next in importance to the *atua* are the *taua* (*kaula*), 'seers', who are said to be closely allied to them in office and reputation. They are, however, more numerous, and it is certain individuals of this class who "venture to usurp the dignity and name of the *atuas*".[3] Women as well as men are said to belong to the class of *taua*. The *taua* claim to possess a hereditary gift of inspiration, and the power of causing a god to dwell within themselves. Their manifestations of divine inspiration are given chiefly at night, when they cry out in a shrill voice in wild and unnatural sounds, and then give the answers in their usual tone, claiming to be conversing with a god within them. During their ecstasy they become convulsed and prophesy in a squeaking voice, with all the usual manifestations of a dissociated condition. At such times they frequently run about, foretelling death to their enemies in this squeaking voice.[4] They were held in the highest honour by the whole population,[5] and were believed to become gods after their death.[6]

The third class here, as in Hawaii, are the *tuhuna* (*tohunga*), who are more numerous, but less influential than either the *atua* or the *taua*. The

---

[1] Stewart, *Visit* I, p. 249 ff. With the passage from Crook we may compare the account of the *tuhunas*, Christian, *E.P.L.* p. 168 f. Christian's information was obtained from three old 'sages'; but it would seem that in this account all three classes mentioned by Crook are included without distinction. See also Clavel, pp. 43, 68, 162.

[2] *E.P.L.* p. 168 f.   [3] *Loc. cit.*

[4] So in Mangaia and elsewhere the priests habitually speak in a squeaking voice when 'possessed' by a god. Is it in imitation of the voices of birds, the 'messengers' of Tane? According to Mangaian tradition "the god first spoke to man through the small land birds; but their utterances were too indistinct to guide the actions of mankind. To meet this emergency an order of priests was set apart" (Gill, *Myths*, p. 35). We may compare the omen birds of the Sea Dyaks, p. 478 below.

[5] See Christian, *J.P.S.* IV, p. 202.   [6] Stewart, *loc. cit.*

office is not necessarily hereditary, and their chief functions are priestly, consisting of the chanting of the *fagu*, or sacred chants, which, as we have seen (cf. p. 309 above), embody much of the antiquarian and cosmogonic learning of the islanders. The *tuhuna* are chiefly responsible for the education of the Pacific, and the intellectual life generally.

The Paumotu Archipelago offers interesting evidence for the existence of prophetesses.[1] Père Laval heard much of a woman named Toapéré, who lived just before the arrival of European ships, and who is said to have been a noted prophetess.[2] Her 'prophecies' were current in four islands, and Laval tells us that he had heard them referred to a hundred times in public. He obtained much information about her from a chief who is said to have lived in her particular confidence.[3] Many of her 'prophecies' are specifically recorded by Laval.

The evidence of Easter Island is especially interesting. There appear to be no priests, but there are said to be certain men known as *koromake*, who practised spells which would secure the death of an enemy. We have seen that in the Marquesas the *taua*, when possessed by the god, were in the habit of prophesying death to their enemies, and when one of these men turned *moke* (? *make*) they retired into the solitude as *atua*. It would seem possible, therefore, that in the *koromake* Easter Island has preserved the *atua*, as well as the *taua*, but not the *tohunga*, or sanctuary priests. Ngaaru, one of these *koromake*, who was still living when the Routledges visited the island in 1914, was the chief guardian of the ancient traditions. In addition there are also said to have been a class of men and women known as *ivi-atua*, who also possessed second sight and prophetic gifts, and the power of communicating with spirits.[4]

In the Central Pacific,[5] notably in the Cook Group, the higher orders of *tohungas* seem to have commonly[6] been men subject to fits of divine inspiration, and known as *taura* (Hawaiian *kaula*, Marquesan *taua*). Indeed, we have a tradition from Mangaia of the banishment of an order of priests of Tane by Rangi, who was traditionally stated to have been the first ruler of the island, because they could not lay claim to such

[1] See Caret, *Annales* XIV, p. 335.
[2] *Ib.* p. 222 ff.   [3] *Loc. cit.*
[4] Routledge, pp. 142 ff., 239.
[5] We call attention here only to a few outstanding features of the priesthood which have a special bearing on the intellectual life of the islanders, and more especially on its literature. For a fuller treatment, see Williamson, *S.P.S.* II, p. 405 ff., and the references there cited.
[6] According to Buck the 'form of procedure' assumed by a priest in a condition of frenzy was universally adopted by the priests of Mangaia. See *M.S.* p. 177.

divine inspiration[1]—an interesting testimony to the genuine belief of the *taura* in his own 'possession', for had he not been sincere, how easy to assume the semblance of inspiration for his own advancement! As a result of his resolute action, Rangi, so says tradition, obtained from Rarotonga the priest named Motoro, the first of his order, who spoke their responses 'from a foaming mouth', i.e. in a condition of frenzy (see below).

So far tradition. In the same island it was the custom for anyone wishing to consult the oracle of Motoro to bring a present of the best food and a bowl of intoxicating *piper mythisticum* (*kava*), which served as a stimulant to the priest, who delivered his oracles 'from a foaming mouth'[2]—an ambiguous expression, but the general meaning is clear, for the drink induced a dissociated condition in which the oracle was delivered. The responses thus delivered were intelligible to 'the initiated' only,[3] by which are doubtless meant the minor temple officials, as in Tahiti (see below). These responses were, of course, believed to be spoken by the god dwelling temporarily within the priests, who were accordingly known as *pia atua*, 'god boxes'.[4] Their office was hereditary, and their power great. In the eighteenth century Mautara, priest of Motoro, succeeded in raising himself to the temporal rule of the entire island, and the importance of this great priest-king, whose family governed the destiny of Mangaia from c. 1720 to 1821, appears throughout Gill's writings.[5] But in this island all kings were *ex-officio* high priests of Rongo.[6]

The important part played by the priests and their families in the intellectual life of Mangaia is difficult to overrate. The great priestly clan of Mautara and his descendants practically transformed the island into a school of poetry during their supremacy, not only by their own active production, and high standard of poetic art, but also by fostering the periods of peace, and encouraging the great festivals for which much of the best poetry was composed (cf. p. 352 ff. above). It was from Numangatini, king of Mangaia and high priest of Rongo, and from Tereavai, the last priest of the shark-god Tiaio, that Gill obtained a large part of his historical and chronological data, and his knowledge of the esoteric lore and mythological traditions.[7] In Rarotonga, another

---

[1] Gill, *Myths*, p. 19. [2] *Ib.* p. 35.
[3] *Loc. cit.* [4] *Loc. cit.*
[5] See e.g. *L.S.I.* p. 13f.; *D.L.P.* p. 212ff. For Motoro, see p. 327 above.
[6] Gill, *A.A.A.S.* (1890), p. 635.
[7] Gill, *Myths*, p. xx; *A.A.A.S.* (1890), p. 635; *D.L.P.* p. 315.

island of the same Group, the last high priest, Te Ariki-tare-are, to whom reference has already been made (p. 322 above), has furnished us with some of the most important genealogical and historical material which has been recorded from the Pacific.[1] The office of high priest had been hereditary in his family for many centuries. He himself stated that he had been taught the sacred history and traditions by his father, and that he had been "kept in a cave by his mother apart from all others, and from his infancy was taught these...precious truths".[2]

Tahiti also has its prophetic class, in addition to other *tohungas* who are more or less official priests, and who lay no claim to divine inspiration. Sometimes the priest slept all night near the idol, and received his communication in a dream; at other times the message was divined in the cry of a bird, or in the shrill squeaking articulations (cf. p. 449 above) of some of the priests. The most interesting and important manner of delivering the oracle, however, was when the god "entered the priest, who, inflated...with the divinity, ceased to speak as a voluntary agent, but moved and spoke as entirely under supernatural influence".[3] At such times his dissociated condition seems to have been complete. With shrill cries and foaming mouth he revealed the will of the god, which the attendant priests received and interpreted to the people.[4] Sometimes the possession lasted two or three days. Mama, a chief of Eimeo in this Group, assured the missionaries that although he sometimes feigned the fits of inspiration, yet at times they came on him unawares and irresistibly.[5] In the island of Niue the 'prophetic' priests were known as *taula-atua*;[6] but the *patu-iki*, or 'king', had certain duties of a similar nature.

A number of notices of priestesses have been recorded in the Tahiti Group, and in the Marquesas and elsewhere. It is uncertain, however, if such notices can be safely regarded as proving the existence of any class of priestesses in the strict sense of the word, except in so far as

---

[1] See *J.P.S.* VIII, p. 61; cf. also Gill, *A.A.A.S.* (1890), p. 616.

[2] Smith, *J.P.S.* VIII, p. 61. With this period of seclusion during education we may compare the stories of the youth of Aukele and of Honoura, p. 279 above. A similar custom prevailed also in regard to the segregation of the royal heir in Mangareva and neighbouring islands. See S. P. Smith, *J.P.S.* XXVII, p. 120f.; Caillot, *Mythes*, p. 150. See also p. 431 above. We may compare the reference to a similar custom in the Hawaiian version of the story of Hiku. See Andersen, p. 302.

[3] Ellis[1] II, p. 234.

[4] *Ib. loc. cit.*   [5] Tyerman I, p. 124.

[6] *J.P.S.* XI, p. 197; Thomson, *S.I.* p. 95 ff.

these laid claim to prophetic inspiration. In general our authorities do not distinguish between the priestess, or temple official, and the female seer. We have not found any satisfactory ground for supposing that any women of the former class have existed in Polynesia in historical times,[1] except possibly in Samoa.[2] On the other hand, women claiming possession by a divine spirit have been by no means rare. These conclusions seem to be supported also by the evidence of the sagas. We know of no clear instances in the traditions of temple officials who were women, though instances are not lacking of women gifted with second sight, and described as 'prophetesses' and 'sorceresses'. An early Hawaiian saga refers to a renowned seeress of this class called Kukelepolani as having been employed by Kila in Tahiti to help him to find his brother La'a-ma-i-kahiki. We are also told in the same saga that Olopana had been wont to consult her.[3]

In general the distinction between the priest and the prophet which we have noted for the northern and eastern Pacific seems to underlie the systems in Samoa and Tonga also. In Samoa there were at least four classes of priestly and mantic persons who were known as *taula-aitu*.[4] Here also the god was supposed at times to enter into the *taula*, and here also female *taula* are not unknown. Indeed, according to Stair, certain *aitu*, or gods, are said to have been served by women priests,[5] but we have in general little reason to suppose that the custom in regard to women priests differed from that of the eastern Pacific.

In Tonga the priesthood constituted a numerous and powerful body whose support taxed the people very heavily.[6] We hear of priests of such power that no one dared refuse them anything.[7] According to West they were divided into two classes, the *taula*, 'or priests inspired

---

[1] A number of instances which have been recorded are mentioned by Williamson (*S.P.S.* II, p. 425 ff.), but we are inclined to suspect that these have reference in reality to women of prophetic class, or to rare instances in which women's names have become attached to the priestly class, owing to some other circumstance, such as the descent of a priestly line from a female (see e.g. Buck, *M.S.* p. 114 f.), or because a woman has become for some other reason the repository of the lore of the priests (see e.g. Stimson, *T.R.* p. 5 f.).

[2] Stair, *J.P.S.* v, p. 40 f.; cf. also Williamson, *S.P.S.* II, p. 408 and the references there cited.

[3] Emerson, *L.V.* p. 22; *Fornander Collection*, vol. IV, p. 124 ff.; cf. also p. 252 f. above.

[4] Stair, *J.P.S.* v, p. 40 f.

[5] For further information and some references, see Williamson, *S.P.S.* II, p. 408 f.   [6] West, p. 257.

[7] Bays, p. 110; cf. p. 118. We may cf. the reputation of the Irish *filid* (cf. Vol. I, p. 604) and of the Brahmans of India (cf. Vol. II, p. 613).

16

by the gods', and the *feao*, who offered the sacrifices, and maintained the temples in good order and repair.[1] According to Mariner, the priests are hardly ever drawn from the chiefs, but more often from the landed class, or even the peasants; but this observation seems to have particular reference to the *taula* class. Such people are said to have differed in no respect in regard to their status or way of life from other people, but to have been more taciturn and given to reflection, and more observant of what was going on.[2] The priesthood is generally hereditary. Finau, the young prince with whom Mariner lived, was sometimes inspired by the tutelary spirit of his family, but was not on this account regarded as a 'priest'. Only those were considered as such who were frequently inspired by a particular god.[3] Such sporadic divine visitations are here most commonly attributed to females.[4]

Among the Maori also we find classes of men who correspond to the inspired person and the official priest of the Central Pacific, though here again the distinction is not generally noted by our authorities; and indeed the priest and the inspired person are often one and the same, as we have seen to be commonly the case in the Central Pacific also. The term *kaula* does not appear to be used in this sense, but we find a class of men known as *waka* or *kauwaka* who seem to correspond in all respects to the *kaulas*, acting as the medium of the god, whose oracle they received in trance or dream, and also acting sometimes as the guardian of his sanctuary.[5] They also acted as a medium of communication between the living and the dead.[6] The mantic gift was often hereditary, and shared alike by women and men. Gudgeon refers to a great *tohunga* of the early European period who could boast a long line of mantic ancestors on both sides. His mother was a renowned 'sorceress', and his wife even more famous, being descended from a tribe of 'spirits'.[7]

The sketch of the career of Uhia, the first great *tohunga* of the Maori tribal war-god Te Rehu-o-Tainui, is full of interest, both in itself, and for the parallel which it offers to the Zulu prophets, to whom brief reference will be made later (p. 635 f. below). The first manifestations of the god's power over the *tohunga* were seen in his causing him to climb

---

[1] West, p. 254 ff. The distinction drawn by West is not brought out clearly in Mariner's (Martin's) narrative, but it seems to underlie his general remarks.

[2] Mariner[3] II, p. 129.

[3] *Ib.* pp. 87, 125 ff.   [4] *Ib.* I, p. 102 ff.

[5] See Best, *J.P.S.* VI, p. 41.   [6] Dieffenbach II, p. 67.

[7] *J.P.S.* XVI, p. 74. Cf. further Angas II, p. 83; Best, *J.P.S.* VI, p. 43.

a high tree and throw himself down uninjured, and to swim under water for a great distance. "All this time Uhia was in a strange condition, as of a deranged person, and appeared quite ignorant of ordinary affairs. When he recovered his usual senses he found himself possessed by the *atua*."[1] He next entered into the sacred sleep, in which the oracle spoke to him in a poem which he afterwards recited and expounded to the people. The *atua* had spoken, and the tribe marched against their foes, marshalled under the warrior priest Uhia, who performed his incantations while they fought. This was the beginning of his martial career, during which he several times led his tribe successfully to battle, having obtained the guidance of his *atua* in the sacred sleep, and by means of second sight.[2] "Uhia, the warrior priest, had supreme command of the force, and his word was law in regard to all arrangements respecting the *taua* and mode of attack. This was agreed to on account of the great success which had attended the manifestations of Te Rehu-o-Tainui, as given through the seer, the wisdom of whose counsels was admitted by all. Even the leading chiefs gave way to the priest and were silent."[3]

It is instructive to observe that it was the fame of this *tohunga* which made an otherwise obscure god renowned: "After the death of Uhia other *tohungas* became mediums for Te Rehu-o-Tainui, but they never acquired the marvellous power and prestige of the *atua*'s first *waka*, Uhia of Tame-kai-moana, and so the strange powers of that famed war-god gradually waned."[4] The career of Uhia as recounted by Best in his illuminating paper affords a rare opportunity of tracing the origin and development of a tribal god.

A remarkable feature of Maori religion is the absence of evidence for the use of temples, altars, or formal structures.[5] This is all the more remarkable in view of the elaborate nature of the Maori forts, and the excellent quality and artistic appearance of Maori house architecture. The explanation doubtless lies in the comparatively recent occupation of the islands, and the break with the old home sanctuaries. This circumstance must have tended to develop the mantic qualities rather than those of the pure official; it is therefore not surprising that our evidence for private and family manticism appears to be fuller from the Maori than elsewhere in the Pacific.

Traces of family and individual manticism are, nevertheless, common in other island Groups. Fornander was of the opinion[6] that in Hawaii,

---

[1] Best, *J.P.S.* VI, p. 44.
[2] *Ib.* p. 62 ff.
[3] *Ib.* p. 54.
[4] *Ib.* p. 65.
[5] Best, *M.M.R.* p. 170f.
[6] *P.R.* I, p. 109.

and indeed everywhere in the Pacific, the priesthood was not originally a separate class or caste, but a prerogative of chiefs and heads of families. Ellis[1] tells us that even in modern times the king was in the habit of personating the god, and uttering the responses of the oracle from his concealment in a frame of wickerwork. It has already been mentioned (p. 451 above) that in Mangaia the kings were *ex-officio* priests of Rongo. In Rarotonga we are told that the chiefs of the Makea clan, in whose hands the ruling power of the island has been since the thirteenth century, have always had important priestly functions to perform.[2] In Niue Smith was present at a ceremony in which the king himself acted in the capacity of high priest.[3] In Samoa also the chief frequently acted as the officiating priest.[4] The same practice is referred to also in the sagas.[5]

The priests are constantly spoken of as having taken an active part in the long voyages of the Migration Period, when, if we may trust the evidence of tradition, it appears to have been the custom for a *tohunga* to accompany every migration in the capacity of authority on the stars and the weather. The great high priest Paao (cf. p. 254 above) is believed to have led a migration to Hawaii from Samoa early in this period. The great Oahu navigator Paumakua is said to have brought back with him from one of his voyages two *kahunas* and a *kaula*, from whom in later times several priestly families claimed descent.[6] Even in modern times the *tohungas* have shown themselves men of enterprise and travel. Haamanemane, an important priest of Tahiti, and a *tiaio* or friend of Captain Wilson of the *Duff*, built a schooner for himself during his residence in Eimeo with a little assistance from the Europeans, and was in the habit of making pleasure cruises from Eimeo to the neighbouring Groups.[7]

For our purpose, the most interesting aspect of the priests and sanctuaries is their importance in the intellectual life of the Pacific. Naturally the opportunities for studying the intellectual life of the sanctuaries at first hand are comparatively few, since Christian missionaries, our best and earliest witnesses, sought their immediate and complete destruction. By comparing the large amount of information which they have given us, however, with the references to sanctuaries

---

[1] Ellis[1] II, p. 235.
[2] S. P. Smith, *J.P.S.* XII, p. 219; cf. *ib.* VIII, p. 61.
[3] *Ib.* XI, p. 198.
[4] Pritchard, p. 110.   [5] See e.g. *J.P.S.* XIX, p. 153.
[6] *Fornander Collection*, Third Series, vol. VI, p. 248; cf. Emerson, *L.V.* p. 13; Fornander, *P.R.* II, p. 25.   [7] Ellis[1] I, p. 79f.

in the sagas, we are able to realise that they were the great repositories of learning and of the arts.

The most important of the sanctuaries of the Central Pacific (*maraes*) is the great island sanctuary of Ra'iatea[1] or Opoa, 'the grand emporium of idolatry to Tahiti, the Society, and the surrounding islands',[2] which served for the East Pacific much the same purpose as Delphi for the ancient Greek world. Here was situated the great temple of Oro or Rongo. Being considered as the birthplace of the god,[3] as well as of the race,[4] it was among the most celebrated oracles of the people, and was the centre of a widely extended and most sanguinary worship. It is believed to have been the first island colonised in that neighbourhood.[5] It is intimately connected with the most important traditions of the Pacific.[6]

From the traditions of the islanders we gather that in the past the sanctuaries served as the chief repositories of learning, and the chief centres of the intellectual life. Any new discoveries are said to have been at once reported at the temples, and any newly discovered foodstuffs, fruits, seeds, or vegetables handed over to the priests. Kupe on his return from New Zealand presented the greenstone which he found there, and the seeds of the *kumara* or sweet potato at the sanctuary of Ra'iatea. He also reported there the sailing directions, by which he succeeded in reaching New Zealand from Rarotonga, and these directions were preserved by the *tohungas* of Rarotonga down to our own day. At a later period, when Toi wished to sail from Rarotonga to New Zealand, he consulted the Ra'iatean priests, from whom he was given the sailing directions left by Kupe.[7] It is said that the Maori priests have even preserved by oral tradition the course to be steered to attain Tahiti from Hawaii.[8] This course is a difficult one—unlike the course in the reverse direction—and the fidelity of the traditional instructions is remarkable when we reflect that regular communication between Hawaii and Tahiti is believed to have ceased in the twelfth century, and that between New Zealand and the Central Pacific during the fourteenth. The information thus handed over to the priests was sometimes preserved by them in the form of chants (cf. p. 393 f. above). It may be added as a significant fact in regard to the antiquarian interests of the

---

[1] For a general note on this sanctuary, see Smith, *Hawaiki*, p. 255 f.
[2] Williams, *M.E.* p. 55 ff.   [3] Ellis[1] II, p. 234.   [4] *Ib.* p. 39; cf. p. 12.
[5] Gill, *L.S.I.* p. 23.   [6] Ellis[1] II, p. 12; cf. p. 51.
[7] See p. 248 above; cf. also *J.P.S.* XIX, p. 207; cf. also Smith, *Hawaiki*, p. 135.
[8] *J.P.S.* XXII, p. 60.

priests that in Mangaia the only tribe which managed to preserve its genealogies until the European period was that of the Ngati-Vara, the family to which the priestly ruler Mautara belonged.[1]

In regard to physical science and meteorics the knowledge of the *tohungas* was hardly less remarkable, and was equally valuable both for navigation and for native time-reckoning. It is believed that the Maori *tohungas* knew that the earth was round from the reports of the great navigators of the Migration Period, who had sailed beyond the horizon. They knew all the principal stars and constellations, with the times of their rising and setting at different periods of the year.[2] They knew the ocean currents, and had names for all the winds with their chief veering points, and the principal kinds of waves. Gill gives a plan of the winds of the Cook Group, which he took down from the lips of the old priests. With slight variations it holds good for many other Groups in the Pacific.[3] Moreover, the charts[4] and the calabash[5] which served to guide the navigators on their course—the latter serving as combined sextant and compass—were in all probability the work of the *tohungas*, for we have seen in the saga of Rata (p. 275 above) that the priest succeeded in guiding Rata's vessel safely past all dangers by means of his calabash.

In order to secure the best conditions for the preservation and transmission of oral traditional learning, certain institutions have been developed in various island Groups, known as *whare*, such as the *whare wananga*, *whare kura*, etc. The word *whare* means literally 'house', but the existence of a *whare* does not necessarily imply the existence of a building, though such buildings are said to have existed in some cases, and this was doubtless the original intention. In practice the *whare* was in the nature of a 'school', or course of instruction in native learning. The word *wananga*, as we have seen, means inspired knowledge, knowledge which is a part of the divine or spiritual experience of an inspired person; but in fact all knowledge was regarded as *tapu* or in some measure sacred by the Polynesians in general. The association of the *tohunga* and his spiritual and intellectual experience is very close. In other words, the Polynesians do not distinguish, as we do, between secular and spiritual knowledge and experience. Among the Taranaki tribe the *whare kura* is said to have been a house in which tribal lore

---

[1] Buck, *M.S.* p. 57.   [2] Best, *Maori* II, p. 205 ff.; cf. *ib. P.V.* p. 43.
[3] Gill, *Myths*, p. 319; cf. also p. 321.
[4] See e.g. *B.M. Handbook, Ethn. Collect.* p. 176; Andersen, p. 31; Smith, *Hawaiki*, p. 187.   [5] Andersen, p. 42.

was taught, while the *whare wananga* dealt only with knowledge of more advanced types, and presumably of wider bearing; but this distinction does not appear to have been universal.

Our fullest information relates to the *whare wananga* of the Maori,[1] in which the traditional oral learning of the Maori was carried on by *tohungas* who appear to have belonged to several orders. The learning itself was guarded with the utmost jealousy and secrecy,[2] being regarded as exceedingly *tapu*. The desire was to hand on the traditional lore with as little change as possible. Great ceremony attended the courses, while the pupils were subject to much ritual and *tapu*. Whatever place was set apart, temporarily or permanently, for these classes was *tapu* while the session lasted, which was generally for a month or more, sometimes for a whole winter.[3] It is said that the pupils had to undergo a preliminary teaching amongst their own tribe before entering the *whare wananga*. The scholars were selected from among the 'young lads' who showed a disposition towards learning, and had been observed to be accomplished in telling stories. Only young lads belonging to families of good standing were taught by the *tohungas* the higher knowledge which was regarded as fitting for the chiefs and priests, especially knowledge relating to religion, cosmogony, traditional history and other antiquarian matters.

We are singularly fortunate in having in our hands a record of what was one of the last genuine sittings of the Maori *whare wananga*. This record was made in the late fifties of last century, when at a large gathering of east coast Maori, it was decided that the most learned of the *tohungas* present should instruct the assembled tribes as to how and when New Zealand was first peopled by the Maori race. It was decided that Te Matorohanga should lecture, assisted by two other *tohungas*, who should recall matter which he might omit, or supplement his knowledge where their own was fuller. It was also decided—and herein lay an innovation—that the lectures should be written down by a 'scribe' as they were delivered, in order to ensure the knowledge being preserved; and this was done by two young men, named Te Whatohoro and Te Kumeroa, who had been educated at the mission schools. In all other respects the conditions under which the lectures were delivered, and the subjects dealt with were the same as those which

---

[1] Our principal sources of information are *Mem. P.S.* III, IV; Best, *M.S.L.*

[2] For the necessity felt by the *tohungas* of guarding their knowledge as a jealous secret, see pp. 239, 392 above, and cf. Gill, *Myths*, p. xx. See further Wilkes IV, p. 121.   [3] Best, *M.S.L.* p. 11.

had prevailed in the *whare wananga* in the past. For more than half a century the traditions thus put on record were considered of too sacred a nature to be disclosed to Europeans; but the advance of civilisation among the Maori, and the knowledge of the risk which the papers ran of being destroyed by fire, induced the owner of the MS. to allow it to be printed, and early this century this invaluable document was published, together with an English translation, by S. P. Smith.[1] The whole procedure, as we see it in the original document, is strikingly similar to that described in the early Norse prose work known as *Gylfaginning*,[2] and here also the lecture is interrupted and carried forward, as it were, by questions from the interlocutor, who corresponds to the Maori 'scribe'.

It should be mentioned that in addition to the *whare wananga*, dedicated to the teaching of the higher types of knowledge, there existed also in some districts (i.e. among some tribes) other *whare*. Thus among the Takitumu Maori we hear also of *whare maire*, devoted to the teaching of the arts of black magic. Such teaching appears to have been given at night, and to have been sacred to the god Whiro, who among the Maori is opposed to Tane, and seems to represent disease and death.[3] Among the Tuhoe Maori, however, the *whare maire* was devoted to the teaching of racial and tribal history.

Both on the ground of tradition and of distribution the *whare wananga* appears to be an ancient institution. The divine prototype is ascribed by high class Maori tradition to the uppermost of the twelve Heavens, the abode of the great god Io (see p. 308 above); and in this same Heaven is also the 'house' from which our earthly knowledge is derived. This house is known as Rangiatea, which is apparently the earlier form of the name Ra'iatea.[4] The first institution of this kind to exist on earth is traditionally placed in Hawaiki,[5] the home of the race. It was apparently an edifice known as the *whare kura*, which, generally speaking, seems to have been an alternative name of *whare wananga*, and its form and semblance are said to have been obtained by Tane and two of his brothers from the second Heaven.[6] A number of other names of *whare wananga* of the past are on record, among the most interesting of which

---

[1] *Mem. P.S.* III, IV.   [2] See p. 902 below.
[3] Best, *M.S.L.* p. 10; cf. however, p. 312 above.
[4] *Mem. P.S.* IV, p. 275 f.
[5] Best, *M.S.L.* p. 7; cf. Cowan, *F.F.T.* p. 28 f.
[6] See *Mem. P.S.* IV, p. 276. For another reference to the *whare kura*, see *J.P.S.* VII, p. 35 f.

is that of the *are vananga* of Rarotonga, concerning which some interesting notes have been preserved.[1]

Institutions similar in many respects to those which we have been discussing can be traced elsewhere in Polynesia. A school of learning is said to have existed formerly on the Marquesas,[2] and Handy's accounts[3] of the manner in which the traditional learning was taught by the *tohungas* to both young people and adults is strong confirmation of this. The address of the last high priest of Rarotonga at the opening of the traditions which he himself placed on record also looks like a formula used in connection with a similar system of teaching.[4] In Samoa the three great divisions of the island of Upolu each possessed a set of traditions which were preserved by companies of old men who constituted a *fale tala*, or 'house of record', and here, as in New Zealand, the members are said to have cherished their records with great care, handing them down from father to son with the utmost scrupulousness.[5] One of the Paumotu chants of Taaki (Tawhaki) contains an allusion to *fare-kura i te Po*, i.e. the *whare kura* in Po, or the realm to which the dead are destined to go, and where the gods dwell, according to Paumotu teaching.[6] Maori (Taranaki) tradition knows a similar institution in Po presided over by Miru.[7]

Even apart from the intellectual importance of the great sanctuaries, and of institutions such as the *whare wananga*, where the *tohungas* form a responsible intellectual body, it would be difficult to overrate the importance of the *tohungas* as individuals to the intellectual life of the islanders in other respects also. Handy refers to great chanting festivals in the Marquesas,[8] which are held on occasions of family or tribal importance, such as the completion of a canoe or a house, or the birth of a firstborn heir. On such occasions the various branches of the families of important chiefs meet together, and, led by the *tohunga*, who makes himself responsible for the earlier portions of the genealogies, the families recite their ancestral lines, often beginning with the Creation, and coming down to the various modern lines and subdivisions. Each chanter is led, or given his cue, and checked by the *tohunga*. Sometimes these Marquesan chants are recited by 'old women skilled in the art'.[9] In Hawaii and Samoa we have seen (pp. 238, 391 above) that the

[1] *J.P.S.* XII, p. 219.
[2] Best, *M.S.L.* p. 11.
[3] *M.L.* p. 20; cf. also *N.C.M.* p. 318.
[4] *J.P.S.* VIII, p. 62.
[5] Stair, *J.P.S.* IV, p. 53.
[6] Stimson, *L.M.T.* p. 74.
[7] See *J.P.S.* VII, 59 ff.; and cf. Cowan, *F.F.T.* p. 28 f.; cf. also p. 295 above.
[8] *N.C.M.* pp. 314 ff.; 322 ff.
[9] *Ib.* p. 341.

genealogical activities of the *tohungas* are no less prominent, and that the importance of such genealogical material for a people without charters or written documents of any kind gives to their custodians the prestige of legal referees.

On the other hand the intellectual activities of the *tohungas* are by no means confined to scientific, historical and antiquarian matters. We have seen that the political preoccupations of the Hawaiian 'prophets' have resulted in ambitious *wananga* or political 'prophecies' extending to 800 lines. In the Marquesas even the *utas* or ceremonial love poems chanted by the members of the *are kaioi*, or *tattoo* groups, are composed for them by the *tohungas*. We have seen that the best saga material throughout the Pacific, and the most ambitious chants, whether pertaining to the gods or to the great heroes of the past, have been recorded from the *tohungas*. Where such chants and sagas have been recorded only after the death of the last of the great *tohungas*, as among the Moriori,[1] the results are apt to be very fragmentary. The preoccupation of the *tohungas* with exact knowledge is the more surprising when we reflect on the large part which 'revelation' and occult knowledge also plays, and the high prestige accorded to the inspired *kaula*, or 'seer'. This intellectual life is, as we have seen, centred in the great permanent local sanctuaries, as well as in institutions, such as the *whare wananga*, and the *whare karioi*, which are, on the whole[2], less rigidly localised, and of a more temporary character, like our own 'summer schools'. It would be interesting to know in what relationship the two latter Polynesian institutions stood to one another. The evidence of the sagas suggests that they were not wholly independent.

We have already referred to the poetical contests by means of which the standard of knowledge and of poetry was maintained among the islanders of the Pacific, as elsewhere where written texts are unknown. The evidence of the Marquesas is particularly interesting in this respect, and shows once more the high standard of intellectual culture and artistic life of this Group. Here we are told of a form of extempore dialogue known as the *u'i*, which consisted of the matching of wits by two *tohungas* (not necessarily priests), held in the form of a dialogue, during which a judge would sit between them, while they 'cross-questioned and recriminated each other'. The contestants were *tuhuna o'ono*, 'masters of myth, legend, and genealogies'. The one outwitted was considered as 'defeated and overthrown by the victor', and it is

---

[1] See Shand, *J.P.S.* VII, p. 74.
[2] See, however, the *are kariei*, or *karioi* of Rarotonga, *J.P.S.* XII, p. 219.

even said that 'formerly a *tuhuna* was defeated and killed', while even to-day it is believed by some that 'those who pretend to knowledge they do not possess will die'.[1]

A favourite occasion for the recitation of an *u'i* is the visit of a party from one valley[2] or island to another, when, before landing, and unless sure of a welcome, the visiting party would sing an *u'i* in the form of a chant of defiance, in reply to which the local tribe would sing a chant called *vave*. It is doubtless in accordance with this custom that Teohu and the orators of the *areoi* are described by the missionaries of Tahiti as parleying from their canoes before landing, while Pomare and his orators were ranged in line on the seashore, listening attentively. In this 'parley' the new arrivals are said to recapitulate certain articles of their belief, such as the origin of their forefathers, etc.[3] The sagas make constant reference to the chant of the *tohunga* of a landing party from the prow of the canoe, which is doubtless the *u'i*.

The practical bearing of such disputations is aptly illustrated by a curious saga from Aitutaki,[4] which relates to a contest in words carried on partly in verse and partly in prose, between the severed head of Tauto, the son of Iro, a hero of the Migration Period (cf. p. 312 above), and two *tohungas* on behalf of their chief Puna. The gist of the contest is really a legal pleading, the head demanding in righteous wrath to know why it has been severed. As the head overcomes three pairs of *tohungas* successively in dialectic, Tauto cries triumphantly to the chief: "I have vanquished you in argument, and tomorrow...your head will be taken off by my brother Iro."

Not the least interesting feature of this remarkable story is the employment by Puna of the *tohungas* to act as spokesmen for him.

In conclusion a word must be said on the subject of oratory, which in Polynesia is cultivated to a remarkable degree. Moerenhout was of the opinion that in the past this art was held in higher esteem than among any other people in the world. He tells us that in Tahiti there were formerly masters of rhetoric and schools where the art of speech was taught; the art was regarded as essential to a ruling chief, whose subsequent reputation is said to have rested more on his eloquence than on his deeds of valour.[5] Certain classes of orators are denoted by special

---

[1] Handy, *N.C.M.* p. 340.
[2] Before roads were made by Europeans the natives almost invariably journeyed from one valley to another by sea.   [3] *L.M.S. Trans.* I, p. 249.
[4] *J.P.S.* XII, p. 136.   [5] Moerenhout I, p. 406ff.

names, and have specialised functions. Moerenhout and Ellis speak of a class of men known as *rautis*, whose duty it was to urge on the warriors to battle, and encourage them throughout the combat with words full of eloquence. Their diction was bombastic and grandiloquent, and was evidently highly artificial and cultivated.[1]

The most interesting and important class of orators of Tahiti were a class of men known as *orero*.[2] One or more of these officials are said to have been attached to the *maraes*, or native temples, as members of the staff,[3] and every district had one or two of them.[4] They were highly respected and generally belonged to the families of the chiefs.[5] Their office was generally hereditary.[6] Their education was long and elaborate,[7] and they are said to have been the most learned men in the community, and to have acted as both teachers and general instructors,[8] and also as record keepers (oral).[9] They acquired their learning largely in the form of songs, which they are said to have learnt *verbatim*, and transmitted in turn to their pupils.[10] Their learning consisted of religious and antiquarian matters, natural science and navigation, the divisions of time[11]—in fact all the matters which have already been enumerated as in the province of the *tohungas*, of whom the *orero* doubtless formed one class. Their memories, we are told, were astonishing, and they could recite their oral traditions for whole nights at a time.[12]

All writers emphasise the dignified bearing and grandiloquent manner of these men when delivering their speeches. They acted as spokesmen at political and religious ceremonies, and were accustomed to declaim before the *marae* to an immense crowd with astonishing volubility.[13] According to the London Missionaries, at the installation of Pomare II of Tahiti the *taata orero*, or public orator, opened the ceremony with a long address;[14] and they mention that all public business was transacted by them. They describe the respective speakers of Pomare I and Tu

---

[1] Moerenhout, *loc. cit.*; Ellis[1] II, p. 488.

[2] Williamson (*S.P.S.* II, p. 424) has shown grounds for identifying the class of people described under the name *orero* by de Bovis, G. and J. R. Forster and others, with the officials described by Moerenhout (II, p. 419 f.) as *harepo*. The work of de Bovis has not been accessible to me. My references are from Williamson.

[3] De Bovis, pp. 217, 279 f.   [4] G. Forster II, p. 154.

[5] J. R. Forster, p. 528 f.; G. Forster II, p. 148.

[6] De Bovis, p. 279.   [7] De Bovis, p. 280 f.; J. R. Forster, p. 528 f.

[8] G. Forster, *loc. cit.*

[9] De Bovis, p. 280, notes.   [10] Caillot, *P.O.* p. 85.

[11] G. and J. R. Forster, De Bovis, *loc. cit.*; Moerenhout I, p. 507.

[12] Moerenhout, *loc. cit.*   [13] De Bovis, p. 280.

[14] Caillot, *P.O.* p. 85.

(Pomare II) as seated on the ground opposite each other on the occasion of the ratification of peace, and haranguing on the subject of their meeting.[1] It will be seen that in their office and status, as well as in their intellectual equipment and their oratorical delivery, the *orero* bear a close resemblance to the *tohungas*, and also to some of the male leaders and other senior members of the *areoi*, the *hoki*, and the *hula*, and we have little doubt that they are identical with certain of these officials.[2]

Oratory is equally highly developed in Samoa. Here a class of men who seem to have had official standing as orators, and who have something in common with the *orero* and the *rautis*, are known as *alataua*.[3] These men are said to have been keepers of traditions and genealogies in early times. They were held to be in touch with the gods, and their counsel was always sought at important gatherings, especially in times of war. They were associated to some extent with certain villages,[4] which were exempt from fighting, but had special religious duties at such times. Williamson regards them as hereditary priestly orator-chiefs, intimately connected with the great royal families of Samoa.[5] Space will not permit us to enter into details in regard to the speeches delivered at the assemblies. It must suffice to say that these were long and very elaborate, couched in highly polished diction and delivered in a peripatetic manner. It is probably safe to say that nowhere in Polynesia, perhaps nowhere in the world, has the art of public eloquence been so highly cultivated as in Samoa.

In New Zealand a high degree of technique is observed in public oratory, and the orations delivered on state occasions (*taki*) are said to be composed according to certain recognised laws regulating their form and arrangement.[6] The speaker generally begins by chanting a song which has reference to the subject under discussion, after which follows a speech in which the subject is set forth. Another short song follows, illustrating further the matter in hand, followed by the con-

---

[1] *L.M.S. Trans.* i, p. 116.

[2] The identification is rendered even more probable if we accept Williamson's equation of the *orero* with the class of officials whom Moerenhout calls *harepo*, but who do not seem to be identical with the *harepo* mentioned by other writers. Even if these two classes are actually distinct, this hardly affects our theme, which is the high development of oratory, and the high status of orators, of whatever class, in Tahiti and elsewhere.

[3] For important references and conclusions relating to the *alataua*, see Williamson, *S.P.S.*, Index, *s.v.*

[4] See Turner, pp. 234, 316.   [5] Krämer I, p. 476.

[6] Shortland, p. 186 ff.

clusion of the speech. While he is delivering the more emotional parts
of the speech, the orator walks or runs a short distance during each
sentence, sometimes concluding the period by a leap to give emphasis,
and accompanying his words with graceful motions of the arms and
body. Shortland quotes a letter from a Christian chief to another of a
hostile tribe written in the form and manner of one of these public
speeches, and illustrating the use of songs. A similar practice evidently
prevailed in formal speeches in Tahiti, for the London Missionaries
mention that during their stay there seven men (one of whom was a
priest), five women, and two children were driven ashore in a canoe,
and at their interview with Pomare, the speaker, after delivering a few
words, began singing, all the rest, except the priest, joining in. They
continued speaking and singing alternately till the oration was concluded.[1]

We have already seen (p. 414 above) that Hawaiian saga recognises
the important part played by rhetoric and the art of disputation, known
here as *hoopaapaa* or *hoopapa*, and that proficiency in this art is regarded
as a safe and rapid step to acquiring wealth and fame. We have seen
also that proficiency in all matters pertaining to facility in literary
expression is fostered by literary contests and disputations. In oratory,
as in all other intellectual matters, the Polynesians are outstanding
among peoples ignorant of the art of writing for their high intellectual
level, and the cultivation of a technical literary standard. We shall see
later that a similar development of oratory has taken place among the
Galla, who in this respect come near to the Polynesians, and who like
them recognise the importance for political purposes, as for entertainment and intellectual and religious instruction, of polished and ordered
speech and eloquence.

[1] *L.M.S. Trans.* I, p. 56.

LIST OF ABBREVIATIONS[1]

AUTHOR AND TITLE OF BOOK	ABBREVIATION
ANDERSEN, J. C. *Myths and Legends of the Polynesians.* London, 1928.	Andersen.
—— 'Maori Music with its Polynesian Background.' In *Mem.P.S.* x. New Plymouth, N.Z. 1934.	Andersen, *M.M.P.B.*
ANGAS, G. F. *Savage Life and Scenes in Australia and New Zealand.* 2 vols. London, 1847–.	Angas.
ARBOUSSET, J. T. *Tahiti et les Îles adjacentes.* Paris, 1867.	Arbousset.
TE ARII TAIMAI, E. (Mrs SALMON). *Memoirs of Arii Taimai.* Paris, 1901.	Arii Taimai.
ASTON, W. G. *Shinto, the Way of the Gods.* London, 1905.	Aston[1].
—— *Shinto, the Ancient Religion of Japan.* London, 1907.	Aston, *Shinto*[2].
BASTIAN, A. *Inselgruppen in Oʒeanien....* Berlin, 1883.	Bastian.
BAYS, P. A Narrative of the Wreck of the Minerva Whaler.... Cambridge, 1831.	Bays
BEST, ELSDON. *Some Aspects of Maori Myth and Religion.* Dominion Museum Monographs, No. 1. Wellington, 1922.	Best, *M.M.R.*
—— *The Maori School of Learning.* Dominion Museum Monographs, No. 6. Wellington, 1923.	Best, *M.S.L.*
—— *Polynesian Voyagers.* Dominion Museum Monographs, No. 5. Wellington, 1923.	Best, *P.V.*
—— *The Maori.* 2 vols. Wellington, 1924.	Best, *Maori.*
British Museum. Handbook to the Ethnographical Collection. 2nd ed. 1925.	B.M. Handbook, Eth. C.
BUCK, P. H. (TE RANGI HIROA). *The Material Culture of the Cook Islands (Aitutaki).* New Plymouth, N.Z. 1927.	Buck, *M.C.C.I.*
—— *Samoan Material Culture.* B. P. Bishop Mus. Bulletin 75. Honolulu, 1930.	Buck, *S.M.C.*
—— *Ethnology of Tongareva.* B. P. Bishop Mus. Bulletin 92. Honolulu, 1932.	Buck, *E.T.*
—— *Ethnology of Manihiki and Rakahanga.* B. P. Bishop Mus. Bulletin 99. Honolulu, 1932.	Buck, *E.M.R.*
—— *Mangaian Society.* B. P. Bishop Mus. Bulletin 122. Honolulu, 1934.	Buck, *M.S.*

[1] See Note, Part I, p. 219 above.

AUTHOR AND TITLE OF BOOK	ABBREVIATION

BURROWS, E. G. *Ethnology of Futuna*. B. P. Bishop Mus. Bulletin 138. Honolulu, 1936. — Burrows.

CAILLOT, A. C. E. *Les Polynésiens orientaux aux Contact de la Civilisation*. Paris, 1909. — Caillot, *P.O.*

—— *Histoire de la Polynésie Orientale*. Paris, 1910. — Caillot, *H.P.O.*

—— *Mythes, Légendes, et Traditions des Polynésiens*. Paris, 1914. — Caillot, *Mythes*.

—— *Histoire des Religions de l'Archipel Paumotu*. Paris, 1932. — Caillot, *Religions*.

CHARTIER, H. LE. *Tahiti*. Paris, 1887. — Chartier.

CHRISTIAN, F. W. *The Caroline Islands*. London, 1899. — Christian, *C.I.*

—— *Eastern Pacific Lands: Tahiti and the Marquesas Islands*. London, 1910. — Christian, *E.P.L.*

—— *Mangaian Vocabulary*. B. P. Bishop Mus. Bulletin 11. Honolulu, 1924. — Christian, *M.V.*

CHURCHILL, L. P. *Samoa Uma*. London, 1902. — Churchill.

CHURCHWARD, W. B. *My Consulate in Samoa*. London, 1887. — Churchward.

CLAVEL, C. *Les Marquisiens*. Paris, 1885. — Clavel.

COOK, J. *A Voyage towards the South Pole and round the World...in the years 1772–1775*. 2 vols. London, 1777. — Cook[1].

—— *A Voyage to the Pacific Ocean...in the years 1776–1780*. 3 vols. Vols. I and II written by J. C., Vol. III by Captain J. King. 2nd Ed. London, 1785. — Cook[2].

COWAN, J. *Maori Folk-Tales of the Port Hills*. Wellington, 1923. — Cowan, *P.H.*

—— *Fairy Folk-Tales of the Maori*. Wellington, 1925. — Cowan, *F.F.T.*

CUZENT, G. *Voyage aux Îles Gambier*. Paris, 1872. — Cuzent.

DE BOVIS. *État de la Société Taitienne, à l'arrivée des Européens*. Papeete, 1863. — De Bovis.

DE ROCHAS, V. *La Nouvelle Calédonie et ses Habitants*. Paris, 1862. — De Rochas.

DICKINS, F. V. *Primitive and Medieval Japanese Texts*. Translated into English. Oxford, 1906. — Dickins.

DIEFFENBACH, E. *Travels in New Zealand*. 2 vols. London, 1843. — Dieffenbach.

DUMONT D'URVILLE. *Voyage au Pôle Sud et dans l'Océanie*. Paris, 1842– . — Dumont d'Urville.

ELLIS, W. *Polynesian Researches*. 2 vols. London, 1829. — Ellis[1].

—— *Polynesian Researches*. 2nd ed. 4 vols. London, 1832–4. — Ellis[2].

(Both editions have been used in the present work.)

Author and Title of Book	Abbreviation
EMERSON, NATHANIEL BRIGHT. *The Long Voyages of the Ancient Hawaiians.* Papers of the Hawaiian Historical Society, No. 5. Honolulu, 1893.	Emerson, *L.V.*
—— *Unwritten Literature of Hawaii.* Smithsonian Institution, Bureau of Ethnology, Bulletin No. 38. Washington, Columbia, 1909.	Emerson, *U.L.*
FLORENZ, K. *Die historischen Quellen der Shinto-Religion.* Göttingen, 1919.	Florenz, *H.Q.*
FORNANDER, ABRAHAM. *An Account of the Polynesian Race.* 3 vols. London, 1878, etc.	Fornander, *P.R.*
Fornander Collection of Hawaiian Antiquities and Folklore . . . as gathered from original sources. By A. Fornander. . . . With translations . . . revised and illustrated with notes by Thomas G. Thrum. 9 pts. Memoirs of the B. P. Bishop Museum. Vols. IV–VI. Honolulu, 1916–.	*Fornander Collection.*
FORSTER, J. G. A. *A Voyage round the World in His Majesty's sloop 'Resolution', commanded by Capt. James Cook, during the years 1772, 3, 4, and 5.* 2 vols. London, 1777.	G. Forster.
FORSTER, J. R. *Observations made during a voyage round the world on physical geography, natural history, and ethic philosophy. . . .* London, 1778.	J. R. Forster.
FRAZER, Sir JAMES GEORGE. *The Belief in Immortality and the Worship of the Dead.* London, 1913, etc.	Frazer, *Belief.*
GIFFORD, E. W. *Tongan Place Names.* B. P. Bishop Mus. Bulletin 7. Honolulu, 1923.	Gifford, *T.P.N.*
—— *Tongan Myths and Tales.* B. P. Bishop Mus. Bulletin 8. Honolulu, 1924.	Gifford, *T.M.T.*
GILL, WILLIAM. *Gems from the Coral Islands.* London, 1856.	Gill, *Gems.*
GILL, WILLIAM WYATT. *Life in the Southern Isles.* London, 1876.	Gill, *L.S.I.*
—— *Myths and Songs from the South Pacific.* London, 1876.	Gill, *Myths.*
—— *Historical Sketches of Savage Life in Polynesia.* Wellington, 1880.	Gill, *S.L.P.*
—— *Jottings from the Pacific.* London, 1885.	Gill, *Jottings.*
—— 'The Fountain of "The Mist"—a Rarotongan Myth.' In *A.A.A.S.* p. 616 ff. Sydney, 1890.	Gill, *A.A.A.S.* (1890), p. 616 ff.
—— 'The Genealogy of the Kings of Rarotonga and Mangaia.' In *A.A.A.S.* p. 627 ff. Sydney, 1890.	Gill, *A.A.A.S.* (1890), p. 627 ff.
—— *The South Pacific and New Guinea.* Chicago, 1893.	Gill, *S.P.N.G.*
—— *From Darkness to Light in Polynesia.* London, 1894.	Gill, *D.L.P.*

AUTHOR AND TITLE OF BOOK	ABBREVIATION
GORER, G. *Bali and Angkor*. London, 1936.	Gorer.
GREY, the Rt Hon. Sir GEORGE. *Polynesian Mythology and Ancient Traditional History of the New Zealanders*. . . . A reissue. Auckland, 1929.	Grey.
HANDY, E. S. CRAIGHILL. *Tattooing in the Marquesas*. B. P. Bishop Mus. Bulletin 1. Honolulu, 1922.	Handy, *T.M.*
—— *Native Culture in the Marquesas*. B. P. Bishop Mus. Bulletin 9. Honolulu, 1923.	Handy, *N.C.M.*
—— *Polynesian Religion*. B. P. Bishop Mus. Bulletin 34. Honolulu, 1927.	Handy, *P.R.*
—— *Marquesan Legends*. B. P. Bishop Mus. Bulletin 69. Honolulu, 1930.	Handy, *M.L.*
—— *History and Culture of the Society Islands*. B. P. Bishop Mus. Bulletin 79. Honolulu, 1930.	Handy, *H.C.S.I.*
HAVEMEYER, L. *The Drama of Savage Peoples*. London, 1916.	Havemeyer.
HENRY, TEUIRA. *Ancient Tahiti*. B. P. Bishop Mus. Bulletin 48. Honolulu, 1928.	Henry, *A.T.*
HOSE, C. and MACDOUGALL, W. *The Pagan Tribes of Borneo*. . .with an appendix on the physical characters of the races of Borneo by A. C. Haddon. 2 vols. London, 1912.	Hose and MacDougall.
JOHNSTONE, J. C. *Maoria*. London, 1874.	Johnstone.
BECKWITH, M. W. *Kepelino's Traditions of Hawaii*. B. P. Bishop Mus. Bulletin 95. Honolulu, 1932.	Kepelino.
Kojiki. See List of Abbreviations to Part I.	*Kojiki.*
KOTZEBUE, OTTO V. *A Voyage of Discovery into the South Sea and Beering's Straits, for the purpose of exploring a North-East Passage*. . .*in*. . .*1815–1818*. 3 vols. London, 1821.	Kotzebue.
KRÄMER, Prof. Dr AUGUSTIN. *Die Samoa-Inseln*. 2 Bd. Stuttgart, 1901–2.	Krämer.
KRAUSE, G. and WITH, K. *Bali*. Hagen-i.-W. 1922.	Krause.
LAMONT, E. H. *Wild Life among the Pacific Islanders*. London, 1867.	Lamont.
LAWRY, W. *Friendly and Feejee Islands: a missionary visit*. . .*in the year 1847*. London, 1850.	Lawry.
LENWOOD, F. *Pastels from the Pacific*. Oxford, 1917.	Lenwood.
LESSON, R. P. *Voyage autour du monde*. . .*sur la corvette 'La Coquille'*. 2 tom. Paris, 1839.	Lesson.
MACDOUGALL, W. See Hose, C.	
MALO, DAVIDA. *Hawaiian Antiquities*. Honolulu, 1903.	Malo.
MANING, F. E. *Old New Zealand*. London, 1884.	Maning.

Author and Title of Book	Abbreviation
MARINER, WILLIAM. *An account of the natives of the Tonga Islands in the South Pacific Ocean* . . .compiled . . .from the . . .communications of W. M. . . .by J. Martin. 2 vols. London, 1817.	Mariner[1].
—— *Tonga Islands.* 3rd ed. 2 vols. Constable's Miscellany, Vols. 13, 14. Edinburgh, 1827.	Mariner[3].
MARSHALL, P. *Geology of Mangaia.* B. P. Bishop Mus. Bulletin 36. Honolulu, 1927.	Marshall.
MELVILLE, H. *Narrative of a four months' residence among the natives of a valley of the Marquesas Islands.* London, 1846.	Melville.
MOERENHOUT, J. A. *Voyages aux îles du Grand Océan.* . . . 2 tom. Paris, 1837.	Moerenhout.
Nihongi. See List of Abbreviations to Part I.	*Nihongi.*
PORTER, Capt. DAVID. *Journal of a Cruise made to the Pacific Ocean* . . .*in the United States Frigate 'Essex', in the years 1812, 1813 and 1814.* 2 vols. 2nd ed. New York, 1822.	Porter.
PRITCHARD, W. T. *Polynesian Reminiscences.* London, 1866.	Pritchard.
REEVES, W. PEMBER. *The Long White Cloud.* . . . 3rd ed. London, 1924.	Reeves.
RICE, W. K. *Hawaiian Legends.* B. P. Bishop Mus. Bulletin 3. Honolulu, 1923.	Rice.
RIVERS, W. H. R. *The History of Melanesian Society.* 2 vols. Cambridge, 1914.	Rivers.
SCORESBY ROUTLEDGE, K. *The Mystery of Easter Island.* London, 1919.	Routledge.
SHORTLAND, E. *Traditions and Superstitions of the New Zealanders.* 2nd ed. London, 1856.	Shortland.
SIBREE, J. *Antananarivo Annual,* Vols. XIII, XIV.	Sibree, *A.A.*
SMITH, STEPHENSON PERCY. *Hawaiki: the original home of the Maori.* 4th ed. Auckland, 1921.	Smith, *Hawaiki.*
STAIR. '*Old Samoa.*' London, 1897.	Stair.
STEWART, Rev. C. S. *Private Journal of a Voyage to the Pacific Ocean, and Residence at the Sandwich Islands, in the years 1822, 1823, 1824 and 1825.* New York, 1828.	Stewart, *Residence.*
—— *A Visit to the South Seas in the U.S. Ship 'Vincennes'—during the years 1829 and 1830.* . . . 2 vols. London, 1832.	Stewart, *Visit.*
STIMSON, J. F. *Tuamotuan Religion.* B. P. Bishop Mus. Bulletin 103. Honolulu, 1933.	Stimson, *T.R.*
—— *The Cult of Kiho-tumu.* B. P. Bishop Mus. Bulletin 111. Honolulu, 1933.	Stimson, *Kiho-tumu.*

AUTHOR AND TITLE OF BOOK	ABBREVIATION
STIMSON, J. F. *The Legends of Maui and Tahaki.* B. P. Bishop Mus. Bulletin 127. Honolulu, 1934.	Stimson, *L.M.T.*
TAYLOR, R. *Te Ika a Maui: New Zealand and its Inhabitants.* 2nd ed. London, 1870.	Taylor.
THOMSON, Sir B. H. *The Diversions of a Prime Minister.* Edinburgh and London, 1894.	Thomson, *Diversions.*
—— *Savage Island.* London, 1902.	Thomson, *S.I.*
THURNWALD, R. C. *Profane Literature of Buin, Solomon Islands.* Yale University Press, 1936.	Thurnwald.
TREGEAR, EDWARD. *The Maori-Polynesian Comparative Dictionary.* Wellington, N.Z. 1891.	Tregear, *Dictionary.*
TURNER, Rev. GEORGE. *Samoa a Hundred Years Ago.* London, 1884.	Turner.
TYERMAN, Rev. DANIEL. *Journal of Voyages and Travels by the Rev. D. Tyerman and G. Bennet, Esq. in the South Sea Islands...between the years 1821 and 1829...compiled...by* J. M[ontgomery]. 2 vols. London, 1831.	Tyerman.
WALEY, A. *Japanese Poetry.* Oxford, 1919.	Waley, *J.P.*
WEST, T. *Ten Years in South Central Polynesia.* London, 1865.	West.
WESTERVELT, WILLIAM DRAKE. *Legends of Ma-ui the Demi-God.* Honolulu, 1910.	Westervelt, *L.M.*
—— *Legends of Old Honolulu.* London, 1915.	Westervelt, *L.O.H.*
—— *Hawaiian Legends of Volcanoes.* London, 1916.	Westervelt, *H.L.V.*
WHITE, J. *Ancient History of the Maori.* 6 vols. Wellington, 1887–90.	White.
WILKES, CHARLES. *Narrative of the United States Exploring Expedition during the years 1838, 1839, 1840, 1841, 1842.* In 5 vols. Philadelphia, 1845.	Wilkes.
WILLIAMS, H. W. *Dictionary of the Maori Language.* Wellington, N.Z. 1917.	Williams, *Dictionary.*
WILLIAMS, JOHN. *A Narrative of Missionary Enterprises in the South Sea Islands....* London, 1837.	Williams, *M.E.*
WILLIAMSON, ROBERT W. *The Social and Political Systems of Central Polynesia.* 3 vols. Cambridge, 1924.	Williamson, *S.P.S.*
—— *Religious and Cosmic Beliefs of Central Polynesia.* 2 vols. Cambridge, 1933.	Williamson, *R.C.B.*
WILSON, WILLIAM. *A Missionary Voyage to the Southern Pacific Ocean...in the years 1796, 1797, 1798, in the ship 'Duff', commanded by Capt. James Wilson...compiled from the journals of the officers and missionaries....* London, 1799.	Wilson.

AUTHOR AND TITLE OF BOOK   ABBREVIATION

WOOD, C. F. *A Yachting Cruise in the South Seas.*   Wood.
London, 1875.

PERIODICALS

Annales de la Propagation de la Foi. Lyon, 1834, etc.   *Annales.*

The Antananarivo Annual and Madagascar Magazine.   *A.A.*
Ed. J. Sibree, etc. Antananarivo, Madagascar,
1875–92.

Australian Association for the Advancement of   *A.A.A.S.*
Science.

The Journal of the Polynesian Society, etc. Ed. by E.   *J.P.S.*
Tregear and S. P. Smith. Wellington, N.Z. 1892,
etc.

Man. Published by the Royal Anthropological Insti-   *Man.*
tute.

Memoirs of the Polynesian Society. New Plymouth,   *Mem. P.S.*
N.Z., 1910, etc.

The Journal of the Royal Anthropological Institute.   *J.R.A.I.*
London, 1871, etc.

The Journal of the Royal Asiatic Society, Straits   *J.R.A.S.*
Branch. Singapore, 1878, etc.   (Straits Branch.)

The Sarawak Museum Journal. Singapore, 1912, etc.   *Sarawak M.J.*

Transactions of the London Missionary Society. Lon-   *L.M.S. Trans.*
don, 1804–18.

A Note

ON
THE ORAL LITERATURE OF THE IBAN
OR
THE SEA DYAKS OF NORTH BORNEO

THE ORAL LITERATURE OF THE IBAN
OR SEA DYAKS OF NORTH BORNEO

It has been shown that considerable similarity exists between the Polynesian stories which relate to the journeys of heroes to the Heavens and the Underworld, and the practice and poetry of the Altai shamans and of the poets of the Abakan Tatars. An even closer analogy to the latter is to be found in the literature of the Ibans, or Sea Dyaks of North Borneo; and this literature also offers so many points of similarity to that of Polynesia that it is undoubtedly of the greatest possible assistance in helping to explain much which is obscure in the latter. In fact the literature of the Sea Dyaks and that of Polynesia supplement one another in a very valuable degree, as is natural in two literatures embodied in kindred languages. Unfortunately our reference to the literature of the Sea Dyaks can only be very tentative, since very few texts appear to have been recorded; and it is doubtful if the material exists at the present time for more than a very slight sketch of the subject.[1]

The Sea Dyaks possess a large body of oral literature handed down from ancient times. This literature contains a number of legends and traditions, some of which are embodied in prose, while others are set to a peculiar rhythmical measure, and sung to a monotonous chant. A story recited in plain prose is known as *ensera*; and a story sung as *kana*. The latter relate to 'mythical heroes', and these are believed to constitute the most genuine native traditions.[2] These chants are commonly recited on ceremonial occasions, and in some of the most famous ones the heroes of old and the *antu*, or 'spirits', especially nature spirits, make journeys to the Heavens and the abodes of the dead in the Underworld, and then return to earth. The gods also are represented as visiting mankind at certain festivals. Sometimes the same person is depicted as making journeys to both the Heavens and the abode of the dead. We will consider briefly the few texts which we have, especially in their relationship to the literatures already considered, so far as this is possible from the slender evidence at our disposal.

So far as we are aware, no *kana* have been recorded from the Sea Dyaks which relate to the exploits of historical heroes. The recorded répertoire consists chiefly of the following: (1) Chants composed on subjects closely resembling those of Polynesian mythical heroes, especially the adventures of Tawhaki, and kindred themes. (2) Stories relating to the visits of gods to the dwellings of men, especially to the dwellings of Klieng the great Dyak hero of the past. These stories have a certain resemblance to a class of poetry and

---

[1] Our chief sources of information in regard to the oral literature of the Ibans, or Sea Dyaks, are a series of papers by Archdeacon Perham, originally contributed to the *Journal of the Straits Branch of the Royal Asiatic Society* (1878, etc.), partly reprinted in an abridged form by Ling Roth in his book on *The Natives of Sarawak and British North Borneo*, 2 vols. (London, 1896); and a paper by the Rev. W. Howell, entitled 'A Sea-Dyak Dirge', in the *Sarawak Museum Journal* I (1911).   [2] Perham, *J.S.B.* XVI (1885), p. 265.

saga common in Samoa and Tonga, in which the gods are depicted as visiting this earth. (3) Elegiac poetry bearing a strikingly close resemblance to that of the shaman of the Altai and other Tatar tribes. As in the Polynesian island of Mangaia, and other neighbouring Groups, the poetry of which we have record is chiefly recited on occasions of important social ritual, in the presence of a considerable body of people; and it thus bears, like Polynesian dramatic poetry, a distinctly ritual character. Among the chief occasions of such ritual are the feasts held to celebrate the acquisition by the tribe of a human head—for the Sea Dyaks are, or were until recently, inveterate head-hunters—and the celebrations of the memorial ceremonies for the dead. But formal recitations of what we may describe as a purely secular character no doubt also took place for purposes of entertainment.

The Dyaks possess a large body of tradition relating to a hero of the far past known as Klieng.[1] This hero is not known to have had a historical existence, and is not localised. He is sometimes spoken of as an inhabitant of the spirit world,[2] but in accounts given by Perham, which represent Dyak literature at its best, there is no doubt that he is a mortal, though he has been revered since his death, as many other mortals have been among these people. Perham's pronouncement on this subject is deliberate:

"The greatest hero of Dyak mythical story is Klieng. . . . He is supposed to belong to this world of ours, but is not now visible to human eyes as in the good times of yore. . . . He is without pedigree. . . . Klieng is not, so far as I know, called Petara;[3] but in Dyak estimation he holds the position of a tutelary spirit, and is sometimes presented with offerings, and often invoked as a helper of men."[4]

It will be seen that Klieng has something in common with the Polynesian hero Tawhaki, who among the Moriori is also invoked with chants on certain occasions (p. 338 above), and with whose adventures those of Klieng are also closely analogous.

Supernatural beings also play a large part in the chants of the Sea Dyaks.[5] These fall for the most part into two groups, which are not in practice very clearly defined, or consistently distinguished. The first group are known as *petara*.[6] The exact limitations of the word are very difficult to determine. There can be no doubt that the word is the Sanskrit *pitaras* (pl.), 'fathers', which is current also in the island of Bali to denote 'the shades of the dead',[7] and the fundamental meaning of the Dyak term is doubtless 'our forefathers',

---

[1] Klieng, also spelt Kling, appears to be the same word as the Bali name for India (*Kling*), *J.R.A.S.* IX, p. 69.

[2] E.g. by Brooke Low. See Ling Roth I, p. 332.

[3] Sea Dyak gods, or deified ancestors. See below.

[4] Perham, *J.S.B.* XVI, p. 266; Ling Roth I, p. 311f.

[5] For interesting accounts of the religion of the Sea Dyaks, see the papers published by Perham, *J.S.B.* V, p. 287ff.; VIII, p. 133ff.; X, p. 213ff.

[6] The form is the same in both singular and plural.

[7] For the Bali *petara*, see Friederich, *J.R.A.S.* IX (1877), p. 86.

i.e. ancestral spirits. In a sense every Dyak, and perhaps even inanimate objects, have their *petara*, or tutelary spirit who watches over them, and acts as a good genius, a protecting spirit. But the word *petara* is also used of the gods of the skies, and even of the Christian God. In fact the word seems to be synonymous with 'god', so far as this term is understood in a beneficent sense. The bewildering clash of evidence as to singularity and plurality in regard to the *petara*[1] corresponds exactly to that relating to the *jajan*[2] of the Tatars. In addition to the *petara* there are also the *antu*,[3] spirits of nature, of the forest, the trees, the river, and demons of the Underworld. These also are at times anthropomorphic, or again zoomorphic, and often, though by no means always, demonic and fearful. There are, however, no temples, altars, or priests. The intermediaries between the human and the spirit world are the *manangs*, sometimes men, sometimes women, who correspond closely to the shamans and *shamankas* of Siberia, and who act as the sages and physicians of the community. The *manangs* profess special knowledge of the *petara*, and of the secrets of the Underworld, and claim to exercise a magic influence over the spirits which cause disease. They are much given to chanting incantations, and are, of course, good poets.

The most important and the most picturesque of the supernatural beings who play a part in Dyak chants is Singalang Burong,[4] who dwells far away in the highest Heaven. He is the Dyak war god, and the Iban trace their descent from him. His form is that of a bird; but he has the face of a young man, though his hair is white. Birds in general are spoken of as his sons-in-law, and are said to act as his messengers and attendants, accompanying him on his frequent journeys to earth. But while they fly like birds, they also speak like men, and are thought of as spirits.[5] Singalang Burong is represented as saying of birds in general:

"These birds possess my mind and spirit, and represent me in the lower world. When you hear them, remember it is we who speak for encouragement or for warning."[6] And again: "I am *Singalang Burong*, and these are my sons-in-law, and other friends. When you hear the voices of the birds (giving their names), know that you hear us, for they are our deputies in this lower world."[7] Perham also gives us an elaborate poem in the form of a prayer or invocation to the birds and to certain ancestors who have been specially favoured by the birds named:

> These I call, these I beckon,
> These I shout to, these I look to,
> These I send for, these I approach,
> These I invoke, these I worship.[8]

---

[1] Perham, *J.S.B.* VIII, p. 134.   [2] See Chadwick, *J.R.A.I.* LXVI, p. 103.
[3] *Antu*, 'ghost', 'spirit', 'demon', Haddon and Start, p. 47.
[4] The name seems to mean 'Bird Chief'. See Howell and Bailey, *S.D.D.* p. 157.
[5] Ling Roth II, p. 180.   [6] Perham, *J.S.B.* X, p. 240; Ling Roth I, p. 200.
[7] Perham, *loc. cit.* p. 237; Ling Roth I, p. 197.
[8] Perham, *loc. cit.* p. 236; Ling Roth, *loc. cit.*

Communication between earth and Heaven is very active in the poems of the Sea Dyaks, and is commonly undertaken by other supernatural beings who carry messages from earth to Heaven, as we shall see. The most important of these messengers is Salulut Antu Ribut,[1] the wind god, whose personality and general behaviour bear so close a resemblance to those of the Japanese wind and rain-storm god Susa-no-wo, as these are depicted for us in the *Kojiki*, that there can be no doubt as to their identity, though Antu Ribut is sometimes represented as feminine—not always—while Susa-no-wo is a male god.

A word may be said at the outset as to the method of chanting. We are told that the songs and incantations of the Dyaks are not set to any particular melody. They are 'sung to a kind of chant', which probably signifies some kind of recitative, and long sentences are often sung on a single note.[2] But we are also told that the singers have several distinct settings for the different songs and incantations, and that these have a definite emotional relationship to the contents of the recitals. Thus a mourning chant sounds sad, even to one who is ignorant of the language.[3]

Dyak chants are very long, and it is by no means unusual for a wailer to continue her chanting for fifteen hours with only one, or at most two, brief intervals for rest. The form is generally largely that of narrative, but a large amount of dialogue is also introduced. In fact the speeches form a considerable portion of the whole recital, and these are introduced as pure dialogue, without any transition from oratio obliqua to oratio recta. The result is an interesting and perhaps unique form of literature—a combination of narrative and dramatic poetry, of epic and dialogue; but of course the speeches are by no means confined to two people. Each character speaks, as it were, for himself, and his part was doubtless, to some extent, spoken by a different member of the Dyak assembly (cf. below). The result is somewhat as if we were listening to a recital of Homer, not by one minstrel, or singer, but by several, each of whom speaks a part, while the narrative portions are carried on by the leader, who is responsible for the greater part of the recital as a whole.

The dramatic effect is further heightened in the English translation by the fact that the present tense is used throughout for the narrative portions. The language of the Sea Dyaks, like that of the Polynesians, has no tense system, but only aspects, and translators are in the habit of rendering the Dyak narrative form of the verb by the English present as its nearest equivalent, just as we found in the *Tawhaki* fragment from Hawaii (cf. p. 298 above). The effect of sustained narrative in the present tense naturally strikes the English reader as strange at first sight. To the Dyak, however, the question of tense or the 'time' at which the action takes place does not present itself

---

[1] For the word *antu*, see p. 478 above.
[2] This statement seems to us to be of considerable importance, and may be true also of pure narrative poetry elsewhere, possibly in e.g. Anglo-Saxon.
[3] Gomes, *S.Y.* p. 229.

at all. He projects himself in imagination into the situation depicted, and the narrative consequently assumes a dramatic quality which, as we have said, is further enhanced by the absence of a narrative tense and the presence of dialogue. The English reader is at first a little bewildered as to when he is supposed to be looking back, as a modern spectator, to events which have taken place in the past, and when he is supposed to be taking part in a drama which is actually in process of being enacted. Owing, however, to the supreme gifts of the Dyak poet in the vivid presentation of his subject, we soon come to realise as we read that it is as if we were listening to the Homeric poems chanted by a poet to an audience already familiar with the subject, and ready to be transported in imagination into the milieu depicted in the poems, and even, in certain chants, to take part in the recitation.

As an example of the first class of our stories—those in which human beings are represented as visiting the Heavens—we will take the song of 'Klieng's War Raid to the Skies'. An epitome of the song is given by Perham,[1] who tells us that if it were given in full it would take nearly a whole night to sing, especially by a good Dyak poet, who would amplify it with extempore additions of his own as he proceeded. The Dyaks, like other reciters of long narrative poems, delight to repeat the same thing over and over again in different words. "The singer", we are told, "lies on a mat in the dim light of the verandah of the long Dyak house,[2] and rehearses the poem in a slow monotonous chant whilst his audience are sitting or lying around, listening to his periods, and commenting or laughing as the mood suits them."[3]

The song opens with the arrival of Klieng, who is significantly disguised as a black man (lit. 'the sooty, crooked one') but grey-haired, at his own dwelling where he is not recognised. He enlists Ngelai and Bujang Bulan Menyimbang to go with him to ask Tutong for the hand of his sister Kumang in marriage. Tutong replies that he will only give her to the man who will lead him to rescue his father and mother 'from Tedai in the halved deep heavens':

> One who can lead me to wage war where the dim red sky is seen.

Klieng is delighted. The commission is one after his own heart:

> I am the man, cousin Tutong.... Tomorrow we carry war to the halved deep heavens...
> I can lead you to wage war to the zenith of the roomy heavens.

---

[1] *J.S.B.* XVI (1885), p. 265 ff.; Ling Roth I, p. 311.

[2] The Dyak house, although a single structure, is in reality a family village or hamlet, built under one roof, raised above the ground, and divided into compartments communicating by means of a single verandah which runs along the entire length of the building.

[3] Perham, *loc. cit.* p. 324.

The companions get ready for the war-path:

> And away they marched with feathers of the hornbill
>   tossing in the sheaths.
> Away down the ladder of evenly notched steps.
> Holding the long rails converging at the bottom.
> So started the three setting forth from thence.
> In the day time they pushed on following the sun.
> By night they used flaming torches of light.

They march along a pathway till they come to a house:

> A long house which a bird could only just fly through in a day,
> A short house through which a little tajak flies in a day.

Here they pause to rest, while Klieng commands the winds to collect an army:

> the great mass of the army,
> Numerous as the unknown spirits.
> And the army went forward.—
> The foremost were not within hearing of a calling voice,
> As the hindmost were just bending to rise and advance.

After some preliminary fighting, which allows for the introduction of episodes, the main body of the army arrive at the hill Perugan Bulan,[1] close to the precincts of the wise old woman, Ini Manang.[2] A curious and obscure passage then describes the heroes as throwing up balls of blue and red dyed thread,[3] which are able to ascend to the stars, while a spirit's tooth becomes a ladder by which they themselves are able to ascend to the house of Ini Manang, where they again take rest and refreshment.

[1] The word *Bulan* means 'the moon' (Haddon and Start, p. 148).

[2] *Ini*, lit. 'grandmother'. *Manang* is the name of the Dyak medicine-man or woman. For a detailed account of their important office and functions see Perham, *J.S.B.* VIII, p. 136; Gomes, *S.Y.* p. 52ff.; see also above. In the passage in our text, the reference is to a mythical *manang*, who lives in the skies, and has in her keeping the 'door of Heaven'. See Perham, *J.S.B.* XVI, p. 276, footnote. In their journeys to the spirit realms the Polynesian heroes are commonly met by supernatural female beings, who assist them in finding the way. We may compare the *gýgr* encountered by Brynhildr in the *Helreið Brynhildar* (cf. Vol. I, p. 27 of the present work), and the female who meets the soul of the departed on the 'Bridge of the Separator' in the *Avesta*.

[3] It will be remembered that the Mangaian hero Ngaru, who also ascends to the Heavens, learns the art of keeping several balls in motion in the air simultaneously from the supernatural *tapairu* (cf. p. 376 above). The coloured threads of the balls are probably to be connected with the multi-coloured ribbons which play a part in Buryat shamanistic ceremonies (see p. 205 above), and both may be connected with coloured kite-tails or strings, and ultimately with the cult of the rainbow, such as we know to have existed in parts of Polynesia, notably in the Marquesas. In both Polynesian and Cheremis myths p. 131, footnote, above, the rainbow is the regular path by which the gods descend to earth, and the strings of the kite and the coloured balls may perhaps represent the attempts of mortals to ascend by a similar path.

Again they pursue their course, and Klieng asks:

> "Which is our way, cousin?
> I know not: hitherto when on the war-path, I have
> only come as far as this."
> And Bungkok went forward, and growled like a
> Melanau building a boat,
> Muttered like a Sebaru man upside down.[1]
> And lo! the way at once was clear and straight.

Spies are sent out who return unsuccessful, though their adventures are described with great vividness and much detail. Then Klieng decides to go, and with him Ngelai and another, and they approach Tedai's house as friends. They arrive to find a festival to Singalang Burong in progress. While taking part in the festival they climb to an upper room, where they find Tutong's father and mother confined in an iron cage, destined by Tedai for a sacrifice.

The three friends rescue them and call up the army. Tedai discovers that the friends whom he has been entertaining are in reality enemies, and flees, carrying off his wife and children. He returns, however, with a mighty host, and a series of single combats follows in which supernatural elements are not wanting, though the narrative is predominantly that of heroic warfare.

> Then Sampurei came face to face with Tedai,
> And was struck by Tedai from the shoulder even to the loins.
> Forward rushed Laja, and met the like fate,
> And many were slain by Tedai.
> Then for the first time Tedai met Bungkok face to face.
> *Klieng*. What is your title, cousin, when you strike the snake?
> What is your title, cousin, when you smite the boa?

Both the heroes proudly boast their titles and a deadly encounter follows.

> And Tedai rushed forward and threw at him a spear, the beak of the white
> kingfisher,
> And hurled at him a lance with double-barbed head,
> And pierced was Bungkok in the apron of his waist-cloth,
> Grazed were the ribs of his side:
> When off dropped the disguise covering his body;
> Away fell the sweat-preventing coat.
> Then it was they recognised him to be Klieng, seeing he was handsomer than
> before.
> And Klieng paid back: he aimed at him a spear newly hilted with horn.
> And Tedai was struck and fell; and was seized by Tatau Ading.
> He fell against the palm tree of Bungai Nuying.

[1] This phrase occurs constantly in Dyak poetry, and appears to be a poetical expression for 'muttering a charm'. We may compare the Tatar songs chanted by the smith as he forges the mail coat of Manas (p. 73 above).

Klieng. Tedai's head do not strike off, Sampurei, lest we have no more enemies
to fight with.
And the great army drew back to return.
Rushing and rustling they marched along the highway.
They filed through the gloomy jungles, sounding like an army of woodmen:
Through solitudes uninhabited, full of weird sounds.
Those in front arrived at the house of Manang Kedindang Arang.
There they stopped a night to inquire the way of grandmother Manang.

Grandmother Manang let them down to earth by the curious device of an
enormous tub[1] which she lowered to the earth.

It was the country of Ngelai where the army found footing.
Klieng and his company returned to Tinting Panggan Dulang.

It will be seen that in this poem heroic and non-heroic elements are
combined in an almost equal degree. The main adventure, however, is
supernatural—the journey of a party of human beings to the skies. The
theme is practically identical with certain Polynesian motifs; and even in
details of incident and treatment resembles closely certain versions of the
journey of Tawhaki to the Heavens (p. 272 ff. above). The heroic elements
in particular are closely similar in the two stories. Among the Tatars the
journeys of heroes to the Heavens generally seem to be undertaken by single
individuals rather than by large armies; but apart from this particular there
is a general resemblance between the two groups of stories.

This Dyak song is said to be very widely known. Chambers mentions
that he once chanced to quote to an old woman the first line of the lament
uttered by Indai-Tutong whilst suspended in the iron cage, which was
overheard by Nating:

"She at once took up my words, and went on in a clear, loud, natural
voice to the end of this passage from the Dyak Iliad, 'The Adventures of
Nating in his expedition to the sky', which few can repeat except in a
peculiar monotonous chant, in which forgotten words are slurred, and
sometimes a word is prolonged for twenty seconds whilst the next is recovered."[2]

The poem referred to as 'The Adventures of Nating' is apparently the
one to which Perham gives the title 'Klieng's War Raid to the Skies'.

Yet another Dyak story relating the journey of mortals to the Heavens is
that of Siu.[3] Siu has married a divine wife, but one day he offends her, and
she disappears. He sets out with his son to seek her, and after travelling for
three or four days they come to the sea-coast, and eventually succeed with
the help of an enormous spider in crossing the sea. The spider then directs

[1] We may compare the basket in which the gods and heroes sometimes pass
between earth and Heaven in Polynesian stories.

[2] Ling Roth I, p. 338.

[3] Perham, *J.S.B.* x (1882), p. 237 ff.; Ling Roth I, p. 198. For a fuller but slightly
variant version, see Gomes, *S.Y.* p. 278 ff.

them on their way, and they soon find themselves in the house of no less a personage than Singalang Burong, who, as it transpires, is Siu's father-in-law. The story is a long and elaborate one, and of especial interest for its close similarity to the stories of Polynesian mythical heroes who marry 'fairy' wives.

There follow a series of ordeals in which Siu's son is made to show his identity and superiority over his uncles, the sons-in-law of Singalang Burong. After his miraculous feats there can be no room for doubt, and he is acknowledged by all as the true grandson of Singalang Burong. Eventually, however, father and son are allowed to return to the lower world. Before their departure they are taught many useful arts of warfare, agriculture, hunting and fishing, and above all the good and bad omens. "These birds", says Singalang Burong, "possess my mind and spirit, and represent me in the lower world. When you hear them, remember it is we who speak for encouragement or for warning." They depart, loaded with presents, and are transported through the air to their own home.

It will be seen at once that this story also bears a close resemblance to a well-known Polynesian type, in which a mortal husband marries a supernatural wife, and after her premature departure, follows her to her spirit home. In these stories, as in that of Siu, the home of the supernatural wife is depicted as a centre of culture and learning, and of practical handicrafts, at the head of which is the bride's father. In Dyak and Polynesian stories alike, the hero returns to earth, bringing with him many useful arts, and improved methods of agriculture and new foodstuffs for the benefit of mankind. In stories of this kind it would seem that the distinction between the abode of the gods and that of the 'fairies' is not always observed in the Pacific.

The second class of Dyak composition consists of chants relating to gods and other supernatural beings or spirits. Our most important example is the *Gawe Pala*, the song of the Dyak 'Head Feast', also known as the *Gawe Burong*, or 'Bird Feast'. The first name is no doubt due to the fact that the ceremony is performed in connection with human heads taken in war; the second, to the fact that the feast is held in honour of Singalang Burong, whose form is that of a hawk, and whose messengers are birds. Accordingly, at the beginning of the feast, a large figure of a bird—not, however, a hawk but a hornbill—is set up high on a post outside the verandah. Some human heads are placed in large brass dishes on the verandah, and to these offerings of food and drink are made, and round these and other war trophies the performers march, chanting the *mengap*.[1] There are generally two principal singers, each followed by five or six others, and we are told that the leaders generally sing a few lines in turn, the rest joining in the chorus at the end of each verse. They all hold long walking-sticks in their hands, and stamp their

---

[1] In Balu Dyak the word *mengap* is equivalent to singing or reciting in any distinctive tone, and is applied to Dyak song or Christian worship; but in Saribus dialect it is applied to certain kinds of ceremonial songs only (Perham, *J.S.B.* II, p. 135; Ling Roth II, p. 183).

feet as they walk.[1] It will be seen that the arrangement and grouping has
something in common with the Polynesian ritual dances. At the close of the
recital the principal reciter actually assumes the rôle of Singalang Burong
himself, and bestows blessings on all present. The *mengap* begins about six
in the evening, and continues till nine or ten the next morning.[2]

In the 'Song of the Head Feast' the most important person is Singalang
Burong. The human hero, who is again Klieng, does not mount to Heaven
himself, but sends his invitation by the wind spirit, Salulut Antu Ribut, and
the gods in response come down to earth. The principal personnel, therefore,
are not the heroes but the supernatural beings. This poem is comparable with
Mangaian ritual and dramatic poetry, both in regard to the subjects treated,
and also in regard to its ritual function. The gods and heroes whose actions
are described are, indeed, spoken of as actually present in the house in which
the recitation takes place. But their parts are not exactly acted by anyone.
The recitation resembles the Mangaian *kapas*, in which, to some extent,
gods and heroes of the past are similarly referred to as actually present during
the performance. The effect is somewhat as if reciters and audience projected
themselves into the past, and imagined themselves as present at Klieng's
Gawe Pala, or Head Feast. This effect is, no doubt, chiefly due to the
introduction of dialogue, and to the use of the present tense in the English
translation (cf. p. 479 above). But the device of chanting of Klieng's Head
Feast at a Head Feast of the present day is a poetic convention quite independent of the tense question, and exactly parallel to the Mangaian poetical
custom in the *kapas*. The Dyak chant in question, like the latter, is chiefly
recited on important ceremonial occasions, and is, in some measure, an
invocation to the spiritual guests to present themselves at the ceremony, and
at the same time it is also a song of welcome and honour to those guests.

Let us explain the matter a little more fully. It has been shown above that
in Mangaia a recent event is often celebrated by ritual chants of which the
contents refer exclusively to events in the far past. It is thus that the dirge for
Vera refers ostensibly, not so much to Vera himself, as to Veêtini, a mythical
hero who was traditionally stated to be the first to die a natural death. So it is
also among the Sea Dyaks. When a Dyak performer wishes to invite Singalang Burong to descend from Heaven and grace the Head Feast with his
presence, he walks up and down the verandah of the long Dyak house,
singing the *mengap*. But this chant does not embody an invitation expressed
as such. Instead it describes the Head Feast given, according to tradition, by
the hero Klieng, to which Singalang Burong was invited. The Dyaks who are
present identify themselves in imagination with Klieng and his people; their
feast becomes Klieng's feast, and so, virtually, the recitation of this ancient
narrative acquires the character of a ritual, and conveys in itself an invitation
to Singalang Burong to be present at the feast given by the reciter or reciters
and their audience.

---

[1] For these details, see Gomes, *Sea-Dyaks*, p. 47f.
[2] Perham, *J.S.B.* II (1878), p. 135.

But the recital is not a simple narrative of past tradition. As in the Mangaian ritual chants, a slight dramatic element is introduced in two ways. The first is by various members of the audience taking up the recital at a given point in the narrative, and carrying it forward, probably as fresh speakers or scenes are introduced. The second is by the ceremony of the reception of the invisible guests, and the offering of food or sacrifice to them, as if they were indeed guests being entertained at a feast by those present.[1] We will give a brief summary of the *mengap*, or 'chant', referring the reader to Perham's paper[2] for a fuller account of the ceremony which accompanies it.

In this *mengap* the scene appears to be laid in Klieng's house, and the performer begins by describing the preparations which are being made for a Head Feast. Kumang, Klieng's wife, chides her husband with tardiness, and he decides to send *Kasulai* (the moth) and *Laiang* (the swallow) to fetch Singalang Burong, who is here said to live on a hill top. "With one bound they can clear the space between the earth and the 'clouds crossing the skies'." Midway to the skies they come to the house of *Ini Manang* ('Grandmother Doctor'),[3] from whom they enquire the way to the country of Salulut Antu Ribut (the spirit of the winds). On they go again and beg Antu Ribut's assistance to convey Klieng's invitation to Singalang Burong. In the *mengap* Antu Ribut is a female spirit. She agrees to convey the invitation, and climbs a high tree,[4] and sets off, and arrives in the farthest Heaven in the form of a hurricane. The domestic occupations of Singalang Burong's household are described with great picturesqueness as the wind searches its way through every corner of the dwelling. The whole scene is depicted with much humour and humanity.

Singalang Burong summons his sons-in-law, the omen birds, from the jungle by means of a great gong, at the sound of which all the birds flock at once to the house of their father-in-law. Here they are told that Antu Ribut has brought an invitation to a feast in the world below, and Singalang Burong places himself at their head, and together they set off to the feast, which henceforth centres in him and the inferior birds who accompany him; hence the alternative title of this feast—*Gawe Burong*, 'Bird Feast'. The sounding of the gong as a summons to the feast recalls the drum of peace which heralded the performance of the Mangaian *kapa*, while Singalang Burong and his attendant birds are reminiscent of the warning birds of Tane, the god under whose auspices the *kapa* was especially held; their parts in one of the dramas were actually acted by men dressed to represent birds (cf. p. 375 above). It has already been remarked that Singalang Burong himself resembles Tane in a special degree.

The course of the Dyak narrative is interrupted and enriched by episodes.

---

[1] Ling Roth II, p. 175.
[2] Perham, *J.S.B.* II (1878), p. 123 ff.; Ling Roth II, p. 174ff.
[3] For this supernatural female being, cf. p. 481 above.
[4] We may compare the procedure of the Siberian shaman who climbs a tree as a preliminary part of his journey to Heaven.

The divine party on its journey to the lower world passes through various mythical countries on the way, and the doorway guarded by Ini Manang (cf. p. 481 above), till they alight and rest on a projecting rock somewhere in the lower skies. Then they go down the path which leads to Klieng's house. At this point in the recital the performer[1] walks to the door of the house and receives the divine guest with great ceremony. His coming is attended with benefits to all concerned. The paddy bins become filled, the sick are made well, etc. There follows the blessing on all present by those who are conducting the *mengap*, and this is believed to convey an actual blessing from Singalang Burong and the bird spirits. Comic relief follows, in which the god is made drunk, his turban falls off, and out of it rolls a human head, which is secured by Klieng's wife as a supreme treasure. Finally, the god and his companions return to the skies. We have already seen that crude humour is also found in the closing portions of the Mangaian *kapas*, while the Altai shaman also makes Erlik Khan, the god of the Underworld, drunk, when in dramatic monologue he represents himself as visiting the latter in the land of the dead.

Other stories are also current in which Singalang Burong and his attendants are represented as visiting the feasts of mortals and leaving favours in return. One of these stories relates how, on one occasion, some Dyaks on the Batang Lupar river make a great feast, and as they sit awaiting the guests a party of strangers arrive unexpectedly. The hosts are full of surprise, but they treat the guests well, and on their departure these guests declare themselves to be Singalang Burong and the omen birds. They leave their hosts, in return for their hospitality, the knowledge of the omen system.[2] Perham also gives details of other feasts with the accompanying *pengap*, or *mengap*, in which the *petara* of the skies, together with those of the hills and lowlands and forests, are invited to attend, and grace the ceremony with their presence. He refers to the *pengap* of the *Besant*,[3] a ceremony which is performed over children, and, occasionally, over invalids. The worldly vanity and human weaknesses of the divine community are as vividly portrayed here as in the 'Song of the Head Feast', and here also the dramatic quality of the chant is marked by the liberal introduction of dialogue. This *pengap* is chanted by *manangs*.

There is among the Sea Dyaks another group of motifs which also claim comparison with many of the Polynesian stories, and which are also comparable with the recitals of the Tatar shamans. We refer especially to the recitations which take place immediately after a death, and again at subsequent ceremonies held some time after the funeral, and once more at the *Gawe Antu*, the 'Festival of Departed Spirits', the greatest of all the observances held in regard to the dead. These recitations or chants are performed by a woman, or, rarely, a man, called a 'wailer'. A professional wailer may be a

---

[1] This is doubtless the leader of the reciters, who is also the principal reciter himself, as well as the master of ceremonies.

[2] Perham, *J.S.B.* x (1883), p. 237; Ling Roth I, p. 197.

[3] Perham, *J.S.B.* VII, p. 133 ff.

man or a woman, a *manang* (see above), or an ordinary Dyak. But she or he must be appointed by one of the gods in a dream, and unless so appointed, death will be their punishment. It is reserved for those who are divinely inspired to pass to and fro between the material and the spirit world. It is said, however, that the *nyuran*, or dirge proper, can be monotoned by any woman who is gifted with poetry, 'provided that her soul does not go beyond this world', i.e. provided that she does not venture into spiritual regions. "A professional 'soul'", as the professional wailer is called, "carries herself to Hades."[1] A dirge recited by a professional wailer occupies about twelve hours.[2] With certain tribes who do not employ a professional wailer when death takes place, all the women in the house, and friends from far and near, chant the *nyuran* over the corpse, which recalls the custom of the Mangaian 'death-talks'. The dirge is monotoned, and during its process no musical instrument of any sort is allowed.[3] The wailer sits during the recital on a swing beside the corpse (see below).

The first dirge is recited before burial takes place, immediately after death, in order to assist the soul of a dead person on its journey to the land of the dead. An example of this dirge, the *nyuran*, is recorded by the Rev. W. Howell,[4] in which we have the essential parts of the text of a single recital, written down during its actual recitation. This particular dirge was recited by a well-known professional wailer called Lemok, who was blind, and whose memory is said to have been extraordinarily good. The language in which it is composed is described by Howell as 'most classical', and he adds that although he had been thirty-two years among the Sea Dyaks, he nevertheless had to have several learned Dyaks to explain to him the meaning of much of its archaic diction and phraseology before he was able to translate it.

The first part of the dirge consists of accusations against the house on the part of the mourning relatives for not 'availing' to prevent the death.[5] The second part consists of the defence made by the house and all its contents. This dirge is a veritable keen, and corresponds in style and function to the Mangaian *tangi*.

The second type of festival takes place shortly after burial, generally about three days later. These days are spent in a partial fast. The festival which marks their termination is known as the *Sabak Nerengkah*, 'the Festival to settle the dead in Hades'. The Sea Dyaks believe that the souls of all the dead return to the original home of man, vast in extent, whence all come, and whither all must go, while this world, so they say, is merely 'a borrowed one'. But the roads which lead from this world are very numerous, and without the wailer's help the soul of the dead person would be lost in space

---

[1] Howell, *Sarawak M.J.* 1 (1911), p. 6.
[2] Perham, *J.S.B.* xiv, p. 289; Ling Roth 1, p. 203.
[3] Howell, *loc. cit.*   [4] *Loc. cit.*
[5] *Loc. cit.*; cf. also Gomes, *Sea-Dyaks*, p. 26ff. We may perhaps compare the *eva toki*, or 'axe dirge' of Mangaia, in which the mourners strike the earth with wooden axes. See p. 359 above.

between this world and its final abode among its former friends and relatives. The purpose of the *Sabak Nerengkah* is to conduct the soul along the right 'way' till it reaches its final goal in safety. This is accompanied by a more ambitious, and a more interesting chant than the *nyuran*. It probably fulfils the same function as the Mangaian *kakai*, or 'death-talk'. The recital, how-ever, is given solely by the wailer, whose function and performance bear a close resemblance to those of the Tatar shaman. The wailer monotones the dirge, seated in a swing in the room of the deceased. This is doubtless to symbolise her incorporeal function as a spirit, a psychopompos, who, like the Siberian shaman, can fly through the air like a bird. The wailer is 'on the wing'.

The recitation must be preceded by an offering of eatables and chewing ingredients to the dead. When all is ready, the wailer begins by asking Antu Ribut, the wind spirit, to herald the arrival of the new-comer in the land of the dead. The wind in response blows so boisterously that the trees are blown down. The wailer next asks the *emponyat*, a kind of beetle, to carry the food and chewing ingredients to the land of the dead; but the *emponyat* declines to go. The bird *kuang kapong* is next requested to carry the offerings; but he also excuses himself. At last the bird *burong raya* sets off, and the dead receive the offerings, and eat the food and chew the betel-nut, etc. The dead spirit, on arriving among its ancestors, is at first overcome with panic, and endeavours to escape and return to earth; but the dead, pleased with the offerings brought to them by the new-comer, are now ready to be friendly, and proceed to convince it that return is impossible.[1]

The length of the dirge depends on the wishes (and doubtless also on the financial means) of the bereaved persons. If the dirge is a long one, it is expanded by the introduction of many incidents and adventures through which the dead person is represented as passing on his or her way to the land of the dead. This is the case in the *Sabak Nerengkah* of which the text has been recorded by Howell, which is a very interesting and ambitious literary (oral) production, but which is unfortunately too long to quote here. It corresponds indeed in content to the ceremony described by Perham as the *Pana*, in which food is conveyed to the dead, and it seems clear that in Howell's account the ceremonies of the *Sabak Nerengkah* and the *Pana* are combined in a single recital. The *Pana* as described by Perham will be referred to more fully below. In Howell's text of the *Sabak Nerengkah* several episodes are introduced and developed with great fulness. Antu Ribut, the wind spirit, is despatched to the household of Jiram, the chief of the dead in 'Hades', to announce the coming of a dead woman named Lebah. The course of this journey of the Wind Spirit is described in great detail, and here, as in the 'Song of the Head Feast', we have a vivid picture of Dyak domestic life transposed to the land of the dead, as the wind searches out every corner of the abode of the dead to give the alarm and arouse the inmates. We then have a minute description of the preparations made by the dead to receive the new-comer. Mentong and Lepang—two fine athletic ghosts—are despatched

[1] Howell, *Sarawak M.J.* I, p. 19 f.

to bring areca nuts and other provisions destined for the reception of the dead from 'the ancient abiding place where man.first dwelt'—the Dyak equivalent of the Polynesian Hawaiki—and a fascinating description of their journey follows. On their return all is once more bustle and excitement, as the householders receive and congratulate the return of the successful messengers, the 'male swallows', as they are admiringly hailed by their friends.

The dirge is somewhat obscure at this point, and it is not impossible that while the wailer has been reciting the journey of Mentong and Lepang to procure provisions, the living Dyaks, friends and relatives of the dead, have been themselves busied in collecting the *pana*, the gifts which the dead must take as offerings to the land of the dead. This, as we have seen, would be quite in accord with Dyak ritual and poetical technique (cf. p. 485 f. above), and it is also suggested by a comparison of Howell's introductory remarks and text of the *Sabak Nerengkah* with that of Perham; but it is evident that great variation exists in these dirges, and the point need not be pressed. The last part of the dirge consists of a description of the great journey of the corpse to the land of the dead, this time in a boat sent from 'Hades', manned by the wailer and the spirits of the dead. Again the course of the voyage is described minutely—the scenery and reaches of a great Borneo river with its rapids and treacherous submerged tree-trunks, and the habits and daily life of the people along the banks. And as they come to each fresh settlement on their journey through the shades, the same question is asked:

> Whom brought ye from the glorious sun,
> Whose rays are ever piercing?
> Is it a mere *manang* or an exalted one?

And the answer is somewhat as follows:

> It is Lebah, the mother of Tipah, the moonlight kite;
> But we also brought an iron bar for stretching the chest,
> We also brought a tiny lump of cotton to wipe the eyes.

Or perhaps:

"Whence came thou?" And the people answered readily:
"We have come from the glorious sun to bear the dead away to the people who live in the shadow behind the posts."

At times the warlike tribes on the banks challenge them to combat; or again:

The boat of those who died long ago had arrived at the shallow still water where fish hooks are being let down.

At last they draw near to the last great peril of the voyage:

The people in the boat began to hear the sound of the Mandoh waterfall ever so loud...

Wong Mandoh that sounds ever so loud is the place where people are arranged who died long ago when shooting waterfalls.

The chant is obscure in many parts, but is of absorbing interest and charm on account of its vivid and picturesque detail and compelling movement. The wailer by her poetic talent takes us as well as her listeners on her long journeys. Gradually, as the voyage proceeds, we realise that the scenes through which the wailer is guiding the soul are a series of states in which the dead in the shades are represented as carrying on the occupations in which they were engaged in this life. But as the dead Lebah is convoyed safely past them all to the final goal among her dead friends, we may perhaps regard these as states of the unblessed, like those referred to among the Tatars and in Buddhist Hell. It is clear that both the wailer and the boat of the dead aim at saving the newly arrived soul from a sojourn among these groups. Finally the boat comes to the end of its long voyage and the wailer to the end of her song:

My voice has been heard at the landing place...
The sweetness of my voice has travelled gracefully along the made batang path and
    has been heard on the made steps...
And has echoed on the eighteen-stepped ruan staircase of the people at Hades...
Aye even has thundered towards the reception room of Jiram...
The utterance of my tongue has lodged up in the long straight house;
After my continual calling all have come in and are seated in a row.

A brief summary of the recitation of the wailer is also given by Perham.[1] His account differs considerably from that of Howell. This, however, may be due in part to the brevity of Perham's description, though he mentions that the wailer's recital occupied about twelve hours. A comparison of the two accounts suggests that the wailer's song was not rigidly stereotyped, but that within a limited range of themes the artistic performances varied considerably and were extemporised on conventional lines.

Perham's account opens with the efforts of the wailer to induce a messenger to take the announcement to the land of the dead that a new-comer is about to join them. In vain she calls upon bird, beast, and fish; none of these can pass the boundary which separates the regions of the living from those of the dead. She then calls upon the wind spirit, who is here represented as male, as in Japan (cf. p. 479 above). At first the wind spirit is reluctant, but at last consents, and speeds on his journey over hill and dale, river and gorge, till at last he is overtaken by night, and stops to rest, weary and hungry. Presently he goes to the top of a high tree to try to discover which course he shall take next. This, it will be remembered, is also the great problem which the Siberian shaman must solve, and in Polynesian stories we have seen how often the heroes lose the direct path in traversing the route from the material to the spirit world.[2] The finding of the right way is always the greatest

---

[1] *J.S.B.* XIV (1885), p. 289; cf. Ling Roth I, p. 203 f.
[2] In Tibet a ceremony exists known as *De-lok*, 'the ghostly returning', in which the lamas go through a ritual, representing themselves as guiding the soul of the dead person to its abode in the land of the dead on a kind of temporary pilgrimage during this life. The theme is common in Buddhist pictorial representations, in which the lamas are seen guiding the spirits by means of scarves that they may not

difficulty which they have to overcome. In the same way without the guidance of the wailer, here symbolised by the wind spirit, the Dyak soul would never reach its destination, but would remain suspended somewhere, and find no rest.[1]

From his position on the tree-top, the wind spirit finds himself surrounded by darkness. He changes his human form for that of a rushing wind, and announces his arrival in the land of the dead by a furious tempest, which sweeps everything before it, rousing the inhabitants to anxious questioning. They are told the cause of the commotion. They must go, they are told, to the land of the living, to fetch so-and-so, 'and all his belongings'. Joyfully the dead set out in a boat, rowing with such zeal that all the fish are killed with the strokes of their oars. On arriving at the landing place they rush for the house, and seize the corpse 'like soldiers who fly upon the spoil'. The soul of the dead cries out in anguish at their violence; but long before the party has reached the land of the dead, it has become reconciled. The wailer has completed her present task; she has convoyed the spirit in safety to its new home.

There is, however, a further ceremony held at a later date which is called a *Pana*, and which according to Perham takes place a short time after burial, though in the text recorded by Howell the *Pana*, as we have seen, seems to be combined with the *Sabak Nerengkah*. The *Pana* is the ceremonial by which food is conveyed to the dead. Until this ceremony has taken place the soul of the dead is not given food or water by the occupants of the spirit world, or received with full rights as a member of their community. The wailer is again present at the *Pana* ceremony, and by her chanting effects the transmission. She calls upon the adjutant bird—'the royal bird which fishes the waters all alone'—and she commands him:

To carry the *pana* of tears to the departed one at the clear mouth of the Potatoe river;
To carry deep sighs to those sunk out of view in the land of the red ripe *rambutan*;
To carry pitying sobs to those who have fallen unripe in the land of empty fruiting limes.

The bird sets out, and after resting, like the wind spirit, on a tree-top, he arrives at the realm of the dead. Again his reception is described with picturesque detail and naïve realism. Not recognising their visitor, they enquire his errand:

"Do you come to look at the widows? We have thirty and one; but only one is handsome. Do you come to seek after maidens? We have thirty and three; but only one is pretty." "No," says the bird; "We have widows and maidens plenty in the land of the living, all beautiful and admired of men." "What is it that you have brought with you so securely covered up?" Then the bird bids them bring a basin, and into it he pours the *pana*. But the tears and sobs of the living mourners have become gold and silver and jewels, and

go astray. In these pictures, however, the spirits may be those of persons actually dead. See Waddell, *Lamaism*[2], p. 99.

[1] Perham, *loc. cit.* p. 290; Ling Roth, *loc. cit.*

the dead do not know what they are.[1] They accuse one another of stupidity, and begin to squabble. But at this juncture an ancient native of the land of the dead, who has never been in the land of men, makes her appearance. She seems to be a person of authority, like Miru (cf. p. 314 above), and like the old woman in charge of the region occupied by the 'fairies' in Maori tales. She scolds the spirits for quarrelling, and explains to them that the bird has come from the world with presents from their living friends. The dead are seized with a passionate desire to return to their old homes, but they are told that this is impossible. With characteristic vividness of imagination, the Dyak conception of death is translated into concrete terms.

> The notched ladder is top downwards,[2]
> Their eyes see crookedly,
> Their feet step the wrong way,
> Their speech is all upside down.

Their limbs and faculties will no longer function in the world of the living. They must remain in the land of the dead. But the desire to return to earth is so strong that great ingenuity must be exercised to amuse the souls who are not yet long established among the dead. Meanwhile the bird wings its way back to earth, and the wailer's song once more comes to an end for this occasion.

Yet another observance is described by Perham, which is said to be carried out at varying periods after death. The symbols and trophies of a head-hunting raid are taken, and in this ceremony the wailer once more procures the service of the spirit of the winds to convey them to the dead, whose abode, before full of darkness and discomfort, is now, at sight of the trophies, filled with light.[3]

The most important ceremony in regard to the settling of the soul in the land of the dead, however, is the *Gawe Antu*, 'the festival of departed spirits', which is held a year or more after the ceremonies described above.[4] The living guests arrive at the festival during the day, and the feasting takes place at night. The dead are supposed to be present in great numbers at this feast. The wailer is also once more present, intoning the chant from her swing on the verandah,[5] and again the entire pageantry takes place in the poetry chanted by her.

As before (p. 489 above), numerous animals, one after another, are called upon to convey the invitation to the dead to come to feast with the living; but none are equal to the journey. Even Salampandai, the maker of men, is

---

[1] In the same way the Maori 'fairies' are said to be indifferent to the jewels of the hero in Maori tradition, handing them back to him after examining them and retaining only the shadows. See p. 344 above.

[2] In order to prevent the spirits of the dead from returning to earth and injuring the living the Dyaks sometimes make a notched stick ladder and fix it upside down in the path near the cemetery. See Perham, *loc. cit.* p. 291 f.

[3] Perham, *loc. cit.* p. 295; Ling Roth I, p. 206 f.

[4] Perham, *loc. cit.* p. 295; Ling Roth, p. 207 f.   [5] Gomes, p. 49.

unable to undertake it. Once more it is conveyed by the spirit of the winds, who urges the dead to accept it by enlarging on the excellence of the feast. A boat has already been sent to convey the dead to the world of life. By the help of the king of all the fish it reaches the first landing stage of the river of death—the river which the wailer has already navigated in a previous chant (cf. p. 490 above). As soon as the boat arrives at the landing stage, the river becomes swollen and overflows. The dead are puzzled by the appearance of the ship, but its purpose is explained by a spirit, which rises from the river, and the dead joyfully rush forward to embark.

> Their shouts reach beyond the clouds.
> They incite each other like men preparing the drums.
> With joy they thump their breasts,
> With gladness they slap their thighs.
> "We shall soon feast below the star-sprinkled heavens.
> We shall soon eat where the roaring thunder falls,
> We shall soon feed below the suspended moon.
> We shall soon be on our way to visit the world, and march to the feast."...

Their behaviour on arriving in the world of men is in all respects like that of Dyak guests at a feast. They eat, and drink, and rejoice in the gay atmosphere of the living world. Like true Dyaks, they have brought their fighting cocks with them, and they indulge in cock fights with their living friends. A division of the family property is made, the dead receiving their share, except that the dead are badly cheated by the living. Finally, at the close of the feast, the dead bid sorrowful and affectionate farewells, and take their final departure to the land of the dead. Such, we are told, is the esoteric meaning of the festival according to the wailer's chant.[1]

Many prose stories and allusions point to the widespread currency of these and similar themes. We may mention the story of Kadawa[2] who strayed to the region of disembodied spirits in a kind of state of suspension between life and death. His wife dies of grief, and Kadawa sees her in the midst of a long procession marching along the line of hills before him to the boat awaiting them on the edge of the Stygian lake. One is reminded cf the Mangaian ritual chants referring to the journeys of the dead, first overland, and then by canoe over the sea; and of the dramatic poem of Ngaru, in which the daughters of Miru are represented as carrying the body of their 'husband' over the mountains to the abode of the dead (cf. p. 378 above). Kadawa enters the boat, though they try to keep him out; but presently the boat sticks on a rock and cannot be pushed off so long as Kadawa remains inside. The living man is an insuperable obstacle to the train of the dead.[3]

---

[1] Perham, *J.S.B.* xiv, p. 297f.; Ling Roth i, p. 208f.

[2] Ling Roth i, p. 211.

[3] We may compare the Irish saga of the *Adventures of Nera*, in which the procession of dwellers underground is represented as commenting on the fact that 'the track is the heavier' owing to the presence of a living man in their midst. See *Revue Celtique* x, p. 212ff.

The ceremonies and performances described above are not confined to the Sea Dyaks. Hose and McDougall tell us that the Punan[1] recite or sing a story in blank verse descriptive of the journey of the soul to the spirit world. "It is sometimes sung in very dramatic fashion, the performer acting the principal incidents and pitching his voice in a doleful, though musical minor key. Such a recitation of the passage of the soul, delivered by a wild and tragic figure before an intently listening group of squatting men and women illuminated by flickering torchlight, is by no means unimpressive to the European observer."[2] The short extract which follows suggests dramatic dialogue poetry of the kind which we have found to be current among the Sea Dyaks.

It will be seen that the wailer's function bears a striking resemblance to that of the Siberian shaman who conducts the soul of the dead to the realm of Erlik Khan. Like the shaman, the wailer is responsible for the whole recitation, or rather chant, and like him she conducts her audience ritually to the realm of the dead and back to earth by the sheer force of her imaginative presentation. She does not dance, as the shaman does, however, and it is not generally stated that any pantomimic action takes place, though we have just referred to mimetic action by the Punan reciter. The Sea Dyak wailer sits on her swing, like a bird in the air, however, and in this bird form she also resembles the shaman.[3] It is difficult to believe that these two performances—that of the Siberian shaman and that of the Dyak wailer—are of independent origin.

The Dyak evidence is, in fact, of special interest and importance for the way in which it helps us to link together certain literary themes in the oral literatures of the far East, and also certain features in the ritual and forms of recitation in which this literature is current. We have seen that it has many points of contact with the oral literature of Polynesia, especially with the non-heroic saga and the ritual and dramatic poetry, and that some resemblance is also traceable in regard to the various stages in which the ritual commemoration of the dead takes place. On the other hand the resemblance of this Dyak poetry to that of the oral literature and ritual of the shamanist Siberian Tatars is perhaps even closer. Again we refer in particular to the non-heroic sagas, and the poetry recited by the shaman, as well as the ritual in which the latter is embodied. The resemblance between the Tatar and the Dyak is particularly arresting, for neither racial contact, nor any kind of direct communication seems possible. Similarities between the Tatar and Polynesian 'non-heroic' themes have already been commented on, and here also any kind of contact or direct communication is impossible.

To discuss here the nature of the relationship of these three oral literatures to one another is, of course, out of the question. There is, however, one

---

[1] The Punan are a hunting forest tribe of the interior of Borneo.
[2] Hose and McDougall II, p. 44 f.
[3] See the paper by Chadwick, 'Shamanism among the Tatars of Central Asia', *J.R.A.I.* LXVI (1936), p. 75 ff.

ancient text which contains many literary themes and motifs which have a close resemblance to those in all three literatures. This is the Japanese chronicle, the *Kojiki*, which is believed to have been compiled about the year A.D. 712. Reference has already been made several times in the foregoing pages to these literary parallels and variants in the Japanese texts, and a more detailed study has also been made elsewhere[1] of some few of the identical themes found in the Japanese text and in Polynesian oral literature. But the subject deserves fuller treatment, which would, we believe, bring to light many more parallels.

The evidence suggests that the literary motifs of the Tatars, the Polynesians, and the Dyaks were already current in Japan by the early eighth century, and that they have radiated out from some centre on the Asiatic mainland at a period shortly before this time. The claim is made in the early pages of the *Kojiki* that the work is a compendium of native myths and traditions, and in this respect it has usually been contrasted with the *Nihongi*, a parallel Japanese chronicle, which, though believed to have been completed only about eight years later, is manifestly under much stronger Chinese influence, and written in Chinese characters. It may, however, be pointed out that, in the first place, the similarities in the subject-matter contained in these two chronicles are, in general, much greater than the differences, and to a considerable extent are to be accounted for as variant traditions which have been orally transmitted. In the second place, and this is all important for our interpretation of the native literatures discussed in the foregoing chapters, many of the themes and motifs contained in these literatures, and the ritual associated with the songs and chants, are to be found in the ritual of Hindu Bali, and in Travancore in south-eastern India, as well as in the Buddhist and pre-Buddhist art of Tibet. In the latter country they can be traced back for many centuries. It seems to us, therefore, that here at any rate the theory of independent development is out of the question, and that certain themes of the oral literatures of modern Siberia, Polynesia, and North Borneo, together with that of early Japan, have their origin in some earlier civilisation of southern Asia, and are to be found wherever Hinduism or some kindred culture[2] has existed or exercised a strong influence, though this influence may extend merely to individual literary motifs, as the influence of ancient Persian civilisation is known to the majority of people chiefly through the *Arabian Nights*.

[1] Chadwick, *J.R.A.I.* LX (1930), p. 425 ff.

[2] It is impossible to speak with certainty as to the exact source of this particular phase until we have fuller knowledge of the relationship of early Hinduism to other cultures of southern and eastern Asia, such as Taoism, and the culture which prevailed among peoples speaking the Mon-Khmer languages.

LIST OF ABBREVIATIONS[1]

AUTHOR AND TITLE OF BOOK	ABBREVIATION

BAILEY. See Howell and Bailey. *S.D.D.*

BROOKE LOW, H. See Ling Roth.   Brooke Low.

GOMES, E. H. *The Sea-Dyaks of Borneo.* London,   Gomes, *Sea-Dyaks.*
1907.

—— *Seventeen Years among the Sea Dyaks of Borneo.*   Gomes, *S.Y.*
London, 1911.

HADDON, A. C. and START, L. E. *Iban or Sea Dyak*   Haddon and Start.
Fabrics and their Patterns. Cambridge, 1936.

HOSE, C. and McDOUGALL, W. *The Pagan Tribes of*   Hose and
Borneo. 2 vols. London, 1912.   McDougall.

HOWELL, W. 'A Sea-Dyak Dirge.' In *S.M.J.* Vol. I,   Howell.
1911.

HOWELL, W. and BAILEY, D. J. S. *A Sea Dyak Dic-*   Howell and
tionary. Singapore, 1900–2.   Bailey, *S.D.D.*

Kojiki. [See List of Abbreviations to Part I, *s.v.*]

ROTH, H. LING. 'The Natives of Borneo.' In *J.A.I.*   Ling Roth,
XXI (1892), p. 110 ff.; XXII (1893), p. 22 ff.   *J.A.I.*

—— *The Natives of Sarawak and British North*   Ling Roth.
Borneo. 2 vols. London, 1896.

LOW, H. BROOKE. *Sarawak...* London, 1848. See   Low.
also in Ling Roth.

McDOUGALL. See Hose and McDougall.   McDougall.

Nihongi. [See List of Abbreviations to Part I.]   *Nihongi.*

PERHAM. *Journal of the Straits Branch of the Royal*   Perham, *J.S.B.*
Asiatic Society.

ST JOHN, Sir SPENCER. *Life in the Forests of the Far*   St John.
East. 2 vols. London, 1862.

START, L. E. See Haddon and Start.

WADDELL, L. A. [See List of Abbreviations to Part I.]   Waddell,
    Lamaism[2].

PERIODICALS

Journal of the (Royal) Anthropological Institute.   *J.(R.)A.I.*
London, 1872–.

Journal of the Royal Asiatic Society of Great Britain   *J.R.A.S.*
and Ireland. London, 1834–.

[See List of Abbreviations to Part I.]   *J.S.B.*

Sarawak Museum Journal.   *Sarawak M.J.*

[1] See Note, Part I, p. 219 above.

PART III

NOTES ON THE ORAL LITERATURE
OF SOME AFRICAN PEOPLES

INTRODUCTION TO PART III

THE material which Africa has to offer us for the study of oral literature is not nearly so full or so important as that of the parts of the world which we have hitherto studied. It is possible that this is due in part to the nature of the records. There can be no doubt that questions of sociology, of material culture, and above all of ethnography and racial history have occupied the minds of travellers and scholars alike far more than questions of mental culture and oral tradition. This is natural enough, since Africa opens up a field of research which is perhaps richer than any other continent in regard to these matters. On the other hand the literary and intellectual life of Africa has been studied only very sporadically and arbitrarily. There are abundant signs that a change is taking place in this respect, and that scholars are waking up to the importance of these studies in Africa, as in other countries;[1] but at present it must be confessed that our available published material is relatively meagre, and must not be regarded as representative of the scope of the subject.

It is to be suspected, however, that the relative paucity of material for the studies in which we are chiefly interested here is not by any means to be attributed wholly to the defective and partial nature of our records. We have, in fact, no reason to think that Africa possesses such rich literary material as the regions already studied. The literary types which call for the most sustained efforts on the part of composer or reciter appear to be little developed, or indeed wholly absent. We have not found any trace of developed narrative poetry in Africa, and oral prose saga rarely rises above the level of folk-tale. The memorisation of exact verbal tradition is seldom widespread or long-lived, and though the composition of extempore poetry is very general, the quality is not such as demands great artistic powers from the reciter or composer.

It has not seemed worth while, therefore, to treat comprehensively any single area in Africa, or to enter into detail comparable to that which we have devoted to the other literatures already considered. We have preferred to select a few areas for which the published literary material offers scope for study, and for comparison and contrast with

[1] We may refer, for example, to such publications as Varley's *African Native Music, an Annotated Bibliography*; and the periodical, *Bantu Studies*.

the other literatures in which we are interested. In these areas we shall not attempt an exhaustive treatment of all the available forms and genres of the literature current, but we shall concentrate in each case on those aspects of the literature which are most striking in themselves and most significant for our purpose. It is hoped that in this way it will be possible in the small space available to indicate some aspects of the native oral literature of Africa which are of importance for the general study of oral literature as a whole.

1. ABYSSINIA[1]

IT is important to make clear at the outset that in the following survey we are concerned with the literature, not of a race or a single linguistic group, but of a complex civilisation whose only unity is that of a limited geographical area, and a central government. It may be said that in a very special sense the geographical conditions of Abyssinia have been the predominant factor in shaping the economic and social life of the country, and its linguistic and intellectual history. This may mean no more than that the mixture of peoples is comparatively recent, or that the record of such admixture is preserved with special clarity here, in contrast, for example, to that of Polynesia. In the following pages, therefore, the literature under discussion represents not only that of the 'Abyssinian' tradition, but also that of Galla settled within the country, either recently or at some period in the past, perhaps in the sixteenth century. We are here concerned, in fact, not so much with Abyssinians or Galla, as with Abyssinia.

The literature of Abyssinia which we are about to consider has been collected for the most part, though not exclusively, from within the limits of the country as it existed before the conquests of Menelek. That is to say, we are concerned chiefly with the province of Tigre in the north, Amhara (including Godjam) in the west and south-west, the various central provinces, including Wallo, settled long ago by Galla, and Shoa in the south. The vast Galla areas occupied by the Arussi and other Galla confederations south of Shoa, which were conquered by Menelek and added to Abyssinian territory at the close of last century, will be considered separately in the next section. It must be borne in mind, however, that numbers of Arussi have been resident in the capital of Adis Ababa, and have lived among the Abyssinians proper for many generations, and that Galla penetration of Abyssinia, both peaceful and warlike, has been going on since the beginning of history. Any distinction between the oral literatures of the two peoples, therefore, can be only partial.

The language of ancient Abyssinia was Ethiopic, or, as it is more correctly called, Ge'ez. It is no longer current as a spoken language,

[1] The following account was written shortly before the recent Italian conquest of the country, and must be understood as applying to the condition of the country at that date.

though it still remains the language of the church and of ecclesiastical and legal literature, much as Latin was used in Europe in the Dark Ages. A considerable literature has been preserved of the ancient northern form of early Ethiopic, but nothing has survived of the southern group. Several languages are current orally in modern Abyssinia, of which the provenance corresponds roughly with the geographical and political areas outlined above. The languages of the north, including Tigre, are known as Tigre and Tigrinna, both Semitic languages, the latter derived directly, the former only indirectly, from the ancient Ethiopic.[1] The official language of Abyssinia, as a whole, however, is Amharic, a language which is indigenous not only in Amhara proper, but also over a large part of Central Abyssinia[2] and Shoa. Its affinities have not been clearly established. Its structure is perhaps a Semitic (Ethiopic) superimposition on a Hamitic basis. Clearly it stands in a definite relationship to ancient Ethiopic. Our only written records of early Amharic are a group of panegyric poems composed on four Abyssinian kings from the fourteenth to the sixteenth century, to which we shall refer later. Various dialects of Galla, which belongs to the Hamitic group of languages, are spoken by the numerous peoples of Galla origin settled in various parts of the country.

The civilisation of Abyssinia is, as everyone knows, an ancient one.[3] Our earliest information relates to the brilliant period of the dynasty at Axum in the north of Tigre, the southernmost outpost of Greek culture. Axum itself must have been a halting place for caravans, and an important market from very early times.[4] The Greek city is thought to have arisen as an extension of the Sabean colonies founded on the west coast of the Red Sea from Yemen in the south-west of Arabia at the beginning of the first century A.D., and to have reached the height of its power in the middle of the fourth century.[5] Inscriptions from Axum make it clear that the art of writing Greek was known and practised in northern Abyssinia at least as early as the first century,[6] while inscriptions of Ezana, the greatest of the Axumite kings, show that even Ethiopic was written during the first half of the fourth century,[7]

[1] Littmann, *Z.f.A.* xx, p. 155.

[2] For an account of Amharic see the works of C. H. Armbruster, especially the Introduction to his *Initia Amharica: An Introduction to Spoken Amharic* (Cambridge, 1908).

[3] For a critical account of the history of Abyssinia based mainly on native records, our chief authority is Budge, *History of Ethiopia*. [4] Budge I, p. 235 f.

[5] See Kammerer, p. 59; cf. Rathjens, *J.A.* cxiv–cxv (1929–30), p. 145; Budge, *loc. cit.* [6] Budge, *loc. cit.* [7] Budge I, p. 242.

and that Christianity was introduced into the country about A.D. 340.[1]
But this brilliant period was of short duration. The series of Mohammedan conquests which began in the seventh century destroyed the
access to the Red Sea, and about 950 the Axumite kingdom was
destroyed by a queen whose name was probably Eve.[2] She belonged
to the great Zagwe tribe of the Agaw, which occupied the mountainous
district of Lasta, today the principal district of the Falashas, a 'tribe'
scattered throughout the country and practising the Jewish religion
(cf. p. 507 below). Eve was probably herself of the Jewish persuasion,
and a period followed in which the Christians were heavily persecuted,
and the Christian churches were laid in ruins.

For some three centuries (till 1270) the predominant power over the
country was in the hands of these central Abyssinians; but at least
the last four of their rulers were Christians, the most famous being the
great Christian king Lalibala, to whom is attributed the building of the
monolithic churches of Lasta. During the twelfth century the greatest
of all Abyssinian saints, Takla Haimanout, is believed to have been
instrumental in reinstating the Axumite line, who are traditionally
stated to have taken refuge in Shoa in the south when the Zagwe
destroyed their power in the north. The following centuries saw a
series of wars against the Arabs, which appear to have been on the whole
successful, and some slight contact with the outside world was once
more established through Egypt. In the middle of the fifteenth century
an attempt was made to join the Abyssinian church to that of Rome,
and in the year 1515 the famous mission under Alvarez was sent from
the Portuguese king. In 1527 the country was overrun and occupied
by Ahmad, better known by his nickname Grañ, 'the left-handed',
who was emir of Harrar, and for twelve years the Abyssinians waged
unceasing war with the Mussulman host for the independence of their
country. In these battles the enemy were successful in every engage-
ment, and it was not till 1543 that the Abyssinians, under the Negus
Claudius, with the help of 400 Portuguese who had been sent to his
assistance, succeeded in crushing the invaders. In the great battle which
saw the defeat of the Mussulmans, Grañ himself was slain, and Christian
Abyssinia was saved.

In the seventeenth century the focus of power shifted to the south,
and the Negus Susenyos, who reigned from 1607–1632, founded a new
capital at Gondar near Lake Tsana. The town preserves many traces
of the culture and refinement of this great period in its history, and the

[1] *Ib.* p. 258.   [2] See *Ib.* I, p. 215.

architectural remains still bear witness to the residence of the Portuguese in the country till their expulsion in 1633.

From the time of Fasiladas, who succeeded Susenyos, to the reign of Menelek the culture of Abyssinia declined. In the eighteenth century the country was torn by factions. The government fell to which-ever of the *rases* of the larger provinces happened to be strongest at the moment, and the royal family were virtually prisoners, powerless and almost forgotten, living in total seclusion in the palace at Gondar, like the Merovingian kings in the hands of the mayor of the palace. By the middle of last century the disruption was complete, and Abyssinia was wholly given over to anarchy and civil wars. The usurper Theodore succeeded in making himself *negus*, but he had neither the family interests nor the character to develop the country economically. The disastrous story of the concluding years of his reign, and of the British expedition against Magdala are well known to all, as are also the events of the reign of his successor, Menelek II, who obtained the throne in 1889, and whose accession represented a return to the ancient royal line. By his decisive and able military measures Menelek succeeded in crushing the invading Italian army at the Battle of Adowa, while his conquests abroad enriched the country with vast new territories. His daughter Judith, and his grandson, the present emperor, have shown themselves progressive and enlightened. The modern changes are, however, not apparent at any great distance beyond the new capital founded by Menelek at Adis Ababa in Shoa. The country as a whole is as yet hardly affected.

In studying the oral literature of Abyssinia, therefore, we are studying the literature of a country which for the most part is still barbaric. It is clear that even down to the end of last century society as a whole was largely of a heroic character. It could not be otherwise. The history of the country is the history of a fight for life. As one reads the pages of the chronicles, of the diaries of travellers, or of careful and learned critical historians such as Budge, one is equally struck by the wearisome iteration of invasions and defensive wars, and the constant return of the upper classes, more especially of the court, to the pursuit of intellectual life and of the arts, in the brief intervals permitted by the constant activity and vigilance necessitated by the disturbed conditions.[1] The

---

[1] In recent times we may refer, among innumerable instances which might be cited, to the statement of Charles Johnston who travelled through Shoa in 1842, that the usual occupation of the *dabteras* in the principality was to transcribe MSS. for the Negus 'who has a most extraordinary desire to be possessed of all the works

society which began so brilliantly with the Greek culture at Axum is now a nation of soldiers making its last stand for the civilisation which it has struggled for two thousand years to defend against foreign rapacity and aggression. We have only to consider their libraries, their churches and ecclesiastical art, and the number of literate people still to be found among the native population in order to realise how much of their ancient civilisation they have still managed to retain.

Northern Abyssinia, that is to say Abyssinia as it was before the conquests of Menelek extended its borders over Galla land, has been a Christian country[1] since the conversion of the Axumite king Ezana. The form of Christianity which has always prevailed is the Coptic. The majority of the Hamitic tribes annexed to the country by Menelek are Mohammedan, though many are still heathen, as we shall see when we study the Galla. Mention has already been made of the Falashas (p. 505 above) who practise the Jewish religion. Their chief home is in Semyen, the highest and most mountainous part of Abyssinia, and it is thought that they may be the modern representatives of the ancient religion of the country before its official conversion to Christianity. The Christian Church of Abyssinia is virtually independent, though the chief bishop, known as the *abuna*, is always a Copt. In the past he rarely left the ecclesiastical palace at Gondar. Beneath him are the priests. There is yet another class of educated men in the country, who are known as *dabteras*. These are intermediate between the clergy and the laymen. They are neither ordained nor under ecclesiastical supervision, but it is said that no religious service can properly be held without them. It is their chief duty to chant the psalms and hymns. They have at all times been mainly responsible for the learning and the written literature of the country.[2] They generally act as clerks and secretaries to anyone who may require their services.

Such traditional culture as has been handed down from early times has been almost exclusively the possession of the Church. How far back the general use of writing goes, as distinct from such inscriptions as those of Adulis and Axum[3], is uncertain; but writing appears to have been used even for literary purposes from an early period. Some of

in the Ge'ez language, and to procure copies of which, or, if possible, the originals themselves, he expends annually a considerable sum'. Cf. also Griaule, *A.J.* p. 77 f.

[1] For an account of the Abyssinian Church and its organisation, the reader is referred to H. M. Hyatt, *The Church of Abyssinia* (London, 1928).

[2] Hyatt, p. 59.

[3] Littmann, *T.G.A.* IV, p. 76 ff.; cf. I, *passim*.

the actual manuscripts in the d'Abbadie collection date from the thirteenth century,[1] and Littmann suggests[2] the last quarter of the thirteenth century as the upper limit for the earliest MSS. which have come down to us. We have every reason to suppose that the writers of the chronicles and other works contained in these manuscripts were frequently utilising earlier written sources, as we know to have been the custom later.

The framework of these early chronicles is that of Eusebius, which no doubt reached Abyssinia from Greek sources. The form is roughly annalistic, and the starting-point is generally the Creation of the World. The chronicles themselves are manifestly of learned origin. On the other hand, as time goes on they tend more and more to expand the narrative elements with wealth of detail and fulness of description.

We have no reason to suppose that the art of writing was ever at any period at all general. With the exception of the *Songs of the Emperors* (cf. p. 522 below), preserved in MSS. in the Bibliothèque Nationale at Paris and in Oxford, no native literature of any of the Abyssinian dialects has been preserved in written form. The memory of persons and events of the past is kept alive, as it has been for centuries, by oral tradition, and the native[3] science of the stars, plants, etc., together with a certain amount of mythology and tribal tradition, is transmitted by the same means.

Oral prose saga does not appear to have attained to any great development. This is doubtless to be accounted for by the wealth of written historical and learned literature in the country. D'Abbadie speaks of 'historiens, hommes sages', who, he tells us, 'connaissaient les légendes', and to whom the prince of Godjam undertook to introduce him.[4] Parkyns also speaks of accounts given to him by native Abyssinians—"men of learning, and who were supposed to be good at relating stories of the past reign or two";[5] and Rossini speaks of oral traditions of the great Mussulman conqueror of the sixteenth century,

[1] Chaine, *Catalogue*, p. ix.

[2] Littmann, *G.ä.L.* p. 204.

[3] By native science we mean those branches of popular knowledge which are commonly called 'lore', as opposed to such Greek or Arabic learning as is to be found in books in Abyssinia. Into the question of ultimate Arabic influence, orally transmitted, on the astronomy of the North Abyssinian tribes it is not proposed to enter here. Cf. Littmann, *Sternensagen*, p. 298 ff.

[4] D'Abbadie, p. 243; cf. also p. 215 f.   [5] Parkyns II, p. 103.

Mohammed Grañ (cf. p. 505 above), which he says are still current in
Adowa.[1] Indeed we hear not infrequently of men who are said to be well
versed in the legends of the past. But apart from legends embodying
local antiquarian speculations,[2] there is no reason to suppose that
ancient traditions have been preserved wholly independently of written
records. Indeed the testimony of Plowden, who was doubtless well
informed in matters of this kind, is definitely against such a supposition.
In his experience the oral traditions of Abyssinia extend back little
more than two hundred years.[3]

The art of telling a story, or at least of 'reporting', seems to be
cultivated to a considerable extent, however, as is to be expected from
a people which is largely unlettered. Travellers speak frequently[4] of the
fondness of men of all classes for telling a story, or reporting an anecdote, and of their skill in this art. A particularly striking example is
the narrative of the relations of the two chiefs, Ras Oubié and his uncle
Walda Jesus, narrated to Lefebvre by his dragoman.[5] The perusal of
such few written diaries as we possess from the pens of Abyssinians
who have travelled abroad also shows their skill in detailed and vivid
narrative.[6] More important is the witness borne by the chronicles to
the art of prose story-telling, especially such as relate to comparatively
modern times. We may refer to the Chronicle of King Theodore,[7] which
is simply a vivid biography of the king; or to that of John IV,[8] in which
the annalistic style of the earlier chronicles is combined with the saga
style of the later biographies. We know that this art of reporting recent
events in vivid and detailed narrative has been deliberately cultivated
by the rulers. Salt tells us that Ras Welled Selassé of Shoa presented
him with a manuscript containing an account of his last campaign
against the Galla, written by a 'scribe' of his court, "which", says Salt,
"is filled with more adulatory compliments than facts". Parts of this
account, he adds, were occasionally read in the prince's presence to
his great satisfaction.[9] In our own time Griaule noted that Ras Hailou

[1] *S.L.D.* p. 635, footnote 1.
[2] See e.g. Combes and Tamisier II, p. 333 ff.; Griaule, *J.A.* CCXII (1928), p. 19 ff.;
Rossini, *G.S.A.I.* XIV, p. 41 ff. (cf. Littmann, *J.A.O.S.* XXIII, p. 52).
[3] Plowden, p. 32.
[4] See e.g. Littmann, *P.E.* II, p. 12; Sundström, *J.A.O.S.* XXIII, p. 54 f.;
Plowden, pp. 79, 82 f.; Eadie, *passim*; Griaule, *A.J.* p. 220 f.
[5] Lefebvre I, p. 55 ff.
[6] Littmann, *J.A.O.S.* XXIII, p. 51 ff.; cf. *ib.* *G.ä.L.* p. 260; also Lefebvre I, p. 149 ff.
[7] *Theodoros.*
[8] Chaine, *R.S.* (1913), p. 178 ff.   [9] Salt, p. 364 f.

of Godjam kept communities which "spent their time exalting his merits on parchment chronicles": "scores of sheep", he adds, "gave their skins every year for this end."[1]

The form of oral tradition with which we are most familiar is that of poetry. Abyssinian poetry is generally sung, often to the accompaniment of a stringed instrument. The poems never attain to great length. Few consist of more than a hundred lines, while the majority are quite short. This fact leads one to suppose that such poems as attain to any circulation will be transmitted with only slight verbal variations. Indeed in the case of the highly elaborate and artificial poetry of the *dabteras*—the educated 'clerical' class—which is often satirical in character, and in which the alteration or misplacement of a word may completely reverse the sense of the entire poem, any licence on the part of the reciter is inconceivable. On the other hand, among the more popular types of composition, frequently extempore, generally ephemeral in character, and only sporadically memorised and given a wide currency, it is natural to suppose that a considerable amount of laxity will prevail in regard to verbal exactitude. This, as a matter of fact, appears to be the case in the few duplicate versions which have come under our observation.[2]

The secular poetry of modern Abyssinia is heroic, and this literature is comparable in many respects with the heroic poetry of the Galla. On the other hand the literature of the ecclesiastical tradition and of the *dabteras* in Abyssinia has practically precluded the development of a non-heroic literature, such as we shall find flourishing today in those communities of the Galla to the south which have still preserved their heathen faith. On the whole, therefore, we have thought it best to adopt in relation to the oral poetry of Abyssinia only the broad classification into ecclesiastical and secular. Only the latter class will be considered here in any detail. The special interest of this secular poetry lies in the fact that it represents the intellectual efforts of a heroic society which is the heir to a civilised tradition from the past, and which still cherishes in its Christian ecclesiastical and monastic institutions a civilised community in its midst.

It will be convenient to notice briefly at this point the poetry of the *dabteras* before passing on to examine somewhat more in detail the secular poetry of the unlettered Abyssinians, who are, of course, the vast majority of the population. The *dabteras* are, by the nature of their

[1] Griaule, *A.J.* p. 77f.
[2] We may refer, e.g. to Cerulli, *Canti*, nos. 3, 8, 20, 35, etc. (p. 566f.).

office, all poets, and apart from their long religious poems—which are commonly written down when composed, and which therefore need not detain us here—they are also called upon to improvise hymns in the church on days of festivals, and other great occasions. These more or less extempore poems are generally not more than eight or nine lines long, and are often shorter.[1] A favourite form of composition among the *dabteras* is the short witty poem, very artificial in style, known as the *qene*. There are said to be at least ten types of the *qene* alone.[2] The locality in which they are mostly cultivated is that of Godjam, immediately to the south of Lake Tsana, and more especially in the monastery of Dima.[3] It may be added that the province of Godjam is at once the most conservative and the most artistic province in Abyssinia.[4]

The schools for the composition of *qene* are in fact schools of rhetoric.[5] A collection of *qene*, consisting of little poems composed by *dabteras* to be sung after certain verses of the Psalms, is published by the Italian scholar Guidi.[6] These poems abound in metaphors and allusions to names and characters of the Old and New Testaments. Considerable obscurity of style often results, and this is further increased by the extreme condensation and love of puns. A type which is greatly admired is one in which the alteration of a single word reverses the entire sentiment of the verse. Such poems are, of course, only preserved in writing when some special excellence commends them as suitable to be written down and learned by young disciples.

It will readily be understood that this particular genre, potentially double-edged, is admirably suited to purposes of encomium and of satire. It is, moreover, by a natural transition from either, a highly effective medium for purposes of begging, and the *dabteras* are not above using it for all these purposes. Indeed the *dabteras'* songs are frequently composed for secular purposes, sometimes in the form of addresses to kings and great men from whom they would beg money, sometimes for the purpose of ridiculing, abusing, or injuring those who have incurred their displeasure.[7] D'Abbadie tells us that when he was in the entourage of Guoscho Biro, during his campaign against the

---

[1] Cf. however, Rossini, *J.A.* 2nd ser., Vol. VI (1915), p. 222.
[2] For an account of the *qene* see Guidi, *R.R.A.L.* IX, p. 464; cf. Littmann, *G.ä.L.* p. 229. [3] Mondon-Vidhaillet, p. 3191.
[4] *Ib.* p. 3181; Chaine, *R.O.C.* p. 422. [5] Mondon-Vidhaillet, p. 3191.
[6] *R.R.A.L.* IX, p. 463 ff.; cf. also Chaine, *R.O.C.* p. 401 ff.
[7] Rossini, *J.A.* (1915²), p. 223.

Galla, the clergy met him on the triumphal return march, chanting 'hymns in Ge'ez composed in his honour'.[1] These would no doubt be *qene*, and similar to the verses composed by the 'priests of the four churches of Angobar' in honour of Ras Sāhla Selassé, which were recited by a 'coryphée'. They are said to have been composed on the same day as that on which they were recited, and to have contained allusions to the most recent events.

Rochet d'Héricourt has left a translation of one of these poems:

"Sáhla-Selassé est le plus grand de tous les rois qui ont jamais paru: aucun ne peut lui être comparé. Son intelligence et sa bravoure sont sans rivales; parler de lui, c'est donc instruire. L'empire de Sáhla-Selassé est semblable à un vaisseau. Prions comme le prophète Élie, afin qu'il demeure longtemps à Angobar; sa présence remplit toute la ville de joie."[2]

The same writer also records[3] a similar panegyric composed in his own honour, and recited in his presence by three *dabteras* of Shoa because he had taken prisoner three Galla.

The long love poem or love letter in verse quoted by Eadie in his Amharic Reader may be the work of a *dabtera*. The Biblical tone, allusions and diction, as well as the liberal sprinkling of Ge'ez, all point in this direction. The allusion to writing also rather suggests that the author was an educated man, though of course if it was composed in Adis he need not have been a *dabtera* necessarily. The following lines are strangely like the Anglo-Saxon poem of the Husband's Message:[4]

> Go you paper which is sent by me . . .
> My love having taken you out of the envelope, let her look at you,
> You having finished the work, and spoken the message,
> Do not stay, come back quickly.[5]

It is probably from the *dabteras* that the secular poets have borrowed the form of the short, allusive, punning poem which they compose for similar purposes, and which is so convenient a vehicle for political satire. Instances are quoted by Chaine.[6] The collections of popular verse in various modern Abyssinian dialects published by European scholars contain a large number of such poems, referring in veiled terms to such subjects as the severity of Theodore, the attack on Magdala, the campaigns of Menelek, the war against the Italians and the Battle of Adowa, etc., etc.

[1] D'Abbadie, p. 325.
[2] D'Héricourt ii, p. 231.
[3] *Ib.* p. 214f.
[4] See Vol. i, p. 425.
[5] Eadie, p. 264.
[6] Chaine, *R.O.C.* p. 413.

We will now pass on to consider briefly the literature of the unlettered poets of Abyssinia. It has been remarked as strange[1] that no
trace of epic poetry, or indeed of narrative poetry of any kind, has been
recorded from Abyssinia. Even the numerous longer poems collected
both by Rossini and by Littmann from Tigre[2] contain no narrative,
though they are rich in allusions to past events. Nor have we been
able to find in the writings of any earlier travellers the slightest indication that they ever heard epic or narrative poetry of any kind recited.[3]
But as we have noted above, this absence of narrative poetry seems to
be common to the whole of Africa.

The evidence of books of travel leaves no doubt that the commonest
form of poetry is panegyric. Probably no traveller in Abyssinia, from
Poncet at the close of the seventeenth century to Rey in our own time,
has made a journey to the country without having heard, whether on
the march to battle or at the feast in camp or at home, some minstrel
singing in honour of their host or the more important of his guests. In
all ranks of society it is the custom for one or more minstrels to be
present on such occasions and to recite their encomia to the accompaniment of harp and fiddle. Instances are too numerous to be cited in any
detail, and may be found throughout the works of men who have lived
long in the country, such as Pearce, d'Abbadie, and Plowden. We may
refer also to the panegyrics recited on Ras Sāhla Selassé of Shoa,
recorded by Harris;[4] to those recited in the presence of Combes and
Tamisier on the Samu-Negus by groups of women after his victory
over the Wållō Galla;[5] to the panegyrics recited by a single minstrel to
the music of his small harp at the evening meal in the tent of the same
travellers in southern Abyssinia;[6] and to the improvised panegyric of
the *azmari*, as such minstrels are called, which was recited to the music
of the 'quaint guitar' outside the house in the village of Ambo Derbo
in Tigre, where the English traveller Bent was entertained.[7] The poems
so composed are said to be extempore, but it often happens that,
becoming popular, they pass from mouth to mouth, and are handed
down for several generations.[8] Naturally in Abyssinia, as elsewhere,

---

[1] Chaine, *R.O.C.* p. 306; Littmann, *Kaiserlieder*, p. 8.

[2] Rossini, *Z.f.A.* XVII, XVIII, XIX; cf. nos. 117 ff.; Littmann, *Princeton Expedition*, Vols. III, IV; *Z.f.A.* XXVII, p. 112 ff.

[3] Plowden's summaries of the 'exploits' recorded of 'now living warriors' give
no indication that he had obtained them from poems of a narrative character, nor
do we believe that this was so.

[4] Harris II, p. 283.   [5] Combes and Tamisier II, p. 322 ff.

[6] *Ib.* p. 352.   [7] Bent, p. 69.   [8] See Littmann, *Z.f.A.* XXVII, p. 112.

the purpose of these panegyrics is to beg. Littmann's collection of poetry from Tigre furnishes many examples of this practice.[1] It may be added that many European travellers have been made the subject of panegyrics. In addition to those already mentioned Ferret and Galinier quote a poem which was composed in their honour by the young people of Diksa in Tigre,[2] and Parkyns complained with mock bitterness on his return to England: "The men will not look after me with admiration, nor the girls make songs about me here."[3]

Songs of welcome are often in fact panegyric poems, and these are sung by the women on the arrival of a distinguished person in the district. Plowden could not get rid of the 'poets' and 'poetesses' who flocked to welcome him on his return to Adowa.[4] D'Abbadie mentions[5] the cries of joy and the 'villanelles' with which the girls welcomed the prince of Godjam as he returned with his army from the campaign against the Galla referred to above (p. 511 ff.). Such a welcome is naturally intensified when the prince returns victorious from a battle. D'Abbadie tells of the 'chanteurs ambulants', the 'chœurs de jeunes filles', and the 'filles de champs, nos chanteuses et improvisatrices en titre' who took part in welcoming the returning Godjamite army after this same campaign against the Galla.[6]

A hero who returns from the slaying of a lion or an elephant is as highly qualified to receive a panegyric poem as a hero returning from battle. Littmann and Rossini quote the text (and translation) of a poem celebrating the return of a hero from a successful elephant hunt:

1st Chor.   He has slain, he has destroyed him.
2nd Chor.   Whither went he when he slew him?
1st Chor.   As he went hence did I see him at all?
All.   Perhaps on the bank of the river he has stricken him down.
             Destroyer and slayer art thou called,
             Hurrah, Hurrah, doubly a slayer.[7]

The chief of one of the Tigre tribes was hailed on his return home from a plundering raid by a singer as follows:

> What sort of a terrifying man is this? Like
> a lion he fought the opposing army!

[1] See e.g. Littmann, *Z.f.A.* XXVII, p. 112.
[2] Ferret and Galinier I, p. 401.   [3] Parkyns II, p. 311.
[4] Plowden, p. 372.   [5] D'Abbadie, p. 255.
[6] *Ib.* p. 325. We may compare the dance and song of welcome of the women of Israel before Saul and David after their victory over the Philistines, I Samuel xviii. 6, 7.
[7] Littmann, *G.ä.L.* p. 267.

And what sort of a Leopard is this?
He watched while powder and match he
held ready.

And what sort of a thunder ross (*sic*) is this?
Annihilating he passed through
village and open country.[1]

As in other heroic communities we also hear of poems of abuse.
Bruce tells us that on a day on which the *abuna*[2] excommunicated the
great Ras Michael, about thirty poets and poetesses of Gondar
"abused, ridiculed, and traduced Michael in lampoons and scurrilous
rhymes, calling him crooked, and lame, old, and impotent, and several
other opprobrious names, which did not affect him nearly so much as
the ridicule of his person: upon many occasions after they repeated this,
and particularly in a song they ridiculed the horse of Sire, who had run
away at the battle of Limjour."[3] Pearce also refers to the custom of
singing denunciatory poems in case the poets are of opinion that their
panegyrics have not been adequately rewarded. When Ras Michael
fell from his horse, and the poets in his train were trying to put
a good face on the matter, we are told that they repeated by turns a
number of verses in which they made out the fall to be a lucky omen,
asserting that Ras Michael and, after him, Ras Welled Selassé, fell on
the same spot, while exhibiting their address in the same exercise on the
commencement of their power; but the young women and girls
belonging to the town were singing the adventure outside in verse in a
very different style.

"It is a general custom, with the Abyssinians", adds Pearce,
"especially with the females, to sing verses of this kind, merely to show
their esteem or contempt for one person more than another. The Ras
and his soldiers were obliged to listen without showing their anger, as
it would only make matters worse to fall out with the women; the only
way to put an end to such songs is to be generous and give each gang
a cow. On all great holidays the women go to the premises of the
different chiefs, where they sing in praise of each, till he gives them a
cow, but if he does not, the song is changed to some kind of abuse or
ridicule; and if a chief has ever done anything to the prejudice of his
character, such as shewing symptoms of cowardice, or what not, they
will make it the subject of a song, which they will sing over and over

---

[1] Littmann, *G.ä.L.* p. 267; Rossini, *Z.f.A.* XVIII, p. 351.
[2] The *abuna* is the head of the Ethiopic Church; cf. p. 507 above.
[3] Bruce VI, p. 17 f.

again for days together, after their domestic work is done. Should a chief have no blemish upon his character they touch him up with stinginess, and all are obliged to bear it with patience or comply with their demands. They will even make a sham cry[1] if he pays no attention to them, holding a cloth up to resemble the customary cry for the dead.... Very few deny them, in case it be upon a regular holiday, and it is customary to give on such a day."[2]

Hints of a "fearful castigation given by the women in their songs to niggardly chieftains" are also to be found in the writings of Plowden,[3] who adds that "Songs adapted always to passing events, and often witty and apt, are the 'Charivari' of the Abyssinian, and dreaded as much as the lash of the chiefs."[4] A very interesting description of a performance by the court hermaphrodite of Godjam in the presence of Ras Hailou in our own day is published by Griaule, in which the reciter chants a diatribe against the Ras and his European visitors. The diatribe is in reality a caricature and a piece of political criticism in one:

> Gouverneur du pays du Nil, toi, restes sur ton héritage,
> L'autre, le neveu de Ménélik, Tafari-les-Mains-Fines
> Est allongé sur le trône de la Reine de Sabá,
> Et toi tu dors tranquille,
> Collé à ton lit royal comme une galette brûlée.[5]

Poetry which embodies an appeal or prayer to some individual is also common. We have seen that panegyric poetry often contains a frank appeal for largesse. Poetry which contains a call to arms is very widespread. Pearce, who spent many years in the service of the Ras of Tigre during the early part of the nineteenth century, tells us that when the armies marched to battle it was the custom for poets to ride before their chief, descanting in poetry in a loud voice in order to stimulate the courage of the soldiers.[6] They sing of the reward of bravery, and the redemption of the sins of a soldier who dies in the presence of his master in the field of glory, and the curse which God sends on those who flinch or run away. D'Abbadie tells us that on one occasion the army attributed their victory in battle against the Galla to one of their poets, and he quotes the concluding lines of his appeal:

[1] A keen, or elegy as for the dead.
[2] Pearce II, p. 223 ff.
[3] Plowden, p. 215.
[4] Ib. loc. cit.
[5] Griaule, A.J. p. 109.
[6] Pearce I, p. 271; cf. Griaule, A.J. p. 106.

O frères, vous avez faim et soif! O véritables fils de ma mère,
N'êtes-vous pas des oiseaux de proie? Allons, voilà les viandes ennemies!
Et moi, je serai votre écuyer tranchant! En avant!
Et, si l'hydromel vous manque, je vous donnerai mon sang à boire![1]

Elegiac poetry is very common, and is composed by both men and
women, and when such poetry is composed for nobles or princes it is
sometimes preserved in oral tradition for a long time, even, it is said,
for several centuries. We may instance the famous elegy for Saba Gadis
which Gobat heard sung by the servants of Kidam Maryam, a chief of
a caravan of Gondar:

"I heard the servants of Kidam Maryam singing an air which
touched me even to tears: it is the only agreeable air that I have heard
in Abyssinia. I asked him what his people were singing; to which he
replied with tears in his eyes, 'It is a dirge over Saba Gadis, which the
people sing every evening, weeping, in all the Amhara country'. These
are the words:

Alas! Saba Gadis, the friend of all,
Has fallen at Daga Shaha, by the hand of Oubeshat!
Alas! Saba Gadis, the pillar of the poor,
Has fallen at Daga Shaha, weltering in his blood!
The people of this country, will they find it a good thing
To eat ears of corn which have grown in the blood?
Who will remember [St] Michael of November [i.e. to give alms]?
Maryam, with five thousand Galla, has killed him [him, i.e. who
     remembered to give alms]
For the half of a loaf, for a cup of wine,
The friend of the Christians has fallen at Daga Shaha."[2]

Personal and occasional poetry is very common, and is found in all
parts of the country. Representative collections have been published
by Littmann and Rossini from Tigre and the various tribes of northern
Abyssinia, by Cerulli from Amhara, and by Cohen and Eadie from the
south (Adis Ababa). By no means all these poems are composed in
the first person. Sometimes they have the form of dialogue. The subject
which predominates is love, but other emotions, such as scorn, contempt
and hostility also find expression. One poet sings the praises of a
mistress; one complains of the obduracy of parents who oppose the
union of two lovers; a little triplet in the third person quoted by
Littmann expresses the proud reply of Gendefli to his sons, who ask
him what possessions he has in his solitary abode on the hill-top:

[1] D'Abbadie, p. 298; cf. p. 438.   [2] Gobat, p. 250f.

18

A chief is Gendefli, high is the top of his [mountain] throne;
Its wood is never cut, its paths are never trod upon!
Pshaw, ye children, ye will [not] become like him.[1]

Poems which embody a challenge to battle are also very numerous, and boasting and challenge are often combined in the same poem. Such a poem is known as a *gerara*. It may be addressed either to the enemy or to the warriors whom the poet is inciting to battle, or it may be chanted by the hunter to the animal he is about to slay. An Amharic challenge recorded by Mittwoch is modelled on a hunter's poem of this class:

Hippopotamus, come, we will fight, you and I.
With what lance shall I fight? With my zagar-lance;
May the little zagar-dart pierce your father.
If I pierce you, you will become bloody,
The foam of your blood will froth up, etc.[2]

We shall see in the next section that similar poetry is known also among the Galla.

As examples of poetry of a more personal character we may refer to the complaint of the Godjamite woman recorded in the Chronicle of Theodore:

Lorsqu'on pilla le Mêtch'â,
    les maraudeurs déchirèrent mes
        vêtements et s'en revêtèrent

Les fusiliers poussèrent mes
    bœufs devant eux et les égor-
        gèrent....

Roi! il ne vous reste plus que
    quelques mots d'amharique
        à prononcer;

Pourquoi ne saccagez-vous pas
    les entrailles, qu'enfin je
        repose en paix![3]

Stereotyped forms of personal poetry proper to occasions of social ritual, are frequently referred to in books of travel, and numerous examples are included in the collections recorded from all parts of the country. We may instance the wedding songs recorded by Cerulli,[4] and the 'birth song' recorded by Rossini.[5] Perhaps the commonest form is the boasting poem, the poem in which the warrior makes his *doomfata*,

[1] Littmann, *Princeton Expedition* II, p. 53.   [2] Mittwoch, *M.S.O.S.* p. 214.
[3] *Theodoros*, p. 48.   [4] *Canti*, p. 641 f.   [5] *Z.f.A.* XVIII, p. 377, no. 121.

his boast either of what he has done, or what he will do. Such *doomfata* are regularly made by the chiefs and their retainers as they assemble before their lord in anticipation of battle, or to celebrate the victory and to present the trophies.[1] They are also recited by a hunter after a successful lion or elephant hunt.[2] Poems embodying these *doomfata* are known in the south as *faqara*.[3] Chaine observes that the Homeric warriors boasting before the Trojan camp are modest in their pretensions compared with the Abyssinians, who make no scruple to refer to themselves as lions and sons of lions. The people of Tigre and of Godjam, he tells us, are particularly notable for the boldness of their hyperboles in such poems.[4]

In recent years poems have been recorded in Adis Ababa which may be described, on the whole, as post-heroic. The form and style of these poems are just such as are everywhere applied to heroic poetry, but the outlook of the poet has changed. The contact with foreigners, and the changes in material culture which are daily before the eyes of the people of the new capital have brought about a revolution in ideas quite independently of writing or of books. The majority of the people are still uneducated, and we have therefore a rare opportunity of studying the popular oral poetry of a post-heroic phase. This poetry is chiefly contained in the collections of Cohen and Eadie from Adis, the former chiefly recorded from natives who can read and write.

In these collections it is interesting to note that the first post-heroic features to appear are a spirit of criticism—criticism both of the Abyssinians and of the foreigners; a sense of national responsibility; a serious political morality; and an appreciation of the advantages to be derived from education and foreign culture. One is especially struck by the impression which the superior education, etc. of foreigners has made on the natives, and by the shrewd native wit which is brought to play on the characteristics, and especially the foibles, of the various European peoples resident in Adis Ababa. We may refer to the following trifles published by Cohen:

> Disant: "Bonjour, Monsieur" entre le Français.
> "Comment vas-tu, Dasseta?" [c'est] l'affaire des Grecs![5]

[1] See e.g. Bruce VI, p. 116; Lefebvre I, p. 99; Harris II, p. 219.
[2] See e.g. Plowden, p. 62f. No doubt the 'Song of triumph' chanted by the successful slayer of the elephant mentioned by Major Powell-Cotton was a poem of this class. See Powell-Cotton, p. 336. [3] Mondon-Vidhaillet, p. 318I.
[4] Chaine, *R.O.C.* p. 409f. Chaine (*loc. cit.*) quotes three examples.
[5] Cohen, p. 27.

And again:

> Si le Français se fâche, moi en colère, moi en colère;
> Je ne sache pas avoir trouvé celui qu'il y a comme toi, mon enfant.[1]

Another begins also with a glimpse at the Abyssinian's view of the French, and then passes on to refer to the English, Italians, and others:

> Comme les Français, je n'ai pas beaucoup d'argent, etc.[2]

The Japanese figure as the high-water mark of versatility and industry in the opinion of the Abyssinians.

Abyssinian personal poetry is essentially occasional in character. Cohen's specimens in particular closely resemble the work of Archilochos in their terse and trenchant, if somewhat sardonic, humour.

> La souris en ribote a mis la dent au malt;
> A voulu tuer mon chat, lui a mordu la nuque.[3]

Or this:

> Pendant que les Grecs t'arrosent de leur argent,
> Pendant que les Italiens t'arrosént de leur argent, . . .
> Que vais-je devenir, moi, ton misérable amant?[4]

An interesting change of tone from the earlier panegyric poetry of the old régime is observable in two comparatively long poems from Adis recorded by Cohen[5] and Eadie.[6] Their outward form is that of conventional panegyric poetry, the former addressed to a lady, the latter to the deposed Emperor, Lidj Iyasu. The framework and all the stereotyped formulae of panegyrics are here—the fulsome and gross flattery, excessive exaggeration, idealisation. But into this heroic outline the poets have introduced passages which remind us of the work of Solon and of the Anglo-Saxon post-heroic poems. The nation is reminded in detail of its past history, is urged to review the moral and social condition of the present time, to look around at other nations, and to consider in what the true health and strength of a nation consists. Industry and enlightenment are inculcated—sometimes in a manner rather naïve. The catalogue, gnomic utterance, the vignette—all are utilised in these two interesting compositions.

The light and trifling character of many of the subjects (e.g. those of Cohen, nos. 5, 7, 9, 10, 18, 25, 28), and the tone of disillusionment and frank realism (nos. 6, 13) are characteristics which we venture to think

---

[1] Cohen, p. 31.   [2] *Ib.* p. 48.   [3] *Ib.* p. 41.
[4] *Ib.* p. 33.   [5] *Ib.* no. 21.   [6] Eadie, p. 229 ff.

are a new element incident upon the growth of town life, and contact with the outside world. Probably the little moral narrative poem of a baboon and a wolf recorded by Eadie[1] is due to the same influences. This poem tells of a baboon who cried 'wolf', or rather 'man with dog' so often to her husband that he grew callous, and when the catastrophe fell, he was caught off his guard. The 'keen' of the baboon family is hit off with a light humour and satire on the current panegyrics for the dead which argues the widening outlook of the new capital, and are in strange contrast to the panegyric on Lidj Iyasu just referred to, which immediately precedes it. The capital seems to have passed from a 'heroic' to a 'post-heroic' stage.

The literature of native (heathen) learning is naturally unrepresented in Christian Abyssinia; but some of the conventions proper to learned and didactic literature are found widespread in the secular oral literature which we have been discussing. Particularly common is the convention of the catalogue. These are found in great numbers throughout the heroic poems, as well as in the poetry of post-heroic character recorded in Adis Ababa. We may refer to the material collected by Littmann from the Habāb,[2] etc. and elsewhere in Tigre.[3] One of the most frequent devices is an appeal made by the poet in the first person to a series of villages, districts, or tribes, which are named categorically. Examples occur in Rossini nos. 142, 154.[4] One of these poems recorded by Rossini from Tigre enumerates places in which markets have been set up.[5] The catalogue form is even found in heroic elegiac poetry. In an elegy recorded by Rossini, a series of villages are questioned categorically as to whether they will send representatives to the funeral of the dead hero.[6] With this we may compare also the catalogue of villages in *ib.* p. 360 f. The same form is prominent in many of the other poems recorded by Chaine, Littmann, Cerulli, Rossini, and Eadie.

Littmann records two interesting gnomic catalogue poems. The first[7] consists of a list of animals which the poet tells us in the first line were created by God. It reads very much like a census of the inhabitants of Noah's ark. The second,[8] which is more interesting, is avowedly composed for the purpose of imparting information: "Man does not know

---

[1] Eadie, p. 244. [2] *Z.f.A.* xx, p. 151 ff.
[3] Littmann, *Princeton Expedition* IV, *passim.* Cf. Nöldeke, *Z.f.A.* xxxi, p. 12.
[4] *Z.f.A.* xix, p. 319f.
[5] *Ib.*; cf. however, Rossini's note *ad hoc.*
[6] Rossini, *Z.f.A.* xviii, p. 380.
[7] Littmann, *Princeton Expedition* ii, p. 87. [8] *Ib.* p. 88.

it; for these wild animals are hard to understand." A list of animals with their characteristic habits or attributes follows, the whole forming a poem of observation comparable to the Cottonian collection of gnomic verses in Anglo-Saxon.[1]

The popular poetry of Abyssinia is not a new development. Alike from distribution, diction, treatment, and poetical conventions, as well as from the large number of technical terms by which poets and various types of poetical compositions are referred to, it is clear that a long history lies behind it. We have fortunately, however, more explicit evidence for the antiquity of poetry closely resembling that which is current in Abyssinia today. A happy accident has preserved for us eleven little poems addressed to and celebrating four Abyssinian emperors, namely, Amda Seyon (1312–1342, or 1314–1344); Isaac, surnamed Gabra Maskal (1414–1429); Zara Yakob (1434–1468); and the great Claudius who defeated Mohammed Grañ, and who reigned from 1508 to 1540. These songs are composed in the old Amharic language, and are preserved in a small MS., doubtless written by an ecclesiastic or *dabtera* about the time at which they were composed, or shortly afterwards. They have been edited and translated by the German scholar Littmann[2] with the help of an old Abyssinian resident in Jerusalem. They are all composed in the form of addresses, and are addressed or directed to the reigning emperor, generally by name. Their contents differ little from the oral poetry of the *azmari* and other popular poets of modern Abyssinia. Panegyric constitutes the greater part, and this may take the form of pure encomia, or of allusions to past exploits and battles of the emperor, or of adverse reflections on the conduct of his enemies. Catalogues are also prominent, as is usual in poetry of this kind in Abyssinia. The following little poem takes the form of a call to arms addressed to the Emperor Isaac by the soldiers who are anxious to take the field again against their enemies now that the winter season has passed and the grass is again long and rich enough to pasture their horses.

> Come, Isaac Negus, come.
> Where are you now?
> Your harp is resounding,
> The animal world has grown strong and vigorous,
> The grass sways fragrant in the wind,
> The east is your footstool,

[1] See Vol. 1, p. 380 of the present work.   [2] Littmann, *Kaiserlieder.*

The west is your throne,
Your banner is aloft,
The period of warfare has begun.
Where now are you?
Isaac Negus, come.[1]

We must now give a brief account of the poets and minstrels who compose and sing the oral poetry which is current in Abyssinia today, and which we have just shown to have been current in a similar form for many centuries. The composition of poetry, and the singing of poetry to the accompaniment of a stringed instrument are very widespread among the people as a whole, while there are, and have been for many centuries, a number of different classes of professional poets and poetesses in the country. On the other hand it has been shown that no developed saga has been recorded in oral form in Abyssinia. The extent to which this is to be attributed to the existence of a lettered class throughout the country may be gauged by reference to the passage already quoted (p. 509 above) in which Salt mentions a manuscript which contained an account of the Ras Welled Selassé's last campaign against the Galla, written by a scribe of the court, and which was read from time to time in the Ras's presence. With this we may compare the passage from the *Haralds Saga Harðráða*, ch. 99, cited in Vol. 1, p. 581 of the present work, which describes King Harold listening to the stories of his own campaign recited by an Icelander at his court in Norway.

Space will not permit us to give any detailed account of the minstrels and reciters of religious poetry, of whom Christian Abyssinia has retained many classes. The wandering monks who sing religious verse while soliciting alms[2] need not detain us, as their work has little to do with popular poetry in the strict sense of the term. Of the *dabteras*, whose poetry is frequently composed on secular and occasional subjects, something has already been said. The *lalibalas*, however, call for a fuller notice. These constitute a strange corporation of beggars and cripples, who wander about the streets at night and sing outside the houses of the great and the wealthy for alms. Their companies consist of both men and women, and are believed to have been instituted by the famous king Lalibala, who built the monolithic churches still existing in the mountainous district of Central Abyssinia. They sing entirely without accompaniment, and traces of their ecclesiastical origin

[1] *Ib.* p. 16f.   [2] Chaine, *R.O.C.* p. 314.

are perhaps to be seen in the fact that they sing in harmony, the voices of the men and women mingling in two or three parts: "les femmes chantant d'abord, puis les hommes. Ce n'est plus de la musique homophone. C'est une harmonie simple, généralement basée sur la tierce, dominée par une mélodie de vocalises parfaitement exécutées."[1]

It will be seen that the *lalibala* resembles closely the Russian *kalêki* (cf. Vol. II, p. 270 of the present work), and it can hardly be doubted that they are of a contemporary, if not of a common origin. It is to be noted, however, that the *lalibala*, unlike the *kalêki*, are said only to sing before sunrise. They must disappear with the appearance of the morning star.[2] The most important and most numerous class of professional poets and minstrels in Abyssinia are the *aẓmaris*. These men compose short extempore poems which they sing to the accompaniment of the *leqso*, a one-stringed instrument like a fiddle.[3] They are found everywhere, whether in the entourage of princes or wealthy men, in the houses of men of humbler rank, or wandering along the roads, and attending at all public gatherings, like the medieval minstrels to whom they are constantly compared by all travellers who have seen them. They live entirely by their wits, and have in consequence developed a quick and lively ability to hit off the foibles of their audience, to incorporate topical allusions, and to introduce puns and various other witty sallies into their poems.

The subjects of the songs of the *aẓmaris* are generally contemporary events, or the characters or personal appearance of some prominent person in their audience. Their allusions are of the most outspoken, and, if they should chance to be offended, of the most outrageous character. More often they are complimentary, since this is the type of song most calculated to produce the desired reward. Witty and amusing allusions are liberally introduced and much appreciated by the audience, and the poetry in general represents a highly developed diction and art, if a somewhat limited range of form. The subjects, however, are by no means jejune, for they change from day to day as new events occur, and the *aẓmari* composes his running comment on them, like our own ballad-makers in the past. Mondon-Vidhaillet calls him the 'gazette chantante de l'Éthiopie', and Chaine expresses the regret that all the compositions of the *aẓmaris* have not been preserved, for they consti-

---

[1] Mondon-Vidhaillet, p. 3181.

[2] *Loc. cit.* For a curious parallel, cf. p. 375 above.

[3] A detailed account of Abyssinian musical instruments and of the *aẓmaris'* method of singing is given by Mondon-Vidhaillet, *loc. cit.*

tute, he says, a literature of actuality, being a perfect reflection of contemporary public opinion. "*L'azmari* est une gazette ambulante, ses œuvres seraient une véritable source pour l'histoire de l'Abyssinie."[1] Reference has already been made (p. 516) to the court hermaphrodite of Ras Hailou of Godjam, who during Griaule's visit chanted verses full of political and personal criticism against the Ras at a feast at which the Ras himself was present. In this performance the hermaphrodite was accompanied by an attendant who played on a one-stringed fiddle.

The *azmaris* are met with everywhere, on the march and in the camp, among military retinues and at feasts, and wherever we find them they appear to have no difficulty in obtaining an appreciative audience and an honourable reception. This probably accounts in a large measure for the general uniformity of Abyssinian poetry to which Littmann calls attention.[2] Their persons are held sacrosanct, and it is said that in battle no one will touch them.[3] According to d'Abbadie, both the male and female professional poets at the court of the prince of Godjam were appointed for the year. Some, he tells us, had the right of entrance on ordinary days, while others were only admitted at festivals.[4] Pearce mentions the fact that they usually have an estate assigned to them for their maintenance.[5] It is evident that the professional poet is a person of considerable importance and standing. We read in the Chronicle of King Theodore of an *azmari* being present at the royal feast and composing extempore poetry.[6]

The *azmaris* resemble closely the *skomorokhi* of earlier times in Russia (cf. Vol. II, p. 261 ff. of the present work). It would seem that, like the *skomorokhi*, the entertainment of the *azmaris* is not, or has not always been, limited to poetry and minstrelsy. Pearce classed them together with Tottamasey, the head harlequin of Ras Michael,[7] and Bruce is clearly referring to the *azmaris* in a story which he related of the massacre of the poets by Ras Michael.[8] He describes them as 'a sort of mummers, being a mixture of buffoons and ballad-masters', who, he says, run about the street on all public occasions. And on private

---

[1] Chaine, *R.O.C.* p. 412. Cf. also Plowden, p. 215. [2] *G.ä.L.* p. 260f.
[3] Pearce I, p. 271; Plowden, pp. 54, 406; cf. Nöldeke, *Tigre-Lieder*, p. 8.
[4] D'Abbadie, p. 367. [5] Pearce I, p. 271.
[6] *Theodoros*, p. 28. [7] Pearce, *loc. cit.*
[8] Any violence offered to an *azmari* was looked upon with horror, and was only of very rare occurrence. When Ras Michael massacred the poets and poetesses of Gondar for singing scurrilous rhymes about him Bruce tells us that all the people present, though most of them were hardened warriors, were shocked and disgusted at the deed (Bruce VI, p. 17f.).

occasions, such as marriages, they come into the courtyards and dance and sing songs of their own composition in honour of the day, 'and perform all sorts of antics'.[1] Ferret and Galinier record the presence at Gondar of *azmaris* who combined the arts of music and the improvisation of poetry with dancing and the art of painting.[2] There can be little doubt that the *azmaris*, like the *skomorokhi*, are derived from an ancient corporation of public entertainers who were patronised, and indeed actually supported, by the courts. Their history was already ancient in the sixteenth century, and they were probably the authors of the royal Ge'ez (Amharina) chants which have survived from that period.

Women are among the most proficient poets and minstrels in Abyssinia. In his essay on Amharic poetry Chaine makes brief reference to 'des femmes troubadours et poètes',[3] and Pearce, who lived for many years in Chelikut in the north, refers to both men and women who get a living by making rhymes and attending at funerals. The more proficient, he tells us, receive high pay in corn, cattle, or cloth. It is also clear from what he says that even wealthy women practise the art. He states that he was acquainted with a very handsome middle-aged woman, who, though she had a large estate, had studied poetry from her infancy, and gave her services free at all large funerals.[4]

Professional women poets are known by the name *mungerash* (*manzaratchs*), at any rate in the Galla districts of Abyssinia proper and in Shoa. They are commonly attached to some chief, to whom they are indispensable, especially in time of war, for they extol the deeds of the brave in a kind of rapid chant, and pour abuse on the cowards.[5] It is said that their praise or blame will make or mar a reputation. They are especially proficient in war poetry, and heroic poetry is said to be chiefly composed and recited by them.[6] According to Plowden they share with the *azmaris* the reputation of being dissolute courtesans.[7] Certain individuals among them enjoy an extraordinary reputation at court, and Mondon-Vidhaillet describes a lady named Tadigê who, although no longer young, was greatly admired and much sought after. She figured in official ceremonies, mounted on horseback, and a most imposing figure she must have been, her long blue mantle floating in the wind, as she chanted heroic lays and panegyrics on Menelek and his

---

[1] Bruce VI, p. 17; cf. Ferret and Galinier II, p. 387f.   [2] *Loc. cit.*
[3] Chaine, *R.O.C.* p. 312, footnote.   [4] Pearce I, p. 195.
[5] Griaule, *A.J.* p. 106. The word *mungerash* is not used by Griaule, but there can be no doubt that it is of them that he is speaking. See also d'Abbadie, p. 435.
[6] Plowden, pp. 55, 407.   [7] *Ib.* p. 407.

illustrious guests, and accompanied her recitations with ample gestures. She was also to be found at the feasts of great nobles, where she did not hesitate to stimulate her art with hydromel. She played on several instruments.[1]

The position of honour in which the poets and poetesses of Abyssinia are held is by no means a recent or passing phase. In the annals of Iyasu II (1730–1755) we are told that the *ite agrod*, together with *daraba bete*, sang the praises of Queen Mentewwab.[2] The *ite agrod*, according to Guidi, is a woman who sings and dances on various occasions,[3] and the *daraba bete* are troops, apparently of public entertainers.[4] The reference is probably to the predecessors of the *mungerash* and the *aẓmari* of our own day. Poncet, writing about 1700, tells us that at Enfraz on Lake Tsana he heard a concert composed of a harp and a sort of violin to which verses were sung in honour of the person to whom the minstrels addressed themselves.[5] Again the reference is doubtless to the *aẓmaris*. In the annals of John I we are told that at his proclamation in 1667 the *ite agrod* sang songs in honour of the new king.[6] Earlier in the same century Père Paez mentions the *ite agrod* among the officials of the royal household whose function it is to turn back by their scorn and castigations soldiers who flee from battle.[7] In that most interesting document known as the *History of the Gallas*,[8] written by an Abyssinian monk at the end of the sixteenth century, the *aẓmaris* are specified by name as constituting the ninth class of the population of Abyssinia. The passage suggests that they were numerous, and without doubt even then of great antiquity.

Further interesting references to minstrelsy occur in the seventeenth century. We hear of 'officers of the crown' who followed the Emperor when Poncet was in his train (1699 and 1700), "singing the praises of the Emperor and answering as it were in choirs". The same author makes mention of four or five hundred women whom he saw round about the princess Helicia, sister of the Emperor, "singing verses in her praises and playing upon the tabor after a brisk manner, not disagreeable".[9] We have already seen that a little poem in old Amharic addressed

---

[1] Mondon-Vidhaillet, p. 3183. [2] See Guidi, *M.S.O.S.* x, p. 167.
[3] *C.S.C.O.* p. 347 *s.v.* [4] See Guidi, *Vocabulary*, p. 658[2].
[5] Poncet, p. 94. [6] Guidi, *C.S.C.O.* p. 4; cf. *ib. M.S.O.S. loc. cit.*
[7] Paez II, p. 54.
[8] Schleicher, p. 34. See further p. 539 below, and the reference there cited.
[9] Poncet, p. 54.

to the Negus Isaac, better known from his surname Gabra Maskal, who reigned from 1414–1429, makes mention of the playing of the harp, apparently as an instrument summoning the warriors to battle.

In modern times minstrelsy, combined with the composition and chanting of poetry, is an accomplishment commonly found among Abyssinians of the upper class. Educated amateurs are known as *nataq*.[1] In the Chronicle of Theodore we read that, upon the death of his wife, while preparations were being made for the funeral, the king composed an elegy which is quoted in the text.[2] In the same work an elegy is also quoted which was composed by Ras Ali on the death of his daughter. Such recitations are commonly sung by the aristocracy and the wealthy to the accompaniment of the *baganna*, a large harp or lyre,[3] which is sometimes four feet in height.[4] The same instrument is also sometimes used to accompany the recitation of occasional poetry. King Theodore II was an accomplished performer on the *baganna*.[5] The great hero of the Abyssinian soldiery at the close of the eighteenth century, Dejaj Farris, is said to have been a much admired player on the 'harp'.[6] Women of the aristocracy also compose poetry. Chaine quotes a poem of seven lines attributed to the daughter of Ras Oubié, and another of six lines attributed to the wife of King Theodore at the time of his suicide, after his defeat at Magdala.[7] These laments composed by people of the upper classes are more cultivated in language and diction than the popular laments, and are called *leqso*, a name which suggests derivation from the *leqso*, a kind of fiddle, though elegiac poetry is said to be generally recited to the accompaniment of the *kerar*, a small lyre with six or ten strings.[8]

Funeral laments are composed by both men and women of all classes, but chiefly women. Poncet noted at the close of the seventeenth century that when anyone died, verses were recited in his praise.[9] Reference has already been made to the professional poets, both men and women, who make a living by composing rhymes and attending at funerals; and the laments attributed to King Theodore and Ras Ali cited above, as well as innumerable instances which might be added,

---

[1] Chaine, *R.O.C.* p. 419. [2] *Theodoros*, p. 26f.
[3] Mondon-Vidhaillet, p. 3182. [4] Pearce I, p. 322.
[5] Theodore's *baganna* is preserved in the Victoria and Albert Museum, South Kensington. [6] Plowden, p. 82. [7] Chaine, *R.O.C.* p. 407.
[8] Plowden, p. 54. Heroic panegyric poetry is also commonly chanted to the *kerar*. For further information on the subject of Abyssinian secular music, see the works cited by Varley, p. 28. [9] Poncet, p. 108f.

bear witness to the popularity of this class of composition among amateurs. Mondon-Vidhaillet mentions the fact that he has himself witnessed the recitation of compositions of this kind among members of the family of the deceased,[1] and Lefebvre describes the funeral of a young girl which was attended by a troop of maidens, her companions, who took part in the funeral procession to the cemetery, and interrupted the funeral prayers and the chanting of the *De Profundis* with improvisations and the dance of death. They formed themselves into a circle, and one of their number, advancing into the middle, expressed by gestures all the signs of despair, after which she improvised a hymn, and her companions responded by dancing like herself, and weeping in a most touching manner.[2]

It may be said in conclusion that the composition of oral poetry among men and women of the middle and lower classes—if we may use the terms of Abyssinia—is universal. The soldiers recite extempore verses on the march, one member composing a couplet, and the rest of the party joining in the refrain.[3] The women compose at their household tasks, and indeed one gets the impression from accounts of travellers that this is almost their only form of intellectual exercise.[4] Instances are too numerous to cite. Such poetry is commonly sung, as one would expect, without musical accompaniment; but there can be no doubt that the men at least always procure a *kerar* or *leqso* if possible. Marcel Cohen mentions the fact that his two servants insisted on taking a *kerar* and a *leqso* to beguile the tedium of the long caravan journey from Adis Ababa to Asmara.[5]

In comparison with the oral literature of the Galla which we are about to study, the oral literature of Abyssinia offers little variety. This is largely due to the presence in Abyssinia from early times of a large body of people who are able to read, and who are therefore preoccupied with a common and an alien literary tradition. This foreign literary tradition has precluded the development of many oral forms with which we are familiar elsewhere, such as theological and historical literature, and the literature of native learning. The oral literature of Abyssinia is almost wholly ephemeral in character, and we have seen that both the

---

[1] See e.g. Mondon-Vidhaillet, p. 3181 f.

[2] Lefebvre I, p. 106 f.   [3] See e.g. Salt, p. 235.

[4] Chaine, *R.O.C.* (p. 309) and Mondon-Vidhaillet (p. 3180) lay special stress on the part played by women in the composition and recitation of popular poetry; cf. also Pearce II, pp. 224, 236; Plowden, p. 215 ff.; D'Abbadie, p. 345, etc.

[5] Cohen, p. 13.

literary forms which are most widely employed and most fully developed today, and the types of professional minstrels who recite them, have remained unchanged for many centuries. The country as a whole has been untouched by modern developments of thought in the world outside. We have seen, however, that there are signs of a changing outlook in the capital. The enlightenment, so long delayed, threatens soon to dispossess the illiterate minstrel and force him to lay aside his harp and fiddle. This changing and 'progressive' outlook in the capital can best be gauged from a poem recorded in Adis Ababa from an educated Amhara in 1913:

> Let counsellors abound, that our mind may not be undecided,
> So that the enemy may not win on the day of our encounter.
> Let us examine history, let us read the newspaper,
> Let us learn languages, let us regard maps;
> 'Tis this which opens the peoples' eyes.—
> Darkness has gone; dawn has come.[1]

[1] Eadie, p. 199.

LIST OF ABBREVIATIONS[1]

ABYSSINIA AND THE GALLA

Author and Title of Book	Abbreviation
D'ABBADIE, A. *Douze Ans dans la Haute-Éthiopie.* [With a map.] Tom. I. Paris, 1868.	D'Abbadie.
ANNARATONE, C. *In Abyssinia.* Rome, 1914.	Annaratone.
ANNESLEY, GEORGE, 2nd Earl of Mountnorris. *Voyages and Travels to India, Ceylon, the Red Sea, Abyssinia, and Egypt, in the years 1802–6.* By George, Viscount Valentia [and H. Salt]. 3 vols. London, 1809.	Annesley.
ARMBRUSTER, C. H. *Initia Amharica: An Introduction to Spoken Amharic.* Cambridge, 1908.	Armbruster.
BENT, J. T. *The Sacred City of the Ethiopians, being a record of travel and research in Abyssinia in 1893.... With a chapter by Prof. H. D. Müller on the inscriptions from Yeha and Aksum, and an appendix on the morphological character of the Abyssinians. By J. G. Garson. London, 1893.*	Bent.
BORELLI, J. *Éthiopie Méridionale.* Paris, 1890.	Borelli.
BRUCE, J. *Travels to discover the Source of the Nile, in the years 1768–73.* Third edition, corrected and enlarged [edited by A. Murray], etc. 8 vols. Edinburgh, 1813.	Bruce.
BUDGE, Sir E. A. WALLIS. *A History of Ethiopia, Nubia and Abyssinia.* 2 vols. London, 1928.	Budge.
BURTON, R. F. *First Footsteps in East Africa, or An Exploration of Harrar.* London, 1856.	Burton.
CASTANHOSO, M. DE. *The Portuguese Expedition to Abyssinia in 1541–3....* Translated and edited by R. S. Whiteway. Hakluyt Society, Ser. II. Vol. X. London, 1902.	Castanhoso.
CASTRO, L. DE. *Nella Terra dei Negus.* 2 vols. Milan, 1915.	De Castro.
CECCHI, A. *Da Zeila alle Frontiere del Caffa.* 3 vols. Rome, 1886.	Cecchi.
CERULLI, V. 'Canti Popolari Amarici.' In *R.R.A.L.* Ser. va, Vol. XXV (1916).	Cerulli, *Canti.*

[1] See *Note*, Part I, p. 219 above.

Author and Title of Book	Abbreviation
CERULLI, E. 'The Folk-Literature of the Galla of Southern Abyssinia.' *Varia Africana* III. *Harvard African Studies* III. Published by the African Department of the Peabody Museum of Harvard University. Cambridge, Mass. U.S.A. 1922.	Cerulli.
CHAINE, M. *Catalogue des Manuscrits Éthiopiens, de la Collection Antoine d'Abbadie.* Paris, 1912.	Chaine, *Catalogue.*
—— *Histoire du Règne de Johannes IV, Roi d'Éthiopie (1868–89).* In *R.S.* 1913.	Chaine, *R.S.*
—— 'La Poésie chez les Éthiopiens.' In *R.O.C.* XXII (1920–1).	Chaine, *R.O.C.*
COFFIN. See Pearce.	Coffin.
COHEN, M. *Couplets amhariques du Choa.* Paris, 1924.	Cohen.
COMBES, E. and TAMISIER, M. *Voyage en Abyssinie, dans le Pays des Galla, de Choa et d'Ifat, précédé d'une excursion dans l'Arabie-Heureuse.* . . . Par E.C. et M.T. 1835–37. 4 vols. Paris, 1838.	Combes and Tamisier.
[See Powell-Cotton.]	Cotton.
EADIE, J. I. *An Amharic Reader.* Cambridge, 1924.	Eadie.
FERRET, P. V. A. and GALINIER, J. G. *Voyage en Abyssinie, dans les provinces du Tigre, du Samen, et de l'Amhara.* 3 vols. Paris, 1847.	Ferret and Galinier.
GOBAT, S. *Journal of a three years' residence in Abyssinia, in furtherance of the objects of the Church Missionary Society.* . . . *To which is prefixed, A brief history of the Church of Abyssinia.* By Professor Lee, etc. 2nd ed. London, 1847.	Gobat.
GRIAULE, M. 'Mythes, Croyances et Coutumes du Bégamder (Abyssinie).' In *J.A.* CCXII, 1928.	Griaule, *J.A.*
—— *Abyssinian Journey.* London, 1935.	Griaule, *A.J.*
GUIDI, I. *Vocabolario Amarico-Italiano.* Rome, 1901.	Guidi, *Vocabulary.*
—— *Annales Johannis I. Corpus Scriptorum Christianorum Orientalium.* Paris, 1903.	Guidi, *C.S.C.O.*
—— 'Quĕnē o inni Abissini.' In *R.R.A.L.* Ser. Va, Vol. IX.	Guidi, *R.R.A.L.*
—— 'Strofe e Brevi Testi Amarici.' In *M.S.O.S.* X.	Guidi, *M.S.O.S.*
HARRIS, W. C. *The Highlands of Ethiopia.* 3 vols. London, 1844.	Harris.
[See Rochet d'Héricourt.]	D'Héricourt.
HYATT, H. M. *The Church of Abyssinia.* London; New York, 1928.	Hyatt.
ISENBERG, C. W. and KRAPF, J. L. *Missionary Journals of Isenberg and Krapf* . . ., *describing the*	Isenberg and Krapf.

AUTHOR AND TITLE OF BOOK	ABBREVIATION

proceedings in the Kingdom of Shoa and journeys in other parts of Abyssinia in . . . *1839, 40, 41 and 42.* To which is prefixed, a geographical memoir of Abyssinia and South Eastern Africa, by J. McQueen, etc. London, 1843.

JOHNSTON, C. *Travels in Southern Abyssinia.* 2 vols. London, 1844. — Johnston.

KAMMERER, A. *Essai sur l'histoire antique d'Abyssinie. Le royaume d'Aksum et ses voisins d'Arabie et de Meroe.* Avec. . . 4 cartes. Paris, 1926. — Kammerer.

KRAPF, J. L. *Travels, Researches and Missionary Labours, during an eighteen years' residence in Eastern Africa.* . . . With an appendix respecting the snow-capped mountains of Eastern Africa, . . . and a concise account of geographical researches in Eastern Africa up to the discovery of the Uyenyesi by Livingstone in September last, by E. G. Ravenstein. With portraits, maps and illustrations, etc. London, 1860. — Krapf.

—— See also Isenberg.

LAVIGNAC. *Encyclopédie de la Musique* (see Pt. 1, p. 222 above). Partie 1, Vol. v, p. 3181. C. Mondon-Vidaillhet, ' La Musique Éthiopienne '. — Lavignac.

LEFEBVRE, TH. *Voyage en Abyssinie exécuté pendant les années 1839–43* par une commission scientifique composée de MM. T. Lefebvre, A. Petit et Quartin-Dillon Vignaud. . . 6 vols. Paris, 1845–54. — Lefebvre.

LITTMANN, E. ' Semitische Volkspoesie in Abessinien.' In *Verhandl. des XIII. Internat. Orient. Kongr.* Hamburg, 1902. — Littmann, *S.V.*

—— *Geschichte der äthiopischen Litteratur.* Leipzig, 1907. — Littmann, *G.ä.L.*

—— ' Preliminary Report of the Princeton Expedition to Abyssinia.' In *Z.f.A.* xx (1907). — Littmann, *Z.f.A.* xx.

—— ' Sternensagen und Astrologisches aus Nordabessinien.' In *A.f.R.* xi (1908). — Littmann, *Sternensagen.*

—— *Pennsylvanian Expedition to Abyssinia.* 2 vols. Leyden, 1910. — Littmann, *P.E.*

—— ' Ein Nordabessinisches Heldenlied.' In *Z.f.A.* XXVII (1912). — Littmann, *Z.f.A.* XXVII.

—— ' Popular Literature of Modern Abyssinia.' In *J.A.O.S.* XXIII. — Littmann, *P.L.*

—— *Die Altamharischen Kaiserlieder.* Strassburg, 1914. — Littmann, *Kaiserlieder.*

AUTHOR AND TITLE OF BOOK	ABBREVIATION

LITTMANN, E. *Publications of the Princeton Expedition to Abyssinia.* 4 vols. Translated into German and English by the author. Leyden, 1910–15. — Littmann, *Princeton Expedition.*

—— *Galla-Verskunst. Ein Beitrag zur allgemeinen Verskunst nebst metrischen Übersetzungen.* Tübingen, 1925. — Littmann, *Galla-Verskunst.*

LITTMANN, E. and VON LÜPKE, T. 'Reisebericht der Expedition.' In *Topographie und Geschichte Aksums.* Berlin, 1913. — Littmann, *T.G.A.*

MARKHAM, SIR C. *History of the Abyssinian Expedition.* London, 1869. — Markham.

[See de Salviac.] — Martial de Salviac.

MITTWOCH. 'Proben aus amharischen Volksmunde.' In *M.S.O.S.* x (1907). — Mittwoch.

MONDON-VIDHAILLET, C. See Lavignac. — Mondon-Vidhaillet.

NÖLDEKE, TH. 'Tigre-lieder.' In *Z.f.A.* XXXI–XXXII (1917–19). — Nöldeke, *Tigre-lieder.*

PAEZ, P. P. *Historia Aethiopiae ed. C. Beccari, Rerum Aethiopicarum scriptores occidentales inediti a saeculo XVI. ad XIX. cc.,* etc. Vol. II, etc. Rome, 1905, etc. — Paez.

PARKYNS, M. *Life in Abyssinia: being notes collected during three years' residence and travels in that country.* 2 vols. London, 1853. — Parkyns.

PAULITSCHKE, P. *Ethnographie Nordost-Afrikas: Die Materielle Cultur.* Berlin, 1893. — Paulitschke, *M.C.*

—— *Ethnographie Nordost-Afrikas: Die Geistige Cultur.* Berlin, 1896. — Paulitschke, *G.C.*

PEARCE, N. *The Life and Adventures of Nathaniel Pearce, written by himself during a residence in Abyssinia from the years 1810 to 1819, together with Mr Coffin's account of his visit to Gondar.* Edited by J. J. Halls. 2 vols. London, 1831. — Pearce.

PLOWDEN, W. C. *Travels in Abyssinia and the Galla Country, with an account of a mission to Ras Ali in 1848.* From the MSS. of the late W. C. Plowden.... Edited by...T. C. Plowden. London, 1868. — Plowden.

PONCET, C. J. *A Voyage to Æthiopia, made in the years 1698, 1699 and 1700. Describing particularly that famous empire....With the natural history of those parts....Translated from the French original.* London, 1709. — Poncet.

AUTHOR AND TITLE OF BOOK	ABBREVIATION

POWELL-COTTON, P. H. G. *A Sporting Trip through Abyssinia*. London, 1902. — Powell-Cotton.

RATHJENS, C. 'Exploration au Yémen.' In *J.A.* CCXV, 1930. — Rathjens.

REY, C. F. *Unconquered Abyssinia as it is to-day* .... With illustrations and a map. London, 1923. — Rey, *U.A.*

ROCHET D'HÉRICOURT, C. E. X. *Second Voyage sur les deux rives de la Mer Rouge dans le pays des Adel et le royaume de Choa*. Paris, 1846. — D'Héricourt.

ROSSINI, G. CONTI. 'Canti popolari tigrai.' In *Z.f.A.* XVII, XVIII, XIX. — Rossini, *Z.f.A.*

—— 'Storia di Lebna Dengel Re d'Etiopia.' In *R.R.A.L.* III (1894). — Rossini, *S.L.D.*

—— 'Tradizioni Storiche dei Mensa.' In *G.S.A.I.* XIV (1901); translated into German in *Orientalische Studien Th. Nöldeke zum siebzigsten Geburtstag.* Herausgegeben von C. Bezold. Bd. II, p. 941 ff. — Rossini, *G.S.A.I.*

—— 'Notice sur les Manuscrits Éthiopiens de la Collection D'Abbadie.' In *J.A.* Sér. II, Tom. VI (1915). — Rossini, *J.A.*

—— 'Æthiopica.' In *R.d.S.O.* IX (1921–3). — Rossini, *R.d.S.O.*

SALT, H. *A Voyage to Abyssinia, and Travels into the interior of the country, executed . . . in the years 1809 and 1810*. London, 1814. — Salt.

SALVIAC, P. MARTIAL DE. *Les Galla*, 2nd ed., Paris, 1902. — De Salviac.

SCHLEICHER, A. W. *Geschichte der Galla* . . . . Text und Übersetzung. Berlin, 1893. — Schleicher.

SOLEILLET. *Obock, Shoa, Kaffa; Récit d'une Exploration commerciale en Éthiopie*. Paris, 1886. — Soleillet.

SUNDSTRÖM, R. 'En Sång på Tigrē-språket.' In *Skrifter utgifna af K. Humanistiska Vetenskaps-Samfundet i Uppsala*. VIII. Uppsala, 1902–4. — Sundström.

[See Combes.] — Tamisier.

WĀLDA MĀRYĀM. *Chronique de Théodoros II*, etc. Edited and translated by C. Mondon-Vidhaillet. Paris, 1904. — Theodoros.

[See Annesley.] — Valentia.

VARLEY, D. H. *African Native Music*. Royal Empire Society Bibliographies, no. 8, 1936. — Varley.

PERIODICALS

Archiv für Religionswissenschaft. Leipzig, 1898, etc.   *A.f.R.*
Giornale della Società Asiatica Italiana. Firenze, 1887, *G.S.A.I.*
  etc.
Journal Asiatique. Paris, 1822, etc.   *J.A.*
Journal of the American Oriental Society. New York, *J.A.O.S.*
  1843, etc.
Mitteilungen des Seminars für Orientalische Sprachen. *M.S.O.S.*
  Berlin, 1898, etc.
Rivista degli Studi Orientali.   *R.d.S.O.*
Rendiconti della Reale Accademia dei Lincei, Classe *R.R.A.L.*
  di Scienze morali, storiche e filologiche. Rome,
  1885, etc.
Revue de l'Orient Chrétien. Paris, 1896, etc.   *R.O.C.*
Revue Sémitique d'Épigraphie et d'Histoire ancienne.... *R.S.*
  Paris, 1893, etc.
Zeitschrift für Assyriologie. Strassburg, 1884, etc. *Z.f.A.*

2. THE GALLA[1]

IN the present Note, which is devoted to the Galla,[2] as being the purest representatives of the ancient Hamitic race, we propose to give primary attention, wherever information is available, to those groups which are still independent, and to those which have remained outside the Abyssinian borders till their inclusion in the empire of Menelek in the latter part of last century (cf. p. 506 f. above). For the social life of the Galla as a whole, our principal source of information is *Les Galla*, by P. Martial de Salviac. Other sources of information will also be referred to. For the native oral literature of the Galla, and for details as to their personal and tribal history, we are almost entirely dependent on the texts, translations, and commentaries furnished by E. Cerulli in *The Folk Literature of the Galla of Southern Abyssinia*, published by the African Department of the Peabody Museum of Harvard University in 1922.[3]

Our excuse for much which is defective in the following pages is contained in the opening sentence of de Salviac's work, *Les Galla*, where the author observes that the Galla are one of the least known peoples in the world, though in their numbers and the extent of the country which they occupy, they are one of the most considerable peoples of Africa. They are a comparatively homogeneous Hamitic people, extending from Somaliland in the Horn of Africa in the east to the R. Sobat in the watershed of the White Nile, due north of Lake Rudolf in the west, and from the south of Kenya till they merge gradually into Abyssinia in the north. The name *Galla* is a general term applied by the Abyssinians to these barbaric tribes—both the tribes

[1] For titles of books and periodicals cited in the present section, see the List of Abbreviations at the conclusion of the section on Abyssinia, p. 531 above.

[2] The following account was written shortly before the Italian conquest of Abyssinia, and must be understood as applying to the condition of the country at that date.

[3] In general, where Cerulli is our source of information, we have adopted his system of transliteration. In our ignorance of the Galla language we have not ventured to normalise the forms, or to bring his system into any consistent relationship with that of other scholars. Forms which have already appeared in the Abyssinian section are, however, generally retained here to avoid confusion, even where the spelling differs from that of Cerulli. Cerulli's system, being somewhat unusual and difficult, has not been introduced into the Abyssinian Note.

which are included within Abyssinian territory, the occupants of the southern and south-eastern districts of their empire, and also those beyond its borders, east, west, and south. The Galla themselves say that the word means 'immigrant',[1] but according to de Salviac it is an 'epic' term having relation to the warlike nature of the people.[2] The Galla do not use the name. They call themselves *Orma* or *Oroma* (*Oromo*), i.e. 'Strong Men', and they all claim to be descended from a common ancestor of that name.[3]

Gallaland, as their territory is called, is a varied country, with mountains and forest in the west and desert in the east. A great part of the country, however, consists of lofty, rolling parklands, grasslands studded with great forest trees, eminently suited for cattle nomads, such as the original Hamites no doubt were, and the majority of the Galla are today. Their institutions are derived from a pastoral tradition.

The Galla language belongs to the easternmost group of the Hamitic family of languages, and is closely akin to the language of the Somali.[4] The Galla themselves are divided into a number of separate groups which are known by different names.[5] Among the most characteristic representatives of the ancient Hamitic stock are the Arussi Galla, inhabiting the mountains in the northern parts of the Galla area, immediately to the south of Shoa. They are pastoral nomads, jealous of their rich grasslands. The Bōránā tribes[6] occupy an extensive territory southwest and south of the Arussi, extending almost from the edge of Italian Somaliland to Lake Rudolf and Kaffa. They are shepherds and hunters, and carry on a commerce in ostrich feathers, etc.[7] West and south-west of the Arussi many of the smaller groups are as yet comparatively untouched by outside influences. The Wallabou and Bōránā Galla of the extreme west, who inhabit the slopes of the mountains immediately to the north of Kaffa and south-west of Adis Ababa, are believed to be the purest remnants of the ancient Galla, and the region which they

---

[1] Budge, I, p. 13.   [2] De Salviac, p. 7.   [3] Budge, *loc. cit.*
[4] For the area in which the Galla language is spoken, and its affinities, see W. Schmidt, *Sprachfamilien und Sprachenkreise der Erde* (Heidelberg, 1926), p. 60 f.; and Atlas, Karte II.
[5] Many of the group names and place names, and the geographical features referred to in the following pages will be found in the maps of Abyssinia published in 1935, by *The Times*, and the *Daily Telegraph*, as well as in our larger atlases.
[6] Cerulli warns us (p. 169) of the danger of confusing the Bōránā proper, a branch of the Galla tribes in general (including the Máčča or Mecha situated on the Gogäb River) with the Bōránā confederations, which include the Harrari, the Ittu, and the Arussi. See below.   [7] *Ibid.*

occupy today is regarded by Martial de Salviac[1] as the ancient home of the race, whence the others have migrated. Of these western Bōránā Galla one branch is the Mecha on the R. Gŏğäb. Most of the literature of the Galla which will form the basis of the following section consists of texts composed in the dialects of the Mecha Galla, especially those of the north-eastern group: the Liêqā, the Límmu, and the Gúmā Galla situated in the mountains to the north of Kaffa and south-west of Adis Ababa.

Like all the contemporary heroic peoples whom we are studying the Galla are a people on the down-grade. They are a people with a finer past than present. But of their past very little is known. They are believed to be the purest remnant of the ancient Hamitic stock in existence—not a nation, or a people, but a race, of whom the Semites of Asia are only a younger branch. At some early period infiltrations of people of the same stock have also made their way down through eastern Africa, and left their blood and traces of their language as far south as the Cape. It was probably warlike bands of Galla who supplied chiefs and dairymen to many of the Bantu peoples in the neighbourhood of the Victoria Nyanza in the past. It would seem therefore probable that the southward trek of the Hamites which had begun in early times has had a continuous history, for it is not likely that the Bahima could have retained not only their racial, but also their cultural purity comparatively uncontaminated among the agricultural Bantu for any great length of time. In the north also there are indications of Galla movements in comparatively recent times. According to Abyssinian traditions there were Galla settled in ancient Ethiopia from early times.

Very little is known of the history of the Galla. The little work which claims to be a history,[2] and to which reference has already been made (p. 527 above), is little more than a collection of antiquarian speculations relating to the western Galla, together with a list of their recent *luba* ('magistrates', cf. p. 557 below), and some facts of ethnological rather than historical interest. It is, however, of importance as giving a number of traditions current among the Galla relating to their early home and migrations. It places the origin of the Galla in the country where they are found today in their purest form—the country now occupied by the Wallabou and Bōránā Galla in the extreme west—whence they are said to have expanded in the reign of Lebna Dengel (1508–1540).

---

[1] *Les Galla*, p. 2.
[2] For an account of the various editions of this curious little work, and a translation of the text, see Budge, II, p. 603 ff.

There can be no doubt that it is largely from these regions that the great irruption of Galla referred to above issued forth in the sixteenth century in the wake of the various tribes of Mussulmans, such as the Somali and Afars, who for two hundred years had been harassing Abyssinia in the east. We have seen how, in 1527, under the leadership of the famous Aḥmad, nicknamed 'Grañ', the 'left-handed', who was Emir of Harrar, they began a war of extermination against the Christian country of Ethiopia. After a series of victories over the Emperor David III, the Mussulman armies conquered the country as far north as Tigre, ravaging and burning all that lay in their course. The tide of war was turned, as we have seen, by the Negus Claudius, with the help of the Portuguese, and Christian Abyssinia was saved; but only just in time. While Mohammed Grañ was ravaging the country, other Galla hordes, accompanied by their wives and families, their flocks and herds, made inroads into the southern parts of the country, and settled in Shoa, Godjam, Beghemeder, Amhara, making themselves masters of the country occupied today by the Wållō Galla, who, according to Galla tradition, are derived from Arussi stock.[1] The invaders were driven back from the central plateaux, but settled in the southern and western districts, and along the mountains fringing eastern Abyssinia. From this occupation the Galla never withdrew, and thus it came about that Ankober and the surrounding territory became isolated from the rest of Abyssinia. This southern advance was something different from the fierce but transient sweep of the armies of Grañ. It was a systematic occupation of the choicest parts of the country, and henceforth the history of the Galla settled in Abyssinia becomes inextricably bound up with Abyssinian history.[2]

Under Nour, the successor of Mohammed Grañ on the throne of Harrar, the tribe of the Barentu Galla began to make attacks on the emirate, and Nour was obliged to fortify the city. After his death the power of the realm of Adal and the Somali declined, and the Galla spread eastwards, and about 1700 they occupied the upper and more fertile plains which surround Harrar. The ancient population disappeared or were absorbed, and the old trade routes vanished. The town of Harrar alone escaped the general disaster, and the Galla, masters of the surrounding country, held the Harrari prisoners in their own refuge. In time the emir was able to come to terms with the surrounding tribes, and

[1] Cecchi 1, p. 513. See however Cerulli, p. 13.
[2] For a brief résumé of the part played by the Galla in Abyssinian history, see de Salviac, p. 34 ff.

the Galla were induced to permit the passage of caravans in return for heavy imposts. The conquest of Harrar by the Amhara in 1887 restored to the Empire of the Negus one of the finest provinces, which had been cut off for three and a half centuries, and dealt a decisive blow to the realm of Adal, whence the first flood had swept over Abyssinia. Henceforth the Galla became the chief enemy of Abyssinia. But the same campaign put an end to Galla independence also. The conquest of the Bōránā confederacy was begun by Menelek in 1882, and completed in 1896. Since that time the Galla have been included in the Empire of the Negus, and for political purposes form a part of Abyssinia.

The native Galla constitution is patriarchal. It has been called a perfect republic. Every tribe, and every section of a large tribe is self-governing, and is divided into five political units known as *gada*.[1] Each *gada* rules in unvarying rotation for a period of eight years, and is directed by a kind of chief magistrate, known as the *Abbā Boku*, the 'Father of the Sceptre', and by the *Abbā Dulu*, 'Father of War'. These officials are assisted by a council of elders. Each *gada* is composed of the male members of the tribe who are initiated at the same time. This initiation is not undergone individually, but collectively by members of the *gada*. In comparatively recent years royal authority has been introduced among the tribes between Godjam to the south of Lake Tsana and Kaffa in the south-west.[2] Even here, however, the *moti*, or 'king', has not displaced the *Abbā Boku* in his right to preside over the council of elders.

During the years 1855 to 1870 the Mecha Galla beyond the R. Gibîe were converted to Islam[3], and many of the tribes immediately to the south of Shoa still remain Mussulmans. On the other hand Menelek imposed Christianity on a great part of the tribes of the Bōránā confederation. Nevertheless many of the Galla tribes are still heathen, and even of those who have adopted Christianity or Islam, it is clear that many still remain heathen at heart. They are ignorant of all save the outstanding observances of their religion, and have only a very rudi-

---

[1] Much has been written on the *gada* system, but even yet it still remains obscure and difficult. De Salviac calls the system simple, but he does not expound it with any fulness. The most satisfactory treatment seems to be that of Cerulli (p. 167), who frankly admits the difficulty and complexity of the subject, and points out some of the contradictions among the chief authorities. He also gives a list of these authorities (p. 172), to whom the reader is referred for further information.

[2] De Salviac, p. 192f.

[3] Cerulli, p. 22f.; cf. also 'L' Islam nei Regni Galla Independenti' by the same author in *L'Africa Italiana* (Naples, 1916), Vol. xxxv, p. 113ff.

mentary notion of their creeds. Many heathen festivals and observances are still retained among them, as we shall see.

The hereditary avocation of the Galla, and the chief source of their wealth is cattle-keeping. They are the chief pastoral people of Africa. They are also great hunters of big game, and the glory of the chase is second only to the glory of battle.[1] As warriors they are magnificent. Every Galla is a warrior by nature, by training, and by tradition.[2] He is bold and fearless and a brilliant horseman. His supreme achievement consists in collecting javelins from the ground at a gallop, his leg hanging over the backbone of his horse, and his hand hidden in its floating hair. In this position he extends himself in the twinkling of an eye, and again raises himself, ready to cast again the shaft which he has just picked up. Such, says de Salviac, were the terrible hordes of northern Galla horsemen, mounted bareback, who broke the Italian regiments at the Battle of Adowa in 1896, and pursued the fugitives implacably.[3]

The Galla are illiterate almost to a man. Practically none can read or write. The vigour with which the slave trade has been carried on, especially from the big markets and centres of population, such as Ennarea, have kept foreign mercantile enterprise at bay in the past, and left the Galla as a whole singularly free from foreign knowledge and foreign culture. In their eyes books contain the secrets of magic, and are regarded with suspicion.

On the other hand the Galla have a flourishing oral tradition, both of prose and poetry, which their ignorance of letters makes especially valuable for the student of native oral literatures. It is greatly to be regretted that so little of this oral literature has been collected and transcribed. The only considerable collection which we know is Cerulli's *Folk Literature of the Galla of Southern Abyssinia*, to which reference has already been made. Several of the songs contained in this Section are also published by the same author among the 'Canti Popolari Amarici' in *Rendiconti della R. Accademia dei Lincei, Classe di Scienze morali, storiche e filosofiche*, Vol. xxv, Pt. vi (Rome, 1916); and a few little Galla songs are published by Marcel Cohen in *Couplets amhariques du Choa* (Paris, 1924), and by A. Werner, 'Two Galla Legends', in *Man*, Vol. xiii (1913). Further examples are quoted by Martial de Salviac in *Les Galla*. Cerulli also refers to a considerable collection in the *Galla Spelling Book*, which was published in 1894 by Onesimos Nesib, a native Galla, and printed at the Swedish mission at Massowa.

[1] De Salviac, p. 270 ff.   [2] *Ib.* p. 268 ff.   [3] *Ib.* p. 276 f.

From this book he obtained some of the pagan religious poems in his collection.

But the literature of the Galla is fast disappearing. Martial de Salviac noted (p. 249) as early as 1901 that the rising generation no longer learnt the 'pilgrims' songs', or remembered the heroic poetry, except such pieces as related to hunting. Cerulli also has observed the rapid decay of oral prose saga in recent years, and the loss of oral tribal genealogies, and there can be no doubt that under the present progressive government at Adis Ababa, where a considerable foreign element is settled, the traditional oral poetry also will rapidly disappear.

Cerulli's collection of texts contains a very varied assortment of poetical[1] and prose forms. Nevertheless it is almost confined to t he répertoire of one man, Loransiyos by name, a native of Shoa, who for a time was resident in Naples. Unfortunately Loransiyos was obliged to return to Africa shortly after reciting his poems, and when his prose recitals had only just begun; but Cerulli was convinced that he had a considerable prose répertoire at his disposal. As Loransiyos was by profession a soldier, and not a minstrel or a sage, the extent and variety of his poetical répertoire as represented by Cerulli's collection is very striking testimony to the preponderant part played by oral literature in the intellectual life of the Galla.

No heroic narrative saga appears in Cerulli's collection. This is indeed hardly to be looked for in view of what has just been said. On the other hand there can be little doubt that such saga exists, and that it was flourishing until the close of last century. Cerulli has recorded an oral chronicle relating to the kings of Gúmā which consists of a series of summaries of sagas, some of which are undoubtedly heroic. Fuller reference to this chronicle will be made when we come to consider antiquarian poetry and saga. We may refer here also to the 'genealogy of the kings of Gúmā, with anecdotes about some of the kings', published by Cecchi, and referred to by Cerulli (p. 158) in this connection. Cerulli refers further to a 'long historical text relating to the cruelty of King Fáysā Lamú', which he was in the act of recording from the recitation of Loransiyos, when the latter was recalled. This text also is probably a heroic saga.[2]

Cerulli emphasises the historical nature of these stories, and their preoccupation with individual Galla chiefs. Since the loss of Galla

---

[1] For a general survey and classification of Galla poetry the reader is referred to Paulitschke, *G.C.* p. 181 ff.   [2] Cerulli, p. 148 f.

independence, following on the conquests by the Amhara on behalf of Menelek, these historical stories are no longer composed. Loransiyos declared that "the struggle of the Amharic chiefs, their rise and fall, and their disagreements, are not subjects dealt with in the stories of the sons of Orma". On the other hand the traditions relate to surprisingly early times. They are said to contain references to a certain Sipenhao, i.e. Sapenhi, governor of Ennarea in the reign of Malak Saggad (1563–1597), and to the Emperor Theodore I (1411–1414).[1]

Very little information is as yet available regarding the structure of Abyssinian poetry. According to Littmann,[2] however, the metre is quite definite, and is syllabic in form, each line having a fixed number of syllables. This scheme is rigidly adhered to, the only exceptions being at the beginning and end of a given poem, certain particularly outstanding lines of the song, and the refrain. From what he says it is clear that the metre consisting of a line of seven syllables is by far the commonest. De Salviac[3] speaks of the prevalence of rhyme in Galla poetry, the same word often reappearing to sustain it. The Galla, he adds, love the *rime kyrielle*, which consists of repeating the same line at the end of each couplet.

Apart from such poems as are purely occasional or emotional in character the majority of Galla poetry recorded by Cerulli is heroic. Reference is frequently made to tribes and kingdoms, especially in poems dealing with warfare, but the poetry can never be regarded as purely national or even tribal in character. References to the leaders and individual heroes are more prominent than references to the tribes, and the poems rarely show any conception of the issues at stake in the warfare, while allusions to single incidents, accidents and achievements abound. Moreover it is clear from what we know of the Galla that the heroic style of the poems is not a mere tradition here, as in Russia, but a direct reflection of the cast of thought of the people to whom they relate. The economic conditions which the literature implies correspond in all essentials to those which we know to have prevailed in the Galla lands last century. We have no indication that, with the exception of a few individuals converted to Islam or Christianity and in direct touch with foreigners, any class in the community had acquired more civilised ideas, or had learned to express itself in any more advanced forms of art than those which we are about to consider.

[1] See Cerulli, p. 149, and the references there cited.
[2] *Galla-Verskunst*, p. 3.
[3] De Salviac, p. 249.

This heroic poetry resembles that of Abyssinia very closely in its general classification, its subject matter, and its style, as well as in that peculiarly allusive quality which to a European makes a running commentary absolutely necessary for the comprehension of the simplest poem. There is nothing elementary or 'primitive' in Galla poetry. On the contrary it makes a heavy demand on the intellect of both the reciter and the audience, and great speed of thought and a well-stocked memory are necessary even to a Galla who would appreciate to the full the witty allusions, *doubles entendres*, and artificial figurative diction. We are, in fact, in the presence of court poetry composed sometimes directly under court patronage, sometimes merely in the courtly tradition. In view of this general similarity to Abyssinian poetry, we shall treat this part of our subject comparatively briefly, reserving as much space as we can spare for religious and mantic poetry, and the poetry of native learning, which are naturally practically unrepresented in Christian Abyssinia.

As in Abyssinia, narrative poetry is wholly absent. Instead we have a kind of narrative shorthand—a convention extremely common in poems of celebration and impersonal poetry. Allusion is made to events, exploits, people, history. These allusions are frequently made in a series. Narratives are thus conjured up before the mind of the audience by mnemonic symbols. A carefully glossed *fârsā* or *gūerārsā* —the tribal and personal boasting poems respectively—would convey as much information as an epic. It would, however, differ from an epic in that the events would be found to be arranged artificially, so as to form a gradual crescendo. We should miss the strictly relative chronology and accidental character of the events which we find in epic style.

Dramatic poetry, and poetry embodying speeches in character, also appear to be lacking, unless we include poems actually composed by minstrels but purporting to be spoken by other individuals, such as a boasting song referred to by Cerulli (p. 74), and said to have been composed by a minstrel for Ras Gobanâ,[1] the famous leader of the Amhara in the wars against the Galla under Menelek II. The first line of this poem is quoted by Cerulli:

Gobanâ rides the belly of his steed—

[1] An interesting account of him is given by Soleillet (p. 139 ff.), who visited him at his residence at Gimbiči in Shoa in 1882. Ras Gobanâ was regarded as the chief warrior in Shoa in his day. He was put in charge of all the Galla countries by Menelek.

a reference to Gobanâ's expert horsemanship. As in Abyssinia, the great majority of Galla heroic poems will be found to consist of personal poems and addresses or challenges, boasts and taunts, and perhaps most numerous of all, panegyrics.

Panegyric and elegiac poetry is especially common, and resembles Abyssinian poetry in its figurative and allusive character, and in its extremely condensed style, to which we have already referred. One of the most ambitious of the panegyrics (no. 24) is that composed by a Galla minstrel on Firrisâ, the Mohammedan heir to the crown of Gúmā, who for about two years waged a holy war against Ras Tasammâ of Amhara. The poem consists almost exclusively of heroic exclamations and reminiscences, and happy allusions to the deeds of Firrisâ, his ancestors, and immediate relations. This poem consists of 131 lines; but frequently the Galla panegyrics are quite brief, sometimes consisting of only four lines.

Galla elegiac poetry does not differ in form from panegyric. Indeed elegies are almost invariably panegyrics on a dead warrior, and consist of allusions to his prowess and heroic deeds, and frequently to those of his relatives and ancestors. We may refer to the *Elegy on the death of Firrisâ*, the hero of the panegyric referred to above, and of the *Request* to which we shall refer below. A striking little elegy is that on Grāzmăč Garasú Bĭrrātu, killed at the Battle of Adowa (no. 64), in which the poet skilfully keeps his hero in the centre of the piece while referring to great names like Menelek and the Empress Tāytu.

> The hero (son) of Bĭrrātu (son) of Golê;
> His wife was Ayântu,
> His horse was Dalaččo,
> His emperor Menelek,
> His empress Tāytu (l. 16 ff.).

In no. 109 we have an elegy on a woman, the mother of Fitāwrâri [1] Simâ and Diêntā.

In contrast to panegyric poetry the Galla very frequently compose poems in which they taunt or abuse the objects of their dislike. Cerulli gives a poem (no. 35) of nineteen lines composed in the third person expressing contempt of Hábta Giyorgis, to whom at that time the Sulú Galla paid tribute. Hábta Giyorgis had attempted to substitute a wer-gild for the blood feud, a measure which was so bitterly condemned and resented among the Galla that Menelek had to remove Hábta

---

[1] *Fitāwrâri* is a title, and signifies a general or commander-in-chief.

Giyorgis from his command, and the vendettas were allowed to continue. In the poem, Hábta Giyorgis is referred to as a slave, a harvester of sprouts, the food of the poorest Abyssinians, while his successor who re-established the blood feud is 'He who is born from the stock of the ancient kings:

"Hit with the point!"
the lord has said.'

No. 49 is a long and ambitious poem (85 lines) reproaching Ras Gobanâ for discouraging the ancient Galla customs in regard to the treatment of prisoners. The minstrel is probably himself a warrior, for he refers to his horse, Disô. Sometimes, as in Abyssinia, these poetical taunts gain a wide currency, and are equivalent to our libel and blackmail. Such was the case with a little poem of four lines (no. 85) in which Wāqô Sibillú, a chief of a Sulú clan, is denounced. The unhappy chief was obliged to make an appeal to the Emperor, who issued a proclamation prohibiting the refrain.

Poems are also composed with the object of making a request. In no. 56 a minstrel of the court of Ras Makonnen prays the Emperor Menelek to reward his master's prowess in the expedition against the Danakil (1878–9) with a higher feudal title. Incidentally he expresses his disapproval of Ras Dārgiê, the son of Sāhla Selassé of Shoa, who is believed to have been using his influence with the Emperor against Makonnen. In no. 27 a pagan minstrel, hearing that Firrisâ, the last prince of Gúmā (already referred to) is condemned to death by the victorious Amhara, pleads with Ras Tasammâ their chief for the King's life. As is not unusual in such poems, the minstrel introduces threats of vengeance from Heaven on the Ras if Firrisâ is executed. Some poems of this class are very brief. No. 10 is a little request in three lines by some prisoners that the ransom of four cows be paid for them:

O Abbā Bárā[1] of times past,
Turn your head and redeem me!
The ransom is four cows.

Among the commonest forms of Galla poetry are the *fârsā*, the tribal boasting poem, and the *gīerársā*, the boasting poem of the individual. These are often long and ambitious compositions. The *fârsā*[2] are often composed in short lines, and have the form of catalogues. The

---

[1] Abbā Bárā was a famous seer and governor of Hánnā, a district of the pagan Galla to the north-west of Gúmā (cf. p. 567 below).

[2] An account of the *fârsā*, followed by four examples, is given by Cerulli, p. 58f.

principal heroes of the tribe are named successively, and their deeds and prowess are extolled individually by the minstrel of the tribe. The *gīerārsā*, or *gheraera*, the boasting poems of the individual, seem to be universal among warriors and hunters. They are sung after individual exploits, whether of battle or hunting, and are composed either by the hero himself, or by a minstrel. Cerulli in his introduction to poem 142 tells us that at the ceremony of the *buttâ*, an important element in the series of initiation ceremonies among the Galla:

"Beside the sacrifice of the ox... the account is given of the victories obtained by the warriors of the tribe in wars and hunts, followed by the assignment of decorations.... The warrior whose victims are to be reckoned up comes forward towards the elder and enumerates his deeds one by one, prefacing every statement with the cry: 'Sararará'."[1]

It is possibly to this ceremony that we owe the high development of boasting poetry among the Galla.

Immediately after the above passage Cerulli cites one of the boasting songs recited by a warrior at a *buttâ*, which consists of sixty-eight lines. The opening boasts relate to the slaying of insignificant and ignoble animals, such as baboons and porcupines, and pass in a crescendo movement to enumerate more difficult feats:

"O thou, etc., I have killed a lion. I have killed a lion and I shall kill more. A lion that looks like me have I killed", and so works up to the climax:

"O thou, etc., I have killed a foot-soldier, a warrior who wore a lion's skin. A foot-soldier who resembled me have I killed.... O thou, etc., I have killed some Amhara. I have made Wåldīe spend the day fasting. I have kept the fold closed. O, thou, etc., the Amhara of Wåldīe have I killed."

And with this proud boast the song ends. De Salviac quotes (p. 275 f.) a fine example of a *gīerārsā* on the slaying of a lion, and another on an elephant hunt.

The foe are unsparingly reviled in these poems, especially when an enemy has been successfully overcome in the presence of a large company. An interesting example is given by Cerulli, no. 3, where the circumstances are related as follows:

The rich court of Tullú Abbā Ǧifâr in Ǧimmā attracted all the most celebrated Galla minstrels. On one occasion Tolâ Mamûd, a Mussulman warrior and famous elephant hunter, wagered against Qiṭṭiêssā Gállō, governor of a province in the Ǧimmā kingdom, that he could

[1] Cerulli, p. 141.

kill an elephant with his sword single-handed in the presence of the whole court of Ǧimmā. The stake was a famous horse Sardô. This feat was performed successfully, though Sardô was killed. The Galla minstrels chanted several songs on this occasion as the assembled court watched the encounter from the hillside. Whether Tolâ himself composed the victory song which is attributed to him we cannot be certain, though it is possible that he did. The poem consists wholly of expressions of contempt against Qiṭṭiêssā who had of course lost his wager.

Songs of defiance or of obloquy, couched in terms of vainglorious boasting, often take the form of challenges, and a regular 'flyting' sometimes takes place between two armies. According to Cerulli (p. 33), in the war which took place in the early 'nineties of last century between the pagan and the Mussulman Galla, both armies before the battles sang songs of defiance and challenge. In no. 21 of Cerulli's collection a warrior of these pagan Galla recites his challenge to the Mussulmans of the tribe of Límmu to meet the pagans in battle. The poem contains personal reminiscences of the league which had been formed among the various pagan tribes against the Mussulmans, and promises much spoil, including 'the drum and the dwarf'.[1]

> When the spring has broken forth,
> When the dirt has become dry,
> The Nónnō[2] will tell wonderful tales,
> The Límmu afterwards will weep....
> And you, what can you do?...
> Give food to your horses.
> Then await us!
> Even if you confederate with the seven Gudrú
> And with the six Ǧimmā...
> We will await you!

Nos. 52–55 of the same collection form quite a little anthology of such insults and girdings which the opposing armies hurled at one another during the expedition of the Amhara under Ras Dārgiê, son of Sāhla Selassé of Shoa, against the Arussi Galla. Even when extensive engagements are actually taking place between considerable bodies of people, it is common for chiefs to challenge one another individually.

---

[1] Dwarfs were a much prized source of entertainment among the wealthy Galla.
[2] The Nónnō, Límmu, Gudrú and Ǧimmā are tribes to the south-west of Shoa— 'the tribes beyond the Gibîe', as the Shoans call them, who had been converted to Mohammedanism.

Such challenges are frequently, if not usually, couched in the form of poetry:

> Our appointment is for Sunday...
> Let us bring our wealth and our women (as stakes of the combat).
> You will lead your Rás Darasô.
> I will lead my Gobanâ Danči...
> We will call Abbā Čāffiê.
> You will pray to your genius, Ǧiǧǧô Baččô.[1]
> We will meet twice in the week.
> Those who fear death cannot escape from it.
> I have paid my tribute to the Emperor.
> Except him (the emperor) I will fight (lit. make trenches) against all.
>
> (Cerulli, p. 57)

The most ambitious and sustained of the heroic poems of a purely personal character is Túfâ Rôbā's farewell to Gúmā (no. 15), where he had been appointed governor of a district near the frontier. The poem is composed in the first person, and may well be the work of Túfâ Rôbā himself. It is a kind of manifesto, called forth no doubt by the fact that his departure was necessitated by slanderous accusations. In the poem he rebuts these accusations, states his reasons for having settled in Gúmā, recalls the deeds of his ancestors, accuses his detractors in his turn, calls to mind the warning which he had received from a diviner against living in Gúmā, and finally declares his resolution of returning to his native land:

> Come! We also have a country!
> Returning to one's own country is good.
> Then we will return there this year,
> If God has spoken (thus) in our behalf.

A large number of love songs are given in Cerulli's collection. The most striking little group of such poems are three which, according to Cerulli, were inspired by a love adventure which befell the Liêqā. A girl betrothed to a young warrior called Ayāniê fell in love with another warrior called Wâq Kiênnê. The families met together to decide whether the bride-price might be returned to Ayāniê or whether, according to Galla law, the girl must marry her betrothed. A poem is quoted at this point (no. 94) in which both lovers implored their judges for mercy. It concludes with the lines:

> Speak, O kinsmen!
> Do not separate us from each other!
> Decide and end the matter!

[1] Abbā Čāffiê and Ǧiǧǧô Baččô were famous seers. See p. 551 below.

The decision of the meeting was that Ayāniê was lawfully betrothed to the girl, and she must marry him. She protested by singing a little song (no. 95) which concludes:

> To cause sorrow is natural to one's relatives.
> I weep! What can we do?

Wâq Kîennē answered his beloved in a song (no. 96) which derides her betrothed and expresses himself as heart-broken:

> Come! Let us go away from Naqamtê.

The song is too obscure to quote in full, but was clearly understood by the girl, for she fled with Wâq Kîennē, and the decision of the court was useless. If we are to believe, as the wording of the whole passage suggests, that these songs were actually composed and sung as a part of the transaction, we must conclude that not only Galla law, but Galla legal proceedings are carried on in poetical form, at least in part. This is not surprising, for we have already seen that among many peoples who have a flourishing oral literature formal speech is commonly couched in poetical form.

Non-heroic sagas appear to be current, though few texts have been recorded. The allusion to Abbā Ôdā—

> The ancient matter is finished,
> Abbā Ôdā is really dead—

in the opening couplet of a heroic poem (no. 35) shows that traditions of the famous seer, Ğiğğô[1] Kurâ, otherwise known as Abbā Ôdā, 'the lord of the sycamore', who had prophesied the submission of the Galla to the Amhara, are still current and widely known. The text of the tradition on which his fame rested is given by Cerulli (p. 188), and appears to be an interesting though confused antiquarian saga of the actual origin of a tree sanctuary. Traditions also exist of the famous seers Ğiğğô Galatê (Cerulli, p. 189) and Ğiğğô Bāččô (ib. pp. 181, 188), but unfortunately we do not possess any narrative texts relating to them.

One or two prose texts of quite a different kind are also printed by Cerulli (p. 190 f.). These consist of brief humorous anecdotes, which express in narrative dress the critical and reflective elements sometimes at work even in a heroic society. The narrative form is ill-suited to these

---

[1] Ğiğğô is the title of many famous seers. See Cerulli, p. 183, and cf. p. 567 f. below.

little prose passages. They are the outcome of a satirical spirit, a humorous observation, and a sophisticated taste, and, slight though they are, they suggest that short anecdotes of this kind are not rare among the Galla.

Non-heroic poetry consists chiefly of songs connected with religious functions and ritual poetry. Especially interesting is the poetry connected with the great pilgrimage made annually by the men of all authentic Galla tribes to the dwelling of the Abbā Muda, the 'father of Unction', the religious head of the heathen Galla. The Abbā Muda is looked upon as the chief repository of the law and the traditions, and the chief representative of the people in the eyes of Waqa, the supreme God. The Galla of Harrar make their pilgrimage to Mormoro, but all the rest of the Galla tribes repair to the foot of Mount Wallal in the territory of the Wallabou Galla, this being the traditional home of the race, and the starting-point of their original migrations. When the men arrive at their destination, the Abbā Muda questions them on the law of Waqa and on Galla custom, and exhorts them to the simple pastoral life. Sacrifices are offered, and, as the central feature of the ceremony, the Abbā Muda anoints the pilgrims with butter.[1]

According to de Salviac the songs of pilgrimage contain some of the finest specimens of Galla poetry. The example which he has recorded falls into three parts. The first part, which is the longest, consists of eleven stanzas, each concluding with an invocation to the Abbā Muda: "O, my perfume, O, sweet-scented priest." The song opens with the departure of the caravan amid the songs of birds; the huts and wives are left behind, the low-caste and the foreigners are excluded, yet the pureblooded Galla who set out are as numerous as an army, nay a legion. They depart waving scented branches amid the sighs of their mothers and the good-will of their people. The distance is terrifying, but 'le pays du Wallal nous appelle'. Does not the whole race aspire to unction? Were not their ancestors anointed? The four concluding stanzas of this part contain a picturesque account of the mode of travel and the conditions of life among the pilgrims, and of the peoples through whom they must pass, which is full of ethnographic interest. The rest of the poem is quite brief. The second part relates to the arrival of the pilgrims, and voices their address to the Abbā Muda. The third part relates to their return, and touches on the length of the journey, the imminence of the rainy season, and the hardships which they have endured, and concludes with a stanza of jubilation.

[1] De Salviac, p. 152 ff.

Among the poems of religious ritual we may include also songs sung at religious festivals, such as the song sung by the heathen Galla at the festival of Atêtê (Cerulli, no. 133). This song is composed in the form of an invocation to Friday, the day sacred to the heathen goddess Atêtê, and to Mary, whose name has been substituted throughout the poem for that of the goddess. A number of further ritual poems are couched in the form of advice to women—especially, but not exclusively, to those who are childless, e.g. no. 132. These appear to be recited in private where a group of women are assembled in connection with the feast of Atētê, the goddess of fertility.[1] Sometimes, as we have seen, this advice is couched in the form of general reflections, as, e.g. no. 130, in which the folly of girls who are unwilling to marry is pointed out in gnomic form.

No saga or narrative poetry relating to heathen deities appears to have been recorded, but we have a number of hymns and prayers from among the heathen Galla. De Salviac quotes (p. 151) an extract from one of the communal hymns to Waqa sung in thanksgiving for rain by the assembled Galla. He also quotes a prayer of the *Abbā Boku* on entering office (p. 185). Cerulli tells us (p. 136) that the true Galla prayer, which, according to their belief, places man in contact with divinity, is the *wâdâğā*, which consists of propitiatory songs, preceding and following the sacrifice of a sheep. The *wâdâğā* is directed by the father of the family or an invited elder. The most considerable example of these *wâdâğā* recorded by Cerulli consists of a poetical dialogue between the elder and his family, or group of worshippers, forming a kind of liturgy in which the elder imparts scientific and moral instruction, the congregation assenting and praying for help.

(Head of the *wâdâğā*): O wonder! O wonder!
(Chorus): What are the wonders?
(Head of the *wâdâğā*): The wonders are six:
The hornbill complains without being sick;
The plant *hiddi* flourishes without nourishment;
The water runs without being urged;
The earth is fixed without pegs;
The heavens hold themselves up without supports;
In the firmament He (God) has sown the chick-peas of Heaven (the stars),
These things fill me with wonder.

[1] The name Maryam, the Virgin Mary, is frequently substituted for that of Atētê.

After this follows the liturgy:

> (Head of the *wàdâ̆gā*): Let us all pray to God.—
> O God, who hast caused me to pass the day,
> Cause me to pass the night well.
> (Chorus): Cause us to pass the night well,[1] etc.

It will be observed that the statements of the Head of the *wàdâ̆gā* are in the nature of a series of gnomic utterances on the wonders of nature, and thus form what we may call a brief lecture on natural science, preparatory to the prayers which follow. These gnomes, like the Anglo-Saxon gnomic verses, resemble the answers to riddles, combined to form a sequence. Like the Russian and Norse riddles, their chief preoccupation is with physical science. The subjects touched on are the animal and vegetable world, water, land, the sky, and the stars. It is interesting to find such literature composed for ritual purposes. The Galla, it would appear, combine instruction with worship, and require that the supplicants shall be informed before they pray.

We know of no Galla antiquarian poetry, but antiquarian prose is highly developed. Even local traditions are common. In the prose texts quoted by Cerulli (p. 184 ff.) the kings of Shoa are referred to as kings of Bokkahâ. Bokkahâ is a mountain in the territory of the Gombičču Galla to the south-east of Adis Ababa on which stand the ruins of the ancient castle of the kings of Shoa, and would seem to be identical with a mountain mentioned by Cecchi in the Gombičču territory on which are found the ruins of ancient dwellings of emperors. According to Cecchi (see Cerulli, p. 186) "these ruins are connected by local traditions with the legend of King Theodore".

It has already been observed that the Galla are rich in genealogical traditions. Although Cerulli was prevented by the return of his informant, Loransiyos, to his own country, from recording many examples of such traditions, nevertheless references to them abound throughout the notes and introductory matter affixed to the poems in the collection published by him. Thus he tells us (p. 140) that "As among the Lièqa tribes, those of Billô have a position inferior to the others...on account of less noble genealogical traditions, so within each tribe there is a distinction made between the *bōrantičcâ* who boasts of his origin from Babbô, the ancestor of the Lièqa, and the *gabartičcâ* who cannot prove such an origin by means of genealogies."

[1] Cerulli, p. 137.

Again (p. 141) he tells us that the military colonies recruited by the Emperor of Ethiopia among the Galla tribes and frontier populations, who afterwards acquired all the rights of their former chiefs, made legendary genealogies for themselves.[1] Further (p. 38) we are told that the Límmu Sobâ and the far distant Límmu tribes are brothers according to the Galla genealogists. It is not quite clear whether the traditions of the Ǧimmā Abbā Ǧifâr which connect them with the five other Ǧimmā tribes (see Cerulli, p. 38 f.) are genealogical, antiquarian, or historical, but the traditions of the Lièqa—that they are related to a tribe living in Wårrā Himânō in Wållō, and that they were expelled by Mohammed Grañ (cf. p. 505 above) to their present position—are to be remembered in this connection, as well as the claim made by certain royal Galla and Sidama families that they are descended from the Portuguese (Cerulli, p. 157).

The most important piece of Galla antiquarian oral prose which we know is the *Chronicle of Gúmā* (p. 148 ff.) to which we have referred above. We are, however, assured by Cerulli that many others exist. Such chronicles, he says (p. 149), are known only to the elders, and he adds that one of the principal reasons for their existence is to exalt the noble origin and deeds of the reigning dynasty. Here, then, we have heroic material selected and arranged by the 'elders' of the tribe. The result is a series of brief narratives of saga type, arranged in order according to relative chronology, beginning with the primitive heroic story of Adam, and passing on, as we are told—for the Chronicle is incomplete[2]—to the saga of Ončo Ǧawê, which is clearly based on an advanced type of heroic saga.

The opening story in the chronicle gives an account of Adam, who is here represented as the first king of the dynasty. In spite of Mussulman elements—easily detachable from the main fabric of the story—we have here a personal saga analogous to the story of Heracles in Greek, and that of Kintu in Uganda (cf. p. 587 f. below), a story of the kind which may be called the 'mythical ancestor type'. The saga relates that Adam was a wild man of superhuman strength who lived in a cave in the woods, slaughtering wild animals for his food, and partially domesticating them. The king of Gúmā, hearing of Adam's strength, sent a body of men to try and capture him. They failed, but the king's

---

[1] Cf. Carlo Conti Rossini, *Principi di diritto consuetudinario dell' Eritrea*, p. 89 f. Roma, 1916.

[2] The latter portion of the Chronicle is not given by Cerulli, the recall of his informant preventing him from recording it.

daughter offered to try to deliver him into their hands. She went to live with Adam in his cave, after which Adam's strength deserted him little by little, till at last he was unable to roll the big stone which protected the door of his cave, and the king's men were able to capture him and deliver him bound before the king as a slave. Adam, however, challenged the king to a single combat, and having defeated and slain him he reigned in his stead.

We know of no Galla poetry of pure gnomic form. It is, however, not rare to find poems which are almost wholly gnomic in content, though the framework is that of some other type of poetry. Among the most striking examples is the discourse of the elder at the sacrifice of the *wådå ̆gā* to which reference has been made above. Further examples occur in two versions of a caravan song (nos. 145, 146), which open with general statements about the life of a merchant, and pass swiftly to gnomic utterances on the evils of poverty, which occupy the rest of the poem.

Poverty is a terrible disease;
It penetrates the sides,
It bends the vertebrae,
It dresses one in rags,
It makes people stupid;
It makes every desire remain in the breast;
Those who are long, it shortens;
Those that are short it destroys wholly.
Not even the mother that has borne (the poor man) loves him any longer!
Not even the father who has begotten him any longer esteems him!

(No. 146)

No. 132, on the other hand, opens with general reflections—'The word of God is providence'—and passes rapidly into a picture poem of the childless woman (cf. p. 553 above), though the song appears to have been composed actually for ritual purposes. So also no. 141 appears to be a rain charm in form, but is virtually a little philosophical poem on the effect of rain. Many other poems contain incidental gnomic utterances, e.g. no. 114, a love poem which concludes as follows:

Behind us there is death;
Before us there is old age.
I will come to a decision!
Therefore, I will win (her).

Sometimes, as in 70, the device is adopted which is common enough elsewhere, of disguising by the use of the second person utterances which are virtually gnomic:

> By vigorous ploughing, certainly (they can obtain a harvest);
> (Otherwise) how could they eat the corn?
> By vigorous fighting, certainly (you can gain renown);
> (Otherwise) how could you distinguish yourself from other men?

Proverbs are frequently gnomes detached from any context, and are often found in poetical form.[1] No. 20 of Cerulli's collection (p. 191 ff.):

> He who has despised the poor man will not grow rich—

may be compared with the gnomic utterance in poem no. 133, ll. 97, 98:

> The man who stoops, O Mary,
> Gathers what he has sown, O Mary.

Among the Galla the laws are for the most part enshrined and handed down in 'metrical' form.[2] Travellers speak of the difficulty of finding anyone who can expound them,[3] and from the manner in which they are transmitted we may suppose that they are in part esoteric. Fortunately examples given by de Salviac and Cerulli enable us to form some idea of their nature. We may refer to the resolution passed by the assembly of the Gullalliê tribe and recorded by Cerulli (p. 70), in which it is resolved to resist the Amhara:

> Do not take away the harness from the horse.
> Do not take away the addû[4] from your head.
> Do not take away the miēdičča[5] from your hand.
> I have struck the law,
> I have cut the law,
> The law of the fathers lubbâ.
> This is the sceptre,
> This is the parliament,
> The parliament of the Galla fathers.

Cerulli's analysis of this verse is interesting. The first part (ll. 1–3) constitutes the introduction, commanding everyone to be ready for

---

[1] Paulitschke, *G.C.* pp. 164, 217.
[2] *Ib.* p. 52; Cerulli, p. 70; Littmann, *Galla-Verskunst*, p. 52.
[3] See de Salviac, p. 212.
[4] The *addû* is the skin of a she-goat or a bull's head with which the Galla cover their heads (ED.).
[5] An armlet of she-goat's skin (ED.).

war; the second part (ll. 4–9) is the formula of all Galla laws passed by the assembly. The phrase 'I have struck the law' refers to the custom of the president of the assembly, after the vote, striking on the ground with his sceptre as a sign of the approval of the law. The phrase 'I have cut the law' means, according to Cerulli, that the law has been agreed upon, 'to cut' being the idiom often used for 'to decide'. The *lubbâ* or *lûba* refers to the members of the *gada* whose *Abbā Bokkû*, 'Father of the Sceptre' (cf. l. 7, and see p. 541 above) is in power.

De Salviac observes that a compilation of Galla laws would form at least a large volume. This is because, in regard at least to the laws of more general import, the text is expanded with a considerable amount of circumstantial detail and illustrative matter. For example the law of homicide is set forth initially with a triad:

> Three secret homicides;
> Three overt homicides;—
> First of all the nocturnal homicides:[1]

This type of homicide is then defined more fully, and it is interesting to find that, as in Anglo-Saxon law,[2] the necessity of a shout to announce the approach of anyone coming with honourable intentions is insisted upon:

> He who calls out is a friend;
> He who omits to call out is to be regarded as an enemy.

In conclusion the law sets forth a practical instance as an example of justifiable homicide, insisting on the necessity of witnesses and of circumstantial proof of the guilty intentions of the slain person.[3]

Here, as elsewhere in early laws, there is a general tendency to express the laws in negative terms. That is to say, instead of adjuring the public to do certain things, the law adjures them not to do the opposite: e.g. 'Do not take away the harness from the horses', i.e. no doubt 'Harness your horses'. The same tendency is referred to by Cerulli as a characteristic of Galla solemn oaths, which take the form of renunciation formulae. That is to say, instead of swearing to do a thing one swears not to do the opposite. Only one such formula is quoted by Cerulli in full (p. 144). The use of such formulae is an elaborate piece of ritual, and it must be confessed that with only one brief and very

---

[1] An interesting parallel is offered by the Welsh legal triads; cf. Wade-Evans, *Welsh Medieval Law* (Oxford, 1909), p. 264 ff.

[2] See the Laws of Ine, cap. 20 (Attenborough, *Laws of the Earliest English Kings*, Cambridge, 1922, p. 43).   [3] De Salviac, p. 208 f.

obscure text we cannot obtain a very clear idea of their character. Probably the formula is an old one, since Cerulli's informant, Loransiyos himself, could not suggest any meaning for three lines out of six.

Gnomic literature occurs also in prose form, and here again we find the love of triads. A little text recorded by Cerulli (p. 190 ff.) on *The Three Misfortunes of the Universe* resembles the *Triads of Ireland* (cf. Vol. I, p. 397 of the present work) in its opening formula:

"In the whole world there are three misfortunes. Of these three misfortunes, one is wealth when it is great and increases. The second is thy wife. The third is God, who has created us."

The reciter then passes on to expand each of his statements in a cynical vein: e.g.

"Thy wife...falls in love with a valiant warrior, and then, if this warrior loves her, he kills thee, marries her, and flees away to another country."

The text is evidently the utterance of a court 'jester', quoted verbatim (cf. p. 566 below). The sophisticated tone is strongly at variance with the heroic tone of the majority of Loransiyos' texts.

On p. 198 f. Cerulli gives a brief collection of seven riddles. No information is given about them, but elsewhere incidents are related in which the asking and answering of so-called riddles forms a part of the procedure. Thus Cerulli records a 'riddle' (no. 9) which the Galla sang to the Amhara:

Come on, divine! Is the bone distressed in the pot?

which Cerulli explains thus: As a pot protects a bone against the dogs who will not risk rushing into the pot, and cannot get the bone except by breaking the pot, so Hasan, a Galla chief, was protected by the Gallas against the Amhara, who would not risk their lives by coming among them to seek for Hasan.

Again, on one occasion Abbā Ǧubîr, King of Gúmā, and a famous seer, is said to have assembled all the princes and officers of his kingdom, and to have recited to them this riddle with reference to the various Mussulman Galla tribes who were acting as his allies in the war against the pagan tribes towards the close of last century.

Abbā Ǧubîr: A riddle! A riddle!
Abbā Diggá: Come on!

Abbā Ğūbîr: A calladium moves the leaves (literally, the ears) in the plain,
There is a great family of cowards.
The very hot pepper,
A handful (of it) kills the people.
(There is) a lion at my side,
There is a buffalo at my right hand,
There is a leopard at my feet.
Divine this. (Literally, know this.)

Abbā Diggâ, the brother of Abbā Ğūbîr, replies, interpreting each of the cryptic statements in order:

My Lord, I will tell (it to you),
The calladium which in the plain
Moves its leaves (literally, the ears), as you have said,
My Lord, is Límmu.
The great family of cowards
Which you have mentioned, O my Lord, is Ğimmā (Abbā Ğifâr).
The very hot pepper,
A handful (of which) kills the people,
As you have said, O my Lord, is Gómmā, etc.[1]

This scene recalls the motif with which we are familiar in folk-tales, in which a king is represented as asking riddles of his courtiers, frequently with reference to affairs of state, or the royal household. We may compare also the dream of Nebuchadnezzar and its interpretation by Daniel.

Cerulli also gives a list of riddles (p. 198 f.) which differ from those just mentioned in that they are of general rather than of specific application, and also in that the answer in each case is a simple noun. These riddles are descriptive in character; that is to say, they are intended to convey information, whereas the riddles just considered are calculated rather to veil and obscure information which the hearers already possess. This second class of riddles may be compared with the Russian riddles and with the riddles of Gestumblindi,[2] and like these they are extremely brief. Like these also they are principally concerned with physical science. The Galla answers are (in order): the fowl, the earth, a man in bed, fire (*bis*), the sun, the handle of a lance. The last one does not appear to me to be satisfactory. Of the other six, four are identical with the subjects of gnomic utterances, and the remaining two (man, the sun) are so close to these that they may well have formed part of the same gnomic sequence.

[1] Cerulli, p. 40.   [2] Cf. Vol. II, pp. 212, 410, 560 above.

The Galla possess a considerable amount of poetry and prose relating to unspecified individuals. The prose consists of brief stories, which, like similar literature elsewhere, depend for their effect on wit and finish and shrewd observation, rather than on sustained literary effort. They may be divided, roughly speaking, into two classes. The first consists of what de Salviac calls 'didactic apologues', brief narratives, manifestly fictitious, relating to purely hypothetical people, and composed expressly for the purpose of suggesting or expounding some maxim. De Salviac gives two examples, one of which relates how a father sent his three sons forth to spend the day each in a different spot, bidding them come to him in the evening and tell him what they had seen. Their experiences are briefly narrated, and the story concludes with the father's moral reflections on each incident, quite in the manner of Mr Fairchild. The second class consists of folk-tales closely resembling those of Aesop and La Fontaine, and like them tending to exalt intellect and physical weakness above the heroic virtues of courage and valour. Animal folk-tales abound.[1]

Apart from ritual poetry, most of the Galla poetry of this class is identical in all respects with heroic poetry, and need not detain us. Some account has also been given of the poetry of military ritual, such as the *gīērársā* and the *fârsā*, and the poetry relating to religious functions. Poetry of social ritual is also widespread, and like similar poetry among other peoples, such as the Russians and the Tatars, it no doubt plays a more important part in the intellectual life of the community than would seem obvious from the small amount which has been recorded. Cerulli records a cradle song consisting of seventy-three lines,[2] which is a surprisingly ambitious and sustained address to one who, as we are reminded in a variant,[3] is merely a 'little, little finger of a man'.

Wedding songs form an important part of Galla ritual poetry. As in Russia, the various stages of the marriage ceremony are accompanied by appropriate songs. It does not appear, however, from the collection before us that these are sung by the bride and bridegroom, but only by the relatives and friends of the bride. Thus in nos. 118, 119 they rail at the prospective bridegroom and warn the bride against the evils which will ensue from the union:

> Knock him down with the gun!
> "I have slaughtered!" you have said;
> O ugly son-in-law,
> Where is the skin?

[1] De Salviac, p. 244f. [2] Cerulli, no. 126. [3] *Ib.* no. 125.

"I am a fine young man!" you have said ;
O ugly son-in-law,
Where is the flesh of the cheeks?
. . . This is a sorcerer;
He will eat you (O girl)![1]

(No. 118, l. 5 ff.)

When the husband has taken his place beside the bride, her friends
address her in songs of encouragement (no. 121) and advice (no. 122).
The latter is especially interesting. It is composed in the second person,
and is a remarkable example of a didactic poem, parallel in form to the
'advice' poems of Irish, Norse, Anglo-Saxon, and Russian, a type
which persisted in our own country down to the fifteenth century and
is represented in Furnivall's *Babees Book*, and by such poems as *How
the Goodwife taught her Daughter*. As Cerulli points out, the poem
consists of pieces of advice as to what the bride must do (clean, cook,
attend upon her husband's needs at table) and what she must not do:

O girl, O my friend,
These things I recommend to you:
To take away the dust (from him);
To break the bread (for him);
To help (him) at the table.
These things I recommend to you:
To stay out of the court-yard . . .
Not to laugh with the sister-in-law.
Do not perfume (your body) in the house;
(Otherwise) you will be a coarse woman, etc.

Finally, in nos. 123 and 124 the relatives who have accompanied her
part of the way to her new home take leave of her and express their
grief at parting.

Prophecy is a very important class of literature among the Galla.
Unlike the Greeks, the Galla compose their prophecies in prose form,
if we may judge from the specimens published by Cerulli, though
allusions to prophecies, and quotations from them abound in the songs.
We may refer to no. 44 in Cerulli's collection (l. 43 f.), where the
prophecy of Abbúkkō of the Lięqā Billô is quoted and refuted. In their

---

[1] Both the Abyssinians and the Galla are fond of throwing out dark hints that
seers and those who practise magic are fond of drinking human blood; but how far
these hints are intended seriously is uncertain. We may, however, recall the habits
attributed to a similar class of men in Polynesia (e.g. Mangaia and the Marquesas),
pp. 258, 448 f. above.

general form, however, the Galla prophecies offer a close analogy to those of Jeremiah, though the hortatory tone is usually absent. Like the *wanana* of Hawaii also (see p. 340 above) they are intellectual rather than moral pronouncements, and appear to be the outcome of careful thought on political matters. It is to be suspected indeed that the Galla prophets are the soundest and most influential politicians in the country.

Like the Hebrew prophets, the Galla sometimes prophesy the triumph of a strong neighbour over their own countrymen. Thus Abbā Ôdā continually prophesied the triumph of the Amhara over the Galla, and urged submission. Such prophecies, we may believe, were not well received by a brave and warlike people, and the allusion in poem no. 35 testifies to their unpopularity. We refer to a song in which the poet cries 'Abbā Ôdā is really dead', meaning that his prophecies have proved false. Soleillet found a prophecy very widespread among the Galla of Jemma that the crown would pass into the hands of Europeans, in consequence of which belief the French traveller received a cold welcome from the king and his council, who were pursuing an uncompromising anti-foreign policy.[1]

Like the Welsh prophecies, all the Galla prophecies recorded by Cerulli have reference to great political, and what we may call national affairs. One text (p. 184 f.) is devoted to the second coming of the Emperor Theodore I (1411–1414)—a prophecy which is said to be very widespread among both the Amhara and the Galla. The most important series are the so-called prophecies of Ğiğğô Báččô, which relate in regular and chronologically correct sequence the history of the Galla and Kaffa, and their relations with the Amhara, etc., as well as many events of Abyssinian history. The first included by Cerulli begins and ends with an exhortation:

"Let not the word of Ğiğğô Báččô go forth from thy head, let it not go forth from thy heart."

But apart from these formulae the entire prophecy would be identical with prose saga if the tense were not future throughout. By the substitution of the past for the future the prophecies become history.

"The king of Kaffa will sell the Amhara for a piece of salt; at the price of a *barču* he will sell the mules: this I prophesy. But in the end, the Amhara will occupy the country of Kaffa. The kingdom of Kaffa will not pass to the son [of the present king].... The emperor will make the slaves and the Galla, the blacksmiths and the Amhara, like brothers,

[1] Soleillet, p. 218.

and will have them marry. Such an emperor will come. When this emperor shall reign, the times will become better.... He will reign twenty-seven years...."[1]

We have no doubt that the prophecies have generally been composed after the event, whether by the distinguished Galla seer Ǧiǧǧô Báččô himself, or by someone else who attached the prophecy to his name. We do not know how widespread this literary type may be, or whether it was confined to Ǧiǧǧô Báččô; but it seems probable that we have here to do with a Galla convention for narrating history, which is virtually saga.[2] It should be added, however, that this is not invariably the case. Cerulli mentions (p. 183) an instance of a prophecy which was fulfilled under his own eyes. In any case the convention would only be likely to have arisen as a result of the general importance and soundness of the pronouncements of the Galla seers on political matters.

Charms and spells are represented in the collection of Loransiyos by invocations to rain. According to Cerulli 'there exist special ceremonies for asking the divinity for rain'. The two examples cited, however, are not prayers to a divinity, but invocations to rain itself, and the Mandiyó referred to in the following example (no. 140) as having withheld the rain is Abbā Mandó, the čāmsitu, or 'rainmaker'. This invocation is recited as part of an elaborate ritual in which rain is invoked.

> O grass *kusurrú* of the Gibiê!
> O storm of Mandiyó!
> Where art thou shut up?
> Rain! Rain!

No. 141 consists of a series of reflections on the qualities and effects of rain, but Cerulli tells us that it is recited on similar occasions, and it also contains invocations:

> O rain...
> O rain, rain down!

The existence of further spells is to be suspected also from the conventional invocations to the sun, mist, Friday, etc. which form the framework of, and are especially prominent in the opening lines of some of the ritual songs, and songs which probably had a ritual origin.

---

[1] Cerulli, p. 182.
[2] We may compare the Anglo-Saxon poem *Beowulf*, ll. 2032–66, and the Welsh prophetic poems contained in the *Red Book of Hergest*, no. 1, *passim*. For the latter, see Vol. 1, p. 456f. of the present work.

The Galla share with the people of the Central Pacific a gift for oratory which is very highly developed. De Salviac observes that it is not uncommon for a Galla speaker to hold the interest of his audience with a polished speech lasting for three hours, and to be listened to with polite attention throughout, even though the views expressed may be quite contrary to those held by his audience. Their orators are aware of the full value of tone, gesture, accent, pause, and other devices unknown to our orators.[1]

Of the circumstances under which the composition and recitation of prose sagas is carried on among the Galla we know almost nothing. Cerulli's informant, Loransiyos, as we have observed, was a soldier, and it may be regarded as certain that here, as in Abyssinia, the sagas which he related were known and recited by soldiers round the camp fires, and by caravans at the evening bivouac. Cerulli tells us that the native oral chronicles are now known only to the elders of the tribes.

While these oral prose chronicles have preserved traditions of at least five generations, none of the poetry of Loransiyos appears to be older than his own generation. From this it would appear that extempore composition is still more natural to the Galla, and more prevalent among them, than memorising. We may point here to the relatively large amount of poetry which is composed on official and even routine and mundane subjects. Thus on the one hand we have seen that the laws are given a 'poetic' form. On the other hand we have evidence for the composition of a large amount of occasional and personal (private) poetry, as in Abyssinia. The unstudied character of much of this poetry, and the spontaneous manner in which it appears to be uttered, makes it clear that the art of extempore composition is widely cultivated.

The highly figurative diction of Galla poetry appears to be no less sustained in these trivial and occasional poems than in the longer and more elaborate ones. It is plain therefore that such diction is largely static in quality, and consists of stock epithets, formulae and phraseology. Such conventionality of diction, phrase, and formulae naturally reduces the intellectual effort of poetical production to the minimum. It is to be remembered, moreover, that such Galla conversation as we have heard reported also abounds in figurative speech.

The professional minstrel appears to constitute an important class of persons at the little Galla courts. Cerulli notes (p. 20) that all the most celebrated Galla minstrels gathered together to produce their songs in the literary and commercial centre at the court of Tullú Abbā Ğifâr at

[1] De Salviac, pp. 190f., 248.

Gíngō in Ğimmā. We have seen also that heroic panegyric and elegiac poetry, and poetry composed for the purpose of making a request, or of inciting the warriors to battle, is commonly the work of court poets. The longer and more sustained heroic poems seem to be largely the work of professional minstrels. The *fârsā* are composed by the tribal minstrels.

Cerulli refers very frequently in his notes to the 'singing' and 'reciting' of poems by minstrels,[1] but unfortunately we know very little as to their manner of chanting their poetry, or how far they are in the habit of accompanying their songs with instruments. Musical instruments are common, however, and appear to resemble, and indeed to be to some extent identical with those of Abyssinia. During his travels in the neighbourhood of Margi Mr L. C. G. Clarke met several minstrels who had come down from Abyssinia far to the north-east. Soleillet also met a youthful minstrel from Godjam in Ğimmā—'un petit violon pendu au col, qui vient jouer, chanter et danser pour me distraire.'[2] It will be remembered that Godjam has long been a centre of native art and minstrelsy in Abyssinia. De Salviac has published a wood-cut of some Galla 'harps', and a small instrument resembling a viol.[3]

A further class of professional artists in the Galla courts are the so-called jesters on whom Cerulli has an interesting note (p. 190): "The Galla", he says, "delight in the humour of professional jesters, who are maintained at the expense of the small courts. The wittiest sayings of these jesters are quickly learned by heart and spread abroad. Thus there has sprung up among the Galla a distinct literary form." Reference has been made above (p. 559) to their type of wit and their *bons mots*. Men of this class appear to be widespread in north Africa. We may refer to the famous jester Tottamasey who was attached to the court of Ras Michael in Tigre in Abyssinia during Pearce's sojourn in the country. And in our own day we may perhaps refer to the court 'hermaphrodite' of Godjam (cf. pp. 516, 525 above). We may compare also in West Africa in our own day Tabanjama, the court jester of the Emir of Katsina, who closely resembles the medieval court jesters, and who, in various humorous guises, follows his royal patron in state processions, attended by two small boys, his pages and apprentices.[4]

Mantic literature is cultivated, as we have seen, by a class of men who are called variously by Cerulli 'sooth-sayers', 'magicians', 'prophets',

[1] E.g. pp. 68, 74.   [2] Soleillet, p. 224.   [3] De Salviac, p. 143.
[4] See Welsford, *The Fool* (London, 1935), p. 192.

'sorcerers', but who seem to correspond more or less closely to the people whom we have referred to in Vols. I and II as 'seers', or 'sages'. They are said to be quite distinct from the *čamsítu*, who appear to be rain-makers.[1] In some cases the seers clearly are—or were in the not remote past—identical with the rulers. According to Cerulli (p. 113), Šonâ, a district in Nónnōland, was governed by the famous seer ('sorcerer') Aḃbā Ofâ. Elsewhere (p. 25) the same writer tells us that "in many Galla and Sidama states there is a general belief in the magical powers of a king". The heroic poems make frequent reference to this belief. The three generations of rulers of the kingdom of Gúmā during the latter half of last century—Ončo Ǧílčā, Ončo Ǧawê, the father of Abbā Ǧubîr, and Abbā Ǧubîr himself—were all famous both as rulers and as seers.[2] This is the more remarkable since all three were Mohammedans, and Abbā Ǧubîr was in addition a great warrior, who waged a holy war on behalf of Islam against the heathen Galla towards the close of the century. On the other hand the kingdoms which remained heathen were also governed by royal seers.[3] We may refer, for example, to the famous seer Abbā Bárā, the ruler of Hánnā, a country of the Ilû, who opposed Abbā Ǧubîr in his holy war.

It is clear that the seers of whatever status are held in very high repute among the Galla, and enjoy a high authority. Cerulli speaks of them (p. 118) as the richest men in the community. Their abodes were objects of pilgrimage, and their pronouncements are frequently handed down from generation to generation in the memories of the Galla. De Salviac tells us (p. 169) that the most formidable adversary with whom the missionaries were confronted was a 'prince of magic' in Ennarea. The king himself bowed before him, and his authority was recognised even by neighbouring republics. Long caravans streamed up to consult him, and were ready to wait several days for their turn for an audience. A great female 'magician' in Gudrú is said to have been constantly surrounded by hundreds of visitors who had come from a distance, their arms loaded with presents.

Very little is known of their habits or general manner of life. They seem to live on high places. Of the three chief ones mentioned by Cerulli, two live on hill-tops and one on a plateau. It is interesting to observe that the celebrated prophet Ǧiǧǧô[4] Galatê, the author of the prophecy on King Theodore to which we have referred above (p. 563),

---

[1] See Cerulli, pp. 22, 140; cf. de Salviac, p. 166f.
[2] See Cerulli, Index of proper names, *s.v.*, and the references there cited.
[3] See Cerulli, p. 24.   [4] For the title *Giǧǧo*, see p. 551, footnote 1 above.

eats only vegetables, though other magicians eat the flesh of the victims sacrificed. Ğiğğô Galatê is credited with the power of quelling buffaloes with his glance, and 'using them as horses', while Ğiğğô Kurâ appears to have claimed close communion or affinity with a sycamore tree.[1] The prophets are spoken of as offering sacrifices, themselves generally partaking of the meat sacrificed. Ğiğğô Kurâ is said to have been a rich man who had no children. He used to sacrifice oxen on a mountain; "He called people to a banquet; he gave them to eat and drink", most probably at the sacrificial feast.

Beyond these few scattered facts, and the texts of the seers' utterances already referred to in connection with mantic literature (p. 562 ff. above), we know very little of this most interesting class of people. It would have been of importance if we could have known by what power or inspiration the prophecies are uttered. It does not appear from the texts that the seers claim to be in touch with a divinity; but on the other hand it is not specifically stated that they claim any special inherent power. We are not even told of association with sanctuaries, though this is doubtless implied from the association of Ğiğğô Kurâ with the sycamore (p. 188). That the seers were regarded and treated as oracles also seems to be clear from the same story, and from what has been said above; but again we know nothing of the precise circumstances under which their oracles are delivered. The seers seem to have affinities with the earlier Hebrew prophets, and the sycamore claims comparison with the oak sanctuary at Dodona; while their wealth and prestige, and their preoccupation with politics recall the oracle at Delphi. There is perhaps no class of people mentioned in this work regarding whom fuller information would be more welcome than the Galla seers.

[1] We refer to the expression: "Come, go and ask questions of the sycamore tree", with reference to this seer. See Cerulli, p. 188.

LIST OF ABBREVIATIONS

(For the abbreviations used throughout the Section on the Galla, see List of Abbreviations at the close of the Section on Abyssinia.)

3. THE NORTHERN BANTU

THE Northern Bantu peoples offer peculiarly favourable conditions for the study of oral literature in Africa, on account of both their geographical position and their history. In the past they were even more isolated from the stream of European civilisation than the Galla or the Abyssinians. The Uganda Protectorate in particular was surrounded by impenetrable barriers, consisting partly of natural features, partly of hostile tribes. The warlike Masai on the east were dreaded by the coast people, while the difficulty of the southern route into the country deterred the ordinary trader from the long journey into the interior. The hostile territory of Unyoro lay between Uganda and the valley of the Nile to the north, and westwards lay the less advanced Bantu tribes and the highlands which separated the Great Lakes from the forests of the Congo Basin. It has been stated that it was not until 1849–50 that Uganda was first visited by a man from the outside world, one Isan Bin Hussein, a Baluchi soldier.[1] But even the name of the country was practically unknown to Europe till in 1861 Speke and Grant made their way to the court of Mutesa, the grandfather of the present king, Daudi Cwa, on their journey to discover the source of the Nile.

The Northern Bantu cover the greater part of east-central Africa in the neighbourhood of the Great Lakes. Within this area the most important peoples for our purpose are the Baganda, that is to say the peoples of Uganda to the north-west of the Victoria Nyanza; the Banyoro or Bakitara immediately to the north and west of them, and east of the Albert Nyanza; the Banyankole to the south-west, between Lake Edward and the Victoria Nyanza; and the Basoga due east of Uganda, along the north-eastern shore of the Victoria Nyanza. It will

[1] Johnston, *U.P.* I, p. 216; Treves, p. 219. Cf. however Crabtree, *Manual of Lu-Ganda*, p. xiv, footnote 1. The *katikiro*, or prime minister, Sir Apolo Kagwa, in his history of the country, mentions (p. 105) the arrival of Swahili and Arabs among the earlier events of Suna's reign, while a native tradition recorded by Roscoe (*Baganda*, p. 225) states that plates, cups, saucers, and glass had been first introduced into Uganda by King Kyabagu, the father of King Semakokiro, and great grandfather of Suna. If this tradition is to be trusted, it is difficult to believe that such articles could have been brought into the country except by foreigners experienced in packing and carrying fragile goods.

be seen that these countries lie almost entirely between 1° N. and 1° S. lat., and 30° E. and 34° E. long. The equator passes through Uganda. All these peoples, and a number of less important neighbouring peoples, have been united under British rule since the close of last century, and are known as the Uganda Protectorate.

Among the population of this region[1] two elements are easily distinguishable. The first, which is believed to be the earlier, is the negro or negroid agricultural element, which is found everywhere, and constitutes the warp and woof of the population as a whole. The second consists of the fairer-skinned, tall, and well-built cattle nomads, known as the Bahima, who are believed to have invaded the country in the not remote past from the north-east, and to be related to the Galla. In Unyoro, and still more in Ankole and in Karagwe, to the south-west of the Victoria Nyanza, these Bahima (Bahuma) form the aristocracy, and have kept themselves practically uncontaminated by negro admixture. Their fine features and light complexions form a strong contrast to those of the negroid population whom they have subjugated, and who form the proletariat in these parts. The Bahima regard fowls, eggs, fish, and vegetables with abhorrence as articles of diet, subsisting wholly on milk and meat. The courts of the *mugabe* ('king') of Ankole, and of the *mukama* ('king') of Unyoro, are, or were a few years ago, little more than royal dairies. In Uganda the Bahima have been merged to a greater extent than elsewhere with the earlier negroid population. This is especially noticeable in the *kabaka* ('king') and in the rest of the royal family, who, while finer in features and lighter in colour than the people as a whole, are nevertheless darker than the royalty among the Banyoro or the Banyankole, and who, unlike the latter, do not subsist on the products of the dairy, having no objection to eating vegetables. They are, in fact, less pure-blooded than many of their subjects. Even in Uganda, however, the care of the cattle is entirely in the hands of the pure-blooded Bahima, who hold themselves aloof from the rest of the population in their way of life, and it is impossible to doubt their physical superiority to that of their Baganda overlords. No-one is more aware of this superiority than the Bahima themselves. Their contempt for the vegetable-eating Baganda is emphatic and undisguised. Even the king, being of mixed descent, comes within the range of their scorn. "The king", said Roscoe's herdsman to him one day in a voice full of contempt, "is merely a slave; he eats bananas!"[2]

[1] For a brief survey of this subject, see Roscoe, *Immigrants*.
[2] Roscoe, in conversation.

The languages of the Bantu peoples in general form a closely related group, and of these the language of Uganda is one of the purest and most archaic. It bears a very close resemblance to the languages of Unyoro, Ankole, and the neighbouring peoples, the differences being no greater than between the Romance languages of Europe.[1] Swahili is a nearly related language belonging to the east coast, but much mixed with Arabic. Its wide currency in the country is due to Arabic traders.

One of the most distinctive features of all the Bantu languages is their employment of prefixes. The prefix *bu-* denotes 'land of'. *Bu-Ganda* is the native name of the country, 'land of Ganda'. *U-Ganda* (*Uganda*) is the corresponding Swahili form. *Mu-*, or *m-* (the Swahili form) is a very common personal prefix, the plural of which is *ba-* (*wa-*). *Mu-Ganda* is a person (male or female) of *Bu-Ganda*, *U-Ganda*, or *Ganda*; *Ba-Ganda* (plural) means 'people of *U-Ganda*'. *Lu-Ganda* is the native name of the language of the country. Other common prefixes are *ki-* and *ka-*. It may be observed that early travellers commonly used the Swahili forms, both for the peoples and the countries, e.g. *Waganda*, *Wanyoro*; *Uganda*, *Unyoro*; while recent writers more often use the native forms, *Baganda*, *Banyoro*; *Buganda*, *Bunyoro*. But few writers attempt consistency, and the forms which we have employed in the following pages are governed for the most part by current oral usage.

Of the countries which have been mentioned we shall concentrate more especially on Uganda proper, partly because our evidence is fullest and most valuable for this region, and partly because the Baganda represent the zenith of northern Bantu culture. The fullest and in every way the most helpful source of information which we have found for our purpose is Roscoe's book on the *Baganda*. But the author also published several other books and studies on the social life of the Baganda and the neighbouring Bantu peoples, which are hardly less helpful. Roscoe spent more than twenty-five years in the country, and for some years taught King Mwanga, son of Mutesa. His books are written with intimate knowledge, as well as sympathetic insight, and a historical sense only too rare in books dealing with a country which has no history save oral tradition. Besides Roscoe's books, however, there is a wealth of literature relating to the social life of the country, written by other early missionaries, such as Ashe, and by British officials,

[1] See Crabtree, *Lu-Ganda*, p. xiii, and the references there cited. For a classification of the Bantu languages, and a detailed bibliography of the subject, the reader is referred to P. Schmidt, *Die Sprachfamilien und Sprachenkreise der Erde* (Heidelberg, 1926), p. 85 ff.

such as Portal, Lugard, and Sir Harry Johnston. There are also many books of travel, some of them early enough to be very valuable for our purpose, such as the works of Speke, Grant, and Stanley, and of men who accompanied them, as well as more recent travellers, such as Cunningham, Treves, etc. Fuller references to these will be found in the List of Abbreviations at the close of the present Section.

Unlike the other non-European countries which we have been studying, the history of Uganda seems to be that of a rising civilisation, even before the advent of Europeans. Captain Speke, who was the first European to visit the country, found it more advanced in material culture than any other East African state. There are clear indications that for at least the last five reigns peaceable relations with the outside world had been developing.[1] Suna, the grandson of Semakokiro, encouraged the Arabs to settle at his court for purposes of trade, and began the slave trade and commerce across the Victoria Nyanza which his son Mutesa expanded and developed.[2] It is probably due to this growing trade, as well as to the aggressive wars against Usoga, Unyoro, and Ankole, that Uganda became the most enlightened and powerful state in Central Africa.

In its modern conditions under British protection Uganda has, of course, undergone much change, especially in regard to internal political organisation and social life. With these changes we are not concerned here. We are attempting to give some idea of the native oral literature and traditions of Uganda as she was before the changes came about, and of their relationship to the social conditions under which they developed. When the present tense is used, therefore, it is to be understood as having relation here to the latter half of last century, and in particular to Uganda as she was when Speke and Grant and Stanley visited her, and when the early missionaries settled in the country.

The population of Uganda is largely engaged in agriculture, but great herds of cattle graze on the uplands and the plains, and before the advent of white men the country was entirely self-supporting. Broad roads intersect it on all sides, rendering communication easy, and facilitating social intercourse. From the time of Suna, and no doubt earlier, the government has been largely that of a militarist régime. Indeed the aristocracy of Suna's and Mutesa's courts practically formed a heroic comitatus. Guerrilla warfare, which had been a static condition of affairs on the borders of Unyoro, Ankole, and Usoga, was now

[1] See Roscoe, *Baganda*, p. 225.   [2] *Ib.* p. 226.

organised into an aggressive policy by a strong central government. But the kings no longer fought in person, and in general even the conduct of the wars of aggression resolved itself into a series of individual enterprises on the part of the chiefs. These heroic elements seem to have been more or less confined to the upper classes, though it is interesting to note that the ages of children and the dates of other events are fixed by reference to battles. The agricultural peasantry were apparently unaffected, and the territorial chiefs, when not actually in attendance at court, had other interests and responsibilities. The most powerful organisation in the country, the Baganda priesthood, was frequently, if not habitually, in direct opposition to the heroic spirit. It would seem that the internal life of the country pursued its course almost regardless of the militarist régime which ensured its peace and prosperity.

The predominant tone in Uganda was therefore non-heroic. Intellectually and economically the influence of the priesthood predominated in all classes of society. Until the time of Mutesa not even the kings were intellectually independent of their tutelage. We shall see later that the financial resources of the country were largely expended on the support of the hierarchy. The temples and the temple estates resembled the great medieval abbeys of Europe, and the number and size of these, together with the staffs required for immediate attendance upon the temples, and for the upkeep of their territories and the herds dedicated to their support, must have given a similar ecclesiastical orientation to national effort.

The preoccupations of the priesthood were with the past. The most outstanding features in the national religion were ancestor worship and the belief in metempsychosis. The belief in ghosts was a living and universal faith. Even the great national gods, Mukasa and his family, are believed by good observers to have been originally human beings whose ghosts still retain their prestige. Kibuka, the war god, was apparently a real man.[1] The gods of the elements and of death, though worshipped to some extent, never attained to anything like the prestige of Mukasa and his family. On the other hand the ghosts of all the kings from the earliest times to the present day were honoured under the heathen régime, though the more recently dead kings claimed precedence over those of the past.[2]

It is probable that writing was first introduced into Uganda by Arab

[1] See Roscoe, *Man*, VII, p. 161.
[2] According to Miss Werner (*Mythology*, pp. 118, 180), in most of the Bantu states a ghost becomes obsolete after three generations.

traders. It seems clear from Stanley's narrative that the Arabic script was known to many of the more intellectual members of Mutesa's court. In a passage of great interest he tells us:

"Nearly all the principal attendants at the court can write the Arabic letters. The Emperor and many of the chiefs both read and write that character with facility, and frequently employ it to send messages to one another, or to strangers at a distance. The materials which they use for this are very thin smooth slabs of cotton-wood. Mutesa possesses several score of these, on which are written his 'books of wisdom', as he styles the results of his interviews with European travellers. Some day a curious traveller may think it worth while to give us translations of these proceedings and interviews."[1]

We have not heard if this suggestion of Stanley's has ever been carried out, but there can be no doubt that Mutesa's version of these interviews would be a document of unique value and interest. It is probable that the art of writing only became general at the court shortly before Stanley's visit, for Speke had to explain to Mutesa what a letter (i.e. epistle) was, and it is certain that outside the court the art of writing was practically unknown.[2] All literature was purely oral.

Unfortunately there do not seem to be any collections of the native oral poetry of Uganda, or any extensive collections of such poetry from any of the Northern Bantu, so far as we are aware. Little attention has been given to this aspect of their culture by either travellers or anthropologists,[3] and it is extremely difficult to obtain precise information about customs and forms of composition which must have come within the daily observation of all Europeans who have visited the countries during the last seventy years. The native style of minstrelsy and literature is fast dying out before the infiltration of European fashions, and native modes of thought are rapidly changing under the enlightenment of Christianity and education. It will probably not be easy to obtain such collections in the future. The late Canon Roscoe wrote to the best authorities whom he knew on our behalf to try to obtain collections of native oral literature in 1923 or 1924, but without success. It cannot be too strongly urged that every effort should be made to collect specimens of such literature, and information with regard to methods of composition, recitation, and minstrelsy, before the older generation passes away. In view of the absence of any such collections,

[1] *T.D.C.* p. 259.　　　　　　　　[2] See Crabtree, *Lu-ganda*, p. xiiif.
[3] For a chapter on the oral literature of the Southern Bantu, see Schapera's book on *The Bantu-Speaking Tribes of South Africa*, pp. 291 ff., 443 f.

we have been entirely dependent for the following brief and partial account of the poetry and minstrelsy of Uganda on descriptions of recitation and composition as these have been written down by eye-witnesses. Such accounts are, of course, generally merely incidental, and occur scattered throughout various books of travel, etc. In addition we have been fortunate enough to have had opportunities of conversation and correspondence with the late Canon Roscoe, and of questioning him on these matters, and much of our information has been derived from these conversations and letters.

Oral tradition has a long history in Uganda. The stories of the kings cover a period of some seven centuries or more, and some of the histories of the clans relate to a period even further back, though we do not know if their traditions continue in an unbroken line down to the present day, as do those of the kings. The authenticity of these traditions varies considerably, as we shall see, and perhaps none relating to the earliest times can, interpreted literally, be regarded as actually historical. We shall see reasons, however, for concluding that literal interpretation of Uganda traditional prose is often misplaced.

The most reliable sources for oral tradition are the genealogies. These have been collected by Roscoe for the royal line with collateral branches for twenty-three generations from Kintu, the so-called founder of the present dynasty, down to Daudi Cwa, the reigning king.[1] This royal family tree is a wonderful feat of memory, rivalling some of the best Maori pedigrees. It is not alone however. Roscoe also gives the family tree of the Oribi[2] and of the grasshopper[3] clans for some eighteen and sixteen generations respectively, and we have no reason for supposing that they are in any way unusual. He tells us that he selected the pedigrees of these two clans to show how the mother's clan is disregarded, and that the clans are careful to retain the name of the male ancestors and claim descent through the male line only.[4] Elsewhere also he tells us that the oldest family of 'peasant princes' trace their descent back to a prince named Keya, who was said to be one of Kintu's sons.[5]

It has been mentioned that in Uganda, in addition to the royal genealogies, there were also a large number of traditions attached to the

---

[1] *Baganda*, p. 175 ff.   [2] *Ib.* p. 181 ff.
[3] *Ib.* p. 184 ff. This is the clan to which belonged the late Sir Apolo Kagwa, the *katikiro*, or prime minister of the country.   [4] *Ib.* p. 173.
[5] *Ib.* p. 140. 'Peasant Princes' is the name given to the king's brothers after a king's son has reached an age to be eligible as heir to the throne.

kings. We shall consider these more fully later; but it is important to note here that these traditions were cultivated and preserved with the most jealous care at the Uganda court. The oral dynastic histories were recited in recitative—'in a sort of rhythmical chant'—by a court minstrel at the coronation of a new king or at a state function, and so rigidly were these oral 'texts' preserved that a single error in their recitation on a formal occasion is said to have been punished by death.[1]

Among the surrounding Bantu peoples similar lists of kings have been obtained. These will be referred to more fully when we come to consider antiquarian literature (p. 596 f. below). Roscoe informed us[2] that in Uganda the actual genealogies were preserved in the form of poetry, and handed down by oral tradition, and that the king had a certain chief at the court who was responsible for the preservation in poetical form of these royal genealogies, and whose duty it was to recite them at set times, such as feasts. Each clan also had a member who was similarly responsible for the memorising in poetical form of the genealogies of important members of the clan.[3]

This brings us to the subjects of metre and minstrelsy. Unfortunately we have very little information regarding African metres. If we understood Roscoe aright in regard to the chanting of the traditions, it was the musical accompaniment of the voice, rather than any defined metre as the term is generally understood, which distinguished the recitations from ordinary prose. It would seem possible from this that poetry in Uganda, at least in regard to narrative, has no existence apart from music. Poetry is, in fact, speech which is sung. Livingstone, however, refers to a Batoka song as composed in a sort of blank verse, each line consisting of five syllables.[4]

---

[1] Roscoe, in conversation. A similar practice still prevails in Ashanti. Rattray tells us that there is a class of minstrels known as *kwadwumfo*, who are trained from childhood in the history of the clan, and whose duty it is to chant the titles and deeds of dead kings with a curious nasal intonation, as they stand behind the stool of the reigning chief.—"The recital of these greatly affects the chief and often moves him to tears." Rattray adds that they are still to be found at the courts of the great *amanhene*, or 'paramount chiefs' (*Religion*, p. 143, footnote 1). Elsewhere the same writer tells us that these *kwadwumfo*, who "drone like a hive of bees in the chief's ear" the names and deeds of the departed kings, must become 'word-perfect' at their task. And he adds that at one ceremony which he attended, at which two old women had to recite the titles of the great ancestral spirits as far back as there was any record, he was informed that in the old days two executioners would have been detailed to stand behind them, and that if they made a mistake they were 'taken away' (*Ashanti*, p. 219). The *kwadwumfo* appear to chant generally in pairs.

[2] In a letter.   [3] Roscoe, in conversation.   [4] *N.E.Z.* p. 236.

The harp has always been a favourite instrument in Uganda,[1] and is in common use in both Uganda and Usoga to accompany songs and recitals. These harps are of two kinds. The old harp of Uganda, used at the court of the kings and chiefs, is a vertical harp of eight strings formed on the same principle as the Irish harp, though differing widely from this in shape. This was the instrument chiefly in use for court poetry, such as panegyrics, and for accompanying "the older and more popular songs...the traditions and legends of the nation, sung in the minor key".[2] This harp has recently been superseded in Uganda by the Basoga harp, which is a horizontal harp, also of eight strings, and formed more after the fashion of a Greek lyre, though apparently held at a different angle. This harp is employed chiefly to accompany lyrical poetry, such as love and drinking songs.[3] It seems to be a more domestic and informal instrument than the old native harp of Uganda. According to Kollmann this type of harp is also in use in the Sese Archipelago.[4] Roscoe mentions the interesting fact that one of the accessories of the war god Kibuka was a harp named *Tanalabankondwe*, which was placed in front of the dais in his temple.[5]

Apart from the evidence mentioned above, we have no knowledge of narrative poetry in Uganda. What does this evidence amount to? It is clear that the older songs of Uganda, that is to say, songs which have been handed down by exact verbal tradition, consisted to some extent of the traditions and legends of the nation and of the kings. These were sung by court minstrels to the accompaniment of a harp. The latter seems to be of the same fundamental type as the harp which was used to accompany narrative poetry in ancient Greece and in medieval Europe. No texts of these early narrative poems of Uganda— if such they were—have come down to us. From what Roscoe says it is clear that poetry of this kind was already becoming a thing of the

[1] Wilson and Felkin II, p. 214; Roscoe, *Baganda*, p. 33 f. For the various types of instruments in use in British Central Africa, see Werner, *B.C.A.* p. 221 ff. A full account of the musical instruments of the various Bantu peoples round the Victoria Nyanza, with numerous illustrations, will be found in Kollmann, *V.N.* p. 37 ff.

[2] Roscoe, *Baganda*, p. 35. A picture of this harp is given in *ib.* fig. 10. Harps similar in shape occur also among the Dinka tribe (Sayce, fig. 22 *b*) and among the Azandeh in the Congo (*H.E.C.* fig. 211).

[3] For pictures of this harp, see Roscoe, *Baganda*, fig. 10; Sayce, fig. 22 *a*.

[4] *V.N. loc. cit.*

[5] *Baganda*, p. 305. For further information on the minstrelsy of the Northern Bantu, see Varley, p. 58 ff.

past when he first went to Uganda, and it has therefore not been possible to enquire into its relation to other forms of poetry on similar themes. From the prose sagas of the kings which have been recorded, and from the forms of poetry other than narrative, there is ground for believing that some at least of these narrative 'poems' or songs were heroic in character. In this connection the occurrence of the old Baganda harp in the temple of Kibuka, the war god, is especially interesting.

Occasional poetry is evidently very common among the Northern Bantu. In his account of the customs of the Baganda the *katikiro* has devoted a chapter (XXVIII) to an account of the songs and music of his people. Many examples of the songs are quoted. From this chapter it is clear that songs were composed by all classes of the population, including the king himself.[1] They were sung with and without musical accompaniment, and were often handed down for considerable periods of time. Many of them claim to be contemporary with kings who reigned several centuries ago, such as a little ditty on the amours of King Mawanda, the thirteenth king before the present ruler, Daudi Cwa. This ditty was played by private musicians in Mawanda's honour, and so pleased him that he ordered the court musicians to play it.[2] Another little song is recorded in which playful reference is made to the baldness of King Kyabagu, the third king after Mawanda, which is also said to have pleased the king.[3] The humorous side is, in fact, singularly prominent in these songs, and we are constantly reminded of Speke's phrase, 'the laughter-loving Waganda'. It is clear also that these songs, full as they are of allusions to public and private events, immediately acquired a wide circulation, and served as running commentaries on Baganda history. We shall see later that this habit of registering contemporary opinion on current events is very widespread, if not universal in Africa.

The most ambitious panegyric known to us is one which is traditionally stated to have been sung by 'the people', on the accession of Suna and Mutesa. Mutesa was much admired by the people, who were weary of Suna's cruelties:

> Out of a cruel thing (Suna) came forth a precious thing.
> He who does not know the precious thing, it is Mutesa.
> Out of a cruel thing came forth a precious thing.
> Banda the city of Mutesa,
> Which we inhabit—receiving salt and meat from him.
> Out of a cruel thing came forth a precious thing.

[1] Kagwa, *Customs*, pp. 145, 147.   [2] *Ib.* p. 141.   [3] *Loc. cit.*

The Baganda minstrel makes a liberal use of refrain, for he continues:

> He who does not know the precious thing, it is Mutesa.
> Out of a cruel thing came forth a precious thing.
> Those who build the city really do build.
> Those who build another palace really do build.
> Oh,
> Out of a cruel thing came forth a precious thing.[1]

Panegyric poetry was evidently very much cultivated at the court of Uganda, as well as in the households of chiefs. The early missionaries, Wilson and Felkin, mention songs in praise of the king or great chiefs as extemporised to the accompaniment of the harp by the court minstrels of Uganda, and quote the following panegyric on Mutesa:

> Thy feet are hammers,
> Son of the forest.[2]
> Great is the fear of thee;
> Great is thy wrath;
> Great is thy peace;
> Great is thy power.[3]

Roscoe also refers to songs sung to the accompaniment of the old harp at the court of the king and the chiefs, "belauding the king's power and benevolence, praising him, and belittling his enemies. The words", he adds, "were made up to fit the tunes at a moment's notice, and were suited to passing events."[4] It is to these songs that Speke makes reference when describing his visit to the *kamraviona*, or commander-in-chief:

"I found him sitting on the ground with several elders; whilst Wasoga minstrels[5] played on their lap-harps, and sang songs in praise of their king, and the noble stranger who wore fine clothes and eclipsed all previous visitors."[6]

Panegyric poetry is equally common among many other Bantu peoples[7]. We may refer to a song which was improvised in Stanley's honour by the 'choragus' of the Banyamwezi in his caravan.[8] Among the Zulu also panegyric poetry is highly developed. Shooter quotes a

---

[1] Kagwa, *Customs*, p. 145.
[2] A synonym for the lion, which is the symbol of royalty in Uganda.
[3] Wilson and Felkin I, p. 215.   [4] *Baganda*, p. 35.
[5] The Wasoga, or Basoga, are the chief minstrels in this part of the world, and are frequently mentioned as performing at the court and elsewhere in Uganda.
[6] Speke, p. 344.   [7] For the Southern Bantu, see Schapera, p. 295 f.
[8] *H.I.f.L.* p. 621 f.

very simple address to Chaka,[1] and also a long and ambitious poem on Dingan[2] which far surpasses in scope any poetry which we have seen from Uganda.

Elegiac poetry was cultivated at the court and elsewhere in Uganda no less than panegyric poetry. Kagwa tells us that some time after the burial of a king a beer feast was held in mourning. An instrument was played and all the mourners wept, and the following song was sung, first by the men, and then the women joined in:

> A little mushroom,
> I have fallen, and remained there
> As a mushroom.[3]

Roscoe tells us that when a king died his successor visited his shrine frequently, taking his wives with him, to sing the departed monarch's praises.[4] Wilson and Felkin include dirges and laments for dead chiefs and warriors among the songs said to be extemporised to the harp by the court minstrels. A number of elegies are recorded in Kagwa's collection.[5] The following lamentation over a dead chief recorded by Wilson and Felkin illustrates the crudity and simplicity of these dirges:

> Oh, separator![6]
> Oh, Sematimba!
> They tied goats;
> They tied goats for him in vain.
> Son of a king,
> He has no pride.
> He freely gives plantain wine.
>
> Luhinga! Luhinga!
> Him of whom I speak,
> He has no pride.
> For he freely gives plantain wine.
> Mkwenda! Mkwenda!
> Whose home is Chikongi[7]
> Him of whom I speak,
> He has no pride,
> For he freely gives plantain wine.[8]

---

[1] *Kafirs*, p. 268. [2] *Kafirs*, p. 310.
[3] Kagwa, *Customs*, p. 111.
[4] *Baganda*, p. 112; cf. p. 284.
[5] See e.g. Kagwa, *Customs*, p. 142. [6] A synonym for death.
[7] Chikongi is the place where he is buried.
[8] Wilson and Felkin I, p. 214.

Miss Kidney quotes an elegiac poem which she heard in Nyasaland, and which she tells us is sung unaccompanied during the final ceremonies of mourning among some of the mountain peoples:

"On the night of a full moon the chief singer stands on the top of a hill, and with his hands raised to direct the sounds from his mouth across the valley below, he sings the 'Lament', with high voice and declamatory manner, while at the foot of the mountain hundreds of villagers sit huddled among the trees to sing a refrain between the sentences of the lament:[1]

> 1. There death now has come to the homestead,
>   Enter not, my brother.
>   Ho-ya-ho-ya-ho.
>   A maiden, alas, there is sleeping.
>   Ho-ya-ho-ya-ho.
>
> 2. Her rest is dark and unending.
>   She returns no more.
>   Ho-ya-ho-ya-ho.
>   Her spirit has passed on a journey.
>   Ho-ya-ho-ya-ho."[2]

Poetry celebrating contemporary or past events is also widespread elsewhere among the other Bantu peoples. Such poems, like those of the Baganda, are rich in allusion, and when composed on important events or great chiefs they serve as historical records of the first importance. Bishop O'Ferrall noted down the complete text of one of these poems from a native of the Ba-bemba tribe of north-eastern Rhodesia in 1925.[3] The form is that of narrative, though the action is represented as taking place before our eyes—a kind of historic present. The action is rendered somewhat difficult by the rapidity of the transitions, and the tendency to use pronouns where proper names would have given greater clarity. In all this the usage resembles that of a similar class of poems among the Abyssinians and the Galla, as described above. The type is evidently widespread in East Africa. As has been observed already, the relationship of poetry of this class to the traditions and legends of the nation and of the kings requires investigation when fuller material allows of it. Miss Werner also mentions

---

[1] Mr Fraser tells us that this manner of chanting or conversing from hill to hill, or across valleys, is common also among the Zulu, who can make their words carry an astonishing distance in the still mountain air.   [2] Kidney, *Songs*, p. 126.
[3] *B.S.O.S.* IV, iv, p. 839 ff. With this poem we may compare 'The Ballad of Saole' of which Miss Werner gives some verses in *J.A.S.* XXXI (1932), p. 183 ff.

that she noted down several songs in British Central Africa which are full of unexplained allusions to local chiefs and events.[1] We may refer further to the statement of Junod that the songs of the Baronga of Delagoa Bay contain allusions to the historical events of the country.[2] There is doubtless a close relationship between all these classes of poetry.

Martial and hunting poetry is frequently recorded. Miss Kidney notes a number of poems of this class from Nyasaland. These poems are communal rather than individual in their interest, like the *fârsā* of the Galla. The following is the opening stanza of one of these Nyasaland poems:

> Fight now! Come and fight now!
> Slay them! We'll brandish spears!
> Straight forth doth speed your arrow.
> Tremble! Yes! *They* tremble!
> When *we* draw near,
> And *far* they'll flee as we approach them! etc.[3]

The following are the opening lines of a little hunting song from the same collection:

> Come, my people—come for fresh meat.
> Come, my brothers—come and seek food.
> Come, my people—come to cut meat.
> Distant going—runs the wild buck,
> Horns upraised, and eyes a-glowing,
> Come and find him, quick, we'll slay him.[4]

Personal poetry is frequently referred to, but such poetry appears to be generally slight in character, and purely extempore, and is rarely recorded by travellers, though numerous instances are quoted by the *katikiro*.[5] Roscoe refers to love songs as sung by the women of the Banyankole to the accompaniment of the harp, but only at home and in private;[6] he did not remember to have heard these songs himself.[7] Among the Basoga love and drinking songs are also said to be sung to the accompaniment of the harp. But strangely enough Miss Kidney says that she does not remember ever to have heard during sixteen years' residence in Nyasaland a song which might be classed as analogous to the civilised 'love-song'.[8]

[1] *B.C.A.* p. 219.   [2] Junod, *Chants*, p. 43.
[3] Kidney, *J.A.S.* xx, p. 126.   [4] *Ib.* p. 122.
[5] Kagwa, *Customs*, p. 140 ff.
[6] *Northern Bantu*, p. 140; cf. *Banyankole*, p. 81.
[7] Roscoe, in conversation.   [8] Kidney, *Songs*, p. 123.

Occasional poetry appears to be universal, and no subject is too slight to call forth an extempore song. Stanley quotes a song of triumph extemporised by a member of the Unyamwezi in his caravan on reaching the Victoria Nyanza.[1] When Grant lay sick in Karagwe he was constantly entertained with songs celebrating his own person and the state of his health:

"At night my few men would gather round their fire, and, particularly after having an extra allowance of plantain-wine, sing a ditty about my health. Frij on the single-stringed zeze or guitar would commence:

> I am Frij, I am Frij;
> My brother Grin,[2] my brother Grin,
> Is very sick, is very sick,
> We'll get a cow, we'll get a cow,
> When he gets well, when he gets well."[3]

Roscoe tells us that at the court of Uganda the minstrel made it his business to learn all the gossip of the day, and to retail it in his songs. Their recitations, however, invariably have reference to the king or great chiefs.[4] Stanley observes that among the Wanyamwezi of Unyanyembe, who are great improvisers—

"The latest scandal, or political news or personal gossip is sure, if it is of sufficient public interest, to find expression in village music.... The Musungu, or Muzungu,[5] as it is sometimes pronounced, was also a favourite subject upon first arrival, but this soon lacked novelty."[6]

By far the commonest form of poetry is undoubtedly extempore poetry, sung or recited at recurrent social ceremonies, or as an accompaniment to physical action or employment. Miss Werner noted that natives nearly always sing when engaged in concerted work. She quotes a corn-pounding song from Blantyre.[7] Songs are also sung on the march,[8] when hauling a heavy log,[9] and above all to accompany the rhythmical movement of the paddles of a canoe. Among the Baganda this is one of the most widely practised and highly patronised forms of native literature. Roscoe tells us that the canoe-men are the acknowledged 'songs-men' of the country.

"It was their invariable habit to sing when paddling. They seldom put in more than a few strokes, before someone started a song, to keep

[1] *T.D.C.* p. 92.   [2] I.e. 'Grant', the author's name.   [3] Grant, p. 153.
[4] *Baganda*, p. 34; and in conversation with ourselves.
[5] I.e. Stanley himself.   [6] *H.I.f.L.* p. 449 f.
[7] *B.C.A.* pp. 216, 219.   [8] Kidney, *Songs*, p. 122.
[9] Werner, *loc. cit.*; cf. Roscoe, *Baganda*, p. 29.

time for the paddlers; all the men joined in the chorus.... The King often sent for the canoe-men to come and sing their songs; when they came, they marched round and round in one of the courtyards, working their arms as though paddling, and singing at the same time."[1]

Stanley quotes snatches of the song of his Wajiji canoe-men on Lake Tanganyika,[2] and J. E. S. Moore transcribes a bar of the music of one of the boat-songs of the canoe-men of the same lake.[3] In Nyasaland[4] and among the tribes on the Zambezi[5] the boat-song is equally popular.

It would be a mistake to infer from the slender nature of our records that poetry plays a small part in the social life of the Baganda. It is clear from the texts recorded by the *katikiro* that here, as among the Basuto, the Ba-ronga, the Zulu, the Yoruba, and many other African peoples, the composition of occasional poetry is a universal accomplishment. The kings appear to be the great patrons of both poetry and minstrelsy. Incidental references and quotations also make it clear that the kings have been in the habit of composing poetry themselves. The *katikiro* quotes poems attributed to both Suna and Mwanga,[6] while Mutesa was an accomplished musician.[7] All these Baganda compositions are, however, so slight in character, and the weight laid on the musical accompaniment is so marked that they are really perhaps to be classed as part of the artistic and social rather than the intellectual life of the people. The thought is simple and superficial, and the poems quoted never exceed a few lines, which even in this limited compass make extensive use of repetition. In this they are in marked contrast to the comparatively long and elaborate poems of the Basuto and the Zulu.[8] Grant noted during his visit to Uganda that instrumental music was much commoner than singing.[9]

A number of heroic stories have been recorded in summary form from Uganda and elsewhere. These have come to us, not in the form of independent sagas, but as forming a part of an oral history of the kings of Uganda. This great oral memorial of the past is known both

[1] *Baganda*, p. 37; cf. also pp. 279, 300.
[2] *H.I.f.L.* p. 568.   [3] Moore, p. 95.
[4] Kidney, *Songs*, p. 119f.; Werner, *B.C.A.* p. 217f.
[5] Livingstone, *N.E.Z.* pp. 30, 419.
[6] See Kagwa, *Customs*, pp. 145, 148.   [7] Grant, p. 245.
[8] It is very possible that the Baganda evidence is defective on this point, or that longer poems have been recorded which have escaped our notice. From the high level of Baganda culture in other respects we should think this very probable.
[9] Grant, p. 245.

to courtiers and to the priests, in variant forms reflecting the natural bias and preoccupations of the milieu in which it is preserved. The version current at the court of Mutesa was recorded by Stanley[1] from the recitation of Sabadu, at that time a page at Mutesa's court. The version which was current among the priests and mediums was recorded by Roscoe.[2] A further version has also been recorded by Sir Apolo Kagwa, the *katikiro* or prime minister of Uganda, "in consultation with many old men of the old times who had learned these things by heart and had not forgotten them."[3] The version current at Mutesa's court is perhaps connected to some extent with the version of the stories of past kings referred to by Roscoe, which were recited by court minstrels at important functions (cf. p. 576 above). In the form in which this oral chronicle has come to us it is, of course, a product of antiquarian learning, and will be referred to more fully when we consider anti-quarian literature later. But it is clear that it has embodied in summary form a large number of oral stories, both heroic and non-heroic, and a brief mention may be made of these at this point.

An early hero whose exploits are related in heroic fashion by Sabadu is Kibaga (Kibuka), whom Sabadu describes as a warrior of King Nakivingi (Nakibinge), but who is worshipped as the god of war, and whom we shall refer to later among the stories of the gods. One of the most typical of Sabadu's heroic stories is that of Wakinguru, the mighty single champion of King Chabagu (Kyabagu), who is reckoned as the thirtieth king of Uganda on Stanley's list.[4] It is said that it was entirely due to the exploits of the daring Wakinguru that Chabagu was able to conquer the country of Busoga. The hero is said to have crossed alone over Jinja, 'the Falls', at the north end of the Victoria Nyanza, and shouted his challenge to the Basoga to fight him singly or all together. The enemy came on, first in small numbers, then in ever increasing bands, and hurled their spears, but Wakinguru merely laughed at their efforts, and hurled his own spears with such deadly aim that by nightfall six hundred of the Basoga lay slain, and he was able to return to Uganda across the Falls, and 'refreshed himself with the milk and bananas of his own country', and received the congratulations of the king and army.[5]

It is an important element in the claim of Sabadu to be regarded as a

---

[1] Stanley, *T.D.C.* p. 218 ff.   [2] Roscoe, *Baganda*, p. 214 ff.
[3] Roscoe, in conversation. Kagwa's version is published at length in *Ekitabo*, while a much shorter version is contained in *Customs*, p. 18 ff. by the same author.
[4] Stanley, *T.D.C.* p. 240.   [5] *Ib.* p. 227.

serious historian that as we approach modern times his narratives become fuller and more detailed, and, of course, less extravagant. His narrative of the reign of Suna, the son of Kamanya and great-grandfather of the present king, is a summary of a saga Cycle rather than a single story. But in spite of their brevity the stories have retained the true saga style in their vividness and attention to details. The scene, for example, in which the warrior Kasindula, having surpassed all other chiefs in heroic exploits, presents himself in victorious humility before the mighty Suna, is a masterpiece of vivid narrative in summary form.

In spite of the individualism of the stories the heroic element is preserved consistently in the later stories of Sabadu's narrative. No personality is developed except those of Suna and Mutesa. The chiefs are differentiated, not by individual traits, but by their exploits. Reflection also is absent. The narrative is that of continuous action, with rapidly shifting scene and personnel. Exaggeration plays a large part, and a tone of exaltation characterises the sagas. The heroes boast and taunt and defy, they perform feats of superhuman strength, and the conquered are subjected to unbelievable tortures. But it is not only bearable but enthralling when related by Sabadu, because he succeeds perfectly in preserving the heroic atmosphere. All is on the grand scale. The illusion created by the heroic atmosphere may be realised by the shock which the reader would experience if reflective and unheroic elements were introduced. These would instantly make such deeds as those of Suna intolerable reading, as one sees by turning to Ashe's account of the persecutions of the native Christians under King Mwanga.[1]

Unfortunately we possess no considerable body of sagas of the priests or of priestly families. Some information is to be gleaned from the accounts of the gods and temples, and something is known also of the relations of individual priests with the kings. But we have not found complete sagas of which the priests are the leading figures, and no continuous history bearing directly on priestly traditions, though from incidental references in the *katikiro's* book on the Customs of Uganda it is clear that a large body of such saga is current. Many of the stories related of the gods clearly refer to their 'mediums' or mantic representatives. We may refer, for example, to the story[2] of the visit of four 'gods', headed by Mukasa, to advise King Semakokiro, who 'was

[1] *Two Kings*, p. 136 ff. [2] Kagwa, *Customs*, p. 116.

suffering from indigestion, and had sent for the god'. Unfortunately the translator does not always make clear what was the exact technical function of the persons—for they clearly are persons in this and other similar stories—who represented the gods; but they were evidently mantic, for it is interesting to note that three priests of Mukasa are also mentioned as present on this occasion, in addition to the 'four gods'. The absence of fuller records of this class is the more to be deplored as the priests were in all probability the most intellectual men in Uganda, and the most learned men in matters relating to the past. Indeed the priestly seal has set itself completely on the whole of the oral prose of the country in sacerdotal preoccupations and colouring. In Mutesa's day heroic prose was still a living form, but with the disappearance of the heroic court it has vanished, or so it would seem, and the same traditions collected by Roscoe have assumed a priestly bias.

In contrast to the heroic stories which we have been considering, the non-heroic stories are confined in Sabadu's narrative to the earlier kings of the chronicle. On the other hand the entire account of all the kings obtained by Roscoe, chiefly from priestly sources, is told in the interests of the heathen priesthood, and is therefore essentially non-heroic in character. The stories represent the evils which in the past befell kings who violated sanctuaries or insulted priests, who disregarded oracles or fetishes, or did not observe the accepted marriage tabus of tribe or family. Nothing is said of any of the heroes of whom the heroic stories are related by Stanley. Of course stories are told of the same kings in both accounts in almost every case; but the anecdotes and stories which are related of these kings are frequently different, and in the great majority of cases they are different in tone even when relating identical occurrences.

The most interesting Cycle of non-heroic stories told in the early part of Stanley's narrative is that of Kintu, who figures as the first king of Uganda in both Stanley's and Roscoe's narratives. According to the former he was a priest, while according to the latter he was descended from the gods. His wife was the daughter of the sky god Gulu. It is clear that the tradition of Kintu and of the majority of the other early kings is that of peace kings. They are distinguished in Stanley's narrative by their long absence on great journeys in wild and solitary places, such as hills and woods, rather than by prowess in battle. In this and other respects their affinities are with mantic rather than with heroic persons, and in these stories relating to early times, in contrast to those of later times, superior cunning is exalted above prowess.

Kintu himself is stated to have disappeared frequently, no one knew where.[1] This disappearance is narrated by Sabadu as a strange and individual feature, for which the reciter knew of no parallel; but in Roscoe's version it appears to be rationally explained as an early burial custom of Uganda which differed from those of later times in the absence of the royal tomb. Several of the kings of Unyoro are similarly said to have disappeared. Isaza, the fourth king, tried to cheat Death who wished to make blood-brotherhood with him; but one day, in following a certain heifer, he wandered to an island and there met Death sitting in state like a king. He was reproved for his deceit and detained, and though he often tried to return, he was never again seen by his subjects.[2]

In Stanley's narratives of the Uganda kings a certain unifying element is introduced by the recurrent theme of a search which was instituted for the lost Kintu. His son Chwa (Cwa) and his grandson Kimera, as well as many of the succeeding kings, are said to have sought in vain for Kintu and to have sent messengers far and wide upon the same quest. Only once, in the reign of King Mawanda, the twenty-seventh king of Uganda,[3] was Kintu seen for a brief space.[4] A peasant discovered him surrounded by his court in the forest. Kintu commanded him to bring the king for an interview with him, but on no account to bring anyone else or tell what he had seen. The king obeyed the summons and followed the peasant till he stood before the ghostly court. Unknown to the king, however, he had been secretly followed by his *katikiro*, or 'prime minister'. When Kintu observed him he reproved the king for disobeying his injunctions to come alone, and forthwith disappeared. The king speared the *katikiro* in wrath for his having deprived him of his interview with Kintu. An interesting variant of this story is also given by Roscoe[5] in a brief note on the same king. The same writer further tells us that Cwa, Kintu's son, is also said to have been lost, like his father, when quite an old man; but there is no mention of the motif of the search. We have, however, some interesting reminiscences which seem to echo this motif. In Roscoe's note on the war of Nakibinge against Unyoro[6] we are told that the king

---

[1] See e.g. Roscoe, *Baganda*, pp. 136f., 214. Stanley, *T.D.C.* p. 218ff.; Werner, *Mythology*, p. 155.   [2] Roscoe, *Bakitara*, p. 323ff.; cf. p. 88.

[3] According to Stanley's list. In Roscoe's and Kagwa's he is the twenty-second king.

[4] *T.D.C.* p. 222f.; cf. Roscoe, *Baganda*, p. 222f.

[5] *Baganda*, p. 222f.   [6] *Ib.* p. 217.

was advised by a medicine-man to go to Magongo and consult his fore-father Kintu about the war with his cousin Juma. Though Nakibinge followed his advice, however, and followed out the instructions of the oracle, he perished in the war against Unyoro.

Two curious stories are related by Roscoe of Ndaula, the nineteenth king of Uganda.[1] Ndaula is said to have stipulated on ascending the throne that he should not be made the medium of the god Mukasa. Accordingly the people appointed Juma, one of the sons of King Tebandeka, to be priest. From that time onwards one of Juma's descendants was always priest, instead of the reigning king. Whenever a new king came to the throne, a new prince was made priest, and succeeded to the estates of Juma, while the former priest retired into private life. The story is not quite clear as we have it, for no distinction seems here to be made between the priest and the medium of Mukasa;[2] but as Ndaula's father had been made medium of Mukasa, the implication seems to be that from the time of Ndaula a substitute acted as medium.

Roscoe's other story of the same king bears a close relation to the story of Mawanda narrated above. According to the story of Ndaula, the king, acting on the advice of a medicine-man, went and hid himself in the forest; but a hunter saw him, and led the *katikiro* to the spot. The king was angry with the hunter for betraying his hiding-place, and killed him. We are told that the king acted as he did on the advice of the medicine-man because of an infirmity under which he was suffering, and that he was cured in consequence. It is to be suspected that the two stories of Ndaula point to an ecclesiastical controversy between the priesthood of Mukasa, the god of the Nyanza, and the medicine-men, who in this instance seem to stand for the cult of Kintu and ancestor worship generally, which is doubtless much older in Uganda, and is certainly much more widespread in this part of the world (cf. p. 601 below). The same controversy can be traced in the story of Tebandeka, Ndaula's predecessor, and elsewhere in the stories of the kings.

Before leaving the subject of Kintu attention may be called to its affinities with the story of the death of Malumbe, the son of Mungalo, the first ancestor of the Basola chiefs of Northern Rhodesia, who is stated to have entered the country from the far east. Mungalo had a daughter Chintu, which is said to be the southern form of the northern

---

[1] *Baganda*, p. 220f.

[2] According to Roscoe, the chief priest of the war god Kibuka was also the medium (see *Man* VII, p. 162). Perhaps the same is true of Mukasa's medium.

Kintu. She is the ancestress of the Basola chiefs. Her brother, or, according to a variant tradition, her son, Malumbe, is said to have been distinguished for supernatural rather than for military powers. He worked miracles, and won the submission of the Ba-Ila peoples (by whom he is reverenced as a *muzhima*) by the fear which he inspired. He is said to have struck his opponents with blindness, and he had also the power of creating and drying up springs. He is represented as having entered into a contest of power with Munyama, a rival *muzhima*. It is expressly recorded by a consistent tradition, however, that the contest was not one of arms, but of skill in a game, which, according to one tradition, Malumbe had introduced himself. Finally he is said to have disappeared suddenly and the manner of his death remained unknown. His dress and weapons were found by the side of a deep pond, but he himself was never seen again.[1]

We are not aware that any poetry relating to gods or spirits has been recorded from among the Northern Bantu. On the other hand, prose stories of the gods are common. In the form in which such stories were obtained by Roscoe in Uganda, chiefly from old men and women and from priests,[2] they generally assume the form of antiquarian tradition or speculation rather than of entertainment; but similar stories recorded by Stanley and others are often comparatively free from antiquarian elements. The great majority of stories of the gods are about the family to which belonged Mukasa, the god (*lubare*) of Bubembe Island in the Victoria Nyanza. This great pantheon constituted a family group stretching over at least four generations. The greatest of the family were Mukasa and his brother Kibuka. According to Cunningham[3] the sex of Mukasa is uncertain, some traditions making the god feminine, some masculine. It is clear from Kagwa and Roscoe, however, that the god is masculine, and Cunningham's uncertainty is probably to be explained by the fact that the medium was a woman.[4] Cunningham reproduces a photograph of Mukasa (i.e. the 'medium') and the court.[5] The relationship between Kibuka and Mukasa, whether twins, or born on different occasions, is still uncertain, as is also their relationship to their 'so-called forefathers', Wanema and Wada, and to Bukulu, who is said to have come from the skies.[6] Katonda is spoken of as the 'father

---

[1] Smith and Dale II, p. 182f.
[2] In a letter to ourselves; cf. also *Man* v (1907), p. 161.
[3] Cunningham, p. 79, footnote 1.   [4] See Kagwa, *Customs*, p. 115.
[5] Cunningham, p. 75.   [6] Roscoe, *loc. cit.*

of the gods', while Namuluwere, who is not stated to have belonged to the divine family, is said to have been the servant of the other gods.[1]

Mukasa is a peaceful god whose worship is very widespread and whose temples are many. He is the tutelary deity of the Victoria Nyanza, and is said to be able to control its waters as well as to exercise great influence over the welfare of the whole of Uganda.[2] Interesting stories are told of his boyhood.[3] He is said to have been called Selwanga as a child,[4] which is interesting as being also the name of the python god, whose sister Nalwanga was Mukasa's wife, and whose temple was in Budu by the shore of the Victoria Nyanza.[5] The infant Mukasa refused ordinary food when he had been weaned, but ate the heart and liver of an ox and drank its blood. In his childhood he disappeared and was found on the Island of Bubembe. As it was concluded that he must have come from the Island of Bukasa he was called Mukasa. A hut was built for him and a chief called Semagumba took charge of it. The nature of his diet convinced the people that he was a god, and Semagumba became his priest. According to some traditions Mukasa continued to live in his hut for fourteen generations. He married three wives. The stories differ as to the manner of his death, some saying that he died and was buried on the island in the forest near the temple, while others affirm that he disappeared as suddenly as he had come.

The god of whom the largest number of stories are told is Kibuka, the war god, Mukasa's brother. According to Stanley's version of the best known of these stories he was a warrior of King Nakivingi (Nakibinge), who in Stanley's list is said to have been the twelfth king of Uganda.[6] Kibuka[7] possessed the art of flying. When Nakibinge was engaged in war against Unyoro he sent for Kibuka from the Islands of the Lake to fight against his enemies. Kibuka came, and by his power of flying in the air he was able to shower great rocks down upon the people of Unyoro and so defeat them. As a part of the spoil, however, Kibuka was given an Unyoro woman as his wife, and this proved his undoing, for, Delilah-like, she "set herself to watch him, and one morning, as he left his hut, she was surprised to see him suddenly mount into the air with a burden of rocks slung on his back". She hastened to betray him to her own people, who shot into the air, and the dead body of the hero was afterwards found by Nakibinge entangled

---

[1] *Baganda*, p. 317.   [2] Wilson and Felkin I, p. 206.
[3] For the legends of Mukasa, see Roscoe, *Baganda*, p. 290ff.
[4] *Baganda*, p. 291.   [5] *Ib.* p. 322.   [6] *T.D.C.* p. 221.
[7] The form of the name in Stanley's version is *Kibaga*.

in the branches of a tree. Nakibinge was himself killed also by the people of Unyoro, so this saga, like the Battle of Kosovo (see Vol. II, p. 313 above), is the story of a heroic defeat.

Roscoe cites a large number of versions of this story.[1] Although Kibuka is described by Stanley as 'a warrior of King Nakivingi', the current belief in Uganda is that the feats were performed by the god himself. According to one version given by Roscoe,[2] Nakibinge consulted the ghost of Kintu in regard to the war which he was waging against Unyoro; according to another version, Wanema, the father of Mukasa.[3] Wanema consented to send Mukasa, the peaceful god, but Nakibinge begged that his brother Kibuka, the war god, might be sent instead, and to this Wanema consented. In this version Kibuka appears to have behaved like a general.

"When he arrived in Uganda the army was organised and taken to the seat of war and there Kibuka communicated his plans to the troops and gave his instructions for the battle. He then went up into a cloud and took up his position over the contending armies." Here also we are told that Kibuka was shot in his cloud by the Banyoro, and alighted on a tree and died.[4]

It is not difficult to account for the variation which makes Kibuka alternately a god of war and a great general. When we reflect that in modern times he had forty mediums, and three priests who were accustomed to accompany him to battle,[5] it will be seen that Kibuka and his attendants formed a body of advisers not unlike the General Staff of a modern War Office.

Mukasa and his relatives would seem to have spread at some period to the mainland from the Sese Archipelago.[6] Wanga, Mukasa's grandfather, and one of the oldest of the gods, is said to have been brought over from his original home on the Sese Islands to Uganda by King Juko to restore the sun to its place in the heavens whence it had fallen. In consequence of his success, the king granted him an estate in Busiro where he remained, and where a temple was afterwards built and provided with priests and a medium.[7] We have just seen that an earlier member of the same family—Kibuka the war god—had been brought over at an earlier date by King Nakibinge.

---

[1] *Baganda*, pp. 217, 302f. Some practices in regard to the worship of Kibuka are also mentioned by Wilson and Felkin I, p. 207.   [2] *Baganda*, p. 217.

[3] *Man*, VII (1907), p. 161. Elsewhere, however, Wanema would seem to be a brother or half-brother of Mukasa. See *Baganda*, p. 314.

[4] *Loc. cit.*   [5] *Loc. cit.*

[6] See Roscoe, *East Africa*, p. 138.   [7] Roscoe, *Baganda*, p. 313; cf. p. 219.

It is also related that Wanema, Mukasa's brother, left Sese in consequence of a quarrel with his brother and that he migrated to Singo in the north of Uganda,[1] 'taking his water-skin with him'. We have already seen that the principal gods of the mainland are related to Mukasa, and it is a significant fact that Mukasa's emblem, the paddle, which Speke observed in the great island sanctuary of 'Mugussa' in Murchison Creek in the Victoria Nyanza,[2] is to be found with scant appropriateness in many mainland temples, e.g. that of Kibuka, the war god.[3] The 'water-skin' of Wamala, brother of Wanema, may be a reminiscence of his original home, and its association with the River Wamala, which flows into the lake of that name, is also interesting.

It will be seen that the gods of the Sese Archipelago form a divine community, like the gods of the ancient Greeks or the early Norse peoples. How far these gods are identified in the stories related above with their priests and mediums, as well as with other human beings,[4] is often difficult to determine. In many cases there can be no doubt that the traditions are at variance as to whether a particular god was of human or divine origin. Kaumpuli, the god of plague, for example, is according to one version, the misshapen offspring of the union of King Juko's brother and a woman of the Civet-Cat Clan, which the gods had forbidden; according to another, he is identified with King Ndaula, Juko's son, who was said to be worshipped as the god of plague (cf. p. 595 below). On the other hand, a number of other gods also exist in Uganda who do not appear to form a part of any community. It is interesting to note that in general these latter gods have not the same wealth of stories attached to them. We have little doubt that a closer scrutiny of the stories of the community of the gods of the Sese Islands, in connection with the traditions of the kings of Uganda, would lead to the conclusion that some at least of these divine stories had their origin in stories relating to the priests and mediums of the temples of these gods.

The Baganda are rich in antiquarian literature. Local legend is found everywhere. Even stories of the origin of place-names occur in the south, though we have not found any among the Baganda. Livingstone relates[5] a local legend very like the Irish *Dindsenchas*, the object of

---

[1] Roscoe, *Baganda*, p. 314.   [2] Speke, p. 394f.

[3] *Baganda*, p. 305.

[4] The remains of the war god Kibuka have been found to contain parts of a human being. See Roscoe, *Baganda*, p. 308, footnote 1; *Man* VII, p. 161 ff.

[5] *M.T.R.* p. 327.

which was to explain the name of Lake Dilolo on the upper Zambezi. Roscoe tells us that most of the rivers of Uganda were thought to have originated from a human being. He relates stories of the origins of the rivers Mayanja, Sezibwa, and the river which flows into Lake Wamala.[1]

Stories from the Northern Bantu which purport to explain the origin of the Universe and of the Heavenly bodies are generally of a puerile character, as is common also elsewhere. In Unyoro stories of the nature of folk-tale are current which purport to explain the functions of the sun and moon. We do not know of any exact parallel from Uganda, but among the Basoko[2] mankind is said to have been created in an imperfect form by a large toad. The moon had intended to create mankind in a perfect form, but, having been forestalled by the toad, he was only able to improve them. In the Basoko story the moon is said to have created the day and night and the seasons, and to have taught mankind the knowledge and use of plants and fruits, and the domestication of animals.

Many of the stories contained in the oral chronicle of the kings referred to above are related in order to explain the origin of certain customs and institutions, and also of places, temples, shrines, etc. Thus Kintu is credited with having introduced domestic animals into Uganda. His grandson[3] or great-grandson[4] Kamiera (Kimera), who was born in Unyoro, is said to have brought with him when he first entered Uganda two peasants, a man and a woman, and the *namasole* or queen mother,[5] as well as two dogs. This looks also like a 'first pair' story. Other antiquarian features appear in Roscoe's version of the story. Thus the place where Kimera's mother rested on her way to the capital became the traditional site of the *namasole's* palace.[6] According to Cunningham, the use of charms is believed to have been first introduced into Uganda by Kimera.[7]

Instances of antiquarian stories of this kind might be multiplied indefinitely. The explanatory element is by no means confined to the lower classes. The story which purports to account for the custom of removing and preserving the lower jaw-bone of the king may well be

---

[1] Roscoe, *Baganda*, pp. 314, 318.
[2] A tribe on the banks of the Aruwimi River which flows into the Congo from the north.
[3] Stanley, *T.D.C.* p. 220f.   [4] *Baganda*, p. 215.
[5] The *namasole* has always been the most important person in the country after the king, by whom she is held in the highest esteem.
[6] *Baganda*, p. 215.   [7] Cunningham, p. 66.

of priestly origin. According to this story Kalimera, the son of King Cwa, died as he was on a journey from Unyoro to Uganda. His followers did not know what to do with the body, but as they would have to prove that he was dead, they took his lower jaw-bone back to Uganda as the principal part to be saved. Henceforth kings and important people have had their lower jaw-bones removed and preserved.[1]

An interesting story is told of Kintu to account for the existence of Death in the world. Kintu, as we have seen, is said to have married a daughter of the sky god Gulu, who lived in Heaven. Her brother Death is said to have followed them to Earth, and to have succeeded in remaining there hidden in a hole in the ground from which he emerges at intervals, despite the efforts of his brother Kaiguzi to capture him and bring him back to Heaven. This appearance of Death is said to have been due to the disappearance of Kintu's wife, who failed to carry out her father's instructions on leaving Heaven.[2] A story is told of a hunter named Mpobe who followed his dogs into a hole and finally came to a settlement of people in the midst of whom was Death.[3] It is a significant fact that the god of Death had a temple at Ntanda in Singo in the north, where there was a deep ravine, and a medium and a priest in attendance.[4] Stories of this kind are very widespread. Emin Pasha relates a story of the 'Great Magician' and his dealings with mankind, the purpose of which is to explain the origin of mankind, and the presence of Death in the world.[5]

With this story we may compare the story of the origin of the temple of Kaumpuli, the god of plague, which is said to have been established between the borders of Uganda and Unyoro on a tract of country which was practically No-Man's Land, in the reign of King Juko. The god is said to have been the misshapen offspring of a marriage between King Juko's brother and a woman of the Civet-Cat Clan, which the gods had forbidden. The woman and her child are said to have been driven from Uganda to Busoga, but the Basoga sent them back to Uganda. They were driven back from each place where they attempted to settle till at last they were allowed to settle in the tract above mentioned. After Kaumpuli's death he was declared by the gods to be the god of plague, and a temple was built for him and his remains placed in it. According

---

[1] Roscoe, *Baganda*, p. 112.
[2] *Ib.* p. 460 ff.; for a variant version of this tradition, see Kagwa, *Customs*, p. 112 f.　　　[3] *Baganda*, p. 465 f.
[4] *Ib.* p. 315 ff.　　　[5] Emin Pasha, p. 92 f.

to some traditions, Kaumpuli is identified with King Ndaula, Juko's
son, who was worshipped as the god of plague.[1] The god was said
to reside in a deep hole in the temple which was covered by skins
securely fastened down to prevent his escape. King Juko was forbidden
to look in the direction of the temple because it was believed that he
would die if he did. For years it was the duty of one of his wives to
hold a bark cloth before his eyes to prevent the catastrophe; but one
day when she was ill the king looked towards the hill on which the
temple stood, and died shortly after.[2]

By far the most important body of antiquarian tradition among the
Baganda, however, relates, as we have already seen, to the origin of
their royal family, their gods, and their clans, though of the clan
traditions unfortunately very few have actually been recorded. The
stories embodying such traditions are largely associated with the names
preserved in the genealogies and lists of kings and chiefs. These
genealogies and lists are retained, as mentioned above (p. 576), in the
memory of specially trained officials, and are preserved with such care
that they serve as valuable material for the history of a country which
is entirely without written records.[3]

The lists of the kings, together with the stories attached to them, are
arranged in chronological order, and thus form what are virtually oral
dynastic chronicles of the kings of Uganda. Of these chronicles we are
fortunate in possessing three versions. Two have already been discussed
to some extent. Of these the longest list of kings was obtained by
Stanley[4] from King Mutesa, while the stories were supplied by an official
of his court. This list contains the names of thirty-five kings down to
and including Mutesa; but Stanley remarks that it is probably incomplete. A second list of kings, together with a large amount of traditional
matter, chiefly in narrative form, was obtained by Roscoe[5] from a
variety of sources, chiefly the priests and mediums of the temples, who
were recommended to him for the purpose by the *katikiro* during the
early years of the present century. This list contains thirty-four kings,
down to and including Daudi Cwa, who is still reigning. The third of
these oral chronicles was published by the *katikiro*, Sir Apolo Kagwa
himself, in his history of Uganda in 1912.[6] As his book is published in

---

[1] See Wilson and Felkin I, p. 206; cf. Roscoe, *Baganda*, p. 219.

[2] *Baganda*, p. 309; cf. *ib.* p. 219.

[3] For the methods used in training the memory and transmitting historical
tradition, see p. 622 below.

[4] *T.D.C.* p. 218 ff.   [5] *Baganda*, p. 214 ff.   [6] Kagwa, *Ekitabo*.

Luganda we have not been able to do more than compare the names of the kings, and the relative chronology and lengths of reigns, with those of the other two lists. His book enumerates thirty-five kings, including Daudi Cwa. It should be mentioned that Wilson also obtained from Mutesa a list of kings,[1] but this naturally does not differ very substantially from that of Stanley. A few kings of Uganda and some stories attached to them are also given by Speke.[2]

It will be seen that these versions of the oral dynastic chronicles of Uganda have been obtained from very different sources, and at wide intervals of time. The amount of correspondence between them is therefore very remarkable. They all contain the same names, with a few exceptions, though they show variations both in regard to the order and the number recorded. These variations are, however, not great. A comparison of the stories in all these versions would be extremely interesting, and would no doubt yield important results for the reconstruction of the history of Uganda.

It has already been made clear that the stories related in the narratives of Stanley and Roscoe are in general very different in tone, even when the stories are founded on identical occurrences. Not infrequently also the actual stories related of a certain king are entirely different. It is important to emphasise the fact, therefore, that the stories have nevertheless enough in common to make it clear that the general nature of the traditions of the kings has been consistently adhered to. Generally speaking the same kings play an important part in both narratives, whereas those of whom no stories are told by Roscoe are generally passed over with a bare mention by Stanley also.[3] Frequently the same event can be detected behind two widely different narratives in the accounts of Stanley and Roscoe. The variations are to be accounted for quite easily in many cases by the difference of the milieu in which the stories have been preserved. It is clear that a large body of historical tradition existed in regard to the kings of Uganda from which the reciter was accustomed to select such episodes and incidents as suited his fancy or his purpose. The general consistency of the relative chronology—no dates are given, of course—speaks strongly in favour of the fundamental reliability of the tradition.

Similar lists of kings, and some few traditions associated with the

[1] Wilson and Felkin I, pp. 197, 219 ff.　　　　[2] Speke, p. 251 ff.
[3] There does not appear to be so much correspondence between the length of narrative apportioned to the respective kings in the *katikiro's* account and those of the other two.

names which they contain, have been obtained also from certain other of the Northern Bantu peoples. Among the people of Ukerewé, on the south-eastern shore of the Victoria Nyanza, Stanley obtained a list of fifteen kings, and a brief antiquarian saga relating to the founder of the dynasty, Ruhinda I, who is described as having led his people into the country in an invasion, and as having introduced the plantain and banana plants.[1] A list of twenty-three kings has also been obtained by Roscoe from Unyoro, and in the majority of cases the names of the mothers and their clans are also recorded.[2] In some cases stories are told of the kings, those which refer to the earliest kings bearing a striking resemblance to the stories of the early kings of Uganda. Other royal lists, such as that obtained by Roscoe from Ankole,[3] and that procured by Kollmann from the 'sultan' of Ussindja,[4] immediately to the south of the Victoria Nyanza, are less reliable.

We have seen that the custom of reciting dynastic chronicles in which the kings are enumerated in chronological sequence with brief sagas was current also among the Galla, and the custom prevails also among the Yoruba and in Ashanti. Similar chronicles also exist among the southern Tuareg. The similarity of these oral dynastic chronicles to the early Norse *Ynglinga Saga* referred to in Vol. 1 (p. 307) of the present work is striking, and is certainly not fortuitous.

In both Unyoro and Uganda antiquarian speculation has been active with regard to the period prior to the dynasties which we have been discussing. Roscoe tells us that the Banyoro claim that the Bachwezi (who, as we shall see, are divine beings represented by priests claiming descent from them) formed a dynasty of kings who reigned for a time and then left the country. "Four other names are also given as being those of kings who formed one dynasty, but these are names only, and nothing at all seems to be known of them: they are Hangi, Nyamenge, Ira, and Kabangera."[5] The Civet-Cat Clan have a tradition that a king called Ntege was reigning in Uganda when Kintu arrived (cf. p. 602 below). In Uganda a monster python called Bemba is said in popular tradition to have been among the early kings of Uganda. The only

---

[1] *T.D.C.* p. 160. [2] *Bakitara*, p. 87 ff.
[3] Roscoe, *Banyankole*, p. 35. When Roscoe first visited the country the people could not furnish him with any information as to the names of their previous rulers; but eleven years later, when he again visited the country, a list of twenty-one rulers was produced. It seems likely that the list had been prepared in the interval in emulation of the royal lists of the Baganda and the Banyoro.
[4] Kollmann, *V.N.* p. 108. [5] Roscoe, *Bakitara*, p. 87.

stories related of him are of the nature of folk-tales, however, and his name does not appear in the list of kings obtained from serious historians. The story of Bemba was related to Cunningham to account for a groove in a rock resembling a python at Kitala.[1]

Antiquarian saga is also widely distributed among the clans in the form of clan histories. According to these traditions five clans were already in the country before the arrival of Kintu. Fifteen are said to have come into the country with Kintu, or to be descended from his sons, while eight are regarded as new-comers, and as having entered the country subsequently to Kintu's arrival.

Mingled with what appears to be genuine tradition is a large amount of antiquarian speculation of an explanatory character. Thus the origin of the clans and their totems is attributed to Kintu, who, when game was becoming scarce in the land, is said to have made a rule that certain kinds of animals should be taboo to certain families.[2] The Lion Clan explain the choice of their totem by a story to the effect that soon after Kintu ascended the throne he killed a lion and left a chief named Sabaganda to flay it and dry the skin. When it was ready, Kintu stood on the skin in the presence of a large crowd and announced to his children that henceforth the animal was to be regarded as sacred.[3]

It is not easy to state briefly, in the space at our disposal, the precise historical value of the oral saga of Uganda. The question resolves itself largely into one of the interpretation of literary (oral) diction, and the comparison of variant versions. It is clear in the first place that several streams of oral traditions relating to the royal line have long been current in Uganda, one of which was preserved by the temple staffs, the other by the more intellectual officers and officials at the court. In addition to these there are also the clan histories, which would no doubt be invaluable as supplementary material. At present very few are available. It is natural that discrepancies will arise between these variant versions. Side by side with the sacerdotal and moral bias which is the predominant characteristic of the stories recorded from the priests and mediums, we find also a strongly-marked credulity. This is incidental to their transmission through an ecclesiastical milieu. On the other hand the element of the marvellous and supernatural, as divorced from divine power, is hardly present. The stories are more sober on the whole than those of the court tradition. The latter, at least in the version

[1] Cunningham, p. 170.
[2] Roscoe, *Baganda*, p. 137.
[3] *Ib.* p. 141.

of Sabadu, have passed through the medium of the professional enter-
tainer, and are bizarre and picturesque at the expense of verisimilitude.

A comparison of Roscoe's and Stanley's versions is especially interesting as showing the widely different complexions which one and
the same story takes when related by men of priestly and courtly preoccupations. Perhaps the most striking instance of this difference of
attitude is afforded by the accounts of Suna's reign. The heroic character
of Sabadu's sagas has already been discussed. The only story related by
Roscoe of this, the greatest of Uganda's kings, is that of the punishment
which befell him for insulting the medium of a god, and of his subsequent repentance and ample amends. But the variant versions of the
story of King Kamanya, and of many of the other kings, are equally
significant. On the other hand a comparison of the Uganda legends of
the early kings with those of neighbouring countries often show surprising similarities. The traditions of Kimera, the grandson of Kintu,
are very similar to those of the early Bunyoro king Ndaula, while
Ndaula's predecessor, King Isaza, is said to have disappeared, like
Kintu himself, after a vain attempt to elude death.

A close scrutiny of the oral traditions as a whole can hardly fail to
convince one that a solid substratum of fact lies behind these variants,
despite their discrepancies. We have seen that the actual genealogies of
the kings are preserved in a form substantially authentic for many
centuries, not only in a direct line, but in the collateral branches also;
and on the basis of these genealogies Roscoe places the Kintu period
about a thousand years ago. Oral tradition in Uganda is thus as old as
in Polynesia. It is important to note therefore that a comparison not
only of one tradition with another, but also of the variant currents of
tradition—priestly, courtly, and clan—show on the whole consistencies
which are more striking than the discrepancies, and which supplement
one another in regard to the general outline of events in a way which
carries conviction.

There can be no doubt that much which strikes us as manifestly
unhistorical in the early stories is really due to our own unfamiliarity
with the court diction, and the general intellectual and cultural, and
especially the spiritual tradition of Uganda. This is nowhere clearer
than in regard to the Kintu Cycle. At first sight this Cycle, as related by
Sabadu, appears to be nothing more or less than a piece of brilliant
fiction. Yet the more one examines it the clearer does its significance
become, if not for the history of individual kings, at least for the history
of the nation.

We have seen that Kintu is represented among the earliest names of both the Baganda and the Ba-Ila lists of rulers. In the former it is the name of a man, in the latter of a woman. It is probable, therefore, that it is not a proper, but a common noun, referring to original ancestors, or progenitors, especially those whose names have been forgotten. It is important to remember that in Uganda in the past, as in Ankole today, it was not the custom to say that the king was dead. He 'went away', or 'went into the forest', like the lion spirits of the Ankole kings. Moreover there is reason to believe that in the past it was the custom in Uganda that when kings grew old or ill, their lives were ended, either by their own hands, or those of their wives or chief ministers or medicine-men, also as in modern Ankole and in ancient Unyoro.[1] Possibly he retired voluntarily, and ended his life in seclusion. Such a custom might well give rise to stories like that of Kintu and some of his successors. It may be that, again as in modern Ankole, their names were soon forgotten. On the other hand it may be that, as in the neighbouring country of Busoga, in early times each royal jaw-bone, instead of having a temple to itself, as is the custom in Uganda, made way for its successor, the superseded jaw-bones, and with them the spirits of the dead kings, being taken to the forest. Whichever explanation we adopt, there can be little doubt that the story of the disappearance of Kintu and of some of his successors is closely connected in some way with early Bantu funeral practices. We have little doubt that the constantly recurrent theme of the search for Kintu is equally closely connected with similar customs.[2]

Kintu is said to have led his people into Uganda from the north-east, crossing the Nile, according to one tradition, at Foweira, and arriving on the borders of the Victoria Nyanza.[3] There is also a tradition that the Baganda came to Uganda by lake, and for years lived on the shore of the great lake in the vicinity of Jungo near their first landing place.[4] These stories, as Roscoe points out,[5] agree with the traditions of other pastoral tribes, who state that their forefathers came from the north-east, and that they have a common ancestry. It is also to be noted that the Baganda speak the same language as the Sese Islanders. Now we

---

[1] Roscoe, *Bakitara*, p. 121.

[2] In this connection we may refer to the Unyoro custom referred to by Roscoe (*Northern Bantu*, p. 16), according to which after a king's funeral, his successor mounted a rock, attended only by a few princesses and his wives; but should any man accompany them, he was captured and speared to death.

[3] Felkin, *Notes*, p. 764.

[4] Roscoe, *East Africa*, p. 138.   [5] *Loc. cit.*

have shown reason for believing (p. 592 above) that the great family of gods of whom Mukasa was the head came to Uganda from the Sese Islands in the Victoria Nyanza. Moreover there is a legend which relates that the sons of Gulu, the sky god—Kintu, and Musisi, the father of Mukasa and Kibuka—came to the earth together.[1] It seems probable on the whole, therefore, that these legends of Kintu and of the family of Mukasa reflect antiquarian traditions of the simultaneous appearance of the ruling families and of the divine community from the north-east, whether by land or water.

An examination of the clan histories shows that these also contain valuable historical data. Like the stories of the kings, these traditions often supplement one another in a manner which carries conviction, and many of them appear to be of considerable antiquity. Some of them refer to times earlier than those recorded in the royal and priestly traditions. While both these represent Kintu as the first king, the Civet-Cat Clan have a tradition that Ntege, the head of their clan, was ruling the country prior to Kintu, and was deposed by him.[2] But the tradition relates that Kintu nevertheless gave him several estates with permission to retain the title of king (*kabaka*), and that when Kintu died his son Cwa married Ntege's daughter. It is further stated that from that time onwards each king has taken a wife from this clan.

It is interesting to observe that of the five clans which are traditionally stated to have been in the country before the arrival of Kintu, the Reed-Buck Clan are believed to have been from a very early date hunters in the Mabira forest in Kyagwe in the east of the country, and to have continued to inhabit the same territory down to the present day.[3] There is no reason to doubt the soundness of this tradition. To this region their hereditary avocation as elephant hunters doubtless gave them an undisputed claim, and it would have been both impracticable and uneconomical to displace them. The Jackal Clan, who claim to have come originally from the island of Nyende in the Nyanza, have the care of the royal canoe, *Namwige*.[4] One branch of the Lung-Fish Clan claim to have come originally from the northern shore of the Nyanza, and to have been connected with canoes and the fishing industry from that time onwards.[5] Many other stories connected with the origin of various clans point to an authentic historical tradition.

The quality of the traditions as a whole cannot claim to be so high as those of Polynesia. On the other hand we have seen that many of the

[1] Roscoe, *East Africa*, p. 137.   [2] Roscoe, *Baganda*, p. 145.
[3] *Ib.* p. 168.   [4] *Ib.* p. 165.   [5] *Ib.* p. 148 f.

elements which at first sight appear to be supernatural, such as the disappearance of Kintu and his successors and the subsequent search, turn out on a closer examination to be in all probability genuine traditions of native customs couched in the characteristic figurative Luganda terminology. Many of the stories of the gods and their intercourse with men are probably referable to their priests or mediums who are thought of as in much closer union with the divinity than is easily conceived by the European mind.

We have seen also that the general tone of the narrative is sober and unusually free from gross exaggeration or the miraculous. We are inclined on the whole therefore to believe that a fuller understanding of the diction of Luganda and of native customs, as well as the customs and traditions of neighbouring peoples, would make it possible to write a sound history of the country based on a comparative study of the great wealth of Baganda genealogical data, and the various schools of oral prose saga—royal, ecclesiastical, aristocratic, and popular. The body of such saga is very much slighter in bulk than is the saga of Polynesia. This is due in part to the smallness of the area, in part to the fact that the material has never been systematically collected. Apart from this, however, we doubt if the relative historical value of the material in the two areas would be found to be very disparate.

Riddles are common, but we have no evidence that as such they possess any distinctive literary form. Their mantic associations in Uganda are made clear by the fact that in the list of mediums of the gods given by the *katikiro*, we find that of Nabagasere, who is described as 'the interpreter of the king's riddles'.[1] This may have reference to the oracles which were often sought by the kings. Miss Werner tells us that at Likoma, an island in Lake Nyasa, riddle contests take place which open with a formula much like that which Griaule heard among the Abyssinians in his caravan[2] and that which Cerulli records among the Galla (cf. p. 559 above). It is interesting to note that the penalty for failing to guess a riddle is said to be quite a heavy one, and consists of oxen.[3]

---

[1] Kagwa, *Customs*, p. 122.   [2] Griaule, *A. J.* p. 221 ff.

[3] Werner, *B.C.A.* p. 214. According to R. S. Rattray, the natives of Angoniland in the Nyasaland Protectorate have a similar custom in regard to riddles, he who is able to ask an insoluble riddle having the right to claim that someone's cattle shall be killed for him. This is done 'in pretence', and he eats the cattle and divulges the answer. See Rattray, *Folk-Lore*, p. 153.

Very little gnomic literature has been recorded, though we suspect that this is due to accident. Roscoe told us that he had heard strings of what sounded like proverbs recited in sequence, each 'proverb' occupying one 'line'. The series was recited without a break for two or three minutes. The performance has the appearance of something like a recitation of the Cottonian or Exeter Book series of Anglo-Saxon gnomic verses discussed in Vol. 1, p. 380 ff. above.

Important indirect evidence for the existence of gnomic sequences in Uganda is furnished by a story related to Stanley by Saruti, an officer of Mutesa's court. This story, to which fuller reference will be made below (p. 612), purports to relate the adventures of Saruti himself as he is returning home from Unyoro, whither he had been sent on a mission by Mutesa. The most interesting of these 'adventures' is an account which Saruti gives of his meeting with 'a very old man with a white beard' who is described as 'a great man at riddles', of which he asked Saruti a great many. Saruti's report of his conversation, however, suggests that his répertoire consisted, not of riddles, but of a wealth of gnomic and mantic utterances, and the old man was evidently a sage.

"That old man was a very wise one, and among some of his sayings was that...'When the old moon is dying, the hunter need never leave home to seek game; because it is well known that he would meet nothing.'

"And he further added, that at that time the potter need not try to bake any pots, because the clay would be sure to be rotten....

"He also said: 'When you see a crookback, you do not ask him to stand straight, nor an old man to join the dance, nor the man who is in pain, to laugh.'

"And what he said about the traveller is very true. 'The man who clings to his own hearth does not tickle our ears, like him who sees many lands, and hears new stories.'"[1]

An interesting combination of gnomic and mantic utterances is recorded by Livingstone from the Makololo on the Zambezi. In describing the effects of smoking *bang*, or Indian hemp, he writes:

"The smoke causes violent coughing in all, and in some a species of frenzy, which passes away in a string of unmeaning words, or short sentences, as, 'the green grass grows', 'the fat cattle thrive', 'the fish swim'. No one in the group pays the slightest attention to the vehement eloquence or the sage or silly utterances of the oracle, who stops abruptly, and the instant common sense returns, looks rather foolish."[2]

[1] Stanley, *Companions*, p. 270. [2] *N.E.Z.* p. 286f.

It is significant that these gnomic utterances were made under the influence of a stimulating drug, which no doubt accounts for the outburst, but could hardly be responsible for originating the exact form in which this 'natural philosophy' is expressed. It is also significant that the impression made on Livingstone was not that the speaker was talking random nonsense. Something in the manner or the matter suggested to him an oracle delivering himself of sage utterances.

It is not stated that the utterances to which Livingstone refers were made in verse, though they were evidently very brief. It seems clear, however, that such mantic utterances were sometimes couched in poetical form. Writing of the Echewa tribe on a tributary of the Zambezi west of Lake Nyasa, Livingstone has the following entry in his diary:

"Last night a loud clapping of hands by the men was followed by several half-suppressed screams by a woman. They were quite eldritch, as if she could not get them out. Then succeeded a lot of utterances as if she were in ecstasy, to which a man responded 'Moio, moio'. The utterances, as far as I could catch, were in five-syllable snatches—abrupt and laboured. I wonder if this 'Bubbling or boiling over' has been preserved as the form in which the true prophets of old gave forth their 'burdens'? One sentence, frequently repeated towards the close of the effusion, was 'linyama uta', 'flesh of the bow', showing that the Pythoness loved venison killed by the bow. The people applauded, and attended, hoping I suppose, that rain would follow her efforts. Next day she was duly honoured by drumming and dancing."[1]

To this passage the editor[2] adds an interesting footnote, which suggests that predictive prophecy formed an element in the mantic utterances of the 'Pythoness':

"Chuma",[3] runs the footnote, "remembers part of her song to be as follows:

> Kowé. kowé. n'an dambwi,
> M'vula léru, korolé ko okwé,
> Waie, ona, kordi, mvula.

He cannot translate it, as it is pure Manganja, but with the exception of the first line—which relates to a little song-bird with a beautiful note—it is a mere reiteration 'Rain will surely come today.'"

Apart from the brief indications mentioned above, evidence for the existence of mantic literature among the Bantu peoples of East Africa is

[1] *Last Journals*, p. 153.   [2] The Rev. H. Waller.
[3] Chuma was in Livingstone's service.

scarce though again we suspect that this is due to the defective nature of our records. Kagwa mentions that at the ceremony known as the 'capturing of ghosts' to cure a sick person, the party of ghost-catchers sat on the floor and sang songs, as a result of which one of their number became possessed by the ghost and spoke in his person, as it were.[1] Roscoe told us that spells and charms were common in the past. Spells were recited by travellers as they crossed a river, but in this case we have no evidence that they contained more than a few words, or that they had any claims to literary form. Such spells were provided by the prophets or priests.[2] On the other hand there is ample evidence for the currency of mantic literature among the southern Bantu. Junod mentions the widespread use of exorcism among the Ba-ronga, especially in the case of sick persons:

"Ces singuliers guérisseurs chantent: ils lui parlent, le flattent, le supplient sur des airs à la fois sauvages et doux dont les paroles ne manquent point de poésie.

> Viens (disent-ils), viens t'ébattre dans la plaine;
> Dehors déjà les oiseaux chantent et jouent.
> Viens aussi jouer, ô Esprit."[3]

The writer tells us that there is a whole anthology of exorcism chants. Rattray has also recorded a lengthy spell from the Angoni which is chanted by the medicine-man as he stirs the concoction used for the poison ordeal.[4]

Prose stories of the kind which we commonly call folk-tales are very numerous everywhere among the Northern Bantu.[5] The chief examples of stories of this class from the Baganda and the neighbouring peoples are animal folk-tales; but before passing to a consideration of these we should like to call attention to a remarkable series of stories which relate to men and women who are apparently not unknown to the narrator apart from the particular stories in which they figure, but which in other respects correspond to European folk-tales. These stories appear to be especially common among the Basoko, on the upper Congo; but examples have been found also among other tribes in this

[1] Kagwa, *Customs*, p. 127.
[2] We may compare the ceremonies at the ford of the Tano River in Ashanti described by Rattray, *Ashanti*, p. 199 ff.
[3] Junod, *Chants*, p. 52. [4] Rattray, *Folk-Lore*, p. 87 ff.
[5] The chief collection of such stories with which we are familiar is contained in Stanley's volume, *My Dark Companions and their Strange Stories*.

region, e.g. among the Manyema. The heroes and heroines are represented as the local chiefs and their families; but similar stories are also
told of persons of whom the historical existence is very doubtful.

These stories are among the purest type of narratives related solely
for the purpose of entertainment of which the actual texts have been
recorded among the Northern Bantu. The perfunctory moral which is
sometimes tacked on at the end is due to the demands of the audience,
and obviously forms no part of the original story, as the narrator tells
us quite clearly.[1] It is a remarkable fact that the interest of these stories
is exclusively feminine, and although they frequently relate to people
of chiefly rank, they are markedly non-heroic in character. They are
concerned exclusively with domestic and marital relations. None of
them deal with warfare, or the relations between clan and clan, or even
between village and village.

The *Story of Maranda* tells how a wife is ill-used by her husband, and
is finally rescued by signalling from a tree-top to a passing canoe which
quickly bears the tidings to her father. *The Queen of the Pool* is also a
story of an ill-used wife who escapes and lives as a hermit in the woods,
surrounded by the birds and beasts which she has tamed. In both cases
the wicked husbands are duly punished.

King Gumbi's Lost Daughter is based on the well-worn motif of a
king's daughter who is saved from death in childhood and secretly
brought up against the king's orders by her grandmother. It relates the
joyful reunion of the daughter and her parents, her marriage, and the
death of the bridal pair in the cataracts. Even the story of *Kitinda and
her Wise Dog* is a purely domestic story of marketing and local gossip.
It will be seen that, as in our own folk-tales, the cruel and oppressive
come to a bad end, or are at least defeated. Cunning and feminine beauty
are exalted without discrimination or individuality. The men and
women are hardly humanised. They are the stock properties of the
village social organisation.

In many respects the animal folk-tales are in marked contrast to these
village domestic stories. They are full of individuality and careful
observation. The habits and peculiarities of the different species of
animals are noted with the eye of an expert field naturalist. This is
particularly noticeable in the stories of the two Waganda, Kadu and
Sabadu. Kadu himself explains how he has come by his knowledge of
their ways and appearance:

"'Master', began Kadu, after we had made ourselves comfortable

[1] Stanley, *Companions*, p. 96.

before a bright and crackling fire, 'some men say that animals do not reason, and cannot express themselves, but I should like to know how it is that we perceive that there is great cunning in their actions, as though they calculated beforehand how to act, and what would be the result. We Waganda think animals are very clever. We observe the cock in the yard, and the hen with her chickens; the leopard, as he is about to pounce on his prey; the lion, as he is about to attack; the crocodile, as he prepares for his rush; the buffalo in the shade, as he awaits the hunter; the elephant, as he stands at attention; and we say to ourselves, how intelligent they are! Our legends are all founded on these things, and we interpret the actions of animals from having seen their methods; and I think men placed in the same circumstances could not have acted much better. It may appear to you, as though we were telling you mere idle tales to raise a laugh. Well, it may be very amusing to hear and talk about them, but it is still more amusing to watch the tricks of animals and insects, and our old men are fond of quoting the actions of animals to teach us, while we are children, what we ought to do. Indeed, there is scarcely a saying but what is founded upon something that an animal was seen to do at one time or another.'"[1]

It is a striking fact, however, that the animals, true to nature as they are, are far more human than the human beings. Combined with keen observation of the habits and instincts of the animal world is an imaginative projection of the narrator's sympathy on the situation and its possibilities, as they appear to a human being. When Dog is cloyed with the delicious repasts of fresh meat supplied by his mistress Leopardess, by whom he and Jackal are employed in the capacity of domestic servants, he pleads with her as follows:

"'Well, you see, mistress, I fear you do not understand the nature of dogs very well. You must know dogs delight in marrow, and often prefer it to meat. The latter by itself is good, but however plentiful and good it may be, without an occasional morsel of marrow it is apt to pall. Dogs also love to sharpen their teeth on bones and screw their tongues within the holes for the sake of the rich juice. By itself, marrow would not fatten my ribs; but meat with marrow is most delectable. Now, good mistress, seeing that I have been so faithful in your service, so docile and prompt to do your bidding, will you not be gracious enough to let me gnaw the bones and extract the marrow?' 'No', roared Leopardess decisively, 'that is positively forbidden....And you, Jackal, bear what I say well in mind', she continued, turning to that

[1] Stanley, *Companions*, p. 198.

servile subordinate. 'Yes, mistress; I will, most certainly. Indeed, I do not care very greatly for bones', said Jackal, 'and I hope my friend and mate, Dog, will remember, good mistress, what you say.'"[1]

The success of the Waganda animal tales lies in the humanity of the animals. As Kadu points out, they behave as we should behave if we were situated as they are. A sympathetic and keenly observant attention has noted how different is the situation of each class of animal and bird —how different are the problems which each must solve for himself, how disparate are their appearance, their needs, and power of aggression and defence. The creatures are individualised into a convincing personality which is lacking to the human beings of the Basoko stories. The rabbit, because he is small and weak, is cowardly, but he manages to survive by means of his wits. The elephant is powerful and almost invulnerable. He is therefore dignified and nonchalant. It is not worth his while to be the aggressor, and besides, he does not require meat. But the leopard is hungry for blood, especially the blood of small defenceless animals, such as abound near human habitations, and therefore he is cruel, and every man's hand is against him.

It may be said that the Waganda deliberately combine an imaginary representation of how human beings would act with a picture of how animals do act in given situations. Both Sabadu and Kadu, the two Waganda story-tellers, were men of Mutesa's court. They have had exceptional opportunities of watching men and manners, and have lived in an atmosphere where a good joke is appreciated. The result is that their animal stories are not only veiled pictures of humanity, but they are also social satires, redolent of wit and humour. Kadu's story of the council of the larger animals is an admirable parody of a human palaver. Every beast says his say, and each says exactly the same thing as his neighbour, only each says it in his own words and his own way. Each is careful to make his speech in set terms and formally, all are aware of the dignity of the occasion. All are sententious and consequential. Again, the picture of leopardess in her relations with dog and jackal is an admirable satire of a well-to-do fussy mamma, desiring to pose as a beneficent mistress, but actually living solely for herself and her pampered cubs. And in the background is the sleek, well-fed, deceitful but not ill-natured servants' hall, represented by dog and jackal.

There is a philosophy behind the best of the Waganda animal tales, perhaps behind all African animal tales. They imply a full acceptance

[1] Stanley, *Companions*, p. 164.

of the fact that knowledge is power. They are not only non-heroic. They are strongly and deliberately anti-heroic. They are the outcome of a belief and a teaching that no social organisation, and no brute force, however great, can triumph over activity of brain. The animals, in the story of *Kibatti the Little*, attempt a combine of all their heaviest weights in concerted action against mankind, but they are defeated by man, or rather by a clever little boy. Stork, from her strategic position on a high tree, seems safe from her enemy tortoise; but she goes to sleep, while tortoise thinks out, not how he can attack her himself, but how he can utilise the qualifications of serpent for the business. Dog is not so strong or so brave as leopardess, but he knows where his best interests lie and flees to those who give him good protection—and this although he is certainly in the wrong, and leopardess has good cause of complaint against him.

This philosophical conviction of the superiority of brain to everything else is especially interesting because it is even stronger than morality. Kadu's story of the animals makes this clear. For the attack of the animals on mankind, it is to be observed, is a righteous attack. The animals are fussy to get their consciences clear on this score at the preliminary meeting. It is not because man is their enemy that they are out against him. As lion remarks, the animals themselves have their own mutual feuds and grievances, but they are up and above board and without malice. "Friend Buffalo and our family have sometimes a sharp quarrel, but there is no malice in it." The real grievance against man is twofold. In the first place, his mode of attack is not gentlemanly, not 'heroic'. Lion admits that "The four-footed tribes have much cause of grievance against me and mine. However, none can accuse my family of having taken undue advantage of those whom we meditate striking. We always give loud warning, as you all know, and afterwards strike....But these pestilent two-footed beasts—by net, trap, falling stake, pit, or noose—are unceasing in their secret malice, and there is no safety in the plain, bush, or rock-fastness against their wiles." The second and perhaps the greater grievance is the wantonness of human cruelty and bloodthirstiness. Again we quote lion: "For what I and my kin do there is good motive—that of providing meat for ourselves and young; but it passes my wit to discover what the son of man can want with all he destroys. Even our bones—as, for instance, thy long teeth, O Elephant—they carry away with them, and even mine. I have seen the younglings of mankind dangle the teeth of my sister round their necks, and my hide appears to be so precious that the king of the village wears it over his dirty black loins." Leopard is of the same mind: "We have our own quarrels in the woods—as ye all know—and they are sharp and quick while they last, but there is no premeditation or malignity in what we do to one another; but Man, to whom we would rather give a wide berth, if possible, pursues each of us as if his existence depended upon the mere slaying, though I observe that he has abundance of fruit, which ought to satisfy any reasonable being of the ape tribe."

Was ever the animal point of view more convincingly stated? But right is not might. For it is man who triumphs, even though the animals unite and make war with all the strategy of a human army and conquer for a brief space. This philosophy of the African folk-tales is an important factor of African reasoning. The Waganda are more aware than we are ourselves that it is not by superior organisation or military strength that we wave a union jack over a black king with a lion skin hung about him, but by superior knowledge.

It is not only in virtue of their philosophical meaning that the Waganda sagas are more advanced than the Basoko anecdotes. Kadu's stories also show an advanced artistic technique. His manipulation of dialogue is masterly in its economy and concentrated wit. The humour of a situation is never lost on him, nor the pathos. And he knows by heart all the ignoble ruses by which humanity try to gain their own ends at the cost of their fellows. He knows that although Miss Crane and young Terrapin may make a bargain, in the pangs of hunger, to eat their 'mas', yet young Terrapin, once his appetite is satisfied, will feel filial compunctions and dishonour his bond. But Kadu does not hurry to the point. He opens up in a leisurely way, chatty and amiable-like: "How is your family to-day, Miss Crane?"

"Oh, very well. Mamma, who is getting old, complains now and then, that's all."

"But do you know that it strikes me that she is very fat?" said Terrapin, and so on. Naturally when they have eaten ma Crane and ma Terrapin is not forthcoming, Miss Crane is very angry. The dialogue and the incidents which follow are full of humanity and of humour.[1]

The admirable social and dramatic instincts of the Waganda are seen perhaps in their most advanced form in their inability to blacken their own villains. Humorous sympathy invariably intrudes itself and allows them to escape. The Terrapin's refusal to give up his ma to the pot is indefensible, as he has battened off Mrs Crane; but Kadu is not the fellow to be hard on young Terrapin when his heart yearns to his ma.

[1] Stanley, *Companions*, p. 213.

His cautionary story of Dog and Leopardess is equally distorted in its morality. Leopardess feeds her household so well that they can never fairly complain. When she and the cubs have eaten all they can there is quite enough left over for Dog and Jackal. The cubs too are graciously condescending, nice children to look after. Moreover Dog is warned explicitly by Leopardess, and has three chances, even after his transgression with the juicy bone, before the end comes. His fault costs Leopardess the life of her cub and there is not a word to be said for greedy Dog. But for all that Leopardess is a horrid woman and we are glad Dog gets off unpunished.

All travellers among the Waganda from the time of Speke onwards are impressed by their light-heartedness and love of laughter and jokes. This strongly developed social sense is present everywhere in the stories. They are carefully planned with intent to amuse at all costs. Even the gods are not safe from the irreverent Sabadu's love of fun. When Rabbit can think of no better way of getting the animals to help him to drive home his cow, he claims that he has been commissioned by the god Mukasa to drive the cow home to his feast, whereupon all lend a ready hand.[1]

It is clear both from their setting—the circumstances under which they were told to Stanley—and from internal evidence, that the animal stories, like the village histories, traditions, and anecdotes of the Basoka, are stories worked up for purposes of entertainment. Such was probably not their origin however. We have seen that Kadu received his moral and intellectual education largely in this form from the 'old men'. Their origin is didactic, and the didactic is never wholly lost sight of. It is, in fact, demanded by the audience as sanctioned by tradition, and few of the story-tellers forget to add the moral to their tale. Stanley tells us that "Whenever a real aborigine of the interior undertook to tell a tale of the old days, we were sure to hear something new and striking; the language became more quaint, and in almost every tale there was a distinct moral."[2]

Apart from these stories we have little didactic literature from Uganda. We may, however, include here the *Adventures of Saruti*, referred to above (p. 604). This saga is narrated by Saruti, an officer of Mutesa. It purports to relate a series of adventures and experiences which befell the reciter on his return from a journey to Unyoro. The framework of the story is reminiscent of the oral chronicles in that the whole resembles a series of saga summaries. A string of villages is

[1] Stanley, *Companions*, p. 250.　　　　[2] *Ib.* p. 2.

named in sequence, each having one brief story related of it. It probably represents Saruti's répertoire, from which he would know how to select, and which he would no doubt expand as occasion demanded. The list is most varied, from antiquarian speculation and marvellous stories of beasts and birds, to simple anecdotes of village life, and huntsman's adventures. Some of them are so palpably mendacious that Saruti saw fit to enlist Mutesa's favour with a compliment half-way through. "Knowing that I was on the king's business, they did not dare tell me their fables."[1] The most interesting of Saruti's adventures is his account of the old man with a white beard, who recited to him the gnomes already mentioned.

Before leaving the subject of the animal stories of the Northern Bantu and of the education of the young, we should like to call attention to a passage from Casalis which has reference to the educational methods of the Basuto. The passage refers especially to the instruction given to youths as a part of the teaching which accompanies the exercises and discipline of the young initiates. These are said to cover a period of about six months.

"The young scholars are made to learn a number of little compositions which generally consist of descriptions of animals or narratives of hunting and military expeditions. The metre is perfectly regular, and the style not wanting in poetry...."

The author then gives us an example of a verse descriptive of carrion birds:

> These white birds,
> Streaked with black,
> What do they eat up there?
> They eat fat,
> The fat of a zebra,
> Of a coloured zebra,
> Of striped colours,
> With noisy nostrils,
> With resounding feet.
> Far off, yonder far off,
> The haze is thick.
> When it is dispersed
> There is a breast which will resound (that of the lion).

"In this rustic academy", adds Casalis, "they employ themselves with the study of the principal phenomena of nature, and the lack of scientific explanations is supplied by the most attractive allegories."[2]

[1] *Ib.* p. 269. [2] *The Basutos*, p. 265.

Again the same writer tells us:

"These wondering youths are taught that the sun is a man and the moon a woman. Peals of thunder are compared to the flapping of the wings of a gigantic bird. The...earth is likened to a prodigious animal, on which beings infinitely smaller are sporting about. The rocks are the bony framework of the monster, the vegetable earth his flesh, and the rivers his blood."[1]

Our information relating to the art and technique of the Baganda story-teller is exceptionally rich. The collection of stories which we have been considering was recited by Stanley's men round the camp fire in the evening after the day's march. Kassim and Baruti, two of the Basoko, tell us something of the native conditions under which such stories were told and handed on, and these evenings round Stanley's camp reminded Baruti of the evenings spent in story-telling in his own village. When the Basoko were accused by a Zanzibari of having invented their stories, Baruti replied with an indignant look:

"We heard them of course...for how could Kassim or I imagine such things? I heard something each day almost from the elders, or the old women of the tribe. My mother also told me some, and my big brother told me others. At our village talk-house, scarcely a day passed but we heard of some strange thing which had happened in old times. It is this custom of meeting around the master's fire, and the legends that we hear, that reminds us of what we formerly heard, and by thinking and thinking over them the words come back anew to us.... When our old men were in good-humour, and smoked their long pipes, and the pot of wine was by their side, and we asked them to tell us somewhat about the days when they were young, they would say, 'Listen to this now', and they would tell us of what happened long ago. It is the things of long ago that we remember best, because they were so strange that they clung to the mind, and would not altogether be forgotten."[2] From Kassim we learn that it was from his mother and the old women who used to come and sit with her that he had first listened to the recital of stories.[3] Kadu, the Muganda, as we have seen, learned them from the 'old men' as a part of his education.[4]

How much in the animal stories of the Baganda is really due to the skill of Sabadu and Kadu may be gauged by glancing at the collection of animal tales in the summary form given in the Appendix to Roscoe's

[1] *The Basutos*, p. 266.
[2] Stanley, *Companions*, p. 327f.
[3] *Ib.* p. 297.
[4] *Ib.* p. 199.

Baganda. It is clear that the Baganda had developed the art of telling animal stories to a high standard. The art was not confined to Kadu and Sabadu, for Chakanja, also a Muganda lad, tells the story of the Elephant and the Lion with all the merit which we have noted in the tales of the other two, and moreover with an elaborate preamble in which he claims that to hear good news, or a lively story, is one of the three things of which the Baganda are most fond, the other two with which it is equated being to have a nice wife and a pleasant farm.[1] Chakanja himself recognises how much the merit of his tale will depend on his powers as a raconteur.[2]

We have no doubt that the high standard of the art of story-telling in Uganda is due in part to court patronage. Bujomba, one of Stanley's retinue, represents Mutesa as hanging on the words of a man recounting his travels with the keenest attention.

"Mutesa was ever fond of a good story, and loved to question those whom he sent to distant countries, until you might say that there was nothing left in a man worth hearing after he had done with him. But Saruti did not need any questioning. He talked on and on without stopping, until Mutesa could not sit up longer for sheer weariness.... He was very amusing, and Mutesa laughed heartily many times as he listened to him."[3]

Stanley has told us something of the artistic devices by which Sabadu gave life to the narratives of the Baganda and held the interest of his audience:

"Sabadu was unequalled in the art of story-telling; he was fluent and humorous, while his mimicry of the characters he described kept everybody's interest on the alert. To the Rabbit of course he gave a wee thin voice, to the Elephant he gave a deep bass, to the Buffalo a hollow mooing. When he attempted the Lion, the veins of his temple and neck were dreadfully distended as he made the effort; but when he mimicked the dog, one almost expected a little terrier-like dog to trot up to the fire, so perfect was his yaup-yaup. Everyone agreed as Sabadu began his story that his manner, even his style of sitting and smoothing his face, the pose of his head, betrayed the man of practice."[4]

In his prefatory remarks to the story of *Kibatti the Little who conquered all the Great Animals* Stanley says that he "despairs of rendering

[1] *Ib.* p. 64. [2] *Ib.* p. 65.
[3] *Ib.* p. 260 ff.
[4] *Ib.* p. 244 f.

the little touches and flourishes which Kadu knew so well how to give with voice, gesture, and mobile face."[1]

Speaking of the natives of Nyasaland Miss E. Kidney remarks: "Any one who has heard a native telling stories to his companions round a camp fire at night will know of the subtleties of expression and change of voice that he puts in, and the cute way he portrays each character in the yarn he is telling."[2]

The story-tellers have their own conventions, one of which is an affected shyness or reluctance to begin. "Like a singer who always professes to have a cold before he indulges his friends with a song, Chakanja needed more than a few entreaties; but finally, after vowing that he never could remember anything, he consented to gratify us."[3] The trick was not peculiar to the Baganda however. It is shared by the Basoko.[4]

Felkin draws a distinction between the treatment of the 'text' of what he styles professional and non-professional story-tellers:

"The Waganda are very fond of reciting, and in this way legends have been handed down from generation to generation, and one notices that the same story told by an old man and a young one, although having one and the same main idea, yet varies considerably in detail and style. This is less the case when the stories are told by professional story-tellers or sung by the bards. In such cases almost identical sequence is followed, the same sentences and modes of expression being preserved as accurately as the incidents themselves."[5]

Something has already been said of the composition and recitation of occasional and choral poetry, and more especially of the widespread prevalence of the custom of chanting poetry to accompany any physical movement or manual labour which calls for rhythmical communal action. We have seen that songs of this kind are generally extempore, and that the verses are composed by a coryphaeos, while the rest of the men join in the refrain. The coryphaeos is usually the same person, who has specialised in the art.[6] Among some of the Ba-ronga he is regularly paid for his task,'[7] and is, in fact, a professional poet in his

[1] Stanley, *Companions*, p. 221.
[2] E. Kidney, *Songs*, p. 116.
[3] Stanley, *Companions*, p. 64. [4] *Ib.* p. 4; cf. pp. 31, 44.
[5] Felkin, *Notes*, p. 763 f.
[6] See, e.g. Stanley, *H.I.f.L.* pp. 351, 621 f., 276 f.
[7] Junod, *Chants*, p. 49.

own line. Songs of this kind are generally unaccompanied, but among some tribes, such as the Batoka, the coryphaeos accompanies his chanting to the music of a primitive stringed instrument such as a *sansa*, or one-stringed fiddle.

More interesting for our purpose are the higher types of individual minstrelsy, such as are practised by court and other professional minstrels and by cultivated amateurs. The recitation of poetry to the harp is widespread among the Northern Bantu, and is of the nature of a polite accomplishment. We have already seen (p. 582 above) that among the Basoga love and drinking songs are commonly sung by the men to the accompaniment of the harp.[1] In Ankole the harp is used by the women in their houses to accompany the love ditties which they sing to their husbands;[2] and in his description of a 'sitting dance', Roscoe mentions that the women, who were too fat to dance, "sat together inside the kraal, and one of them played a harp and sang, while the others moved their bodies and arms."[3] Among the Bagesu also, a tribe of Mount Elgon, the harp is used to accompany songs indoors, but is not used in public songs and dances. The girls are said to sing love poetry to the accompaniment of small instruments of reeds after the pattern of a zither.[4]

The most interesting instance of the composition of poetry by women among the Northern Bantu is recorded by the *katikiro* from Uganda. We are told that when King Mwanga, aided by the Europeans in Uganda, was fighting against his brother Kalena, the ladies in Suna's temple[5] heard of it, and composed a derisive song against Mwanga. We shall see later (p. 628) that these ladies were the 'permanent' occupants of the temple-tomb of the dead king. It is therefore especially interesting to find that they took an active interest in the politics of a reign considerably 'after their day', as we may say, and that they continued to share the intellectual and artistic life of Uganda, composing poems on contemporary events, and even 'taking sides'. It is also relevant to their official position as wives of Suna, long dead, and also it would seem of his predecessor Kamanya, that their

[1] Roscoe tells us that this is only report. He never heard these obscene songs sung.

[2] Roscoe, *Northern Bantu*, p. 140.

[3] Roscoe, *Banyankole*, p. 81, where a picture of the performance is also given.

[4] Roscoe, *Northern Bantu*, p. 189.

[5] The word used in the translation is 'palace', but the reference is undoubtedly to Suna's temple enclosure. See p. 628 below. Suna became king in 1810, Kamanya in 1790 (Kagwa, *Customs*, pp. 42, 50).

poem has primary reference to Suna himself, and even to Kamanya
also:

> Let Suna be told, where he is at Wamala.... [1]
> And also Kamanya at Kasadja,
>   Let him be told
> Kabaka Mwanga spends his days at Kampala.
> He will suffer the consequences.... [2]

The Baganda are said to be especially musical as a nation, and to be
very fond of singing to the *nanga*, or harp. The ancient type of Baganda
harp, and the smaller Basoga harp which has largely taken its place in
recent years, have already been described. The kings and important
chiefs have regular private orchestras of stringed instruments, which
are led by conductors. Some of these bands are said to have numbered
as many as forty or fifty performers; but they are mostly composed of
the Basoga, who are said to be the best harpists in Central Africa.[3]
When Mutesa's envoys accompanied the Rev. W. Felkin to England,
they brought their harps with them, and the missionary tells us that he
was often surprised to hear them, after they had retired for the night,
persevering until they had reproduced some catching melody which
they had heard during the day.[4] They are said to be very clever at
picking up new tunes.[5]

The professional minstrels about whom our information is fullest
are the court poets of Uganda. These men were privileged members of
the court whom the king frequently admitted into his councils. Roscoe's
account of them is as follows:

"The old harp used at the court of the King and chiefs used to be
accompanied by songs belauding the King's power and benevolence,
praising him, and belittling his enemies. The words were made up to
fit the tunes at a moment's notice, and were suited to passing events.
Both the King and the chiefs had musicians, who were expected to come
forward and play, especially when the evening meal was ended. The
bard was usually a man who had been deprived of his sight, that he
might not look upon the court ladies,[6] or fall in love with them, and
who made it his business to learn all the gossip of the day, and to retail

---

[1] This is possibly a reference to a myth associated with the god Wamala, son of
Musisi, the earthquake god (cf. p. 593 above), in which a quarrel takes place between
Wamala and his brother (see Kagwa, *Customs*, p. 114).

[2] Kagwa, *Customs*, p. 114.

[3] Wilson and Felkin I, p. 216; Felkin, *Notes*, p. 749.

[4] Felkin, *Notes*, p. 751.   [5] Felkin, *ib.* p. 749.

[6] See, however, p. 619 below.

it in his songs. In this way he would entertain his hearers as they sat together in the evening. The older and more popular songs were the traditions and legends of the nation sung in the minor key."[1]

Ashe notes that most of the Baganda minstrels were blind. He tells us that it was the custom to put out the eyes of the court performers, as it was believed that they thus became more proficient in their art.[2] Grant mentions that the queen generally had a blind minstrel performing to the harp in her court.[3] At the courts of the chiefs also blind minstrels were regularly to be met;[4] but this feature is not confined to Uganda, or apparently to court minstrels. Grant also refers to a blind minstrel of Ukuni in Karagwe who used to entertain him with songs.[5] In Karagwe the minstrels seem to have been frequently old women who performed to the *nanga* like men. Some of these appear to have been good musicians. Grant mentions one whose instrument had seven strings, of which six were a perfect scale, only the seventh being faulty.[6]

Reference has already been made (p. 576 above) to the court minstrels who recite the oral dynastic histories at state functions. Roscoe told us that there would generally be at least two official minstrels at a time at the court of Uganda. It was by no means unusual for a minstrel to perform continuously for three hours, and that beginning about six, he would continue to play and sing till eleven in the evening. He also told us that he had heard of poetic contests having taken place between them. Nothing is known of their training for their office, but boys were always in attendance on them as their pupils. The minstrels themselves were in the habit of absenting themselves for considerable periods of time from the court, and he believed that on such occasions they were in the habit of visiting the courts of other chiefs. During their visits to neighbouring courts they learned the songs current there, and repeated them to their own people on their return. Thus a Baganda minstrel on a visit to Unyoro would bring back with him fresh songs from Unyoro with which to entertain his Baganda audience, and the similarity of the various Bantu languages greatly facilitates such a practice. Similarly Junod makes constant reference to the adoption on

---

[1] Roscoe, *Baganda*, p. 35 f.
[2] *Two Kings*, p. 107. We believe that the Baganda are right, and that a person plays the harp better blind, or in the dark, or blindfold than when using his eyes.
[3] Grant, p. 245.
[4] *Baganda*, p. 35.
[5] Grant, p. 83.
[6] *Ib.* p. 183.

a large scale of Zulu songs by the Ba-ronga of Delagoa Bay.[1] Living-stone's Batoka minstrel composed extempore songs in which he re-hearsed their deeds ever since they left their own country, and his songs contained "a history of everything he had seen in the land of the white men and on their way back".[2]

The blind minstrel whose photograph is given by Roscoe in *The Baganda* (p. 35) does not appear to have any unusual features in his dress, but other accounts suggest that a certain type of costume was favoured by the Basoga minstrels, which aimed at representing old men, and perhaps primitive men also. As Emin Pasha was on his way to the capital of Uganda he met a minstrel dressed in the fleece of a long-haired Usoga goat, and disguised by a long pointed beard, which partly covered his mouth. He seated himself in the midst of a circle of spectators and began to play on his seven-stringed instrument, com-mencing with a short prelude, and passing into a "recitative of simple rhythm, praising the beads and the generosity of the white man".[3] Felkin also mentions that one day, as he was dining with the *katikiro*, three or four musicians played pleasing melodies at the door of the hut, after which a minstrel ornamented with a fantastic head-dress, and having a long goat's beard attached to his chin, played and sang to the harp in the courtyard outside.[4]

When not engaged in actually performing, the minstrels of the Northern Bantu appear to stand apart from their fellow-men by certain striking peculiarities of behaviour. Roscoe told us that when one of these minstrels was met on the road he was immediately recognisable by his excited and apparently uncontrolled manner. He waved his arms about and muttered, and his behaviour resembled that of a man possessed. Grant also was struck by the wild and excited manner of the minstrel sent to entertain him when he was ill in Karagwe.[5]

"The man boldly entered...and looked a wild, excited creature. After resting his spear against the roof of the hut he took a 'nanga' from under his arm and commenced. As he sat upon a mat with his head averted from me, never smiling, he sang something of his having been sent to me, and of the favourite dog Keeromba. The wild yet gentle music and words attracted a crowd of admirers, who sang the dog-song for days afterwards, as we had it encored several times."[6]

[1] Junod, *Chants*; see especially p. 40. Cf. Werner, *B.C.A.* p. 220.
[2] Livingstone, *N.E.Z.* p. 236.
[3] Emin Pasha, p. 32.
[4] Felkin, *Notes*, p. 719.
[5] Grant, p. 183.
[6] Grant, *loc. cit.*

In general the minstrels of Karagwe seem to have resembled those of Uganda very closely. Here also they were generally blind. Grant tells us that during his stay in the country one blind man used to visit him periodically, and, without even the aid of a dog, knew every turn in the village; he was welcomed everywhere, and would stand by moonlight singing for two hours at a time with a crowd of a hundred people, men and women, the Sultan amongst them, all round him, joining in a chorus. Yet another blind man used to gather the village boys around him and teach them the songs of their country, while he beat time with his foot.[1]

Enough has been said to show that the art of extempore composition is very widely cultivated among the Northern Bantu, both by amateur and professional minstrels. We have seen also that ephemeral songs were very frequently repeated by all classes of the population for some time after their first recitation—so long, in fact, as the novelty of the subject excited any interest. Far more often, it would seem, the song perished after a single recitation. What is of more interest and importance, however, is the fact that there is ample evidence that a considerable body of more serious and ambitious poetry has been handed down from past times, and is preserved by a verbal tradition which is more or less word-perfect.

A striking instance of this verbal exactitude is given by Bishop O'Ferrall in connection with the song discussed above (p. 581) from the Ba-bemba of Northern Rhodesia. The bishop heard it recited by a man of thirty-five years of age who had heard it in his youth in his own village, and had himself sung it many times. This man could repeat the song again and again with hardly any variation in the words. He himself had only heard it sung round the camp fire; though he says it was originally sung by warriors dancing round the heads of the slain. The song was never accompanied by any instrumental music.

In his discussion of the court minstrelsy of Uganda Roscoe tells us that in reciting the past history of the country the minstrel invariably repeated with scrupulous exactitude precisely the same incidents in each repetition. When, however, he was reciting incidents which had taken place during the régime of the king reigning in his own day, he selected incidents at pleasure, reciting one day one incident, another day another incident. That is to say, the narration of past history had become static,

---

[1] Grant, p. 83f. With this we may compare Miss Werner's account of the 'itinerant poet' or 'dancing man' among the tribes on the Shire River in Nyasaland who teaches the children the chorus of his songs, and then carries on a dialogue of song with his audience. Werner, *B.C.A.* p. 221.

that of contemporary history was still dynamic. So far as we can re-collect, however, from Roscoe's (verbal) account, an incident once recited by a court minstrel on a formal occasion at the court was fixed for all time. Whenever that particular incident was selected for poetical celebration in future, it must be recited in the same form. Felkin also observed that "when the stories are told by professional story-tellers or sung by the bards...almost identical sequence is followed, the same sentences and modes of expression being preserved as accurately as the incidents themselves".[1]

The system is of peculiar interest as it seems to form a primitive official history on which the royal seal was set by the first hearing. We would gladly have known more of the matter. Are we, for example, to suppose that the composition of this official history was a monopoly, or was there competition among the royal minstrels? And in any case, as the many incidents of a contemporary reign must have formed more numerous themes than those of past reigns, which we are told were invariably repeated at each recitation, on what principle was a selection made in the succeeding reign from all these incidents for the static history? These are only a few of the many questions that call for further elucidation in this remarkable form of public record office.

Before leaving the subject of historical tradition, however, it should be mentioned that we have from the *katikiro* himself an interesting note on the methods employed for the training of the memory of those who were responsible for handing on traditions, and of the methods used in private for their transmission. These men, we are told, were trained from childhood by their parents. They were made familiar with state procedure, and with the traditions, including the names of the kings, their wives, chiefs, and so forth.

"The father would cut a number of pegs, and name each after some important historical personage. Then before his sons he would call out the name represented by each, expecting them then to be able to tell him what they stood for. Thus it was possible to preserve the history of the country without writing."[2]

It is very rarely that we are thus privileged to go behind the scenes and observe the native technique of education actually at work. It is greatly to be hoped that when the *katikiro's* collection of Ganda stories has been translated into English we may be able to learn, by direct statement or allusion, a little more of the native methods of teaching oral traditions.

[1] Felkin, *Notes*, p. 763.   [2] Kagwa, *Customs*, p. 78.

It has been observed that we have practically no texts of gnomic or prophetic literature from Uganda, no hymns or prayers—though the former are known to have existed—and no charms or spells. These also are known to have existed, and we know that they sometimes took a literary form. Antiquarian poetry is also absent. Antiquarian prose is highly developed, but we are uncertain which class of people are primarily responsible for its cultivation. We have not found any prophecies or oracles, blessings or curses.

It will thus be seen that we are almost wholly ignorant of the particular forms of the literature of Uganda which we are accustomed elsewhere to associate with the learned, the priestly, or the mantic class. It would therefore be otiose for us to enquire into the intellectual classes here were it not for the existence of a remarkable system of manifestations of inspiration, and an equally remarkable method of recording the past, which seem at once to precede and to supersede oral tradition. We refer to the mediums of the gods and of dead kings, and to the royal cemetery at Emerera in Busiro, in the neighbourhood of the capital.[1] The importance of the royal mediums and of the temple-tombs for historical tradition becomes apparent at once when we turn to Usoga and Ankole which have no royal temple staffs, and where the traditions appear to be inconsiderable. A brief discussion of the professional classes of Uganda and the surrounding countries may therefore not be out of place.

These consist chiefly of the medicine-man, the rain-maker, the priest, and the medium.[2] Among many of the Bantu peoples, including those of the north, the kings and important chiefs themselves exercise priestly functions, and, like those of the Galla, are described as 'magicians', 'rain-makers', etc. Thus Stanley tells us that Lukongeh, King of Ukerewé, was supposed to be endowed with supernatural power, "and Lukongeh seizes every opportunity to heighten this belief. He is believed to be enabled to create a drought at pleasure, and to cause the land to be drenched with rain."[3] Emin Pasha says of the *kabarega*, or king of Unyoro: "Kabrega[4] himself is at this time (i.e. the new moon) occupied in preparing his magic powders, his amulets and talis-

[1] See Cunningham, p. 224f.; also p. 628 f. below.

[2] We have followed Roscoe's classification, because, though other classes of persons are mentioned in the *katikiro's* book on the Customs of Uganda, such as 'diviners', 'fortune-tellers', 'ghost-catchers', etc., we are not clear as to the exact significance of these terms, or how far the translator intends them to refer to distinct classes of persons.   [3] *T.D.C.* p. 160.

[4] Emin Pasha was apparently under the impression that this was a proper name.

mans, and no doubt also dabbles a little in the art of divination, as is the custom with all Wahuma chiefs during the first few days of the new moon."[1] Roscoe also gives full accounts of the important part played by the kings of Unyoro in the same ceremonies,[2] and Speke describes Mutesa as similarly employed.[3] It is clear from Roscoe's accounts that their functions are sacerdotal. Moreover these royal 'magicians' acted *in propria persona*. It does not appear that any remarkable paroxysms or afflatus accompanied their efforts, and we have no doubt that, as in many other parts of the world, the priestly functions which the kings of Central Africa[4] fulfil on ceremonial occasions are inherent in their kingship. On the other hand Speke's account[5] of the pretensions to supernatural power of the kings of Karagwe, notably Rumanika and his father Dagara, as well as his brother, give a particularly striking picture of a royal line which combined intellectual and mantic gifts.

The medicine-man never acts as a medium of the gods in Uganda. His knowledge is his own, and seems to be acquired by normal means. He has no shrine or temple, and apparently no official status; at any rate he appears to receive no state recognition or office. The power which the medicine-men possess is probably greater with the common people than with the aristocracy, and rests on their real skill in medicine and surgery, their reputed skill as exorcisors, and their monopoly of the manufacture of charms and fetishes. They are the most intellectual men in the country, and among the most important.[6]

The status of the priest is well defined, and it is clear that in Uganda the sacerdotal and prophetic functions are kept apart when means permit. The priest probably belonged in general to a higher social class than the medium—in the majority of cases to the ranks of the chiefs. In many cases the head-man of his clan (*mutaka*) was himself the chief priest, and was responsible for the safety and good conduct of the god's slaves and cattle, and for the general upkeep of the temple and the temple estates.[7] The priest of Mbadjune, a snake deity, was the chief of the district.[8] Some temples had four priests, and it was common for

[1] Emin Pasha, p. 66.

[2] *Northern Bantu, passim; Bakitara, passim.*   [3] Speke, p. 441.

[4] Cf. also Livingstone, *Last Journals*, p. 49. See also Stevens, p. 89. For the non-Bantu people, see Baker II, p. 5.

[5] Speke, p. 221 ff.

[6] Roscoe, in conversation. See also *ib. Central Africa*, p. 212; *East Africa*, p. 139; cf. Wilson and Felkin I, p. 208.

[7] See e.g. Roscoe, *Baganda*, pp. 134, 321; *East Africa*, p. 140.

[8] Kagwa, *Customs*, p. 123.

the chief priests to have inferior priests under them, who acted as assistants. It was the priest's function to act as an official intermediary between the medium and the people, and to interpret the oracle given through the medium which was often expressed in utterances which the priest alone claimed to understand.[1] In short the priest was a temple official. He possessed no supernatural power, and did not partake of the sanctity of the god. In these and many other features he resembled the Icelandic *goði*. But we are told that the priests were highly revered, sometimes more than the gods whom they represented.[2]

Mediums appear to have been numerous in Uganda. There were mediums of gods and spirits, as well as of kings and other members of the royal family. Even the river gods had their mediums, and we hear of a tree which prophesied.[3] There were mediums who personated lions, leopards, and snakes, in addition to the more usual mediums who personated dead human beings. At every ford on any big river stood a temple with never less than two inmates—sometimes men, sometimes a man and a woman—who seem to have been the priest and medium of the river god.[4]

The mediums were officially recognised and regulated. When a person became suddenly possessed by the god, and began to utter secrets and to predict future events, which apart from divine influence it would have been impossible for him to do, it was generally recognised that a god had selected him to be his medium, and he was at once taken to the temple.[5] With the exception of the gods of war, only one medium was attached to a temple. In the case of the medium of a god, a priest was appointed to act as intermediary between the medium and the people.

The medium of a god might be either a man or a woman, and was sometimes of high rank. The medium of the River Mayanja (see below) was the son of a princess, while the medium of Mukasa (see p. 590 above) has always been of princely rank since the time of King Ndaula, who figures in Roscoe's list as the nineteenth king in succession from Kintu.[6] Mediums are said to have had only one duty to perform—that of being the mouthpiece of the god.[7] The oracles were delivered at times in response to a definite enquiry from someone who had approached

[1] Roscoe, *Baganda*, p. 274 f.
[2] Kagwa, *Customs*, p. 124.   [3] *Ib*. p. 123.
[4] Roscoe, *Baganda*, p. 318 f.; and in conversation.
[5] *Ib*. p. 275.
[6] *Ib*. p. 220; cf. Cunningham, p. 84.
[7] Roscoe, *Baganda*, p. 274.

the temple for the purpose, at others spontaneously and without fore-warning.

When the medium of a god was a woman, she was not allowed to marry. She was looked upon as the wife of the god, and allowed to see no man except the priest. Her person was sacred. She was not allowed to enter the temple, however, if we may judge from the instance of Mukasa's medium.[1] She might have as many girl slaves as she wished, and a number of young girls, who bear a striking resemblance to the Vestal Virgins of ancient Rome, were also attached to most of the temples. It was their duty to attend to the sacred fire, and to the daily needs of the temple.

The medium, when under the influence of a spirit, assumed the bearing, age, and manner of speech attributed to the god or dead person whom he or she was impersonating. When Speke accompanied Mutesa to interview the medium of Mukasa, he found that although not an old man, he "affected to be so, walking very slowly and deliberately, coughing asthmatically, glimmering with his eyes, and mumbling like a witch". His wife when speaking imitated the croaking of a frog.[2] Cunningham also tells us that when the day of Mukasa's sacrifice came round, i.e. once every three months, the medium "became possessed of the Spirit of Mukasa, and became a bow-legged contorted wizard".[3] When the spirit of Selwanga, the python god, came upon his medium, he "went down on his face and wriggled about like a snake, uttering peculiar noises, and using words which the people could not understand".[4] The mediums or priests of Musisi, the earthquake god, shook their bodies as he was supposed to shake his.[5] The River Wajale and the River Katonga were said to be possessed by spirits which were worshipped under the form of a leopard, and the medium gave his oracle in gruff tones and made noises like a leopard, growling and rolling his eyes about like an angry beast, being under the influence of the leopard ghost.[6] On the Island Damba a sacrificial place Kitinda was dedicated to crocodiles, with a temple and a medium, who, when possessed, "worked his head about, opening his mouth and snapping it, as a crocodile moves its head from side to side and snaps its mouth to shut it. The medium gave oracles."[7] An ecclesiastical congress of heathen Baganda would have been very much like Noah's Ark.

---

[1] Roscoe, *Baganda*, p. 297; cf. Kagwa, *Customs*, p. 115.
[2] Speke, p. 394. Further details of Mukasa's medium will be found in Wilson and Felkin I, p. 206.   [3] Cunningham, *loc. cit.*   [4] Roscoe, *Baganda*, p. 322.
[5] Kagwa, *Customs*, p. 113.   [6] Roscoe, *Baganda*, p. 318.   [7] *Ib.* p. 336.

Roscoe has given us an interesting description of the manner in which oracles are delivered by the medium of a god:

"When a medium wished to become possessed in order to give the oracle, he would smoke a sacred pipe, using in most instances the ordinary tobacco of the country. Sometimes a cup of beer was also given him before the pipe was handed to him to smoke. He sat in the temple, near the fire, and after smoking the pipe, remained perfectly silent, gazing steadily into the fire or upon the ground, until the spirit came upon him. During the time that a medium was under the influence of the god he was in a frenzied state, and his utterances were often unintelligible to anyone except the priest, who was the interpreter. A priest often had to tell the medium afterwards what he had been talking about. As soon as the spirit of the god had left the medium, he became prostrated, and was allowed to sleep off the effects."[1]

The similarity of the oracle to that of Delphoi is striking. The intoxicating fumes, the stimulating drink, the sacred fire, the frenzied and unconscious state of the medium, the cryptic utterances interpreted by the priest, and the subsequent sleep of exhaustion, all recall in a remarkable degree the Pythia.

According to Kagwa, Mukasa's medium spoke her oracle from behind a curtain which divided the house into two parts. She invoked the god by reciting the following chant:

> God, God, the Great, come today and help me to judge.

Then, we are told, the assembled people took up the shout and drums were beaten, and after quiet had been re-established she would begin her prophecy. It would seem probable that the medium, like the Siberian shamans, possessed voice-throwing powers, for it was believed by the people that Mukasa had spoken out of the air.[2] The *katikiro* also gives us the interesting information that there must have been some sort of understanding among the 'gods', because they often gave identical prophecies.[3]

The gods of the surrounding countries also had mediums, who seem to have resembled in their main features the mediums of Uganda, imitating the personality and bearing of the divine being. In Unyoro the medium of Wamala, the god of plenty, is said to have mixed with the crowd at the sacred feast, bellowing like a bull,[4] while the female medium of Mugizi, the god of Lake Albert, wore a fringe of cowrie

[1] Roscoe, *Baganda*, p. 275.   [2] Kagwa, *Customs*, p. 115.
[3] *Ib.* p. 116.   [4] Roscoe, *Bakitara*, p. 23.

shells which was made to move about like the waves of the lake when she walked.[1]

In order to understand the relationship of the royal mediums to the mediums of the gods it will be necessary to say a few words on the elaborate funerals of the kings of Uganda.[2] When a king died his body was laid with much ceremony on a couch in a grass hut built specially for the purpose, and a number of his retainers were slaughtered, and "sent to attend upon the king who was supposed to have need of them in the next world". Actually a complete private domestic establishment on generous lines met death with its royal master. Five months later, the grass hut, known as the royal tomb, was again entered, and the skull or the jaw-bone freed from the body and cleaned and decorated with great ceremony. A temple was then built to receive the royal jaw-bone, and was permanently staffed with the most important relatives and officers of the dead king, or official representatives of them who were appointed to take their places. Each king had his own temple. The ghosts of kings were placed on an equality with the gods, and received the same honours and worship; they foretold events concerning the state, and advised the living king, warning him when war was likely to break out. The king made periodical visits to the temple, first of one then of another, of his predecessors.

The temple of the jaw-bone is a close approximation to the royal court of Uganda, with all its ceremonial relationships, conventions, and offices. Those who had held important offices during the dead king's lifetime took the more important sites near the temple, and retained their old titles. The *katikiro*, or prime minister of the dead king, and the *kimbugwe*, or king's private chaplain[3]—the highest ecclesiastical officer in the country—took up their permanent abode here. The former now became prime minister, the latter no doubt chief priest of the dead. The widowed queen dowager became the chief guardian of the temple, and moved her abode to be near the entrance.[4] Several of the dead king's widows went to take charge of the temple, and they had houses inside the temple enclosure, some of them sleeping inside the temple as guardians. The principal wife and a few other wives held definite offices. An important chief, on whose estate the temple had been

---

[1] Roscoe, *Bakitara*, p. 24.

[2] For the details of the funerals of the kings of Uganda, see Roscoe, *Baganda*, p. 283 ff.; *East Africa*, p. 149 ff; Cunningham, p. 224; Ashe, *Chronicles*, p. 66, footnote.   [3] For the *kimbugwe*, see also p. 631, footnote 5 below.

[4] Roscoe, *Baganda*, pp. 111, 114, 283.

built, was responsible for the upkeep of the temple, and had an official residence.[1]

The most interesting figure in these courts of the dead, however, is the medium, the living embodiment of the spirit of the dead king. "The medium first chosen for office was a man who had been in the deceased king's service, and who therefore knew many of his peculiarities; this man was found to have the spirit of the king upon him, causing him to act as the king had done, to speak as he used to speak, and to imitate his gestures and mode of walk; this was the sign that he was possessed by the ghost, and he was then set apart for this work of a medium and lived in the temple."[2] He was not always under the influence of the ghost, nor was he restricted to the temple enclosure; there were periods when he moved about in his natural way; but when he was required to give an oracle, he went through a form of preparation: "he sat near a fire in the sacred chamber of the temple, smoked a special pipe, and gazed into the fire, until at length he began to speak in the tones of the late king and to utter the words of the oracle; he was then said to be under the spirit of the king."[3]

The medium of the king, like the medium of the god, actually impersonated his master.[4] When he was under the influence of a ghost, his whole bearing and behaviour corresponded in the most minute particulars with those of the person whom he represented. It is said that King Kigale, who was the fifth king of Uganda, died as an old man in his dotage, with the saliva running from the corners of his mouth. His medium was a young man; but at such times as the spirit of the dead king came upon him, he became tottering in his walk, his bearing was that of a decrepit old man, and the slaver ran from his mouth.[5] It is perhaps as a medium, and certainly in his mantic capacity that Dagara, who was king of Karagwe before his son Rumanika—the latter the host of Speke and Grant, and later of Stanley—is said to have "turned sometimes into a young man, and then an old one, alternately, as the humour seized him.[6]

When Roscoe was interviewing[7] the old men and women of Uganda who had lived in the days of Mutesa and Suna on the customs and traditions of the past in Uganda, the *katikiro*, Sir Apolo Kagwa, sent

[1] With Roscoe's account of these courts of the dead, cf. Ashe, *Two Kings*, p. 80f.
[2] I.e. in one of the huts of the temple enclosure; cf. Roscoe, *Baganda*, p. 283.
[3] Roscoe, *East Africa*, p. 151.   [4] Roscoe, *Baganda*, p. 283.
[5] *Ib.* p. 217; and in conversation.   [6] Speke, p. 235.
[7] Roscoe, in conversation.

an old man to him who, though Roscoe did not know it at the time, was the medium of King Semakokiro who reigned five generations before the present king. As they sat talking together on the verandah of Roscoe's house, the old man suddenly lowered his head and began to talk continuously in an unknown tongue. Roscoe questioned the man several times but received no answer, though the man continued to talk. Finally, after endeavouring in vain to silence him, Roscoe sent him away; but the old man still remained oblivious and went on talking, as it were to himself. Roscoe then went to the *katikiro* to ask why such a crazy fellow had been sent to him. But when the *katikiro* learnt what had happened, he remarked in awe-struck tones, though he himself was a Christian: "How I wish I had been there. The king had him by the head!"[1] The most curious thing about the whole incident is that the medium was actually speaking in the archaic dialect current in the reign of King Semakokiro, hence Roscoe's inability to understand what he said.[2]

A perfectly rational explanation is, however, not far to seek. We have seen that the first man to become the medium of a dead king was always someone who had been very close to his person during his lifetime. It is probable that the mediumship was hereditary (cf. p. 625 above), or confined to the clan of which the first medium was a member (cf. p. 631 below). The Baganda are admirable mimics, and their dramatic sense is very highly developed. Once the first medium of a king (or a god) had established the traditional bearing and form of speech to be assumed in impersonating him, it would be comparatively easy for these to be handed on to all succeeding mediums, and the clan responsible for providing the mediums of a particular king would preserve the traditional technique of the mimesis as a normal piece of professionalism. An obsolete dialect might easily be handed on from generation to generation in this way, as the Siberian shamans sometimes speak in ecstasy a language with which they are unfamiliar in ordinary life, but of which they have doubtless learnt a little as a part of their professional equipment.

The actual person of the dead king is represented by the jaw-bone. The person of the medium in itself counts for nothing, and no ceremony appears to be due to him. When, however, the spirit of the dead king comes upon him, when 'the king seizes him by the head', as the ex-

---

[1] *Kukwata ku mutwe*, 'being seized by the head' is the Luganda expression for a fit of divine possession. Roscoe, *Baganda*, p. 275.

[2] Roscoe, in conversation.

pression is, the utmost reverence is paid to his utterances. He is in fact the national oracle. In a royal temple the deceased king held daily receptions, and from time to time the medium sent some special message to the nation, while every three or four days he sent the king important messages about matters of state, or warned him of invasions which were being planned.[1]

The most significant feature of this ceremonial is the provision which is made for continuity. The temple-tomb of every king from Kintu down to Mutesa is known and is said to be kept up,[2] and in the province of Busiro, in the neighbourhood of the capital, there were still thirty-six in addition to Mutesa's in 1905[3], though the pomp of the older temples is not so great as that of the more recent ones. In these temples the office of queen dowager was perpetuated, and when one princess died, another was appointed to succeed her.[4] The *katikiro* and *kimbugwe*,[5] who also retired on the death of a king to continue their duties in the ghostly court, were replaced on their death by other members of the clans responsible for furnishing men for the office.[6] The wives of the dead king—they were not called or thought of as widows—had to be replaced by other women of their clans trained to fulfil the office in the event of their death or remarrying.[7] The clans which supplied the early kings with *katikiros* and other chiefs have continued to do so to the present time in unbroken continuity.[8] In illustration of this Roscoe told us (in conversation) that he had a native woman gardener at Entebbe who insisted that she was the aunt of a certain king who had reigned many generations before.[9] The truth was that she was a member of the family responsible for furnishing official aunts, first to the living, then to the dead king for all time (cf. also p. 628 above), and she happened to be then 'in office'.

A glance at the neighbouring tribes suggests that, while burial

[1] Roscoe, *Baganda*, p. 112f.; *East Africa*, p. 151.
[2] Roscoe, *Baganda*, p. 285. According to Cunningham, these were already in a more or less dilapidated condition in 1905.
[3] Cunningham, p. 230.   [4] Roscoe, *Baganda*, p. 284.
[5] The *kimbugwe* was a royal officer next in importance to the *katikiro*. He had the care of the king's umbilical cord and the royal fetishes (Roscoe, *Baganda*, p. 235).
[6] Roscoe, *Baganda*, p. 111f.
[7] *Ib. loc. cit.*; *East Africa*, p. 150.
[8] *Ib. Baganda*, pp. 111f., 283. It is probable that in origin the royal temple was simply the palace which the king had occupied during his lifetime. See *ib.* p. 141; cf. Wilson and Felkin I, p. 176.
[9] This sense of continuity is shared to a great extent by all classes of the population. See Roscoe, *Baganda*, p. 3.

customs are far less elaborate and expensive, the attitude to the dead is the same. In Unyoro to the north, the kings received very elaborate funerals, and although the name of a dead king passed from the language and must never be mentioned, a temple and an oracle with a priest and medium were established at the grave, and a court of the dead king was established similar to that of Uganda.[1] Among the Basoko to the east also, a medium, who is, or was, a woman, has a special house and shrine, and is established as an oracle in charge of the dead king's jaw-bone.[2] Among the Lusaka of Northern Rhodesia the chief had a shrine built for himself during his own lifetime where he kept his most valuable property—drums, guns, and hunting-trophies. It was not built over a grave, and is therefore not a tomb but a temple, like those of the Uganda kings.[3] It may throw some light on Rumanika's 'museum' in Karagwe, described by Stanley.[4]

In Ankole the name of a king immediately passed out of the language on his death, while his spirit, as well as that of dead princes and princesses, passed into animals which were guarded in a sacred forest by a man who seems to have combined the office of priest and medium.[5] The 'priest' of the lions, which represented the dead kings, held communion through them with the departed kings,[6] and gave messages to the reigning king.[7] Among the Ba-Ila of Northern Rhodesia each community has a grove which is sacred to the *muzhima*, the god or spirit of the first ancestor of the chief,[8] and which is under the guardianship of a man whose office seems to correspond to that of the custodian of the sacred grove of Ankole. The will of the *muzhima* is made known to the people by mediums.[9]

The sense of continuity which lies behind this system of ancestral mediums, and which has reached its most elaborate form in Uganda,

---

[1] Roscoe, *Northern Bantu*, pp. 5, 52 f.; *ib. Central Africa*, p. 200; *Bakitara*, p. 126. In the latter the oracle is not mentioned.

[2] Roscoe, *Northern Bantu*, pp. 204, 227 ff. We may compare also *Bagesu*, p. 131.

[3] Smith and Dale II, p. 169 f.

[4] *T.D.C.* p. 301 f.

[5] For the medium, see Roscoe, *Banyankole*, p. 23; *Northern Bantu*, p. 128. A similar belief and custom existed also in Karagwe; see Speke, p. 221.

[6] Roscoe, *Northern Bantu*, loc. cit.

[7] *Ib. East Africa*, p. 214; cf. *ib. Central Africa*, p. 80; *Northern Bantu*, p. 132. For a general account of the beliefs and customs regarding the kings of Ankole, see Roscoe, *Banyankole*, pp. 27, 50 ff.

[8] May we compare the forest to which Kintu retired in Uganda tradition (pp. 588, 601 above)?

[9] Smith and Dale II, p. 187 f.

implies a conception of time which is not easy to grasp at first sight. The past is clearly conceived as continuous and ever-present. It is re-enacted—not allowed to die. In the crystallising of court function and personnel at the moment of death, as well as in the person of the medium, time is, as it were, caught on the wing and held back. It loses its dynamic force and becomes static. There is no past. It is still present.

It may be suspected that the conception of history implied by this re-enactment of the past is an earlier one than tradition, and it is because of its relation to oral tradition that we have considered it here. We know of no country where the picture is so complete; where the celebrations, the receptions, and the ceremonials at the tombs or temples of the dead are enacted against a background of continuous make-believe. With the intermittent phenomenon we are all familiar. Can it be that in this system we have the precursor of oral tradition and of heroic drama in one?—a system which in its break-up would naturally lead to inter-mittent celebrations at the tombs of the dead?

The relationship of the system to oral tradition in Uganda is obvious. We have seen that it was the office of a certain chief of the court to be responsible for recording the genealogies of the kings and the order of succession, while the court minstrels were responsible for recording the national traditions. There can be no doubt that a constant aid to accuracy would be to hand in the temples, courts, and mediums of the dead, as well as in the royal tombs. Indeed the entire system of com-memoration was recognised by Roscoe as being invaluable for purposes of history.[1] Its importance can be gauged from the fact that in Ankole, where the system did not admit of temples or tombs, no genuine royal lists are available, and dynastic tradition is wholly absent.

Mantic and prophetic persons are found among many of the Bantu peoples further south. Among the Ila-speaking peoples of Northern Rhodesia, seers are by no means rare. Smith and Dale distinguish between seers who are mediums, and seers whose manifestation takes the form of ecstasy; that is to say, whose spirit is in the habit of leaving the body temporarily and going on long journeys, and then returning to tell what it has seen and heard. The mediums appear to resemble in many respects the mediums of Uganda. The ghost of a dead person, or some powerful spirit, or even a god, may possess the medium per-manently or only intermittently or temporarily, causing him (or her) to speak 'prophetically', and in some cases to identify himself with a

[1] *Baganda*, p. 3.

person long dead. As in Uganda the ghost is said to 'seize' the person possessed. The Ila seers may be either men or women, and some enjoy a very wide reputation. Stories are still told of the marvellous feats of a seeress named Longo, who was captured by the Makololo in the time of Sekeletu, the son of Sebetoane, the great Makololo chief who flourished during the early years of last century.[1]

Reference has already been made (p. 605 above) to the woman of the Echewa tribe whose strange gnomic utterances were spoken while she was in a frenzied and apparently unconscious condition under the influence of Indian hemp. Among the Makololo on the upper Zambesi the seer was a man of great importance. He was called a *senoga*, 'one who holds intercourse with the gods'.[2] Like some of the rulers of the Northern Bantu whose functions are also prophetic, he was in the habit of retiring to a sequestered spot, such as a cave. Here he remained in a hypnotic state till the full moon, when he returned to his tribe, emaciated and excited, to prophesy in a state of ecstasy. The prophet Tlapone is said to have warned the great Makololo chief, Sebetoane, against danger from the east (presumably from the Portuguese), and to have urged him to march westwards against the Barotse. His recorded prophecies are almost exclusively political, and so impressed Sebetoane that he followed his advice implicitly, and with complete success.[3]

During the latter part of the eighteenth century and the early part of the nineteenth, there ruled over the Basuto on the head waters of the Orange River the mystic and seer Mohlomi. Mohlomi is said to have been the greatest figure in Basuto history, greater even than Moshesh,[4] their most distinguished chief, and to rank among the greatest names in South African history. He is said to have had a vision as a young man, in which he saw the roof above him open, and he himself was carried to the skies,[5] where he received a command to rule by love and to regard his people as his brothers. Certain it is that throughout his life Mohlomi consistently followed these precepts. He lived at peace with all men, both his own people and neighbouring princes, whom he was in the habit of visiting. He was indeed a great traveller, and took the keenest

[1] Smith and Dale II, p. 136 ff. [2] Livingstone, *M.T.R.* p. 87.
[3] *Ib. loc. cit.*; cf. Ellenberger and Macgregor, p. 312 f.
[4] So the Rev. E. W. Smith. See A. Werner, *J.A.S.* XXXI, p. 183, footnote.
[5] It is an interesting fact that King Rumanika of Karagwe claimed to have been raised up to Heaven by supernatural means as one of the ordeals which he underwent before ascending the throne (Speke, p. 222). The motif occurs also in African folktales of seers, and is no doubt a stock property of the mantic experience.

intellectual interest in other tribes and their customs. He was an excellent raconteur: "the adventures which befell him in the course of his travels in distant lands and among strange peoples forming his theme."[1] His reputation as a physician and as a rain-maker was very great, and his name is still invoked in the traditional invocations for rain.[2]

Perhaps on the whole our evidence relating to seers and mantic persons generally among the Southern Bantu is fullest for the Zulu of Natal. These seers profess to enjoy the peculiar favour of the spirits, from whom they claim to have received the gift of inspiration. Like the prophets of the Basuto and the Makololo, they are astute observers of men and manners, and generally have one or more assistants who keep them primed with information on contemporary affairs. The prophet may be either a man or a woman, and the office is often hereditary and held in the highest honour by all, even by the chief. Shooter, who is our principal early informant on these matters,[3] draws a sharp distinction between the prophet and the rain-maker. The prophet, who is often erroneously called a witch-doctor by Europeans, is essentially the spiritual and intellectual leader of the community.

Among these people the early stages of inspiration, and the condition of ecstasy or transport in which the prophecies are delivered, bear a very striking resemblance to those which prevail among the shamans of Asia. Symptoms believed among the Zulu to indicate an individual's coming inspiration are mental depression, a disposition to retire into solitude,[4] severe attacks which to an observer appear to resemble epilepsy, and extraordinary and numerous dreams. The young prophet, on returning from his period of solitude, appears terribly emaciated, and declares that he is under the influence of spirits, including the spirits of his dead ancestors. Becoming more and more excited, he dances and sings, while his eyes glare, tears roll down his face, and his chanting is interrupted by loud cries. The men and women around him join in singing responses. It is of interest to note that the women are instructed beforehand as to the part which they are expected to play in such a

---

[1] Ellenberger and Macgregor, p. 297. We may compare 'The Adventures of Saruti' as related by the *muganda* envoy Saruti, pp. 604, 612 above.

[2] For a detailed account of Mohlomi, see Ellenberger and Macgregor, p. 90 ff.

[3] Shooter, p. 167 ff.

[4] Again we may compare the practices of the mantic kings of Karagwe. King Dagara, the father of Rumanika, is said to have been in the habit of retiring underground for periods of ascetic and solitary contemplation (Speke, p. 235).

performance, and it is clear that the whole ceremony, for all its wild and casual semblance, follows a recognised procedure.

More remarkable than the religious ecstasy of these prophets is their intellectual curiosity and acumen, and their political insight. In the conflicts between the Southern Bantu and the British which took place early last century, several of these prophets adopted a national policy, and, claiming divine inspiration for their mission, rallied the Amaxosa clans, and led them to the attack with a confidence and gallantry which were entirely justified by their military talent. The prophet Makanna, who led the attackagainst the British headquarters at Grahamstown in 1818, had previously been in the habit of visiting the garrison on friendly terms, and had shown insatiable curiosity and an acute intellect in discussing matters of war and mechanics with the officers, and theology with the chaplain. In a later war the principal chiefs were glad to consult Umlanjeni, a young prophet of the Gaika tribe, who had gained fame on account of his austerities, and to leave the decision of peace and war in his hands. Many other great prophetic names, such as that of Umhlakuza, are still remembered in the annals of this war.[1]

It will be seen that the most striking feature of the Zulu prophets, and those of neighbouring peoples, such as the Amaxosa, as well as of the other prophets of the Southern Bantu, is their preoccupation with politics, especially such important political matters as affected the relations of their people with powerful neighbours. Their influence seems to have been unlimited, and their insight and sagacity frequently equal to their prestige with their tribes. The analogy with the prophets of Hawaii, of the Galla and of the ancient Hebrews is extremely close. The intellectual attainments of these men, their powers of scientific observation, and their preoccupation with worldly matters on the grand scale, cannot be too strongly stressed, and are in no way subordinate to their mystical and mantic functions.

[1] For a recent note on the prophets of the Bantu-speaking tribes of South Africa, see Schapera, p. 253 f., and the references cited.

THE NORTHERN BANTU

LIST OF ABBREVIATIONS[1]

AUTHOR AND TITLE OF BOOK	ABBREVIATION

ASHE, R. P. *Two Kings of Uganda, or Life by the Shores of the Victoria Nyanẓa.* 2nd ed. London, 1890. — Ashe, *Two Kings.*

—— *Chronicles of Uganda.* London, 1894. — Ashe, *Chronicles.*

BAKER, Sir S. *The Albert Nyanẓa.* 2 vols. London, 1866. — Baker.

CASALIS, E. *The Basutos.* London, 1861. — Casalis.

CRABTREE, W. A. *A Manual of Lu-Ganda.* Cambridge, 1921. — Crabtree, *Lu-Ganda.*

CUNNINGHAM, J. F. *Uganda and its Peoples.* London, 1905. — Cunningham.

ELLENBERGER, D. F. and MACGREGOR, J. C. *History of the Basuto Ancient and Modern.* London, 1912. — Ellenberger and Macgregor.

SCHWEINFURTH, etc. *Emin Pasha in Central Africa.* (Being a Collection of his Letters and Journals.) Edited by Schweinfurth, etc., and translated by Mrs Felkin. London, 1888. — Emin Pasha.

FELKIN, R. W. 'Notes on the Waganda Tribe of Central Africa.' In *P.R.S.E.* (1886). [See also *s.v.* Wilson and Felkin.] — Felkin, *Notes.*

GRANT, J. A. *A Walk across Africa, or Domestic Scenes from my Nile Journal.* London, 1864. — Grant.

British Museum. *Handbook to the Ethnographical Collections.* 1910. — H.E.C.

JOHNSTON, Sir H. *The Uganda Protectorate.* 2 vols. London, 1902. — Johnston, *U.P.*

JUNOD, H. A. *Les Chants et les Contes des Ba-Ronga de la Baie de Delagoa.* Lausanne, 1897. — Junod, *Chants.*

KAGWA, Sir APOLO. *Ekitabo kya Bakabaka Bebuganda.* London, 1912. (History of the Kings of Buganda, Bunyoro, Koki, Toro, and Ankole in the Luganda Language. The book is not translated.) — Kagwa, *Ekitabo.*

—— *The Customs of the Baganda.* Translated by E. B. Kalibala, edited by M. Mandelbaum (Edel). New York, 1934. — Kagwa, *Customs.*

KIDNEY, E. 'Songs from Nyasaland.' In *J.A.S.* Vol. XX. — Kidney, *Songs.*

[1] See *Note*, Part I, p. 219 above.

Author and Title of Book	Abbreviation
Kollmann, P. *The Victoria Nyanza.* London, 1899.	Kollmann, *V.N.*
Livingstone, D. *Missionary Travels and Researches in South Africa.* London, 1857.	Livingstone, *M.T.R.*
—— *Narrative of an Expedition to the Zambesi and its Tributaries.* London, 1865.	Livingstone, *N.E.Z.*
—— *Last Journals.* Edited by the Rev. H. Waller. London, 1874.	Livingstone, *Last Journals.*
Moore, J. E. S. *To the Mountains of the Moon.* London, 1901.	Moore.
O'Ferrall, Bishop R. S. M. *B.S.O.S.* IV, iv, p. 839 ff.	O'Ferrall, *B.S.O.S.*
Rattray, R. S. *Some Folk-Lore Stories and Songs in Chinyanja.* London (S.P.C.K.), 1907.	Rattray, *Folk-Lore.*
—— *Ashanti.* Oxford, 1923.	Rattray, *Ashanti.*
—— *Religion and Art in Ashanti.* Oxford, 1927.	Rattray, *Religion.*
—— *Akan-Ashanti Folk-Tales.* Oxford, 1930.	Rattray, *Folk-Tales.*
Roscoe, J. *The Baganda.* London, 1911.	Roscoe, *Baganda.*
—— *The Northern Bantu.* Cambridge, 1915.	Roscoe, *Northern Bantu.*
—— *Twenty-Five Years in East Africa.* Cambridge, 1921.	Roscoe, *East Africa.*
—— *The Soul of Central Africa.* London, 1922.	Roscoe, *Central Africa.*
—— *The Banyankole.* Cambridge, 1923.	Roscoe, *Banyankole.*
—— *The Bakitara.* Cambridge, 1923.	Roscoe, *Bakitara.*
—— *The Bagesu.* Cambridge, 1924.	Roscoe, *Bagesu.*
—— *Immigrants and their Influence in the Lake Region of Central Africa.* (The Frazer Lecture in Social Anthropology, 1923.) Cambridge, 1924.	Roscoe, *Immigrants.*
—— Various articles in *Man.*	Roscoe, *Man.*
Sayce, R. U. *Primitive Arts and Crafts.* Cambridge, 1933.	Sayce.
Schapera, I. *The Bantu-Speaking Tribes of South Africa.* London, 1937.	Schapera.
Shooter, J. *The Kafirs of Natal and the Zulu Country.* London, 1857.	Shooter, *Kafirs.*
Smith, E. W. and Dale, A. M. *The Ila-Speaking Peoples of Northern Rhodesia.* 2 vols. London, 1920.	Smith and Dale.
Speke, J. H. *Journal of the Discovery of the Source of the Nile.* Edinburgh, 1863.	Speke.
Stanley, H. M. *How I found Livingstone.* London, 1872.	Stanley, *H.I.f.L.*

Author and Title of Book	Abbreviation
STANLEY, H. M. *Through the Dark Continent.* 6th Ed. London, 1887.	Stanley, *T.D.C.*
—— *My Dark Companions and their Strange Stories.* London, 1893. Some of these stories appeared in the *Fortnightly Review*, LIII (New Series, 1893), p. 797 ff.	Stanley, *Companions.*
STEVENS, T. *Scouting for Stanley in East Africa.* London, 1880.	Stevens.
TREVES, Sir F. *Uganda for a Holiday.* London, 1910. [See List of Abbreviations to ABYSSINIA.]	Treves. Varley.
WERNER, A. *The Natives of British Central Africa.* London, 1906.	Werner, *B.C.A.*
—— *African Mythology.* London, 1925.	Werner, *Mythology.*
WILSON, C. T. and FELKIN, R. W. *Uganda and the Egyptian Soudan.* London, 1882. 2 vols.	Wilson and Felkin.

PERIODICALS

Bantu Studies.	*Bantu Studies.*
Bulletin of the School of Oriental Studies. London Institution. IV (1926–8).	*B.S.O.S.*
Journal of the African Society, 1901, etc.	*J.A.S.*
Man, 1901, etc.	*Man.*
Proceedings of the Royal Society of Edinburgh.	*P.R.S.E.*

4. THE YORUBA

IN the three oral literatures from eastern Africa which we have briefly examined, the most interesting development is that of the chronicles relating primarily to the reigning kings and dynasties. Among the Galla and the Northern Bantu, these chronicles have been carried on by oral tradition. Among the latter peoples they are recited by the royal bards at the king's court, and we have seen that in Ashanti in the west a similar practice prevailed down to our own day. Traces are to be found among other peoples. The evidence as a whole leads to the belief that among the more highly developed of the African peoples several bodies of historical and antiquarian traditions were carefully preserved in various milieus—the 'official' text by the 'bards' or chanters at the royal courts, a variant series representing a more sacerdotal point of view by the temple priests, while yet another series seems to have been current among the chiefs. It is only rarely, as in Uganda, that the two latter series are recorded, except as isolated sagas and anecdotes; but the royal texts, with their dynastic interests, have attracted more attention, both among the educated natives, and among Europeans resident in Africa. It is largely on antiquarian records of this kind that the histories of the Southern Bantu, notably the Basuto, have been based. From West Africa we are fortunate in possessing a written history of the Yoruba compiled by two Yoruba from their own traditions.[1] This circumstance, combined with the high development of antiquarian interests, and the great wealth of saga which the book shows to exist among these people, have suggested to us that a brief examination of their literature will be of interest, both for its own sake, and also for comparative purposes.

The Yoruba-speaking peoples[2] constitute one of the three great West African negro kingdoms, and include the Yoruba proper, the Egba, the Ibandans and Ijebus, the Ijeshas, Ondos, and Benin people. They lie between the 6th degree of east longitude and the kingdom of Dahomey, and stretch inland from the Bight of Benin and the Slave Coast on the south as far as to the tableland in the north through which

---

[1] S. and O. Johnson, *The History of the Yorubas* (London, 1921).
[2] For details of the Yoruba and their civilisation, see Talbot's references to these people throughout the four volumes of his work, *The Peoples of Southern Nigeria*.

the Niger flows from west to east. The southern and eastern portions of the country are forest land, but the northern, western and central portions for the most part form an undulating plain—the heart of the kingdom, or Yoruba proper—which is almost entirely pasture land. The soil is rich, and the people are largely engaged in agriculture, though several industries are carried on. The Yorubas are indeed to some extent a town-dwelling people, with a highly developed city life. Several of their towns have a population of over 40,000, and many of them are walled. It is believed that these towns have arisen from the need for strong protection against the Dahomey slave raiders. The houses of the chiefs often contain fifty rooms, and are well built. The government is monarchical, but the power is in the hands of a council of chiefs. In political and administrative matters, as well as in the organisation and regulation of town life, the Yorubas are very far advanced, and during the eighteenth century the Yoruba kingdom was far more powerful than at any later time, surpassing both Dahomey and Ashanti.[1] Until the introduction of the missions, however, writing was unknown. All laws and records of the past were carried on orally. The 'History' of the Yorubas to which we have referred is based wholly, for its account of past times, on the traditional oral literature of the people themselves.[2]

In the preface to the book some hints are given as to the principal sources from which the oral traditions have been drawn. Expressing a wish that the traditions of the lesser known parts of the country should be investigated, the writer observes:

"It may be that the oral records are preserved in them which are handed down from father to son, as in the case of the better known royal bards of the Metropolis."

And again:

"With respect to the ancient and mythological period he (i.e. the author) has stated the facts as they are given by the bards."

In the body of the work we again read:

"As the Yorubas have no knowledge of letters, their learning consists chiefly in oral traditions. The historians are the king's cymballists and ballad singers, the chief of whom is called the *ologbo* or *arokin*."[3]

[1] Farrow, p. 8.
[2] For some account of the history of the Yoruba from outside sources, mainly European, see Talbot I, p. 28 ff. Cf. further for more general historical matter Lady Lugard, *A Tropical Dependency*.
[3] Johnson, p. 125.

The word *ologbo* is said to mean 'one who possesses the old times', and the word *arokin* seems to mean 'a chronicler'. There is a Yoruba proverb, '*Ologbo baba arokin*', 'The *ologbo* is the father of chroniclers'.[1] According to Ellis, the *ologbo* is the chief of the *arokin*, and also a chronicler, and the same writer tells us that several *arokin* are attached to each king or paramount chief. These men may be regarded as the repositories of the ancient chronicles.[2] The royal *arokin* chant in the king's presence the history of the nation and details of the reigns of former kings. Their office is hereditary, and they are kept in the royal service and well supported.[3] Johnson adds the interesting statement that the *arokin* have an apartment to themselves, where they repeat daily in songs the genealogy of the kings, the principal events of their lives, and other notable events in the history of the Yoruba country.[4]

The *ologbo* is sometimes more astute than his fellow councillors, and a clever observer of men. When King Abipa was deceived by a trick played on his credulity by a disaffected party of nobles, the deception was 'shrewdly suspected' by the *ologbo*, who exposed it to the king. The nobles poisoned the *ologbo* in revenge; but the king, in order to show his love and esteem for his faithful subject, ordered for him a semi-state funeral.[5] These officials bear a striking resemblance to the *kwadwumfo* or minstrels of Ashanti to whom reference has already been made (p. 576, footnote 1 above). There can be no doubt that in both countries they act as the record-keepers and national historians and genealogists, carrying on the historical traditions by their songs, and preserving their texts by daily recitations, which serve to refresh their own memories and instruct their audience. We shall see as we look more closely at the 'History' that the authors have had many other oral sources of information besides the chants of the royal bards; but there can be no doubt that here, as in Ashanti and Uganda, it is these official oral records which form the foundation of the national traditions.

In the Yoruba history, as in the other oral histories which we have already considered, the early part of the work consists of antiquarian speculations on the original home of the Yoruba, and the origin of the various tribes, customs, places, and titles. As the authors themselves observe, it is not difficult to discount the few comparatively modern Mohammedan allusions in favour of the large body of native traditions. From these speculations the history passes to purely dynastic record, giving a list of kings, and one or two anecdotes of each reign. These

---

[1] Ellis, p. 243 f.   [2] *Loc. cit.*
[3] Johnson, p. 125 ff.   [4] *Ib.* p. 58.   [5] *Ib.* p. 165 t.

are chiefly of a personal nature, especially in the early portions, and are apparently selected with a view to presenting a personal history of the royal family. So exclusively regal is the interest of this portion of the 'History' that although in the reign of King Ojigi[1] we are told that "one of the most famous men in Yoruba history, Yamba, was a Basorun[2] of this reign", no further information is given about him. This list of kings with the brief anecdotes attached is so closely analogous to the oral history of Uganda that we have no doubt that the official court chronicle of the Yoruba has here been incorporated more or less in its entirety as it was recited by the official bards.

From the time of Abiodun, whose reign closed with the eighteenth century,[3] the character of the narrative changes. The record becomes more coherent and congruent, and the relation of cause and effect appears to be more natural and less artificially 'arranged'. The short anecdote of the early part of the history is frequently supplanted by long and detailed continuous narrative of the important events in the history of the Yoruba and the subject or allied tribes. These narratives are no longer confined to the reigning king, but relate the course of battles, the adventures of chiefs, and the part played by important state officials.

The history, however, remains a history of individuals down to modern times, and is largely made up, at least from the reign of Abiodun, from the personal stories of great men. Of these stories variant versions are sometimes introduced, as in the case of the birth and childhood of Prince Atiba.[4] When the war chiefs are the subject of a story the narrative becomes heroic in character, as in the story of the chief Dado, whose career is sketched in detail.[5] We hear much also of palace intrigues; of the youthful escapades of the Crown Prince Adewusi;[6] we follow the personal career of the war chief Dekun,[7] or of some important official such as the Basorun Gáhà,[8] whose functions resemble those of the Mayor of the Palace under the Merovingian kings. The personality of Gáhà stands out as clearly as that of the Icelander, Snorri Goði, who figures prominently in the saga literature of the Viking Age; and in spite of his cruelty Gáhà commands the interest and admiration of the European reader by his astute judgment, his surpassing mastery of intrigue, and his penetrating wit.

[1] Johnson, p. 174.   [2] I.e. the chief statesman.
[3] Farrow, p. 8.   [4] Johnson, p. 274 f.
[5] Ib. p. 236 f.   [6] Ib. p. 212 f.
[7] Ib. p. 228 f.   [8] Ib. p. 178 ff.

It is clear that much more is known from oral tradition of the history of the country than has found its way into the narrative. The wealth of saga which lies behind the recorded traditions can be gauged in several ways. We may refer to the brief mention of Yamba as one of the most famous men of Yoruba history, though practically nothing is said of him here. Again, variant versions of the traditions are referred to not infrequently, and sometimes more than one version is related.[1] The selective process which has governed the choice of traditions, may be partly Johnson's own, but the similarity of the outline and scheme of the whole to the dynastic accounts of Uganda as we have them in both Stanley's and Roscoe's versions suggest that, when due allowance has been made for the ambitious scale of the work, the form is that of traditional oral chronicles handed down by native chroniclers, both the court bards, and native antiquaries.

Apart from the wealth of antiquarian and personal saga, as well as heroic or dynastic chants and genealogies, to which the work bears witness, we learn both from the 'History' and from other sources that many other forms of literature were current among the Yoruba. Stories of the gods are sometimes referred to, both in the history and elsewhere,[2] and many of these appear to have been current in an anti-quarian or learned form. The most important of these are, of course, the cosmogonic speculations, for which the 'History' is again our chief source. But 'origin' stories of all kinds seem to be widely cultivated. Stories which account for the origin of the universe[3] and of the gods[4] and of sanctuaries,[5] of sacred animals,[6] and of customs connected with divination[7] and worship are alike common. It is said that even the social and political organisations of the country are based historically on principles of theocratic autocracy, and that the gods are the deified leaders of the prehistoric migrations of the Yoruba from the Nile.[8] From all this it is clear that the influence of the priesthood on the intellectual life of the people is very great. This is noticeable even where we should hardly look to find ecclesiastical influence. Thus Dennett

[1] E.g. Johnson, pp. 32, 171.
[2] Ellis, *passim*; Dennett, *N.S.*; Farrow, *passim*.
[3] See Frobenius I, p. 282 ff.; Farrow, p. 19.
[4] Dennett, *N.S.* p. 88 ff.; Farrow, pp. 36 ff., and *passim*.
[5] Dennett, *N.S.* p. 75 (cf. pp. 19, 24); Farrow, p. 17.
[6] Dennett, *N.S.* p. 35.
[7] Dennett, *B.M.M.* p. 269.
[8] See *The Times, British West Africa* Number, Oct. 30th, 1928, p. xviii; cf. Farrow, pp. 17, 37.

records a tradition in which the origin of the four days of the Yoruba week are ascribed to the god or goddess Odudua,[1] and the same writer received a story of the origin of Orishala and Yemuhu from an old priestess who spoke through a near relative, also connected with the priesthood.[2]

The god of the Yoruba of whom we hear most is Ifa, the god of divination and prophecy. He is the great oracular deity, and is commonly invoked under the name of Ela.[3] His responses are generally given in the form of veiled sayings, as is sung of him in one of the many current poems in which he is celebrated:

> Ifa speaks always in parables—
> A wise man is he who understands his speech.[4]

The word which Johnson and Dennett generally translate 'parables' seems to mean something in the nature of a maxim or precept, sometimes a veiled utterance, but sometimes merely a reflection. Dennett gives two instances:

"There is never a morning when a Babalawo or a consulting priest does not consult his Opele, as there is never a morning that a blacksmith is not called upon to sharpen a cutlass for a farmer."[5]

"The possibility of tomorrow not being like today in regard to the events which may transpire in it, is what induces a Babalawo to consult his Ifa and sacrifice to it every fifth day."[6]

Proverbs are said to be very numerous.[7]

It will be seen that these 'parables' make reference to the divining priests, and give us an indication of the large part which oracles and divination play in the functions of the Yoruba priesthood.[8] So far as we can judge from a present poem recorded by Dennett, the influence of the oracle seems to be a good one, inculcating virtue, and urging the avoidance of evil:

> In purpose be thou true,
> Not given to perfidy;
> For the work of the perfidious will o'ertake him,
> The evil of the wicked shall slay him.[9]

The hymns to Ifa[10] likewise show him as a beneficent and friendly god,

[1] *N.S.* p. 77. Tradition varies as to the sex of Odudua; see Dennett, *loc. cit.*; cf. further Farrow, p. 94.
[2] *N.S.* 17.   [3] Farrow, p. 41.   [4] Dennett, *B.M.M.* p. 249.
[5] *Ib.* p. 251.   [6] *Ib. loc. cit.*   [7] Farrow, pp. 28, 31.
[8] Dennett, *B.M.M.* p. 249.   [9] *Ib. N.S.* p. 87f.   [10] *Ib.* p. 255.

who is not above visiting his worshippers and partaking of the yam feast with them:

Our friend of the past year has come again to observe the yearly festival,
The anniversary has returned.... Ela has reappeared.[1]

The longest and most important text of Yoruba poetry which we have seen is a hymn to Ifa, which is believed to be very old, and which was recorded by a Yoruba clergyman from an old priest of Ifa.[2] The following is a brief chant to Shango, the lightning god, who is believed to have been introduced into the country from the Niger territory:

> O Shango, thou art the master!
> Thou takest in thy hand the fiery stones,
> To punish the guilty!
> To satisfy thy anger!
> Everything they strike is destroyed.
> The fire eats up the forest,
> The trees are broken down,
> And all things living are slain.[3]

The *babalawo* or diviners, to whom reference is made above, constitute one class of the priests[4] of Ifa. There are said to be three grades of priests, the grades corresponding, apparently, to the number of years of preparation during which the disciple imbibes the oral teaching of his preceptor. An important part of his education consists in learning the traditional stories associated with the divinities who are subordinate to Ifa. There are said to be 1680 stories attached to each of these divinities, and a pupil is nominally expected to commit all these to memory in addition to a number of other stories associated with other divinities. How exactly the selection is made is not very clear, but in any case the numbers are presumably merely used figuratively. The important thing for us is the statement that the pupil does in fact learn by heart a very large number, and from these, in combination with a divining bowl, he delivers his oracular responses as they appear to suit the case put to him.[5] The division into grades, and the importance attached to the acquisition of an extensive répertoire of prose stories, remind one of the Irish *fílid*,[6] though among the Yoruba there seems

---

[1] Dennett, *N.S.* pp. 255, 256. Invocations to Ela are also quoted by Farrow, 41.
[2] See Farrow, p. 161 ff. [3] Farrow, p. 50.
[4] For an account of the priesthood, see Frobenius I, p. 245 ff.; Farrow, p. 103 ff.
[5] Dennett, *B.M.M.* pp. 249, 266.
[6] Cf. Vol. I, p. 602 f. of the present work.

to be an implication that the stories are connected with the gods, whereas among the *filid* the répertoires are essentially secular.

Another interesting class is that of the mediums, known as *awon abukosoro*, 'speakers with the dead', who profess to speak with the dead, and to act as channels of communication between them and the living. Unfortunately we hear very little of them, though Johnson makes the curious statement that their deliverances have 'generally been found to be true'.

The Yoruba are lovers of popular tales and popular poetry. The *akpalo kpatita*, 'one who makes a trade of reciting stories', is a person held in great esteem and in great demand for social gatherings. He is, of course, to be sharply distinguished from the *arokin*, for he is not attached to the entourage of any king or high chief, but wanders from place to place, and his stories are recited purely for entertainment. As among the Ewe tribes, the professional story-teller very often uses a drum, with the rhythm of which he fills up the pauses in the narrative. When he has gathered an audience around him, he cries out: "My *alo* ('story') is about so-and-so", mentioning the name of the hero or heroine of the tale; or "My *alo* is about a man (or woman) who did so-and-so", and after this preface, proceeds with the recital.[1] The Yoruba stories published by Ellis[2] are probably fair specimens of his répertoire; but numbers of other stories recorded in the pages of Frobenius and Farrow illustrate the great popularity of oral saga among the Yorubas. The elaborate art with which these stories are narrated is aptly illustrated by the story of Edjur and Oju related by Frobenius.[3]

Mention has already been made of the popularity of extempore topical poetry, which among the Yoruba, as among the Abyssinians and Galla, appears to be composed by all classes of the population. Extempore poetry is sung in the streets in recognition and celebration of any important event.[4] Such poetry indeed serves admirably to express the popular opinion of the more important political events, and of the people who take part in them, and while the Yoruba are without a printing press or representative government, they contrive to give very effective voice to popular opinion by this telling and frequently

[1] Ellis, p. 243 f.   [2] *Ib. loc. cit.*   [3] I, p. 236 ff.
[4] Clapperton records an interesting pantomimic performance among the Yoruba which may possibly have had a topical element in the burlesque of a white man, and choral songs are said to have been sung by the 'king's women' between each 'Act', while the assembled crowd also chimed in (*S.E.* p. 53 ff.).

highly embarrassing method. Indeed this form of composition is a political weapon by no means to be disregarded, and Johnson's 'History' shows that, in the absence of written records, the usual way of estimating the impression that a person or event has left on a given generation is to turn to the popular songs. In spite of their ephemeral character, these songs are often carried on for several generations by oral tradition.[1]

This facility in poetical composition is equally evident in private life. Mrs Hinderer, the missionary's wife, overheard a young girl singing to herself an extempore song about her occupation as she was washing clothes in the river.[2] Elegiac poetry is also recited at the funeral feast, both by the women of the household, and by their friends. An example recorded by Ellis shows that this consists of a simple theme.

"I go to the market; it is crowded. There are many people there, but he is not among them. I wait, but he comes not. Ah me! I am alone....

"Alas! I am alone. Alone in the day—alone in the darkness of the night. Alas! my father (or husband) is dead. Who will take care of me?"[3]

The simplicity of this utterance is characteristic of African lyrical poetry, and in strong contrast to the elaborate and sustained imaginative chant of the Dyak wailer (see p. 487 ff. above). Yet we are told that among the Yoruba also there are professional mourners who are 'chosen for their poetical turn of expression', who are engaged by well-to-do households, and who often contrive to work up the real mourners to a condition of frenzied grief. A professional mourner, we are told, sings in a sad tone, which rises and falls in a modulated wail:

"He is gone, the lion of a man. He was not a sapling, or a bush, to be torn out of the earth, but a tree—a tree to brave the hurricane; a spreading tree, under which the hearts of his family could rest in peace", etc. etc.[4]

[1] Some of the songs of the Yoruba and neighbouring peoples are said to be so old that the meanings of many of the words have been forgotten. See Talbot III, p. 808.
[2] Hinderer, p. 142f.   [3] Ellis, p. 157f.   [4] *Loc. cit.*

LIST OF ABBREVIATIONS[1]

AUTHOR AND TITLE OF BOOK	ABBREVIATION
CLAPPERTON, H. *Journal of a Second Expedition into the Interior of Africa*. London, 1829.	Clapperton, *S.E.*
DENNETT, R. E. *At the Back of the Black Man's Mind; Notes on the Kingly Office in West Africa*. London, 1906.	Dennett, *B.M.M.*
—— *Nigerian Studies; or the Religious and Political System of the Yoruba*. London, 1910.	Dennett, *N.S.*
ELLIS, A. B. *The Yoruba-Speaking Peoples of the Slave Coast of West Africa*. London, 1894.	Ellis.
FARROW, S. S. *Faith, Fancies and Fetich, or Yoruba Paganism*. London, 1924.	Farrow.
FROBENIUS, L. *The Voice of Africa*. 2 vols. London, 1913.	Frobenius.
HINDERER, A. *Seventeen Years in the Yoruba Country. Memorials of A. H. . . . gathered from her journals and letters*. With an introduction by R. B. Hone. London, 1872.	Hinderer.
JOHNSON, S. and O. *The History of the Yorubas from the earliest times to the beginning of the British Protectorate. . . .* Edited by Dr O. Johnson. London, 1921.	Johnson.
LUGARD. *A Tropical Dependency*. London, 1905.	Lady Lugard.
MEEK, C. K. *Tribal Studies in Northern Nigeria*. 2 vols. London, 1931.	Meek, *T.S.N.N.*
—— *A Sudanese Kingdom*. London, 1931.	Meek, *S.K.*
TALBOT, P. A. *The Peoples of Southern Nigeria*. 4 vols. Oxford, 1926.	Talbot.

[1] See note, Part I, p. 219 above.

5. THE TUAREG

PERHAPS no literature of which we have taken account in these volumes is composed against so picturesque a background as that of the desert Tuareg.[1] Left behind by time, they have lingered on in the security of their great natural mountain fortresses, defended by the 'Desert of Fear', the 'Desert of Death', and other arid and lifeless barriers, till their very existence was forgotten by all save the inhabitants of the fringing oases, who lived in perpetual fear of their raids and exactions. Yet their civilisation is neither exotic nor remote from that with which we are familiar in Europe. It is only more archaic. Making due allowance for desert conditions, it will be seen that the Tuareg have retained many of the customs and much of the culture of our own Middle Ages, perhaps also of our Dark Ages. Their literary coteries, and their preoccupation with 'courtly love' are such as we might have found in the Provençal courts of the twelfth century, and their poetical forms and formulae are such as flooded Europe during the Moslem invasion of Spain, and have lingered on in our own lyrical poetry down to the present day.[2]

But the Tuareg are not a fossil people, crystallised in an ancient and moribund tradition. Like all peoples who have remained in comparative isolation for centuries, they have developed their own customs and their own literary conventions till these have reached a degree of individuality well adapted to the needs, and expressive of the personality of a people in a specialised environment. Their way of life is that of a predatory heroic society.[3] They have maintained themselves by plundering the rich lands on their borders, and by defending and guiding those who pay them blackmail through their desert territory. In accordance with these, their only means of existence, they have developed a lofty standard of personal valour and of heroic honour. The women, left

---

[1] The Hon. F. J. R. Rodd refers (*The Times*, Nov. 3rd, 1922) to "the melodramatic atmosphere with which the Sahara has been invested"; but he admits (*P.V.* p. vi) the 'fascination' of the Tuareg, and there can be no doubt that, despite his sober *caveat*, it is largely the world of romance still lingering in the western desert which caused Rodd to describe his nine months' sojourn among the Tuareg as "the happiest he had ever spent" (*ib.* p. vii).

[2] For a recent study of the history of the Sahara, see Bovill.

[3] As elsewhere, we are speaking of conditions which prevailed before the spread of European influence.

much alone in charge of their worldly goods, enjoy an amount of freedom and a high social status to a degree almost unknown anywhere else.[1]

The Tuareg are a nomadic race; the nobles do no manual work, and the leisure afforded by their way of life, combined with the prominence of feminine society, has resulted in a love of poetry and a habit of extemporising lyrics which has reached a higher standard here than anywhere else among the peoples whom we have investigated. This is the more remarkable since the Tuareg are familiar with the art of writing, and have retained their native script. These traces of a more ancient civilisation, combined with the glamour and romance attached to heroic nomadism, have made the Tuareg a singularly interesting and attractive people to students of oral literature, and of literature which lies on the border line between minstrelsy and the written word.

In speaking of the customs and the literature, we shall use the present tense in general, for the Tuareg have retained their individuality, and in a great measure their independence, down to the last few years. It was not until 1900 that the French effectively penetrated the Sahara, nor until the Great War that the southern and western Tuareg were finally subdued. At the time when these pages were first drafted the Azger tribes behind the Italian territory of the Fezzan were still a free and unconquered people. But the French, and perhaps others also, have laid a heavy hand on the 'terror of the desert'. The Tuareg have been formed into a camel corps, their written literature has been dispersed. Since the Great War the European powers have turned their attention to the effective development of the Sahara, and we have little doubt that with the rail and motor enterprises of which our tourist agencies and newspapers apprise us from time to time, the face of the desert and its inhabitants is changing rapidly. It is probable that even yet much of the native culture remains. In 1928 the effects of European penetration were hardly apparent, except in the neighbourhood of the European forts; but we have no doubt that with modern methods change has been more rapid.

The Tuareg are a desert people of the central Sahara. Their territory is a larger continental area than that of any people whose literature we have examined, covering as it does some 1,500,000 square miles—a large area of the land surface of the world. Until last century the country was

---

[1] We may compare the relatively high status of women among the Arabs in pre-Islamic days. See Basset, *P.A.A.* p. 33 ff.

very little known and almost unexplored. Even the name of its inhabitants was still unfamiliar to many educated people in Europe, while a general impression prevailed that the entire area consisted of an unending and almost uninhabited waste of sand-dunes. In reality the country presents very varied geographical features, ranging from great masses of mountains, the peaks of which attain in some cases to an altitude of more than 10,000 feet, while elsewhere the elevation sinks through undulating valleys and foothills, to sandy waterless wastes. It is now generally recognised that the Sahara was in remote times a fertile area, rich in vegetation and animal life, stunted and degenerate remnants of which are still to be found in the upland pools and rivers.[1] The desert itself today, both in the Ahaggar mountains and in the east, presents the desiccated skeleton of a vast river system, and a once fertile country.[2] It is computed that the Sahara supports an average of only one individual to every 60 square miles.[3]

The Tuareg[4] who inhabit these great mountain masses of the Sahara are not a tribe but a 'people'. They are divided into several groups[5] of which the principal are: (1) the Aulemmiden, whose confederation occupies the Adrar[6] massif and the low-lying desert of the south down to the north bank of the Niger;[7] (2) the inhabitants of the mountains of Air (or Asben, as the name is known in the South), north of the Nigerian equatorial zone; (3) the Ahaggar, or, as the French call them, the Hoggar, who inhabit another great mountain group north-west of Air; (4) the Azger, occupying the mountain groups east of the Ahaggar, and across the low sandy waste of the north into the Fezzan, and along the northern foothills of the Ahaggar and Air mountains; (5) the Ifoghas in the south-west and in the central massif of the 'Adrar'. Roughly

---

[1] Kilian, p. 139 ff. *et ante*.

[2] For an account of the geological changes in the Sahara, see Bovill, *J.A.S.* xx (1921), p. 174 ff.; Rodd, *G.J.* LXVII (1926), p. 42 ff.; Gautier, *G.R.* XVI (1926), p. 387; Abadie, p. 79 ff.   [3] Buchanan, *Sahara*, p. 67.

[4] The best general account of the Tuareg published in recent times, though concentrating chiefly on Air, is that of Francis Rennell Rodd, *The People of the Veil*. The best earlier account for all except the Ahaggar tribes is that of Barth. Duveyrier was the first to give a detailed and valuable account of the Ahaggar.

[5] For the classification adopted above, see F. R. Rodd in *The Times*, March 19th, 1928, p. 16. See also *ib. P.V.* p. 17.

[6] *Adrar* means 'mountain'. This mountain group between Air and the Niger, and south of the Ahaggar, has no name. It is called the 'Mountain of the Ifoghas' (Rodd, *P.V.* p. 18, footnote).

[7] For a list of the tribes in the neighbourhood of the Niger, see Campbell, *W.W.A.* p. 78 f.

speaking the Ifoghas and the Aulemmiden Tuareg may be said to lie behind the French, the Air behind the British territory of the Niger Valley, the Ahaggar Tuareg behind the French of Algeria, and the Azger behind the Italian territory of the Fezzan. The latter are fairly closely associated with the Ahaggar Tuareg, though traditional feuds between individual tribes and groups also exist, as the French found to their cost in 1917. For the most part, however, the various groups are independent of one another.

These groups are by no means uniform. Air[1] is a mountain group, surrounded by desert on all sides. The mountains contain a number of permanent settlements with patches of cultivation, but true nomadism over wide ranges is practised in and around the hills. The Ahaggar[2] is somewhat more barren, and nomadism in a restricted sense is here the custom, though it is not usual for camps to move in a greater radius than about twenty-five miles.[3] The Azger mountains, being the highest, have a comparatively rich vegetation, though much of the territory of the Azger Tuareg[4] north of the mountains consists of low sand-dunes. Much of the territory of the Aulemmiden is almost devoid of either mountains or rivers, but the undulating plains are intersected by valleys which become watercourses in the rainy season, producing abundant grass. The Aulemmiden are the only Tuareg who, in addition to the camel, use horses, chiefly for purposes of warfare. Like the Ahaggar tribes, they move in a given area with extreme regularity.[5] The Ifoghas in the south-west and the central Adrar are all nomads, even their prince.

Physically the Tuareg are very distinctive. Unlike the Arabs of the western desert, they are tall in stature, tough and strong. They are well proportioned and graceful in carriage, slow and stately in movement. Their ankles and wrists are extraordinarily small, their hands long and delicate. The face is long and pointed, the nose straight and never

[1] See p. 652, footnote 4 above. The work of Jean is also valuable.
[2] For accounts of the Ahaggar, see the works of Duveyrier, Gautier, Bazin, Masqueray, Kilian, etc.
[3] Bazin, pp. 215 f., 294; Gautier, *G.R.* XVI (1926), p. 390.
[4] Interesting recent accounts of journeys through the country of the Azger Tuareg are given by Vischer, and by Harding King. For earlier accounts, see Richardson, Denham, etc.
[5] For a description of the country of the Aulemmiden, see Richer, p. 8 ff. An account of their nomadism will be found in *ib.* p. 5 ff. Richer's book, already referred to, and Palmer (*B.S.S. passim*) are our chief recent authorities for these tribes. For earlier accounts see also the work of Barth.

flattened, the eyes horizontal. The skin is fair, varying from 'white' to all shades of brown. But the complexion of the Tuareg men is extremely difficult to study, owing to the habit of wearing a *litham* or veil. This veil is never laid aside, even at night, or when eating, or even in the presence of the family. It is, however, never worn by women, who move about quite freely and invariably with the face uncovered. Whatever may have been the origin of this custom,[1] the rigidity with which it is adhered to is phenomenal. The desert is surely the most conventional society in the world.

The language is one of the Berber group, but the racial affinities of the Tuareg are much disputed, and the only conclusion which seems to be generally accepted is that they came originally to their present homes from the north,[2] having been probably driven into the desert by the Arabic invasion of north Africa during the seventh and eighth centuries of our era. They are certainly not the aborigines, but they are the ruling race wherever they are found, acting both as military protectors and proud masters to the various classes of darker-skinned people with whom they have contact. All Tuareg tribes are divided into three main classes, which consist of (1) the *Imajeghan* or nobles, the pure-blooded Tuareg, who are engaged solely in warfare and transit, and who do no manual work; (2) the *Imghad* or serf class who are akin to the *Imajeghan*, but less pure-blooded and darker in colour, and who are engaged in agriculture and the care of the flocks and herds; (3) the slaves. We may add the *marabouts* or priestly caste, and the offspring of mixed unions between Tuareg men and *Imghad* women. The Tuareg profess the Mohammedan faith, and the *marabouts* are the native clergy, who, though mostly drawn from special clans, are distributed throughout all the tribes.[3] The social organisation of the Tuareg as a whole is tribal. Each tribe, whether noble or serf, is governed by a leader who is rather the representative than the governor, and who may, upon occasion, be a woman,[4] though this is not usual. Groups of tribes in more or less close relations with one another form confederations for the conduct of affairs and for warfare, headed by a paramount chief known as an *amenokal*.

[1] One is inclined to suspect that it arose as a protection from sun and sand; but it is commonly believed to be derived from some forgotten ritual.

[2] A careful study of the subject will be found in Gautier's *Maghreb*; see especially p. 214 f.

[3] For accounts of the *marabouts* and the desert monasteries, see Richer, p. 4; Duveyrier, *Touareg*, p. 332; Harding King, p. 255 f.

[4] See Rodd, *P.V.* p. 169.

The Tuareg have no considerable towns, no developed industries, no made roads. They have supported themselves in the past, chiefly by the slave trade, partly by plunder,[1] and partly by acting as guides and convoys to the trans-Saharan traffic. They are not traders in the true sense of the term; they are convoyers. No caravan could safely pass through their territory without their protection and safe conduct. The ways and wells were known to themselves alone, and the lives of all travellers and caravans were in their hands.[2] As guides and protectors they are a peerless people; their code of honour is superb. Their manners are those of polished gentlemen,[3] and their pride is immense.[4] Many of their proverbs are significant of their aristocratic pretensions: 'Shame enters the family that tills the soil'; and again: 'Hell itself abhors dishonour'.[5]

All recent travellers in the Sahara are of the opinion that the civilisation of the Tuareg was at one time much richer than it is at present.[6] Many dry stone monuments strew the Ahaggar, some at least of which are believed to have belonged to Ahaggar dignitaries.[7] Many deserted villages, ascribed by tradition to the Itesan tribes, who are believed to be the first invaders of the country, show a superiority in point of building and architecture to the modern dwellings. The best wells are ascribed to the same early culture.[8] It is, of course, a question whether many of these features may not have been due to the earlier occupants of the desert, perhaps a darker-skinned negroid people akin to some of

[1] For a vivid account of the Tuareg exactions from the northern oases, especially Ghat, see Richardson II, pp. 37 f., 195 ff., 215 ff. Richardson's account of his travels in the Sahara deserves to be better known than it is for its interesting account of the Tuareg. See also Barth I, p. 181. For an account of the Tuareg as the dominant people in Timbuctoo, see *ib*. IV, p. 398 ff.

[2] See Gautier, *Conquête*, p. 202 ff.

[3] Rodd, *G.J.* LXII (1923), p. 88; *ib*. *P.V.* p. 420.   [4] See Bazin, p. 236.

[5] There has been much unintelligent and somewhat controversial matter written on the vices and virtues of the Tuareg in his relations with Europeans in the past. We would therefore stress the importance of the sober pronouncements of men like Rodd and Gautier. The latter in a brief review (*Conquête*, p. 195, *G.R.* XVI, 1926, p. 381) offers an estimate which is especially valuable on account of the intelligent character of its sympathy—a sympathy enlightened by an acute sense of the geographical and ethnological factors involved.

[6] See e.g. Jean, p. 82 ff.; Rodd, *G.J.* LXVII (1926), p. 29 ff.; Bovill, *J.A.S.* XX, p. 115; Buchanan, *Sahara*, p. 56 ff. For some account of the flourishing condition of the western oases in the fourteenth to sixteenth centuries, see Ch. de la Roncière, *R.D.M.* Feb. 1923, p. 653 ff.

[7] Gautier, *G.R.* XVI, p. 383.

[8] Rodd, *P.V.* pp. 377 f., 393; Buchanan, *Sahara*, p. 57 f.

those who today occupy the valley of the Niger. But apart from these relics of material culture, there can be no doubt that the Tuareg has lost ground, even in comparatively recent times. In the eighteenth and nineteenth centuries they exercised a paramount influence in Bornu. In the early part of last century they were the rulers of Timbuctoo. Assode, the chief city of Air, in the past, is believed to have numbered some 8000–10,000 inhabitants. When Barth passed close by it in 1850 it was said to contain over 1000 houses in ruins, only about 80 being still inhabited. It was said, moreover, to contain seven mosques.[1] Today it is quite deserted. Agades, the southern outpost, the 'port' of Air, is the largest town today. It is believed to have numbered 12,000 inhabitants in the past. Today there are less than 3000.[2]

The Tuareg has maintained possession of the desert for centuries by force of arms. His method of warfare is essentially the *razzia*,[3] the surprise raid. The men fight mounted on their camels, and their technique consists in swift and sudden attack and surprise movements. Indeed with the smallness of their numbers, and the vastness of the desert distances, it is difficult to see how they could have survived by any other method. Their arms are of the simplest,[4] consisting of a raw-hide shield, an iron broad-sword, and a spear and dagger. Bows and arrows they despise as dishonourable weapons.

One of the most interesting and distinctive features of their civilisation is the freedom and high status of the women.[5] The Tuareg are matrilinear. Descent is invariably counted through the female line.[6] A Tuareg woman inherits and possesses property in her own name, even after marriage, and after managing it entirely according to her own wishes during her life, married or other, she bequeathes it also as she wishes at her death.[7] She moves about freely and unattended, and travels without the need of male escort. She has men friends, etiquette demanding that she shall have a number at once, and not single out any

[1] Barth 1, p. 375 f.
[2] Buchanan estimated the population of Agades in the past at 50,000, today at about 2000 (Buchanan, *Sahara*, p. 67 f.). Rodd estimates it at 3000 (*P.V.* p. 402); Jean (p. 177) at less than 1000. Cf. further, Richer, p. 47.
[3] See Rodd, *P.V.* p. 235 ff.; Jean, p. 259 ff.
[4] Rodd, *loc. cit.*; Jean, p. 237 f.
[5] This feature of the Tuareg civilisation has been noted by all travellers, and it would be superfluous to multiply references.
[6] See Gautier, *Conquête*, p. 191.
[7] For a general account of the status and habits of the Tuareg women, see Rodd, *P.V.* p. 167 ff.

one for special preference.[1] On the members of her circle of men friends she is in the habit of bestowing favours in the form of some token, frequently inscribed with a verse or motto, like the ladies of the Middle Ages in Europe. It may be a piece of silk, a bracelet, or a garment embroidered as a token of remembrance or compact. These tokens are frequently referred to in the letters written by the Tuareg men when far from the lady to whom they have vowed allegiance and friendship (cf. p. 671 below). It should be added that the marriage tie is usually respected, and married women are expected to behave with decorum and modesty. On this matter public opinion is said to be strong.[2] Owing to the prolonged absence of the husbands from their homes, necessitated by the great distances of the desert, the women are generally the best educated people in the community, and many of them are taught by the *marabouts* to read and write.

The use of writing is widespread among the Tuareg, though it is rapidly dying out.[3] Their alphabet is peculiar to themselves, having nothing in common with that of the Arabs or of any other known peoples. They are indeed the only ancient people of north Africa who have kept an individual script. It is known as *tifinagh*, and is believed to be descended from an early Libyan alphabet of north Africa. As Rodd observes, the fact that a nomadic people should have retained a distinctive script when their way of life renders writing almost superfluous is in itself one of the many indications which we have that the Tuareg were once possessed of a far higher civilisation than they now display.[4] We have, however, no indication that it was at any time much used for literary purposes. Like the runic alphabet, it was chiefly used to inscribe names on objects, e.g. on rocks, weapons, musical instruments, and even dress.[5] It does not appear to have been much used for funerary inscriptions, but it is employed for correspondence.[6] No books or considerable manuscripts have been found written in *tifinagh*, and the Tuareg declare that there are none.[7] This is probably correct (though see p. 676 below).

[1] Duveyrier, *Journal*, p. 185.

[2] Rodd, *P.V.* p. 175 f. Rodd also gives a translation of some delightful passages from the *Travels* of Ibn Batuta, the great Arabic traveller who visited Air in the middle of the fourteenth century, and who writes most interestingly of the freedom of the habits of the Tuareg women.   [3] Rodd, *P.V.* p. 268 ff.

[4] *Ib. G.J.* LXVII, p. 33.   [5] Duveyrier, *Touareg*, p. 389.

[6] Rodd, *P.V.* p. 268; Masqueray, *passim*.

[7] Denham, etc. I, p. 121; Duveyrier, *Touareg*, p. 389; Richer, p. 44f.; Harding King, p. 285.

Books in the Arabic script are not rare among the Tuareg, and were probably much commoner in the past. Campbell[1] and Rodd[2] visited libraries preserved in caves in the mountains of Air, and both speak of manuscripts still to be found lying in the ruined mosques. These appear to contain chiefly the Mohammedan scriptures, and perhaps tribal histories and tribal genealogies (see p. 673 ff. below). Richer speaks of large numbers of manuscripts among the Aulemmiden.[3] Historical matter is preserved for the most part, however, in oral traditions. Many of these traditions refer back to the Tuareg migration into the Sahara from the north; and some of them may refer back to a period as early as the Arab invasion of north Africa in the seventh century. But Richer observes that—among the Aulemmiden at least—tradition is not to be trusted for more than four or five generations unless reinforced by written records.[4] There is always the possibility of the Tuareg historical records having been affected by the reading of the marabouts from written sources not yet investigated, and possibly also by later movements from the north. We shall discuss this subject more fully later.

Apart from the marabouts, the reading and writing of tifinagh, and such Arabic as is known, is chiefly an accomplishment of the women. Indeed the superior intellectual achievements of the women over those of the men have arrested the attention of all travellers.[5] We have seen that the same is true also of the nomad Tatars, though here the learning is purely oral in character. Among the Tuareg the men, and in particular the nobles among the Aulemmiden, are said to feel a haughty contempt for letters; but Duveyrier observed that the better educated among the Azger women would put to shame the Arab women of Algeria.[6] Like other forms of native Tuareg culture, the art of writing and the knowledge of Arabic are declining, and in Air the women are said to be comparatively ignorant of Arabic, though not of Tuareg lore.[7] There can be no doubt, however, that in general the women are chiefly responsible for the intellectual and artistic life of the Tuareg.

All Tuareg, men and women[8] alike, are poets. The women indeed excel in this art. If we exclude narrative and dramatic poetry, which are

---

[1] *T.V.T.* pp. 1 ff., 183 f.   [2] *P.V.* p. 302.

[3] Richer, p. 44 f.   [4] Richer, p. 13 f.; cf. also *ib.* p. 43.

[5] See e.g. Gautier, *G.R.* XVI (1926), p. 383; Rodd, *P.V.* p. 173.

[6] Duveyrier, *Touareg*, p. 420; *Journal*, p. 188 ff.; cf. Harding King, p. 315.

[7] See Jean, p. 230; cf. however, Rodd, *P.V.* pp. 173, 268.

[8] It will be remembered that many women poets were famous in pre-Islamic Arabic literature. See Basset, *P.A.A.* p. 37 f.

not found among the Tuareg, it may perhaps be said that they have practised the art of extempore composition more widely than any other people whose literature we have studied. They excel in personal and occasional poetry. The names of some of their poets have been remembered for several generations for the excellence of their works.[1] We never hear of professional poets or minstrels, however. The art of poetical composition is in the nature of a polite accomplishment, common to all, and enjoyed by all, and the love of poetry and song is one of the most characteristic and striking features of Tuareg social life. Poetry is sung, chanted, or recited, with or without music. In general the art of extemporising appears to be more widely and highly cultivated than that of memorisation, and examples of poetry relating to the past are comparatively rare in the collections, though the Rodds heard a poem recited in Air which had reference to past events,[2] and F. R. Rodd refers to "traditional poems of their race which are so old that their origin has been forgotten".[3] Bazin also refers to "poems that have been handed down in the family or tribe from generation to generation".[4] It is by no means rare for poems to be composed in private, and memorised for subsequent recitation.[5] F. R. Rodd mentioned to us two poems composed by a native of Air which were not extempore, but memorised by the composer, and afterwards recited to F. R. Rodd himself and his brother Peter Rodd. It is an interesting and rare circumstance in composition of this kind that although the same poems were recited on several successive days, the Rodds noticed that the wording did not vary.[6] The process of verbal memorising is evidently not wholly undeveloped in Air, and we must conclude that the rarity in our collections of poems undoubtedly ancient is due to the wealth of contemporary poetry, and the widespread art of extempore composition; probably also in part to the absence of research by travellers.

The recitation of poetry is commonly accompanied by the *amẓad*, which is the only stringed instrument in use among the Tuareg,[7] and which is one of the stock articles of the furnishings of a Tuareg tent.[8] It is composed of half a calabash, over the hollow of which a skin is

[1] See e.g. Campbell, *T.V.T.* p. 208f.; Haardt and Dubreuil, p. 227f.; Rodd, *P.V.* p. 271; Bazin, p. 277.
[2] F. R. Rodd mentioned this to us in conversation.
[3] *P.V.* p. 271.   [4] Bazin, p. 237.   [5] *Ib.* p. 283.
[6] The notes on the composition and recitation of these poems were given to us by F. R. Rodd in conversation.
[7] A detailed account of the *amẓad* is given by Rouanet, together with a picture. See Lavignac v, p. 2925.   [8] Jean, p. 211; Bazin, p. 237.

stretched, pierced with one or two holes. It has only one string, and is played with a curved bow, and is used solely to accompany the human voice. Tuareg music is mainly vocal.[1] The *amẓad* is played principally by women, whether to accompany the songs of the men or their own recitations. Although, according to Rouanet,[2] it is not usual for women of noble birth to sing themselves, Duveyrier noted in his *Journal* that in Ghadames when a woman sings the men seat themselves in a circle and listen,[3] and it is clear that women of all classes sing and play the *amẓad*. This accomplishment is a part of their education, and is taught to the young people by their parents in their leisure moments.[4] Indeed the part played by the *amẓad* in the social life of the Tuareg is of unique importance, and we may gather from the following lines in what high esteem it is held:

> I humbly adore the acts of the most High,
> Who has given to the fiddle[5] what is better than a soul,
> So that when it plays, the men are silent,
> And their hands cover their *lithams*[6] to hide their emotions.
> The troubles of love are pushing me into the tomb,
> But thanks to the fiddle, O son of Aicloum,
> God has given me back my life.[7]

A brief notice on the relationship of Tuareg poetic metres to the musical accompaniment is given by Rouanet in his account of Tuareg music. Though Rouanet wrote from Algiers, he had presumably some facilities for studying Tuareg music, and his observations are important, both for Tuareg and for other African poetry. He tells us that the basis of the songs is a *tiouit*, an air, or rather a 'timbre' to which the poetical compositions are adapted by means of contractions, elisions, and every kind of grammatical compromise. Poetical metre does exist, but musical metre is the governing factor, and so poetry is made subservient to music. The Tuareg have, Rouanet adds, according to the confederation to which they belong, a variable number of *tiouit* to which they adapt all their poetical compositions.[8]

We have no doubt that Rouanet is right in his main conclusion—that musical measure is the basis of Tuareg poetical metre. And his

---

[1] Rouanet; see Lavignac v, p. 2893.   [2] *Loc. cit.*
[3] *Journal*, p. 183.   [4] Rouanet, Lavignac v, p. 2893.
[5] The word *amẓad* is translated 'fiddle', 'violin', or 'mandoline' by English and French writers. As it is played with the bow, the two former words give the nearest equivalent.
[6] The *litham* is the veil worn by all noble Tuareg men (see p. 654 above).
[7] Haardt and Dubreuil, p. 231.   [8] See Lavignac v, p. 2893.

observation is supported by Hanoteau's statement that when the latter asked some Tuareg on what rules their prosody was based, they seemed astonished at the question, and assured him that in composing poetry, their ear was their only guide.[1] Nevertheless Rouanet's statement that poetical metre as such does not exist certainly requires some modification, for Hanoteau[2] and Rodd[3] both agree that while the prosody is not strict, yet a certain amount of formality is observable. This formality results in what is virtually a poetical metre, and this may be, and probably is, ultimately based on musical rhythm, as Rouanet observes. Iambic verses of nine, ten, or eleven syllables are the most usual forms of scansion, with a regular caesura, and rhyme or assonance. In regard to the latter there is somewhat wide licence. Sometimes both rhyme and assonance are absent. Most commonly the same rhyme is continued throughout a whole poem. Sometimes the assonances are much mixed, and such terminations as those in 'pen', 'mountain', and 'waiting' would be permissible.[4]

Hanoteau makes some observations[5] on the general character of Tuareg poetry which are especially interesting for the close similarity which they show to the poetry of the Galla, to whom the Tuareg are possibly racially akin. The poetical compositions of the Tuareg are generally addressed to individuals of the same tribe as the poet, who are perfectly well acquainted with both the persons and the events to which allusion is made. In consequence the idea is generally hinted at rather than fully expressed. The author always seems afraid of insulting the intelligence of his public by developing it *in extenso*. These remarks might be made with equal truth of the poetry of both the Galla and the Abyssinians, as will readily be seen from examples of the poetry of all three peoples cited in the present volume.

Although the men do not practise minstrelsy, they are all poets and fond of singing. As is natural in a heroic people, songs of love and war are among the favourite types of composition. Panegyrics on the successful warrior, boasting poems in which the hero extols his own deeds, and hortatory poetry are widely cultivated. Panegyric poetry is perhaps the commonest, and is composed by all classes, men and women, from the highest *amenokal* to the poorest woman on the verge of starvation, and is called forth by the generosity of the Frenchman as readily as by the prowess of the *Imajegh*. When Lieut. Vella, a young French officer, risked his life among the flying bullets at the battle of

---

[1] Hanoteau, p. 201.
[2] *Loc. cit.*
[3] *P.V.* p. 271.
[4] Rodd, *loc. cit.*
[5] *Loc. cit.*

Assakoa to rescue an Ahaggar chief who was mortally wounded, carrying him from the field on his shoulders, the grateful Tuareg celebrated his act of gallantry in the following lines:

> None go to Assakoa but men of courage.
> Lieutenant Vella has killed hundreds of men among the enemies.
> He defeated Sultan Ahmoud, whose thoughts were but of women expert on the fiddle,
> He pushed them to the foot of the mountain where they died. . . .
> His memory will never be forgotten among the women who play the amʒad.[1]

We have a number of such poems composed by the Taitoq in Algiers in praise of the French officer Masqueray.[2]

The finest example of a panegyric which we have seen was composed in 1894 by a Tuareg of the Ahaggar celebrating a successful raid by Musa Ag Amastane, the great Ahaggar chief who attached himself to the French and remained loyal to their cause throughout the Senussi revolt till his death in 1916. The poem opens with a picture of the hero as he rides forth to the raid on his high camel:

> Musa, son of Amastane, rides amidst the sand-hills.
> We follow him as, with his foot, he urges on his enlisted *mehari*,[3]
> Which has a (high) hump and is girthed with white muslin.
> On its flank rests his rifle.
> Musa has given him a great number of horses as companions.[4]

The poet then goes on to upbraid another tribe which has not joined Musa:

> You have no honour left, O bad Imrad.
> You have rejected Musa and let him go alone into Ahnet, the country of violins, to recruit his companions.
> In none of your men has awakened the sense of honour.
> Look, all men follow Musa, even the lame and the one-armed, but not you.
> The lame Akamadu with his white-footed camel rides close by the side of Musa's,
> Kaima, the one-armed, with his bundle tramps side by side with Musa and his men.

The poem concludes characteristically with a reference to the women

---

[1] Haardt and Dubreuil, p. 234. [2] Masqueray, p. 204, etc.
[3] A riding camel of fine breed.
[4] Musa is evidently supplied with horses and arms by the French. None of the Tuareg except the Aulemmiden keep horses, and few are able to afford a rifle (cf. p. 656 above).

left behind at the well, and a tribute from the hero to their beauty, and protestations of his love.[1]

Women readily compose panegyric poetry. De Foucauld records a panegyric on the *amenokal* Amud composed by a woman of the Ahaggar,[2] presumably of noble birth; but the practice is not confined to the rich, for the same writer also gives a poem of thanks recited by a poor woman to a French officer who had given her alms, in which her poverty is expressed in plain terms:

> Hungry, exhausted, crying...
> I went to the captain who had pity on me,

and in which she does not forget to thank the benevolent young officer 'Valorous in war', because

> He makes women shout with joy and wins merit in the eyes of God.[3]

In Air also the generosity of the French is much admired by the women and frequently made the subject of extempore poetry.[4] And in their panegyrics the Tuareg, like other heroic people, such as the Turkomans and the Kara-Kirghiz, do not forget the companions of their rides, among the Tuareg the camel:

> Instead of wings, I have my *mehari*.
> Praise to God the Mighty One,
> Who gave me my *mehari*, brown with white spots,
> To carry me where love calls.[5]

A little panegyric on the *amẓad* has already been quoted above (p. 660).

Hortatory poetry is very popular, and the women are again among the foremost composers. The women were largely responsible for the obstinate resistance which the Ahaggar Tuareg offered to the French, sometimes interposing their own bodies between their husbands and the enemy to prevent the latter from firing. The reward of the brave in these poems is again the praise of the *amẓad* and honour from the women;[6] but the chief practical aim in the forays is, of course, plunder. It is the same in the boasting poems of the men:

> We bore off their swords with beautiful sheaths, and their shields white as
> cream,
> And grey camels worthy of praise,
> Fit to be saddled for fair ladies to ride.[7]

---

[1] Bazin, p. 274.   [2] *Ib.* p. 277.   [3] *Ib.* p. 278.
[4] Jean, p. 212.   [5] Haardt and Dubreuil, p. 232.
[6] For examples, see Masqueray, pp. 195, 248.
[7] Translated from the French translation of Masqueray, p. 247; cf. Duveyrier, *Touareg*, p. 450f.

The men frequently make the most extravagant claims of the havoc which they have wrought among the enemy, and of the devastating wounds which they themselves have received. "Lances are sticking out of my body", cries a hero of the Kel Fadei tribe, "like the horns of a cow."[1] One of the Ahaggar who had fought against the Aulemmiden in 1895 boasts of his deeds to 'all women who go to gallant parties',[2] and urges them to shower down curses on any man whom they find near them who—unlike himself—has absented himself from the fray.

> When the enemy fled, I took my sword in my hand,
> I struck at their legs, which flew off like jerjer stalks,[3]
> I defy them to use them hereafter on the march.[4]

Another boasts after the Battle of Tit, one of the French disciplinary rounds in the Ahaggar, and like the last poet, he also addresses his boast to the women at the evening parties:

> The young women who gather round the violin will not hear it said of me that I hid in the rocks.
> Is it not true that after falling three times they had to lift me up,
> And that they bound me unconscious on a camel with cords?
> On that account defeat is not dishonour.
> Even against the Prophet himself, pagans have won the victory in days of yore.[5]

These men fight, like the Anglo-Saxon heroes, for *dom*, the honour of fair fame; but there is a difference. The Anglo-Saxon hero thinks of the reputation which will live on and do honour to his name after he himself has passed away. The Tuareg hero thinks of the ladies with their violins, with whom he would win favour and credit during his life, for it is in their songs that his reputation lies.

Warlike poetry and epigrams are sometimes recited in poetical contests by people of opposing parties. A gibe or poetical diatribe calls forth an answer from the person or some poet of the party attacked, and a poetical duel results. In such cases the pieces of verse, the attacks and replies, follow one another in great numbers. It is said that in wars

[1] Abadie, p. 396. The Kel Fadei are said to be related to the Taitoq, one of the noblest and proudest of the tribes of the Ahaggar (see p. 671 below), from whom they are believed to have come, though they are now in the south-west. They are reputed the greatest robber nomads of Air (Abadie, p. 159).

[2] I.e. the *ahal*; see p. 666 below.

[3] A plant, the stalks of which are carried away by the wind of the desert (ED.).

[4] Bazin, p. 275.

[5] *Ib.* p. 275. Instances of boasting poems will be found also in Masqueray, no. 45 ff.; Abadie, p. 396, and throughout the other collections cited.

poetical hostilities always accompanied armed hostilities.[1] In these poetical hostilities the women are as proficient as the men, and sometimes compose diatribes against one another. Campbell records a poem in which a Tuareg lady pokes fun at a woman of their hereditary enemies, the Chaanba, a tribe which is much mixed with Arab blood, and has in some measure adopted Arab customs, such as the veiling of the women:

> Ah, there she goes, the woman of the veil.
> She is afraid to show herself because she is so ugly;

—and more to the same effect.[2]

It is not necessary to dwell on the innumerable examples of occasional poetry of this kind, which is immensely popular among the Tuareg. A few suffice to give a general idea of their style and scope, though it should be added that the variety is considerable. In addition to the subjects mentioned above, we have poems, both panegyric and abusive, composed, not only on individuals, but also on tribes[3]—a class of poetry of which the Tuareg are especially fond. This tribal interest is the less surprising in view of the fact that the tribes are small, every individual of noble rank being known over a wide area of the desert. Another large class of poetry which is widely represented in the collections consists of occasional poems, which record incidents of the journey,[4] or register the events of a raid impersonally. Poems of this kind give a series of rapid impressionist pictures.[5] They serve as poetical journalism in countries where oral poetry is the principal vehicle for rapidly conveying news. The Tuareg offer a rich field for studying the slighter forms of topical poetry which are rarely recorded from those peoples among whom heroic narrative poetry has been recorded, such as the Tatars and the Russians.

Amid so much raiding and plunder, it is surprising how little poetical record we have of the deaths of heroes.[6] Elegiac poetry is hardly represented in the collections which have come under our notice.[7] This may be due to accident, though so long as the Tuareg fought only among

---

[1] Bazin, p. 273; cf. Rouanet, Lavignac v, p. 2893.   [2] Campbell, *T.V.T.* p. 223.

[3] See e.g. Masqueray, p. 234; Duveyrier, *Touareg*, p. 351f.; Campbell, *T.V.T.* p. 223; Bazin, p. 14.

[4] P. R. Rodd, *B.S.O.S.* v, pt. i (1928), p. 112.   [5] *Ib.* pp. 109ff., 111f.

[6] In this respect Tuareg poetry appears to differ from pre-Islamic Arabic poetry, where elegiac poetry is prominent, especially among the poems composed by women. See Basset, *P.A.A.* p. 37.

[7] A brief example is recorded by Haardt and Dubreuil, p. 232.

themselves, the simplicity of their arms perhaps precluded the possibility of much loss of life. For despite their proud boasts of slaughter inflicted, and wounds received (p. 664 above), plunder rather than bloodshed was the avowed object of their raids, which were necessitated by poverty rather than by hatred. Annur, the chief of the Air Tuareg at the time when Barth passed through the country in the middle of last century, considered the Europeans dreadful barbarians for slaughtering without pity such large numbers of people with their guns, instead of fighting with spear and sword, 'the only manly and becoming weapons'.[1]

The art of poetry and minstrelsy is stimulated and fostered by an attractive custom which prevails throughout the Sahara, and which has already been referred to in some of the quotations given above. This is the custom of holding evening parties, known as *ahal* or *diffa*.[2] Such parties are attended by the young men and the young unmarried women and widows.[3] According to Jean, who writes chiefly of Air, married women do not go to the *ahal*;[4] but this rule does not seem to be universal.[5] Such a party is generally presided over by a woman famous for her beauty and wit, her minstrelsy or her gift of improvising poetry; and such women are sometimes famous throughout the Sahara as the greatest poets of their time.[6] The men also take part, often composing verses beforehand in preparation for the *ahal*. Witty and cultivated conversation and story-telling form an important element in the evening's entertainment.[7] It is said that a young man will sometimes go from sixty to a hundred and twenty miles to be present at the *ahal* of a woman famous for her beauty and wit.[8] A rigid etiquette governs the entire conduct of the function, even the dress.[9]

These gatherings have been constantly compared to the Provençal Courts of Medieval Europe, where the compositions of the troubadours were recited, and where courtly love and Platonic friendship between men and women were in fashion, and formed the chief inspiration of the artistic and intellectual life. The comparison is rendered closer by the great freedom which women enjoy, and the custom of having men friends. Great freedom of speech prevails, and it is not surprising that

---

[1] Barth I, p. 294; cf. Rodd, *P.V.* p. 235 f.; Jean, p. 237 ff.
[2] For a description of the *ahal*, see Denham, etc. I, p. 59; Haardt and Dubreuil, p. 227; Duveyrier, *Touareg*, p. 363; Bazin, p. 316 f.; Kilian, p. 152; Rodd, *P.V.* p. 271 f.
[3] Bazin, p. 237.   [4] Jean, p. 211.
[5] See Duveyrier, *Journal*, p. 183 f.; cf. also Rouanet, Lavignac v, p. 2893.
[6] Rodd, *P.V.* p. 271.   [7] Denham, etc. I, p. 126.
[8] Bazin, p. 237.   [9] *Ib. loc. cit.*; Bazin cites Gautier, *Conquête*.

the *ahal* is sometimes looked askance at by the graver sort of parent, as we may gather from the following poem:

> My parents had stopped me from starting for the *ahal*...
> I remained, I shed tears, I went back to the tent;
> I wrapped myself up and hid my face and lay down;
> Even that seemed to increase my sorrow.
> I could not rest; I put on my crossed sash; I ran to the place where the camels were crouching;
> I seized a well-trained one;
> I put the saddle on the top of his hump where the hair ends;
> I was evenly balanced on him, and made him go down into the valley of Isten.
> When I stopped short, on getting near the *ahal*, they said to me: "What has happened?"
> I replied: "Nothing has happened
> But depression and a gloomy face."
> And now, there is but one God! it is written;
> I shall see the maiden with the white teeth.[1]

De Foucauld, the Trappist monk and missionary to the Ahaggar Tuareg, who has left us one of the best pictures of the *ahal*, naturally frowned on the custom, but among the young people it is immensely popular. Consternation was widespread among the Ahaggar Tuareg when a rumour spread that the French general Laperrine meant to put an end to these parties. By a strange irony, when Laperrine turned to look for an interpreter to contradict the rumour, the task fell to de Foucauld himself, who happened to be standing beside him.[2] The relief to the young Tuareg must have been intense, for there can be no doubt that with the suppression of the *ahal*, the poetry and minstrelsy, the witty conversations, and all that goes to make up the cultivated intellectual life of the desert nomad would have vanished; and nothing could have taken its place, for the *ahal* is a relic of a practice once common in the south of France and in north Africa whence it was doubtless derived. It is a survival in the desert from the Middle Ages, like the poetry which it inspires:

> Last night we tethered our camels
> Under the walls of the village.
> We made a shelter with our garments.
> Suddenly I heard an air of music
> Played by beautiful maidens who held their fiddles on their knees.[3]

[1] Bazin, p. 276. [2] *Ib.* p. 283.
[3] Haardt and Dubreuil, p. 233.

The influence of the *ahal* on the life and thought of the Tuareg is seen perhaps most clearly in the letters written by the Tuareg prisoners in Algiers to their friends and relatives in the desert, and in the replies which they received. The homesick dreams of these exiles are never of home and family, but always of the *ahal*. The messages are not messages of homely solicitude, but of courtly love to Tuareg ladies of their acquaintance. Their hopes and their boasts are that they will be celebrated in the songs of the Tuareg girls to the notes of the *amẓad*. Their greatest fear is the scornful song. In a letter to the French officer Masqueray, one of these writers declares roundly: "I am going to war for fear of the curse of hell, and for fear of the parties of young girls and their violins."[1] When the Tuareg ladies write messages to them in return, the greatest compliment they can pay them is the promise that they will not again touch the *amẓad* till the heroes return from Algiers.[2] The boast after a successful raid or expedition is the same:

I boast of it among the violins.[3]

The fashion of friendship and courtly love between men and women, and the highly developed art of extemporising produce numerous amatory poems in a highly adulatory style and embroidered diction. These poems are not necessarily intended to convey the sentiment of personal affection, but rather of the kind of courtly love which the Provençal poets express for the lady to whom they offer homage. Such poems are very commonly composed to be recited to the accompaniment of the *amẓad* before the assembly at the *ahal*, whether the poem in question refers to the lady who happens to be presiding, or another. A number of such poems are addressed to a lady whose name is Rakhma Oult Fenda:

Rakhma Oult Fenda, what she does, I do.
If she fly to Orion, I go there.
If she return to earth, I am there.
If she plunge into the uttermost desert, I have my *mehari*[4] to join her.[5]

Poems such as this are very often composed in praise of ladies famous for their beauty and wit, and the pages of de Foucauld, Haardt and Dubreuil, Masqueray, and others who have recorded Tuareg poetry contain many examples, some of them composed by men in responsible

---

[1] See Masqueray, p. 116; cf. p. 104.   [2] *Ib*. p. 88.
[3] See Masqueray, p. 255; cf. *ib*. p. 252.
[4] For the *mehari*, see p. 662, footnote 3 above.
[5] Haardt and Dubreuil, p. 234.

positions. The *amenokal* Musa Ag Amastane, to whom reference has been made above, was not above composing such a poem in honour of Dacine, a famous Tuareg beauty, which opens with the usual adulatory phrases:

> Dacine is the moon;
> Her neck outshines the neck of the colt,
> Tethered in a field of oats or wheat in April, etc.

And concludes as follows:

> She is free and gracious. She plays the violin,[1]
> And she sings pleasingly.
> I should give in alms the people and the herds who go up into the
>   mountains,
> And all the pasturage which fattens men and goats,
> From Gougueran hither, and as far as Bornu, . . .
> If thou, Dacine, dwelt in my heart as the sun among the stars. . . .
> As for me, she no longer turns her head towards me;
> She pays no heed to me.

This poem was recited at an *ahal* "in a pure, clear and well-modulated voice by quite a young girl". According to custom the entire assembly joined in at the end of each verse in a humming chorus.[2]

Women compose these poems of facile love as readily as men, and with something of the grace and light touch of the Elizabethans:

> Shall I compare thee to a white *mehari*, to a camel of Termai?
> To a herd of Kita antelopes? To the fringe of Jerba's red scarf?
> To grapes which have just ripened?
> In a valley where alongside of them ripens the date?
> Amûmen is the thread on which have been strung the pearls of my
>   necklace.
> He is the cord on which are hung the talismans on my breast.
> He is my life.[3]

This facility in composition, and the constant habit of extemporising have been aided by, and in their turn tend to perpetuate, a highly stereotyped form of diction, a conservative turn of expression, a static phraseology. Metaphors and figures of speech, once fresh, have become trite, though the Tuareg has never lost the art of concluding his effusion with a climax, generally reserving his choicest phrase, his most daring and delightful extravaganza, for the closing lines. He makes his exit

[1] I.e. the *amẓad*. [2] Haardt and Dubreuil, p. 228.
[3] Bazin, p. 278.

with éclat. The constant practice afforded by the *ahal*, with its circle of exacting critics, themselves all composers and musicians in their own way, ensure that he shall never be out of form, never at a loss. An amusing example of the readiness with which a Tuareg can produce a poem suited to the occasion at a moment's notice is recorded by Hanoteau. A Tuareg noble named Bedda, during his stay in Algiers, was asked to write some verses in the album of a young French lady. Being, like most Tuareg, an excellent improviser, Bedda was by no means at a loss, and at once wrote the following verses:

"It is I who have spoken: 'Your name, Angelina, has kindled in my soul a love which cannot be extinguished, and for your love I would go as far as France. Your eye slays by its brilliance and takes away the reason from the heart of man. If your value could be measured, I would give six thousand pieces of gold for you; I would give my horse for you.... He who shall possess you will find sweet repose. Before this young lady had attained to a marriageable age, we did not imagine that the gazelle had assumed human form; but now we have seen this marvel. If this young lady came into our country of the plains, there is not a man who would not hasten to look at her.'"[1]

The facility with which Bedda composed his poem, despite the conventionality of its phraseology, proves that a *höfuðlausn*[2] would not keep a Tuareg awake at night.

It will be seen that a striking feature of this poetry is the refinement of language and sentiment, the courtly tone—a courtliness and refinement which we know governs in general the intercourse between Tuareg men and women. There is a total absence of coarseness of speech or reference. The Tuareg has no company manners. He is always a gentleman. The poetry is composed to be recited to, or by, ladies in public, and is never guilty of impropriety. Its chivalry of thought and expression are based, not merely on literary conventions, but also on the social usage and institutions of Tuareg society. It is perhaps hardly necessary to quote examples in illustration of a feature which is obvious everywhere in their poetry; but we would like to call attention to one poem in particular in which refinement of feeling and of touch have left a charming record of a situation which in more fumbling hands would have become coarse or ludicrous. The poem is addressed by the Tuareg prisoner, Moumen, in the hospital in Algiers

[1] Hanoteau, p. 208.

[2] For this poem, composed in one night by the Norse poet Egill Skallagrímsson, see Vol. I, p. 343 of the present work.

in 1899, to a lady, probably Sister Joseph, the nun who nursed him and his fellow prisoners—Tuareg nobles of the Taitoq tribe—through an attack of small-pox. It describes, allusively and more by implication than by direct statement, the advances which the noble Tuareg had made to Sister Joseph, whom he likens to a gazelle pasturing on fresh grass in the valleys all alone:

> but she fled from me;
> She said to me: "I have nothing to say to you, you are a man...."
> She is the nourishment of the life which is in my breast.
> But we cannot 'go in company'; she will not come alone with me.
> But I shall remember her until I die of waiting.[1]

It is not easy to convey in English the aloofness and delicacy of Masqueray's translation of the Tuareg text, or the noble prisoner's uncomprehending respect for the withdrawal of the lady. Naïvely enough the concluding lines of the poem were added by Mastan, a fellow Tuareg, also nursed by Sister Joseph. In these the nurse is compared to the fine grass, the moonlight from a cloudless sky:

> She even surpasses the gardens in In-Salah.[2]

In-Salah is a group of oases in southern Algeria, and its gardens would be the most restful and delightful thing known to the Tuareg in his native land. The charm of the whole incident lies in the fact that the Tuareg were doubtless thanking Sister Joseph in the only way dictated by their own code of good manners. Both made the effort; both would no doubt have said that she would expect it of them.

It is clear from a comparison of this and other poems written by the noble Taitoq prisoners in Algiers with the letters[3] written by the same men to their friends at home, and to the French officers and others with whom they came in contact, that it is much easier and more natural for them to compose any kind of formal address in poetry than in prose. These letters, and the letters which the prisoners received from their friends in the desert, are written, like the poems, in *temajegh*,[4] and are therefore a characteristic development and expression of native thought. Their diction resembles that of the poems closely, and is equally conventional; but we miss the easy self-confidence of the extempore poems. The letters are laboured, and unlike the facile flow of the Tuareg verse, they are generally brief. The customary opening formula is: 'I Chek-

---

[1] Translated from Masqueray, p. 221.   [2] See Masqueray, p. 222.
[3] A collection of these letters was published by Masqueray, p. 67 ff.
[4] The language of the Tuareg is called *temajegh*.

kadh (Moumen, Mastan, etc.) speaking: Sign, the gold ring which we received from you', or the mention of some other token or action or event common to both the writer and the receiver of the letter. Then follow a few brief personal sentences. The letters generally end with the formula: 'I, Kenan, etc. speaking', and protestation of gratitude, etc.

As is to be expected in the literature of a people professing the Mohammedan religion, literature of native learning appears to be almost unknown among the Tuareg. In particular gnomic poetry or prose seems to be rare. De Foucauld mentions 'epigrams' as among the 'usual subjects' of verse, among the northern Tuareg,[1] and it is said that in the past laws were handed down orally.[2] According to tradition in Air, laws which were promulgated in the past were made known by a camel crier, who "visited groups of nomad tents, and proclaimed each law in the name of the king and people".[3] Descriptive catalogue poetry is apparently not very rare. An example recorded by P. R. Rodd from Air bears a striking resemblance to the Anglo-Saxon poem on the *Endowments of Men*, referred to in Vol. I, p. 418 of the present work.

> Behold a community of Tuareg
> camped at Terezeren.
> Some have camels and goats;
> some have horses and cattle;
> some cut down trees,
> they work at the carpenter's craft;
> some drill;
> some patrol the country and are anxious,
> they tighten their saddle girths;
> some dig the ground
> to give them corn in plenty;
> some work at the chase and trapping,
> they ride on the watch for game.
> There are some who know no work;
> They sit and tidy their veils,
> they pull out the ends and tighten them.
> The camel herd is like a varied pattern
> of white camels and black.
> A pretty face with a smile showing the teeth
> finds no enemies,
> a slave prepares a funeral and the wood for the bier.[4]

[1] Bazin, p. 273. [2] Duveyrier, *Touareg*, p. 427. [3] Campbell, *T.V.T.* p. 195.
[4] *B.S.O.S.* v, Pt. i, p. 111. With this poem we may compare another of similar type recorded by Hanoteau from the northern Tuareg, p. 215.

It has been observed that while the Tuareg are exceptionally proficient in the art of extemporising poetry, we have comparatively few examples of ancient poems in the collections, and therefore little evidence of sustained memorising or exact verbal poetical tradition among them. The explanation which most readily suggests itself is that the Tuareg, possessing the art of writing, have no great need of cultivating the memory. But this explanation hardly meets the case, for it does not seem likely that the Tuareg were much in the habit of writing their poems at any time,[1] and the more probable explanation is that they have never abandoned the universal African habit of extemporising their poetry. On the other hand, the presence of a written prose literature in all probability accounts for the fact that little saga of value has been noted among the Tuareg. This manuscript literature is entirely written in Arabic script, and largely composed in the Arabic language, while a very large proportion of it consists of works on Arabic learning and the Mohammedan religion. The learned Tuareg *marabouts*, therefore, and their pupils, both men and women, who are able to read and write, have, for the most part, been familiar with only such written prose as embodies an alien tradition. At the same time the presence of this body of prose literature in their midst must have militated here, as in other Mohammedan and Christian communities, such as Abyssinia, against the cultivation of traditional oral prose.

A certain amount of traditional prose has, however, been preserved. This consists in a great measure of (1) geographical and place-name speculation and brief stories, generally of purely local interest, in which the supernatural plays a large part;[2] and (2) tribal history and genealogical matter. The first have originated in some cases among the *marabouts* and *mallams*,[3] but have doubtless been circulated largely by guides and caravan leaders and attendants, who seem to be the chief purveyors of popular antiquarianism in the desert. These prose traditions and speculations are for the most part similar to the stories of this class which we have found in all countries, and they do not call for special study here. The historical traditions and native records are important, however, and though they belong properly to the study of history, such records

---

[1] It is true that European writers sometimes speak as if the Tuareg are in the habit of writing their poems down even today. And it is also true that the Tuareg do sometimes write them down, as we have seen; but we do not think that this is their usual practice.

[2] Examples will be found in Masqueray, p. 159 ff.; Campbell, *T.V.T.* p. 185; Haardt and Dubreuil, p. 247 ff.   [3] Buchanan, *Sahara*, p. 104 f.

have a direct bearing on the study of oral literature, especially in a country which, like the Tuareg, may be said to be on the borderline between the literate and the unlettered.

Many tribes are stated to have preserved their genealogies, some in written, others in oral form. There are also tribal traditions which narrate how a particular tribe came into a given district, and from what district it came. Such traditions also are said to be preserved in both oral and written form, the oral traditions being handed down by the chiefs and the rest of the tribe, the written records by chiefs and by *marabouts*. It is not always easy to gauge how far these two streams of record are independent of one another. We will examine a few examples for which we have specific evidence.

Duveyrier tells us that among the Azger Tuareg he received much traditional matter on the origin of the tribe in a letter from the Sheikh Ibrahim Ult-Sidi, who was reputed to be the most learned among the Tuareg. The contents of this letter were accepted by the Tuareg as the expression of their common views. Duveyrier mentions further that Azger popular tradition adds to the contents of the note certain details on the formation of their confederation and on the division of the lands among the different tribes.[1] Possibly therefore, both written and traditional sources were available for information regarding the history of the Azger, and each was probably reinforced at times by the other.

Among the Aulemmiden Richer tells us that the knowledge of the past history of their tribe is carried on only by oral traditions,[2] and that these traditions are practically valueless for the period before the sixteenth century.[3] By implication we may assume that from this period they have a solid historical value. No documents written in *tifinagh* have, of course, been found among them, but the existence of documents written in Arabic is very probable, for some of the more learned of their *marabouts* possess extensive libraries, which will probably be found to possess 'des documents précieux pour l'histoire'.[4] Here, therefore, as among the Azger in the north, the interchange between written and oral tradition is to be suspected. A flourishing antiquarian saga seems to have been current among all classes,[5] reinforced and possibly inspired by lettered *marabouts*.

Jean refers to tradition in Aïr as "des souvenirs imprécis, transmis de géneration en géneration, mais sans fidélité et se réduisant de plus

[1] Duveyrier, *Touareg*, pp. 318, 323.
[2] Richer, p. 44.
[3] *Ib.* p. 43; cf. p. 13.
[4] *Ib.* p. 45.
[5] *Ib.* p. 13.

en plus".[1] We have, however, three manuscript documents relating to the history of Air which appear to be based on native sources. Two of these were sent by the sultan of Agades, the principal town of Air, to the sultan of Sokoto, and have been recently translated into English.[2] The first is a brief *Treatise concerning the People of the Kingdom of Ahir and the Kingdom of Bornu*. It is an extremely interesting document. It opens with an account of the conquest of Air by four Tuareg (*Imoshag*) tribes from the original inhabitants, who are described as Sudanese, i.e. presumably black people.[3] The bulk of the document, and its main purpose, however, is to account for the peculiar character of the sultanate of Agades, and to justify and rationalise the Imoshag dominion and imposts in the kingdom of Air. Although the document has possibly had a long history in written form, its material cannot be said to rank as history in the strict sense of the word, but appears to be based on learned speculations and perhaps a certain amount of learned tradition.

The two remaining manuscript documents consist of two sets of annals of the dynasty and history of the kingdom of Air. The first, the *Chronicle of the Sultanate of Ahir*, was sent direct from Agades to Sokoto; the second, *An Asben Record*,[4] was procured by a Hausa *mallam* at Katsina in 1908.[5] The first is a brief document and consists of little more than a list of the rulers of Agades. The second is longer. It opens with a brief prose version of the story which is widely current among the Tuareg tribes, and which seeks to account for the peculiar parentage of the sultan of Agades. It then passes on to a series of annals of Air, which relate, besides the royal succession, a certain amount of detail of Air history, and especially the wars and battles in which the people engaged from time to time. The work is a series of Arabic notes compiled by a Hausa *mallam* from Tuareg sources, probably from Tuareg manuscripts which may still be extant.[6] It is possible that the *mallam* actually made his notes from memory, for he makes no reference to his originals; but there seems no reason to doubt that the annals are derived, either immediately or ultimately, from written records.

[1] Jean, p. 82 ff.; cf. p. 231.

[2] Sir Richmond Palmer, *The Bornu Sahara and Sudan* (London, 1936), p. 55 f.

[3] The word *Sudan* comes from an Arabic root meaning 'black'.

[4] The titles here given are those used by Sir Richmond Palmer in his translations of the documents in question; *B.S.S.* p. 57 ff.   [5] Palmer, *B.S.S.* p. 58.

[6] For a translation and discussion of the document see, in addition to Palmer, *B.S.S.*, an article by the same author in the *J.A.S.* IX (July, 1910), p. 388 ff.; and cf. Rodd, *P.V.* p. 362.

The important fact for us, however, is that in Air and the Sudan written documents have been found relating to the history of Air, and have therefore been available—perhaps others also—to the *mallams* of Agades, the 'Sudanese' city of Air. In all probability they are derived from a Chronicle of Air compiled by these very *mallams*. F. R. Rodd heard during his stay in Air of two books on tribal lore and history, one of which had belonged to the family of a chief dwelling in Auderas village, and which had 'long been in the possession of his forefathers'; the other kept by a woman of Agades, and quoted by the Kel Geres[1] as their authority for the nobility, etc. of the tribes of the south.[2] The same writer tells us that in the past the practice arose of keeping book records or tribal histories in Arabic, designed to establish the nobility of origin of the various clans.[3] Most of these books are now lost. His informant was doubtless the chief referred to above, and the other natives who related to him the oral traditions which follow in the same chapter of his book.

F. R. Rodd tried hard to press his informants regarding any written history or literature in the *temajegh* language and recorded in *tifinagh* script. He was assured that the only *tifinagh* book was a Koran the whereabouts of which he failed to trace. His informant added that the *marabouts* had frowned upon the Koran being transcribed into *tifinagh* since it was not proper for the holy book to be used in any other form than Arabic! Among the documents in Arabic script which exist in Tuareg country, it is nevertheless possible that there may be some in *temajegh* recorded in Arabic script which lends itself to use for this language. Written history is however probably not of great antiquity in such form as it may survive. The best historical sources, as yet unexamined, are probably Arabic texts in Southern Nigeria, Tripolitania, and Nigeria, where material is gradually coming to light, as the confidence of Nigerian Emirs and *mallams* is being gained.

There can be no doubt, however, that in Air, as among the Azger and probably among the Aulemmiden, written historical traditions have been carried on side by side with oral traditions. The latter seem to be abundant in Air. Rodd has recorded much, and he says specifically that he has supplemented the information derived from the 'Agades

---

[1] *Kel* means tribe. The Kel Geres are a branch of the Air Tuareg who have migrated southward and are now living north of Sokoto.

[2] Rodd, *P.V.* p. 361 f.   [3] *Ib.* p. 360.

Chronicle' and Sultan Bello[1] with information derived from numerous conversations with the older men whom he met in Air. "By repetition and sifting it[2] acquired sufficient consistency probably to represent, somewhat approximately, the truth."[3] It is clear that in Air, as among the Tuareg generally, we have a certain amount of interplay between written and oral record, as is natural among a people who have a small lettered class, and who practise the art of writing but sparingly. A closer study of these historical records could hardly fail to be both interesting and instructive, for comparative purposes in regard to form, to students of the early written chronicles of Europe.

[1] Sultan Bello was Emir of Sokoto during the visit of Denham and Clapperton in 1824.

[2] I.e. the material thus obtained.

[3] Rodd, *P.V.* p. 362.

THE TUAREG

LIST OF ABBREVIATIONS[1]

AUTHOR AND TITLE OF BOOK	ABBREVIATION
ABADIE, M. J. J. *La Colonie du Niger, etc.* Paris, 1927.	Abadie.
BARTH, HEINRICH. *Travels and Discoveries in North and Central Africa: being a journal of an expedition ...in the years 1849–55.* 5 vols. London, 1857–8.	Barth.
BASSET, RENÉ. *La Poésie Arabe anté-Islamique.* Paris, 1880.	Basset, *P.A.A.*
BAZIN, RENÉ. *Charles de Foucauld, hermit and explorer....* Translated by Peter Keelan. London, 1923.	Bazin.
BOVILL, E. W. *Caravans of the Old Sahara.* Oxford, 1933.	Bovill.
BUCHANAN, A. *Out of the World, North of Nigeria.* (Exploration of Aïr)....London, 1921.	Buchanan, *O.W.N.N.*
—— *Sahara.* London, 1926.	Buchanan, *Sahara.*
CAMPBELL, D. *On the Trail of the Veiled Tuareg.* London, 1928.	Campbell, *T.V.T.*
—— *Wanderings in Widest Africa.* London, 1930.	Campbell, *W.W.A.*
CLAPPERTON, Capt. See Denham.	
DENHAM, DIXON. *Travels and Discoveries in Northern and Central Africa, in 1822, 1823 and 1824.* By Major Denham, Captain Clapperton and...Dr Oudeney. 4 vols. London, 1831.	Denham, etc.
DUVEYRIER, H. *Sahara algérien et tunisien.* Journal de route de H. Duveyrier, publié et annoté par C. Maunoir et H. Schirmer. Précédé d'une biographie de H. Duveyrier par C. Maunoir. Paris, 1905.	Duveyrier, *Journal.*
—— *Exploration du Sahara: Les Touareg du Nord.* Paris, 1864.	Duveyrier, *Touareg.*
GAUTIER, E. F. *La Conquête du Sahara.* Essai de psychologie politique. Paris, 1910.	Gautier, *Conquête.*
—— 'The Ahaggar: Heart of the Sahara.' In *G.R.* XVI (1926).	Gautier, *G.R.*
—— *Les Siècles obscurs du Maghreb.* Paris, 1927.	Gautier, *Maghreb.*
HAARDT, G. M. and AUDOUIN-DUBREUIL, L. *Across the Sahara by Motor-Car.* London, 1924.	Haardt and Dubreuil.

[1] See Note, Part 1, p. 219 above.

AUTHOR AND TITLE OF BOOK	ABBREVIATION
HANOTEAU, A. *Essai de Grammaire de la Langue Tamachek*. Paris, 1896.	Hanoteau.
KING, W. J. HARDING. *A Search for the Masked Tawareks*. London, 1903.	Harding King.
HORNEMANN, F. C. *The Journal of F. Hornemann's travels from Cairo to Mourzouk, the capital of the kingdom of Fezzan*. London, 1802.	Hornemann.
HOURST, E. A. L. *French Enterprise in Africa: the personal narrative of Lieut. Hourst of his exploration of the Niger*. Translated by Mrs A. Bell. London, 1898.	Hourst.
JEAN, C. C. *Les Touareg du Sud-Est. L'Aïr. Leur rôle dans la politique saharienne*. Paris, 1909.	Jean.
KILIAN, C. *Au Hoggar. Mission de 1922*. Paris, Bruxelles, 1925.	Kilian.
Encyclopédie de la Musique. Edited by Lavignac. Our references are to the article by Rouanet, Partie I, Vol. v, p. 2893 ff.	Lavignac.
MASQUERAY, E. *Observations grammaticales sur la grammaire Touareg et textes de la Tamahaq des Taïtoq*. Paris, 1896.	Masqueray.
OUDENEY. See Denham.	
PALMER, Sir RICHMOND. *The Bornu Sahara and Sudan*. London, 1936.	Palmer, *B.S.S.*
RICHARDSON, J. *Travels in the Great Desert of Sahara, in 1845 and 1846*; including a description of the oases and cities of Ghat, Ghadames and Mourzuk. 2 vols. London, 1848.	Richardson.
RICHER, A. M. J. *Les Touareg du Niger: Les Oulliminden*. Paris, 1924.	Richer.
RODD, Hon. P. R. *B.S.O.S.* [See Periodicals.]	P. R. Rodd, *B.S.O.S.*
RODD, Hon. F. J. R. *People of the Veil: being an account of the habits, organisation and history of the wandering Tuareg tribes, etc.* London, 1926.	Rodd, *P.V.*
—— Articles in *The Times*, Nov. 3rd and 4th, 1922, and March 19th, 1928.	Rodd, *Times.*
ROUANET, M. J. See Lavignac.	Rouanet.
VISCHER, H. *Across the Sahara from Tripoli to Bornu*. London, 1910.	Vischer.

PERIODICALS

Geographical Journal, formerly the Royal Geographical   G.J.
     Society's Proceedings. London, 1893, etc.
Geographical Review. New York.   G.R.
Journal of the African Society. London, 1901, etc.   J.A.S.
Revue des Deux Mondes. Paris, 1831, etc.   R.D.M.
School of Oriental Studies, London. Bulletin. London,   B.S.O.S.
     1917, etc.
The Times. London.   *Times.*

A Note

ON

ENGLISH BALLAD POETRY

We should have liked to include in our survey an account of English oral literature in medieval and later times, most of which is generally known as 'Ballad' poetry. This poetry supplies many interesting analogies to the literatures we have discussed; and to these we shall have to refer from time to time in the summary of our conclusions which follows. But the subject is too complex and difficult to be treated as a whole except by those who have devoted more time to it than we have been able to do. We shall therefore confine our attention to a few features which affect more closely the objects of our survey.

English ballads, like those of northern Europe in general, fall into two main classes. The first consists of ballads which are of native origin and of purely native connections, the second of those which have international connections and are, mostly if not wholly, of foreign origin. There are a number of ballads the position of which is not clear; but on the whole this classification is without doubt correct.

Ballad poetry is believed to be of southern origin and to have made its way to northern Europe chiefly through France. Its introduction into Denmark can be dated to the twelfth century. It was accompanied by dancing and doubtless by dance music, and soon became extremely popular. The earliest events which form the subjects of Danish historical ballads occurred shortly before 1150; and a number of such ballads seem to have been composed in the thirteenth century.

There are a few Danish ballads (*Folkeviser*) which may be derived from the Norse (or possibly Danish) poetry of earlier times by oral transmission. 'Tor av Havsgaard'[1] would seem to be connected—remotely—with the Thrymskviða, and there is an undoubted connection between 'Ungen Svejdal'[2] and the 'Svipdagsmál' (cf. Vol. I, p. 432), though even here the resemblance is somewhat remote. Another ballad, 'Havbor og Signelil',[3] shows a closer resemblance to the story of Hagbarðr and Signý, related by Saxo, p. 231 ff. (p. 278 ff., Engl. transl.)—a story of the Heroic Age, which in extant early Norse literature is known only from frequent allusions. Other ballads relating to persons of the Heroic Age are derived from German sources, whether through written or oral channels we are not clear. Others again seem to come from Norse 'Sagas of Ancient Times'.[4]

Early Norse literature is much more largely represented in the ballads of the Faroes. These are still in common use and accompanied by dancing.[5] Some of them contain references to a 'book from Iceland' as their source, a MS. (*skinnbók*) either of sagas or—perhaps more probably—of *Rímur*, or

---

[1] Grundtvig, *Danmarks Gamle Folkeviser*, I, 1 ff.

[2] Olrik, *Danske Folkeviser i Udvalg*, I, 143 ff.

[3] Olrik, *op. cit.* I, 97 ff.

[4] E.g. 'Alf i Odderskær' (Olrik, *op. cit.* I, 105 ff.). A closely related ballad is transl. by Kershaw, *Stories and Ballads of the Far Past*, p. 188 ff.

[5] For an account of Faroese ballads in general, with translations, see Kershaw, *op. cit.* p. 153 ff.

rhyming paraphrases of sagas, such as were current in Iceland in the fourteenth and following centuries. But Faroese ballads relating to stories of the Heroic Age are commonly derived from the German versions of these stories—a fact which seems to point to the influence of merchants, either from Germany direct or through Denmark.

If Scandinavian ballads of Norse derivation, whether in Denmark, the Faroes, or elsewhere, be compared with their prototypes in the earlier literature, one cannot fail to be struck by the greatness of the contrast they present, not only in language and style, but still more in thought and outlook. The difference is, broadly speaking, much the same as the difference between books specially written for young children and books intended for ordinary circulation. To take an instance, 'Ungen Svejdal' looks very much like an edition of the 'Svipdagsmál' prepared for use in the nursery. The extremely 'primitive' features shown by many Faroese ballads may be ascribed in part to the poverty and remoteness of the islands; but there can be no doubt that Scandinavian ballads in general were intended for a society on a lower intellectual plane than that which produced the Norse literature of earlier days.

In this country we know of no survivals in ballad poetry from earlier native literature. The oldest historical ballads which have been preserved date from the fourteenth century; and it is doubtful whether any ballads of native origin can be traced further back than this.[1] Some ballads indeed contain historical names of earlier times, e.g. 'Queen Eleanor's Confession' (156)[2] and 'King John and the Bishop of Canterbury' (45); but these seem to be ballads of international currency—sometimes derived from folk-tales—which have adopted English names.

English ballads of international currency may have been in circulation at an earlier date. The evidence for this country is less definite than for Denmark; but, since ballad poetry came from the south, it is not likely to have reached Denmark before England. The literary history of this period, however, is somewhat obscure, owing to the fact that English was little used by the upper classes before c. 1250. It is doubtless for the same reason that we cannot trace the existence of historical ballads before this time.

The 'international' and the historical ballads as a rule differ from one another greatly in character. With the exception of a few theological pieces, the former may be regarded as belonging properly to the 'unspecified' or

[1] The verses on Canute's visit to Ely, contained in *Hist. Eliensis*, II, 27, are thought by many scholars to be the beginning of a very early ballad. Cf. Gummere, *Cambr. Hist. of Engl. Lit.* II, p. 397f. The *cantilenae* referred to by William of Malmesbury, who wrote c. 1130–40, may have been ballads; but he gives no information as to their form. It has been suggested that much earlier evidence for the existence of ballads is to be found in an obscure passage in the Ang.-Sax. poem 'Deor' (14 ff.); cf. Kemp Malone, *Journ. Eng. Lit. Hist.* III, 253 ff. But we regret that we cannot regard the proposed interpretation of this passage as probable. Cf. also Norman, *London Med. Stud.* I, 165 ff.

[2] The figures in brackets denote the number of the ballad in Child's *English and Scottish Popular Ballads*.

'timeless nameless' category,[1] whatever their ultimate origin, although most of them have adopted English names—sometimes historical names—in this country. Native ballads on the other hand belong as a rule to the heroic and 'post-heroic' categories. The former very frequently have a refrain, which is believed to be a reminiscence of choral singing, accompanied by dancing. In the latter, at least in ballads which are clearly of native origin, refrains seem to be less frequent, though by no means unknown. In the former the diction is commonly of a more primitive and childlike character, and the repetitions more frequent, than in the latter. Women are much more prominent in the former; a much larger proportion of these ballads are concerned with love affairs, though other motifs are sometimes involved. The chief difference between the two series, however, lies in the outlook. In the international ballads this is much the same as in folk-tales; we may note especially the frequence of supernatural elements, the absence of decorum, the free play allowed to the passions and the unrestrained and unreasonable savagery. The native ballads depict a very rough society and many brutal deeds; but they do not give the impression that one has left the world of reality.

The force of these comparisons is impaired to a certain extent by the fact that there are a not inconsiderable number of ballads as to the provenance of which we are in doubt. They may be either international ballads which have adopted English names, or native ballads which have retained only a few names, and these perhaps not without change. The ballads in question are mostly concerned with love stories; and, if the second alternative is correct, it would seem that they have sometimes been influenced by the international type. Indeed it is quite possible that ballads of originally historical character were affected by such influence in much the same way as heroic stories were affected by folk-tales. Yet, in spite of this doubtful element, the contrasts pointed out above may be accepted as in general correct.

The great majority of ballads, whether international or native, are narrative poems (Type A),[2] though ballads consisting of speeches or dialogues in character (Type B) are not rare. As instances of the latter we may cite 'Lord Randal' (12) among the international ballads and 'Lord Maxwell's Last Goodnight' (195) in the native series. Elegies (Type D) also are occasionally found in the latter series, as in one version of 'The Bonny Earl of Murray' (181 A).[3] Matter of impersonal interest is represented only in speeches contained in ballads which have a personal theme. The examples consist chiefly of strings of riddles, usually in the briefest possible form (e.g. 1, 46, 47) and

[1] So far as we know, there are no ballads relating to the Teutonic Heroic Age. There are, however, a few ballads connected with Arthurian and other romances. These are presumably derived, though perhaps indirectly, from written sources.

[2] This type perhaps tended to encroach upon the others. At all events it is clear (e.g. from 'Ungen Svejdal') that narrative ballads sometimes took the place of earlier poems of Type B.

[3] Version B is a narrative poem, much occupied with speeches. The two versions would seem to have been independent poems originally, though the surviving text of A has borrowed one stanza from B.

very similar to what we have found in various other languages, both ancient and modern.[1] It may be noted that, just as in Russian (cf. Vol. II, p. 211 f.), these dialogues are commonly connected with proposals of marriage or love. They belong, in part at least, to the international series; we are not certain that any of the riddle ballads are of native origin.

Beyond this point we are not prepared to discuss the international series. They present too many problems, social[2] as well as literary, which can be dealt with only by specialists. Some of the native ballads, however, seem to be less obscure.

First we will take a small group of historical ballads relating to the fourteenth and early fifteenth centuries. The most interesting of these are 'The Battle of Otterburn' (161) and 'The Hunting of the Cheviot' or 'Chevy Chace' (162). Both relate to the same event, which took place in 1388, but are believed to be of independent origin; the former is known from six texts, the latter from two. Both in interest and in milieu these poems differ as much as possible from international ballads. Indeed they seem to us to have nothing in common with the latter except metre; and we cannot but think that the practice of including them under the same term is misleading. 'Chevy Chace' was a minstrel poem in the sixteenth century; the oldest text is derived from a minstrel, and it was from minstrels that Sir Philip Sidney heard it. Both poems are typically heroic, apart from one section of 'Chevy Chace' (st. 59-64 in A), which shows national feeling and is obviously an addition. Close analogies are to be found in Montenegrin poems of last century, especially perhaps 'The Sack of Kolašin' (cf. Vol. II, pp. 376, 392) and 'Omer Pasha's Attack upon Montenegro' (ib. 334, 430).

In 'Durham Field' (159) the heroic element is by no means so prominent. The first part of the poem is largely occupied with speeches in which the Scottish king promises to grant various desirable possessions in England to his leading men; and for this analogies are to be found in Montenegrin poems, where Turkish rulers are represented as distributing beforehand the territories they are about to conquer. But in general the emphasis is laid, not on the exploits of individuals (heroes), but on the superiority of the English, especially the English yeomanry, to the Scots. The same national interest pervades other English poems, except in stories of outlaws.

In Scotland the heroic element was probably stronger. 'The Knight of Liddesdale' (160) may have been a heroic poem,[3] though only one stanza is preserved. The same element, however, is well marked in 'The Battle of Harlaw' (163), which celebrates the defeat of the Highlanders under Donald of the Isles (Macdonell) in 1411—though the poem survives only in what seems to be a late and abbreviated form.

[1] Cf. Vol. II, pp. 212f., 410, 560f.; and below, p. 835.

[2] E.g. the system of courting, which is alien to Teutonic tradition. Is it a custom derived from a servile population, or is it Celtic, or due to foreign (Mediterranean or Oriental) influence? This can hardly be a purely literary question.

[3] In view of the later ballads relating to Liddesdale; see below.

The term 'heroic' may also be applied to ballads which are concerned with outlaws, such as 'Adam Bell' (116) and the large group of poems relating to Robin Hood (117–54). Such ballads doubtless owe their popularity in the first place to the feeling against the forest laws. But the popularity of Robin Hood rests upon a stronger motif even than this. He and his followers are not only poachers, but also highwaymen who devote special attention to wealthy ecclesiastics. In the fourteenth century the rapacity of the latter seems to have been deeply resented; and stories which depicted their discomfiture evidently made a wide appeal. We need not discuss the origin of Robin Hood—who may at first have been a person of merely local celebrity; but his exploits appealed to the prevailing sentiment of the day. The growth of his fame may be compared to a certain extent with that of Marko Kraljević; but the adventures attributed to the latter are in general of a more extravagant character and more obviously derived from alien sources.

A far more typically heroic series of poems comes from the borders of Cumberland and Scotland in the sixteenth century. This 'Heroic Age' is doubtless a continuation of what we find in 'Chevy Chace', though little or nothing seems to have been preserved from the intermediate period; but the action is usually on a smaller scale. The poems relate to a limited area, of which the centre is Liddesdale, and most of the heroes belong to a few leading families, especially the Armstrongs, Elliots and Halls on the northern side, and the Scroopes, Musgraves and Grahams on the southern. There are, however, a few heroes whose origin is unknown, notably 'Hobie Noble' (189), an English outlaw in the service of the Armstrongs, and 'Dick o the Cow' (185), who seems to have been Lord Scroope's jester.

These poems are purely heroic. The interest is centred in the exploits of individuals, usually the chiefs of the clans or their sons, with their families and adherents. There is hardly any national feeling, at least on the Scottish side. In 'Johnie Armstrong' (169), which appears to be the earliest poem of the series, King James V is represented as inviting the leaders of that clan to a parley and then treacherously slaughtering them. The tragedy took place in 1530; but it is clear that the king regarded them—not without good reason— as brigands, who owed him no allegiance and rendered the country unsafe. In point of fact individuals and even whole families sometimes transferred their allegiance,[1] or lived in full independence. Most of the poems belong to a later period, towards the close of the century, when the border was controlled by the Wardens of the Marches. But even then both the chiefs of clans and lesser individuals often took the law into their own hands. It may further be noted that, although these poems relate to a period when both England and

---

[1] The leading families on both sides seem often to be in close relations. Johnie Armstrong's page is a Musgrave; Hughie Grame at his execution presents his sword to an Armstrong, with a request that he will 'remember' his death, when he comes to the Border.

Scotland were deeply stirred by the Reformation, they apparently contain no reference to it. The Borderers would seem to have taken no interest in religious questions at that time.

The poems of this period as a whole bear a rather striking resemblance to Yugoslav heroic poems of the time of the *hajduci*—the sixteenth and seventeenth centuries, after the Turkish conquest—a number of which were noticed in Vol. II, p. 326 ff. The resemblance is doubtless due to the prevalence of similar political conditions, along a border which was not effectively controlled. One of the favourite subjects is the rescue of prisoners, as in 'Kinmont Willie' (186), 'Jock o the Side' (187), and 'Archie o Cawfield' (188)—which may be compared with the stories of Ivo of Senj. In the roughness of the life which is depicted there is little to choose between the two series of poems. In both cases the heroes have their homes in towers or small castles; cattle-raiding and love of adventure are their guiding principles. For brutality the story of the *beg* Ljubović is matched by 'The Death of Parcy Reed' (193). On the other hand a much more favourable impression is conveyed by 'Lord Maxwell's Last Goodnight' (195), a speech-poem by a clan chief who has been exiled owing to a feud.

We do not know whether any of the events celebrated in these poems can be dated later than 1608, the year of Lord Maxwell's exile. But in any case the Heroic Age was soon brought to an end by the union of the crowns (in 1603); Border raids and feuds were no longer tolerated. Lawless conditions continued on the fringe of the Highlands, north of the Tay,[1] for another hundred and fifty years, and form the subject of many poems—several of which are concerned with the abduction of girls. But the poems themselves cannot be regarded as heroic; they come from the more civilised people of the Lowlands, who suffered from these exploits. Internal evidence suggests that they are for the most part the work of women, at least from c. 1700.

There are a number of interesting poems relating to the court and the high nobility of the sixteenth century, which have certain heroic affinities. But they are not concerned with the celebration of exploits; their attitude is usually unsympathetic. The interest, however, is exclusively personal; and they show no definitely non-heroic or 'post-heroic' features—no patriotic feeling or interest in political or religious questions. The absence of these features is specially curious if the poems originated, as one would naturally expect, in Edinburgh. Their personal sympathies are rather clearly marked. Queen Mary (the 'queen of France'), Bothwell, Huntly and the Douglases are evidently regarded with disfavour, Darnley ('the king') and the (younger) earl of Murray with favour. One of the most interesting poems is 'Northumberland Betrayed by Douglas' (176), in which a sister of William Douglas learns of her brother's treachery by second sight, and endeavours thereby to save the exiled earl, Thomas Percy, who is under his protec-

---

[1] A few poems from this region relate to earlier times. 'Captain Car' or 'Edom o Gordon' (178) surpasses even 'Parcy Reed' in brutality.

tion.[1] Mention may also be made of 'The Laird o Logie' (182), which offers a pleasing relief to an otherwise tragic series.

Characteristics of a definitely post-heroic nature appear in the course of the seventeenth century. The poems are largely occupied with battles; but the interest is no longer centred in heroic exploits, but in the fate of armies and in the principles which are at stake. In 'The Battle of Philiphaugh' (202) Sir David Leslie is advised by an old man (unnamed) how to arrange his forces against Montrose. In 'Loudon Hill' (205) Claverhouse's own cornet emphasises the merits of the Covenanters, while in 'Bothwell Bridge' (206) the same commander is bitterly censured for massacring the fugitives against the Duke of Monmouth's orders. The contrast between these poems and those of the previous century is very marked. Apart from the military poems, we may cite 'The Earl of Errol' (231), a typically post-heroic piece, concerned with a legal dispute (in 1659) about the payment of a bride's portion.

English historical ballads are in general much inferior to the Scottish in interest. The most striking feature perhaps is their exuberant patriotism and sense of superiority to all opponents, whether Scottish or French. We have already noticed this in 'Chevy Chace' and 'Durham Field'; and it recurs also in 'King Henry V's Conquest of France' (164), 'Flodden Field' (168) and 'Musselburgh Field' (172), as well as in poems dealing with sea-fights. This feeling of patriotism seems to carry with it a devotion to the kings, which does not appear in the Scottish ballads. Personal interest in the court, however, is limited to a very small number of ballads; and these cannot be discussed apart from other records of the time.[2]

The poems last mentioned belong presumably to London; but most of the English ballads evidently come from the north. 'The Rising in the North' (175) represents that stage in narrative poetry, in which the action is swallowed up by the preliminaries. 'The Earl of Westmoreland' (177) is believed to have been influenced by a romance. The best narratives are 'Sir John Butler' (165) and 'Rookhope Ryde' (179). The former is the story of a tragic family quarrel; the scene is laid at a castle near Warrington in 1463, but the circumstances are obscure. The latter describes the brave repulse of a raid by Borderers—English, not Scottish—upon Weardale in the County of Durham in 1569. It is a typical example of 'post-heroic' war-poetry, comparable with the Perast poems noticed in Vol. II, p. 351 ff. The interest lies in the struggle of the local community as a whole; the commander's name is never mentioned, though he is evidently a courageous and competent leader.

---

[1] This poem should perhaps be referred to the northern English series (see below). Relations between the ruling classes of the two kingdoms seem to have been very close in the reign of James VI. The betrayal took place in 1572.

[2] Thus 'Thomas Cromwell' (171) should be taken in connection with a series of controversial poems, of marked post-heroic character (cf. Percy's *Reliques*, II, i, 11), which seem not to have been preserved as ballads. It would appear to be due to accident that this poem, and this only, passed into circulation as a ballad.

Taking the evidence as a whole, the country may be divided into three areas. In the Borderland heroic poetry—a Heroic Age—persists in full vigour down to 1603. In eastern Scotland and the north of England we find a good deal of poetry, which is either post-heroic or in course of transition from heroic to post-heroic. In the south of England and the Midlands oral poetry would seem to be more or less moribund from the fourteenth century.

It is to be remembered, however, that the groups of poems discussed above include only a minority of the ballads. Many of what are commonly called the 'romantic' ballads are doubtless of native origin, but of unknown date and provenance. In this class of poetry we have to take account not only of international ballads which have assumed English names, but also of native poems which have borrowed motifs and themes from the international stock. Even historical ballads relating to well known people contain adventitious elements, as we have seen in 'The Earl of Westmoreland' (p. 688). 'King Edward IV and a Tanner of Tamworth' (273) would seem to be a widespread popular story,[1] which has become attached to that king. Poems relating to less illustrious persons are obviously more liable to change, both to the loss of personal and local names—which in fact often vary greatly in the different versions of a ballad—and to the admission of new elements from alien sources of every kind. It is to these causes, we believe, that the difficulty of determining whether a ballad is of native or foreign origin is due.

The study of ballad poetry has been much obscured by the fact that many scholars have failed to distinguish between the special features of the ballad and those which are generally characteristic of oral poetry, other than learned or highly cultivated court poetry. The special features apparent to the reader are the metre (including rhyme and stanza) and the simplicity of the diction. But the completeness with which the ballad displaced other forms of oral poetry shows that it must have possessed some exceptionally attractive quality, which is less apparent to us. There can be little doubt that this lay in the music. We have no satisfactory evidence that anything which we should call singing was cultivated before this time either in England[2] or in the North, except in church music and spells. The success of the ballad was presumably due to the new facilities for enjoyment which it afforded even to the youngest and least expert singer, both for social festivities, in combination with dancing, and also for private amusement. In particular it seems to have appealed to girls and young women. In one of the very earliest references to a

---

[1] For a somewhat similar story told of Peter the Great see Vol. II, p. 177f. We need hardly mention that unhistorical elements abound even in the historical ballads. Discrepancies between different versions of a ballad often show that these have arisen in the course of oral transmission.

[2] According to W. Malmesbury (*Gest. Pontif.* iii, 116) Abp. Thomas of York (1070–1101) was in the habit of adapting minstrel tunes (*arte ioculatoria*) to ecclesiastical purposes. This is the earliest definite evidence known to us for the development of secular music. It was presumably French, rather than English.

ballad (Barbour's *Bruce*, xvi. 520 ff.) it is said that whoever wishes may hear

> Yhoung women, quhen thai will play,
> syng it emang thame ilke day.

The reference is to a Border fray which took place about the year 1315; but nothing more seems to be known of the ballad. Again, even in the last days of ballads, when collectors were hunting for them, a very large proportion of the material was obtained from women.

Very many ballads, especially those of the international series, correspond in general to the Yugoslav *Ženske Pjesme*, or 'Women's Poems', and might well have been composed by women. But many others, as we have seen, are heroic, and correspond to the Yugoslav *Junačke Pjesme* (cf. Vol. II, p. 306). And there is no evidence, so far as we know, that in actual usage any distinction like that of the Yugoslavs was recognised in this country. The ballad referred to by Barbour was probably a heroic poem.

According to the prevailing view ballad poetry was 'poetry of the folk', as opposed to minstrel poetry. Actually there is an appreciable amount of evidence that in the sixteenth century it was cultivated by minstrels. For 'Chevy Chace' this has been noted above. We may also refer to Puttenham, *Arte of Poesie*, ii. 9, who speaks of 'Adam Bell' as a typical item, along with 'Bevis of Southampton' and 'Guy of Warwick', in the répertoires of 'blind harpers or such like taverne Minstrels'. Occasionally too, as in 'Rookhope Ryde', a ballad ends with a minstrel's epilogue, such as we find in the oral narrative poetry of other peoples, both ancient and modern. More frequently we meet with preludes of the same origin, such as "listen, lively lordings all," or "now lith and lysten, gentlemen"—which seem to point to performances in the halls of squires.

It is commonly held, however, that very few ballads are derived from minstrels; and, so far as the immediate derivation of our texts is concerned, this is quite correct. We may agree also that 'Adam Bell' is not likely to have often belonged to the same répertoire as 'Guy of Warwick', at least in early times. The first is an oral poem; the second a poem dependent on a written text. It is improbable that book-minstrels had much to do with the production of ballads.[1] But unluckily many writers on this subject seem not to have thought of any other kind of minstrel, and consequently to have assumed that the origin of ballads is to be found in a kind of spontaneous production by 'the folk',[2] at their gatherings. The existence of the unlettered minstrel, who

---

[1] But it should be borne in mind that neither the book minstrel nor the literary troubadour can be traced back much beyond the twelfth century. Before that time—when all minstrelsy was still oral—there were already doubtless great differences, in rank, remuneration, etc., between one minstrel and another. But we are not convinced that the ballad had an essentially different ancestry from the poetry of the troubadours.

[2] It may be remarked here that analogies drawn from the (supposed) procedure of very primitive peoples in the composition of poetry would seem to be rather out of

in other lands, as we have seen, is of the greatest importance in oral literature, has here commonly been ignored.

It is to be borne in mind that ballads often had a very wide currency, sometimes as far as from London to Aberdeen, and also that ballads of quite different kinds were often known to, and sung by, the same persons, whether men or women. But it cannot be assumed from this that these different kinds of ballads had the same origin. It will be enough here to note the international (foreign) and the Border heroic ballads. The former were perhaps introduced by travellers—who in early times cannot as a rule have been professional minstrels in the strict sense; for a livelihood was hardly to be gained from English poetry before the fourteenth century. We have to think rather of persons who had some other occupation, but were ready to entertain for some slight remuneration, or even for drinks, as in Yugoslavia. For the most part they may have been traders, craftsmen or soldiers. Or, as an alternative explanation,[1] we would suggest that such ballads belonged to the oral poetry brought to this country by the illiterate Normans, especially the ladies, at the Conquest; and that their conversion into English was due in the main to the servants of the chiefs, who in the course of the following century became amalgamated with the native population. In any case we think that the diffusion of these ballads is to be attributed largely to the servant class, both men and women, together with traders, etc. But the origin of the Border ballads must be sought in the Borderland itself, especially perhaps in towers and small castles like that of Mangerton, while the poets can hardly have been any other than the members and dependants of the landowning families. The conditions, as we have seen, were apparently very similar to those of Yugoslavia in Turkish times.

We cannot prove that the authors of the Border ballads were minstrels. Most of these poems belong to a late period, and it may be that the harp or crwth had then gone out of use in the district; but we do not think that this can safely be inferred from the silence of the poems.[2] For the earlier period— the thirteenth and preceding centuries—when ballad poetry began to be

place in the consideration of ballads, in view of their late date and pronouncedly southern form.

[1] This is the explanation to which we are ourselves inclined. But we have no special knowledge of the period, and consequently give it only for what it is worth. It is difficult to doubt that ballad poetry was old in France, though nothing seems to have been recorded from early times.

[2] In Yugoslavia heroic poetry is hardly ever recited without instrumental accompaniment; but this is very seldom referred to in the poems themselves. On the other hand the accompaniment has been discarded in the greater part of Russia. It may be observed here that there is evidence for harpers on the Scottish side of the Border in the sixteenth and seventeenth centuries. We may refer, e.g. to 'The Blind Harper of Lochmaben', to the accounts of James IV (at Lochmaben and elsewhere) —see the citations published in Armstrong's *Irish and Highland Harps* (1904)—and to the story told by Sir W. Scott in Note lxiv to 'The Lay of the Last Minstrel'. We do not know what evidence there is for crowthers or fiddlers.

cultivated in this country, definite information seems to be almost wholly wanting. But we find it difficult to believe that an innovation of this kind can have been introduced without the aid of instrumental music.[1]

It is to be borne in mind that the ballad is neither a subject category nor a formal type of poetry. Various categories and types are represented in ballad poetry, as we have seen; and the distinctive element in the latter must lie in a kind of 'treatment', which could be applied to any of these. Even the international ballads, which have been introduced from abroad, are by no means uniform; and it would seem that no oral poetry of any kind survived in this country, except in ballad form. The difference between this form and that of earlier English poetry is to be seen in the substitution of French for English metre—the rhyming stanza or couplet in place of the alliterative uniform line—but the essential element in the innovation, which involved the change of metre, must be sought in the music.[2]

It has been remarked that English ballad poetry, unlike that of Denmark and other Scandinavian lands, seems to have preserved no themes from earlier times. The life of English literature, or at least the secular literature, was brought to an abrupt end by the downfall of the native nobility and the native culture. Yet it is difficult to believe that all traces of the past can have been obliterated at once, especially in view of the references to *cantilenae* relating to Saxon times, which we find in records of the twelfth century. Something must have survived, especially in the more remote parts of the country; but it is hard to trace, owing to the poverty of our information. Such poetry may never have been written down.

In point of fact formal traces of the older poetry are not rare in the earliest northern ballads. 'The Battle of Otterburn' and 'The Hunting of the Cheviot' show a good deal of alliteration, though it is irregular and sporadic. Survivals of the older diction also occur, e.g. "Whylle I may my weppone welde", and especially static epithets like 'doughetie Doglas'. Such phrases are enough to show that at least in the far north the break with the past was not complete and instantaneous. Beside the new foreign poetry, i.e. the true ballads, some of the old native poetry must have been remembered long enough to preserve the traditional form; and this would seem to have been only gradually transformed or assimilated to the new poetry. At the end of the twelfth century Giraldus Cambrensis (*Descr. Walliae*, I. 12) speaks of

[1] We may refer to the customary derivation of the word *jig* ('ballad, dance') from early French *gigue*, 'fiddle'. This derivation, however, is regarded with scepticism in the *New English Dictionary* (s.v. *jig*), apparently owing to the absence of evidence for the word before the sixteenth century. The meaning of 'fiddle' seems not to be found in English, though *gigours* ('fiddlers') occurs in 'King Horn' (1510).

[2] We regard the origin and early history of the ballad as a problem for the historian of music, rather than the student of literature. The date of any given tune —say 'Flying Fame'—or any type of music may be known, or obvious, to the musician. But we are wholly without such knowledge; and both the evidence and the principles involved are unintelligible to the non-expert.

alliteration as characteristic of English (as also of Welsh) poetry. It is not clear whether he is thinking of oral or written poetry; but in any case, if we could recover an oral poem of his time, we should probably find its metrical form to be in a state of fluctuation, much as in Lawman's 'Brut' or 'The Proverbs of Alfred'. The traditional form was of course preserved far more purely in literary poetry of a religious or didactic character, for which we are probably indebted to the country clergy. But continuity may also be claimed for the oral poetry to the extent which we have noted. For the process of transformation we may compare the Dalmatian poems noticed in Vol. II, p. 338.

In conclusion we may note that English ballad poetry supplies abundant and interesting material for the study of variants. Some ballads are preserved in a considerable number of texts, which differ from one another in varying degree. Sometimes the differences are slight and merely verbal. Sometimes again one text seems to be a modernised paraphrase of another, as in the two texts of 'Chevy Chace'. The variations here are comparable with those between the texts in the two Perast MSS. noticed in Vol. II, p. 423 f. On the other hand the differences between two texts are occasionally so great that one is inclined to doubt whether they have had a common origin. Thus, in 'The Bonny Earl of Murray' (181) Text A is an elegy (Type D), while Text B consists mainly of speeches in character, with brief connecting narrative. In A st. 2 is obviously borrowed from B; but it is not clear to us that there is any original connection between the two. A is doubtless contemporary; but is there any valid reason for supposing B to be much later? Again, to take another case, 'The Battle of Otterburn' and 'Chevy Chace' are believed to be different poems. They certainly have different openings, and indeed show great differences throughout. But 'Chevy Chace' in st. 9 follows the Otterburn opening, not its own, while st. 30 ff. cannot be independent of 'Otterburn' 49 ff. Are the two poems really variants, or are these common features due to secondary influence—as seems to be the case with 'Chevy Chace' 57 and 'Otterburn' 67?

PART IV

A GENERAL SURVEY

Note. In the following chapters reference will frequently be made to certain types of literature which were defined in Vol. 1 (pp. 28, 42, 60, etc.) and Vol. 11 (p. 2). It will be convenient therefore to repeat these definitions here. Type A: narrative poetry or saga, intended for entertainment. Type B: poetry (very rarely prose) in the form of speeches in character. Type C: poetry or prose intended for instruction. Type D: poetry (seldom prose) of celebration or appeal, especially panegyrics, elegies, hymns, prayers and exhortations. Type E: personal poetry (very rarely prose) relating to the author himself and his surroundings. These types apply only to literature relating to persons, not to impersonal literature.

By 'saga' we mean prose narrative preserved by oral tradition.

CHAPTER I

WRITTEN AND ORAL LITERATURE

ORAL literature is found under three different sets of conditions:
(1) In communities where the art of writing is entirely unknown. As instances of such communities we may cite the Polynesian peoples down to the beginning of last century and most of the northern Bantu until quite late in the century.

(2) In communities where writing is known and used for certain purposes—e.g. for denoting ownership, for correspondence, and perhaps for purposes of trade or magical purposes—but where written literature is unknown. Such conditions may now perhaps be found among the Tuareg; in ancient times instances are frequent. Such was the case with the Teutonic peoples in the period when they were acquainted only with the Runic alphabet—a period which in the North must have lasted at least seven centuries. Analogous conditions would seem to have prevailed in Ireland, in the times when only Ogam writing was known. Among the ancient Gauls the use of writing may have been more general; but there is no evidence for a written literature. The earliest Italian and Greek inscriptions point to the prevalence of similar conditions. In all these cases the use of writing for literary purposes—to any appreciable extent—was probably rendered impracticable by the absence of serviceable writing materials.

(3) In communities where written literature is also current. We do not know indeed of any community in which both written and oral literature are equally cultivated by all. The former generally tends to displace the latter. But it is frequently the case that written literature is generally known to a special class, ecclesiastical, official or wealthy, while the rest of the population are familiar only with oral literature. Such conditions are—or were until yesterday—widespread in eastern Europe and in many Mohammedan countries; and there can be no doubt that in medieval times and earlier they were even more widely prevalent.

Sometimes written literature is known only in an obsolete form of language, as was formerly the case in Orthodox Slavonic countries, in Abyssinia, and in India. Still more often a wholly foreign language is employed, like Latin in Catholic Europe during the Dark Ages, or

Arabic in many parts of Asia and Africa. A vernacular oral literature may flourish by the side of these, as in Yugoslavia, where Ecclesiastical Slavonic, Latin and Arabic have been known as literary languages for centuries. But when the living native language comes to be used for written literature it would seem that oral literature is bound to suffer. It becomes more and more restricted to the more backward elements in the population; and its creative power tends to be impaired, though old themes may still be cultivated. This is what can be seen in Russia during the nineteenth century. Somewhat similar conditions may have prevailed in Teutonic and Celtic lands many centuries before, though here the influence of written literature upon the laity was probably indirect in the main. Under modern conditions, when printed books are more plentiful and accessible, the disappearance of oral literature, e.g. in Africa and Polynesia, is much more rapid.

In Christian and Mohammedan lands the spread of written literature is favoured by the religion, which is vitally dependent upon it. But in some countries, where the religion is native and existed before the time of written literature, its influence is on the other side. The most noteworthy case is India, where oral literature has been maintained in the most perfect form known to us. We may note also what Caesar[1] says of the ancient Gauls. He states that the Druids did not think it right to commit their learning to writing. In his opinion this was due partly to a feeling that their learning should not be made accessible to the general public, and partly to a desire not to neglect the training of the memory. Presumably he had some grounds for his opinion, at least as regards the former reason; but it is uncertain whether the Gauls had what can properly be called a written literature, though they employed writing freely in their public and private transactions.

In Vol. I, p. 500f., it was noted that in ancient Europe the writing of vernacular native literature commonly begins with laws and legal documents. In Christian countries the written laws were due to the same foreign (Roman) influence which brought about the conversion. There seems to be no doubt that the Laws of Aethelberht date from within a few years after the conversion of Kent (A.D. 597), while the Laws of Ine

---

[1] *Gall.* VI. 14: *Neque fas esse existimant ea litteris mandare, cum in reliquis fere rebus, publicis priuatisque rationibus, Graecis litteris utantur. Id mihi duabus de causis instituisse uidentur—quod neque in uulgum disciplinam efferri uelint, neque eos qui discunt litteris confisos minus memoriae studere,* etc. The whole chapter is of great importance for the study of oral tradition.

(c. 690) followed the conversion of Wessex by hardly more than half a century.[1] There is no clear evidence in the seventh century for anything else which can properly be called literature, written in the vernacular, apart from laws, though the survival of archaic forms in glossaries, especially the Épinal Glossary, shows that the writing of English was known at this time. Indeed it is probable that some kind of educational work, involving written translation into English, was carried on from the arrival of the missionaries—primarily of course for religious purposes.

In the Norse world written literature had apparently very similar beginnings. Both in Norway and in Iceland the interval between the conversion and the writing of the laws was longer than in England; but the latter seems to have preceded any other form of written literature in either country. Here also, however, we may probably assume the existence of some kind of religious educational activity, even before the publication of the laws.

For Ireland only indirect evidence is available. But, such as it is (cf. Vol. I, pp. 489, 663), this seems to indicate that laws and legal tracts were at least among the earliest—perhaps the very earliest—of the works written in the native language, though the interval between the conversion and the beginning of these writings seems to have been much longer than in either England or the North.

In Russia the course of events was apparently much the same, although the book-language introduced at the conversion differed but little from the Russian of the time (cf. Vol. II, p. 13 ff.). The conversion is said to have taken place in 988; the first written laws seem to have been issued by Yaroslav, who reigned from 1015 to 1054. Religious literature in Russia would seem to have begun about the same time. The Ostromir Gospels, the most famous of the early texts, were written about two years after Yaroslav's death.

We do not mean of course to propound it as a general principle that written literature begins with laws. It is not clear that such was the case with either the Britons or the Yugoslavs. For the former case it will be sufficient here to refer to Vol. I, p. 501. As for Yugoslavia the differences between the Ecclesiastical Slavonic book-language and the native language must have been negligible when the former first came into use. Yet we know of no laws and of hardly any literary activity of any kind in this region for some centuries afterwards—apart from some Latin in the west.

[1] The conversion can hardly have been complete at Ine's accession. His predecessor was unbaptised.

In ancient Greece no foreign religious influence comparable with Christianity can be traced; yet such evidence as we have seems to indicate that here also the writing of literature began with laws. We should perhaps add treaties and agreements of various kinds. Indeed the evidence rather suggests that the use of writing for such purposes may have begun in an earlier phase, when only wood and stone were available (cf. Vol. I, p. 494f.), though it is not clear that any extant inscriptions antedate the introduction of papyrus. In ancient Italy the evidence of tradition seems to point to the same conclusions.

In Palestine the history of writing is long and complicated. Hebrew records refer the writing of the (sacred) national Law to the earliest times, and state that it was at first written on objects of stone and rocks (cf. Vol. II, p. 633). There is at all events no need to doubt that writing was applied to law at an early date. For India on the other hand we have no satisfactory evidence. Some of the Dharma Sūtra are believed to go back to the fifth century (B.C.); but it is not known when they were written down. No edicts of kings earlier than the third century are preserved.

Among those peoples who have acquired the art of writing only in modern times from Europeans its introduction seems as a rule to have been due to missionaries; and consequently the first written, or printed, books have usually been of a religious character. Where colonisation or annexation has taken place the native laws have been largely superseded by European laws. But where independence has been maintained for a time the native laws, sometimes at least, have been committed to writing at an early date, just as in ancient times. In Hawaii writing was introduced by missionaries about 1820–22; the native laws were codified and published in 1839–42.[1] We are under the impression that events have followed a similar course in protectorates which have been established in recent times.[2]

We may now leave the subject of writing and consider the question what genres of literature are found to be cultivated where writing is unknown or not used for literary purposes.

[1] Cf. W. D. Alexander, *A Brief History of the Hawaiian People*, pp. 175, 178f., 229f.

[2] Thus in Uganda writing probably began soon after the arrival of the first missionaries in 1877. The protectorate was established in 1894. From the beginning of this century the (native) legislative council seems to have issued various laws; the marriage laws were published in 1903. We suspect that similar evidence could be obtained from other protectorates; but such information is not easily accessible to us.

In each of the literatures which we have discussed we have classified the material according to 'categories'. Some of these categories relate to individuals, specified or unspecified, such as 'heroic', 'non-heroic', etc., while others are of an impersonal or general character—viz. 'antiquarian', 'gnomic', 'descriptive', 'mantic'.[1] The former series have been treated according to 'types'—A, B, C, D, E—a treatment which is inapplicable to the latter.

Some of these categories are represented everywhere, while others are more or less widespread. But it will have been seen that the oral literatures of modern Christian and Mohammedan peoples are poor in the second (impersonal) series. The place of these categories is taken by book-literature of foreign origin. On the other hand they are sometimes fairly well represented in the oral literatures of earlier Christian times, as may be seen from the numerous examples given in Chs. x, xii, xiii and xv of Vol. i. We believe that these are in general to be regarded as survivals of native wisdom from still earlier periods. The encroachment of foreign upon native learning may be seen in an incipient form in Anglo-Saxon gnomic poetry and spells (Vol. i, pp. 380ff., 446f.), in a more advanced form in Anglo-Saxon riddles (*ib.* 412f.) and the piece known as 'a Father's Instructions' (*ib.* 382), or in the Irish *Bid Crinna* (*ib.* 397). Some forms of native learning, however, e.g. cosmological speculations, are practically unrepresented. We may refer to the last section of Ch. x in Vol. i (p. 317ff.), where our illustrations had to be drawn almost exclusively from Greek and Norse sources.

It was noted at the beginning of Vol. i (p. 2) that the vernacular literatures of medieval Europe, in so far as they were independent of Latin influence, were essentially literatures of entertainment and celebration; and the same remark is true of the oral literatures of Eastern Europe down to the present day, in so far as these are independent of Greek, Church Slavonic or Arabic influence. It is only the 'personal' categories—in which entertainment is represented by Types A and B, and celebration by Type D—that we find flourishing in them. The impersonal categories, which are feebly represented, belong in general to the literature of thought; and the same may be said of Type C in the personal categories, which also is of little account, except where it is obviously derived, directly or indirectly, from book-literature. In the

[1] In the last case only spells and declarations of mantic wisdom can strictly be described as impersonal; prophecies often relate to individuals. We have treated the subject, however, from the side of prophecy (in the abstract), not from that of the events prophesied.

British Isles, where the records date from much earlier times, the (oral) literature of thought is far more richly represented; yet even here we can see it being gradually transformed and superseded by foreign (Christian) book-literature. It is in Norse records that we find native literature of thought most fully represented. These records, which come almost wholly from Iceland, date from a period when the new learning had not yet had time to penetrate very deeply.

It will be seen then that for (native) oral literature of thought we are in general dependent upon records dating from pre-Christian times or from times before Christianity (or Islam) has become all-powerful. On the other hand oral literature of entertainment and celebration may thrive under Christianity or Islam. The 'theological' category is not represented—at least not in its native character. And in general everything associated with heathen thought tends to disappear or to be transformed. But literature which is free of such associations, like Yugoslav and Russian heroic poetry, may flourish for a very long period, until its popularity is undermined by foreign influence—due in modern times usually to the school and the bookseller.

The various categories, personal and impersonal, will be discussed in the following chapters. Here only a few preliminary remarks need be made.

Oral literature relating to specified (human) individuals is probably to be found wherever oral literature exists. We have usually divided the material into 'heroic' and 'non-heroic'. The former is literature normally—not invariably—concerned with persons of princely rank—their exploits, adventures and experiences. The latter is most commonly concerned with seers, sages and saints, and their intellectual and spiritual achievements and experiences; but we have also included under this head literature relating to other persons, chiefly princes, if the object of such literature is to illustrate doings or experiences of spiritual interest. Both heroic and non-heroic literature is interested in individuals; but the latter has frequently also a communal or national interest—a feature which is unusual in the former, though it is prominent in modern Yugoslav and Galla poetry.

All the literatures which we have discussed contain both heroic and non-heroic elements.[1] Usually these are clearly distinguishable and, as

---

[1] There may of course be oral literatures in which this is not the case. The ancient traditions of Rome, which are presumably derived from saga or poetry, suggest that the heroic element was here very slight, though not entirely lacking. But it may have been reduced through preservation in non-heroic circles.

we have seen, evidently emanate from different circles. But they are seldom or never wholly uninfluenced by one another. Heroic themes (Type C) come to be cultivated in non-heroic circles, and non-heroic themes, or at least elements from such themes, penetrate into heroic circles. Commonly the tendency is for the non-heroic to encroach upon the heroic. Again in course of time both heroic and non-heroic themes frequently become current among one class of entertainers or among the general public. It cannot be assumed, however, with confidence that heroic and non-heroic elements are always necessarily of different origin. In particular there seems to be no satisfactory evidence that such was the case in Polynesia.

We apply the term 'Heroic Age' to a period, past or present, in which the heroic element is dominant. In the past such a period may be known to us only from literary records, saga or poetry, relating to it, but not necessarily dating from it in their present form. Sometimes, however, it may be seen from independent—perhaps foreign—records that the dominance of the heroic element in saga or poetry corresponds to a dominance of the same element in the society of the times to which the saga or poetry relates. At present—by which we mean within the last century or half-century—the heroic element is, or has been, dominant in part of Yugoslavia, among the Galla and the Tuareg, and in various other countries, both in society and in oral literature relating to the present. We know of no evidence for a Heroic Age as a purely literary phenomenon, without foundation in the life of the times to which the literature relates, though in periods of the far past independent evidence as to the character of the times is sometimes slight or even altogether wanting.

To the Heroic Age and the heroic elements which constitute it we shall have to return in Ch. III. Here we may note that in some countries, as among the peoples just specified, the Heroic Age has lasted down to our own times. In the past, however, the Heroic Age seems often to have come to an end long before the beginning of written literature. In ancient Greece the intervening period must have amounted to at least three or four centuries. To literature dating from, or relating to, such intervening periods we have applied the term 'post-heroic', and sometimes treated it as an independent category. Actually, however, it lacks the unity of the other categories. Sometimes it shows heroic features, sometimes—perhaps more often—non-heroic; but usually it is not much concerned with either princes or séers. The persons who figure in it are of various positions in life—very often connected with seafaring—

but apparently more or less independent. The most widespread characteristic is a feeling for the community, which finds expression chiefly in poetry of Type D. But beside this, though doubtless belonging to a rather late phase, we find in Greek and Norse a considerable body of poetry of Type E, which is often strongly individualistic; and the same feeling is prominent in Norse sagas. This category also will require notice in Ch. III.

Literature relating to unspecified individuals seems to be very widespread; but examples are rare in the ancient literatures, except English. In the modern oral literatures we have examined it is perhaps to be found everywhere. We include of course not only stories and poems which are strictly nameless, but also such as have names invented for the occasion. Even these are rare in the ancient literatures; but we have noticed a number of incidents related of well-known characters in heroic and non-heroic stories which may have been derived from stories of this category. It would seem from the modern evidence that the cultivation of this category belongs primarily to peasants and communities living under primitive conditions. But this question will require discussion in Ch. V; the wide distribution of folk-tales must be taken into account. We may note that nameless stories with a moral (Type C) were utilised or invented by the learned for didactic purposes even in ancient times. In the history of fiction this category would seem to have considerable importance.

Theological literature is in monotheistic communities practically limited to hymns and prayers (Type D) and to mantic and didactic matter (including Type C); and these are probably to be found everywhere. But in polytheistic communities we find also literature of entertainment (Types A and B) widely represented, especially in Greek, Norse and Polynesian. One would naturally expect that the earliest stories were due to seers or priests and had an explanatory purpose; and this may be true. But the widespread conception of a divine community seems to have been freely utilised for imaginative poetry of all kinds. This category also has clearly been of importance in the history of fiction.

Antiquarian literature seems to be found everywhere; but among modern Christian peoples it is of comparatively little importance. Genealogies, catalogues and speculations on the origin of place-names and of nations are apparently the most popular subjects. Speculations on the origin of places and institutions are on the whole perhaps rather less frequent. Speculations on the origin of mankind and the world seem not to occur in the Christian oral literatures; but they are wide-spread elsewhere.

Gnomic literature, chiefly poetic, is widespread, but perhaps not universal. We have found little of it in Polynesia; and in Africa too, except among the Galla, examples seem to be rare, though this may be due to defects in our information. In the modern Christian and Mohammedan oral literatures which we have examined we have found nothing worth recording. For the rest we have classified the material under two Types, (I) gnomes of choice or obligation—the Aristotelian type—which can be converted into precepts, and (II) gnomes of observation. The former are the more widespread, though gnomes of observation relating to human beings (IIa) and to fate, death and the gods (IIb) are frequent and widely distributed. Gnomes relating to animals and inanimate objects (IIc) are prominent in English and Welsh gnomic poetry; but elsewhere they are not frequent, though they occur sporadically in several of the other literatures which we have examined.

'Descriptive' poetry, such as we discussed in Vol. I, Ch. XIII, has a rather wider distribution than gnomic; for it occurs to a certain extent in modern Christian oral literatures. Prose examples of this category seem to be rare. The objects described are as a rule typical, not individualised; and consequently this class of poetry has affinities with gnomes of Type II. Often it is associated with gnomic poetry, though it occurs also in similes and other contexts, as well as in independent poems describing the characteristics of (e.g.) animals, the seasons, natural phenomena and types of men. One of its most widespread and popular varieties is the riddle.

Mantic literature, again usually poetry, is probably to be found everywhere, though in some Christian literatures it occurs only in a debased form and infrequently. The material consists mainly of spells and prophecies, together with blessings and curses, which are intermediate between these two. It is to be noted that by 'prophecy' we mean the declaration of knowledge which cannot be apprehended through the ordinary faculties, but is acquired either by revelation from a deity or by some mantic power inherent in the seer himself, and which may relate to the present or the past, as well as the future. In this category we also include declarations of mantic wisdom and philosophy such as we find in Brahmanic literature and in certain Welsh poems.

CHAPTER II

THE DISTRIBUTION OF LITERARY TYPES

WE have now to discuss the distribution of the Types A, B, C, D, E, in relation to the categories treated in the previous chapter. Incidentally this subject will involve some discussion of the relations between poetry and prose, though we are not prepared to treat that problem as a whole.

First we may take the general distribution of the Types.

Poetry of Type A, i.e. narrative poetry designed for entertainment, has been included in our survey of ancient Teutonic literature (English, Norse and German), of the ancient literatures of Greece and India, and the modern oral literatures of Russia, Yugoslavia and the Tatars. In early Irish literature we have found very little, and that not of the oldest period, practically nothing in early Welsh, and nothing at all in Biblical Hebrew or anywhere in Africa. In Polynesia it is limited to a comparatively small area. On the other hand we know that this type of poetry is current in many modern oral literatures which are not included in our survey, e.g. Albanian, Greek, Finnish and Malay. In the Middle Ages it was current in France and Spain, as also in the 'ballad' poetry of northern Europe. From very ancient times we have evidence for it in Syria and Mesopotamia. In the latter case it may be traced in Sumerian records back to the third millennium (B.C.). It is therefore both ancient and widespread, though by no means universal.

Saga of Type A is more widespread than poetry of the same type. It is probably to be found in all the literatures included in our survey, though in some of them it is preserved only in summaries or translations. In some form or other indeed it may possibly occur everywhere, though we are by no means clear that this is the case. We believe, however, that even highly cultivated saga is more widely distributed than narrative poetry. Its distribution is very different; for it is found in Irish, Welsh, Hebrew, Polynesian and several African languages, as well as in Norse and among the Tatars. In Norse the saga and the narrative poetry relate to different periods; but among the Tatars the difference in distribution seems to be geographical.

Poetry of Type B, i.e. the speech or dialogue in character, is also perhaps more widely distributed than poetry of Type A. We have found it in English, Norse, Welsh, Irish, Russian, Yugoslav, Hebrew, among the Tatars, in India and Polynesia, and perhaps in Africa. It is common in medieval (and later) ballad poetry. Most commonly it occurs in the form of an independent poem, with or without a short introduction in prose or poetry. But verse speeches of the same type are also frequently contained in sagas. We have noted examples in Norse, Irish and Hebrew, and among the Tatars and Polynesians. The same form was without doubt current in early Wales, though the sagas are lost, and perhaps also in England.

Type C, i.e. didactic poetry or saga, relating to individuals, abounds in early Indian and Hebrew literature, and is perhaps to be found everywhere, though with varying frequency.[1] There is no doubt that Type C very frequently arises out of Type A or Type B through the introduction of didactic elements. The tendency to this process seems indeed to be universal where poetry or saga of the latter types has passed into the hands of religiously or academically minded persons or even come under religious influence; and it is not unfrequently a doubtful question whether a poem or saga, as we have it, should be assigned to Type A (B) or to Type C. Some of the poems and sagas of this type, however, were doubtless didactic from the beginning.

Type D was described briefly in the previous chapter as literature of celebration. Actually, however, we have used the term throughout as including 'appeals' (prayers, exhortations, etc.) as well as hymns, panegyrics, elegies, and songs of triumph or of social ritual. The two varieties, e.g. prayer and praise, are so often associated in the same poem that we have not thought it necessary to classify them separately. Type D is probably to be found everywhere, though it is often not well represented in the records which have survived. Poetry seems to be far more frequent than prose.[2]

Type E, i.e. poetry of diversion, relating to the poet himself and his surroundings, is also probably to be found everywhere. In its simplest form it may be seen among the Yoruba (cf. p. 647 f.), in more cultivated forms among (e.g.) the Tuareg, Galla and Amhara. But in ancient literatures, except Greek and Norse, very little poetry of this type has been preserved; and this often consists of brief references to the poet's

---

[1] Occasionally—where closer definition is required—we distinguish between CA, i.e. didactic narrative, and CB, i.e. didactic speech-poetry.

[2] Poems which properly belong to Type D sometimes take, wholly or largely, the form of a narrative or of a speech in character. To these we have occasionally applied the terms DA, DB.

own affairs, which he has inserted in a poem mainly concerned with some other theme. Indeed the interest of poetry of this type is as a rule merely ephemeral. In general it would seem to have a chance of surviving only under certain conditions:

(i) If it is written down at once or very soon after its composition. We may instance the Irish poem on the pet cat (cf. Vol. i, p. 368) or the Welsh poem in the MS. of Juvencus. Both of these doubtless owe their preservation to the fact that they were written in the blank spaces of MSS. containing what was regarded as more important matter.

(ii) If it is incorporated in a poem of general interest, like the personal references in Hesiod's poems, or in a highly developed saga. We may refer to the numerous poems, most of which are believed to be genuine, contained in Egils Saga Skallagrímssonar. Greek, Norse or Irish poems may also owe their preservation to being quoted in treatises on metre.

(iii) If the author is famous for his position or other reasons. We may instance the verses attributed to King Harold the Fairhaired and other kings of Norway (cf. Vol. i, pp. 363, 367f.).

Poems of this type may of course survive when both the author himself and the circumstances of their composition have been forgotten. It is likely that folk-songs of Type B are largely derived from such poems.

We may now pass on to the relationship between the types and the categories. Here we will begin with Type E, which is the least complex of the types in this respect.

Type E is found in the heroic, non-heroic and post-heroic categories, in so far as these are distinguished. Numerous examples from modern non-European literatures have been noticed above. Some of these show marked heroic characteristics (cf. pp. 518 f., 664); but the majority contain little or nothing to indicate their provenance, though this may be known from the collectors. As a general rule the style of the poems is highly conventional; individual traits are seldom apparent.

In the modern European (Slavonic) literatures we have found no certain examples of this type, though we have no doubt that it was cultivated, at least in Yugoslavia.[1]

---

[1] For the cultivation of Type E in Yugoslavia we may refer to Vol. ii, p. 307 and note. It is likely of course that many timeless-nameless poems of Type B, both in Yugoslavia and elsewhere, originated as personal poems (Type E). Even folk-songs may sometimes record actual experiences of the (unknown) authors.

In the ancient literatures also we do not know of any certain examples of heroic poetry of Type E; but we think that the English poems *Deor* and *Widsith*, and perhaps also certain Welsh and Irish poems, contain elements derived from such poetry. At all events it is clear from the story of Gelimer (cf. Vol. I, p. 26) that poetry of this type was cultivated in heroic circles.

For examples from non-heroic poetry we are hardly any better off. We can only refer to certain passages in the Rgveda (cf. Vol. II, p. 506 ff.), in which the seers allude incidentally to themselves. With these may be compared the personal references in the poems of Hesiod and the early prophets of Israel (*ib.* p. 722 ff.), which would seem to follow non-heroic tradition, though chronologically they belong to a late phase.

In 'post-heroic' poetry, at least Greek and Norse, this type is far more fully and satisfactorily represented. For examples we may refer to Vol. I, p. 358 ff. The Greek and Norse poems would seem to be largely independent of either heroic or non-heroic tradition; not unfrequently indeed they show a markedly individual character. Both series date from times of discovery, when new knowledge and new ideas were current. They approximate to modern feeling more nearly than any other class of literature included in this book.

Type D, the poetry (seldom prose) of celebration and appeal, has a much wider scope than Type E. It is found in all the 'personal' categories. In general too it is much more fully represented, though in some ancient literatures it is not well preserved. As the material is of a somewhat heterogeneous character, we will take the different varieties seriatim.

Elegies or dirges seem to occur everywhere. Examples will be found in most of the literatures, both ancient and modern, treated in this book. Most of them belong to the heroic and 'post-heroic' phases; but elegies upon 'unspecified' (nameless) persons are also frequent. Apart from instances which were doubtless intended for actual use, we often find, in heroic sagas and narrative poems, elegies composed as speeches in character. The speakers, both here and in the genuine elegies, are at least as often women as men. Sometimes elegies are pronounced by more than one person—one or more, of an emotional type, by the widow and near female relatives of the deceased, others, of a more formal character, by his military followers in the case of a great chief.

Wedding-songs and other poems of social ritual are perhaps almost as widespread as elegies; but they are seldom preserved in ancient literatures. For examples from ancient India we may refer to Vol. II,

p. 566f. For modern times the Russian material (*ib.* p. 232ff.) is especially abundant. Most of the examples everywhere relate properly to 'unspecified' persons. They may be adapted to special occasions, but usually follow conventional lines.

Songs of triumph, after battle, have been recorded very often in modern times, especially in Africa and Polynesia (cf. pp. 266, 548, above). In ancient literatures such poems are seldom preserved; we may refer in particular to the English 'Battle of Brunanburh' (Vol. I, p. 352f.) and the Hebrew 'Song of Deborah' (Vol. II, p. 658f.). For the (more personal) heroic variety we can refer only to secondary instances contained in narrative poetry.[1] With these we may compare poems (pp. 518, 549 above) which boast of exploits before the event.

Panegyrics are among the most constant and characteristic features of heroic society. A number of instances have been cited in this volume; we may refer to pp. 262 f., 513 f.,[2] and especially to the examples found among the Tatars (p. 58 f.), who have panegyrics upon horses, as well as upon heroes and distinguished visitors. In the ancient literatures not many heroic panegyrics have been preserved. A few are to be found in Welsh (Vol. I, p. 37ff.), and a number of fragments in Irish (*ib.* p. 55f.), while at least one early example comes from India (Vol. II, p. 482). But there is a considerable amount of evidence for such panegyrics almost everywhere, either from references in historical records or from secondary examples contained in sagas and narrative poems. We may refer in particular to the Teutonic evidence noticed in Vol. I, p. 574ff. and to the passages in the Mahābhārata cited in Vol. II, p. 617.

In non-heroic poetry examples are by no means so frequent. In modern literatures indeed we cannot recall any panegyrics which may with confidence be assigned to this category, though we are not inclined to doubt that such poems are composed from time to time. From ancient India we may cite the panegyric on the Vasishtha family in Rgv. VII. 33 (cf. Vol. II, p. 507). Moreover the panegyrics on princes, which occur in numerous poems of the Rgveda (*ib.* p. 482ff.), are in all

---

[1] E.g. *Iliad* XXII. 393, Hamðismál, st. 30. In both cases the heroes, Achilles and Hamðir, use almost the same expression: "We have won great glory" (or "good fame"). Cf. the hero's boast in Beow. 636 ff.

[2] We may refer also to the long and elaborate panegyric upon Dingan, king of the Zulu, given (apparently incomplete) by Shooter, *The Kafirs of Natal*, etc., p. 310ff. (cf. p. 580 above). Among the Basuto, heroes and even kings are said as a rule to compose panegyrics upon themselves, though apparently they are sometimes sung by their minstrels. Examples may be found in Casalis, *The Basutos*, p. 328ff.; cf. Ellenberger, *History of the Basuto*, p. 297. See Postscript on p. 749.

probability to be regarded as belonging here; for it is for their sacrifices and their generosity to priests that these princes are praised. From early Ireland we may cite the 'Eulogy of St Columba' (Vol. I, p. 102), if it is really what it claims to be. In 'post-heroic' literature dating from pre-literary times numerous panegyrics are preserved in the North, though mostly in a fragmentary state. The majority of these were composed by Icelanders who visited or took service at the courts of Norwegian or other kings, under conditions which differed little from those of the Heroic Age (*ib.* p. 345 f.).[1] In Ireland also panegyrics of heroic character continued to be composed down to literary times (*ib.* p. 350); and the same may probably be said of Wales (*ib.* p. 352). For the Greek evidence we may refer to (*ib.*) p. 354.

In connection with panegyrics mention should be made of abusive poems, directed against enemies of the poets or of their patrons, or by one warrior against another. These seem to be a frequent characteristic of heroic society, especially perhaps in its less advanced forms. Modern examples will be found in the present volume, pp. 515, 546. Fragments of early Irish poems of this kind are preserved (cf. Vol. I, p. 350); and it is recorded by ancient writers (e.g. Diodoros, v. 29, 31) that such poetry was much cultivated by the Gauls. In post-heroic times abusive poems were current in Greece (cf. Vol. I, p. 359f.), and examples are not rare in Norse sagas; but they may at least as well be regarded as personal poetry (Type E).

Hymns of praise to deities—which may be regarded as the theological counterpart of panegyrics—were probably current at some time among all the peoples whose literatures we have discussed. Examples from modern peoples have been noticed in this volume (pp. 132, 334, 645 f.); but in general this class of literature has not been well recorded. From ancient times we have a very large collection of poetry of this kind in the Rgveda (Vol. II, p. 529ff.), and smaller collections, mostly of uncertain date, in Hebrew and Greek (*ib.* p. 714; Vol. I, p. 241f.). Among Christian and Mohammedan peoples such poetry has been displaced by book-poetry.

Prayers (to deities) are commonly combined with hymns. Indeed it would seem that hymns everywhere usually contain an element of prayer. On the other hand prayers may occur without any hymnic

---

[1] One difference may be seen in the fact that post-heroic panegyrics are seldom, if ever, composed in honour of persons other than rulers, whereas heroic panegyrics frequently also celebrate the deeds of heroes. The incentive in the later period is of a more obviously mercenary character.

element. Instances will be found in this volume (pp. 132 f., 335 f.); we may also refer to Vol. I, p. 241 f.; Vol. II, pp. 575 ff., 714.

Exhortations and appeals to armies or to the general public seem to be specially characteristic of 'post-heroic' poetry. Literature of political appeal was cultivated in Greece from early times. Instances will be found in the early patriotic poets (Vol. I, p. 355 f.)—with which we may perhaps compare certain Irish references (*ib.* p. 351). The appeals made by the ('literary') Hebrew prophets (Vol. II, p. 721 f.) and the seers of Hawaii (p. 340 above) belong to a similar phase. Such appeals are by no means unknown in less advanced social conditions;[1] but when they occur the milieu seems, usually at least, to be non-heroic, and the authors are often patriotic seers. 'Heroic' appeals on the other hand are as a rule addressed to individuals or, perhaps rather less frequently, to personal retinues[2] or small groups of persons, who are sometimes mentioned by name. Instances of this kind will be found above (pp. 266, 516). In ancient literatures secondary examples are of frequent occurrence, as in Waldhere (*ad init.*), where the hero is exhorted by his lady: "Let not thy prowess fail this day."

Apart from hymns to deities, poems of Type D may in general be assumed to be contemporary with the persons and events celebrated in them. Panegyrics and elegies, and even celebrations of victory, may be composed in later times; but we believe this to be of very rare occurrence, except when the panegyrics, etc., are introduced merely as incidents in some longer composition. On the other hand it is often doubtful whether a poem was composed for actual use as a panegyric or elegy (Type D), or whether it is a speech in character in the form of a panegyric or elegy (Type B, or rather BD), composed as part of a story, and placed in the mouth of one of the characters. Poems of the latter type may of course have been composed at any subsequent time. No one will suggest that the elegies for Hector spoken by Andromache and the others, at the close of the Iliad, or Emer's elegy for CuChulainn (cf. Vol. I, p. 51) are records of actual speeches by these ladies. But

---

[1] We may refer especially to the cultivation of oratory among the Galla, the Maori and the Samoans; cf. pp. 565, 465.

[2] E.g. *Iliad* XVI. 269 ff., where, as in Beowulf and elsewhere, the appeal is to personal loyalty. Incidentally it may be remarked that—as others have noted before—the simile in (*ib.*) 212 ff. seems to reflect the (infantry) warfare of later times. The Myrmidons play no active part in the sequel; Patroclos apparently takes his place among the other Achaean princes.

there are many poems in regard to which doubt is possible. We have treated David's elegy for Saul and Jonathan as an example of Type D, because the majority of scholars interpret it as a genuine elegy; but there are others who take it as a speech in character. The reasons for doubting its genuineness are not clear to us; but the question can only be decided by specialists.

The chief group of poems affected by this question is that of the Welsh heroic elegies and panegyrics noticed in Vol. I, p. 37f. We do not see how the majority of these poems, especially the panegyrics, can reasonably be explained except as contemporary compositions. But it is quite possible that some of the elegies are poems of Type B—speeches in character—which originally formed part of sagas now lost.[1] This question again must be left to specialists, though we would urge that too much weight should not be attached to arguments based on the language or metre of the existing texts,[2] especially in a literature where oral tradition was sometimes so free or so careless as in Welsh. There is some reason for thinking that, just as in Norse,[3] panegyrics and elegies, which were attributed to famous poets, were committed to memory and preserved as part of the poets' training (cf. Vol. I, p. 584); and some of them would seem to have fared rather badly in the course of time (*ib.* p. 526f.).

We suspect that this 'educational' use of poetry of this type was by no means peculiar to Britain and Norway. Evidence to the same effect is to be found in the numerous fragments of such poetry preserved as quotations in works on metre and other learned treatises—Greek and Irish, as well as Norse. In India this was certainly the case with the Vedic hymns. The composition of panegyrics and hymns was doubtless the most remunerative part of a poet's activities everywhere; and hence we may presume that such poetry was the most carefully prepared.

[1] Prof. I. Williams, *Canu Llywarch Hen*, pp. livf., lxiff., explains in this way two poems in the Red Book, Nos XII and XVI, which in Vol. I, p. 38, we took to be genuine elegies. He shows clearly that there must have been a saga relating to Llywarch Hen (cf. p. 718 below). It may be pointed out that the former of these poems is concerned with Urien, rather than Llywarch, though it claims the latter as its author, while the evidence for a saga relating to Cynddylan seems to be very slight. But Prof. Williams is very much better qualified than we are to form an opinion upon the character of these poems.

[2] For instances of poems which have undergone partial or complete change of metre we may refer to the Yugoslav variants noticed in Vol. II, pp. 419ff., 423ff.

[3] We may refer to the quotations from such poems in the Skaldskaparmál and Háttatal (Prose Edda) and to the Prol. to the Heimskringla quoted in Vol. I, p. 581.

The general distribution of Type A, in both poetry and saga, has been noted above (p. 706). Here it may be noted that wherever narrative poetry is found,[1] it seems always, or almost always, to be represented in the heroic category. Usually indeed the great majority of such poems are heroic. Heroic saga is found among almost all the peoples included in our survey which have no heroic narrative poetry, and also in Norse, Russian and Yugoslav; but in the two former[2] it is at least very frequently derived from poetry.

Non-heroic narrative poetry may be said to be found everywhere, or nearly everywhere, where heroic narrative poetry is found, and non-heroic saga wherever heroic saga is found. But it would be hasty to infer from this, at least in the former case, that the two have had a common history. In early Teutonic poetry we know of only one non-heroic story—which is told in the Völundarkviða[3]—while the Greek poems of this class, such as the Melampodia, are generally believed to have been of later origin than the Homeric poems. Yugoslav non-

[1] Narrative poetry is highly developed among the Malays and kindred peoples, whom we have not included in our survey (apart from p. 476 ff. above); to have done so would have required a knowledge of the whole area which it was not in our power to acquire. It seems clear that the literatures of many of the various districts and islands, though they have an individuality of their own, have been greatly influenced by each other, and also that they have been much affected by Indian influence and by Mohammedan influence in general. Of special importance is the narrative poetry of the Achehnese (in Sumatra), an account of which may be found in Snouck Hurgronje, *The Achehnese* (Eng. transl.), Vol. II, p. 80 ff. The poems, some of which are of great length, are mainly concerned with the wars with the Dutch from the seventeenth century to the nineteenth. It seems to be difficult to determine the relations between written and oral records. The older poems are preserved in writing; but the author of the last great poem, dealing with the wars of c. 1880–91, could not read or write. Yet he cultivated strict memorisation; and there is no mention of any instrumental accompaniment. The nearest analogies of these poems seem to lie with the Dalmatian poems discussed in Vol. II, p. 351 ff.; but they are evidently much longer and more ambitious, and apparently also more sophisticated, than the latter. It is to be suspected that, like these, they presuppose the existence of heroic narrative poetry. The same suggestion might be made for some poems of the Sea Dyaks (cf. p. 480 ff.). A comparative study of the literatures, both ancient and modern, of the whole region—the East Indies and the Malay Peninsula—would doubtless lead to interesting results.

[2] Yugoslav saga has not been accessible to us.

[3] The story of Völundr (Weland) would seem to be of non-heroic origin; but Weland is often referred to in heroic poetry, and his son, Wudga, is a famous hero. Elsewhere also smiths have an anomalous position. Amargin, the father of Conall Cernach, is son of a smith; but his wife is King Conchobor's sister. Cf. also the Kazak story of Ak Köbök (p. 59 above), where the hero composes a panegyric upon a smith.

heroic narrative poems seem to be few in number and, unlike heroic poems, relate apparently only to the far past; and both they and the Russian examples are poor in incident and personnel. It is only in ancient India, especially in the Mahābhārata, and among the Tatars that we find non-heroic narrative poetry widely represented. The Mahābhārata, however, contains a large amount of matter which in earlier times was treated in prose. Apart from didactic matter, non-heroic—not heroic—saga is to be found in the Brāhmanas (cf. Vol. II, p. 496 f.). On the whole then there would seem to be good reason for believing that non-heroic narrative poetry is usually a late and secondary development, originating in times when heroic and non-heroic literature had become current in the same circles.

In post-heroic literature narrative poetry is very poorly represented. In England we have the 'Battle of Maldon', which differs very little from heroic poetry (cf. Vol. I, p. 338), and fragments and traces of some other poems, which would seem to have been of a different character. In Norse and Greek we know of nothing at all. In Yugoslavia (on the Adriatic) and in Russia there is a certain amount of such poetry (cf. Vol. II, pp. 348 ff., 63). But in the latter case at least this is clearly connected historically with heroic poetry, and may be regarded as a survival of heroic form, adapted to changed conditions. In general, the vehicle of narrative in post-heroic literature is evidently saga, not poetry.

Narrative poetry relating to unspecified individuals is not known to us from any ancient literature, except in one or two didactic stories in the Mahābhārata (cf. Vol. II, p. 567 ff.). There is a certain amount, however, in Yugoslavia, and apparently more in Russia. In all three cases it may well be due to the versification of prose matter, owing to the popularity of heroic poetry. For the narrative poems of Tonga and Samoa we may refer to p. 346 f. above.

Narrative poetry relating to deities is found in Norse and Greek and in the Mahābhārata. Here again we are not inclined to attach much importance to the last of these. The passages as a rule give the impression of being late and sophisticated; frequently they are at variance with the theology of the Rgveda. There are other passages, however, in which both deities and men figure; and some of these may follow an older tradition. Similar incidents occur also rather frequently in the non-heroic narrative poetry of the Tatars (cf. p. 84 ff. above), as well as in the Homeric poems. From the latter (*Od.* I. 337 f., VIII. 266 ff.) it appears that stories of the gods belonged in Greece to the répertoire of the heroic minstrel. Both the Greek and the Norse poems will require notice in a later chapter.

This survey suggests that in general narrative poetry belongs primarily to heroic literature. At all events there is no doubt that in some countries, especially India, Russia and Yugoslavia, such poetry has encroached upon saga, i.e. that there has been a widespread tendency to convert prose narrative of all kinds into poetry, though the reverse process is also found, at least in Russia. We are not prepared, however, to declare without wider investigation that narrative poetry invariably begins with heroic matter. There may be peoples, not included in our survey, who have narrative poetry but no heroic literature. And the earliest narrative poetry known to us, in Mesopotamia, seems to contain non-heroic and theological, as well as heroic, elements.[1] At present we must perhaps be satisfied with observing that heroic literature is the category in which narrative poetry is chiefly found. This may be due largely to the prevalence of court minstrelsy, as we shall see later. Stories of the gods would seem to come next in importance.

In general saga would seem to be a more natural form for narrative than poetry, and it is certainly more widespread. Between the two, however, we frequently find intermediate forms, in which both prose and poetry are used. Usually it is the speeches, though not all speeches, which are in poetry. Sometimes the poetry is of Types E and D, as in certain 'Sagas of Icelanders', or of Type D alone, as in the story of David (in the Books of Samuel); sometimes it is of Type B, as in other Norse sagas, and also in Irish, Tatar and Polynesian sagas. This latter variety may well be derived from the former.

Some scholars hold that narrative poetry is derived from saga with speeches in character (Type B); but others trace its origin to narrative elements in poetry of celebration (Type D). Both explanations may be correct in individual cases; and we should also not be inclined to doubt that a narrative poem may be derived from a saga without poetry. On the other hand it is clear enough, e.g. from the Yugoslav evidence, that such poetry very frequently comes direct from a poet's personal observation or from contemporary news; indeed we see no reason for doubting that this is the normal origin of narrative poems. But the origin of narrative poetry as a genre—the question how the first narrative poems come into existence—is less clear. To this we shall have to return shortly.

[1] It may be noted also that the theological poems found at Ras Shamra contain narrative elements; cf. Vol. II, p. 712.

Type B is found in the heroic category in Norse, Welsh, Irish, Russian, Tatar, and practically in Yugoslav, though apparently all the examples here contain a slight narrative element. We may perhaps also cite one example from the Mahābhārata (cf. Vol. II, p. 470f.).

In the non-heroic category we cannot cite any true examples, except in Tatar and Polynesian. The form is found in Welsh, Irish, Sanskrit (in the Upanishads) and Hebrew; but all the instances known to us are didactic, i.e. properly CB.

In post-heroic literature Type B is of very frequent occurrence in Norse sagas and by no means unknown in Ireland. For instances we may refer to Vol. I, p. 338ff.

In poetry relating to unspecified individuals this type is best represented in English (Vol. I, p. 423ff.). Examples are also to be found in the Rgveda and in Greek, Russian and Yugoslav, and probably in Welsh. In modern folk-songs it is extremely frequent everywhere.

In theological poetry Type B appears in Norse, Greek[1] and in the Rgveda. The Hebrew examples are probably all didactic (CB).

Type B is what may be called a secondary type, and seems to have more than one origin. Many folk-songs are probably derived from poems of Type E, and it can hardly be doubted that many other poems of Type B, both those contained in sagas and independent poems, are compositions in imitation of Type E poems. Others again are imitations of elegies and other poems of Type D. Poems like Guðrúnarkviða I (cf. Vol. I, p. 27) give the impression of scenes taken from heroic narrative poems (in which elegies are introduced), and developed as studies of emotional situation. Lastly, it is held by some scholars that theological dialogue poems like the Skírnismál or the dialogue between Yama and Yami in the Rgveda (cf. Vol. II, p. 532) may have their origin in mimetic ritual.

Poetry of Type B is sometimes strictly contemporary. As an example we may cite the 'Lament of Princess Ksenÿa', recorded by James (cf. Vol. II, p. 160f.). It seems at least very probable that other Russian poems of the same kind were also composed at the time of the events with which they are concerned. The 'elegies' for various tsars, which also doubtless belong to Type B (BD), are likewise in all probability of contemporary origin.

---

[1] If we may regard the Homeric Hymn to Aphrodite (No. IV) as an example of Type B (cf. Vol. I, p. 244).

The same may be said of poems of Type B in other literatures.[1] This remark applies especially to poems of the nameless variety, if we are right in believing that these often originated as poems of Type E. Some of the 'spurious' poems contained in sagas also may well be contemporary, or almost contemporary, though others are probably much later. But where famous persons are concerned, there can be no question that poetry of this type tends to grow in popularity, as interest comes to be transferred from exploits and events to the persons themselves. Poems in which the speakers are famous heroes, heroines or seers may be derived from narrative poems or sagas, rather than personal records, just as in cases where the speakers are deities. We have little doubt that this is the true explanation of most of the poems of Type B preserved in ancient literatures, when they are concerned with famous persons of the far past. Such poems may have been composed at any time, so long as the stories were remembered.

Poems of this type which were composed after the times of the speakers are usually preserved (as speeches) in sagas; and in general they probably owe their existence to these sagas. Numerous examples occur in Norse and Irish sagas, and in the former their origin is often clear enough; for they are found together with speech-poems which seem to have been composed by characters of the sagas—i.e. poems of Type E (cf. p. 708)—and which doubtless served as models for the later poems. In Vol. I, pp. 34 ff. and 105 f., it was pointed out that there are a number of Welsh poems of this type, both heroic and non-heroic, which seem to presuppose the existence of sagas, though the sagas have not been preserved. Recently Prof. I. Williams in his important book *Canu Llywarch Hen*, p. xli ff., has confirmed this suggestion, and at the same time has shown that many difficulties and apparent discrepancies in the poems[2] are due to the loss of connecting narratives. Some of the

---

[1] For special—perhaps somewhat exceptional—varieties we may cite the Montenegrin poem (Karadžić v. 18) on the funeral of Prince Danilo (Vol. II, p. 335 f.) and the Norse Hrafnsmál (Vol. I, p. 341 f.), which was evidently intended as a panegyric upon King Harold the Fairhaired. Here also we may refer to the Darraðarljóð (*ib.* p. 346 f.).

[2] Especially in certain poems noticed in Vol. I, p. 36. What we said there should be corrected in the light of Williams' explanation. He points out (*Canu Ll. H.* p. xxxix f.) an interesting parallel in the speech-poems (dialogue)—preserved only in late MSS.—from the story of Trystan and Esyllt. In this case a connecting prose narrative has been preserved by two of the MSS.—publ. by him in the *Bull. of the Board of Celtic Studies*, v, 115 ff. The obscure fragments of poetry in the Black Book (No. XXXIV), noticed in Vol. I, p. 34 f., doubtless come from another story of the same cycle.

poems are dialogues, while in others there is no true sequence—the loss of the narrative has brought together speeches and conversations which belonged to different scenes in the stories. The text evidently comes from someone who cared only for the poems, and did not write down or copy the narratives.

We would call special attention to two varieties of this type. One is the debate between two sages, human or supernatural, such as we find in the Vafþrúðnismál or the Irish 'Colloquy of the Two Sages' (Vol. I, p. 97). The subject-matter of such debates is usually antiquarian or mantic; but the form may be noticed here. We see no reason to doubt that these debates reflect actual custom, such as we see in the Upanishads. The other variety is the heroic dialogue, which is sometimes, though by no means always, of a boastful or abusive character. This also we believe to be based upon actual usage in heroic society. There is good evidence that Tatar princes cultivated the art of speaking in poetry on formal occasions (cf. pp. 64 f., 187 above), and the same art seems at least to be implied in various passages in ancient literature.[1] We may refer also to the Polynesian debates described on p. 414 f. above.

It would be difficult to overestimate the importance of Type B in the history of literature. But we cannot attempt here to deal with the subject in all its bearings, e.g. in relation to drama.

In Type C, the didactic type, we may take poetry and saga together. In heroic poetry it is found to an enormous extent, both in primary and secondary usage (cf. p. 707), in the Mahābhārata. It occurs also in Norse, Welsh, Irish and possibly Hebrew.[2] In secondary usage and incidentally it is much in evidence in Beowulf and in many Irish heroic sagas. The lost Greek heroic poems seem to have been much influenced by it. The didacticism is sometimes religious, sometimes antiquarian, sometimes it may be described as rhetorical pedantry. In modern literatures it seems to be much less frequent, though examples are to be found in Russian (cf. Vol. II, p. 276ff.), Yugoslav (ib. p. 314), and elsewhere.

---

[1] E.g. Beow. 630ff. We may compare Diodoros v. 29, where it is stated that Gaulish warriors before the beginning of a battle would rush forward and challenge the enemy to single combat; and whenever anyone would listen to them they would begin to glorify (ἐξυμνοῦσι) the valour of their forefathers and boast of their own prowess, and deride and belittle their opponent.

[2] Certain stories in the Book of Judges may possibly be of this origin; cf. Vol. II, p. 654.

In non-heroic literature this type is probably to be found almost everywhere. The Mahābhārata again supplies the largest store of material. The didacticism is sometimes moral, sometimes designed to illustrate the superiority of the Brahman caste. Hebrew literature furnishes much religious material.

In post-heroic literature Type C seems to be extremely rare. Didactic literature of general reference was widely cultivated in these periods; but it is only seldom, as in the 'Works and Days', that we find anything relating to specified individuals.

In literature relating to unspecified individuals this type is rather widespread. It is not well represented in ancient literatures; but examples from the Mahābhārata and from Hebrew will be found in Vol. II, pp. 568f., 742f. In modern oral literatures it is known in Russian and Yugoslav and in parts of Africa.

In theological literature it is also widespread. The didacticism may be moral or antiquarian, as well as religious. Examples are to be found in Norse, Greek, Polynesian and especially Hebrew. It is also very frequent in Vedic poetry, though the poems have the form of Type D.

Poems and sagas of Type C usually, if not always, date from times much later than those to which they relate. There may be exceptions; but we cannot recall any examples which we should be inclined to regard as contemporary. Literature of this type will require further discussion in the next chapter.

Of the five literary types discussed above two (D and E) may be described as primary. They are perhaps to be found everywhere; in some of the African literatures, which we have noticed, they seem to be the only forms of poetry known, at least in poetry relating to persons.

Actually both these types are represented in prose, as well as in poetry. But their prose usage is in general less developed, except in oratory and prayer. We suspect that one of the chief sources of poetry[1] is to be sought in these types—on the one hand in formal public speech, including address to deities, on the other in solemn or studied private speech, including the utterance of reflection. The salient characteristics of such poetry—invocation or appeal, emotional emphasis or intonation, and repetition—may in its original form have differed little from those of oratory, or prayer. Indeed we have to confess that we do not know

[1] Other sources are probably to be sought in spells, etc., as we shall see later. Spells, when they relate to individuals or to individual spirits, are closely akin to Type D; but other considerations have to be taken into account.

what is the essential[1] difference between poetry and 'rhythmical prose', unless it is that the former is 'sung'. Yet orations and even recitations of saga are said to be chanted among some peoples (cf. pp. 241, 411 f.). But these speculations lie properly beyond the bounds of our enquiry.

Types B and C are of secondary character. The former, i.e. the speech or dialogue in character, is sometimes derived from, or modelled upon, poetry of Type E or Type D; and examples of this kind may be almost or quite contemporary (cf. p. 717 f.). Sometimes on the other hand it is derived from narrative poetry or saga; and in such cases may be separated by centuries from the origin of the story. Type C, the didactic type, is derived from, or modelled upon, narrative poetry or saga, or poetry of Type B, and usually dates from times considerably later than the events with which it is concerned.

Narrative poetry and saga (Type A) require further discussion. Both these forms of narrative are sometimes, as we have seen, strictly contemporary, while at other times they show features which point to the lapse of a long period between their origin and the events which they profess to relate. Here, however, we are concerned with the relationship between poetry and saga.

For the purpose of narrative, as we have remarked, prose (saga) would seem to be a more natural vehicle than poetry; and it may perhaps be assumed that the use of the latter has everywhere been preceded by something in the nature of saga, though not necessarily cultivated to any appreciable extent. But, if so, how did the change come about?

It is commonly held, we believe, among Sanskrit scholars that the stories of the Mahābhārata were originally related in prose; and there is some evidence to that effect for the non-heroic, though not, so far as we are aware, for the heroic stories. The change from prose to poetry would seem to be part of a general tendency to employ poetry for didactic purposes—which can be dated approximately to the last five centuries before the beginning of our era. Even the teachings of Yājnavalkya, which we have cited (Vol. II, p. 585 ff.) from the early (prose) Brhadāranyaka Upanishad, are treated in poetry in the Mahābhārata. But it cannot safely be assumed that narrative poetry was unknown in India before this time (cf. *ib.* p. 617 ff.). More probably, when the Brahmans took over the heroic stories, they took over with them the form in which they were told.

---

[1] Rhyme, alliteration, stanza, and the regulation of the number of syllables in a period (line) are of course non-essential. We may refer to the 'metres' of the Russian *byliny*, noticed in Vol. II, p. 19 ff.

For the northern literatures a somewhat different explanation is current, viz. that narrative poetry is derived from saga interspersed with poetry of Type B, i.e. speeches in character, such as we find in Irish heroic sagas.[1] Some of the more archaic Edda poems consist wholly of dialogue, with brief connecting narratives in prose; and in one case a poem of this kind seems to be definitely more archaic than a narrative poem on the same subject (cf. Vol. 1, p. 524). But such evidence is insufficient to establish any general principle.[2] There can be no reasonable doubt that Teutonic narrative poetry was current several centuries before either of these poems existed, at least in anything like its present form.

We are not inclined to doubt that individual narrative poems have from time to time arisen out of saga, either with or without speech poems, by conversion of prose into poetry. But we see no reason for believing that narrative poetry in general originated in this way anywhere. It is assumed in both the explanations cited in the preceding paragraphs that the stories themselves were already in existence when the change from prose to poetry took place—i.e. an already existing body of narrative literature was transformed. Indeed we believe that those who have put forward these explanations have thought of the stories as old at this time. Yet it is strange that such a change should have taken place among so many peoples, especially if we bear in mind the rather close resemblance shown by the heroic narrative poetry of the different peoples, both in its general character and in its production. The Yugoslav evidence leaves no doubt that narrative poems—not merely individual poems, but the whole body of such poetry—can undergo a change of metre. But, in spite of this, we cannot regard as satisfactory any explanation which everywhere involves a conscious and deliberate change from prose to poetry in the whole existent body of stories.

Apart from the derivation from saga noticed above, the only explanation of narrative poetry that we have seen is that it is an offshoot of poetry of Type D, e.g. hymns, panegyrics and songs of triumph. It has been pointed out that poems of this type not unfrequently contain

[1] Speech poems (usually didactic) are found also in the Brāhmanas and the prose Upanishads.
[2] We have noticed that in variant forms of Yugoslav poems speeches occasionally show a closer resemblance than the narrative itself. But we do not see how—in such poems—this can mean more than that speeches were sometimes more carefully memorised.

narrative passages. Examples from hymns may be found in the Rgveda and the Psalms; a good instance occurs in the 'Song of Deborah' (Judges v), which is partly a hymn and partly a song of triumph. Further, it is of importance to note that such hymnic and panegyric poetry is to be found almost everywhere and in all periods, and that, like narrative poetry, it belongs chiefly to the theological and heroic categories.

We are not inclined to attach much importance to songs of triumph in this connection. Such compositions properly, though not universally, make use of the first person, whereas narrative poetry regularly employs the third, and its derivation should be sought in compositions where this is customary. Songs sung in chorus by a number of persons may of course be left out of account in this connection. Heroic narrative poetry is recited almost everywhere[1] by a single performer, usually accompanied by a stringed instrument.

If derivation from Type D in any form is correct, the chief source of narrative poetry must be sought in the heroic panegyric. In this connection we may refer again to a passage in Beowulf (867 ff.), where very soon—not more than a few hours—after the overthrow of Grendel, one of the Danish king's squires produces a poem celebrating the hero's exploit. This passage was quoted in Vol. 1 (p. 574), but in view of its importance it may conveniently be repeated here: "Now one of the king's squires, a man full of grandiloquent phrases and intent upon poetry, who remembered a very great number of stories of the past—(wherein) one expression led to another in due sequence—(this) man in his turn began to describe Beowulf's exploit in skilful style, declaiming with success a well constructed narrative, with varied phraseology. He related everything that he had heard told of Sigemund and his deeds of prowess," etc. This would seem to be a panegyric (Type D); but it evidently contains a considerable element of narrative, since it includes a full account of Sigemund's exploits—presumably by way of comparison with those of Beowulf. Indeed the passage rather gives the impression that what the poet is describing is the genesis of a heroic narrative poem.

---

[1] Ballad poetry is exceptional; but true ballad poetry was not originally 'heroic' in character, though it came to be applied to heroic themes. The short lines also which occur in some early Yugoslav poems (*Bugarštice*) may have been sung by the audience. In two passages relating to the Teutonic Heroic Age we hear of two performers, though it is not stated whether they recited together or alternately; but these passages—which are quoted in Vol. 1, p. 574 ff.—probably refer to panegyric poems (Type D).

For our purpose the value of the passage is perhaps somewhat impaired by the fact that it comes from a milieu in which narrative poetry is fully developed. The use of (detailed) narrative in the celebration of an exploit which has just taken place, and in the same locality, can probably be paralleled;[1] such poetry may well have been composed in similar circumstances last century in Montenegro. But can it be used legitimately as evidence for the genesis of narrative poetry as a genre?

Another, perhaps more serious, objection to this explanation lies in the fact that it cannot apply in general to narratives other than those of successful exploits. The themes chosen by Phemios and Demodocos for their recitations in the Odyssey I. 326f., VIII. 73 ff., could hardly have formed the subjects of panegyrics—or indeed of any poems of celebration. And the same may be said of the story of Sigurðr's death and that of the death of Gunnarr and Högni. Indeed numerous instances of this kind might be cited. If the derivation from Type D is correct, we must infer that poems dealing with such themes belong to what we may call a secondary phase in the history of narrative poetry. This in itself is of course by no means impossible; but the fact that such themes occur everywhere, or almost everywhere, where heroic narrative poetry is to be found gives some reason for hesitation. On the whole therefore we are inclined to doubt whether this explanation by itself is sufficient to account for the rise of narrative poetry, though the importance of the passage quoted above from Beowulf is certainly not to be overlooked.

At this point we ought perhaps to raise the question whether narrative poetry is of independent origin among the various peoples which cultivate it, or whether it has been acquired by one people from another. It is certainly of interest to note that in modern times it has flourished among three neighbouring peoples, the Yugoslavs, Albanians and Greeks, whose languages differ from one another very greatly. Yet, if we apply the theory of borrowing to the literatures included in our survey, we are confronted by serious chronological difficulties. Narrative poetry appears first in one language, then in another, at intervals throughout the last 2500 years. That of the Tatars is hardly known before last century, that of the Russians and the Yugoslavs from the sixteenth

---

[1] Russian poems of celebration which would seem to have been composed immediately after the events sometimes contain an element of narrative. Apart from the 'Laments' for various emperors, we may refer in particular to the poem on the entry of the Patriarch Filaret into Moscow (transl. by Chadwick, *Russ. Her. Poetry*, p. 252), which was recorded by R. James within (at most) a very few months of the occurrence (1619). But we have not met with any case in which the scope of the narrative is comparable with what is indicated in the passage from Beowulf—unless the 'Slovo o Polky Igorevê' is to be mentioned here.

century, or a little earlier; but Teutonic narrative poetry can be traced back at least to the sixth, while the Greek must have been in existence more than twelve centuries before that time. In France and Spain it appears at some time in the interval between the Teutonic and the Yugoslav, in India at some time between the Greek and the Teutonic. In Mesopotamia it is said to occur at a much earlier date—apparently as far back as the third millennium (B.C.).

It would be folly of course to assume that narrative poetry was a new thing at the time when it is first recorded; for the dates given above—so far as the literatures included in our survey are concerned—invariably fall within times for which detailed information is wanting, or only just beginning; and our observations have led us to the conclusion that this is no accident. For anything that we know to the contrary, narrative poetry may have flourished among the Teutonic or the Slavonic peoples or the Tatars for ages before we first hear of it. It may also have flourished among many neighbouring peoples who have left no records.

Yet it is sufficiently clear that intervals occur, during which such poetry ceases to be cultivated. Probably no one will maintain that oral narrative poetry has had a continuous history in Greece—from Homeric times to the War of Independence. In India similar intervals seem to occur. Among the Teutonic peoples the creative period ends with the sixth century, though old poems were remembered and recast. It is dangerous, as we have frequently seen, to draw conclusions from the absence of evidence;[1] but there are gaps in the history of narrative poetry in this country, which are not easy to bridge.

It may be that narrative poetry originated in one region, perhaps Mesopotamia, some four thousand years ago or more, and that it spread thence in different directions largely, though not wholly, through the Indo-European languages. For an analogy we may compare the rhyming narrative poetry, which spread, in ballads and otherwise, over a great part of Europe in the twelfth and following centuries. If this explanation is true,[2] its origin may be due to special conditions, which it is impossible for us now to trace.

On the other hand, if narrative poetry originated independently among many different peoples, it must be capable of some explanation

[1] Thus many scholars deny the antiquity of Russian and Yugoslav narrative poetry; but the reasons alleged do not seem to us satisfactory, especially in the former case.

[2] One of the two authors is inclined to this explanation, the other to the explanation suggested in the following paragraph. The former of the two alternatives is stated rather more fully in a paper shortly to be published in the *Journal of the R. Anthr. Inst.*

which will apply generally. The simplest and most obvious explanation would be that it arose from saga, not by a conscious and deliberate transformation of existing material, as postulated in the theories noticed above, but gradually, by a mechanical and unconscious change in the method of recitation, possibly involving the introduction of some kind of rhythm. What we mean is that among various peoples, though not universally, the method of reciting stories for the purpose of entertainment may gradually have become assimilated to the method of recitation employed for the purpose of celebration (Type D).

It may be questioned whether such a mechanical change, from prose to poetry, is possible. We have heard of the intonation of saga in various parts of the world. References to its use in Polynesia and in West Africa will be found above (pp. 411 f., 641 f.). We are under the impression that the 'Dynastic Chronicle' was recited in this way[1] at the court of Uganda, and that the reciters were the court minstrels. We have heard also that the Basuto, and perhaps other Southern Bantu peoples, are—or were until very recently—in the habit of reciting stories at great length and accompanying them on the native 'harp',[2] both at social gatherings and to themselves alone, e.g. for the purpose of whiling away the time on a journey. If all this information is correct, it would seem that at least among many African peoples saga is—or was—actually in the process of passing into narrative poetry.

Unfortunately we do not regard the evidence at our disposal as wholly satisfactory. Possibly we have inferred too much from what we have read and heard. We will therefore take this opportunity of publishing two questions, in the hope of obtaining more definite information from those who have first hand knowledge of African peoples:

(1) Are formal recitations of saga in West or Central Africa ever accompanied by a stringed instrument?

(2) Do the recitations of the Southern Bantu, accompanied by the native harp, consist of—or include—saga?

We should also like to know (3) in what respect, if at all, such recitations differ from recitations of panegyric poetry. It has been noted above (p. 710, note) that a special form of panegyric is much cultivated by the Basuto.

---

[1] The late Canon Roscoe told us that the Chronicle was declaimed 'in a kind of recitative'. Unfortunately we did not at the time appreciate the significance of this expression, and consequently omitted to ask him for further information, e.g. as to whether the recitation was accompanied on a musical instrument.

[2] The bow with calabash attached. We understand that nowadays an empty petrol can is commonly substituted for the calabash.

CHAPTER III

HEROIC AND NON-HEROIC

THE largest and probably the most important class of literature with which we are concerned is that which relates to specified human beings, i.e. to men and women whose names are given. In such literature we have throughout our survey distinguished two elements, heroic and non-heroic, each of which has usually been treated as a separate category. We have applied the term 'Heroic Age' to periods for which the records are of a heroic character, whether these records themselves are contemporary or date from later times. To literature relating to times later than the Heroic Age, so far as it comes within the scope of our survey, we have applied the term 'post-heroic', though we have not, except in Vol. I, devoted special chapters to this category.

Heroic literature consists partly of stories, prose or verse, of exploits and adventures, and partly of poems, panegyrics or elegies, in which exploits and adventures are celebrated. The outstanding feature is a pronounced individual interest, both as shown by the poet or narrator, and as attributed to the characters themselves. The primary element in heroic literature is probably to be found in the celebration or narrative of an exploit performed by someone (the 'hero') by his courage or strength, and by which he acquires fame. But it is only in the simplest form of heroic literature that we find this element alone. The scope tends to be extended in one direction or another. Sometimes a secondary interest is shown in the exploits of the community to which the hero belongs. Sometimes the interest is extended, and indeed often transferred, from the exploit to the hero himself and his surroundings. In literatures which show the latter tendency we usually find that all the heroes belong to a royal or princely class. In such cases heroic literature tends to become a literature concerned with the exploits, adventures and experiences of members of a princely class, both men and women, including perhaps their noble followers; in short heroic literature becomes court literature. This description seems to be true of all ancient heroic literatures, though not of some of their modern counterparts. The explanation of the tendency may lie in the obvious fact that persons of princely rank stand a better chance of having their doings

remembered—in a widespread court literature—than persons whose celebrity is merely local. Exploits of the latter may of course sometimes be
recorded in 'nameless' literature after their names have been forgotten.

The Heroic Age is essentially a barbaric period. Indeed the conditions
requisite for the exploits, adventures and experiences which form the
subjects of heroic literature could hardly be found—as normal conditions—in either primitive or civilised society. The beginnings of
'heroism' are doubtless to be traced to primitive times, and it may
persist into civilised times; but in both cases it is exceptional. The
periods and conditions reflected in heroic literature are of a character
intermediate between these two.

Here perhaps some definition of our use of these terms is required.
By 'primitive' we mean the conditions of a local community which is
sufficient for itself and dependent upon its own resources, whether it
live by hunting or by cultivation of the earth. It may be wholly independent, or it may be subject, perhaps tributary, to some dominant
power—which itself may be barbaric or civilised; but no external
relations are necessary for its own sake. By 'civilised' we mean the
conditions of a society which is dependent for its existence—for the
maintenance of its civilisation—upon relations with the wide world.

'Barbaric' society, as we understand it, lies between these two
extremes. The local community is one of a number of similar communities, which are grouped together under a king or political organisation. Each community contains an element which is in intimate and
necessary relation with elements in other local communities. These
elements are the more typically barbaric elements; sometimes they form
an upper class. External relations, with other groups, vary both in
character and in degree, but are never entirely wanting. When external
relations become a permanent necessity and widespread, the result is
what we call civilisation.

The Heroic Age is, as noted above, a barbaric period. But 'heroic' is
of course not synonymous with 'barbaric'. Account is also to be taken
of non-heroic literature, which often relates to the same period as
heroic. Under this term we must include any literature which is not
heroic. But in actual fact we find that the persons with whom such
literature is concerned are either princes or persons of the same class as
those who figure in heroic literature, regarded from a different point of
view, or else, and more frequently, seers, saints and sages—three classes
who are as a rule not clearly differentiated in barbaric society. The point
of view from which both princes and seers are treated is that of the

latter. Princes are praised for their piety and generosity (to seers), and censured for the reverse qualities. Communal interest is far more frequent than in heroic literature, and is very often expressed even in ancient records; but it is usually bound up with the national religion.

Stated briefly, heroic literature may be said to represent the warrior—in ancient times the princely warrior or the princely class in general—while non-heroic literature represents the seer and the religious interest. No other class or interest seems to be represented, at least in ancient literatures, before post-heroic times—indeed not before the phase of transition between barbarism and civilisation. In this latter phase the warrior and the seer are still prominent; but the former is now frequently a soldier of fortune, who serves under a temporary contract, like Archilochos or Egill Skallagrímsson.[1] Beside him there appear new classes—the merchant, especially the merchant-shipowner, the independent landowner and the city official. Now too we meet with lawyers or legislators and philosophers who, at least in Greece, do not claim to be seers.

The times in which these new classes first appear are separated from the Heroic Age by several centuries in Greece and in the North. Roman tradition seems to have preserved no memory of a Heroic Age. It is clear then that this term cannot be applied to barbaric times in general; there must have been 'non-heroic ages', as well as heroic ages. For such periods in ancient times we have usually but little information. But there is evidence that sometimes, as among the Old Saxons in the eighth century and in many Greek states, kingship was non-existent, while elsewhere the power of kings is said to be limited.[2] In both cases the supreme power rested with an assembly, connected with the national religion. Hebrew literature preserves traditions that before the establishment of kingship Israel was ruled by a seer, who seems to preside over a religious national assembly. Somewhat similar conditions are known to have prevailed in Mangaia (cf. p. 451).

It is clear then that there were both heroic and non-heroic periods in

---

[1] In the Heroic Age also mercenary service seems to have been very common. But then the nucleus of the force apparently consisted of a prince with his personal following. In later times these troops were evidently chance gatherings of adventurers brought together by an attractive proclamation; cf. Egils S. Skall. cap. 50.

[2] An interesting illustration may be found in Rimbertus, *Vita Anscharii*, cap. 26f., where a king of the Swedes states that he cannot give permission to missionaries to preach without first consulting the wishes of the assembly (*populus*). It is added that all public business depends *magis in populi unanimi uoluntate quam in regia potestate*. The king's position would seem to have been not too secure (cf. cap. 19).

barbaric times. In almost all ancient literatures, however, we find both heroic and non-heroic traditions relating to the same period; and among modern barbaric peoples also both elements, heroic and non-heroic, exist contemporaneously, both in literature and in actual life. It would seem indeed that the two elements were always present in some degree. Sometimes we find them in friendly relations with one another, under religious kings; sometimes—and perhaps more frequently—they are more or less strongly opposed. Numerous instances of both kinds are to be found in the Mahābhārata and the Books of Samuel and Kings.[1]

So too in literature we may find 'heroic' elements in times other than the Heroic Age. We have seen that Norse panegyrics upon kings of Norway and other countries in the Viking Age hardly differ in substance from heroic panegyrics. No doubt they followed traditional lines to a large extent. But heroic elements are by no means rare also in the 'Sagas of Icelanders'; and we see no reason for doubting that in actual fact many of the characters were at times, especially on their expeditions abroad, engaged in occupations which had much in common with the life of the Heroic Age. Yet it is a serious error to regard the Icelanders of the Viking Age as a heroic community. The same persons whose desperate deeds abroad are related in the sagas generally spent the greater part of their lives at home as respectable and law-abiding farmers. Iceland offered little opportunity for 'heroism', except in family feuds and cases of outlawry. We may instance the difficulties which long prevented Gunnlaugr Ormstunga and his rival Hrafn from fighting out their quarrel.

On the other hand we think it would be an equally serious error to regard the period to which the Indian heroic stories relate as a 'Non-heroic Age', in spite of the enormous amount of non-heroic matter in which they are enveloped. This matter is doubtless the product of a long period; and we do not question the existence of non-heroic elements in the times of the heroes. But the significant fact here is, that though non-heroic characters are usually present, they do not influence the course of events. At the time when the stories first took shape—or rather when the original poems were composed—Brahmanism can hardly have possessed the influence to which it attained not much later.

Heroic elements then are probably to be found in all barbaric communities; but we apply the term 'Heroic Age' only to periods in which

[1] In Israel the conditions are often complicated by the presence of different non-heroic elements, which are opposed to one another. But we need not enter into this question here.

these elements were dominant. In principle we may probably describe the Heroic Age as a warlike Age, and the heroic community as a warlike community, while non-heroic ages and communities may be regarded as essentially peaceful. But this description must not be pressed too closely. There are many heroic stories—we may instance Beowulf, the Odyssey and the story of Nala—which are not concerned with times of warfare. On the other hand there is plenty of non-heroic poetry and saga relating to warfare, especially in Hebrew literature. Usually no doubt this warfare is defensive, or occasioned by a revolt against oppression, as in the 'Song of Deborah'. Sometimes, however, it takes the form of an aggressive 'holy war', as in the traditions of the conquest of Palestine. Such warfare seems to be of an essentially different kind from heroic warfare. It is represented as a warfare of extermination, sometimes involving the destruction of livestock and goods, as well as all human beings. The difference is well illustrated by the story of the quarrel between Saul and Samuel. It is the prophet who requires the total destruction of the captives and the booty.[1]

A more accurate description of the Heroic Age is to be obtained from a consideration of the literature, as noted above (p. 727). It is not necessarily a time of continuous warfare, but a time when the warrior, or warrior prince, is dominant. Similarly, the heroic community is a community in which this element is dominant. Warfare from time to time, however, is doubtless an essential condition, or at least an essential preliminary, of such ages. When travellers describe a certain people or tribe as warlike, it may usually be inferred that it contains a considerable heroic element. The warfare for which they gain their reputation is as a rule of an aggressive and predatory character. Indeed this seems to be true of all Heroic Ages, both ancient and modern. We may refer (e.g.) to the series of Irish heroic sagas which are entitled 'Cattle-raid'; and similar incidents occur in the Iliad and Odyssey, the Mahābhārata, and the modern heroic poetry of the Yugoslavs and Tatars. Frequently also we hear of other booty and of trophies.

The predatory habit must not be regarded as an accessory, but as an essential, of heroic life (cf. Vol. 1, p. 91 f.) In heroic stories which are concerned with warfare the raid is indeed on the whole the most frequent and characteristic feature. Many other motives are of course involved— often it is the desire to avenge a personal wrong or insult—but the

[1] Similar practices are known among the ancient Celtic and Teutonic peoples (cf. especially Diodoros v. 27; Tacitus, *Ann.* XIII. 57). These were clearly connected with religious vows, though we cannot say that the warfare was 'non-heroic'.

thought of booty is never to be ignored. In the simplest form of heroic society a local chief or influential man gathers together a band of the young men of his district. Whatever his motive may be, if the raid is successful, his followers must be rewarded; and in one form or another this principle persists throughout the Heroic Age. Society comes to be dominated by a restless element, mostly young, which prefers a predatory life to more settled conditions.

In one or two cases the origin of a Heroic Age is attested by fairly recent tradition. The Lango,[1] a Nilotic people in the north of the Uganda Protectorate, are said to have had an essentially military organisation at the beginning of this century, when they came under British authority. Each village was under a leader of a company, several of whom were grouped under a petty chief, while several of the latter again were subject to a greater chief. The greater chiefs were engaged in constant strife with one another. All the chiefs owed their position mainly to prowess in war, aided perhaps by liberality in beer; and their functions were almost entirely military. But this system had apparently been in existence only for about half a century. Before that time, according to tradition, the country had been so peaceful that even unaccompanied women could pass safely from end to end of it. The change is said to have been due to the influence of the Banyoro, who had a well-developed military organisation, and who for a considerable time past had been accustomed to employ bands of Lango as mercenaries, both in their internal wars and in raids against the Baganda. It was apparently about the middle of last century that some of these mercenaries, especially a certain Akena, began to establish themselves by force as chiefs in their own land. The warfare was of a heroic character, depending more upon individual prowess than military organisation; and it was accompanied by shouts of defiance, celebrations of triumph, etc., such as we commonly find in heroic warfare. On the other hand non-heroic features were not wanting. Raids were preceded by a religious ceremony and sacrifice, at which the warriors were exhorted and their weapons blessed.

Somewhat similar records come from the Pacific. When the Tonga Islands first became known, at the beginning of last century, they were under a military organisation of a rather more advanced and centralised character than that of the Lango. But it was believed to be of recent origin. It had been the custom for the young men of Tonga to visit Fiji, where they had been employed as mercenaries, in much the same way as the Lango had been employed by the Banyoro. The establish-

[1] Cf. Driberg, *The Lango*, pp. 106ff., 205ff.

ment of military organisation in Tonga was said to have been due to these mercenaries.

It would seem then that the militarisation or 'heroisation' of barbaric society sometimes arose from a kind of contagion, much like the militant nationalism of modern times. Economic and geographical conditions are doubtless to be taken into account; but in such cases as these the primary factor is apparently a social disease.

One cannot perhaps assume with safety that this is always the case. In Yugoslavia and the neighbouring lands the Heroic Age had a long history, and its origins are obscure; but its continuance in certain districts down to about half a century ago was certainly due to geographical, economic and political conditions, which were beyond the control of the inhabitants. These conditions were quite different from those of the earlier Yugoslav period. The Montenegrins are as poor as the Lango—though far more advanced intellectually—and their warfare was not essentially different. It consisted mainly of raids carried out by war-bands gathered together for the occasion, commonly without the knowledge of the bishop or prince. The chief difference between the two cases is that in Montenegro the raids were usually directed against external foes; but in Albania, we believe, this was by no means always the case.

A more advanced phase of heroic society is represented where we find kings and princes maintaining permanent bodyguards (*comitatus*) of young warriors. Instances are to be found in Africa, e.g. among the Banyoro and Baganda, and in various other parts of the world. At least in the more primitive form of this phase raiding is a necessity, in order to provide for the warriors. This is the type of society which Tacitus (in his *Germania*) attributes to the Teutonic peoples. Like the more primitive phase, it may often be due to the influence of neighbouring and more advanced peoples, e.g. in this case to that of the Gauls.

A still more advanced phase[1] of heroic society is depicted in ancient heroic poetry almost everywhere. The ideal of heroic kingship is stated

[1] In the following pages, for the sake of brevity, we shall speak of this phase as 'more advanced' and of the others, without distinction, as 'less advanced' or 'more primitive'. Actually Irish heroic society seems to be intermediate between the two phases, approximating apparently to the more advanced in the earliest period and to the less advanced later. Ancient Teutonic heroic society, if we may judge from incidental references, as against Tacitus' general description, may really have been in a state of transition from the less advanced to the more advanced. Gaulish society was clearly more advanced. Russian heroic society may have belonged to the more advanced phase; but the poetry has been so long preserved by peasants that this has been disguised.

in the opening lines of Beowulf, where Scyld, the mythical ancestor of the Danish royal family, is said to have attained to such a glorious position by his conquests that all his neighbours across the sea obeyed him and paid tribute. In Teutonic, Greek and Indian heroic poetry, and in the earlier heroic poetry of the Yugoslavs, the cattle-raid is less prominent than in early Ireland; tribute has largely taken its place. Each king maintains a bodyguard of warriors, who are ready for all emergencies and adventures; but we commonly find them at their ease and feasting. Young and restless princes can always count on support from the *comitatus*, and often dominate the political situation. Wars and fights arise almost invariably either from personal quarrels between the kings of neighbouring kingdoms or from dissensions within one royal family itself. Very frequently, however, we find friendly relations between kings. Agamemnon brings together princes from all parts of Greece, when he goes against Troy. In the great battle which forms the climax of the Mahābhārata princes from the whole of northern India take part, on one side or the other. Marriages also between different royal families are the regular custom in the Teutonic, Greek and Indian Heroic Ages, as well as in Celtic Britain, Israel, and elsewhere. Even wars are sometimes terminated by such marriages, as in Beowulf, where Hrothgar gives his daughter in marriage to his defeated enemy.

As a result of these conditions we find everywhere in this final phase of heroic society a princely class which is international in its interests and feelings. This is reflected in the literature, which is almost always free from local or tribal prejudices. The heroes celebrated in the English poems are, with rare exceptions, not English, while the Norse poems are occupied with Continental far more than with Scandinavian heroes. The absence of local feeling in the Homeric poems has been a source of perplexity to scholars from the earliest times—many cities claimed Homer as their own—but it is normal in this kind of literature. Heroic poetry and saga—the latter perhaps not quite to the same degree—had an 'international' circulation; it could acquire a currency wherever the language was understood.[1] Occasionally we even find heroes who were of wholly alien nationality. Attila was a well-known figure in heroic poetry throughout the Teutonic world; but he is not regarded as an

---

[1] The different Teutonic languages were probably mutually intelligible to a certain extent down to the sixth century. Real linguistic barriers are not often passed. But some Irish heroic stories seem to have been known in Britain; and there are common elements in Yugoslav and Albanian poems, though we are not certain as to the provenance of these (cf. Vol. II, p. 399).

alien. Several of the most prominent and popular heroes celebrated in the earlier Yugoslav poems were Magyars; but the fact that they were not Yugoslavs is seldom, if ever, noticed in the poems themselves. Neither does Russian poetry recognise that Mikhailo Potyk was a Bulgarian.

We have described the characteristics noticed above as heroic; but it must be borne in mind that they are not common to all heroic poetry and saga, or to all heroic communities. The milieu of modern Yugoslav poetry, especially the Montenegrin poems composed in the middle of last century, is wholly different from that of the earlier poems. The latter are concerned with princes, the former with poor mountaineers—the bishop or prince is not a prominent character.[1] The Montenegrin poems cannot have had much circulation beyond the principality itself and the neighbouring Turkish districts. Moreover these poems, apart from the exploits of the heroes, show a very marked communal interest, which is absent from the earlier poems. Communal interest, though of a somewhat different kind, is even more marked in the heroic poetry of the Galla (cf. p. 547 ff. above). Often indeed these poems are as much concerned with local patriotism or the glories of a family or clan as with the exploits of the heroes themselves. In some war-songs, both here and elsewhere in Africa, individuals are ignored, just as in European post-heroic poetry.

It is clear that we have to distinguish throughout between different types of Heroic Ages, both in literature and in real life. One is restricted in area and in its relations with the outer world. Its heroic poetry is almost exclusively occupied with raids and fighting. Communal interest is strong. Even the chief men are not wealthy. In Africa kings may have great herds of cattle and numerous wives; but they are—or were until recently—too remote from the civilised world for such wealth to procure for them a standard of life essentially different from the rest of the community. At the other end of the heroic scale we find Heroic Ages extending over vast areas, perhaps nearly half a continent, and sometimes in contact with more civilised peoples. The literature is not exclusively concerned with fighting; the interest tends to shift from the exploit to the hero himself. Communal interest is slight. Everywhere we find a wealthy princely (Kshatriya) class, in whom the interest of the literature is centred. The princes seem to have more intimate relations

[1] It is noteworthy that very little is said of Bp. Peter II, who was a remarkable man and a very distinguished poet. Prince Danilo is more prominent, but only on public occasions, e.g. in poems relating to his accession, marriage and death.

with princes of other states than with the mass of their own subjects, and are far removed from the latter in their standard of life. In short the princely class tends to form a kind of international society.

We have defined the term 'barbaric' above as covering all phases of society intermediate between the primitive and the civilised. It would seem that almost as much difference is to be found in heroic literature and society. The former of the groups noticed above may be said in general to belong to the 'lower barbaric', though it is far removed from the primitive, while the latter approximates to the civilised, so far as the princely class is concerned. The Tatars seem to occupy a position intermediate between these two groups. Their heroic literature, especially the poetry of the Kara-Kirghiz, bears a rather close resemblance to that of the more advanced group; and the interest lies in the individual, not in the community. But the culture of the Tatars is essentially nomadic, and consequently difficult to compare with that of other peoples.

It is natural to expect that the more advanced form of heroic society normally developed out of the more primitive; but we have little definite information as to the antecedents of ancient heroic ages. No poetry or saga seems to have survived from earlier times in any of the areas which we have discussed, except India and Palestine; and in both these cases what has been preserved is wholly of non-heroic (religious) provenance. In the latter, however, David is represented as a typical heroic chief—of the less advanced type—before he became king; and the story of Jephthah suggests that such heroic war-bands had long been known in Israel. Again, as we have seen, the account given by Tacitus in his *Germania* seems to indicate a less advanced form of heroic society than what we find in Teutonic heroic poetry. It is true that the *comitatus* is already a permanent body and that the leaders are usually, if not always, princes; but national or communal feeling is emphasised, and the standard of culture depicted is obviously lower than in later times, even if we make allowance for the fact that the description comes from a foreigner. The British Heroic Age might at first sight seem to suggest a different origin; for Britain had long been a Roman province. But the traditions derive most of the royal families from regions beyond the frontier.

Among the more advanced Heroic Ages there is a striking similarity. In some cases—Teutonic, Greek and Indian—this may be due in part to a similarity in the form of the records. But even where there is no such similarity in form—in British, Irish, Hebrew and the earlier

Yugoslav—the resemblance in the life and the characters portrayed is hardly less striking. The explanation must clearly be found in the conditions (and the antecedent history) of the periods. And these, where we know them, show a general resemblance; but unfortunately we are without definite information in several cases.

In the fifth century the Teutonic peoples, or rather Teutonic princes with their armies, had acquired dominion over the greater part of Europe; and their advance to power can clearly be traced in the preceding century. The Yugoslavs became dominant in the Balkan peninsula in the thirteenth and fourteenth centuries, and were not completely overthrown until after the middle of the fifteenth. David seems to have secured supreme power between Egypt and the Euphrates. The British Heroic Age belongs mainly to the sixth century; but the rise of the royal families is probably to be dated back to the early part of the fifth, when the Roman power collapsed. In the north, to which most of our records relate, they seem to have maintained their position against the English until the beginning of the seventh century. An important element in all these cases is that the rising powers had previously been brought into contact with a higher civilisation, especially, it would seem, through military service.[1]

Elsewhere definite evidence is wanting. It may be noted, however, that the Indian heroes, except in one story, belong to a region—the upper basins of the Ganges and the Jumna—which is barely known to the Rgveda, though it was the centre of Indian learning and civilisation in the following period, and probably in the Heroic Age itself (cf. Vol. II, p. 519f.). There is good reason therefore for believing that the Aryan kingdoms in this region were of comparatively recent origin, or at least that they had only recently become powerful. As regards Central India, the scene of the story of Nala, there can be no doubt that this was the case.

For Greece and Ireland we are wholly dependent upon the evidence of heroic poetry or saga and the antiquarian traditions and speculations current in later times. These traditions have been variously interpreted, and there is still great diversity of opinion as to their value. According to our view, which has been set forth elsewhere,[2] the background of the

---

[1] The Roman armies of the fourth century, and even the commanders, were largely Teutonic; and there can be little doubt that the northern Britons and the Yugoslavs had been employed in a similar way. The early part of the story of David suggests the prevalence of similar conditions in Palestine.

[2] Cf. Chadwick, *Heroic Age*, Ch. XVI–XIX.

Greek Heroic Age was closely parallel to that of the Teutonic, though
the area was of course much more restricted. In Ireland the conditions
seem to have been similar in principle, though less advanced. The
kingdoms and dynasties were in general probably of older standing,
though we suspect that one very important dynasty, the Clann Rudraige,
had only recently risen to power.

From a survey of the records as a whole we may describe heroic
society of the advanced type as a society in which the power lies in the
hands of military princes, supported by retinues of armed followers.
Very often these princes have established themselves in cities or territories which they have conquered. Often too this conquest has arisen
out of military service under the—usually more civilised—states which
they have subsequently overthrown. But most of the records relate to
a phase in which their power has already become established, or perhaps
inherited for one or two generations. They are represented as wealthy
people, endowed with all military virtues, but arrogant and quarrelsome.
They are of importance for us because they were usually liberal patrons
of poetry and minstrelsy. Almost everywhere it was their great desire
to have their glory celebrated in poetry; and an impetus to the art must
have been given thereby, such as in later phases of civilisation architecture, sculpture and painting owed to the patronage of the wealthy.

There is one feature in this heroic literature—the advanced type, not
the primitive heroic—which deserves special notice here—the prominent part played by women. Norse heroic poetry is more concerned
with women than with men, Indian on the whole hardly less so. But it
is noticeable in all the literatures we have been considering, except
English and Welsh. In the former case this may well be due to the
paucity of the material which has survived, in the latter to the fact that
what remains consists largely of Type D; the evidence of the Triads
suggests that the sagas had much to say about women. In a large
proportion of the stories which we have noticed women supply the
leading motif; and as a rule they play a by no means passive rôle. The
'heroines' of the various literatures have much in common, so much
indeed that one can almost speak of a heroic type of woman.[1] They tend
to take the initiative, for good or ill, and are usually stronger characters
than the men. In general they are represented as resourceful rather than
cunning, but cultured according to the standards of their milieu, loyal,

[1] We do not mean of course that this type was a purely literary creation. Such
women are known from contemporary historical records. We may refer e.g. to the
Frankish queen Brunichildis, who was killed (in old age) in 613.

proud, resentful and quick to foment strife. Desire for vengeance is a widespread motif. But some Indian heroines and all Tatar heroines are far superior to the heroes in every way. It may be added that the leading heroines are as a rule young married women, usually it would seem without children.[1]

A good number of poems and stories, especially Norse, Indian and Hebrew, seem to represent a woman's point of view. We have suggested that these were composed either by women or for the entertainment of women. The former alternative cannot be regarded as intrinsically improbable; for it was clearly a heroic custom everywhere, except perhaps in Palestine, for women to compose—or at least to recite—elegies for their husbands or near male relatives. The evidence seems to us rather to indicate that women had more scope for intellectual activity in heroic society than in later times. This is apparently the case even in some more primitive heroic societies; we may refer especially to what has been said above (pp. 658 ff., 663 ff.) with reference to the poetry of the Tuareg. In other societies of this kind, however, both poetry and saga are almost exclusively concerned with fighting, and women are seldom mentioned. The contrast between the earlier and later poetry of the Yugoslavs in this respect is most remarkable.

Some of the princely heroic societies of which we have been speaking came to a disastrous end through foreign conquest. Such was the case in Yugoslavia, and to some extent in Britain and perhaps in Greece. But in the majority of the cases there is no evidence for such widespread catastrophes. Normally the Heroic Age would seem to have perished from internal causes. It had come into existence and flourished in times of unrest, and can hardly have been well adapted to more settled conditions. Actually we find in post-heroic times either that kings have disappeared or, more frequently, that their power has been more or less subordinated to some kind of national authority. In the older kingdoms the change may often have been in the nature of a return to previous conditions; in new kingdoms, which had been established in conquered territory, the kings' power tended to pass into the hands of their followers. The forms of government which resulted vary from case to

[1] Among those who have no children, at least at the time of the action, we may cite Emer, Derdriu, Brynhildr, Hildr, the heroines of the Helgi poems, Sāvitrī, Vukosava and Barbara, the wife of Fiery Vuk, all the Russian heroines, and the Tatar Kanykäi. Later speculations tended to invent children, as in the case of Brynhildr. It is to be suspected that in the original form of the stories Draupadī and Etain, the wife of Eochaid Airem, had no children.

case, as may be seen from a survey of early Teutonic or Greek political institutions. But everywhere the disappearance or subordination of the heroic element seems to have been accompanied by a growth or recovery of the power of the religious or mantic element. In proportion as conditions became more settled the influence of this element was bound to increase, owing to their intellectual superiority and, in particular, their knowledge of the national law. The struggle between the heroic and non-heroic (mantic) elements is well illustrated in Indian and Hebrew literature; and the comparison of the two cases is made the more interesting by the difference in the character of the manticism.

In Christian countries the non-heroic or mantic element was soon displaced by the Church—which, in so far as it was in touch with the centres of civilisation and with civilised thought, both present and past, does not come within the scope of our survey. We see no reason, however, for believing that the attitude of the Church towards the heroic element differed in principle from that of native non-heroic elements. There have been Heroic Ages in Christian countries; but the warfare has been almost always against non-Christians. Among the Celtic peoples, owing to their remoteness and the fact that they were long cut off from the rest of the Church, the resemblance to the mantic element of heathen times seems to have been much stronger. The 'Lives' of Celtic saints present many interesting analogies to the stories of Brahman saints, preserved in the Mahābhārata.

The Irish Heroic Age differs in several respects from the rest of the group discussed above. The society, though princely, is rougher and cruder; and the later stories are almost always concerned with fighting, though all the combatants are Christians. Moreover the best and most detailed stories are those which relate to the earliest times; later they seem gradually to become shorter and rarer. Lastly, it is not easy to determine when the Heroic Age came to an end. We have taken the Battle of Allen (c. 721) as the latest heroic story; but it is clear from the annals that raiding and heroic warfare continued for several centuries after this time. The explanation of these peculiarities lies, we think, in what has been pointed out above—the remoteness of the country and the special characteristics of its Christianity. The decline of the heroic element was extremely slow, and in general this element was not greatly influenced by the Church; but heroic exploits ceased to form the themes of sagas. The native intellectual element, represented by the *filid*, preserved its vitality longer than elsewhere; but its sympathies lay more with the Church than with the princes. Even in the Battle of Allen the interest is centred in the poet Donn Bo far more than in the high-king Fergal, while Christian influence is very marked.

It will have been observed that in most of the literatures which we have discussed, non-heroic poetry and saga are not so well represented as heroic. It is only in India and in Israel that the former exceeds the latter; and in both these cases a large proportion of the non-heroic material is believed to be of late date. This predominance of the heroic in early records is of course in no way surprising. A seer or sage is less likely to have his doings celebrated in his lifetime than a successful prince; and his doings themselves are less likely to make an appeal for purposes of entertainment. He may of course acquire great fame; in II Kings viii. 4, the king of Israel wishes to hear of Elisha's great deeds, while the prophet is still alive. But the literary form in which his fame is preserved would seem usually to be due to later generations.

Yet it would be a serious mistake to regard the heroic element as more important than the non-heroic in the history of literature, even in its earliest phases. The influence of the latter cannot be estimated merely by the literature which we have treated under the title 'non-heroic poetry and saga'. In this category we have included only stories and poems relating to persons. But account is to be taken also of the 'impersonal' categories—antiquarian, gnomic, descriptive, mantic. The works included in these categories sometimes have the names of seers attached to them, rightly or wrongly; more frequently perhaps they are anonymous. But there can be no doubt that as a rule they are of non-heroic origin. Information of special interest in this respect is supplied by the Upanishads; but much evidence is also to be found in Hebrew and early Irish records, and indeed almost everywhere.

To the non-heroic element we may also attribute most of the poetry and saga relating to deities. The material, which belongs chiefly to Types C and D, will require discussion in a later chapter; but, apart from certain stories and poems designed for entertainment, such as we find in Norse and Greek, it is probably almost entirely of non-heroic provenance. The same remark applies in general to Type C (the didactic type) in other categories.

In heroic poetry and saga of Type C we see the encroachment of the non-heroic upon the heroic. But this is a somewhat complex question, as we have already noted (p. 707). Such poems as the Norse Sigrdrí-fumál were doubtless of non-heroic provenance from the beginning; the heroic setting is merely a framework for a discourse on mantic and

25

gnomic lore. And the same is in all probability true of the whole Trilogy (cf. Vol. I, p. 27f.) to which this poem belongs.[1] Again, there are certain Irish stories, such as 'The Phantom Chariot of CuChulainn', which are just as clearly of non-heroic origin, though they are of a wholly different character from this Trilogy; they were composed doubtless for the purpose of reconciling heroic saga with the teaching of the Church. Yet a third variety is of very frequent occurrence in the Mahābhārata, where the object of many stories is to illustrate the piety of Yudhishthira and his eagerness for Brahmanical learning.

On the other hand the Mahābhārata as a whole requires a different explanation. There can be no doubt that both the main story and several of the subsidiary stories are of heroic origin, and that the non-heroic elements which they contain are secondary. The nucleus clearly consists of a number of heroic poems, which have come into the hands of Brahmans and been more or less transformed by them, in varying degree. Analogies are probably to be found in Hebrew, e.g. the story of Jephthah, though as a rule the examples are less certain. In Russia also we have a parallel in the cultivation of heroic poetry by the Kalêki, who are properly to be regarded as a non-heroic class, at least in origin. Their versions of the poems often betray a religious interest, as we have seen (Vol. II, pp. 190, 248). Here too we must take account of the *filid* of early Ireland, who cultivated heroic saga very extensively (cf. Vol. I, p. 602ff.). They were sometimes attached to the service of kings, and entertained them with their recitations. They have little in common with the Kalêki; but in origin they were clearly a mantic class, as their name implies (*ib.* p. 606), and to some extent they preserved their mantic functions. It is to them doubtless, or to their influence, that we owe the large antiquarian element and the frequent etymological speculations contained in the sagas—perhaps also the rather excessive interest in portents and similar phenomena. Many early texts of sagas are generally believed to come from *filid*.

The transformation effected by non-heroic influence is of course very frequently only partial. Very many of the poems and sagas of which we have been speaking, including considerable portions of the Mahābhārata, remain primarily works of entertainment. They cannot fairly be regarded as examples of Type C—i.e. the didactic element has not become the predominant interest—though the changes, so far as they go, tend

---

[1] It is possible that our text may be derived from different sources, though we are not at all certain that the variety in metre requires such an explanation. But we cannot discuss the question here.

in that direction. The same process, with the same limitation, is to be seen in Anglo-Saxon heroic poetry. The religious and moralising elements in these poems, especially Beowulf, are commonly treated as an isolated problem; but there is no reason for regarding them otherwise than as a variety of the widespread phenomenon we are discussing. In this case indeed we have no evidence that the poems had been taken over by a different class of poets from those by whom they had been originally composed. The religious elements may be due to a change in the outlook of the heroic poets themselves and their audiences, consequent upon the acceptance of Christianity. In such cases we should properly speak of the 'influence', rather than the 'encroachment', of the non-heroic upon the heroic. Analogies are probably to be found in the Tatar poems relating to Manas, especially in that version of the story of his death in which he is restored to life by angels (cf. p. 169 above). Such analogies are not confined to heroic poetry. We may refer e.g. to the curiously irrelevant religious passages found in certain Welsh mantic poems, and more especially to the variants of modern Yugoslav poems noticed in Vol. II, p. 405.

The non-heroic elements in the Anglo-Saxon poems are clearly for the most part of Christian origin; some of them at least could not have existed in the heroic poetry of heathen times. In the Irish sagas, this is not so clear; for here the non-heroic elements are usually not of a religious character. Some scholars hold that the recitation of sagas was one of the functions of the *filid* from the beginning.[1] But this view seems to us improbable; we find it difficult to believe that 'seers' can have been employed regularly as court entertainers before their character as a class had undergone some change, presumably as a result of the change of faith. We suspect—though this would be difficult to prove—that the 'encroachment' of which we have spoken did not generally take place until towards the close of the Heroic Age.[2] In the other literatures we have been considering such evidence as is available seems to point in the same direction. At all events most of them preserve a good deal of heroic poetry which is unaffected, or very slightly affected,

---

[1] A knowledge of sagas formed part of their education; but this may have been required merely for the purpose of antiquarian study (cf. Vol. I, p. 606).

[2] The Book of Druim Snechta, the earliest known written collection of sagas (c. 700–750), is thought to have been the work of a *fili*. Only one of the twelve sagas and poems, which it is believed to have contained, is heroic; and this (the Courtship of Étain) is perhaps not wholly of heroic origin. For this text see Thurneysen, *Ir. Heldensage*, pp. 17f., 72; Bergin and Best, *Ériu*, XII, 137 ff.

by non-heroic influence. Such is the case with the Norse heroic poems (except the Trilogy), the earlier Yugoslav poems, the Homeric poems (except *Od.* IX–XII), and even with some parts of the Mahābhārata, especially the story of Nala. The scarcity of non-heroic elements in the Homeric poems is noteworthy, because Greece was prolific in non-heroic poetry relating to heroes; but this (lost) poetry is generally believed to have been of later date.

In the literatures of less advanced peoples, especially in Polynesia, the distinction between heroic and non-heroic is by no means so clearly drawn (cf. p. 245 f. above). Even among the Tatars we find heroic stories and stories of mantic interest included in the same poem (cf. p. 34 f.), though the treatment of the latter in such cases is not usually didactic. The complete severance of heroic from non-heroic interests appears to be characteristic of the more advanced heroic literatures. The audiences for which they catered evidently required entertainment, not instruction, and took but little interest in mantic subjects. The encroachment of the non-heroic would seem normally to be characteristic of a later phase.

We see no reason for doubting that these literary movements reflect a process of change in the outlook of heroic society. Towards the close of the Heroic Age and later the royal seer (*rājarṣi*) or intellectual prince becomes a familiar figure. Such persons appear of course from time to time in all phases of heroic society; as representative instances we may cite Rumanika, king of Karagwe (cf. p. 624 above), Cormac mac Airt (according to Irish tradition) and Solomon. But it is only when the Heroic Age is coming, or has actually come, to an end, that such persons are to be found frequently. We may refer especially to the royal seers who figure in the Upanishads. As Western examples we may cite the Irish king Mongan (cf. Vol. I, p. 468 ff.), the Northumbrian king Aldfrith and—in spite of Gregory of Tours—the Frankish king Chilperic.

The effect of non-heroic encroachment or influence upon heroic literature is commonly to be seen in the introduction of didactic elements, religious, moral or antiquarian, such as properly belong to the impersonal categories. Sometimes, however, we find personal stories of heroes which are clearly of the same origin. Of these the most widespread are stories of marvel relating to the birth or childhood of heroes.[1] Instances occur practically everywhere; yet it is much to be doubted whether true heroic poetry or saga, when unaffected by non-heroic

[1] It is hardly necessary to give instances from non-heroic stories. They are especially frequent in Polynesia (cf. p. 277 ff.).

influence, showed any interest in the subject. The Homeric poems seem to know nothing of the kind, except that certain persons have a divine father or mother; but later Greek literature revels in such stories. In Beowulf we hear only that the hero's mother is a daughter of King Hrethel, that he himself was brought up at that king's court from the age of seven, and that his father had sought the protection of the Danish king in consequence of a feud. But in Hrólfs Saga Kraka Bjarki—the same hero—is the son of a bear. In the main story of the Mahābhārata[1] hardly any of the chief characters have normal births; but their marvellous origins are of no significance for the story, except in the case of Karna, the son of the god Sūrya. In Ireland such stories are sometimes more deeply interwoven with the heroic sagas; but they are so inconsistent with one another, e.g. the different accounts of CuChulainn's birth, that they leave no room for doubt that they are of the same origin as the rest. The whole series represent a form of speculation closely akin to antiquarianism, and doubtless cultivated by the same class of persons.[2]

Stories relating to the dead, especially stories of visits to the underworld and consultations of the dead, form a widespread series in non-heroic literature. Occasionally also they are found in a heroic milieu, though less frequently than the last series. One of the favourite themes is a visit to the underworld under the guidance or direction of a witch or seer. Sometimes the object of the journey is to bring someone back to the land of the living, sometimes to consult one of the dead; but other motives also are found. Such stories are popular among the Tatars, the Polynesians and the Sea Dyaks; among the Tatars they are found also in a heroic context, e.g. in the latter part of the story of Joloi (cf. p. 87 f.). Yet the non-heroic affinities of this part of the story will be seen by a comparison with the poems from the Abakan steppe and neighbouring districts cited on p. 88 ff. Greek parallels may be found in Odysseus' visit to Hades (*Od.* XI) and in the story of Alcestis. It may be noted that in Norse mythology deities visit Hell for similar purposes. In Mesopotamia stories of this kind, relating to deities, can be traced back to very ancient times. We may refer also to the Japanese chronicle cited on p. 292.[3]

---

[1] It may be noted that the story of Nala, where Brahmanical influence is very slight, has no instance of this kind, except that Bhīma obtains his children as a blessing from a Brahman.

[2] These stories will be noticed again in the next chapter (p. 763 f.).

[3] To the subjects treated in this and the following paragraphs we shall have to refer again in Ch. IX.

Visits to Heaven are less widespread, though they are of frequent occurrence among the Tatars and the Polynesians, as also in Japan (cf. pp. 103 f., 272 ff.). In the Mahābhārata III. 42 ff. the hero Arjuna visits the home of Indra, to obtain weapons from him. We may compare the story of CuChulainn's journey to Mag Mell, noticed in Vol. I, pp. 205, 257.

Stories describing the experiences of heroes or heroines after death occur sporadically in many countries. At the close of the Mahābhārata (XVI. iii and XVIII) Yudhishthira makes his way to Heaven; but the episode is obviously late and of non-heroic provenance. The Helreið Brynhildar describes an encounter between the dead Brynhildr and an ogress, which is more in the heroic vein; but here again the underlying idea is non-heroic. In this connection we may refer to the arrival of the slain suitors in Hades, related in *Od.* XXIV—with which may be compared the account of Prince Danilo's arrival in Paradise, described in the Montenegrin poem cited in Vol. II, p. 335. Some Irish stories, especially the 'Voyage of Connla', may also be cited. For a Polynesian parallel we may refer to p. 290 f. above.

The above are probably by no means the only imaginative elements which heroic literature in its later phases owes to non-heroic influence. We do not mean of course to suggest that the marvellous or supernatural is necessarily of non-heroic origin. Heroic literature has its own conventions, which allow not only gross exaggeration (e.g.) in the feats performed by heroes, but also a free use of supernatural elements, especially the personal intervention of supernatural beings. We have seen that Yugoslav poets of last century often introduced such beings in accounts of contemporary events,[1] though they can hardly be said to affect the course of the action. Again, chronological errors and unhistorical associations occur frequently in late heroic literature; but these are due to lapse of time and forgetfulness, not necessarily to any non-heroic influence. In spite of all this, however, our survey tends to show that in general unhistorical and imaginative elements are more characteristic of non-heroic than of heroic literature.

There is still one more aspect of non-heroic influence which requires notice—what we may call an academic, or perhaps rather pedagogic, tendency. It is in Welsh heroic literature that this is most pronounced. The Dream of Rhonabwy, a very late work, consists largely of descriptions of the appearance of heroes and their horses, which seem hardly explicable except as mnemonic exercises. The same is true of

[1] To this subject we shall have to refer again in the next chapter (p. 759).

certain poems which may originally have been composed as panegyrics or elegies, but which have been reduced to something little better than nonsense. In Culhwch and Olwen this tendency takes the form of catalogues—a feature which is characteristic of non-heroic literature everywhere.[1] We may instance the series of animals and birds, each of which is older than the last preceding—a remarkable (non-heroic) parallel for which is to be found in Mahābh. iii. cxcix. 3 ff. (cf. Vol. ii, p. 572 f.). Catalogues occur frequently in the Norse Trilogy, as indeed in Norse poems of Type C in all categories. But catalogues of an informative character occur elsewhere in a purely heroic context, e.g. in Widsith and in II Sam. xxiii. Catalogues of troops, in stories of warfare, are especially widespread as we shall see later; they are to be found e.g. in the Iliad, which is almost free from non-heroic influence, the Mahābhārata, the Tain Bo Cuailnge and a Yugoslav poem noticed in Vol. ii, p. 408.

The non-heroic origin of such catalogues must not be pressed too far. The last series reflect and no doubt result from the intellectual training of their authors, and illustrate their power of forming a comprehensive survey and synthesis of their material; but they have nothing mantic about them. It is the academic or educational side of non-heroic activities which is here involved. In a system of education which is wholly, or almost wholly, oral, catalogues naturally play an important part. It is probable that the informative catalogues of which we are speaking belong as a rule to a late phase in the history of the stories, when some information as to the personnel was thought to be necessary. But even in the Heroic Age itself such education as was available must have followed the lines set by seers, even if it was not obtained directly from them; for seers were the leaders of thought in barbaric times.[2] Non-heroic literature would doubtless appeal to heroic audiences[3] as little as a book of this kind to patrons of sensational fiction. It was intended for academic audiences, and for instruction rather than entertainment. But if a heroic minstrel or saga-teller had to supply informative matter, the form he employed could hardly be independent of the educational methods current in his day.

[1] Including folk tales of Type C; cf. pp. 780, 784.

[2] The *filid* (and Druids) and the Brahman seers were often teachers; and in Greek and Norse tradition there are hints of similar activities on the part of seers, e.g. Cheiron and Reginn. In Christian times their place was presumably taken by the clergy.

[3] Catalogues, however, may appeal to such audiences; cf. Radlov's interesting statement noticed on p. 185.

The chief change which took place at the end of the Heroic Age, both in society and in literature, was the re-assertion of communal, as against individual, interest. But this change seems rarely to have influenced heroic literature.[1] Presumably the latter was becoming unreal, and recognised as a thing relating to the past. The counter movement, to individualism again, which took place in a more advanced phase (cf. p. 704), probably affected Norse heroic poetry; but we think that the main lines of the latter were inherited.

It may now be convenient to summarise briefly the results arrived at in the course of this chapter.

(1) In barbaric society we find usually, if not always, two elements, which we have called heroic and non-heroic. The former element is attached to warfare, the latter to religion or manticism and law. In the former the chief figure is the warrior, in the latter the seer. We apply the term 'Heroic Age' to a period in which the heroic element is dominant.

(2) Each of these elements has its own literature. Heroic literature is concerned with persons ('heroes'), sometimes also with the family, locality or tribe to which they belong. It is intended chiefly for celebration or entertainment. Non-heroic literature is also concerned in part with persons (especially seers); and here the communal interest is usually stronger. But the literary activities of the non-heroic element are mainly concerned with religion and with the impersonal subjects treated in our antiquarian, gnomic, descriptive and mantic categories. The literature is largely didactic in character.

(3) Two kinds of Heroic Age must be distinguished. In the more primitive type the heroic and non-heroic elements have something in common. Heroes may be drawn from any class, and communal interest (in family, locality or tribe) is frequently expressed. But the poems and stories are concerned almost exclusively with exploits, not with the heroes themselves. Women play little part.

The more advanced type is more or less free—often almost wholly—from non-heroic influence. Heroes are drawn from the princely class; communal interest is wanting. Poems and stories are concerned practically with persons of the princely class alone. The interest tends to shift from the exploits to the characters. Women are often as prominent as men.

---

[1] A striking instance occurs in the modern (Karadžić's) version of the poem 'Musić Stefan' (cf. Vol. II, p. 366 ff.). It is significant that the earlier version contains no trace of this.

There is a remarkable resemblance in the general characteristics of the more advanced type of Heroic Age and its literature among the peoples we have discussed. The same phase is to be found in the history of other peoples, though we do not know how far the resemblance goes. It would seem indeed that most of the civilised peoples of Europe and western Asia had passed through a phase of this kind; where evidence is wanting it may be due to the lack of records. But we are not prepared to propound the doctrine that a phase of this kind is a necessary antecedent to civilisation.

In the history of literature this phase is important, because heroic princes were generous patrons of minstrels, partly in order to get their own fame celebrated. A great incentive was doubtless given to the art thereby. The audiences may well have been critical; for princes frequently cultivated minstrelsy themselves. Where narrative poetry was in use, it was evidently the chief entertainment of the courts; and it attained a perfection which has not since been equalled.

(4) The Heroic Age in its advanced form seems usually to have been a transitory period, lasting not more than a few generations. Sometimes it ended in catastrophe; more frequently the non-heroic element appears to have recovered its authority. In the following period heroic literature was often preserved for the purpose of entertainment; it was also adapted to didactic purposes. But the new literature which was composed was predominantly non-heroic, and the prevailing interest was either communal or impersonal. In maritime countries which were most in touch with the outer world the non-heroic element tended in course of time to lose its mantic character; the seer was succeeded by the secular law-giver and philosopher. These changes were accompanied by new movements in literature of individual, though not heroic, interest.

Postscript. An interesting illustration of heroic life of the less advanced type (cf. p. 735) is given by Mr F. R. Paver in *The Times* of 20 August 1938, in an account of an interview with a very old warrior of the Bechuana. This man related *inter alia* how a wounded enemy had once begged him to kill him, but first to allow him to sing his *dithako*, or 'praise-song', which, he adds, "every Bechuana of consequence had ready for great occasions". The following may be quoted:

"Even as a youth I was a fighter in the cattle-raids,
I trample on people before Sebegwe son of Makaba," etc.

It seems probable that self-panegyrics of this kind are derived from boasting songs and songs of (individual) triumph (cf. p. 710 and notes)—which doubtless go back to the very beginnings of heroic literature. On the other hand, we may compare the speeches of the dying hero in Beowulf (especially 2732 ff.).

HEROIC NARRATIVE POETRY

THE importance of the heroic story in narrative poetry has already been noticed. Heroic narrative poetry may be said to dominate the oral literature of the Russians, the Yugoslavs and the Kara-Kirghiz; and the same is probably true of the Albanians and of a number of peoples in Asia. Among the ancient English it must have held a similar position; for, although comparatively little has been preserved, its form and diction were regularly employed for the treatment of Biblical and hagiological stories. In ancient Greece it was regarded as the foundation of literature. In ancient India it may seem at first sight to have been less prominent; but that is largely due to the fact that only the literature current in ecclesiastical circles has survived.

It is time now to discuss the characteristics of this kind of poetry, noting incidentally where saga and non-heroic (and post-heroic) narrative poetry differ from it. But saga and narrative poetry relating to unspecified persons and to deities will be reserved for notice in the following chapters.

The leading characteristics of heroic narrative poetry in each of the literatures in which we have found it have been noted and stated in tabular form in the course of the survey of the various literatures; cf. Vol. I, pp. 20ff., 29ff., Vol. II, pp. 68ff., 337ff., and above, p. 40 ff. It will be seen that in general there is a very close resemblance everywhere in this kind of poetry, in both ancient and modern literatures.

The first four characteristics are invariable. These poems are (1) narrative, (2) occupied with adventure (under which we include both exploits and disasters). The second characteristic is not necessarily true of non-heroic stories, the object of which may be to illustrate the knowledge or mantic power of a seer. (3) The object of the poem is to provide entertainment—which is our definition of Type A. Heroic narrative poems the object of which is to provide instruction[1] of various kinds (Type C) are not unknown; but with these we are not concerned here. We believe that such poems are due to the encroachment of non-heroic elements, as we have already indicated (p. 741 ff.). In non-heroic

---

[1] Among these may be included 'poems which have been converted or adapted to purposes of instruction'; cf. p. 707.

stories the didactic element is of course vastly more frequent. (4) The poems relate to a definite period, which we call the 'Heroic Age' (cf. p. 727 ff.). This period may have extended almost down to our own times, as in Yugoslavia; or it may have come to an end thousands of years ago, as in Greece and India.[1] Non-heroic stories have no such limitation.

These four characteristics hold good also, at least in general, for heroic saga, which in many lands takes the place of heroic narrative poetry. The encroachment of non-heroic elements is perhaps more frequent in saga. Possibly too the end of the period is sometimes less clearly defined. Creative narrative poetry usually ceases with the end of the Heroic Age—though this is apparently not the case in Yugoslavia—whereas saga often flourishes in post-heroic times. But the question is complicated in several cases by an extended use of writing.

(5) Anonymity seems to be universal, as in all narrative poetry and saga dating from pre-literary times. Karadžić actually records the names of several poets who composed heroic poems, published by him, on recent events (cf. Vol. II, p. 441 f.). But no claim to authorship is made in the poems themselves; nor do we think that the poets would be regarded, or even regard themselves, strictly as authors—any more than a man who brings news is regarded as an author. In times of oral tradition saga and narrative poem are regarded as statements or accounts of events—not necessarily to be believed implicitly—which anyone may repeat with such expansions or changes as he may; but he is a reporter or recorder, rather than an author. We hear at times of persons who can tell a story well, but not of authors. The attribution of narrative poetry and saga to authors would seem to date from times when these kinds of literature had lost their vitality and flexibility. This question, however, will require notice in the last chapter. The most interesting record in this connection is the Irish story of the recovery of the Tain Bo Cuailnge.

(6) Narrative poetry usually employs a uniform verse (line). In the ancient literatures—Teutonic (English, Norse, German), Greek and Indian—there seem to be practically no exceptions. The same is true of modern Yugoslav narrative poetry. The older (MS.) poems also commonly employ a uniform line, which is different from the modern; but in other poems this metre is interrupted, at regular or irregular intervals, by very short lines.[2] Russian narrative poetry is governed apparently

---

[1] An exception should possibly be made in the case of the Tatar poems, for which no chronological data have been accessible to us.

[2] Cf. Vol. II, pp. 304, 339.

by rhythm rather than by metre.[1] The universality of the uniform line in the ancient literatures deserves notice, because metres with non-uniform line were also in use from the earliest times, at least in India and the North, and probably also in England.

(7) There is much diversity in regard to the use of strophe or stanza. It is unknown in Anglo-Saxon—which, we think, represents early Teutonic usage—and in Greek narrative poetry, and so also in Russian and modern Yugoslav. In the older (MS.) collections of Yugoslav poetry, from the Adriatic coast, we find both stanzaic and non-stanzaic narrative poems (cf. Vol. II, p. 339). English narrative ballads are all stanzaic, except a very small number which are in couplets. For the Norse and Indian evidence we may refer to Vol. I, p. 30, and Vol. II, p. 478 f. If we bear in mind that the non-stanzaic (i.e. uninterrupted) form is rather exceptional in other types of poetry, it would seem likely on the whole that this is to be regarded as the normal form for narrative, and that the stanza, where it occurs, is due to the influence of other types, whether native or foreign. In that case we must conclude that the narrative form tended to become generalised in some languages, e.g. Greek (in the earliest times) and Anglo-Saxon[2]—where it is used even in gnomic poetry—whereas other languages, e.g. Norse (cf. Vol. I, p. 61), appear to have moved in the opposite direction. The uninterrupted form of narrative poetry is most marked in Anglo-Saxon, where the sentence very frequently ends in the middle of the line. Internal breaks are of course to be found also in Greek and elsewhere; but they are usually of less importance, and seldom occur, as in Anglo-Saxon, in positions where the translator would begin a new paragraph.

In connection with metre reference may be made to the very wide-spread custom of accompanying narrative poetry on a stringed instrument—harp, fiddle or guitar. The evidence for this practice has been stated in Vol. I, pp. 568 f., 572–7, Vol. II, pp. 256 ff., 434 ff., 605 f., 617. It would seem to have been known almost everywhere, but to have been discarded in various countries. We shall have to return to this question, however, in Ch. x. For the Tatars we may refer to pp. 175, 189 f. above.

(8) Speeches are introduced everywhere, and often occupy a considerable proportion of the poems. This is a feature which narrative

[1] Cf. Vol. II, p. 19 f. For the metres of the Tatars cf. p. 19 ff. above.

[2] In Anglo-Saxon gnomic poetry the sequence of the uniform line is sometimes interrupted by pairs of short lines. Although there is no stanza, these passages rather suggest a connection with metres used in Norse gnomic poetry; cf. Vol. I, p. 399 f. The true stanza occurs (rarely) in late ecclesiastical poetry; cf. Flower, *Brit. Mus. Quart.* VIII. 131.

poetry shares with saga, though speeches are usually shorter in the latter. Norse and Irish sagas frequently contain speeches or dialogues in verse; and the same practice probably prevailed in Wales. For these we may refer to p. 718 above.

(9) The detailed and leisurely description of proceedings, even commonplace proceedings, is characteristic of heroic narrative poetry almost everywhere. Instances will be found in the references cited on p. 750 (cf. p. 40 ff.). The Norse poems are exceptional, owing to their conciseness, though they are able to convey a good deal in a few words. Such leisurely descriptions are in general less characteristic of saga. In their place a larger amount of space is occupied by conversations, other than formal speeches.

(10) The diction of heroic narrative poetry tends everywhere to abound in static epithets, descriptive circumlocutions, kennings, repetitions and recurrent formulae. The Norse poems are the most restrained in this respect, those of the Kara-Kirghiz perhaps the most luxuriant. Such diction is characteristic of all types of heroic poetry, and in some languages it pervades all kinds of poetry, though the conventions observed in other categories are usually somewhat different. In general it is unusual in saga, including even heroic saga.

(11) The length of time covered by the action varies greatly between one poem and another. Sometimes it is limited to a few weeks or days, or even to one day; sometimes it extends over a good number of years. In the latter case, however, the action invariably falls into two or more scenes, each of which is treated in some detail—though the first may be quite brief—while the intervals are passed over in a few words. We have not met with any heroic narrative poems which can properly be regarded as biographical. The same may be said of heroic sagas, though in these the action seems often to be less concentrated around one or two events.[1] But non-heroic and post-heroic sagas frequently take the form of biographies, doubtless owing to the aggregation of stories, including stories of secondary origin.

(12) Heroic narrative poems seldom indicate whether an event happened recently or long ago. The Norse poems, all of which relate to the far past, are exceptional in this respect; several of them begin with the formula 'long ago'. On the other hand no great significance need be attached to Homeric comparisons between the present day and the

---

[1] The story of David, as we have it in the Books of Samuel, amounts to a biography; but we think it is properly to be regarded as a collection of sagas, not wholly heroic, which have been brought together in later times.

times of the story (cf. Vol. I, p. 23 f.). Yugoslav poems regularly use the same language in speaking of recent events and those of the fourteenth century. We do not think that the usage of saga in general differs in this respect from that of narrative poetry.

The milieu of heroic poetry and saga and its characteristic individualism have been discussed in Vol. I, Chs. IV and V, and in the chapters devoted to these subjects in the various literatures treated in Vol. II and the present volume. The results of the evidence have been summarised in the preceding chapter.

Now we may consider briefly the historical and unhistorical elements in heroic stories, whether these are preserved in poetry or saga. The evidence bearing upon this subject has been discussed in Vol. I, Chs. VII and VIII, and in various chapters in Vol. II and the present volume.

The Heroic Age, as we have seen, is usually a period for which little or no good historical information is available; sometimes it is prehistoric, sometimes it belongs to the twilight of history. This is of course not merely an unfortunate accident. Historical records involve the existence of some kind of civilised conditions, which are hardly compatible with a Heroic Age. Luckily for our purpose, however, there are regions, more or less cut off from the civilised world, yet not wholly inaccessible, where heroic conditions have maintained themselves down to our own times. From one of these, the western highlands of Yugoslavia, a large amount of valuable material is available. Indeed the Yugoslav evidence as a whole is of the greatest possible importance for this subject. Many even of the earlier stories, relating to the fourteenth and fifteenth centuries, are concerned with persons and events well known from historical records; and they are invaluable as illustrations, not only of the origin of such stories, but also—and perhaps more especially—of the growth of fiction and myth. The same may be said, in a somewhat less degree, of Russian heroic stories relating to the sixteenth and later centuries.

The earlier Russian, the Teutonic, the British, the later Irish and the Indian Heroic Ages belong to the 'twilight'. Where we can check the stories, they show—in varying degree of course—a combination of historical and unhistorical elements, very similar to what is found in the earlier Yugoslav stories. Hygelac's disaster is a historical event, as we know from trustworthy records of not much later date. The personnel of the Danish court, as described in Beowulf, may also be regarded as historical, in view of the agreement between English and Scandinavian tradition. But Beowulf's adventures at this court—as described in the poem—are of a less convincing character. They may be compared with the Yugoslav story of Sekula's death, summarised in Vol. II, p. 318 f., though the latter is more extravagant. Sekula transforms himself into a flying snake at Kosovo, and in that form fights with the Turkish king and is accidentally shot by his own uncle, Janko of Sibinj (John Hunyadi). Whatever may be the explanation of this, it is known that Sekula did accompany Hunyadi to Kosovo (in 1448), and that he was killed in the battle.

The earlier Irish, the Greek and the Hebrew Heroic Ages are 'prehistoric'. We have no historical records—whether contemporary or anything like contemporary—relating to even the greatest men of these Ages, e.g. Conchobor, Agamemnon or David. But it is sheer folly to assume from this that such persons are products of myth or fiction. Some of the stories relating to Irish heroes, especially CuChulainn, are of a fantastic enough character, but not more so than stories told of Sekula or of the Serbian prince Vuk Grgurević, who died in 1485 (cf. Vol. II, p. 321 ff.). We see no reason whatever for doubting that the 'prehistoric' stories are historical in the same sense as those which belong to the 'twilight' and later times. The degree of historicity doubtless varies much from case to case. One of the chief considerations is the length of time during which the preservation of the story depends wholly upon oral tradition. We think that the story of David is nearer to historical fact than what we hear of Agamemnon or Conchobor—largely for this reason. The first story may have been committed to writing within two centuries of David's time; but we can hardly allow less than five centuries for the second, and perhaps considerably more for the third.

The attitude to heroic stories commonly adopted by modern historians is by no means satisfactory. Last century great currency was attained by a theory which regarded heroic stories as myths and derived many of the leading characters from deities. We need not discuss this theory here, for we think that few scholars, at least in this country, would now venture to uphold it, except in a very attenuated form. We need only remark that, so far as our knowledge goes, no derivation of a 'hero' or 'heroine' from a deity has ever yet been substantiated. But, though the theory itself is now more or less dead or moribund, it has left behind it a feeling that heroic stories, whatever may be their origin, cannot be used for historical purposes; and it is this feeling we wish to combat. We need not accept the stories as literal records of fact, in the sense in which they were regarded by ancient Greek, Hebrew or Irish scholars. What is required is an understanding of the nature of heroic poetry and saga, just as much as of that of literary records.

It is essential to bear in mind that heroic narrative poetry or saga (Type A) is intended for entertainment, not for instruction. Moreover in each story there is as a rule one outstanding character, in whom the interest is centred. In describing the exploits of this hero the poet's imagination is allowed free play, within certain limits. But such freedom does not extend to the setting or milieu of the story; for both the hero himself and his connections are known to the audience. Liberties of this kind are possible only when a poet is handling a very old story which has largely been forgotten. Consequently when we meet with a heroic poem or saga at a date not too far removed from the times to which it relates, we need not in general doubt the incidental information which it affords, whatever we may think of the exploits attributed to the hero.

In references to events of 'twilight' periods the scanty information given by historical records may often be corrected or supplemented, more or less safely, by the evidence of heroic poems and sagas. Thus, when Frankish historians describe Hygelac as king of the Danes,[1] we need have no hesitation in preferring the evidence of Beowulf, where he is king of the Geatas (Gautar). Again, the poem states that the enemies by whom Hygelac was overcome were both Franks and Frisians; but the historical records ignore the latter, though they make it clear enough that the raid took place on the Frisian frontier. Here too we need not hesitate to accept the evidence of the poem; parallels may be found in the common defensive action taken by the English and Welsh against Scandinavian raids in Alfred's time and later. Such evidence is not to be regarded as invalidated by the absurd feat attributed to the hero (Beowulf) after the battle.

But the historical value of heroic poetry and saga is by no means limited to events which happen to be mentioned in early written records. We believe that normally they are to be accepted as having at least a foundation in fact, except in the case of very well-known heroes— which will be noticed below. But the value of the available evidence varies from case to case. Where two independent traditions are preserved it may be almost as good as that of a contemporary written

---

[1] Only the 'Liber Monstrorum' describes him as *rex Getarum*. The passage is quoted in Klaeber's edition of Beowulf, p. 253, and quoted and translated (together with the passages in the Frankish histories) by M. G. Clarke, *Sidelights on Teutonic History during the Migration Period*, p. 43 f.

record (cf. Vol. 1, p. 133f.). Such is the case with the Danish kings who figure in Beowulf. An equally secure example is to be found in the English kings who reigned in Angel before the invasion of Britain, in spite of the fact that only meagre references to their story are preserved in early poetry. This story is of special interest from the fate it has received at the hands of historians. It carries English history back well into the fourth century; yet it was wholly ignored in practically all 'Histories' until the last few years, and even now its significance is by no means fully appreciated. The explanation lies in the fact that historians of last century, who had no knowledge of the native poetry, assumed that the English had no kings before the invasion of Britain; and their successors were slow to admit that they had been mistaken. On the other hand all historians have given great prominence to certain records which are obviously based to a large extent upon antiquarian speculation.[1] We may instance the story of the foundation of Wessex, whether the speculation here be the work of the original annalist himself, or derived by him from antiquarian saga. In either case the story possesses a certain interest, even if inferior to the one we have just been considering; but as historical evidence it stands on a wholly different, and decidedly lower, plane. Such failure to recognise the relative value of authorities is of course a natural result of modern academic distinctions, wherein history and literature—so far as English antiquity is concerned—are deemed to belong to different departments of thought. One set of scholars do not know the records; the other know them, but have no appreciation of their historical value.

In the study of Greek and Indian antiquity these unintelligent distinctions have fortunately never been allowed to gain such sway. We doubt if anyone would undertake a serious study of early Greek history without first obtaining some acquaintance with the Homeric poems. The trouble here lies partly in the exclusiveness of Greek scholarship—an unwillingness to take account of analogies in other (barbaric) literatures —and partly in the fact that Greek scholars, owing largely to this exclusiveness, have too often allowed their judgement to be warped by fantastic theories. The Heroic Age lies wholly beyond the limits of what are recognised to be historical times; but we think there is a good deal

---

[1] There would seem to have been a good deal of antiquarian speculation current in England even before Bede's time; and we think that he draws from this not unfrequently, though he shows no knowledge of heroic poetry. An instance is to be found, we suspect, in the famous classification of the invaders, given in *Hist. Eccl.* 1. 15, which historians generally take as the foundation of English history.

of traditional evidence relating to this period which is independent of the Homeric poems, and by means of which it is possible, as suggested in Vol. I, p. 181 ff., to test and often to establish the historicity of the latter. The same remarks apply in general also to the Indian poems; but the external evidence (cf. Vol. II, p. 513 ff.) seems to be less abundant, though some of it is of higher value.

The Irish Heroic Age is, in its earlier phases, the one for which the least satisfactory data are available.[1] Irish scholars in general apparently still cling to a mythical, or at least unhistorical, interpretation of the earliest stories, though a historical existence is now usually conceded to Cormac mac Airt, in the third century. We have discussed the evidence in Vol. I, p. 166 ff., to which we may refer the reader. Here it will be enough to repeat that we see no ground for believing the earlier stories to be of a different origin from the later ones or from the heroic stories of other peoples. Note may be taken of the fact that the earliest stories indicate the prevalence of political and social conditions very different from those of historical times. If these conditions once really existed—and it is extremely unlikely that they are purely imaginary— the memory of them can hardly have been preserved except in connection with traditional narrative.

Thus far we have been speaking of historical elements. It is to be borne in mind, however, that all heroic poetry and saga contains also unhistorical elements; and these must now be noticed.

It is essential to distinguish between unhistorical statements and motifs which can be introduced in a contemporary narrative and those which can only make their appearance after a lapse—perhaps a considerable lapse—of time, or in a story relating to persons living in a distant country. To the former class belongs the exaggeration of a hero's prowess, which is a more or less constant feature of heroic narrative. Instances may be found in the Montenegrin poems on the 'Sack of Kolašin' (cf. Vol. II, p. 392), which were published within seven years of the event. But one would like to know how far a contemporary poet could go in the supernatural sphere. Probably such feats as are attributed to Beowulf could be accepted only after a long lapse of time, or when the story had travelled across the sea; but we have not seen enough of strictly contemporary poems to speak with confidence. We do not know when Sekula was first made to take the form of a flying snake; for it cannot be shown that the earliest existing

[1] We have no chronological data for the poems of the Kara-Kirghiz; but such evidence may exist, though it is not accessible to us.

poem on the subject is anything like contemporary. The Russian poem which relates how Frederick the Great transformed himself into a grey cat and other forms (cf. Vol. II, p. 130) is not likely to be much later than his time; but Frederick lived far away.

Foreboding dreams are of very frequent occurrence, especially in Yugoslav poetry; and poems which contain them may often be contemporary. A typical instance, on conventional lines, occurs in a poem (Karadžić v. 16) on the death of Prince Danilo, in 1861.[1] It was probably composed very soon after the event—certainly before 1865, when this volume was published. Another favourite convention in Yugoslav poetry is the arrival of two ravens, which bring news of a tragedy. In Vol. II, p. 337, we cited an instance dating from 1914.

Of all conventions of this kind the most widespread and striking is the introduction of divine beings. This is a frequent occurrence in the Homeric poems, and has been much misunderstood by modern scholars —who take the view that a story in which a deity is introduced is ipso facto discredited. "Homer says that Achilles slew Hector with the aid of Athene. We are not entitled to omit Athene, and still to affirm that Achilles slew Hector." This statement,[2] by a distinguished scholar of the last generation, well illustrates the Classical attitude to barbaric studies. The motif we are discussing is a common feature of barbaric narrative poetry and saga, both heroic and non-heroic, almost everywhere—instances have been given above from Norse, Irish, Yugoslav, Indian, Hebrew and Tatar literature—and it can by no means be assumed that a story in which it occurs is fictitious. We may refer to a Yugoslav poem cited in Vol. II, p. 332, in which Kara-Gjorgje—the ancestor of the reigning dynasty—is interviewed first by one Vila, and then, later, by another. The circumstances are historical, and relate to the years 1813–14; and the poem was probably composed not long afterwards. Another instance occurs in a poem cited ib. p. 378, in which two Vile act in concert to warn Prince Danilo of an impending surprise attack by Omer Pasha. The second Vila interviews the prince, who is at first unwilling to believe her. Here again the circumstances are historical; Omer's attack took place in 1852; and the poem was published in 1865. For instances in ancient poetry and saga, where historical persons and circumstances are involved, we may refer to Vol. I, pp. 206, 210. The personal intervention of deities must be recognised as a more or less regular convention of barbaric literature; and it is as barbaric, not as

---

[1] The dreamer is Stana, mother of the late King Nikola.
[2] Jebb, *Introduction to Homer*, p. 147.

Classical, literature that the Homeric poems should in our opinion be treated—though Classical scholars would doubtless not assent to this view.

It may be observed in this connection that heroes may have relations of various kinds, including conjugal relations, with deities; or they may be the offspring of divine fathers or mothers, though not of both. But the distinction between human and divine beings is never obliterated. As noted above, none of the literatures which we have surveyed furnishes any evidence for the theory that heroes were themselves originally deities.[1] In non-heroic tradition—and doubtless also in mantic and popular thought—kings may be credited with divine characteristics, or may represent and in some sense be identified with deities, while heroes may in course of time come to receive semi-divine honours; but such ideas are seldom if ever to be found in heroic poetry or saga.

We are not in a position to determine the degree of intimacy between heroes and deities which is permissible in contemporary poetry.[2] The amount of strictly contemporary material at our disposal is limited; and it is to be remembered that the Yugoslavs of last century, in spite of their Vile, were Christians. In other respects, however, we are somewhat better able to trace the growth of unhistorical elements.

The growth of a hero is well illustrated by the two poems—or rather two variants of one poem—on the death of Smail Aga, abstracts of which have been given in Vol. II, p. 413 ff. In the first poem, which was sent to Karadžić in 1846, within six years of the tragedy, the honours are about evenly distributed among the three leaders of the attack. Novica Cerović is not more prominent than the others, though he may be the most important man. It is Mirko who kills the Aga, and cuts off his head. But in the second poem, which is not dated—though both were published in 1862—Novica has definitely become the hero and central figure of the story. It is he who kills the Aga, though Mirko gets his head. It would seem that even within his own life-time Novica gained more credit than was his proper due from the exploit.[3]

[1] In Indian and Irish tradition a deity can be born or reborn as a human being, and in the former a hero may be an avatar of a deity; but these are mantic ideas, different from what is meant by the advocates of the theory referred to.

[2] Marko Kraljević is in one story the son, in another the husband, of a Vila; but the poems are doubtless much later than his time. It would seem that conjugal relations with deities were recognised in the North down to the end of heathen times (cf. Chadwick, *The Heroic Age*, p. 402); but the evidence is derived from saga.

[3] The substitution of one hero for another may be seen in the Border ballad 'Jock o the Side' (Child, No. 187). In one version Hobby Noble gets the whole

The fame of a popular hero does not cease with his death. If he has luck with the poets, it may continue to grow indefinitely; and he may gain credit, not only for actions in which perhaps he played only a minor part, but also for exploits which he never performed at all—just as in our days famous wits of the past are credited with many sayings of which they were probably quite guiltless. We have not the material to trace the steps, by which the process was carried out; but there can be no question that, in addition to the 'primary' stories of (real) exploits by which they first acquire fame,[1] most of the great heroes of the past have a number of 'secondary' or fictitious stories attached to them. With the lapse of time, when the true circumstances have been forgotten, the recitation of 'fact' is supplemented or succeeded by romance.

Sometimes the source of these secondary stories can be traced with more or less confidence. It would seem that some of them have been transferred from persons who are little known to more famous heroes. We may instance the modern Yugoslav poem, noticed in Vol. II, p. 381, which relates how the famous hero Miloš Obilić threw a heavy club over a church, with disastrous results. In a much earlier poem (*ib.* p. 353) the same story is told of a certain Montenegrin, who is otherwise unknown, but who lived about a century after Miloš' time. There can be little doubt, as we have seen, that this latter is the original story. It may have had a foundation in fact. An instance of a different kind may be found in the poem (*ib.* p. 324f.) which relates how the brothers Jakšića are enticed by Vile into a quarrel which proves fatal to them both. This story is quite irreconcilable with what we hear of these heroes elsewhere, and would seem to be derived from the story of Mujo and Alija (*ib.* p. 399)—which is itself perhaps based on a Mohammedan folk-tale. The stories which relate how a hero—Marko Kraljević, or his father, or Novak—marries a Vila (*ib.* p. 377) may also show the influence of folk-tales.

Some very famous heroes, in both medieval and ancient times—we may instance especially Marko Kraljević and CuChulainn—have a very large number of exploits attributed to them; and it is not always easy to determine which of these are 'primary'. We have examined the stories of Marko (*ib.* p. 384ff.), in order to see if it is possible to ascertain

credit for the exploit; in the other the chief hero is 'the laird's Jock' (apparently a son of Lord Mangerton), who is not mentioned in the former.

[1] A hero may of course have more than one primary story to his credit. Novica Cerović shares the chief honours in the 'Sack of Kolašin', as well as in the 'Death of Smail Aga'.

which of them has the best claim to historicity; and we decided in favour of 'Marko and Mina of Kostur', though even in this the historical facts seem to be greatly distorted. Nearly all the rest are probably, or certainly, fictitious. But they have had the effect of producing a myth, viz. the conception of Marko as a—more or less superhuman—national hero. In the poems themselves the tendency in this direction is by no means complete; for it is seldom or never forgotten that he was loyal to the Sultan, though he frequently treats other Turks in no friendly way. But in popular belief the myth was complete, as may be seen from the incident which is said to have occurred at the battle of Prilep in 1912 (cf. Vol. II, p. 389). Myth[1] is the last—not the first—stage in the development of a hero; and its growth is specially interesting in the case of Marko Kraljević, owing to the very unpromising circumstances of his (real) history.

We have taken our examples from Yugoslav poems because these relate to times for which some historical data are available. In Russian heroic poetry of the Kiev cycle we frequently find different heroes credited with the same exploit; but hardly any external evidence is to be obtained. Poetry relating to later times seems to have been less prolific in producing secondary stories. But unhistorical elements of other kinds are abundant. We may instance the poem in which Ivan IV resolves to kill his son, but relents—which must apparently be regarded as a primary story, though it may possibly have been influenced later by a similar incident in the life of Peter the Great. But in both cases the son was actually killed. For further examples we may refer to Vol. II, p. 128 ff.

One of the most distinctive features of the secondary story is chronological confusion—the introduction of characters who properly belong to different periods. This is of course one of the unhistorical features which are not permissible in primary stories—nor indeed in secondary stories until long after the hero's time; it is a definite proof of late date. Prince Danilo may be allowed to meet with heroes of the past when he arrives in Paradise, but not in his lifetime. When we find Marko Kraljević associated with Janko of Sibinj, we may know that the poem, or at least the passage in which the association occurs, dates from long after their times. References to a number of similar cases will be found

---

[1] By 'myth' we mean a concept or story which we ourselves do not believe, but which is, or has been, widely believed by others. We do not think that fictitious (secondary) stories can normally be taken or intended too seriously when they are first produced; but the belief in them may grow with the course of time.

in Vol. II, pp. 375 f., 383 f. But, except perhaps in 'Marriages', such confusion is by no means general in Yugoslav poetry, even in poems relating to the earlier periods. In Russian poems of the Kiev cycle it is apparently much more deep-seated. Vladimir's entourage (*ib.* 112 ff.) would seem to be drawn from different quarters and different generations.

The prevalence of such confusion may within certain limits serve as an index of the length of time during which poems and sagas are current, before their form becomes more or less fixed. It was perhaps in Russia that this period was longest—as against the view of some recent writers. In Germany, where it was not appreciably shorter, the medieval poems represent Eormenric, Attila and Theodric the Ostrogoth as contemporaries (cf. Vol. I, p. 199). In the North, where heroic poetry is preserved in an earlier form, the confusion is not so great. For the earlier Irish stories historical data are lacking; but there seems not to be much serious confusion between the different cycles (*ib.* p. 203 f.). In Greek, Indian and English heroic poetry there is hardly any evidence for such confusion;[1] but in the non-heroic parts of the Mahābhārata and the late additions to the Rāmāyana famous seers have apparently no limits to their lives.

The unhistorical relationships noted above are sometimes apparently due in part to an impulse to connect famous heroes or their stories with one another. Marko Kraljević and Janko of Sibinj are brought together both as friends and foes; and the same is true of Teutonic heroes in late stories. The story of Sigurðr and Guðrún is extended in both directions, by making Helgi Hundingsbani a half-brother of Sigurðr and Svanhildr a daughter of Guðrún. The grouping of a number of heroes and their stories round a central figure, such as Vladimir or King Arthur, is another variety of the same tendency. All these associations of course belong to a late stage in the history of heroic stories.

Lastly, among the secondary elements in heroic stories—or, perhaps we should rather say, in stories about heroes—we must also include stories relating to the birth and childhood of such persons, and to their experiences in the home of the dead. Actually these stories are seldom to be found in poems which can properly be called heroic, as we noted in the last chapter (p. 744 f.). They belong to the literature which grows up round the memory of a hero, when he has become famous; and they are clearly of non-heroic provenance. For an account of Beowulf's birth we must turn to the late story of Bjarki. The Iliad tells us that

[1] For certain passages in Waldhere and Widsith see Vol. I, p. 200 f.

Achilles' mother was a goddess; but we must look to later sources for the adventures of his childhood. In modern (European) oral poetry such stories are rare, owing doubtless to the weakness of the non-heroic element; but a good instance is to be found in the story of the birth of the Serbian prince Vuk Grgurević (noticed in Vol. II, p. 322), who died in 1485. It is significant that those scholars who hold that heroes[1] are of mythical origin base their theory very largely upon this class of stories. They prove nothing of the kind; but the theory contains this amount of truth, that such stories clearly have affinities with myth. They are products of a phase when the hero is passing into myth.

Stories of visits made by heroes to the underworld or to Heaven, or of the arrival of heroes in the land of the dead, are less frequent than birth-stories, but usually seem to be of the same provenance. For examples we may refer to the previous chapter (p. 745 f.).

The groups of secondary poems which we have been considering sometimes consist of a number of more or less independent units, which have no special relationship to one another. Such is the case with the poems relating to Marko Kraljević. There are other groups, however, in which relationships are distinctly traceable; one poem serves as a preliminary or a sequel to another which may itself be 'primary', and must either have been composed for that purpose or subsequently adapted to it.

First we may take the group of poems relating to the first battle of Kosovo, in 1389. It can hardly be doubted that the poem (*bugarštica*) which describes the quarrel of Miloš' and Vuk Branković's wives (Vol. II, p. 315 f.) was composed as a preliminary and explanation of the long poem on the battle (*ib.*). Again, the poem (*ib.* p. 316) in which Milica converses with the dying Miloš must have been composed as a sequel to an account of the battle, though it belongs to a different tradition from the other two.

A similar process of composition may be traced in some of the poems in Karadžić's collection, though no poem on the battle itself is preserved here. Thus (e.g.)[2] 'King Lazar and Queen Milica' (No. 45) and the fragments contained in No. 50 are 'preliminary' poems, while 'The

---

[1] E.g. Achilles, CuChulainn, Sigurðr (and many others). For Sigurðr we may refer to *The Heroic Age*, p. 144 ff.

[2] Most of these poems are noticed briefly in Vol. II, pp. 314 f., 341 f. Translations will be found in Subotić, *Yugoslav Popular Ballads*, p. 61 ff.

Girl of Kosovo' (No. 51) and 'The Death of the Mother of the Jugovići' (No. 48) are 'sequels'. There is no special relationship between any of these poems, except possibly Nos. 50 and 51. No. 45 is unconnected with No. 48, though both of them are concerned with the Yugovići, Milica's family. It is incredible that such a group of poems could be derived from a literary unit, whether epic or romance (cf. Vol. ii, p. 433). They are clearly independent compositions, presumably by different authors, designed to lead up to, or follow, a poem—or perhaps various poems—on the battle. We see no reason for doubting that poems were composed on this battle, just as on later events, from the time when it took place. The 'preliminary' and 'sequel' poems may have been composed at any subsequent date.

We do not mean of course to suggest that contemporary poetry relating to the heroes of Kosovo was limited to narratives of the battle. 'Banović Strahinja' (No. 44; cf. Bogišić, No. 40), which deals with a different event, is clearly a 'primary' poem; and the same may possibly be true of certain poems relating to the battle itself, e.g. 'Musić Stefan' (No. 47), an analysis and discussion of which was given in Vol. ii, p. 420f. The greater part of this poem is typical 'preliminary' matter; but it goes on (only in Karadžić's text) to describe the hero's fate in the battle. We do not think that this latter part is inconsistent with a 'preliminary' origin; but such an origin is less certain here than with highly imaginative pieces like Nos. 48 and 51.

Another group of 'preliminary' and 'sequel' poems is to be found in the *bugarštice* relating to the second battle of Kosovo, in 1448 (*ib.* p. 319f.). Like 'Musić Stefan', these poems usually contain an epilogue (or opening) relating to the battle itself; but their imaginative and unhistorical character renders it improbable that they are contemporary compositions. An investigation of the history of this cycle would probably produce very interesting results; but it cannot be attempted here.

In Russian *byliny* also, which relate to the earlier periods, 'preliminary' and 'sequel' poems are by no means unknown; but the literary history is more complicated, owing to the very large number of variants and the paucity of historical data.

In Ireland 'preliminary' sagas (*remscéla*) connected with the Tain Bo Cuailnge were recognised by scholars in the twelfth century, if not earlier. From the lists of such sagas given in the Book of Leinster and elsewhere[1] it is clear that the term was used in a wider sense than that in

[1] For these lists see Thurneysen, *Irische Helden- und Königsage*, I. 248 ff.

which we have used it. It is applied apparently to all sagas relating to the heroes who figure in the Tain Bo Cuailnge and to times anterior to the events narrated therein. Some of these sagas, e.g. the Tain Bo Regamain (cf. Vol. I, pp. 91, 236), seem to have been composed as preliminaries to the. Tain Bo Cuailnge. But others, e.g. the stories of the births of Conchobor and CuChulainn (*ib.* p. 216), are preliminaries, not to this saga itself, but to the Ulster cycle as a whole, while others again are stories of gods, only indirectly and remotely connected with either the saga or the cycle.

Sagas or poems which are preliminary to a cycle deserve special notice, as they are rather widespread. Usually they are of a different character from sagas or poems preliminary to other sagas or poems. They are often concerned with the births of heroes; but their affinities would seem to be non-heroic (cf. p. 744 f.). The curious (unhistorical) poem on the birth of Janko of Sibinj, noticed in Vol. II, p. 317, is apparently a poem of this kind, composed as a preliminary, not to any one poem on the second battle of Kosovo, but to the cycle of poems relating to Janko as a whole.

'Sequel' stories are not recognised, as such, in Irish MSS. Many modern scholars, who believe the whole of the Ulster cycle to be a product of fiction or myth, would probably regard all stories which are concerned with events later than the Tain Bo Cuailnge as 'sequels' to that saga. But those who are, like ourselves, sceptical as to the fertility of (constructive) imagination attributed to the ancients, would speak with less confidence. It seems to us not unlikely that some of these stories may be 'primary' heroic sagas of the usual type, though many others may well be fictitious. But we are not prepared to deal with their connections.

A number of secondary heroic poems, both preliminary and sequel, are preserved in the Edda collection. They consist mainly or wholly of speeches, and are concerned with situations rather than with action, though some of them tell a story in retrospect. For a brief account of these poems we may refer to Vol. I, p. 26 f.

Guðrúnarkviða I is obviously a sequel to an account of Sigurðr's death, perhaps the poem (Sigurðarkviða hin meiri), of which the last part is preserved in the MS. immediately before Guðrúnarkviða I, or a variant not far removed from it. The Helreið Brynhildar is also to be regarded as a sequel, though of a very different kind (cf. p. 746 above), of a poem on the same subject. The relationship here may be with Sigurðarkviða hin skamma, which precedes the Helreið in the text. The two poems on the hero's death are very different, as we have them; but it can hardly be doubted that they originated as variants.

The second part of Guðrúnarahvöt is a sequel, or rather epilogue, to the 'cycle of Guðrún', as contained in the poems on Sigurðr and Atli, together with the story of Svanhildr. The first part, however, is a variant of the first part of the Hamðismál (cf. Vol. 1, p. 515 f.). The latter poem itself may also be regarded as a sequel (not epilogue) to the same cycle; but originally it was independent, and not connected in any way with the story of Guðrún. As to the relationship of the original elements in the latter, i.e. the stories of Sigurðr and Atli, we are not prepared to speculate. Both of them may very well be primary stories, though they have largely the same personnel.

A preliminary, or rather prologue, to the story of Sigurðr is to be found in the Trilogy (ib. p. 27 f.). Like the Irish remscéla, this begins with a story of gods, and then passes on to the youthful adventures of the hero. But the poems themselves are of different character from the Sigurðarkviður. They consist wholly of speeches, and are mainly didactic, with non-heroic affinities. Another prologue to the same story is provided by the (probably very late) poem Grípisspá (ib. pp. 119, 451), in which the whole course of the hero's life is prophesied to him in detail.

The first of the Kara-Kirghiz poems on Manas, noticed above (p. 28 f.), is obviously in the nature of a prologue to the story of that hero. It gives an account of his birth, the prophecies of his future greatness, and the feats performed by him in his childhood. Radlov suspected that the reciter was making the story up; but if so, he was clearly following traditional lines. The sixth poem in this series would seem properly to be a sequel to the story of Manas, rather than a portion of it, and the seventh poem, again, a sequel to the sixth. A similar extension to the next generation occurs also in the story of Joloi (p. 34 f.); and here there is a marked change in the nature of the theme, though the whole story is treated in one poem.

The cycle of Manas shows another feature which deserves notice. The third and the fifth poems cover in part the same ground—the hero's marriage and his subsequent murder and resuscitation—and here, in spite of important differences, the two accounts seem to be variants. But the first part of No. 3 is taken up by an account of his warfare with Er Kökchö, which is lacking in No. 5, though it is mentioned in No. 4. It would seem then that the various incidents in the story of Manas could either be treated separately or combined (seriatim) in one poem.

The poem on Joloi rather suggests that the process of combination has been at work here also.

This combination of several poems (seriatim) in one poem is to be found also in Yugoslav heroic poetry, as we have seen. In particular we may refer to the *bugarštica* on the first battle of Kosovo, an analysis of which was given in Vol. II, p. 419 ff. Here we have (1) the departure of Busić Stjepan, corresponding to Karadžić II. 47; (2) a very brief version of Milica's request that one of her brothers should be left behind (*ib.* 45); (3) the banquet (*ib.* 50, iii); (4) the battle, which has nothing corresponding to it in Karadžić's collection. The last section is the primary theme, and the poem as a whole is made up by prefixing to it three 'preliminaries', one after another.

For the extension of a poem by suffixing a 'sequel' we may probably refer to the story of the *beg* Ljubović, noticed in Vol. II, p. 329 f. The last part of the poem—the Sultan's appeal for a champion against the black Arab and Majković's response thereto—is a conventional theme, which has little connection with the rest of the story. It is perhaps a Christian minstrel's addition to a Mohammedan poem.

MSS. of Irish sagas frequently contain scenes and episodes which are lacking in other MSS. We may instance the wager between Medb and Ailill which forms the introduction to the Tain Bo Cuailnge in the Book of Leinster and related MSS., and a number of episodes which occur in some only of the MSS. of Bricriu's Feast. It is commonly held now that these interpolations are the work of scribes; and this may sometimes be true, though we distrust the view that oral tradition came to an end as soon as the sagas had been written down. But in any case the scribes were merely continuing a usage which they had inherited from earlier times. The episode of Fer Diad in the Tain Bo Cuailnge is doubtless of the same origin, though it is found in all the complete MSS. now existing. We suspect that the process of accumulation is very old. From the analogy of other literatures we should be inclined to doubt (e.g.) whether the feats of CuChulainn's childhood belonged to the earliest stratum, though the textual authority for this section seems to be as good as for any part of the saga.

The Norse heroic poems on Helgi, Sigurðr, Atli and Hamðir were eventually paraphrased in continuous prose narratives; but this took place in the days of written literature. All that can be said of earlier times is that, in the last three cases, the poems themselves sometimes adumbrate a combination of the stories, by means of prophetic and retrospective speeches. In post-heroic and romantic sagas, however, a similar process of accumulation had been operative long before they were written down.[1]

In the Nibelungenlied the stories of Siegfried (Sigurðr) and Etzel (Atli) are combined, together with much 'preliminary' and other new matter, in a continuous epic. And other medieval German poems show a somewhat similar treatment of old heroic stories; thus the story of Hilde (Hildr) has had a long imaginative sequel attached to it. We think that the formation of these epics is probably to be explained by the process we are considering; but unfortunately their history cannot be traced with confidence. We do not know how far the process had advanced before the poems were written down; and consequently, in view of the very strong foreign influence by which they are pervaded, their evidence can be used only with considerable reserve.

Evidence of a similar character may be obtained from Beowulf. The second part of this poem (from l. 2200 onwards) has—apart from the episodes—no satisfactory historical or heroic setting and no personnel except the hero and Wiglaf; and one may perhaps suggest[2] that it was composed as an (imaginative) sequel. Its attachment to what precedes seems to be rather slight and superficial. Again, the introduction to the poem is in the nature of a prologue which might be made use of in any poem relating to kings of the Danes; it has no special appropriateness for this poem, especially as the hero himself is not a Dane. And there are other passages which may well not belong to the oldest stratum; we may instance the swimming contest in the hero's boyhood.

The story of David is more of a biography than any of the examples noticed above. It is in fact a biographical saga, similar in form to many of the Sagas of Icelanders, e.g. Egils Saga Skallagrímssonar, and like them constructed out of a number of short sagas—originally no doubt a collection or cycle—which deal with incidents or short periods (cf. Vol. II, p. 647f.). In one case at least (ib. p. 635) saga variants have been included as different stories. At the beginning of the cycle we find two stories relating to the hero's youth (ib. p. 652f.), which are of a 'preliminary' character and clearly of non-heroic provenance.

Not one of the poems discussed above—apart from the German epics—is of such a length that it could not have been recited in the course of an evening. We shall see in Ch. x that this may be regarded as

---

[1] Cf. Kershaw, *Stories and Ballads of the Far East*, p. 58 (with reference to Hrómundar Saga Greipssonar).

[2] The two authors are not in agreement upon this subject. A different explanation may be advanced later.

the normal limit for recitations. But examples which exceed it are not very rare either in poetry or saga. The Odyssey would have required at least four evenings, the Iliad at least five, the Rāmāyana—even without the late Books I and VII—at least a dozen. It may be, however, that these poems were recited in the daytime, as well as the evening, especially at festival gatherings. Indeed the Rāmāyana itself (VII. 106 f.) claims to have been first produced at a festival, during which it was recited continuously throughout the day. Sometimes too we hear of recitations adjourned from one evening to the next, as in the story of the Icelander who was instructed by King Harold Hardrada to make his recitation extend over twelve successive evenings (cf. Vol. I, p. 581). The frequence and length of preliminaries and sequels would rather lead us to infer that the latter was the more usual, or at least the earlier, process—we mean that these were originally composed as recitations for the preceding and following evenings. But in any case the growth of great sagas and epics—again like the story of the Icelander—involves a good deal of expansion in the treatment of the original matter, apart from these and other adjuncts.

The Odyssey obviously contains a very large amount of 'preliminary' matter.[1] In Vol. I, p. 533 f. we distinguished three elements of this kind, each of which may well have formed a separate poem or recitative unit, suitable for a long evening's entertainment. None of these poems in itself possessed a complete heroic theme, without the implication of a dénouement to follow. But the same is true of some of the poems on the first battle of Kosovo, noticed on p. 764 f., e.g. 'King Lazar and Queen Milica'. We think that the formation of the Odyssey as a whole is due to the combination of these three preliminaries with the original poem, which was the source of the story, and that in principle the process is the same as was observed in the *bugarštica* on the same battle. But the length of the Odyssey is also due largely to expansion, especially in the original part, whereas the *bugarštica* seems to have abbreviated its constituent elements.

We suspect that the formation of the Iliad is to be explained in a similar way; but the constituent elements are less easy to distinguish. It is possible that these poems were shorter and more numerous, and also older. The matter too as a whole is less obviously fictitious, and less directly connected with the main theme. It has often been remarked that some of the incidents related, e.g. the single combat between

---

[1] 'Sequels' also were composed for the Odyssey, though they did not find admission into the final text; cf. Vol. I, p. 535.

Menelaos and Paris, might have been expected to take place long before the quarrel of Achilles and Agamemnon. What we would suggest is that the poems which followed the first preliminary, down to the intervention of Patroclos (i.e. between Books I and XVI), were largely derived from earlier poems relating to all stages of the war,[1] not excluding variants; and that some of these (earlier) poems were preserved more or less complete, while others were already disintegrated. We see no reason for doubting that the composition of heroic narrative poetry on the war began from the time of the war itself. But the existence of fictitious elements, mostly of later date, is not to be ignored (cf. Vol. I, pp. 230f., 233).

The Homeric poems contain no birth-stories or other non-heroic matter of any kind, except in *Od.* XI, though such matter seems to have been well represented in some of the Cyclic poems, especially the Cypria.[2] On the other hand, it can hardly be doubted that there has been much expansion, especially in those parts of the poems—say the last nine books in each—which are concerned with the original themes. As we have unfortunately no variants of early Greek poems, it may be of some interest here to note that the nineteenth-century versions of Yugoslav heroic poems in Karadžić's collection are sometimes twice, sometimes even four times the length of their counterparts (*bugarštice*) in earlier MS. texts. Thus in Karadžić's versions 'Marko Kraljević and Mina of Kostur' and 'Banović Strahinja' amount to 336 and 810 lines respectively, while the corresponding *bugarštice* contain only 161 and 131 lines.[3] Yet the two versions cover much the same ground in each case. Along with this process of expansion we may take account of the inclusion of stock scenes, like the games in *Il.* XXIII, a close parallel to which is to be found in the fourth poem of the Manas cycle (cf. p. 32 f.).

In the Rāmāyana the late books (I and VII) consist wholly of non-heroic matter—mostly of a speculative character—and form a prologue

[1] Some scholars hold that various characters and incidents of the Iliad have been transferred to the story of Troy from other parts of the Greek world. The evidence adduced in support of this theory seems to us unconvincing; cf. Vol. I, p. 228f.

[2] This poem would seem to have been composed as a preliminary to the Iliad, while some of the other lost poems (Aithiopis, etc.) may have been composed or adapted as sequels to it. They seem to have possessed some late features, though they may well have contained a good deal of primary matter.

[3] We may reckon two of the normal (long) lines of the *bugarštice* as equivalent to three decasyllabic lines (as in Karadžić's versions). But in the former poem one line in every three is so short that its equivalent in decasyllabics would not be more than 180 lines.

and epilogue to the original story. In the older portion (Books II–VI) the non-heroic elements are slight, except in passages which are generally regarded as interpolations. But the amount of expansion is amazing. The ground covered in these books is the same as in the version of the story contained in the Mahābhārata; and, except in a few passages, they do not give much additional information. Yet the Rāmāyana version amounts to over 35,000 lines, the Mahābhārata to only about 1300.

We cannot of course attempt to trace the history of the Mahābhārata as a whole. The (subsidiary) heroic stories of Rāma, Nala and Sāvitrī are of normal length, all appreciably shorter than Beowulf. Non-heroic elements are slight in the third, and apparently lacking in the two former, except in one 'preliminary'.[1] The main story has been swollen to an enormous extent, partly by expansion of the heroic element itself, especially in the account of the battle (Books VI–IX), but much more by the intrusion of non-heroic elements. The 'preliminaries' (in Books I–III) are mainly non-heroic; but at least one of them—the marriage of Draupadī—would seem to have a heroic kernel. In Book IX the heroic element is reduced to very small proportions; after Book XI it disappears altogether, apart from the personnel of the framework. What follows is partly (imaginative) sequel, partly epilogue, but wholly non-heroic.

The poem itself frequently speaks of the recitation of the Mahābhārata as a whole; but we have not noticed any passage in which the length of time required for this purpose is stated. It was evidently intended for people of leisure. Even if the recitation lasted the whole day, it must have occupied several weeks.

[1] iii. 273–5, which is to be regarded as a non-heroic 'preliminary' to the story of Rāma.

CHAPTER V

POETRY AND SAGA RELATING TO UNSPECIFIED INDIVIDUALS

THIS category is much more fully represented in modern oral literatures, especially perhaps those of Europe, than in antiquity. To a certain extent, however, this is probably due to the character of our records. If the ancient literatures had been as well preserved as the modern, we should perhaps find poetry and saga of this kind everywhere.

We will begin with narrative poetry and saga. In this we may distinguish three formal varieties:

(i) The story is purely 'timeless nameless'; no characters have names attached to them. The subject of the story is described as 'a man' or 'a girl', or perhaps 'a prince' or 'a peasant'. In some countries, e.g. Lithuania, this variety is very common. In the ancient literatures which we have discussed we have found it seldom, and only in narratives which have a didactic purpose (Type C).

(ii) One or more of the characters may bear names of a common kind, which supply no clue for identifying them with persons known from other stories or records. We mean such names as 'Jack' in English prose stories and 'Lady Isabel' or 'Lord William' in ballads. It may be observed that not infrequently we meet with stories of which one variant contains names of this kind, while another is strictly nameless. Names derived from a character's circumstances or origin, like 'Cinderella' or 'Bear's Son', may also be mentioned here, though perhaps they belong more properly to the first variety.

(iii) Even stories in which some of the characters bear names known from other stories or records cannot always be left out of account. Sometimes a story relating to well-known characters is an obvious variant of a nameless story, and may be derived from it, though the alternative explanation—viz. that the latter has lost its names—is also possible. And even when two stories relating to different sets of well-known characters are obvious variants, account is to be taken of the possibility that both are derived from a nameless story, though other

26

explanations may be possible. On the other hand, a story which contains perhaps only one personal name, if it is unfamiliar, or even only a place-name, may quite possibly point to definite associations in the past.

Saga in this category consists largely of folk-tales. We restrict the use of the latter term to timeless-nameless stories which have an international circulation; but, in addition to these, we must include stories of the same kind which have only a local and perhaps temporary currency. In one form or another timeless-nameless saga is perhaps to be found everywhere—even in modern civilised society it is cultivated by wags and bores—but the amount of attention paid to it varies very greatly.

Narrative poetry seems to be much less widespread. Apart from one or two didactic stories in the Mahābhārata, we have not met with any examples—which can properly be called timeless nameless—in the ancient literatures we have treated. Neither have we found any satisfactory instances among the Tatars or in modern Africa. In western Polynesia, however, stories which have the appearance of folk-tales are treated in narrative poetry (cf. p. 346 ff.). In Russia also and in Yugoslavia we find a somewhat similar poetry. It has the metre and to some extent the diction of heroic poetry; but the affinities of the stories themselves lie with folk-tales (cf. Vol. ii, pp. 216 ff., 398 ff.). In Yugoslavia most of these poems are customarily reckoned among what are called 'Women's Poems' (*ženske pjesme*), though they are not exclusively recited by women.

But the chief store of timeless-nameless narrative poetry known to us is to be found in the (international) ballad poetry of western and northern Europe. The history of this poetry can be traced to a certain extent (cf. p. 682 f.). It was introduced into Denmark in the twelfth century, into this country possibly somewhat earlier, together with dancing and dance music. It is clearly of southern origin; many of the themes have Mediterranean and Oriental connections. In the north of Europe it seems to have acquired new themes from various sides; in Scandinavian lands many ballads are derived from early Norse poems and sagas. Indeed its metrical forms (the couplet or four-line stanza, with rhyme) in course of time displaced all native metres in oral poetry—though in England this may not have taken place before the fourteenth century. In consequence of this vitality ballads not infrequently contain names, such as 'Earl Brand' or 'Lord Douglas', which may point to associations of some kind in the past. Yet in general the true ballads retained their timeless-nameless character; if they contain any names, they are of the unidentifiable kind.[1]

The characteristics of these poems are very similar to those of folk-tales. Their attraction for us lies in their extreme simplicity and naïveté, though in their own days their popularity was probably due more to the music which accompanied them than to any other cause. Their most striking feature is the prominence of women, or rather girls, and of the love motif in various forms. On the other hand, they are often crude and savage; and, although they are largely concerned with lords and ladies, they show little knowledge of social conventions. These features would seem to be incompatible with an aristocratic origin of this poetry. Yet there is external evidence that, especially in Denmark, it was patronised by the ladies of the nobility. That can hardly have been the case in this country before—at least not much before—the fourteenth century, because the language of the nobility down to this time was French. There can be little doubt that in the twelfth and thirteenth centuries the romance was the entertainment of the hall, the (English) ballad that of humbler circles. Eventually the latter also found its way into the hall; but we think it must have entered through the back door.

Who brought the ballads to the north of Europe? In this country at least the influence must have come direct from France—German influence is obvious enough in Scandinavian ballads, but not in English. Many French minstrels doubtless made their way here after the Norman conquest. Those who were attached to the court or the great nobles were presumably educated men, and possessed written copies of the romances. But it is quite possible that there were also itinerant minstrels of a poorer class, who came to seek a livelihood by entertaining the dependants of the nobles, as well as the traders and craftsmen (builders, etc.) who flocked to this country during the following period. It is still more probable that the latter not seldom had some knowledge of popular minstrelsy themselves. At all events there is no doubt that these poorer French frequently married English wives, and that their families soon became English. We suspect that this was the milieu in which ballads made their first appearance in English, and that eventually they won their way into the hall through the servants (cf. p. 691).

We believe that the folk-tales of western and central Europe have had a somewhat similar history. Folk-tales were no doubt current in

---

[1] It must be understood that in this chapter we are speaking of the true (international) ballads, and not of the native oral poetry in ballad metre, which has been discussed in the Note on p. 682 ff.

these regions long before the Middle Ages; but it is not clear that they were the same folk-tales as we find later. One of the features of twelfth-and thirteenth-century literature is the production of collections of stories, which often show affinities with stories of our category, in spite of the names which they contain. It is very probable that a new influx of folk-tales—bearing much the same relationship to these literary stories as ballads bear to romances—took place about the same time. The impulse doubtless came from the increased facilities for travel and communication which were afforded by the formation of large dominions, like those of Henry II.

The resemblance between folk-tales and ballads is very close, as noted above. The former share practically all the characteristics of the latter—simplicity, naïveté, coarseness, gruesomeness, savagery, the absence both of aristocratic conventions and of intellectual interests, the dominance of the love motif. They are indeed the prose equivalents of ballads,[1] and can hardly be of a different origin. In this case, however, there is no need of either musical instrument or professional training. Skill in reciting stories can be acquired by persons of poor education. The diffusion of folk-tales may well be due to traders and emigrant craftsmen.

In Thiðreks Saga af Bern, cap. 394, the author—or rather redactor—states that he obtained his knowledge of German heroic stories from men of Soest, Bremen and Münster; and elsewhere he frequently refers to German stories and poems. It is generally agreed that his informants must have been traders whom he met with in Norway. These stories were of course not folk-tales, but oral literature of a more advanced character; but the passages are of interest as evidence for the diffusion of oral literature through traders. Unfortunately, evidence as to how folk-tales are diffused seems difficult to obtain. In Europe, both east and west, they have long been preserved mainly by women. In modern times their chief function has been for the amusement of children by their nurses; but in the past, at least in Russia, when books were rare and the knowledge of reading limited, grown-up people were also commonly

---

[1] They have of course special features of their own: (i) One of the chief characters, either the 'hero' or the 'heroine', is usually a peasant; (ii) the ending is almost invariably happy; (iii) the fantastic is much more widespread, indeed practically universal. These features are presumably due to the fact that—though both are of democratic origin—the folk-tale did not, like the ballad, gain admission to the hall. But it is probable also that folk-tales have had a longer history in the north of Europe than ballads (as such) have had.

entertained by them (cf. Vol. II, p. 289f.). For the introduction of new folk-tales, however, such little evidence as we have (*ib.*) seems to point to traders and travellers.

The growth of fairs and markets probably contributed most of all to the diffusion of such literature; for they brought together traders from different lands, who could exchange their stories, like their merchandise. There is no need of course to suppose that the stories told on these occasions were always timeless-nameless; Thiðreks Saga af Bern is evidence to the contrary. But the stories in the Saga were written down by a man who heard them from the foreign traders themselves. If they had not been written down, but preserved (and retailed) by oral tradition, there can be no doubt that the foreign names would soon have been lost or become unrecognisable. Folk-tales, like international ballads, must be timeless-nameless, though of course timeless-nameless stories are not necessarily folk-tales.

We have yet to consider stories which seem to be folk-tales, but which are attached to the names of persons known from other stories or from historical records. A good instance occurs in a Yugoslav poem relating to the Jakšiéa, noticed in Vol. II, p. 324f. The two brothers, who elsewhere are married men, are here represented as unmarried and meeting with their deaths at the instigation of a Vila. The story seems to be derived from 'Mujo and Alija' (*ib.* p. 399f.), which is probably a folk-tale. Where a story is told of different persons, in different environments, it is likely to be derived from a folk-tale or other timeless-nameless story; but such an explanation is of course by no means necessary. The Yugoslav story of the throwing of a club over a church is told of two different persons, who lived in different periods (cf. p. 761). We see no reason here for assuming the existence of a third (timeless-nameless) version of the story. The incident may have happened to the first man, and been transferred from him later to the second, who was a famous hero. But the case is different when the story is incredible in itself and conforms to a traditional type, like stories of the slaying of dragons. In such cases one story may of course be derived from another; but the influence of a folk-tale—ultimately of foreign origin—is to be suspected at some point in the tradition.

It is only through stories which have been transferred to well-known heroes or seers that we can trace the existence of folk-tales in ancient times. The Mahābhārata contains many instances of this kind, while in the Odyssey (IX–XII) the hero appropriates a series of such adventures. The story of Beowulf's fight with Grendel is of special interest because we think we can trace different strata in its history (cf. Vol. I, p. 436 ff.), as also in that of the folk-tale which influenced it. 'Bear's Son' usually contains a number of incidents which are unknown to Beowulf or Grettis Saga, e.g. the rescue of the three princesses. Though one cannot speak with confidence on a subject for which the ancient evidence is limited, it seems not unlikely that this incident is an addition to the old folk-tale, due to the influence of the later folk-tales, which were introduced in the Middle Ages. The story of Beowulf's adventure in its original form—before it was influenced by the folk-tale at all—would seem to have been very like that of Bhīma and Vaka, noticed in Vol. II, p. 569 f., though Vaka is more human than Grendel; like the Rākshasa of other stories, he suggests derivation from a cannibal savage rather than a wild beast. Beowulf, like Heracles, specialises in beast monsters.

Timeless-nameless stories may be described as the vagrants of oral literature. Some of them—what we call folk-tales—have wandered far and wide, through many countries, while others are not found beyond the limits of one country. Most, if not all, of them have presumably once possessed names and associations of their own; but these have been forgotten,[1] partly through the lapse of time, partly through their migrations and consequent transference from one language to another. In modern times they are known in their true form chiefly, though not exclusively, as peasant literature; but in ancient times, from which no peasant literature has survived, we hear of them only when they have assumed secondary associations.

Timeless-nameless poetry of Type B, i.e. the speech in character, has in modern times much the same distribution as the timeless-nameless story. But in ancient literatures it is sometimes preserved in its true form.

The modern poems are mostly folk-songs. A large proportion of them are love poems. In poems which consist of monologues the speaker is more often a woman or girl than a man; in dialogues the speakers are usually a youth and a girl. This class of poetry is very widespread, and has given birth to an immense amount of popular

---

[1] In Polynesia the same stories are often told both of well-known characters—men or gods—and of nameless persons; and the question arises whether the names have been forgotten in the latter case, or whether they are secondary in the former (cf. p. 343). In Europe the occurrence of a place-name in a story may sometimes give a clue to its origin; but these also are doubtless frequently due to secondary localisation.

poetry in recent times; but true folk-songs are not limited to love poetry.

Poetry of this kind seems to be best represented in Russia (cf. Vol. II, p. 223 ff.; cf. p. 215), where the form and diction hardly differ from those of heroic poems of the same type. The corresponding poetry of Yugoslavia (*ib*. p. 402 ff.) seems to be of a less ambitious character; and on the coast it is sometimes more sophisticated. Indeed the earliest poem, 'Majka Margarita', which dates from c. 1600, is apparently in the nature of a parody on effusions of this kind.

In (international) ballad poetry, as represented in this country, Type B is not rare, though much less common than narrative. Dialogue poems are more frequent than monologues, and tragedy than the love motif, though women are usually prominent. As examples we may cite 'Lord Randal', 'Edward' and 'The Maid freed from the Gallows'—Nos. 12, 13 and 95 in Child's collection. Here also we may refer to dialogue ballads, the point of which lies in answering riddles, or similar contests. Instances occur in the first three ballads in the same collection. It may be observed that two of the three are concerned with proposals of marriage—for which close analogies are to be found in Russian folk-songs (cf. Vol. II, p. 211 f.).

With these last poems we may compare the early Norse Svipdagsmál (Fjölsvinnsmál), the greater part of which consists of a contest of wisdom in the prosecution of a love-suit (cf. Vol. I, p. 432). The theme of this poem is preserved in certain Danish and Swedish ballads; but the speech-poem has been converted into a narrative of adventure, and the 'wisdom' element has almost disappeared (cf. p. 683 above). The case is of special interest as illustrating the contrast between ancient and medieval literary tradition, though the actual difference in date between the Norse poem and the ballads, both Scandinavian and English, may not be very great.

The English poems discussed in Vol. I, p. 423 ff. stand out above all other ancient speech poems of this category. They are obviously not folk-songs, but studied and careful compositions. Two of them are concerned with love affairs, but the others have different interests; and most of the speakers are men. Perhaps the nearest approach to these is a poem in the Rgveda (x. 159), in which a wife triumphant over her rivals expresses her feelings (cf. Vol. II, p. 562). But most of the Vedic poems noticed in connection with this seem properly to be spells; and such an interpretation is not impossible here. The type is known also in Hebrew poetry (*ib*. p. 744). We may note especially the Song of

Songs, which seems to be a collection of love songs in dialogue form.

There can be little doubt that most of the poems of this type, whether folk-songs or poems which have retained an individuality of their own, are derived from personal poetry (Type E). Some of the poems we have noticed may have been composed as personal poems—concerned with the feelings and experiences of the authors themselves—by men or women whose personality has been forgotten. And many others have doubtless been composed on the model of such poems. But this explanation will hardly hold good for all the cases noticed above. In particular the Svipdagsmál and the riddle ballads belong to a different literary tradition, which is in reality didactic, though their form is that of Type B. The model which they follow is that of the contest in 'wisdom', which will require notice in Ch. x.

Didactic literature (Type C) relating to nameless individuals is widespread, though apparently not very common. Strictly we ought perhaps to include here the speech poems we have just mentioned. Apart from these the material consists of narratives. Folk-tales and narratives of similar character often contain a didactic element. Sometimes this is essential; the story itself seems to have been composed for a didactic—explanatory or moral—purpose (cf. p. 784). Often, however, it is an obvious addition—a casual remark added for the purpose of explaining a characteristic of something which has been mentioned, usually an animal or inanimate object.

As an instance of the former class we may cite the Hebrew story of the Fall, the original object of which was perhaps to explain the enmity between mankind and snakes (cf. Vol. II, p. 709f.). Sometimes, however, nameless stories of this type[1] are conscious fictions, invented for the purpose of inculcating a moral. As an example we may cite the prophet Nathan's story (II Sam. xii. 1 ff.) of the rich man who robbed the poor man of his only lamb (cf. Vol. II, p. 742). Some of the stories from the Mahābhārata cited ib. 568 f. may be of similar origin. In such cases again illustrations taken from animal life are of frequent occurrence.

[1] In non-didactic narrative (Type A) we think that conscious fiction is much less frequent. Its existence may be inferred from the false account of himself given by Odysseus in *Od.* xxiv. 303 ff., where he describes himself probably as 'son of Unsparing, son of Very Wealthy, from Silvertown'—and indeed fiction of other kinds is employed very freely in the Odyssey—but the invention of complete stories, with all their characters, for the purpose of entertainment, seems to belong to a more sophisticated age; cf. Vol. I, p. 444.

Timeless-nameless poetry of celebration (Type D) is extremely widespread, especially in connection with marriages and funerals. It is usually, if not always, of a conventional and ritual character. Very little has been preserved in ancient records, except in India; but we doubt if it is legitimate to infer from this that such poetry was not in use. We suspect that the silence of the records is to be explained in the same way as in narratives; this class of literature relates primarily to unimportant people. Such poetry had little chance of being preserved, except in a priestly tradition like the Indian, where more importance was attached to the ritual itself than to the persons for whom it was employed.

First we will take elegies or dirges. For these we have found by far the largest amount of material in Russia; cf. Vol. II, p. 229ff., where a number of examples are quoted. The diction is that of heroic poetry, exalted, but highly conventional. The speaker seems usually to be a woman—the widow, mother, daughter or cousin of the deceased—and the poems are largely occupied with her own destitute situation and feelings. Yugoslav dirges are somewhat similar (*ib.* p. 406), though in general the diction seems to be less ambitious.

The only English dirge[1] which has been preserved, so far as we know, dates from the seventeenth century, and is of a different character from these. It is concerned, not with the feelings of the relatives, but with the experiences through which the soul of the deceased is to pass. The ideas are by no means wholly Christian; he will have to traverse 'Whinny-muir' and the 'Brigg o' Dread', before he comes to Purgatory Fire. It is interesting to note that the dirge is said to be sung by women.

We have no doubt that dirges are in use among most of the modern peoples whose literatures have been discussed in this volume. For our purpose it is necessary of course to distinguish two classes of dirges— one heroic, for princes and heroes, whose 'glories' are celebrated, more or less specifically, the other of a general character, for undistinguished persons. The former are more likely to be recorded, just as we find in ancient Europe; but we are concerned here only with the latter. For illustrations we may probably refer to the elegy for a girl in Nyasaland quoted on p. 581 and to Wyatt Gill's very brief account of funeral ceremonies in Mangaia, quoted on p. 349 f.

The Vedic funeral hymns or dirges were noticed briefly in Vol. II, p. 564f. Like the English dirge mentioned above, they are usually more

---

[1] Recorded by Aubrey, *Remaines of Gentilisme*, etc., p. 31 f.; cf. Scott, *Minstrelsy of the Scottish Border*, p. 401.

concerned with the soul of the deceased than with the feelings of the
relatives. Much is said about Yama and the 'Fathers'. One poem
(Rgv. x. 18), however, gives a somewhat detailed account of the
funeral; and a considerable part of it is addressed to the widow and the
other mourners. It may be observed that all the Vedic dirges belong to
our present (nameless) category, though it is clear from Gandhārī's
elegy in the Mahābhārata (xɪ. xviff.) that the heroic (specific) variety
was also known in ancient India (cf. Vol. ɪɪ, p. 482). In this last case the
elegy is sung or recited by a queen for her sons; in the Vedic examples
the singers were presumably priests.

Poetry connected with marriages likewise seems to be more fully
represented in Russia than elsewhere. Russian peasant marriages have
an elaborate and complicated ceremonial, and there are appropriate songs
to be sung at each stage in the proceedings—the match-making, the
betrothal, etc.—by all the various persons concerned in the transaction.
Quotations from such poems are given in Vol. ɪɪ, p. 232ff. As in the
elegies, the diction is conventional and highly formal; and some of the
traditional expressions employed seem absurdly inappropriate to the
circumstances of the very poor people by whom they are now used.
Somewhat similar marriage poetry is found among the Tatars and the
Yugoslavs and other Slavonic peoples, though perhaps not quite so
elaborate.

We do not know whether marriage poetry of this kind is current in
modern Africa and Polynesia. Marriage poetry is found in both areas;
but the references we have met with are to the marriages of chiefs, and
the songs sung are of a 'specific' character—panegyrics on the bridegroom or his family. Very little material seems to be preserved in
ancient literatures. For the Indian evidence (from the Atharvaveda) we
may refer to Vol. ɪɪ, p. 567. In Hebrew one marriage hymn (Ps. xlv)
has survived; but it would seem to have been composed for the marriage
of some king. The Song of Songs may also be mentioned again here
(cf. p. 779 f.).

A number of Vedic poems, especially in the Atharvaveda, are concerned with social ritual relating to other ceremonies, e.g. the blessing
of a child, the 'coming of age' of a youth, the opening of a new house
(cf. Vol. ɪɪ, p. 566f.). For the last, which is specially interesting,
analogies are to be found elsewhere, e.g. in Polynesia. All these poems,
like those relating to marriages and funerals, contain a large religious
or mantic element (prayer or spell). They are doubtless of priestly
origin, and intended in the main for recitation by priests. It is to this

that we owe their preservation; for the Vedas are ecclesiastical literature. Here also we may refer to poems connected with the proclamation of a new king, which are found both in the Rgveda and in the Atharvaveda (*ib.* p. 565 f.). With these may be compared the early Irish 'Instructions' to kings (Vol. 1, p. 393 ff.), which likewise seem to be connected with the assumption of office, though they are of a hortatory character. Unlike the Indian poems, these latter always have names attached to them, sometimes those of famous heroes. Yet they are of pronouncedly non-heroic character.

Lastly, mention may be made of 'occupation' songs, though these can hardly be described as poetry of celebration. They are found among various peoples in connection with work which involves motion of a rhythmical nature. We may instance boatmen's songs, especially the paddling songs current among the Bantu peoples (cf. p. 583 f. above) and the hauling songs found in New Zealand (p. 350f.) and in south Russia. An interesting song or short poem connected with the pressing of soma is preserved in the Rgveda, ix. 112 (cf. Vol. ii, p. 550f.). Grinding songs and weaving songs are probably widespread; but in the literatures we have examined they are represented only by adaptations, like the Norse Grottasöngr and Darraðarljóð, or even by fragments of such adaptations (cf. Vol. i, pp. 346f., 429, 448f.). The Norse adaptations are in the form of spells—which suggests that the original occupation songs may have had the same character. On the other hand, the Greek children's begging songs noticed *ib.* p. 428f. seem to be relics of true celebration poetry, connected with popular festivals.

It will be seen that the literature discussed in this chapter is in the main of plebeian provenance. Where this is not the case, apart from the Anglo-Saxon poems noticed on p. 779, its associations are usually, if not always, 'non-heroic'—by which we mean that it is the work of seers or priests, as in some of the examples cited under Types C and D. Heroic associations are almost negligible, except that its influence has sometimes affected heroic stories, as in Beowulf and the Odyssey. On the other hand, it would doubtless be erroneous to assume that this literature was exclusively a product of peasant society in its ultimate origins. Much of it is certainly 'vagrant'—carried from one country to another by travellers or traders. But both the vagrant and the native elements are probably derived ultimately to a large extent from heroic and mantic circles. Even where it is best preserved, as in Russia, traces of the former may be seen in the diction of the poetry.

Much of the literature is clearly the work of women. This is true especially of speech poems (cf. p. 778 f.) and elegies; but it is likely that in narratives (of Type A) also the process of transition from one social class to another took place largely through women.

Didactic saga (Type C) of this kind has been cultivated by seers and sages in many lands. It would even seem that some folk-tales have such an origin and that they have circulated among 'the wise' of distant countries. We may refer especially to the story of the 'Wise Counsels', which is attached to the names Fithal in Ireland and Höfundr in the North (cf. Vol. 1, p. 396). An indication as to how such literature may travel is to be found in the interesting story of Saruti (pp. 604, 612 above).

The Anglo-Saxon poems noticed on p. 779 stand somewhat apart from the rest of the literature treated in this chapter. It is true that they have much in common with nameless poems of Type B in Russian and other literatures; but they differ from these in the fact that, except in the 'Seafarer', their affinities are heroic and their milieu aristocratic. For such studies of emotion or emotional situation other literatures choose scenes from heroic stories, as in the Norse poems Guðrúnarkviða I and Guðrúnarhvöt, and in certain Welsh poems (cf. p. 718 f.). An equally close analogy is to be found in the Russian 'Laments' of princesses (Vol. 11, p. 160 ff.), some of which are contemporary. The peculiarity of the English poems is that they have chosen a form derived from popular literature for the presentation of such studies. Their literary connections and approximate date are indicated by the fact that one such study occurs in Beowulf (Vol. 1, p. 423), and also by their obviously close relationship with descriptive poetry in Beowulf and elsewhere (*ib.* pp. 408 f., 404). It would seem that during a certain period, perhaps the seventh and eighth centuries, English (secular) poetry, including heroic poetry, was deeply influenced by a tendency to generalisation and general reflection, which found expression in a widespread use of gnomes and typical descriptions. The adoption of the nameless form by poetry of Type B with heroic affinities was perhaps connected with this tendency. The phase has something in common with the post-heroic poetry of Greece. It is as if the latest Homeric poets had come under the influence of Solon, though without losing their aristocratic connections. But this explanation is not wholly satisfactory.[1]

---

[1] The 'Wanderer' group, as also the 'Ruin etc.' (Vol. 1, pp. 404, 408), seem to have an underlying affinity—in motifs, not in form—with poems attributed to Llywarch Hen (cf. p. 718 above). But the question is too complex for discussion here.

CHAPTER VI

THEOLOGICAL LITERATURE

THEOLOGICAL literature consists mainly of invocations addressed to deities (Type D) and didactic matter of various kinds, intended for the instruction of those who worshipped or recognised the deities (Type C). In the former the elements of praise and prayer are commonly combined. The prevailing form in the literatures which have come within our survey is poetry. Most of the compositions may be described as hymns.

There is evidence enough to show that invocation-poetry is very widely distributed; but it has been very unevenly preserved. Among peoples who have been converted to Christianity or Islam it has of course been displaced by book-literature of foreign origin; and very few traces of it are usually to be found. In Norse we have only one or two fragments, while in English and Irish survivals of such poetry may perhaps be traced in a few spells. In ancient Greek the remains are more numerous, though largely fragmentary. On the other hand India possesses a very large amount of hymn poetry, dating from the earliest times, while a good deal has also been preserved in Hebrew. Among modern peoples a considerable amount of such poetry has been collected from the Tatars, and much more in Polynesia. But we have seen nothing from the Bantu, and have not met with much among the other (heathen) peoples of Africa, though examples from the Galla and Yoruba have been cited in this volume. This may be due in some cases to defects in our information. Prayers to deities and ancestral spirits are certainly in use among many peoples; but we do not think that hymn poetry can be much developed.

Narrative elements occur from time to time in hymn poetry, especially perhaps in the Vedic and the Homeric Hymns. But apart from hymns we find narrative poetry relating to deities in Norse, Greek and Sanskrit (the Mahābhārata), and among the Tatars. Saga relating to deities is found in Irish, Norse, Polynesian, Luganda, and—to a limited extent— in Hebrew; but not much scope is allowed for narrative in a mono-theistic religion. Both the poems and the sagas usually belong to Type C, rather than Type A, i.e. they are intended for instruction rather than entertainment. But there are a good many exceptions; in Norse, Irish,

Greek and Polynesian, and among the Tatars, we find a number of stories in which no didactic element is evident. In early Greece, as we have seen, stories of deities formed part of the répertoire of heroic minstrels.

Two varieties of these stories may be distinguished. In one the scene is laid in the world of the gods, all the characters are deities, and the interest is—usually at least—centred in their relations with one another. In the other a deity, or perhaps more than one deity, comes to visit men; in such cases the interest is usually centred in the human characters. Both these varieties are found in almost all the literatures mentioned above, but perhaps only the latter variety in Hebrew. A third variety, in which a man or woman visits the world of the gods, is represented in many Tatar stories,[1] as well as in those of the Sea Dyaks and the Polynesians. This is found also in Irish; but elsewhere it seems to occur only in dreams and visions. Here again the primary interest usually lies in the human beings concerned. In all these varieties elements of various origin are doubtless to be traced. Some stories seem to be derived from traditional myths of unknown antiquity, others from the mantic experiences of seers; in others again, especially perhaps in those of the first variety, allowance is to be made for free use of the imaginative faculty. It is to this variety perhaps that stories of entertainment (Type A) chiefly belong. But there are a good number of stories, concerned with visits both of deities to men and of men to deities, in which no didactic purpose is obvious.

Speech poetry attributed to deities is also widespread. Examples have been cited from Norse, Welsh, Irish, Hebrew and probably Greek literature, from the Rgveda and from Polynesia. Prose speeches are frequent in Hebrew, but very rare elsewhere. Nearly all the instances we have met with may be regarded as in some sense didactic, and belong therefore properly to Type C (CB), rather than to Type B. The subject of the didacticism varies greatly; it may be religious, moral, antiquarian, or merely rhetorical. Among poems of this class we ought also to include prophecies which claim to be utterances of deities; these also commonly contain a didactic element. Poems in which no didactic or mantic elements are traceable, i.e. poems which belong strictly to

---

[1] These stories frequently deal with visits to the supernatural rulers of the underworld (cf. p. 92 ff.). Such stories have of course much in common with the visits to the home of the dead, noticed in Ch. III (p. 745). But we are speaking now of stories in which the persons visited are divine. In Norse stories, just as in ancient Mesopotamia, gods sometimes visit the underworld.

Type B, appear to be quite rare, though we have noted a few instances above.[1]

The origin of these speech poems, or at least the monologues, is probably to be sought partly in oracles and mantic utterances by seers. Down to quite late times, at least in Greece and Palestine, such prophecies seem to have been widely accepted as utterances of deities, though we need not doubt that—somewhat inconsistently—the form was recognised as a literary convention. Even impromptu mantic utterances must be taken into account; we may instance the discussion (quoted on p. 444 f.) between a prophetess of Pele and the missionary W. Ellis—which is of the utmost importance for the understanding of mantic literature. It hardly needs pointing out that this might well have formed the basis of a (dialogue) speech poem of Type B (CB). Apart from such mantic usage, speech poems here may have the same origins as in other categories (cf. p. 717 f.)—in which doubtless much is due to the imaginative faculty. Wisdom contests between deities or between a deity and some other supernatural being, like the Vafþrúðnismál, may be regarded as reflections of debates between (human) seers or sages. The object of the Skírnismál is apparently to illustrate the potency of a spell. But there are a certain number of poems, like the dialogue between Yama and Yamī (Rgv. x. 10) and the Lokasenna, which we find it difficult to account for.

Apart from consideration of the formal types, it is not easy to discuss the history of theological literature without entering into problems of mythology, which lie of course beyond the scope of our survey. The origin of religious cults cannot be wholly ignored; but we shall deal with the subject as briefly as possible.

Among the literatures which we have discussed that of ancient India is perhaps the one which throws most light upon this subject. The origin of some of the chief deities celebrated in the Rgveda is obvious enough. In Agni ('Fire') and Soma (or Indu) the process of personification is far from complete. The poets almost always have in mind real fire—commonly the sacrificial fire—or the exhilarating juice of the soma plant;[2] and hymns to either of these deities are often closely akin to spells, for the kindling of fire or the purification of the juice

[1] The comic poem about Vrshākapi (Rgv. x. 86) can hardly be regarded as a 'theological' dialogue. It would seem to be a satire on some prince, to whom the name 'Indra' is applied.

[2] We may compare the Samoan and Hawaiian hymns to Kava noticed on p. 349.

respectively. The nature of Ushas ('Dawn') and Sūrya ('Sun') is just as apparent, though the hymns to these deities have nothing in common with spells. On the other hand, there are a number of gods, such as Varuna and Vishnu, whose origin is much debated.

In the northern Pacific we find a deity called Pele (Pere), who is clearly a personification (and in fact an incarnation) of volcanoes. In Hawaii she is regularly identified with the volcano Kilauea (cf. p. 324). Yet throughout the Polynesian area there are many other deities, such as Tane and Rongo, whose origin is quite uncertain.

In Europe the origin of deities is seldom so clear as in the cases noted above. Dionysos may have been 'Wine' originally; but, unlike Soma, he has become completely anthropomorphic. And most of the others show even less to betray their origin. Everywhere, however, we find a god who is connected with thunder or the thunderbolt. Sometimes he is called 'Thunder', as in the Teutonic languages. Yet everywhere he seems to have become more or less fully anthropomorphic, and has assumed what we may call 'human' features—of age, position, character, etc.—which differ greatly between one people and another. In Iceland Thor's connection with thunder was quite forgotten, and even in early Norse literature it is very seldom to be traced, though it was clearly remembered in Sweden. Zeus also has become fully anthropomorphic; but he is a person of quite a different kind from Thor.

Some deities are clearly of local origin. Among these we may note in particular those who bear the names of rivers. Several examples of such goddesses occur in Ireland, and they seem to have been known in Britain. In early India, Sarasvatī (cf. Vol. II, pp. 504, 531) became the goddess of wisdom and eloquence, and one of the most important deities. In Yugoslavia each Vila has her own mountain; but in the past they were sometimes apparently attached to rivers (ib. pp. 344f., 390).

Sometimes again we meet with family deities. Such was evidently the case with Thorgerðr Hölgabrúðr, who was not recognised as a member of the Norse pantheon. Her cult would seem to have been introduced from the far north by the family of the earls of Hlaðir. The cult of Frey was widespread, but was connected more especially with the ancient royal family of the Swedes, who claimed descent from him. In this and similar cases it may be suspected that the deity originated in a divine king, who was perhaps not so much an individual as a composite picture of the kings of the past. But this question cannot be discussed here.

More important for our purpose are the deities of different social classes or castes. In Indian literature it is possible to some extent to observe the evolution of such cults. In the Rgveda Indra is the chief deity. He is the wielder of the thunderbolt, but is most frequently invoked as the giver of victory. In heroic (Kshatriya) poetry, as preserved in the Mahābhārata, he seems to preserve his position; he is also said to have a kind of Paradise, to which slain princes pass at their death. But in the non-heroic (Brahmanic) portions of the Mahābhārata he is often treated with aversion and contempt. He is regarded as a Kshatriya and inferior to Brahmans. His slaying of the demon Vrtra, the exploit for which he is most celebrated in the Rgveda, has now come to be a case of Brahmanicide, the worst of crimes. In his place the Brahmans have brought into being a new chief deity Brahmā (nom. sing.) out of the term *brahma*, 'prayer' or 'spell', or rather the priestly or mantic power expressed in prayers and spells. Tentative beginnings of this theological revolution may be traced in the Rgveda itself, where we sometimes find priestly gods, Brhaspati or Prajāpati, later often identified with Brahmā. For further details we may refer back to Vol. II, p. 583 ff.[1]

In early Norse literature we again find different deities worshipped by different classes; but the line of division is not the same. Thor was the deity whose worship was most widespread in the North, especially among the (non-royal) landowners; but there is very little evidence for his worship by the princely class.[2] Othin was the deity chiefly worshipped by the latter; and there is little satisfactory evidence that he was worshipped by any lower class, though he figures much in poetry. In mythology he is the chief of the gods. Like Indra he is the giver of victory, and has a Paradise for slain warriors (Valhöll). But the remarkable fact is that, in spite of all this, Othin is not a heroic but a mantic character: he carries out his purposes not by valour, but by spells and mantic wisdom. In position, as chief of the gods, he corresponds to Indra and Zeus; but in character he is wholly different from either of them. Whatever may be his origin, he is a typical seer or wizard.

[1] In other passages of the Mahābhārata the chief deity appears to be Vishnu or Çiva; but these need not be discussed here. It may be observed that Indra is helpless against Çiva.
[2] The evidence of the sagas is borne out by that of personal names. Names compounded with *Thór-* are very rare in royal families, but extremely numerous in other classes of the population.

Other instances might be cited of differences of cult as between different classes of a population. We may refer to Herodotos v. 7, where, it is stated that the kings of the Thracians worship Hermes above all other gods, but the rest of the Thracians worship only Ares, Dionysos and Artemis. The name 'Hermes' suggests a deity of the same kind as Woden (Othin), who is commonly translated by 'Mercurius'.

In New Zealand the same deities were recognised as elsewhere in Polynesia. But the Tohungas, or priestly class, of New Zealand, the Marquesas, and the Paumotus cultivated a loftier form of religion, centred in a god called Io (cf. p. 308 f.). His name was apparently not unknown in the Central Pacific also (e.g. in Mangaia). The evidence, so far as it can be ascertained from the teaching of the Maori Tohungas and the recently published Paumotu chants, suggests a division between cults on the same lines—in principle—as in India.

It would seem then that sometimes we find different deities worshipped by the princely class and inferior classes, while sometimes the division lies between the princely class or lay society in general and a priestly or mantic class. One could doubtless point out instances of other cults characteristic of special classes, especially perhaps those of agricultural deities; but the distinctions noted above are probably the most important for the study of literature.

The difference between these two lines of division is perhaps not quite so fundamental as might appear at first sight. It is evident from the early anonymous (Edda) poetry that the cult of Othin must have been shared by the mantic class with the princely. We may note especially the latter part of the Hávamál (from st. 111 onwards), which is a typical collection of mantic lore. Othin is the speaker; but here he appears in his proper milieu as a seer and wizard. The natural inference is that the mantic class have imposed their own deity—a divine reflex of themselves—upon the princely class. Among the latter he has assumed the attributes of kingship, without losing his original character. It is another case of the encroachment of the mantic element upon the heroic. But the encroachment must have taken place in ancient times; for the god seems to have had the same composite personality among the other Teutonic peoples (cf. Vol. I, pp. 254, 640)—indeed perhaps even in Tacitus' time.

For such an encroachment analogies are not wanting elsewhere. The Thracian parallel has already been mentioned; but unfortunately the evidence available here is all of a legendary character, though it points clearly enough to the dominance of mantic elements.[1] Historical evidence, however, is available for Iran, where the cult of Ahura Mazda was the religion of the Persian court from the time of Dareios I (521–485). There can be no doubt that this cult had superseded a polytheistic system, more or less identical with that of Vedic India. The revolution in thought was clearly of mantic origin and comparable with that which we find in India after the Vedic period, though it was more of an ethical than purely intellectual character. Indra was here degraded to a subordinate position in the evil hierarchy. It is still matter of dispute when this revolution took place, and whether it was the work of one prophet (Zoroaster) or a gradual process, as in India. But some time seems to have elapsed, whether generations or centuries, before the new religion became fully established.

A similar revolution in theology would seem to have taken place in Israel in earlier times. Jehovah was evidently recognised as the national deity before—apparently long before—the establishment of kingship. Other deities also were worshipped; but they were regarded as alien and condemned by Jehovah. Some of them, however, had long been recognised in the land; the view that they were foreign must be taken in connection with the tradition that the Israelites themselves were immigrants. If the tradition of a migration en masse is mistaken, the worship of these other deities may sometimes be attributed to conservatism—as a survival from the time when Semitic polytheism prevailed. We may refer e.g. to the story of Gideon, where Baal is worshipped by one of the leading families. On the other hand, there is reason for suspecting that the origin, or at least the generalisation, of the cult of Jehovah is due to seers. The story of Moses points in this direction; and so do various features which the cult has in common with that of Ahura Mazda. Like the latter it seems to represent a revolution in theology, rather than a departmental outgrowth. It is exclusive, and recognises no other deities; it has no sexual side; and its appeal is wholly intellectual and mantic. The deity may have been known in earlier times;[2] but if the cult had been widespread, we should expect to find some evidence for it in the Amarna letters or other records of the

[1] We may refer to the stories of Salmoxis, Dicineus, etc., and to Vol. I, pp. 611, 643 ff.

[2] A monument to El, with likeness of the deity, has recently been found at Ras Shamra, in a stratum dating from early in the twelfth century; cf. Schaeffer, *Illustr. Lond. News*, 20 Febr. 1937 (p. 293 f.), where the monument is figured. The same deity is mentioned in the poetic texts found in an earlier stratum at the same site (cf. Vol. II, p. 712).

Eighteenth dynasty. Palestine was by no means an unknown land in that period.

From the instances given above it will be seen that cults of mantic origin are sometimes grafted upon existing systems of theology; sometimes they assume an exclusive character, and eliminate all other cults. In the former case the deity is a member of a society, and consequently has a more human personality, though he is a seer; in the latter, where personal associations are wanting, his associations must be with abstract ideas and principles.

There is indeed a third variety of deity, in which abstract ideas themselves are personified, e.g. Vár ('Covenant'), Themis ('Law'). Several such personifications occur in the 'Works and Days', especially Horcos ('Oath') and Dice ('Justice'), and in later Greek records they become common. We may compare also the attendant spirits of Ahura Mazda, e.g. Aša ('Right'), Vohu Manah ('Good Thought'). These abstract deities are important in the history of thought; but the personification seems never to go very far, nor is the worship paid to them (as personalities) very widespread. It will be seen that Brahmā approximates very nearly to this class; and in his case also personification is limited.

Mantic deities of a personal character who are incorporated in pantheons are not necessarily unassociated with abstract ideas and principles. In the latter part[1] of the Hávamál Othin gives utterance to a series of precepts, which contain ethical elements, though caution and prudence are the predominant features. So also in the oracles of Apollo, the chief mantic deity of the Greeks, ethical elements are not wanting. But in general the attitude of such mantic deities, like that of other deities, is governed by their relations to devotees or favourites. A man wants to have a deity as his 'friend', to help him in his difficulties and undertakings. One man may seek one deity, another man another deity, as in the Iliad and the story of the battle at Upsala (c. 990) between Eric the Victorious and Styrbjörn. Often the relationship is inherited. Sometimes however a supreme deity who is not necessarily a mantic deity can stand for ideas and principles, without regard to persons. In the 'Works and Days' Zeus is represented in this aspect, which is not far removed from monotheism.

On the whole the difference—in polytheistic communities—between

---

[1] The first part (down to st. 110) contains much cynical humour, which must not be taken too seriously; cf. Vol. I, p. 382 ff. In st. 110 Othin gloats over his violated oath.

mantic and non-mantic deities is more noticeable in mythology than in actual cult. Deities who are not (primarily) mantic may be consulted at sacrifices, or even have regular oracles. Thus in the Eyrbyggja Saga, cap. 4, Thórolfr sacrifices to his friend Thor, and consults him as to which of two courses he ought to follow. The circumstances are similar to those of I Sam. xxiii. 9 ff. Zeus also had oracles, at which the future could be ascertained, though they were not so numerous as those of Apollo. The explanation is probably to be found in the fact that the personnel of important sanctuaries commonly included seers or seeresses, or at least persons who were credited with mantic power. The oracle of Zeus at Olympia was under the care of the Iamidai, the most famous mantic family in Greece. They claimed descent from Apollo.

We have spoken above of deities individually and in their relations with men. But a large proportion of the theological literature which we have reviewed relates to deities themselves, in their relations with one another and with other supernatural beings. Literature of this kind is widespread, if not universal, among polytheistic peoples. Not much, however, seems to have been obtained from Africa, or even from Polynesia; and it is not so well represented as one might have expected in the earliest (Vedic) period in India.

In the ancient literatures of Europe and Asia the deities form a community, which consists, wholly or mainly, of one family. Sometimes we hear of more than one divine community. But in such cases the interest is centred in one of them; the others—e.g. the Norse Vanir or the Side of Munster—receive notice only incidentally, and through their relations with the first community. Usually also we hear of other supernatural communities, who are not regarded as deities. The most frequent and important of these is of the type best represented by the Norse Jötnar (commonly translated by 'Giants'). They are less civilised than the gods, and often include monstrous and theriomorphic beings. Their relations with the gods are usually hostile, but not invariably so; their women are not unfrequently married to gods.

The divine community everywhere seems to be modelled upon a human family. In the ancient literatures of Europe, which supply our best material for this subject, there is in general a close resemblance between these communities; similar, though not identical, types of humanity occur more or less everywhere. As there is a considerable variety of these, it may be well first to note the chief forms of human life which are not represented.

Children are virtually ignored;[1] indeed they are less in evidence even than in heroic stories. In contrast with ancient Egypt, mothers appear only in relation to grown up sons or (less frequently) daughters. In fact only two periods of life seem to be represented in the women—youth and (fairly advanced) middle age. The ages of the men, however, show more variety.

More striking perhaps is the—practically complete—absence of 'heroic' characters. There is a strong man, usually middle-aged or older, who is derived from the thunder-god, and who destroys Jötnar or demons with the thunderbolt or some rather primitive weapon in place thereof; but this person, who is sometimes the head of the community, has nothing in common with 'heroes' of heroic stories. The young gods are almost always either mantic or amorous. Ares is an isolated example of a warrior; but he is an unsympathetic character and unsuccessful. Lug wins a battle by skill; but he is primarily mantic. The chief god, who is either elderly or old, is sometimes, but not always, mantic; but he is always extremely amorous, with love adventures in all directions.

The women are likewise without 'heroic' characteristics. The young goddesses, like the young gods, are always either mantic or amorous. The wife of the chief god is generally not on the best of terms with her husband, though their disagreements never lead to a deadly quarrel.

There is no doubt that deities individually were often regarded with great devotion by their worshippers. But it must be confessed that the divine communities, as they appear in the stories, present rather unattractive pictures. Thor and the Dagda are enormously heavy eaters, Frey and Aengus completely helpless through love-sickness; and most of the deities are quarrelsome and faithless in their love affairs, and inclined to be tricky and dishonourable in other respects. As a rule they are far inferior to the men and women of heroic stories.

We have seen that stories of the gods were included in the répertoire of Greek heroic poets; and there is no reason for supposing that this was a custom peculiar to Greece. At all events a good number of the Norse and Irish stories are obviously intended for entertainment. This may go some way, though not very far, towards explaining the characterisation of the divine community. The gods are often portrayed in a lifelike manner—sometimes more lifelike and intimate than the pictures we get of heroic society; but the treatment is different. The

[1] We mean children represented (and acting) as children. But in any case the Hom. Hymn to Hermes must be regarded as one of the rare examples.

same respect is not shown to them as to heroic characters; not seldom they supply a comic element. At times it may very well have been safer to make fun of gods than of princes. But why should a poet wish to represent them as untrustworthy, greedy and contemptible? We may contrast the representation of the gods in Greek sculpture, though this belongs to a later and more advanced period. It would seem that the material at the disposal of the poets was not promising—that their knowledge of the deities was accompanied by characteristics and associations which called forth no great respect.

Herodotos (II. 53) thought that the Greek pantheon was the work of Hesiod and Homer, though he gives this as his own private opinion. The context shows that he was thinking primarily of 'theogonies' and poetry dealing with the relationships of the gods; and we do not doubt that he was right in believing that such speculations were largely the work of poets. But we suspect that he was much mistaken in his estimate of their antiquity and in supposing that they were the product of one generation. We know from a letter of Bishop Daniel of Winchester (Vol. I, p. 325 f.) that the learned heathen, English or German, of his time were much occupied with very similar speculations. We know also from Tacitus (*Germ.* 2) that these speculations were cultivated seven centuries earlier, that even then they formed the subject of ancient poems, and that owing to their antiquity they showed much variation. It may be suspected then that Hesiod was working over themes which had occupied his predecessors for perhaps a thousand years or more.

So also with stories of the adventures and experiences of the gods. We do not doubt that great latitude was allowed for fiction in such themes—greater than in heroic stories, at least such as related to comparatively recent times, and perhaps greater than in any other category. But in principle the poets were subject to the same limitations as heroic poets; they could not come into conflict, at least not into direct conflict, with what was generally accepted. They were governed and checked by traditions inherited from the past. They could not make a heroic warrior of Apollo or Frey.

It may be noticed that in all the divine communities which we have discussed above the life depicted is on a small scale. There are no royal courts, with hosts of servants and warriors. Othin is sometimes said to have a host of warriors; but these play no part in the stories. He has seldom more than one or two companions in his adventures; and the same is true of Thor, and likewise in general of the Greek gods. The community indeed seems to consist of little more than one family, with hardly any servants except one or two girls, whom they employ as messengers. The Greek deities have a smith, who is a member of the family, and the same is true of the Irish deities; but the Norse deities, though they are said to have a smithy, are usually dependent upon the dwarfs for weapons or treasures. The Norse deities are constantly getting into difficulties, and have to resort to an entirely untrustworthy character—it is not clear whether he is a servant—to help them out. When they want to have their home fortified, they have to call in a Jötunn, who drives a hard bargain with them. Indeed both the Norse and the Irish deities seem to lead a rather precarious existence.

Not seldom we meet with crude and brutal features, which may probably be regarded as an inheritance from less civilised times. But even when these are lacking, the picture presented is usually that of a backward and not too wealthy society. Its prototypes are clearly to be sought, not in kings' courts, but in those circles which were most intimately concerned with theological lore, i.e. in priestly circles. And here we are not to think of Delphoi in the time of its wealth and splendour, nor of any temples in cities, or attached to kings' courts. The origin of the divine communities is rather to be sought in sanctuaries of a less advanced type—possibly in such as we hear of at the homes of landowners in the North,[1] in which they themselves acted as priests, or perhaps rather in secluded sanctuaries, in woods or upon mountains, which may originally have been the homes of seers. In view of the prominence of manticism in the stories,[2] the latter would seem to be the more probable derivation.

It has been noted above that the description of Ásgarðr seems to be derived from a sanctuary. We may add here that in the Völuspá, st. 7, the gods are said to build temples and shrines, while Snorri in the Ynglinga Saga, cap. 2, says that their duties were to keep up the sacrifices and judge between men. In short they are thought of as priests. Mantic elements, however, are always in evidence. We may refer (e.g.) to the springs beneath the Ash Yggdrasill.

Ásgarðr cannot be identified with any known sanctuary in the North; very likely the picture is a composite one, with features drawn from various sanctuaries. Frey's home is at Upsala—which was his chief

---

[1] In the Viking Age many of these, at least in Iceland, were temples; but the earlier type of sanctuary was a *lundr*, or sacred grove.

[2] Even in stories relating to deities, like Frey, who are not obviously mantic. We may instance the Skírnismál (Vol. 1, p. 248), where Frey's messenger is evidently an adept.

sanctuary—and Gefjon's probably at Leire; but most of the homes of the gods bear fictitious names. On the other hand, the Irish deities are usually associated with known places, especially with the Brug na Boinne, but also with barrows in other parts of Ireland (Vol. 1, p. 255 ff.). Unfortunately we have very little information with regard to Irish sanctuaries.

Greek deities are almost always associated with known places, often with more than one, though one is generally regarded as the favourite home. At these places they had temples in historical times. Their collective home, properly one of the homes of Zeus, is on Mt Olympos, in Thessaly—which is evidently an early Aeolic conception. But we do not know whether any temple or sanctuary existed there. If so, it would seem to have been deserted before historical times.[1]

An interesting parallel for the home of the gods is to be found in Uganda (cf. p. 592 f.). The chief family of deities had sanctuaries in many parts of the land; but their home, from which they came, was in the Sese Islands, off the west coast of the Victoria Nyanza. Here the sanctuary of Mukasa, the chief god, was occupied by his medium with his household down to recent times.

Every sanctuary doubtless cherished its own traditions; but these cannot be assumed to have been of a simple and uniform character. Quite probably they included elements from different ages and different sources. As remarked above, crude and brutal features in the stories may be survivals, often misunderstood, from the far past. But above all we cannot assume that sanctuaries were isolated in their intellectual life, and uninfluenced by one another. The traditions of one sanctuary had to be known and taken account of, if not necessarily accepted, at others. Identifications or family relationships might result from such knowledge. New deities too might have to be accommodated—whether deified seers or princes, or deities introduced from other lands or districts.[2] There is indeed abundant evidence that the pantheons were not impervious to change. Thor cannot have been a son of Othin from the beginning; Njörðr has apparently changed his sex; Artemis is some-

---

[1] The mountain seems to have been little known in ancient (historical) times; but we have no records from Thessaly except inscriptions. We do not know whether the inhabitants of the mountain were Greeks.

[2] For instances of both kinds—the deification of a Swedish king named Eric, and the dedication of a temple to the alien goddesses Thorgerðr Hölgabrúðr and Irpa (cf. p. 788) in association with Thor—we may refer to Chadwick, *The Heroic Age*, pp. 255 f., 410 f. Cf. also Bede, *Hist. Eccl.* II. 15, where the East Anglian king Redwald has an altar to Christ and another to heathen deities in the same temple.

times, but not always, a twin sister of Apollo; Hera seems usually, but not everywhere, to have displaced Dione; the obscurities in our knowledge of the Irish gods—e.g. as to who was the real head of the community—may be due to inconsistencies in the pantheon itself, almost as much as to defects in our information. It would doubtless be easy everywhere to accumulate much material in support of Bishop Daniel's statements regarding the activities of the learned heathen.

It is worth remarking that the Rgveda, although it is the largest collection of theological poetry surviving from antiquity, gives us very little information about a divine community. We learn hardly anything from it as to a home or homes of the gods, or as to their home life and their relationships with one another. Moreover goddesses are not often mentioned, and very seldom in relation to gods or other goddesses. In short the humanising of the deities seems to be much less advanced than in Europe. These facts are surely to be interpreted[1] in connection with the absence of permanent sanctuaries, which is one of the most striking features of the Rgveda. The deities themselves, except perhaps Sarasvatī, seem to have practically no local associations—which may possibly be due to the fact that the Aryans had not been settled very long in the country.

On the other hand, later Sanskrit literature, especially the Mahābhārata, abounds in references to holy places (*tīrtha*), many of which are said to have been the abodes of famous seers of the past, or of incidents in their history. We have seen that the Mahābhārata is very largely occupied with stories of these seers, a few of which are summarised in Vol. II, p. 497 ff. They may fairly be said to form a new mythology; many of them indeed have a human interest, which is quite comparable with that of stories of the gods in Europe. It is worth noting therefore that nearly all these stories are related to Yudhishthira by seers in sacred forests, and many of them at the actual places where the events are said to have happened.

Parallels may be found in the stories of the Hebrew patriarchs. We are not much attracted by the theory that these persons were originally gods; but the stories have much in common with theological stories. We think they are rather to be taken in connection with the stories of seers in the Mahābhārata, many of which, fantastic as they are, certainly relate to real persons. The patriarchs are not people of exactly the same

[1] The absence (or loss) of all narrative literature from this period must of course be taken into account. But we do not think that this by itself is a sufficient explanation.

type—they are chiefs, as well as seers;[1] but the stories have the same essentially personal interest. It is incredible to us that they, any more than the Indian stories, can be products of a highly organised religious system, such as is involved in the following books of the Hexateuch, from Exodus to Joshua. We suspect that they took shape in sanctuaries, such as Beth-el, Shechem and Beer-sheba, which claimed the patriarchs as their founders.

A further analogy may be found in stories of British saints. In spite of the severe censorship to which they have been subjected by the professional hagiographers of later times, it can be seen that these stories were largely of personal interest, and not always of too serious a character. For instances we may refer to the Lives of St Cadoc and (more especially) St Kentigern (cf. Vol. I, pp. 102, 108 ff.). Many features, especially the mistakes in chronology, indicate that the stories were long preserved by oral tradition; and there can be little doubt that it was in the sanctuaries founded by the saints—say at Nantcarfan and Glasgow—that they took shape.[2]

In this connection we may refer to the Polynesian evidence. Here the pantheon is no more developed than in Vedic India; and it presents special difficulties, which have been noted above (p. 311 ff.). But we may observe that for two islands from which we have comparatively full information, New Zealand and Mangaia, the evidence comes from priests, who were accomplished narrators. The last high-priest of Rarotonga is also said to have supplied much information about his sanctuary.

The theology of the (non-Mohammedan) Tatars differs essentially from those of the other polytheistic peoples we have discussed. If the term 'pantheon' is applicable at all in this case, we must grant them two independent pantheons, one located in the heavens above, the other beneath the earth. These are said to represent the powers of light and darkness (or good and evil) respectively, and to be in constant opposition to one another. But in the oral literature which has been accessible to us the two never come into contact; the community in the heavens is concerned with life, the underground community with death (cf. p. 82). Each body consists of a chief with a number of subordinates,

---

[1] Interesting parallels may be found among the mantic chiefs of the Galla (cf. p. 567 f.). It may be observed that the homes of these chiefs seem themselves to be regarded as holy.

[2] It is to be borne in mind that our records date from five or six centuries after the times of the saints. The beginnings of such traditions may be seen in Adamnan's Life of St Columba.

both male and female. The 'pantheon' of life would seem to be derived, not from a family community, but from a kind of mantic college or society under a great seer. It is to be borne in mind that the Tatars have no permanent sanctuaries. The 'pantheon' of death, which is the more lifelike of the two, looks more like a collection of Jötnar than anything else.

There would seem to be some connection between this system and the theology of the Avesta, whether direct or through some intermediate system, such as Manichaeism. But, if this is its derivation, there has been much simplification, and the conceptions have in general been materialised.[1] On the other hand, it may be that a kernel of native mythology has been overlaid by successive waves of foreign influence from the south and south-west, and possibly also from China. At all events both Iranian and Buddhistic elements are traceable.[2]

A far closer resemblance to the theologies of ancient Europe is to be found in the early records of Mesopotamia and Egypt—to which we may now add the documents recently discovered at Ras Shamra. In all these cases we find pantheons, which consist apparently of family groups of deities; and imaginative literature seems to be very largely occupied with their adventures, experiences and quarrels. But the records present difficulties which can be faced only by specialists. We are not qualified to deal with the subject.

In conclusion the question may be raised whether the theologies of the various peoples we have discussed, including the conception of divine communities, are connected with one another. In particular it may be asked whether the rather striking general resemblance among the ancient European theologies is to be explained in this way. Such questions are of course easier asked than answered. Most of the Indo-European languages have the same word for 'god' (Sanskr. *deva*, etc.), which would seem to indicate that this conception goes back at least to the third millennium (B.C.). To the same period we may perhaps assign a personification of the sky, represented in Greek by Zeus, though in India the personification is not carried very far. Other equations on linguistic evidence are less clear. Yet in the third millennium the theologies of Egypt and Mesopotamia seem to have been more or less fully developed.

---

[1] Moral ideas are not very prominent in the literature of entertainment, which is our chief source of information; but they are emphasised in the ritual of the Altai Tatars, and also in that of the Yakut and the Buryat.

[2] One of the authors intends to deal with the subject more fully elsewhere.

Somewhat more definite evidence may perhaps be obtained from sanctuaries. Over a great part of Europe the god of the sky and thunder was associated with the oak, and had his sanctuary in an oak-grove.[1] Even more widespread was the association of a mantic goddess or goddesses with the sacred spring (cf. Vol. I, p. 648 ff.). These and other common features in the religion render it probable that the resemblances in theology were in part the outcome of resemblances in the sanctuaries. But it is not to be doubted that the process of personification was furthered by the influence of more advanced theologies in the south and east, or that deities were at times introduced (ready-made) from those quarters.

It is of course difficult and unsatisfactory to treat a subject of this kind, however briefly, without reference to cults and rites, which lie properly outside the scope of our work. But, viewing the subject, as we do, from the side of literature rather than religion, the general principle to which we would call attention is the widespread distribution of certain phases or currents of theological thought. Divine communities and theogonies seem to be the outcome of one such phase—in which the paramount influence is, we suspect, that of the sanctuary and the social life connected therewith. On the other hand, the rise of systems which are more or less monotheistic is to be attributed to a phase in which the governing force is the personality of the seer. The dominance of one or other of these phases may perhaps be compared with Heroic or Non-heroic Ages. But they are often found side by side; and their relations are sometimes hostile.

[1] Cf. Chadwick, *J.R.A.I.* xxx, 22 ff.

CHAPTER VII

ANTIQUARIAN LEARNING

ANTIQUARIAN learning is found in some form or other among almost all the peoples whose literatures we have discussed. It would seem indeed to be the most widespread of all forms of intellectual activity. Its distribution, however, is very uneven. Among modern Christian and Mohammedan peoples it is very little cultivated except by persons who derive their information from books—whether ecclesiastics or those who have received a modern education. The oral literature which is cultivated among these peoples is intended for entertainment or celebration. Learned literature of native origin, whether didactic or speculative, ceased to be cultivated, sooner or later, after the introduction of the new religion; and intellectual activities were diverted into the new channels which were opened thereby. From these oral literatures we can obtain little beyond rudimentary speculations and a débris of learning, most of which is ultimately derived from books.

On the other hand, antiquarian learning is often well represented in Christian literatures of the past, dating from times when native tradition and speculation had not yet died out. The introduction of Christian learning seems to have acted not infrequently in such times as an incentive or supplement to the study of native learning; and much activity was devoted to the task of bringing the latter into connection and harmony with the former. Theological and cosmological speculations, incompatible with Christian doctrine, were commonly, though not always, suppressed; but genealogies and speculations on the origins of names, places, peoples, etc. were frequently committed to writing. Evidence from this phase must of course be treated with caution; for the representation of native tradition is liable to be influenced by the new learning. But the extent to which this influence is felt varies greatly in different countries and periods, and even between one author and another. Those who write in Latin are in general more affected by the new learning, and consequently less trustworthy for native tradition.

Among modern peoples who have not come under the influence of Christianity or Islam until very recently a large amount of antiquarian learning has been found in Polynesia, and a varying, though much smaller, amount among the Tatars and in Africa. The relative barrenness of antiquarian learning in our chapters relating to the latter is probably due in the main to defects in our information, though in certain cases the influence of Islam may be responsible.

Throughout this work we have included in the chapters on antiquarian learning not only works which are primarily of antiquarian character, but also passages of the same character which occur in works devoted in the main to other subjects; and the same plan will be followed here. Very often doubtless such passages have been added in later times, when a poem or saga has come into the hands of the learned.

In the classification of the material we follow the scheme adopted in Vol. I, p. 270 ff.

I. Genealogies, especially of royal families, but often also of priestly or mantic families, were preserved among all the ancient peoples whose literatures we have discussed (cf. Vol. I, p. 270 ff.; Vol. II, pp. 541 f., 687). They are seldom found in heroic poetry or saga, but more frequently in non-heroic and post-heroic saga. Most commonly, however, they are preserved only in lists of genealogies or in short tracts of purely antiquarian interest.

The family genealogies, especially those of royal lines, seem as a rule to be trustworthy for a certain number of generations before the time when they were first committed to writing, though occasionally they may be confused with lists of kings. Beyond a certain point suspicious names usually appear; and the genealogies are extended into mythical elements. The mythical genealogies which will be noticed in Sections VI and VII, below, are doubtless modelled upon the historical genealogies. They are of more frequent occurrence in learned poetry; and much ingenuity has often been expended upon them.

We have not met with any genealogies in the oral literature of modern Christian or Mohammedan peoples. But what has been said above with reference to the ancients would seem to be true in general of those modern peoples, included in our survey, who are still—or were until recently—heathen. In particular this is the case in Polynesia (cf. p. 236 ff. above), where numerous genealogies are preserved. They are often chanted in the form of ritual poetry; and many of them are of immense length. The earlier names are clearly mythical; but the historical element seems to extend over a surprising number of generations. The existence of similar genealogies in Africa is shown clearly enough by the 'dynastic chronicles' of the Baganda and the Yoruba (pp. 575 f., 641 f.) and by the traditions of clans; but we do not know whether any formal texts of genealogies have been recorded. The same remark applies to the southern Bantu, from whom many genealogies have been collected.[1]

From the absence of genealogies in oral literature it is not safe to assume that they are not preserved. We have met with no genealogies worth mention in the literature of the Tatars; yet every male child is said to know his ancestry for seven generations. Genealogies have a practical, as well as an antiquarian interest, as may be seen from the story of the Maori (p. 235 f.) who occupied the attention of a court for three days by his recitation of genealogies. Parallel instances, though not on such an ambitious scale, might be cited from the Sagas of Icelanders. We may compare also the Hyndluljóð (cf. Vol. 1, p. 278f.). Indeed illustrations might probably be obtained from many lands. In the times before oral tradition has been displaced by documents every man of position must know his genealogy. But the long genealogies of the Irish, the Indians, the Hebrews and the Polynesians are, usually if not always, products of mantic learning or revelation. In Ireland it is the *filid*, in Polynesia the *tohungas*, who are responsible. The genealogies of the Mahābhārata and the Purānas are ascribed to Vyāsa and other famous seers. It is from the (supernatural) witch Hyndla that Óttarr the son of Innsteinn learns his ancestry, which includes most of the famous legendary families of the North.

II. Catalogues, other than genealogies, are not much more frequent than genealogies themselves in heroic poetry and saga, except among the Tatars. Moreover, when they do occur, there is often some reason for suspecting that they did not form part of the original matter.

The most widespread variety of heroic catalogue is the list of heroes, or of princes with their followers, which is introduced usually in connection either with a battle or a ceremony. Examples of such lists in connection with battles may be found in the Iliad and the Tain Bo Cuailnge (Vol. 1, pp. 276, 281); in the account of the great battle in the Mahābhārata they are of prodigious length. We may refer also to the lists given in the Norse story of the battle of Brávík (*ib.* p. 278), which is practically of heroic character, and to a Yugoslav poem—unhistorical and doubtless late in its present form—relating to the first battle of Kosovo (Vol. ii, p. 314). Instances in connection with ceremonial occasions have been cited from Yugoslav and Tatar heroic poetry,

---

[1] E.g. Ellenberger, *History of the Basuto*, p. 331 ff. Some of the genealogies go back to the thirteenth century, and even earlier.

ib. p. 407f., and in the present volume, p. 32; others will be found in the Mahābhārata (e.g. II. xxxiv. 5 ff.) and elsewhere. We may also refer here to the lists of David's heroes (Vol. II, p. 687), of the Gothic heroes ('Eormenric's household-force') in Widsith, and of Arthur's heroes and followers in 'Culhwch and Olwen' and the 'Dream of Rhonabwy'.

The introduction of lists of heroes in stories of warfare may be regarded as a necessary, or at least useful, supplement to the narratives. But in point of fact such catalogues often contain a good deal of matter which has little or no bearing upon the narratives; and in general they may be explained as encroachments of antiquarian learning upon poetry or saga of entertainment. Sometimes the encroachment may be almost contemporary—and in such cases the catalogues may be more or less trustworthy—but in others it must have taken place at a much later date. In the Welsh stories just cited the heroic element would seem to have been subordinate to the bardic or 'professional' interest from the beginning; and the same may be true of Widsith.

Catalogues other than those of heroes are not of frequent occurrence in heroic literature. The poetry of the Kara-Kirghiz is exceptional in this respect: we may refer e.g. to the lists of nations and their characteristics, and more especially to the long list of horses noticed on p. 72 above. The examples which occur elsewhere are not always of antiquarian interest. Thus Welsh panegyrics and elegies sometimes contain lists of exploits and victories of the princes whom they celebrate; and the object here is doubtless to enhance the princes' glory—though other poems contain similar lists in which the interest seems to be antiquarian. The list of Phaeacian athletes in the Odyssey (Vol. I, p. 276) is an exercise in the formation of names, like the lists of names in the Rígsþula (*ib.* p. 420); but the list of mermaids in the Iliad—which may be compared with the list of dwarfs in the Völuspá (*ib.* p. 278)—has 'non-heroic' connections, though ultimately it may be of similar origin. But other catalogues are of a more definitely antiquarian character; we may instance the list of famous women in the Odyssey (Bk. XI) and the lists of place-names in Irish heroic sagas (Vol. I, p. 282). On the whole it may be said that most, though not all, of the catalogues which are found in heroic poetry and saga seem to be due to learned (non-heroic) influence. It can hardly be due to accident that a large proportion of them occur in late works and in passages and episodes which are commonly thought to be late additions to earlier works.

In works which are primarily of antiquarian interest, as also in nonheroic and (didactic) theological poetry and saga, catalogues are of far more frequent occurrence; indeed many such works may be said to abound in them. For extreme examples we may refer to the Norse poems Grímnismál and Rígsþula (Vol. I, pp. 278, 420). Hesiod's Theogony and the 'Catalogues' and other fragmentary poems attributed to the same poet are largely composed of such matter. Here also we may cite the Welsh 'Stanzas of the Graves', with which may be compared certain Irish poems (*ib.* pp. 279, 282). The famous Irish saga called 'The Destruction of Da Derga's Hall' is largely in the form of a catalogue. The non-heroic portions of the Mahābhārata contain numerous examples, of which a few are noted in Vol. II, p. 543; as further illustrations we might add the list of snakes in I. xxxv. 5 ff., the lists of seers in II. iv. 10 ff., vii. 10 ff., of wise kings ('royal seers') in (*ib.*) viii. 9 ff., and of rivers and various supernatural beings in the following chapters (ix ff.). Many more examples may be obtained from similar Hebrew literature (Vol. II, p. 687 f.) and from the oral records of peoples treated in the present volume, especially the Polynesians (p. 393 f.).

The catalogues which occur in such works as we are discussing are not always of strictly antiquarian character. Lists of (e.g.) rivers and peoples sometimes contain names which can only have become known recently; and examples could probably be found in which the antiquarian element is wanting. Strictly speaking, the use of the catalogue is a characteristic of didacticism,[1] rather than of antiquarianism. It is probably an indispensable feature of oral teaching everywhere (cf. p. 747). The Upanishads abound in catalogues, though they are seldom or never concerned with antiquarian interest. We may refer also to the list of spells in the Hávamál and the lists of gnomes and precepts which are to be found among so many peoples. The ubiquity and prominence of the antiquarian catalogue is probably due to the prominence of antiquarian learning in oral tradition. It would seem that where writing is unknown or little used the intellectual and didactic activities of the learned are usually more concerned with the past than with the present, and with the origins of things rather than with the observation of their characteristics.

The connection of the catalogue with antiquarian learning may be illustrated by the close relationship between the Norse words þula, 'catalogue poem', and þulr, 'learned poet' (cf. Vol. I, p. 618). The latter word seems also to mean 'prophet' or 'oracular medium'; and this can

---

[1] It may be observed that several of the heroic instances of catalogues noticed above (e.g. Widsith and the Welsh sagas) belong to the didactic type of heroic literature (Type C), which is commonly of the same origin as non-heroic literature.

hardly be a mere accident; for antiquarian learning is closely connected with manticism, as we shall see below. The Irish *filid* also were originally seers, as well as learned (antiquarian) poets; and catalogues of future kings were composed, in the form of prophecies, both in Ireland and in Wales (*ib.* pp. 455 f., 462 f.), just as in India (Vol. II, p. 540), down to comparatively late times. Some similar connection of ideas may underlie the fact that early Greek poets frequently appeal to the Muses when they are about to introduce a catalogue (cf. Vol. I, p. 635 f.).

III. The explanation of names, especially names of places, is an extremely widespread form of antiquarian learning. It is perhaps to be found among all the peoples included in our survey; for the few cases where it has not been noted may well be due to defects in our information.

In Ireland both place-names and personal names were made subjects of systematic study, the former at least from early times, in the form of catalogues, both verse and prose, which may fairly be called explanatory dictionaries (cf. Vol. I, p. 283 f.), although not many of the explanations would appeal to modern criticism. We have not met with evidence for such systematic study elsewhere; but explanations of names, especially place-names, occur sporadically almost everywhere in non-heroic and theological literature. For illustrations we may refer to Vol. I, p. 286 ff., Vol. II, pp. 408, 543, 688 f., and to pp. 142, 394 f., 593, in the present volume. In heroic literature instances seem to be rare, except in Irish heroic sagas (Vol. I, p. 285), where we may probably attribute their introduction to the influence of *filid*.[1] It may be observed that the desire to explain names appears to be one of the most fertile sources of myth. Apart from the Irish examples, we may refer in particular to the absurd story told in Mahābh. I. iii. 24 ff., which seeks to explain how the famous philosopher Uddālaka Āruni obtained his name (cf. Vol. II, p. 504.) Still more striking evidence to the same effect may be found in the marvellous stories told of the Yugoslav prince Vuk the Fiery, who died in 1485 (*ib.* p. 408).

'Linguistic antiquarianism' was cultivated among other ancient peoples at least as intensively as in Ireland; but it took different directions. In India a more or less scientific classification of sounds was evolved at quite an early date; and the study of metres and of archaic words seems to have begun still earlier. The impulse to these activities

[1] For the activity shown by this class in the study of place-names we may refer to an interesting story of the great *fili* Mac-Liag (d. 1016) recorded by O'Curry, *Manners and Customs* II, p. 99 f. (cf. Hull, *Textbook of Irish Literature* I, p. 176 f.).

arose from the study of the ancient hymns, especially those of the Rgveda, which, owing to their sanctity, it was desired to preserve exactly in their original form—an extreme kind of memorisation, which involved the preservation of many obsolete words and pronunciations. In the Upanishads (cf. Vol. ii, p. 587) the study of phonology and of metres takes a mystical turn, with strange results, while speculative etymologies of a fanciful kind are introduced incidentally.

The study of metres was cultivated elsewhere, especially perhaps in Ireland and in the North, as well as in India. In the North, however, attention was chiefly directed to the study of poetic synonyms and periphrases (kennings). A good example is to be found in the poem Alvíssmál, where the dwarf Alvíss, interrogated by Thor, declares the (synonymous) terms applied to various objects (the earth, sky, moon, etc.) by mankind, gods, dwarfs, elves, and other beings. Later the subject was treated comprehensively by Snorri Sturluson in his Skaldskaparmál, or 'Diction of Poetry', a portion of the Prose Edda. Contests in poetic diction are of course widespread.

IV. Traditions and speculations relating to the origin of institutions, customs and ceremonies are found among most of the peoples included in our survey. But the evidence comes in the main from sporadic and incidental notices; we have not met with any attempt of native learning to deal with the subject comprehensively, as in the Irish works on place-names referred to above. The nearest approach to such an attempt is to be found in the Hebrew Hexateuch (Vol. ii, p. 691 f.); but most of the matter is said to be derived from a source which is generally believed to be late.[1] In India (ib. p. 543 f.) probably a good deal more material is obtainable than we have been able to find. In ancient Europe (Vol. i, p. 289 ff.) our fullest information comes from Greece and Ireland, though much of the Greek material is derived from late authorities. It may be added that a good deal is probably to be found also in the traditions of early Rome, which we have not included in our survey. In modern times Polynesia is again by far the richest area (cf. p. 398 above). In Africa we have met with evidence here and there (pp. 594 ff., 644) which suggests that its paucity is due to defects in our information.

On the whole the subjects which seem most to attract speculation are the origin of (specific) festivals and religious ceremonies and that of

---

[1] It may well be that 'P' sometimes draws from early sources; but the material is thought to have been systematised and edited or interpreted according to the ideas of a sophisticated age.

exceptional customs relating to marriage, kinship and inheritance. We have found examples of the former in Ireland, the North, Greece, Rome, Palestine, India, Polynesia and Central Africa; of the latter in the British Isles (relating to the Picts), Greece, India, Central Africa and among the Tatars. In some cases of course these speculations may be founded upon genuine tradition.

In this connection we may note the stories of 'Culture-heroes', which are widespread in Africa, Polynesia and parts of Asia. The term is not a happy one, for the milieu of such stories is essentially non-heroic; the characters thus described are benefactors of mankind who invent or introduce fire, useful arts and crafts and (animal or vegetable) food-stuffs. For such stories among the Polynesians and the Sea-Dyaks, and also the peoples of Central Africa we may refer to pp. 397 f., 484 and 594 above. In the ancient literatures which we have discussed we have found no satisfactory analogies, except possibly in the story of Prometheus.[1]

Speculations upon the origin of the priesthood are perhaps not so widespread as one might expect. The reason may be that among the peoples with whom we are concerned—excluding those which are Christian or Mohammedan—the priesthood seems usually to be here-ditary, at least in the sense that priests are taken from certain families or clans. The traditions or speculations therefore take a genealogical form. The Brahman families of India claim descent from famous seers, some of whom are authors of poems preserved in the Rgveda, but others seem to be wrapped in myth. The Hebrew evidence is probably similar, but much more complex and obscure, especially with regard to the Levites. In Europe the priesthood was usually bound up with the possession of a sanctuary, which perhaps always had mantic associa-tions. Rulers were sometimes priests, sometimes priests belonged to ruling families, sometimes divine descent may be involved; but we do not know how widespread such conditions were. Among modern peoples the Polynesian evidence (p. 453 ff.) deserves special attention, owing to its variety. We may refer also to what we have found in Africa (pp. 623 ff., 646).

V. Among traditions and speculations which relate to localities the most widespread are those which are concerned with the origin of

---

[1] The pigs presented to Pryderi by Arawn (in the Mabinogi of Math) are said to be a new species of animal. But we cannot regard Pryderi—or any other character in the Mabinogion—as a culture-hero.

sanctuaries. We have met with these in the North, in Greece, India, Palestine, Polynesia, Central Africa and among the Yoruba, perhaps also in Ireland and among the ancient Teutonic peoples of the Continent (Vol. I, p. 617). Reference may also be made to the legends connected with the sanctuary of the heathen Prussians at Romove (*ib.* p. 611).

We see no reason for doubting the substantial truth of the stories which describe the establishment of sanctuaries in Iceland during the period of colonisation, although these stories must have been preserved by oral tradition alone for well over two centuries. A good instance may be found in the account of the sanctuary at Thorsnes in the Eyrbyggja Saga, cap. 4. Some of the Indian sanctuaries mentioned in the Mahābhārata may also be cited in this connection. These sanctuaries (*tīrtha*) seem as a rule to have consisted of little more than a grove or glade, with a river or pool in which pilgrims bathed. Many of them derived their sanctity from visits of deities, but others from their having been the abodes of famous saints and seers. We may refer to places associated with the ancient religious poet Vasishtha (e.g. III. cxxx. 9, 17) and with the much later philosopher Çvetaketu (*ib.* cxxxii. 1 ff.; cf. Vol. II, p. 504). Many churches in this country, both English and Welsh, have doubtless had a similar origin. Croyland is a good example. The initial stages in the growth of such sanctuaries may perhaps be seen among the Galla, where the homes of famous seers seem to be regarded practically as sanctuaries during their lifetime (cf. pp. 551 f., 567 f. above); but we do not know whether these places retain their sanctity after the seers are dead. On the other hand, many sanctuaries are said to commemorate the occurrence of a vision or supernatural appearance on the site, as in the case of the Temple at Jerusalem, according to II Chron. iii. 1.

Many other sanctuaries, however, especially royal and national sanctuaries, are of immemorial antiquity. The foundation of the royal sanctuaries at Leire and Upsala was attributed by Norse tradition to deities, at a time when they lived on earth. A similar origin was claimed for certain Greek sanctuaries and for that of Pele in Hawaii (cf. p. 324). We may also compare the traditions relating to the great sanctuary in Ra'iatea (pp. 318, 457) in the Society Islands, and possibly those relating to certain African sanctuaries (p. 591 f.). In all these cases doubtless speculation was active from early times. The story of the sanctuary was usually connected with the festivals which took place there. Often too the history of a priesthood—which may be, as at Upsala, that of a divine kingship or divine ruling family—is involved.

It may perhaps be taken for granted that speculations upon the origin of sanctuaries will usually reflect to some extent the customs and ideas of the times when they originated. But in the case of ancient sanctuaries complications arise, not only from changes due to the lapse of time, but also from the fact that sanctuaries may change either their human or their divine owners. In historical times Icelandic sanctuaries, which were the homes of leading families, might be sold. But in older lands even more serious disturbance may arise through conquest or political changes. Many English churches—far more perhaps than is commonly supposed—were originally British. Usually the traditions of the past were lost; but here and there something was preserved, as at St Albans and in Cornwall. The church of Glasgow would seem to have survived two successive changes in the nationality and language of its owners; yet the traditions of its founder were by no means wholly forgotten. For a change of faith we may refer to Pope Gregory's injunctions to Augustine—to convert heathen sanctuaries to Christian use. We do not know whether these injunctions were carried out; but there are certain churches, e.g. Thunderley (the 'Grove of Thunder') in Essex— now destroyed—and Goodmanham in the East Riding, which may quite probably occupy the sites of heathen sanctuaries. At (Old) Upsala the foundations of the heathen temple have recently been found beneath the church. Again, it is related in the Landnámabōk, ii. 16, that when Queen Auðr of Dublin settled in Iceland she used to go to certain hillocks to pray; for the Christian settlers brought no priests with them, and built no churches. Her descendants, who were heathen, treated this spot as a place of great sanctity. We may refer also to the Christian altar which, according to Bede, *Hist. Eccl.* II. 15, the East Anglian king Redwald set up in his temple. Parallels to such incidents could doubtless be collected from many lands. No wonder then need be felt at the discrepancies and contradictions which are to be found in the traditions of ancient sanctuaries.

Next to sanctuaries, tombs seem to be the most widespread subject of speculation. In Ireland indeed the two were not unconnected; for the gods were believed to inhabit barrows (*side*), especially the great chambered barrows of the Brug na Boinne (Vol. 1, p. 302). There was apparently some confusion between these prehistoric tombs and souterrains, the use of which may have lasted down to the Viking Age. Yet the nature of the former can hardly have been altogether unknown; for the huge grave from which St Patrick is said to have raised a dead man —as related in the story noticed *ib.* p. 661 f.—would seem from its description to be a long barrow of the earliest period. The graves of heroes of the sagas are noticed in more than one antiquarian poem (*ib.* pp. 282, 301). This latter subject is treated still more fully in the Welsh 'Stanzas of the Graves' (*ib.* pp. 279, 299). Among the graves enumerated in this poem are some of unknown persons, perhaps prehistoric tombs. From modern names, such as 'Taliesin's Grave' (*ib.* p. 298), it would seem that the chamber tombs of the Bronze Age (and earlier) were known to be graves, though they were associated with persons of a later period. In England we know of evidence only from the names of Long Barrows, especially 'Woden's Barrow', near Alton Priors, and 'Wayland's Smithy', near Lambourne. The former points in the same direction; but the latter suggests a different association. In Norse sagas and learned poetry it is commonly stated where great men of the past were buried or burnt. We hear too of attempts to rob the tombs of famous men of the Heroic Age and (from Saxo) even that of the god Balder. Many of these statements and identifications must be due to speculation; but a remarkable case of apparently genuine tradition has been noted in Vol. I, p. 294. We do not know of any references to tombs of the Bronze Age or earlier, unless some reminiscence of them is to be traced in the rocks inhabited by dwarfs. The Greek evidence is very similar to the Norse; note may be taken of what has been remarked about Mycenai (*ib.* p. 293). The Hebrew evidence (Vol. II, p. 693f.) is also on the whole similar; we may compare the 'pillars' with the Norse *bautarsteinar*. We know of no evidence from ancient India.

Among modern peoples the most interesting evidence comes from Russia (the Ukraine) and from Uganda. In the local traditions of Kiev, Ilya of Murom and other ancient *bogatyri* are identified with the bodies buried in the crypts beneath the cathedral; but according to another tradition they are buried at Pereyaslavl, and connected in some way with big stones which lie in the cemetery there (*ib.* p. 210f.). The evidence from Uganda is far more definite and striking (cf. p. 631 above). Every king of the past had a temple and court, which lasted for centuries. As the officials died off, they were replaced by successors from the same tribes. Speculation hardly comes into consideration here. The whole institution would seem to indicate an extremely conservative form of tradition. We do not know how far parallels are to be found among other African peoples. Comparison with ancient Egypt is of course tempting.

Speculation upon the origin of ancient buildings and constructions in general is apt, when the names of the true builders are forgotten, to fix upon the most famous names of antiquity. Sometimes the names are those of ancient and vanished peoples, such as Huns, Vandals and Pelasgoi, sometimes those of mythological communities. Anglo-Saxon speculation seems in the main to have followed these lines in relation to the remains of earlier civilisations in this country. Sometimes, however, names of individuals were adopted. These were usually names either of deities or, more frequently, of persons of the Heroic Age—whether heroes or seers—presumably because this was as a rule the earliest period of which anyone except a professional antiquary had any knowledge. Arthur is by far the most widespread of such names in this country—for megalithic tombs, as well as later structures and natural features—but his popularity hardly goes back beyond the Norman period. From earlier times we have Woden in Wansdyke, etc.; but English human names chosen on this principle seem to be uncertain, though Wales has Gwrtheyrn, Taliesin, and others. It may be observed that foreign names are not accepted in speculations of this kind, unless they have previously become naturalised through literature of entertainment. Caesar (*Casere*) seems to have been the only Roman name with which the ancient English were familiar, except through books. The Germans attributed the ancient buildings of Rome to Theodric the Ostrogoth; and in the same way the ancient Greeks attributed the prehistoric palace of Cnossos to Minos, who was presumably an Achaean. The names of the earlier owners were unknown or forgotten.

In some countries it is often very difficult to distinguish between speculation and genuine tradition. In Ireland and in Greece almost every locality has stories attached to it. Greece is doubtless exceptionally rich in speculation, owing to the fact that antiquarianism was exploited there on a large scale and for a very long period. The same persons and events are frequently claimed by several different localities. In Ireland, owing to its conservatism and comparative isolation, it is probable that the proportion of the genuine traditional element is much greater.

Polynesia is rich in antiquarian traditions and speculations. We may refer to what has been said above (p. 396) about the *marae* of Tahiti and elsewhere, the trilithon (*Hamonga*) in Tonga, the octagonal building (*Fale o le fe*) in Samoa, the forts in New Zealand, and antiquities of various kinds everywhere, as far east as Easter Island. Here also we may refer to the megalithic structures in Hawaii and in the Caroline Islands. In this area too it is sometimes not easy to distinguish between speculation and genuine tradition; but both elements are doubtless well represented. A feature of special interest may be noted in what has been said above (pp. 328, 400) about the *Menehune*. In Hawaii—though not elsewhere—these are said to be a vanished dwarf race, who do building operations by night. We may compare the story of the nocturnal building of the road by the god Midir's followers in the 'Courtship of Etain' (Vol. i, pp. 52, 303).

Apart from the tombs in Uganda, the only material of much interest which we have found in Africa comes from Abyssinia, and this may be due to literary influence. We suspect, however, that material is to be found among the Galla and Bantu peoples, if we had more information. From the Tatars there is probably less to be obtained.

VI. Speculations upon the origin of nations have been discussed in Vol. i, pp. 304 ff., Vol. ii, pp. 544 ff., 695 ff., and in the present volume, pp. 143, 398 ff., 601 f. It will be seen that the speculations or traditions usually consist in part of genealogies, in part of a story of migration and settlement. A declaration of the establishment of some institution or institutions by a deity sometimes enters into the story.

The genealogies commonly contain the following elements: (i) genealogies of royal families, such as have been noticed above (p. 803 f.); (ii) eponymoi, often including eponymoi of neighbouring nations; (iii) deities or mythological beings. But there is a good deal of variation. In Welsh genealogies the place of the mythological beings is sometimes taken by Roman emperors or (non-insular) saints. This element can be seen increasing; it appears in the later versions of genealogies when it is wanting in the earlier versions. Eponymoi also can be seen creeping in, e.g. *Dimet* (i.e. Dyfed) in the genealogy of Dyfed, except the earliest version. But there can be no doubt that some of the Welsh eponymoi are historical persons, i.e. kings whose kingdoms derived their names from them.

In English genealogies we find two kinds of eponymoi—those of royal families and those of kingdoms. We need not doubt the historicity of Icel and Wuffa, from whom the Iclingas and Wuffingas (the Mercian and East Anglian royal families) traced their descent; but it would require courage to maintain this for Gewis and Beornic, whom the kings of the Gewisse (Wessex) and the Bernicians claimed as their ancestors.[1]

---

[1] The absence of an eponymos for the Engle (English) as a whole may be noted. The same remark applies to other ancient Teutonic peoples, the Goths, Franks, Swedes, Burgundians, etc. Latin Danish historians have an Angul as a brother of Dan (Danr); but this is doubtless an idea of later times.

The Danish royal family (Skjöldungar) have two eponymoi, Skjöldr and Danr. The former, well known to the English as Scyld, is obviously more ancient than the latter, though we are not prepared to maintain the historicity of either. Danr seems to have been unknown to the English.

We would call special attention to the Frankish genealogy noticed in Vol. I, p. 305 f., which had a very long history. In its earliest form, as recorded by Tacitus, it contained mythological elements, as well as eponymoi. It bears a rather close resemblance to the Greek genealogy of Hellen's family, as given in the Hesiodic 'Catalogue' (*ib.* p. 304). The three ancestral brothers are also found in Ireland,[1] among the Scythians, and elsewhere. The Indian genealogy of Manu's descendants (Vol. II, p. 544ff.) may likewise be compared, though here there are five eponymous brothers. In this case, as in Ireland, the royal genealogies are of immense length, and bear striking witness to the activity of their authors. Some of them apparently contain elements which point to an ancient and good tradition; but others, e.g. that of Ayodhyā, would seem to be almost wholly works of the imagination. The most complete scheme, however, is that of the Hebrew genealogies—represented most fully in I Chronicles i–viii—which gives a considerable number of eponymoi, both for Israel and for the neighbouring peoples. The genealogies of the leading families in the tribes of Israel, which follow, are in some cases very detailed; and there can be little doubt that they preserve much old tradition, although we have no early evidence, like that of the Rgveda, wherewith to control them. It would seem that in Israel much attention had been paid from early times both to genealogical speculation and to the preservation of family traditions.

Polynesian genealogies (cf. p. 236 f. above) are sometimes as long as the Irish and Indian; and in some groups of islands they seem to be remarkably trustworthy for at least five or six centuries. There can be no doubt, however, as to the widespread prevalence of speculation in the earlier portions.[2] Many of the names suggest mythological associations, while many others are obviously unhistorical. But we have not been able to trace eponymoi among any modern peoples—though we are not prepared to deny their existence. In Africa the nearest approach to the Polynesian genealogies known to us is the list of the kings of

---

[1] For the (prehistoric) Irish and Norse genealogies we may refer to (*ib.*) pp. 312ff., 306f.

[2] For yet other unhistorical elements in the Polynesian genealogies, see p. 391 above.

Uganda (p. 575); but the affinities of this list lie still more closely with that of the early Swedish kings, as given in the Ynglinga Saga (Vol. 1, p. 307). It would be of considerable interest if we could ascertain definitely whether national eponymoi are really unknown to African and Polynesian speculation. Islands and rocks sometimes figure in the early stages of the Polynesian genealogies (cf. p. 401 above).

Stories relating to the origin of nations are at least as widespread as genealogies—with which they are very often bound up. So widespread indeed are these stories that, if allowance be made for defects in our information, it would seem probable that they exist everywhere among peoples who have attained a certain degree of civilisation or intellectual development. See p. 901.

The most striking feature in these stories is the prevalence—one might almost say the ubiquity—of invasion or migration. Here again allowance must be made for defective records. We have hardly any information as to the English conquest of Britain. Traditional records must have existed in the seventh century; but it would seem that none of those who had acquired the new learning were sufficiently interested in this subject to write anything down except a short summary of the story of Hengest and Horsa. Sometimes, however, account must be taken of a lapse in tradition itself. Although many poems in the Rgveda depict a state of warfare between Aryans and natives, apparently in the eastern Punjab, we have practically no record of the conquest of the Ganges and Jumna basins, any more than of that of north-west India. In place of these conquests 'Puranic' learning has a long and imaginative history connected with the 'Four Ages'. It would seem that before the rise of this learning antiquarian study had been in abeyance—intellectual activity had been diverted into other channels. Again, an early Irish record—apparently good—states that the dynasty of Dyfed came from Ireland, and gives it an Irish ancestry (cf. Vol. 1, p. 312). Welsh records, as we have them, know nothing of this story, and give the family a genealogy which excludes any such origin.

Far more striking, however, than such lapses in tradition is the fact that many peoples have stories—sometimes detailed stories—of invasion for which no corroborative evidence is to be found, whether in history, archaeology or language. We may instance the invasions of Ireland in the 'Book of Invasions', the settlement of the Aesir in Sweden in the Ynglinga Saga, the migrations of the Goths, Lombards, and other peoples from Scandinavia. We do not mean of course to deny that Ireland was ever invaded in prehistoric times, or that movements took place to and fro across the Baltic; but we see no reason for believing that invasions on a great scale corresponding to these occurred within times to which antiquarian tradition could extend. We regard these invasions as products of speculation, partly based upon foreign analogies, but also partly founded upon real movements of small bodies of adventurers—say a prince with his personal followers—such as frequently take place under heroic conditions. The Hebrew invasions present a different problem; for in this case the probability of invasion cannot be denied. But the records give accounts of two different invasions by the same people, separated from one another by a considerable interval of time, during which they had withdrawn from the land. For a discussion of this problem we may refer to Vol. II, p. 698 ff.

Among stories of this kind perhaps the best examples of antiquarian tradition are to be found in those which relate to the Norse settlement of Iceland and the Maori invasion of New Zealand. Speculative elements are present in both stories; yet in general they may be regarded as historical records, although some 250 years of oral tradition are involved in the former, and perhaps five centuries in the latter. The merits of the former may be appreciated by a comparison with the Norse accounts of the Scandinavian invasion of England. This invasion took place only a few years before the settlement of Iceland; but the accounts are legendary and untrustworthy. They are clearly derived, not from local antiquarian learning, but from reports wandering from one coast to another, and finally worked up into saga form in Iceland.

VII. Speculations upon the origin of mankind, the world and the gods are to be found in all the ancient literatures included in our survey, except those which have eliminated native learning incompatible with Christianity. Traces of such speculations may perhaps occur even in these; but they are of uncertain value, owing to the influences to which they have been subject. In general therefore we will confine our attention to the Norse, Greek, Hebrew and Indian records.

The subjects with which such speculations are chiefly concerned are: (1) the origin of mankind; (2) the destruction and restoration of mankind; (3) the origin of the gods and other supernatural beings; (4) a warfare between the gods and other supernatural beings; (5) the origin of the earth. These subjects are, however, not fully represented everywhere. In India nos. (1) and (2) are not clearly distinguished. In the North nos. (2) and (4) are confused. In early Hebrew literature nos. (3) and (4) are entirely wanting, though something like no. (4) appears in very late times.

It may be doubted whether no. (2) is a true product of native speculation in any of the ancient literatures which we have discussed. The Greek, Hebrew and Indian stories of the Flood seem to be derived from a common source in Mesopotamia; there is no evidence that the story was known in the period of the Rgveda (Vol. II, p. 546f.). In later times Greek and Indian thought contemplated another destruction in the future, which was perhaps to be recurrent at intervals of 10,000 years (*ib.* p. 622). In India the idea was bound up with the doctrine of the Four Ages; but in Greece this doctrine appears to be earlier.[1] In the North we know of no satisfactory evidence for the first destruction —Noah's Flood—but Norse antiquarian literature has much to say about the second (future) one (Vol. I, p. 321ff.). Two human beings (apparently) are to survive; but attention is much less centred on the fate of mankind than upon that of the deities, most of whom are doomed to perish. As noted above, this destruction is combined with the fight between gods and demons. There is some evidence, though not quite so definite as might be wished (*ib.* p. 328), that the Druids of Gaul also taught the doctrine of a coming destruction (or destructions) of the world—by fire and water, just as in the case of Ragnarök. If this is correct, it would seem probable that there was some connection, not only between these two doctrines themselves, but also between them and the Greek and Indian doctrines—in other words, that these speculations had a common origin, presumably somewhere in the Near East, from which they travelled far and wide. Possibly the doctrine in its original form was not uninfluenced by the old story of the Flood.

Speculations as to the origin of mankind may be said to fall into two series. In the first they are created by a deity or deities. This is the doctrine taught in Genesis (ii. 7ff.); and practically the same is true of the Norse story, at least according to Snorri's version (Vol. I, p. 324)— viz. that the first human pair were transformed by deities from logs into living beings. In Greece there is some evidence for a somewhat similar story of creation by Prometheus and Athena (*ib.* p. 319). But the more usual Greek account seems to be that of the Hesiodic 'Catalogues', according to which Prometheus is the ancestor of mankind, through his son Deucalion. This means that gods and men spring from the same family; for Prometheus and Zeus are first cousins—their fathers

---

[1] We regard Hesiod's 'Race of Heroes' as no part of the original scheme, but a later addition; cf. Vol. II, p. 546.

Iapetos and Cronos are brothers. It is apparently not made clear how or at what point the differentiation took place; but it seems to be connected in some way—whether as cause or effect—with the enmity between Prometheus and Zeus. The original family are perhaps better described as supernatural beings (of various kinds) than as deities. Again, Manu has something in common with Prometheus, and not only as institutor of sacrifice; his father Vivasvat belongs to a group of supernatural beings which includes some at least of the gods. But Manu is not involved in any hostility with deities, so far as we know. In the Rgveda, which shows no knowledge of the Flood, he is the ancestor of the Aryan peoples, but not of the Dasyu or natives.

Certain resemblances are to be found in these stories; but they lie not in the actual creation or origin of mankind, but in the fate of the first man, or in some incident connected with him, which had a permanently injurious effect upon the race. Thus there is undeniably an underlying, though not superficial, resemblance between the incident of Pandora and the Hebrew story of the Fall. Both are probably derived from folk-tales, yet not from the same folk-tale—snakes play no part in the Greek story. The question whether anything more than chance coincidence is involved is rendered difficult by the antiquity of the speculations and by the probability that they have undergone considerable modifications in the course of time. We can in fact trace different strata in the speculations. Manu comes to no trouble, as Adam and Prometheus do; but he is connected in some obscure way—indeed presumably identical in origin—with Yama, the god of the dead (cf. Vol. II, p. 547). The latter is in the Avesta the progenitor of mankind, and forfeits immortality through a decline in virtue.

Common to all these speculations is the idea that the earliest age of mankind was the best. The Four Ages both in Greece and in India show a continuous decline in virtue and happiness. In the North we hear only of a Golden Age, which is said to have been destroyed by the arrival of certain women from Jötunheimar;[1] but the reference is to the gods rather than to mankind. In the Avesta Yima's (Yama's) time is an age of perfect bliss, like Adam's life before the Fall. Here again we may ask how far these speculations are independent. The Golden Age in the North rather suggests external influence.

The origin of the gods and other supernatural beings is in Greek speculation bound up with that of the world. What is doubtless the

[1] Cf. Völuspá, st. 8 (Cod. Reg.); Gylfaginning, cap. 14. The story implied in this passage of the Völuspá is not known to us; and it is not clear that Snorri knew it.

oldest genealogy (Vol. I, p. 317) begins with the widespread conception of Heaven and Earth as the original parents. Cronos and Iapetos are among their children, Zeus and Prometheus among their grandchildren. To this family belong all the deities, together with the Sun and Moon, and many 'Giants' who correspond more or less to the Norse Jötnar. In Hesiod's Theogony, where Earth is the mother, as well as the wife, of Heaven, we find also an independent genealogy from Chaos, consisting of natural phenomena and abstract conceptions; but this is obviously a later speculation. In India some similar scheme may once have been known; at all events several hymns in the Rgveda are addressed to Heaven and Earth jointly, though the personification is not carried very far. But our knowledge of the genealogy and relationships of the (earlier) Vedic gods is far from complete. In later literature, and indeed to some extent even in the Rgveda itself, we find a considerable number of what are apparently new deities, arising from abstract conceptions and epithets, the most important of whom is Prajāpati (see below). Speculation was active in constructing genealogies both for these and for various other classes of beings, both natural and supernatural (cf. Vol. II, p. 548).

It is known that genealogies of the gods were cultivated among the ancient Teutonic peoples (Vol. I, p. 325 f.). Woden is credited with an ancestry of five generations in the ancient English genealogies—much more in later times; and the 'ancient poems' cited by Tacitus (*Germ.* 2) stated that Mannus, the father of the three eponymous brothers (cf. p. 815), was son of a god Tuisto, who was son of Earth (or sprung from earth)—a genealogy which may be compared with that of Prometheus, son of Iapetos, son of Earth. Otherwise we have little information, except for the North, where we find two distinct communities of gods, the Aesir and the Vanir, in addition to various other supernatural beings. Of the Vanir we know little; but the Aesir are not all of one family, like the Greek gods. Both Aesir and Vanir intermarry with the Jötnar. The only genealogy recorded is that of Othin, whose grandfather, according to Snorri, grew out of the licking of ice-blocks by a cow (cf. Vol. I, p. 323). The Jötnar are sprung from Ymir (see below), the owner of the cow.

The fight between the gods (collectively) and the demons is placed by Greek speculation in the far past. Zeus and his party are victorious and establish their power for ever. But all the combatants in reality belong to one family. The Norse counterpart of this fight, however, is to take place in the future, and is connected with the—not final—destruction of the world. The result is at best hardly more than a drawn battle; for all the chief gods are slain, as well as some of the leading Jötnar. We do not know whether any true analogies to these conflicts are to be found in Indian mythology, though fights between individual gods and demons, especially Indra and Vrtra, are a common theme in the Rgveda. The hostility between the Deva and the Asura sometimes comes to pitched battles in what seem to be late stories in the Mahābhārata (e.g. III. ccxxx); but we have not the knowledge necessary for discussing these. The same hostility, viewed from the opposite standpoint, is much more prominent in the Avesta, where the decisive conflict is to take place in the future. An analogy is also to be found in a very late phase of Hebrew thought; but this would seem to be due to external influence, possibly to that of the Avesta.

It is clear that the conception of a collective conflict between gods and demons, or between friendly and hostile supernatural powers, was rather widespread in the ancient world, though the evidence relates to different periods. Reference may also be made to a somewhat similar Mesopotamian story, which can be traced back to early times. The conception is curious; and one is naturally inclined to ask whether it can have arisen independently among the various peoples—suggested presumably by human warfare—or whether its distribution is due to the interchange and travelling of thought. Those who are more familiar with the ancient literatures of the Near East may perhaps be able to further the solution of the problem. See p. 901 f.

The origin of the world is treated in Greek antiquarian poetry merely as a genealogical subject. Heaven and Earth, the Sun and Moon, the Sea, etc. are personifications, regarded as members of a human family. From the beginning of the sixth century, however, or slightly earlier, Greek speculative thought, doubtless under foreign influence, discarded mythology and personification, and set out to explain the origin of the world on principles which may be regarded as those of organic development. The Hebrew account, the older version of which is given in Gen. ii. 4ff., agrees with the later Greek in discarding personifications; but in place of organic development it has creation by Jehovah, who is eternal, or at least existed before the creation of the world. Norse and Indian speculations show a good deal of variety; but all of them fall between these three extremes, or compromise between the three principles. Personification is frequent, but not carried out systematically, as in Hesiod's Theogony; for examples we may refer to Vol. I, p. 322, Vol. II, p. 549; cf. p. 401 above. Illustrations of 'organic development' and 'creation' will be found in the same context (Vol. I, p. 321 ff., Vol. II, p. 548f.).

In general it may be said that creation is the more important element in the North, if we may judge from the fragments of poetry which survive. It is the gods, Othin and his brothers, who at least bring the world into order, according to the Völuspá. But Ymir, from whom the Jötnar were descended, was in existence before them; he lived in the 'yawning abyss'—perhaps Hesiod's Chaos. The Vafþruðnismál states that he was the result of a kind of spontaneous growth from the waters trickling there. According to Snorri's interpretation of the passage, this locality consisted of moisture arising from its position between ice and heat—recalling Anaximandros' theory. In another passage in the same poem—preserved more fully in the Grímnismál—the earth, sea, sky, trees, etc. are formed from various parts of Ymir by the gods, who according to Snorri had slain and dissected him. It is remarkable that the same fantastic idea occurs in the Rgveda x. 90, where the gods sacrifice the primeval Purusha ('Man') and create all things from the various parts of his body. Elsewhere in the Rgveda and later literature we meet with various speculations which compromise between creation and organic, or rather spontaneous, growth. A few examples are referred to in Vol. II, p. 548f., among which we may perhaps note especially the hymn (Rgv. x. 121) which derives the creator Prajāpati from the 'Golden Germ'.

It is clear enough from the variety of theories that the origin of the world was a subject of free speculation in ancient India. Indeed one poem (Rgv. x. 129) recognises that the problem is incapable of solution. There can be little doubt that the same is true of the North, for which unfortunately the early evidence is of a fragmentary character. It is often doubtful whether passages, especially in the Völuspá and the Grímnismál, stand in their original context; and one should hesitate before utilising the evidence of one poem to supplement that of another. It is worth noting, however, that where 'creation' is introduced the chief person is always the mantic god Othin, while in India it is Prajāpati or Brahmā, who are likewise themselves creations of mantic thought.

The Tatars have elaborate cosmogonic myths, some of which have been noticed on p. 143 ff. All the five elements which we have noted above can be traced in these stories. But there can be no doubt that much of the matter is derived from foreign, including Buddhist, sources;[1]

[1] What was said above (p. 800) as to Iranian connections applies to cosmology as much as to theology.

and it is not at all clear how far even the main features were generally accepted. Genealogies of the gods are found, at least among the Yakut.

A great and very varied amount of cosmological speculation has been recorded from Polynesia (cf. p. 400 ff.). Sometimes the world is said to have been created by the supreme god Kiho or Io; sometimes the whole subject is treated genealogically; at times the germ of the idea of evolution is distinctly traceable. A special feature of the genealogies, which are of great length, is that they include plants and even rocks and islands. In this last feature the Polynesian cosmological speculations bear a striking resemblance to those of the ancient Japanese, as these are to be found in the *Kojiki* and the *Nihongi*. The Polynesians would seem to have devoted more attention, and to have exercised greater intellectual activity, in connection with the whole subject than any other peoples included in our survey, and the evidence is especially interesting for two reasons: In the first place, the various ideas (genealogical, creative, and evolutionary) are here easily referable to the different milieus in which they circulate.[1] In the second, it is easy to trace the tyranny of traditional diction (e.g. the terminology proper to genealogical material, and that which has been formulated in connection with anthropomorphic conceptions) in the expression of abstract concepts. This traditional diction is probably even more in evidence in the usage of Polynesians when they are speaking to Europeans than among themselves, for it is more difficult to translate abstract than concrete ideas; and it is necessary therefore to be on our guard against a facile assumption that the Polynesian has made us familiar with the whole range of his intellectual activity and his speculative thought.

Cosmological speculations seem to be widespread among the (non-Mohammedan) peoples of Africa; cf. pp. 594, 614, 644 above. One or two examples, of a popular character, have been noted on p. 594. But to treat the subject satisfactorily as a whole would require a special study, extending over a wider area than has been included in our survey.

---

[1] For cosmogony as a subject of ritual drama see pp. 373 f., 429. Similar practices seem to have been known in ancient Mesopotamia and elsewhere, and may have influenced the speculations noticed above, though definite evidence to this effect is not easy to find, at least in Europe.

CHAPTER VIII

GNOMIC AND DESCRIPTIVE LITERATURE

THE ancient literatures of Europe, as we saw in Vol. I, Chs. XII and XIII, preserve a good deal of gnomic and descriptive poetry, which is varied in character and often very interesting. But the poetry belonging to these categories which we have found in preparing Vols. II and III of our survey is on the whole somewhat disappointing. The modern European (Slavonic) literatures yield little material, except riddles; but this is what might be expected from the character of these literatures. Hebrew and Sanskrit records preserve a large amount of such poetry; but most of it is of uncertain date, though not very early, and as a whole it is less varied and interesting than its European counterparts. What is more disappointing, however, is the paucity of the material available from modern peoples outside Europe. Descriptive poetry is richly represented in Polynesia; but otherwise we have found very little in any of the areas treated in this volume.

It is clear that in Christian and Mohammedan communities the native gnomic literature has been displaced or transformed by external influence. We suspect, however, that among other modern peoples—those which have retained their native faiths and culture—the apparent absence of literature of this kind is to some extent due to accident. We have been brought to this conclusion partly by isolated snatches of song and by casual remarks in our authorities, which place its existence beyond doubt where we have not been able to find any further information. Partly too we have been influenced by the collections of proverbs which have been made in various countries—which would seem rather to imply that gnomic composition of some kind is cultivated. It is quite possible of course that we have unfortunately overlooked material which has already been published. But we cannot help thinking that these subjects have been somewhat neglected by collectors; and we rather suspect that the collection of such literature may be attended by peculiar difficulties. May we take this opportunity, however, of suggesting to those who are in touch with native thought that attention should be given to it before it is too late? For the study of literature gnomic compositions are of far greater value than isolated proverbs.

In Vol. I, p. 377f., we distinguished two types of gnomes. Type I, the type recognised by Aristotle, comprises 'gnomes of obligation'; they express what should be. Such gnomes are often associated with precepts, and commonly are convertible into precepts. Type II, not recognised by Aristotle, comprises 'gnomes of observation'; they express what is. Such gnomes are not convertible into precepts, and are not often associated with them. On the other hand, they are very frequently associated with descriptive poetry; and it is often difficult to decide whether to apply the term 'gnomic' or 'descriptive' to a poem or passage, especially when it consists of a catalogue (*ib.* p. 416ff.). In fact gnomes of this type often are descriptions, expressed as briefly as possible.

Gnomes of Type I most commonly imply a moral standard, though occasionally the governing principle is prudence. Under the same type, however, we include also gnomes relating to industries, magic, etc. In Type II we distinguish three varieties of gnomes, relating to (*a*) mankind, (*b*) Fate (death) and the gods,[1] (*c*) animals, inanimate things, and in short everything which does not come within (*a*) or (*b*). Gnomes of Type II*a* are not always easy to distinguish from those of Type I, as may be seen from the Anglo-Saxon sentence quoted *ib.* p. 378.

The material for the study of gnomes is to be found partly in poems which consist wholly or mainly of collections of gnomes—in Ireland there are also prose collections—and partly in series of gnomes which are introduced into poems which are mainly concerned with some other subject. In some poems, e.g. Hesiod's 'Works and Days' and the second part of the Hávamál, the gnomic and non-gnomic elements are more or less evenly balanced. But descriptive passages commonly occur even in poems which otherwise are wholly gnomic. Single gnomes are of course to be found, with varying frequency, in poems and prose works of all kinds; but here we shall confine our attention in the main to collections and series of gnomes.

In Vol. I, Ch. XII, we noticed a remarkable difference between the ancient literatures of Europe. Greek, Norse and Irish gnomic poetry consists of gnomes of Type I and Type II*a*, sometimes combined with precepts. Type II*b* occurs occasionally, but II*c* is wanting. On the other hand, the gnomes contained in the English and Welsh gnomic

---

[1] Gnomes of this variety are quoted by Aristotle, though they do not come strictly within his definition of a gnome.

poems[1]—we mean the poems which consist wholly or mainly of gnomes—almost all belong to Type II, and the majority of them to Type II*c*, while precepts are wanting. This difference is significant for the purpose of gnomic poetry. In Greek, Norse and Irish the purpose is to state rules—especially, though not exclusively, relating to moral and social duties. In English and Welsh it is to state observations— especially, though by no means exclusively, relating to natural history. The difference is perhaps the more interesting because there would seem to be some relationship, however distant, between English and Norse gnomic composition; the same formula—*sceal, skal*—is regularly used in both languages, and for gnomes of both types.

It should be noted that these remarks apply only to poems which are primarily gnomic. Gnomes of Type I occur in other English and Welsh poems, not only singly but also, especially in English, in series, in combination with gnomes of Type II*a*, just as in the other languages. Norse analogies to gnomes of Type II*c* are to be found even in series, apart from gnomic poetry; we may instance the formula of outlawry cited in Vol. 1, p. 386f.—in which the short description of the hawk should be noted. Gnomes of this variety were evidently known; but the cultivation of gnomic poetry took a different direction from what it did in this country. Gnomes relating to animals, etc. are admitted only in illustration of human life, as e.g. in Háv. st. 21: "Cattle know when they ought to go home, and then they leave their pasture. But a foolish man never knows the measure of his own appetite." It is not the habits of cattle that the poet is concerned with, but those of greedy men.

In English and Norse heroic poetry we find gnomes of a heroic character, e.g. Beow. 24: "Success is to be attained in every nation by deeds which evoke praise" (i.e. generosity). But the gnomic poems which we are discussing show little or no heroic influence. Even in the Irish 'Instructions to Kings', in which the speakers are sometimes famous heroes, it is the maintenance of justice which is regarded as the king's chief duty. In the other languages princes are sometimes treated with friendly interest, sometimes with suspicion or hostility; but only a comparatively small amount of attention is paid to them. The chief interest everywhere lies in people of less exalted position, especially

---

[1] For the Welsh gnomic and descriptive poems a critical text, with commentary, has recently been made available by K. Jackson, *Early Welsh Gnomic Poems*; also greatly improved translations in *Studies in Early Celtic Nature Poetry* (pp. 50–76) by the same author.

farmers; and there can be no doubt that it was in such a milieu—non-royal and non-heroic—that the poems originated. The Greek and Norse poems have mantic associations.

From ancient India we have a few gnomic poems—besides numerous isolated gnomes—in the Rgveda and one in the Atharvaveda (cf. Vol. II, p. 550ff.). The gnomes as a rule relate to human activities and experiences; the prevailing form seems to be Type IIa. The poems differ from those of Europe in the fact that the gnomes are usually much more closely connected, so that as a whole they give the impression of being 'descriptive' (e.g. of a certain type of man or quality), rather than gnomic. Both precepts and gnomes of Type IIc occur occasionally. For the latter we may refer especially to an interesting poem (Rgv. IX. 112), quite different from the rest, which seems to be an occupation song, sung by a boy who is engaged in the pressing of soma.

In later times the Vedic schools developed the use of gnomic form to an immense extent in the Sūtras, which consist of rules for various purposes. From these the gnomic form passed into the law-books.

The Mahābhārata also contains a very large amount of gnomic poetry (cf. Vol. II, p. 553ff.). Occasionally, as in the speeches of Vidulā, the gnomes are 'heroic', like the isolated gnomes which occur in English and Norse heroic poetry. But in general the gnomic series belong to those parts of the work which are clearly of Brahmanic origin; and the gnomes themselves are of the usual (non-heroic) character. Both types are represented; but, like the Greek and Norse gnomes, they relate apparently only to human affairs. At least we have not noticed any examples of the variety (Type IIc) relating to natural history, etc.

In early Hebrew literature gnomic poetry is represented by the Proverbs and many of the Psalms. Both collections are of uncertain date, though we have included the former in our survey (Vol. II, p. 733ff.). The prevailing form of gnome is Type II; but precepts are also very much used. The arrangement is often of a studied character; and descriptive passages are fairly frequent. In general the gnomes are concerned only with human interests; references to animal life occur only by way of illustration, as in the Hávamál. Cap. xxx, however, which is generally believed to be a late supplement to the collection, contains a number of 'natural history' gnomes (Type IIc).

The Pentateuch contains a large amount of gnomic matter, chiefly ritual gnomes of Type I; but most of it is believed to be late. The laws in Ex. xxiff. are also largely expressed in gnomic form. The Commandments in (*ib.*) cap. xx are chiefly moral precepts, while those in cap. xxxiv, which are believed to be older, are ritual precepts. Apart from the Pentateuch gnomes are only of incidental, and not very frequent, occurrence in the books included in our survey.

Gnomic poetry seems to be much cultivated among the Tatars. Examples from most of these peoples will be found on p. 147 ff. of this volume. They are of considerable interest owing to their varied character; both types, as well as precepts, are in use. Gnomes of the 'natural history' variety (IIc) seem to be especially popular. As in English and Welsh, they are commonly found in association with gnomes relating to human life (mostly Type IIa). Very often, as in Welsh, a series begins with one or more gnomes of the former kind, and then passes on to the latter. Sometimes there is a common word or idea running through the series; but this does not seem to be invariably the case.

Some special features deserve to be noticed. Sometimes gnomes are expressed in the form of questions, as in the passage quoted on p. 150. Gnomic advice given by older people to younger relatives seems to be rather common, and may be compared with the instructions of Cormac, Fithel, Vidulā, Lemuel's mother, and possibly Hesiod; but we may note the references (p. 150 f.) to such advice to brides, to boys at their naming ceremony, and to young heroes who are setting out on a journey. In particular we would call attention to the precepts given by the old shaman to the young shaman noticed on p. 197. The most remarkable feature, however, is the fashion of beginning a conversation with—apparently quite irrelevant—poetry, which often consists of gnomes (p. 148 f.).[1]

Gnomic poetry was evidently cultivated to some extent by the Polynesians,[2] at least in New Zealand, though we have not been able

---

[1] An interesting analogy to this is to be found in the Welsh poetry of Type B, e.g. in the speech-poems contained in the story of Trystan published in the *Bull. of the Bd. of Celt. Studies* v, 115 ff. (cf. p. 718, note). Translations of two passages will be found in Jackson, *Studies in Early Celtic Nature Poetry*, p. 184 f. Other striking instances occur in the older fragments from the same cycle in the Black Book, No. xxxiv (cf. Vol. I, p. 34 f.). In poetry of general reference such irrelevances or unconnected observations are of course far more widespread both in Welsh and elsewhere; we may refer e.g. to the Norwegian Runic Poem noticed in Vol. I, p. 415.

[2] Reference may here be made to an interesting series of moral precepts (including enthymemes) publ. in the *Reports of the Cambridge Anthropol. Expedition to Torres Straits*, Vol. v, p. 208 (quoted by Hambly, *Origins of Education among Primitive People*, p. 142 f.).

to find much of it. The most important piece is an old Maori poem (p. 404 f.), in which a newly born boy is 'instructed' by his grand-uncle in morals and agriculture, combined with much anti-quarian lore, and which bears a curious resemblance to the 'Works and Days'.

In Africa too the gnomic compositions we have met with are few in number; but they are varied, and some of them quite interesting.

Among the Galla we may note, first, the precepts addressed to a bride by her friends at the wedding (p. 562), for which analogies are to be found among the Russians and the Tatars, as we have seen. Much more remarkable is the preamble to the sacrificial ceremony noticed on p. 553 f., in which the elder addresses the worshippers in a series of 'natural history' gnomes. The caravan song (p. 556) on the evils of poverty consists of a series of gnomes, which amount to a detailed description, like the Vedic poems mentioned on p. 827. Laws and decrees often seem to contain much gnomic matter arranged in the form of triads (p. 558), very like what are found in the Welsh laws.

For gnomic composition among the Bantu we are in the main dependent upon passing remarks by travellers. The most interesting of these is Livingstone's statement, quoted on p. 604 f., about the ravings of people (on the Zambesi) who were suffering from the effects of smoking Indian hemp. The sentences which he records are typical gnomes of the 'natural history' variety. Among some of the southernmost Bantu, e.g. the Basuto and Bechuana, moral precepts in the briefest and simplest form are inculcated upon boys as part of the training connected with initiation or coming of age rites, e.g. "Amend your ways! Be men! Fear theft! Fear adultery! Honour your parents! Obey your chiefs!"[1] Each precept is accompanied by the blow of a switch upon their backs. Sometimes, however, among the Basuto, gnomic poetry of a rather elaborate character seems to be learned during the training. We may quote one stanza from one of these poems:[2]

> Let not the herdsman allow his herd to be captured, before he has been pierced by a barbed spear which sheds his blood.
> When a traveller comes to you, my young friend, give him water to drink.
> Fly not from the Bushman, young friend, that man of might who disappears as soon as he has shot his arrow.

[1] Casalis, *The Basutos*, p. 263 f.
[2] Ellenberger, *History of the Basuto*, p. 282 f.

The form would seem to be that of the precept, so far as one can judge without a knowledge of the language.

It will be seen that, limited as it is, the African evidence as a whole supplies valuable information as to the purpose and the milieu of gnomic compositions. Note should be taken both of their religious and mantic associations and of their connection with the training of the young. Further, the African evidence, together with that of the Tatars, tends to show the wide distribution of 'natural history' gnomes (Type II*c*), in spite of their restricted use in ancient literatures, except English and Welsh. The affinities of this variety—as indeed of Type II in general— seem to lie with descriptive poetry, as we shall see below. On the whole we are rather inclined to suspect that gnomes of observation (Type II), including natural history gnomes, and gnomic precepts are the earliest forms of gnomic composition, and that gnomes of obligation are later.[1]

As regards the purpose of such compositions, the most frequent and widely distributed usage is that of advice by an older to a younger member of the same family.[2] Instruction of some kind is implied in the opening words of the Exeter Gnomes, quoted in Vol. 1, p. 382; and a gnome in the same collection (*ib.* p. 381) speaks of the instruction, discipline and exhortation of a boy. Some kind of educational usage may be suspected, as in South Africa. In the Sigrdrífumál a young hero is instructed by a Valkyrie. In the Hávamál the speaker is the god Othin. In Ireland the instructors are sometimes heroes, sometimes *filid*. In India they are doubtless Brahmans. Among the Tatars the instructors are sometimes shamans; but there are indications in the narrative poems that precepts are also attributed to divine beings (see p. 92 above). In Africa the instructors seem to be the local headmen. Religious or mantic connections are evident in the North, in Greece and among the Galla; and a tradition of such connections is perhaps implied where the speakers are *filid* or Brahmans. On the other hand, there is little connection between gnomic and mantic literature in early Hebrew.

---

[1] But it may be noted that an interesting series of moral gnomes, including enthymemes, is quoted by Hambly, *Origins of Education*, p. 152 f., from Hill-Tout, *The Natives of British North America* (relating to the Thompson Indians). Each gnome begins with the formula "It is bad..." (to steal, etc.).

[2] Cf. p. 828. Egypt has preserved a number of ancient 'instructions', largely gnomic, which profess to have been composed by kings or statesmen for their sons. Actually they were in use as school-books during the 18th and 19th dynasties, and perhaps much earlier. The oldest collection is attributed to the vizier Ptahhotep, who seems to have lived not long after the middle of the third millennium.

One can only say therefore that the connection is frequent but not universal.

We have employed the term 'descriptive' to poetry which is concerned, wholly or mainly with descriptions—whether of persons, animals, inanimate objects, places, times, natural phenomena, or even abstract conceptions. Sometimes such descriptions occupy whole poems, though these are as a rule not long. Sometimes they occur incidentally in poems which are mainly concerned with other interests. Such passages vary of course in length; occasionally we have spoken of even a few words as descriptive. It is perhaps in gnomic poetry that these passages occur most frequently; but they are to be found also in narratives and other poetry of various kinds, sometimes as similes, sometimes as observations or reflections of the poet or one of the characters. Such passages are to be found also in sagas and other prose works; but here they are usually less distinctive. Mention must also be made of riddles, which have a very wide—perhaps world-wide—distribution. They are commonly expressed in poetry, and may be regarded as descriptive poems in the form of questions.

In Vol. I, Ch. XIII, we observed that in the ancient literatures of Europe descriptions of typical objects (persons, places, etc.) appear to be much more frequent than those of specific objects. The same remark is true of the literatures discussed in the two later volumes. It would seem that in oral literature specific features—the distinctive features of an individual object—tend to be forgotten, unless they are very remarkable or very familiar.

The description of Solomon's buildings in I Kings vi f. need not be taken into account here; it can hardly be derived from oral tradition, at least in its present form (cf. Vol. II, p. 739f.). Some passages in the Psalms, however, especially such as relate to Jerusalem, may probably be cited as specific descriptions of places—preserved owing to their familiarity. Here also we may refer to certain Irish poems (cf. Vol. I, p. 404), though they are usually less specific and nearly all of late date. It is in Polynesia, however, especially the western islands, that poetry of this kind is most widely cultivated; examples are quoted on p. 405 ff. above. In particular we may note poems of an emotional character which are attributed to exiles or to persons leaving a country,[1] and which commonly consist of descriptive topographical catalogues. We may

---

[1] Cf. the Tatar poems noticed on p. 155.

instance Tangiia's 'Farewell' to Tahiti, quoted on p. 268, with which may be compared the (late) Irish poem 'Deirdre's Farewell to Alba' (in 'The Fate of the Children of Uisnech') and the ballad 'Lord Maxwell's Last Goodnight'.

Descriptions of persons seem to be brief and rare almost everywhere. Where they occur, as in Ireland, they usually tend to be conventional, varying only according to the age and standing of the person described; the exceptions tend to the grotesque. But in Norse sagas, especially 'Sagas of Icelanders,' the case is otherwise; the descriptions frequently show marked individuality, which is sometimes confirmed by contemporary poems.

The chief descriptions of specific objects we have found are those of weapons, and especially shields—for which we may refer to Vol. I, p. 405 f. The Norse descriptions definitely claim to be specific, whatever we may think of the possibility of executing such designs. The Greek descriptions may doubtless be taken as representing the finest things that the poets could imagine in the way of shields.

Descriptions of typical objects are far more frequent and widespread. Under this heading we may include different types of men—or rather men in different positions and circumstances. Sometimes descriptions of the same situation are to be found in more than one literature, e.g. the English and Greek descriptions of the man consoled by minstrelsy, noticed in Vol. I, p. 407. Further examples of this kind of descriptive poetry will be found *ib*. pp. 381, 408f., and in Vol. II, pp. 215, 411, 556f., 740f. Perhaps the most striking pictures are those of the bereaved father in Beow. 2444ff., the gambler in Rgv. x. 34 (cf. Vol. II, p. 557), and the storm-tossed mariners in Psalm cvii. 23 ff. Examples in a lighter vein may be found in the Russian descriptions of the Dandy and the Belle (*ib*. p. 215) and the Yugoslav descriptions of the married and unmarried men (*ib*. p. 411). In the same series we may of course include descriptions of abstract conceptions relating to human life, like the English and Greek descriptions of old age (or the aged man) quoted in Vol. I, p. 408f.[1] In particular we may refer to the Galla description of poverty quoted on p. 556 above—with which may be compared the description of the name of the letter W (*wyn*, 'joy') in the English Runic Poem.

It may be observed that these descriptive poems are closely connected

[1] The description of the aged man in the 'Seafarer' may be compared with the introduction to the 'Instructions' of Ptahhotep (later text), which presents a very similar picture; cf. Erman, *Literature of the Ancient Egyptians*, p. 55.

with gnomes of Type II *a*—the variety relating to human activities or experiences. Such gnomes may be regarded as epitomes of 'descriptions', though as a rule they express only one (salient) characteristic of the subject. A similar connection may be seen between the 'descriptions' which we have next to consider and gnomes of Type II*c*, the variety which for short we have spoken of as 'natural history' gnomes, though they apply to much more than natural history.

Descriptions of animals, birds, etc. are found in English (e.g. the Runic Poem) and Irish (cf. Vol. I, p. 411), in the Rgveda and the Hebrew Proverbs (Vol. II, pp. 556, 741), and among the Tatars and the Bantu (cf. pp. 151 and 613 in the present volume).[1] The horse is described at great length in the Rgveda and among the Turcomans, and very briefly in the Runic Poem. But perhaps the most interesting poem of this kind is the description of the frogs in Rgv. VII. 103. We would also call attention to the fragments of Basuto songs quoted on p. 613. Descriptions of trees and plants occupy a good part of the English Runic Poem, owing to the fact that several letters of the alphabet have names of this kind. In I Kings iv. 33, Solomon is credited with compositions—presumably poetry of this kind—relating to both trees and animals.

Descriptions of natural phenomena, etc. are well represented in the English Runic Poem; those of hail and ice (the names of the letters H and I) are quoted in Vol. I, p. 415. Ice occurs again, and also storm in the Cotton Gnomes. The Rgveda has poems descriptive of wind and night (cf. Vol. II, p. 556); for the former we may refer also to the 'Works and Days', 506ff. Poetry of this kind is probably more widespread than would seem to be suggested by the few examples which we have noted. We have found it even among the Eskimos of Greenland. But among the peoples included in our survey it appears to be cultivated most of all by the Polynesians. A good example from Hawaii is the description of rain quoted on p. 406f. above. In this group we may also include the Welsh and Irish poems descriptive of winter and summer (cf. Vol. I, p. 409ff.), which have much in common with some of the poems cited above. The Polynesian calendar poems (cf. p. 405 above) may likewise be mentioned here.[2]

---

[1] We may compare also the Yugoslav poem on the thieving tom-cat (cf. Vol. II, p. 411). But this is a speech poem (Type B).

[2] The evidence would seem rather to suggest that poetry relating to natural phenomena is cultivated more especially by coastal populations who are engaged in fishing or hunting.

Descriptive poetry relating to inanimate objects occurs in the English Runic Poem and doubtless elsewhere, just as in riddles; but it is probably not very frequent. The Vedic poems on the chariot, the drum, the plough, etc. are spells or prayers rather than descriptive poems; but we may perhaps cite here a poem (Rgv. VI. 75) on the warrior's equipment (cf. Vol. II, p. 557).

Riddles[1] are perhaps to be found everywhere; and riddle poetry, of a more or less elaborate character, is very widely distributed. Riddles which are expressed in any detail, whether as complete poems or incidentally, are closely related to the descriptive poetry we have just been considering. Often indeed the only difference is that a request for interpretation takes the place of the name of the object.

The distribution of subjects, however, is somewhat different. Riddles in which the answer is a human being are rare. The 'Riddles of Gestumblindi' (cf. Vol. I, p. 412) contain no examples; in the riddles of the Exeter Book there are only two or three—all somewhat doubtful. Riddles on old age, however, are found (*ib.* p. 413); we may refer too to the riddle of the Sphinx. Riddles drawn from animal life are more common; Gestumblindi has eight examples, and the Exeter Riddles about a dozen, while instances occur also among the Tatars and the Galla (cf. pp. 153, 560 above; cf. also p. 613), though they are very brief, like most of the riddles found among these peoples. Riddles on natural phenomena, the elements, etc. are also fairly well represented in both the English and the Norse collections, while in Welsh one long and elaborate example, on wind, has been preserved (cf. Vol. I, p. 413f.). Such riddles are current also in Russia (cf. Vol. II, p. 211), among the Galla, and in Ladakh. Riddles on the seasons apparently do not occur in our collections. But the year itself was a favourite subject in India; several examples are found in the Vedas, and at least one in the Mahābhārata (cf. Vol. II, p. 558ff.). The same subject

---

[1] It is impossible of course to attempt a comprehensive treatment of this subject here. Riddles, like folk-tales, are current among many modern peoples, who otherwise have practically no oral literature; and some of the riddles which are found in ancient collections (e.g. Gestumblindi's 'cow' riddle) are widely known today. Here we can attempt no more than to note the literary form of riddles in the languages which come within our survey, and the chief classes of objects with which these riddles are concerned. We fear that even in these respects our record is far from complete, more especially for the modern peoples.

is represented in Greek (Vol. I, p. 414).[1] Riddles on inanimate objects, e.g. anchor, shield, plough, are more numerous even than those on animals in the English and Norse collections.

It will be seen that the riddles preserved in ancient literatures are in general much fuller and more detailed than those we have found current among modern peoples. They are poems complete in themselves, however short they may be, and aim at a more or less comprehensive description of the subject. The Exeter Riddles have doubtless been affected by the influence of written literature; but this can hardly be the case with Gestumblindi's riddles. Moreover such material as has survived from early times in Wales, Greece and India shows—at least usually—the same characteristics. On the other hand, modern riddles, so far as they take any definite 'literary' form, are most commonly expressed in sequences or catalogues. As a rule only one characteristic of the subject is stated; and consequently their affinities lie with gnomes of observation (Type II), rather than with descriptive poetry. Indeed a series of such gnomes might well serve as answers to a sequence of this kind.

Such sequences are not unknown in ancient literatures. Gestumblindi has one example, which has already been quoted: "What lives in high mountains? What falls in deep valleys? What lives without breathing? What is never silent?" Each question has a separate answer: 'raven', 'dew', 'fish', 'waterfall'. We have noted one somewhat similar sequence in early Irish (Vol. I, p. 414) and one single short sequence and a long dialogue containing numerous such sequences in the Mahābhārata (Vol. II, p. 560f.). Among modern peoples, however, such sequences seem to be very widespread. They are very much cultivated in Russia (*ib.* p. 212f.) and among the Tatars (cf. p. 152 ff.[2] above)—though single, more detailed riddles are also known—and we have found them in Yugoslavia (Vol. II, p. 410), and in English (international) ballads.[3] Similar riddles are current among the Galla (p. 560) and the Bantu peoples (p. 603), though we do not know whether they are grouped in sequences, or indeed whether they make use of any fixed literary form. The Galla, however, also cultivate elaborate riddles relating

---

[1] One of the Exeter Riddles (No. 23) seems to mean 'month' (or possibly 'December'); cf. Tupper, *The Riddles of the Exeter Book*, p. 117, where analogies from various languages are cited.

[2] Cf. also the sequences of riddles and answers current in Ladakh, referred to on p. 154.

[3] Nos. 1, 46, 47 in Child's collection. The last also contains some slightly longer riddles.

to specific persons or tribes; instances are quoted on p. 559 f.[1] On the other hand, Polynesian riddles (cf. p. 407), though they are very short, seem rather to resemble the riddles which are characteristic of the older literatures.

Among some peoples riddles are said to be the subject of serious contests between sages. Such is the case with the Tatars and the Polynesians, at least in stories (cf. pp. 152 f., 407 f.); and the same custom is implied in the story of Yudhishthira and the Yaksha in the Mahābhārata (cf. Vol. ii, p. 561) and possibly also in that of Solomon and the queen of Sheba (*ib.* p. 742). The story of Yudhishthira may also be compared with that of Gestumblindi (and the related ballad 'King John and the Bishop'), in which a man is required to ask (or answer) riddles, in order to save his life. In another story in the Mahābhārata (*ib.* p. 560) the boy Ashtāvakra is tested in riddles by the king, before he is allowed to enter upon the dangerous contest with Vandi. More widespread is the custom of asking riddles in connection with proposals of love or marriage—which we have found in Russia (*ib.* p. 211 ff.) and among the Tatars and in Ladakh and Polynesia (pp. 153 f., 408 above), as well as in English (international) ballads and in folk-tales.[2] The idea seems to be that of an 'education test', as we pointed out in Vol. ii, p. 214. We suspect that in communities which have no writing riddles must play a not unimportant part in the education of the young; but actually we have found no positive evidence for this, except perhaps among certain Bantu peoples.

On the subject of 'descriptive catalogue' poetry we have not much to add to what was said in Vol. i, p. 416 ff. In early Indian didactic literature one could of course find plenty of material superficially resembling these catalogues; but we have not noticed any true analogies. The Greek and English poems are products of observation and reflection, whereas the catalogues of (e.g.) the Upanishads are of a speculative or mystical character. It is quite possible, however, that better analogies may occur in the Mahābhārata; in view of the immense volume of that

[1] Such riddles occur elsewhere—e.g. there are two instances, relating to mythological subjects, in Gestumblindi's collection. In general, however, we have treated questions of this kind as antiquarian speculation.

[2] We may compare the Norse poem Alvíssmál, in which Thor questions the dwarf Alvíss, who is a suitor for the hand of his daughter. The dialogue, however, consists not of riddles, but of questions on poetic diction and synonyms. The Fjölsvinnsmál may also be compared (cf. Vol. i, p. 432).

work we may have overlooked them. Again, we have not been able to find any good analogies in the Proverbs or other early Hebrew works. Such poetry, however, is cultivated by the Tatars; in particular we may note an analogy to Solon's poem on the 'Seven Ages of Man' (cf. p. 151 above). And a Tuareg parallel to the English poem on the 'Endowments of Men' will be found on p. 672. Apart from the literatures included in our survey, compositions of this kind were known in ancient Egypt. We may note especially the 'Instruction of Duauf',[1] a work dating from towards the close of the third millennium, but much used as a schoolbook under the nineteenth dynasty. This work describes briefly the occupations of various classes of men—the smith, mason, barber, bricklayer, etc.—in a manner much like the English poems discussed in Vol. I, p. 419. But in this case it is the misery and hardships of the life which are emphasised. The object of the catalogue is to point out the attractions of the scribe's position as against all others—a favourite theme in works of this kind.

In conclusion we would call attention to the brief summary of the varieties of poetry treated under this category which we gave in Vol. I, p. 421 f. Here we wish in particular to note the close connection between descriptive and gnomic poetry. The two are commonly combined or associated; and it is often difficult to decide whether a sentence should be regarded as a 'description' or as a gnome of Type II. Indeed gnomes of this type may in general be regarded as abbreviated descriptions (cf. p. 825). Again, riddles of the longer variety are usually descriptive poems converted into questions, while those of the shorter variety are gnomes of Type II treated in the same way—or, perhaps one should say, the answers required are gnomes of this type. It is hardly necessary to point out again the gnomic affinities of the 'descriptive catalogue'.

There can be no doubt that the affinities of both categories are primarily non-heroic. From time to time they make their appearance in heroic literature, especially in Beowulf and the speeches of Vidulā, and here we sometimes find a distinctive 'heroic' variety of gnomes. We need not doubt that this represents the usage of real life; but it is not very widespread.[2] More frequently their associations are mantic, as in

---

[1] Transl. by Erman, *Literature of the Ancient Egyptians*, p. 67 ff.

[2] In the Homeric poems the descriptive similes are probably among the latest elements (cf. Vol. I, p. 407 f.). We have not noticed any examples of the heroic variety of gnome.

Norse and Greek poetry, while in India and probably in Ireland[1] they were chiefly cultivated by classes of persons (*filid* and Brahmans) whose traditions at least were mantic. But in early Hebrew works and among modern peoples such association appears to be rare. This question, and also that of the educational use of gnomic and descriptive poetry, will require notice in a later chapter.

[1] For the Irish 'Instructions'—two series of which are attributed to famous heroes—we may refer to Vol. 1, pp. 393 ff., 603.

CHAPTER IX

MANTIC LITERATURE

IN the individual literatures we have recognised two main divisions of this subject—spells and prophecies. Blessings and curses occupy a position between these two. They may be regarded either as spells which are of permanent operation or as prophecies which carry their own fulfilment with them. In addition to the above we have recognised as belonging to this category certain compositions which in Vol. I (p. 471) we described as 'declarations of mantic lore'. The Indian evidence (cf. Vol. II, p. 590) has shown that these are very closely akin to prophecy, and perhaps properly to be regarded as a variety of it.

For the study of spells early Indian (Vedic) literature supplies abundant material, especially in the Atharvaveda. A brief conspectus of this was given in Vol. II, p. 574ff. Anglo-Saxon and early Irish records also preserve a good number—though the latter are extremely obscure—and a few are to be found even among the very sparse remains of the earliest German literature. For all these we may refer to Vol. I, pp. 446ff., 466f. On the other hand, it is rather curious that no early Norse spells seem to have been preserved in their original form, though examples are known from later times. References to the use of spells, however, are frequent in the early literature, in both poems and sagas; and some early poems are evidently adaptations of spells (*ib.* 448ff.). The ancient Greek evidence is similar to the Norse, though less in quantity (*ib.* 471f.). In early Hebrew spells are rare, and as a rule not clearly distinguishable from prayers (cf. Vol. II, p. 715). All the spells known to us from ancient literatures seem to have been in poetry.

The material available from modern oral literatures is much less full and satisfactory. In Russia we have not met with any spells, though we understand that they exist and that a collection, which unfortunately has not been accessible to us, has recently been made of them. Among the Yugoslavs also spells seem not to be much in use; those of which we have heard are in prose (cf. Vol. II, p. 411). The Slovenians and Bulgarians, however, have spell poems. For the Tatars (cf. p. 133ff. above) the evidence is apparently similar to the Norse. Spells are clearly much used, though few have been accessible to us in their original form. For the Bantu peoples discussed in this volume we can only say that spells of some kind were known; we have not been able to obtain any precise information as to their character. Lastly, for Polynesia, especially New Zealand, the evidence is again abundant (cf. p. 336 ff.). Spells are, or were, in very common use, and many of them have been recorded.

From this brief survey it will be seen that the use of spells is extremely widespread, if not universal. Among Christian peoples they have tended to be forgotten; where they are found they may be regarded as survivals from earlier forms of religion.[1] Among non-Christian peoples both spell and prayer are commonly in use. It is not always easy to distinguish between the two; sometimes they seem to be combined. Under Christianity, however, prayer has tended to oust the spell.

As regards the form of spells, poetry is apparently far more common than prose, though we are quite uncertain as to whether this is true of Africa. In Europe, and perhaps in Asia, spells seem to have exercised a most important influence on the history of music, as we shall see in the next chapter.

The purposes for which spells are used are very various. Perhaps the most widespread of all is the cure of diseases and injuries, and of evils of every kind which are attributed to witchcraft. We have found spells for the well-being of the crops, for the recovery of lost cattle, and for the birth of a child both in this country and in ancient India, the last also among the Tatars; for success or safety in battle in the North, India and Polynesia; for quieting the winds among the Moriori of the Chatham Islands; for safety and success on journeys in the North and in India; for success in love in the North, Greece, India and Polynesia. But these are only a few of the objects for which spells are used. One of the most interesting series is that of the spells for success in gambling, contained in the Atharvaveda (cf. Vol. II, p. 577).

The recitation or chanting of a spell is very frequently accompanied by the use of some accessory, such as a herb, or by the performance of some symbolic act; but it is not clear to us that such accessories or performances are necessary for all spells. Written spells are very frequently mentioned in early Norse records; indeed Runic writing came to be intimately associated with manticism in the North, and probably

[1] It is strange that the study of spells continued to form part of the training of the Irish *filid* in Christian times (cf. Vol. I, p. 603); but the system was doubtless extremely conservative. Some Anglo-Saxon spells are more or less Christianised, with curious effects.

among the Teutonic peoples in general. There is some evidence for a similar use of Ogams and other forms of writing among the Celtic peoples; and among other peoples of antiquity such usages would seem to have been rather widespread. Modern analogies are not unknown (cf. Vol. II, p. 411).

Blessings and curses are closely akin to spells, and should perhaps be treated as varieties thereof. Unlike other spells they are, usually at least, not prescriptive, but vary according to the speaker's wishes. We are uncertain, however, how far this distinction can be pressed. Spells may have been invented for special occasions; and on the other hand we are not prepared to deny the existence of prescriptive blessings or curses. Blessings and curses are usually, though apparently not always, irrevocable and permanent in operation. The use of accessories seems to be exceptional, though not unknown.

It follows from what has been said above that most of the evidence to be considered here is secondary, i.e. the examples are chiefly to be found in speech poems (Type B) or incidentally in narratives. The Atharvaveda, however, preserves a number of curses which seem to be intended for actual use, partly against thieves, partly against demons (cf. Vol. II, p. 580f.). And the Norse declaration of outlawry, quoted in Vol. I, p. 386f., is probably to be taken as a curse. Further examples could probably be found, especially in inscriptions. But in the records with which we are concerned secondary instances are more frequent.[1] We may refer to the passages in the Mahābhārata cited in Vol. II, p. 581, and to the Hebrew passages cited *ib.* 716f., to which many more might be added. Similar curses are to be found in early Irish records (cf. Vol. I, p. 466), though the actual words are seldom given. But the most detailed and interesting example we know is the curse pronounced by Skírnir upon Gerðr in the Skírnismál, st. 25 ff. (*ib.* p. 449). In this case a magic wand is used as an accessory; the curse too is presumably revoked when Gerðr gives way. The story belongs to mythology; but we may compare the account of Egill Skallagrímsson's cursing (*ib.* p. 451f.), where a horse's head[2] is used as an accessory.

For instances in modern oral literatures we may refer to the Yugoslav

---

[1] We are not quite clear whether the curses contained in Hebrew religious poems, such as Ps. cix, are to be taken as primary examples.

[2] Behind the soldiers depicted on the silver bowl found at Gundestrup there are three figures carrying horses' heads on poles, which may be intended for a similar purpose. The bowl of course belongs to a much earlier (La Tène) period.

poems cited in Vol. II, pp. 366, 411 f., and to the Tatar and Polynesian poems noticed on pp. 135 f., 339 f. above. Note may also be taken of the mesmeric effect said to be produced by the curse of a Tungus shaman in the reference cited on p. 136.

In ancient literatures we hear not seldom of solemn imprecations pronounced upon those who shall violate oaths or appropriate objects which have been devoted. These correspond to the Norse declaration of outlawry cited above. Interesting examples will be found in the Iliad III. 298 ff., relating to the violation of an oath, and in Joshua vi. 17 ff., relating to the spoils of Jericho. With the latter may be compared Beow. 3069 ff., where a curse is said to be imposed upon anyone who should disturb the buried treasure. The curse proclaimed by the Serbian prince Lazar (cf. Vol. II, p. 366) perhaps belongs properly to the same series. Here also we may refer to imprecations pronounced against an enemy's host in challenges to battle, as in the 'Battle of the Goths and Huns',[1] st. 25: "Your host is panic-stricken, your leader is doomed... Othin is wroth with you." The devotion of an enemy to Othin is of frequent occurrence in Norse tradition;[2] and vows of this kind, followed by wholesale massacre and destruction, are sufficiently attested by historical records for both the Teutonic and the Celtic peoples.

'Blessings' seem not to be in such general use as curses, though prayers for blessings are to be found almost everywhere. We have not met with any formal pronouncements of blessings in modern oral literatures; but this may be due to accident. In ancient literatures on the other hand they are not rare. There would seem to be a rather curious difference of usage in this respect between East and West. In ancient Oriental literatures, as among the modern Tatars, blessings are pronounced by seers—with whom we may reckon the Hebrew Patriarchs —as well as by deities and other supernatural beings; in the West they seem to be restricted to the latter, though we are not prepared to speak with any great confidence on this point.[3]

For examples of Indian blessings we may refer to Vol. II, p. 580. The most frequent variety is the granting of offspring. Thus Sāvitrī is the

---

[1] Ed. and transl. by Kershaw, *Anglo-Saxon and Norse Poems*, p. 142 ff.

[2] For examples see Chadwick, *The Cult of Othin*, p. 7 f.

[3] Some such idea seems to be implied (e.g.) in Thorfinns S. Karlsefnis, cap. 4. Leifr Eiríksson (the discoverer of America) is returning from Norway to Greenland; and King Ólafr Tryggvason tells him he must introduce Christianity there. He remarks that that will be a difficult task, but the king says he will have luck in it. Then he replies: "That depends solely on whether I have your help." The idea is clearly non-Christian; but there is no formal pronouncement of a blessing.

gift of the goddess Savitrī. But Drupada is indebted to two Brahmans for his children; they are produced from the altar, but there is no reference to any deity. In Mahābh. III. liii. 6ff. Damayantī and her three brothers are a gift from the Brahman Damana, though in this case there is no formal pronouncement of a blessing. Similar examples occur in Hebrew. Sometimes, as in the births of Isaac and Samson, the child is a gift from Jehovah; sometimes, as in the case of the child born to the lady of Shunem (II Kings iv. 13ff.), the blessing seems to come from the seer himself. More important for our purpose, however, are the formal blessings pronounced in poetry by the Patriarchs Isaac and Jacob for their sons and by Moses for his followers (cf. Vol. II, p. 716). With the two former we may compare the story of Yayāti and Pūru, related in Mahābh. I. lxxxv (*ib.* p. 498f.). Such blessings seem to be irrevocable; and they are always pronounced by speakers who are approaching the end of life. Here also we may refer to the story (*ib.* p. 716) of the seer Balaam, who is invited to curse Israel, but actually blesses them, in a series of poems. The story is of importance as showing that the pronouncement of curses, if not of blessings also, was regarded as a regular function of the seer.

For Europe the Norse evidence is, as usual, by far the most interesting. Apparently blessings are pronounced only by supernatural beings. The declarations of the Norns at the birth of a child[1] seem to be regarded in this light, as (e.g.) at the beginning of Helgakviða Hundingsbana I (cf. Vol. I, p. 208). In some stories, however, only the first two Norns confer true blessings; the third out of spite imposes some disadvantage, or limits the benefits conferred by the others. Blessings are bestowed also by the god Othin upon his favourites.[2] In the Hyndluljóð, st. 3, he is said to give victory to some and wealth to others; eloquence and wisdom he grants to various persons. In the (legendary) Gautreks Saga, cap. 7, the gods assemble in a forest-clearing to determine the future of Starkaðr, who is present with them. Othin pronounces upon him a series of blessings; but each of these is qualified or marred by Thor, who cherishes a grudge against him. Thus (e.g.), when Othin declares: "I grant him the gift of poetry, so that he shall be able to compose as fast as

---

[1] The custom of pronouncing blessings of some kind at the naming of a child seems to be widespread. We may refer to the account of the naming of Manas (cf. p. 28 above), where the child receives blessings from the various guests present. Something of the kind seems to be implied also in the Polynesian story of the naming of Maui (cf. p. 283f.), where the effect of the *karakia* is spoilt by the father's forgetfulness. [2] Cf. Chadwick, *The Cult of Othin*, pp. 51ff., 68ff.

he can speak", Thor rejoins: "He shall not be able to remember what
he composes". The evidence from other parts of Europe is somewhat
slight, though we hear not rarely of blessings bestowed by Zeus and
other deities, or by the Muses.

Prophecy, as we remarked in Vol. I, would seem at first sight to have
little in common with spells; but a connecting link[1] is supplied by the
subjects we have just been considering. In particular the Norns make
known the destiny of a child, and are consulted as an oracle for this
purpose. But the destiny which they make known is determined by
themselves, and the operation (weaving) by which it is determined is
clearly in the nature of a spell. Here also we may refer again to the
passage of Dion Cassios (LV. 1) relating to the death of Drusus, which
was quoted in Vol. I, p. 453. As he was approaching the Elbe, a woman
of superhuman size called out to him: "The Fates forbid thee to advance.
Away! The end of thy deeds and of thy life is at hand." Is this a
prophecy or a curse?

We have repeatedly[2] called attention to the fact that prophecy may
relate to the present and the past, as well as to the future—or, in other
words, that ancient literatures draw no clear distinction between prophecy (in the modern sense) and declarations of mantic knowledge
relating to the past or present. Among many modern peoples too
prophecy relating to the present is one of the chief functions of the seer
or medicine man. This faculty is applied to many different purposes.
Among the most widespread are those of indicating what has become of
lost animals and of ascertaining and removing the causes of various
evils, such as a plague, the illness of a chief, or other calamity, which, in
Africa at least, are commonly attributed to malignant witchcraft.

In ancient records, as we have seen, the use of spells for the former of
these purposes is very frequently mentioned. But seers were sometimes
resorted to, as in the story of Samuel and Saul's lost asses (cf. Vol. II,
p. 717).[3] For the latter purpose we hear mostly of divination by the
casting of lots. Instances occur especially in stories of ships endangered
or hampered by bad weather. Thus in Gautreks Saga, cap. 7, when
Víkarr's fleet is held up, it is ascertained by divination that Othin

---

[1] Another link may be found in necromancy, which is extremely widespread. It
is commonly accompanied by spells, but the most frequent object is to obtain
knowledge of the future.

[2] Vol. I, p. 473, and elsewhere in the first two volumes.

[3] For a somewhat similar story among the Tatars see p. 85 above.

requires a victim; and the lot falls upon the king himself. We may compare the story of Jonah. Sometimes, however, both the cause and the remedy of the trouble are declared by a seer. The sacrifice of Iphigeneia at Aulis, as related in the 'Cypria', provides a rather close analogy to the story of Víkarr; but it is the seer Calchas who declares the cause of the trouble and orders the sacrifice. And in the Iliad i. 68 ff. the same seer announces the cause of the plague, and shows how the deity is to be appeased.

The seer's faculty of knowing what cannot be known by ordinary means may further be illustrated by the story, published by Castrén (cf. p. 198), of the three brothers who encountered a shaman. The latter says that he "knows the future, the past, and everything which is taking place in the present, both above and below the earth". One of the heroes then asks him, "what our people are doing far away in our own home". From ancient literatures we may compare with this the stories of Elisha and of Math son of Mathonwy (cf. Vol. ii, p. 717)—in both of which cases the seer knows what is spoken at a distance. To the same faculty may also be attributed the power of instantaneous counting, possessed by the seer Mopsos and by King Rtuparna (cf. Vol. i, p. 474, ii, p. 591). Other stories again turn upon the knowledge of something which has happened in the past, but has now come to be unknown or known incorrectly. An interesting example of this kind is to be found in the dispute between King Mongan and his *fili* Forgoll as to the scene of the death of the ancient king Fothad Airgthech (cf. Vol. i, p. 98). With this may be compared Herodotos' story of the question put to the Delphic Oracle about the burial-place of Orestes and the response given thereto (*ib.* p. 473).[1]

Prophecy relating to the past, however, is more usually concerned with antiquarian speculation upon genealogies and the beginnings of things.[2] In the Hyndluljóð the goddess Freyja appeals to Hyndla, who is obviously a (supernatural) witch, to recount the ancestry of Óttarr, her devotee. The Völuspá, or 'Prophecy of the Seeress' (or

---

[1] An interesting parallel occurs in the Welsh 'Stanzas of the Graves' (Black Book, No. xix), st. 42 f. The speaker says that Elffin has brought him to prove his 'bardic (i.e. mantic) lore' (*bartrin*, for *barddrin*)—by identifying an unknown grave. It has been shown by I. Williams, *Canu Llywarch Hen*, p. xlviii f., that the speaker must be Taliesin, and that the passage would seem to be derived from an earlier form of the story of Taliesin—where Elffin is required to prove the superior skill of his bard (cf. Guest's Mabinogion, in 'Everyman', p. 269).

[2] Including doubtless the personnel of the divine communities (cf. p. 795 ff.).

'Witch') is concerned with cosmogony—the origin of the world and the gods and other supernatural beings—as well as with the catastrophe which is to come. Hesiod's 'Theogony' is doubtless to be taken in a similar sense. He says (31f.) that, when the Muses called him on Mt Helicon, "they inspired me with a voice divine to celebrate both the future and the past". Of the Muses themselves (cf. Vol. II, p. 624f.) he says that they tell of "the present, the future and the past". In the Iliad (I. 70) the same description is given of Calchas: "he knew the present, the future and the past." It is probably a static description of a seer. For ancient India the evidence is perhaps not quite so explicit; but there can be no doubt that antiquarian speculation, whether in the Purānas or in the cosmogonic poems of the Rgveda, was the work of authors who claimed to be seers, and were regarded as such. Such may also have been the case with the Hebrews, though here we suspect that in general the influence of sanctuaries was stronger than that of individual authors. For the Tatars we may refer again to Castrén's story cited above. The shaman here claims the same powers which are attributed to Calchas—perhaps even more, for he adds "both above and below the earth".

Prophecy relating to the future, i.e. prophecy in the ordinary sense, is found in all the ancient literatures we have surveyed, except English. In modern times it is found among the Tatars, in Polynesia and in some parts of Africa; in Slavonic oral poetry we have met with very little. In general it will perhaps be sufficient here to give references to the chief passages in which we have discussed this subject—viz. Vol. I, pp. 445 f. (Greek), 451 f. (Norse), 453 ff. (Welsh), 462 ff. (Irish); Vol. II, pp. 579 f. (Indian), 719 ff. (Hebrew); Vol. III, pp. 340 (Polynesian), 562 ff. (Galla). It will be seen from these references that prophecies differ greatly in character, even among the same people. Sometimes they are specific and detailed, sometimes obscure and veiled; sometimes they hardly amount to more than vague forebodings. Sometimes they are a result of dreams or visions, or are uttered under ecstasy. Sometimes they seem to be due to some faculty inherent in the seer himself, sometimes to revelation or inspiration from a deity or other supernatural being, in which case the seer may be merely the mouthpiece of the latter. This question was discussed to some extent in the last chapter of Vol. I.

Two special varieties of prophecy may be mentioned in passing. One is what may be called 'prophetic history', i.e. history related as future by someone, usually a seer or supernatural being, who is represented as speaking at a time long anterior to the events. The history as a rule consists largely of a succession of kings. This variety of prophecy is well represented in Wales, Ireland and India (the Purānas). The second variety we would refer to is political prophecy; and this is more widespread and important than the other. Such prophecy is usually of a strongly patriotic character. It was much cultivated in Wales during the eleventh and twelfth centuries, when the Normans were trying to establish their power, though many of the prophecies were attributed to Myrddin (Merlin), who lived on the Scottish Border some five hundred years before. The early Hebrew prophets, especially Isaiah, reflect a somewhat similar situation, and are likewise markedly patriotic in feeling; opposition to foreign influence is a constant feature in Hebrew prophecy. We know also that patriotic prophetic poetry was current in Greece at the time of the Persian invasions, though not much of it has been preserved. A prophetic movement of the same kind took place in South Africa, among the Amaxosa and neighbouring Bantu peoples, during the early part of last century, when the penetration of the country by white colonists was becoming intensified.[1] Something similar happened about the same time in New Zealand; but prophecy of a patriotic character has long been current in intertribal disputes also among the Polynesian peoples and was especially highly developed in Hawaii (cf. p. 340). We may note too that the only prophetic Yugoslav poem which we have seen (cf. Vol. II, pp. 334f., 366) shows a very strongly developed feeling of nationality.

Lastly, we may refer to the curiously widespread prophecies relating to an elemental catastrophe, sometimes connected with the end of the world. Instances are to be found both in the Mahābhārata and in the Hebrew prophets (*ib.* pp. 622, 731), though we are not clear as to their date in either case. Such prophecies occur also among the Tatars (cf. p. 137f., above), by whom they may perhaps have been derived from India. But it is not so easy to account for the Norse doctrine of Ragnarök;[2] and there is a trace of a similar doctrine among the Druids (cf. Vol. I, p. 328). Obscure as the question is, there would seem to be

---

[1] Cf. Shooter, *The Kafirs of Natal*, etc., p. 195 ff.; cf. also p. 636 above. Reference may also be made here to the 'mullahs' or 'mad mullahs' who have often caused trouble to European governments in North Africa; but we do not know whether any of their prophecies have been preserved.

[2] In Ragnarök, as depicted e.g. in the Völuspá, the elemental catastrophe is combined with a battle between the gods and demons (*jötnar*), which has something in common with the Greek battles between gods and demons. But the latter are referred to the far past, not to the future.

enough resemblance between these various ideas to suggest the possibility of derivation from a common source, presumably in some volcanic region. The Indian doctrine is, sometimes at least, combined with the story of the Flood; but it is not clear that this connection is original.

We have yet to consider (cf. p. 839) the class of compositions which in Vol. I we described as 'declarations of mantic lore' (or 'bardic wisdom'). In Vol. II we discussed another series of compositions, which we were inclined to describe as 'timeless-nameless prophecies'. In the present volume we have met with other compositions, which seem to have something in common with one or other of these. We are now inclined to regard all these compositions as prophecies—relating not to events, whether future, present or past, in the material world, but to an unseen world. This unseen world may consist of beings—commonly, though not necessarily, of human form and character—or merely of abstract ideas or conceptions. It may be real enough to the seer, though it is seldom, if ever, a creation of his own mind; it is a possession which he has inherited from his teachers and predecessors.

In some sense seers may doubtless be said to be occupied with an unseen world everywhere. But the extent to which this forms the subject of their utterances varies between one people and another. The Hebrew literature which has survived from the earliest times is for the most part primarily religious. Yet little is said of Jehovah, apart from his messages to men, especially the people of Israel; such visions as those of Micaiah (I Kings xxii. 19 ff.) and Isaiah (cap. vi) are merely incidental or preliminary to messages to men. A polytheistic religion like that of the Rgveda might be expected to afford more scope for utterances of this kind. Yet the hymns give hardly any information about the divine community or the relations of the deities with one another; the poets' attention is practically always concentrated upon their own needs. The Zulu prophet who visited the home of the dead (cf. Vol. I, p. 221) seems to have given a much more detailed description; but his 'vision' was subsidiary to a message to Tchaka, the Zulu king. From the Tatars also (cf. p. 92 ff.) we have graphic accounts of visits to Heaven and the abode of Erlik Khan; but in these again the chief interest lies in the mortals who undertake these visits. Here we are concerned more especially with visions and mantic utterances in which the interest lies in the other world itself.

We have not met with any detailed first-hand descriptions of gods or their abodes, though such are probably to be found.[1] Secondary examples are not rare. We may cite the Grímnismál, st. 4 ff., where the disguised Othin is revealing himself: "Holy is the land which I see extending to the Aesir and the Elves", etc. What follows is a description of the homes of the deities, their sanctuary, the Ash of Yggdrasill and, finally, of Othin himself. We may compare the long *fagu* from the Paumotu Archipelago (cf. p. 308 f.), in which the god Kiho (Io) describes himself. Perhaps we may also refer here to some of the Irish Mag Mell poetry, especially the second poem in 'The Voyage of Bran' (cf. Vol. I, p. 468), where the god Manannan mac Lir is the speaker. Such poems may very well be modelled on first-hand 'prophecies', though they are naturally subject to expansion and elaboration for the purpose of entertainment or instruction—as may be seen clearly enough both in the Grímnismál and in the Mag Mell poetry. Indeed it is likely that mantic utterances of this kind were one of the chief sources of theological poetry (cf. p. 787).

Visions of the home of the dead are of more frequent occurrence; and even first-hand descriptions are not very rare. We may instance Shortland's account of the experience of a Maori woman, whose nephew was in his service (cf. p. 290 f.)—an experience apparently by no means unique in New Zealand. We may compare the story of Naciketas (cf. Vol. II, p. 602). The shaman of the Tatars visits Erlik Khan in the course of his duties, and gives a detailed account, in dramatic form, of what he sees and hears in his abode (cf. p. 206 ff. above).[2] We have referred above to a South African story which—even if the incident itself was an imposture—shows that knowledge of the home of the dead was regarded as not unattainable by prophets. The mediums of Uganda (cf. p. 629 f.) must owe their existence to a belief not very remote from this; we may compare also the story of Kintu noticed on p. 588. On the other hand, the evidence afforded by ancient literatures is less satisfactory. Except where necromancy is practised for a specific purpose, the mantic element has given way to a more or less purely imaginative treatment, though the stories may imply the former existence of such visions. The Mag Mell poetry should be mentioned again here.

Next we may take 'prophecies' or mantic declarations relating to the powers of the seer himself. Supernatural powers are commonly claimed by seers and witches; and formal declarations of such claims have been

---

[1] We may refer to Verbitski's account of the sacrifice to Bai Ülgen (cf. p. 200 ff.), the latter part of which seems to have been abbreviated.

[2] We may compare the dirges of the Sea Dyaks, noticed on p. 487 ff.

recorded at first hand, perhaps not unfrequently, in modern times. Sometimes a seer claims identity with his deity. For a most interesting example of this kind we may refer to the incident noticed on p. 445 f., where the seeress repeatedly states that she is Pele (the volcano goddess), and assumes full responsibility for what the goddess has done and will do.[1] Another interesting example—though not strictly first hand— occurs in a Maori story of an interview between Bishop G. A. Selwyn and a *tohunga* called Unuaho[2]. The latter claims power over the elements, the waters of a lake, the trees, the earth and mankind, and, as a challenge to the bishop, withers a tree and then brings it to life again. The same man was credited with being able by his will-power and spells to choke or paralyse an enemy, to kill a bird in mid air, to quell a storm, and to cause lightning and thunder.

We think that it is in the light of such declarations as these that the series of early Welsh poems discussed in Vol. i, p. 459ff., should be interpreted. These poems, as we have seen, contain long lists of questions on the laws of nature, etc. and rhetorical catalogues introduced by the formulae 'I have been', 'I am', 'I know'—catalogues which imply not merely supernatural knowledge, but also some kind of transformation into animals of various kinds, and even into inanimate and incorporeal things. It is uncertain whether these poems are directly derived from first-hand declarations, or whether they are speech poems in character modelled upon such declarations; but certain passages seem to point to an origin in contests of 'wisdom', as suggested in Vol. i, p. 105. Further, we have seen (*ib.* p. 466f.) that similar features, including the catalogues, occur in some early Irish poems, and, again (*ib.* p. 468), that in the second poem in 'The Voyage of Bran' it is prophesied of the mantic prince Mongan that "he will be in the shape of every beast", etc. With all this we may compare the claims of the Tatar shaman, who not only knows the past, the present and the future, but can transform himself into bird, beast or inanimate object—perhaps even the wind and other elements.[3] Similar powers of transformation are attributed to Brahman seers (especially into the form of deer), to the mantic

---

[1] It is to be observed that this claim was made on more than one occasion, and apparently by different seeresses. The evidence comes from two different missionaries, who were present when these declarations were uttered.

[2] Cowan, *Fairy Folk Tales of the Maori*, p. 109ff. Unuaho also uses the expression, "Am not I a god in myself?" But there seems to be no reason for thinking that he was identified with any generally recognised deity, like Pele.

[3] Cf. Chadwick, *Journ. R. Anthr. Inst.* LXVI, 75 ff. (esp. p. 98).

god Othin,[1] and to certain Greek mythical beings, e.g. Proteus and Thetis, who have the faculty of prophecy. It is clear then that the declarations of which we are speaking, however absurd they may seem, represent a very widespread type of mantic thought.

In conclusion reference must be made here to the Upanishads, which in Vol. II, p. 590, we ventured to describe as examples of 'timeless-nameless prophecy'. These works, which we discussed *ib.* p. 584ff., consist of pronouncements and debates upon certain abstract problems with which intellectual people in India, princes as well as Brahmans, were deeply concerned, especially it would seem in the period between the eighth and the fifth centuries (B.C.). The connection between these doctrines and the declarations discussed in the last two paragraphs is, we think, not quite so remote as might appear at first sight. The conception with which the sages are chiefly occupied is that of *brahma*, which may be defined as a power which pervades and comprehends the world and is itself self-existent. But the term originally meant 'spell' or 'prayer', from which it came to denote 'holy power' or, perhaps we should say, 'spiritual power'—often in contrast with *kṣatra*, 'princely power'. The declarations discussed above expressed the claims of the (personal) seer to a power over nature; the evolution of the term *brahma* proceeds along lines not very remote from this—the idea being that the seer's power (in the abstract) is the dominant force in the world.

This abstract thinking was not for everyone. In the Mahābhārata, as indeed in some of the Upanishads, the impersonal *brahma* has become a personal Brahmā (masculine), a new supreme deity and creator. Sarasvatī, originally the name of a (sacred) river, then identified with Vāc, 'Speech' (personified), eventually comes to be his wife. Many of the sages who figure in the Upanishads appear also in the Mahābhārata, and the difference in their characterisation is interesting and instructive.

We have seen that the associations of the Upanishads, as well as the literary tradition from which they are derived, are mantic. They may perhaps best be described as prophecies relating to the abstract.[2] Sometimes indeed they show a tendency to pass into something which is little more than rhetoric, as we have remarked (*ib.* p. 587). But this is

---

[1] Especially in the Ynglinga Saga, cap. 6 f., where he is represented as a wizard, and said to become bird, beast, fish or snake at will.

[2] This term seems, on consideration, to be preferable to 'timeless-nameless prophecies'. We have as a rule used the latter expression in relation to unspecified (human) individuals. But the Upanishads are much more concerned with abstracts.

not a peculiarity of Indian manticism. The Irish 'Colloquy of the Two Sages' (*ib.* p. 589) is also clearly mantic in its associations and its literary tradition; but it can hardly be regarded otherwise than as an exercise in rhetoric. The same tendency is observable in prophecies of all kinds, probably everywhere, and is natural enough in subjects where definite knowledge is unattainable—more especially where the tradition is so purely academic as in India. In Europe Othin, the mantic god, is the giver of eloquence and poetry; and the same is true of Apollo and the Muses.

The classification of mantic literature adopted in this chapter must not be regarded as exhaustive. Other forms of mantic activity might have been illustrated, though they are probably less important from the literary point of view.

Mention should be made of the interpretation of omens. To the modern mind this is merely a variety of popular wisdom or folklore. But it was once in high esteem as a branch of mantic knowledge; at sacrifices in particular the observation of omens was maintained in official use down to comparatively late times, even at Rome. In literature which comes within our scope the best example perhaps of a composition of this kind is to be found in the Reginsmál, st. 19 ff., where the disguised Othin gives instruction in omens to Sigurðr. We may also cite here Hesiod's calendar of lucky and unlucky days, in the 'Works and Days' (765 ff.). But instances are probably to be met with everywhere. In particular we may refer to the 'Omen Birds' of Singalang Burong, which play a very important part in the religion of the Sea Dyaks (cf. pp. 478, 484 ff.).

The interpretation of dreams is another form of mantic activity, to which importance has often been attached. Here again instances are perhaps to be found everywhere. They abound in Norse poetry and saga; for interesting examples we may cite the interpretations given by Ósvífr Helgason in Ari's Íslendingabók, cap. 4, and by Gestr Oddleifsson in the Laxdoela Saga, cap. 33. We may also refer to the story of Joseph in Genesis.

More important perhaps is the fact that hymns are often regarded as mantic works. According to Indian scholastic tradition every hymn in the Rgveda was the utterance of a seer, to whom it was revealed. We have seen (Vol. II, p. 607 ff.) that most of the Rgveda is derived from collections of hymns by priestly families. But a good number of hymns profess to be the work of the famous seers from whom these families claimed descent; and there seems to be no adequate reason for doubting their statements. We may compare the evidence from Hawaii, quoted on p. 446 ff. above. The significance of these facts is that the seer here appears in a different position from that which he occupies in spells, prophecies, etc. Here he speaks, not as the mouthpiece of a deity to men, but as a man to a deity, though he is inspired by the latter. His position is practically that of the shaman of the Tatars when he is visiting Bai Ülgen or Erlik. In necromancy the principle is the same; for examples see Vol. I, p. 450 f. (and p. 445, note); Vol. II, p. 667; and in this volume pp. 129, 454, 629 ff., 902.

The seer then is in a double sense the intermediary between men and deities; he is employed by men in order to approach the deities, and by deities to announce their messages to men. His position differs from that of priests—who commonly inherit from him—only in the fact that he owes it to his personal mantic power or inspiration, whereas priests owe theirs to traditional rights. We may refer here to what Diodoros (v. 31) says of the Gauls. He states that it is their custom never to offer a sacrifice except in the presence of a 'philosopher' (i.e. Druid); for they say that offerings acceptable to the gods must be presented through those who are acquainted with the nature of the gods, since they only know their language. The Druids seem to have been priests who adhered to the cultivation of manticism (cf. Vol. I, p. 609 ff.). Their character was evidently very similar to that of the philosophers who figure in the Upanishads.

It may be observed that seers or mantic priests may preserve their manticism, even when the gods have disappeared or lost their vitality. In post-Vedic India the old prayers and rites retain their potency; but the mantic power (*brahma*) is no longer derived from deities, but inherent in the words themselves and in the persons (Brahmans) who use them (cf. Vol. II, p. 583, 585 f.).[1] In principle the manticism of this period tends to approximate to the form in which it usually appears among the peoples of northern Europe (cf. Vol. I, p. 638 ff.), and perhaps also among the Tatars; the 'inspiration', if such it can be called, comes from within.

[1] This remark applies strictly of course only to the Vedic schools, and perhaps only to some of them. The Mahābhārata shows a great variety of theistic conceptions.

CHAPTER X

RECITATION AND COMPOSITION

IN this chapter we have to discuss (1) the circumstances under which literature of various kinds is produced, and (2) the methods of production. In the former case we have to take account not only of the original production, but also of subsequent recitations; in the latter case the chief questions to be considered are those of improvisation and memorisation and of the use of the voice, with or without instrumental accompaniment. Literature intended from the beginning for reading does not come within our scope.

(1) In discussing the circumstances of production it will be convenient in the personal categories to arrange the material according to the 'types' which we have employed throughout our work.

Poems of Type D—i.e. panegyrics, elegies, hymns, prayers and exhortations—are as a rule intended for use in the presence of the person who is celebrated or appealed to; and the same is doubtless true of prose compositions of the same type, though these are seldom preserved. Hymns and prayers to deities cannot be regarded as exceptions; for the deity is thought of as present in some way, or at least accessible to the words of the poet. Such compositions are of course frequently capable of being adapted to use on future occasions, or even utilised without change.

Elegies or dirges are, as we have seen, among the most widespread forms of oral literature; and it would seem that everywhere, so far as our information goes, they are as a rule intended for use at a ceremonial mourning.[1] This need not take place at the actual funeral—very often it is held subsequently—but the frequent use of 'thou' and the Vocative shows that, at least by literary tradition, the deceased was regarded as present in some sense. The preservation of elegies in their original form is probably to be ascribed in general to the fame either of the poet or of

[1] Exceptions occur, e.g. the Hákonarmál and 'The Bonny Earl of Murray' (Child (No. 181 A), though in the former (cf. Vol. I, p. 344 f.) changes may have been made later. The Russian 'laments for tsars' (cf. Vol. II, p. 67) are not elegies in the strict sense, but poems of Type B in imitation of elegies. True elegies from Russia will be found *ib.* p. 229 ff.

the person celebrated; but it is very likely that elegies which met with favour were often copied or adapted to use for other occasions, as we know to have been the case in Polynesia (cf. pp. 370, 417).

Panegyrics are concerned either with the achievements of heroes or with the power and generosity of kings. In both cases they seem to be composed normally for recitation in the presence of the person celebrated; in the former this takes place very soon after the achievement. For instances we may cite the references to the panegyrics upon Beowulf (Beow. 867 ff.) and David (I Sam. xviii. 6 f.); modern examples are frequent (cf. pp. 58 f., 546, 578 ff. above). Ancient panegyrics are preserved in Welsh, Irish, Norse and Vedic Indian (cf. Vol. I, pp. 38 ff., 55, 343 ff., 350; Vol. II, p. 482 f.), while references to the recitation of such poems are widespread, especially in records (English, Greek and Latin) of the Teutonic Heroic Age and in the Mahābhārata (cf. Vol. I, p. 574 f.; Vol. II, pp. 605 f., 617). Modern examples and references will be found in this volume (pp. 513 f., 618).[1] As in the case of elegies, the ancient examples must owe their preservation to the fame either of the poet or of the person celebrated. It would seem, especially from Norse records,[2] that more care was spent on their composition than upon that of any other kind of poetry, and that panegyrics composed by famous poets were studied as models by later generations. Almost all the Norse and Irish examples which have survived consist of fragments, which are quoted either as illustrations of poetic diction or for their historical interest. The preservation of the Welsh poems is probably due to their use in the training of bards. In other ancient literatures panegyrics are seldom preserved, though references to them are frequent. The scene of the first recitation is—in panegyrics upon kings—almost invariably the king's hall.

Hortatory poetry, or at least political oratory in poetic language, is much cultivated among the modern peoples included in our survey; instances will be found on pp. 463 f., 516 f., 582, 663 above. The scene is usually either the assembly or the battle-field. In ancient literatures we have found very little poetry of this kind (cf. Vol. I, pp. 348, 351,

---

[1] We may include the peculiar panegyrics of the Basuto (cf. p. 710, note), in which the person celebrated seems to be the poet himself, though he sometimes has them recited to him by minstrels.

[2] We may refer e.g. to Egils Saga Skallagrímssonar, cap. 59, where the composition of Egill's panegyric upon King Eric Blood-axe is described (cf. Vol. I, p. 343). When advised to compose the poem, Egill at first replies that he has never occupied his mind with composing panegyrics upon this king (who was his deadly enemy).

355 f.), from which we may probably infer, not that it was unusual, but that it had only a short life. The little that has survived is mostly the work of famous poets, and dates in each case from near the close of the period.

With regard to the composition and preservation of personal or occasional poetry (Type E) little need be said here. Such poetry is extremely widespread among modern peoples—at least among the peoples treated in this volume—and a good number of instances have been quoted or cited above (pp. 187, 268, 550 f., 582 f., 667 ff.) in connection with the circumstances of their composition.[1] From ancient times on the other hand we have very little material except in Greek and Norse (cf. Vol. I, p. 357 ff.). Yet it must not be inferred that such poetry was less cultivated than among modern peoples; it has perished doubtless because its interest is as a rule ephemeral. The circumstances under which it can be preserved have been discussed above (p. 708); we may note that almost all the Greek and Norse examples are attached to the names of famous poets. Sometimes we hear of references to the composition of such poetry in countries or periods from which no texts have survived. Interesting examples may be found in Gelimer's letter (cf. Vol. I, p. 576) and the story of Ibro Nukić (cf. Vol. II, pp. 329 and 337, note 3).

Apart from poems composed by the author for his own amusement or consolation, we have to take account also of dialogue or conversation poems, in which speeches are improvised by two persons alternately. These also are rather widespread, especially in the form of sparring between a youth and a girl. Examples may be found in an incident related of Egill Skallagrímsson in his youth, and quoted in Vol. I, p. 366 f. and in a Yugoslav poem noticed in Vol. II, p. 403 f.; and they are common among the Tatars (pp. 152, 157 above). Somewhat similar instances may be found in the other literatures treated in this volume. Some of these are doubtless secondary, i.e. speeches in

---

[1] It is quite possible that such poetry, like that of social ritual in Russia (cf. Vol. II, p. 286), is often composed by experts for a fee, though we have not noted this custom in our survey. For some very interesting observations on the composition of poetry of this kind in the Solomon Islands (Buin) we may refer to Thurnwald, *Yale University Publications in Anthropology*, No. 8 (especially p. 6). The poet may spend three or four weeks preparing his work, fitting together phrases and melody, and perhaps retire to the forest for the purpose. Then he brings it to the man who is employing him, who may suggest improvements. When completed, the song is sung at a feast. Lampoons are often produced in this way, sometimes with serious results.

character (Type B), but they may be taken as evidence that such improvisations were widely cultivated.

Narrative poetry and saga (Type A) require somewhat more detailed notice. We will begin with the latter.

It will be convenient to distinguish between first-hand stories, in which the narrator speaks from personal knowledge, and second-hand stories, for which he is indebted to others. As an example of the former we may refer to the description, contained in Njáls Saga, of the Christmas party given by Earl Sigurðr of Orkney in 1013—an account of which will be found in Vol. 1, p. 580. In response to a request from the king of Dublin, the story of the murder of Njáll is told by Gunnarr Lambason, one of those who had taken part in the attack. On the same page we cited a passage in the Fóstbroeðra Saga, where a certain Thorgrímr narrates to an assembly in Greenland how he had slain Thorgeirr, the friend of Thormóðr Kolbrúnarskald. With these references we may compare II Kings viii. 4 f., where the king of Israel (Joram) requests Gehazi, the servant of Elisha, to give him an account of all the great things which the prophet had done.

For a good example of the second-hand story we may refer to Vol. 1, p. 581, where King Harold III of Norway is entertained with an account of his own exploits in the Mediterranean by an (unnamed) Icelander. This man had heard the story in his own country from one of Harold's followers; but he tells it in such a way as to please the king, and at such length that it extends over the twelve evenings of a Christmas festival. Among modern peoples instances of second-hand saga which is just assuming a definite literary form must have been met with not unfrequently; but we have not noted any cases in which the relationship of the narrator to the story is pointed out. We may, however, perhaps cite Mr James Cowan's interesting story, 'The Bishop and the Tohunga',[1] which recounts the visit of Bp. George A. Selwyn to a famous Maori seer named Unuaho. The story was related, apparently with much picturesque detail, by the seer's grandson after the lapse of some considerable time—perhaps half a century or more—after the interview.

It will be seen that several of the recitations noticed above take place at the courts of rulers; and we hear too of such recitations to Irish kings in ancient times (cf. Vol. 1, p. 586) and to kings of Uganda in modern times (cf. p. 615 above). But it must not be assumed that the cultivation of saga was usually dependent upon patronage of this kind. There is

[1] *Fairy Folk Tales of the Maori*, p. 109 ff.; cf. p. 850 above.

not the slightest doubt that the 'Sagas of Icelanders' were composed primarily for recitation in Iceland itself, i.e. in the houses of farmers or small landowners. They seem to have been the chief form of entertainment provided at social gatherings; the saga-teller's greatest opportunities lay in the entertainment of the concourses at national and district assemblies. In some countries, especially Ireland, royal patronage was no doubt very important. So in Israel, we have given reasons for believing that the story of David, in its original form, had its home in the court. But the stories of Elijah and Elisha would seem to be intended for prophetic, rather than court, circles, while the story of Samson suggests a milieu different from either. Perhaps the cultivation of saga was general in Palestine; and the same may be true of Polynesia. From Mr Cowan's *Fairy Folk Tales of the Maori*, p. 11 ff., it appears that saga-telling is still the regular evening occupation of Maori sheep-farmers in certain mountainous districts of New Zealand. On the evening described at least three men recite; people of all ages and both sexes listen and ask questions.

We have chosen our examples of saga-telling as near as possible to the time of composition. But it is to be remembered that in most countries saga-tellers have stories of long ago in their répertoire. This is the case throughout Polynesia, as we have seen. The first story told in the Maori entertainment just mentioned relates to the time when that people first landed in New Zealand, some six centuries ago. One of the Irish saga-tellers referred to in Vol. I, p. 586, recited stories from the earliest times down to his own day. The Icelander who entertained Harold Hardrada had previously exhausted a répertoire which had lasted for several weeks. He kept this story to the last, because he was afraid to tell it in the king's presence. It is to such stories of the past that we are indebted for what we know of early Hebrew tradition; and the same seems to be true of the Baganda and other African peoples.

For the recitation of narrative poetry we have abundant evidence from Russia and Yugoslavia, summaries of which were given in Vol. II, pp. 238 ff., 434 ff. In both countries such poetry is still recited in remote and backward districts. In Russia, however, the poems all relate to the past, and more especially to the far past. For more than two hundred years creative narrative poetry has been on the down grade; in the early part of last century it was already moribund. Its circulation has for a long time been restricted to the poorest classes in the forest region; yet expert reciters are still to be found. In parts of Yugoslavia, however, such poetry retained its vitality until late in last century. Old poems, relating to the fourteenth and fifteenth centuries were still recited; but numerous new poems on current events were composed. Most of the minstrels were poor and illiterate; but this poetry was also cultivated by such educated persons as there were in the border districts—Mohammedan squires, Orthodox ecclesiastics and the leading men of Montenegro. Several members of the episcopal-princely family were themselves poets; and the majority of the poems we have seen dating from the reign of Danilo (1851–1861) appear to be the work of high officers in the prince's household. Unfortunately we are without information as to the places and circumstances in which these poems were first produced, though in general we hear of minstrelsy (chiefly heroic) in the houses of people of all classes, in monasteries and at festival gatherings. Such evidence as we have suggests that poems were commonly composed immediately after the events which they celebrate; but they soon passed into general circulation, and the names of their authors were often forgotten in a few years. Indeed authorship as such seems not to have been recognised.

Recitations of heroic narrative poetry among the Tatars have been described above (p. 178 ff.). The audiences are drawn from all classes; the 'sultans' or men of the highest class are among the most eager listeners. We do not know, however, whether this poetry is still creative; the few poems which have been accessible to us relate to past times.

The most instructive of the ancient literatures in this respect are Greek and English. In both the Odyssey and Beowulf we hear of heroic narrative poems recited by minstrels in kings' halls, where they clearly form the normal evening's entertainment of the court. The recitations described in the former poem relate to recent events. In *Od.* 1. 351 f. Telemachos remarks that the newest poems are those which are liked best, and by this he obviously means poems which deal with the most recent occurrences. In Beow. 867 ff. one of the king's squires composes a poem on the hero's exploit within a few hours of the event. This is no doubt a 'poem of celebration' (Type D), as we have seen; but the description shows that it is of a kind which could—and naturally would —soon be converted into a narrative poem.

Other Greek and English (and also Continental Teutonic) records show that heroic narrative poetry was recited also in less exalted circles —in Greece especially at public festivals (cf. Vol. 1, pp. 568 f., 573, 575). Yet the milieu and the conventions of the poems point, as we have seen (*ib.* p. 64 ff.), to the courts as their place of origin. We believe the same remark to be true of Indian heroic narrative poetry, in spite of the fact that in the Mahābhārata most of the stories are related by Brahmans in the forest. Most of the later Yugoslav poems, like the heroic Border ballads of the Elizabethan period, are concerned with heroes of lower rank, though in both cases this phase of poetry was preceded by an earlier series, relating to the doings of princes or great earls. What we would emphasise here, however, is that in both ancient and modern times narrative poetry—which is usually heroic—is largely occupied with recent events. We believe that, if fuller information were to hand, this would be found to be true everywhere.[1]

With regard to speech poems in character (Type B) we have little to add to what was said on p. 717 f. Some poems of this type, such as the Russian 'Laments' discussed in Vol. II, p. 160 f., must have been composed, and presumably recited, within a very few years, at most, of the occurrences; but we have no records as to where and how they were recited. Poems of the same type, which survive in Russia today, are recited, we believe, in the same manner and by the same persons as narrative poems. And we have not heard of any peculiarities in the recitation of such poems in Yugoslavia or among the Tatars. In ancient literatures the only record we have found of the recitation of such poems is in Nornagests Saga, cap. 9, where an unknown visitor (Nornagestr) recites the Helreið Brynhildar (cf. Vol. I, p. 27) to King Ólafr Tryggvason and his court. Nornagestr is a skilful harper, though it is not clear whether he accompanies this poem on the harp.

In connection with poetry of this type we may refer to the performances of the Tatar shaman, described on p. 199 ff. above, when he represents himself as visiting heaven and hell. These performances may be regarded as in some sense dramatic, though he is the only actor; for he speaks in the character of the beings of the upper and nether worlds, and even simulates their movements. In Polynesia we have found more developed forms of drama, especially in the funeral celebrations and the *kapa* of Mangaia (cf. p. 372 ff.), for which island we have unusually detailed information. The poetry sung on these occasions must be regarded in general as ritual poetry; but there is much dialogue, and the speakers often speak in the characters of persons of the past and of

---

[1] Thus we have little doubt that the Border ballads of the Elizabethan period were composed and sung soon after the events; but we know of no definite evidence to this effect. 'Dick o the Cow' (Child, No. 185) had found its way to the south of England before 1596; but the date of Dick's adventure seems to be unknown. 'Captain Car' (No. 178), a ballad relating to the Highland border, is found in a MS. which is believed to date from before 1600. The tragedy itself took place in 1571.

mythical persons. At times they employ dramatic action, as well as speech. Indeed the performances may best be described as ritual drama.

Poetry of Type B has of necessity something in common with drama. And it is not unlikely that in ancient times the recitation of poetry of this kind was 'dramatised' to some extent, especially in dialogue poems, though how far this was done is very difficult to determine. It is clear from Widsith and from Priscos' account of his visit to Attila[1] that among the early Teutonic peoples panegyrics were sometimes recited by a pair of poets or minstrels. But we do not know whether these panegyrics were in the form of dialogues, or whether the two took turns in reciting a continuous theme. The Edda collection contains a good number of poems which consist wholly or mainly of dialogue, and in which the speakers are usually supernatural beings. Some of these are obvious reflections of the 'contests of wisdom', of which we shall have to speak below, while others are contests in repartee, consultations of witches, etc. It is quite possible that such poems were recited in some kind of dramatic form; but we do not know of any definite evidence to this effect. In the only reference to the recitation of Edda poetry known to us (see above) the Helreið Brynhildar, a dialogue poem, is clearly recited by one man; but the authority is late.

At present many scholars are inclined to attach great importance to the influence of dramatic representations of a ritual character, especially such as are associated with the 'sacred marriage' and other fertility rites. It seems to us not unlikely that poems of Type B may occasionally owe their origin to dramatic ceremonies; but here again definite evidence is extremely difficult to find. We may refer to certain Vedic poems noticed in Vol. II, p. 532 f., especially the curious dialogue of Yama and Yamī (Rgv. x. 10). This may have been connected with a ceremony such as appears to have been known among the Areoi of Tahiti and perhaps elsewhere in the Pacific (cf. p. 429 above), though little has been recorded by the missionaries, who naturally had little sympathy with such rites. A somewhat similar explanation[2] has been proposed for the Edda poem Skírnismál (cf. Vol. I, p. 248). For the rite involved in this case—the marriage of the god Frey—evidence is to be found in

---

[1] Translations of these passages are given in Vol. I, p. 574 ff.

[2] Cf. Phillpotts, *The Elder Edda and Ancient Scandinavian Drama*, p. 13 ff. This book should be consulted for a full statement of the evidence for drama in the Edda poems. We suspect that the Skírnismál is connected in some way with Frey's human wife. Possibly its object is to account for her existence.

the story of Gunnarr Helmingr,[1] though this story itself points to mimetic ritual proceedings extending over a considerable length of time, rather than to speech-drama. It may be added that Saxo Grammaticus, p. 228 (Eng. Transl.), speaks of *mimi*[2] in connection with the sacrifices at Upsala—Frey's chief sanctuary—but does not make clear the nature of their performances. His words might mean either true drama or mimetic ritual.

Funeral and memorial ceremonies may also be taken into account; but here again the evidence is not free from ambiguity. In the Edda (dialogue) poem Helgakviða Hundingsbana II (cf. Vol. I, p. 513 f.) the wife's elegy is followed by the hero's reception in Valhöll, and this again by a subsequent visit to his wife. Helgi is a hero of the far past; but it is possible that the poem is here following the programme of a funeral or memorial ceremony.[3] Indeed a contemporary example of the 'reception in Valhöll' is preserved in the Eiríksmál, a dialogue poem, which is said to have been composed (about the year 954) at the request of Eric Blood-axe's widow. We have treated this poem (Vol. I, p. 344) as an elegy; but perhaps it was composed as an item to follow the true elegy (or dirge), which would presumably be pronounced by the king's widow or one of his near relatives. In any case we cannot prove that the recitation was dramatised, or that there was more than one reciter. It is true that only a portion of the poem is preserved; but the very closely related Hákonarmál (*ib.*) contains narrative and other elements which are difficult to reconcile with a dramatic origin. The ultimate affinities—or rather perhaps analogies—of these poems are to be found, we think, in the funeral recitation of the Tatar shaman (p. 206 ff.), when he is conveying the soul of the deceased to Erlik's abode, and in the long funeral oration pronounced by the seeress of the Sea-Dyaks (p. 488 ff.), when she describes the journey of the soul to the land of the

---

[1] Flateyjarbók I. 337 ff. (cf. Chadwick, *Origin of the Eng. Nation*, p. 241 f.). Gunnarr was an exiled Norwegian, who took refuge at Frey's sanctuary in Sweden, which was under the charge of the god's young wife. When the time comes for Frey to tour the country—in order to secure a fertile year—his carriage sticks in the mud, owing to bad weather, and is abandoned by the rest of his attendants. Gunnarr fells the god—who is said to be an image in the text, as we have it—and then personates him for the rest of the winter. In course of time Frey's wife is seen to be with child, which is interpreted as a good omen for the year.

[2] *Effeminatos corporum motus scenicosque mimorum plausus*, etc. (p. 185, ed. Holder).

[3] This poem also is taken to be of dramatic origin by Phillpotts, *op. cit.* pp. 144, 147 f. (*q.v.*); but a different interpretation is given of its significance.

dead. In the former of these cases a large amount of dramatic action is involved; but in both the performance is carried out by one person. It seems to us likely that the Norse poems may have had their origin in a convention derived from somewhat similar orations; but the treatment has been formalised, and the mantic element has more or less disappeared.[1]

Lastly, some kind of dramatic representation may perhaps be traceable in the story of Balder's death, as told in Snorri's Gylfaginning, cap. 49, though here the connections would seem to lie with some public festival,[2] rather than with funeral or memorial ceremonies. But in this case hardly any speech-poetry (Type B) has been preserved; and consequently the derivation of the story is perhaps to be sought in mimetic ritual of some kind, rather than in true drama.

All other kinds of literature—both personal literature of Type C and impersonal literature—may be treated together, so far as production and recitation are concerned. Very often elements of different genres— antiquarian, gnomic, descriptive and mantic—are to be found in one poem. Thus Hesiod's 'Works and Days' includes antiquarian, gnomic and mantic lore, and descriptive elements are not wanting; and a similar combination of interests is to be found in the Maori poem noticed on p. 404 f. above. Mantic, antiquarian and gnomic lore are all included also in the Edda Trilogy (cf. Vol. 1, p. 27 f.), which is properly to be regarded as a single heroic poem of Type C. The common element is usually instruction. Thus in the Trilogy Othin gives instruction in omens, the snake Fáfnir in antiquarian lore, the Valkyrie in magic and gnomic lore. Instead of instruction, however, we sometimes find a contest in 'wisdom'.

References to recitation are not very frequent in connection with these forms of literature; but the poem (or prose work) itself often gives indications of its origin. Thus among many peoples we find collections of gnomes which claim to be addressed by a father to his son; the father is sometimes a famous sage or king. Whatever we may think of such

---

[1] Another analogy to the Norse poems may be found in the last scene of the Montenegrin poem on the funeral of Prince Danilo (Karadžić, v. 18; cf. Vol. II, p. 335). We are not in a position to discuss this case, because we do not know whether the theme—the reception of the prince in Paradise—was a recognised convention at Montenegrin funerals, or an original idea of the author's. Also we do not know what sort of education the author had received (ib. p. 336). We suspect that ultimately the theme is derived from ecclesiastical sources.

[2] Neniae are mentioned in connection with the great sacrifice at Upsala by Adam of Bremen, IV. 27.

claims in individual cases, they may at all events be taken as evidence for the widespread use of paternal 'instructions'. A number of such works have survived from ancient Egypt, where they were used as schoolbooks under the eighteenth and nineteenth dynasties.[1] The works themselves, however, claim to have been composed by kings and viziers of much earlier times—from the third to the twelfth dynasties.

Among the literatures included in our survey we have found instructions from fathers in Irish (Vol. i, p. 395 ff.), Norse, English, and in the Hebrew Proverbs (Vol. ii, p. 733 f.); but the English precepts (Vol. i, p. 382) are not in the line of native tradition. We may perhaps add the fragment of Simonides noticed ib. p. 416. The only one of these passages which gives any information as to the circumstances of production is the Norse instance cited ib. p. 385 f.; but the affinities of this lie with folk-tale. It is somewhat curious that we have found no instructions from fathers among modern peoples; but we are inclined to suspect that this is due to accident.

Instructions from a mother are given in the Proverbs, cap. xxxi, from an uncle in the Tatar story referred to on p. 151, from a great-uncle in the Polynesian poem cited on p. 404 f. In the last case the instructions are addressed to a baby; but the instructions themselves have much in common with Hesiod's 'Works and Days'.

The 'Works and Days' itself may be regarded as instructions from a brother, perhaps an elder brother. This case differs from those discussed above, owing to the introduction of special circumstances—a quarrel between the two brothers over the division of their property, which has led to a lawsuit (37 ff.). But a distinction[2] may be drawn between different parts of the poem. The precepts and gnomes in the first part are all connected with the quarrel, while the antiquarian matter is chosen to account for the depravity of society. But from 327 onwards—perhaps somewhat earlier—the gnomes and precepts are of a general character, unconnected with the quarrel, first moral, then agricultural, then nautical, etc. This latter part of the poem, apart from two passages relating to the poet and his father, is quite in accord with the 'instructions' from fathers noticed above. The first part, however,

---

[1] Cf. Erman, *Literature of the Ancient Egyptians*, p. 54 ff.

[2] This distinction was overlooked in Vol. i (p. 390). The two elements—the public speech and the typical 'instructions' which follow—have of course been fused together, as usual in oral tradition; and we are not clear where the first ends and the second begins. But the division lies somewhere between 273 and 327.

would seem to be a—somewhat heated and bitter—appeal for justice to a court of law. Some of it is addressed to the princely judges.

To public recitations of didactic matter we have found few references except in Hebrew literature, and these are in general believed to be late.[1] Elsewhere the recitations seem to be addressed to rather small groups of young people, e.g. in the Marquesas. We may refer to the gnomic poems taught to the young Basuto during the training connected with initiation (cf. p. 829 above) and to the address of the Prussian Weydulut quoted in Vol. i, p. 617. It would seem, however, that individual instruction is more usual among peoples who have no written literature —whether it is given by a member of the family or by someone whom we might regard as a professional teacher.[2] See p. 902.

On the other hand, didactic and mantic elements sometimes enter largely into what we should call political oratory. Such is the case with the Hebrew prophets and the early political poets of Greece, especially Tyrtaios and Solon. The use of poetry for this purpose seems strange to us—just as in the first part of the 'Works and Days', if this is really an address to a court of law. And a passage in one of Solon's poems (i. 2) perhaps suggests that it was unusual in his day. But analogies are by no means wanting. We may refer especially to the political poetry current in Yugoslavia during the last century (cf. Vol. ii, p. 355). Among the Galla laws and resolutions of assemblies are said to be expressed in poetry; and the frequent occurrence of poetry in early Scandinavian laws, especially those of Sweden and Gotland, gives some ground for suspecting that this was the case here also in heathen times.[3] Oratory, like the language of laws, seems to develop on different lines in different countries; in Polynesia, where it is much cultivated, it is chanted, but not sung. What we would note here, however, is that among many peoples both oratory and laws give scope for the public expression of doctrine, whether antiquarian, gnomic or mantic.

Contests in 'wisdom' of various kinds are very widespread. We have

---

[1] The opening words of the Völuspá suggest an address to an assembly, perhaps a festal gathering. But what follows seems to be addressed—apparently by the witch—to Othin. Unfortunately the poem is too ill preserved to allow any safe inferences to be drawn from it in a question of this kind.

[2] We may note the 'genealogies' of doctrines recorded in the Upanishads; cf. Vol. ii, pp. 503, 542.

[3] We may refer to the strings of alliterative phrases, often containing verses, which abound in legal language (cf. Vol. i, p. 386f.), and made their way into English in the late Saxon period.

found them in the early literatures of Ireland, the North, Greece and India, and in the oral literature of the Tatars; and they are at least implied in certain Welsh stories (cf. Vol. I, p. 103 ff.). We may perhaps cite Hebrew parallels from Exod. vii f. and I Kings xviii. 21 ff. We have little doubt also that such contests were known in Polynesia. Actually the only example we have found there is a contest in poetry (cf. p. 414 f. above); but Mr Cowan's story, 'The Bishop and the Tohunga', cited on p. 850, seems to indicate that contests in magic were not unfamiliar. Moreover we have met with instances among peoples not included in our survey. We suspect that contests in wisdom in some form or other are to be found almost everywhere. To some extent they are reflected in the riddle dialogues still current in peasant communities, in Russia and elsewhere.

It will be seen that the contests differ greatly in nature. Sometimes they consist in the performance of supernatural feats by magical power or divine aid, as in the Hebrew examples cited above, and also in Mr Cowan's story and stories from the Tatars and other peoples in the north of Asia referred to on p. 108. Sometimes the feat is mantic, as e.g. the power of instantaneous counting in the story of Calchas and Mopsos (Vol. I, p. 474; cf. Vol. II, p. 591) for which an interesting parallel is to be found in the Tatar story of the Two Princes (cf. p. 107 above). Sometimes again it consists in a knowledge of antiquarian lore, as in the Vafþrúðnismál (Vol. I, p. 321 f.). Contests in mantic and antiquarian lore often tend to become contests in rhetoric, as in the Irish 'Colloquy of the Two Sages' (ib. pp. 97, 467), the Alvíssmál (p. 808 above) and the story of Ashtāvakra (Vol. II, pp. 505, 587). The same tendency is observable in the contests in mystic lore described in the Upanishads (ib. pp. 584, 587).

Many of the examples cited above relate to the far past, and would seem to be more or less legendary; sometimes, especially in Norse poetry, the disputants are supernatural beings. But the evidence of the Upanishads leaves no room for doubt that such contests were of frequent occurrence in ancient India. Sometimes they were held at great public gatherings, in the presence of kings; and rich prizes were offered for success. We see no reason for questioning that the examples drawn from other countries reflect more or less truly a custom of the past; indeed we think it by no means unlikely that such contests may yet take place in remote and backward regions. Where other means of publication are lacking, they afford to the intellectual man—the seer or sage—his best chance of acquiring fame and wealth. They do not differ essentially from the contests in poetry which we find in ancient Greece (e.g. 'Works and Days', 655 ff.) and other lands (cf. p. 188 above).

A curious feature which recurs in many of these stories is that a defeated competitor loses his life; and it is remarkable that this is found occasionally even in the Upanishads (cf. Vol. II, p. 584)—apparently when a line of argument is carried too far. The cause and method of death differ from case to case; in the Upanishads it seems to be due to the successful competitor, presumably through the operation of a curse. Sometimes, however, the defeated competitor merely pays a heavy penalty. Instances of this occur in the poetry of Tonga (p. 406 above), and in Bantu custom and saga (p. 603).

Riddle dialogues may perhaps be regarded as a degenerate or popular variety of the contest in wisdom. The most interesting feature is their use in proposals of marriage, as noted on p. 836 above. The connection with the contests in wisdom discussed above may be seen in the Alvíss-mál and the Fjölsvinnsmál, which are likewise 'courtship' dialogues; but the subjects here are questions on diction, antiquarian lore, etc.

Both memorisation and improvisation are employed in the preservation of oral literature. Sometimes the exact words of a poem may be remembered for hundreds of years, even when the language has become more or less obsolete and unintelligible. Sometimes only the barest outline of a theme or story may be preserved. All possible varieties between these two extremes are found.

From Yugoslavia we have a very full and interesting body of evidence bearing upon this subject, which is illustrated and discussed in Vol. II, pp. 413–26 (cf. p. 437). From Russia there is an even greater amount of material, hardly inferior in variety, except perhaps in early MS. collections, which we have treated *ib.* pp. 134–63. In both these cases the tradition is on the 'free' side—i.e. improvisation seems to be more prominent than memorisation. The same is true of the Tatars—see especially pp. 179–186 above. The most striking example known to us on the other side is the Vedic literature of ancient India; in the Rgveda variants are extremely rare, though the poems must have been preserved by purely oral tradition for several centuries. Yet in the Mahābhārata ancient India shows traces of a tradition which must have been almost as free as that of the Russians and the Yugoslavs; and even in Vedic literature there is some evidence that complete rigidity had not always prevailed. The Indian evidence as a whole has been surveyed very briefly *ib.* pp. 593–602. Among other ancient literatures early Norse poetry is especially interesting, owing to the variety which it shows as between free and rigid tradition (cf. Vol. 1, pp. 508–25). Among the modern peoples included in our survey memorisation is best represented in Polynesia (cf. p. 236 f. above)—by antiquarian traditions, especially genealogies; but in Polynesian poetry exact verbal tradition is said to be almost wholly absent.

On the whole we must regard the free variety, which allows more or less scope for improvisation, as the normal form of oral tradition, and strict memorisation as exceptional. The latter would seem to take place under the following conditions:

(1) In poetry intended for collective singing. This subject will be noticed briefly below.

(2) In poetry—less frequently prose compositions—which have come to be regarded as sacred. This was the case with the Rgveda; here, as elsewhere, the actual words were believed to possess some inherent power.

(3) In poems of carefully studied diction, especially panegyrics, and perhaps also poems composed for contests in poetry, such as the *mele inoa* of Hawaii (see p. 414 f. above). It is clear from the Norse evidence (cf. p. 713) that such poems were learnt and studied as models by later poets, especially if they were the work of famous authors. There is some Welsh evidence (cf. Vol. 1, p. 584) which perhaps points in the same direction, though actually the memorisation of such poems would seem often to have been very defective.

(4) In poetry which has complicated metres. Norse ('Skaldic') poetry which employs internal rhyme seems often to have been carefully preserved, since not unfrequently it points to an obsolete pronunciation. Such poetry coincides largely with the poetry treated under the last heading; and consequently the memorisation may be due to either of these causes or to both combined. The same remark is probably true of Greek lyric poetry. One would naturally expect that Greek poetry even in the hexameter and elegiac metres would be preserved more rigidly than Norse poetry in the older (rhymeless) metres or than Yugoslav poetry, since these obviously allow more freedom; and such material as we have for the study of variants in Greek poetry tends to show that this was the case. But unfortunately it is too small in amount to be conclusive.

We have an impression—by no means distinct—that variant versions of oral narrative poems sometimes show a closer resemblance in speeches than in the actual narrative. If this observation should prove to be correct on further examination, it would mean of course that there is a stronger tendency to memorisation in speeches. This would be in accord with Radlov's observation noted on p. 181 above, that the minstrels of the Kara-Khirgiz regularly employ two melodies, one in slow tempo and as a solemn recitative for the speeches, the other in quick tempo for the course of the action. See also p. 903.

In the preservation of prose works we have not found much evidence for the use of verbal memorisation, though it was doubtless employed for laws and legal formulae. In ancient India it seems to have been used, at least to some extent, in didactic and speculative works, since the differences between one text and another are sometimes very slight (cf. Vol. II, p. 595 ff.); but it is not certain that writing was unknown. Saga seems as a rule to show quite as much freedom as narrative poetry; and in course of time the current versions of a story come to differ quite as greatly. For examples we may refer to Vol. I, p. 536 ff. (Norse and Irish), Vol. II, p. 747 ff. (Hebrew), and more especially the variant forms of the dynastic chronicle of Uganda (p. 596 f. above). A detailed study of the different versions of stories which are known throughout Polynesia would doubtless be of interest in illustrating the growth of variants.

For collective or choral singing we have not found very much evidence which can be called satisfactory. Ancient records often state that a number of persons sang; but it is not made clear whether they sang collectively or in turn. This difficulty applies more especially to Norse records (cf. Vol. I, p. 579 f.); it may be observed that all the passages in question relate to spells. Choral singing was known in ancient Greece, certainly in the seventh century, and perhaps in much earlier times (ib. p. 588). In early Hebrew literature we hear much of singing (cf. Vol. II, p. 759 f.); but the question how far this was collective or choral is one which we must leave to specialists. The same remark applies to ancient India. So far as the singing of the Vedas is concerned, the question affects only a very small group of priests; but it is possible that collective singing on a larger scale is meant in some passages in the Mahābhārata (ib. pp. 605, 617). Among the modern peoples included in our survey collective singing is known everywhere, especially in songs sung during an occupation which involves collective rhythmical movement. Boatmen's songs are known from Russia, Polynesia and Central Africa. War-songs (or their refrains) are sung collectively at social gatherings by some of the southern Bantu peoples. At certain

29

Polynesian festivals (cf. p. 353, etc.) we hear of collective singing by alternate halves of a chorus.

If collective singing was not native in the north of Europe, it was certainly introduced in the Middle Ages with the ballad, in the form of refrains. From Yugoslavia we hear of collective singing in 1547, in a poem about Marko Kraljević (cf. Vol. II, p. 444). Here the reference can hardly be to a refrain; more probably it is to be connected with the short lines which frequently occur in the texts of poems preserved in early MSS. (*ib.* p. 339). References to collective singing occur also in the Slovo o Polky Igorevê and in the *byliny*; but we are not aware that collective singing is in use for heroic poetry in modern times, either in Yugoslavia or in Russia.

In Polynesia singing, even by one individual, is distinguished from chanting or recitative. Both singing and chanting are in use for poetry —of different kinds—the latter also in oratory and in the recitation of saga (cf. p. 411 f.). We believe that some such distinction is commonly recognised among modern peoples, though the difference is not easy to grasp where no regular stanza is in use. For the chanting of saga there seems to be some evidence also in Africa (cf. p. 726). In Russia and Yugoslavia we understand that the form of recitation employed (for *byliny* and *narodne pjesme*) is what we should call chanting, rather than singing. But there are said to be differences in Yugoslavia, though we are not clear as to their nature; it may be that some kinds of *ženske pjesme* (cf. Vol. II, p. 306) are sung. In Russia it was stated last century that as a rule even good reciters know hardly more than two or three 'tunes', often only one; but Yakushkov, the best reciter of recent times, is said to have had a different tune for almost every poem (*ib.* p. 243 f.), and it may be suspected that the ear of early recorders was untrained to distinguish different tunes.

For ancient times a good deal of evidence is available from Greek sources, and a little from Norse. The former, however, is too technical for comprehension except by experts, though there is no doubt that elaborate singing, both individual (solo) and choral, was cultivated in the seventh century, if not earlier. The Norse evidence, which has been summarised in Vol. I, p. 579, limited as it is, seems to indicate that singing was used for mantic purposes, and perhaps exclusively for these before church music was introduced. An interesting example may be found in Thorfinns Saga Karlsefnis, cap. 3 (cf. Vol. I, p. 537), where it is clear that the object of the singing is to summon spirits. Thorbjörg, the Greenland witch, is unable to attract them, until she has obtained the help of Guðríðr, who is a good singer. We may add that the metres employed in mantic poetry, the *ljóðaháttr* and the *galdralag* (*ib.* p. 30), are those which would seem to be best adapted to singing. For the close connection between manticism and music we have found evidence elsewhere—among the Hebrews (Vol. II, p. 754 f.), the Polynesians (p. 337 above) and the Tatars (pp. 23 f., 210 f.). Among the Tatars at least the object of the singing is to attract spirits,[1] just as in the story of Guðríðr. We may also refer to the Muses (cf. Vol. I, p. 635 f.). The antiquity of the connection, at least in Europe, seems to be indicated by the fact that our word 'song' is almost identical with the Greek word ὀμφή, 'mantic utterance' ('voice of a deity', etc.).

We do not know what method of recitation was employed in Norse for other kinds of poetry—whether it was chanted or merely declaimed. It is likely, however, that chanting was in use in early times, just as in England.[2] We do not know of any evidence for the chanting of saga.

The difference between 'chanting' and 'singing' is a question which we must leave to experts.[3] We suppose that the former was more monotonous, and that the latter allowed more variation, though the difference may be one of degree. It seems clear that some kind of musical revolution took place in the North in the twelfth century, with the introduction of the ballad. By this time the stanza had already become established in all kinds of poetry; but the choral refrain after the stanza seems to be an innovation. We are under the impression too that the new style of poetry, with rhyme instead of alliteration, and often accompanied by dancing, was 'sung' much more than the old. This new style came into general use throughout the north of Europe (cf. p. 682 ff.), and is used even for heroic narrative poetry. Its main features may be preserved in some of the ballad tunes which still survive, and which probably go back to the sixteenth century. On the other hand, the old style is maintained in the east of Europe, at least in Yugo-slav and Great Russian oral poetry, which is still chanted and has no rhyme, stanza or refrain.[4]

---

[1] Cf. Chadwick, *J.R.A.I.* LXVI, 297 ff.

[2] Ang. Sax. *sang, singan,* etc. mean both 'singing' (of church music) and 'chanting' (both of heroic poetry and of the Bible, e.g. the Pater Noster). In Norse, however, the corresponding words (*söngr, syngva*) are very seldom applied to secular poetry, except where there is some affinity with spells.

[3] The most familiar characteristics of the latter, e.g. division into equal periods and the recurrence of the air, would seem not to be essential.

[4] All these are to be found occasionally in modern Yugoslav folk-songs. The stanza occurs also in early MS. poems from some places on the Adriatic coast, together with short lines which may have been sung collectively, like refrains (cf. p. 870).

The accompaniment of poetry by stringed instruments is found in most parts of the world,[1] in both ancient and modern times. Harps were found in the royal graves of Ur, dating from early in the third millennium, and there is evidence for something of the kind in the Greek islands not many centuries later.[2] It is difficult of course to determine from archaeological evidence whether instruments were employed with or without the voice; and the same is true sometimes even of literary records—we may refer e.g. to I Sam. xvi. 16 ff. But we will summarise briefly such information as we have been able to obtain.

Heroic poetry, narrative, panegyric and personal was accompanied among the ancient Teutonic peoples; for the evidence, both English and Continental, we may refer to Vol. i, p. 573 ff. For the North information is wanting, except from Nornagests Saga (cf. p. 860). In early Wales and Ireland we know that the harp was much cultivated; we know also that saga-telling and harp-playing were cultivated by the same persons in Ireland, and by the same class of persons (the bards) in Wales. It seems natural to infer that heroic panegyric poetry, and perhaps also the poetry (Type B) introduced in sagas, was accompanied by the harp; but we have not found any positive evidence to this effect (cf. Vol. i, p. 583 ff.). In ancient Greece heroic narrative poetry, and also narrative poetry relating to deities, was accompanied on the *citharis*; but later the accompaniment was abandoned (*ib.* p. 568 f.). In ancient India heroic panegyrics are regularly accompanied on the lute, while heroic narratives, in the Mahābhārata, are unaccompanied (cf. Vol. ii, pp. 606 f., 616 f.). The circumstances of the recitations, how-ever, as recorded, are abnormal; and we suspect that the narratives also are derived from minstrel poetry. At all events, it is clear from the Rāmāyana, vii, 106 f. that heroic narrative poetry was sometimes accompanied; Vālmīki's poem is recited to the accompaniment of a stringed instrument by Rāma's two sons, Kuça and Lava.[3] Among the ancient Hebrews there is evidence for the accompaniment of heroic panegyric poetry (*ib.* p. 753).

In modern times no instrumental accompaniment seems to be in use for Great Russian heroic poetry, though we believe it is found in Little Russia. We have seen, however, that there is good reason for believing

---

[1] Polynesia, apart from Hawaii, is an exception.

[2] Cf. especially the statuette of a harper found in the island of Keros (Cereia) and figured in Ebert, *Real-Lex. d. Vorgeschichte*, Bd. vi, Taf. 4.

[3] These names are believed to be derived from the word *kuçīlava*, 'bard, actor' (cf. Macdonnell, *Sanskr. Literature*, p. 304f.).

that the former was accompanied in the past on the *gusli*, an instrument which is now extinct (*ib.* pp. 22, 257 ff.). Yugoslav heroic poetry of all kinds is still regularly accompanied either on the *gusle*—a different instrument from the Russian *gusli*—or on the *tambura* (*ib.* pp. 303, 435 f.). An instrument similar to the *gusle* is also used in Albania (*ib.* p. 456). For the Tatars we have very little information; but we are under the impression that heroic poetry is accompanied on stringed instruments, at least in some parts (cf. pp. 175 f., 189 f., 903). This is also true of the Tungus. In Africa 'harps' of various kinds are very widely used for the accompaniment of heroic poetry (cf. pp. 527 f., 577, 662 ff.). It would seem that among some of the Bantu peoples even the recitation of heroic saga is accompanied (cf. p. 726). This is one of the questions upon which we should be most glad to have further information.

From what has been said above it is clear that the accompaniment of heroic poetry—narratives as well as panegyrics—is extremely widespread. Indeed unaccompanied poetry of this kind would seem on the whole to be rather exceptional. We have noted, however, that the accompaniment has sometimes apparently disappeared. This may be due to various reasons; but we think that the cause is in some cases to be found in poverty and the inability to make or procure instruments —conditions which themselves are due probably to the loss of royal or noble patronage. The form of the instrument varies greatly—from fiddle to harp—between one country and another; but as a rule it seems to be of a more or less primitive character. Among modern peoples, where records or descriptions have been obtained, the recitation appears to be in the nature of chanting rather than of singing.[1]

It is hardly possible to discuss in detail the use of minstrelsy in connection with other kinds of poetry; for the records, especially for ancient times, seldom specify the character of the poetry, unless it is heroic. In England, during the Saxon period, minstrelsy was widely cultivated; but the subject of the poems or songs is hardly ever stated. In Wales and Ireland, during the twelfth century, the use of the harp was perhaps even more widespread; but it is not clear to us whether this was usually minstrelsy or instrumental music alone. In Iceland the harp must have been extremely rare, if we may judge from the sagas; but in Norway

---

[1] The tunes traditionally associated with some of the heroic Border ballads may be regarded as 'song' tunes; and some of them would seem to date from the time of the poems themselves, or not much later. But in this country all oral poetry in the Middle Ages apparently came under the influence of the true (international) ballad.

and elsewhere in the North we hear of it both in early and late times, though usually without any specific information as to its use. In ancient Greece an improved instrument, the lyre of seven strings, is said to have been introduced in the seventh century. It was used for the accompaniment of various kinds of (sung) poetry, choral and solo, religious and secular. For Palestine the evidence is similar; there seems to have been a considerable variety of instruments in use. For India, on the other hand, we have found few references; but the use of the *vīnā* was probably not limited to heroic poetry.

In modern times the *balalaika*, a kind of primitive guitar, is used in many parts of Russia for the accompaniment of folk-songs, not *byliny*. In Yugoslavia the same instruments are used for all kinds of oral poetry; but it is only for heroic poetry that they are regarded as indispensable. Among the Tatars several instruments are in use; but we have no detailed information. In Africa stringed instruments of more or less primitive character are widespread. In Abyssinia and to a certain extent among the Galla more advanced instruments are also found. In Uganda and elsewhere in Central Africa the primitive native harp (*nanga*) has largely been displaced in recent times by an instrument from the Basoga, which seems to be used to accompany singing rather than chanting. For further information we may refer to pp. 577, 579, 582 above.

Instrumental music accompanies the singing of religious poetry among some peoples, e.g. the ancient Greeks and Hebrews. Among the latter it was used even with religious gnomic poetry (e.g. Ps. xlix. 4). By the prophets of early times it seems to have been much cultivated for the purpose of producing inspiration and ecstasy (cf. Vol. II, p. 754 f.), though the literary prophets apparently seldom use musical instruments. We have not noted any references to the cultivation of instrumental music by the seers of ancient India; but the divine seer Nārada once appears with a lyre (*ib.* p. 606, note).[1] The Greek mantic god Apollo commonly has a lyre. For an instance among the Tatars we may refer to p. 85 above, where the supernatural woman Bek Toro says that she has touched the ear of Kudai by playing on her *komus* (cf. also p. 23). But we have not found much evidence for the use of a stringed instrument to accompany spells, in spite of the widespread prevalence of singing in this connection.[2]

[1] Minstrelsy is practised by the Gandharvas at Indra's court (*ib.*); but the picture is probably derived from a king's hall.

[2] A number of instances of the use of stringed instruments by shamans are cited by Czaplicka for various peoples of Northern Asia, including some Tatar tribes.

Musical instruments of all kinds, including the pipe[1] and drum are commonly used among the Tatars in order to summon spirits;[2] and some similar usage may possibly be traceable in certain Greek mythological stories. In some of the Polynesian islands the drum, which is the only native instrument, is used for the same purpose. For Mangaia we may quote a passage from one of the ritual dramas translated by W. Wyatt Gill:[3] "Spirit-land is stirred to its very depths at the music of the great drum. The fairies...have come up. Lead off the dance..."

The combination of dancing with some kind of choral singing, and often also with instrumental music, is very widespread. Very frequently, as in this case, it is connected with religion or the spirit world. There is no doubt that in some countries, e.g. in ancient Greece, as well as in Polynesia, this custom has greatly influenced the history of poetry. On the other hand, we have not found any satisfactory evidence for such influence in the north of Europe before the introduction of the ballad, though 'dancing' of some kind was doubtless known in the amusements of young people, and perhaps also in religious and other solemnities.[4] For the other peoples included in our survey we are not prepared to speak with any confidence. Incidentally, however, we may refer to the interesting passage relating to the Yakut quoted on p. 158 f.

But the evidence is sparse and not very satisfactory, and sometimes it is even conflicting, while most of the works to which reference is given are inaccessible. This is a matter on which further evidence would be welcome.

[1] We are under the impression that poetry has not been much influenced by wind instruments among any of the peoples included in our survey, except perhaps the ancient Greeks, among whom elegiac and some forms of lyric poetry were accompanied by a flute, or rather clarionet. Some kind of pipe music was used among the Hebrews, both for social festivities and also by companies of prophets. Among the northern peoples such instruments seem to have been introduced from the south, in not very early times.

[2] Cf. Chadwick, *J.R.A.I.* LXVI, 299 ff.

[3] *Myths and Songs from the South Pacific*, p. 259 ff.

[4] We know of no early evidence, except for the southernmost Teutonic peoples; but the history of the words *lac* and *plega* has to be taken into account. A tempting analogy to the Polynesian belief may perhaps be seen in the dancing of the elves in modern folk-lore. But there is no evidence, so far as we know, that the elves of heathen times danced.

CHAPTER XI

AUTHORSHIP

FIRST we may consider the conditions under which an author's name is preserved in oral tradition.

At first sight there would seem to be great difference of usage in this respect between one people and another. Yugoslav oral poetry is almost wholly anonymous; it is only in the case of poems which have been published within a few years of their composition that the author's name is known, and not always even then. In Russia, where oral poetry is concerned only with the past, except in 'celebration' poems, we have found no evidence of authorship. The same remark applies to the Tatars, except the Turcomans, though here we cannot speak with as much confidence, owing to the defects of our information. On the other hand, Polynesian poems usually have the names of authors attached to them, even when they are believed to be centuries old; but sagas are anonymous. The Abyssinians and Galla also usually preserve the names of poets.

The same difference appears in ancient literatures. Anglo-Saxon poetry is almost wholly anonymous;[1] but in ancient Greece and India an author's name is assigned to almost every poem. The latter tendency is found also in Hebrew poetry, though the prose works, including the saga which they contain, are anonymous. Early Norse, Welsh and Irish literature lies between the two extremes in this respect. The sagas are as a rule anonymous, but the poems vary, though only a few early Welsh poets are recorded. It is to be observed, however, that the claims to authorship made by a good number of poems, especially Welsh and Irish, are not to be taken too seriously; many of them are doubtless speeches in character (Type B).

The reason for these differences between one people and another is to be found to some extent in the nature of the poetry cultivated by them. Saga, which is very poorly represented in ancient Greece and India, seems to be as a rule anonymous everywhere. We hear from time to time, in Norse records and elsewhere, of persons who could tell a

---

[1] Cynewulf's poems are almost the only examples which contain an author's name; and these need not be taken into consideration here, since the acrostics would seem to show that they were written by the poet.

certain story well; but it is very seldom that an author is mentioned—and perhaps only when the story is said to be fictitious. As a rule saga is regarded as an account of what has actually happened, however much latitude the reciter may allow himself in the way of embellishment. Exceptions are doubtless to be allowed in the case of didactic saga (Type C), which may often have its origin in speculation or fiction and also perhaps in the case of 'secondary' stories (cf. p. 761 ff.), which have been transferred from one hero of the past to another; but even such stories in course of time usually tend to be regarded as narratives of fact. Saga relating to deities, even when its character is imaginative rather than didactic, belongs to the same series.

Narrative poetry is likewise anonymous among the modern peoples included in our survey, i.e. the Russians, Yugoslavs and Tatars, who cultivate such poetry. The author of a poem may be known for a few years after its composition—though this is apparently not always the case (cf. Vol. II, p. 440 f.)—but he has no 'copyright' in it; any minstrel who hears it may reproduce it with such changes as he wishes. English ballad poetry seems to have been governed by the same principles. Among the ancient literatures narrative poetry is strictly anonymous in English and Norse; and in the latter at least the evidence of variants shows that it was treated in much the same way as in modern oral literatures (cf. Vol. I, p. 514 ff.).

We have seen reason for believing that narrative poetry is everywhere, or almost everywhere, concerned in the main with heroic themes—as against saga, which has a wider provenance. Apart from this we need not doubt that both have an identical history. The primary function of both is to give an account of events—in the first place very recent events. The transference of stories from one hero to another and the invention of didactic stories and of imaginative stories relating to deities are secondary features which arise in both in the course of time. The narrative poem is as a rule more highly embellished than the saga, owing to the character of the milieu in which it is produced; but the poet is not regarded as an author, any more than the saga-teller. His merit is to give a good account of what has happened or to tell a familiar story well, so as to entertain—or in the case of didactic stories to instruct—his audience. However inventive he may be, he seems to be regarded as a reciter or artist rather than as an author, so far as our evidence goes.

We have yet to notice that in ancient India and Greece narrative poems, like all other poetry, have authors assigned to them. Vyāsa is said to be the author of the Mahābhārata, as also of the Purānas, Vālmīki of the Rāmāyana, Homer of the Iliad and Odyssey and various other poems, mostly now lost, though these latter were sometimes attributed also to other poets.

Vyāsa is frequently introduced in the Mahābhārata as a great seer and grandfather of the heroes, whom he often visits. He also visits his great-great-great grandson Janamejaya, and orders his disciple Vaiçampāyana to recite to that monarch the Mahābhārata, which he has himself composed. It is now generally held, we understand, that Vyāsa is a fictitious character. We ourselves are not convinced of this: we think he may well have been a learned seer of the far past—perhaps of Janamejaya's time—and that his reputation as an authority on Puranic (i.e. antiquarian) learning may be derived from very old tradition. But that is a different matter from admitting his authorship of the Mahābhārata, or of any portion of it, except that the Puranic elements which it contains may owe something ultimately to his influence. The stories of the Mahābhārata, both heroic and non-heroic, must be regarded as a collection of anonymous narrative poems, just as much as those of the Edda. Probably no one would suggest that the reciters, such as Markandeya or Brhadaçva, were other than characters chosen for the purpose.

The Rāmāyana, on the other hand, is commonly believed to be the work of a single author, Vālmīki, though considerable portions of it, including practically the whole of Books I and VII (the first and last books), are thought to be additions of much later date. Vālmīki's authorship of the poem is definitely stated in the first few chapters of Book I and frequently in Book VII; and references to the poem under his name occur elsewhere (e.g. Mahābh. VII. cxliii, 66 f.), though these may be due to what is stated in the Rāmāyana itself. Vālmīki is thought to have lived in the sixth or fifth century (B.C.), and long after Rāma's time, though nothing seems to be known of him except from the poem itself. In the poem, however, he is said to be a contemporary of Rāma and a holy hermit. In I. 1–4 he is instructed in the story of Rāma by the divine seer Nārada, and encouraged in his task by Brahmā; and he teaches the poem to Rāma's two young sons, who recite it in the city and in the king's presence. His education of the boys is treated more fully in Book VII (cf. Vol. II, p. 473). All this would seem to suggest that Vālmīki is a legendary character, similar to Vyāsa. On the other hand, the Rāmāyana itself has a unity which is quite lacking in the Mahābhārata—a unity not only of theme but also of treatment. The theme is a heroic story which is just passing—or perhaps rather has already passed—into romance; but the treatment is of a studied character, in which the interest in the action tends to be subordinated to diction and description. The speeches too are often of a highly academic nature, curiously inappropriate to the exciting situations in which they are sometimes introduced. As compared with the Mahābhārata, the poem bears the marks of a distinctive hand, though it may be open to question whether this poet composed or merely transformed it, and whether he was called Vālmīki or not.

The short version of the story of Rāma preserved in the Mahābhārata, III. 276–90[1] (cf. Vol. II, p. 471) is believed by many scholars to be derived from the Rāmāyana. It certainly agrees very closely with the latter in the course of the narrative; and in some places it seems to presume a more detailed knowledge of the story. But the characteristics noted above are absent; the story is treated in a simpler and more natural style, like the other heroic stories in the same work. We are inclined to the view that its relationship to the Rāmāyana dates from a time before the latter, even in the older portions, had acquired its present form; but the question is one which must be left to specialists. There is no reference to Vālmīki in this version of the story.

At present, in reaction against the views prevalent last century, it is commonly held that the Iliad and probably also the Odyssey are the work of one poet. But comparatively few scholars, we think, would be inclined to put much faith in any of the 'Lives' of Homer, or even to claim that we have any authentic information relating to him. In this respect modern opinion is in agreement with that of the ancient Greeks of historical times, before the Alexandrian period. Homer was indeed sometimes identified with the blind man of Chios, who speaks in Hom. Hymn I; but nothing more seems to have been known about the latter. And the identification cannot have been generally admitted; for the honour of being Homer's birthplace was claimed by a number of cities in various parts of Greece. Such information as the 'Lives' furnish can have had no more than local currency, if it existed at all, before Alexandrian times. Even as to the poet's date wide difference of opinion prevailed. As a personality Homer must be regarded as 'the Unknown' in ancient, as well as in modern, times.

In early times many poems were attributed to Homer—perhaps indeed all narrative poems which had come down from the past, except those which were of antiquarian (catalogue or genealogical) character.

---

[1] The story begins in III. 273, but it is interrupted by an account of the origin of the Rākshasa, which may be compared with Rām. VII. 2f., 9ff.

Herodotos (II. 117, IV. 32) questions Homer's authorship of the Cypria and the Epigonoi—in the former case owing to a discrepancy with the Iliad—but his words seem to imply that he is contesting a commonly held view. Later we find various authors assigned to the poems which are now lost. But there is little agreement among the authorities; most of the poems are attributed to more than one author. A few of these names are found elsewhere associated with what seem to have been antiquarian poems; but others are quite unknown—possibly they may be the names of reciters (rhapsodists). At all events they may be taken as illustrations of the (late) Greek feeling that every poem should have a known author—a feeling which is doubtless to be traced also in the numerous attempts which were made to bring ancient poets into relationship, and even into competition, with one another. In early times, however, it would seem that 'Homeric poems' (τὰ Ὁμήρεια ἔπη) meant no more than (old) heroic narrative poetry, and that no care had been taken to preserve any tradition of the poet himself or the scope of his work. When criticism made its appearance, and it was inferred from discrepancies between the two that the Iliad and the Cypria could not be of the same authorship, the reasons for allowing the former to Homer, rather than the latter, were derived presumably from internal evidence—perhaps its superior merit or greater length.

Modern scholars are spared from a decision on this question. The question before us is one which did not, and could not, occur to the ancients. The two poems which now survive were regarded as unities doubtless long before Herodotos' time. There is no evidence that scholars of his day had any acquaintance with a living, variable, anonymous narrative poetry, such as we have found flourishing among many other peoples. Reciters had ceased to improvise; and variants were regarded as errors. Laws which governed the poetry produced in the seventh and sixth centuries were believed to apply to poetry inherited from the past.

To those who deny that the laws which govern the poetry of barbaric peoples can apply to Greek poetry, and hold that a great poem must necessarily be the work of a creative genius, inspired by the Muse, the origin of the Homeric poems is of course a superfluous question. There are others who may regard Homer as a 'Vālmīki', who transformed an existing body of poetry; but we do not see any trace of such academic influence. Homer may have been the man who 'unified' one or both of the poems, and brought them into their final form. But we are inclined to doubt if this last stage in their history was of exceptional importance. Except in length we cannot find any essential difference from the heroic narrative poetry of other peoples. The composition—both the diction and the treatment of the story—is in general on a higher level than elsewhere; but the story of Nala will bear comparison with the Odyssey, at least in its general treatment, while Beowulf, though it is occupied with unpromising themes, contains a number of scenes[1] which are presented quite as impressively as anything in the Greek epics. To us, who claim no first-hand knowledge of the Muse's gifts, it would seem that the merits of the Homeric poems, like those of their counterparts elsewhere, may best be accounted for, not by a great creative genius, but by a poetic tradition, long and intensively cultivated under favourable conditions—more favourable doubtless than are now to be found in any land where oral poetry is still current. In both Greece and India we believe that the 'authors' of narrative poems are products of later (literary) conditions.

We have been speaking above primarily of narratives, both poetry and saga, which are intended for entertainment (Type A). But the same seems to be true in general also of didactic narratives. Perhaps the only real exceptions are to be found in timeless-nameless stories invented by a seer or sage—the authorship of which may be remembered either on account of the author's fame or in connection with the circumstances of their production. We may refer e.g. to the prophet Nathan's story in II Sam. xii. 1 ff. Narrative poems of this kind occur in the Mahābhārata (cf. Vol. II, p. 568 ff.), where they are attributed to famous seers or sages; but we need not take these attributions seriously.

Poems which consist of speeches in character (Type B), whether preserved in sagas or independently, are likewise as a rule anonymous. Here again exceptions may occur in poetry of a didactic character (Type CB), though we cannot recall any.

It is to be borne in mind, however, that poems of Type B are often difficult or impossible to distinguish from genuine personal poems (Type E), and that in the latter anonymity is practically excluded by our definition (cf. p. 707). Indian scholastic tradition indeed does not distinguish between these two types; it treats the speakers in poems of Type B in the Rgveda as authors, even when they are deities—though

---

[1] We may instance the descriptions of Scyld's funeral (26 ff.), the arrival of Grendel (702 ff.), the demons' lair (1357 ff.), the burial of the treasure (2231 ff.). The introduction of the (non-Christian) supernatural is usually more impressive in Beowulf. Resemblances in individual passages are quite frequent; cf. Chadwick, *The Heroic Age*, p. 320 ff.

this is perhaps merely a traditional convention. But there can be little doubt that many timeless-nameless poems of Type B were originally produced as expressions of personal feeling by forgotten authors.

The various classes of poetry which we have grouped together under Type D differ in respect of known and unknown authorship. The authors of panegyrics and elegies are usually known (cf. p. 713); their names may be preserved for centuries, in regions as far apart as Iceland and the islands of the Pacific. Exceptions again occur in the case of timeless-nameless elegies, for which a traditional form may continue in use for a long period.[1] In hymns to deities there is much variety of usage. In the Rgveda the poet himself often records his name in a hymn, while all the rest of the hymns have names attached to them by scholastic tradition, the value of which is very doubtful. The Greek hexameter hymns were ascribed by the ancients to Homer; but actually they are anonymous—apart from the reference to the blind man of Chios in Hymn 1 (cf. Vol. 1, p. 357)—and now generally believed to date from various periods. The authors of hymns in other metres are usually known from trustworthy literary tradition. Anonymity is the rule in Hebrew hymnal poetry. Biblical tradition attributes certain hymns to famous rulers, including Hezekiah, David, and even Moses, while later scholastic tradition gives authors for all the Psalms; but hardly any of these attributions would now be generally accepted. Polynesian hymns also are for the most part anonymous. The hortatory poetry which has come under our notice dates from times little, if at all, anterior to written records; and, probably for this reason, the authors are usually known.

Antiquarian literature, both poetry and prose, is for the most part anonymous; but there are a good many exceptions in Greek, Norse and Irish poetry. In the two latter cases these occur chiefly in poems which are intended for the glorification of the ancestry of the prince for whom the poem is composed (cf. Vol. 1, p. 271 f.). In intention therefore, though not in content, such poems are akin to panegyrics; and we need not doubt that, like them, they were duly rewarded. The early Greek antiquarian poems were products of a different political and social milieu; but it is not clear that the impulses to which they were due were essentially different. Many of them were composed in honour of

[1] In various parts of the world those whose duty it is to pronounce elegies for relatives often obtain them from persons who are (more or less) professional poets. We have noted this custom in Russia (Vol. 11, p. 286f.), and in Polynesia (cf. p. 357 above).

families or states (i.e. city communities) by poets, not necessarily natives, who worked for rewards, sometimes in the form of prizes. Most of this poetry is lost; but the genealogy and legends which were treated would seem to have been those of the family which was, or had been, dominant in the state. And even when the panegyric element is lacking, as in Hesiod's Theogony, the prospect of a prize—in a poetic contest—is probably to be taken into account. It may be doubted, however, whether many of the attributions of authorship—we may instance Hesiod's 'Catalogue'—are due to anything more than literary speculation of later times. Among other peoples, both ancient and modern, it seems to be quite exceptional for authors to be remembered. Such antiquarian speculation as meets with approval soon passes into the current body of local or national tradition.

Gnomic poems and collections of gnomes frequently bear the names of authors; but these are usually sages or kings of the far past, sometimes even supernatural beings. The number of authors who would be generally accepted is very limited—Hesiod[1] and Theognis in Greece, one or possibly two of the Irish authors mentioned in Vol. I, pp. 395, 397, and perhaps the old Maori poet quoted on p. 404 f. above. Few scholars now would be willing to admit that Solomon was the author of the Proverbs, or that Cormac and Fithal and Vyāsa were responsible for the collections attributed to them. It is possible of course in such cases that some kernel or germ of the collection may be derived from the reputed author. But even this can hardly be allowed for the non-heroic gnomes attributed to famous ancient heroes like CuChulainn and Conall Cernach, any more than for those which come from the Valkyrie Sigrdrífa and the god Othin. Anonymity must be regarded as the rule for gnomic poetry, whether there be a framework of Type B, as in these cases, or complete impersonality, as in English and Welsh, and elsewhere. In this connection it may be observed that little in the way of rewards is likely to be got out of poetry of this kind, however much it may be used for educational purposes.

The same remarks apply to descriptive poetry of various kinds—which, as we have seen, is very often combined with gnomic. Perhaps the only genuine authors whose names have been preserved—as apart from attributions of Type B—are certain Greek poets, especially Simonides of Amorgos and Solon, whose poems were probably written down either by themselves or very shortly after their time. In general

---

[1] We see no reason for doubting that the author of the 'Works and Days' is the Hesiod of the 'Theogony', though it would be difficult to prove their identity.

it would seem that the authorship of poetry of this kind was soon forgotten.

In mantic literature we have, first, to distinguish between spells and prophecies. The former are commonly of general application; and their authors are seldom recorded. The latter relate usually to specific persons and events; and they nearly always have the names of seers attached to them. These seers may be persons of the far past, like Myrddin, who could not possibly have composed the prophecies attributed to them; and they may even be supernatural beings. This use of Type B is not rare. But there are many others whose claims to authorship cannot, or need not, be doubted—seers who belong to modern times, such as those of Hawaii, or whose prophecies were soon committed to writing. There is, as we have seen, a third class of mantic literature—often combined with prophecy (of the future), especially in Hebrew—consisting of declarations of mantic wisdom or of the divine will, which may also be described as timeless prophecies or prophecies relating to the present. These are sometimes attributed to authors, sometimes anonymous. Both forms are found side by side in the Upanishads, while of the early Welsh poems discussed in Vol. I, p. 459 ff., two or three claim to be the work of Taliesin, and the rest are anonymous. In general it may be said both of these compositions and of prophecies of the future that, where the authorship stated is not genuine, it is due to the desire to claim the credit of a famous name; but it is often difficult or impossible to determine whether the claim is true or not.

We may next consider the social classes or positions in life to which authors belonged. This can sometimes be determined with more or less confidence even in the case of anonymous literature.

First we will take heroic narrative poetry. We have seen that in Montenegro last century minstrelsy was very widely cultivated; but authors seem to have been much less numerous than reciters. Those whom we can trace were members of the episcopal-princely family or high officers in the prince's household (cf. Vol. II, p. 441 f.). For other modern peoples we have no evidence. But the evidence of ancient literatures, so far as it goes, points in the same direction. In English, Greek and Indian heroic poetry princes themselves recite; Bhīshma recounts at length the story of his experiences in the dispute with Ambā. But we suspect that the authors are usually to be sought in the knights and high officers in the royal household—such persons as the 'minstrel' whom Agamemnon left in charge of his queen. In Beow. 867 ff. (cf.

p. 723) we have an account of the genesis of a heroic poem, composed by one of the king's squires. It is true that this seems to be a panegyric or poem of celebration, rather than a narrative, though it must run to a considerable length, as it contains a full account of Sigemund's adventures, by way of illustration. But we see no reason for thinking that the panegyric and the narrative poet were different persons in the Heroic Age. 'Widsith', who accompanies the princess Ealhhild to the court of Eormenric, is not actually said to recite anything except panegyrics: but the lists of famous kings and heroes contained in the poem distinctly imply that he has a répertoire of heroic stories. Heorrenda, who displaces Deor in the service of Heoden (Heðinn), would seem to be a person of similar position, in view of the part which he plays in the German version of the story. The *sūta*, whom we find in the Mahābhārata as charioteer and even as commander-in-chief, figures also both as panegyrist and reciter. His position at court seems to be the highest after the princes. We hear also of the *māgadha* and others, of lower social rank;[1] and similar persons are to be found elsewhere—Demodocos, Phemios, etc.—and are doubtless to be taken into account. But the evidence suggests that the higher rank were the more important force in creative poetry, probably owing to their wider knowledge of the heroic world.

In ancient Ireland, as we have seen (Vol. I, p. 586 f.), heroic saga was recited at kings' courts and elsewhere both by *filid* and by persons who apparently were not *filid*. Among the latter we may note Fedlimid (in the 'Exile of the Sons of Uisliu'), who has a recognised position in Conchobor's service and is well enough off to entertain the king and his court. In the Tain Bo Cuailnge stories (of CuChulainn's childhood), which seem to be early, are recited to Medb and Ailill by princes, including Fergus mac Roich and Cormac son of Conchobor. In Vol. II, p. 761 f., we saw reason for suspecting that a considerable part of the story of David comes, at least indirectly, from the queen (Bath-sheba).

There can be little doubt that all types of heroic literature are of 'heroic'—usually aristocratic—origin, except the didactic type (C), the affinities of which are clearly non-heroic. The origin of non-heroic literature itself seems to be more complex. As the various elements occur also in theological literature and in 'impersonal' literature (anti-

---

[1] In South India similar duties are now performed by the Bhāts or Bhatrāzns, who are apparently sometimes called Māgada; cf. Thurston, *Castes and Tribes of S. India* I, 223 ff.

quarian, gnomic, descriptive, mantic), it will be convenient to take these all together.

A priestly origin is probably to be sought for the whole of early (pre-Buddhist) Indian literature which has survived in these subjects. Even heroic literature owes its preservation to Brahmans;[1] but the rest would seem to have been the property of Brahman families from the beginning. We hear frequently of intellectual princes and of their doctrines; but they are known to us only through Brahmanic records. Intellectual activities on the part of persons of lower rank, such as the *sūta*, were apparently regarded with disfavour, except when they were devoted to heroic and Puranic subjects. In early Hebrew literature also the priestly element seems to be very considerable, at least in the Hexateuch; the other narrative books also may owe to this class their preservation and at least an appreciable amount of their contents, especially where matters of antiquarian interest are concerned.

Elsewhere this element is less easy to detect. The responses of the Delphic oracle are presumably due in the main to the priests who interpreted them. Antiquarian tradition too, in Greece as elsewhere, was mainly preserved at sanctuaries; but the antiquarian poets known to us seem not to have been priests. Even hymns to the gods were composed by secular poets, so far as our records go. For peoples who have become Christian, whether in ancient or modern times, information is difficult to obtain. There is reason, however, for believing that antiquarian learning and law were cultivated by the ancient Teutonic and Celtic priests. In Polynesia also antiquarian learning was chiefly in the possession of the priests. From Uganda one version of the 'dynastic chronicle' comes from the priests (cf. p. 587). There too it was the priests' function to interpret the responses of the mediums.

It would seem that in general priests are responsible for traditions of their deities and for antiquarian learning relating both to their sanctuaries and to the institutions and origin of the community to which

---

[1] 'Brahman' is the anglicised form of Sanskr. *Brāhmaṇa*, which means not only 'priest', but also a member of the priestly caste, who is not necessarily a priest himself, though the priesthood is open only to this caste. The word would seem to have a double derivation—in the former sense from *brahman* (neut.), 'spell, prayer, worship', in the latter from *brahman* (masc.), 'priest'. In the latter case the original meaning was presumably 'descendant of a priest'. We do not know how far Brahmans were engaged in secular life in ancient times. Most of those mentioned live by charity or hospitality; but we hear occasionally of warriors, and even rulers. We are using the term here in the narrower sense.

they belong.[1] Sometimes, though not always, hymns to the deities are composed by them. Where mediums or other oracles are employed it is the duty of the priests to interpret the responses.[2] Sometimes the administration of the law is in their hands or under their supervision. This variety of usage is doubtless connected with a corresponding variety in the position and attributes of the priest. Sometimes, as (usually at least) in the North, he is also the temporal head of the community; but this would seem to be on the whole rather exceptional. Usually he is attached to sanctuaries, most commonly to one special (permanent) sanctuary; but this is apparently not true of ancient India, at least in early times, nor of the Tatars. Sometimes he is also a seer or 'medicine man'; but very often his mantic powers are limited to divination from sacrifices, or he may act merely as the interpreter of the seers who belong to his sanctuary.

The great Brahman families claimed descent from famous seers; and there can be little doubt that priesthoods elsewhere are frequently of similar origin (cf. p. 451 f.). In such cases the mantic functions of the priest are inherited from his ancestors or predecessors, who were essentially mantic; but the priest may employ a medium. It may be observed that among the Tatars, who have no organised priesthood and no permanent sanctuaries, the seer (shaman) acts as priest. He is not only the mouthpiece of deities, but also the representative or agent of men, when they appeal or sacrifice to deities. Indeed he would seem to be in process of transition from seer to priest; and, like the Druids, he is a necessary intermediary between deities and men.

Oral literature on the whole probably owes more to the seer than to the priest, though perhaps not so much to the professional seer, who is an official, like Calchas, or who imparts information for a fee, as to the non-professional—who may be a man in apparently any rank of life. A large amount of Hebrew (non-heroic) saga relates to seers or prophets—we may instance the stories of Elijah and Elisha—and is probably derived from their followers. The Mahābhārata contains

---

[1] Cf. p. 796 f. We may also refer to Sections IV–VI (possibly also VII) of the chapters on 'Antiquarian Learning' included above, e.g. Vol. 1, p. 289 ff.

[2] As at Delphoi. In such cases the priests are usually persons of higher rank and education than the mediums. In Bali (E. Indies) last century there were often inspired persons of the lower castes attached to the temples. It was one of the duties of the priests (who were Brahmans) to edit and check their utterances; cf. Friederich, *J.R.A.S.* (1877), p. 80 ff. We do not know whether the same custom is found in India. As regards Uganda we may refer to p. 624 f. above for information as to the rank of the priests and mediums.

numerous stories of seers, most of whom are Brahmans; but it is as seers, rather than as priests, that they figure. The same remark applies to stories of Christian (English, Welsh, Irish and Russian) saints. For stories of Irish and Welsh seers, other than saints, we may refer to Vol. I, pp. 97 f., 103 ff., for similar Greek stories to (*ib.*) p. 116 f., for Tatar, Polynesian and South African stories to pp. 84 ff., 454 f., 634 f., 850 above. It will be seen that the Tatar examples mostly relate to princely seers; and similar cases occur in the Mahābhārata.

The influence of the seer is doubtless to be traced in all the 'impersonal' categories—antiquarian, gnomic, descriptive, mantic. As regards the first of these it is to be borne in mind that the seer's function is to prophesy of the past, as well as the present and the future (cf. Vol. I, pp. 451 ff., 473). Norse (supernatural) seeresses prophesy both of genealogies and of cosmogony; and we need not doubt that the latter subject at least usually falls within the seer's activities (cf. p. 198 above). The *awen* (Vol. I, p. 636 f.) is the source of poetry, as well as prophecy.

We have used the terms 'seer' and 'mantic' (as applied to persons) in a rather wide sense, which perhaps calls for some explanation here. To discuss the question in detail would of course require a knowledge of psychology, to which we make no claim. But we may observe that 'dissociation', more or less complete, seems to be known among many of the peoples with whom we are concerned. We may refer to the mediums of Uganda (p. 629 f.), the prophets of the southern Bantu (p. 634 f.), the *kaula* (*taua*) of the Polynesians (p. 449 ff.) and some of the shamans of the Tatars (p. 214), and for earlier times to the Welsh *awenyddion* and perhaps the medium at Delphoi (Vol. I, pp. 636, 657), and to the prophets and others referred to in the Hebrew passages noticed in Vol. II, p. 772.

Manticism is of course not a hereditary profession, like the priesthood, though it is commonly said to run in families. Everywhere it seems to be cultivated on traditional lines; but these differ a good deal between one people and another.[1] Among the Tatars and some African peoples the seer is believed to receive a 'call', usually rather early in life. This may be the voice of a deity or an ancestor, or an impulse from within. He then betakes himself to some solitary place, perhaps a forest or cave, where he starves himself for a while and behaves in an eccentric

---

[1] It should perhaps be remarked that we have followed the accounts given by writers of last century, who were inclined to generalise. We suspect that specialisation in different forms of manticism is very frequent, and that what is said here is not necessarily true of all mantic persons even in one community.

way, perhaps (in Africa) twining snakes round his neck.[1] Then he comes home in an excited or exalted state, and may—or may not—obtain recognition as an inspired person. After this he attaches himself to the service of an expert seer, from whom he receives instruction in manticism. See also p. 903.

Similar phenomena were known in antiquity, both in Europe and elsewhere—and they are not unknown in modern life. Sometimes the 'call' is said to take the form of a dream or vision, as in the case of Myrddin. But we doubt if this can have been very widespread in the North; otherwise we should hear more of it in sagas, where manticism is everywhere in evidence. Intellectual life seems usually to take a mantic form—which may include the power of knowing, and occasionally of seeing, things which are unknown or invisible to other people. In early Norse literature we hear that persons with such endowments were accustomed to spend much time alone; but we hear nothing of asceticism or eccentric behaviour. Such men were often statesmen and leading authorities in law; and they were much in demand as advisers and arbitrators. There are some indications too that people of this kind were frequently entrusted with the education ('fostering') of children, and that the preservation of learning was largely due to this practice.[2] On the other hand, professional seers or wizards are mentioned only in connection with harmful witchcraft, which generally brings them to a bad end. Seeresses or witches, however, are sometimes received with great honour—presumably those who avoid injurious practices. We hear even of ladies of high position going for instruction to the Lapps, who were regarded as experts in witchcraft; but this was viewed with disapproval. We may refer to the story of Gunnhildr, the wife of King Eric Blood-axe.

In Palestine and in India we hear much more of dissociation—ecstasy in the former case, asceticism in the latter. But it is not clear that the great prophets of Israel, e.g. Elijah and Elisha, practise ecstasy, though they receive inspiration through visions and from music. It is also not clear that the great philosophers of the Upanishads practise asceticism, at least before the time when, at an advanced age, they retire to the forest. Some of them, like Yājnavalkya, are men of considerable

---

[1] Cf. Shooter, *The Kafirs of Natal*, etc., p. 191 ff.

[2] Cf. Vol. I, p. 582. For Norway we may probably refer to Haralds S. Hárf. 26 and S. af Haraldi Gráfeld 8. It may be noted that Guðríðr had learned spells from her fostermother. Wizards are found as fosterers in legendary stories, e.g. Yngl. S. 38 and the Reginsmál.

property. In both cases, however, the educational tradition is prominent. Elisha acts as servant to Elijah, and receives his training from him; and the same practice seems to have been regularly followed by the Indian seers. The latter also clearly occupied much of their time in meditation or reflection.

We are inclined to doubt if any of the prophecies which we have found recorded in literature are products of strict dissociation, such as is attributed to the *awenyddion* and the seers of the modern peoples noted above—unless they have been recast by the seers themselves or their interpreters. But the importance of such utterances for the history of mantic literature must not be overlooked. Mantic thought, like all thought, necessarily follows traditional lines; and this is doubtless true both of dissociation itself—even in the strictest sense—and of mantic utterances. We see no reason for doubting either that dissociation is cultivated by seers everywhere, including—to a certain extent—even the wise men of the North, or that prophecies and mantic declarations are everywhere, at least usually, the products of such studied and partial dissociation. The *kamlanie* of the shaman (cf. p. 200 ff.) is an artistic performance, which can only be produced as a result of training, as long and intensive as that of an actor or musician; and the same may be said of performances of a medium in Uganda, when he is representing a king of the past or a water-deity. We see no reason for seeking an essentially different explanation for the utterances ascribed to seers, witches and mantic philosophers everywhere. They inherit traditional beliefs and ideas, traditional methods of concentrating and stimulating thought, and traditional formulae and (figurative) diction. Their training enables them to adapt this inherited material to new situations and speculations; and for this purpose they use the time of silence or reverie, which they commonly require. Their duties call for the maximum of mental effort. Specialisation is of course very frequent; but in many lands they may be required to act alike as physicians, detectives, lawyers, intermediaries with deities, and experts in all varieties of antiquarian lore—we might almost say 'general knowledge'—and consequently they must amass as much information as possible from every quarter, and also develop an acute faculty of observation. Imposture is of course inevitable, when they have to do or explain things which are beyond their power or knowledge; they must use their imagination or cajole their interrogators. And this is most likely to happen when they are faced with foreigners who have inherited superior knowledge, and their interests and reputation are consequently threatened. Yet in spite of all the limitations we have noted, they must be regarded as the essentially intellectual element in a barbaric community, and their influence upon its intellectual life must be rated accordingly.

Spells stand on a somewhat different footing from prophecies; they belong properly to the province of the 'medicine man', rather than the seer. In most of the ancient literatures which we have discussed, these two would seem to have been identical; but among some modern peoples, e.g. the Baganda, the 'medicine man' is quite distinct from the medium. In its first use a spell may involve some kind of dissociation, as in II Kings iii. 15; but the form in which they have generally been preserved is one which is crystallised by use. Presumably they were at first preserved by the families or pupils of the seers who composed them. We have seen that the genealogy of a spell is recorded in the Brhadāranyaka Upanishad vi, iii. 7 ff.

In ancient India the (Brahman) seer passes into the philosopher; the philosophy of the Upanishads is of mantic origin. In Ireland the *fili* must originally have been a seer;[1] but in early historical times he had become a scholar and (professional) intellectual man, versed in the cultivation of learned poetry. The growth of the native philosophy was cut short by Christianity; but there is evidence enough to show that, like the Welsh, it was essentially mantic. It may be noted that both the Indian philosopher and the Irish scholar, in spite of their intellectual attainments, adhered to a certain extent to the use of spells; and both seem to have been credited with the power of killing by a curse. The (more popular) account of the Indian philosophers given in the Mahā-bhārata resembles the stories of seers which we find in ancient Europe and elsewhere. Both Yājnavalkya and Çvetaketu meet with the goddess Sarasvatī and receive instruction from her (cf. Vol. ii, p. 504); and the story of the boy Ashtāvakra (*ib.* p. 505) shows a rather close analogy with that of Taliesin (Vol. i, p. 103 f.). Even in the Brhadāranyaka Upanishad itself the genealogies of doctrines given at the end of the second, fourth and sixth chapters are traced back to deities and supernatural beings—though in principle they may doubtless be accepted as evidence for the method by which such doctrines were pre-served.[2] We may compare the learning of the *tohungas* (p. 458 ff. above).

Gnomic poetry is sometimes closely connected with mantic, more

---

[1] Cf. Vol. i, p. 606. For the Welsh bard see p. 903 below.

[2] For comparison we may again refer to the 'genealogy' of Ari's historical information given by Snorri Sturluson in his Preface to the Heimskringla (cf. Vol. i, p. 582).

especially in Greek and Norse literature. Hesiod uses the language of a seer, inspired by the Muses; and the 'Works and Days' contains both gnomic and mantic elements. The same combination occurs in the poems Sigrdrífumál and Hávamál; in the former the speaker is a Valkyrie, in the latter the mantic god Othin. Elsewhere, however, such connection seems to be wanting. The Hebrew Proverbs have no mantic features; they contain religious elements, but obviously represent a school of thought different from the prophets. The gnomic compositions of early Egypt, which have much in common with the Proverbs, claim to be the works of sages—kings and royal officials —rather than seers. Early Indian gnomic poetry is presumably the work of Brahmans; but it is without mantic characteristics, so far as we have observed, and stands quite apart from the mantic philosophy noticed above.

Gnomic literature in general may be regarded as literature of the experienced and elderly, though it is frequently intended for the benefit of the young. It seems to be derived partly from precepts, partly from descriptions, both of which are probably of educational origin (cf. p. 830). Collections of precepts (and even gnomes also) among many peoples often take the form of instructions by a father or other near relative; and it is hardly possible to doubt that this is in fact the chief origin of precepts, though account is also to be taken of their use at initiation rites (cf. p. 829), and at the ceremonies held when a youth comes of age or enters upon some office. The origin of 'descriptions' is less clear to us; but these too seem to be in use at initiation rites. Examples have been cited above (p. 613) from the Basuto, by whom both precept and description, though retaining their practical character, have been cultivated so as to acquire a certain literary form; but we do not know whether this is widespread. We are under the impression that the cultivation of gnomic composition, whether of preceptual affinities (Type I; cf. p. 825) or of descriptive origin (Type II), belongs in general to a more advanced stage of culture than that of the Bantu peoples. Among the peoples treated in this volume it seems to be much less well developed than in the ancient European literatures discussed in Vol. 1; and neither the Indian nor the Hebrew evidence suggests that it is characteristic of a very early phase of literary history.

The essential element in gnomic composition is the formulating of generalisations. The change from precept to gnome means that the place of the instructor, whether relative or village headman, is taken by the sage or philosopher—though the speaker usually preserves the characteristics of an experienced and more or less elderly person.[1] This is the phase which is commonly represented by the gnomic poetry of ancient Europe and Asia. But where the reference is to human affairs the change is commonly accompanied by an encroachment of the descriptive element. The sage's work therefore is not only to formulate principles, but also to illustrate them in the best form he can; and gnomic composition tends to rhetoric. Compositions relating to nature remain of course descriptive; and little change takes place, except in the way of elaboration and perhaps expansion.

Literary tradition often ascribes the authorship of gnomic and descriptive poetry to kings and supernatural beings. But the only definite information we have comes from Greece,[2] where the authors are men of independent position, varying from small landowners, like Hesiod, to the leading statesmen of the day, like Solon. The period during which poetry of this character flourished—from the eighth to the sixth century—might well be called the Age of Wisdom;[3] at this time it would seem to have been the poetry most cultivated by those who did not work for pay. Among the northern peoples, where such poetry seems to have been cultivated under somewhat similar, though slightly less advanced conditions, we have no information as to the real authors. But there is little evidence, except perhaps in Ireland, for rewards to be obtained for such poetry,[4] and consequently we have some reason for suspecting that it was cultivated by persons of independent means, who gained a reputation for wisdom thereby. And the first part of the Hávamál is clearly intended for an audience of this class. In Ireland the reputed authors are kings, heroes and *filid* of the past; but actually there is some reason for thinking that *filid* did compose such poems (cf. Vol. I, p. 603). The contest in wisdom—doubtless for rewards, just as

---

[1] Sigrdrífa seems not to be an elderly lady, even if she is not to be identified with Brynhildr. But she is a mantic character (witch), to be compared with the Irish Scathach. The Sigrdrífumál is half mantic, half gnomic.

[2] We do not know how far the Egyptian tradition, which attributes the authorship of the various 'Instructions' to statesmen and kings, is to be trusted. At first sight it does not look improbable.

[3] We may refer to the 'Seven Sages', a term borrowed from Oriental mythology —cf. the Indian 'Seven Seers' (*saptarṣi*)—but applied to leading Greek thinkers and statesmen who (Thales, Solon, etc.) were living about 600 B.C.

[4] It is clear enough that contests in wisdom of various kinds were widespread in early times (cf. Vol. I, pp. 97, 105, 412, 474, 590); but we are inclined to doubt whether such contests lasted into the period of which we are speaking, except perhaps in peasant circles (cf. Vol. II, p. 211 ff.).

in India—may have lasted here down to historical times, though we do not know of any definite evidence to this effect.

The attribution of gnomic and descriptive poetry to the independent land-owning class is not incompatible with the fact that such poetry is often associated with mantic elements. Many Norse landowners, including leading statesmen of the tenth century, are credited with something of mantic power, though they would have scorned to practise as seers or medicine-men. For instances we may refer to Vol. I, p. 658 f.; but many more could be cited. We may refer too to the god Othin, who in mythology is a typical medicine-man, an expert in spells, necromancy and magic of every kind; but in the first part of the Hávamál he is the exponent of worldly wisdom, such as an intellectual landowner, with a gift of cynical humour, might well be expected to propound. In Greece most of the 'wise men' who flourished about 600 B.C.[1] would probably have repudiated the possession of mantic power. But Greek thought at this time was a little in advance of that of the Viking Age. Somewhat earlier the conditions may have been more similar; at all events Hesiod claims direct inspiration from the Muses. Even among the Hebrews, where the mantic and gnomic schools of thought were quite distinct and possibly opposed, the latter can hardly have disclaimed manticism from the beginning. For they evidently looked to Solomon as their founder; and Solomon's wisdom, which expressed itself in descriptive poetry, including perhaps riddles, was a divine gift received, like Caedmon's, in a dream.

The prevailing anonymity of oral literature renders it difficult to estimate the part played by women in the composition of either poetry or saga. Even in regard to the cultivation and recitation of literature a difficulty is caused by the fact that the great majority of modern collectors have been men—who naturally have found it easier to obtain recitations from their own sex. For an illustration of the uncertainty which may arise from this we may refer to Vol. II, p. 254 f. The most recent Russian collectors believe that the proportion of women among the reciters has increased very greatly in the last sixty years. But they went to the houses of the peasants to hear recitations, whereas the older collectors were as a rule content with sending out general invitations to reciters to come to them. It is natural to suppose that these invitations

[1] But Epimenides and perhaps Anacharsis are exceptions. Possibly also we may refer to Plutarch's story of Solon's behaviour when he was rousing the Athenians to take Salamis. Was this a traditional pose?

would not and could not be so readily responded to by the women as by the men.

Actually we have seen that the cultivation of oral literature by women is both frequent and widespread in modern times. For Russian and Yugoslav examples we may refer to Vol. II, pp. 229 ff., 244 f., 289 f., 306 f., and probably also 400 ff. It will be seen that all these references are concerned either with recitation or with composition on traditional lines, between which it is not always easy to distinguish. In the present volume a good number of examples have been cited from Polynesia and North Africa (pp. 413, 515 f., 526, 663, 668); and here the evidence is for composition rather than recitation. On the other hand we have found very little direct evidence from the Bantu and Tatar peoples, though we are inclined to suspect that this may be largely due to the defects of our information. For the former we may refer to p. 617 f. above. As regards the Tatars the poems give some reason for thinking that women have, or have had, a good deal of intellectual life —perhaps not less than among the Tuareg. There can be no doubt that this is true of the Yakut, as also of the neighbouring Tungus (cf. p. 195). Among the Sea Dyaks mantic poetry at least is cultivated by women perhaps even more than by men.

From ancient times we have very little definite evidence for the cultivation of oral literature by women. A little poetry, almost entirely fragmentary, is ascribed to women in Greek, Norse and Irish records; but the Greek poems belong to the very end of our period, and were probably written down by the authors themselves. The other ancient literatures included in our survey, English, Welsh, Sanskrit and Hebrew, have preserved nothing, so far as we know, which is generally accepted as a woman's composition. All of them, however, together with Norse and Irish, preserve speech-poems in character (Type B) in which the speaker is a woman or female supernatural being; and these may usually be accepted as indirect evidence, of varying value, for the composition of poetry by women. Moreover, reasons have been given for suspecting that certain Norse and Hebrew sagas are derived from women (cf. Vol. I, pp. 542, 600, Vol. II, p. 761 f.).

Taking our survey as a whole we may point to certain genres of literature which seem to be more especially cultivated by women.

Evidence, direct or indirect, for elegies (dirges) sung by women is found in almost all the ancient literatures we have discussed.[1] Every-

---

[1] It is only in Hebrew that we have found no satisfactory instance. For Irish examples, which are fairly numerous, we may refer to Vol. I, p. 54 f., 340, 585, for an

where, it is true, we find also elegies by men. But it is clear from some of our authorities, e.g. Iliad XXIV. 723 ff., Beow. 1117 f. and Guðrúnar-kviða I, that elegies by women were customary, at least in heroic society —though these may have been followed, either immediately or on a subsequent day, by elegies (of a less emotional character) by men. The same custom is represented also among almost all the modern peoples we have considered. For Russian and Yugoslav examples we may refer to Vol. II, pp. 229 ff., 406, and especially to the poem on Prince Danilo's funeral (*ib.* p. 335 f.)—where the speeches of the senators and generals follow the laments of the prince's widow and his sister-in-law. For instances among the Tatars, Polynesians, Sea Dyaks, Abyssinians and Yoruba we may refer to pp. 60 f., 265, 487 f., 517, 648 of the present volume. In particular we would call attention to the funeral of the Maori chief described on p. 265; here apparently the speeches of the warriors precede his sister's lament. It is only among the northern Bantu that we have failed to find examples;[1] and this may be due to defective information.

In Russia the elegies recited by women are sometimes composed for them by other women, who are professionals in social ritual, though this seems to be rather exceptional (cf. Vol. II, p. 286 f.). We have no doubt that the same practice is to be found elsewhere (cf. p. 882, note). But this cannot have been the original custom; and, so far as our evidence goes, it would seem that usually, where literature is purely oral, women who make any claim to education are expected to be able to compose elegies.

The cultivation of mantic poetry by women is also widespread. Its distribution is certainly more limited than that of the elegy; but this is probably due in part to the fact that it is more or less suppressed or discouraged among Christian and Mohammedan peoples. The fullest evidence comes from Norse literature, where it is attributed to both human and supernatural women (cf. Vol. I, pp. 451, 537, 639). Examples may also be found in Irish, Greek and Hebrew literature (*ib.* pp. 635 f., 641, 645 f.; Vol. II, p. 763 f.), though in the two latter (human) seeresses (like Cassandra) are less frequent and important than seers. In modern times examples may be found among the Tatars, the Polynesians, the Sea Dyaks and the Bantu (cf. pp. 192 ff., 445 ff., 452 f., 487 ff., 625 ff. above).

Indian example to Vol. II, p. 482. A Welsh example is to be found in *R.B.H.* XVI; cf. Vol. I, p. 38, where the sex of the speaker was overlooked (cf. I. Williams, *Canu Llywarch Hen*, p. lxi f.). In Guðrúnarkviða I (cf. Vol. I, p. 27) the widow is at first unable to pronounce the elegy owing to her emotion.

[1] For the Basuto examples are given by Ellenberger, *History of the Basuto*, p. 299 f.

The mantic activities of women vary a good deal, not so much in character as in the scope which is allowed to them. Among many peoples women are credited with mantic faculties superior to those of men, i.e. with a receptivity to spiritual experiences and impressions, whether derived from an external (supernatural) source or from within. We may refer e.g. to the note on p. 194 and to the ancient Teutonic peoples (cf. Vol. I, p. 640 f.). The existence of an influential priesthood or priestly class, as in Christian and Mohammedan lands, in India, or in sanctuaries like Jerusalem and Delphoi, would seem commonly to act as a deterrent upon the cultivation of such activities; yet in the last two cases the mantic faculties of women were evidently recognised (cf. Vol. II, p. 764), though they were probably controlled. On the other hand where, as in the North in heathen times,[1] there is no strong priestly influence, the seeress or witch may act with full independence and receive great honour, like Thorbjörg, the Greenland witch referred to in Vol. I, p. 537. Similar conditions prevail in parts of Polynesia (cf. p. 450) and on the eastern Steppe, and also, we believe, among some of the Bantu; for ancient times we may compare the story of Deborah. Indeed there can be little doubt that witches are often an important factor in the intellectual life of unlettered communities; and it is unfortunate that their utterances have been so seldom recorded. Except for the Sea Dyaks, we are practically dependent upon Tatar and Polynesian stories and upon inferences from Norse and Greek mythology.

Apart from elegies and mantic poetry, we are inclined to think that the various chapters of this book which are concerned with literature relating to 'unspecified individuals' contain much which is of feminine authorship. This remark applies more especially to poetry of social ritual, such as the wedding poetry we have discussed in Vol. II, p. 232ff. But we suspect also that poems of the kind which in Yugoslavia are conventionally known as 'Women's poems' (ženske pjesme), including timeless-nameless narrative and speech poems, are everywhere largely of this origin, though they may sometimes be sung by men. Among these we may include a considerable proportion of the unhistorical (international) ballads. And the same may be said of timeless-nameless prose narratives. Indeed for the cultivation of saga in general by women there is evidence enough from both Polynesia and Africa (cf. pp. 411, 614, above).

[1] In the North, as elsewhere, witches or wizards who used harmful spells went in danger of their lives. Instances are not rare in sagas. But there is no reason for thinking that such witchcraft was of very frequent occurrence, except perhaps in warfare, or that the dread of it dominated life, as it is said to do in modern Africa.

Lastly, as regards heroic literature—there is no doubt that heroic poetry of Type D in more or less elementary form, including panegyrics and exhortations, and also taunting and vituperative poems, as well as elegies, is widely cultivated by women. Examples will be found in the chapters dealing with the Abyssinians, the Northern Bantu and the Tuareg, above (pp. 514 ff., 526 ff., 617 f., 663, 668), and also among the ancient Hebrews (cf. Vol. II, p. 656) and the ancient Teutonic peoples.[1] For heroic literature of a more advanced character we are dependent upon inference. Reasons have been given for thinking that the story of David is largely of feminine provenance (*ib.* p. 761 f.); and we are inclined to the same explanation of several of the Norse heroic poems (cf. Vol. I, p. 599) and also for some of the Yugoslav *bugarštice*, which are much occupied with the feelings of women (cf. Vol. II, p. 448). It has been noted too (*ib.* p. 623) that certain stories in the Mahābhārata would seem to have been composed in the first place either by or for women; in any case they represent women as intellectually active.[2]

The Norse poems, as we have them, date from times long after the Heroic Age, though they may owe something to old literary tradition. For India and Israel, however, we have quite good evidence for the intellectual activities of women in the Heroic Age itself (*ib.* pp. 623, 761). This, together with the modern evidence, especially for Abyssinia and the Tuareg, would seem to justify the inference that 'heroic' conditions are rather favourable to such activities. It may be observed that not all the women to whom these references apply belong to 'heroic' (aristocratic) classes; the same freedom is enjoyed by women of other (professional and poorer) classes. But the underlying cause may perhaps be that the women of the heroic class were often better educated than the men.

The question how far the growth of literature is determined by occupational causes is one which we can only answer very briefly. Aristocratic (heroic) literature has already been considered, and so also the literature of the professional intellectual (mantic and priestly) classes. In modern times the travelling trader and craftsman are influential factors in the dissemination of literature from one district or country to another; and the same may be true of antiquity, though we do not know of any evidence. But do they also produce literature?

[1] Cf. Priscus in C. Muller's *Fragm. Histor. Graec.* Vol. IV, p. 85. We may perhaps compare Tacitus, *Germ.* 7 f., though it is not stated that the eulogies and exhortations here mentioned were expressed in poetry.

[2] We may refer also to what has been said of the Yakut on p. 186, above.

In general the problem before us may be restricted to occupations followed by the community as a whole, i.e. it may be treated as a geographical problem. Of the peoples whose literatures we have discussed some may conveniently be described as 'continental', others as 'maritime'. The life of the former is centred in agriculture or cattle or sheep-farming, that of the latter on the sea, though they may also practise agriculture or sheep-farming. Urban communities were not unknown in the periods covered by our survey—in Greece and Palestine even true urban communities, independent of a king's court—but they seem to have left no specifically urban literature, except in Greece.

Among the 'continental' peoples we have found little or no literature which is not of either heroic or mantic derivation. Both the heroic and the mantic poets frequently betray the fact that the society to which they belong rests ultimately upon a pastoral basis—upon the possession of livestock—but we cannot point to any poem of more than a few lines[1] or to any story in which the interest is centred, wholly or primarily, in agriculture or sheep-farming, or in the experiences of a farmer as such. 'Bucolic' poetry belongs to a more advanced stage of literature. Hesiod gives advice on agriculture, as on other things; but the interest is centred in 'wisdom' of all kinds, especially mantic wisdom; and this would seem to be the normal opening for intellectual activity in 'continental' communities. With mantic wisdom we must of course associate the mantic story, which is perhaps better represented among the Tatars than in any of the ancient literatures.

'Maritime' peoples have, in addition to heroic and mantic literature, a third opening for intellectual activity. In Vol. I we treated under the term 'post-heroic' a class of literature, best represented in Greek and Norse, which is primarily of individual interest, but commonly has no heroic features, while mantic connections are also usually absent. The nearest approach which we could find in Vol. II to this literature was a number of poems (ib. p. 348 ff.) from the Adriatic coast.[2] In form these have nothing in common with the Greek and Norse poetry—they are

---

[1] Such as riddles and other short descriptive poems (cf. p. 833 f.). Such poetry seems to be less frequently concerned with agriculture and domestic animals than with wild life and natural phenomena. This would seem to indicate that, like poetry descriptive of natural phenomena (cf. p. 833), with which it is sometimes associated, it belongs primarily to people whose living is derived from fishing and hunting, rather than from cattle-keeping.

[2] We are inclined to think that parallels are also to be found in the East Indies (cf. p. 714, note); but we have not the knowledge for discussing the subject.

almost wholly narrative—but they show the same absence of heroic and mantic features, and seem to be the products of a similar society. In the present volume widespread resemblances are to be found in Polynesian literature. In one respect an important reservation is to be made in this case. The Greek, Norse and Dalmatian poems, and also the Norse sagas, all show frequent evidence of contact with higher civilisations, which is of course wanting here. There remains, however, a considerable common element, due partly to the freedom of movement which is open to a maritime population, partly to intellectual activity, and partly also to an interest in the doings of people (individuals) of ordinary flesh and blood, who are neither idealised heroes nor persons of princely rank. It would seem that the life of small and scattered maritime communities is that which allows most independence to the ordinary person, and also the best chance of having his memory perpetuated.

It is in the literatures of maritime communities which are in communication with more civilised lands that the transition from barbarism can most easily be traced. Among Continental peoples, where this transition begins with a ruling class, its effects on the individual seldom leave a literary record. What constitutes perhaps the chief interest of the early Greek and early Norse literatures is that they illustrate the process of transition.[1] The records of the latter are much fuller; but those of the former belong for the most part to a more advanced phase. By a comparative study of the two we are able to see how mankind can pass from the heroic and mantic worlds of thought into one which is more or less identical with ours today.

The process of transition is perhaps of a rather more subtle character than might appear at first sight. Intellectual progress would seem to be not wholly governed by material civilisation; we may bear in mind what the intellectual activities of the Polynesians achieved with a material culture which was inferior to that of our neolithic age. In the tenth century (A.D.) we see the northern peoples assimilating the civilisation of Western Europe, which was more advanced than their own. Similarly, in the seventh century B.C. we see the Greeks assimilating the civilisation of Egypt and the East, which was more advanced than theirs. But how far are we justified in believing that the intellectual life of Western Europe was more advanced, or nearer to ours, than that of

---

[1] In modern times the introduction of European influence usually brings about a rapid submergence of the native culture. Evidence for a phase of transition, however, has been given for Abyssinia (pp. 519 ff., 530) and could probably be obtained for various other parts of Africa.

the North—or that the intellectual life of Egypt and the East was more advanced, or nearer to ours, than that of Greece? All that one can say with confidence is that the more advanced civilisations possessed superior knowledge in many respects. It would seem rather that the intellectual progress made in Europe was only in part taken over from the higher civilisations; otherwise the native thought would have been wholly displaced, as in fact has often, though not always, been the case. We have also to take account of the stimulus derived from contact with a new world of thought.

We may here rectify certain omissions in the last few chapters.

P. 816 f. In connection with the discussion of stories of 'national origins', it may be noted that in many parts of the world such stories, usually combined with —more or less speculative—genealogies, serve as introductions to national or dynastic (oral) histories. These latter are themselves derived partly from speculation, partly from genuine tradition. Examples from Africa have been noted above (pp. 575 f. and note, 584 ff., 640 ff.). In ancient Europe the existence of similar works is traceable in Sweden and Norway (cf. Vol. I, p. 306 f.). There can be little doubt also that the Danes had an oral history of this kind—which was presumably the source of the opening lines (1–56) of Beowulf. Works of the same character have been used by the Latin historians of the Goths and the Lombards (cf. Vol. I, ib.). In this country not much has been preserved; but the existence of such works, both English and Welsh, is attested (e.g.) by the story of Hengest and Horsa and by the genealogies in Harl. 3859, ad fin. (ib. p. 309 ff.). For Ireland the material is more abundant; we may refer especially to the legendary history of the kings (high-kings) of Tara, which is doubtless derived in the main from an oral dynastic history. It is clear enough too that somewhat similar works existed in early times among the Greeks (ib. p. 304 f.) and the Hebrews (cf. Vol. II, p. 695 ff.). For further analogies we may perhaps refer to the Russian 'Chronicle of Nestor' (ib. p. 23 f.) and to the Japanese 'Kojiki' (cf. p. 496, above), and possibly also to the early traditions of Rome.

Some of these oral histories, especially perhaps those of the Irish, the Hebrews and the Baganda, seem to have been among the most noteworthy achievements of oral literature. And in general the importance of such works for the history of literature must not be overlooked; for it is from them in the main that the study of history is derived. The earliest literary historians in Greece probably did little more than commit the work of their predecessors to writing; and the same may be said of other countries where historical literature was of native origin.

P. 820 f. In connection with the war between gods and demons it may be added that interesting analogies to the demons and demon-fights of Ragnarök will be found in A. Olrik, *Aarbøger f. nord. Oldkyndighed*, 1902, 157 ff., and *Danske Studier*, 1913.[1] Olrik held (*Aarbøger*, p. 216 ff.) that the 'Second Battle of Moytura' (cf.

---

[1] We are indebted to Miss H. R. Ellis for calling our attention to these articles.

Vol. I, p. 258) was originally concerned with a theme similar to Ragnarök and, like it, relating to the future; and it may be noted that the story ends with a short prophecy of the evils which were to precede the destruction of the world. But we suspect that this story had a very complex origin. For Ragnarök reference may also be made to Neckel, *S.B. d. Heidelberger Akad. d. Wiss.*, 1918.

It may be observed here that Greek antiquarian learning distinguished two collective fights between gods and—different sets of—demons. The later of these (the Gigantomachia) shows the closer resemblance to the Norse. But better parallels are to be found elsewhere for individual fights.

P. 853. A very interesting case of necromancy occurs in Þorleifsþáttr Jarlsskalds, cap. 8, where a shepherd habitually visits the barrow of the poet Thorleifr, whose death has been brought about (by witchcraft) by Earl Haakon the Great (c. 990). He sleeps on the barrow, hoping to obtain inspiration by composing an elegy on the poet; but he can never get further than "Here lies a poet." Eventually he sees the barrow open; the poet comes out and grants him his wish. The passage is translated in Kelchner, *Dreams in Old Norse Literature*, p. 129—where many other interesting examples of Norse mantic dreams are collected. The passage may be compared with the story of Caedmon's inspiration.

P. 865. Reference should have been made here to the sitting of the *whare wananga* described on p. 459 f. and also to the Gylfaginning, cap. 2. Owing to an oversight no account of the latter has been given in this work; and it may be convenient to add a few words on the subject here.

The Gylfaginning[1] is the first part of the 'Prose Edda', written by the Icelandic scholar and statesman Snorri Sturluson, who died in 1241. In cap. 2 a king named Gylfi makes his way to Ásgarðr in disguise, and calls himself Gangleri, which perhaps means 'Weary Traveller'. He enters a hall and sees there three 'high-seats', occupied by persons called Hár, Jafnhár and Þriði.[2] He questions these persons on cosmogony and on the characteristics and doings of the deities, and they reply at length (cap. 3–53). The replies amount to what may perhaps be called a systematic exposition of Norse theology; Hár is the chief speaker. At last (cap. 54) Gylfi hears crashes around him, and finds that the hall has disappeared and that he is standing alone out in the open.

The Gylfaginning is followed by the Skaldskaparmál, or 'Diction of Poetry', and the Háttatal, or 'List of Metres'. The Prose Edda as a whole seems to have been designed as a handbook for the study of poetry. But the question which interests us here is how far the Gylfaginning preserves a tradition of the method of teaching practised in heathen times. In any case the resemblance to the session of the *whare wananga* described on p. 459 f. is noteworthy. We may also compare the Irish 'Ecstasy of the Champion', referred to in Vol. I, pp. 206, 462.

---

[1] The name is sometimes transl. 'Beguiling (or Deception) of Gylfi'; but *ginning* means rather 'hallucination', with an approximation to the sense of 'ecstasy', 'mantic vision'.

[2] These names are words which usually mean 'high', 'equally high', and 'third'; but all of them occur in the list of names borne by Óthin in the Grímnismál, and therefore were not made up by Snorri.

P. 869. In connection with improvisation reference may be made to the traditional phraseology, static descriptions, and conventional openings and scenes of heroic narrative poetry, as described on p. 180 f. and in Vol. II, pp. 246 f., 427 ff. These conventions without doubt materially facilitate the improvisation of such poems, and commonly form a not inconsiderable portion of them.

The passage on the same page relating to early Indian prose works applies primarily to the Upanishads. If the archaic language of the Brāhmanas was preserved without the use of writing—which seems to be the prevailing view (cf. Vol. II, p. 463 f.)—the power of memorisation involved is very remarkable.

P. 873. It is curious that Radlov makes no mention of an instrumental accompaniment, when he describes the recitations of heroic narrative poetry among the Kara-Kirghiz (cf. p. 179 ff. above). But Vambéry (*Das Türkenvolk*, p. 272) states definitely that these poems are accompanied on the two-stringed *koboz*.

P. 885. It may be added that the best story-tellers of Uganda—Sabadu, Kadu and Saruti—were members of Mutesa's court; cf. pp. 585, 604, 609.

P. 888 f. For inspiration and the call of the seer we may refer to Vol. I, Ch. xx, Vol. II, pp. 624, 776, and to pp. 197 f., 212 in this volume; and also to the vision of Balaam (Numbers xxiv. 15 f.), the dream of Caedmon (Bede, *Hist. Eccl.* IV, 24), and the story of Thorleifr and the shepherd cited above. For the 'inspiration' which comes from within (the *awen*) see Vol. I, pp. 636 f., 657 f.

P. 891. It should have been mentioned that the early Welsh bards seem in general to have resembled the Irish *filid*, though we have much less information relating to the former. We may refer to Vol. I, pp. 601 and 614, and to p. 845, note, in the present volume.

INDEX